James Henderson

the Ca‍‍‍‍‍‍‍‍‍ ‍‍‍las

G000111464

About the Author

For nearly ten years, James Henderson has studied the Caribbean, from the window of tiny island-hopping planes, through scuba-diving masks and from some of the smartest hotels in the region. He travels there as much as possible, braving flash tropical downpours and droughts, *coups d'état*, 'jerk', drunken bus drivers and posses of mad Californians; dodging safari buses of cruise-ship passengers and the attentions of over-zealous aloe masseuses, jumbies and machete-flourishing coconut salesmen. Half English and half Scots, he has wandered all over Britain, Europe, the USA and Australia, sometimes taking part in madcap cross-continental sporting events.

He has lingered longest in the Caribbean, still watching for the Green Flash and writing features for the *Financial Times*.

About the Updaters

Simon Calder (Cuba) is travel editor of the *Independent*. He first visted Cuba in 1989 and since then has returned to the island every year. He is co-author, with Emily Hatchwell, of *Travellers' Survival Kit: Cuba* (Vacation Work) and *Cuba in Focus* (Latin American Bureau).

Rodney Bolt (Puerto Rico) is the author of the Cadogan guides to Germany, Bavaria, Amsterdam and Madeira, as well as other books and numerous articles. In 1994 he won the German National Tourist Office's 'Travel Writer of the Year' award. He lives in Amsterdam.

We would also like to thank Kathy Matusik (Turks & Caicos), Doreen Kralick (Aruba), Julio Cesar Mordan (Dominican Republic), Suzanne Seitz (Haiti), various Jamaica Tourist Board offices across the island, the Bahamas Tourist Board and Bahamasair in London, the Bonaire Tourist Board, and all the tourist offices across the Caribbean who supplied the very latest information for this guide.

Please help us to keep this guide up to date

Keeping a guide to the Caribbean up to date is a daunting task—you need to start again as soon as you've reached the end. The region has a multi-million dollar tourist industry and things are constantly changing. Each year new hotels open up, a new chef arrives at a restaurant or moves on, PR companies embellish island-histories yet further, crowds drift from one bar to the next...even beaches migrate in the Caribbean (sounds silly, but they really are seasonal in some places). It is hard to keep track of the changes, impossible to test them all out (and even then it might be a particularly good or bad night). But someone proposed marriage with the help of the second edition and that is surely a coup.

We need your thoughts to create as complete a picture as possible for each update. If you had a particularly pleasing (or unpleasant) experience, or if you know any new acronyms for LIAT (*see* p.11) we would like to hear about it. Similarly, if you feel that you have some ideas for the guide, send them in. Be as opinion-ated as you like. Writers of the best letters each year are awarded a complimentary guide of their choice from the series.

Contents

Maps

Acknowledgements

For the fourth time, my thanks go to all West Indians, native and adoptive, who make travelling in the islands such fun; for all the lifts (cars, bikes, boats and planes), beers, beds for the night and impromptu lessons in French Creole; to all the voluble taxi-drivers, limers and tourism officials who responded so kindly to hours of questions, and then replied to urgent and demanding faxes. Thanks also to those at Cadogan who pulled this edition together and were (more or less) unfazed by the author's sudden departure for another continent.

Introduction

When you first arrive in the Caribbean you find that people walk very slowly. But then, after a few days, island atmosphere gets to work on you, and gradually those people begin to catch up with you. The Caribbean is an ideal place to slow down and relax. It's an easy life in the islands: with reliable warmth, strikingly new and beautiful tropical scenery and, of course, magnificent sea and sand.

The islands have an enchanting atmosphere; for centuries they have captivated travellers from the temperate zones. It is a wonderful experience to be surrounded by islands; they sit serenely on a sea horizon and the glare of the sun makes the surface of the sea glint as though it were sprinkled with diamonds. You will be bombarded by vibrant unfamiliar sensations: the sweet flavours of ripened fruits—mango, soursop or sweet banana—and the fragrance of jasmine and frangipani on the night air. Only the strongest colours stand out in the glare of the Caribbean sun—the impossibly bright plumage of a scarlet ibis and the shimmering fluorescence of a hummingbird. And rhythms familiar from elsewhere—*reggae*, *steel pan* and Latin *salsa*—suddenly take on a different feel.

The Caribbean is known as a hedonist's destination, the place for an all-over body holiday. You can simply lie back and absorb the sun's warmth; dive in euphoric, suspended animation, feasting your eyes on a glittering seascape of corals and tropical fish; savour the taste of *piña colada*; take a trip on a catamaran, or feel the surge of a windsurfer beneath you as you race off on the trade winds—it's the ultimate 20th-century rest cure. There are beach bars from paradise here, made of just a few rickety struts and a deck standing on the sand.

But beyond the beach and body culture, the coconut oil and ganja, you will discover a West Indies that pulses to a different beat, a land of *creole*, *callaloo* and *calypso*, rhythmic, vibrant and compelling. There is such variety on the islands, and there are so many places where it feels good to be. There are so many variations on the tropical theme. The pace of life is laid-back, shambolic and often infuriating, and at times service is so absurdly slow that you feel like an unwitting player in a farce. But if you make a fuss, the islanders will just look on in bemusement at the worries of a slave to the minute-hand.

Caribbean life is demonstrative and always lively. There is a theatre of the street which turns a bus trip or a visit to the market into an adventure. It's also an easy place for travelling; if you want company, you simply stop and talk to somebody. The West Indians are masters of street talk and you can expect to be on the receiving end of a 'limer's' quip or two. It is difficult for a visitor even to understand at first, let alone respond in kind, but, whatever your reaction, you can guarantee peals of distinctive West Indian laughter all around you. Music is played everywhere, loudly, and people set up vast speakers in the road and dance just for the hell of it. Practically every island has its own rhythm—*soca, salsa, ska*.

Since its discovery and colonization by the Europeans, the Caribbean has become an extraordinary melting pot of cultures, with echoes from all over the world: Parisian chic, parish churches from rural England, American-style cable TV and large cruising cars, Hindu prayer flags and Moslem minarets, and of course the strongest reminders of Africa in the faces, the spirit religions and the relentless drum-based rhythms. And yet the flashes are only momentary, because they have metamorphosed, creolized into something uniquely West Indian—Christmas carols to a reggae or calypso beat, faces with Dutch features and ebony black skin, Martinican *créole*, which sounds so like French, but which evaporates as soon as you think you have understood it. Each island has its distinctive characteristics and the variety is striking, even across just a few miles of sea. If you are island-hopping, it is interesting to work out the common strains across the islands.

It is difficult to imagine how wealthy the Caribbean was two hundred years ago. The fertile islands were turned into sugar factories—the wealth of the West Indies was enough to kick-start the industrial revolution—and the imperial armies would come thousands of miles to fight over them, erecting the vast fortresses that still litter the islands. But that heyday is long past.

Today the islands struggle to keep afloat financially and their economic mainstay is tourism, an industry which has changed the face of the islands over the last twenty years—many islands are now highly developed, and most are continuing to build. On some islands it can be quite difficult to find an isolated beach, but then again, here you can also find some of the smartest and most exclusive resorts in the world.

Guide to the Guide and a Little Geography

To get a mental picture of the Caribbean islands, imagine a dinosaur skeleton, standing between the North and South American continents, facing left. The body is made of the Greater Antilles, perched in the middle of the Caribbean Sea; its trunk at Hispaniola, supported by feet in Jamaica and stretching out its head and neck (Cuba) towards the Gulf of Mexico. In the east, the arc of the Lesser Antilles makes up the links of its prehensile tail, of which the final vertebra, Trinidad, is firmly embedded in South America.

The area has a variety of names: 'Caribbean' comes from the indigenous tribe of American Indians, the Caribs, who inhabited the Lesser Antilles (*see* p.45) until the arrival of the Europeans; the origin of the term 'West Indies' lies with Columbus himself, who found the islands while trying to find a route via the west to India; and the 'Greater' and 'Lesser Antilles' derive from Antillia, supposedly a corruption of 'Atlantis', the lost continent that was presumed to lie beyond the Azores. The string of islands encloses the Caribbean Sea, separating it from the Atlantic Ocean, and over the millennia active volcanoes have sprouted along the rift between the Atlantic and Caribbean tectonic plates. The Tropic of Cancer cuts through the middle of the Bahamas, passing just a few miles north of Havana in Cuba.

There are 28 different political units in the Caribbean and the Bahamas, among them independent countries, crown colonies, overseas departments, a territory and a commonwealth. This guide book approaches them in a rough geographical order, tracking along the island-chain from the southeast to the northwest, but collecting them according to language and nationality and the old groupings of the colonial administration. For convenience and in order to emphasize their cultural unity, the French West Indies are treated as one group (even though they are scattered among other islands and spread over 300 miles), as are the two groups of the Netherlands Antilles, which are separated by some 600 miles of the Caribbean Sea. Strictly speaking the archipelago of the Bahamas is not geographically in the Caribbean itself, but is included in this book as the islands and their people have a similar heritage, and visitors of course have much the same reasons for going there as they do to the Caribbean.

Introductions to the different island groups are given in the text. Each island is then divided up according to the same format: leading with an introduction and history, followed by any 'topics' that are particularly striking about the island. Then, for each island, there are the practical, 'getting around' sections, followed by information on beaches, beach bars and flora and fauna. Next comes a description of island sights, a selection of the best hotels, restaurants, bars and nightlife. Finally there is a practical directory for each island, with details on 'getting there', tourist information, festivals, money and shopping, a section on watersports and lastly sports based on land and spectator sports.

The Caribbean at a Glance

Here is a thumbnail sketch of the islands, including recent changes.

Anguilla

With an ultimately laid-back atmosphere and magnificent beaches, Anguilla is still uncrowded and has a string of excellent places to stay, some at the very top of the range, others affordably cheaper. The restaurants are also excellent, if a little pricey, and you can eat in serious gourmet style or in rickety beachfront shacks on superb sand.

Antigua

Some smart hotels and some laid-back retreats for independent travellers. But Antigua also has a large package-tourism industry. It is fairly expensive, but is easy to reach and has some busy beaches with watersports as well as countless miles of undisturbed, superb sand. Antigua is known for its sailing, out of English Harbour and Falmouth Harbour in the south.

Aruba

Aruba has fantastic beaches, developed in very American style, with a string of high-rise hotels. Big names such as Holiday Inn and Hyatt Regency are continuing to build. Not the place for a quiet, off-beat holiday, it has international standards of comfort and is well organized with cabarets and casinos. Aruba is easily accessible from the USA (although it is more difficult from the UK).

The Bahamas

Nassau, Cable Beach and Paradise Island are the principal tourist resorts and cruise ship terminals. They are crowded and hardly relaxed (unless you are in one of the expensive private enclaves such as Lyford Cay). They have lively bars and good restaurants and everything you might want in the way of watersports. Most package holidays end up here.

Freeport/Lucaya is a purpose-built resort area with big hotels and some good beaches.

The **Family Islands** consist of hundreds of cays and sandbars. They are some of the least explored islands in the whole area—scattered with occasional hotels, each isolated on its own magnificent strip of sand. They have superb sailing, deep-sea fishing, bonefishing and scuba diving.

Barbados

Barbados is the gentleman of Caribbean tourism and is second home to a crowd of English sophisticates; it has some of the Caribbean's best-known hotels and restaurants along the west coast. The south coast offers a lower-key atmosphere with riotous nightlife. It boasts excellent beaches, and it is easily accessible. It caters well for all tastes, making it a good option for a first visit to the Caribbean. The Bajans are among the most charming people in the West Indies.

Barbuda

Attached to Antigua, tiny Barbuda is one of the least-known islands in the Caribbean. It has superb sand, a couple of outrageously expensive hotels and a lazy Caribbean life that has not changed in about fifty years.

Bequia

Bequia is a charming and pretty island in the Grenadines, well developed, with small hotels and restaurants along the waterfront around the main bay, and scattered in the small coves. It also has an airstrip.

Bonaire

A slumberstruck coral outcrop with little except excellent diving, Bonaire is an ideal quiet retreat. It has great diving lodges to stay in and a surprising string of good restaurants. The island is however developing fast.

The British Virgin Islands

The BVI are easygoing and pretty expensive islands with the feel of a sophisticated playground. There are good restaurants and bars on **Tortola** (the main island) and a nautical feel with all the passing yachts—the Virgin Islands have excellent sailing. Across Francis Drake Channel are the nearly deserted **Norman Island, Cooper Island** (nothing but a beach bar) and the second island, **Virgin Gorda**, with a string of excellent hotels and beaches. **Jost van Dyke** and **Anegada** are very low-key.

Carriacou

A classic, small island of Caribbean life in the Grenadines, Carriacou has superb beaches, ideal sailing and some hip bars.

The Cayman Islands

Grand Cayman is highly developed and fairly American in style—the hotels are big and modern. It is a well-organized rest-cure, easily accessible from the USA, with charming islanders and superb scuba-diving. The Caymanians are a charming people. **Cayman Brac** and particularly **Little Cayman** have a castaway island atmosphere, good small hotels and more excellent diving.

Cuba

Cuba is selling its tourism hard at the moment and building extensively. If you are prepared to be a dutiful package tourist, spending your time in the resorts and on packaged bus tours, then the island offers a typical Caribbean beach holiday. As an independent traveller's destination, Cuba can be frustrating but very rewarding.

Curaçao

Easily accessible and extremely cosmopolitan, Curaçao is the senior Dutch Caribbean island and has a string of good bars and restaurants and a lively crowd. The beaches are not brilliant, but there is good diving. The island has some nice, small hotels.

Dominica

Least developed and poorest of the Windwards, Dominica has a natural charm of its own. It has supreme natural life above and below the waterline—a rainforest with over 100 species of birds, whale-watching in season and excellent scuba. There are just a few golden-sand beaches and life is extremely low key.

The Dominican Republic

Spanish-speaking, the Dominican Republic is one of the largest Caribbean countries. It has a huge tourist industry (over 1 million visitors each year), but beyond the tourist ghettos are cool coastal towns on superb beaches and lively island life. It is also relatively cheap.

Grenada

Grenada has volcanic peaks and rainforests, fruit and spice plantations and easy-going islanders. It is less developed than St Lucia and has good beaches in the south of the island. It is easy to reach, with some good small hotels: a full range from luxury to budget. *See also* **Carriacou.**

The Grenadines

Strung between St Vincent and Grenada, the Grenadines boast fantastic sea, beaches and sailing; a good mix of attractive tourist islands—including island-enclaves of super-luxury—and accessible West Indian life. Island-hopping is possible. **Canouan** has fine anchorages and hidden coves; **Mayreau** is secluded with beaches on all sides; the **Tobago Cays** are uninhabited islets in paradise. **Union Island** is the local transit point for the Southern Grenadines. *See also* **Bequia, Carriacou, Mustique, Palm Island, Petit St Vincent** and **Young Island.**

Guadeloupe

Guadeloupe is a highly developed French island, with a large tourist industry, particularly Grande-Terre in the east (for the beaches). Less crowded, Basse-Terre has golden sand beaches in the north west, but also rainforest for walking. The charming offshore islands, **Marie Galante** and **La Désirade,** are very low key; **Terre de Haut** in **The Saints** is pretty and well developed.

Haiti

Haiti is hardly a typical tourist island, as politics prevent it. For the traveller, however, Haiti is quite simply one of the most compelling countries in the world, with its French and African influences, naïve art, markets, tap-taps and voodoo.

Jamaica

The largest of the former British Islands, Jamaica is easily accessible and has a full range of tourist hotels (super-luxury to friendly guest houses), good bars and restaurants. Beyond the coastal resorts, it has fascinating island life in music and a vibrant culture.

Martinique

Martinique is the most developed French Caribbean island. Martinicans are chic and their restaurants excellent—in town and in the resorts. The beaches are best in the south, where most of the tourist industry is concentrated.

Montserrat

Montserrat is a charming, slow and sedate island, held to ransom for the moment by its angry volcano, making it difficult to recommend.

Mustique

Mustique is best known as an exclusive holiday domain for the rich and famous. It is just a series of luxurious, privately owned villas, with one hotel, one beach bar and an airstrip.

Nevis

A gradually developing Leeward Island, just waking up from its slow and gentle, small-island life. It has just a few bars and restaurants, with some excellent beaches and several classic Caribbean plantation hotels.

Palm Island

An island-resort in the southern Grenadines, reached by boat, Palm Island is comprised of just a few villas, a beach and an easy life.

Petit St Vincent

An island-resort in the southern Grenadines, reached by boat or by helicopter, Petit St Vincent has just a few villas, where you communicate by flag and call room service to your beach-hammock.

Puerto Rico

The smallest of the Greater Antilles (but still a large island by Caribbean standards), Puerto Rico is a Spanish-speaking American territory (English is also spoken). It has a large tourist industry on the northern shore, with good bars and restaurants in San Juan, National Parks, mountains and rainforest. There are also delightful offshore islands: **Vieques** and **Culebra**.

Saba

Saba is a tiny outcrop with gentle, easy-going islanders. There is not much to do, but the diving is a good option. Development continues, but without beaches it is a quiet, reliable retreat.

Saint Barthélemy (St Barts)

St Barts is a champagne playground, as only the French could conceive. It has some charming hotels and fine restaurants, and is very expensive. There is barely any West Indian culture to distract you from the essentials of gourmet dining, sunning and posing.

St Kitts

The larger and marginally more developed partner of Nevis in the Leeward Islands, St Kitts has an easy-going West Indian atmosphere. Its beaches and the traditional Caribbean resort hotels are in the south; the north has some of the Caribbean's best plantation hotels.

St Lucia

The most developed of the volcanic Windwards, St Lucia has some very smart and comfortable hotels along its good beaches. It is lively in the main centres, but has some lovely and luxurious hideaways to stay in among the coves of the leeward coastline.

Saint Martin

Saint Martin is the larger and (marginally) less developed French half of the island shared with Dutch **Sint Maarten**. Quite expensive, it has good beaches, some smart hotels, a number of nice (if expensive) guest houses and excellent restaurants, all with a Gallic atmosphere.

St Vincent

St Vincent is an unspoilt, quite poor, English-speaking Windward Island; it has grand natural fertility and just a few comfortable, family-run hotels. It is a good starting point for a tour of the Grenadines.

Sint Eustatius

A tiny outcrop, whose heyday was really two centuries ago, Sint Eustatius is a very peaceful, writer's retreat.

Sint Maarten

Sint Maarten is the more developed (Dutch) half of an island shared with French **Saint Martin** with a large tourist industry. It has excellent beaches and good sports facilities, casinos and shops. There are also great restaurants (with an endless choice of others in the French half) and bars. It is strong on package tourism and too developed for some, but the locals swear by the island.

Tobago

Partnered with Trinidad, Tobago is a lovely, low-key tropical island. Tourism, which developed rapidly over the last few years, is concentrated in the southwest, but elsewhere idyllic spots are still to be found in isolated coves beneath the tumbling rainforests.

Trinidad

Trinidad is industrialized, crowded, and strong on culture—lively home to carnival, steel pan and calypso. Also spectacular natural life—over 400 species to be found in the rainforest and the coastal swamps. Some quiet coastal retreats in the east.

The Turks and Caicos Islands

At the southeastern limit of the Bahamas, the Turks and Caicos Islands lie in two groups. Providenciales is the most developed and most accessible; the rest are in varying states of undevelopment and are ideal for a lazy retreat. There are spectacular beaches throughout and the diving is superb.

The United States Virgin Islands

St Thomas is highly developed and easily reached from mainland USA. There are big hotels and endless shopping in Charlotte Amalie. The island gets crowded, but it has great restaurants and bars and is a good transit point. The island has recovered from Hurricane Marilyn. **St Croix** is larger and less developed, but still has some nice hotels and restaurants. **St John** is the least developed of the US Virgins—much of it is National Park. There are good bars and restaurants on the coasts. The island is also frequented by passing yachties.

Young Island

Young Island is a tiny, forested blip just a couple of hundred yards off St Vincent's southern coast. It has just one, charming West Indian hotel.

The Best of the Caribbean

Backchat: rude boy stands, Trinidad (any cricket International); Coronation market, Kingston, Jamaica.

Beaches

Beaches to sail to: Tobago Cays in the Grenadines; Stocking Island, off Great Exuma in the Bahamas; the cays off Jost van Dyke.

Isolated beach: Anse de la Roche, Carriacou.

Walking beaches: Seven-Mile Beach, Grand Cayman; Negril Beach, Jamaica; north coast of Providenciales, Turks and Caicos Islands.

Windsurfing beaches: Silver Sands, Barbados; Cabarete, north coast of the Dominican Republic.

Botanical gardens: St Vincent; Andromeda in Barbados; Jardins de Balata in Martinique.

Day's sail: Sir Francis Drake Passage, BVI.

Dive sites: Cayman walls; Turks and Caicos walls and caves; and Bonaire slopes; Saba.

Drinks: *bastidas* (fresh fruit milkshakes) in the Dominican Republic; Barbadian fruit punches.

Duty-free ports for shopping: Philipsburg, Sint Maarten; Charlotte Amalie, St Thomas, USVI.

Factories: Hacienda Buena Vista coffee factory, Puerto Rico and Mavis Bank, Jamaica; Nutmeg Cooperative, Gouyave, Grenada; cigar factories, Cuba; the salt flats of Bonaire; Curaçao Liqueur Factory, Curaçao; Appleton sugar and rum factory, Jamaica.

Forts: the Citadel in Haiti; Brimstone Hill in St Kitts; El Morro, Santiago de Cuba; El Morro, San Juan.

Great houses: Greenwood and Good Hope, Jamaica; Habitation Clement, Martinique.

Islands

Island-resorts: Petit St Vincent in the Grenadines and Peter Island, BVI (both for high luxury); Young Island off St Vincent (for its West Indian charm).

Islands to be marooned on: Jost van Dyke, BVI; Mayreau in the Grenadines (when the cruise ship's not in the bay).

Small but developed islands: Bequia, Grenadines; Terre de Haut, in the Saints off Guadeloupe; Harbour Island, Eleuthera, Bahamas.

Markets: Port au Prince, Haiti; St George's, Grenada; floating market, Willemstad, Curaçao.

Natural wonders: the evening flight of the scarlet ibis, Caroni Swamp, Trinindad; bio-luminescent bay, Vieques, Puerto Rico.

Picturesque ports: Admiralty Bay, Bequia, Grenadines; English Harbour, Antigua; Gustavia, St Barts; St George's Grenada; Hope Town, Abacos, Bahamas.

Plantation-house hotels: Rawlins Plantation, St Kitts (and others on St Kitts and Nevis); Hacienda Gripiñas, Puerto Rico; Caribbee Inn, Carriacou; Good Hope, and Strawberry Hill, Jamaica.

Rainforest retreats: Asa Wright Nature Centre, Trinidad; the whole island of Dominica; El Yunque rainforest, Puerto Rico.

Restaurants

Gourmet: Blanchard's, Anguilla; The Cliff, Barbados; Norma's, Montego Bay, Jamaica.

Local: Timberline, north coast, Trinidad; Casita Blanca, Puerto Rico; Bistro Nu, Saint Martin; Miss June's, Nevis; El Conuco, Santo Domingo, Dominican Republic.

Waterfront charm: Pisces, Barbados; Maya's, St Barts.

Secluded bay: Marigot bay, St Lucia.

Towns: Colonial Havana, Cuba; Old San Juan, Puerto Rico; St George's harbour, Grenada.

Views: from Firefly, Noel Coward's House in Jamaica; Sir Francis Drake Channel from Virgin Gorda, BVI; from Fort Charlotte, St Vincent, across the Grenadines; the Pitons, St Lucia.

West Indian fast food: Jamaican jerk centres; Store Bay, Tobago for crab and dumpling; Baxter's Road, Barbados (night only) for battered kingfish; Trinidad Breakfast Sheds for rice 'n' peas; Plaza Biejo, Willemstad, Curaçao for a *toetoe* or iguana soup.

Travel

humming bird's nest

The first thing to consider on your trip to the Caribbean is whether to travel independently or on a package. Most visitors from the UK and Europe do buy a 'package', although the word itself should be treated with a certain circumspection in relation to the Caribbean, which does not necessarily conform to the stereotypical image (a week-long nightmare of knobbly knee and wet T-shirt competitions). Caribbean packages can be exclusive, personally tailored and extremely expensive. Basically though, tour operators can put together the whole trip for you, including flights, airport transfers, accommodation for the duration of your stay and often a variety of meal plans and other optional extras. Their fee will be less than the rate you would pay if you were to arrange the whole thing yourself because they are able to block-buy aeroplane seats and hotel rooms at a discount and then pass some of the difference to the customer.

If you style yourself a traveller rather than a tourist, you might want to consider whether to travel independently, or possibly use the advantages of the package format by buying one at a knock-down price, staying at the hotel for a couple of nights, and then taking off independently. Independent travel offers much greater flexibility and possibilities for exploration and most importantly it enables you to reach places that most operators cannot offer (e.g. some charming hotels which are too small or too cheap to have arrangements with a tour operator).

In the USA packages are available from tour operators in the same way but there is a much larger market for independent travellers because there is much greater flexibility in the flights and because the cost is not discounted drastically, particularly if you are balancing the convenience of an extended weekend trip against the constraints of travelling on pre-organized charter schedules. A good travel agent should sort through the options for you.

Sourcing Information

The single most vital ingredient of any successful holiday is an informed choice. The Caribbean has amazing variety. Something, somewhere, will be just right for you. This book will provide leads, but there are many other sources of information and it is best to use them in combination. The best source is by word of mouth, of course, but if you are going to travel with a tour operator on the basis of details published in a brochure, do not be scared to ring them up (even if a travel agent is handling the actual booking for you). Of course they're only going to sell you the hotels in their brochure, but you'll soon discover their level of knowledge. Also look at newspapers and magazines. Increasingly there is information about the Caribbean available on the Internet: many hotels have home pages and some tourist boards have set up websites too. These are really brochures put to screen and provide no critical opinion. However, on the user groups you will occasionally be able to ask questions of somebody who knows the area. Treat information found in this way with a healthy scepticism.

Getting There

By Air

From the UK

The Caribbean is quite well served from the UK, both by scheduled and charter flights. The transatlantic flight takes 8 or 9 hours and so with the time change (chasing the sun around the earth) you usually arrive in good time to catch onward flights to almost all the Caribbean islands or just to settle down and watch the sunset. There is no reason to fly via the States unless you particularly want to. Fares are at their peak in the weeks around Christmas, and between July and September. This is slightly curious because it does not coincide with the Caribbean's own high season (the winter in the northern hemisphere), which runs from about mid-January to mid-April. The main hubs for travel from the UK are Jamaica, San Juan, Antigua, Barbados and Trinidad, but many other islands do have direct connections either on scheduled or charter services.

British Airways (✆ (0345) 222 111) has the widest range of services to the Caribbean from the UK, with direct flights to Antigua, Barbados, Grenada, St Lucia, San Juan in Puerto Rico, Jamaica, the Cayman Islands and Nassau in the Bahamas. Concorde flies to Barbados during the winter season, cutting the journey time nearly in half. All BA flights except Concorde depart from Gatwick (*see* individual island sections for regularity of service). **BWIA** (✆ (0181) 577 1100), the airline of Trinidad and Tobago, has a number of flights, departing London Heathrow for Port of Spain in Trinidad, sometimes touching Barbados, St Lucia and Antigua en route. From Port of Spain there are easy onward connections to Tobago and Guyana. **Air Jamaica** (✆ (0181) 570 7999) runs several weekly flights from London Heathrow to Kingston and Montego Bay.

Generally speaking, standard scheduled flights from the UK to the Caribbean are pretty expensive. Peak season **fares** (a scheduled economy return) cost between £800 and £1000 and in the low season they drop to between £700 and £800. Prices do not vary that much between the airlines and vary little according to your destination. These fares may require 7 days or 21 days' advance booking and sometimes have a minimum length of stay. There are also penalties for changing reservations. There are slightly more expensive fares available if you want a bit more flexibility. The trip on Concorde will set you back a cool £5500. Lower fares (than the official published rates above) are almost always on offer as the airlines sell off block-bookings of seats. Here it is a case of shopping around to get the deals; seats are subject to availability. Go through the travel agents mentioned below.

Charter airlines: Caledonian Airways, Thomson and Airtours also offer seats on a flight-only basis and these are probably your best bet for a cheap ticket, but there are very tight restrictions (usually one- or two-week returns are available, though sometimes you can pay a little extra for more time; they are also non-refundable, etc). Contact your travel agent, or the Caribbean travel specialists mentioned below. With luck and a bit of shopping around, you can find a return fare to the Caribbean for as little as £300.

UK travel agents specializing in flights to the Caribbean, on scheduled and charter airlines, include **The Caribbean Experience**, 70 Pembroke Road, London W8 6NX (✆ (0171) 602 4021), **Calypso Gold**, 1, Kingston Lane, Teddington, Middelesex TW11 9HL (✆ (0181) 741 8491), **Caribbean Travel**, 367 Portobello Road, London W10 5SG (✆ (0181) 969 6230), **Newmont Travel**, 85 Balls Pond Road, London N1 4BL (✆ (0171) 254 6546) and **Stoke Newington Travel**, 168 Stoke Newington Road, London N16 7UY (✆ (0171) 254 0136).

Beyond London (mainly in the areas that West Indians have settled), you will find local travel agents specializing in travel to the Caribbean. In Birmingham, contact **Diamond Travel**, 178 Dudley Rd, Edgbaston B18 7QX (✆ (0121) 454 6990). In Manchester try **Miss Eena's Travel**, 18 Upper Charlton Rd, Old Trafford, Manchester M16 7RN (✆ (0161) 232 9979). Some of these companies will also book (usually cheap) accommodation for you for your arrival.

There are two flights clubs in the UK. You join for a minimal fee and then are sent information about fares at considerable reductions (subject to the usual availability). BWIA's **Sunjet Reunion Club** can be contacted at Central House, Lampton Rd, Hounslow, Middlesex TW3 1HY (✆ (0181) 570 4446) and the **Reunion Club** run by tour operator Caribbean Connection can be reached at 93 Newman Street, London W1P 4DT (✆ (0171) 344 0101).

From Europe

Scheduled fares are expensive, but they can often be discounted. There is also a number of European charter operators which offer discounted fares.

Lufthansa (✆ (01803) 803 803) flies from Frankfurt to Antigua, San Juan (both twice weekly) and Port of Spain (weekly). **BWIA** (✆ (069) 962 16410) flies to Antigua, St Lucia, Barbados and Trinidad from Frankfurt in Germany. **Air France** (✆ (0802) 802 802) from Paris to Martinique, Guadeloupe and Sint Maarten. **AOM** (✆ (0149) 79 12 34) flies from Paris Orly to Martinique, Guadeloupe, St Maarten, Cuba and the Bahamas. **KLM** (✆ (0181) 750 9000) flies from Amsterdam to Aruba, Bonaire, Curaçao and St Maarten. **Maartinair** (✆ (020) 60 11 310) flies from Amsterdam weekly to Montego Bay in Jamaica, Barbados, Cuba, Puerto Rico and three times a week to the Dominican Republic. **Iberia** (✆ (902) 400 500), Spain's national airline, flies from Madrid to Spanish Caribbean countries, with flights to San Juan (Puerto Rico), Santo Domingo (the Dominican Republic) and Havana.

From the USA

American Airlines (✆ (1 800) 433 7300) have the most extensive service from the States to the Caribbean. They fly direct to all the Greater Antilles and to a selection of the smaller islands in the Eastern Caribbean, usually in time to catch onward flights. Many services originate in New York (JFK) or Miami (there are often two flights a day), or touch them en route. Increasingly, though, American Airlines have routed their flights via their Caribbean hub at San Juan in Puerto Rico, from where their subsidiary American Eagle has onward flights to the smaller islands. **Continental Airlines** (✆ (1 800) 525 0280) fly from Newark, New Jersey to Barbados, Antigua, the Virgin Islands, St Maarten, San Juan in Puerto Rico and Santo Domingo. **Delta** (✆ (1 800) 241 4141) flies regularly from Atlanta (with other services from Orlando) to Nassau, San Juan, St Thomas and St Croix (in the USVI), also Fort Lauderdale to Nassau. **US Air** (✆ (1 800) 428 4322) flies from a variety of cities on the east coast (Baltimore, Boston, Philadelphia, Charlotte) to Nassau, Grand Cayman, San Juan, St Thomas, St Croix and St Maarten.

Air Jamaica (✆ (1 800) 523 5585) has flights from a number of major cities around the US (Miami, New York, Newark, New Jersey, Baltimore, Philadelphia, Orlando and Fort Lauderdale) into Kingston and Montego Bay. They have recently added some flights out of New York to Antigua, St Lucia and Barbados. **ALM** fly from Miami and Atlanta to Jamaica, Haiti, Santo Domingo in the Dominican Republic, Havana in Cuba and their home base, the ABC islands off the South American coast (✆ (1 800) 327 7230). **Air Aruba** (✆ (1 800) 882 7822) flies from Newark, Baltimore and Miami to Aruba with onward flights to Curaçao and Bonaire. **BWIA** (✆ (1 800) 538 2942) runs flights from New York and Miami to Port of Spain in Trinidad, some of them touching Antigua, St Lucia and Barbados en route.

Viasa, the Venezuelan national carrier, makes some stops in the Caribbean as it flies south to Caracas. Santo Domingo in the Dominican Republic is well served from Central and South American countries, but otherwise connections can be made in Miami.

Fares from the USA vary little from one carrier to another. The seasons are strictly observed: mid-December–mid-April is high season, late June–mid-September is the summer peak, and the rest of the year is low season. Sample scheduled single fares from Miami to Jamaica are $250 and to Antigua $400, from New York to Jamaica $350 and to Antigua $450 in low season. From the Midwest add around $100, from the West Coast $200. These fares require advance booking and there is usually a minimum stay of a week; supplements are payable for weekend travel and cancellations. Charter flights are also available through travel agents and this may mean as much as a third off the scheduled price. Check the newspapers and your travel agent.

From Canada

Air Canada (✆ (1 800) 268 7240) flies direct, usually out of Toronto but occasionally touching Montreal, to a number of destinations in the Caribbean, including Jamaica (Montego Bay and Kingston), Antigua, Guadeloupe, St Lucia, Barbados, Port of Spain in Trinidad and Nassau in the Bahamas. Another alternative is to connect with American or Caribbean carriers in New York or Miami. **BWIA** (✆ (905) 676 8382) also fly from Toronto in Canada to Port of Spain, stopping over in Antigua and Barbados. Once again, there are plenty of charter flights from Canada servicing the vacation packages.

Further details on flights to and between the islands are listed under 'Getting There' in each island directory.

By Sea

A popular way of travelling around the Caribbean is by cruise liner, which enables you to visit as many as four or five different islands in a week, without the hassle of delayed flights or even packing your suitcase. Most depart from Miami or Fort Lauderdale and a few are based in San Juan, Puerto Rico. They sail all year round.

The best place to start is in a travel agent, where you can find brochures. Cruise-ship companies include: **Celebrity Cruises** (UK ✆ (0171) 412 0290, ✆ 412 0908, USA toll free ✆ (1 800) 437 3111), **Cunard** (UK ✆ (0171) 839 1414, ✆ 839 1837, USA toll free ✆ (1 800) 221 4770), **Norwegian Cruise Lines** (UK ✆ (0990) 906 060, ✆ (0171) 938 4515, UK (0800) 181560, USA toll free ✆ (1 800) 327 7030).

The possibilities of independent travel to the Caribbean by sea are more limited and may not be convenient anyway because of the time involved. However, many cargo ships make the crossing to the Caribbean and Central and South America and some of them do take passengers. An agency with details of a large number of ships, some of them banana boats, to the Caribbean is **The Cruise People** at 88 York St, London W1H 1DP (✆ (0171) 723 2450, ✆ 723 2486, cruise@dial.pipex.com, http://members.aol.com\cruiseaz\freighters.htm). Passages are quite expensive; reckon on around £1000 each way. It no longer seems possible to work a passage out to the islands, even swabbing the decks, unless you have a merchant marine card.

A large number of yachts make the Atlantic crossing to the Caribbean towards the end of the year (after spending the summer in the Mediterranean), arriving in time for the winter sailing season. You might be able to pick up a yacht on the south coast of Britain, in the south of France, in Gibraltar, or even in the Canaries any time from September (just after the hurricane season). Try the yacht club noticeboards and yachting magazines. The **Cruising Association**, CA House, 1 Northey Street, Lime House Basin, London E14 8BT (✆ (0171) 537 2828, *www.cruising.org.uk*), has a crewing service, connecting skippers and crew in a monthly newsletter (£20 to have your name on the list). You negotiate from there with the skipper.

Experience is not necessarily required. Most yachts will charge you just enough to cover food or nothing at all, but there are one or two sharks around who have been making outrageous charges for what can be quite a hard three-week sail. If you are worried about the crossing, catamarans are more comfortable. The return journey eastwards across the Atlantic generally takes place at the end of April, fairly soon after Antigua Race week, and the ports of Antigua are the best places to look.

In the same way the American yachting community migrates down to the Caribbean over the winter. Once again, try yacht club noticeboards, the yachting magazines and the ports on the eastern seaboard.

Entry Requirements and Customs

As a British citizen you do not need a visa to any of the Commonwealth Caribbean countries or the French or Netherlands Antilles or to the Dominican Republic or Haiti. To enter Cuba you must have a tourist card (£10). Americans and Canadians travelling as tourists do not need a visa to enter any Caribbean country, but they must buy a tourist card when entering the Dominican Republic (US$15), and Cuba (US$10). Citizens of other countries do not usually need a visa, except sometimes for Puerto Rico and the US Virgin Islands (same regulations as USA). In most of the Caribbean islands, proof of identity is enough, though a passport is the best document for Europeans. Business visitors should consult the embassy before departure.

The Caribbean may be known for being laid back. Their immigration authorities, however, are most definitely not so. Invariably they will demand to see an onward ticket and they will hold your passport until you produce one. Some islands may require proof of funds. On the immigration form you will also be asked to give a local address: this is almost a formality as they rarely check up, but it eases entry to put something down. Addresses of hotels and guest houses are in each separate island chapter.

It is worth remembering to keep some change for when you leave, because most countries levy a **departure tax**, usually payable in US dollars, but sometimes demanded in local currency (listed in the separate island sections).

Drugs not issued on prescription are illegal in the Caribbean and people do occasionally end up inside for possession of user quantities. Customs officials operate a strict policy against them and they search bags going in and out of the countries. While on an island you will probably be approached by 'oregano salesman' with an offer of marijuana (weed, ganja etc.) and occasionally cocaine. You will not be popular if you are caught. Alcohol and tobacco allowances vary from island to island.

Specialist Caribbean Tour Operators

Most holidays to the Caribbean are sold as packages, and with these you can get anything from a two-week, two-destination package at two different luxury resorts at opposite ends of the Caribbean Sea with transatlantic legs on Concorde, through the proliferation of wedding and honeymoon packages (complete with nuptial underwear if you want), to the charter holidays that take advantage of the low-season rates and give you a return flight and two weeks' accommodation for less than the price of a normal scheduled return airfare. Many of the tour companies include obligatory **insurance** in their packages, but travel agents will always sell you a policy. Check your existing policies—it is worth insuring against medical problems, cancelled flights and lost luggage.

Tour Operators in the UK

There is a number of specialist Caribbean tour operators working at the top of the market in the UK. They can be a little more expensive, but their sales staff know the hotels better than those in the larger, worldwide companies and they are more flexible when it comes to tailor-making holidays around the islands. It is possible to deal directly with them without the need to go through a travel agent.

Caribbean Connection, Concorde House, Forest Street, Chester CH1 1QR (✆ (01244) 341131, ✆ 310255, brochure line ✆ (01244) 329556). A wide-ranging selection of hotels in most of the Caribbean islands at a range of prices, including all-inclusives (special brochure), some villas and some special-interest trips including test matches.

Elegant Resorts, The Old Palace, Chester CH1 1RB (✆ (01244) 329671, ✆ 341084). Top-of-the-range packages to most of the Caribbean's smartest hotels, three brochures (general, villas and yachts).

Caribtours, 161 Fulham Road, London SW3 6SN (✆ (0171) 581 3517, ✆ 225 2491). A small and friendly operator with a broad range of prices, including some all-inclusives.

Harlequin Worldwide Travel, 2 North Rd, South Ockendon, Essex RM15 6QJ (✆ (01708) 852780, ✆ 854952, *harlequin@harlequin-holidays.co.uk, www.harlequin-holidays. co.uk*). The broadest selection offered by UK companies; all the top-of-the-range hotels but also some off-beat gems; specialist brochures for villas and eco/nature holidays.

Caribbean Expressions, 13 McCrone Mews, Belsize Lane, London NW3 5BG (✆ (0171) 431 2131, ✆ 431 4221). A newcomer with a small selection of top hotels on offer.

Powder Byrne, 4 Alice Court, 116 Putney Bridge Rd, London SW15 2NQ (✆ (0181) 871 3300, ✆ 871 3322). Their Hideaways programme has a small selection of hotels at the top of the market.

The Owners' Syndicate, 79 Balham Park Rd, London SW12 8EB (✆ (0181) 767 7926, ✆ 767 5328). Originally a villa company which has expanded to include a number of carefully selected hotels, which tend to be small and charming and often do not feature in larger companies' brochures.

Carib Inns

Some of the smaller hotels (too small to deal with the large tour operators) have recently banded together to form the Carib Inns, to help them with marketing to the UK. For information and bookings, contact: **Unique Hotels** (✆ (0800) 317185). Also **Valigo**, 10 The Wharf, Bridge St, Birmingham B1 2JS (✆ (01706) 212333, (0121) 683 0050, ✆ (01706) 831420), and **Thomas Cook** (✆ (01733) 330300, reservations (01733) 332255), address below.

If you wish to spend even less, some Caribbean specialist travel agents can book hotels at the cheaper end of the range: **Caribbean Experience**, 70 Pembroke Road, London W8 6NX (✆ (0171) 602 4021, ✆ 603 6101), offer transatlantic flights and bookings in a number of smaller and more off-beat Caribbean hotels. The **Caribbean Centre** (✆ (0181) 940 3399, ✆ 940 7424, *jan@caribean.itsnet.com*) will also book hotels for you with good savings, either for a full two-week period or for a (minimum) three-day stay before you set off travelling; also some private homes. Also see the flight specialists above, some of whom have connections to island hotels.

Other, more general tour operators, who often offer the same hotels at a slightly less expensive rate, but do not usually give the same level of service, include:

British Airways Holidays, Astral Towers, Betts Way, London Rd, Crawley RH10 2XA (✆ (01293) 723 161, ✆ 722 624). A broad selection of upper range hotels (in their Premium Collection) and some mid-range ones (in their Worldwide brochure) including a number of all-inclusives.

Calypso Gold, 178b High Street, Teddington, Middx, TW11 8HU, ✆ (0181) 977 9655, ✆ 977 9225. Tailor-made breaks including cricket holidays.

Thomas Cook Holidays, PO Box 36, Thorpe Wood, Peterborough, Cambridgeshire PE3 6SB (✆ (01733) 332255, ✆ 505784). Mid- and upper-range hotels around the islands.

Silk Cut Faraway Holidays, Meon House, Petersfield, Hants GU32 3JN (✆ (01730) 265211, ✆ 230398). Concentrate on small hotels, some top of the range, others less expensive.

Kuoni, Kuoni House, Dorking, Surrey RH5 4AZ (✆ (01306) 742222). A broad selection of mid-range and some more expensive properties in a good selection of islands.

If your main desire is to get to the West Indies for as little money as possible, you can travel with one of the charter package companies and the best prices are in summer. Some of the cheapest are offered by **Airtours** at Wavell House, Holcombe Road, Helmshore, Rossendale, Lancs BB4 4NB (✆ (01706) 260000), and **Thomson Holidays** (brochure line ✆ (01509) 238 238, reservations ✆ (0990) 502 399, ✆ (0121) 236 7030), who reach most of the major Caribbean islands, departing Heathrow, Gatwick and Manchester.

Villas

Many of the specialist tour operators have villa programmes, but there are also villa specialists. As a rule you can expect daily maid-service in the package and services to stock the villa with food and leave flowers for your arrival. Most companies will offer car hire, but it is worth noting that often you will usually have to arrange your own flights (*see* above). It is also possible to contact villa companies in the islands direct (*see* under separate island).

The Owners' Syndicate. A broad range of villas around the islands (*see* above).

Caribbean Chapters, 102 St John's Wood Terrace, London NW8 6PL (✆ (0171) 722 9560, ✆ 722 9140, *info@villa-rentals.com, www.villa-rentals.com/*). Luxury villas throughout the Caribbean, most with pools and usually staffed.

Exclusive Villas (✆ (0181) 947 7300, ✆ 947 9712). Luxury staffed villas in Barbados, Mustique and St Lucia; will arrange car hire and flights.

Palmer and Parker Holidays, The Beacon, Penn, Buckinghamshire HP10 8ND (✆ (01494) 81411, ✆ 814184). Work exclusively to large (minimum four-bedroom) villas in Barbados, Jamaica and St Lucia.

special-interest holidays

Honeymoon packages (with wedding included if you want) get ever more popular and most of the tour operators above will arrange one for you.

In general specialist-interest holidays are not arranged through the regular tour operators, but there are some smaller operators in contact with outfits in the Caribbean itself who will put together something for you. You can arrange **scuba diving** through the **Barefoot Traveller** at

204 King St, London W6 0RA (✆ (0181) 741 4319, ✉ 741 8657) in the islands of Tobago, St Vincent, Dominica, Cayman, Bonaire and the Bahamas and some birdwatching holidays in Trinidad and Tobago; or **Hayes and Jarvis**, Hayes House, 152 King St, London W6 0QU, (✆ (0181) 748 5050, diving dept ✆ 222 7840, ✉ 741 0299), who cover Grenada, St Kitts, Tobago, Antigua, Barbados, the Cayman Islands, Cuba and more, and who also do non-diving Caribbean trips. **Broadway Music Tours**, 1 Chapel Court, Holly Walk, Leamington Spa CV32 4YS (✆ (01926) 332266, ✉ 831578), has packages to the annual music cruise on the SS *Norway* in October or November and will arrange tailor-made tours to festivals around the islands, for instance the St Lucia Jazz Festival held each year in May. When the England **cricket** team tours the West Indies there are a number of companies offering tours, often with former players as guides. Contact the tourist boards of the islands you wish to visit.

A wide range of **sailing** holidays are available. Here there are basically two options: 'crewed yachts', in which there is a captain and usually a crew, even wall-to-wall flunkies in white shorts who communicate by whistle if that's what you want, and 'bareboats', in which you look after yourself (though it is possible to have the yacht provisioned and if you are not too confident you can have a skipper for a couple of days to get you started). For a bareboat you can contact the big charter companies direct or go through the major UK tour operators above, any of whom will put together a complete package, including flights, yacht and possibly time ashore. Contact **The Moorings**, Middle Wall, Bradstowe House, Whitstable, Kent CT5 1BF (✆ (01227) 776677, ✉ 776670) or **Sunsail**, The Port House, Port Solent, Portsmouth, Hants PO6 4TH (✆ (01705) 219847, ✉ 219827, *sales@sunsail.com*, *www.sunsail.com*).

Booking a crewed yacht is a little more complicated, because they are usually handled by brokers, who have the details of a number of yachts and their crews around the islands on their books. These brokers usually leave you to arrange your own flights, but offer a personal service direct often to owner-operated charter yachts. Crewed yachts are available through **Yacht Connections**, The Hames, Church Road, South Ascot, Berks SL5 9DP (✆ (01344) 624987, ✉ 626849) and **Tenrag**, Tenrag House, Wingham, Canterbury, Kent CT3 1AR (✆ (01227) 721874, ✉ 721617). If the only answer is a huge gin palace, then a small selection of luxurious yachts is available through **Camper and Nicholsons**, 25 Bruton St, London W1X 7DB (✆ (0171) 491 2950, ✉ 629 2068, *info@lon.cnyachts.com*).

Tour Operators in the USA

Many Caribbean hotels have a booking agent in the United States or a dedicated reservation number, so you may choose to arrange your bookings direct and fix your own transport through your travel agent. Tour operators working out of the USA include **Caribbean Concepts**, 575 Underhill Boulevard, Syosset, NY 11791 (✆ (516) 496 9800, ✉ 496 9880, toll free ✆ (1 800) 423 4433), a small operator catering to the upper end of the market, who will arrange flights, car hire and hotel accommodation; **Aiken Tours** 1661 Norstrand Ave, 2nd Floor, Brooklyn, New York, NY 11226 (✆ (718) 856 7711, ✉ 282 1152, toll free ✆ (1 800) 224 6222); **French Caribbean International**, 5662 Calle Real, Suite 333, Santa Barbara, CA 93117–2317 (✆/✉ (805) 967 9850, US and Canada toll free ✆ (1 800) 322 2223, *fci@frenchcaribbean.com*, *www.frenchcaribbean.com*), specialists in the French Caribbean islands as the name suggests, who arrange mostly accommodation in hotels and villas, but not usually flights; and **Fling Vacations**, 999 Postal Road, Allentown PA 18103 (✆ (215) 266 6110, ✉ 266 0280, toll free ✆ (1 800) 523 9624). Big Caribbean operators include **American Express Vacations** (toll free ✆ (1 800) 241 1700), **GoGo Tours**, with offices all over the country (head office ✆ (201) 934 3500 or toll free in New York City ✆ (1 800) 526 0405) and **Travel Impressions** (toll free ✆ (1 800) 284 0044).

Bahama Out Islands Promotion Board, 1100 Lee Wagener Boulevard, Suite 204, Ft Lauderdale, Florida 33315-3564, ✆ (954) 359 8099, 📠 359 8098 toll free ✆ (1 800) 688 4752, unifies 74 hotels in the islands and can help to match you to your ideal locatuion.

special-interest holidays

Most tour companies will arrange a **honeymoon** for you in the Caribbean. **Caligo Ventures** at 156 Bedford Road, Armonk NY 10504 (✆ (914) 273 6333, 📠 273 6370, *margaret@ caligo.com, www.caligo.com*), arrange birding trips and natural history tours of Trinidad and Tobago centred on the Asa Wright Nature Centre. **The Moorings** can be reached toll free at (✆ (1 800) 437 7880). **Sunsail**, Landing Marina, 908 Awald Rd, Annapolis, MD 21403 (✆ (410) 280 2553, 📠 280 2406, toll free ✆ (1 800) 327 2276, *sunsailusa@sunsail.com, website: www.sunsail.com*, arrange yacht charter through their fleets around the Caribbean. **Camper and Nicholsons'** US address is 450 Royal Palm Way, Palm Beach, Florida 33480 (✆ (561) 655 2121, 📠 655 2202, *info@pal.cnyachts.com*).

Getting Around

Island-hopping is one of the great pleasures of a Caribbean holiday and the Lesser Antilles particularly has a grand variety of islands within a relatively short distance of one another. In the chain of the Eastern Caribbean islands (which are visible one from the next for the 500 miles from Grenada in the south to Anguilla in the north), 20 minutes' flying can get you from a French overseas *département* or a Spanish-speaking island to independent islands that have a strong British heritage, from busy, developed countries to tiny, comatose blips with just a few shacks and palm trees.

Most of the big Caribbean tour operators will arrange an island-hopping itinerary for you, with flights between hotels. If you wish to travel more independently (and less expensively) you can take off on your own with one of the island-hopper tickets issued by the local Caribbean airlines (*see* below). The specialist Caribbean travel agent **Caribbean Experience** (✆ (0171) 602 4021, address above) is the most knowledgeable agent in the UK and they will make suggestions and book itineraries for you. If you do not want to arrange an actual island-hopping itinerary, it is perfectly possible to make short day or weekend tours (some by sailboat, others by plane, bookable on the islands themselves with local tour operators) to the islands near to the one on which you are staying. Barbados, St Lucia and Martinique offer many trips to the Grenadines and there are endless trips to the islands around Sint Maarten— Saba, Statia, St Barts and Anguilla. Travel is very easy from the USVI to the BVI and vice-versa. Cuba has also opened up for weekend hops to and from the surrounding islands: Jamaica, the Bahamas and the Cayman Islands.

By Air

Most island-hopping nowadays is by **aeroplane** (often Twin Otters or Islanders and increasingly DASH 8s). Some of these planes, the smaller ones at least, do look a bit like coffins with wings on and when they take off they have so much lift that it feels almost alarming, but they are very safe and reliable. The pilot will position the plane at the start of the runway and run the engines hard until the control panel becomes a blur and the plane thrums like an outsized tuning fork. Then he lets off the brakes and puts the props in drive. Flight can be a bit of a novelty (some people actually pay for rides like this in the funfairs). Planes this size tend to bounce off clouds—there are vertical streams of air within them which will leave your stomach a hundred feet above you in a matter of a second or so. If you do come across a penetrable cloud, you might find it coming through the overhead blowers. In calmer moments the views of the islands and the sea from 3000ft are fantastic.

Island-hopper planes are affectionately known as the islands' bus service. They tend to run along the island-chain and will simply miss out a destination if nobody wants to get on or off. The main centres for travel around the Eastern Caribbean are San Juan in Puerto Rico, Sint Maarten, Antigua and islands down to Trinidad. Generally, island-hopping by plane is a good and reliable way of travelling. A couple of words of warning, however. Booking can be a little haphazard. Planes are sometimes oversold, and those booked in advance may well leave half-empty. Travelling standby often works. And it is worth reconfirming obsessively. If you miss one flight you may find that the whole of the rest of the itinerary is cancelled. A dose of judicious anger in the airline office sometimes helps you get what you want. Most airlines are usually quite amenable when it comes to excess luggage, except when the plane is full.

The biggest carrier in the Eastern Caribbean is **LIAT** (officially this is Leeward Islands Air Transport, but the number of acronyms it has gives an idea of how fondly it is thought of: 'Leave Island Any Time', 'Likeable Interested Attentive Tolerant', 'Lost in Air Transit', 'Luggage in Another Town', 'Likely to Irritate Another Tourist' and 'Lord It's Awful Transportation'!). Many LIAT flights originate in Antigua and they fly as far south (usually at least two a day) as Barbados and Port of Spain, Trinidad, and to Puerto Rico in the north (with some flights to Santiago in the Dominican Republic). There is also a link from St Lucia to Caracas. LIAT has three hopper tickets which are ideal for people travelling around the Caribbean. The *Super Caribbean Explorer* ticket allows you unlimited stops in one direction (though you are permitted to return to a destination to make a connection) for a period of a month, with return to point of origin, price US$449. The *Caribbean Explorer* lasts for a 21-day period and allows three stops (none repeated except for connections), with return to point of origin, price US$249. The *Eastern Caribbean Airpass* allows stops in between three and six LIAT destinations over a 21-day period, each leg being charged at US$80. There are some restrictions. Super Explorer tickets may be bought in the Caribbean, but the other two must be bought before departure from your country of residence, in conjunction with a ticket to the Caribbean (any carrier will do, despite what some airlines assure you).

BWIA (pronounced Beewee), the Trinidad and Tobago airline, has the *Intra-Caribbean Airpass* which allows you one stop at any BWIA destination in the Caribbean; connections are allowed (maximum stay 24 hours) over a 30-day period, with return to the original point of departure, price US$356. This is particularly interesting because it includes Jamaica, which is not covered by LIAT. Other BWIA destinations are Antigua, Barbados, Grenada, Guyana, Trinidad and Tobago. **Air Jamaica** has also recently introduced some hopper fares from its hub in Jamaica. **ALM** (the airline of the Netherlands Antilles) also has a number of hopper tickets: the *ABC Pass*, which enables you to fly between Aruba, Bonaire and Curaçao, three coupons US$135; the *Sint Maarten Pass*, which includes the return flight to Sint Maarten as well, five coupons US$249; and the *ALM System Pass*, which enables you to fly to all ALM destinations (only one stop on the mainland USA), eight coupons US$695. Some tickets must be issued in conjunction with transatlantic tickets or before leaving the USA.

Many islands have their own, individual airline. **Air Martinique** (local ✆ (596) 51 11 11, ☏ 63 61 75) flies south from Martinique to Barbados and to St Lucia, St Vincent and several of the Grenadine islands. **Air Guadeloupe** (✆ (590) 82 47 00) radiates north and south from Guadeloupe, flying south to Dominica and north to Antigua and Sint Maarten. **Winair** (✆ 599 552002), the airline of the Dutch Windward Islands, is based in Sint Maarten and flies to all the neighbouring islands.

There are plenty of smaller airlines, usually linking a smaller island to the nearby hub for international flights. **Mustique Airways** (UK ✆ (01453) 835801, ☏ 835525, local ✆ (809) 458 4380, ☏ 456 4586) connects Barbados and the Grenadines. Many airlines link the British Virgin Islands to the US Virgin Islands and to San Juan, Puerto Rico, also the French islands of St Barts and St Martin to Guadeloupe and San Juan. For details, *see* the separate islands.

The last option is to **charter** a small plane, which can work out at a good price if there are enough of you. All Caribbean airports have a charter company (five-seaters, nine-seaters and sometimes helicopters) on call (*see* the separate island directories).

The Caribbean also has some pretty hairy airstrips. Some are very short—you will know about this just after landing when the whole plane shudders because the pilot applies reverse thrust. Others are hairy because there is an obstacle course on approach to landing. At St Barthélemy near Sint Maarten, there are two approaches: from the sea (marginally preferable) where you get a close inspection of some second-degree jungle and the local cemetery just before you land; and over land, for which the traffic stops on the road in case the plane's wheel takes off a driver's hat (and for the view of the planes landing of course). But the most spectacular of them all is the strip on Saba, just 400 yards long (shorter than any self-respecting aircraft carrier) and with a 100ft drop at either end. Taking off is exciting; landing has a stress quotient. People say: 'they only use half the runway'. Just pray that it is the first half.

By Sea

Until 30 years ago all the islands of the Caribbean were linked by elegant old sloops and schooners once or twice a week. These have mostly gone now, but it is still sometimes possible to hitch a ride on the **freighters** which bring provisions and manufactured goods into the islands. Go to the dock and ask around and they might sign you on as 'crew'. There is a regular service out of Barbados to St Vincent, Trinidad and South America. If you are travelling between Grenada and Trinidad, you might be able get a lift on one of the magnificent sloops that tie up in St George's harbour, Grenada. Boats from the Grenadines go as far north as Sint Maarten, though they won't necessarily stop at other islands en route.

Ferries connect all the Virgin Islands; Grenada, the Grenadines and St Vincent; the French island of Guadeloupe to Martinique (via Dominica) with the occasional onward trip to St Lucia; the Guadeloupean mainland to all its small offshore islands; and some of the islands around Sint Maarten (*see* separate island sections). Another possibility is to travel by hitching a ride on a **yacht**, which you can catch at the main centres (BVI, USVI, Sint Maarten, Antigua, Guadeloupe, Martinique, St Lucia and some of the Grenadines). If you go down to the marina and ask around, you may come up with something: the crews are often happy to take along the occasional passenger who is prepared to help out.

By Road

For details of car hire, public transport, taxis, etc., *see* 'Getting Around' at the beginning of each island section.

Practical A–Z

Beaches

If the 20th century's ultimate quest is the finest sun-drenched, palm-fringed curve of satin-soft, ankle-deep sand, washed by warm waves, gin-clear shadows and set in an aquamarine sea, all of course with a perfect sunset view, then the Caribbean offers happy hunting grounds. The best sand tends to be on the low-lying islands like the Bahamas and the Leeward and Grenadine Islands, which because of their coral base have the bright white sand, but you will also find magnificent, often secluded coves tucked between the vast headlands of the mountainous islands in the Eastern Caribbean and the Greater Antilles. Swimming is safe in most places, but do not swim alone, and beware the undertow on the Atlantic side of the Lesser Antilles.

If all you want from the Caribbean on your holiday is a beach, then the best islands for being alone on uninterrupted miles of sand are Anguilla, Antigua and Barbuda, the Family Islands in the Bahamas and the Caicos Islands in the Turks and Caicos. A bit better known, and often more crowded, are the British Virgin Islands, Barbados and the Grenadines. As a general rule, beaches in the Caribbean are usually public up to the high water mark (basically the top of the sand) and so, as long as there is access (which there may not be, though you can always swim in of course), you are permitted onto them, though the facilities will usually be limited to hotel guests. This means that there are not that many 'public beaches', but some islands do have a system of lifeguards and rangers. Most islands will have at least one popular beach which is known for its watersports and activity.

You should note that not every Caribbean hotel is set on a picture-postcard beach, particularly at the lower end of the price range, and that not every beach is necessarily that nice. If the most important ingredient of your holiday is the beach, you should ensure that it is good enough by quizzing the tour operator on its nature and facilities. Most hotels of any size will have some watersports, but again this is not necessarily the case. If in doubt, find out. For more information, *see* 'Beaches' in the individual island sections.

Bookshops

In the UK, the following London shops have a wide selection of travel books with special sections for the Caribbean:

Daunt's bookshop at 83 Marylebone High Street, London W1M 4DE (✆ (0171) 224 2295). They will send you a reading list.

The Travel Bookshop at 13 Blenheim Crescent, London W11 2EE (✆ (0171) 229 5260).

Stanfords at 12–14 Longacre, London WC2E 9LP (✆ (0171) 836 1321). This is also a specialist map shop.

Nomad Books, 781 Fulham Road, London SW6 5HA, ✆ (0171) 736 4000.

In the USA, try:

Book Passage, 51 Tamal Vista Blvd, Corte Madre, CA 94925 (✆ (415) 927 0960, ✉ 924 3838, toll free ✆ (1 800) 999 7909).

Rand McNally, 150 East 52nd Street, New York, NY 10022 (✆ (212) 758 7488).

Rand McNally Map Travel, 444 North Michigan Avenue, Chicago, IL 60611 (✆ (312) 321 1751).

The Complete Traveller, 199 Madison Avenue, New York, NY 10016 (✆ (212) 685 9007).
Traveller's Bookstore, 22 West 52nd Street, New York, NY 10019 (✆ (212) 664 0995).

Calendar of Events

The biggest festivals in the Caribbean are the various carnivals. These are usually held just before Lent (Dimanche, Lundi and Mardi Gras and in some islands *Mercredi des Cendres* or Ash Wednesday), but are sometimes staged in the summer at the end of the sugar harvest, usually in late July or early August (called *Cropover* in Barbados and the *zafra* in Cuba). The summer months are a popular time of year for festivities anyway (the West Indians think the weather is warmer then): there are many official celebrations and general blow-outs in the British islands (around Emancipation Day, 1 August) and religious festivals in the Catholic islands (the *fiestas patronales* of Martinique and Guadeloupe, Puerto Rico, the Dominican Republic and Haiti). Many islands have slightly more formal events commemorating Independence days and National Memorials (even military parades in some islands).

As you would expect in the Caribbean there are many other less formal get-togethers (many of them staged in order to increase numbers of tourists at the low point in the season) and these are centred around music—calypso, steel pan, merengue, reggae and most recently jazz (*see* below)—and around sports, particularly centred around the sea, with local and open sailing regattas and fishing competitions and latterly a few more conventional events: tennis and golf competitions sponsored by big international companies, and some triathlons and some cycling competitions. Finally, there are some island cultural events, from dance in Jamaica and story-telling in St Lucia and Dominica to Indian festivals in Trinidad and gastronomic blowouts in the French islands.

Whatever the official reason for the celebration, almost all Caribbean festivals are also an excuse for an organized party and so they invariably involve a *jump-up* (more Caribbean dancing) which will spontaneously appear in the streets or in a field or on the beach. It is often a bit like an oversized picnic, with cook-ups on the sidelines, where a half oil-barrel is turned on its side to make a brazier. Here chicken and fish are barbecued and then sprinkled with hot pepper sauce and soldier crabs are roasted in their shells.

The summer months are the best if you want to see the West Indians at play and there is a number of festivals in June, July and August. Things also get booked up then. Generally speaking you will have no problem joining in the festivities in any Caribbean event: you will find that the islanders make you welcome.

January

At **New Year** singers and musicians known as *Dande* stroll chanting from house to house on Aruba, and in Curacao there is a *tumba* music festival. The end of Christmas is celebrated on 6 January in Puerto Rico and the Dominican Republic as **Three Kings' Day**, and with gastronomic flair in Martinique as **La Fête des Rois**. St Croix's Crucian Christmas Festival culminates in early January with carnival-like parades: later in the month they hold a rhythm and blues festival. Grenada holds a fishing tournament and a sailing regatta and there are windsurfing competitions in Barbados and the Dominican Republic. Early in the month there is a **Maroon** festival in Jamaica, commemorating events from the 18th century, and then there is a thoroughly modern sprint-triathlon in Negril. St Barts holds a Music Festival and Barbados a jazz festival, **'Paint it Jazz'**, with international musicians.

January also sees the culmination of the St Kitts Carnival and the start of the Bahamas **junkanoo** celebrations, with street parades quite similar to the carnival masquerades. But most of the pre-Lenten **Carnivals** are just warming up, with weekend fêtes and the early stages of calypso and carnival king and queen competitions.

February

Grenada holds its **Independence Day** celebrations on 7 February, with *jump-ups*, followed by St Lucia on 22 February and the Dominican Republic on 27 February, where there are national parades interspersed among days of carnival activity. The Holetown Festival in Barbados commemorates the first settlement of the island in 1627. There is a **jazz festival** in Havana in February or March.

Most Caribbean **Carnivals** culminate in February, in a three-day *jump-up*, with calypso and steel band competitions and masked parades in the streets on Shrove Tuesday (Mardi Gras) or Ash Wednesday: Aruba, Bonaire, Carriacou, Curaçao, Dominica, Dominican Republic (on the weekend closest to 27 February), Guadeloupe, Haiti, Martinique, St Lucia, Saint Barthélemy, Saint Martin, Tobago and of course Trinidad.

March

Montserrat celebrates **St Patrick's Day** on 17 March and in Trinidad **Phagwah** sees street parades in which people spray each other with bright red dye. Late in the month there is a yachting competition in St Thomas and then at the end of the month, on 30 March, the USVI commemorate the anniversary day of the islands' transfer to American ownership.

April

The Netherlands Antilles commemorate Queen Beatrix's official birthday with parties on 30 April and there are also celebrations for **Easter**, including a **Fish Festival** in Oistins Town on Barbados and **goat and crab races** in Tobago (yes, men and women with goats on leads). Easter sees kite-flying all over the Caribbean: more formal events include **Food Festivals** in Martinique and St Barts, a three-day **Easter Opera Season** in Barbados and carnivals in St Thomas and Jamaica, where you can also see the Jamaican National Theatre Dance Company perform their programme. Many of the **sailing** competitions get under way, including the Spring Regatta in the BVI, the Family Islands Regatta in the Exumas, Bahamas, the Bequia Regatta in the Grenadines (sometimes March) and two regattas in Antigua: the Classic Yacht Regatta and then the famed International Sailing Week or Race Week. The Cayman Islands also hold a regatta and a carnival: **Batanabo** (sometimes late March).

May

St Lucia holds a Jazz Festival for three days early in the month and St Martin stages a **Food Festival** with *jump-ups* as well as classic cooking; Aruba also holds a culinary exhibition and competition. **Abolition Day** is remembered with picnics and fêtes in the French islands on 27 May. Early in the month a triathlon is held in St Croix. There is a sport fishing tournament in Antigua.

June

The **Bomba y Plena** festival of African music and dance is held in Ponce, Puerto Rico at the beginning of the month and the **Goombay** festival kicks off with street parades and reviews in the Bahamas. In the Cayman Islands there is **Aviation Week**, which sees planes flying in from all quarters; they also hold Million Dollar Month (a fishing competition). There is also an annual billfishing tournament held in the Turks and Caicos Islands. Regattas include a week's sailing in Tobago and **Regatta Time** in the Abacos in the Bahamas. In Aruba it is the Hi-Winds amateur world champions windsurfing competition: they also hold a triathlon and a **Jazz and Latin Music** festival. **Vincie Mas** takes place towards the end of the month in St Vincent and the Grenadines.

July

The Bahamas celebrate **Independence** on 10 July and the USVI commemorate 4th July with fireworks and their own carnival. Martinique has a **Cultural Week** with performances of classical art and in Nevis there is a more Caribbean cultural event in **Culturama**—carnival parades and island-wide festivities. The big events in Cuba are around 26 July, when the anniversary celebrations of the Moncada Garrison attack and then **Carnaval** are held. Saba's **Summer Festival** runs for a week with carnival events. Late in the month a number of other islands get their carnivals moving, St Eustatius, Antigua, the Turks and Caicos (Provo Summer Fesitval) and Barbados (*Cropover*), so that they culminate in the first few days of August. Music is strong in July, with **Reggae Sunsplash** and **Reggae Sumfest** in Jamaica and the **Merengue Festival** in the Dominican Republic. Dominica's **Domfesta** stages Caribbean cultural activities in July or August. The **Bimini Blue Marlin Tournament** takes place towards the end of the month.

August

Most of the former British islands have festivities on 1 August, the date of emancipation, which in Jamaica also coincides with the **Independence Day** celebrations on the first Monday in August. **St Barts** celebrates its saint's day on 24th and *Pitea Day*, commemorating their connection with Sweden. Trinidad celebrates Independence on 31 August; in Tobago they stage the Tobago Heritage Festival. In Guadeloupe the extraordinary and colourful **Fête des Cuisinières** takes place on 11 August, St Laurent's day (the patron saint of cooks), with parades of dishes and blow-outs. St Thomas holds a game fishing tournament for blue marlin. Anguilla holds its **carnival week**, with a **regatta** running concurrently, at the start of the month, and Grenada stages **carnival**, in which the masqueraders drag the carnival floats over the hills of St George's. In Jamaica the reggae festivals mentioned above may be held in August rather than July; in Curaçao there is a **Salsa Festival**. There are plenty of regattas with the **yoles rondes** sailing races in Martinique, the **Carriacou** regatta, races at **Canouan** in the Grenadines, the **Anegada** race in the BVI late in the month and in the **Turks and Caicos**. St Lucia's **Rose Festival**, held on 30 August, has a mock court, ball and music.

September

St Kitts and Nevis celebrate **Independence** on 19 September and St John, USVI, holds its **carnival** near the beginning of the month. **Foxy's Wooden Boat Regatta** is held early in the month in tiny Jost van Dyke in the BVI.

October

There are annual **regattas** in Bonaire (mid-month) and in North Eleuthera in the Bahamas. St Lucia holds a bill-fishing tournament. The Cayman Islands stage **Pirates' Week** with all sorts of festivities towards the end of the month. Puerto Plata in the Dominican Republic has a **merengue festival** in the second week, in Antigua there is a jazz festival and the area of St Lawrence in Barbados holds a music festival. In St Lucia the festival of the Marguerite is held on 17 October, also **Jounen Kweyol** on 28 October, a day of creole festivities. Dominica celebrates local island culture at this time, with a **Creole Week and** a Heritage Day. Trinidad stages a **steelband competition** early in the month and **Diwali**, the very colourful Hindi festival of lights, is held in October or November.

November

Dominica celebrates **Independence** on 3 November and Barbados on 30 November. Sint Eustatius commemorates the first salute to the American flag on 16 November and nearby Saint Martin/Sint Maarten get together and hold joint festivities on **Concordia Day** on 11 November. Trinidad holds the yearly **Pan Jazz Festival**. Late November sees the beginning of the Antigua sailing season with the **Nicholson's boat show**. The Jamaica Festival Opera Season is held in November or December.

December

Saba celebrates its flag day on 7 December and St Lucia's **National Day** is on 13 December. The **ARC** Rally arrives in the island about the same time after an Atlantic crossing. In much the same way **Route du Rosé**, in which yachts bring over bottles of rosé wine, culminates in St Barts and there are celebrations at the arrival. There are jazz and guitar festivals in alternate years in Martinique. St Kitts starts **Carnival Week** on about 20 December and the Bahamas set **junkanoo** into motion, a carnival-like celebration which lasts into the New Year. All Caribbean islands celebrate Christmas; **St Croix** in the USVI starts a month-long calypso and carnival jamboree. **Nine Mornings** in St Vincent sees a week of celebrations in the run up to it; and of course the New Year itself is yet another good excuse for another *jump-up*. In Trinidad and a little in Grenada, you may come across **Parang**, a special style of Christmas singing. Elsewhere they play out island gossip in dance and song, as in St Eustatius on Boxing Day. Well worth a visit to see the Puerto Ricans in a riot of excess is the **Hatillo Festival of the Innocents** on 28 December.

Children

Despite its reputation as a honeymooners' and couples' destination, travelling with children in the Caribbean is perfectly possible and you will find that in most islands the locals are indulgent and friendly towards them (they might be invited to join the screaming little-persons' posses that chase around the beaches and countryside). The majority of hotels will accept children, though they will have only limited facilities for them. Children are sometimes allowed to stay for free in the same room as their parents and baby-sitters are usually on call in any hotel.

A few hotels at the top of the range have a policy of not accepting any children below a certain age; usually 12, and often only in the winter season; others have built special playgrounds for them (notably Malliouhana in Anguilla, Sandy Lane in Barbados, the Half Moon Hotel in Caneel Bay in St John, Jamaica) and provide nannies so that you can sun yourself in peace. Just a few hotels actually specialize in looking after children, providing all-day entertainment (finger-painting lessons, Nintendo, local dancing and mini-watersports) to keep them off your hands. One worth looking into is Boscobel Beach in Jamaica.

If you have a large family it might be easiest to opt for a two- or three-room flat in an apartment complex of which there are many around the islands. Here there will usually be hotel facilities including watersports concessions and a restaurant. If you are happy to look after yourself, then you might take a villa. Children are accepted happily in restaurants, and the tendency towards American food means you can always find a burger and chips to keep them quiet. The Caribbean islands have few museums or daytime activities designed with children in mind, but of course their stock in trade, beaches, are quite suitable for keeping them happy.

Climate

Colonists once knew the Bahamas as the 'isles of perpetual June' because of their fair and clement weather. Generally speaking the climate over the whole Caribbean area is impeccable. As islands, their temperature is kept constant by the sea and so the climate is far gentler than that in the continent that surrounds them. Frost is unknown and it is rarely even cold. The sun is hot year-round, of course, but you will find that in 'winter', the edge is taken off the heat by a breeze. Conversely it can get quite hot, and humid, during the 'summer' months and it can be quite hot and sticky into the evening. Air-conditioning is not really necessary most of the year; if you are staying in a breezy traditional style of building, fan ventilation is all you need. The recent style of building in concrete, without a through-flow of air, means that you may want air-conditioning between about June and October.

The temperature varies just a few degrees across the year and across the geographical area, from Nassau, the capital of the Bahamas, in the north to Port of Spain in Trinidad, which lies more than 1000 miles farther south, just off the South American coast. In the larger islands it will occasionally reach 100°F. Temperatures drop at night; in summer there is no need to cover up, but you might need a thin jersey on a winter evening, particularly at high altitudes.

Average winter and summer temperatures, °C (°F)

	Nassau (Bahamas)	Kingston (Jamaica)	San Juan (Puerto Rico)	St John (USVI)	Port of Spain (Trinidad)	Willemstad (Curaçao)
winter	21 (69)	25 (77)	26 (78)	25 (76)	26 (79)	27 (80)
summer	27 (80)	28 (82)	28 (82)	28 (82)	27 (80)	28 (82)

Caribbean seasons do not follow those in the temperate zones. There are two main seasons in the islands: wet, in which tropical showers pass by, offload thousands of gallons of water in seconds, and then the sun comes out to dry it all up again; and the dry season, in which it still rains but less frequently or heavily. The seasons vary very slightly in timing between Nassau in the north and Port of Spain: the wet seasons are in May or June and October or November. A tropical shower will drench you (with warm rain) in a matter of seconds. You may consider taking a waterproof, but remember that the sun will dry you out almost as quickly as you got wet. Of more concern are cold fronts which spin off the continental weather system up north, putting a blanket of cloud over the islands for three or four days at a time. They seem to have been a bit more frequent in recent years.

hurricanes

Hurricanes are the severest natural disaster in an area of otherwise benign weather. Turning anti-clockwise in the northern hemisphere, hurricanes rise near the coast of Africa as evaporating and then falling seawater begins to spiral. Fed by warm winds over the ocean, they get a couple of thousand miles' run-up before they slice their way through the islands, blowing with sustained speeds of up to 200mph. At this speed they sound more like explosions and massive percussions than winds. They uproot telegraph poles, bend roadsigns horizontal, hurl tin roofs around in the air at a couple of hundred miles an hour and disturb the sea as much as 200ft below the surface (causing considerable damage to the corals). They also deliver massive deluges of rain, which cause yet more destruction sweeping away roads and bridges: Hortense, which came through in 1996, was only designated a tropical storm, but it dropped 16 inches of rain on St Croix in about as many hours. After a hurricane, an island looks like a grey moonscape, with every leaf stripped off the trees in what is normally an overwhelmingly green area.

If you hear that a hurricane is on the way, find the strongest concrete bunker possible and shelter in it with everybody else. If all goes quiet at the height of the storm, then you are in the eye (the very centre of the hurricane): batten down the hatches because it will start again in a few minutes. If you are in a sailing boat, the best place to head for is a mangrove swamp. The most likely month for hurricanes is September: statistically the most likely week is between 10th and 20th. The traditional rhyme runs:

> *June too soon, July stand by,*
> *September remember, October all over.*

There has been a string of pretty bad hurricanes over the last ten years or so: Hurricane Gilbert swept through in 1988, wasting Jamaica and the Cayman Islands, and Hurricane Hugo in 1989, the worst this century, carved a swathe through Guadeloupe and then handsomely trashed Montserrat and St Croix. Most recently, 1995 was a bad year, with Hurricanes Luis and Marilyn, which arrived within a week of each other and flattened several islands in the Northeastern Caribbean. Luis destroyed 1200 yachts and ships in Sint Maarten (many apparently from smashing into one another after breaking loose from their badly laid moorings) and a whole lot of hotels besides, paint-stripped every building in Anguilla (the sand and other debris in the air literally does strip the paint) and washed away Sandy Island. Further south it buffeted Antigua and created seas rough enough to wash away a major road as far south as Dominica (which wasn't really considered to have been in the firing line). Hard on Luis's heels came Marilyn, which caused most damage in the US Virgin Islands and dumped fearsome amounts of rain. St Croix got off lightly this time, but in St Thomas and St John a quarter of the houses were destroyed.

Electricity

In most Caribbean islands the electrical supply is 110 or 120 volts at 60 cycles, and so American electrical appliances need no adaptor (British and French visitors will need to take one). The French islands work to 220 volts and the Dutch islands at 110. The British islands are mixed; those that have developed recently tend to be on the American standard (BVI and Anguilla), but some of the British Caribbean islands have a 230 or 240 volt supply at 50 cycles per second. Even then, some individual hotels work on the American system, so it may be worth checking before you go. If hotel rooms are not fitted with electrical appliances, ask at the front desk, where they may well keep some stashed away.

Food and Drink

When visiting the Caribbean on his trip to write *The Traveller's Tree*, Patrick Leigh Fermor decided that: 'Hotel cooking in the island is so appalling that a stretcher may profitably be ordered at the same time as dinner'. Admittedly this was in the late forties, but Caribbean food, particularly hotel food, is often pretty unadventurous, and has a universal and lacklustre 'international' style. A former British colonial influence might just have something to do with it, but responsibility should probably be shared by the Americans who are only too happy to eat burgers and chips. A quick trip to the French Antilles will tell a different story entirely. If you're a type for whom food can be heaven, then unless you choose carefully and spend a fair bit of money, the Caribbean is likely to be 'burger-tory'.

On the restaurant circuit things have improved recently and you will find at least one good and often adventurous restaurant in every island now. Some chefs and restaurateurs have taken the best of West Indian traditions and applied Continental techniques (and often also imported ingredients) to produce a sophisticated and satisfying Caribbean cuisine. Many have a French or Continental American training, but they tend to adapt this to the Caribbean, creating a lighter fare to go with the climate and also to accommodate the many travellers with special diets. You will find an eclectic mishmash of tastes (there was even a case of 'Thairibbean' food in 1997). Such is the popularity of certain restaurants that in order to make sure of their favourite table, people will fax their reservations months in advance. You can expect to pay as much or more to eat in these restaurants as you would at home.

Have no doubt, running a restaurant in the Caribbean is hard work. There are problems of supply, particularly with regard to regularity if the fishermen decide that they just don't want to go out that day...or Customs decides that they're holding on to today's delivery of food for inspection...). A few restaurants import their food fresh on a daily basis, but the majority of restaurants serve frozen food (jokingly people will tell you that the delays in local restaurants are because they only start unfreezing it when you place your order; it's not entirely untrue). As for hotel dining rooms, they say the most difficult meal to cater for is breakfast, mainly because no self-respecting West Indian would ever eat two eggs over-easy and a bucketful of weak coffee.

Dress codes for dinner have almost entirely died out in the Caribbean and only a couple of hotel dining rooms will request that you wear even a jacket and tie. Service, on the other hand, is often a problem. It is one of the hardest things to get right and often the most notice-able difference between the islands and home. Even in quite smart restaurants and hotel dining rooms it can be haphazard and sometimes it will border on the macabre. There seems little point in complaining in most cases (though it's notable that tourists often have to grin and bear an attitude that West Indians would never dream of putting up with). The settings, though, are magnificent. You will dine on beachfront decks with the waves washing beneath you and on verandas surrounded by tropical greenery, with tree frogs peeping on the night air (in the evenings you always eat in the dark because it is invariably dark by seven). Wine is available in the smartest restaurants, but it does not take well to the heat (nor does it comple-ment the stews of West Indian food too well) and not all restaurants have cooled cellars.

Islands to look out for are: **St Barts** and French **St Martin** for their French heritage, which is then tailored to the climate. Of the former British islands, **Barbados** is in excellent form (there is even a string of wine bars there which serve such unlikely fare for the Caribbean as deep-fried Camembert) and, unexpectedly, there are some superb restaurants in **Anguilla**. It has the advantage of importing fresh ingredients daily from Dutch **Sint Maarten**, which also has some good restaurants serving mainly international fare. **Martinique** and **Guadeloupe** stand in their own right for their indigenous *créole* food and **Puerto Rico** and **Trinidad** are inter-esting places, the latter for its Indian-influenced tastes.

Local Food

A week's worth of curry goat or stew fish might be more than any newcomer could take, but it is worth getting out in search of West Indian food. It has its own distinctive flavours, it is cheaper and the restaurants are often more fun. It is also worth seeking out the beach bars, where you will have barbecued local fish and vegetables.

Gastronomes should really head for the French islands, where there is a strong tradition of creole cookery with luxurious sauces, served with meticulous attention to detail both in the preparation and in the service. Like their metropolitan counterparts, the French Antilleans treat their food with a little more ceremony than other West Indians. You will have a surprise in the Dutch Caribbean islands (particularly in the ABC islands), where there are echoes of Holland in dishes made with Edam cheese, but more curiously Indonesian food (the Dutch West Indies meets the Dutch East Indies) in *rijstafel.* The tastes of India have come through strongest in Trinidad, but curry goat and *roti* (an envelope of dough with a meat or vegetable filling) have reached everywhere now. The Spanish islands are known for their aromatic sauces and stews.

Caribbean food is traditionally quite spicy and West Indians can be quite liberal with pepper in their cook-ups. Beware of bottles marked *Hot Pepper.* Fish is abundant, and often delicious, as are seafoods such as lobster and crab and an island favourite, conch. Other foods that have become popular are made of ingredients that were originally hardship foods, often fed to the slaves, because they were cheap at the time. The Jamaican national dish is *ackee and saltfish*; now that there is refrigeration and food is no longer salted in order to preserve it, salted cod is expensive and difficult to get hold of. *Rice 'n' peas* (or peas 'n' rice depending on which island you are in) is another standard meal in the cheaper restaurants in the British islands and is particularly good when served with coconut milk. *Callaloo* is a traditional West Indian soup made from spinach (also look out for pumpkin soup, which is often excellent) and *oil-dung* is a pot of vegetables cooked in coconut oil.

West Indian food is universally heavyweight with stews and rice or a volley of tropical vegetables, or 'ground provisions' which are mostly starchy and often sweet. Try breadfruit, yam, fried plantain (like a banana) and cassava (originally an Arawak food) and the delicious christophene. Then of course there are the more familiar 'Irish' and sweet potatoes and avocados. The Caribbean is famous for its **fruits**—mango, banana, pineapple, soursop and papaya among others even more exotic; these taste especially good in the ice creams.

It is not usually necessary to make a **reservation** in Caribbean restaurants, except at the most popular in the high season. Under the 'Eating Out' sections in this book, restaurants are divided into three **price categories**: *expensive, moderate* and *cheap.* As some islands are generally more expensive than others, the pricing of these categories will vary a little according to the island, but basically a main course at US$20 or more is *expensive,* US$10 to $20 is *moderate* and US$10 or less is *cheap.* Steak, shrimp and lobster tend to be about 30 per cent more expensive than the standard fish or chicken dishes and so they are not included within the different pricing categories. Eating out in the Caribbean is not cheap, and you can expect service and government tax or recently VAT to be charged on top.

Cocktails

The Caribbean is famous for its cocktails and many were invented here, making the best use of the exotic fruits. The *Piña Colada* (pineapple and coconut cream and rum) supposedly originated in Puerto Rico and the *Daiquiri* (crushed ice, rum and fruit syrup whisked up like a slushy sorbet) in Havana. The *Cuba Libre*, mixed after the Cuban Revolution in 1959, is made of rum with lemon and cola, and Hemingway's *Mojito* is made with white rum, fresh mint and Angostura bitters. The *planter's punch*, traditionally drunk all over the Caribbean, is made from rum and water with a twist of lime and sugar, topped with ground nutmeg. Unfortunately many barmen will use over-liberal dashes of bright red, sticky sweet Grenadine syrup, obliterating the tastes of the other fruits. Almost every bar has a speciality, if not an actual cocktail list, and so you will find plenty to keep you amused.

Rum and Red Stripe

Rum is the Caribbean 'national' drink—50 years ago bars kept their bottles of rum on the counter free of charge and it was the water you had to pay for. Distilled from sugar molasses, rum is produced all over the islands and though it often tastes like rocket fuel, it gives the West Indians their energy for dancing, so it cannot be all bad. The most popular local variety of rum and the quickest to produce is 'white rum', which is drunk in the rum bars and at local dances. Gold rums are a little mellower; their colour comes from caramel which is introduced as they age in wooden barrels; some are blended. As you would expect, the French West Indies treat their rums with admirable solemnity and seriousness: the *petit ponch* is drunk as an *apéritif:* brown sugar is heaped into a measure of white rum, a lime is squeezed within an inch of destruction, and then it is downed in one; chilled water is used as a chaser. Alternatively some restaurants hold a series of *ponch à fruits* in which fruits are steeped in bottled rum, giving it their flavour. For after dinner, older rums are drunk as a *digestif,* in much the same way as brandies are in Europe; they are laid down to mature for years and there are even vintages (*see* Martinique and Guadeloupe).

Look out for *Appleton's* in Jamaica, *Mountgay* in Barbados, *Barbancourt* in Haiti and the varieties of *Trois Rivières*, *Rhum Bally* and *Rhum St James* in Martinique. Guadeloupe also has plenty of home-grown rums.

Far more than wine, the West Indians prefer a cool beer to combat the heat and nowadays almost every island brews its own, usually a lager, some under licence from the major international drinks companies. The best known is *Red Stripe* from Jamaica of course, but you may also recognize *Banks* from Barbados and *Carib* from Trinidad (*Chill And Relax, It's Beer time!),* also *Stag* from Trinidad. Cuban beers include *Hatuey.* St Vincent has been brewing *Hairoun* and *EKU,* passable but not brilliant, for many years and St Lucia now produces *Piton (La Bière Sent Lisi)* and Dominica *Kubuli.* Antigua's contribution is a mediocre brew, *Wadadli,* and the Cayman Islands went for the unlikeliest idea, a dark beer, *Stingray,* which is probably best left untouched. Perhaps the best of all the Caribbean beers is produced in the Dominican Republic, a light lager called *Presidente. Heineken* and American beers such as *Bud* are almost universally available. Only *Red Stripe* and occasionally *Carib* can be found outside their own islands.

Soft Drinks

Caribbean fruits make excellent non-alcoholic drinks: fruit punches are particularly good in Barbados and in the Windward Islands you will find that they make the best of their fruit juices—papaya, mango, passion fruit, lime, even humble orange tastes delicious; often they are spiced. In the Dominican Republic they make *bastidas,* delicious fresh fruit concoctions with ice, quite like milk-shakes.

Life in the Caribbean sun is hot work, and so, besides the bottled drinks available in the shops, the West Indians have an array of drinks on sale in the street. *Snow cones* and *Sky juice* are made with crushed ice (scraped off a huge block), water and a dash of fruit concentrate and put into a bag or cup. You swill it around with a straw and the effect is something like a cold ribena. You have to be careful not to drink the water and the concentrate too quickly otherwise you are just left with a mound of ice crystals. In some islands you get weird and wonderful toppings with condensed milk and crushed peanuts.

Each island has its own system. In Jamaica the vendors walk around pushing brightly painted handcarts and they present the drink to you in a little plastic goldfish bag rather than a cup. In Trinidad they use silver carts like mobile soup-kitchens and they crush the ice by machine, and in the Dominican Republic and Haiti they have tricycles mounted with an ice-box and a whole armoury of concentrate bottles (the water is often dodgy here, so you could go for a *bastida* instead). Gradually these traditions are dying out, as people settle for canned and bottled drinks instead. The usual international soft drinks, Coke, Fanta, Sprite etc, are sold all over the Caribbean, alongside some more Caribbean ones like *Ting*. A particularly good Trinidadian drink is a *Bentley*, lemon and lime with a dash of bitters. Other popular West Indian drinks are sorrel, the red Christmas drink not unlike Ribena, ginger beer and mauby juice, a disgusting bitter concoction made from tree-bark. If in doubt, fresh lime juice is an excellent choice for a soft drink, though not all places have fresh limes in stock all the time.

Another option available in all the islands is coconuts, which are often sold in the street. Do not be alarmed when the vendor pulls out a 2ft machete, because he will deftly top the coconut with a few strokes, leaving just a small hole through which you can drink. Get an older coconut if you can, because the milk will be fuller and sweeter. Once you have drunk the milk, hand it back to the vendor, who will split it for you so that you can eat the delicious coconut slime that lines the inside (it eventually turns into the white coconut flesh). You will also be offered sugar-cane juice, either as a liquid, or in the sticks themselves, which you bite off and chew to a pulp (very sweet).

Health

In the 18th century if you were caught in a cholera epidemic you could have looked forward to a tonic of diluted sulphuric acid and tincture of cardamom or ammoniated tincture of opium as treatment. There are references to 'this fatal climate' on gravestones and memorials throughout the Caribbean. Today, however, the Caribbean is basically a pretty healthy place and unless you are unlucky there is no reason why you should experience health problems.

You should check that your polio and tetanus inoculations are up to date and you may wish to have yourself immunized or take precautions against the following diseases. **Malaria** is still a problem in Haiti and a little bit in the Dominican Republic, so you are advised to take preventative medicines when visiting those countries—the course usually begins a week before you arrive and continues for four weeks after you leave the area. **Hepatitis** occurs rarely: you can have an injection giving some cover against Hepatitis A, which is caught mainly from water and food. **Dengue fever** has occurred from time to time in the larger islands. There has been some incidence of **cholera** in South America over the last few years, but the threat to the islands seems to have receded. If you are travelling to the less-developed islands and wish to take sterile needles (and possibly plasma), make sure they are packed up to look official otherwise customs might begin to wonder.

There is quite a high incidence of venereal diseases around the Caribbean, including **HIV**, which some reckon started in Haiti (there is little evidence that this is true, though it is prevalent there). The risks from casual sex are obvious.

warnings

Sunburn can ruin your holiday and so it is worth taking it easy for the first few days. You are recommended to keep to short stints of about 15–20 minutes in the hottest part of the day (11am–3pm). Be particularly careful if you go snorkelling, because the sun and the cooling water together are lethal. Take care all day if you are sailing: the reflection off the sea and the white decks and sails are a fearsome combination. Take sunglasses, high-protection-factor suncream or total block. Sun-hats are easily found. Traditional West Indian methods of soothing sun-burn include the application of juice of **aloe**, a fleshy cactus-like plant, which is used a lot in cosmetics anyway. Break a leaf and squeeze out the soothing juice. After-sunburn treatments include calamine lotion. And if you will be spending most of your time in and out of the water, you might take some talcum powder for your feet.

There are very few poisonous things in the Caribbean, but you may well come across the **manchineel tree**, which often grows on the beach. These are tall, bushy trees with a fruit like a small apple, known by Columbus's men as the apple of death (*manzana* means apple in Spanish). Do not eat them! Steer clear of the tree itself because the sap is poisonous. You should not even shelter under them in the rain because the sap will blister your skin. A palm tree may seem the ideal place to shade yourself in the height of the sun, but beware: people have been killed by falling coconuts.

Mosquitoes are a plague, though many tourist areas are treated to get rid of them. They can cause dengue fever (in the Greater Antilles) and malaria (in Hispaniola only). Most of all, they are irritating at night and if you're awake you'll hear them dive-bombing with a high-pitched squeak. Burn mosquito coils. Some hotels have mosquito nets for cosmetic reasons (they look pretty). Off the beaten track you might consider taking one (there will probably already be nails in the walls where others have had the same idea). There are many insect repellents, including Autan, Jungle Formula and *OFF!*.

Less potentially harmful, but equally irritating, are the tiny invisible **sand-flies** which plague certain beaches after rain and towards the end of the afternoon. In 1631, Sir Henry Colt wrote: 'First you have such abundance of small knatts by ye sea shore towards ye sun goinge down yt bite so as no rest cann be had without fyers under your Hamaccas'. For a barely visible insect, they pack a big bite. There are one or two poisonous centipedes and only certain islands have poisonous snakes (or snakes at all for that matter).

Swimming holds very few dangers in the Caribbean, though among the reefs and rocks you should look out for fire coral and particularly for spiny sea urchins (little black balls with spines up to 6 inches long radiating in all directions). If you stand on one, the spines break off, and give you a very unpleasant and possibly infected injury. Sharks are occasionally spotted in Caribbean waters by divers, but have hardly ever been known to attack humans. Swimming is generally safe on most recognized beaches. If you are off the beaten track, ask around.

water

The **water** in most islands in the Caribbean is drinkable from the tap, but to make sure, particularly in the larger islands, you might want to drink the water served by the hotel to begin with. However, in Haiti and the Dominican Republic you should definitely only drink bottled water. Do not drink iced drinks off the street in these two countries, because the ice will not have been made with purified water. Get a soft drink or a coconut instead.

There is a shortage of water in many of the flatter islands, and so, even in expensive hotels, you may find that nothing comes out when you turn on the tap. You are always asked to conserve water where possible.

Insurance

You may find that insurance is included in your holiday package. If you are travelling independently, you should make sure that you're covered. Read the small print. A good policy should give full cover for your health: medical costs, hospital benefits, permanent disabilities and the flight home. There is usually a 24-hour contact number in the event of medical emergencies. Also your possessions: in case of loss or theft, it should recompense you for lost luggage, money and valuables. Finally, most policies will cover you for travel delay and most importantly personal liability. You may find that certain sports, most notably scuba diving, are excluded from general policies, so you will have to arrange special cover on top.

If your own bank or insurance company hasn't an adequate travel insurance scheme (they usually have), then try the comprehensive schemes offered by **Trailfinders** (✆ (0171) 938 3939) or **Jardine's** (✆ (0161) 228 3742), or the 'Centurion Assistance' policy offered by **American Express** (✆ (01444) 239900). Tour operators often include insurance in the cost of a luxury tour, but this is not always adequate.

Should anything be stolen, a copy of the police report should be retained. It will be required by your insurance company when making a claim.

Language

English is spoken in the tourist industry in most Caribbean countries, partly because many of the islands have a former colonial connection with Britain and partly because of the large number of American visitors. Most islands also have a local *patois*, an everyday language based on the original official colonial language, but these are often incomprehensible to the foreign visitor.

English is the official language of all the British Commonwealth Caribbean countries— Barbados, Trinidad and Tobago, the Windward Islands (Grenada, St Vincent and the Grenadines, St Lucia, Dominica), the Leeward Islands (Antigua, Montserrat, St Kitts and Nevis and Anguilla), the British and United States Virgin Islands, Jamaica, the Caymans, the Turks and Caicos and the Bahamas.

French is the official language of the French Antilles, Martinique, Guadeloupe, St Martin and St Barts, but English is widely spoken in the hotels. French is also the official language of Haiti, though few people speak it outside the main towns because they talk *kreyol*. English is spoken in the bigger hotels.

Dutch is the official language of the Netherlands Antilles, but *Papiamento* is spoken in the Dutch Leeward Islands (ABC Islands) and English is traditionally the language of the Dutch Windward Islands.

Spanish is the language of Puerto Rico, the Dominican Republic and Cuba. English is widely spoken in Puerto Rico because of the American connection, but few people speak it outside the hotels in either Cuba or the Dominican Republic. If you are intending to go off the beaten track it is well worth learning some Spanish.

Living and Working in the Caribbean

Like sailing around the world, setting up in the Caribbean is a lifetime's dream for some. Beware! Things are not necessarily what they seem during a short visit. Battling with bureaucracy and local prejudices is a perennial problem (small island communities are notoriously inward-looking and once you scratch the surface of the West Indies you will find things are little different from elsewhere) and island inertia can get people down too (West Indian plumbers may not be on call quite as you are used to at home). There is a heartless expression which says that people arrive with a container full of belongings and (after a year's frustration) leave with a suitcase. Perhaps it is best to rent for six months or a year to learn the ropes and see if you like the way of life before you put money in.

Having said that, many people do adapt to the West Indies and certain islands do encourage investment. Buying rights vary from island to island, but most require that if you buy a plot of land you must build within a certain period, and often that you employ a local person. Details are available from the individual High Commissions and Embassies.

Working in the Caribbean is also not as easy as it might seem because most islands impose strict quotas of foreign workers on businesses, ensuring that the work remains for the islanders. Casual work is almost impossible to find. If you are lucky, you might find some work in the bars in islands where there is a large expatriate community or in islands with a large sailing contingent, where crews are sometimes needed. Americans have equal employment rights in Puerto Rico and the Virgin Islands of course, and EC members can work (officially at least) in the French islands, but the British have no special rights in the few remaining British Crown colonies.

Maps and Publications

There are just a few general Caribbean maps and they are available from any good bookstore or map store. Really detailed maps of individual islands are not generally available (either on island or at home). You might find them at a map specialist, but they are not really needed when on island unless you are going walking in remote areas. In most places it is enough to get a photocopied map at the tourist offices (or you can tear one out of the many tourism magazines—see 'Tourist Information', p.35).

Most islands have their own newspaper; these tend to be dailies in the larger islands (islands such as Jamaica and Trinidad will have a broadsheet and some tabloids) and perhaps two or three times weekly in the smaller ones. Many American papers and magazines are on sale (usually a day or so late), but not so many papers make it over from Europe. There are just a couple of pan-Caribbean papers, including *Caribbean Week* and a sailing magazine for the Eastern Caribbean called *Compass*. The BWIA inflight magazine, *Caribbean Beat*, covers Caribbean-wide affairs and is a good read.

Generally speaking the Caribbean is pretty expensive. Flights are often expensive to begin with and if you stay on the tourist circuit you will find yourself paying prices not unlike those in Europe or the USA. However, if you get off the tourist track and stay in local West Indian guest houses in town and eat local food, it is possible to live more cheaply in most islands. All the same, do not expect to stay anywhere for much less than US$20.

A few Caribbean countries have their own currency, but many of the smaller islands share a denomination, often according to their colonial past. The US dollar, however, is the currency in universal demand around the area and at the moment it is permitted to circulate more or less freely in all the islands. Many countries have pegged their currency to it and so there is not much of a black market.

Consequently, prices in the tourist industry almost throughout the Caribbean are quoted in or fixed to US dollars: it is quite possible in places to spend a couple of weeks working exclusively in that currency (in tourist hotels and their watersports concessions, restaurants and shops). However, if you go off the beaten track, it is a good idea to have local notes and change. It is also sensible to take small denominations.

From a Caribbean perspective, tourism is about getting money into the country, and so there is a plethora of taxes to contend with. In hotels there is usually a government room tax, which varies from 5% to 10% (with service at 10% or even 15% this can mean that your bill is supplemented by a fifth or even a quarter when you come to pay, so it is worth bearing this in mind). In restaurants there is usually a government tax too. Service charges are an accepted system around most of the islands (except the French Caribbean, where, as in France, *service* is *inclus*). Usually it is charged at 10%, unless otherwise indicated. In the shops a sales tax is sometimes charged on top, but it is usually included in the price. Less visibly, many islands do not actually have a system of income tax and the burden is passed to the consumers in the form of sales taxes.

On a less formal scale, hustling is fairly widespread in the Caribbean. All visitors are presumed to have a few dollars that they would not mind releasing (they could afford the air fare after all) and some islands have a band of opportunists who will try to persuade you to do so in return for a variety of services, anything from an errand to collect a box full of different fruits from the local market to drugs, or just as a gift. You are vulnerable particularly in the first 48 hours or until you have a bit of colour. The hustle factor varies from island to island, but in some islands you can expect to be accosted if you go to the downtown area and on any public beach. A firm and polite no to whatever is offered is the easiest way to guarantee your peace.

official currencies

You will need to check the exchange rates before you travel only for those countries whose currencies float on the international exchange:

Barbados—Barbados dollar, fixed to US dollar (US$1 = BDS$1.98), US currency also accepted.

Trinidad and Tobago—Trinidad and Tobago dollar, fluctuates on the open exchange (presently US$1 = TT$6 approx), US currency accepted.

Windward Islands and **Leeward Islands** (the former British islands of Grenada, St Vincent and the Grenadines, St Lucia, Dominica, Antigua and Barbuda, St Kitts and Nevis and the

Crown Colonies of Montserrat and Anguilla)—the Eastern Caribbean dollar, fixed to US dollar (US$1 = EC$2.65), US currency also accepted.

French Caribbean (French Antilles: Martinique, Guadeloupe, St Martin, St Barthélemy)— French franc (US$1 = Fr5.5 approx), US dollar also accepted in tourist areas.

Dutch Caribbean (Netherlands Antilles: Sint Maarten, Saba, Statia, Curaçao and Bonaire)— Netherlands Antillean florin or guilder, fixed to US dollar (US$1 = NAFl 1.78), US dollar freely accepted.

Aruba—Aruban florin, fixed to US dollar (US$1 = AFl 1.77), US dollar freely accepted.

British and **US Virgin Islands**—US dollar official currency.

Puerto Rico—US dollar.

Dominican Republic—Dominican peso (US$1 = RD$14.02 approx), floats on the international exchange, US dollars accepted in all tourist areas.

Haiti—Haitian dollar, made up of 5 gourdes; US$1 = 16.25 gourdes. US dollars are accepted by tourist hotels and under the counter by many businesses.

Cuba—Cuban peso, fixed artificially to US dollar in tourist areas (US$1 = Cuban $1). There is a black market, with the US$ trading at Cuban $20 approx.

Jamaica—Jamaican dollar (US$1 = J$35 approx) floats on the open market. US dollars are accepted currency in tourist areas.

Cayman Islands—Cayman Islands dollar, fixed to US dollar (US$1 = 80 Cayman cents or CI$1 = US$1.25).

Turks and Caicos Islands—US dollar official currency.

Bahamas—Bahamian dollar, fixed at par to US dollar, which is freely accepted.

exchange

The banks give the best rate of exchange. At hotels you usually receive a lower rate. The exchanges in most islands will accept hard currency **traveller's cheques**—sterling, French franc, Deutschmark and Canadian dollar, but the most popular is the US dollar, particularly if you are going to a country where the dollar is an acceptable alternative currency. You will also get a better rate of exchange. Some banks charge for the exchange of traveller's cheques, however. Take some small denomination cheques and remember to record the number so that they can be replaced if you lose them. Generally, banking is quite sophisticated in most islands, but service is often slow.

Credit cards are widely accepted for anything that is connected with the tourist industry—in hotels, restaurants and tourist shops. If you need to, you can draw cash on a credit card at the bank—there are AMEX and VISA representatives on all the islands. **Personal cheques** are rarely accepted.

Packing

With such pleasant weather and such an informal air in the Caribbean, you can take a minimalist approach to packing. There are just a couple of restaurants and hotel dining rooms in the whole area which require even a jacket and a tie for men (though most do like trousers and a shirt with a collar). Daytime wear is a skirt or shorts and a light shirt, evening wear about the same, perhaps a longer skirt or trousers. Jeans are too warm in the summer months, so you might consider taking cotton trousers. Also pack a sunhat, sunglasses, suncream and a swimsuit (though they can be bought on arrival).

Photography

You will find that many West Indians either dive for cover or start remonstrating violently at the very sight of a camera. Some will talk about you stealing their soul and others about the money you will have to pay. If you see a good shot and go for it, you can usually talk your way out of trouble, but if you stop and chat first then most people will allow you to photograph them.

In the middle of the day, the brightness of the Caribbean sun bleaches all colour out of the landscape except the strongest tropical shades, but as the afternoon draws in you will find a stunning depth of colour in the reds, golds and greens. The plants of the Caribbean are bright and colourful and particularly good after rain.

Film is very expensive in the islands and the heat can be a problem too (you might put it in the hotel fridge). The officials will swear that no damage will be done by the X-ray machines at the airports, and this is usually true, but you may prefer that it goes through in an X-ray proof bag, or is searched by hand.

Post Offices

Post can take anything from 2 days to 3 months to get from the Caribbean to Europe or North America. Don't depend on it. You will probably have no need to go anywhere near a post office anyway because hotels usually have postcards and stamps and once you have written them they are happy to post them for you. Opening hours vary from island to island.

Shopping

Shopping is one of the Caribbean's biggest industries, but hardly any of the things that are sold here originate in the area. There are objects of cultural value to be found, particularly in the larger islands, but most of it is shipped in to satisfy the collector passions of long-distance shoppers (some of whom actually go on the same cruise year after year to take advantage of preferential customs allowances). On the shelves of all the air-conditioned boutiques and the newer shopping malls that have begun to infest the area you will find jewels and precious stones, perfumes, photographic equipment, clothes, Cuban cigars etc.

The islands follow roughly speaking the historical patterns of their nation, with the French the leaders in perfumes and designer clothes and the Dutch, always great traders, with well-priced photographic equipment from the Far East. St Thomas, a traditional and particularly attractive port in the US Virgin Islands, where almost anything is on sale, is in danger of becoming one outsize emporium. The lure is, of course, the reduced prices (in comparison to the mainland) and every shop announces itself as 'duty-free' or 'in-bond'. The best duty-free shopping-centre islands in the Caribbean (some have been trading like this for hundreds of years) are Sint Maarten, St Thomas in the USVI and Nassau and Freeport in the Bahamas.

There is quite an active art scene now in many of the islands: galleries exhibiting work by local and expatriate artists are mentioned in the text. There are occasionally things of interest in the craft markets, but particularly on the bigger islands—Jamaica, Haiti and the Dominican Republic—you will find some highly original work. The best known is the *naïve* art from Haiti.

diving

The Caribbean and the Bahamas have some superb corals and fish, the best in the Western hemisphere. The variety is stunning, from the world's third-largest barrier reef just a few miles off the coast of Andros in the Bahamas, to the colourful seascapes of Bonaire and the Caymans, to warm water springs and bubble outlets under the sea off the volcanic islands.

The reefs are incredibly colourful. You will see yellow and pink tube sponges and purple trumpet sponges, sea feathers and seafans (gorgonians) that stand against the current alongside a forest of staghorn, elkhorn and black coral and the more exotic species like the domes of startlingly white brain coral, star corals and yellow pencil coral. Near the surface the corals are multicoloured and tightly bunched as they compete for space; as you descend, the yellows and the reds and whites fade, leaving the purples and blues of the larger corals that catch the last of the sunlight at depth (until you shine a light and see them in their full glory).

Many islands have laws to protect their reefs and their fish (there are hardly any places left in the Caribbean where you are allowed to use spearguns) and this is more or less successful. In certain islands you are asked not to buy coral jewellery because it will probably have been taken illegally from the reef. One of the few dangerous things on the reef are fire corals, which will give you a nasty sting if you touch one. Do not annoy Moray eels and watch out for sea urchins, whose spines will cause a nasty injury.

Other underwater life includes a stunning array of crustaceans and of course tropical fish. On the bottom you will find beautifully camouflaged crabs that stare at you, goggle-eyes out on stalks, starfish, lobsters, sea anemones and pretty pink and white feather-duster worms. Around them swim angelfish, squirrelfish, surgeonfish, striped sergeant majors, grunts and soldierfish. Above them little shoals of wrasses and blue tang shimmy in the bubbles. If you get too close, puffer fish blow themselves up like a spiky football, smiling uncomfortably. And beware the poisonous stonefish. If you hear of lobsters migrating (as many as a hundred following one another in a line across the sea bed), then make sure to go out and look.

At night a whole new seascape opens up as some corals close up for the night and others open up in an array of different colours. While some fish tuck themselves into a crevice in the reef to sleep (eyes kept open or in a sort of sleeping-bag of mucus so that they cannot be detected by their scent), starfish, lobsters and sea urchins scuttle around the seabed on the hunt for food. Stop breathing for a moment, and you will hear the midnight parrotfish crunching on the coral polyps, spitting out the broken-down fragments of reef that eventually turn into sand.

The best areas for diving in the Caribbean are Bonaire off the coast of South America (for its slopes with excellent and colourful corals), the Cayman Islands (noted for their sheer walls), some of the remoter Bahamas and particularly the Turks and Caicos Islands. There are also a number of live-aboard dive boats based around the Bahamas and the Caymans. Other islands with good reputations are Saba and Dominica. Most dive-shops in the Caribbean are affiliated to PADI (many also to NAUI) and they will expect you to present a certificate of competence if you wish to go out on to the reefs straight away, but all islands except the smallest have lessons available in the resorts if you are a novice. An open-water qualifying course (which allows you to dive in a pair with another qualified open-water diver) takes about a week, but with a resort course you can usually get underwater in a morning. You will have a session in the swimming-pool before you are allowed to dive with an instructor in the open sea. It is often possible to do 'referral' dives, in which you complete the open-water section of a diving course in the Caribbean after you have completed the classroom and swimming pool parts of the course at home.

The **snorkelling** is also good off many of the islands and most hotels have equipment for their guests and on hire to non-residents. Beware, if you go snorkelling on a sunny day soon after you arrive, because the water and the sun make a fearsome combination on unprotected skin (wear a shirt, perhaps). In most places you can arrange glass-bottom boat tours and snorkelling trips. For those who would like to see the deeper corals, but who do not dive, there are submarines in Barbados, St Thomas in the USVI, Grand Cayman and the Bahamas, St Barts and St Martin.

fishing

A sport that is traditionally renowned in the Gulf Stream (between Key West and Havana, and between Florida and the Bahamas), but which is now possible throughout the Caribbean, is **deep-sea** or **big game fishing**. Docked at the yachting marina, the deep-sea boats are huge, gleaming cruisers, slightly top-heavy because of their tall spotting towers, usually equipped with tackle and bait and 'fighting chair'. Beer in hand, you trawl the line behind the boat, waiting for a bite and then watch the beast surface and fight as you cruise along, giving line and steadily hauling it in.

The magnificent creatures that you are out to kill are fish such as the blue marlin, which inhabits the deepest waters and can weigh anything up to 1100lb and measure 10ft in length. Giant or bluefin tuna can weigh up to 1000lb. Wahoo, around 100lb, is a racer and a fighter and the white marlin can weigh up to 150lb. Perhaps the most beautiful of them all is the sailfish, with a huge spiny fan on its back, which will jump clean out of the water and 'tail' (literally stand upright on its tail) in its desperate attempts to get free. Smaller fish include blackfin and allison tuna, bonito, dorado and barracuda.

The best known areas are the ports off the Gulf Stream, on Bimini, and traditionally around Havana (though things are quieter there now), but you can easily charter a boat from the north coast of Jamaica and from Puerto Rico and the Virgin Islands (there are deep waters offshore). The most famous story about fishing is *The Old Man and The Sea* by Ernest Hemingway, which is set in a small fishing village east of Havana. There is another excellent description in Hemingway's *Islands in the Stream*.

Bonefishing takes place in the shallows not far from the shore, particularly in the Bahamas, but also in some other Caribbean areas. They say, that pound for pound, bonefish are the best fighters of all fish.

sailing

For many people a **sailing trip** is the most memorable day of a Caribbean holiday. There is a marina on most islands where you can find a crewed yacht. They are usually quite well publicised, but be careful because they can vary very much in style, from a crowded rum-soaked booze-cruise to a day's full-on sailing on a racing yacht. Lunch will often be included in the price and there may well be an open bar. They seek out coves and isolated beaches where you can have a picnic. The volcanic islands are particularly good for this, because as you sail along the coast, you see the vast and fertile landscape move gradually above you, but there are many popular sailing areas in the Caribbean and the Bahamas. Tried and trusted are the Grenadine Islands between St Vincent and Grenada, Antigua, the British Virgin Islands (centred around

Sir Francis Drake Passage, one of the most beautiful spots in the whole area) and many of the Family Islands in the Bahamas. For sailing holidays *see* 'Travel', special-interest holidays, pp.8–9, and sections under the **Virgin Islands** and the **Grenadines**.

windsurfing

Because of the warmth and the constant winds off the Atlantic Ocean, the Caribbean offers superb windsurfing, particularly when the winds are at their highest in the early months of the year. The sport is well developed—a number of championship competitions have been held in the Caribbean—and you can hire a board on any island. Instruction is usually available. The best places to go are Aruba, the southern coast of Barbados, the north coast of the Dominican Republic (Cabarete) and the windward coasts of the French islands, where the sport is very popular.

miscellaneous watersports

On the smaller islands there is usually at least one beach where you will find all the **watersports**: anything from a windsurfer and a few minutes on waterskis to a parasail flight, a trip on a pedalo or a high-speed trip around the bay on an inflated sausage (it'll keep the kids quiet anyway). Glass-bottom boat tours are usually available and in most hotels you are able to hire small sailboats such as hobie cats and sunfish. Jetskis (standing up) and wetbikes (sitting) have made their mark in the West Indies and are available for hire at most major centres (though some islands have banned them recently) and a recent arrival are kayaks, which are fun on waves and good for reaching remoter snorkelling areas around a rocky coastline. Hotels set on their own beach will invariably have a selection of watersports, though not usually as complete as above. Prices vary considerably across the Caribbean. Most things can be booked through the hotels or their beach concessionaires. There is not really that much beach culture in the Caribbean islands, but there are some beach bars where you can hang out. Rum cruises and sunset tours aboard a resurrected galleon complete with boozatorium and lots of walking the plank are available on the larger and more touristed islands.

The mountainous islands of the Caribbean literally create rain as the water-filled Atlantic winds race over them. They have rivers worthy of continents and all over the islands you will find waterfalls and rockpools that make for excellent **river bathing**. There is a problem in some islands with bilharzia (in lakes and slow-flowing rivers) so you are advised to take official advice before swimming there. In Jamaica, where there is good river bathing, you can also take a **rafting** trip on the larger rivers—quite expensive, but good fun (*see* p.731).

other sports

Sports based on land include **tennis**, which is well served all over the Caribbean. There are courts in many of the hotels and in island clubs. There are occasional pro-am competitions. If there is no court at your hotel, arrange with another through the front desk, or simply wander in and ask. Hotels generally charge a small fee and they usually have racquets and balls for hire. **Riding** is also offered on the majority of the islands and this is a good way to see the rainforest and the sugar flats if you think that your calves might not be up to the hike. In Jamaica and the Dominican Republic you can even get a game of polo.

Golf is available on the larger islands and those with a developed tourist industry. Courses are usually open to visitors on payment of a green fee (which is often extremely steep: if it is important to you, do some research because in some hotels the green fees are included in the package). If you decide to play, be flexible because the courses will often give priority to hotel guests. Most courses have equipment for hire.

There is good **walking** in the Caribbean islands, which are cut and crossed with traditional trails originally used by the likes of the *porteuses* (*see* **Martinique**) and the farmers of today. The rainforest is fascinating to walk in because the growth is so incredibly lush. Many of the Eastern Caribbean islands have an active volcano in whose crater you can climb—or you could make the walk to the boiling lake in Dominica's Valley of Desolation.

The heat will be most bearable between dawn, usually at around 6am, and 10am, before the sun gets too high and then between 4pm and dusk. However, the higher you go, the cooler it gets, and the temperature in the forest is not bad anyway. It gets dark quickly in the Caribbean, so be careful to be back by 6pm otherwise you may find yourself stranded, at the mercy of such fearsome spirits of the Caribbean night as the *Soucouyant* and *La Diablesse* (*see* **Trinidad**, p.95). It often rains, of course, so take a waterproof coat and high up in the hills you will need a jersey underneath because the winds can make it cold. Big heavy boots are not necessary. Gym shoes or sneakers are usually enough, unless you are headed into very steep and slippery country, when you should have some ankle support—perhaps a pair of light tropical boots. Increasingly there are guides who are well informed and can tell you all about the flora and fauna.

There are a number of islands with extensive **cave** systems which have been carved out of the limestone rock by the dripping of water. The best caves are in the Greater Antilles, though some have been overdeveloped (with electric buggies, hard hats and probably even canned music by now) and not all are open to the public. For hard-core speleologists there are good but unstructured opportunities for exploring uncharted potholes in the larger islands, where whole rivers disappear underground in the karst limestone country.

Telephones

Communications in the Caribbean are quite good. Many hotel rooms are fitted with direct dial phones as standard, though in both the less developed and the larger countries getting through can be a bit haphazard. Public phones are quite dependable and there are usually booths at the marinas and in the towns. Calls seem to cost a about quarter in almost every Caribbean currency and many islands have a system of phonecards. The former British islands and remaining British Crown colonies have an extensive network run mainly by Cable and Wireless (with the advantage that a cardphone bought in an EC$ country can be used all the way along the chain between Grenada and the BVI). There are no coin phones on the French islands, where you will need a *télécarte*, which is also valid on all other French islands. If you are having trouble placing a call you can always wander into the nearest hotel, where they will help you out for a fee.

Time Zones

Travelling to the Caribbean from Europe is particularly satisfying. You reach the island in the afternoon, usually in time to take an onward flight or skip down to the beach and watch the sunset and then you're fit to drop by the end of an early supper. Going to bed early in a strange bedroom with the sound of the sea outside is usually enough to wake you up early the next morning. Dawn is the best time of the day in the Caribbean. It is cool and calm. Be sure to get up and walk around.

Apart from Club Med enclaves (which have their own time schedule for some reason), the whole of the Eastern Caribbean (Barbados up to the Virgin Islands) and Puerto Rico and the Dominican Republic are 4 hours behind GMT. Haiti, Jamaica, Cuba, the Caymans and the Bahamas work to Eastern Standard Time (5 hours behind GMT). There is no 'Summer Time' in the islands, so the difference will vary around the year according to whether there is European or North American Summer Time in effect.

'Caribbean Time', on the other hand, is an expression you will come across all over the islands. It refers to the West Indians' elastic and entirely unpredictable schedules. Businesses can be punctual, but in restaurants and shops they will have little sympathy with a slave to the second hand. The Jamaicans say 'soon come', which means any time from now to tomorrow.

Tourist Information

The Caribbean tourist industry generates a huge volume of paper, from sleek, advertising-driven glossies found in hotel rooms down to humble leaflets left at strategic points for yachties and other passers-by. There is always a tourist information office at the airport, and they are happy to help out with accommodation, maps, directions and pertinent local advice and gossip. There is usually an information office in the main town and on larger islands there will be tourist offices in the major tourist spots. For those who want more detail there is usually an information department in the Department of Tourism itself. Opening hours vary across the islands; basically they follow island business hours, with respect for local traditions (such as a two-hour lunch break in some places). If you cannot find a tourist office, do not be reticent about asking information or directions of a West Indian because they will almost always go out of their way to help you.

All the Caribbean islands publish some sort of tourism magazine to help with orientation when you arrive on island. These usually include lists of accommodation, restaurants and shops (generally listed even-handed without selection or recommendation) and some feature articles as well as general advice about how not to get sunburned. Recommendations for watersports and tours tend to be advertising-driven in magazines such as these, so if you have a specific requirement (e.g. for a trained guide who can take you hiking in the rainforest) ring up and chat with the tourist board. Interpretation boards are sometimes in evidence at 'sights' of local interest and if you do visit a local museum there is usually printed material on sale.

Where to Stay

The Caribbean has some of the finest and most luxurious hotels in the world. You can stay at island resorts so remote and quiet that you communicate by flag, on endless beaches which are deserted at dawn, in 18th-century plantation splendour with a view across the canefields, and in high-pastel luxury in the Caribbean's newest resorts. And then there are suites and cottages rather than rooms and even villas and villa resorts; there are specialist eco-resorts, scuba resorts and a few hotels that specialize in children. Many of the islands offer topnotch hotels, but try the Grenadines and the Virgin Islands for isolated island settings, Barbados for grand and long-established hotels set in magnificent gardens, St Kitts and Nevis for plantation estate elegance, St Barts for chic and luxury, Anguilla for distinctive style and sumptuous, small-island charm and Jamaica for reliable luxury.

When you reach the Caribbean, it is easy to imagine that you have arrived in some remote corner of paradise, but these hotels are businesses and they operate under quite difficult circumstances. To get an idea of what goes on behind the scenes, make sure to read Herman Wouk's *Don't Stop the Carnival!* It is 30 years old, but still killingly accurate. It is hard to look a hotelier in the eye after reading it.

The newest Caribbean hotels tend to be large, humming palaces with blocks of rooms decorated in a symphony of bright pastel colours set against white tile floors, the regimented dreams of international hotel corporations. However, there is a grand variety of places to stay in the Caribbean and the ultimate Caribbean setting, perhaps a private beachfront cabin with a personal hammock hanging between two nearby palm trees, can be found all over the area.

Choosing Where to Stay

If you arrange your trip through a tour operator, you are quite likely to select your holiday on the basis of the hotel, perhaps because of its reputation, or because of a deal on offer through the tour operator. It is worth asking around and listening to what others say about it. Hotels are selected for this book on grounds of value (within their price category), but also for other reasons such as setting, service, friendliness and general management. Many of the big names in Caribbean hotels are included, but smaller, more off-beat places are included too. Hotels and guest houses are listed in the following six categories:

luxury	US$400 and above for a double per night
very expensive	US$250–400
expensive	US$150–250
moderate	US$75–150
cheap	US$35–75
very cheap	under US$35

In almost every Caribbean island the hotels will add an obligatory government tax (usually between 5% and 8%) and a service charge, usually 10%.

Note: Unless otherwise stated, all prices quoted in this book are for a double room in the peak winter season (without a meal plan).

Plans and Seasons

MAP means Modified American Plan (with breakfast and dinner included in the price) and **EP** means European Plan (no meals). You may also come across **CP**, Continental Plan, with room and breakfast and **FAP**, or Full American Plan, with a room and all meals. See also **all-inclusive**, below.

The Caribbean high season is traditionally mid-January until mid-April, with a small peak just before this at Christmas and New Year. Prices are highest then. 'Off-season' travel will bring reductions of as much as 30% in some cases, making some of the idyllic places suddenly affordable. One serious problem with the Caribbean is that holidays invariably seem to revolve around the couple and so single travellers will often find themselves paying the same as a couple for a room. You can try bargaining, but it is unlikely to do any good.

All-inclusive Hotels

The all-inclusive hotel plan has become increasingly popular in recent years and has spread to most Caribbean islands now. As the name implies, once you have paid the initial bill you do not have to pull out your wallet again. It is easier to budget of course and to a large extent it is the solution for people who want nothing more than a beach and barely care what country they are in, but it has had the effect of discouraging people from leaving the hotel and exploring, and going out to try the restaurants for dinner (which in turn means that in some islands there are very few good restaurants left). There is now quite a wide variety of standards and prices within the all-inclusives and some have gone upmarket, offering champagne and *à la carte* dining instead of the traditional buffet-style meals. Jamaica, Antigua, St Lucia and increasingly Barbados have the most all-inclusive hotels and the Sandals chain has many resorts throughout the Caribbean; there are also all-inclusives that specialize in looking after children. Originally the concept was a Caribbean version of Club Med, with a permanently ongoing diet of sports and entertainment for those who wanted it. This has altered in some cases recently, with some hotels offering a straight all-inclusive plan (all meals and drinks paid for) and less of the activities. It is worth checking what facilities are included in the package.

There is still a holiday-camp atmosphere about some all-inclusives, however, and their names often give a good indication of their theme—for example, Hedonism II or Couples (with the symbol of a pair of lions humping). These high-pressure fun factories seem to encourage riotous behaviour—with as much alcohol as you can drink, dancing on the tables, mirrors on the bedroom ceiling and crash courses in marriage. They are well worth a look, at least for a couple of days, after which you might suddenly feel like immersing yourself in a book.

Inns

Dotted sporadically around the Caribbean are some magnificent old gingerbread-style homes, often former plantation houses, that have been converted into inns, ideal for the independent traveller with a bit of cash. Usually they will offer a more personal style than the bigger hotels. Some of the best are the *paradores* in Puerto Rico, often family-run hotels in charming old buildings hidden in the rainforest or in the towns, and the inns tucked into the hillsides of Charlotte Amalie on St Thomas.

Villas, Apartments and Condominiums

In addition to the many hotels there are also **villas** all over the islands, most of them relatively modern and well equipped. You can cater for yourself or arrange for a cook, and the smarter ones will have a pool. Contact them through the individual island villa-rentals organizations or the tourist boards. The Caribbean now copes reasonably well with self-catering or efficiency holidays and so there are a large number of **apartments** on all the islands, some grouped together in one building like a hotel, others scattered in landscaped grounds. Some apartment complexes will have a restaurant or bar and some watersports facilities. Finally, **condominiums** are also springing up in many islands, answering to those who wish to invest in their vacation.

Guest Houses

These are the cheapest option and they are more fun, cheaper, and have far more character than bottom-of-the-range tourist hotels. They are usually presided over by an ample and generous mother figure (something of a West Indian institution, she has not changed much for about 200 years, *see* **Barbados**, 'Where to Stay', pp.68–9) and staying in them can be a good way to be introduced to local West Indian life in just a few days. You may notice a remarkable turnover of guests, as some guest houses often rent rooms out by the hour as well as by the night.

In the major yachting centres you can sometimes persuade the yachties to give you a berth on the charter boats while they are in dock. Simply go down to the marina and ask around and you may come up with something.

Camping

Rules vary throughout the islands and although it is generally not encouraged, particularly on the beaches, there are camp sites on the larger islands (the French Antilles and Cuba are quite well organized for camping). As a general rule, permission should officially be obtained from the police before camping, but you will probably get away with it.

Women

West Indian men are quite macho by nature, so visiting women can expect a fair amount of public attention—matador poses in the Latin islands, or in the British islands the *soots* (soups, tss!), a sort of sharp hiss between the teeth. Advances of this sort are usually laughed off or ignored by local women and visitors can do the same; they are often quite public and loud, but they are not usually persistent and are verbal rather than physical.

There is quite a big thing going between local lads and visiting women in the Caribbean. West Indians are quite forthright about sex anyway. Male staff in some surprisingly smart hotels will make a pass at a single woman, or one whose man happens to be absent.

West Indian women are quite modest when it comes to showing their bodies in public. It is almost unknown except in the French islands for a West Indian to go topless on the beach (though they do often go naked when washing in rivers, so be careful when out walking). They expect foreigners to observe the same rules. They also expect women to wear more than a swimsuit when out and about or in town, so you might take a cotton wrap.

Topics

Columbus greeted by Arawak Indians on San Salvador

Caribbean Fruits and Nuts

Perhaps the most striking thing about the tropics is the strength and variety of new sensations—the smells of trees in bloom, reds, greens and yellows reflected in the setting sun, the evening warmth. But tastes too have a fascinating newness and the best of these can be found in the sweet and exotic Caribbean fruits and nuts. A good idea is to go down to the market and collect a box of all the fruits in season and then gorge yourself on the new tastes.

Perhaps the best-known fruit in the Caribbean is **coconut**, which grows everywhere in the islands. Coconut is extremely versatile; the milk can be drunk (see 'Soft Drinks', pp.23–4) or used for flavouring in cooking and the inner flesh is turned into desiccated coconut for flavouring in confectionery. It can also be used as soap and as oil to burn. The fronds of the palm are used for weaving and palm thatch. A fruit that fascinated early Caribbean visitors was the **pineapple**, which grows on a stem at the centre of a small explosion of cactus-like leaves. So exotic was it considered in the 17th century that it became a symbol of welcome (you had to be generous to give your guests pineapple brought all the way from the Caribbean) and people placed stone pineapples on their gate-posts. The taste of **soursop** is both sweet and slightly tart, and at moments it can seem like a cross between a citrus fruit and a banana. Soursops are large, irregular and green, with dark hooks on their leathery skin. Inside the sweet white flesh is filled with big black pips. Of the many 'bush teas' drunk by the West Indians, soursop tea is one of the most popular. **Sweetsop** (also known as sugar apple) is smaller and shaped like a green pine cone. It is so full of sugar that when it is ripe the sweetness feels almost crystalline. **Mango** is perhaps the most exotic and luxurious of them all. Fist sized, mangos start off green and ripen to startling yellows, oranges and flushing pinks. There are many different sorts of mango including the Julie and the Number 11 (the sweetest around). Eating a mango from the skin is a hands-on business; the juice runs everywhere and the strands from the flesh get stuck in your teeth and can stay there for days, but the taste is of course uniquely delicious. The **papaya** (also known as pawpaw) is also widespread around the Caribbean. Green papaya is used in cooking; it steadily ripens and sweetens to a bright orange colour and a more fruit-like taste. Another well-known Caribbean fruit is of course the **banana** (see p.127), which comes in many different varieties, only a few of which are found in Europe and the States. Look out for the tastiest, small variety called the sweet banana.

Lesser-known fruits seen around the islands include **guava**, a pip-filled mush of sweetness with a hard skin, often used in jams; the distinctively shaped **carambola** or star apple (it looks like a five-pointed star in cross section), which has a crisp, juicy flesh usually yellow in colour; the **golden apple**, a small round and slightly golden-coloured fruit which looks not dissimilar to a pomegranate and has an aromatic flavour; and the **guinep**, a hard green lump just smaller than a golf-ball; inside there is a large pip covered in sweet white flesh not unlike a lychee. Yet more exotic varieties include **tamarind**, an extremely bitter taste extracted from a pod like a brown, knobbly broad bean; and **jackfruit**, foot-long fleshy lumps of fruit covered in hooks. **Watermelons** also grow huge around the Caribbean, and you will see them displayed cut open to reveal their bright red flesh. You can even eat **sea grape** found along the beach, best once they have turned purple, although these are something of an acquired taste. Finally, if you see

Bird of Paradise

someone selling **cocoa pods** at the roadside, stop and get one. Inside there is a white flesh, a delicious sweet and tart silky stickiness which you suck off the cocoa beans.

There are many citrus fruits: **oranges** (often green here), **lemons, grapefruits, tangerines** and **nectarines**. There are even some citrus crosses: the **ortanique** is a mix of orange and tangerine and the **ugli fruit**, whose name derives from its unfortunate skin which has come out in an uncontrollable riot of bumps, a cross between a grapefruit, an orange and a tangerine. But perhaps the finest of the Caribbean citrus fruits is the small, green **lime**, which is used in hundreds of the best Caribbean drinks. British sailors became known as *Limeys* because of their daily ration of lime-juice, given to them to keep away scurvy.

Flora and Fauna

Columbus himself was the first European to be captivated by the extraordinary beauty of the West Indies. The volcanic islands of the Lesser Antilles and the windward coasts of the Greater Antilles are incredibly fertile, watered by constant showers from the Atlantic winds. There are many rainforests in the Caribbean islands. A gardener's most useful tool is a machete, to keep back what used to be known as the *green hell*. Growth is so rampant that fences turn into hedges and even telegraph wires fur up in no time.

Trees

There are many varieties of palm tree in the Caribbean and you will see coconut palms everywhere, including the beaches of course—beware of sitting under them, though, because people have been killed by falling coconuts. In many Caribbean gardens you will often find the golden palm, which looks like a spray of greenery like a fountain, and the sago palm, very dark green, with scratchy fronds like a comb. In St Barts they use the sabal palm (*latanier* in French) for weaving rushwork. But the most impressive palms of all are the tall cabbage, and particularly the royal palm, both of which grow to over 100ft in height and cast off a spike that points directly upwards. The royal palm is cultivated for the heart of palm that is put into salads. There are some date palms in the islands and the odd curious one like the fish-tail palm, with ragged fronds looking like torn fish-tails.

There are many trees which come out in a riot of colourful blooms: the flamboyant turns scarlet in June and July, the African tulip tree (or flame of the forest) comes out in rich red blooms between December and May, and the immortelle tree (or *madre de cacao* in Spanish because it was used to protect cocoa trees) bursts into orange blooms in January and February; yellow and pink pouis are called so for obvious reasons, and they leave the ground smothered in their colourful blooms; frangipani have blooms of yellow and white and lignum vitae and jacaranda bloom a lilac colour. The cannonball tree has huge wooden fruits like cannonballs and yet small and delicate flowers. They drop to earth at dusk, unlike the night-blooming *cereus* (a flower), which dies with the daylight.

In the forests you will see clumps of bamboo (brought to the Caribbean from the Far East for its versatility as a farm material) that reach up to 60ft, sometimes grown in alleys. Gourds are made from the orange- to football-sized fruits of the bushy and spiky-branched calabash tree. The bearded fig tree has a shaggy collection of aerial roots that hang from branches like a beard. In the dry ABC islands look out for the lopsided divi-divi tree, whose branches blow over and grow in the direction of the wind. In lowlands and mid-range forests you will find gommiers (used by the Caribs to construct their canoes), mahoe and mahogany as well as more exotic species such as the spiky-trunked sand-box tree, locust trees and silk cotton, also known as kapok, whose trunk has buttresses. In the branches of higher trees you will find mosses, cycads, bromeliads, creeping vines and lianas on an endless cycle moving from the forest floor up into the top branches, and ferns as much as 10ft long that explode out of the treetops. Back at sea level you will find silver-backed ferns which will leave their pattern like a stencil when you slap them on your skin.

Many of the fruit-bearing trees that grow so well in the islands' fertile soil were imported in the 18th century, as a commercial proposition, or to provide food for slaves. The banana and some of its many relatives, the plantain and green fig, came from the Indian Ocean area. In the southern Caribbean they still grow nutmeg and cocoa (*see* p.132), which was made fashionable in Europe by Marie-Thérèse d'Espagne when she became Queen of France.

Breadfruit, with fruits like vast green cannonballs (also its relation the breadnut), was unpopular with the slaves at first, but has since become a staple. The fruit of the ackee tree tastes a bit like scrambled egg and is eaten at breakfast. Christophene (known in some islands as chow chow), a crisp and light green vegetable the shape of a pear, grows on a creeping vine. 'Ground provisions', staple **vegetables** grown locally, include yam, tannia, eddoe, sweet potato and 'Irish' potato, cassava (used by the Arawaks), all of which you will see at markets.

Flowers

The Caribbean is perhaps most famous for its flowers and gardens and you will see explosions of tropical colours all year round: the orange, pink and purple blooms of bougainvillea grow in long spindly fingers; there are some 200 species of brightly coloured hibiscus (one of which is known as *choublac* in Haiti, and is used to blacken shoes); and poinsettia, whose green leaves turn bright red at Christmastime. More exotic flowers are passion flowers, heliconia, shaped like a lobster claw, the chenille plant (also called red-hot cat tail because of its shape) and the bird of paradise flower, like a bird's face with topknot plumage. You will see the ubiquitous plastic-looking *anthurium* everywhere. There are also hundreds of orchids in the Caribbean, one of which is grown commercially to produce vanilla. The local names for plants vary of course from island to island and between the languages, but there are some colourful names: *mother-in-law's tongue* grows in a sprout of fearsome twisted green spikes.

There are **botanical gardens** throughout the islands. Originally they were used for the propagation of food and of important medicinal and commercial plants (quinine, arrowroot, camphor and spices such as cinnamon, clove, allspice). The oldest and most famous are the gardens in St Vincent, but there were gardens in most islands at one stage; many can be visited and a few of them are still in commercial use.

Fauna

The animal life of the Caribbean is quite limited and all the domestic animals that you see were imported by the colonists—including the ubiquitous goat. Only a few indigenous land animals survive and it is rare to see an armadillo, an agouti or a jutia (a rat-like creature). Reptiles of all sorts exist, from the tiny little tree frogs that keep you awake at night chirruping, toads that croak so loud that they sound like a generator, to the prehistoric, tank-like 5ft iguanas and the crocodiles that live in the swamplands. There are a few snakes, but only one or two of them are poisonous—if you see a pair of eyes glowing at night in Martinique or St Lucia watch out, because it will be the venomous *fer-de-lance*. There are plenty of insects, including mosquitoes, marching columns of termites and on the beaches irritating tiny sand flies that appear towards dusk. Fireflies, which flash bright green, on for a second, off for a second, can be seen all over the islands. Trinidad has much the widest selection of animals and particularly birds because of its proximity to South America.

Birdlife

The birds of the Caribbean are spectacular and incredibly varied. Not only are there plenty of indigenous species, many with plumage of startling tropical colours, but the islands are on migratory routes and so other species pass through as they keep away from the winter cold (both north and south). In the gardens you will find small and daring tanagers and bananaquits (which will have a go at the food on your table if you look away) as well as the yellow orioles and noisy characters called grackles. There is also a large number of hummingbirds. Trinidad alone has about 15 species: you will see these beautiful creatures in the rainforests and in the gardens. The 'doctor bird' or red-billed streamertail (it has a long double tail) is the Jamaican national bird.

Many of the Windward Islands have their own parrots that hide high up in the rainforest; sadly these have been hunted nearly to extinction and exported as pets. Other forest dwellers are the black and yellow trogons and fluorescent green honeycreepers. There are woodpeckers, cuckoos and warblers in the larger islands. Shore birds include pelicans, which you will see offshore, perched on a rock digesting their meal, boobies, terns, scissor-tailed red-billed tropicbirds and magnificent, sleek and speedy frigatebirds.

Swamps have the greatest diversity of birdlife and here you will find many sorts of herons, waders and ducks as well as sandpipers and the odd tiny water-tyrant. Oddest of all are the purple gallinule and the wattled jacana, with overlong toes that allow it to walk over lilies.

One of the most spectacular sights that you can witness in the West Indies is the evening flight of the scarlet ibis, which only takes place in the Caroni Swamp in Trinidad. Another fine sight is the pink flamingo, which nests only in Great Inagua in the Bahamas and on Bonaire in the ABC islands.

For the birdlife, Trinidad is undoubtedly the most exciting island to visit (it supposedly has more species than Canada, which is not that unlikely because most Canadian birds probably spend the winter here), but all the Greater Antilles also have an excellent variety. Over the last few years there has been an increase in awareness of the natural habitat in the countries of the Caribbean, along with the establishment of natural parks or increased powers for those that already exist. There should be excellent opportunities for enthusiasts, but not all islands have the organization to cope well with visitors. The best islands to visit for a general impression of the flora and birdlife are Trinidad (rainforest and swamplands), Dominica (rainforest) and Puerto Rico.

The Green Flash

Every fan of the Caribbean pursues the Green Flash—one of the islands' most ephemeral moments, best sought on a palm-backed beach, rum punch in hand. The Flash occurs over the sea, only rarely, during a totally cloudless sunset, at the very moment that the last tip of the sun disappears over the horizon. It usually lasts for about half a second, and never for more than a second and a half; a green strip the width of the sun on the surface of the sea.

Caribbean Indians

Virtually no indigenous Caribbean Indians survive today, but when the Europeans first arrived in the New World there were two principal races of Amerindians living in the islands. In the north were the tribes of the Arawaks, spread over the Greater Antilles and the Bahamas, and to the south the islands of the Eastern Caribbean were inhabited by the Carib Indians, who had worked their way up along the chain of the Lesser Antilles from South America as far as the Leeward Islands.

The Amerindians are thought to have made their way over from Asia to the American continent about 40,000 years ago, fanning out into different areas to become Eskimos, the North American Indians and the settled tribes of South America. A few hundred years BC, the Arawaks (from South America's coastal area) started to island hop along the Lesser Antilles, settling the Windwards and the Leewards, and eventually the Greater Antilles. The Arawaks were to live in peace on the islands for a thousand years or so, until the Caribs, a belligerent tribe who originated in the Amazon jungle, started to follow them up the chain and force them out. When Columbus arrived, the Caribs had got as far as the northernmost of the Lesser Antilles and were just starting to make raids on Puerto Rico. If the Spaniards had not arrived and set about killing the Arawaks, the Caribs would probably have done so.

Arawaks

The Spaniards found different tribes of Arawaks: on Puerto Rico the *Borinquens*, in Hispaniola, Jamaica and Cuba the *Tainos* (the Indians shouted this word, supposedly meaning peace in their language, when they first saw the Spanish ships) and in the Bahamas the *Lucayans*. A tribe called the *Guanahatabeyes* had already found their way to Cuba, probably from Florida, and lived in the caves inland, but very little is known about them.

The Arawaks were the first to discover the tropical island idyll. They led a very peaceable existence in their hammocks, fishing occasionally and snorting tobacco at three-day dance parties. They lived off the food they could catch—fish, manatee, doves and parrots, animals like iguana and fruits—and grew a few crops like cassava and maize. They were adept hunters. To catch ducks they would allow gourds (fruits like wooden footballs) to float downriver into a flock so that it would become used to them, and then they would swim down with gourds on their heads, grabbing the ducks by the feet and pulling them under as they floated past. They also used to attach a cord to a remora, a little sucker fish with a grip so tight that it could hang on to a turtleshell while they pulled it in.

The height of beauty in an Arawak was a pointed skull with hair worn in a topknot, and so babies' heads were pressed with slats of wood, giving them huge foreheads. This reputedly made their heads so hard that they could stop a Spanish sword. Like the Caribs, Arawaks had thick and glossy black hair which they oiled and wore long. They wore few clothes but they decorated themselves with feathers, tattoos and beads. Only married women would cover themselves at all. Their only domestic animal was a little dog, an *alcos*, that could not bark. Possessions meant little to them, so they happily gave away what they had to the early Spanish visitors. In their simplicity they were fascinated by the mirrors and bells that they were given in return. Theft was regarded as the worst of crimes and those caught were slowly skewered to death with a pole.

They lived in small communities near the sea, in conical thatched shelters and they were led by a *cacique* or chieftain. The cacique, who was also the spiritual leader, would preside over the religious ceremonies, calling his people together on a conch shell and then forcing himself to vomit so that he would be pure enough to communicate with the gods. Then began day-long sessions of dance, stupor and games (some played with a shuttlecock and others like volleyball), all fired by maize alcohol and the Arawak drug, a powder blasted up the nostrils through a metre-long, double-pronged tube called a *tabaco*. The Arawak for tobacco was *cohiba*, and the habit of smoking comes from them—the Spaniards were terrified to see these people with firebrands hanging out of their mouths. Tobacco, syphilis and the hammock, the potato and maize are some of the few Arawak bequests to the Europeans.

All the tribes had similar spiritual beliefs, in a male and a female God. They worshipped them in the form of *zemes*, figures of animals or humans carved in wood and stone, which also represented the forces in their lives—rain, wind, fire and hurricanes. They believed that after death they went on to *coyaba*, a plentiful land without sickness or hurricanes, where they feasted and danced all day long.

Columbus noted that the Arawaks were gentle, generous and honest. Today there is nothing left of them, except a few Arawak features in the faces of the Cubans and the Dominicans. In their search for gold, the Spaniards managed to wipe them out within 50 years. They took them off to work in their gold-mines and in the pearl beds off South America. The Arawaks, who believed firmly in an afterlife, preferred to commit suicide.

Caribs

History has been pretty mean to the Caribs (the European powers had to justify their act of genocide), but these people were hardly liberal or philanthropic towards their fellow Indians the Arawaks or the Europeans. They were widely accused of being cannibals (for which there is in fact not really much evidence: the eating was probably more ceremonial than for nourishment). Their love for alcohol, however, was so great that they would have no qualms about killing the crew of a ship which might have brandy aboard. And they were a fearsome enemy—in their *piragua* canoes, which could hold as many as 100 men, they could paddle as fast as a sailing ship and they would attack on the high seas.

The Caribs never harmed women, merely taking them to live with them, but for men they reserved a special ceremony—the barbecue. They would prepare the unfortunate captive by slitting his legs and back, stuffing the cuts with pimentoes and herbs before despatching him with a club and putting him on the spit. A Carib victim would insult his captors by saying that he had done for so many of the others' relatives that barbecuing him was tantamount to cooking up their own flesh and blood. There was even reckoned to be a pecking order of tastiness among the Europeans. The French were regarded as the most delicate and tasty, followed by the English and Dutch, but Spaniards were so stringy and disgusting as to be almost inedible (a rumour presumably put about by the Spaniards themselves).

On land the men were expert hunters and excellent shots with bows and arrows. They could split a coin at 100 yards and astonished early visitors by the speed with which they fired arrow after arrow in succession. They would capture parrots by burning hot pepper beneath them until they suffocated and they could entrance an iguana out of its hole by whistling monotonously. Fish were shot or poisoned with dogwood bark and simply collected when they floated to the surface.

The Carib features were similar to those of other South American Indians and they were stocky. They painted their skin bright red and adorned themselves with parrot feathers and necklaces strung with the teeth of their victims. But their pride was their long blue-black hair which was oiled by the women after breakfast.

While men fished and hunted, the women worked around the *carbet*, a round palm-thatch house and living area. They tended crops such as yucca (cassava) and sweet potato. Many of the women were Arawak captives and so they spoke a different language among themselves. The Caribs had a hazy conception of good and evil spirits in the world but were completely uninterested in religious matters. Missionaries gave up in the end—the Caribs got baptized simply for the presents that they would receive.

Columbus

Columbus is famous as the discoverer of America. One Caribbean calypso singer objected in song that this view was simply Eurocentric arrogance because American Indians clearly beat him to it by just a few thousands of years. However, his voyages were to have an importance that changed the world. Certainly he gave the West Indies their name. In fact he was sailing for India, Cathay (China) and Cipangu (Japan), as mentioned by Marco Polo, to reopen the spice trade with the East. Discovery of other islands—the existence of islands in the Atlantic, including Antillia (later used in the word Antilles), had been suspected since Biblical times—was a secondary concern for him. Strictly speaking he failed in his quest, but it was clear to all, even by the time that he died, how significant his discoveries in the New World were.

Cristoforo Colombo (or Cristobal Colon in Spanish) was born in the 1450s in Genoa, the son of a weaver, but he chose his career as a sailor while still a young man and travelled throughout the Mediterranean on trading voyages. Eventually he sailed further afield, to Iceland and along the coast of West Africa.

Columbus was largely self-taught. He was obviously an intelligent and forceful man, but he was inflexible and jumped to illogical geographical conclusions. He decided at one stage that the world was pear-shaped. All the same, he was a bold and accomplished explorer and a fine navigator. He was persuasive and even charismatic in court, impressing Queen Isabella so much that she helped him despite the advice of her courtiers. But he was domineering in authority and this was his downfall. He may have carried it off on board ship, persuading his lieutenants to 'see' land and allaying a potentially mutinous crew, but he was a hopeless administrator of the colonies.

If he was a visionary, and he stuck to his plan for years before he was granted the opportunity to carry it out, his dreams also tipped into fantasy and self-delusion. He considered himself chosen by God, with a mission to bring Christianity to the New World, and he was paranoid about others encroaching on what he considered his domain. He was vain and he insisted on huge public honour in reward for his service to the Crown of Spain. He was ennobled, granted the titles of *Admiral of the Ocean Sea* and *Viceroy of the Indies*, as well as huge financial rewards from any future trading with the area. But he fulfilled the dreams of the age. The world was outgrowing its Mediterranean confines as the Portuguese began to explore the coast of Africa. And the ancient spice routes to the east had been closed with the fall of Constantinople in the 1450s. Columbus was a master mariner who had sailed all the seas and was acquainted with all available maps from his cartographic work. Slowly the plan evolved. He would try to reach the east by sailing west.

He tried all the major European kings for a sponsor and had to attend the Spanish court for six years before Ferdinand and Isabella granted him a commission to sail. Freed of the last of the Moors and in confident mood in 1492, they gave him three caravels, the *Santa Maria*, the *Niña* and the *Pinta*. On 3 August 1492 Columbus set off from Palos, touching the Canaries and then heading off into the ocean, navigating due west. According to his calculations (which he had massaged to his favour), he expected to come to Japan or China after about 2500 miles (about where America is). They sailed with the wind behind for over a month, through the Sargasso Sea, into the unknown. Steadily the crew became more rebellious (fearing they might not get home). On 12 October 1492, they sighted land, one of the Bahamian islands.

Columbus called the island San Salvador in honour of the Saviour, but clearly he had not found Japan, so after a few days he set off in search of it, asking along the way for gold. He touched Cuba and then his flagship was wrecked off Hispaniola and he was forced to leave about forty men behind when he sailed for Spain, where he announced that he had reached Asia. On Palm Sunday 1493 Columbus was received with all the pomp and glory that he craved. He was treated almost as an equal to the monarchs in court.

A second expedition was sent the same year, with 1500 settlers to colonize the island of Hispaniola. Administrative problems began almost at once and were compounded when Columbus left his brother Diego in charge during his exploration of Cuba and Jamaica.

Columbus led a third voyage in 1498, arriving in Trinidad in the south, narrowly missing the continent of South America. From here he sailed to Hispaniola by dead reckoning (no mean feat: a journey of 800 miles through uncharted waters). He found the colony in disarray and was forced to treat with the rebels. Eventually his viceregal authority was revoked and he was shipped back to Spain in chains.

He was treated kindly by Ferdinand and Isabella and eventually he was permitted to return to the New World on a fourth journey in 1502, on the express understanding that he was not to set foot on Hispaniola. In some ways his last trip was the most successful—he made contact for the first time with the more developed Indian cultures of the Central American seaboard and he discovered gold in larger quantities there (the shape of things to come). However he was shipwrecked on the coast of Jamaica and had to wait a year before he was rescued and made it back to Spain.

Columbus died in Spain in 1506, faintly ridiculed because of all his problems in the Indies, his eccentric behaviour and his excessive claims against the Crown. Though his experience as a seaman had probably told him otherwise, he maintained to his death that he had discovered the Far East. Columbus (his remains at least) made yet more journeys after his death. He was brought to Santo Domingo in 1544 by his daughter-in-law and then removed (or not, as the case may be; *see* **Hispaniola**) to Spanish soil (Cuba) at the time of the Haitian invasion in 1796, perhaps returning to Seville a century later. In honour of the 500th anniversary of the discovery, Columbus has made yet another journey to a specially constructed crypt in the enormous Faro a Colon, a megalithic lighthouse in the shape of a cross in Santo Domingo.

Pirates, Buccaneers and Privateers

The Papal edicts or 'Bulls' that quickly followed the discovery of the New World by Columbus ordained that all land, discovered or undiscovered, west of a line 100 leagues beyond the Azores, should be an exclusive Spanish preserve (the line cuts off the eastern tip of Brazil and so the Portuguese were allowed to settle there). *No peace beyond the line* was declared, and any ships found in American waters were regarded by the Spaniards as pirates. The crews would be killed if captured. But this did not stop sea-rovers from other European nations, who had heard of the massive riches that the Spaniards were pillaging from the Indian settlements on the Spanish main. Already by 1540 many of these 'privateers', working under contracts to their governments, had started to creep into the Caribbean.

Jack Hawkins (son of a seafaring father who had brought an Indian chief from South America to the English court) made three voyages to the Caribbean in the second half of the 16th century. On his final voyage he took the young Francis Drake. He was working a trade route via Africa that was later to become very familiar—he collected Africans to sell to the Spaniards in the New World as slaves. Others, including French pirates *Pie de Palo* (Timberleg) and Jacques Sores, were less interested in trade as privateers and more interested in what they could seize by besieging and ransoming Spanish settlements. Drake returned at the end of the century, as did Walter Raleigh, on his search for the Golden King, *El Dorado*.

In the early 1600s large numbers of pirate ships operated in the Caribbean and some of the sailors ended up settling the north coast of Hispaniola, killing cattle and curing it for sale to passing ships. They were called **buccaneers**, because of the *boucan*, the oven in which they smoked the meat. Searovers, misfits and deserters came to join them, jumping ship or deserting from their indentureships on the plantations. They lived in small groups, sharing all their property (even wives if they had them) and wore loose clothes with a leather belt that was slung with knives. They were renowned for their shooting. As the century progressed they moved across to the island of Tortuga off the north coast of Haiti, overlooking the Windward Passage between Cuba, Hispaniola and the Bahamas, which became their stronghold and from where they would set off in search of Spanish ships.

They called themselves the *Brethren of the Coast* and they took to sea as pirates, ranging as far afield as Madagascar and the Indian Ocean. The lure of this life on the edge was, of course, easy money, and when the money from the previous expedition ran out, they were ruthless and cunning about getting more, attacking any ships that they could find, taking the loot and selling it in their ports at St Thomas in the Virgin Islands, Port Royal in Jamaica and later Nassau in the Bahamas. They were fearsome fighters, putting the fright into professional soldiers and sailors and they were renowned for their cruelty. Once again they worked in small crews, with laws amongst themselves.

Père Labat tells of a French *filibuster*, a privateer rather than a pirate, for whom he said Mass in 1694. During the service, they fired a salvo of cannons at the Elevation of the Holy Sacrament and at the Benediction and then contributed handsomely to his coffers from the profits of their latest venture. These privateers divided the prizes equally amongst themselves, with a slightly larger share for the captain, quartermaster, surgeon and pilot, and a bonus for the man who first sighted the prize. Money was put aside for a wounded member of the crew and compensation was paid—600 ecus for a limb, 300 for a finger or an eye—and they were cared for out of captured loot.

Henry Morgan was one of the most colourful of the privateers/pirates and he worked out of Port Royal at the height of its infamy in the late 1600s. He soon became the 'admiral' of the buccaneers (elected by them). He developed a strategy of attacking towns far inland and he even took the most fortified Spanish city, Puerto Bello (by using a human shield of monks and nuns to storm the walls). His men would then loot, ransack and rape their way through the town and, loaded down with pieces of eight, they would return to Port Royal for more revelry.

Morgan was notoriously cruel and became hugely wealthy. Eventually, after double-crossing many of his buccaneers, he became Lieutenant Governor of Jamaica and had a hand in stamping out piracy in the region.

Edward Teach or Blackbeard was the most notorious pirate of the 1700s and one of the 'sweet trade's' greatest showmen. He dressed outrageously and cultivated a monstrous appearance with a huge black beard and fuses fizzing in his hair when he went into battle. At one stage he led a whole squadron of boats around the islands. He was known occasionally to fire on his companions just to keep them guessing, while quaffing his favourite drink *rumfustion*, a mix of beer, gin, sherry, rum and gunpowder.

Stede Bonnet was a gentleman and a man of letters of Barbados, a Justice of the Peace who actually bought his own ship and provided for his family before taking to the seas. Jack Rackham had two women in his crew, Anne Bonney and Mary Read, who were reputed to be just as violent as their male colleagues. A man could be killed for cowardice and the captain lose his command if the crew thought he had failed in attacking a prize, so the pirates were always bold and brave, and they would regularly take on ships far larger than their own. One Captain Moidore loaded up his cannons with gold coins when he ran out of shot. L'Ollonois, a Frenchman, executed the whole crew of a ship at one point, licking their blood off his sword and then tore out the heart of a man and ate it. He himself was dismembered and roasted in the end.

The Slave Trade

As the sugar industry developed in the Caribbean, there was a massive demand for labour to work the canefields. Indentured servants from Europe were tried but did not cope well in the heat, and so the planters decided on Africans instead. The Spaniards had imported Africans in the 16th century, but it was not until sugar cultivation started in Brazil and the Caribbean islands that the slave trade grew. A triangular trade route grew up between the ports of Europe and the southern-facing coastline of West Africa, with manufactured goods making their way to Africa on the first leg, as payment in kind for the slaves they took on board. The last stretch, from the West Indies back to Europe, was made with a cargo of sugar hogsheads.

The most notorious leg of the journey was the fearsome *Middle Passage*, from the African coast to the West Indies, which lasted anything from six to twelve weeks. The slaves, from the Coromantee, Eboe, Mandingo and Yoruba tribes, were taken from their villages in night-raids or sold into slavery as prisoners of war and then held captive in the vast fortresses that lined the Gold and Ivory Coasts. Once on board they were chained to one another in the hold, each with a space so cramped that they could not sit up. As the ship pushed off, the crew stood by with lighted torches, threatening to set light to it and all the people on board if the slaves rebelled. Once out of sight of land, the slaves were allowed to exercise for just a few minutes each day, still chained in pairs, before being returned to the festering hold again. On average, about 12 per cent died on each trip, some from disease but others preferred to commit suicide by jumping overboard to certain drowning in their pairs.

In the last few days before arriving in the Caribbean, they were fattened up and as the ship drew into port, the frightened slaves were brought up on deck, where they were oiled to make them look healthy. They were then paraded through the streets singing on the way to the market where they were auctioned.

People joke that the West Indians change the roll of their gait as they walk along the street, switching rhythm to each successive stereo system that they pass. A bit of an exaggeration, but music has been central to Caribbean life since slave days when it was a principal form of recreation, and you will hear it everywhere, all day, every day. You'll see three-year-olds in the first throes of dancing and sixty-year-olds who will take a turn on the living-room floor with lightning footwork and an easy grace. In Santo Domingo the shoeshine boys will strike up on their boxes with brushes and tins of polish. Buses are like mobile discotheques. At Carnival they dance for days. There are almost as many beats as there are islands in the Caribbean and they go on changing and developing over time. The roots are audible in many cases—you will see marching bands dressed in their red tunics playing 'O, when the Saints' *reggae* style, Indian flourishes appear in Trinidadian *calypso*, the Latin beat is clear in Cuban and Puerto Rican *salsa* and the vocals of rap appear in calypso and Jamaican *dancehall*. But in all the Caribbean sounds, the rhythm is relentlessly fast and the beat is as solid as the African drums from which it is derived.

The West Indians will use anything to make music. At carnival the crowds shuffle along to the sound of a couple of drums, a car wheel-rim, a cheese-grater and a cowbell. Even garden forks have been tuned up in Curaçao. But the best example of them all is the steel drum in Trinidad, which was invented in the yards of Port of Spain after the last war. Discarded biscuit tins and oil drums were bashed out and then tuned up and an orchestra was created.

As you travel around the islands, you will see speakers set up in the street just for the hell of it. Cars practically bulge with the beat and they can often be heard before they can be seen coming along the road. If you are invited to a *fête*, go, because they are a wild side of West Indian life. Dance is all lower carriage movement, shuffle-stepping and swaying hips, and is incredibly energetic.

The rhythms of one island often spread to another. The main popular rhythms and their countries of origin are as follows:

Soca (soul-calypso)—Trinidad, where calypso itself started (*see* p.87). Barbados and other islands nearby also produce their own calypsonians, some of them very good.

Zouk—Martinique and Guadeloupe, with a bustling double beat.

Salsa—two different sorts, one each from Cuba and Puerto Rico, the latter influenced by the 'Neo-Riceñans' (Puerto Ricans in New York).

Merengue—the Dominican Republic, also a strongly Latin sound. Another local rhythm, *bachata*, has recently been revived and become popular.

Compas—Haiti, a bit rougher, but not dissimilar to the zouk of the French Antilles, also echoes of West Africa.

Any of the Caribbean **carnivals** is worth attending if you happen to be on the island. You can often join in if you do go by asking around (usually for a small fee to cover the cost of the costume). It is worth crossing half the world to get to the **Trinidad Carnival** (many Trinidadians do), which takes place at the beginning of Lent. Also there are steel band and calypso competitions. Other music festivals include the Cuban **Jazz Festival** in February (Cuba is good for music, because of the many different sorts) and the **Merengue Festival** in Santo Domingo in July. At around the same time, reggae fans cross the world for **Reggae Sunsplash** in Montego Bay, Jamaica.

Barbados

villa Nova

Barbados stands alone, out in the Atlantic, about 100 miles beyond the rest of the Eastern Caribbean, a coral island with some of the finest golden sand beaches anywhere and perhaps the most agreeable climate in the West Indies. The island is long established as a winter getaway and has had a trusty following of wealthy visitors over the last 50 years. Barbados is one of the Caribbean's most popular destinations.

'The whole place has an appearance of cleanliness, gentility and wealth which one does not find in any other island.' So thought Père Labat, a Dominican monk and roving gastronome who visited Barbados at the height of its prosperity in 1700. The spirit of his opinion still stands in the graciousness and hospitality of the late 20th century. Education, literacy and health care, the social services in general, are the best in the English-speaking Caribbean (with the present exception of the Cayman Islands) and the poor are better off in Barbados than in most of the neighbouring islands. Barbados commands a position of influence out of proportion to its size within the Caribbean. This is the source of the renowned Bajan (native Barbadian) self-esteem, and quite a bit of mockery from other islanders. Altogether, the national motto 'Pride and Industry' is quite appropriate for the Bajans.

Just 21 miles by 14, Barbados is occasionally dismissed as small, crowded and flat, but away from the built-up areas the cane-covered hinterland rises gently to 1000ft heights at Hackleton's cliff above the Atlantic. It is true that the island is populous, though; its 260,000 inhabitants make it the most densely inhabited in the area. Most Bajans live along the sheltered west coast of the island and in the massive and ever-expanding suburb that runs from the capital, Bridgetown, all along on the south coast. Just a few villages are tucked away inland. The Barbadians are over 90 per cent of African descent, but there are small communities of white Bajans (a visible and influential business community) and the 'poor whites', descendants of indentured servants who have scraped a living from the land for centuries. There are not that many Bajans of mixed race, and if the island has a problem, it is the residue of a rigid system of colour prejudice.

Barbados's British heritage, which is stronger than in any other Caribbean island, once led the island to be called 'Little England' and even 'Bimshire'. The British influence is hardly strong now, but the 300-year connection has left a delightful and often old-fashioned charm in the manners, the buildings and even the language (you can hear distinct traces of a West Country accent in Bajan speech). Classically beautiful plantation houses stand in the swathes of sugar-cane; cricketers in whites play beneath palm trees and there is even an isolated area of rugged hills in the northeast familiarly known as Scotland. At times, though, it seems that Little England has managed to inherit some of the worst British foibles: pomposity and cliquish social attitudes. Functionaries will address you in clipped and hushed tones about a dress code (jacket and tie) in some clubs, which comes as a bit of a surprise in the Caribbean. The island's

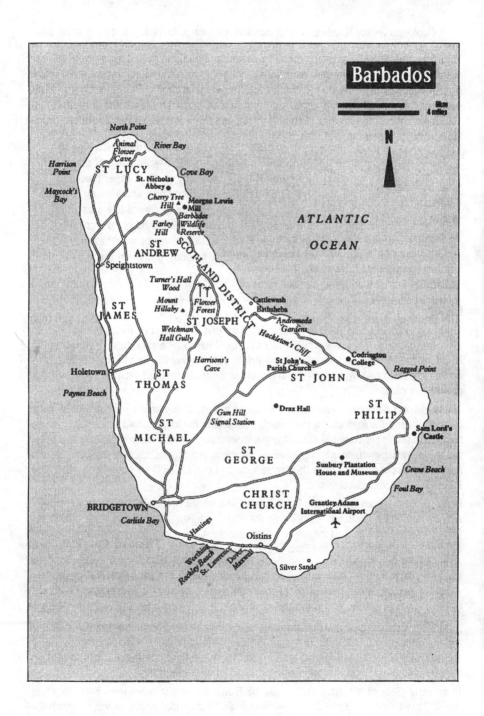

colonial legacy is fading now (since Independence in 1966) as it thrusts on and modernizes. As elsewhere in the Caribbean, the strongest influence now is that of the United States.

With its charming islanders used to visitors and a long-established, broad-based tourism industry, Barbados is rightfully a top Caribbean destination, to which guests return year after year. It is fairly crowded, so if you are looking for beach-bound Caribbean seclusion this is hardly the place to come, but it is easy to have a good holiday here and it is ideal for a first visit to the islands—in whatever price category you choose: interspersed between some of the Caribbean's most expensive hotels there are many much cheaper places to stay. Things have sharpened up recently, with lively bars and a string of excellent restaurants, even gourmet delis with reliable supplies of foie gras and champagne. The famous west coast of Barbados, second home to a crowd of international sophisticates (people measure themselves by whether they arrived on Concorde or by First Class in the season), has given it the nickname 'the millionaires' playground'.

History

The history of Barbados is bound inextricably with that of England and with the fortunes of West Indian sugar. In an area where islands changed hands with almost every war, colonial Barbados had 300 years of uninterrupted British rule. It was the first in the Caribbean to exploit sugar successfully, and even today many of the roads are lined each side with curtains of tall green cane.

The island was supposedly named by Portuguese visitors who passed by in the 1580s. They called the island *los Barbudos* or the 'bearded ones' after the long, matted and straggly shoots thrown off the upper branches of the banyan trees that grew near the coast. There had been native Amerindian settlements on Barbados—recent archaeological discoveries at the site of a marina development show that they were here as early as 1500 BC—but by the time the Europeans arrived none remained.

Barbados was claimed for England in 1625, and was settled two years later, in an expedition sent by Sir William Courteen. They found the island uninhabited except by some wild boars (left by early visitors as food for shipwrecked mariners). After wrangling and intrigue in the court of King Charles I, with the Earls of Pembroke and Carlisle in dispute over rights of colonization (and after a parallel armed battle on the island itself between the Windward and the Leeward men), the settlement flourished, assisted by a family of 40 Arawaks from Guiana who demonstrated how to cultivate tropical plants such as cotton, tobacco and cassava.

The colony exploded, and within 30 years Barbados was overcrowded. Fortune-hunters flooded in; indentured servants put themselves in servitude for years with a promise of land at the end of their term. Refugees came from the Civil War in England; others were deported by the notorious Judge Jeffreys for their part in the Monmouth Rebellion and sold into slavery. To be 'Barbadosed' was a recognized punishment in 17th-century England.

In an early piece of industrial espionage, the Dutch brought sugar-cane to Barbados from Brazil. They taught the Barbadians how yield could be increased by *ratooning*, in which the cane was planted not sticking out of the ground but laid flat and buried; and they introduced boiling techniques. At first the crop was used only for producing rum, but it soon became clear how profitable sugar was for export to Europe. By the 1650s the whole of Barbados was planted with cane, even to the exclusion of growing provisions—cultivating sugar was so profitable that the Barbadians were happy to pay the price of imported food. *Good merchantable muscovado sugar* was used as currency for barter, even for the Governor's salary. Willoughby Fort in Bridgetown was constructed as a defence against pirates in 1656 at a price of 80,000 pounds of sugar.

Whistler, a soldier, visited Barbados in the 1650s and described the population like this:

> *The island is inhabited with all sortes, with English, French, Dutch, Scotes, Irish, Spaniards, they being Jues, with ingones (Indians) and Miserabell Negors borne to perpetual slavery thay and theyer seed...This Iland is the dunghill whar our England dost cast forth its rubidg. Rodgs (rogues) and Hors and such like peopel are those that are generally broght heare.*

The whores and rogues were sent out to provide manpower for the cultivation of sugar. Many of them moved on, leaving the 'Miserabell Negors', the African slaves who were already being brought over in their thousands from the west coast of Africa and whose descendants make up the majority of the Bajan population today.

The empire builders were so successful with their sugar that Barbados came to be called 'the brightest jewel in the English Crown' at the end of the 17th century. The monopoly did not last, despite Barbadian efforts to protect their markets, as other islands started to cultivate the crop. Expensive equipment forced out the smallholders and the plantations became fewer, larger and more profitable. Their fortunes waxed and waned with war and peace in the 18th century, as Britain, France and Spain vied for supremacy. Fortunes were handsomely augmented by the usual Caribbean trade of smuggling, avoiding port taxes. Père Labat wrote that the captain of his barque worked hard unloading during the day, but far harder at night.

Barbados's unconquered history was due mainly to its position out in the Atlantic. Ships had to beat upwind towards it and could be seen from miles off, and it was formidably protected by a string of forts down the west coast. The island was the headquarters of the British forces in the Caribbean for many years. But it was not only from outside that the island was threatened. The plantation slaves plotted rebellion from the beginning and they were ruthlessly treated when found out. The most famous revolt was Bussa's Rebellion, in 1816, caused by thoughts of freedom at the time of the abolition of the slave trade in 1807. It was initiated by torching the canefields and was put down with the loss of nearly 300 lives. Many more rebel slaves were deported to Honduras.

In 1838 the slaves were finally freed (after a four-year 'apprenticeship' period in which they were paid minimally, but had to remain on their plantations) and the industry faltered. Many of the freed slaves emigrated because there was no land for them other than on the plantations. As sugar beet was developed in Europe, the sugar industry nearly collapsed, but after fifty years in the doldrums, West Indian sugar was given preferential treatment and it was profitable again by 1910. Sugar and the rum produced from it are still very important to Barbados. The national coat of arms shows a fist grasping two canes, and the Bridgetown coat of arms has three rum puncheons.

The 20th century brought pressure for political change with the growth of trades unions in the twenties and thirties. Eventually universal franchise came in 1951. Barbados was a member of the West Indian Federation, but when it failed in 1962, the island opted for Independence on 30 November 1966. Barbados remains within the British Commonwealth.

Life has changed radically since Independence and the influence of the United States is steadily replacing that of Britain. There is still a small sugar (and rum) industry as well as a manufacturing sector which produces garments, stainless steel and paper products. Amazingly, Barbados produces over half of its oil requirements at the moment. Off-shore finance services are expanding and there is some data processing, but by far the biggest earner is tourism. The Bajans felt the recession in the early 1990s quite badly but life has begun to improve. Today the island is led by Prime Minister the Right Hon. Owen Arthur of the Barbados Labour Party Party, which was elected with 19 seats in September 1994, with the Democratic Labour Party (8 seats) in opposition with a single member of the National Democratic Party. Elections are next due in September 1999.

Cricket and the Constitution

The two most hallowed institutions to be adopted during 300 years' association with Britain are cricket and Parliament. As with so many other things, Barbados exerts an influence in cricket out of proportion to its small size. The island has won the regional championship, the Red Stripe Cup, more times than all the other islands combined. It has also provided a string of extremely gifted players to the West Indies side, including men like Sir Frank Worrell (the first black captain of the West Indies team), Sir Clyde Walcott, Sir Everton Weekes ('the three Ws'), Sir Gary Sobers and more recently Joel Garner and Gordon Greenidge. Current and recent players include Desmond Haynes, Sherwin Campbell, Roland Holder and Courtney Brown. If a Test Match is being played while you are visiting, be sure to go along (you will find that most of Barbados life stops for it anyway).

Although the first inter-island cricket matches were played here in 1865, Barbados has an even longer-standing association with Parliament. Founded in 1637, the Barbados Assembly is the third-oldest parliamentary body in the British Commonwealth, after Bermuda and Westminster itself. The destruction of its official building, the State House, in a fire in 1668, meant that the Legislative Assembly spent 60 years conducting its business in taverns. For centuries the institution was dominated by white Bajans, but in 1843 the first non-white member was elected. The late 19th century turned out to be a time of political crisis throughout the West Indies because Britain was keen to impose direct rule from London, bypassing the islands' assemblies. However, Barbados was the only Caribbean colony to keep its legislative powers intact.

Barbados has a bicameral parliamentary system, with elections held every five years to the 28-seat House of Assembly. Senate members, of which there are 21, are appointed by the Governor General (currently Sir Clifford Husbands) on the advice of senior politicians. The recently restored parliamentary buildings in Bridgetown can be visited.

Barbados has quite a good **bus** system, emanating mainly from Bridgetown and reaching most areas of the island. It is a cheap way to get around and gives a good exposure to Bajan life. People say good morning when they board the bus and if you are sitting, someone may well hand you a package to hold for them. There is a mixture of public and private buses, most of them painted in Barbadian national colours, yellow and blue. Then there are minibuses known as **Z-vans**. These have something of an image problem with the Bajans because they will happily stop in the middle of the road and hold up all the traffic in order to pick up a passenger. Some Z-vans still have massive on-board stereos and delight in playing the latest *soca* and Jamaican *dub*, which makes them fun to travel on (actually stereos were banned a while ago because schoolchildren used to play truant and spend their lunch-money on a ride).

Private minibus terminals are next to the public terminals in Bridgetown, but out in the country all services use the same bus-stops, with a red and white circle on a pole like an 8ft lollipop. Wave frantically. For services **south** and **east**, the main public bus terminal is in Fairchild Street, just across Charles Duncan O'Neal Bridge from Trafalgar Square. If you are travelling **north**, then you leave from near St Mary's Church, the Lower Green Station or the Pelican van stand. The public system runs to a vague schedule (West Indian time); private buses leave when they are full or when the driver gets the urge. All fares are Bds$1.50.

As a good tourist, you are really expected to travel by **taxi**. These can be arranged in any hotel foyer and at key points around the island—airport, downtown Bridgetown and at certain taxi stands: Sunset Crest Taxi Service in Holetown (✆ 432 1006), Rockley Beach Stand (✆ 435 7328), the Maxwell Taxi Stand (✆ 420 4067), St Lawrence (✆ 428 7292), Lower Green Taxi in Bridgetown (✆ 426 4749) and the Barbados Transport Co-op Society (✆ 428 0953) at the airport. Make sure to establish the price beforehand, though, because taxis are not metered in Barbados. Sample prices are: **airport** to St Lawrence Gap—Bds$20, Bridgetown—Bds$30, Holetown —Bds$40, Speightstown—Bds$48; and from **Bridgetown** to St Lawrence Gap— Bds$18, Holetown—Bds$22, Speightstown—Bds$30 and Bathsheba—Bds$38. A taxi driver would be only too pleased to give a tour of the island, for around Bds$35 per hour.

There is plenty to explore in Barbados for two or three days and so more formal island tours by bus and car—a day trip taking in some of the undeveloped north of the island and the wild and ragged east coast with its fantastic views—can be arranged through Island Tours (✆ 437 9389) or a less expensive option, Topaz Tours (✆ 435 8451). Most companies will pick you up at your hotel and include lunch on a full day tour. A personalized tour by car is available through Custom Tours (✆ 425 0099); Island Safari (✆ 432 5337) offer four-wheel-drive to remoter spots around the island. If you wish to go sightseeing by helicopter, that too can be arranged. Contact Bajan Helicopters (✆ 431 0069) for a tour which follows the coastline or cuts across the dramatic centre of the island.

A good way to explore the countryside is by **hire car**, jeep or by the trusty favourite, a moke (formerly the Mini-moke, now a variety of Suzukis and Subarus). If you do set off, make sure to have a good road map because it is surprisingly easy to get lost in

Barbados's endless fields of sugar-cane. In the winter season there is often a waiting list for vehicles (up to three days), so consider arranging a car when you book your holiday. Firms give better deals for a three-day hire. Expect to leave a hefty deposit with the hire company unless you present a credit card. Most companies will deliver the car to your hotel. Car hire is pretty expensive in Barbados; rates start at US$50 per day for a mini-moke, plus taxes and CDW, and are marginally more for a large car. There are cheaper options, but you are advised to check the fine print very carefully. Reliable companies include Corbin's Car Rentals (✆ 427 9531), Dear's Garage in Bridgetown (✆ 429 9277) and Hastings (✆ 427 7853), Drive-A-Matic (✆ 422 5017), Courtesy Rent-a-Car, head office near Bridgetown (✆ 426 5871) and Sunny Isle Motors in Worthing (✆ 435 7979) and Sunset Crest Rent-A-Car in St James (✆ 432 1482) and on the south coast (✆ 426 1763). **Scooters** can be hired through Fun Seekers (✆ 435 8206) in Christ Church and **bicycles** through Irie Mountain Bikes (✆ 424 4730) and Fun Seekers above.

To drive in Barbados (this takes place on the left as a rule) you need a special visitor's driving licence, which can be purchased on presentation of a valid driving licence at the car hire companies, at the airport on arrival, or at any police station, cost Bds$10.

Beaches

The beaches of Barbados are excellent and they offer something for every taste, from the fine golden sand and calm water of the protected west coast, round the southern point where the water is livelier and the sand becomes coral pink, to the windswept surfing beaches of the east coast, where the sea is positively rough and huge breakers bring in the full force of the Atlantic. There is a more or less continual stretch of sand on the west coast, running north from Bridgetown. It is an excellent place to walk. The whole 10-mile tourist stretch is redolent with the aroma of bodies gently sizzling in coconut oil, but it only gets crowded in clusters around the hotels and the public beaches. Here you will find general watersports operators (often attached to the hotels), offering anything from snorkelling gear to wetbikes and waterskiing trips. Be careful of the tall and bushy manchineel trees all along the coast. Their fruit was called the apple of death by Columbus, because it causes a nasty rash and swelling.

South of Bridgetown the sand is fantastic too and there are plenty of active beaches with bars and watersports. Once you reach the southern tip the sports get more adventurous with rougher water and the wind—windsurfing is best in the south and there is surfing on the east coast. For an out-of-the-way beach go to the southeast, where there are some delightful coves cut into the cliffs with pink sand and fantastic aquamarine water—well worth the effort of a visit. Or go north, beyond hotel country. On the Atlantic side the surf comes pounding in and swimming is often dangerous, but the coast is spectacular to view, from Ragged Point in the southeast to Bathsheba, where crowds come to watch the surfers.

Hotels are usually happy for you to base yourself on their beach for the day if you want to use their facilities and have lunch there. All beaches in Barbados are public below the high-water mark anyway. There are lifeguards on some beaches and NCC rangers dressed in blue on most established beaches. There are only a few hucksters, who will offer the traditional array of services, including hair-braiding, tropical shirts and African carvings. They can be very persistent (and quite persuasive) when they get going, so if you do not want to buy you may have to do a bit of stonewalling. Barbadian modesty prevents nude and even topless bathing.

best beaches

Payne's Bay: Popular west coast beach with hotels and bars, some watersports. Other stretches of west coast sand include **Brighton Beach** (popular with the Bajans at weekends), **Paradise Beach** and **Treasure Beach**.

Folkstone: Marine Park area for snorkelling and swimming off Holetown, popular with the locals at the weekends; some facilities.

Mullins Bay: Active beach backed by casuarina pines, with a bar and some sports.

Heywood's Beach: Just north of Speightstown. Beyond the hotel strip you will find relative seclusion at **Six Men's Bay**, where Bajans build fishing boats or at **Maycock's Bay**.

Accra Beach: Popular south coast beach in hotel territory, crowds sizzling in lines.

Sandy Beach: Worthing, a huge and gradually expanding stretch of sand, beach bars and hotels.

Dover Beach: Culmination of the beaches at St Lawrence Gap; active, some watersports.

Miami Beach: Just beyond Maxwell, backed by casuarina pines.

Silver Sands Beach: Just short of the airport, one of the liveliest beaches on the island at (windsurfing) competition time; attracts a crowd of the Barbados body beautiful and a winter influx of nut-brown poseurs and straw-haired surf bums.

Foul Bay, Harrismith Beach and **Bottom Beach**: (the first named because of its reputation as an anchorage rather than its setting, which is charming), three charming coves cut into the cliffs, secluded with excellent sand and quite large waves.

Crane Beach: Just beneath the surreal hotel of the same name, whose facilities you can use (*adm*), a superb stretch of sand, where there is good boogie boarding.

Bath: Atlantic coast, safe swimming because of an offshore reef, popular with the Bajans on their weekend outings, which involve a cook-up on the beach and general fun and games; some simple facilities. Other beaches for outings include **Barclays Park, Gay's Cove** and **River Bay** close to the northern tip of the island.

beach bars

If you do not want to base a beach visit around a hotel, there is a number of excellent beach bars, some easy-going, others a little smarter where you can expect to eat well. On Paynes Bay south of Holetown you will find **Bomba's**, a rustic wooden, red, gold and green affair which resonates to a rumble of reggae and other Caribbean sounds. Easy atmosphere, a cocktail list as long as your arm—Bomblaster, Rasta Sling and Bomba Mama—and simple fare; mixed crowd and lively in the early evening as a crowd of Bajans catch a beer and a chat on the way home. Not far off, the **Bamboo Beach Bar** has smartened itself up and has lost a bit of character, but it offers a retreat from the sun for lunch or a sunset drink. North of here, where the sand breaks the cliffs near Speightstown, **Mullins Beach Bar** is a popular gathering point by day and evening. It has a very pretty setting with a white gingerbread terrace facing on to the sunset. Monkey murals and lively music, very popular and quite expensive. Burgers, salads, soups, even a pepperpot to go with the cocktails—Mullins Twister and Heart Attack.

Within walking distance of Central Bridgetown heading south is the **Boatyard**, now sexed up with a bar and restaurant beneath the sea almond tree right on the sand at the head of Carlisle Bay. There is a nice bar and restaurant at Accra Beach, the **Sugar Reef**, all dressed up in white wood and parasols. In Worthing on the south coast you will find a mixed crowd of Bajans and visitors under the parasols and palm trees at the **Carib Beach Bar**: snacks by day and often lively after dark. There is a bar on **Silver Sands** Beach, which is at its most active when the windsurfers are on-island in the winter.

Flora and Fauna

When the Europeans first arrived in 1627, Barbados was entirely forested, but the trees were stripped within 20 years as the cultivation of sugar went ahead. Turner's Hall Wood in the north of the island is the only place where the original forest remains. Around the island, however, you will see examples of the huge *ficus citrifolia* or 'bearded fig tree', a gnarly-trunked colossus with a curtain of aerial roots that resemble straggly beards, from which the island took its name.

Particular pleasures in Barbados are the hotel and private gardens, which are excellent (talk to any gardener for an introduction to tropical flora) and where you will find at least some plants in flower at all times of the year. Besides the many palms there are flowering trees, like the flamboyant that explodes into scarlet in the summer and the poinsettia, whose leaves turn scarlet in December, and of course limitless flowering bushes such as bougainvillea, ixora and heliconias including lobster claw and bird of paradise. There is a number of public gardens and parks on view in the island: **Andromeda** in Bathsheba, **Grenade Hall Forest** in the north and the **Flower Forest** in St Joseph.

There are few wild animals in Barbados, though you will come across green monkeys (more brown with green patches), which were brought over from Africa 300 years ago. Other animals can be seen in the **Barbados Wildlife Reserve** in the north of the island. Birdlife is more varied. In the remote northern areas you can see three hummingbirds—the Antillean crested hummingbird, the purple-throated carib and the green-throated carib, as well as colourful tanagers and kingbirds. In the inland swamps you can see sandpipers, terns and warblers (the endangered yellow warbler is endemic to Barbados), and along the coast you will see solitary pelicans digesting their meal on an isolated rock.

Bridgetown

Set on the broad sweep of Carlisle Bay on the southwest coast of Barbados, Bridgetown is a thriving Caribbean capital with a population of over 100,000. Grand old colonial structures with filigree metal balconies jostle with purposeful glass-fronted shops and modern pastel offices, while out in the street-markets hucksters tout their wares from trays to passers-by.

The heart of Bridgetown has always been the old harbour at the **Careenage**, an inlet that takes its name from the process of *careening*, in which a weight would be tied to a boat's mast to upturn it, revealing the hull so that it could be cleaned and painted. The lighters that once loaded the ships at anchor in the bay are now gone because Barbados has a deep-water harbour, but the jetties of the careenage have some café life in the old warehouses and there are still local fishing craft and pleasure boats at dock. It is all quite picturesque nowadays, but about 300 years ago it was an offence worthy of prosecution to disturb the waters of the Careenage because the smell was so bad.

Presiding over the scene from Trafalgar Square on the northern shore of the Careenage is a statue of **Lord Nelson** in full uniform, erected in 1813 following his death at the Battle of Trafalgar. Nelson had been based in the West Indies for several years, and the Barbadians were grateful to him as the 'preserver of the West Indies'. The Barbadian tribute to him preceded the statue in London by 27 years. Traditionally he faces any danger that threatens Barbados and so in the past he has always faced the sea. In a recent redevelopment, however, he was inexplicably turned around. In the present economic difficulties, Bajan wags claim that he now faces the twin threats of the government buildings and the Central Bank.

Trafalgar Square was originally known as **The Green** in English fashion and was once home to the pillory and the ducking stool (quite some punishment, evidently, with the foul waters of the Careenage). Now there is a waterfall supported by the tails of dolphins. On the north side of the square are the **Public Buildings**, home of the Barbados Parliament, which were recently cleaned up to reveal bright Barbadian coral rock. Opened in 1874, the two long rounded Italian renaissance-style buildings have been adapted to the tropics with green-louvred shutters and red tin shades. In the **House of Assembly** there is a stained-glass window commemorating the monarchs of England, from James I to Victoria, including a portrait of Cromwell, interesting in itself because of Barbados's royalist sympathies during the Civil War.

Two minutes' walk east of Trafalgar Square is **St Michael's Cathedral**, rebuilt with money raised in a lottery in 1789 after the early wooden structure was destroyed in the hurricane of 1780. It became a cathedral when William Hart Coleridge arrived in 1825 as the first Bishop of Barbados. Among the sculpted memorials and tablets is a font that dates from 1680 and is decorated with a Greek palindrome: ΝΙΦΟΝ ΑΝΟΜΗ ΜΑΜΗ ΜΟΝΑ ΝΟΦΙΝ, meaning: *Wash the sin, not just the skin.*

On Magazine Lane, leading up to the functional buildings of the Law Courts and the Public Library, presented to Barbados by Andrew Carnegie in 1906, is the recently restored 19th-century **Synagogue** (*adm or Nat Trust Heritage Passport, see* p.79). It occupies the site of the original 17th-century building constructed by Jews who had escaped from Brazil and obtained permission to settle in Barbados on hearing that Cromwell had granted freedom of worship. Just inside the graveyard can be seen the bemusing headstone commemorating a certain Benjamin Massiah, no doubt a local celebrity, who 'performed the office of circumciser with great Applause and Dexterity'.

Now behind Nelson is **Broad Street**, Bridgetown's main thoroughfare and business street, where elaborate colonial edifices with metalwork balconies that might belong in an English south coastal town are interspersed with modern shopping centres and banks. Parallel to

Broad Street is Swan Street, a popular local market, and on the other side is the seafront road, which leads to the deepwater harbour and cruise ship terminal. Opposite the fish market is the **Rasta Mall**, with rastaman stalls painted in red, gold and green with anything from the speeches of Haile Selassie to sandals and herbal medicines on sale; close by is the **Pelican Village**, an artisan's mall selling paintings, wickerwork and clothes.

Headed south from Trafalgar Square you cross the Chamberlain Bridge and join **Bay Street** which heads southeast, skirting Carlisle Bay, where yachts lie at anchor off the beach and the esplanade. A hundred years ago this area was a poor quarter renowned for smuggling and so the government bought it out and built the esplanade. Bay Street itself is still a tatty area of old wooden buildings, nightclubs and poky bars that works by night as Bridgetown's red-light district, but there are also some very elaborate townhouses with gingerbread pointings as intricate as lace.

The Barbadian flag was first raised in place of the Union Jack on the **Garrison Savannah**, a 50-acre park surrounded by trees a couple of miles from central Bridgetown. It takes its name from its original use as a military training ground, and barracks in varying states of repair still surround the Savannah—today's military, the Barbados Defence Force, occupies the 18th-century St Anne's Fort across the road on the south side. The original Guard House, with its green-domed clock tower, is occupied by the **Savannah Club**. Nowadays, as well as the parades, the Savannah hosts sports such as racing, rugby and cricket.

In the handsome setting of the former garrison jail is the **Barbados Museum** (✆ 427 0201; *open Mon–Sat 9–5, Sun 2–6; adm or Nat Trust Heritage Passport*), which gives an enlightening view of Barbadian history from its start as a coral-encrusted shelf, inhabited by various Amerindian tribes, to the archetypal sugar island and on to 'Bimshire' and Independence. There are some particularly good displays in the Aall maps and prints gallery, and some peep-in views of old-time Barbados. Naturally there is an exhibit of a prisoner's cell. The temporary exhibition gallery has revolving exhibits of local contemporary artists and there is a hands-on children's gallery.

The West Coast—North to Scotland and St Lucy

Highway 1 leads out of Bridgetown to the north, along the west coast of the island, to Speightstown, Barbados's second town. Winter home to transient millionaires, the west coast is all hotels and expensive villas muscling in for frontage on the 10-mile strip of extremely fine beaches. Interspersed you will find local clapboard houses, rum-shops, restaurants and the best sunset beach bars. Barbados's most expensive and exclusive hotels are situated here. It is odd to think that until the Second World War people would avoid this area and make the journey by boat. It was considered unhealthy because of the coastal swamps and the road was awful. But since the fifties, people have flocked here from all over the world. In tourist jargon it is referred to as the Gold Coast, recently updated to the Platinum Coast.

Just north of the deepwater port and cruise ship terminal you can see the story of Barbados rum in a number of different places. At the **Mount Gay Visitor Centre** (✆ 425 9066; *open Mon–Fri, 9–4; adm*), a tin-roofed Bajan house, you will see the processes of ageing, blending and bottling (the rum is actually distilled in the north of the island), and, most interesting, barrel manufacture. You can have lunch if you want it, and of course you can have tastings. Video presentation and guided tour (45 mins). At the West Indies Rum Distillery, the **Malibu**

Visitor Centre (✆ 425 9393; *open 9–11 and 12–4; adm*) takes you through the same production of Barbados's famous coconut-flavoured rum, with video presentation and then a guided tour through the different processes. The centre is set on Brighton beach, so you can make a day of it, among all the cruise ship passengers, if you want. Lunch tour available and of course rum tasting. Headed out of town on the Spring Garden Highway, where the Parade of Bands is held at *Cropover*, and where you will find the Kensington Oval (the island's main stadium and home of the cricket internationals), you come to the **West India Rum Refinery** (✆ 435 6900; *open Wed; adm Bds$55*); here you can take the Cockspur 'Where the Rum Comes From' tour, with a look at the production process, lunch and yet another rum-tasting session. The Spring Garden Highway joins Highway 1 at the Cave Hill Campus, one of three that make up the **University of the West Indies**. The other two are in Jamaica and Trinidad.

In the outskirts of the town you will find an excellent example of a private Barbadian home at **Tyrol Cot** (✆ 424 2074; *open 9–5; adm or Nat Trust Heritage Passport*), built with stone and ballast brick, painted white and orange with green louvred windows. It is a little bigger than the cottage that 'cot' implies and it has a very attractive interior with antique furniture and personal collections of porcelain and statuettes. Built in 1854, the house belonged to Sir Grantley Adams, first premier of Barbados and Prime Minister of the ill-fated West Indies Federation, and was the boyhood home of Tom Adams, who later became the second Prime Minister of independent Barbados. Tyrol Cot is surrounded by a small assembly of Bajan chattel houses, painted in traditional island colours (more subdued red and yellow or cream and brown than the bright turquoise, sky blue and lime green that you see nowadays). Each one is the workshop of a traditional Barbadian artisan—pottery, leatherwork and sweets— with products on sale of course. There is a rum shop with island rum and local fare.

Following the west coast road, which runs behind the seafront stretch of houses and hotels, winding over the small headlands and occasionally touching the seafront, you come to **Holetown**, 7 miles north of the capital. This is where the first European settlers made their home. It is apparently called so because it reminded sailors of 'the Hole' on the River Thames. It was here that Captain John Powell claimed the island for England, nailing a sign, 'James K. of E. and of this island', on a fustic tree in 1625. The proclamation has disappeared of course, but the event is recalled by a memorial in the town. Originally the town was called Jamestown, a name which still remains in the Parish and in the Holetown church, **St James's**, the oldest on the island, 'erected here, on God's Acre, in the Olde Towne, 1629'. The church has recently been restored, revealing the bright coral rock.

On the cliff above Holetown you will find the **Sugar Museum** (✆ 432 0100; *open Mon–Sat, 9–5; adm or Nat Trust Heritage Passport*) at Portvale. In the restored boiling house of the old estate there are sugar artefacts from across the ages—boilers, crushers, steam engines, with models and old prints. The museum stands in the grounds of the **Portvale Sugar Factory**, which is well worth a visit during the cane-cutting season between February and May.

Speightstown (pronounced rather like 'spoikestong') is about 12 miles north of the capital. Very early on the town was a thriving port, used to land goods for the northern part of Barbados, before good roads were built. The town was known as Little Bristol because it had links with Bristol, then England's second-largest port. Its name even derives from a Bristol man, William Speight, a member of the Barbados Parliament in 1639. The town has not developed as much as other areas of the island and so there are some charming old buildings and a certain easy-going air.

If you follow Highway 2, which leads inland from Bridgetown, you come to **Harrison's Cave** (© 438 6640; *open 9–4; adm exp or Nat Trust Heritage Passport*), a series of underground rivers and limestone caverns hung with stalactite shark teeth that drip on to glutinous stalagmites, due to join up in a couple of million years. It is all a bit overplayed, with hard hats, strict guides, fat-wheeled buggies, and yet another handicraft shop, but the 500,000-year-old caverns are genuinely a stimulating sight.

Welchman Hall Gulley (© 438 6671; *open 9–5; adm or Nat Trust Heritage Passport*), a couple of miles farther along Highway 2, is a cleft in Barbados's limestone cap that drips with tropical greenery, a canopy that nearly blocks out the sun and drops lianas down on to the array of shrubs and trees (about 200 species in all). On the short walk through the gulley you might think that you have descended to the depths of the island, but when you come out into the open you are presented with a fantastic view over northern Barbados and the Atlantic. The gulley and the caves were used by runaways and escapees of all sorts.

Scotland and St Lucy in the North

The imposed sophistication of the west coast evaporates with the last hotel just north of Speightstown, giving way to fishing villages in the bays and unfortunately an industrial plant amidst the simple attractive parish of **St Lucy**. Among the dramatic scenery of the northern tip of the island is **Animal Flower Cave** (*adm*), a series of caverns thrashed out by the force of the waves. There are some blow-holes and you might see an 'animal flower', a flower-like sea anemone which snaps back when disturbed. In the nearby Pirate's Tavern, you can get a drink and escape the heat. It is possible to visit the **Mount Gay Rum Distillery**, where you will see huge vats of fermenting molasses and water and the stills of the distillation process.

Inland from Speightsown and St James the land rises quickly up a cliff on to a less developed plateau covered in sweeping plains of sugar-cane, that breaks and folds into the rugged and mountainous Scotland District in the centre of the island. Here there are gulleys filled with mahogany trees and grand and steep hilltops that tower above the sparsely grassed east coast slopes. It was to Scotland that the Catholics, 'barbadosed' by Cromwell, were sent to keep them out of the way. Their descendants lived here for centuries, in communities of 'poor whites' as they were known, but not many are left now. Escaped slaves would come to lie up here in the hope of casting off for St Vincent, 100 miles directly downwind and just visible on the clearest days from Mount Hillaby. Finally, the area also found favour with the planters, who built some of the finest plantation houses here. The roads are rough in the remoter areas of Scotland District, but it is worth making the effort to go there just for the views.

There is a magnificent view in all directions from the **Grenade Hall Forest and Signal Station**, which was once a look-out and a link in the semaphore communication chain that could signal around the island in minutes. The original building has been excavated and restored. There is a short historical audio tape and descriptions of how the signalling functioned. Beneath is a small forest where there is a series of trails with signs which illustrate the complexities of the eco-system and indicate plants used in local medicine: *spiritweed* and *broomweed* were used as diuretics and *briny roots* against scurvy and as a purgative. Close by is the **Barbados Wildlife Reserve** (© 422 8826; *open daily 10–5; adm*), a small zoo with animals free to roam around a small wood, including native Barbadian tortoises, agoutis and spectacled caiman, an alligator, raccoons and armadillos.

Close by, **Farley Hill** is a park and garden set around the shell of a 19th-century mansion that was renowned as the smartest in Barbados in the late 1880s. It is a little sad since it was gutted by fire in the sixties, but the gardens, with their magnificent royal palms and other labelled trees and plants, are peaceful and pleasant. *Gardens open until dusk; adm.*

A couple of miles away is **St Nicholas Abbey** (© 422 8725; *open Mon–Fri, 10–3.30; adm to house and gardens or Nat Trust Heritage Passport*), one of the two oldest mansions on the island and among only three Jacobean houses surviving in the whole of the Americas (along with Drax Hall, also in Barbados, and Bacon's Castle in Virginia, USA). Built around 1650 by a Colonel Berringer, it is not really an abbey but a fine stone building with an arched façade topped with curved gables (a reminder of Dutch influence in the early days of settlement). Inside, the private house has some antique furniture and you will notice a curiosity in that the house has fireplaces, as though the inhabitants feared cold nights in the hills of Scotland. It is still a working plantation. Do not miss the film, shown twice daily (*11.30am and 2.30pm*) of Barbados in the 1930s, which includes footage of the Bridgetown Careenage, loading rum puncheons, mauby ladies pouring drinks from barrels on their heads and shots of Barbados's windmills turning in the wind.

One of the finest views of Scotland District is from **Cherry Tree Hill**, from where one can look north to St Lucy and south over the island as far as Hackleton's Cliff in the parish of St Joseph. Just beneath Cherry Tree Hill is a cool avenue of casuarina pines and mahogany trees where the Bajans come to take their picnics. Old prints of Barbados show the island dotted with windmills and at one time about 500 of them were employed in crushing cane. As you descend the steep hill towards the coast you come to the only one that survives intact, the **Morgan Lewis Mill** (*open Mon–Sat, 9–5; adm or Nat Trust Heritage Passport*). Its original crushing gear is on view.

Back on the main road you pass St Andrew's Parish Church. The parish is the least populous in Barbados and boasts the highest point on the island, **Mount Hillaby**, 1160ft above sea level. It also has Barbados's only untouched forestland, **Turner's Hall Wood**, on a ridge leading from Mount Hillaby, the last remnant of the forest that once covered the whole of the island. The wood has a variety of trees including the sandbox, the buttressed locust tree, which has a pod with foul-smelling but reasonably tasty flesh, and the jack-in-a-box tree that takes its name from its seed which stands erect in a pod. You might also see a grey kingbird or a carib grackle. Not far off is the **Flower Forest** (*open 9–5; adm*), with paths through tropical splendour and views of Scotland in the distance. Tropical plants include breadfruit, golden apple and mango, as well as spices and citrus.

The Sugar Heartland—Bridgetown to the Atlantic Coast

Highways 3 and **4** leave Bridgetown to the northeast, struggling through the increasing suburbs before they pass into Barbados's sugar-cane heartland, where they disappear between curtains of the 12ft grass-like crop. Following the track of the old railway (now defunct), the land rises steadily from west to east, culminating in a cliff that gives broad and sweeping views of the east coast and Atlantic ocean, and then descends through the stations on the coastline and its terminus at Belleplaine, where the Bajans liked to escape for their picnics earlier this century. In the uplands, the roads are a maze linking small villages of colourful clapboard houses, *chattel houses* to the Bajans, though these are gradually disappearing now as the

Bajans move into larger and more comfortable concrete housing. You will also come across some of the island's finest plantation houses.

The first important landmark on Highway 4 out of Bridgetown is the **Banks Brewery** (✆ 429 0474; *open Mon–Fri, 10–4; adm or Nat Trust Heritage Passport*), where you can see the award-winning beer created with malt, hops, local water, local yeast and a touch of local cane-juice, through brewing, boiling, fermentation and lagering. **Francia** Plantation House (✆ 429 2113; *visits Tues, Thurs 10am and 1pm*), set in open tropical gardens with a panoramic view of the west coast, is a Bajan family home with echoes of Brazil in some architectural features and in the imported hardwood. There are West Indian prints and maps as well as a three-way seat for a pair of lovers (the third seat is for the girl's chaperone) and a dripstone, which provided clean and filtered water.

Gun Hill Signal Station (*open Mon–Fri, 9–4; adm or Nat Trust Heritage Passport*) is one of a string of semaphore stations that could link the whole of Barbados within minutes. Set up in 1818, it was designed to warn of impending trouble from the sea, by using flags by day and coloured lanterns at night, and able to advise that ships had arrived safely in port with merchandise or even pass the message quickly of an uprising among the slaves. The communication tower at Gun Hill has been restored and provides a fine view of the island all around, as well as a map of the other stations in the network and some military memorabilia. Gun Hill was also used for convalescence for troops suffering from malaria and yellow fever. They tended to recover because the climate was fresher away from the sea and there were no mosquitoes at this height. On approach to the signal station you will see an odd-looking white lion, sculpted by a Colonel Wilkinson during his convalescence (hardly a masterpiece).

Hackleton's Cliff runs parallel to the coastline and commands another of Barbados's fine panoramas with views both north and south along the windward coastline from about 1000ft above the sea. Just inside the parish of St Joseph is a former signal station, the **Cotton Tower**, a link in the semaphore chain from Gun Hill. It stands above a gully, the Devil's Bowling Alley, and has cracking views over Scotland to the north.

The windward coast of Barbados is lined with reefs sometimes up to 3 miles offshore, making it impossible for all but the smallest ships to put in here. But the reefs have little effect on the Atlantic breakers that barrel in and crash on the poised rocks the size of houses on the coastline, eroding it at the rate of 1ft a year. A typical windward coast settlement is **Bathsheba**, a slightly ragged fishing village dotted with houses and windblown palm trees. There is a good mix of locals and tourists—fishermen still make their way out to sea through the reefs, but it is also popular with surfers because it offers the best waves on the island.

Andromeda Gardens (✆ 433 9348; *open daily 9–5, special tour Wed 10.30am, otherwise self-guided; adm or Nat Trust Heritage Passport*) above the village are well worth a visit. They are full to bursting with plants from all over the tropical world, ranging from tiny orchids to the tree that gave Barbados its name, the banyan, or bearded fig tree. Started in 1954, there are grassy walkways through a valley alive with the smells and colours of a tropical explosion (the plants are labelled), and bowers where birds flit. You will see the native *frangipani*, with bright red and yellow petals, a wonderful variety of palm trees, heliconias by the hundred, including *heliconia hirsuta*, or 'Twiggy', orchids that look like five-winged purple and white butterflies and *Ravenala madagascariensis*, the traveller's tree, which has a fan of broad leaves similar to a banana tree.

To the south of here, there is an extremely fine view from **St John's Parish Church**, which stands on the cliff 800ft above the Atlantic coast. The original church was constructed at a cost of 100,000 pounds of sugar in 1667 and was rebuilt in 1836 after the 1831 hurricane. St John's also has a strange history concerning its early vestryman Ferdinando Paleologus, who came to Barbados as a refugee after fighting on the side of the Royalists in the Civil War. His ancestors had been the Christian Emperors of Constantinople until they were driven out by the Turks in the 15th century. His remains were discovered in the destruction of the 1831 hurricane, head pointing west according to the Greek custom, and they were moved and re-interred in a vault with Greek columns.

To the southeast, on a shelf in the descending cliff is **Codrington College** (© 433 1274; *adm or Nat Trust Heritage Passport*), a magnificent coral-stone seminary with an arched portico and views down to Consett Bay. Approached through an avenue of mighty cabbage palms, living columns up to 100ft in height, it is set in a garden of tropical plants with a lake. It was built in the early 18th century with money from a bequest from Christopher Codrington, a Governor General of the Leeward Islands whose grandfather was one of the earliest settlers of Barbados. A story is attached to two of the cabbage palms in the avenue, planted in 1879 by Prince Albert and Prince George who were on a visit to the island. One palm flourished, but the other did not. When the news came that Prince Albert had died, the local Bajans showed no surprise and said, 'We knew he die soon. His cabbage die!' It is still a working theological college, but the grounds are accessible and there is a nature trail.

Suburbs and the South Coast

Like the west coast, the south coast of Barbados is gilded with beaches, mounds of golden sand on which the waves clap and rush. Just behind them are apartment blocks and hotels jostling for space in the extended suburb that contains the homes of the Bajan *bons bourgeois*. **Highway 7** runs from central Bridgetown, to Oistins Town (about 5 miles), throwing off lanes that seek out the gaps and the coves, like St Lawrence Gap, the hub of south coast nightlife. The suburbs have names like Hastings, Worthing and Dover, perhaps a reminder of home for nostalgic colonists in centuries past, but certainly less demure than their British counterparts. The hotels and restaurants of the south coast do not have the sophistication of the west coast, but there is a lively, relaxed atmosphere and good nightlife. Eventually the road passes into country, past the airport, though this itself is now prime development land and is steadily being gobbled up by the endless sprawl of concrete suburbs.

Oistins, where the sea flashes with colourful Barbadian fishing boats, is a fishing centre and Barbados's third-largest town. The market at the roadside comes alive each day in the late afternoon when the catch is brought in and sold, continuing into the evening. According to Ligon, a visitor in the 1650s, it was called 'Austins Bay, not in commemoration of any Saint, but of a wilde mad drunken fellow, whose lewd and extravagant carriage made him infamous in the Iland'. It was in Oistins Town in 1652, at Ye Mermaid's Inn, that the 'Magna Carta of Barbados', the articles of capitulation, were signed by the Royalists, surrendering Barbados after a long siege to the Commonwealth Commissioners sent by Cromwell.

Past the southern point of the island and the airport you come to the Foursquare **Rum Factory** (© 423 6669; *video presentation and tour, open Mon–Thurs 10–6, Fri, Sat 10–9, Sun 12–6*), a modern installation on the site of an old sugar estate that produces white and dark rums. The tour includes the old sugar factory (it closed in 1988 and the molasses for distillation is now brought from elsewhere) with its grinding mills, vacuum boilers and centrifuge, and then the distillery itself. Here you will see the process of rum, from mash, a mix of molasses, local water and yeast, through fermentation to alcohol and then to distillation in the mash column and the rectifier, and the resulting white rum. Also the ageing in barrels made of American white oak, which are scorched on the inside to encourage colouring. You will even learn about the fusel oils and alcohol esters which cause hangovers. In the old coral-stone still house is the Art Foundry, where there are exhibition rooms and some working artists' studios and a print shop where they produce the labels for the rum bottles.

Farther along the coast is a notorious house in Long Bay, the crenellated **Sam Lord's Castle** (*open in the day; adm*), solidly built in 1820 (it was undamaged in the 1831 hurricane but scaffolding on the walls ended up 3 miles away). It is now surrounded by a hotel complex, but it is famous for the legend that surrounds its first owner, Sam Lord, a story that becomes more embellished with each telling. Lord was a greedy man, who was suspected of murder to gain inheritance and who was found out mistreating his wife cruelly, but he is also credited with causing shipwrecks on the reefs below his house, luring ships in to land by hanging lanterns in his windows, his palm trees, the horns of his cattle, or the antlers of his deer (delete as applicable). Then, so the story goes, he would offload the booty and bring it to his castle by way of an underground passage (conspicuously absent today).

He became an extremely rich man, favoured by a series of sudden deaths, but he was busily chasing yet another inheritance when he was uncovered. He had locked up his wife before a journey to England to talk her family into giving him some of her money, but she escaped and managed to get there before him and so he was arrested. However, a case brought against him was inconclusive. He is remembered in a book by Lieutenant Colonel Drury, *The Regency Rascal*: whatever the legend that surrounds him, he was undoubtedly an extravagant rogue whose only bequests were debts, an impressive £18,000 in 1845, to go with his magnificent castle. It is suitably and lavishly decorated according to the period, with plasterwork ceilings and mahogany trimmings, Regency furniture and an extremely fine staircase. (It is often crowded because it works as the hotel lobby as well.) **Ragged Point** is the most easterly point on the island, a limestone cliff thrashed by the Atlantic.

Off Highway 5, the direct route back towards Bridgetown, is the **Sunbury Plantation House and Museum** (✆ 423 6270; *adm*), where the pleasant lawned garden is set with coaches and iron farm machinery. The house, originally constructed in the 1660s, is restored in Georgian style to the state of a plantation house at the height of the island's sugar prosperity. It was burned in 1995 but has been restored. There is a café in the grounds, operated by the Barbados National Trust.

✆ (1 246)–   **Where to Stay**

As the nerve centre of the British presence in the Eastern Caribbean, Barbados has a tradition of hotels going back 200 years. The best known was the 19th-century 'Ice House', patronized because it brought the first cooled drinks to Barbados, but most were famous for a series of prodigious creole landladies who kept houses of varying states of disorder: Sabina Brade, Hannah Lewis who would complain of her lumbago and Betsy Austin, a lady of massive size and earthy language, who would become violent if her bill was questioned. For many of the tavern girls 'of erect figure and stately carriage...without shoes or stockings, in a short white jacket and thin short petticoat...a white turban on the head, neck and shoulders left bare', it was a business profitable enough to buy their freedom from slavery. But the most popular image is that of the gargantuan Rachel Pringle, an expansive matriarch, dressed in voluminous silk, of almost unmovable disposition, whose caricature by the cartoonist Rowlandson can be seen around the island.

Such seaminess belies Barbados's current clean-cut and efficient image. The island offers one of the best ranges of hotels in the Caribbean. Prices are very high in the smart hotels in season because of its reputation, but there is an excellent breadth of prices year round and it is possible to find a good deal in the summer months, particularly in hotel rooms and self-catering flats. If you are happy to look after yourself there are plenty of villas are available for hire along the west and south coasts. Contact **Realtors Limited** (✆ 432 6930, ✉ 432 6919) and **Bajan Services Ltd** at Seascape Cottage, Gibbs, St Peter, Barabados (✆ (809) 422 2618, ✉ 422 5366), with options between one and eight bedrooms. Operators in the metropolitan countries (who will put together a whole package for you) can be contacted through the Tourist Boards: also see **Travel** for Caribbean-wide villa rental companies who cover Barbados.

The smart set head for the Platinum Coast, which runs north along the west coast from Bridgetown up towards Speightstown. Some of the smartest and most expensive hotels in the Caribbean are situated here—some people actually wear their jewellery on the beach—set in gardens of tropical splendour and giving on to the gentle bays with golden strands, a fine place to see the Green Flash at sunset. The south coast is generally less luxurious and less expensive (most of the hotels work with high volume package companies and there are also lots of guest houses there too) but it is more active and has a less exclusive feel. Bear in mind that all accommodation bills in Barbados will be supplemented with a 7.5% VAT and, in almost all cases, a 10% service charge as well.

luxury–very expensive

The **Sandy Lane Hotel** in St James has long been renowned as one of the Caribbean's best-known and most luxurious hotels. Limousine service will whisk you from the airport to this classical, coral-stone enclave of sumptuousness with north and south wings either side of an amphitheatrical courtyard and set on 300 yards of delightful beachfront on Payne's Bay. Soft shades of pink and white run throughout the resort in the coral stone and pickled oak fittings and lend the resort an air of just-so elegance. All imaginable concessions to luxury—24-hour room service by bellmen in cream suits, mock-antique cutlery in the dining room, afternoon tea in the tropics—right down to the chilled towels at the beach. Also all the modern essentials—swimming pool, watersports, fitness centre and children's centres. A large and busy hotel with 120 rooms, dress codes at dinner, soigné, swanky and slightly self-important (✆ 432 1311, ✉ 432 2954, *www.sandylane.com, sandy@caribsurf.com*, booking agents Leading Hotels of the World: UK ✆ (0800) 181123, US ✆ (1 800) 233 3800).

A charming, smaller resort is **Cobbler's Cove** (✆ 422 2291, ✉ 422 1460, *www.ttg.co.uk, cobblers@caribsurf.com*, UK ✆ (0181) 367 5175, US res ✆ (1 800) 890 6060, on the coast just south of Speightstown. There are 40 very elegant suites, each decorated with wicker, rattan, Barbadian clay tiles and dark-stained louvres, and each with a balcony or terrace looking out on to the hotel's charming gardens of golden palm, banana and travellers' trees. Next to the beach (which took a bit of a beating in 1996) are the very pretty dining room, the central drawing room, which lends the hotel a congenial air, and the two most special suites, the new Colleton Suite and the Camelot Suite. An excellent retreat, Cobbler's Cove is one of the Caribbean's few *Relais et Chateaux* (character, courtesy, calm, charm and not least, particularly important in the Caribbean, cuisine); MAP in winter.

The **Royal Pavilion** (℗ 422 4444, ✉ 422 0118, *twithycombe@princesshotels.com*, UK res ℗ (0171) 407 1010, US res ℗ (1 800) 223 1818), farther south, in the Parish of St James, has a feel of manicured luxury in its Mediterranean-style central building, decorated throughout with pink marble and terracotta tiles. There is a certain formality (no children in winter), but it is not overplayed. The charming dining room is set on a veranda right above the waves and all 72 elegant rooms look on to the ocean from deep balconies. Guests have the use of the facilities at **Glitter Bay**, the larger and less formal sister-hotel next door.

Guests return year after year to the **Coral Reef Club** (℗ 422 2372, ✉ 422 1776, UK res ℗ (0800) 964470, US res ℗ (1 800) 525 4800) nearby, a family-run hotel with the stately grace of old-time Barbados. The 75 individually decorated rooms and suites are set in cottages scattered around luxuriant gardens of casuarina pine and mahogany trees and are ranged behind the elegant coral-rock foyer and dining room on the seafront. MAP. You might also consider the 45 slightly more casual suites and rooms of the Coral Reef's friendly sister-hotel nearby, **The Sandpiper** (℗ 422 2251, ✉ 422 0900), which are neatly situated in blocks in a charming garden, wrapped in bougainvillea and other tropical blooms.

Treasure Beach (℗ 432 1346, ✉ 432 1049, UK res (0800) 373742, US res ℗ (1 800) 223 6510) has 25 very comfortable suites in staggered two-storey blocks running down to a fine stretch of the west coast beach. Each suite has a bedroom and a large sitting room with a view onto the pleasant gardens and pool. A quiet and friendly hotel.

expensive–moderate

Elsewhere on the island there are some good hotels with settings just as attractive in their own way. The **Crane Beach Hotel** (℗ 423 6220, ✉ 423 5343, *cranebeach@ sunbeach.net*) stands in St Philip on the southeast coast of the island, in a truly dramatic setting on the clifftops. A surreal shade of turquoise runs as a leitmotif through the hotel, from the absurdly rich colour of the sea to the clifftop pool with its classical columns and balustrades. There are 18 very comfortable rooms and suites (four set in a miniature castle). It is quite busy during the day as people come to the restaurant on the clifftop.

moderate

For all the outrageously expensive hotels in Barbados, the island also has an excellent range of less expensive places to stay and there are even a number of (less lavish) options on the island's famous west coast where you can stay without taking out a mortgage. If you are happy to cater for yourself, you can try **The Beachcomber** (℗ 432 0489, ✉ 432 2824), where there are huge studios and two-bedroom apartments, each well furnished and with a large balcony looking on to an excellent section of the beach. There is no restaurant, but each apartment has a full kitchen. At **Smuggler's Cove** (✆ 432 1741, ✉ 432 1749) there are 20 comfortable studios and one-bedroom apartments in a not terribly attractive block above the pool, but right on Payne's Bay. All have kitchenettes, but there is also a restaurant.

Another haven of old-time Barbadian grace and comfort, also further afield, can be found at Cattlewash on the east coast, at the **Kingsley Club** (✆ 433 9422, ✉ 433 9226). Earlier this century, well-to-do Bajans would escape the (relative) turmoil of Bridgetown to this traditional timber-frame villa. Now it is an ideal writer's retreat and professional's rest-cure, as you can tell by the faded copies of *Architectural Digest* and *Forbes Magazine*. Eight older double rooms and more modern rooms in a new wing.

In the seemingly endless sprawl of suburbia along the south coast towards Bridgetown you will find very well priced places to stay—look in the 'gaps', side-roads in Dover, St Lawrence Gap and Hastings. One pleasant, family-run hotel in Hastings is the **Woodeville Beach Hotel**, WPO 14, Christ Church (✆ 435 6693, ✉ 435 9211, *wdvlle@caribsurf.com*). The 48 big and breezy rooms stand in blocks in a U shape around the pool; they are furnished with bright floral colours and have showers and kitchenettes, also a bar and restaurant. The hotel is not actually on the beach, but Rockley Beach is two minutes' walk away. **Sea Foam Haciendas** in Worthing (✆ 435 7380, ✉ 435 7384, *seafoam@caribsurf.com*) has 12 two-bedroom suites in a building with Spanish colonial touches as the name implies, right on the beach. Very much self-contained and private, with full kitchens. Rates include maid service but cooks and baby-sitters can be arranged.

moderate–cheap

The **Round House Inn** (✆ 433 9678, ✉ 433 9079) has a magnificent setting on the clifftops above Bathsheba on the wild east coast. There are four rooms in an old restored building: they are quite simple but have a great deal of style with louvred doors and windows made of Caribbean woods and straw matting on the concrete floors. This too is quite busy because of the restaurant (*see* below), but the rooms are private and they make for an excellent retreat from the swank of the west coast.

Another good area to head for as an independent traveller is the southern tip of the island around Silver Sands which has a lively feel for part of the year when the wind-surfers are around and otherwise is fairly quiet. There is public transportation. **Peach and Quiet**, Inch Marlow, Christ Church (✆ 428 5682, ✉ 428 2467), has 22 suites in stark white stucco and shingle-tile buildings in a windy seafront setting of palms and casuarina pines. Very relaxed and peaceful and impeccable value; good restaurant, beach nearby. The windsurfers themselves tend to gather at the **Silver Rock Hotel** (✆ 428 2866, ✉ 420 6982), where comfortable studios and apartments are moderately priced; it has a bar and restaurant with a view of all the waterborne activity offshore.

cheap

The **Pink Coral Inn** (✆/✉ 435 3151) uses the best of its setting in a restored wooden colonial house (unfortunately right on the road) in Hastings. There are six brightly painted, fan-ventilated bed-rooms and there is a gracious air about the common rooms, one of which contains an art gallery, and the louvred porches which are ideal for sitting out. You can expect a friendly reception; some share baths and some kitchen facilities. Windsurfers gravitate around **Windsurf Village** on Maxwell Main Road (✆ 428 9095, ✆ 428 2872). Simple rooms with pretty floral décor in a purpose-built block; really a quiet stopover but the windsurfing crowd can make it quite lively.

There is a clutch of small **guest houses** scattered around the Worthing and Dover area. Try the **Rio Guest House** (✆/✆ 428 1546), which is within a shout of St Lawrence Gap: seven very simple rooms, some share baths, some private, small dining and kitchen area. Also try **Kingsway on the Beach** (✆ 428 8202, ✆ 420 4692, *kingsway@caribsurf.com*) which is not actually on the beach but not far from it. Very simple rooms in an extension to an old Barbadian villa. In Worthing try **Shells Guest House** (✆ 435 7253, ✆ 435 7414), seven simple rooms, some with share baths and close by **Crystal Waters** (✆ 435 7514), eight rooms, some shared bathrooms. You can also ask around and negotiate for a room in a family house.

✆ (1 246)–   *Eating Out*

Bajan Food

As in many of the Caribbean islands, some Bajan traditional dishes have a slave heritage. Thus *cou-cou*, a dish made from cornmeal and okra, is served with salt fish, once a hardship food. In Barbados 'peas 'n' rice' is a staple and is often flavoured with coconut. Besides the traditional *pepperpot stew*, a four-day boil-up, there is also plenty of seafood, including crab and *sea-egg*, the roe of the white sea-urchin, which is supposely an aphrodisiac.

The best-loved fish in Barbados is the flying fish, which you may well see if you go out sailing. It is a winged fish that flits and glides over the waves, sometimes for distances up to 100 yards. As well as being a national symbol, it is also something of a national dish, and you can see the daily catch brought in to the Careenage in the late afternoon, in season between December and June.

Bajan Drink

> *The chiefe fudling they make in the iland is Rumbullion, alias Kill Divill and this is made of suggar canes distilled, a hot hellish and terrible liquor.*

Barbados produces some of the finest **rum** in the world. Distilled from molasses, the thick liquid left over from the sugar-boiling process, many rums are left to mature in oak, taking on a darker colour with age. Mountgay is the best known: try their special 5-year-old. Others worth trying are Cockspur Old Gold and VSOR. Local white rums include ESAF, once jokingly called 'Erskine Sandiford And Friends' in reference to a former Prime Minister, otherwise 'Every Sunday Afternoon Free'. There are hundreds of 'rum shops' on the island, mostly small clapboard shacks, where you will find the Barbadians 'liming', passing the time of day. If you would like to see the distillation process, there are tours of distilleries in Bridgetown (*see* p.63).

Besides their good line in rum punches, the restaurants in Barbados serve superb fruit punches, fresh fruit and juices crushed with ice, and usually free of the pints of sticky grenadine syrup that elsewhere obliterate the taste. More traditional drinks include **mauby juice**, a bitter drink made by boiling bark and spices—100 years ago 'mauby ladies' would ply the streets of Bridgetown with urns on their heads, offering drinks to quench a midday thirst. Nowadays you are mainly dependent on canned and bottled drinks, but you may be able to get a **snow-cone** in a plastic cup at the streetside. You will also find delicious home-brewed **ginger beer**, boiled up from grated root ginger, and **sorrel**, a sweet concoction made from the red flowers of the sorrel plant, known as the Christmas drink all over the Caribbean. The Bajan beer is the award-winning **Banks** brew.

Restaurants

Barbados has a steadily growing tradition of fine food, which makes a pleasant change in the British Caribbean, which is not renowned for its cuisine. High quality ingredients are now readily available (both to restaurants and to gourmet delicatessens) and there is an increasing number of chefs on the island with international experience. The Bajans handle service well too, which can also be a problem elsewhere. The result is some excellent restaurants and most recently a string of wine bars (lots of deep-fried camembert and goats' cheese), which offer both fine food and charming locations: terraces on the waterfront just above the waves and the garden settings of Bajan galleries, verandas threatened by explosive tropical flora.

In keeping with the different characters of the two parts of the island, there are elegant restaurants along the coastal cliffs of the west, and most recently a particularly satisfying clutch of good restaurants has appeared in **Holetown** that matches the lively atmosphere of the easy eateries in **St Lawrence Gap** on the south coast. Many of the hotels also have fine kitchens and if you are staying at one of the Elegant Resorts of Barbados you may try the others out. You can even dine out in old-time plantation splendour at Sunbury (✆ 423 6270). No restaurants require a dinner jacket any more, though there may be a dress-code of trousers and a sleeved shirt. There is an encrustation of pizza huts, Chefettes and Barbecue Barns, but you can of course also eat fast-food Bajan style, taking away rice 'n' peas in a polystyrene box or picking up some roast corn at the roadside in the early evening.

Eating out in Barbados is not cheap and annoyingly an already hefty restaurant bill will be supplemented by a huge 15% VAT and a 10% service charge. Charges are made in Barbados dollars, but credit cards are widely accepted. You are advised to reserve a table in the winter season; the most popular restaurants can be booked weeks in advance because people fax their reservations from home long before they arrive.Categories are arranged according to the price of a main course: *expensive*—Bds$40 and above; *moderate*—Bds$20–40; *cheap*—under Bds$20.

The West Coast

expensive

The Cliff (✆ 432 1922) holds pride of place on the island at the moment, in its superb setting on the west coast, literally cut into the rockface of the cliff on a tiny cove with waves lit by floodlight. Tables are arranged in amphitheatrical tiers above an open-air floor with trees and flaming torches of slender metalwork. An eclectic menu takes tastes from around the world to complement Caribbean and international ingredients—try Caribbean shrimp in puff pastry with sweet pepper coulis or grilled vegetable salad with goat's cheese quenelles and balsamic vinaigrette followed by chargrilled tuna (cooked rare) hatched with coriander cream, on garlic mash with capers and mixed vegetables, all neatly presented on huge white china plates. Short but strong wine-list. **Carambola** (✆ 432 0832) has another charming waterfront setting, with tables strung out on a meandering terrace above the gentle waves of St James, under white awnings and umbrellas. The menu is French with an Asian influence—gingered Thai scallops in a ginger, coconut and white wine sauce followed by rack of lamb and breast of duck, braised with carambola and orange brandy. Occasional sting-ray feeding offshore. *Closed Sun.*

Olive's (✆ 432 2112) has a completely different setting in an old Barbadian townhouse in Holetown, but there is the same elegance and attention to detail. Start with an excellent rum punch upstairs in the bar, a drawing room with wicker armchairs and palms and a small terrace and then move down to the indoor dining room with its bare coral walls and open kitchen, or outside under the shelter of a palm tree or a gazebo. Again a varied menu with international flavours: warm shrimps in a creamy garlic dressing over a mixed leaf salad followed by chicken breast in a pecan crackercrumb served on dahl roti with split pea rice. Not far off, **The Mews** (✆ 432 1122) also has a pretty setting in a house. You dine in the garden under the trellises or in the small rooms upstairs. There is a long fish menu—seared yellowfin tuna with garlic butter—and international fare such as a rack of lamb in a herb crust with a minty cranberry sauce. Only the quiet clink of cutlery will rise above the murmur of the night air at **Bagatelle Great House** (✆ 421 6767), where you dine in the coral-stone rooms of one of the oldest plantation houses in Barbados. French cuisine with a twist of the Caribbean in the spices or ingredients; try Dijon steak flambéed in local sugar-cane brandy. Another charming setting is **Mango's Fine Art Gallery and Restaurant** (✆ 422 0704) on a very pretty deck with a palm-thatch roof in Speightstown: green peppercorn paté or a smoked cheese and herb roulade followed by a seafood crêpe with dill sauce or grilled blackened Bajan catch of the day panfried in lime-juice. Finish with a passion-fruit cheesecake or a French orange rum cake.

moderate

In the clutch of restaurants and bars in Holetown make sure to visit **Ragamuffins** (✆ 432 1295), which is set in a brightly painted Caribbean clapboard house with louvres and decorated with fish-nets and brightly painted parrots. A lively bar, but good Caribbean fare too: fish cakes with aïoli dip followed by jerk chicken *escalope* or West Indian chicken or shrimp curry; lastly rum and orange cake. Ragamuffins is a fun place. *Closed Mon.* If Ragamuffin's name belies its pleasant atmosphere, the name **Angry Annie's** (✆ 432 2119) gives a hint of the riotous and lively air of another restaurant nearby which is well worth visiting. Hard to miss, it is bright blue with luscious pinks, outrageous orange and electric green. A mix of Caribbean and international cuisine—Soufrière fish sizzled in citrus and Limer's lobster in garlic and chives.

In a very different style is **Nico's** (✆ 432 6386), which sells itself as a 'Champagne Wine Bar and Restaurant' in Payne's Bay south of Holetown. Through the bar itself, where there are tall stools and waist-high tables, you come to an extended gallery surrounded by garden greenery. Suitable wine-bar (and some more substantial) food: start with bruschetta or deep-fried camembert with a passion-fruit sauce and follow with a simple cottage pie or a chicken breast stuffed with crab and spinach with an orange-ginger sauce.

cheap

You shouldn't expect to find very much that's cheap on the west coast unless you're happy with a bar snack at one of the beach bars or a takeaway. However, you can get a good local meal at the **Fisherman's Pub** in Speightstown, a red and white bar on the road with covered bar and a terrace on the waterfront surrounded by a picket fence. Breadfruit cou-cou, fried chicken or fried flying fish on a revolving menu. It is especially known for its fish, which is fresh daily except Sundays. You might also be able to fix a meal through the many rum shops along the main road.

The South Coast

expensive

The finest restaurant on the south coast, both for its setting in a lovely old Barbadian house (a listed building), and for its cuisine, is the **Mervue House Restaurant** (✆ 435 2888). You dine outside on the gallery hanging with greenery looking out onto the garden or inside in the house with its wooden floors and doorways and louvred windows. The fare is Caribbean and international: seafood crêpe in a white wine sauce or shrimp in grated coconut with a tangy pineapple sauce followed by the Mervue chicken—sautéed slices of chicken breast in a creamy curry sauce with fresh fruit. Another excellent alternative is **Josef's** (✆ 435 6541) in another former private home, made of pink and white coral rock. You dine on a veranda with classical columns looking through the garden towards the sea (you may want one of the four tables in the garden itself). The menu is international: seafood *tempura* served with a teriyaki sauce—with touches of the Caribbean, a jerk pork tenderloin seared and roasted with peach and apple fritters, or some Swedish dishes inlcuding Skagen toast, chopped shrimp with mayonnaise and dill. The best waterfront setting on the south coast is at **Pisces** (✆ 435 6564; *expensive–moderate*), a white wicker dining room wrapped in greenery just above the calm waters of St Lawrence Gap. As the name suggests they have a long fish menu, including snapper caribe, stuffed with shrimp, tomato and herbs and a delicious seafood fettucine, with occasional exotic offerings like chub and sennet, or surf and turf. High pressure, fast turnover, but reliably good. One of the new wine bars that have popped up around the island is **Champers** (✆ 435 6644), which has a charming breezy setting on the waterfront in Hastings. You drink chilled wine to the sound of chatter one side and the breaking waves on the other. A blackboard menu offers a shrimp and mango salad followed by grilled bill-fish in a tomato and sweet pepper salsa and a volley of excellent puddings. Also bar snacks if a full meal is too much. **39 Steps** (✆ 427 0715) in Hastings also has a nice setting upstairs in a modern version of the traditional wooden Caribbean house. Deep-fried camembert followed by blackened fish.

Back in the strip at St Lawrence Gap there is any number of bars that double as restaurants as the evening progresses. A fun place to head for at the start of an evening out (and then remain there possibly for the whole evening, drinking at the barrel chairs looking out on to the road), is **Café Sol** (✆ 432 9531), a Mexican grill and more importantly a margarita bar on the corner. The inside is hung with Mexicalia—sombreros, flags, even chilli-pepper fairy-lights—and of course there is loud Latin music. Nachos and pitchers of sangria to start and if it makes you peckish then there are macho burgers, burritos and taquitos to fill the pit in the stomach. Another good place to head for is the **Carib Beach Bar** in Worthing, where you can find a lively crowd and enjoy some fritters over a Carib beer.

cheap

There is any number of small eat-in/takeaways around Barbados, particularly along the south coast, where you can get a meal for a few dollars. In the day you can grab a local meal of a 'cutter' (a hefty sandwich) or a box of rice 'n' peas from a 'Lunch Box' (a wagon) but during the evening you might try a Caribbean speciality, a roti (*see* **Trinidad**), from the **Roti Den** at the entrance to St Lawrence Gap. Rotis and more regular Caribbean fare, ice creams to take away or eat in.

There is also a number of people selling chickens from braziers at the roadside in St Lawrence Gap itself. It seems that the old favourite late-night eating stop, **Baxter's Road** (on the northern road out of Bridgetown), has lost its charm a little. However, a new institution has been born at the **Fish Market** in **Oistins**, where there are a number of stalls that will sell you a fish meal earlier in the evening. Starting just after dusk Pat's Place, Miss Anne's, Miss June's and Crazy Eddie offer a plate of fried fish with rice and peas or macaroni pie and a beer until late into the evening.

If you are driving over to the **east coast** for the day there is a number of places where you can stop over for lunch. A traditional favourite is the **Atlantis Hotel** in Bathsheba (✆ 423 1526) above the dramatic east coast of the island, but an excellent choice is the **Round House**, which has an equally dramatic setting on a cliff nearby. Superb salt-bread to go with home-made soups and breadfruit chips. Follow with salads and pasta or a more substantial platter such as a fish fillet with rice and peas.

There are also plenty of places to detain you on a day out in **Bridgetown**. A favourite with the businessmen for lunch is **Brown Sugar** (✆ 426 7684) in the south of the town, which is set in a very pretty terrace surrounded by greenery. Right on the Careenage you will find the **Waterfront Cafe** which offers coffee and quick bites—smoked flying fish salad, or larger meals—jerked pork in tomato salsa.

Bars and Nightlife

A French priest who came to Barbados in the 1650s claimed that there were 100 taverns for a population of 2000. The ratio of 1 for every 20 people may have gone down a bit since the 17th century, when even the Barbados Assembly used to meet in the pub, but evenings in Barbados can be very lively. Generally speaking the best areas are Bridgetown and the south coast, particularly around St Lawrence Gap and most recently at Holetown where there is a cluster of lively bars and restaurants. There are some excellent bands in Barbados and they play live in the many clubs: *Spice and Co.* and *Krosfyah* are worth looking out for and you might also come across *Second Avenue, Square One* and *IV Play.*

Bajan entertainment for Bajans tends to be in rum shops, usually local wooden houses with their shutters pinned open. It is worth stopping at one. Try **John Moore**—'John Moore and the Little Man Welcome you to Weston, St James' (otherwise home to some of the most expensive hotels in the Caribbean), where you can catch a game of dominoes. If you're in the Silver Sands area in the south, drop into **Buffy's Bar** for a local experience. If you want something more chichi, there are always the many wine bars, where the Bajan *bons bourgeois* congregate over a chilled glass of Chablis, which would be happy to offer you a drink before you move on to eat. Try **Nico's** in Payne's Bay on the coast road or **Peppers** in Holetown, and on the south coast **Champers** and **39 Steps** in Hastings.

The trick with **nightlife** in Barbados is to bar-hop with the Bajans. Popular with tourists and locals alike is **The Boatyard** in the outskirts of Bridgetown, which has a beachfront setting with an open-air bar with barrel seats and brick and concrete dance floor. A mix of live bands and live music (best nights Fri, Sat, Sun— *'No abusive language, no hats, no arm-hole shirt after sunset'*; also Tues—*'The Toatyard on a Boozeday'*). Also very lively on its days (Fri, Sat, Sun beach parties) is **Harbour Lights** on Carlisle Bay, which is lit with flaming torches and sees plenty of live bands. Just behind the Careenage in Bridgetown you will find **Le Mirage**, a club with local and international music.

The in-place on the **west coast** at the time of writing was the **Crocodile's Den,** known mostly as Croc's, in St James, which sits in a large tin-roofed clapboard house behind a bright yellow picket fence. Concrete floor, bench seats, sports on TV, pool tables and plenty of riotous behaviour from the young crowd. Not far off you will find the **Coach House**, which has live music most days and collects a lively crowd. In Holetown try **Dillons,** a sports bar.

St Lawrence Gap on the south coast is really the most popular area for bars and clubs, and the day's lightly grilled flesh comes in for a night-time roasting here. Start the evening at any of the bars, at **Boomers** or at **Café Sol**, with loud salsa music right on the streetfront. From here you can spill straight into the clubs: **After Dark** is air-conditioned with five bars, one of them 75ft long. It offers live music, sports on the television and mixed Caribbean and international sounds: '*Strict Dress Code Enforce* [sic, ed]: *No men with braided hair, no tracksuit, tank tops, no torn jeans, no bare feet, no men in short pants'.* It's busiest on Friday and Saturday. Next door the **Ship Inn** is also popular, with live music and a sound system. The big nights are Tuesday and Saturday, when visitors and young Bajans dance or pulsate, depending on how much room there is. Dress code: *'Please dress nicely'.* The **Reggae Lounge**, an open-air club strong on reggae as well as local calypso, can get quite lively. Clubs usually charge an entry fee.

A more local club is the **Penthouse** in Bridgetown which plays mostly reggae and dub. For other raw and wholesome Bajan entertainment, you might go to a weekend dance or **Bram**—details in the paper (location, admission price and a picture of the host)—boozing and bit of wining and grinding to the latest *soca* and Jamaican *dub*.

For those who prefer a more formal setting, there are a number of shows depicting Barbadian life and history. The best is probably *1627 and all that...* which celebrates Bajan history from the beginning and takes place on Thursday in the **Barbados Museum**. For Bds$115 you have a tour of the museum, dinner and drinks, and see

Barbados Directory

getting there

Barbados is geographically distinct from the other islands in the Eastern Caribbean, but it is well served by air. As well as regular connections from Europe and North America there are easy links to all the islands nearby and Guyana and Venezuela. All air tickets sold in Barbados are supplemented with a 20% government tax. Departure tax Bds$25.

By air from Europe: British Airways (local ✆ 428 1661) flies almost daily from London Gatwick. During the winter, they run a twice-weekly direct flight on Concorde; a snip at £4500. The journey time is better than halved at 3½ hours and gets you back to the UK on the same day rather than overnight. BWIA (✆ 426 2111) has two or three direct flights each week from Heathrow. There are numerous charter services on which you can buy seat-only tickets through UK travel agents. From continental **Europe,** BWIA have services originating in Frankfurt and a number of charter airlines operate out of Germany (LTU and Condor) and Holland (Martinair).

By air from the USA: The best gateways on the American mainland are Miami and New York, from where there are a couple of scheduled flights each day, on American Airlines or BWIA. Connections are also possible through San Juan on Puerto Rico. Other US cities with scheduled flights include Boston and Philadelphia, from where there is a daily scheduled service on America Airlines. **Air Canada** (✆ 428 5077) has a daily flight from Toronto.

By air from other Caribbean islands: LIAT (✆ 434 5428) has the most services, flying to all the major islands between Trinidad and Antigua, and on to the Virgin Islands and Puerto Rico. Air Martinique (✆ 431 0540) flies to the French island of Martinique and BWIA makes the link to its home island of Trinidad (it is possible to join other trans-Atlantic flights in between islands as they often touch more than one before departing). Flights are also available to Georgetown, Guyana and Paramaribo in Surinam through BWIA and Surinam Air. If you are flying on to the **Grenadines**, Mustique Airways (✆ 435 7009) usually has daily share-charter flights, as does TIA (Trans-Island Air ✆ 418 1654, ✆ 428 0916).

By sea: The MV *Windward* (✆ 431 0449) is a ferry which works a round trip from Barbados to Trinidad, St Lucia, St Vincent and Venezuela. There are cabins and reclinable seats. Eric Hassell & Co. (✆ 436 6102) have a fortnightly sailing to St Lucia and Dominica on which passengers are welcome. Other ships do make the crossing; ask around at the shallow draft dock.

the show (✆ 428 1627). The **Plantation Restaurant** in the old boiling house of the Balls Estate in St Lawrence stages a couple of shows, the *Tropical Spectacular* (Wed, Fri) with fire-eating and flaming limbo, adm Bds$115 for drinks and dinner (for res call ✆ 428 5048).

More formal entertainment, classical concerts and plays, are usually held in the **Frank Collymore Hall** in Bridgetown.

tourist information

UK: 263 Tottenham Court Road, London W1P 9AA (✆ (0171) 636 9448, 🖶 637 1496).

USA: 800 Second Avenue, New York, NY 10017 (✆ (212) 986 6516, 🖶 573 9850) or 3440 Wilshire Boulevard, Suite 1215, Los Angeles, CA 90010 (✆ (213) 380 2198, 🖶 384 2763).

Canada: 5160 Yonge Street, Suite 1800, North York, Ontario M2N GL19 (✆ (416) 512 6569, 🖶 512 6581, toll free ✆ (1 800) 268 9122).

Germany and **Europe:** Staatliches Fremdenverkehrsamt Barbados, Neue Mainzerstr 22, D-60311 Frankfurt/Main (✆ 69 23 23 66, 🖶 69 23 00 77).

Information about Barbados can found at *http://barbados.org.*

Once you are on the island you can get tourist information and assistance with hotels at the main **tourist offices** in Bridgetown: PO Box 242, Harbour Road, Bridgetown (✆ 427 2623, 🖶 426 4080), at the airport (✆ 428 0937, 428 5570) and at the Deep Water Harbour, where the cruise ships dock (✆ 426 1716). There is a toll free number (✆ (1 800) 744 6244). If you need further assistance on current events and tips about where to find shopping bargains, there is a plethora of advertising-led magazines, maps and leaflets, including *Ins and Outs of Barbados* and broadsheets like the *Visitor* and the *Sunseeker*.

The two main Barbadian **newspapers** are the *Advocate* and the *Nation*, which give good coverage of local and international news and list forthcoming events. The *Investigator* will plug you in to the most scurrilous island gossip.

There is an active **National Trust** in Barbados (✆ 426 2421). They organize a walk to a different site of natural and historical interest each Sunday, starting 6am and 3.30pm and lasting about 3 hours (details in the local newspapers or ✆ above, adm free but donations welcomed). They have introduced a programme of 'Open Houses' once á week (usually Wed 2.30–5.30pm, winter season only) which enables you to visit Barbadian houses not normally open to the public—locations published in advance in a leaflet. Their *Heritage Passport* allows you to visit about 15 of the best-known 'sights' of Barbados on one ticket, purchased in advance at Cave Shepherd in town and at National Trust properties, *Bds$70+VAT.*

In a medical **emergency,** contact Queen Elizabeth Hospital, on Martindales Road in the north of Bridgetown (✆ 436 6450) or dial 115.

The **IDD code** for Barbados is ✆ (1 246), followed by a seven-digit island number. On-island dial all seven digits. **Useful addresses**: British High Commission, Lower Collymore Rock, St Michael (✆ 436 6694); US Consul General (✆ 431 0025); Canadian High Commission, Bishop Court, Hill Pine Road (✆ 429 3550).

festivals

The highlight of the Barbadian Festival year is **'Cropover'**, which culminates on the first Monday in August, Kadooment Day (the crop referred to is the sugar-cane harvest). It is a major blow-out along Carnival lines, with calypso-singing competitions, steel band music and carnival 'bands' made up of hundreds of costumed players who strut through the streets to *soca* music. You can 'play mas' by buying a costume and joining the masquerade, or just dance on the sidelines. There is a jazz festival in early January, **Paint it Jazz,** with international players performing in three different venues across the island (in 1997 Patti LaBelle, Grover Washington, Roberta Flack and Al Jarreau among others) and in the middle of the month the Mt Gay International **Regatta** with sailing races. In February the **Holetown Festival** commemorates the first settlement of the island in 1627 with a week's worth of exhibitions, tattoos and general jamboree. The **Holder's Season** is a round of open-air opera performances and Shakespeare plays around Easter-time—in 1997 Pavarotti was the star attraction. In April the **Oistins Fish Festival** celebrates the town's livelihood with blow-outs and the **Congaline Carnival** begins a week of street parades. In May you can see church music performed at **Gospelfest**. In November you can see exhibitions of the visual arts at **NIFCA**, the National Independence Festivities of the Creative Arts.

There is also a number of sporting events which are worth attending for the mix of locals and visitors at play, including windsurfing and sailing competitions in January, polo in February, a triathlon in October, a surfing championship in November, a road running race in December, pro-am golf and cricket tournaments occasionally and horse-racing throughout the year.

money

The Barbados currency is the Barbados dollar, which like many others in the Caribbean is fixed to the US dollar (rate US$ = Bds$1.98) which gives an easy approximate exchange rate of one Bds$ to US50c. All prices (except hotel rates) are quoted in Barbados dollars and so it is worth carrying them, though US dollars will be accepted everywhere. Make sure to establish which currency you are dealing in. Credit cards are widely accepted by the hotels and restaurants and in tourist areas generally.

Banking hours: Mon–Thurs 8 or 9–3, Fri 8–5. You can change money any time at the hotels (usually for a marginally less favourable rate). There is now a number of ATM machines around Barbados which accept credit and banker's cards.

shopping

Opening hours: Weekdays 8–6, Sat 8–noon. For Bajan or Bajan-designed products, try the **Best of Barbados**, with branches throughout the island, or **Fairfield Greathouse Pottery**, set in an old boiling house in St Michael. There are a couple of **'chattel villages'**, in St Lawrence on the south coast and Holetown in the west, with local and imported products on sale. Also the **Foursquare Rum Factory and Heritage Park**, where artists and craftmakers have workshops and galleries.

maps and books

By Barbadian authors: *In the Castle of my Skin,* by George Lamming, is about a black Barbadian boy growing up; *Christopher,* by Geoffrey Drayton, narrates the stifling life of a white Barbadian boy. Edward Braithwaite's collections of poetry include *Rights of Passage.* Good beach material is Thomas Hoover's *Caribbee,* set in the time when Barbados had a tavern for every 20 inhabitants. A publication set in modern times in a mythical hotel on Barbados's west coast is *Platinum Coast,* a steamy tale of international people with unfeasibly large bank accounts and egos to match. There are many well-written histories of the island and lifestyle books. The **bookshops** are stocked with books on the Caribbean and most magazines. Try the Cloister Bookstore on Hincks St or Cave Shepherd on Broad Street.

watersports

You will find general watersports operators on the main beaches on the west and south coasts where you can fix up a kayak, a small sailing boat, a windsurfer, a jetski or arrange a ride on a bouncy banana, under a parasail or go waterskiing. Some shops are hotel concessionaires, but outsiders can usually use them.

Snorkelling: Masks and fins are available at all the watersports shops and many hotels. You will find good reefs in Payne's Bay and at the Folkstone National Marine Park, near Holetown, also off the Heywoods resort near Speightstown. Trips in a glass-bottomed boat on the west coast can be organized through most watersports shops. For a view of deeper Barbados corals without getting wet, contact Atlantis Submarine (© 436 8929); reserve a couple of days in advance in season.

Scuba diving: There are plenty of dive-shops which will take you out and give instruction if you need it. Most of the dive-sites are on the west coast, where the water is the calmest; a reef runs along the drop-off a mile or so offshore— but there are some wrecks in Carlisle Bay and some reefs and wrecks not far from St Lawrence; sometimes there are drift dives down here. Average prices are Bds$90 for a one-tank dive. Companies offering equipment and qualified instruction are Hightide Watersports at the Sandy Lane Hotel (©/☻ 430 0391, *hightide@sunbeach.net, www.world-traveller.com/barbados/high.html,* toll free © (1 800) 513 5763) and the Boatyard Complex in Bridgetown (© 228 3322), West Side Scuba Centre (©/☻ 432 2558) in Holetown. In Bridgetown is a BSAC accredited school: Coral Isle Divers (©/☻4319068, *coralis@caribnet.net, www.caribnet.net/ coral_isle/,* US and Canada toll free © (1 800) 513 5840). On the south coast there are two PADI five-star dive centres: in St Lawrence Gap, ExploreSub Barbados (© 435 6542, ☻ 428 4674); and in Hastings Underwater Barbados (©/☻ 426 0655, *www.ndl.net/~uwb*). Some dive shops have photographic equipment; most will collect you from your hotel.

Windsurfing: A good option in Barbados. It is best along the south coast—experienced windsurfers should head for the southerly point, around Silver Sands, where the 1991 World Championships were hosted and where Mistral keeps an outfit at the Silver Sands Hotel over the winter months (when the tradewinds are at their highest). There is a reef offshore so it is particularly good for waves (jump on the way out, surf back in); if you want to put down a 360, a table-top or a cheese roll, or watch them at it, or simply watch the crowds, this is the place to come. Slightly less extreme, a good place to learn, is at Maxwell Beach, also Mistral (© 428 7277), which offers equipment hire and instruction.

Surfing: Also popular on the island. There are big waves on the east coast at Bathsheba and there is a crowd there most days. It is also quite fun to sit in one of the bars, the Bonito Bar, and watch the surf-gods at it. Other surfing areas are Duppies and Crab Hill in the far north. For the merely mortal there are boogie boards for hire on the south coast beaches, where the waves are gentler; try Accra Beach, Dover Beach or Crane Beach.

Day sails: Snorkelling and cruising up the west coast, or a sunset cruise: plenty of options available (with hotel transfers and a meal usually included). Try the catamaran *Irish Mist* (© 436 9201) and sailing yachts *Secret Love* (© 432 1972) and *Limbo Lady* (© 420 5184). An afternoon of rum-soaked piracy and profligacy can be had aboard the Jolly Roger, with lots of shiver-me-timbers and walking the plank to loud music. For a more stately ride in an old riverboat, try the Bajan Queen (res for both, © 436 6424).

Deep-sea fishing: Charters after swordfish or marlin can be arranged through the boats on the Careenage, among them *Blue Jay* (© 422 2098) or *Billfisher II* (© 431 0741).

other sports

Golf: There are two principal courses on the island, both 18-hole championship courses. They are well kept and have trolleys for hire; the wind is the main complication. The newer is the Royal Westmoreland, designed by Robert Trent Jones, 6870 yards, par 72 (© 422 4635), access restricted to certain hotels (packages available), green fee astronomic at Bds$290. On the west coast is the neatly tended Sandy Lane course (© 432 1145), with green fees around Bds$200 (free for hotel guests).

Tennis: Most hotels have courts, usually for a fee of about US$6 per hour. There are even **squash** courts, some of them actually air-conditioned, in Barbados. Contact the Barbados Squash Club in Hastings (© 427 7913) or Rockley Resort in Christ Church (© 435 7880).

Walking: Walkers can find satisfying hikes in the hilly district of Scotland and along the rugged east coast. If you wish to set off alone, maps are easily available in town. There are various National Trust walks, *see* p.79.

Mountain-biking: At the Canefield Plantation in St Thomas (© 438 8069).

Riding: If you fancy a canter along the beach at dawn, contact the Brighton Stables (© 425 9381) on the Spring Garden Highway in St Michael or Beau Geste Stables (© 429 0139) for a ride through the canefields to Francia Plantation. A ride out in the northern hills can be arranged through Tony's Riding School (© 422 1549).

Spectator sports include the **horse-racing** on alternate Saturdays in the season at the Garrison Savannah south of Bridgetown and even **polo** (Barbados Polo Club, © 427 0022 for schedules) on the west coast. But **cricket** is the Barbadian national sport, and you will come across weekend matches all over the island and less formal games being played by children in the backstreets of the towns—stop and watch, you may even be thrown the ball and told to bowl. Details of forthcoming League matches and international Tests, held in the Kensington Oval north of Bridgetown, can be found in the newspapers or by asking around.

Trinidad and Tobago

The twin-island state of Trinidad and Tobago is an unusual mix of two completely different Caribbean strains. Trinidad has the excitable bustle of a large and busy island, where at times like carnival, with its calypso singing and street masquerades, West Indian exuberance reaches its highest pitch. Equally colourful is the birdlife, unparalleled in the Caribbean. Just a few miles away, Tobago is a classic retreat in the Caribbean mould, a beach-bound idyll of white sand beaches, hidden coves and easy island life. Together they make an unlikely but satisfying combination.

Trinidad and Tobago may be truly Caribbean in spirit, but geologically they are closer to South America. The northern range of mountains in Trinidad, just 7 miles off the continent, was separated from the mainland by rising water levels about 10,000 years ago. Trinidad is the largest of the Lesser Antilles (1864 square miles, about 50 miles by 50). Unlike the other Antilles to the north, it is not volcanic and its heartlands are low agricultural plains. So close to South America, it is home to a surprisingly dense distribution of continental species, particularly birds. Tobago is a cumulus of forested peaks with some small coral-encrusted flatlands in the southwest that broke off from South America millions of years ago. It lies 22 miles off the north-eastern tip of Trinidad and has an area of 116 square miles. Tobago's birdlife is also wonderfully varied.

There are about 1.3 million people on the two islands, which makes it the most populous country in the Lesser Antilles (Tobago has just 50,000 of this population). The islands were unwilling partners when they were first lumped together by the British Government in 1898, but they have grown closer, even if there is occasional dissent. Tobagonians complain that they are politically neglected and joke that Port of Spain is a den of thieves where you need eyes in the back of your head just to survive. In Trinidad, where there is a radically different population, nearly half composed of Indians, they laughingly claim that Tobago is backward, though they then admit that they like it that way because they can go on holiday there.

In fact Tobago is developing fast at the moment. The tourism industry has expanded considerably in recent times and there is much more development scheduled for the future. Trinidad, which traditionally depended more on oil revenues than on tourism (it is an untypical Caribbean island because it does not have many of the palm-backed strands), has also begun to develop a little more and there are guest houses and hotels opening up in the remote coastal villages and the rainforest.

Trinidad and Tobago has long been a political leader in the Caribbean and, until the failure of the West Indian Federation in 1962, Chaguaramas outside Port of Spain was to have been the seat of the Caribbean Parliament. The leader of the country for many years was the charismatic historian and politician Eric Williams of the People's National Movement (PNM), who took Trinidad and Tobago to independence from Britain on 31 August 1962 and remained in power until his death in 1981. In 1976 the country became a Republic, recognizing a President as Head of State (presently A.N.R. Robinson, a Tobagonian former Prime Minister) rather than the Queen, though it has remained within the British Commonwealth.

There are two Houses of Parliament, a 33-seat Upper House and a 38-seat House of Representatives. The country is led by Prime Minister Basdeo Panday of the United National Congress, which is in a coalition with the National Alliance for Reconstruction, holding 20 seats in all (18 to the UNC, 2 to the NAR), as against the opposition PNM's 18 seats. This represented a radical political reversal at the last election. The UNC is dominated by Trinidad's Indian population, whereas the PNM, which had been in power for 23 years, was dominated by Trinidadians of African descent.

Carnival, Calypso, Steel Pan

The country is also a Caribbean cultural leader. *Steel pan* and the *calypso*, a relentless song of stinging social comment, both of which are heard all over the Caribbean, were born here. Carnival or *Mas* is one of the three biggest in the world and is the model for most others held in the area. The 'Trinbagonians' must also take the credit and/or the responsibility for inventing the *limbo* dance.

Carnival

On Shrove Tuesday the streets of Port of Spain seethe with the *bacchanal*—fluorescent satin flashes by as a frenzied army of imps advances, each brandishing a trident. At their head is a massive devil with glowing eyes, a vast black mannequin with a demonic smile held aloft, sparkling with sequins. The Savannah and the length of Frederick Street reverberate to a killing beat—vast articulated lorries stacked 30ft high with speakers, followed by a sea of costumed revellers dancing and shuffle-stepping in waves. It is the Parade of Carnival Bands and at Trinidad Carnival, each band can contain as many as 3000 'players' dressed to a common theme.

The build-up starts right after Christmas. The Trinidadians stage spectacles of calypso, steel bands, costume competitions and 'fêtes' all over the country—all culminating in a four-day jump-up in Port of Spain in which hundreds of thousands of people take part.

Mas (short for masquerade) was introduced by the French settlers who came to Trinidad at the end of the 18th century. At first it was the preserve of the plantocracy and the wealthy traders, who would move in masked processions from one open house to the next; but with emancipation in 1838, the slaves made the event their own. They danced in the streets with lighted torches, celebrating *Canboulay* (from *cannes brûlées*), the burning of the canefields. Drums led the processions and any instrument was used to make a tune: tin kettles, shack-

shacks, even bottles and biscuit tins. In Victorian times the celebrations were frowned upon by the government and many official attempts were made to curb them, but these often ended in rioting (another meaning of the word bacchanal) as bands of revellers and groups of police armed with sticks took each other on.

Early in the 20th century the tradition of dressing up was revived and the drum-driven masquerade once again became the centrepiece of the Carnival. You will still see some of the figures of *Ole Mas*, *moko jumbies* (stilt men), *djab-djabs* (from French *diable*) and the elaborately dressed characters of the sailor bands. Steel bands led the processions in the years after the Second World War and now alongside them you will hear the relentless sounds of *soca* music as the engine-house of the pageant.

Mention Rio or New Orleans to a Trinidadian and they will laugh and assure you that carnival in those cities is just a fashion show. Carnival is more accessible to outsiders here—you do not have to be a member of a club to 'play Mas'. People leave their jobs to get back to Mas, and without exception they get into the Trinidadian spirit of taking it all to glorious excess. If you want, it is possible to dance for four days and nights at a stretch.

The best moments to see are the calypso tents and the calypso competition finals, and the steel band preliminaries and finals. The street-dancing itself begins at 2am on Carnival Monday morning, as party-goers spill out on to the streets for *jouvert* (pronounced jouvay). Players smear themselves with mud, oil and even chocolate sauce (beware if you wander by in smart clothes). After a couple of hours' rest they join the main *Parade of Bands* on Monday afternoon until late (when you can join a night band if you want) and then everyone comes out again on Tuesday. It is a crush and it is deafening, but there is nothing like it. The carnival roadmarch tunes of any particular year become ingrained on your memory as you hear them played over and over again; they will bring back the feeling of Carnival for years. The players continue to dance on *Las'(t) Lap* until midnight on Tuesday, when it all abruptly comes to an end, until next year of course.

If you wish to 'play Mas', you can turn up at a Mas Camp ten days ahead of time and a buy a costume in which to play for between US$50 and $100.

Carnival Calendar of Events

A typical Carnival calendar stages *calypso tents*, *panorama* (steel band) and King and Queen of the Band (the most elaborate and largest costumes) competition heats on the weekends before the beginning of Lent.

Friday before Lent: 'Ole Time Mas' Characters Festival, Piccadilly Green, Arima.
Traditional Carnival Character Festival, King and Queen of the Bands semi-finals.
Extempo Calypso Competition finals.

Saturday: Junior Carnival Parade and Competition, *Panorama* final.

Sunday: *Dimanche Gras*, a day of fêtes followed by the Calypso finals and King and Queen of the Bands finals.

Monday: *Jouvert* (a *jump-up*, 2–10am); Procession of Carnival Bands, starting 1pm. *Night Mas* (mostly steel pan) in St James.

Tuesday: *Mardi Gras*, Parade of Carnival Bands from 9am until late. Las' Lap.

Saturday night, weekend after Mardi Gras: Carnival Champions in concert.

Calypso

The sounds that accompany Carnival—the relentless beat on the *Roadmarch* as the masquer-aders dance through the streets and in the lively sparring in the concert-halls—are *calypsos*. They are Trinidadian-born songs of life, love and lust—witty, lyrical, melodic, full of gossip and often political, but above all entertaining (in their comment or as dance tunes) and with as many styles as there are *calypsonians* (also known as *kaisonians*).

The roots of the calypso are obscure, but the songs were first sung in French creole in Trinidad during the last century. Early this century they became a source of popular entertainment and as they started to reach a larger audience they were sung in English. Since they have become popular in Trinidad, other islands in the area have adopted the form. They are a verbal news-paper of sorts and they deal with contemporary issues, commenting on politics, satirizing life's institutions (anything from love to the IMF) and occasionally descending into plain rudeness (*smut*, as it is known, has been causing controversy recently because it is an easy way of making a mark in a fiercely competitive arena). They are often irreverent and satirical, they have a fearsome cutting edge when it comes to ridicule and they have been known to have a direct effect on politics. Most recently, though, they have come under threat from politicians, who were planning to outlaw certain name-calling in song and in the press.

But the calypsonian is also a performer, daring and outspoken, as seen in the annual calypso competition in the run-up to Carnival. The big calypsonians will spar with each other in song, ridiculing their opponents in their lyrics (there is a special word for personal insult in calypso, *picong*). Singers belong to a *calypso tent* (no longer a tent but a commercial group a bit like a recording label; names include *Spektakula Forum*, *Calypso Revue* and *Kisskidee*) where they perform the songs. Judges select a number of calypsonians from each tent to go on to the National Calypso Monarch Competition.

The finals are something like a variety show as the performers act out their theme. Calypsos must be timely and witty; the style can range from that of a raconteur to a pantomime artist. The repertoire is endless, but they are divided fundamentally into two main categories, both destined for different prizes: the slower and more melodic tunes with more thoughtful lyrics that compete for the calypso monarch title, and the faster, simpler dance tunes that vie for the roadmarch title (won by the song played the most as the bands cross the judging stages in the parade of bands). Very occasionally a single song can win both categories. A third prize is awarded in the *Extempo* competition (from extemporization), in which singers ad-lib, verse by verse in competition with one another (lots of *picong* here), on subjects handed to them seconds before.

After the war, the calypsos were often backed by steel pan, but since the late seventies this has been replaced by *soca* music (from soul-calypso), a much faster beat played on more conven-tional modern instruments. Above the definite African drumbeat can be heard the strains of European rock and often odd blends of Indian or Chinese sounds.

The names of the calypsonians are colourful in themselves: early singers included Attila the Hun, Lord Executor and the Roaring Lion. Another self-appointed Lord includes Lord Melody, who stands alongside Calypso Rose, The Mighty Chalkdust (a schoolteacher), Black Stalin, Crazy and Watchman (a policeman). But the two mightiest (another popular prefix) calypso-nians of them all are Lord Kitchener, famed for his orchestration and steel pan compositions and the Mighty Sparrow, who have both been on the scene for 40 years—Sparrow was first crowned monarch in 1956 and won again as recently as 1992.

Steel Pan

As you walk along the street in Port of Spain, you might hear a rising, tremulous thunder of plinks and clangs. Suddenly you will hear a beat and the rhythm emerges: energetic, compulsive. It is an impressive sight to see a steel band. It is entirely a percussion orchestra and can have have as many as a hundred players all moving in time. At times the music can be raucous and rough, at other time it can sound like notes on velvet.

Steel pan, played on the stretched and tempered lids of oil-drums (literally the discarded drums of the oil industry), was invented in Trinidad and was first heard at the end of the Second World War. It was back-street music that came from the poorest sections of Port of Spain and initially it was frowned upon by the authorities. The *pan-yards* gave themselves names like Desperadoes, Renegades and Invaders and they fought regularly amongst themselves and with the police.

But the movement picked up in popularity and then became more respectable. It soon replaced *tamboo-bamboo* as the music for the Carnival roadmarch, initially as 'pan-around-the-neck' on the streets and later in larger lorry-borne bands. It has been superseded by *soca* only in the last 20 years. Many pan-yards are still active in Trinidad and it is definitely worth going along (just walk in) if you hear them playing. Pan competitions are held annually at Carnival (well worth attending) and every other year at the Pan is Beautiful Festival in October (it alternates with the School Steelband Music Festival). Pan Jazz is a yearly festival also held in November in which steel bands play alongside world-famous jazz musicians. Pan Ramajay (the word ramajay means a combination of display, flair, virtuoso and showing off) is held in May and features pan players showing their finest skills in competition.

Trinidad

In the faces of Trinidad you will see echoes from around the globe; African, (East) Indian, European, Middle Eastern (called Syrian), Chinese and South American. It is an extraordinary mixture, and it has been made yet more complex and exotic as the races have intermingled. You will hear names like Harris Mohammed and Winston Chang and see people wearing saris and African-style suits. On the skyline Hindu prayer flags and the domes of minarets stand among the classically English parish church towers. Even the musical rhythms (*soca* in this area) will be blended, as you can hear in the Indian-sounding strains of *chutney-soca*, which has been popular over the last few years.

The two largest sectors of the population are African and Indian, each of which is about 40 per cent. Other races include a few Chinese, though many have left in recent years, and Europeans, some British, but particularly the descendants of the French settlers of two centuries ago (French creole has become a catch-all term for white Trinidadians). Around 15 per cent of the islanders are of mixed descent. There are the same unspoken rules of colour in Trinidad that exist throughout the Caribbean and here they are further complicated by race (there are terms for the different mixes, such as *Dougla* for an Indian/African combination), but generally speaking it is a benevolent mix.

Nearly half of the population live in the urban east–west corridor that runs between the capital, Port of Spain, and the town of Arima, in the lee of the northern range of mountains, which at the moment is mainly inaccessible and undeveloped (once it was patched with coffee and cocoa plantations). South of here ranges of hills rise periodically out of much flatter land,

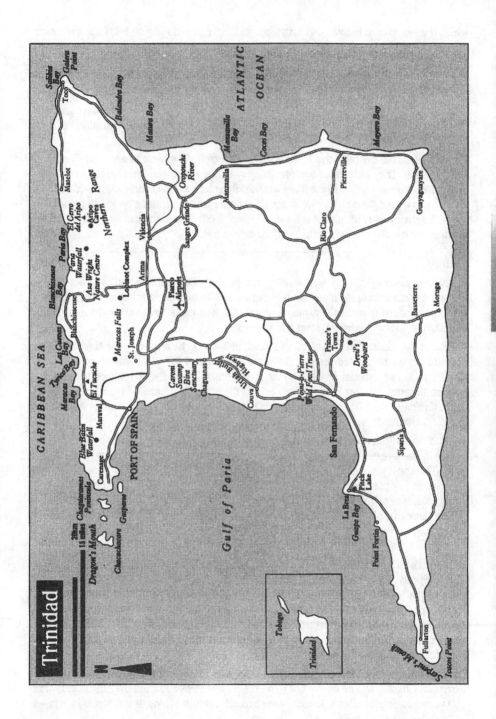

89

which is given over to industrial and agricultural concerns, including oil fields and vast tracts of sugar cane. Because of the nature of the island you are likely to spend quite a bit of time in Port of Spain. However, it is well worth making the effort to get out into the country.

The island is highly industrial for the Caribbean. Oil is still the main earner: after a slump in the early eighties when the OPEC cartel was broken, business has begun to pick up again. Other industries include asphalt and the export of manufactured goods including cigarettes, foods and clothing. Despite the fertile soil, the agricultural sector is small. The intention is for tourism to increase.

For all their mixed heritage, the Trinidadians have a typically expansive and vital Caribbean attitude to life. They have never done anything by halves and so you can expect a lively time, especially if you attend an event like Carnival. But there are also some classic quiet spots where you can see the best birdlife in the Caribbean. Trinidad is not a typical tourist island, but with such a variety of cultural and natural assets, it offers far more than a typical Caribbean beach to the traveller who wants to go off the beaten track.

History

In its early history Trinidad was *Iere* or 'the land of the hummingbird' and was home to Arawak Indians from mainland South America. Unlike their cousins farther north, the Iere Arawaks managed to resist the cannibalizing Caribs who came by in waves about AD 1000, escaping the *boucan* (on which meat was smoked).

The island was christened by Columbus himself in 1498; as he arrived in the New World on his third voyage he sighted three peaks in the southeast of the island and so he called the island Trinidad as a special devotion to the Holy Trinity. The Indians continued to resist any attempts to settle and they kept the Spaniards off the island for a hundred years until 1592. At the beginning of the 17th century, explorers began to use the island as a base for expeditions into the South American jungle in search of El Dorado, the Golden King.

Trinidad was officially a defensive Spanish outpost, but it was usually ignored in favour of the islands in the Greater Antilles and so it did not attract many settlers to develop the fertile lands. There was just a small and beleaguered garrison and the governing *cabildo*, which officially seems to have been called 'Illustrious', could not even afford the ceremonial clothes. A yearly Mass was said when a priest visited, but usually the only visitors to the island were on raiding parties. Insult was added to injury when the island's small trade in tobacco was banned (at one stage the word 'Trinidado' was used to refer to tobacco in the same way that the word 'Virginia' is used nowadays).

In 1783 efforts were made to develop the vast areas of untouched and fertile land in Trinidad and the Spanish king issued a *cedula* (decree) to encourage immigration. Grants of land were given to the 'subjects of powers and nations in alliance with Spain'. Catholics came from French colonies, some of them fleeing the revolutionaries and the slave uprisings in Saint Domingue (now Haiti), and set up cocoa and sugar plantations. Though the language has nearly died out, it is still just possible to hear French creole spoken in the mountains east of Port of Spain.

On 18 February 1797 though, the British fleet sailed into Port of Spain harbour and the Governor, Chacon, had no choice but to scuttle his five ships and hand over the island. After 200 years as a Spanish island, Trinidad now became a British colony. It was already a mix—a mainly French population administered by the British according to Spanish laws. The new British Governor, Picton, tried to develop it into another sugar island, despite the growing lobby against slavery and revolts all over the Caribbean. Next door South America was in turmoil and he had his hands full controlling the lawless population. His solution was to erect on the Government House lawn a set of gallows which he used liberally.

Emancipation came in 1834 and the freed men and women moved away from the cocoa walks and canefields, preferring to live in town or to farm a small plot of land. Large stretches of land were left unworked and so the government encouraged immigration again. In 1845 the first East Indians arrived on indentureships—their return passage paid in return for five years' work on a plantation. In all, by 1917, when indentureship was stopped by the Indian government, 145,000 Indians had come to Trinidad. Some went home when their time was up, but many took up the alternative offer of five acres of land and settled in the remote country areas, where their descendants still live today. The Indian workers were treated far better than their African counterparts had been a hundred years before, and their families were allowed to remain intact.

Adding further to the racial mix, Chinese workers came, renowned for their work in the canefields of Java and the Philippines and conspicuous in their pigtails, blue smocks and broad conical hats. In the 20th century the mix was completed by the arrival of settlers from the Middle East, many of them Syrians and Lebanese.

The energy which expresses itself so visibly at Carnival has a trickier side and Trinidad has suffered sporadic outbursts of political violence throughout the 20th century. Trade unions rallied the workers to confront the colonial authorities over the minimum wage in the thirties, and this culminated in political unrest which eventually led to self-determination. In 1970 the capital was brought to a standstill by Black Power protests and bands of guerrillas took to the hills. A short-lived but widely publicized coup attempt in 1990 foundered when the insurgents discovered that they did not have the anti-government following they expected.

Getting Around

Once you are past the Piarco airport taxi-touts, who are among the Caribbean's most persistent, travel in Trinidad is easy. If you do go by taxi the trip to Port of Spain will cost around TT$120, but it is possible to do it for TT$2 on the public transport bus which leaves every hour. Piarco is 17 miles from Port of Spain and it takes about 45 minutes to cover the distance by car.

There are two **bus** systems on the island: the government-run **PTSC** and the hundreds of private minibuses, or *maxi-taxis* as the contrary Trinidadians prefer to call them. Both systems start running at dawn and continue until late evening. PTSC is extremely cheap and links all the major towns for less than TT$5. As the government transport network, the buses have no plush seats or stereo systems like the private buses and tickets are only on sale during certain hours (they must be bought in the terminal office or in some shops). There is a regular, if infrequent, schedule, leaving Port of Spain from the former railway station on South Quay.

Maxi-taxis, which once were more akin to mobile discotheques than a system of transport, have been quietened down by law recently. Drivers caused so much controversy by playing Jamaican dub music (an insult to Trinidadian self-esteem to be begin with) at such high volume, and supposedly by being irresponsible, smutty and generally corrupting of Trinidadian youth, that music was legislated against. Maxis are crowded and noisy, but still a good exposure to Trinidad life. They will take you to most towns and they are colour-coded according to the route they run. When you reach your destination, shout 'Driver! Stop!' (you will have to shout to be heard above the stereo system).

Faster, more comfortable and a little more expensive are **share-taxis**, private cars that follow (mostly the same) fixed routes to and from the towns. Most leave from the same point as the maxi-taxis: **Independence Square** for the east and west, and **Woodford Square** for St Ann's and St James. Jeeps for the north coast leave from **George Street**. There are no specific stops, so when you want to get out, just tell the driver and for a little extra he will drop you at your door. Drivers leave when the vehicle is full.

Normal **taxis** are in plentiful supply and can be fixed up in the main squares and at all hotels. Some sample prices are: **airport** to central Port of Spain—TT$120, Asa Wright Centre—TT$150; and from downtown **Port of Spain** to Maracas—TT$80, Caroni Bird Sanctuary—TT$70 and Asa Wright Centre—TT$120. To call a taxi you can phone St Christopher's Taxi Co-op (✆ 624 3560), at the cruise ship complex (✆ 623 4419) or the Airport Taxi Co-operative at Piarco (✆ 669 1689).

Tours around Port of Spain and the island can be fixed through Twin Island Tours, 177 Tragarete Road, Port of Spain (✆ 622 7664) or through taxi drivers at the hotels. A 2hr city tour costs about TT$300 (up to four people), over to Maracas—TT$450, to the Caroni Bird Sanctuary—TT$400 and to the Pitch Lake—TT$600 (6 hrs).

Trinidad is a big place and is worth exploring. There are plenty of vehicles for **hire**. The roads are adequate, though if you plan to go off the beaten track it might be worth investing in a four-wheel-drive. Licences from UK, France, Germany, USA and Canada are valid in Trinidad and Tobago, and driving is on the left. When driving, carry your licence with you at all times along with your passport. The authorities were being tough on the wearing of seatbelts at the time of writing. Do not drive in downtown Port of Spain except for sport.

Expect to pay from US$60 per day, tax included, for the smallest car. Rental companies include: Auto Rentals (✆ 623 7368, ✆ 675 2258), on Tragarete Road, Port of Spain; Econo–Car Rentals (✆ ✆ 669 2342, ✆ 622 8074), at the airport and town; Kalloo's (✆ 669 5673, ✆ 645 5182), airport and Woodbrook; and Singh's (✆ 664 5417, ✆ 664 3860) at the airport.

Beaches

Trinidad's beaches do not have the precious picture-postcard feel of other Caribbean islands—try Tobago for that. Here there are fewer beaches to begin with and they are rugged and more spectacular. If you are staying in Port of Spain, you will have to travel quite a few miles to get to one. Some beaches have changing facilities and you can buy a drink and a snack on all except the most remote. The closest beaches to Port of Spain are on the north coast, a short ride over the Saddle. Buses run as far as Las Cuevas (depart George Street, downtown), but only occasionally to Blanchisseuse. Further afield you will need a hire car, but it can be very rewarding because of the scenery and the secluded strands.

Maracas Bay: A huge sweeping strand enclosed by vast headlands, which funnel the waves on to the shelved sand and enormous palm trees. Red flags mean a strong current. At Maracas Bay the thing to have is a 'shark and bake'—a fish sandwich—with a Solo soft drink or a Carib.

Tyrico Bay: Sand OK, waves often big enough to surf.

Las Cuevas Bay: Popular with Trinidadian weekend trippers, named after the underwater caves (changing rooms available)

Blanchisseuse Bay: Remote escape with good sand.

Paria Bay: A couple of miles beyond Blanchisseuse, usually deserted.

Chaguaramas: Beaches are not that nice, but a easy run from Port of Spain, so people often swim here.

Balandra Bay and **Salibia Bay**: Near the northeastern tip of the island, these see the full force of the Atlantic, but there is protected swimming.

Manzanilla Bay, Cocos Bay and **Mayaro Bay**: Miles and miles of palm-backed sand on the east coast running down to the southern corner of the island. The beaches face the Atlantic and so the waves can be big. Island lore explains that a boatload of coconuts from Brazil was washed up here: hence the palm trees.

river bathing

The rivers and rockpools in Trinidad's northern range provide some excellent river bathing if you want a change. Perhaps the easiest to reach is the **Blue Basin Waterfall** in Petit Valley off the Diego Martin Valley, west of Port of Spain. At 300ft high, **Maracas Falls** are worth a visit and can be found 1 mile off the road that runs north out of St Joseph. The **Paria Waterfall**, off the Arima to Blanchisseuse road, can be reached along a track that follows the river into the rainforest for an hour. There is a waterfall and a pool at the **Asa Wright Nature Centre** and there is good swimming in the Caura River at Eldorado Village and in the Oropouche River at the eastern end of the range.

Flora and Fauna

The flora and fauna of Trinidad is related to that of nearby South America and is consequently richer and more varied than on other islands. The vegetation looks neolithic after the explosive lushness of the Windwards—vines and lianas grow to an immense thickness and the trees grow up to 200ft high clinging to the steep land. The rainforest flits and squawks all day long with incredibly colourful butterflies and birdlife and there are equally abundant mangrove and freshwater inland swamps.

Among the yellow and pink pouis, and 100ft bamboo sprouts (which look particularly pretty over remote rivers), you will find heliconia and chaconia (the crab-claw-shaped Trinidadian national flower) and even Venus fly-traps. There are 2200 species of flowering plants and trees.

By comparison mammals are relatively limited, though the 108 species is an abundance for a Caribbean island. They all originate in South America, so you might see an agouti, an opossum, an ocelot and even an armadillo. There are also a number of insects, including over

600 species of butterfly, and reptiles including snakes (47), lizards and the endless tree-frogs that sing their shrill tune on the night air.

But the birdlife on Trinidad is the most spectacular—there are about 425 species that make an appearance during the year. The island is on a migratory route and like tourists they fly down here to escape the cold weather. You will often see parrots flying near the botanical gardens near dusk. Among the kiskidees (called so because of their call, which sounds a bit like *'qu'est-ce qu'il dit'* in French) and bananaquits, motmots and macaws, there are 27 herons and 18 hummingbirds, which flash with fluorescence as they come to suck at a flower on the veranda, and species such as nocturnal oilbirds and white-bearded or golden-headed manikins (which true to their name spend a large proportion of their time displaying).

The swamps have an enormous variety of birdlife and water-borne life (from groupers to spectacled caymans and tree crabs). In among the mangroves, which grow with a complex network of roots like flying buttresses run riot, you will find tree oysters and small sloths. And in the last rays of the sun, the trees in the Caroni Swamp light up with egrets and the colourful scarlet ibis, Trinidad's national bird (*see* p.98).

Trinidad has six Wildlife and Nature Reserves: three swamps—Caroni, Nariva in the east and Point-à-Pierre (*see* p.98), and three forests—El Tucuche (Trinidad's second-highest mountain), Valencia and the Asa Wright Nature Centre (*see* p.97). Two of the most accessible are the **Asa Wright Nature Centre** in the northern range, where you can see toucans, honeycreepers and bell birds and, if a swamp does not sound too outlandish (it is fascinating), the **Caroni Swamp Bird Sanctuary**. Tours to the Caroni Swamp can be arranged through **Nanan Tours**, 38 Bamboo Grove Settlement No. 1, Butler Highway, Valsayn (*©* 645 1305), at about US$10 per person. Birding tours with a knowledgeable guide can be arranged through Geoffrey Gomes (*©* 624 2223)—ring a couple of days in advance. Also **Avifauna** (*©* 633 5614).

There is little coral on Trinidad's shores because of the freshwater outflow from the Orinoco (go to the eastern end of Tobago for coral), but one of the world's largest species of turtle, the leatherback (it can weigh up to 1200lb and is about 7ft long) comes to nest on both islands between April and September—on Matura Beach on the east coast of Trinidad and on Turtle Beach on Tobago.

Trinidad has large reserves of oil beneath its surface and these find odd ways of coming to the surface. The gases seep up through bubbling mud flues and the island has one of the Caribbean's oddest underworld phenomena in the Pitch Lake in the south of the island near La Brea (*see* p.99).

To help you orientate yourself, there is a number of good field guide pamphlets available.

Port of Spain

Like so many Caribbean capitals, Port of Spain (population about 500,000) is set on the sea and is framed by hills. It lies in the northwest of the island on the Gulf of Paria, in the crook of the Chaguaramas peninsula. The downtown area, which is set back from the docks and wharves of the waterfront (much of which has been reclaimed), is a gridiron of tight streets with concrete buildings. It is not particularly attractive, but it is the heart of the island and it buzzes. Just north of here is the Savannah, a huge area of parkland in the centre of the city; scattered around it, the residential suburbs have some of the Caribbean's most elaborate and

Gingerbread House

beautiful gingerbread houses. Beyond here the hills rise steeply in a green backdrop, too steep in places to have houses, but settlements creep along the valleys' floors that head into the hills behind the city.

Downtown the streets are mayhem, with share-taxis stopping at will and buses nosing for position among them; hucksters line the pavements of Frederick Street, their trestle-tables stacked with cassettes and mirror-shades or yards of T-shirts and underpants. Everywhere there is the smell of batter snacks frying and the cry of peanut vendors. As in any large city, you are advised to be careful after dark. For every thousand charming Trinidadians, there is one tricky one. However, you'll need your wits about you to enjoy the city anyway, because it is extremely lively.

The original capital of the island was positioned inland at St Joseph as a defensive measure, but it was moved to the coast in 1757 when the new governor found his residence uninhabitable. The new town expanded rapidly as the island population soared at the end of the century and trade picked up. The town was almost completely destroyed by a fire in 1808 and then laid out anew by Governor Woodford in 1813. Echoes of the British influence remain in the hefty colonial architecture and the spiked metal railings in the squares.

The business centre of the town is just above the waterfront, around **Independence Square.** Known as Marine Square until Trinidad's Independence in 1962, it is not really a square at all, but a long wide street: the pedestrian island in the middle was recently redeveloped and renamed the Brian Lara Promenade, after the island's cricketing hero. The city's two other main thoroughfares, Charlotte Street and Frederick Street, run north from here, the latter touching **Woodford Square**, the heart of Trinidadian politics, where you will see groups of people involved in political and no doubt less committed discussion. Demonstrations have occurred here, but its most important moments were as the 'University of Woodford Square', birthplace of Independence politics in the fifties. On the western side of the square, the **Red House** is the seat of the Trinidad and Tobago Parliament, flights of grand columns, arches and classical pediments all topped by mansard roofs and a cupola. It was first painted red in 1897 for Queen Victoria's Diamond Jubilee and has been repainted and called so ever since. The chamber can be visited during session (*adm free*) and there is a spectacular bright blue ceiling. On the south side is the yellow stone Anglican Cathedral.

At the very top of Frederick Street you will find the **National Museum and Art Gallery** (✆ 623 6419; *open 10–6; adm free*), which exhibits Trinidadian life throughout the ages, from the Arawaks and early Spaniards to angostura, asphalt and oil. It also has a display of carnival costumes and some of the excellent paintings of the Trinidad countryside by Michel Cazabon. Upstairs are more modern Trinbagonian paintings and a display of characters from island folklore, including Papa Bois, a friendly spirit who saves animals from hunters with the blow of a horn, the Soucouyant, an old hag who turns herself into a ball of fire and will suck your blood, and La Diablesse, who leads intoxicated men astray after a party and with a shriek of laughter dumps them in a thorn bush.

The Trinidadian claim that the **Savannah** is the biggest roundabout in the world is probably true—it has a 2½-mile circumference. At any rate it has a special place in the heart of every

Trini and it is a very attractive park, circled with huge trees. Once it was used to graze cattle that would terrorize the inhabitants, but now it is used more as a sports ground. According to C. L. R. James (*Beyond a Boundary*), it is big enough to contain 30 full-size cricket pitches, but at least some of them are now given over to hockey and football. The culmination of Carnival takes place here too. There is always a crowd of vendors at the roadside selling fresh fruit—sliced pineapple, oranges and particularly coconuts, which they slice in the usual manner. At night there are fast-food caravans serving burgers and hot dogs.

On the western side of the Savannah are the **Magnificent Seven**, a row of incredibly elaborate and imposing colonial mansions. Built early this century, they are a hotchpotch of styles, and include a mock Rhineland castle, a Moorish creation called Whitehall, and a mansion in the style of the French Second Empire known as the Gingerbread House.

On the northern corner of the park are the **Royal Botanical Gardens** (*open during daylight hours; adm free*), 70 acres of garden where you can retreat from the bustle of Port of Spain in *Banyan Lane, Raw Beef Walk* (after a famous tree which seeps red sap like a joint of meat when cut) and *Bougainvillea Dell*. The gardens were laid out by Governor Woodford in 1820 and he moved his residence up here because they were so pleasant. Among the pink and yellow *pouis* is a *cannon-ball* tree (with fruit like a wooden cannon ball, but the most ephemeral flowers that drop to earth at dusk) and the oddly shaped *chaconia*, the national flower of Trinidad and Tobago. The official residences of the President of the Republic and of the Prime Minister are in the gardens.

Nearby is the **Emperor Valley Zoo** (*open 9.30–5; adm*), named after a butterfly that once lived here, which exhibits Trinidad's deer and other South American animals like caymans (alligators), which lie frozen still with their mouths open, monkeys, tropical snakes, indigenous agouti and ocelots (a wild cat); other cats include cougar, jaguar, lions and tigers. Toucans and macaws are on display.

The western suburbs of the town are a good place to visit because of the many restaurants and bars and the pretty gingerbread houses (particularly in Woodbrook). Beyond here, the district of St James, on Tragarete Road, is called the 'City that never sleeps' and is very lively. Traditionally it has a strong Indian population and you will know that you have arrived when you see a pink and green arch built in Indian style with minarets. Close by is a monument to the leading Calypsonian, Lord Kitchener.

The heights above Port of Spain are dominated by the usual series of forts; **Fort Picton** and **Fort Chacon** both stand in the east, above the crowded suburb of Laventille. Just beneath Laventille on Beetham Highway (on the road to the airport), the main Port of Spain **market** is one of the liveliest places in town and worth a visit. Dominating St James on the other side of town, **Fort George** is half an hour's drive into the hills and has cannon and ramparts but is now mainly visited by lovers on a day out.

Over the Saddle Road to the North Coast

The Saddle Road runs north out of Port of Spain, from the northwest corner of the Savannah, through the wealthy suburb of **Maraval**, and then winds into the hills of the northern range. The scenery is majestic and makes the drive worthwhile even before you descend to the rural north coast. Maracas Bay, with its palm trees 100ft high, is a popular picnic place at the weekends. It is possible to reach the **Maracas Falls** and Trinidad's second peak **El Tucuche** from here, but it is quite a hike. The villages of **Las Cuevas** and **Blanchisseuse** overlook the sea and their beaches are usually less crowded than Maracas Bay (*see* 'Beaches', pp.92–3).

The Chaguaramas Peninsula

The route west out of Port of Spain follows the coast through the western suburbs and then beneath scrubby hills, passing the vast transhipment terminal (formerly used for bauxite) before coming to Chaguaramas, a popular area for day trips and evening entertainment. There is a number of good bars and nightclubs and the marinas are always full of visiting yachts. Chaguaramas is one of the areas which was leased to the Americans during the Second World War. The American presence on the island had a considerable effect on the Trinidadians because they paid so highly and because they spawned a large entertainment industry. 'Working for the Yankee Dollar' was the catchphrase of a calypso that spoke about the Trini girls deserting their menfolk for the rich American sailors.

Set in its concrete yard, the **Chaguaramas Military History and Aviation Museum** (*open daily 9–6; adm*) has displays of military hardware and planes. Inside there are boards on subjects such as the Spanish in Trinidad, the history of flight in the island, the U-Boat war in the Caribbean (Port of Spain was attacked), Trinidadians who served in the Second World War, general military history and even the coup in 1990. Worth a quick look if that's your interest.

Off the peninsula are five offshore islands in the **Bocas del Dragon** (the Dragon's Mouth), named by Columbus in 1498, where rich Trinidadians have built villas for themselves. On **Gaspar Grande** are some caves (*adm*) with stalactites and stalagmites and the remains of a fortress. **Chacachacare** is the biggest of the islands and has some strange red-brick buildings that once were a leper colony.

The Eastern Main Road

Running out of Port of Spain to the east as far as Arima, the corridor along the Eastern Main Road is the most populous area of the island outside the capital. Just out of the city is the **Angostura** factory, where the famous bitters are produced. An unrevealed number of spices and barks are selected by just four people and then percolated in alcohol to produce the bitters. Tours can be arranged (✆ 623 1841, marketing department; *adm free*). The road skirts the southern side of the lush Northern Range of mountains on the left and as you approach St Joseph, site of the original capital of the island, the St Augustine campus of the University of the West Indies is on the right. Overlooking the plain from 800ft up in the foothills is the Mount St Benedict Monastery. There is now also a school there and a Catholic seminary, and you can stay there in the small guest house.

The **Lopinot Complex** (*open until about 5; adm free*), a restored 19th-century estate, is off the road from Arouca. In 1800, the Comte de Lopinot fled the troubles in Saint Domingue (now Haiti) and he settled the plantation he cut out of the jungle in the Arouca Valley, where he planted cocoa, cashew and coffee. Early in the year the immortelle trees flame bright orange in the valley. Visits to caves on the estate are also possible. **Arima** has a strong Amerindian influence deriving from a community of Arawaks that lived here 200 years ago. There is a small museum devoted to the Indians in Cleaver Woods Park, just west of the town.

One of the island's most appealing spots is the **Asa Wright Nature Centre** (✆ 667 4655; *open to outsiders 9–5; adm US$6 adults, $4 children, accompanied walks*), 1200ft up in the hills above Arima, about an hour and a half from Port of Spain. Built in 1908, the estate house is very popular with naturalists and has some accommodation (*see* p.101), where you can witness the amazing colour and variety of the squawking, screeching rainforest. The veranda at the Nature Centre is one of the most charming places in the whole Caribbean, and you can realistically expect to see 25 species of birds before breakfast.

Five trails (varying between a few minutes and 3 hours) have been cut into the forest around the main house, and you will possibly see species such as the white-bearded or the golden-headed manikin, toucans and honeycreepers, as well as some of Trinidad's 18 fluorescent hummingbirds and its 600 or so butterflies. The most famous inhabitant is the nocturnal oilbird, which comes out only at night and feeds on fruit that it picks from the trees while in flight. They were once hunted by the Arawaks for their oil, but now are protected and live in remote regions in caves.

Not far off is Trinidad's highest peak, **El Cerro del Aripo** (3083ft), its sides mantled with rainforest and home to Trindad's rare piping guan. The Aripo caves are extensive, with a forest of monstrous stalactites and stalagmites, and a colony of oilbirds' nests.

Beyond Aripo the main road turns south, but if you take a left you come to the east coast at Salybia, close to **Matura Beach**, where the leatherback turtle nests by crawling up on to the sand and digging a hole with her flippers before laying about 150 eggs. From here, the road leads to the northeastern point of the island to the rugged Toco coast.

The South of the Island

The southern plains of Trinidad contain the agricultural lands, covered in green swathes of sugar-cane, and the industrial and oil heartland that has made Trinidad rich in the past (you will see the drill heads pecking at the ground like huge metal chickens). You will also find a gentle, laid-back calm more typical of smaller islands around the Caribbean.

Take the eastern main road out of Port of Spain and then turn south on the Uriah Butler Highway towards Chaguanas and San Fernando. The road skirts the **Caroni Swamp**, a wildlife reserve and bird sanctuary, which contains an enormous abundance of birdlife, with around 75 species. One of the island's most spectacular sights takes place here every evening, when the **scarlet ibis**, Trinidad's national bird, flies in to roost. You can take a leisurely tour at dusk as they arrive: for a moment whole trees will seem to be on fire with the scarlet of the ibis in flight. The knowledgeable guides will give you all sorts of anecdotes about swamp life— among the mangroves you might see a spectacled cayman (an alligator) or *Cyclopes didactylus* (a silky anteater) or perhaps a greater ani (tiny) or a pootoo, whose eyes glow in the dark. *The tour starts around 4.30pm, in good time for dusk, and costs around TT$50 per person, depending on the size of your party (restless children not recommended).*

The highway continues to the town of **Chaguanas**, which has mushroomed in recent years. The population is mostly of East Indian descent and in the main street you will find the **Lion House**, once the home of V. S. Naipaul (it is private, so you cannot go in). From here the road passes sugar mills and the factories of heavy industry at Point Lisas and the tangle of silver pipes at Point-à-Pierre, the island's main oil refinery. It was bought by the Trinidad and Tobago government from Texaco in 1984 when the oil company withdrew. On the lakes within the refinery compound, the **Point-à-Pierre Wild Fowl Trust** (© 637 5145; *open weekdays 10am–5pm, weekends 12–4; call in advance*) breeds wild fowl, mainly ducks, and encourages their reintroduction into the wild. It has trails and an education centre.

San Fernando, an urban sprawl with a population of 60,000, is Trinidad's second, slightly calmer city. The San Fernando Hill gives a good view of the city and the surrounding countryside. The **fish market** down by the bus station is worth a visit in the late afternoon.

The Pitch Lake

Open any time in daylight (remember that the round trip is about 6–8 hours by bus from Port of Spain), for a look at the small museum and a guided tour of the lake itself, on which you will learn more fantastic stories from the guide (adm free officially, but it is worth taking a guide, a bargain at TT$30 or so).

In the 'deep south', as it is jokingly known, is one of the Caribbean's most extraordinary phenomena, the **Pitch Lake**. As you approach the Pitch Lake through the town of La Brea, the side of the road is covered with splodges of black goo and an infestation of weeds. The lake itself is 100 acres of tar, slightly springy underfoot, with folds like a cake mix that move very, very slowly. When you step on it you leave an imprint and then very gradually you sink. Stay there for an hour or two and you will be stirred into the mix.

According to a legend of Iere, a chief once killed a sacred hummingbird, which so angered the gods that they punished him by engulfing his village in pitch. Although the 'lake' often turns up old artefacts in its continual stirring—from prehistoric tree trunks to biscuit tins—it has not yet produced a whole village to verify the legend.

More recent history has Sir Walter Raleigh caulking his ships with it—'most excellent good and melteth not with the sun as the pitch of Norway'. However, when he brought it back to England and asphalted Westminster Bridge for the opening of Parliament, it did melt, clogging the carriage wheels and the horses' hoofs. Since then, Trinidad pitch has been used with more success on roads all over the world. Towns as far flung as Cairo, Bombay, Singapore and London were laid with it, as well as Port of Spain. Once it was tried as fuel for street lighting, but the smoke and the stench were so overpowering that it had to be stopped (though it was used to fumigate the town after a smallpox epidemic in 1920). It was even applied as a covering to prevent weeds growing, but it turned out to be such a potent fertilizer that the streets were infested in no time.

Old prints show the 19th-century mining methods. A pickaxe was used, and then a shovel to load up the carts with stringy black goo. Today it is more like a vehicle ballet, with JCBs scooping up the bitumen and dumping it in railway carriages. The railway is run as near to the mining site as possible, but with the lake constantly in motion it is difficult to get close.

The cake mix itself has seeped from the oil sands that lie beneath Trinidad and is apparently 'uniform in composition—made up of celloidal clay (30%), bitumen (54%), salt water (3%) and ash (36%).' As Quentin Crewe points out in *Touch the Happy Isles*, any composition which adds up to 123% has to arouse some doubts.

It is the largest lake of its kind in the world, but stories that this monstrous cauldron is of unfathomable depth and constantly self-replenishing are not true. A hole dug one day may be gone the next as the lake settles, but the level is steadily dropping. The Pitch Lake's main attraction is really in its history and mystery—visiting it is quite like wandering around on a bouncy car park. Take a flat pair of shoes, because high heels might get you swallowed up.

From La Brea, the southern main road continues along the peninsula to Icacos Point, from where you can see Venezuela about 10 miles away. Columbus was supposed to have dropped anchor at Los Gallos when he arrived in Trinidad in 1498. At **Siparia** there is a statue of a black Virgin which has become a focus of pilgrimage for Trinidadians of all religions, not just Christians. Her festival is on the Sunday after Easter when she is carried around the town.

The Atlantic Coast

At Valencia, the eastern main road turns south to Sangre Grande and reaches the Atlantic coast at Manzanilla (the Spanish word for the poisonous manchineel tree which grows here). But this coast is more noted for its coconuts—in all there are nearly 50 miles of palm-trees that stand in a tangled network of trunks behind the coastline, which is a fantastic sight as you drive through them. In the season, the beaches towards **Guayaguayare** are covered in chip-chip shells, which make a favoured local dish, and off the southeastern tip of the island are the oil-rigs which brought Trinidad its wealth in the seventies. From the sea you can supposedly see the three peaks which inspired Columbus to call the island Trinidad.

As you drive back inland towards San Fernando through the canefields, you might pass the villages of Third Company and Sixth Company, named after black American regiments who were brought to Trinidad in the middle of the last century when the island was crying out for settlers. There is no mention of the Second Company because they were lost at sea.

✆ *(1 868)–*   *Where to Stay*

Trinidad does not have many resort hotels in the typical Caribbean mould. Most hotels are in Port of Spain itself, but there are some notable exceptions in the mountains around the town and increasingly along the north coast. A hotel room tax is charged on all rooms at 10% and most places charge 10% extra for service (guest houses usually factor the taxes into their prices). Untypically for the Caribbean, many hotels in Port of Spain keep their rates the same year-round, except at Carnival, when you can expect room prices to rise by anything from 30% to 70%.

Though there are few beach hotels, some Trinidadians have built villas for themselves on the beaches, particularly in the northeast of the island, and it is possible to rent these at the weekend, or during the week when they are more likely to be available. Contact **Eckel and Quesnel Ltd** (✆ 622 4945, ✉ 622 4946). Also check in newspapers.

expensive

For the views alone, the **Trinidad Hilton**, PO Box 442, Port of Spain (✆ 624 3211, ✉ 624 4485, UK res ✆ (0800) 856 8000, US res ✆ (1 800) 321 3232), is worth a visit. It is set on a hill in up-town Port of Spain and many of the rooms look out over the city, over the Savannah and the 'Magnificent Seven' to the hills in the west. It is known as the upside-down Hilton because the reception is at the top and the floors are numbered heading down the hill. International standards of comfort, with 'executive floors' for business travellers, but also facilities for holidaymakers; two restaurants.

moderate

Business travellers headed for downtown Port of Spain can stay at the **Holiday Inn** (✆ 625 3361, ✉ 625 4166). The **Hotel Normandie,** PO Box 851, St Anns (✆ 624 1181, ✉ 624 0108), is close to the Botanical Gardens to the north of the Savannah. Its address at 10 Nook Avenue gives an idea of the cosy setting around a courtyard, where a riot of banana and golden palm surrounds the swimming pool and its friendly atmosphere. One or two rooms are a little dark (there is a range of suites and rooms), but the loft apartments are very comfortable and it is a good place to base yourself in town. There is a busy shopping centre next door. The **Kapok Hotel**, 16–18 Cotton Hill, St Clair (✆ 622 6441, ✉ 622 9677, *kapok@trinidad.net*) is set in a modern building at the northwest corner of the Savannah. Within easy reach of the city centre, it takes its name from a silk cotton tree that grows outside. Rooms are decorated with prints of the West Indies, and there is a pool in a palm courtyard at the back.

If you are looking further afield, to the rainforest and the north coast, you will find some delightful retreats. The **Asa Wright Nature Centre**, Spring Hill Estate, PO Box 4710, Arima (no tel, but ✆/✉ 667 4655 for res), is set in a charming old colonial estate house lost in the rainforest of the northern range. It is famous for its bird-watching and thus many people pass by during the day, but the 24 rooms are very comfortable: most are in the garden but some are in the wooden main house itself. There is a swimming-pool. Take afternoon tea on the magnificent veranda of the main house, amidst the sound of toucans, tufted coquettes (hummingbirds) and silent butterfly wings.

cheap

Guest Houses

'In peace awhile here rest most welcome Guest.' The **Pax Guest House**, Mount St Benedict, Tunapuna (✆/✉ 602 4084, *pax-g-h@trinidad.net*; *moderate–cheap*) is set beside a monastery in the hills above the Eastern Main Road. There are 18 simple rooms, some with shared bathrooms, a self-contained cottage with kitchenette and verandas with a magnificent view of the valley and hills beyond. There is a dining room for meals, including afternoon tea, and walking trails on the 600-acre estate, even laboratory facilities if you want them. Full or part board.

There is a number of good places to stay spread around town. A good option in St Clair is **La Maison Rustique** (✆/✉ 622 1512), a pretty, well-kept modern house ('rustique' comes from the street name, 16 Rust Street) set in a pleasant garden of colourful tropical flora. Tranquillity with attentive service, seven double and single rooms, some share bath, one cottage, all meals available (good home cooking), particularly afternoon tea, to which people come for miles; includes breakfast. In the dormitory district of Maraval is **Monique's**, 114 Saddle Road (✆ 628 3334, ✉ 622 3232), also set in a modern West Indian house. The 19 rooms all have private baths, a/c, cable TV and phones: those in the new block are carpeted for modern comfort and some rooms have kitchenettes. Close by is **Carnetta's House**, Scotland Terrace (✆ 628 2732, ✉ 628 7717, *carnetta@trinidad.net*), just six rooms with private baths and kitchenette on request, also with a pleasant homely feel. The **Pelican Inn**, 2–4 Coblentz Ave (✆ 627 6271, ✉ 623 0978), is right above the bar of the same name (a popular gathering point for young Trinidadian drinkers). 24 simple but adequate rooms with private baths in an old wooden setting, restaurant and of course very lively bar.

very cheap

On Adam Smith Square in Woodbrook is **Mi Casita**, 17 Carlos St (✆ 627 4796, ✉ 627 7355), where you will find a family atmosphere with just six rooms. You can also try **Schultzi's** at 35 Fitt Street, Woodbrook (✆ 622 7521) or **La Calypso**, 46 French Street, off Tragarete Road (✆ 622 4077); 18 very simple rooms, fairly clean, breakfast available.

If you would like to spend a few days over in Blanchisseuse you can stay at **Second Spring**, PO Box 995, Port of Spain (✆ 623 8827, ✇ 623 4328), where a number of suites and a cottage stand in a garden on a dramatic rocky waterfront. Private and self-contained with a charming wooden deck, beaches nearby. **Surf's Country Inn**, PO Box 3429, Maraval (✆ 669 2475), also has a number of small rooms and apartments. There are also extremely simple cabins at **Timberline Nature Resort** (✆ 638 2263, after 7pm), which stands on a finger of land off the north coast road. Very quiet, with an excellent restaurant. In Mayaro in the far southeast of the island you will find the **Whispering Palms** resort (✆ 630 3336), a simple but comfortable stopover.

Bed and Breakfast

Another inexpensive way to stay, with the distinct advantage of seeing the Trinis in their homes, is in the bed and breakfasts, which you will find all over the northern part of the island. Houses are vetted by the Tourism Development Authority and prices start at about US$25 per night for a single and US$15 each in a double. Facilities vary, but all provide breakfast and most can fix an evening meal if requested. Details through the Tourism Office in Port of Spain and at Piarco airport, or the **Bed and Breakfast Association of Trinidad and Tobago**, PO Box 3231, Ground Floor, 1 Wrightson Rd, Port of Spain (✆/✇ 627 (BEDS) 2337).

✆ (1 868)– *Eating Out*

A Tour of Snacks and Sweetmeats

You can live in Trinidad without ever sitting down to a formal meal—snacks are available all day everywhere. You can start right outside the airport when you arrive, perhaps with a *pow!* (the Chinese word for bread), a little white fluffball of dough, colour-coded with a spot for salt or sweet, or with one of Trinidad's most popular snacks, a *roti*, an envelope of unleavened bread with a filling of anything from curry shrimp to lentils. Spices are optional, but when you are asked if you want hot pepper sauce be wary. *Doubles* are similar; they are folded *bara* (more unleavened bread) with *channa* (split peas). *Aripa* is a corn-flour pattie with mince stuffing, and *pastel* is a mix of peppers, raisins and beef wrapped in a dasheen leaf. *Aloo pie* (from the Indian for potato) is a doughy potato mix. Batter snacks include *phulori*, split peas in batter balls and *sahina*, made with dasheen, which you can dip into mango chutney, sweet or hot, or into pepper sauce, firebrand style. The stalls are invariably run by charming and chattering ladies, who do their frying on outdoor ovens.

So much for the first course. You can follow the savoury mouthfuls with a whole volley of sweet snacks. Perhaps go for a *pamie* (pronounced 'pay-me'), sweet coconut in a pattie or wrapped in a banana leaf, or try *pone*, a creation of cassava flour, sugar and coconut. Then there are *bene balls*, crisp lumps of sesame snap in molasses, and for the very brave there are *tamarind balls*, sluggish sugary lumps with unverifiable specific gravity and *salt prunes*, a child's sweet, both of them a torture of bitter and sweet.

Restaurants

If you do decide to sit down to a meal, you will find that Trinidad has a grand variety of styles, in keeping with its mixed heritage—Italian, Chinese, Indian, even Arab, and of course creole. Trinidad's restaurants tend to be active and noisy, full of friendly crowds, but there are one or two quieter spots where couples retreat for an evening out. In general, prices in Trinidad are lower than in most tourist restaurants around the Caribbean as they serve a local clientele, but you will find that bills are supplemented with a charge of 15% for VAT and usually a service charge of 10%.

Categories are defined according to the average price of a main course: *expensive*— TT$70 and above; *moderate*—TT$30–70; and *cheap*—TT$30 and below.

expensive

Solimar (© 624 6267) has a charming Caribbean setting on a covered terrace hung with greenery tucked away in Nook Avenue in St Anns just north of the Savannah. The fare is international with good fish dishes: start with the Solimar salad, 'from the market that day', and lamb loin *en croute* or grouper in a green Thai curry. For creole fare in a fine creole setting you can go to the **Le Chateau de Poisson** (© 622 6087), which is set in the pink, white and green verandas and interior of a charming creole wooden house in Woodbrook, where the eaves are festooned with greenery and gingerbread woodwork. There is a long menu of seafood and fish on offer, including crab meat *amandine*, in a cream sauce with almonds and, in keeping with Trinidad's variety, creole, Spanish, gumbo and tandoori sauces to go with the fish, lobster, shrimp and crawfish. Italian restaurants seem to be popular on the island. **Il Colosseo** (© 623 3654), on Ariapita Avenue, has a subdued air in an air-conditioned dining room of romanesque columns and arches and gathered curtains. Dishes from around Italy including a pasta speciality with plenty of seafood: *gamberoni del ré*, shrimp wrapped in bacon and a honey-mustard sauce. There is also a stylized Italianate air with mock-columns, greenery and garden statues at the **Gourmet Club** (© 628 5115) upstairs in the Ellerslie Plaza in Maraval. The cuisine is southern Italian, with pastas followed by kingfish in an aïoli sauce, or a house steak speciality. For an 'authentic Indian' meal (rather than Trinidadian Indian, which is different), you should go to **Apsara** (© 662 1013) in the Grand Bazaar Mall, just close to the turning south to San Fernando. The large dining room is redolent with burning spices and has tent roofs, alcoves, mock Indian furniture and a decor of puppets and elephants. Real tandoori ovens produce nan breads and tandoori lobster tails, or you might go for a *paneer tikka* with cubes of cottage cheese made from buffalo milk or a *naw rattan kurma*. A top Oriental restaurant, for the view and the food, is the **Tiki Village** (© 622 6441) at the Kapok Hotel. There is a long menu of Polynesian and Chinese dishes: steak Samoa or *jar doi yuk pien* (Szechuan radish). A hip spot around town, frequented by a mainly white crowd, is **Rafters** (© 628 9258) at 6A Warner Street. It is set in an old dry goods store, its shutters and windows still intact, but now modernized inside with glass and fluorescent strip lights; simple snacks one side, with dinner à la carte next door—Rafters ribs, chicken teriyaki and tiramisu.

moderate

There are two excellent spots to get a weekday lunch in the city. Try **Veni Mangé**, at 67A Ariapita Avenue in St James (© 624 4597), where two Trinidadian sisters, Allyson

Hennessy and Rosemary Hezekiah, have a lively restaurant in an old wooden-floored town house now painted bright orange, with elegantly wobbly tables and with window louvres on stilts. Excellent soups and other exotic Trinidadian creations—superb fish grilled in capers and spices or a daily vegetarian dish followed by soursop ice cream. *Lunches; evenings Wed and Fri only, for drinks with informal snacks.* Slightly quieter is the **Verandah**, 13 Rust Street, St Clair (© 622 6287), where the dining tables sit above the garden on a town-house veranda. The fare is home Caribbean cooking— favourites include spiced beef-stuffed dumplings and fish dishes served in their own tomato-based sauces, followed by excellent ice creams. *Lunch only.*

There are also some lively places to eat and drink in the Chaguaramas area out of town. At Crews Inn you will find **The Lighthouse Grub and Grog** (© 634 4384), which sits on an open deck raised above the harbour, tables ranged next to the balsustrades and looking out on to the forest of yacht masts. International fare—coconut shrimp and spag bol along with striploins and sandwiches. Not far off is the **Anchorage** (© 634 4334), where you dine right above the water on a breezy covered deck with another view of yachts. Good West Indian fare—start with a drunken mermaid (squid in batter and white wine) and follow with fish or seafood, perhaps a *run dem soucouyant*, sautéed shrimp in white wine. Watch out for the bats late on. The Anchorage gets particularly lively at the weekends, when the Trinis flood out of town. Some dancing.

Back in town there is a lively restaurant and sports bar at **Flags** (© 628 3000) on the corner in Maraval, marked by all the flags on poles. A/c, TVs permanently running, lots of beers and pool downstairs; upstairs the food follows the theme of the many flags outside: chimichanga chasers, Japanese Honshu snapper and Hawaiian burgers. A **Chinese** meal is a popular evening out in Trinidad. **Hong Kong City** on Tragarete Road is brightly dressed up in Chinese decor of red velvet and golden dragons. The food is straight Chinese, plus a few dishes with West Indian ingredients—dasheen pork, beef with corilie and sweet and sour lambi.

cheap

For a fast-food Indian meal, try **Monsoon** on Tragarete Road. Call 628 ROTI! (© 628 7684). Purple and green neon decor clash and mesmerize you as you sit in; or you can take away such creations such as conch paratha and dhalpuri. Many of the local bars and rumshops will serve you traditional West Indian fare—souse or a curry chicken with rice 'n' peas. For a distinctly local Trinidadian feel there is the **Breakfast Shed** on the waterfront not far from the Holiday Inn Hotel, offering home-style rice 'n' peas with fried plantain at very good prices. It caters for local workers, who come in from the wharf nearby, so opening hours are 5–3, although it's best to get there before 2. You can also get an excellent night-time roti at the stall on the Western Main Road, opposite the Smokey and Bunty rum shop. At Low's, nearby, you can take away a Chinese meal. Alternatively you will find a number of **snack-wagons** on the eastern side of the Savannah where you can pick up a fry chicken or a burger for a few dollars.

Beyond Port of Spain

One of the Caribbean's most original creole restaurants can be found on the north shore at **Timberline** (© 638 2263 after 7pm; *expensive–moderate*). First you crush a bay leaf in your fingers for the smell and drink a fresh local fruit juice, and then there follows a compendium of superb creole dishes (you are asked to guess the ingredients and spices). The menu is set and varied daily. Perhaps you will have a chicken, plantain and hibiscus roll with a tamarind sauce, a creamy pumpkin soup, lightly curried shrimp and steamed kingfish. The ingredients are personally selected and always fresh (many of them from the gardens) and the dishes are not served on plates, but on circles of banana frond, in hollowed-out calabashes and in sectioned bamboo. It's difficult to find, but definitely worth the effort, down an impossibly steep road off the Lookout (the viewing area) on the north coast road before Maracas. Farther along the coast in Blanchisseuse you will find wholesome Caribbean fare in the hillside gazebos at **Surf's Country Inn** (✆ 669 2475; *moderate*). Chicken and fish served with a volley of ground provisions. In **San Fernando** in the south of the island, try **Soongs Great Wall** on the Circular Road (*moderate*), a popular Chinese restaurant in the town.

Bars and Nightlife

 Like the restaurants, Trinidadian bars (often called pubs here) are lively, particularly at the weekends when Port of Spain drops everything for a drink. You will find cocktail bars, where Trinidad-produced Angostura bitters add the zing to the traditional Caribbean rum punch and a profusion of rum shops, fired by VAT 19, and the two local brews, light **Carib** and the darker, malty **Stag** beers.

How do you make the roof of a shopping mall a place worth visiting? Dress it up as a transatlantic liner, with wooden decks with railings and overhead trampolines to keep off the rain. Add live music (Wed–Sat, from jazz to the big names in calypso), and then serve some outrageously strong cocktails to go with the light snacks. Well worth a try: **Moon over Bourbon Street** (closed Mon, Tues) in the West Mall, 10 minutes out of town towards Chaguaramas. The ever-popular **Pelican**, just beneath the Hilton, sees a mixed and lively crowd who roll in after work for a drink or pack in later on for the live bands. You can leave your car number-plate as a memento of your visit if that's your style. A mainly white crowd collects at **Rafters** on Warner Street, where there is a video bar; big after work on a Friday. If you're getting frantic for the NFL and watery beer, then there's a good sports bar at **Flags** in Maraval: pool and TV accompaniment. In the Grand Bazaar Mall, the other direction from town, is the **Parrot**, which also sees a lively crowd after work and on Saturdays. There are any number of rum shops around the town. An approachable one is **Smokey and Bunty** on the Western Main Road in St James.

Many of the bars out at **Chaguaramas** have an 'afterwork lime' particularly at the weekend and then later double as nightclubs—if there's room, people will take a quick turn on the dancefloor late on. The **Anchorage** is a trusty favourite and has a huge area for live music and dancing on the waterfront. Not far off is **Pier 1**, which sees a busy trade at the weekend and close to here is the **Base,** a more regular nightclub in an old warehouse. Back in St Ann's in town, **Club Coconuts** is busiest between Thursday and Saturday and you might also try **Upper Level** in the West Mall.

The **Mas Camp Pub** on the corner of French Street and Ariapita Avenue in Woodbrook is something of an institution. Here you will find anything from ballroom dancing to calypso singing; each night is different and it's well worth checking out for the best in local entertainment.

getting there

Trinidad has some of the best air links in the Caribbean. It has its own airline—BWIA, often referred to as Bee-wee—and is served by numerous others. As well as good links to Europe and the USA, flights are easily arranged to places in South America, such as Guyana and Venezuela. A departure tax of TT$85 is payable.

By air from the UK: BWIA (✆ POS 627 2942, Piarco 669 3000) has several services each week direct from London Heathrow. From **Europe**, BWIA serves Frankfurt direct. It is worth noting that charter airlines such as Caledonian and Condor fly into nearby Tobago.

By air from North America: BWIA flies daily to Miami and weekly to New York, and American Airlines (✆ 669 4661) flies daily from New York via Miami. In **Canada**, Air Canada (✆ 664 4065) and BWIA fly from Toronto.

By air from other Caribbean islands: Between Trinidad and **Tobago** there are about eight services a day on Air Caribbean (✆ reservations 623 2500, Piarco 669 2500). Further afield, BWIA stops off at other Caribbean islands en route for Trinidad, but LIAT (✆ 669 3000) is the major inter-island carrier and it links the island to all the major destinations in the Eastern Caribbean. Airlines linking to the South American continent include Surinam Airways (✆ 627 4747), ALM serving the Dutch ABC islands, Guyana Airways to Georgetown, Guyana and Aeropostal which flies to Caracas, all handled by Piarco Air Services (✆ 623 1073).

By sea: The ferry to **Tobago** leaves from the cruise ship dock every day except Saturday (✆ 625 4906 or ✆ 639 2417 in Tobago). If you are travelling further afield, the MV *Windward* sails to La Guiria or Margarita in Venezuela each week and then to St Vincent, Barbados and St Lucia; the schedule is a little haphazard but basically weekly (✆ 634 4144). You might even try your luck in catching a schooner to Grenada in the Windward Islands.

tourist information

The **Tourism and Industrial Development Corporation of Trinidad and Tobago (TIDCO)** has offices at the following addresses:

UK: Morris Kevan International, International House, 47 Chase Side, Enfield, Middlesex, EN2 6NB (✆ (0181) 367 3752, ✆ 367 9949, toll free ✆ (0800) 960057).

Germany: Touristic Marketing Promotions, Berger Strasse 17, D-60316 Frankfurt/Main (✆ (69) 9433 5813, ✆ (60) 9433 5820, toll free ✆ (0 130) 86 07 94).

Italy: toll free ✆ (1 678) 77530.

USA: Sales, Marketing and Reservations Tourism Services, 7000 Blvd East, Guttenberg, New Jersey 07093 (✆ (201) 662 3403, ✆ 869 7628, toll free ✆ (1 888) 595 4TNT).

Canada: The RMR Group Inc, Taurus House, 512 Duplex Ave, Toronto M4R 2E3 (✆ (416) 485 8724, ✆ 485 8256, toll free as USA).

TIDCO have an **internet** website at *www.tidco.co.tt* and there is an **email** postbox at *tourism-info@tidco.co.tt.*

TIDCO in Trinidad is at 10–14 Philipps St, 3rd Floor, in central Port of Spain (✆ 623 1932, ✆ 623 3848). They will give advice about accommodation and help with arranging trips on the island. On arrival it is definitely worth checking with the very helpful office at Piarco airport (© 664 5196). You can find details of current activities in the free tourist newspaper *Island Information*. You will also find useful information in the small annual magazine *Discover Trinidad and Tobago* and both of the islands have their own small newspapers designed specifically for visitors.

In a medical **emergency**, the Port of Spain General Hospital is on Charlotte Street in the centre of town (© 625 2951).

The **IDD code** for both islands is © (1 868), followed by the seven-digit local telephone number. If you are phoning between the islands dial just the seven figures.

The Trinidadians are occasionally known by other Caribbean islanders as 'Trickidadians' and they have a reputation for being a little rough and cheeky at times (they will always bargain when doing business). You are advised to be careful with regard to **personal security**, particularly in the eastern areas of Port of Spain and around the city at night.

festivals

The most colourful festival outside Carnival is **Divali** (pronounced 'deewali'), the festival of lights, which was brought to Trinidad by Hindus in honour of Lakshmi, the goddess of light. In October, hundreds of thousands of *deyas*, little clay bowls with coconut oil candles (and increasingly electric lights) are kept alight all night to show her the way. People throw open their houses and entertain guests with sitars and dancing and huge vegetarian meals.

Phagwa is the Hindu New Year celebration, which takes place in March. It has taken on the Carnival style of floats in the street with dancing and is celebrated by Trinis of all racial origin now. If you see a band of dancers covered in red food dye, they are out celebrating Phagwa. **Hosay** (Hussein) is a Moslem festival that remembers the martyrdom of Hussein (it brings in the Moslem New Year, but the date varies in the Christian calendar). Processions of tassa drummers follow models of Hussein's tomb through the streets and you will occasionally still see fire-eating and jugglers throwing sticks of fire. The Trinidadian Moslems also celebrate **Eid ul Fitr** to mark the end of Ramadan. Dates vary according to the Islamic calendar.

Another high moment in the Christian calendar is **parang**. This is a special sort of singing that takes place in the run-up to Christmas, when *paranderos* sing their Annunciation songs in outlying villages. Originally from the Spanish *parranda*, parang has absorbed influences from Venezuela and is set to a typically Trinidadian rhythm. Instruments include the guitar, cuatro, maracas, violin and box base.

money

The currency is the Trinidad and Tobago dollar (TT$), which floats on the international exchange, presently at around US$1=TT$6. The US dollar is accepted in tourist areas. There is not much of a black market, but you should retain a (recent) receipt if you wish to change TT$ back when you leave the country.

Banking hours: Mon–Thurs 9–2, Fri 9–2 and 3–5.

Shops: Open weekdays 8–4.30 (often later), Sat 8–noon.

maps and books

The most eloquent form of expression in Trinidad life is probably the calypso, but there is a flourishing literature that first grew in the 1930s. Eric Williams, for a long time Trinidad and Tobago's Prime Minister, was also an accomplished historian and the author of *Capitalism and Slavery, From Columbus to Castro,* also *A History of the Peoples of Trinidad and Tobago,* written at the time of Independence. Together with C. L. R. James (who died in 1989 in London) he changed the perspective of West Indians towards their history and culture, heralding the birth of West Indian Independence. C. L. R. James wrote *Beyond A Boundary,* a charming autobiographical book about cricket and Trinidad life in the twenties. In *The Wine of Astonishment,* Earl Lovelace tells of the changes in town life during the war. *Ways of Sunlight* by Samuel Selvon is a collection of short stories of rural life in Trinidad and 'hard times' in London. Novelist V. S. Naipaul was born in Trinidad of a Brahmin family. His works set in Trinidad include *The Mystic Masseur* and *The Suffrage of Elvira,* two satires of the elections in the forties and fifties, and *A House for Mr Biswas,* which portrays the dissolution of traditional Trinidadian life. *Miguel Street* uses the eyes of a young boy to paint a charming picture of the characters in a Port of Spain street.

The finest Trinidadian painter is Michel Cazabon, who painted many charming scenes of Trindadian town and country life in the middle of the last century, many of which can still be recognized today. His paintings are on view in the Museum in Port of Spain.

watersports

There is not much in the way of **watersports** on offer in Trinidad. A general operator is Ron's Watersports (✆/✉ 673 0549) on the Western Main Road, who offer windsurfing and diving and fishing trips. Windsurfing can also be arranged through the Trinidad and Tobago Windsurfing Association (✆ 637 3667).

Day sails: The Yacht Club (✆ 637 4260) in the Bayshore area west of Port of Spain or Bayshore Charters (✆ 637 8711) will make a trip down-island.

other sports

Trinidad is not as well organized as its sister island to cater for the traditional Caribbean watersports, and most of the popular Trinidadian sports are land-based.

Hiking: Wildways (✆/✉ 623 7332, *wildways@trinidad.net*) will arrange hikes and cycle trips through the mountains and rainforest, also kayaking to isolated coves.

Tennis: Can be arranged through the Trinidad Country Club (✆ 622 3470) in Maraval or the Tranquillity Square Lawn Tennis Club (✆ 625 4182).

Golf: There are three courses on the island, of which the closest to Port of Spain is the 18-hole St Andrew's course at Moka just beyond Maraval (✆ 629 2314). There are 9-hole courses at Chaguaramas and Brighton near La Brea in the south.

Spectator sports: On Saturdays and Sundays the Savannah in central Port of Spain will be crowded with football and hockey matches. **Cricket** is also played on the Savannah, some games more formal than others. If you go to watch a match at the main Queen's Park Oval stadium, you might try to get into the 'rude-boy stand', where the banter is liveliest. **Horse racing,** which used to be held on the Savannah, is now centred in Arima.

Tobago

Tobago is completely unlike its sister island Trinidad. It has none of the press of Port of Spain or the glaring flamboyance of carnival. In Tobago you will find laid-back life in classic Caribbean island style. It is more typical of the rest of the Caribbean in its tourism, which is more established than in Trinidad. The industry has developed considerably in the last few years and it dominates the western end of the island. Beyond here, however—in the secluded coves of the north coast and the fishing villages of the east—you will still find some charming, undeveloped spots with slow-time Caribbean life.

Geographically Tobago is related to Trinidad and South America, but in appearance it is more similar to the Windward Islands. A single spine of thickly forested mountains (up to 1890ft) runs along its length, casting off spurs that reach out as headlands into the sea. Inland, rivers tumble and cascade in waterfalls and on the coast there are huge crescent bays. At the flatter and more accessible western end of the island, the huge Buccoo reef throws up white sand (this is why the hotels have gathered here, of course). The island offers superb natural life to visitors. The scuba diving is excellent and the birdlife is almost unparalleled.

Historically Tobago has been more closely associated with the Windwards too. Like them it was a plantation island and in its 18th-century heyday it was so successful that people would use the phrase 'as rich as a Tobago planter'. As you travel around the remoter parts of the island, you will see the waterwheel and stone buildings of the plantation age poking out of the undergrowth. Tobago was also battled over incessantly in the race for Empire. By the late 19th century, however, when the sugar and cocoa plantations failed, the island was declared bankrupt and it was simply appended to Trinidad for political convenience.

The population of Tobago (about 50,000) is radically different from Trinidad's, as it is almost entirely African in origin. About 10,000 people live in the capital, Scarborough, on the southern shore. There is very little industry on Tobago and the main sources of employment are farming, fishing, the civil service and of course tourism. The shacks of subsistence farmers and the villas of international holidaymakers (many of them from Trinidad) stand side by side in Tobago. The island's heyday may have gone—the cannons at Fort King George point only at windsurfers and yachts now—but her charm lies in her calm and for the moment unaffected manner, just as so much of the Caribbean used to be.

History

Some claim that Columbus sighted Tobago as he emerged through the Dragon's Mouth from the Gulf of Paria on his third voyage in 1498, and called it Bellaforma. Whatever the case, he did not stop there, but continued west along the South American coastline. Tobago never became a Spanish island and until the late 18th century was not really a 'possession' at all. It saw so many settlements and sieges that it changed hands more often than any other in the area.

The Dutch were the first to claim it in 1628, but all their expeditions were harried by canoes full of Caribs and Spaniards from Trinidad. King James I of England then granted the island to his godson Jacobus, Duke of Courland (a principality in modern-day Latvia), but each one of the six Courlander settlements failed too. Working on the same claim, that the English flag had been planted on the island in 1580 by some passing sailors, James's successor, Charles I, decided to grant the island to the Earl of Montgomery. To complete the picture, the French made similar claims, grants and settlements—Louis XIV made the leader of a French-backed expedition, Dutchman Adraien Lampsius, Baron of Tobago.

The settlements were intended to cultivate plantations of tropical produce for Europe and to begin with their main crop was tobacco. Tobago's name derives from the same Carib word as tobacco, though this was not what the Caribs called the plant. (To them a 'tobacco' was a yard-long, double-pronged tube that they used to blast their powdered drugs up each other's noses.) Still, smoking was popular in Europe by the late 1500s and *freighting smoke* was a profitable occupation, even though the shippers had to run the gauntlet of the Spanish navy, who had instructions to root out the trade.

Towards the end of the century, in an attempt to stop the fighting, Tobago was declared a neutral island. The Treaty of Aix la Chapelle in 1684 allowed the island no defences and it was supposedly free for all nations to come and go. Within years the treaty was nicknamed the 'Pirates' Charter' because along with settlers came pirates who were being chased out of their traditional hunting grounds around Jamaica and the Bahamas. Man O' War Bay in the north-east was renowned for its 'safe retreat and commanding situation for cruize and plunder'.

Tobago was an attractive prize and, while some fought for her, others tried to gain the island by legal means. At one stage it was the cause of one of the Caribbean's most touching love stories, set in the court of Marie Antoinette in France. A Swedish diplomat named Staël was wooing a Mademoiselle Necker, a courtesan, and she told him that she would only consent to marry him if he were an ambassador. He turned for support to the Queen, who wrote to King Gustavus requesting that he be made one. The King wrote back saying that he would consent, but that in return Staël must get him an island in the Caribbean, preferably Tobago. Staël bargained at the court, but the best he could do was St Barthélemy in the Leeward Islands, in return for a warehouse in Gothenburg, because the French government would not relinquish Tobago. However, the Queen intervened once again with King Gustavus and secured the ambassadorship. Staël won the hand of Mlle Necker.

The 19th century saw the spiralling decline of the sugar industry, as a result of the emancipation of the slaves in 1834 and the cultivation of sugar-beet in Europe. All the estates on the island became dependent on a single British firm, Messrs A. M. Gillespie and Co., and when it went bankrupt in 1884, Tobago was left ruined. The land was sold off at 10 shillings an acre and so the former slaves were able to buy themselves plots of land on which to grow their crops. Tobago became a very poor agricultural island.

For many years Tobago looked north in political matters. When under British rule in the 19th century, it had been one of the Windward Islands and unlike Trinidad, which had remained under direct rule from London, it had always had some elected representation on its Governing Council. Now that it was in debt, it was simply attached to Trinidad, first as an economic arrangement, but then just placed under its control, as a 'ward', uninvited and largely unwanted. With this heritage, many of the Tobagonians feel that their island has suffered a continual neglect. There was no regular link with Trinidad until a steamer started to make a trip in 1910—before that the mail was rowed the 22 miles over from Toco. Electricity did not reach the island until the 1950s and the Prime Minister Eric Williams himself admitted in 1957 that the problem was 'one of stark poverty'. Many Tobagonians have left the island to look for a better life in Trinidad and elsewhere. Things took an upturn when a Tobagonian, A. N. R. Robinson, was Prime Minister of Trinidad and Tobago from 1986 to 1991, but it has tailed off. The Tobagonians do occasionally talk of secession, but it is unlikely to come to fruition.

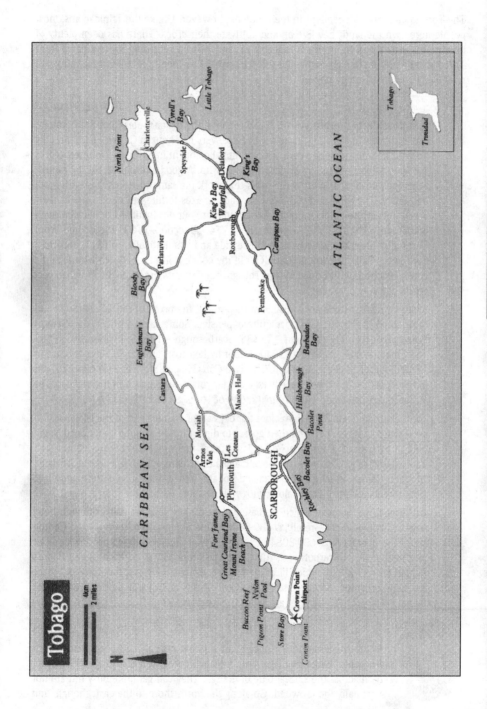

111

The Tobagonians are independent in their outlook, however. Unlike the Trinidadians, most people here own the land they live on and cultivate their crops. There has been plenty of investment recently as the tourism industry expands—from returning Tobagonians, from Trinidadians and from foreign companies—and there has been plenty of building, so things are reasonably positive at the moment.

Getting Around

The government-run **bus** system (PTSC) runs all the major routes from Scarborough. It is extremely cheap and runs to a schedule, every half-hour to Crown Point, but only once an hour or two elsewhere. Tickets must be bought in advance. No ticket offices are open at weekends, so remember to stock up. A good alternative are the **share-taxis** (private cars) and the **maxi-taxis** that work the same roads, usually with more frequency. These pause for the few seconds it takes to fill with passengers at their various departure points in town. Ask around for your destination: from Scarborough to Crown Point—TT$7, Plymouth—TT$4, Buccoo—TT$3, departing from Carrington St on the waterfront, and Speyside and Charlotteville—TT$11, departing from James Park on Burnett Street. Out in the country, flag them down with a frantic wave. **Hitching** works quite well in Tobago, but check whether the driver will expect you to pay before you get in.

Plenty of regular **taxis** are available at the airport, the taxi-stand in Scarborough and through all the hotels. They are quite expensive. Some sample prices are: **Crown Point airport** to Pigeon Point—TT$35, Scarborough—TT$65, Plymouth—TT$65 and Charlotteville—around TT$240. A tour by taxi costs around TT$85 per hour, or TT$250 for a half-day's excursion. The Taxi Cab Co-op at Store Bay (✆ 639 2707) or in town (✆ 639 2659) will happily fix a cab for you. A regular tour of the island can be arranged through Good Time Tours (✆ 639 6816) or Sun Fun Tours (✆ 639 7461).

For maximum flexibility—to explore the bays at the eastern end of the island and to see Tobago in its variety, and then go out to dinner in the evening—you need to get hold of a **hire car**. Four-wheel-drive is useful as the remoter roads sometimes turn into muddy tracks. Driving is on the left, and a licence from the UK, France, Germany, USA and Canada is valid in Trinidad and Tobago. When driving, you are supposed to carry it with you at all times, along with your passport. Also, wear your seat-belt.

Car hire firms, many of which are based at the airport but who deliver to your hotel anyway, include Peter Gremli (✆ 639 8400), Auto Rentals (✆ 639 0644) and Carlton James Car Rental (✆/✉ 639 8084). Expect to pay around US$40–45 per day for a car, plus insurance. In Scarborough: Hill Crest Car Rental (✆/✉ 639 5208) and Baird's Rentals (✆ 639 2528), which hires motorbikes. Banana Rentals at the Kariwak Village has some **bicycles** as well. Also Island Bikes (✆ 639 8587) and Glorious Ride Cycle Rental (✆ 639 7124). Bicycles are about U$5 per day.

Beaches

At the western end of Tobago you will find typical Caribbean picture-post-card beaches: white sand and palm trees with windsurfers cutting a fluorescent dash across the surreal blue of the sea. They can get quite busy but are not usually too crowded. Go along the north shore to the east, though, and there are secluded coves with curves of golden sand where you will find nobody but a few fishermen. The beaches on the south coast are not so nice, but there are a few steep-sided bays where the waves chase one another in to the sand.

best beaches

Pigeon Point: Tobago's liveliest beach. Plenty of soft sand to walk, with shallow water and backed by palms for shade; some watersports on offer—windsurfing, water-skiing, wetbikes—as well as a snack bar and an excellent view of the sunset. The beach is on private land and so you are asked to pay an entry fee of TT$10.

Store Bay: Smaller but also lively, changing rooms and breakfast sheds (local Tobagonian fast-food stores, which will provide food and drink) across the road. Trips can be arranged out to Buccoo Reef from here, departing late morning.

Mount Irvine Bay: Lively in season, watersports and changing facilities.

Stone Haven Bay and **Great Courland Bay:** Hotel beaches, some activity.

Turtle Beach: Also some activity from the hotel, named after the turtles that come there to lay their eggs.

Arnos Vale: A small beach within the arms of massive headlands, and a good snorkelling reef. In hotel grounds.

Castara: Just a few shacks under the palm trees and you can get a snack and a drink.

Englishman's Bay: Probably the most beautiful of them all, a classic West Indian beach in a crescent curve, where the royal blue water stands out against the green forestland and the palms. Very secluded; you will find the path down to it on the straight piece of road half a mile beyond Castara. Take a picnic.

King's Bay: Palm-backed grey sand, some faciilities.

Speyside: Passable, some facilities (also a lovely strip of sand at the Blue Waters Inn on Batteaux Bay just beyond here).

Man O' War Bay: The end of the line, a charming corner of sand (also with some simple facilities) beneath the headlands along from Charlotteville.

beach bars

Pigeon Point has the best-known beach bar and it is an excellent place to come for a day out—you can take a cocktail on to the jetty to watch the sunset. In crowded Store Bay you will find the **Taxi Co-op Pub**, where the drivers take a bit of time off alongside the beachgoers. You might also take a day trip to **No Man's Land**, a beach accessed by water where there is a bar and barbecue lunch laid on. The **Mount Irvine Bay** hotel has a bar and just down from here is **The Waterfront,** a public beach facility where you can lime with the Tobagonians and grab a bite to eat. On Turtle Beach there is a small shed owned by Cecilia, where you can get a burger or a cooked fish with fries. In remoter parts of the island most bays have a waterfront rum-shop. In Speyside you can try **Jemma's** above the water for a fruit juice (she does not sell alcohol).

Scarborough, Tobago's main town, clambers over the side of a hill above Rockley Bay, on the south coast not far from the western tip of the island. With a population of 10,000, it is a little ramshackle, with just a few nice old wooden buildings among the tatty overlay of concrete ones and brighter recent development, and sleepy—most Tobagonians say that they only ever come to town when they have to collect something off the ferry. Even so, Carrington Street can get pretty lively when all the rum shops and roti-sellers are open.

Fort King George stands sentinel 400ft above the town and has commanding views east along the coastline and west as far as Trinidad. The stone and brick barracks, which share the hilltop with the nice wooden creole buildings that are now used by the Tobago hospital, were abandoned in 1854 (after destruction in a hurricane in 1847), but they have been restored and it is quite peaceful now to sit among the cannons and trees. There is an excellent **museum** (*open 9–5 weekdays; adm*) in the old guard house in the former citadel, where you can see Tobago history and cultural life revealed in a series of displays—Amerindian patterned pottery with animal faces (supposedly the animals which barred the way in the afterlife), and a mock-up of an Amerindian burial site; the colonial plantation era including militaria and some cartoons in the priceless series of *Johnny Newcome* (to the Caribbean) and his troubles of creole love and life; musket balls and buttons, a BOAC cocktail pourer and even a bird of paradise (*see* p.116). There is also a fine art gallery nearby with changing exhibitions.

Walking down the hill you pass among the old stone colonial buildings and homes, including the Tobago **House of Assembly** on its small tree-shaded square, which was completed in 1825. On **Gun Bridge**, the railings are made from rifle barrels, flanked by cannon. From here, steep streets and alleys lined with local houses lead down to the waterfront area. The modern concrete official buildings are in the Scarborough Mall, which was thrown up in the sixties. Behind here are the bus station and the new market square, which is quite lively in the mornings with vendors and limers. Modern development has continued along the waterfront, but Carrington Street, where the ferry from Trinidad docks, is still the heart of the town as the taxis tout for business and the breakfast sheds do their daily trade, opening up at 7am and serving snacks all day. Behind the town are the Scarborough **Botanic Gardens** (*open during daylight hours; adm free*), good for sitting out in peace after the (relative) hustle and bustle of the metropolis. If you are interested in batik you might visit the **Cotton House** factory, shop and café in Bacolet, on the road east out of town, beneath the Fort.

Around the Island

The west end of the island is most attractive for its reefs, beaches and natural life, though you may hear elaborate stories about Robinson Crusoe's life (his 'cave' is just below Crown Point airport) from a fellow who claims he saw him there not long ago. The majority of Tobago's hotels are concentrated at Crown Point and along the northwestern coastline, but a considerable population also lives here, in the many 'traces' (like the 'gaps' of Barbados), side roads which seek out the intricacies of the shoreside and interior country.

Not far from Store Bay, the beach and small pedestrianized zone of vendors' stalls (and food stalls) you can see **Fort Milford**, a former fortress with impressively thick walls and a few French and British cannon hanging around (both nations used it, though it was actually built

farm house in Buccoo

by the Dutch in 1777) which now acts as a small park with sea almond trees and flowerbeds in the fortifications.

Offshore from Pigeon Point, once called Flying Fish Point, is **Buccoo Reef**, Tobago's best known underwater sight. It attracts scuba divers, snorkellers and boat-borne non-swimmers alike. In the vast area of coral heads just a few feet below the surface—forests of seafan and staghorn coral and lobes of white brain coral—you will find black and yellow rock beauties, stoplight parrotfish and angelfish loitering and trumpetfish hanging around (vertically). Considerable damage has been done to Buccoo Reef over the years by careless visitors and souvenir hunters, and although there has been legislation for some time it is not properly enforced. However, there are some surprisingly large fish on the reef and it is a fun day out. Organized tours depart from Store Bay and Pigeon Point. some in glass-bottom boats, but times vary, so check beforehand. The **Nylon Pool**, on the way out to the reef, is an off-shore sandbar where the pale turquoise water is waist to thigh deep and the warm sand caresses your toes.

Plymouth, Tobago's second town, developed as a fortification and dwelling on the point covering Great Courland Bay, an excellent natural harbour where yachts still ride at anchor, is a village really, with a few shops and a petrol station. The defence, **Fort James** (named after Jacobus of Courland, who sent settlements to the area in the 17th century) is little more than massive walls and cannons, and a few goats, next to the sports ground.

From Plymouth you can return to Scarborough, or continue along the north coast road which passes into deep forest before emerging periodically on to the coastline. At the fishing villages of Castara and Parlatuvier you will see the fishing boats with their double rods sticking out either side in the bay and the fishermen drying their nets waiting for the tide to turn. Returning via Moriah or Les Coteaux, you will find Tobago at its most rural and traditional. This is the rich plantation land of 200 years ago and you will still see the sugar estate buildings and crushing gear poking out of the undergrowth.

Windwardside

The south coast of Tobago is known as Windwardside because of the Atlantic trades that blow for most of the year. As you head east from Scarborough, the country becomes steadily more rugged and overgrown and the road switchbacks and chicanes as it clambers on the hillsides and drops down into the bays. The settlements get steadily more scarce and you will see just a few houses in a plot of beaten earth with a massive breadfruit tree for shade. In plantation days, workers from each estate would carry its produce down to the nearest bay, from where it would be picked up by ship. The distance to Charlotteville in the northeast of the island is about 15 miles, but it can take well over an hour to complete.

At Studley Park (site of the Prime Minister's residence in the island, Blenheim) you can take a left turn on to a winding road that disappears into the rainforest, passing the Hillsborough dam and then descending to Mason Hall. A mile after you leave the coast, you can walk to the **Green Hill Waterfall** just off the road. Farther along the coast, **Carapuse Bay** takes its name from the turtle shell or carapace, a legacy from the 17th century, when turtlers would come to the island. Turtles were a valuable source of meat, particularly as they could be kept alive on their backs for up to three weeks until the meat was needed. Outside Roxborough is the turning to **The Falls of Argyle Natural Park**, a cascade that tumbles in three falls over a rockface into two swimmable pools. It is a 20-minute walk and guides are available (TT$15).

Speyside, at the eastern end of the island, looks out into Tyrell's Bay and towards the island of Little Tobago. This is also known as Bird of Paradise Island, because in 1909 Mr Ingram, the owner of the island, brought a colony of the birds from New Guinea, where they were becoming extinct. The mating dance was a spectacular sight, with wings held aloft to reveal a golden plumage that was kept constantly shimmering by strutting and sidestepping. No birds are left there now, but there is one on view in the museum.

The road labours over the heavily forested point and drops steeply into a charming, almost amphitheatrical bay, home to **Charlotteville,** a classic West Indian fishing village, where the red-roofed houses are stacked top to toe above one another. The seabirds clamour offshore in flocks and high above them frigatebirds cruise on the winds while the islanders sit waiting for transport and chatting in the shade of the sea almond trees that line the waterfront. The sale of the fishing catch is announced each day with a blow of a conch shell. The road beyond Cambleton to Parlatuvier, which is not surfaced, is passable only in the dry season.

✆ *(1 868)–*   ### Where to Stay

With better beaches, Tobago offers more in the way of typical Caribbean beach hotels than Trinidad—the recent building in Tobago has brought a number of new resort complexes. However, there is a good range of accommodation here—look further afield and you will find some superb West Indian hideaways tucked into a cove or in the hills and there are also plenty of guest houses. If you wish to hire a villa, contact **Tobago Villas Agency**, PO Box 301 (✆/✉ 639 8737). Unlike Trinidad, hotels in Tobago tend to stick to the Caribbean's traditional high (Christmas to April) and low seasons. You can also expect bills in all hotels to be supplemented by 10% for government tax (like restaurants, hotel dining rooms have to charge 15% VAT) and usually 10% for service (guest houses factor this into their prices).

very expensive–expensive

The most elegant and comfortable place to stay in Tobago is in a small collection of villas, the **Plantation Beach Villas** (✆ 639 9377, ✉ 639 0455, *villas@wow.net; expensive for two couples, moderate for three*), which are ranged among the tropical greenery in Stonehaven Bay, where there is a nice beach. Built in a compendium of colonial styles with steeply pitched roofs, balustrades and gingerbread trimmings, each villa has a huge wooden veranda with high-backed wooden chairs. Inside there are spacious rooms with ceiling fans (some bedrooms air-conditioned) and full kitchens. There is a pool and a bar down below; no restaurant, but cooking can be arranged on request. At the **Mount Irvine Bay Hotel**, PO Box 222 (✆ 639 8871, ✉ 639 8800), the rooms stand in blocks overlooking the dining room in the restored sugar mill, or the garden festooned with tropical plants and on to the sea. There are some cottages, and all the standard international comforts. It is quite large, with 105 rooms, but calm and quiet in the expansive setting of its own golf course. A hideaway with great old-time West Indian charm and a long history (the Beatles and Princess Margaret stayed here once upon a time) is the **Arnos Vale Hotel**, (✆ 639 2881, ✉ 639 4629, *arnosval@opus.co.tt*). It is set on a 400-acre estate hidden away on the north coast, dominated by an old plantation house, site of the bar and dining room with its elegant pineapple-backed wooden chairs. From here you walk down the steep path through a tight, luxuriant valley to the pool and beyond to a pretty and very private beach. The 38 rooms, some breezy, others air-conditioned, stand on the verdant hillsides around the old estate house, in a block down by the pool, or overlooking the beach itself. Magnificent birdlife to keep you interested at breakfast.

If you want something a little more upbeat, a resort in typical modern Caribbean comfort and style, you can try **Le Grand Courlan Resort and Spa**, (✆ 639 9967, ✉ 639 9292, US res ✆ (1 800) 223 6510, Canada res ✆ (1 800) 424 5500, *legrand@trinidad.net*; *www.grandehotels.com*). Set on the hillside above on Stone Haven Bay, it is large, brisk and busy with 78 plush, air-conditioned rooms with oriental carpets and all modern conveniences (satellite TV, minibar and safe). Two restaurants, spa and watersports down below. You can also use the facilities of its sister hotel next door, the **Grafton Beach Resort** (✆ 639 0191, ✉ 639 0030), which is slightly less expensive. At Crown Point at the western tip of the island, the **Coco Reef Resort**, PO Box 434 (✆ 639 8571, ✉ 639 8574, *cocoreef-tobago@trinidad.net*, *www.vaxxine.com/cyb/cocoreef*) also offers high-grade comfort in (125) sumptuous rooms and service. Classical pillars and arches in the foyer and the formal dining room give the resort a rarified feel, which is piqued by the rustic beach bar effect of the restaurant down on the sand. Disappointing beach, but Pigeon Point is not far off.

moderate

A simpler and less lavish resort-style hotel on the beach is the **Turtle Beach Hotel** (✆ 639 2851, ✉ 639 1495), which has 125 air-conditioned rooms in long, low blocks overlooking nice gardens and a line of palm-thatched umbrellas on the light brown sand of Great Courland Bay: good watersports and some entertainment.

There is a number of charming places to stay dotted around the western end of the island. At Crown Point near the western tip, there is a very pleasant and friendly atmosphere at the **Kariwak Village**, PO Box 27 (✆ 639 8545, ✉ 639 8441, *kariwak@tstt.net.tt*), where shingle-wood and palm-thatch roofed cabanas stand around a pool and in a superb tropical garden. The 24 rooms are air-conditioned with phones and locally made furniture but have no TVs. There is a TV room, but the resort hopes to take you away from all that, calling itself a 'holistic haven and hotel' and offering yoga, tai-chi and shiatsu massage, and organically grown, some vegetarian cuisine. Kariwak is not actually on the beach, but there is a shuttle to Pigeon Point. It has a library and bar with some entertainment.

If you are happy looking after yourself in splended tropical isolation with a magnificent sea view, then you might well enjoy the seclusion of the suites and apartments of the **Old Donkey Cart House** (✆ 639 3551, ✉ 639 6124) in Bacolet, just outside

Scarborough. Two rooms are in the old wooden house (with the charming restaurant, *see* p.119) and ten behind, in modern buildings either side of a pool—these are very attractive with wooden floors and louvred doors and windows and balconies; some have four-posters made with Trinidadian wood and draped with mosquito nets; all have TV, fridge and phone, excellent penthouse. Another charming spot, behind a stone wall just above the beach at Stone Haven Bay, is the **Seahorse Inn,** PO Box 488 (✆ 639 0686, ✆ 639 0057; *moderate–cheap*). The inn has just three rooms overlooking a small courtyard (also an excellent restaurant, *see* p.119) which is festooned with brightly coloured tropical blooms. Neat and modern in good Caribbean style—wooden interior and a balcony: very quiet during the day, a little activity at night. In the Crown Point area you will find the **Toucan Inn** (✆ 639 7173, ✆ 639 8933, *bonkers@trinidad.net*), another small enclave where five hexagonal cabanas (each with two rooms), tropical greenery and a wooden dining room with a pointed roof are clustered around a swimming pool. Rooms are pretty, with teak furnishings and stark white walls—air-conditioning but no phone or TV. Fun atmosphere.

There are many other small hotels and inns around the remoter eastern part of the island, each with their own West Indian charm and often a magnificent setting. Standing on a hill above Richmond on the south coast, the **Richmond Great House** (✆/✆ 660 4467) echoes with the graciousness of old-time Tobago in an old timber-frame estate house in tropical gardens. The house has been restored by a Tobagonian professor of African history, whose collection of art is on view. Ten rooms lead off the open central dining area and are furnished with locally made pieces, including four-posters. Very quiet, and a variety of prices within this category.

Just beyond Speyside is the **Blue Waters Inn** (✆ 660 4341, ✆ 660 5195, *bwito-bago@trinidad.net*, *www.trinidad.net/bwi-tobago/*) where 38 rooms are ranged on the shores of the charming Batteaux Bay, with wonderful views through the craggy old sea grape trees to the sea and the islands offshore. A variety of rooms, self-catering 'efficiencies' and one- and two-bedroom bungalows (some kitchen facilities). Lots of watersports and onshore activities.

cheap

Yet further afield, overlooking the waves just along from 'downtown' Charlotteville, are the six **Man O' War Bay Cottages** (✆ 660 4327, ✆ 660 4328), which are scattered around a sandy garden in the shade of huge trees. The cottages are relatively simple and quite old in style, but they offer the ultimate in West Indian seclusion.

There are also plenty of **guest houses** around the western end which offer budget accommodation. In Crown Point you will find friendly service and simple rooms at **Wood's Castle** (✆ 639 0803), private baths, TV, a/c, fan, one with a kitchenette, also dining room; and right opposite the airport, **Jetway** (✆/✆ 639 8504), very simple, functional but clean rooms. In Plymouth you will find comfortable rooms at the **Cocrico Inn** (✆ 639 2961, ✆ 639 6565), set in a modern block with restaurant, and a clean and simple place to lay your head at **Gladys Villas** (✆/✆ 639 2604).

For bed and breakfast in private homes, a good way to see Tobagonian life, contact the Tourist Office in Scarborough about the **Bed and Breakfast Association**, c/o Federal Villa, 1–3 Crook's River, Scarborough (✆ 639 3296, ✆ 639 3566). The cost is generally about US$25 per person. In the towns of the eastern end of the island (e.g. Speyside and Charlotteville), you can find very cheap rooms by asking around.

There are some good restaurants outside the hotels in Tobago and it is worth the effort of visiting them. In general dining out in the island is not as expensive as elsewhere in the Caribbean. Categories are arranged according to the price of a main course: *expensive*—TT$70 and above; *moderate*—TT$30–TT$70; *cheap*—less than TT$30. Restaurants must add VAT at 15% and they will usually add service at 10% as well.

expensive

The **Old Donkey Cart House** (© 639 3551) has an alluring and romantic setting in a fairy-lit tropical garden, where tables stand on a veranda and in alcoves under wreaths of tropical plants. Steaks and salads, Calcutta shrimp (with mushrooms) or kingfish sautéed in wine and garlic, washed down with German wine. *Closed Wed.* Another superb setting is at the **Sea Horse Inn** (© 639 0686) on Great Courland Bay. You dine on a terrace surrounded by a stone wall cascading with greenery. A long cocktail list before a meal of creole and international cuisine with plenty of seafood: crab rosette (blue crab meat parcelled in a patchoi leaf) or seafood chowder followed by deep-fried shrimp in a sweet creole sauce or *pastels*—seasoned minced beef steamed in a banana leaf. Try **Eleven Degrees North** (© 630 0996), near Store Bay in a house with double doors open to the air and a wraparound veranda. The fare is Cajun, Mexican and Caribbean: bayou chicken, seafood enchilada or a caroni delight (shrimp in a curry sauce, followed by local 'guava cheese'-cake or 'Something Chocolate'.

You will eat reliably well at **Papillon** Restaurant (© 639 0275) at the Old Grange Inn in Mount Irvine, on the tropical garden terrace or in the air-conditioned interior. A long seafood menu: local conch (seasonal) cooked in coconut, or a seafood casserole in ginger wine, with generous servings of plantain and ground provisions, followed by *Tobago pone* for pudding. There is an excellent Italian restaurant in Buccoo, **La Tartaruga** (© 639 0940), where you sit inside or on a charming deck sheltered by banana plants. Superb home-made pastas with sauces made from herbs in the garden and freshly caught fish. Friendly and efficient. There is a chichi pink and white veranda setting at the **Black Rock Café** (© 639 7625). Plenty of international food, but perhaps start with a beef *pastel* and follow with shrimp in curry sauce.

moderate

In the Crown Point area there is a fun spot set on a wooden terrace which doubles as restaurant and bar: **In Seine** (© 639 9467). Named after a type of fishing net, it is strong on seafood. Start with shrimp wontons or a crab-back and follow with a mussel or conch pasta. You will be welcomed into a classic West Indian setting, on a veranda with trellises and flowers and get the best of local food at the **Blue Crab** (© 639 2737), at the corner of Robinson and Main Streets in Scarborough. Set menu: pumpkin soup or fish chowder followed by the daily catch grilled, curried or creole, or coal-pot chicken. Lots of juices and breads, mangoes, bananas and avocados from the garden and all the local vegetables. You must ring to reserve (and request any dish you want). *Lunch and dinner, closed Thurs.* Not far off, on the road out to Bacolet, is **Rouselle's** (© 639 4738), another favourite with Tobagonians: fine West Indian fare, particularly fresh fish, served with rice and peas, and a spot of liming at the bar.

When you are travelling around the island it is worth stopping at **Jemma's Sea View Kitchen** (*moderate–cheap*), which sits on a series of 'tree house' decks on the waterfront in Speyside. She is a Seventh Day Adventist, so she is closed on Friday night and Saturday and will sell you no alcohol (though you can take your own if you want). Set lunch and dinner menus. Right next door, **Redmans 'Simple Restaurant'** offers similar fare—'fish, tricken, curry beef, pomkin soup, shrimp, conch, some people call it lambi, and wile meat, that is rabbit, manicou an' agouti...' In Charlotteville there is a number of local snack stalls for a roti, but **Sharon and Pheb's** offers a fine chicken or fish, on a small veranda above banana trees.

Finally, at **Store Bay** you will find a clutch of snackettes in the newly spruced-up stalls, where you can take away the famous Tobago crab and dumpling on a polystyrene plate, a callaloo and a coocoo, or curry goat and 'buss up shut' (paratha bread, or 'bust-up shirt')—Miss Esmie, Sylvia, Alma, Joicy's, Miss Trim and Miss Jean, all in a row. *Open until about 10pm.*

Tobago Directory

getting there

By air: Crown Point airport in Tobago is served by some direct international flights from Europe and the USA, most of them charter flights. Scheduled links usually involve a connection in Port of Spain. Most international airlines will endorse tickets to Air Caribbean (✆ 639 2500), who have eight or ten flights a day between Trinidad and Tobago, a connection which takes 12 minutes. There is a departure tax of $TT85.

By air from the UK: There are no direct scheduled services from Europe straight in to Tobago; they are routed via Port of Spain. BWIA (✆ 639 3291) flies daily to Trinidad. Charter operators Caledonian fly direct to Tobago twice-weekly from Britain.

By air from Germany: BWIA flies to Trinidad out of Frankfurt, but the charter airline Condor flies direct to Tobago.

By air from USA: Connections must be made in San Juan in Puerto Rico for the daily flight on American Eagle (✆ 664 4661), or you must go via Trinidad, to which there are daily services from Miami and New York on American Airlines (same ✆).

Other Caribbean Islands: The best scheduled flights to the rest of the Caribbean are on LIAT (✆ 639 0276) who fly on to Barbados, Grenada and St Lucia (also a couple of flights a day to Port of Spain). Air Caribbean have links to Barbados and Grenada. Aerotuy (✆ 639 7461) fly twice-weekly to Margarita island off Venezuela and charter operator TIA (✆ 639 8918) flies in occasionally from Barbados.

By sea: There is also a daily ferry (except Sat) from Port of Spain to Tobago. Return trips leave from Scarborough and are generally overnight. Crossing time is approximately 6 hours. Return prices vary from TT$160 for a cabin on the *Panorama* to TT$50 economy on the *Tobago*. Tickets are on sale until 8.30pm, but not at weekends; information ✆ 639 2417.

tourist information

For **TIDCO** offices abroad, *see* 'Trinidad Directory', p.106. TIDCO have an **internet** website at: *www.tidco.co.tt* and there is an **email** postbox at *tourism-info@tidco.co.tt.*

Bars and Nightlife

The hotels sometimes stage live entertainment which you are welcome to attend and you can always wander into any restaurant or hotel bars, but there are local bars worth a look too. In town the big place is the **Great White** bar (complete with cartoon shark outside) which sees early evening drinkers and then wilder players later on—pool tables on a sandy floor and sports on the TV.

There are one or two **clubs**. In Crown Point the place to go is the **Golden Star**, particularly on Wednesdays when there is a 'Scouting for Talent' night (apparently it is your talent at karaoke that is at issue) and at the weekends when there are general jump-ups. The **Great White** is popular on Fridays for reggae and Saturday for general Caribbean music. In Bon Accord, the **Copratray** is often busy. On Sunday night you should try 'Sunday School' at **Hendrix's Bar** in Buccoo, a jump-up that kicks off late.

℗ (1 868)–

The **Tobago Department of Tourism** office is in the main street in Scarborough (℗ 639 2125, ✆ 639 3566; for information ℗ 639 INFO 6436). There is an information office at Crown Point airport (℗ 639 0509) and at the cruise ship complex in town if there is a ship in harbour. You will also find useful information in the small annual magazine *Discover Trinidad and Tobago* and both of the islands have their own small newspapers for visitors.

In a medical **emergency**, Tobago County Hospital is on Fort St in Scarborough (℗ 639 2551). The **IDD code** for Tobago is ℗ (1 868) followed by the seven-figure island number. If phoning from Trinidad or on the island, dial the seven figures.

festivals

Like its counterpart in Trinidad, the Tobago Carnival is a major blow-out and culminates with Mardi Gras at the beginning of Lent. You can catch a calypso tent for a month beforehand. The end of Lent is celebrated as well, with goat and crab races and a general jump-up in Buccoo on Easter weekend. In August the island hosts the Tobago Heritage Festival, at which you can see an old-time wedding at Moriah among other celebrations of Tobago traditions. There are windsurfing and game fishing competitions across the year and in July or August there is a power-boat race from Trinidad to Store Bay.

money

The currency is the Trinidad and Tobago dollar (TT$) which floats on the international exchange and stands at about US$1=TT$6. Hotels will accept US dollars and most accept credit cards, but it is a good idea to have some TT$ while you are out on the island. A (recent) receipt must be presented if you wish to change money back when you leave.
Banking hours: Mon–Thurs 9–2, Fri 9–1 and 3–5.
Shops: Open weekdays 8–4.30 (often later), Sat 8–noon.

maps and books

The earliest book set on Tobago (and one of the earliest English novels) is *Robinson Crusoe* by Daniel Defoe (published in 1719), which tells the story of a shipwrecked sailor who lives on the island for nearly 30 years.

watersports

Most watersports—snorkelling, kayaks, windsurfing, outings on small sailboats and scuba—can be arranged through the hotels or at Pigeon Point.

Day sails: Try the attractive wooden yacht *Chlöe* (℗ 639 2449), or *Tiercel* (℗ 639 9613) or you can go with Kalina Cats on a catamaran (℗ 639 6306). You can also take a full day trip with a picnic and swimming to No Man's Land.

Snorkelling tours: Many boats take swimming and snorkelling tours to Buccoo Reef; departures from Store Bay and Pigeon Point, price about US$10. Most stop on the way back at the Nylon Pool. Take a swimming costume and make sure that the boat has a mask your size. There are also good reefs at Arnos Vale, and at the eastern end of the island at the Blue Waters Inn and at Charlotteville.

Surfing: Popular in the winter when the waves are at their biggest; alternatively **boogie boards** are available most of the year. If you are travelling independently, there is a general watersports shop at Mt Irvine Bay Watersports (℗ 639 9389).

Deep-sea fishing: Dillon Tours and Charters, aboard *Super Cool* (℗ 639 8765), or through Classic Sportfishing (℗ 639 9389).

Scuba: The best reefs are at the eastern end of the island, where there is a good variety of sites from shallow snorkellable reefs to drift dives on which you can see barracudas and often manta rays. However, there is no need to go that far as there are dive sites on the reefs all along the northern shore. Popular dive-sites include the Sisters, London Bridge and the Japanese Gardens where there are whole slopes of seafans and sponges. Contact Manta Dive (℗ 639 9969, ● 639 0414) on the Pigeon Point Road. At the eastern end of the island, contact Tobago Dive Experience (℗ 660 5268, ● 660 5030, *divemanta@trinidad.net, www. trinidad.net/tobagodive*) and AquaMarine Dive Ltd (℗ 660 4341, ● 639 4416, *amdtobago@trinidad.net, www.trinidad.net/bwi-tobago*), both in Speyside; and in Charlotteville, Man Friday Diving (℗/● 660 4676). Equipment and instruction are available through all operators and it is worth remembering that some hotels offer diving packages in their rates. A single-tank dive costs around US$35-40.

other sports

Golf: There is an 18-hole course at the Mount Irvine Hotel (℗ 639 8871); green fees US$46.

Tennis: Many of the hotels have courts. If yours doesn't it can be arranged at reception.

Hiking: In the rainforests there are trails in the **Tobago Forest Reserve**; try the 3½ mile Gilpin Trace. If you would like to take a bird-watching or plant-watching hike into the rainforest between Roxborough and Parlatuvier or Little Tobago, contact David Rooks at PO Box 348 in Scarborough (℗ 639 4276, ● 639 5448) who will explain the ongoing processes of life in the forest (and how leaf-cutting ants fit into it, for instance) and mangroves. Also contact Man O' War Bay Cottages in Charlotteville (℗ 660 4327). These people will also arrange turtle-watching trips in season if requested.

Horse-riding: Palm Tree Village (℗ 639 4347) for a gallop along the sand at Rockley Beach or a walk into the fertile inland areas.

The Windward Islands

The four independent nations of the Windward Isles stand like a line of Titans in the Southern Caribbean. Each one in sight of the next, these massive fertile peaks soar thousands of feet from the water, separating the Atlantic Ocean from the Caribbean Sea.

The Windward Islands are all similar in appearance and are among the most beautiful and fertile in the Caribbean. They rise sheer from the water to serrated volcanic peaks, usually stacked with rainclouds formed as the Atlantic winds are forced up their slopes. Their height gives them their own micro-climates. The rainfall here is measured in feet, and it crashes down the hills in torrents and waterfalls. It also feeds the dripping, sweltering forest: a monstrous tangle of trees, creepers, bushes and ferns clambering over one another in botanical pandemonium. The islands are so fertile that clumps of bamboo will grow to over 60ft in height, creaking even when there is no wind. The gardener's most useful tool is the machete.

The name Windwards began as a geographical term, describing the islands windward of the usual arrival point for ships in the Caribbean, around Martinique or Dominica, but during the last century it became a political designation within the British Empire. Since then the islands have gone their own way politically but the term still remains in use as a description of their geographical position, particularly among sailors.

In fact the islands are a series of volcanic peaks on a mountain range below the surface of the water. They lie along a fault-line on the seabed, where the Atlantic crust is gradually forcing its way under the Caribbean plate and the magma is throwing up lava through volcanoes. Though the eruptions have calmed down somewhat over the last few million years, the volcanoes are still active, and each of the main *soufrières* blows about once a century and causes earthquakes that reverberate along the whole chain of the Lesser Antilles. On one day in 1867, weird happenings on Grenada in the far south of the chain, where the harbour water swelled and contracted as though the underworld were breathing, were echoed by seismic activity as far north as the Virgin Island of St Thomas.

Each one of the Windwards has its *soufrière*, a sulphurous volcanic vent, and if you go exploring you will be greeted by its smell. The St Vincent volcano and those on nearby Martinique and Guadeloupe are the most violent, tending to blast out volumes of lava and superheated gases that collapse mountains and destroy anything in their path, as well as a plume of gas and a shower of pumice stones. In the last few years it has been Montserrat, one of the Leewards to the north, which has shown the most activity, spewing forth lava and pyroclastic flow and showering the island with ash. In other islands things are usually less extreme: *fumaroles* constantly let off steam through vents above the waterline and below (which makes for interesting dive-sites). In Dominica there is even a volcanic steam-bath that lets off sulphurous fumes so disgusting as to kill off all the plant-life. In the

Grenadines there is an underwater volcano (Kick 'em Jenny), now quite close to the surface, whose activity has been spotted by pilots flying over the area. An American seer predicted that the 1990s were to be an active time for the Caribbean Islands. According to her, one island would disappear during the decade—this happened when Sandy Island off Anguilla was simply washed away in Hurricane Luis in 1995—and a new one would appear. Perhaps it will be Kick 'em Jenny.

The Windwards are smack in the middle of the hurricane belt and in the season are occasionally visited by these outsize whirlwinds, the first point of contact with land after a 2000-mile run-up across the Atlantic. Hurricanes are indescribably destructive—Hurricane Luis destroyed 1200 yachts in the lagoon in St Maarten and Hurricane Hugo caused major damage to over 90 per cent of the houses in Montserrat. Not only do the winds damage the crops and houses (literally sand-blasting them in some cases, stripping off every square inch of paint), but the torrential rains that accompany them sweep away roads and collapse bridges.

The islands are partly agricultural, depending mainly on bananas and other small-scale agricultural industries such as nutmeg in Grenada and arrowroot in St Vincent. They are also industrially undeveloped, in sharp contrast to the nearby French islands, which are more like mainland France.

But the societies are changing. Whereas the older generation has lived a tough farmer's existence attached to the land, the youth of today are unwilling to live like this. Many would prefer to take their chances in town. On an island like St Lucia, a large proportion of the population lives in the capital, Castries. There is a burgeoning middle class and civil service in all the islands, and the largest industry now is tourism, which contributes most of the foreign exchange needed to buy medicines, luxuries and even some foods. The face of the islands is changing too—there has been plenty of building over the last few years, as families build new concrete homes set in a large plot of land instead of the small wooden houses in a yard. The one thing that doesn't change is the friendly welcome you will get from the islanders themselves. If you ever want to talk, you simply stop anyone you come across in the street.

Windward Islands History

Human history in the Windwards is split-second in terms of the volcanoes and plate tectonics and is reckoned to have started about 2000 years ago, when Arawak Indians first touched the islands on their migration north from the South American mainland. For a thousand years they led a peaceful existence centred around agriculture and fishing. Pieces of their pottery are still to be found in the islands today, as are their rock-carvings.

Around AD 1000, their peace was disturbed by the Caribs, another South American Indian tribe, who followed them along the island chain. The newcomers were reportedly cannibals (though there is little evidence of anything more than ceremonial killing) and they made short work of the gentle Arawaks as they bludgeoned their way north, murdering the men and adopting the women as family as they moved. At the time of Columbus's arrival in the New World, the Caribs had island-hopped as far as the Virgin Islands and were beginning to raid Borinquen, now Puerto Rico. On the earliest maps of the Americas, the Windward Islands are marked as the 'Cannibal Isles', such was the terror which they conjured up in the minds of sailors. The Spaniards gave them a wide berth and headed for the bigger and less hostile islands of the Greater Antilles.

But as the age of Empire began, in the early 1600s, so the Europeans encroached on the Lesser Antilles, settling, colonizing and planting and at the same time conducting a war that would lead to the genocide of the Caribs. The mountainous Windwards became the heartland of Carib resistance to the invaders. A treaty of 1660 supposedly ensured that they would be left alone on St Vincent and Dominica on condition that they kept the peace elsewhere, but the governments connived with the colonists' campaign of extermination because the land was proving to be so valuable. The Caribs from Dominica and from St Vincent, where there was a mixed race of Caribs and escaped African slaves, the 'Black Caribs', conducted a desperate campaign to defend themselves right up to the beginning of the 19th century. But the 18th century was also the height of French and British rivalry. Every war in Europe sent shock-waves to the Caribbean and the islands were invaded and snatched. Fleets from the two nations would tear up and down the island chain, ransacking the colonies and annexing them, only to see them back at the next treaty. Despite blockades, the islands were extremely valuable to the colonists as they brought in a vast wealth in sugar. Their importance can be seen in the Treaty of Paris in 1763, when the French traded their rights in the whole of Canada in order to retain a foothold in the islands by keeping Martinique, the most prosperous of their islands. By the early years of the 19th century, the final pattern was fixed—Martinique was French and the Windward Islands were in British hands.

Behind the wars and the empire building, the issues were rather different for the islanders themselves, to whom the colonial armies were an ambivalent presence. There is some French influence in each of the Windwards. Many of the place-names are French, as are the *anses* (bays) and *mornes* (hills), and in Dominica and St Lucia you will still hear French creole, which survives as the first language of the people even though the official language has been English for nearly 200 years.

If the 18th century was a turbulent and prosperous one, the 19th saw a steady decline to obscurity and poverty in the Windwards. Their major industry, sugar, became uncompetitive as sugar beet was grown more economically in Europe, and attempts at other crops met with limited success. A highlight was emancipation in 1834. Unlike Barbados, where there was no unowned land and the former slaves were effectively forced to continue working the plantations to make a living, the freed slaves on the Windwards voted with their feet, preferring to take a plot of land in the hills where they could be their own masters. The islands became backwaters, declining to the point where Dominica had only a fortnightly postal service.

The Windwards (except Dominica, which did not join the Windwards until 1939) were grouped under a governor in St George's, Grenada and in 1874, Crown Colony status was enforced and direct rule was transferred to London. As the political scene changed after the Second World War, universal franchise came in 1951 and internal self-government in 1967. The Windward Islands ceased to exist as a political unit in 1960 as the islands were on the path to Independence. All four nations remain within the British Commonwealth and the Queen is represented by a Governor General. The highest court of appeal is the Privy Council in London.

Attempts to link the islands in a Federation had failed as early as 1763 and again in 1885. The Windwards were a part of the short-lived West Indian Federation in 1958 and since 1981 they have been part of the Organization of Eastern Caribbean States, which promotes economic integration between the smaller Commonwealth countries in the area.

Bananas

A familiar sight in the Windward Islands is the messy swathes of banana trees covering a whole valley floor, their leaves tousled and arched in irregular directions. Look closely and you may see them lashed together for support with a network of string, their dark green fruits, or 'hands', protected by blue plastic bags.

The banana is native to China and Malaya and had made its way to the Canary Islands by 1510. Its botanical name is *Musa sapientum*, or the 'muse of wise men', and according to Indian legend, sages would sit under their huge leaves for shade and savour the fruit. They had lost their popularity with Caribbean colonists by the start of the 19th century, when they were regarded as a suspect fruit because of their colour and shape: they were thought 'to excite urine and to provoke venery'.

There are over a hundred different varieties of banana, the most widely known in Europe being the cavendish, locally known as the *gros michel*, which is large and yellow when ripe. Less known is the smaller and sweeter canary banana or rock fig (considered *l'amie de la poitrine* by Père Labat), which is about 4 inches long. But the most exotic and sweetest of them all is the secret fig, which grows no longer than about 2 inches. There are also many unsweet varieties to be seen in the Caribbean, such as plantain, tasty when fried, and other starchy vegetables, the green fig and the bluggo. Names vary from island to island.

In fact bananas do not grow on trees at all, but on a stem of unripe leaves packed closely like a cigar, growing out of a rhizome underground. As each new leaf forces its way up, it stands erect like a bright green scroll and gently unfurls, bending gracefully as it is superseded by another. The leaves, sometimes 10ft long by 2ft, start off with a beautiful green sheen that makes water dance like mercury, and as they age they become shredded and look like an untidy head of hair.

When a plant bears fruit, it throws out a long trunk with a purple heart at the tip, which opens to reveal little black teeth in rows. These teeth are the end of the fruit, which swell until the bunches appear like so many fingers sticking up. A trunk produces one 'bunch' of bananas, which may have as many as ten 'hands' or 'finger rolls'. Each plant produces fruit only once, after which it dies and another shoot takes its place in the same spot. The blue plastic bags protect the maturing bananas from the scratches of lizard claws, insects and birds. The 'Banana Boat Song', with its 'Day Oh!' chorus made famous in the fifties by Harry Belafonte, was originally sung by banana packers as they loaded the United Fruit Company ships in Jamaica at night: 'Come Mr Tallyman, come tally me banana, Daylight come and me waan go home'.

The banana has been a very important export crop in the Windwards since the 1950s and the trade, under protected agreements mainly with Britain, has been a vital source of foreign exchange. The packing stations are all over the islands and you will see farmers carrying the fruit down the hill in time for the weekly visit of the *Geest* ships that make the three-week round trip from Europe. Over the last few years, though, the protected agreements have broken down in the face of the free markets and competition with the 'dollar banana', which is grown more economically in Central America.

Grenada

Grenada and its Grenadines are strung out over 50 miles or so in the far south of the Caribbean, at the foot of the Windward Islands chain, about 90 miles north of Trinidad and the South American coast. The island of Grenada itself is typical of the Windwards in its tropical beauty, with towering mountains mantled in explosive rainforest, and coastal inlets and bays furred with palms and white sand beaches. To its north Grenada (pronounced 'gre-nay-der') is linked to the island of St Vincent by the Grenadines, a 60-mile string of coral islands and cays, towering peaks that soar out of the water and sandbars that barely make it to the surface. Two of the inhabited Grenadines, Carriacou and Petit Martinique, belong to Grenada, and altogether the three islands are home to a population of about 96,000.

Grenada's capital, St George's, is the prettiest harbour town in the whole Caribbean. It is set in a massive volcanic bowl, and its slopes are lined with red-tiled roofs that descend to the edge of the bay, where yachts and old-fashioned schooners have long lined the waterfront and now cruise ships dwarf the daily activity on the waterfront. Beyond the capital, the island is wonderfully fertile and green. Measuring just 12 miles by 21, Grenada calls itself the Spice Island of the Caribbean because its fertile soil produces spices for markets all over the world. In the valleys of the mountainous interior you will see the fruit and spice plantations and the cocoa walks, where orange immortelle trees stand aflame above the cocoa trees early in the year. Nutmeg, from which come the spices nutmeg and mace, is Grenada's most famous spice and it is important enough to the island to appear on the national flag.

Grenada is quiet and easy-going in true Caribbean style, but it is remembered for an event not so long ago, in October 1983, when it was thrust into the international news. Following a revolution it became the site of an invasion that set the might of the United States on to a tiny Caribbean island. The customary Caribbean quiet did not take long to return, though the event remains in the memory of the Grenadians.

Like the other islands in the area, Grenada is seeing considerable development at the moment as the islanders build homes for themselves. The island is less developed than St Lucia, but it sees a steady stream of tourists to its broad range of hotels. Grenada is also well positioned for exploring the Grenadines, by yacht, by ferry and by island-hopping plane.

History

From the earliest sightings travellers have spoken of Grenada's physical beauty and fertility. To 16th-century Spanish sailors coasting the Windwards it was supposedly a reminder of home, the hills above the city of Granada. However, early attempts to settle 'Camerhogne', as the island was known before their arrival, failed at the hands of the Caribs. Englishmen came in 1609 in the ships *Diana*, *Penelope* and *Endeavour*, but they were chased off, as were later settlers sponsored by the Frenchman de Poincy.

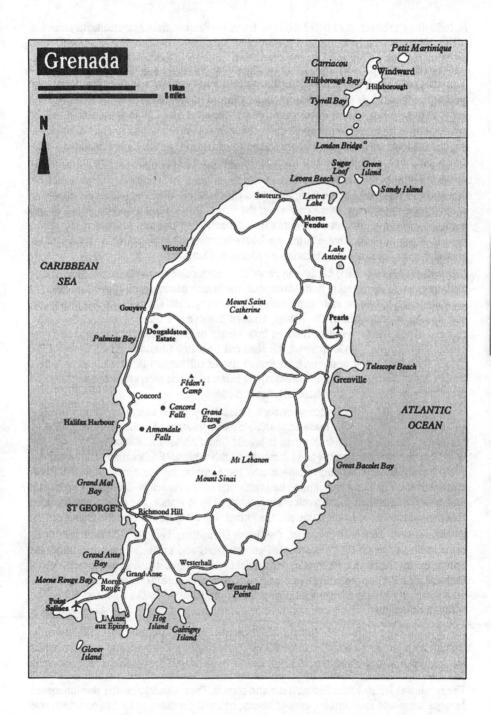

Grenada

10km
8 miles

N

CARIBBEAN
SEA

ATLANTIC
OCEAN

Petit Martinique

Carriacou

Hillsborough Bay

Hillsborough

Tyrrell Bay

Windward

London Bridge

Sugar
Loaf

Green
Island

Levera Beach

Sandy Island

Sauteurs

Levera
Lake

Morne
Fendue

Victoria

Lake
Antoine

Mount Saint
Catherine

Pearls

Gouyave

Dougaldston
Estate

Palmiste Bay

Telescope Beach

Fédon's
Camp

Grenville

Concord

Concord
Falls

Grand
Etang

Halifax Harbour

Annandale
Falls

Mt Lebanon

Great Bacolet Bay

Mount Sinai

Grand Mal
Bay

ST GEORGE'S

Richmond Hill

Grand Anse
Bay

Westerhall

Morne Rouge Bay

Grand Anse

Morne
Rouge

Westerhall
Point

Point
Salines

L'Anse
aux Epines

Hog
Island

Calvigny
Island

Glover
Island

In 1650, the Caribs actually invited the Frenchman Du Parquet, from Martinique, to settle the island. He came with 'two hundred men of good stamina', arriving to a salute of guns and promptly erecting a cross and building a fort. He bought the island from the Caribs for 'cloth, axes, bill-hooks, knives, glass beads, mirrors and two large bottles of *eau-de-vie* (brandy) for the chief himself', but it was not long before the Caribs decided the deal was not a good one after all. By 1654 they were locked in a duel with the French for possession of the island. Reinforcements came for the French from Martinique by ship and for the Caribs from St Vincent and Dominica by canoe.

It was an extremely brutal time. The Caribs roamed the island killing French hunters and then attacked the French settlement. But, armed only with bows and arrows against the guns of the French, the Caribs were eventually forced up to the north of the island where, rather than be captured and killed, they threw themselves off a cliff to their deaths. The settlers didn't have it all their own way, though. A new owner of the island, the Comte du Cerillac, sent a brutal governor who so abused his power that the islanders tried him and sentenced him to be hanged. At this he pleaded noble birth, which gave him the right to be beheaded. There was no executioner on Grenada, so the islanders eventually had him shot.

In the early 1700s the island became an important French colony, as a plantation island and as a refitting station on the route from Martinique, the French headquarters in the Caribbean, to South America. But in the endless rounds of 18th-century wars, Grenada was blockaded and captured again and again as the navies whittled through the island chain. As the island changed hands, the names were changed from French to English and back again; Fort Royal became St George's and Gouyave on the west coast became Charlotte Town. Some of the names stuck, but many of the original French names still remain in Grenada even today. Despite the difficulties brought by the wars, the island remained prosperous and was thought of as 'the second of the English Islands' (after Barbados).

It was not long before the French were back. Grenada was taken almost by mistake because an attack on Barbados was made impossible by bad weather. Admiral d'Estaing entered St George's harbour and the Irish troops of his ally Count Arthur Dillon attacked by land. The island surrendered. Hard on his heels came the British Admiral, Foulweather Jack Byron, but even though some of his ships made it into the harbour, he could not draw the 'mere gasconade of a vapouring Frenchman' into battle and so the French won Grenada again. The British Governor and the island's colours were shipped off to France. The latter were strung up above the High Altar in Notre Dame and the former was eventually returned to Britain.

Once the British were back in control, the British Grenadians were vengeful over their treatment at French hands. They confiscated church lands and made the French Grenadians submit to the 'Test', an oath demanding a rejection of transubstantiation, impossible for a Catholic. Many chose to emigrate to Trinidad, where the Spaniards were crying out for settlers. Much of Trinidad's French heritage dates from these Grenadian refugees. But on the island itself the grievances increased, fired by the harsher treatment of the slaves under the British and by the French Revolution, which was being spread from Guadeloupe by Victor Hugues (*see* p.262). Eventually it erupted into open rebellion in 1795.

Fédon's Rebellion

The revolt was led by Julien Fédon, a mulatto planter. From Guadeloupe the revolutionaries brought 'arms and ammunition, caps of liberty, national cockades and a flag on which was inscribed in large characters, *Liberté, Egalité ou la Mort.*' The rebels overran the whole island, killing prisoners along with suspected collaborators. Their first strike was on the east coast, at La Baye, near modern Grenville, where British settlers were taken from their beds and shot, and at Charlotte Town, where the Governor himself, Sir Ninian Home, was captured trying to return to St George's. He was one of 51 hostages taken to the rebel mountain stronghold, eventually to be slaughtered on Fédon's personal instructions as the rebels came under threat from the advancing British troops.

St George's never fell to the rebels but it took a year before reinforcements under Sir Ralph Abercromby defeated the guerrillas. Their leaders were captured and executed immediately or exiled to Honduras, but Fédon himself was never taken. Some think he drowned in an attempt to escape to Trinidad, but others think that he made it to Cuba. His estate at Belvidere, from where he ran the insurrection, is just below one of Grenada's mountain peaks, now known as Fédon's Camp. By the end of the conflict, Grenada was in ruins.

When the slaves were freed in 1838 they took over small plots of Grenada's fertile land. Unlike the other Windwards, Grenada remained reasonably prosperous during the decline of the 19th century. Agriculture was the economic mainstay; bananas and cocoa were grown, among lesser-known spices such as cinnamon, bay leaf, allspice and ginger.

With the failure of the Federation, when attempts to unite all the British Caribbean islands into one country foundered in 1962, and after a later failure to unite with Trinidad and Tobago, Grenada became an Associated State of Britain in 1967. They were not long in deciding on Independence and Grenada became an independent nation within the British Commonwealth on 7 February 1974. Grenada's first leader was Eric Gairy, a volatile and charismatic man whose political heritage was in the oil-fields of the Caribbean island of Aruba. Elected as early as 1951, he was fondly thought of by many Grenadians as the champion of workers' rights against the colonial government. After Independence his leadership became steadily more corrupt, wasteful and bullying, and he used a secret army called the Mongoose Gang to impose his will unofficially.

In the early seventies the socialist New Jewel Movement was formed. Initially clandestine, to avoid harassment from the overbearing government, the NJM steadily gained ground, allying itself with the disillusioned opposition to Gairy, including the influential and traditionally conservative business class. They also armed themselves in preparation for revolution.

Revolution and Invasion

On 13 March 1979, with Gairy out of the country, 38 armed members of the NJM stormed the army barracks at True Blue on the south coast of the island and in a bloodless coup the NJM attained power. With popular support, they began a social experiment unprecedented in the Commonwealth Caribbean. Considerable improvements were made in health care and in education, and general economic growth came over the next four years. However, the repressive nature of the People's Revolutionary Government's programmes gradually became clearer: the press was stifled, political detainees were held untried and then, when Grenada forged closer ties with Cuba and the Eastern bloc, the Grenadian Revolution began to excite international disapproval.

Under this pressure from outside and facing straitened economic circumstances on the island, the PRG foundered in a split from within. The leader, Maurice Bishop, was placed under house arrest by the other members of the Central Committee, but eventually his supporters brought him to St George's, where they congregated at Fort George. Bernard Coard and others of the opposing faction of the PRG sent down troops who fired on the crowd to disperse it, killing about 60 people, then shooting Bishop and five of his close associates inside the fort. The whole island was placed under a 24-hour curfew for four days. Then, on 25 October 1983, the US 82nd Airborne Division invaded and took the island over.

Massive aid and assistance came in the first couple of years and President Reagan himself made a visit in February 1986, but it has tailed off now that Grenada has acquiesced. Many Grenadians do think of the invasion as the 'rescue mission' and are grateful to Reagan for sending troops. Others will never forgive the USA for what seemed to them an unwarranted show of force against a small country by a big power in whose backyard Grenada happened to be. There is still considerable support for Maurice Bishop, if not for his deputies.

From time to time the issues are brought back into island consciousness. There are still 17 people in jail from the events and in 1997 a 'Mercy Committee' tried to gain the release of two of them—Phyllis Coard (wife of Bernard) and Colville Kamau McBarnette—both of whom were ill. There has also been a certain regional rapprochement to Cuba, but they are considered less of a threat by the United States now.

Grenada remains within the British Commonwealth and has two Houses of Parliament, a 13-member Senate and a 15-member House of Representatives elected for five-year terms. The country is led by Prime Minister Dr Keith Mitchell of the New National Party, which was elected in June 1995 with eight seats. The official opposition is the National Democratic Congress, which has five seats. Two former members of the third party, the Grenada United Labour Party, went over to the Government, so the NNP (jokingly called the No Nonsense Party) leads the country with a majority of ten to five.

The Spice Island of the Caribbean

Grenada is known as the Isle of Spice—the source of the island's prosperity at the turn of the century. Even though Grenada's one-third share of the world market in nutmeg is now lost and market prices are at a low ebb, spices are still a profitable business and you are bound to be offered them for sale in the streets. Otherwise, two good places to visit are the **Minor Spices Society** next to the Market in St George's and **Arawak Islands Ltd**, which is set in a pretty creole house in Belmont just out of town.

Nutmeg is the island's principal spice. In the past it has been used as a charm to ward off illness and today it is used locally in remedies against colds by the islanders as well as in Vicks Vapour Rub. In the Second World War, oil of nutmeg was in demand for aircraft engine oil because it does not freeze at high altitudes. Nutmeg was introduced into Grenada in 1843, supposedly at a party, where it was added as a mystery ingredient to the top of the regular planter's punch—the party was no doubt a success, but more importantly, Grenadians have never drunk a rum punch without nutmeg since.

nutmeg

The tree (which has the botanical name *Myristica fragrans*) is evergreen and grows up to 60ft in height. Its fruit looks like a yellow apricot and the Grenadians will tell you that no part of it goes to waste. When it ripens, the flesh splits open, revealing a brown nut covered with a red wax netting, and it drops to the ground. The fruit must be collected at once to prevent it from rotting and then the parts are separated.

Cocoa beans drying in mobile boucans

The outer flesh goes into making jams or preserves and the nut, which contains the nutmeg itself, is processed to make the spice nutmeg. Finally, the red netting is used for a second spice, mace, which is stored for six months and then graded as the spice itself, or used as a preservative in food or cosmetics, to be exported in tea chests. The 'nut' is put through a crusher which removes the shell and then the kernels are graded by throwing them into water. Those that float are used in pharmaceuticals, but the good ones sink and they make the spice nutmeg that ends up floating on a rum punch. These are then stored in hessian sacks, stencilled with huge brushes and black ink. It is not commonly known that the two spices come from the same plant. A London bureaucrat caused great hilarity among the estate workers when he sent notice that the international market price of mace was on the increase and that of nutmeg decreasing and so cultivators would be advised to grow more of the first and hold on the latter. The two biggest nutmeg factories are in Gouyave and Grenville and they are well worth a visit, *open weekdays* (*see* p.138).

Another tree seen all over the island is the **cocoa** tree, *theobroma* or 'Food of the Gods', with hand-sized, purple pods sprouting indiscriminately from trunk and branches. They grow in cocoa walks, as the valley plantations were called, alternate male and female trees up to 30ft high, which go on producing for up to a hundred years, usually in the shade of the much larger immortelle tree, famed for its orange blooms. The pods are collected and broken open to reveal a (delicious) white sticky-sweet gel and up to thirty cocoa beans. The beans are fermented, piled into a wooden sweating box with a little water and turned regularly, and the white pulp degrades. Next the brown beans are laid out on to huge trays, or *boucans*, where they are dried in the sun, again constantly being turned, or 'danced', by the workers, who shuffle through them in lines. At this stage they begin to smell of bitter unsweetened cocoa. From here they are exported, as Grenada has no large processing plant. For local consumption though, some beans are processed and the oily product is rolled into sticks, which can be grated into boiling water to make cocoa for breakfast.

Other spices cultivated in Grenada are **cinnamon** bark, bundles of which can be bought in the markets rolled up in pink ribbon, **cloves** and **pimento** or **allspice**, so-called because it tastes like cinnamon, clove and nutmeg all at once (outside Jamaica, Grenada is the only island in the Caribbean in which it grows). **Ginger**, **bay leaves** and **vanilla** are also grown. Many are used in confectionery and the flavouring of food or as a preservative. Apart from local use for their alternative medicinal properties (bay rum and lemon grass are used to quell fevers, and corilie for hypertension; oil of ginger is said to reduce pain), many are exported for use in the pharmaceutical industry.

Buses run all the main routes in Grenada and can be flagged down from the roadside with a frantic downward-pointing finger. Rap on the metalwork when you want to get off. On board they are quite crowded and often they give you a good introduction to local music (though this has quietened down a bit recently). They leave from the main Market Square on the Esplanade side of town, starting at dawn and running until about 7 in the evening and infrequently into the night. After the run to church on Sundays, services are less frequent. Some prices are: **St George's** to Gouyave—EC$3, Grenville—EC$4.50 and to Sauteurs—EC$5. To the Grand Anse area and to the top of the L'Anse aux Epines road, the ride costs EC$1.25 and buses run frequently.

The alternative is to go by **taxi**, which is very expensive but easily arranged at a hotel, in town or at the major beaches. Often the drivers are a mine of information and are happy to give you an impromptu tour. Sample rates, set by the Grenada Board of Tourism, are: from **St George's** to Grand Anse—US$7, L'Anse aux Epines—US$12, to Point Salines Airport—US$12, to the Grand Etang—US$30 return, and to Gouyave and Dougaldston—US$40 return. To hire a taxi by the hour costs US$15 and drivers are available for a day's outing. The Grenada Hotels Taxi Drivers Association can be contacted on ✆ 444 4882 and Grencab on ✆ 444 4444.

Car hire is another possibility and a good way to see the island if you are prepared to brave the vagaries of the Grenadian road and can remember to keep to the left. You will need a visitor's licence, which can be bought from the police at the fire station on the Carenage, or from the the rental companies, on presentation of a valid licence from home, for EC$30. Rental cars, from about US$45 per day with taxes on top, are available from Spice Isle Rentals, the Avis rental in St George's (✆ 440 3936, 🖃 440 9009), jeeps also available, David's Car Rentals (✆ 444 3399, 🖃 444 5777), SR Car Rentals (✆ 444 3222, 🖃 444 3639) and Maitland's Motor Rentals (✆ 444 4022, 🖃 440 4119), which also rents out motorbikes.

Beaches

Grenada has plenty of beaches—true Caribbean idylls mounded with silken white sand, and tiny secluded coves bristling with coconut palms that are so typical of the mountainous Windward Islands. Grand Anse is the best known, but there are more secluded strands beyond, towards the western tip of the island.

best beaches

Grand Anse: Two miles of pristine sand where many hotels are located, *see* pp.141–3.

Morne Rouge Bay: Sometimes known as BBC Beach after a defunct discotheque, an attractive stretch of sand in a deep bay with a perfect sunset view most of the year, with two delightful coves, **Dr Groom** and **Magazine Beach,** beyond it.

L'Anse aux Epines: Another popular beach (when spoken, it sounds something more like 'lansapeen'), on the south coast to the south of Grand Anse.

Westerhall Point, **La Sagesse**, **Bacolet Bay** and **Telescope Beach** (near Grenville): These are among the underdeveloped beaches to be found among the finger-like protrusions of the southeastern coast.

Bathway Beach: At the northeastern tip of the island, looking out into the Atlantic. Safe for swimming because it has an offshore reef, but the water at nearby **Levera Beach** is rougher. Take a picnic to this area.

Palmiste Bay, Grand Mal Bay: The Grenadians' favourite stretches, on the west coast.

beach bars

There are some good seaside haunts with secluded bars where you can spend an excellent day sunning and snorkelling. Two of the nicest are on the south-western peninsula, set in high-sided, steep-walled coves: one is the **Aquarium** (✆ 444 1410), just beyond the airport. There is a neat and pretty dining room on an open veranda with pastas and sandwiches for a lazy lunch retreat and some limited watersports. Not far off, **Dr Groom's Café** is also on a superb strip of sand; lower-key, but a nice shady spot among the trees; also some watersports. On the south coast there is a quiet and charming bar and restaurant in the trees at **La Sagesse Bay**, also ideal for a day out in the isolated southeast. Transfers, lunch and a guided walk through the local woodlands for about US$30 (✆ 444 6458). If you are travelling independently there is another bar in **Petit Bacaye** nearby, which is set in a charming cove.

On **Grand Anse** there are any number of hotel and beach bars to retreat to: **Cotbam** is curiously contained within a wall, so the smaller **Umbrella Beach House**, under the police station next door, is a preferable spot for a burger and a beer. In the next bay, on BBC Beach is **Sur le Mer** bar, an ideal liming spot with a cracking view of the sunset through the fishnets and shutters.

Flora and Fauna

Like the other Windward Islands, much of the interior of Grenada is too wild and remote to be inhabited and so there are large tracts of rainforest that are untouched, but which you can explore by a series of trails (many start out from the Grand Etang in the National Park, where no building is allowed anyway). You will see huge gommier and mahogany trees, grappled by creeping vines and lianas that threaten to throttle the path, and if you go higher, beyond the montane forest into the elfin woodland, there are stunted trees and ferns. Living in the forest are a few animals, including mona monkeys, opossum, a species of nine-banded armadillo and many birds, including tanagers and the odd hawk. The Grenadian national bird is the endemic and endangered Grenada dove, of which less than 100 are thought to exist. There are a number of mangrove areas in Grenada, including Levera in the northeast and La Sagesse estuary in the southeast, which have an entirely different bird life. Here you may see coots and flycatchers and the more traditional seabirds such as pelicans and boobies. The national flower of Grenada is the bougainvillea, which you will see around hotels all over the island.

If you wish to go walking on a tour of island wildlife, you can find knowledgeable guides at the Tourist Board (✆ 440 2001) or the Grand Etang National Forest office (✆ 440 6160).

St George's

The capital of Grenada is the prettiest harbour town in the Caribbean. Stacked on an amphitheatrical hillside are lines of warehouses, homes and churches with ochre-tiled and red tin roofs that glow in the evening light against the rich tropical green of Grenada's slopes.

St George's Harbour

St George's is still very much a working port and many ships put into the harbour—cargo vessels, cruise ships, fishing boats and water taxis and of course the brightly painted schooners from the Grenadines which you will see tied up on the wharves of the Carenage.

Named after King George III, the old parts of the town date from the late 18th century, when the original buildings were destroyed in fires. It is sprinkled with fine old creole houses, built of brick in soft shades of rose, yellow and beige and embellished with elaborate ironwork balconies and the occasional porch that was used to keep sedan chair passengers from getting wet in the rain. St George's is built over the backbone of a hill and is split into two main halves: the Carenage, on the inner harbour, and the Esplanade, which fronts on to the Caribbean Sea. The two sides are linked by a network of steep cobbled streets and stepped alleys. At Carnival, when the costumed masqueraders wind through the streets of St George's, the steel band floats have to be winched up the cobbled streets and then held back from running away down the other side.

Once, St George's Harbour was an inland lake, but now it can take ocean-going vessels. It was the crater of a volcano, from which the sides have crumbled. It is extinct, but not entirely dormant, as was shown by a curious and alarming incident in 1867, when volcanic activity was felt throughout the Caribbean. At five in the afternoon the level of the water in the Carenage suddenly dropped by 5ft and the Green Hole started to bubble and steam, letting off sulphurous gases. Moments later, the level of the sea rose to about 4ft above the normal, only to be sucked down and to rise again a number of times.

The statue on the waterfront at the head of the harbour, a replica of Christ of the Deep, was dedicated to the people of Grenada after their efforts to save the passengers of a cruise liner, the *Bianca C*, which burned in Grenada harbour in 1961. Nearby, the island's British heritage is retained in the red telephone boxes. There are plenty of cafés and bars around the waterfront where you can catch a drink and a rest when your feet overheat from walking around the town. One of the best views of the town can be had from a water-taxi trip across the harbour (*price EC$5*).

The **Carenage** is the centrepiece of the town, the very attractive curved waterfront lined with old mercantile buildings which are still used by businesses today. One of the finest and oldest creole houses is the former French military barracks on Young Street, now home to the **Grenada National Museum** (*open weekdays 9–4.30, Sat 10–1.30; small adm*). Here Arawak petroglyphs are on view, alongside Empress Josephine's marble bathtub (she spent her childhood on the nearby island of Martinique), copper kettles, a rum still from the days of sugar, old island maps and some descriptions of the flora and fauna. Worth a visit.

Forts and churches dominate the heights of St George's and many of them stand on Church Street, the ridge road that gives on to both sides of the town. Close to Fort George, which overlooks the harbour mouth, is the **Scots Kirk**, a Presbyterian church erected in 1831. A little farther up is the **St George's Parish Anglican Church**, rebuilt in 1825 on the site of an original 1763 French Roman Catholic church. It contains plaques commemorating the victims of the Brigand's War, or Fédon's Rebellion, and the 51 hostages, including the Governor, Ninian Home, who were murdered by the 'execrable banditti'. Still on Church Street is **York House**, the Grenadian House of Parliament. But the best position of all is commanded by the **Roman Catholic Cathedral** (many Grenadians are still Catholic from French days), built in 1818.

The other half of St George's is the **Esplanade** or Bay Town, which looks on to the Caribbean Sea. It was hard work getting over the ridge to the market from the Carenage and so at the end of the 19th century a tunnel was constructed, linking the two. The Sendall tunnel, named after the Governor, is over 100 yards long and still used now for heavy traffic.

The Esplanade has lines of old warehouses overlooking the sea and on the waterfront itself is the **fish market**, alive when the catch is brought in at the end of the day. The main St George's **market** is a couple of blocks inland from the Esplanade, on open ground between Granby and Hillsborough Streets. There is a typical Caribbean ironwork-covered market building, but most of the activity takes place out on the square, where golf umbrellas shelter the vendors and their produce—root vegetables and tropical fruits (and of course Grenadian spices)—from the sun and from passing rainstorms. The best day to visit is Saturday, in the morning, but it is lively on any weekday morning (it is quiet on Sundays). If you have not been waylaid already by the spice women who ply the streets of St George's, then at the back of the square on Grenville Street you can visit the **Minor Spices Society**, which smells of the cinnamon, cloves and allspice on sale here.

Close by is the **Yellow Poui Art Gallery** on Cross Street. Named after a Caribbean tree, it features West Indian art, particularly impressive for its primitivist paintings, and West Indian scenes by foreign painters and sculptors. Look out for Grenadians Michael Paryag and Elinus Cato, and Carriacouans Canute Caliste and Frankie Francis.

Only two forts remain of what was once a protective ring of defences on the heights above St George's. **Fort George** dominates the harbour mouth, with a fine view of the Carenage and of the open sea, and it is now the main St George's police station. Constructed in 1706, it spent a spell more recently as Fort Rupert (named after the father of Maurice Bishop who was killed in a riot in 1974). It was here that Maurice Bishop himself and his colleagues were shot on 19 October 1983. Cannon still poke over the battlements and underground there is a warren of tunnels and caverns, supposedly leading to a series of underground passageways from one fort to the next (now blocked off). Tours are possible.

On the rising ground that forms the backdrop of St George's harbour, among the homes of prosperous Grenadians, is **Marryshow House**, a creole building that was once the home of the Grenadian political leader and architect of the West Indies Federation, Theophilus A. Marryshow. Now part of the University of the West Indies, it does not have much for visitors to see inside, but it is a pretty creole house with gingerbread trimmings and slanted louvres. Higher still is **Government House**, with a fine view over the harbour and town. Built in 1802 of brick with arches and dormer windows, it is the official residence of the

Governor General and it cannot actually be visited. The most spectacular view of the town can be seen after a stiff climb up **Richmond Hill**, which commands the harbour and the coast as far as Point Salines in the southwest. Once there were four forts in all, started by the French after they captured the island in 1779 and completed by the British. Fort Frederick is in reasonable repair and there is a campaign to restore Fort Matthew.

There are two botanical gardens in St George's. At the foot of Richmond Hill, on the outskirts of the town, are the old **Botanical Gardens**, established in 1886. They are a little tatty now, just a small collection of trees and shrubs around the war memorial. A better bet are the **Bay Gardens** behind Richmond Hill (*open daylight hours; adm*), which are set in the grounds of a former sugar mill, and where you will see a huge range of Caribbean flora—vivid blooms of purple, pink and scarlet among the endless shades of green. It is well worth finding a guide to tell you about the many species on display.

The West Coast

The Grenadian coastline is a series of headlands and bays, spurs of land thrown off from the volcanic peaks and valleys carved out by rivers, where Grenada's spice plantations have grown. The road follows the coastline, all hairpins and switchbacks and overhung by cliffs, initially laid out by the French in the 18th century. The names recount the island's mixed history— Happy Hill, Molinière, Beauséjour Bay and Halifax Harbour.

From St George's the Esplanade road leads up the west coast, passing the ruin of the old communal lavatory on the bayfront and on to **Queen's Park** on the outskirts of the town, site of the new National Stadium and general sports ground. Inland from Concord, following the Black Bay River upstream among the nutmeg and cocoa plantations, are the **Concord Falls**, a series of three waterfalls lost in the forested mountains. It is possible to drive to the lowest one, but the other two must be reached on foot: the first takes 25 minutes, and the next is 1½-hour's walk. However, each fall has a pool in which you can swim after the climb. In high season you will probably not be alone, but it is a pleasant walk. It is even possible to walk up to Grand Etang (about 5 hours' climb). Back on the coast, **Black Bay** is named after its appearance, which is black volcanic rather than white coral sand.

Just outside Gouyave is the **Dougaldston Estate**, a charming old plantation of clapboard and tin-roofed buildings and dilapidated farm machinery, where cocoa and nutmeg are grown among allspice, tonka beans and coffee. In years past the estate would ring to the sound of violins as the workers 'danced' the cocoa beans to dry them evenly in the *boucans*, shuffling in lines and turning the cocoa beans with their feet. The *boucans,* vast trays that are pulled out from beneath the building to catch the sun, are on wheels so that they can be rushed underneath in case of rain. In the main building, heavy with the smells of cinnamon, cloves and nutmeg, the old processes can be seen, worked by the Grenadian women. It is possible to buy the spices on display.

Gouyave (French for 'guava') is a little farther along the coast. Set on a promontory, the town's old creole houses are past their best now, but it is alluring in its faded prosperity. Travelling in the forties, Patrick Leigh Fermor came across a sweepstake here, in which the first prize was a free funeral for the ticket holder or for any friend or relation. The biggest building in Gouyave is the **Grenada Nutmeg Cooperative Association**—floors full of sacks, tea chests and machinery, the air redolent with the sweet-spice smell of nutmeg.

Set on a sweeping bay on the north coast is the village of **Sauteurs**, the island's third-largest town and the scene of one of the saddest moments in Grenada's history, when the retreating Caribs were surrounded by the French troops and reputedly threw themselves to their death in the sea rather than be killed. And so, in French, the place became known as *Le morne des Sauteurs*, Leaper's Hill.

Towards the northeastern point of the island is **Levera Bay**, a strip of golden sand with fine views of the offshore islands. Nearby is Levera Lake, an extinct volcanic crater like Lake Antoine to the south, and at Bedford Point itself are the ruins of an old fort.

The South Coast

With its white sand beaches so close to St George's, the southwestern tip of Grenada is the hotel heartland. The countryside is flatter and drier than the island interior and most of Grenada's sugar was grown here. The southern coastline is a long succession of deep bays and promontories, where many wealthy Grenadians build their homes and where cruising yachts put in for shelter. Farther east the coast becomes more remote, but judging by the names it has a romantic history—*Morne Delice, Mamma Cannes, Perdmontemps*, and *Après tout.*

A couple of miles south of St George's, **Grand Anse** is the most popular beach on the island, with about 2 miles of blinding-white, satin-soft sand. A number of hotels front on to the sand, but the beach does not usually become too crowded. The area has seen considerable building in the last few years, both hotels and private houses. Farther round the point are a number of small bays, pleasant and secluded, though the peace will occasionally be interrupted by planes passing overhead as they come in to Point Salines airport at the island's southwestern tip. On the airport road you will see a monument to the American veterans killed during the Grenada invasion in 1983. Just along the southern coast is another popular bay, once called Prickly Bay by the English, but now usually known by its French equivalent, **L'Anse aux Epines**. It has some fine hotels and apartments, spread out on the thin strip of sand at the head of the bay and on the clifftops. Visible out to sea south of Grenada is Glover Island, operated as a whaling station in 1925 by the Norwegians.

Calvigny Point was the site of the main camp of the People's Revolutionary Army in the time of Maurice Bishop, and the area saw considerable military activity during the American invasion. Beyond the charming fishing village of Woburn, Fort Jeudy, now an expensive housing estate, speaks of earlier conflicts, when a fort used to guard the entrance to Egmont Harbour. A little farther on is the **Westerhall Rum Distillery**, the producer of light and dark rums, including jack-iron, an almost mystical drink in which ice sinks. It is possible to make a tour of the distillery.

The coast road winds through the former plantations and past secluded beaches such as **La Sagesse Bay** and **Bacolet Bay** until it reaches **Marquis**, just south of Grenville. This settlement was the first target in Fédon's rebellion, where the English inhabitants were dragged from their beds and killed.

Over the Grand Etang to the East Coast

To a Grenadian, 'over the Grand Etang' means going over the mountains and through the centre of the island, on roads that wind and switchback as they climb steadily into Grenada's staggeringly lush interior of mountains dressed in ferns, grasses and elfin woodland. The best road to take from St George's goes along the St John's River, past the stadium in Queen's Park, but it is also possible to go via Government House and left at the roundabout. From here you climb to the oddly named Snug Corner and eventually to the Grand Etang itself. Remember to look behind as you climb for some of the island's most spectacular views, as far as Point Salines in the southwest. Just off the road are **Annandale Falls**, a 30ft cascade (only really impressive in the rainy season) that races into a bathing pool, surrounded by tropical greenery. The valley was the scene of considerable fighting in the 1983 invasion.

At the summit of the range is the **Grand Etang** (Great Pond), another extinct volcano crater. Set in a Government Reserve, its water is cold and metallic blue (estimates of its depth vary from 14ft to fathomless). The **Grand Etang Forest Centre** (*open Mon–Sat 8–4; adm free*) has illustrations of local flora and fauna and a description of the Caribbean's geological past: two chains of volcanic islands created by the shifting of the Atlantic and Caribbean tectonic plates. There are also short walking tours around the Grand Etang and into the rainforest in the mountains, where you will see explosions of bamboo, tree-top ferns and creeping vines. You might also see birds like Grenada's hummingbirds, tanagers and the occasional cuckoo, as well as armadillos and opossums.

Some way off is **Morne Fédon**, also called Mt Qua Qua. Much of the fighting in the 1795 rebellion led by Fédon, who owned the estate at Belvidere just below the mountain, took place in this area. The mountain stronghold was situated on the three spurs of the peak, each named after one of their slogans, *Champ la Liberté, Champ l'Egalité* and *Champ la Mort*. It is a couple of hours' hike to get there. Also in this area are the two Mt Carmel falls, cascades which drop 70ft into icy rockpools.

Descending to the windward side of Grenada the road passes among tiny villages clinging to the hillsides down to the cocoa-receiving station at Carlton, where the beans are processed and prepared for shipment. After a short walk off the road in St Margaret's you will find the Seven Sisters Falls, worth a detour for a swim, though you should ask permission to walk over the private land. Eventually you arrive at the coast at **Grenville**, set on a large bay sheltered by reefs. It is still referred to as La Baye, as it is known in French creole. There are a few solid stone structures that speak of its former position of importance, the 'second city' to St George's. The countryside here is known as Grenada's *lifeblood*, the island's breadbasket, and it is dotted with plantation houses. In the town itself, the covered market and fish market are the centres of town activity. Graceful Grenadian sloops can often be seen at the water-front, calling in on their trips between the Grenadines and Trinidad. There is also a nutmeg factory in Grenville that is worth a visit (*see* 'Gouyave', p.138).

North of here is the **River Antoine Rum Distillery**, which functions using old-time Caribbean machinery, its crushing gear still driven by an old waterwheel. You can sample the fearsome rum they produce. Lake Antoine is the crater of a volcano reckoned to be extinct, though underground forces are still at work just beyond here, at the mineral springs, which emit wisps of sulphurous gas from hot springs. Further on, the **Levera National Park** is best known as a picnic area by the Grenadians at the weekends. You may well see doves in the woods and oystercatchers along the shore.

On the road to the north-coast town of Sauteurs is one of Grenada's most charming spots, Betty Mascoll's **Morne Fendue**, an old plantation house full of family memorabilia. It is an enchanting place to visit. Nutmeg shells laid out on the drive give off a heady smell of spice as you drive up. There are three rooms for rent, but it is best known for its lunch, traditional

Caribbean callaloo and island specialities (the pepperpot has been on the go for 14 years, since the much older one was interrupted by the 1983 troubles), taken on the veranda with fine views of the Grenadian landscape.

🕿 (1 473)–

Where to Stay

Most of Grenada's hotels are to be found in the southwestern corner of the island between St George's and the airport. The island has a good range of accommodation, with the large, brisk and humming resorts typical of Caribbean tourism at the moment, all air-conditioning, jacuzzis and satellite televisions, but also some small places, with a little more personal character. If general life in Grenada is expensive, the island offers a good range of places to stay at the lower end of the market. The Grenada Hotel Association has a free booking number in the States (🕿 (1 800) 322 1753). All hotels have to charge an 8% government tax on the bill and most will also add 10% service as well.

There is a number of villas for rent on the island, many of them to be found in the southwestern corner of the island (True Blue, L'Anse aux Epines, Westerhall and Grand Anse). Contact Villas of Grenada, PO Box 218 (🕿 444 1896, 🖷 444 4529) and Grenada Realtors Limited, PO Box 534, St George's (🕿 444 4255, 🖷 444 2832).

luxury–expensive

The most comfortable and elegant hotel in Grenada is the very quiet **Calabash Hotel**, PO Box 382 (🕿 444 4334, 🖷 444 5050, UK res 🕿 (01778) 347512, 🖷 380815, US res 🕿 (1 800) 528 5835) at the head of Prickly Bay (L'Anse aux Epines). There are 30 breezy suites (each with a private pool or a whirlpool) set in an arc of stark white and cottages with shingle roofs that surround an expanse of lawn with coconut palms and calabash trees and give on to the pleasant beach. Inside, the rooms are bright and white in modern Caribbean style, with wicker furniture, a/c and fans, baths, mini-bars and hairdriers. Breakfast is served on your balcony and there is complimentary afternoon tea. The **Spice Island Beach Resort**, PO Box 6, St George's (🕿 444 4258, 🖷 444 4807; *spiceisl@caribsurf.com*; *www.cpscaribnet .com/ads/spiceisl.html*), has pride of place on Grand Anse beach. There are 56 extremely comfortable suites, some right on the mounded sand, others tucked away in their own small walled enclosure with their own pool in the garden behind. There are a weights room and watersports, all modern comforts. **Secret Harbour Resort**, PO Box 11 (🕿 444 4439, 🖷 444 4819, UK booking through the Moorings, who own the hotel, 🕿 (0800) 220 763), lives up to its name; it is a reclusive string of 20 villas overlooking Mt Hartman Bay at the far end of L'Anse aux Epines. The elegant arches of the main house are inlaid with mosaics and the roof topped with terracotta tiles, like a Spanish colonial palace above the harbour. The beach is uninspiring, but there is a pool on the heights and there is a view from your four-poster bed to the bay below, where watersports are available. No children. You can combine tailor-made sailing trips to the Grenadines with a stay in the hotel. **Twelve Degrees North**, PO Box 241 (🕿/🖷 444 4580), is another extremely fine retreat on L'Anse aux Epines Bay, a collection of one- and two-bedroom apartments on the clifftops with fully equipped kitchens. So named because it lies exactly 12 degrees north of the equator, it takes a maximum of 20 people, children not allowed. There is a pool and palm-thatch bar on the beach below.

Grenada also has some bigger beach hotels with international standards of comfort, which include the **Rex Grenadian** (✆ 444 333, ✐ 444 1111), a mock-Mediterranean beach resort, 212 rooms, and **La Source**, (✆ 444 2556, ✐ 444 2561) an all-inclusive resort with an all-over-body holiday agenda (a never-ending diet of spa treatments, light cuisine and watersports). The most preferable is probably the **Grenada Renaissance Resort**, PO Box 441 (✆ 444 4371, ✐ 444 4800), which is set in manicured gardens right on Grand Anse beach. It has a busy feel with comfortable rooms, air-conditioning, television. The **Flamboyant Hotel**, PO Box 214 (✆ 444 4247, ✐ 444 1234; *flambo@caribsurf.com*; *www.cpscaribnet.com/ads/flambo /flambo.html*), sits on the rising ground behind Grand Anse at the far end of the beach. It has a variety of rooms, suites and apartments, the nicest of which are set in the older villas (fans and wooden floors) rather than the newer air-conditioned blocks. All have balconies that view St George's in the distance.

moderate

A nice retreat tucked away in the southwestern peninsula is the small and personable **True Blue Inn**, PO Box 308 (✆ 444 2000, ✐ 444 1247, *trueblue@caribsurf.com*; *www.cpscaribnet.com/ads/trueblue/trueblue*), where the three two-bedroom cottages and four apartments are festooned with bougainvillea. The rooms are comfortable with a good view from the pool and terrace restaurant. There's a passable beach nearby, scuba on the premises. If you are happy to cater for yourself, the comfortable, older-style Caribbean apartments at **Lance aux Epines Cottages**, PO Box 187 (✆ 444 4565, ✐ 444 2802, *cottages@caribsurf.com*, *www.spiceisl.com/cottages/*) offer an excellent deal and comfort in L'Anse aux Epines Bay. Eleven self-catering units in one and two-bedroom cottages with ceiling fans and tile floors (a/c in the bedrooms) are set in a sandy garden above the beach. It's a low-key hotel with no dining room or pool, but good value, with several restaurants nearby.

There are two small getaways hidden in coves in the southeast of Grenada which are well worth considering if you want the best in island charm and isolation. **La Sagesse Nature Centre**, PO Box 44, St George's (✆/✐ 444 6458) is set in the miniature grandeur of an estate house with an arched façade and curious staircase hidden away in tropical greenery just behind the beach. Just four rooms in the estate house and four other rooms in two outbuildings, fan-ventilated (one a/c), and with a charming bar and restaurant in the trees giving on to a nice beach in a classic bay enclosed by headlands; very quiet, and at the lower end of moderate. Not far off, **Petit Bacaye**, PO Box 655 (✆ 443 2902, ✐ 443 2552) is in a different style, with a collection of palm-thatched cottages scattered around a sandy garden of crotons, oleander and bougainvillea in its own bay. It is small, with just two one-bedroom and two two-bedroom cottages (kitchenettes, small porches, mosquito nets over the beds and fine showers built in stone) but very calm and charming. There is a small bar restaurant at the heart of it, where you can get the chef to cook up the fresh fish landed each day by the fishermen who work in the bay. In the north of the island is **Morne Fendue** (✆ 442 9330), also known as Betty Mascoll's Plantation House. The atmosphere is that of a welcoming family home on an old West Indian plantation estate. There are only three rooms, though there are always plenty of people passing by for the renowned Morne Fendue lunch.

A small hotel which retains a certain older Caribbean charm and style in some of its rooms is the **Grand View Inn**, PO Box 614 (✆ 444 4984, ✉ 444 1512, *dovetail@ caribsurf.com, www.caribbean-connexion.com/hotels/granview.htm*). It is set in the former Soviet Embassy compound, complete with guard-post at the entrance, and has a magnificent view as the name suggests, to St George's and the mountains beyond. A mix of large and breezy older rooms and more modern air-conditioned ones; all have kitchenettes and cable TV; 30 rooms in all. There is a commanding view from the terrace of the restaurant, Pirate's Cove, the former embassy building. The **Mount Helicon Guest House** (✆ 440 2444, ✉ 440 7168) is set in its own gardens on the crest of a hill high above St George's. The six rooms are set in the nice old wooden estate house and attached buildings. It is quite far from the activity of the town and the beach, but there is often a crowd in the restaurant in the main house.

At **Roydon's Guest House** (✆ 444 4476, ✉ 444 2444) you can find a comfortable and simple room within a shout of Grand Anse beach. Just six rooms. You might also try **RSR Apartments** (✆ 440 3381) not far off, with full kitchens and a sitting room; both clean and cheap. And there are a couple of very cheap travellers' haunts in town: **Simeon's Inn** (✆ 440 2537) is on Green Street, nine rooms, fan-ventilated, shared baths, bed and breakfast with an excellent view over the town from the communal balcony. Also **Mitchell's Guest House** (✆ 440 2803) on Tyrrel Street, which has eleven rooms sharing bathrooms. If you are exploring the island there are simple reliable stopovers in Victoria, at the **Victoria Hotel** (✆ 444 9367) on Queen St, and, in Grenville, at the **Grenada Rainbow Inn** (✆ 442 7714), which has self-contained units with a local restaurant.

✆ *(1 473)–*   *Eating Out*

It might be that the Grenadians have retained their interest in and flair for cooking from the days when the French owned the island. At any rate, the abundance of island produce makes Grenada a good place for classic West Indian fare: callaloo, breadfruit, christophene and green fig, as well as the more exotic *tatou* (armadillo) and *manicou* (opossum). There is 'international fare' on offer, often in hotels, for those who feel too far from home in the West Indies, but Grenada has plenty of charming restaurants, often taking advantage of good settings, perhaps a view over the Carenage in town or on a bay and beach of the southwest peninsula. Eating out in Grenada is pretty expensive at the moment, and then you can expect a service charge of 10% plus 8% VAT to be added to your bill. Categories are arranged according to the price of a main course: *expensive*—EC$50 and above; *moderate*—EC$20–50; *cheap*—less than EC$20.

expensive

Canboulay (✆ 444 4401) has the top position both for its cuisine and for its setting (looking over Grand Anse and St George's beyond). A strong theme of the West Indies and particularly Carnival runs through the restaurant, in the bright colours of the dining room, the carnival masks, the names of the dishes and the adventurous Caribbean cuisine. Soucouyant and Shango cocktails to start, *tamboo bamboo* (steak and shrimp kebabs in tamarind and peanut sauces) or an untraditional Caribbean callaloo (not a soup, but a coconut milk crepe with creamed crab filling and a puréed callaloo sauce) and *parang poulet,* chicken breast stuffed with sweet potatoes served with a citrus sauce. Daily changing à la carte and set menus (EC$75–110 including starter, salad or a sorbet, main course, pudding, coffee and petits fours), occasional exotic buffets, dinner except Sun, lunch à la carte.

Coconuts Beach restaurant (✆ 444 4644) has a nice setting in a pretty wooden house at the head of Grand Anse Bay. You dine outside on the sand under palm thatch parasols or inside in full view of the working kitchen, which produces Caribbean and French creole fare—chicken breast *à la sauce féroce* or catch of the day in lemon butter, Nantais butter or mango chutney. Simpler food is available during the day. At the other end of Grand Anse Beach you might try **Tabanca** (✆ 444 1300) which is set in a pretty green courtyard just above the sea. Trusty West Indian fare prepared and presented nicely. Mainly fish and seafood: spicy conch or flying fish to start, followed by spiny crab and a chocolate mousse.

In St George's there is a charming restaurant in an old plantation estate setting at **Mt Helicon** (✆ 444 2444), which as the name implies, is set on a point high above the town. The dining room has bare floorboards and chichi drapes and the fare is up-market West Indian: pumpkin and spinach soup, followed by pan-fried flying fish or sautéed mahi-mahi, rounded off with one of a selection of Cuban cigars. There is an excellent setting at the **Aquarium** (✆ 444 1410), which is really more than a beach bar by night, tucked away in the southwest peninsula beyond the airport. You dine in an open-air gallery supported by brightly coloured pillars just above the waves. In l'Anse aux Epines you will find two eateries with international fare and a passing foreign trade: the **Boatyard** (✆ 444 4662), which is set on an open veranda over-looking the yachts at anchor; steak and fish, salads and burgers; and the **Red Crab**, with pub-style décor inside, tropical garden outside.

moderate

Pirate's Cove is set high on the hill in the former Russian Embassy building, an attractive wooden building with a fantastic view from the veranda. Now it is a pirate theme restaurant, but not too bad for that. West Indian and international fare: plantain fritters followed by fish *dango* cooked in a ginger and coconut sauce. For a classic West Indian meal you can go to **Mamma's** (✆ 440 1459), on Lagoon Road heading south out of town. Sadly the inspirational Mamma has died, but her daughter has continued the tradition. The Special (the only order) brings a compendium of local dishes

Grenada Directory

getting there

Grenada has reasonable international air links, both from Europe and from North America, arriving at Point Salines airport in the southwestern tip of the island. The airport has certainly opened the island up for visitors, whatever its military applications might have been—it was one of the stated reasons for the American invasion. If there is no direct flight, it is nearly always possible to make a connection the same day, via Barbados, Trinidad or St Lucia. Departure tax EC$25 and a security charge of EC$10 are payable by all adults who stay more than 24 hours; children aged 5–11 years pay half as much; under 5s are exempt.

(upwards of 16, according to season), from oildown (four or five vegetables boiled in coconut milk), to yam, breadfruit, turtle, booby (a local seabird) and fish broth (one of a number of local aphrodisiacs), followed by a lime or passion fruit sorbet. Specials EC$45, plus taxes, reservations before 3pm—come hungry.

St George's has a number of restaurants and bars that take best advantage of a setting on the harbour (as well as snack bars for a lunchtime roti and a juice). Ever-popular is **Tropicana** (℗ 440 1586) on a veranda right on the road into town, opposite the cinema, serving trusty international fare from fried rice to shrimp and lambi specials, rotis to hamburgers. The **Portofino** restaurant is very visible with its red, white and green colouring. There's pizza and pasta, fish, clams in a cream sauce and key lime pie, all in a pleasant upstairs dining room. **Delicious Landing** serves Caribbean fare with an emphasis on fish and seafood.

cheap

Nutmeg is well worth a stop for a juice and a commanding view of the harbour from upstairs; simple platters followed by nutmeg ice cream if you actually want a meal. **Rudolf's** also attracts a lively crowd, with pub-style benches and an egg-box ceiling; steaks, seafood and omelettes. The **Carenage Cafe** is another nice stopover for a juice and a croissant, a salad or a sandwich, right on the waterfront road.

Bars and Nightlife

Most of restaurants have bars which are worth investigating, but a lively crowd of medical students and visitors turns up for pool and general drinking at **Casablanca** in Grand Anse; liveliest on a Friday night. For a sunset drink any night it is hard to beat the **Sur la Mer** bar on BBC Beach, beyond Grand Anse. There are also plenty of bars in town where you can join the locals in a game of dominoes and a white rum (Clarke's Court of varying percentage proof): **007**, the floating bar on the Carenage, can get quite busy, and there is **Aboo's** nearby, and **Ye Olde Farm House** opposite the Yellow Poui Gallery.

Nightlife in Grenada is generally pretty quiet, but a number of bars and hotels have a special night and some stage entertainment during the season. **Fantazia 2001** over in Morne Rouge can be lively at weekends and in Grand Anse **Cotbam** has been known to pull a crowd in its club **African Nites**. For something very local you can try **Le Sucrier** at the Sugar Mill south of Grand Anse which can get pretty wild (Wed–Sat) or the **Island View** in Woburn.

℗ (1 473)–

By air from the UK: One direct flight a week on British Airways (℗ 440 2796) from Gatwick and there is a weekly flight on Caledonian (same ℗). There are no direct scheduled flights from **Europe**, but there is a weekly charter service from Milan.

By air from the USA: American Airlines (℗ 444 2222) flies daily to their hub at San Juan in Puerto Rico, and BWIA (℗ 444 4134) has twice-weekly flights from Miami and New York.

By air from other Caribbean Islands: LIAT (℗ 440 2797) connects Grenada with Barbados, Tobago, St Vincent and several of the Grenadines, including Carriacou and Union Island. Airlines of Carriacou (℗ 444 3549, ✆ 444 2898) hop through the Grenadines as far as St Vincent. BWIA flies between Grenada and Trinidad and Aerotuy (✆ 444 4732) fly twice weekly from Margarita off the Venezuelan coast. Charter planes are available through Helenair (✆ 444 4101) and Region Air (✆ 444 1117, ✆ 444 1114).

By sea: There are many ferry services each week between Grenada and its major Grenadine island Carriacou, often continuing on to Petite Martinique. The hydrofoil *Osprey* (✆ 407 0740) makes the trip most days in 2hrs. Cheaper and slower boats also make the run most days. Flexible schedule: check at the Carenage in St George's or the Tourist Board. There are occasional (cargo) boats to Trinidad which may allow you to travel as a paying passenger.

tourist information

In **Britain**, the Grenada Tourist Office is at 1 Collingham Gardens, London SW5 0HW (✆ (0171) 370 5164/5, ✆ 244 0177, *grenada@panther.netmania.co.uk*). In **Europe** contact Johanna-Melber-Weg 12, D-60559 Frankfurt, Germany (✆ (069) 62 92 82, ✆ (069) 62 92 64, *msi-germany@t-online.de*).

In the **USA** you can contact them at 820 Second Avenue, Suite 900D, New York, NY 10017 (✆ (212) 687 9554, ✆ 573 9731 or toll free ✆ (1 800) 927 9554) and in **Canada** at 439 University Avenue, Suite 920, Toronto, Ontario M5G 1Y8 (✆ (416) 595 1339, ✆ 595 8278, *assoc@thermrgroup.ca*). You can get information on the **internet** at Grenada's home page, at *www.interknowledge.com/grenada*.

In Grenada itself, the main **Board of Tourism** (✆ 440 2001, ✆ 440 6637, *caribsurf.com*) is at Burns Point in St George's in the cruise ship terminal area on the Carenage. There is a small office at Point Salines airport (✆ 444 4140), whose staff are helpful with accommodation and advice. Open 8–4 in St George's and 7am–9pm at the airport. The *Grenadian Voice*, the *Informer* and *Grenada Today* are the island's weekly newspapers and they list local events as well as covering Caribbean news. The Grenada Board of Tourism puts out a number of complimentary publications: *Greeting*, a glossy magazine with tourist information and a list of options if you are struck with a shopping crisis; and the pocket-sized *Discover Grenada*. A monthly tourist paper, *Spicy Grenada*, covers current events and activities.

In a **medical emergency**, contact St George's Hospital (✆ 440 2051/2/3).

The **IDD code** for Grenada is ✆ (1 473), followed by a seven-digit number.

festivals

Carnival in Grenada is celebrated in August rather than at the beginning of Lent, but it is still three days of dancing in the streets of St George's with carnival parades, steel bands and calypso singing. If you would like to *play mas* (i.e. buy a costume and *jump up* with the parades), contact the Tourist Board for the name of a band. They also have a *jump-up* on the anniversary of Independence Day, **7 February**. **Easter** sees kite flying and during the year the Grenadian towns celebrate their saints' days with plenty of drinking and dancing as well as cultural displays. It is always worth looking to see if there are any celebrations taking place in **Carriacou** and making your way up there. In **November** is *Extempo*, in which singers ad-lib on subjects given to them moments before, or spar with one another in song. Parang is a special sort of Christmas music.

money

The Grenadian currency is the Eastern Caribbean dollar (shared with a number of other British Commonwealth Caribbean countries), which is fixed to the US dollar at a rate of about EC$2.65 = US$1. It is advisable to be sure which currency you are dealing in, as a bargain may suddenly turn out to be nearly three times better or a taxi fare considerably more expensive. Life in Grenada is pretty expensive at the moment, though good prices can still be found for accommodation.

Banking hours: Mon–Fri, 8–1, some until 2; and Fri 3–5.

Shops: Open weekdays 8–4, Sat 8–noon.

watersports

Sailing: The island's ragged southern coastline has endless coves (though inexperienced sailors are requested not to sail here). From here you can run by St George's and coast north beneath Grenada's towering, rainforested mountains to the Grenadines, where the sea, sand and snorkelling are superb and there are islands with just a few palm trees and swim-up bars. A week-long **Sailing Festival** is held out of Grenada in January or February each year, with competitive and less competitive yachting races around the island, starting as far away as Bequia and Trinidad. There are many other regattas during the year—even an 'End of Hurricane Season' regatta in December—of which the liveliest is probably the Carriacou Regatta in August. The Spice Island Game Fishing Tournament (*℗* 440 2198) is staged in January each year.

> **Charter Companies**
>
> **The Moorings** (*℗* 444 4548, *⊜* 444 4819) in the Mt Hartmann Bay behind L'Anse aux Epines, has the biggest selection of yachts for bareboat charter.
>
> **Seabreeze Yacht Charters** (*℗/⊜* 444 4924) works out of the Spice Island Marine Centre in L'Anse aux Epines, where there is a port of entry.
>
> *Psyche* (*℗* 444 4010) arrange day sails.
>
> **Starwind Enterprises** (*℗* 440 3678).
>
> *Rhum Runner* tour (*℗* 440 2198). For an afternoon of fun with the cruise ship passengers or a rum-and-reggae-soaked sunset cruise.

Deep-sea fishing: Bezo Charters (*℗* 443 5021) or Evans Chartering Services (*℗* 444 4422), will arrange a deep-sea fishing trip, trawling the depths to the west of Grenada. About US$500 a full day, $300 for half a day.

Smaller watersports: It is best to go to Grand Anse, where you can fix up a jetski; try World Wide Watersports (*℗* 444 1339), a flight under a parasail or be dragged around the bay on a bouncy banana. Contact Sky Ride (*℗* 440 1568). Waterskiing, kayaks, small sailing craft and windsurfers are available through the hotel concessionaires.

Scuba diving: Also best arranged at Grand Anse, through Dive Grenada at the Grenada Renaissance Hotel (*℗* 444 4371, *⊜* 444 4800), Grand Anse Aquatics (*℗* 444 4129, *⊜* 444 4808) and Scuba Express (*℗* 444 2133, *⊜* 444 1247; *trueblue@cpsnet.com*) at True Blue on the south shore. Grenada is surrounded by reefs on all sides; some of the better known are Boss Reef and Whibble Reef in the southeast, Shark Reef to the south of the airport and

Molinière Point just north of St George's. You can also dive the *Bianca C*, a 600ft liner which was scuttled after a famous fire in the Carenage and is now thought to be the largest wreck sitting upright in the world. Dive the upper decks and then take a turn around the swimming pool. Single tank dives from about US$45; packages and certification available.

Snorkelling: There are good shallow seascapes in L'Anse aux Epines and at Molinière Point north of St George's.

other sports

Walking: It is well worth taking a walk through the tropical rainforests, perhaps to one of the waterfalls. Henry's Tours (✆ 444 5313) offer well-organized walks, reaching off-beat

Carriacou and Petite Martinique

Carriacou and Petite Martinique, the only two other inhabited islands in the country, lie about 15 miles north of Grenada, at the northern limits of Grenadian territory. Strictly speaking, the border with St Vincent slices the north end off the two islands, but they have not come to blows over it recently.

Among the smaller uninhabited islands are Les Tantes and the Sisters and one that even calls itself London Bridge. The underwater volcano by the name of Kick 'em Jenny, perhaps a corruption of the French *Cay qui me gêne*, is so called because the water around it is renowned for being very rough (sea-sickness pills advised if you go anywhere near it). LIAT pilots who fly over here have reported seeing movement under the water and the seismic instruments in Trinidad regularly detect it. Many reckon that it is growing slowly as it belches and that eventually another Grenadine might appear.

Getting to Carriacou is part of the fun—coasting Grenada's leeward (western) side from St George's gives spectacular views of the fertile slopes that tumble from Mt St Catherine, and then there is a horizon dotted with the Grenadines. It is possible to go by yacht or by the hydrofoil or the ferries that leave from the Carenage, best of all on one of Carriacou's own graceful schooners. If you are travelling on through the Grenadines, boats head for Union Island on Monday and Thursday, about midday (*EC$10 (plus departure tax)*.

Alternatively, go by air and experience Lauriston, one of the Grenadines' gentler airstrips (no mountains to negotiate on approach), though you might be surprised to find that the island's main road runs diagonally across the middle of it. Local airlines include Airlines of Carriacou (✆ 443 7362), Region Air (✆ 443 6111) and LIAT (also ✆ 443 7362), with scheduled flights down to Grenada and on to St Vincent. Departure tax is EC$25 plus EC$10 airport security charge (the latter charged if you are flying to Grenada).

Carriacou

Carriacou is gentle and quiet (just 8 miles by 5), with a population of about 6000, who are known as 'kayaks'. It is mountainous, though not high enough to have the tropical lushness of Grenada itself, but it is bordered with the supreme white-sand beaches of the Grenadines.

parts of the island, including *Fédon's Camp*, the summit from which Julien Fédon led his rebellion in the 18th century and Mt St Catherine. You can try Sunsation Tours (*©* 444 1594) for a variety of tours and Telfor Hiking Tours (*©* 442 6200).

Riding: It is possible to tour the rainforest in the dry season, beaches and canefields during the wet—contact The Horseman (*©* 440 5368)

Mountain biking: Try Ride Grenada (*©* 444 1157).

Tennis: There are courts at many of the hotels and in the Grand Anse area.

Golf: Play a nine-nole course near Grand Anse, at the Grenada Golf and Country Club (*©* 444 4128), green fee EC$50.

Tiny islets lie off its shores, nothing more than sand and a few palm trees.

The first settlers of Carriacou (from the Indian Kayryouacou) were French turtlers fishing in the abundant waters or taking the turtles on the island's fine sand beaches as they came to lay their eggs. Soon it was settled as a plantation island, growing mainly cotton, but also supporting two sugar estates that provided the island with rum.

The island is well known for its tradition of boat-building and you will still occasionally see these graceful boats being built here. And it is also known for smuggling, something of a Caribbean tradition. It is so endemic that calls have been made by the islanders to make the island duty free. Shippers, legal or otherwise, are called 'traffickers' hereabouts and they take produce from Grenada down to Trinidad or Barbados, returning with tinned food, snacks and manufactured goods. Cargoes from Sint Maarten and the other duty-free islands and the odd consignment of whisky and foreign brand cigarettes do occasionally go astray in a cove en route. The mainstay of the declared economy is agriculture, vegetables sent to market in Grenada and sheep and goats, looking confused, tied up in bags so that only their heads protrude, on their way to market in the other islands. The island used to be cultivated all over and carefully husbanded, but the cattle and goats get everywhere now. The agricultural concerns are dying steadily as young Carriacouans (as elsewhere in the Caribbean) are not keen to work the land.

You will find almost every conceivable alcohol in Carriacou, but the island's special drink is *jack-iron*, or the jack, which, quite apart from being extremely strong, has the peculiar and disarming quality of making ice sink in it. Not much is distilled here any more; most of it comes from Trinidad.

The liveliest and most spectacular moment in the Carriacouan calendar is the annual **Regatta**, held in early August, to which yachts come from all over, usually to be beaten by sailors from the next-door island of Petite Martinique. There are also celebrations on Independence Day on 7 February and at Carriacou's **Carnival** at the beginning of Lent. If you are on island at festival times and hear of a **Big Drum Dance**, or the Carriacou **parang festival** in December (*see* Trinidad, p.107), it is well worth going along.

It is fascinating to see the skeletal hulls of cedar steadily take shape on the shoreline in Windward, and more recently Tyrrel Bay as the Carriacouan shipwrights create their boats.

traffickers unloading

Not so many big ships are built any more, but many smaller boats are. Most of the wood is white cedar from Carriacou, but the main keel piece is greenheart imported from Guyana. The work is done by hand, following a tradition supposedly bequeathed by a Scots ancestry. The launching ceremony is a major festivity and well worth a visit if you hear of one. The blood of a goat is sprinkled on the boat as it is blessed and then it is launched to the sound of drums, while everybody looks on dressed in their Sunday best.

Carriacou is rimmed with fine white **beaches**, most of which will be deserted. Look normally to the west coast, or on a still day try the windward (east) coast. Beyond the airport is a fine strip called **Paradise Beach** and **L'Esterre**, where you will find **Ali's Bar** right on the sand. On the western side of the island there is a good harbour at **Tyrrel Bay** and strips of sand which make for good sunbathing and sunset viewing. There is even passable sand right off Hillsborough.

The best find of all, though, is **Anse la Roche**, in the northwest. Getting there is half the fun and is something like a treasure hunt. On the track north from Bogles look for a gnarled tree leaning over the road; turn left by the boulders down on a track through the bush to a clearing with a dried pond and a ruin; then right and down the hill at a black rock which you recognize because it usually has a conch shell perched on the top. Anse la Roche is an idyllic cove, but you need to be careful because there have been some petty thefts there. Round the northern point beyond here is another superb beach in Windward Bay, called **Petit Carenage**.

It is also fun to take a trip to one of the sandbars in Hillsborough Bay, tiny islets with just a few palms: **Mabouya** (from the Indian for evil spirits), **Jack A Dan**, whose name is a mystery, and **Sandy Island**, sometimes indistinguishable in the haze, which is supposedly silting away at the moment. A number of boats operate out of Hillsborough, serving day-trippers from Grenada. Ask around for spaces, or contact Snagg's Water Taxi (✆ 443 8293). There is excellent snorkelling on these islands: onshore go beyond the rock of Anse la Roche.

There are two **scuba** shops on the island, Carriacou Silver Diving (✆ 443 7882) just outside Hillsborough and Tanki's Watersports Paradise (✆ 443 8406, ✉ 443 8391) in l'Esterre Bay, from where Tanki is well set to take you to Pagoda City, to the caves at Kick 'em Jenny or to loiter among a school of barracuda. Single tank dives US$50, novice instruction available, sunset trips and deep-sea fishing also available. An island tour can be fixed up through Bullen Tours (✆ 443 8590), US$6 with enough takers, or through the taxi drivers. A rudimentary bus service runs out from Hillsborough to Tyrrel Bay and the other way to Windward.

Stretched along the seafront, **Hillsborough** is the only settlement that constitutes a town. The centre of activity is the jetty, which comes alive on days when the boats bring mail and provisions. The two streets contain all the island's official buildings (including immigration if you come by boat), banks and a small tourism office (✆ 443 7948). There is a museum (*small adm*) in a restored cotton ginnery building, with a display of Amerindian history in zemies and pottery figurines, patterned body stamps and a well casing, a series of bottomless pots placed over a spring; of European heritage are weapons, lime juicers (with spikes like a bed of nails), oil storage urns and even a bed pan. The small botanical garden is now in extreme disrepair, with just a couple of benches beneath the palm trees.

Above the town is the great house of **Belair**, with its windmill tower, from where the view stretches both ways along the chain of the Grenadines, south to Grenada and as far as St Vincent in the north. The area was also used by the PRG as their principal army base during their tenure in the early 1980s. Heading south from the town you pass the airport, which has recently installed electronic gates to hold up the traffic when a plane is coming in, and then l'Esterre, where you can visit the art shop of **Mr Canute Caliste**, whose naïve paintings are now world-famous. Beyond here is the area of Tyrrel Bay.

✆ (1 473)–   **Where to Stay and Eat**

The **Caribbee Inn** (✆ 443 7380, ✉ 443 8142; *expensive*) at Prospect towards the northern end of Carriacou is one of the Caribbean's gems. The atmosphere has the grace and charm of the old West Indies—four-poster beds, muslin nets, ceiling fans that whip the sea breezes through louvred windows. It has just 10 rooms and suites, the newest of which have a magnificent setting on the clifftop and balconies or terraces. Perfect for lazing around in privacy. library and dining room (no shoes inside, please), where the kitchen serves fresh local ingredients in French and creole style. Anse la Roche is a short walk away. Meals $35 per person per day. At **Cassada Bay Resort** (✆/✉ 443 7494; *moderate*), the breezy wooden cabanas are perched on the hillside and have superb views through the southern Grenadines to Grenada 15 miles away. Remote and very quiet, 20 passable rooms, central restaurant on the hilltop. The **Silver Beach Resort** (✆ 443 7337, ✉ 443 7165; *moderate*) is set in a modern building right on the sand in Hillsborough bay. The 16 simple air-conditioned rooms are in garden cottages and a block on the beachfront. Some watersports, some self-catering rooms. There are six comfortable rooms on l'Esterre Bay at **Paradise Inn** (✆ 443 8406, ✉ 443 8391; *cheap*), all air-conditioned and fan-ventilated with tiled floors and wicker furniture and private baths; popular with the diving crowd, meals available at the beach bar.

If you are happy to look after yourself, self-catering villas can be arranged through **Down Island Ltd** (✆ 443 8182, ✉ 443 7086). Otherwise there are a number of very cheap places to stay. In town is the plush **Ade's Dream House** (✆ 443 7317, ✉ 443 8435) a three-storey cream, grey and red-brick giant on Main Street with 23 rooms (some private, other share-baths), some self-catering, some air-conditioned. Also the **Sand Guest House** (✆ 443 7100), nine rooms with kitchenettes, or **Hope's Inn** (✆ 443 7457) on the beach in l'Esterre.

There is a string of guest houses across from the seashore in Tyrrel Bay: **Alexi's Luxury Apartment Hotel** (✆/✉ 443 7179), 13 suites with kitchenettes and simple rooms with private bathrooms, or the **Constant Spring Guest House** (✆ 443 7396), very simple, three rooms and shared kitchen and bathroom.

There are quite a number of **restaurants** outside the hotels in Carriacou, but Carriacou's truly laid-back style extends to most kitchens and so eating out is a little haphazard. You often find yourself waiting for an eternity for literally anything to eat (much of it is defrosted only when you make your order). A charming spot on Main Street in Hillsborough is **Callaloo** (✆ 443 8004), where there is a long list of cocktails to start, followed by callaloo soup of course and then honey ginger chicken breast or local catch in garlic butter. Sailing scenes painted on calabashes on the walls, lunchtime salads and sandwiches, *moderate*. **Kayak** will serve you local rice 'n' peas or a roti to go, *cheap*.

There are a couple of nice restaurants in Tyrrel Bay, where most yachts put in for the anchorage. **Poivre et Sel** (✆ 443 8390; *moderate*) serves French fare on a balcony upstairs; fish *en papillote* followed by crêpes Suzette. **Le Petit Conch Shell** (*moderate*) sits back from the beachfront, soups to start, chops, burgers, chicken or fish, on a small veranda setting, or airco inside. Or there's **Scraper's** for a spicy barbecue chicken and the **Twilight Bar** (*cheap*) for chicken or fish.

There are a number of waterfront bars here too, palm-thatch lean-tos where you can sit with a rum punch and watch for the Green Flash. Try **Stella's**, a small shed right above the waves with a tiny deck or **Alexi's Bar**, with a palm-thatch shelter and a cannon to sit on. Finally there is one of the coolest and most unlikely bars in the islands on the waterfront in Hillsborough. The **Hillsborough Bar** looks like an English pub and disco (it was built by pub-builders from Birmingham). Barbecue dinners take place under the thatch on the seafront, with plenty of drinking and dancing as the mood takes the customers.

Petite Martinique

The inhabitants of this tiny island, which lies about 3 miles east of Carriacou, are also fishermen and boat-builders, reputedly even more closely involved in smuggling than their neighbours. Perhaps as a result, they are supposed to have one of the highest per capita incomes in the Caribbean. In an effort to clamp down on it there has been a joint operation between the Grenadian government and the Americans to build a coastguard dock (officially to help in preventing the drugs trade). They got no help from the Petite Martinicans, who promptly burned it down (they have a history of throwing customs officers off the island during previous attempts). However, it looks as though it is there to stay now.

Altogether the Petite Martinicans are fiercely independent. There is a small and close-knit community of about 1000 islanders. The atmosphere on the island is slightly listless, the main activity being at the dock when a ship puts in. There is a fairly regular crossing (not quite daily) from Hillsborough to Petite Martinique on the *Osprey*. Alternatively, hire a boat in Windward on Carriacou. The island's name (which in grammatical correctness is spelled Petite, but which is pronounced more like 'Petty') is thought to come from the fact that, like the island of Martinique, it has snakes. It is said that rival colonies would introduce snakes on to other islands to make life more difficult for the settlers. You can stay at the **Seaside View Holiday Cottages** (✆ 443 9210, 🖷 443 9113; *very cheap*), just four rooms with a bar and cooking facilities with a fine view of the island of Petit St Vincent and other Grenadines. Simple and low-key. You can also try the **Palm Beach** restaurant for local fare.

St Vincent and the Grenadines

St Vincent and the Grenadines offer a classic Caribbean combination, of local island life and luxurious small-island seclusion. Side by side stand the staggering lushness and friendly way of the Windward Islands, and the slow-time, easy life of the tiny Grenadines, 30 islands strung out over 60 miles of strikingly blue sea, each a short hop from the next. Once the heartland of Indian resistance, where Caribs would ply the waters in their war canoes, St Vincent and the Grenadines are now cruised by more peaceful craft. It has become a sailor's paradise.

St Vincent stands in the north, set between the Atlantic and the Caribbean Sea, like a massive cut emerald with facets of lush forested slopes stacked irregularly, rising to the central mountain range of Morne Garu. At 18 miles by 11, this fertile island is the smallest link in the Windward Islands. It is so rough and mountainous that even now no roads cross the body of the island. In the north St Vincent is dominated by the mighty Soufrière, a distinctly active volcano, which last blew in 1979, showering the island with ash and adding yet more fertilizer to the rich land. A pencil could take root in the deep brown earth of the Mesopotamia Valley. In Kingstown are the oldest botanical gardens in the Americas, 20 acres of spectacular tropical abundance of scarlet, yellow and purple blooms.

Many of the 107,000 islanders live a simple life dependent on the land or the sea. With little industry, there is high unemployment and agriculture is still the economic mainstay. The principal exports are bananas, coconut products and arrowroot, a starch once used by the Indians as an antidote to poisoned arrows and now used in biscuits, computer paper and babyfood. Fruit and vegetables are sent to nearby Barbados, and as far afield as the Virgin Islands. St Vincent itself is still relatively undeveloped: there are not too many tourists and it is unscarred by the high-rise concrete monstrosities of mass development. It doesn't really have the beaches anyway. Some of the Grenadines depend on tourism, though, and an hour's sail will take you from simple island life to the most expensive island luxury. In centuries past, the Grenadines would be leased out for a hundred years on West Indian charters and turned into plantations. Nowadays, developers lease them to create some of the most exclusive resorts in the world.

The tropical island idyll is perfected here, seclusion with a view over dazzling white sand to islands that fade to grey on the horizon. You can be so isolated that you communicate by flag. Two hundred years ago the message might have been 'Bear to leeward, danger, reefs'. Now, with room service just at hand to pamper you, you are more likely to string up: 'Orange juice, coffee and croissants' or 'We do not want to be disturbed'.

History

With little strategic value, inhospitable St Vincent was given a wide berth by the early European visitors. *Hairoun* was wild even among the 'Cannibal Isles'. It was a Carib stronghold, and the newcomers would all too often be confronted by a shower of arrows and the barbecue spit. As the Europeans picked off the other islands in their quest for empire, St Vincent became a sanctuary for the Caribs, left as a European no-man's-land as late as 1750, a place where the Carib race could live out the last of their days.

St Vincent also became a refuge for slaves, who first arrived in 1675, when a slave-ship was wrecked off Bequia. As word got out, escaping Africans made their way from the islands around, St Lucia and Grenada, to join them. From Barbados, slaves would cast off on rafts and drift a hundred miles with the wind in a desperate bid for freedom.

The Africans mixed with the local Indians, the *Yellow Caribs*, to create a 'tall and stout' race known as the *Black Caribs*. This fierce new tribe took over the resistance to the European colonizers and eventually dominated the original Yellow Caribs, taking their land. Faced with extinction at the hands of their cousins, the Yellow Caribs promptly invited the French to settle St Vincent in 1719. The French settlers brought African slaves to work plantations. Fearing for their freedom, the Black Caribs retreated to the hills, where they distinguished themselves from the newcomers with bands around their calves and upper arms and by deforming their babies' skulls in old Carib style with tightly bound slats of wood, giving them foreheads that sloped upwards to a point.

The Black Caribs kept the colonizers at bay for another 50 years. In the Treaty of Aix-la-Chapelle in 1748, St Vincent was too hot to handle and so officially it was left neutral, with an unwritten clause that the European powers would fight over it later. By 1763 it was British. The new owners wanted the Black Carib land for their plantations and so they went in and took it in the First Carib War.

But soon afterwards the French were in control. They came in three sloops of war in 1779, unchallenged by the merchants of St Vincent, who were wide-eyed at the opportunity of trade. The soldiers were all at work on the Governor's plantation up north and the key to the battery was apparently lost in any case, so the invaders just landed and took the place over. In moments the island had surrendered.

Four years later the British were back, and they were faced with another Black Carib uprising in the 1790s in the Second Carib War, or Brigands' War, whipped up by Victor Hugues in Guadeloupe, who was spreading revolutionary fervour around the islands. Duvallé, a violent leader, swept down the east coast, burning the plantations and killing the British planters by passing them through the crushing gear in the sugar-mills. On the west coast the overall chief, Chatoyer (also Chattawar), spared them such destruction, save for a single sideboard which he sliced with his cutlass to show his intentions. Their armies came together like pincers in the south and they fortified themselves on the hills above Kingstown.

Chatoyer was killed in combat with the Militia Colonel Alexander Leith as Dorsetshire Hill was stormed. On his body was found a silver gorget, a present from Prince William, later King William IV, who had met him on a visit to the West Indies in the ship *Pegasus*. Chatoyer had dreamed of forging an island home for the Black Caribs, but his dreams died with him.

For a year the Black Caribs held on, attacking the British from the heights and slinking back into the jungle, but eventually, in 1797, General Abercromby gained the upper hand, razing their settlements and destroying their crops. He threatened them with surrender or extinction and 5000 gave themselves up. They were deported to Roatan Island in the Bay of Honduras (their descendants can still be found there, a thriving community). The Caribs living in the north of the island today are descended mainly from the few Yellow Caribs to survive the wars, forced to the north coast as the settlers took their fertile land.

With the cannon silenced and the colonial map fixed in the early 1800s, St Vincent ended up in British hands and became another quiet agricultural island, growing sugar, Sea Island cotton and arrowroot, of which they held a large share of the world market.

Governed as part of the colony of the Windward Islands, St Vincent and the Grenadines became an Associated State of Britain in 1969 and then took its Independence on 27 October 1979, remaining within the Commonwealth. The present Governor General is Charles

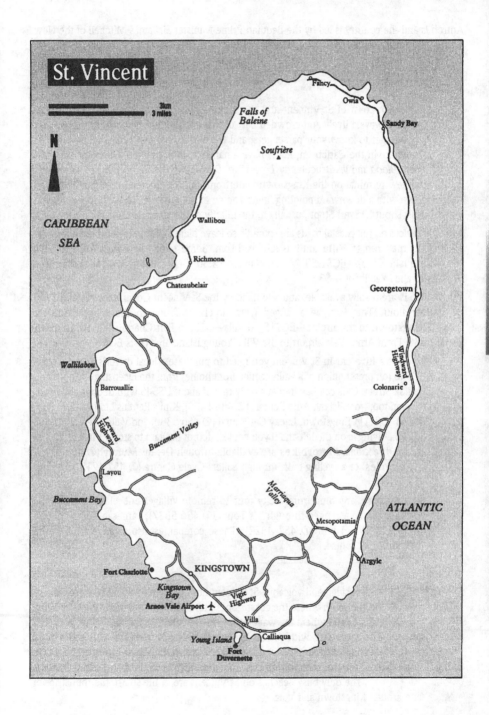

St. Vincent

3km
3 miles

N

CARIBBEAN
SEA

ATLANTIC
OCEAN

Fancy
Owia
Sandy Bay
Falls of
Baleine
Soufrière
Wallibou
Richmond
Chateaubelair
Georgetown
Wallilabou
Barrouallie
Colonarie
Leeward Highway
Buccament Valley
Windward Highway
Layou
Buccament Bay
Marriaqua Valley
Mesopotamia
Fort Charlotte
KINGSTOWN
Argyle
Kingstown Bay
Arnos Vale Airport
Vigie Highway
Villa
Young Island
Calliaqua
Fort Duvernette

Antrobus and the country is led by the Bequian Prime Minister Sir James Mitchell of the New Democrats Party, elected in 1984 and returned to power in 1989 and 1994. His party holds 12 seats and the opposition is Labour MN Unity led by Vincent Beach.

Getting Around

The south coast of St Vincent and the major valleys are well served with **dollar-buses**, always a lively and crowded part of Vincentian life. The buses are cheap and you will get to know your passengers, and the current popular tunes, pretty well. As elsewhere in the Caribbean, many have a name on their bonnet: *Fresh Kid, Hitman, Fresh Blood* and less truculently *Love Vine, Dub Trubb* and *Remixx.* Buses leave from the new terminal on the Kingstown waterfront. Out on the road they can be waved down with a downward-pointing finger and an expectant face. To be dropped off, you must shout 'Driver! Stop!', usually to the hilarity of the other passengers.

Services on the coastal roads are sporadic so leave plenty of time to get there and back, but they run to **Villa** until as late as 11pm. Some fares are: **Kingstown** to Villa (Aquatic Club)—EC$1.50, Mesopotamia—$2.50, Georgetown—$4 and to Layou—$2 and Wallilabou—$3.

Taxis are readily available, at a rate fixed by the St Vincent Government or at EC$40 per hour. They can be arranged from hotels or found in the Market Square. **Kingstown** to the airport—EC$15, to Villa—$20, to Fort Charlotte—$10, Layou—$35. From Arnos Vale airport to the Villa/Young Island area costs EC$20.

To drive a **hire car** in St Vincent you need to purchase a local driver's licence, price EC$40 (on presentation of a valid licence from home) from the Licensing Authority on Halifax Street. Cars can be hired at a daily rate of about US$45 with deposit and insurance on top, from: Island Auto Rentals (© 485 1480), Kim's Rentals Ltd (© 456 1884, © 456 1681) in Kingstown, Lucky Car Rental (© 456 5380) and Valley Rental (© 458 5331). Driving is on the left and if you get lost do not hesitate to stop a Vincentian and ask for directions. **Motorbikes** are available through Dennis Murray (© 457 9113) and **bicycles**, or a cycling tour, through Sailors Cycle Centre (© 457 1712, evenings 457 9207).

Island tours, anything from a city tour to remote villages and plantations or the volcano, can be arranged through T's Tours (© 456 5837), Fantasea Tours (© 457 4477) and SVG Tours (© 457 4322). These companies also arrange trips to the Grenadines, of course.

Beaches

Steep-sided and volcanic, St Vincent has mainly black sand beaches, except in the south where the coast slopes more gently out towards the Grenadine Islands and where the wave action on the coral reefs pushes up whiter sand. The east coast, with the big breakers coming in from the Atlantic, is quite rough and so for seclusion and the afternoon sun it is best to go to the leeward coast with its sheltered bays with black sand and fishing villages. The only busy beaches on St Vincent are in the south, the thin strips of sand around Kingstown and Villa.

Villa Beach on **Indian Bay:** Golden sand with traces of black, sometimes a little stony, popular with the Vincentians at weekends and holidays. There are some watersports shops and bars in the **Villa** strip nearby where you can retreat after a hard day's lying about in the sun. **Beachcombers** is a pleasant beach bar, a timber-frame veranda set back from the beach, where you can get a drink and a pizza or a lime pie.

West coast: The nicest bays are **Peter's Hope, Kearton's Bay** and **Mt Wynne Beach** near Barroualie; also **Buccament Bay** and **Richmond** at the limit of the Leeward Highway. Consider taking a picnic, though it is possible to buy a drink and a snack in the villages along the coast.

Flora and Fauna

St Vincent is extraordinarily fertile and if you visit the upper valleys you will find a whole new world of explosive tropical vegetation. Close to Kingstown is the Mesopotamia (Marriaqua) Valley, where you will see all the produce growing that later makes its way to market. You will see hummingbirds and tropical mockingbirds among the heliconias and anthuriums in the Montreal Gardens at the top of the valley. Vast areas of the island are unsettled, crossed only by farmers' tracks.

Another fertile area is Buccament Valley, inland from Layou on the west coast, where vast forests of bamboo rise to 60ft and the rainforest begins, an infestation of creeping vines and lianas that clamber over gommier and mahogany trees. There are trails in the Vermont area and it is here that you have the best chance of spotting the endangered St Vincent parrot (*Amazona guildingii*) around dawn. Unique to the island, it has a white, blue and yellow head, a tawny brown body with blue wing-tips and a tail of green, blue and yellow. The female is more colourful than the male and usually lays two eggs. There are thought to be only about 450–500 of these protected birds left. Another endemic species seen in the same area is the whistling warbler. It can also be seen in its reserve in the botanical gardens.

In the north of the island is the Soufrière, where the vegetation is different again, as rainforest gives way on the heights to elfin woodland, home to the rufous-throated solitaire. For a tour led by a knowledgeable guide, contact Hazeco Tours (✆ 457 8643) or the Forestry Division (✆ 457 8594) and ask for Mr Johnson.

Kingstown

The capital of St Vincent is set on the mile-wide sweep of Kingstown Bay at the southwest corner of the island. A town of about 16,000, it is surrounded by a ring of steep ridges spiked with palm trees, running from Cane Garden Point in the south to Berkshire Hill, where Fort Charlotte commands a magnificent view of the 60-mile string of the Grenadines. Downtown in quaint cobbled streets, modern glass-fronted shops stand out against the faded grandeur of old stone warehouses in the business centre near the waterfront. Vaulted walkways keep off the rain, the arches supporting the wooden upper storeys of the houses and sloping tin roofs, all strung together by a profusion of telephone wires.

On the higher ground of Kingstown Vale stand the old colonial houses, once majestic in their open tropical gardens. Now they are jostled for space as the Kingstown suburbs encroach. Overlooking the town from their perches on the heights are the modern houses of today's

the fish market St Vincent

wealthy Vincentians, some of whom have returned to their island and built homes after working abroad for years.

Down on the waterfront Kingstown is busy; cargoes of tinned food and timber are hauled aboard and stacked under tarpaulin at the **Deep Water Pier** and the **Grenadines Wharf**, where the boats depart for the journey south to the Grenadines. Along the waterfront are the Financial Complex and the National Bank, a modern colossus towering above the town. Beyond here are the bus terminal and the new **Fish Market**, where men in stained working coats pour out boxes of sprats and slap brightly coloured snappers on the marble slabs. Close by is the main **market building**, from which the bustle spills out on to the pavements of Bay Street and Bedford Street. In the hustle, trays of sweets are thrust under your nose and the market ladies, their skirts rolled up over their knees, remonstrate with buyers, selling their fruits and vegetables from the piles on tables and blankets spread out before them.

Officialdom keeps its distance from all this activity on the other side of Halifax Street, opposite a small grass square with a war memorial, behind the iron railings of the **Law Courts.** The building, with its imposing stone façade, green tin roof and louvred windows with white surrounds, is where the 15-member St Vincent Parliament and six senators meet.

The Kingstown skyline of steep sloping roofs is broken by church towers. The large Methodist church stands nearly opposite **St George's Anglican Cathedral**, a brightly painted Georgian structure with a castellated clock-tower, which was built in 1820 as the cathedral of the Anglican diocese of the Windward Islands, partly from government money that came from the sale of Carib lands. The stained-glass window with the red angel was supposedly commissioned by Queen Victoria for St Paul's Cathedral, in honour of her first great grandson (later King Edward VIII), but she rejected it on the grounds that in the Bible the angels were dressed in white. It was given to Bishop Jackson by Dean Inge of St Paul's and he brought it to St Vincent. Inside, a tablet commemorates Major Alexander Leith, a hero of the Brigands' War of 1795, who killed the Carib leader Chattawar.

The most surprising architectural feature of Kingstown is the **Roman Catholic church**, presbytery and school. Built in 1823 and enlarged in 1877 and 1891, it is a riot of styles in dark brick, a hodgepodge of Romanesque arches and Gothic pointings that would be more at home in deepest medieval Europe.

The St Vincent Botanical Gardens

Gardens open dawn–dusk, museum Wed 9–12 and Sat 2–6; adm. The museum also opens when there is a cruise ship in town and for pre-arranged groups.

Behind the town, on the steep slopes facing into Kingstown Valley, just off the road north to Layou, are the **Botanical Gardens**, the oldest in the Americas and one of the delights of the Caribbean. The walkways and lawns are bordered by an overwhelming abundance of tropical splendour: bushes with fluorescent flowers, trees with heavy aromas and palms that soar and sway overhead.

Founded in 1765, the gardens were run commercially in order to propagate useful species from all over the world in the Caribbean, and were connected to the Botanical Gardens at Kew in London. It was to the West Indies that Captain Bligh was heading on his fateful voyage in the *Bounty* in 1787. He was on a commission for the Society of West Indian Merchants to bring the breadfruit tree from the South Seas to St Vincent, where it could be used as food for the slaves on the plantations. Cast adrift with 18 loyal officers by his mutinous crew, he sailed 4000 miles to Timor without the loss of a life.

Six years later, this time in the ship *Providence*, he succeeded in bringing over400 specimens of the breadfruit tree to St Vincent intact, and offshoots of them still grow in the gardens today. Ironically, the slaves would not touch the new food when it first arrived, but nowadays the huge perennial tree, with its lustrous dark green leaves shaped like medieval flames, can be seen all over the Caribbean. The starchy fruit starts life as a small green lollipop and then turns over with the weight, swelling to the size of a cannonball and dropping to the ground with a thud. Boiled or steamed, it is a popular supplement to the 20th-century Caribbean diet.

The guides are helpful (basically you will not escape without one). In their jargon they offer an 'educational tour', which is probably worth taking because even if their botanical knowledge is often a little shaky, they do know all the amusing plants to show off, telling stories and crushing leaves for the aroma—cinnamon, citronella, camphor and clove. The gardens are open from the early morning until dusk and there is no admission charge, but depending on the number of people, you might give a guide EC$8 for an hour's tour.

The gardens are well worth a visit, a fascinating hour even for botanical novices. They are full of gems like the sandpaper tree, with leaves as rough as emery paper, and the velcro tree, *flambago*, related to flax, to which material sticks. And there is the waterproof lotus lily, on which water rolls in beads like mercury (put them underwater and the waterproof pink leaves take on a silver sheen and then come out dry). There is the tree of life, or *lignum vitae*, whose wood is so hard that it was used to replace iron as bearings for propeller shafts, the sealing-wax or lipstick palm that seeps bright red, love-lies-bleeding and the mahogany tree, whose pods explode, releasing a shower of whirling seeds like a sycamore. At sundown, when the white-painted trunks of the palms loom in the obscurity, the flowers of the cannonball tree that open in the day fall to the ground, and the air is heavy with the aroma of jasmine.

Above the Botanical Gardens today is the house of the Governor General and in a pretty West Indian house in the grounds is the **St Vincent Museum**, with fierce and sublime faces in stone and pottery left by the Arawaks and Carib Indians and later artefacts from the Black Carib wars of the 18th century. The chattering and squawking that rings in the gardens comes from the blue-brown St Vincent parrot, some of which are in a captive breeding programme, after recovery from illegal hunters. There are a couple of other animals on exhibit, including an agouti and a Barbados green monkey.

Fort Charlotte

Open during office hours (roughly speaking); adm.

This lumbering giant on the Berkshire Hill promontory is worth a visit if only for the fantastic view north along the leeward coast, on to Kingstown and over the Grenadine Islands scattered to the south. It is a pleasant half-hour walk from town, mostly uphill. Constructed at the turn of the 19th century and taking its name from George III's queen, Fort Charlotte was once the island's main defence, with barracks for 600 men and 34 cannon. For all this hardware and manpower, the fort saw action only once, an argument between two men just outside the gates, in which a Private Ballasty killed Major Champion in 1824. The perpetrator was tried and hanged on the same spot.

The fort stands 630ft above the sea, and is approached by way of a steep causeway and through an arch. Only three of the cannon remain and the barracks now house a museum of the Carib Wars. It is illustrated with a series of paintings by Lindsay Prescott, picturing important moments such as the death of the Carib Chief Chatoyer and the deportation of the Black Caribs in 1797.

The South Coast

Leaving Kingstown valley to the east, you come to the airport at Arnos Vale. From here the road (the Vigie Highway) leads inland to **Marriaqua**, often known as **Mesopotamia** after a town that is spread along the sides of this extraordinarily lush valley. The steep ground is terraced and the rivers come together at the spectacular Yambou Gorge. Kids play cricket in the road by the pastel-coloured houses perched on the hillsides among a profusion of greens: banana, breadfruit and coconut.

The ridge at **Vigie** (French for 'look out') gives spectacular views of Kingstown from above. The Carib camp was situated here in the war of 1795–6 and it was fortified with earth-filled sugar hogsheads (cone-shaped moulds through which molasses was dripped after boiling). Higher up, lost in the mountains, are the **Montreal Gardens**, with walkways through the tropical foliage, nutmegs and citrus. The gardens specialize in anthuriums, grown here commercially and seen all over the West Indies, with a heart-shaped leaf like a vividly coloured plate and a long thin protrusion.

Following the coastline from E. T. Joshua airport, the Windward Highway leads past the expensive houses of St Vincent's prime residential area to **Villa Point**, a charming line of former family holiday homes built earlier this century. They are all similar in style with tall, gently sloping corrugated tin roofs and they have been converted into restaurants and small hotels, which has given the area a friendly seaside feel.

Opposite Villa, a little way out to sea is **Young Island**, one of the Caribbean's best hotels (*see* 'Where to Stay', p.163). Young Island takes its name from a Governor Young who brought a black stallion with him to St Vincent in the 18th century. The horse was admired by a chief of the Black Caribs, whereupon the gallant Sir William Young said, 'It is yours!' The chief took him at his word and rode off on it. Some time later, the Governor was with the Carib chief again on the balcony of Government House in Calliaqua and he admired the island off the coast. Not to be outdone, the Carib, who owned the island, said at once, 'Do you like it? It is yours!' It has remained Young Island ever since.

The island is private, but visitors are allowed when the hotel is not full—you might go over in the evening for a cocktail. There is a telephone on the dock at Villa Point to call the ferry.

Fort Duvernette, behind Young Island, is an outcrop of rock that rises a sheer 200ft out of the water and is covered in dark green vegetation, marked on old maps as Young's Sugar Loaf. There are two batteries, still with ten mortars and cannon from the reigns of George II and George III, covering the southern approaches to St Vincent, though it is now favoured more for its beauty than for any strategic significance. A staircase to the heights is cut out of the rock, and is worth the climb for the view across to the Grenadines. Visits can be arranged though the Young Island Hotel.

A little farther along the coast is the quiet town of **Calliaqua**, once St Vincent's capital and the residence of the Governor in Sir William Young's day.

The Windward Highway to Georgetown

The Windward road cuts in from the south coast beyond Calliaqua and emerges on the Atlantic at Argyle. Immediately the sea is rougher, with huge ocean breakers. This fertile sloping land originally belonged to the Carib Indians but the European planters steadily ate into it. As the road twists along the coastline the skeletons of the old plantation prosperity are just visible; the buildings and aqueducts are disappearing, overwhelmed by the tropical undergrowth. New plantations, acres of bananas and coconuts, can also be seen at every turn.

Inland from Argyle, a short walk off the road to Mesopotamia that passes through the Yambou Gorge, are some **rock carvings**, squiggles and ghostly faces carved by the Arawak Indians, who lived on the island until about AD 1000.

Georgetown, 22 miles and a good hour's drive from Kingstown, was once a prosperous centre, servicing the plantations of the Windward Coast. Now it is an empty town, its buildings run down. Beyond Georgetown, in the shadow of the Soufrière Volcano, the road crosses the **Rabacca Dry River**, a river course in a rainstorm and the path for lava after a volcanic explosion, and passes into the Orange Hill Estate, at 3200 acres one of the largest coconut plantations in the world. In the villages of **Sandy Bay** and **Fancy** live the descendants of the Yellow Caribs. Even though they have now mixed and have considerable African blood, their Indian heritage of lighter skin and pinched eyes is still clearly visible.

At **Owia** on the isolated northeastern tip of the island, about an hour beyond Georgetown on the rough roads, is a large pond fed by the sea, but protected from it by a barrier of rocks, a good place to stop for a swim. There is an arrowroot factory in the town which may be visited, *adm free.*

The Soufrière Volcano

Dominating the whole of the northern end of the island is the St Vincent **Soufrière** Volcano, 3000ft high and definitely still active, blowing occasionally in a pall of smoke, thunder and flame. Farmers in St Vincent speak of extraordinary abundance following the eruptions—outsize fruits that come out of season because the ash acts as a fertilizer.

The Soufrière spat fire in 1718 and then blew properly in 1812, spewing into the air ashes and sand that floated down on the island, leaving a white covering inches thick like snow. The pall of smoke was illuminated by darting electric flashes and accompanied by violent thunder, an earthquake and a stream of lava overflowing from the boiling crater. The cloud even plunged Barbados, 100 miles away, into darkness. Then it was quiet for another 90 years until 1902 when it blew again (in tandem with the cataclysmic explosion at St Pierre on Martinique), killing 2000 people, mostly the descendants of the Caribs living on St Vincent's northern shore. On this occasion it rained stones for miles downwind, bombarding the fleeing Vincentians. The streams ran thick with ash and the noise was so terrible that people thought the island was sinking.

It was quiet until 1971, when a minor eruption created an island of lava in the crater lake, but on Good Friday, 13 April 1979, the Soufrière blew once more; a vast cloud of ash rose 20,000ft into the sky, and explosive gases boiled over the crater lip and raced down the mountainside, destroying any crops and houses in the way.

The best places to approach it from are the Rabacca Dry River on the east coast, just north of Georgetown, and Richmond, north of Chateaubelair on the leeward coast, which is a gentler climb. It is about three hours' walk to the summit (from where you can descend 750ft into the crater which steams from time to time) and you are advised to arrange a guide and to take some food.

The Leeward Highway to Chateaubelair

The Leeward Highway winds along the west coast of the island, climbing over massive ridges and promontories and dropping into deep coves, good shelters for passing yachtsmen, where small fishing villages of pretty clapboard houses sit on black, volcanic sand beaches. Inland the valleys are steep-sided and draped in greenery.

About 3 miles from Kingstown the road passes the majestic Peniston or Buccament Valley. At the head of the valley there are nature trails that lead up into the depths of the rainforest in the hills. The road rejoins the coast at **Layou**, where there is a petroglyph, Arawak impressions scratched on a 20ft rock. It can be reached on foot by a 10-minute walk, though visitors should ask permission because it is over private land (ask at the Ministry of Tourism and they will arrange a guide). The road then passes on to the fishing village of **Barrouallie**, and just off the road not far up-river from **Wallilabou** you will find a fall that pours into a small rockpool, ideal for a midday dip. Ask around for directions. The road continues through the town of Chateaubelair and eventually comes to an end at **Richmond** where there is an attractive bay and beach with just a few houses. A 15-minute hike inland from here you will find **Trinity Falls**, a stunning area surrounded by lush greenery where you can walk behind the cascade. Take a swimming costume for a dip in the two pools and the hot springs up above.

In the far north of the island are the **Falls of Baleine**. Here, the river, which rises on the Soufrière, races down through the tropical forest on the slopes of the Soufrière Volcano and drops into a rockpool in a 60ft spray of warm water. They are inaccessible by road, so visits are made by boat—a great day out from Kingstown, coasting the leeward side of St Vincent, past all the fishing villages and landing on the northern tip of the island. From there it is a short walk in the river bed to the rockpool and the falls themselves where you can swim. Outings can be arranged through one of the watersports companies and tour operators listed below (*see* 'Watersports', p.167–8).

St Vincent remains relatively undeveloped, untouched by international hotel corporations and their concrete plant. Most of the hotels are small (the largest has just 30-odd rooms) and many have the friendly atmosphere of West Indian inns and are set in attractive old-fashioned houses, family homes or the old warehouses of Kingstown. Apart from the few in Kingstown, the hotels are mainly on the white sand beaches of the south coast, particularly around **Villa**, which is about 10mins' ride from the capital. There is never a problem finding a room in St Vincent (but you are advised to book ahead for the more exclusive retreats like Young Island and trusted faithfuls in the Grenadines) and there are very good prices available too. However, a 7% government tax will be added to all hotel bills and most hotels charge a 10% service charge.

luxury–expensive

Lying 200 yards off the south coast of St Vincent and reached by a wonderful old African Queen style tub, **Young Island**, PO Box 211 (© 458 4826, ✆ 457 4567, UK toll free © (0800) 373742, US toll free © (1 800) 223 1108) offers hospitality in true Vincentian style in one of the Caribbean's loveliest hotels. There are 30 cottages of local stone scattered on the slopes of the tiny island and lost in a profuse and charming tropical garden, where walkways and a salt-water pool meander among the golden palms and ginger lilies. Each room has its own terrace and is screened, with huge louvred windows and ceiling fans to chop the cool sea breeze. Dark stained wood and rattan furniture are offset by bright fittings. You dine under small palm-thatched huts lost in the greenery, looking on to the beach and across to St Vincent. There is a tennis court on the island and some watersports are laid on. You can vary nights in the hotel with nights aboard one of the resort's yachts. Whenever you go do not miss the hammocks on the beach, slung under a palm thatch roof, big enough for two.Off the beaten track in style and location is **Petit Byahaut** (©/✆ 457 7008, *www.outahere.com/petitbyahaut*), which is hidden in a cove on the leeward coast where the emerald water is enclosed by huge headlands. It is accessible only by boat. The 'rooms' are permanent tents with tin roofs, each lost in hillside greenery and invisible from the next, with hammocks and showers, ranged on the hillside above the bay; bathroom walls are usually palm trees and you may have a loo with a view. Plenty of peace and seclusion. Petit Byahaut is a nature-lover's resort and environmentally friendly (solar power) with low-fat, healthy eating on the dining terrace. All meals and watersports (except scuba) are included in the *expensive* daily rate (for two people). The **Grand View Beach Hotel** at Villa Point (© 458 4811, ✆ 457 4174) at the lower end of the price range has superb facilites for a small hotel and is set in eight acres of landscaped garden with wonderful ocean views.

If you want an exec's stopover in town, the **Camelot Inn**, PO Box 787 (© 456 2100, ✆ 456 2233, UK res (0181) 367 5175, US toll free (1 800) 223 6510) is set high on the hill overlooking the town, on the site of the former Governor's residence. Classical features run riot, with white pillars and balustrades around the pool and a mock antique air in the drawing and dining room (which is good); 22 bedrooms and suites with beauty salon and gym; quiet and private.

Beachcombers, PO Box 126 (© 458 4283, ® 458 4385) is a charming small inn set in the sloping gardens of a former private house, where gazebos and cottages sit among mango trees and tropical shrubs running down to a small stretch of beach at the end of Indian Bay near Villa. Very quiet and friendly, 12 comfortable rooms scattered in some pretty wooden buildings around (all phones, fans, terraces, some a/c) and a nice beach bar, even a health spa in the new block. There is still a feel of old-time Villa about the **Umbrella Beach Hotel**, PO Box 530 (© 458 4651, ® 457 4930), which is set behind a screen of flowers in one of the old wooden and tin-roofed houses. There is a small sitting area at the front and all nine fan-ventilated rooms have kitchens, private bathrooms and telephones. The walls are thin but the rooms are good prices. A more modern version of low-key Vincentian seaside comfort can be found at the **Indian Bay Beach Hotel**, PO Box 538 (© 458 4001, ® 457 4777, US res © (1 800) 742 4276); quite a simple spot on the small strip of sand at Indian Bay.

For those who wish to stay in Kingstown itself (perhaps in order to catch the mail-boat early in the morning to get to the Grenadines), there is a clutch of West Indian inns among the columns and arches and the cobbled streets of the capital. The **Cobblestone Inn**, PO Box 867 (© 456 1937, ® 456 1938), is set around a courtyard in a fine old warehouse with a wooden interior. Bright, floral furnishings in the 19 air-conditioned rooms and a rooftop restaurant, with phones, TVs and private baths. The **Heron Hotel**, PO Box 226 (© 457 1631, ® 457 1189), also has an old-fashioned West Indian island charm. The nine rooms have private bathrooms, breakfast is on the terrace above the inner courtyard.

There are a few **guest houses** on the island. There is an odd and friendly charm about the **Bella Vista Inn** (© 457 2757, ® 456 1648), in the Kingstown Park area above town. Simple rooms, some private baths, hot and cold water, fans, breakfast and dinner available. Otherwise you can try **Adam's Apartments** (© 458 4656, ® 456 4728) with 24 very simple apartments with cooking facilities, just next to the airport.

© *(1 809)–* **Eating Out**

Outside the hotel dining rooms (Young Island has a particuarly charming setting) and a couple of restaurants, Vincentian food is solidly West Indian. As always, restaurants also double as bars and occasionally the Villa strip can get lively at night. Some restaurants will take credit cards, but ask beforehand. There is a 7% government tax to add to all bills and most restaurants will charge 10% for service. Categories are arranged according to the price of a main course: *expensive*—EC$50 and above; *moderate*—EC$20–50; *cheap*—less than EC$20.

expensive

The **French Restaurant** (© 458 4972) is set in one of Villa's pretty houses, where you dine on the veranda at candle-lit tables on white linen, as expected on French fare, with a Caribbean touch. There is a long lobster menu in season—lobsters are picked live from the vivier in the garden and served *au basilic et cachuètes*—or also try lime butter chicken in a peppercorn sauce. Some mixed reports about the service.

There is a lively atmosphere at the **Lime 'n' Pub** (✆ 458 4227) not far off, where there are a two dining rooms: a formal one on a raised veranda festooned with greenery, at tables around a central tree, or for snacks, on a covered terrace. Long international menu with seafood—devilled crab back or fillet of fish—with pub specials including fish and chips and cottage pie. Pizzas to take away, some entertainment and a long list of dubious- sounding cocktails—try a *Blow Job* if that's your thing. In town you can try **Basil's Bar and Restaurant** (✆ 457 2713), which is set in the stone and brick surrounds of old-time Kingstown. Popular at lunch for the buffet; dinner is grilled *filet mignon* or a seafood *crêpe*.

moderate

Back in the Villa strip, the **Hairoun Pepperpot** has bench tables inside and a covered terrace outside, where you can taste national dishes from around the Caribbean— *cracked conch* from the Bahamas, *Colombo chicken* from the French Caribbean, *jerk pork* from Jamaica and a *pepperpot* from St Vincent itself, all to a Caribbean musical accompaniment. **Beachcombers** restaurant (✆ 458 4283) is tucked away at the end of Indian Bay, on a pleasant deck looking on to the garden and the beach: daytime sandwiches, burgers and rotis; in the evening stir-fried fish or a fillet of fish in herb butter. **The Attic** (✆ 457 2558) is a disco late on, but serves food as well in stark red and black surroundings: *christophene au gratin* followed by a beef brochette.

A top spot in town, for the setting and popularity, is **Vee Jay's Rooftop Diner** (✆ 457 2845) on Upper Bay Street. Lunch and dinner, with a live band on Fridays. Good West Indian fare—chicken, fish or shrimp with veg, or burgers and a chicken salad. Two excellent local restaurants with lively bars, both on Grenville Street, are **Aggie's** (✆ 456 2110), where you will find a variety of seafood such as whelks and conch, or a grilled fish in a creole sauce, always accompanied by local fruit juices, with a courtyard and upstairs setting; and **Sid's Pub** (✆ 456 2315), which is decorated with the cricketing memorabilia of the owner, who also serves West Indian food and a permanent diet of sports on the TV. On Halifax Street you can grab a roti or a sandwich at lunchtime from the **Bounty** (✆ 456 1776) and for a pizza, try **Tony's Original Pizza**.

Bars and Nightlife

Nightlife is pretty quiet in St Vincent and is centred mainly on the hotels, which stage steel bands occasionally. Villa is a natural gathering place where you will find visitors and passing sailors ashore for a beer and a game of darts and then discotheques at the weekends. Try the **Lime 'n' Pub** and **The Aquatic Club**, which has an occasional discotheque and screens sports some evenings. Karaoke seems to be popular in the island at the moment.

In Kingstown there are any number of bars in which to sit and have a Hairoun or an award-winning EKU beer, both of which are brewed in St Vincent. In addition to the many fresh fruit juices and St Vincent's powerful rums, you might also try a *sea-moss* (made with seaweed, milk and spices) or a *linseed* (as in linseed oil), both slightly sick-sweet drinks that are supposed to be aphrodisiacs. Two popular haunts, **Aggie's** and **Sid's**, collect an amusing crowd of locals, and some go to the **Harbour View**, a top-floor bar on Upper Bay St. Discotheques include **Touch** on Sundays, which attracts a younger crowd, **Level 3**, which goes for an older crowd, and **The Attic**.

getting there

There are no direct flights to St Vincent and the Grenadines from outside the Caribbean, so most visitors travel via Barbados (the best connections), or via St Lucia or Grenada. There is a special transit desk at Grantley Adams airport in Barbados for passengers bound for St Vincent. American Eagle (✆ 456 5000) fly daily to the American Airlines hub in San Juan, Puerto Rico.

Many scheduled hopper flights make their way up and down the Windward Island chain; contact LIAT (✆ 458 4841 in St Vincent), which flies north and south and across to Barbados, and Air Martinique (✆ 458 4528, ✉ 458 4187), which touches Canouan and Union and north to Martinique (they will also charter). Other smaller planes cover the Grenadines (Bequia, Mustique, Canouan, Union and Carriacou, usually two flights a day each way); contact Airlines of Carriacou (✆ agents LIAT, *see* above).

For most travellers from Europe or the USA the most reliable way to get to the many Grenadine islands is to take one of the regular small charter flights, usually from Barbados. (In fact they are regular enough to be effectively scheduled flights, but they are not listed on airline computer networks because they are officially charter airlines.) Contact: Mustique Airways (✆ 458 4830, ✉ 456 4586, UK contact ✆ (01453) 835801, US toll free ✆ (1 800) 233 0599, *mustair@caribsurf.com*) and in Barbados TIA (*see* p.78). Other companies include SVG Air (✆ (809) 456 5610, ✉ 458 4697) and Helenair (✆ 458 4528, ✉ 458 4187).

There are **ports of entry** at Kingstown, Arnos Vale airport and Wallilabou bay in the north-east and in the Grenadines you can register in Bequia and Union Island. There is a departure tax of EC$20.

tourist information

The St Vincent and the Grenadines tourist offices abroad are:

Britain: 10 Kensington Court, London W8 5DL (✆ (0171) 937 6570, ✉ 244 0177).

Germany: Wurmberg Straße 26, D-7032 Sindelfingen (✆ (049) 70 31 80 10 33, ✉ 70 31 80 50 12).

USA: 801 Second Avenue, New York, NY 10017, (✆ (212) 687 4981, ✉ 949 5946, US toll free ✆ (1 800) 729 1726) and 6505 Cove Creek Place, Dallas TX 75240 (✆ (214) 239 6451, ✉ 239 1002, toll free ✆ (1 800) 235 3029).

Canada: 32 Park Road, Toronto, Ontario N4W 2N4 (✆ (416) 924 5796, ✉ 924 5844).

The main tourist office on the islands is in the Financial Complex on Bay Street, Kingstown (✆ 457 1502, ✉ 456 2610), and there is a tourist information desk at **E.T. Joshua airport** in Arnos Vale (✆ 458 4685). For those making connecting flights via Barbados, there is the **St Vincent and the Grenadines desk** at the Barbados International Airport (✆ 428 0961), open from 1pm until the last flight of the day bound for St Vincent has left.

The tourist board puts out two magazines, the *Escape Tourist Guide*, with features and information (including ferry timings to the Grenadines) and standard prices for taxis, etc., and the smaller *Discover* magazine, also with current information.

If you have a medical **emergency**, contact the General Hospital in Kingstown (✆ 456 1185).

The **IDD code** for St Vincent is ⌀ (1 809), followed by a seven-digit local number. On-island, dial the full seven digits.

festivals

Carnival, or **Vincy Mas** as it is called, at the end of June or in early July, is the main event in the Vincentian calendar. A month of calypso competitions culminates in a *jump-up* in the streets of Kingstown, with steel bands and wild pageants of dancers all fired by rum and Hairoun, the Vincentian beer. Christmas gets an early start with the **Nine Mornings Festival**, which runs from 14 December. Vincentians stage nightly dances and parades through the streets with carol singers and steel bands. Many of the Grenadine Islands stage **regattas** (Bequia in March and Canouan in August), after which there are always jump-ups.

money

The currency of St Vincent and the Grenadines is the Eastern Caribbean dollar (EC$2.65 = US$1), but the US dollar and traveller's cheques are widely used in tourist restaurants and hotels. Major credit cards are also accepted in the tourist centres. Be sure which currency you are dealing in, for example in taxis.

Banks: Open Mon–Thurs, 8–1 or 3pm, Fri 8–5. For those passing through the island on their way to the Grenadines, there is a Bureau de Change at E. T. Joshua Airport, open daily except Sun until 5pm.

Shops: Open weekdays 8–noon, 1pm–4pm, Sat 8–noon.

watersports

St Vincent is not that developed and for equipment—snorkelling gear, windsurfers and small sailing boats—you will be dependent on the larger hotels and the dive shops listed below.

Snorkelling: There is very attractive coral off Young Island and equipment is available in Villa. Snorkelling tours and Grenadine Island tours are offered by Baleine Tours in Villa (⌀ 457 4089).

Scuba diving: Contact Dive St Vincent (⌀ 457 4714, ⌀ 457 4948) in Villa. The fish life of the Grenadines is good and there are some excellent coral reefs on the leeward shore of St Vincent, where you will find caves and a wall from 20ft. An excellent option, if you are travelling down the islands, is to buy a ten-dive 'rollover' package, which can be spread between Dive St Vincent, Dive Bequia, Dive Canouan and Grenadines Dive (in Union Island).

Sailing: The Grenadines are among the world's top sailing destinations. The islands are extremely beautiful, dramatic yellow and grey-green colossi that stand out against a bright blue sky and an aquamarine sea. As you cruise, dolphins play at the prow of your yacht and schools of gar fish jump up ahead, twenty silver flashes sewing their way through the water. But the big attraction is to moor in a deserted bay where the water is crystal clear and the beach is pristine white, and the Grenadines can provide this too. As a general rule, the Grenadines are less developed than the BVI and the sailing is more exposed. Many people charter yachts out of Grenada and St Lucia and then make their way to the Grenadines, but in St Vincent you can arrange to charter through Barefoot Yacht Charters (⌀ 456 9526,

@ 456 9238), who have a fleet of bare boats and a sailing school at their base in the Blue Lagoon beyond Calliaqua on the south coast, and through TMM (✆ 456 9608, @ 9917, *sailtmm@caribsurf.com*) who have bareboats and crewed yachts.

There are a lot of companies who arrange **day trips** through the Grenadine Islands; contact Fantasea Tours (✆ 457 4477) and Baleine Tours (✆ 457 4089). Some of the hotels also have yachts on call for their guests.

Walking: Walking in St Vincent's fertile country is a pleasure that has been enjoyed by visitors for more than 200 years. It is an adventurous 3hr hike up through seasonal forest, rainforest, and elfin and montane woodland to the lip of the **Soufrière**, from where there is a cracking view of the steaming crater and across the island. If a 4000ft climb seems daunting, follow instead the **Vermont Nature Trails** in the Buccament Valley off the

The Grenadines

Scattered over the 80 miles between the volcanic peaks of St Vincent and Grenada are the Grenadines, 30 tiny islands and cays that rise dramatically out of the Caribbean Sea and many more reefs and sandbars that barely cut the surface into surf. Here you will find some superb, deserted strips of sand, glaringly white against an aquamarine sea, protected by a rim of offshore reefs, where lines of silver breakers glint in the haze.

The Grenadines are some of the finest sailing grounds in the world—the white triangles of yachts ply from island to island, from the pretty waterfronts to isolated beaches and swim-up bars. An occasional clipper ship will cruise by with a full rig of sails. Each one an hour's sail from the next, the Grenadine Islands are an island-hopper's paradise.

Life for the locals is a much tougher prospect. Many of the islanders are poor, earning as little as US$5 for a day's work when they can get it, with expensive imported food to buy. Unemployment is high and the inhabitants of the Grenadine Islands do feel neglected occasionally, as in 1979, just after Independence, when there was an uprising on Union Island and 40 of the islanders staged an armed revolt. In general, though, you can expect to be welcomed in the Grenadines with customary Caribbean charm.

There is a traditional connection with the sea; the islanders have long gone away to work on the big ships and many more who stay in the islands make their living from fishing. And on the smaller islands there is something of a 'when the boat comes in' mentality. Life revolves around the dock when the mail boat makes its twice-weekly visit, bringing the mail, as well as the weekly supply of soft drinks, beer, gas bottles and sheets of galvanized tin and sacks of cement for building.

There are some charming places to stay, many of them exclusive island resorts, just a few rooms on an isolated cove or cottages ranged around the coastline of a secluded island. And then there are developed islands like Mustique, with luxury villas, and Bequia, with its pretty waterfront with bars and small hotels and robust local community. The Grenadines are not as

Leeward Highway, where there is a chance of seeing the St Vincent parrot in the evergreen forest and the rainforest.

The lush mountainsides of St Vincent are cut with tumbling and waterfalls, perfect for a walk through the forest and a dip. The most spectacular are the **Falls of Baleine** in the north of the island (these must be approached by sea and there are plenty of operators who will take you there), but others can be found at Trinity, up from Wallilabou and inland from here at Hermitage. On the Windward coast there is good walking around Colonarie and there are rockpools which make for good swimming in the South Rivers Valley, unless of course somebody has got there before you to do their washing or to take a bath. Guides are available through the Tourist Board, the Forestry Department or through tour companies listed in 'Getting Around', p.156.

developed as the Virgin Islands and they have a rawer, more natural Caribbean air. Whether you are ensconced in luxurious seclusion in a private island resort or island-hopping by fishing boat and ferry, the Grenadines offer some of the best in easy island living.

Getting Around

Island-hopping by plane is the quickest and easiest way of getting around the Grenadines and most of the islands are well served with flights. You will also get some cracking views along the way. There are one or two slightly hairy airstrips—you can enjoy watching the next plane approach once you are safely on the ground. Canouan and Bequia often have cross-winds, there is a steep descent and sometimes a bouncy landing on Mustique, and even with Union's new strip you still nearly touch the treetops with the right wingtip. But the islands are typically low-key and you may come across nonchalant signs like:

CAUTION—AIRCRAFT

LOOK LEFT

Mayreau, the Tobago Cays, Palm Island and Petit St Vincent have no airstrip at all. Airlines with scheduled services through the islands are listed in the St Vincent section.

But the Grenadines are really about the sea and it is fun to travel by the local mail boat and the many smaller craft that make the island run. The mail boat, the MV *Barracuda* (© 456 5180) makes two sailings a week each way between Kingstown and Union Island, touching Bequia (1 hour), Canouan (2 hours), Mayreau (1 hour) and on to Union Island (30 mins). It travels south on Mondays and Thursdays and north on Tuesdays and Fridays. Fares are impeccable: from St Vincent to Bequia—EC$10–12, to Canouan—EC$13, to Mayreau—EC$15 and to Union Island—EC$20. Once in the Grenadines you can visit other islands on day trips, with picnic and snorkelling gear included. You might also be able to persuade a fisherman to drop you on the next island or hitch a ride on a yacht.

Bequia

Bequia (pronounced Beck-way) is one of the Caribbean's neatest and prettiest island hide-aways. Largest of the St Vincent Grenadines (an irregular splash 5 miles by 2), it lies 9 miles, or an hour's sail, south of Kingstown and the sea approach to the main town of Port Elizabeth is glorious as the rocky headlands glide by on both sides, towering above you.

Bequia is easy to get to. Most people fly in to Paget Farm in the southwest (taxi fare into town EC$30). If you are flying from Barbados, check the Grenadines-based charter services who fly almost every day in the season. At least two **motor vessels** make a daily trip to Kingstown during the week, departing early in the morning and returning soon after midday and late afternoon. The mail boat MV *Barracuda* stops there four times a week too. There is a small **Tourist Office** by the pier in Port Elizabeth (✆ 458 3286). The liveliest times of year in Bequia are Christmas, when Admiralty Bay has barely a square foot of spare mooring space, and at the Easter Regatta.

The island is quite developed—Port Elizabeth is full of pretty pastel boutiques and T-shirts strung up at the waterfront like washing—but it holds it well. It is a pleasure in itself to stroll along the waterfront in the Belmont area, a narrow walkway that passes between the sea and the pastel-coloured wooden villas built in the twenties and thirties which are now bars and restaurants. There is a picture-postcard perfection about Bequia and it is easy to be captivated by the island's charm.

The 5000 Bequians themselves are quiet and independent, still claiming to be a bit wary of 'Vincentians', who might almost come from a world away. There is a small community of white Bequians stuck up on the hill above Mt Pleasant; they have isolated themselves up there for years, but the younger generation have moved down now and are more visible in the community. There is a long tradition of boat-building on the island (and recently model boats for sale in the shops). Though no large boats have been built recently, it is possible to take a day trip on the *Friendship Rose*, an old Bequian schooner (✆ 458 3202).

The best **beaches** on the island lie on the south side of Admiralty Bay. The sumptuous golden sand of **Lower Bay** is easily reached by sea-taxi (contact Iba's Love or just loiter on the jetty, EC$15) or land-taxi, and the more secluded inlet of **Princess Margaret Beach** (once Tony Gibbens Bay) is a little walk over the headland. On the south coast is the huge half-moon of **Friendship Bay**, with passable sand and a view to Petit Nevis (an island still ocasionally used by whalers from Bequia to section their catch). East coast coves worth a visit are at **Industry Bay** (also called Crescent Bay) and **Spring Bay**.

There are **beach bars** on nearly all the beaches on Bequia, pleasant spots to take time out from sizzling and snorkelling. On Lower Bay try **De Reef** and **Theresa's** and on Friendship Bay you will find **Spicey and Herby,** a waterfront bar with chairs swinging from the ceiling to help your balance after a few rum punches. The **Crescent Beach Inn** is a lovely, isolated spot for a day out. People have been known to skinny-dip at Hope Bay.

It is fun to explore Bequia, though 'sights' are limited. As you enter the harbour, Admiralty Bay (chosen by the British Navy as a port, but never occupied because of a lack of fresh water), you will see some dwellings built into the cliffside. Called **Moonhole** after a natural arch in the rock, they are private residences, perched right above the waves. Tours can be arranged (✆ 458 3277). The residents do not take kindly to people poking around uninvited. There is a small fort on the point in Hamilton on the north shore of Admiralty Bay. The east of the island

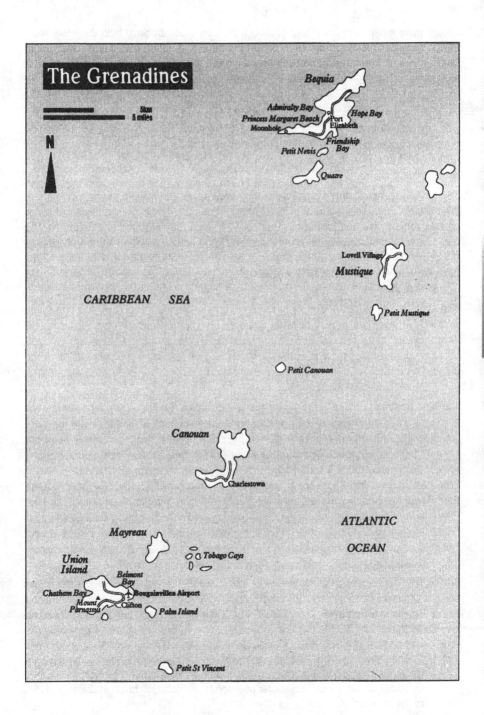

The Grenadines

5km
5 miles

N

Bequia

Admiralty Bay
Princess Margaret Beach
Moonhole

Port
Elizabeth

Hope Bay

Friendship
Bay

Petit Nevis

Quatre

Lovell Village

Mustique

CARIBBEAN   SEA

Petit Mustique

Petit Canouan

Canouan

Charlestown

ATLANTIC

OCEAN

Mayreau

Tobago Cays

Union
Island

Belmont
Bay

Chatham Bay

Bougainvillea Airport

Mount
Parnassus

Clifton

Palm Island

Petit St Vincent

is much more remote and undeveloped, though villas are gradually being built there too: you may come across tropicbirds and the scissor-tailed frigatebird. Irregular dollar-buses (*costing EC$1.50*) ride out from Port Elizabeth down to Paget Farm.

***

✆ (1 809)–   ***Where to Stay***

Many of Bequia's small hotels (only one has as many as 30 rooms) are set in the island's fine old buildings, restored forts or old family holiday homes. They have charm and character, lost in tropical gardens on the heights or down on the seafront in Belmont overlooking Admiralty Bay and the yachts at anchor. As the island becomes more accessible, it is worth reserving a room on Bequia, particularly in the winter season. Villas are available on Bequia, through Bequia Villa Rental (✆ 458 3393, ✆ 458 3417).

very expensive–expensive

The **Friendship Bay Hotel**, PO Box 9 (✆ 458 3222, ✆ 458 3840) is a charming hideaway on the south side of the island. Twenty-seven rooms stand just above the beach and in blocks scattered around the main house (dining room and bar) on the steep hillside and tropical gardens; all are brightly coloured and very comfortable, some with gingerbread fretwork and many with a porch and a fantastic view over Friendship Bay. There is a charming bar and restaurant down on the beach, wooden floor and palm-thatch rusticity, but excellent food. Family run and friendly, quite quiet and low key (no TVs or even telephones in the rooms, but some watersports and yachts for sail-away packages).

The **Plantation House Hotel**, PO Box 16 (✆ 458 3425, ✆ 458 3612, US ✆ (1 800) 223 1108), is peach-coloured pastel prettiness taken to perfection. Scattered around a greathouse in a garden of palms, hibiscus and crotons, there are 27 cabins and beachfront villas decorated in old-time Caribbean style with clay-tile floors and louvred doors, rattan furniture and muslin bed nettings. Phones, TVs, air-conditioning and fans, pool and some sports on the small beach, some evening entertainment; the dining room, on the terrace of the main house, serves international fare.

The small and private **Old Fort Country Inn**, PO Box 14 (✆ 458 3440, ✆ 457 3340) stands in a stone house isolated high on the hilltop in Mt Pleasant, from where there is a fort's eye view of the Grenadines, occasionally as far as Grenada. There are just five apartments in the main house, each with its own individual charm, with wooden floors and big windows—rush mats and muslin nets on the beds—set in a garden with copper boilers and hammocks and a pool. With stone floor and arches and even a fireplace, the open-fronted dining room is charming. It serves French, Italian and creole fare and looks out on to a pretty garden where peacocks, dogs and donkeys roam.

Spring on Bequia (✆ 458 3414, ✆ 457 3305, US reservations ✆ (612) 823 1202) also has a dramatic setting looking over the palms on Bequia's isolated east coast. Just 10 rooms ranged in cottages of local stone on a steep hillside: rooms are louvred all around with hefty wood and have a large stone porch. Studiedly spartan, but ideal if you're happy to be utterly quiet and self-contained, with minimal services and correspondingly lower prices. Freshwater pool and tennis court, all meals available. *Closed in the summer.*

Back in town, in pride of place on the Belmont waterfront is the **Frangipani**, PO Box 1 (℗ 458 3255, ✆ 458 3824, *frangi@caribsurf.com*), an inn which has retained an air of the family house that it once was (it is the house of the Prime Minister, Sir James Mitchell). There are 16 rooms in all; some simple ones in the charming wooden main house and then more comfortable units scattered around the gardens behind, where copper sugar boilers are shaded by mango trees and red and white frangipani. Prices vary considerably. High up on the hillside in Lower Bay, but still within a shout of the beach, is the **Creole Garden Hotel** (℗/✆ 458 3154), recently built in modern Caribbean style with concrete walls and tin roofs and smothered in greenery. There are five quite simple rooms and two one-room apartments with nice views; some self-catering, but a good local restaurant and a friendly atmosphere.

cheap–very cheap

Down below here is a simpler stopover at **Keegan's Guest House** (℗ 458 3530, ✆ 457 3313) in Lower Bay, with three fan-ventilated apartments and 11 rooms; rates include breakfast and dinner.

The **Lower Bay Guest House** (℗ 458 3675) is lost in a tropical garden; eight double rooms, central TV room, some share-baths, meals available. In town, on Back Street just behind the jetty, is **Julie's** guest house (℗ 458 3304, ✆ 458 3812), with 20 simple rooms with private bathrooms, all meals available.

℗ (1 809)– **Eating Out**

There is a surprising variety of dining on offer around Bequia with Italian, French and French creole as well as international and of course local fare. However, eating out is quite expensive and as on the other Grenadines, service is often a little haphazard. Expect a 7% government charge and 10% for service to be added to your bill.

Le Petit Jardin (℗ 458 3318; *expensive*) on Back Street in town serves French cuisine (a Bequian chef trained in France). You sit in a breezy wooden dining room or in the garden. *Poulet aux noix and crevettes* (shrimps) *sauté à l'anisette*, followed by *meli-melo de goyave*. On the Belmont waterfront, the **Gingerbread House** (℗ 458 3800; *expensive*) has an upstairs view of the yachts in harbour through a filigree of gingerbread fretwork. Salads and burgers by day, fancier fare at night—fish chowder or West Indian pumpkin and split-pea soup, speciality curries, spicy or mellow in coconut and a long list of puddings. At the far end of Lower Bay, **Coco's Place** (℗ 458 3463) has pride of position high above the sea, a double terrace dressed in pink, purple, turquoise and orange. International fare and a lively atmosphere. Well worth a visit just below here is **Theresa's Café and Bar** (℗ 458 3802; *moderate*), a typical Caribbean concrete shed with a palm-thatch shelter: sandwiches and salads by day and vegetarian and more senior dishes in the evenings, fun atmosphere.

Some of the best of Bequia can be found in a couple of excellent West Indian restaurants. **Dawn's Creole Garden** (℗ 458 3154; *expensive*) has another typical West Indian setting on the hillside at the end of Lower Bay (close to Coco's). Plenty of varieties of fresh fish in Dawn's creole sauce (clove, ginger and nutmeg), accompanied by breadfruit, sweet potato and plantain. Four-course fixed dinner. Another classic is

Daphne Cooks It (✆ 458 3271; *expensive*), in a side-street opposite the pier in town. Creole food; local soups, curried and creole dishes served with frittered plantain, christophene and yam followed by exotic fruit sorbets or impossible pie. Ring to reserve a table and a favourite dish.

Ever popular, **Mac's Pizzeria** serves the obvious pizzas as well as other dishes such as salads and Macnuggets (codfish balls) on a wooden veranda above a luxurious tropical garden in Belmont. The bamboo-fronted **Green Boley** is right on the waterfront too. Very easy-going, with simple local fare and tropical fruit juices to a Caribbean musical accompaniment. Or you might try **De Bistro** in town (...New York, London, Paris, Bequia...) for chicken plates, pizzas and burgers.

Many of the restaurants double as **bars**. The Belmont waterfront can be quite lively. Try the **Whaleboner** (seats made from whale vertebrae and the bar with a rib) at the Frangipani, where there is a steel band sometimes in season. The **Gingerbread Restaurant** also has live music, a string band, a couple of times a week. The hotels have an occasional *jump-up* and the **Harpoon Saloon**, itself an excellent place to get a drink as the sun descends through the masts, also has a dance from time to time.

Sports and Watersports

Watersports are best arranged through the hotels. **Scuba divers** will find good reefs around Bequia and the smaller islands nearby. A wall drops from to 100ft and there are wrecks at the Devil's Table and Moonhole. The west st of the island has been designated a national park: black tipped sharks have been seen at the wall at West Cay. Dive Bequia (✆ 458 3504, ✉ 458 3886) operates from next to Plantation House Hotel. A one-tank dive costs about US$45. They will also fix snorkelling tours. There is also Sunsports, at the Gingerbread Complex (✆ 458 3577, ✉ 457 3031, and Dive Paradise, in Friendship Bay (✆ 458 3563, ✉ 457 3115).

Sailing trips, day trips to Mustique and along the coast of St Vincent to the Falls of Baleine, sunset tours and the like, can be arranged on the catamaran *Passion* (✆ 458 3884) and on the yacht *Pelangi* (✆ 458 3255) out of the Frangipani hotel.

Mustique

The island of Mustique has a lore all of its own. Its image is one of almost absurd exclusivity, an enclave reserved for the very rich—famous, notorious or anonymous. Personages as incongruous as Princess Margaret and Mick Jagger have made this place their Caribbean retreat.

The island is run as a company, **The Mustique Company**, which over the last 30 years has turned an undeveloped scrubby outcrop infested with the mosquitos of the name into an exclusive enclave of 20th-century luxury. Shareholders invest in the company by buying a villa or by buying one of the 120 or so plots of land and then building on it—a not inconsiderable investment as the going rate is about ½ million US dollars for the plot and then there are the costs of building your dream house. Through a series of committees (made up of interested shareholders), the company takes care of the infrastructure and development of the island (the environmental committee have arranged for the burying of all cables and paving of steep stretches of road to prevent erosion, for instance), including healthcare and the education of the local children. The Mustique Company is the biggest employer in St Vincent.

The direction of the island has changed a little in recent years, since some of the leading lights of the island, including Colin Tennant (now Lord Glenconner) have moved on. It is still extremely expensive nonetheless. Incredibly neat, Mustique has a sedate air, pricked by the occasional character who washes up at Basil's Bar. It is possible to come across the transient millionaires around the island, if you can spot them among the roving sailing-bums.

Just 3 miles by 1½, the island is small enough to walk around in a couple of hours (look out for the iguanas, which are pretty big, and for the mysterious wild cattle which leave their prints when they come to drink at the pools by night, though they haven't been seen recently), but if walking seems too energetic then it is possible to hire a 'mule' (like mini-mokes); enquire at the main office near the airport. Flights to Mustique come mainly from Barbados (on Mustique Airways and others, *see* 'Getting There' in St Vincent, p.166) and from St Vincent: scheduled flights are by Mustique Airways and Air Martinique. There are no boat services to Mustique.

You are quite likely to arrive by air at the pint-sized terminal building. From here roads encircle the island, linking all the villas and the beaches. Lovell Village is the recognizably West Indian part of Mustique with the island church and the police station, and it is here that many of the people employed by the Mustique Company live. Heading down the hill you pass an aviary with some endangered St Vincent parrots and you come to Britannia Bay, really the only busy part of the island. The 75 or so fishermen, some of whom were here for generations before the company arrived, have their huts here and there is a small fish market where you can sometimes get fresh fish. The main jetty for the supply boat from St Vincent is here and Basil's Bar sticks out into the water. Close by there is a foodstore and bakery and Mustique's pretty gingerbread boutiques, Treasure Fashion and Treasure Boutique. There is even an antique shop down there. Britannia Bay is also the best anchorage for yachts.

There are some excellent **beaches** scattered on Mustique and walkways have been built to provide access to some of them. The most protected are in the southwest. **Lagoon Bay** is a gently curving strip of sand with a palm fringe and shallow water: some picnic areas and shelters. From here you can walk around to **Gelliceaux Bay,** a charming and secluded cove. **Endeavour Bay** in the northwest is the busiest beach because of the nearby Cotton House Hotel and Dive Mustique (✆ 456 3486), the scuba diving and general watersports shop; further round to the north **L'Ansecoy Bay** is pleasant but often windswept. The east coast feels the brunt of the Atlantic waves but **Macaroni Bay** has mounds of bright white sand and one or two umbrella shades. There are tennis courts and there is a stable with horses for riding out on the beaches and around the island.

✆ *(1 809)–*   ***Where to Stay***

Visitors to Mustique generally take a villa; about 50 of the 75-odd luxurious piles dotted around the island are for rent. These vary in style from an Etruscan palace to chichi gingerbread cottages, with two rooms and more. All come with maid service, gardeners and cooks, in fact all that is needed to ensure the ultimate rest-cure. With names like *Nirvana* and *Serendipity* you get the idea that this might be as near to heaven as the developed world of the late 20th century can manage. Villas are not cheap. Prices for a two-bedroom villa start at US$4000 per week in winter and $2800 in summer; three bedrooms start at $5000 in winter and at $3000 in the summer. Four-bedroom villas range between $6000 and $16,000 for a week in winter and start at $4500 in summer, and five bedrooms are $8000 or more in the winter. Then you add 5% government tax and 8% administration charge. Contact **Mustique Villa Rentals**, PO Box 349, St Vincent (general ✆ 458 4621, ✆ 456 4565). In Britain they can be contacted at Chartham House, 16a College Avenue, Maidenhead, Berks SL6 6AX (✆ (01628) 583517, ✆ 783379) and in the USA through Wegner Associates (✆ (212) 758 8800, ✆ 935 2797).

The other places to stay on Mustique are a single hotel and a very upmarket bed and breakfast. The **Cotton House Hotel** (✆ 456 4777, ✆ 456 5887, US reservations ✆ (1 800) 223 1108; *outrageous luxury*) is set in rolling lawns and gardens in the northwest of the island, around the old windmill of the sugar estate. The 20 rooms and suites stand in small blocks and are furnished with four-posters with muslin netting. Each has a balcony or terrace overlooking nearby islands, or west for the incomparable sunsets. The pool stands on the hilltop surrounded by the restored walls of an old plantation structure and there is a beach bar on the nearby beach. The heart of the hotel, though, is the main house, a breezy, single-storey stone house with a huge drawing room and bar inside: guests gather for drinks before moving out to the candle-lit tables of the dining room ranged around the veranda.

For those who might feel a little extravagant staying at the Cotton House there is **Firefly** (✆ 456 3414, ✆ 456 3514; *very expensive–expensive*). Perched on a steep hillside overlooking Britannia Bay and the Grenadines to the southwest, it has just four rooms and a great deal of style and charm. The bar, with dining room and general sitting area, is a general gathering place for visitors and islanders who come to drink from the long list of cocktails and listen to whoever's on the piano at the time (it has been Phil Collins and Rolf Harris before now). From here you descend by spiral staircase to the rooms, with four-posters and mosquito nets and huge windows for the breeze and the view (some showers with a view too); very comfortable, fan-ventilated rather than air-conditioned. Stone steps descend through the steep garden to the double-level pool and bar (for snacks by day; they also do picnics if you are going off exploring). The cry goes that you do not have to be a millionaire to stay on Mustique because you can come here, but if you do, be sure to come with plenty of loot even so. Rates include breakfast in your room.

Eating Out

Eating out in Mustique is a little limited, but you will be well fed both at the Cotton House; elegant dining, with an excellent chef at the time of publication who cooks 'international fare with a Caribbean twist'; and at Firefly, where the fare is casual Caribbean; not 'silver service' but friendly and reliable—crab cakes with papaya cream, baked christophene with savoury beef as well as pizzas. Best known, though, is **Basil's Bar** (*expensive*; also a restaurant, despite the name), which has a setting from paradise: an open-sided construction of bamboo slats with a rush-work roof that juts out into the water on stilts. Tables and bench seats surround the dancing area and bar, so you can admire the sunset and the views of the Grenadines over the gin palaces that bob in the bay. The fare is international: cold shrimp platter by day and *filet mignon* or shrimp Vincent in the evenings. Basil's is particularly popular on Wednesdays in season, when the yachts bring their passengers ashore and the millionaires venture out from their villas for the *jump-up*; entry on Wednesday night costs about US$10; drinks will set you back about US$5. By day in season there is a café with juices, coffee, cakes and ice cream, **Johanna Banana**, and in Lovell Village there is a local bar, **Teresa's**, where *cheap(ish)* meals and beer can be found.

Canouan

Crescent-shaped Canouan lies 25 miles from St Vincent in the middle of the Grenadines, a scrubby island measuring 3 miles by 1½. It has a population of about 850, most of whom live on the protected leeward coast of the island. Until recently, Canouan was almost completely undeveloped, with just a couple of very low key places to stay and not so much as a bank or supermarket. For years Canouan was neglected—people expected to 'get their feet wet' when arriving here because there wasn't even a jetty.

Over the last few years, though, Canouan has seen a change. An international company has descended on the island with huge plans and vast investment. And with them the trappings of the modern world have begun to arrive. Roads have been cut around the north of the island, plots have been sectioned off, a golf course has been laid, condos built and there are projects afoot for restaurants and hundreds of villas and condominiums. As usual it has been received with mixed feelings by the islanders as they see outsiders coming in and taking the job and investment opportunities, but there is an upbeat air at the moment in the island. Vincentians, who jokingly thought of Canouan as 'some people on a rock, somewhere', have been quick to come in and claim the jobs that have become available.

The centre of island life is Grand Bay, which is divided into districts—Retreat, Balance, Batchelor's Hall Bay, site of the island electricity plant, and St Ann's Point. There are a few small shops to stock up at if you are passing by on a boat. The island is at its liveliest during the regatta season in July or August, when the different districts compete against one another in sailing races. Before the hurricane of 1921, however, most of the population lived in the 'Village', in the north of the island, where all the development is now taking place. Their old abandoned church, just over the rise as you leave Grand Bay, has now been included in the plans for a revamped modern 'village' with restaurants and boutiques. The northern area is intended to contain 100 villas and as many condominiums. For the moment, the roads are a useful way to explore the forests and secluded bays of the northern part of the island, where on the windward side the Atlantic winds run up the slopes and sculpt the overgrowth into lines and on the calmer Caribbean side iguanas, doves and the occasional feral cat shelter in the undergrowth.

The island has a few hidden coves and beaches to explore. Grand Bay itself has magnificent sand. The snorkelling is particularly good in Windward Bay and Glossy Bay. Hire cars are available through the hotels. For **watersports** you must go to the hotels: Dive Canouan (© 458 8044) works out of the Tamarind Beach Hotel (*see* below) and offers instruction as well as snorkelling trips and day sails to other islands. Canouan can be quite difficult to get to: there is an airstrip, but there are only occasional flights from St Vincent. Otherwise you will have to charter a private plane (*see* 'Getting to St Vincent' p.166). Alternatively, a very good way to get to the island is on the four-times-weekly visits by the mail-boat, the *MV Barracuda*.

The **Tamarind Beach Hotel** (© 458 8044, ☎ 458 8851, UK © (01453) 835801, US toll free (1 800) 223 1108; *very expensive*) sits tucked in to the top end of the huge Grand Bay on a superb strip of sand. There are 42 rooms in three modern and rather disappointing turquoise-roofed blocks (make sure to get a room upstairs, where the ceilings are higher), but they are very comfortable, with stained wooden interiors, louvres and nice balconies. There are two restaurants: the smarter Palapa restaurant for Caribbean cuisine and mock rustic Pirate Cove beach bar; plenty of watersports.

Canouan Beach Hotel, PO Box 530, Kingstown (© 458 8888, 458 8875; *very expensive*) is isolated in the south of the island beyond the airstrip. The 32 rooms are scattered around the sandy gardens on a spit of land with beach on either side and a fine view of the other islands. Full board, watersports and daily catamaran excursions.

There are a couple of small guest houses on the island: the **Anchor Inn** (© 458 8568; *cheap*) is set back from the beach a little way in Grand Bay, in a modern concrete house. There is a friendly atmosphere; guests in the four fan-ventilated rooms (private baths) have the use of a sitting room. Good home Caribbean cooking is available in the dining room. Price includes breakfast and dinner. **Crystal Apartments** (© 458 458 8356, ☎ 458 8001; *moderate*), not far off, also has rooms available sometimes, in some charming old wooden Caribbean houses. Otherwise it is a good place to eat, for a chicken or fish dinner off a bright red tablecloth. Occasionally it is possible to get a room at **Villa le Bijou** (© 458 8025; *moderate*), a seventies dream of a house (sunken video area and rooms off at funny angles) with a magnificent view over the Grenadines; three rooms with share baths. There are a couple of local bars on the high ground above Grand Bay where you can get a meal or a drink. Try the **Hilltop Snack Bar**, which pulses with reggae, and the **Rock Entertainment Bar**.

Mayreau

With just 180 inhabitants and no airstrip, this island blip of 1½ square miles is almost the most secluded of them all (the Tobago Cays nearby win that claim). There are no roads or cars and there is not even a jetty big enough to take the mail boat, so the week's supplies are offloaded into smaller boats. Cows making a journey from Mayreau are winched up on to deck, and if alighting here they are simply herded off into the bay and left to swim for it.

The islanders lead a very simple life, living in the small cluster of houses above Saline Bay. But things are moving on and some money is coming into the island; the rum shops are becoming restaurants and the islanders are rebuilding their houses in concrete rather than in wood. Electricity has just reached Mayreau and telephones have also made an appearance (in January 1995 they had the most modern system in the world). Above the town you will find the tiny Catholic church (most of the islanders are Catholic, because the island was owned, as much of it still is, by a single family, who were Catholic). It is made of stone and painted bright blue, with a small series of calvary paintings and helpful signs like *'Responsibility and Good Behaviour Always Win'*. Beyond here, small trails lead through the scrub down to pastures and cultivations and to the bays from which the local fishermen work.

Getting to Mayreau presents a few practical problems, but it is visited four times a week by the mail-boat, which originates in Union Island and St Vincent. You might persuade a fisherman to take you (they often visit to sell their catch) or pay a water-taxi to carry you over from Union, or possibly even catch a lift on a yacht.

Mayreau has beaches, excellent ones, on all sides. The best known are at **Saline Bay,** just south of the town, and **Salt Whistle Bay** in the north, which is also a particularly good anchorage. But there are many others, including a nice stretch just north of the town, **Twazam** (pronounced Twazane, perhaps from Trois Anes, French for Three Donkeys). Snorkelling is recommended at the northern point and on the windward beaches, where the sand is framed with sea grape bushes. Head windward on the day that the cruise ships put in and dump their passengers in Saline Bay, or alternatively go walking and take advantage of the island's views from the high ground, north to Canouan, east to the Tobago Cays and south to the majestic peaks of Union Island.

The **Salt Whistle Bay Club** (✆ 458 8444, ✉ 458 8944, or call on VHF channel 16 and 68, North America toll free ✆ (1 800) 561 7258; *luxury*), is set on a stunning, crescent-moon bay. It is about as remote as you can get; with 10 very comfortable rooms around a neatly raked sandy garden of palms, sea grape and cedar trees, with hammocks slung everywhere between them. The central area has a bar (and a small library) and a series of circular stone gazebos where you can sit out to eat and take in the evening air. The rooms are quite simple but very comfortable, with tiled floors and polished stone walls, king-sized beds and rattan furniture, ceiling fans, dark stained wooden louvres and window-screens. Bathrooms are open plan and have a large stone shower. There's no need for locks on the doors; phones are available, but nobody bothers to have one. The Club is very quiet and low-key, but there are often yachts in the bay and so there is sometimes a lively crowd at the bar. Some watersports.

Dennis's Hideaway (✆/✉ 458 8594, VHF Channel 68; *cheap*) is the only other place to stay on the island, five plush rooms in modern Caribbean style set in two modern concrete houses in the centre of Mayreau's town, each with a balcony with a view from the hillside. There is a small veranda dining room and bar just below, which collects a crowd of passing yachtsmen in the evenings and where Dennis himself plays guitar (otherwise a steel band sometimes). It is also worth going a little farther up the hill to the **Island Paradise** Bar and Restaurant (call on Channel 68; *moderate–cheap*) which is set on an attractive veranda hung with flags and other nauticalia. Wholesome West Indian food, an occasional string band. Elsewhere on Mayreau, entertainment consists of an occasional discotheque or a film screening in the restaurants and rum shops.

Tobago Cays

The Tobago Cays (pronounced 'keys') are five uninhabited islets set in the circle of Horseshoe Reef, an underwater world as spectacular as the island views above the surface. The islands are furred with scrub and sand and the water is crystal-clear all around, out to the limit of the reef, which is marked by a circle of silver breakers. You will cruise in between the reefs and drop anchor in the shallows of a pristine white sand beach. Devotees of the Tobago Cays talk of them as the closest thing to heaven and somehow it is true.

Or was, because the Tobago Cays are so well known that they have actually become quite crowded, particulary in high season (December until April and especially at Christmas). Day sails come over from Union Island (people fly in from as far away as Barbados). However, if you are yachting through the islands, it is well worth a look to see if it's not too crowded. The islands have recently been granted national park status, so there is no building on the cays and no spear-fishing. Hopefully this will protect the reefs and fish because the snorkelling is still superb—head out towards the Atlantic side. You are asked not to leave any litter (which has been a problem recently) and it is better not to pay anyone to take it away because it is often dumped just around the corner.

Union Island

Midway down the Grenadines is spectacular-looking Union Island, its parched yellow slopes draped down from the sharp peaks of the oddly named Mount Parnassus and Mount Olympus, also known as the Pinnacle. Just over 3 miles square, Union Island has a population of 2000. The island has quite a positive buzz at the moment; the island is clean and money is coming in from the large numbers of tourists, though a large projected development (with a 150-room hotel, a golf course and a 300-slip marina) actually folded recently after some ground had been cut. Union Island is a sailing centre and yachts crowd in the bay off the main town of Clifton.

Union Island is a gateway to the southern Grenadines and the airport serves as dropping-off point for the other islands nearby: Mayreau, the Tobago Cays, Palm Island and Petit St Vincent. The island is well served by air to the new airport outside Clifton: contact LIAT (✆ 458 8230), or Air Martinique (✆ 458 8328). It is also possible to sail from here to Carriacou in the Grenadian Grenadines (twice weekly ferry) for about EC$10, and of course to St Vincent on the mail boat. Union Island is a **Port of Entry** to St Vincent and the Grenadines. There is a small **Tourist Office** in Clifton (✆ 458 8350).

If you have time to explore Union Island, you will find that it has some good beaches tucked away in its tortuous coastline. **Big Sand** beach in Belmont Bay has shallow water and fine sand screened by bushes, but perhaps the best place to go for a secluded day at the beach is over the hill at **Chatham Bay** with miles of (as yet) undisturbed strand. There are no facilities in these places, so be sure to take water and a picnic if you will want them. The island has two main centres: Clifton, a cluster of bars and hotels along a concrete street running down from the airport, and Ashton, on the southern side, a quieter and more local town.

✆ *(1 809)–*   ***Where to Stay and Eat***

The **Anchorage Yacht Club** (✆ 458 8221, ✉ 458 8365; *expensive–moderate*) has 12 air-conditioned rooms in a garden of palms looking out over a passable beach towards Palm Island. There is a constant bustle and turnover, Grenadine style, of yacht crews and passengers, many of them French-speaking from the islands to the north. Be careful after the usual intake of rum punch, as the sharks kept in the pool at the waterfront seem to loom ever larger as the evening draws on. The restaurant, on an open terrace, serves French food. At the other end of Clifton is the **Sunny Grenadines Hotel** (✆ 458 8327, ✉ 458 8398; *cheap*), with 18 rooms in small units with ceiling fans, set among the palm trees with a sometimes lively bar that gives on to a rickety wooden jetty, perfect for lounging in the evening light. Local fare in the dining room, including curry conch and steamed snapper. The **Clifton Beach Hotel** (✆/✉ 458 8235; *cheap; guest house very cheap*) and the nearby Guest House provide simple and clean air-conditioned and fan-ventilated rooms with bathrooms. **Snagg's** Guest House in Clifton (✆ 458 8255) also has a couple of *very cheap* rooms, some cooking facilities. You can hire apartments in Union Island; contact the Clifton Beach Hotel.

There are one or two restaurants in Clifton outside hotels. Try **T. & N. Restaurant** upstairs in Clifton, for local dishes of chicken and fish creole. The **Lambi Supermarket, Bar and Restaurant** is on the waterfront, serving regular Caribbean dishes, including lambi (conch), the pink shells of which are set into the wall. In the centre of town is **Boll Head** restaurant, a simple spot with tables inside and out. Fish, chicken or a lambi dinner, or a roti takeaway. On the road to the airport, **Sydney's** Bar and Restaurant serves sandwiches and fish and chips and in Ashton you will find the **Frigate** Restaurant for local food and **Janice's** for pizzas. The **Eagle's Nest** in Clifton is the local club.

Watersports

Snorkelling on reefs around the island and **scuba diving** off Union Island and Mayreau (where there is the 1918 wreck of the British gunship *Purina*) can be ɪged through **Grenadines Dive** (✆ 458 8138, 🖃 458 8122, Channels 16 and or through **Dive Anchorage** at the Anchorage Hotel. A single-tank dive costs US$50, boat trips available. There are plenty of day yacht trips from Union Island. Try the catamaran *Scaramouche* (✆ 458 8418) or *Capt Yannis* (✆ 458 8513), both about US$60. If you wish to charter a yacht, contact the Anchorage Yacht Club, who also rent out bicycles.

Palm Island

Until recently with a population of just two cows, Palm Island, or Prune Island as it used to be known, has been transformed over the last 30 years into an island resort with a string of private villas and 24 hotel rooms facing out to sea over the magnificent **Casuarina** beach that runs the length of the sheltered west coast. There is an easy air of retreat here, with no telephones or televisions in the fan-ventilated rooms, which are set in stone cottages, each with a small terrace behind a low wall; inside they are furnished with cane furniture on the speckled tile floors and have wide vertical louvres to encourage a breeze; the showers are made of stone and some of them have a view over Union Island, about 15 minutes off by boat. At 130 acres in size, the island has a forest of palm trees standing over the sandy garden. There are two restaurants, a formal one for dinner and the less formal beach bar, the **Sunset Yacht Club**, which sees an easy crowd of sailors who anchor offshore: some watersports, including sunfish and scuba.. The villas, which are ranged along the northern shoreline, are available for rental at slightly lower rates (✆ 458 8824, 🖃 458 8804, US reservations ✆ (1 800) 999 PALM; FAP, *very expensive*).

Petit St Vincent (PSV)

Petit St Vincent, a self-contained island resort (✆/🖃 458 8801, US toll free ✆ (1 800) 654 9326), is the most southerly of the St Vincent Grenadines; from here it is possible to see people walking about on Petit Martinique, part of Grenada. But this is about as close to the crowds as you will get on PSV (as habitués know it), because this island resort specializes in seclusion. You get peace at a price at PSV. You can even have room service at your beach hammock.

Exertion is a walk to the beach and, since the island is completely surrounded by them, even that will not be too far. The cottages are spread out for maximum seclusion, each one isolated from the next. They are extremely comfortable, but they conform to an older Caribbean style of comfort with no phones, no TVs and no air-conditioning. The island's idea is that you should be allowed to shut out incessant modern communication for a while and do nothing but read, walk and swim—in fact you communicate to room service by flag, simply by placing an order in the post box, raising the flag and retiring to further inactivity. If you do wish to stretch some muscles, there is a tennis court and watersports are laid on (windsurfers, hobie cats and kayaks). The central bar and restaurant stands on rising ground in the south of the island, with boutique, library and a sandpit for the owner's many labradors: guests who want to venture out gather there before dinner (outsiders will find that the service is pretty unforth-coming). Finally, day sails are on offer, to the Tobago Cays and to tiny Mopion, the original sandbar with absolutely nothing but a palm thatch umbrella.

If prices are a concern, however, then PSV might not be for you, as such luxury comes at about US$750 per couple per night (FAP with meals and the facilities of the resort) in the winter season and $500 or so in the summer months.

St Lucia

Hold St Lucia, and the rest may perish!

The call to arms on behalf of St Lucia was raised so often that she become known as the Fair Helen of the West Indies. Desire to possess her moved whole armies and led to her changing hands fourteen times. She is a charmed isle, not so much for her strategic value nowadays, but for her people, among the friendliest in the Caribbean, and for her natural beauty: hidden coves, tropical abundance and the Pitons, twin volcanic pyramids from the south seas.

Lying between Martinique and St Vincent, St Lucia (pronounced 'St Loosha') is another island peak in the Windward chain, with slopes that soar from the sea to a central mountain spine crested by Morne Gimie (3117ft) and then fall away in forest-clad hills to lush valleys of bananas, tropical overgrowth and beaches mounded with golden sand. Some 27 miles by 14, St Lucia has a volcanic vent, a fumarole called *la Soufrière*, a bubbling and stinking morass which claims the dubious distinction of being the only 'drive-in' volcano in the world.

The 150,000 St Lucians are mostly descended from Africans who were brought to the island as slaves in the sugar heyday of the 18th century. More than one-third live in the capital, Castries, which shambles over hills above a sheltered harbour in the northwest.

St Lucia is the most developed of the Windward Islands and has some industry, including oil refining, furniture and clothing manufacture. There is a positive air about the island; new homes are springing up everwhere and the island is attracting investment from within the Caribbean area. Agriculture is still important, however, and many of the islanders live a simple West Indian existence, tied to the land, producing sustenance and a small living from produce sold in the markets. Traditionally bananas, grown by St Lucia's 2000 banana farmers, were the biggest export crop and they account for about 70 per cent of export earnings, but now, with the contraction of the industry in St Lucia, this has reduced.

St Lucia has a tangled and romantic history: she was disputed bitterly by the British and French for over a hundred years, and the island is littered with the ghostly fortresses of

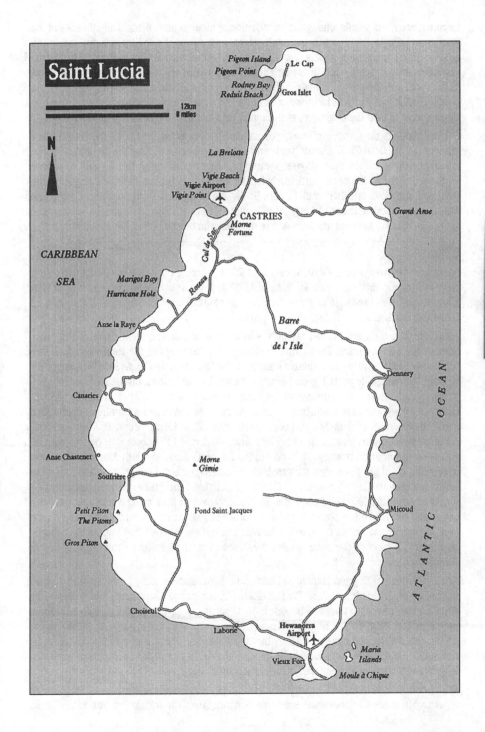

Saint Lucia

12km
8 miles

N

Pigeon Island
Pigeon Point
Rodney Bay
Reduit Beach

Le Cap
Gros Islet

La Brelotte

Vigie Beach
Vigie Airport
Vigie Point

CASTRIES
Morne
Fortune

Grand Anse

CARIBBEAN

SEA

Marigot Bay
Hurricane Hole

Cul de Sac

Roseau

Barre

de l' Isle

Anse la Raye

Dennery

O C E A N

Canaries

Anse Chastenet

Morne
Gimie

Soufrière

Petit Piton
The Pitons

Fond Saint Jacques

Micoud

Gros Piton

A T L A N T I C

Choiseul

Hewanorra
Airport

Laborie

Maria
Islands

Vieux Fort

Moule à Chique

forgotten wars, still visible among the encrustation of modern hotel plant. The influence of the French remains in the *mornes*, mountain-peaks, and *anses*, the sheltered bays, and in the culture—the population is mostly Catholic and there are distinct flashes of French style in the way they act and dress—and in the language. Every visitor will hear the strains of the local patois spoken in the streets, tantalizingly like French for a moment and yet impossible to pin down. English is the official language of St Lucia and so parents will bring up their children in the language to help them 'get on', even though they talk in patois between themselves.

St Lucia is one of the Caribbean's most popular destinations at the moment—the 18th-century war-cry 'To St Lucia! To St Lucia!' has been raised once again and now the air- and seaborne invaders have come in their droves, swamping Castries, storming the heights of Morne Fortune. The island has opted particularly for the all-inclusive format, in which people pay up front and don't pull out their wallet again, hardly venturing forth from the resort compound. This is a pity because the island is good to explore. There are also some small and charming spots hidden away in coves and bays where the calm and beauty of Fair Helen still remains.

History

Santa Lucia first appears on a royal *cedula* of 1511 marking out the Spanish domain in the New World, and then on a Vatican globe of 1520. It is not known who discovered it, or why it was named after the virgin-martyr of Syracuse, but the St Lucians celebrate St Lucy's day, 13 December, as their national day.

Hewanorra, as the Caribs called St Lucia, was a favoured hide-out for the pirates and privateers of the 16th century. They came to scourge the Spaniards in the Indies and men like Frenchman François de Clerc (better known to the Spaniards as *Pie de Palo* because of his wooden leg) would lie up at Pigeon Island in the north of the island, on the look-out for shipping to plunder, just as the admirals of the European navies would 200 years later. In 1553 de Clerc left for a grand tour in which he sacked the major towns in Santo Domingo, Puerto Rico and Cuba.Attempts to settle St Lucia began at the turn of the 17th century. The first, in 1605, really happened by accident, when the *Olive Blossom* limped to St Lucia after being blown off course on the Atlantic crossing. She was headed for the Guianas in South America, but, short of supplies, 67 of her passengers took their chances in St Lucia and bought huts and food from seemingly friendly Carib Indians. The Caribs soon changed their tune, though, and after five weeks of hostilities just 19 of the settlers were still alive, so they made a final purchase of a canoe and paddled off to South America. Another English attempt in 1639 survived for 18 months unmolested before the Caribs attacked. The Indians winkled them out of their fort by burning red pepper in the wind, a trick they used to catch sleeping parrots. Almost all the British were killed.

Just as Charles I of England granted St Lucia and other islands officially in the Spanish domain to the Earl of Carlisle in 1627, so Cardinal Richelieu felt free to offer islands 'not possessed by any Christian prince' to the French West India Company in 1642 and soon the French settlements in the West Indies began to appear. The scene was set for the next 200 years; settlements, battles and treaties, a rivalry that would see St Lucia change hands a ridiculous 14 times. Once the Caribs were wiped out, the island steadily turned from a rabble of deserters, loggers and turtlers to a prosperous colony, cultivating sugar.

With Louis XVI guillotined in January 1793 in Europe, Britain and the Republic of France were at war again in the Caribbean and the revolutionaries raised the *tricolore* in St Lucia. With its revolutionary sympathies and a guillotine erected in the capital, the island became known as *St Lucie la Fidèle*. The British fought their way back into Castries in 1796, but the *Armée française dans les bois* (a forest-based guerrilla force) held the rest of the islanders to ransom for another year. The subsequent war and treaty left St Lucia in British hands and the planters promptly got back to the business of cultivating sugar. The slaves were emancipated in 1834.

In 1885 Castries became one of the two principal coaling stations in the British West Indies, along with Kingston, Jamaica, filling a thousand steam-ships a year and gaining yet more importance when the Panama Canal was opened in 1914. Women would be seen climbing the gangways with 110lb baskets of coal on their heads, smoking pipes or singing shanties.

After the Second World War, as the West Indian islands moved towards political self-determination, St Lucia became self-governing in 1967 and then took Independence on 22 February 1979. The country is still a member of the British Commonwealth, with an elected parliament after the Westminster model and headed by a Governor General, presently Sir George Mallet. The island is governed by the St Lucia Labour Party under Prime Minister Dr Kenny Anthony, who hold 16 of the 17 seats in Parliament. The other seat is held by the United Workers' Party, who were in power for over thirty years until 1997.

St Lucia's economy depends mainly on tourism, but bananas also contribute to foreign exchange earnings. Most are shipped out by Windward Island Bananas and are sold in Britain. The industry has been in serious decline recently as the preferential arrangements with Britain and the European Community have collapsed and their market has been undercut by Central American 'dollar bananas'.

Getting Around

Private **minibuses** run all the main routes around the island. Gros Islet and the north are served frequently and buses continue until as late as 10pm (longer on a Friday night), leaving from Darling Road. Buses heading south leave from around Bridge Street, departing on and off until the late afternoon. For a day trip to Soufrière you must be quite careful because the last bus back to Castries leaves by mid-afternoon, after which time you will have to take the longer route via Vieux Fort. Some sample prices are: **Castries** to Gros Islet—EC$1.50, to Dennery—$3 and to Soufrière or Vieux Fort—$7.

Taxis can be arranged easily enough at hotels, in town or at the airport or through Courtesy Taxi Service (✆ 452 3555) in town and the Gablewoods Mall taxi stand (✆ 451 7521), Rodney Bay (✆ 452 0379), Marigot Bay Taxi (✆ 453 4406) and the St Lucia Taxi Service (✆ 452 2493) in the south of the island; if you are lucky the driver will give you an impromptu guided tour. By the hour a taxi costs about EC$55, and a day tour in a taxi can be shared for about EC$350 between four people. Sample one-way fares are: **Castries** to Vigie airport—EC$12, and to Hewanorra airport, near Vieux Fort—EC$120, to Rodney Bay—$40 and the Cap Estate in the north—$45.

Car hire gives more independence for exploring the inland byways like the rainforest road out of Soufrière and the route to Grand Anse northeast of Castries. A temporary driving licence is required, costing EC$30 on presentation of a valid licence from home to the police at either airport or in Castries. An international driving licence is valid. Driving is on the left, generally.

Many hire companies have desks at the airports and typically they will require a deposit of US$100 or a credit card imprint. Cars cost from US$45 per day, from Avis in Castries (✆ 452 2202), National, nearer to Gros Islet (✆ 450 8721), CTL Rent-A-Car (✆ 452 0732) or S.L.Y. Car Rental (✆ 452 5057). Jeeps are available through Cool Breeze Jeep Rental (✆ 454 7898) and you can hire motorbikes through Wayne's Motorcycle Centre in Vide Bouteille (✆ 452 2059), motorbikes about US$30 a day and scooters US$25.

Island tours around St Lucia can be arranged through Solar Tours in Choc Bay (✆ 451 9041) and Barnards Travel (✆ 452 2214). If you would like to tour the island by helicopter—in half an hour you can fly between the Pitons, hover in rainforested valleys and zoom yachts—contact St Lucia Helicopters (✆ 453 6950) or Eastern Caribbean Helicopters (✆ 453 6952), departure from Point Seraphine. North and south island tours at about US$200 for 10 minutes (max three people).

Beaches

St Lucia's best white-sand beaches lie on the protected leeward coast at the northern end of the island, between Castries and the northern tip. Here you will find the most active beaches, with hotels and watersports. To the south of Castries most of the beaches have black volcanic sand, often in secluded coves where the mountains fall steeply down to the coast. You will find that although there is officially public access to every beach, some of them are effectively closed to visitors because the hotels operate an all-inclusive policy (and would demand a full day's fee to use their facilities). However, Reduit Beach offers most things.

best beaches

Reduit Beach: In Rodney Bay, the island's most popular beach, a 20-minute drive from the capital, and most watersports are on offer. Miles of mounded sand so soft that you stumble trying to get through it. Also bars in case you feel sunstroke coming on.

Pigeon Island: Across the bay from Reduit Beach, a couple of secluded strips of sand.

La Brelotte: A steep-sided bay to the south, towards town (the Windjammer resort is here).

Vigie Beach: A 2-mile stretch starting at the airport and running north; natural and mostly undeveloped, but a couple of hotels and bars.

West coast: The coastline has a number of charming bays, first **La Toc** Bay just south of Castries, where there is a hotel. Some can only be reached by boat.

Marigot Bay: The small stretch of sand is not brilliant, but the setting in the charming bay is magnificent: call the ferry over to take you across. There is a bar there.

Anse Cochon: Accessed by boat, a remote cove a couple of miles south of Marigot Bay, good for an afternoon's snorkelling and lazing around.

Anse Chastanet: Just north of Soufrière on the leeward coast, an idyllic cove with dark sand, sheltered by sheltered massive headlands. **Soufrière** has a passable beach.

Anse des Sables: In the southeastern corner of the island near the airport on the Atalntic side, a shallow, open bay swept by the trade winds, renowned for windsurfing.

St Lucia has some good spots to base yourself for a day's beach activity. On Reduit Beach you will find a couple, of which the more preferable is **Spinnakers,** set on a palm-thatch and wooden deck right on the sand, with a TV accompaniment to your beer and salad or burger. The **Islander,** set back across the concrete car park, is cheaper and offers local as well as international fare. On the Atlantic side, in Cas en Bas, you will find a bar called **Turtle Reef,** which is good for a day out. On Vigie Beach, the area around **D's** is pleasant and never crowded. There are a couple of excellent waterfront bars beneath the palm trees in **Marigot Bay,** where Doolittle's has an excellent setting beneath some tall palms. If you happen past **Anse Jambette**, just further south, while it is open, that is well worth hoving to for (reservations can be made through the Green Parrot, ✆ 452 3399). Close by, **Anse Mamim** has a charming setting in a tiny cove. Finally, **Anse Chastanet** has a fine tropical bar and a superb view over the dark sand to the sunset. In the far south of the island you will find a couple of restaurants and bars on the windy beach near the airport: try **Sandy Beach** for snacks and time out from the sun.

Flora and Fauna

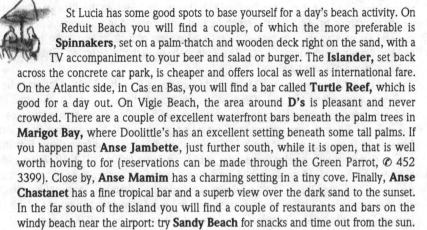

Like all the Windwards St Lucia has exuberant flora; coastal mangrove swamps (near Savannes on the southeast coast) where you can see the mangrove cuckoo and the tropical mockingbird and warblers, and plains flown over by hawks and herons. The white bird that keeps a silent vigil by the grazing cows is the cattle egret, which found its way over from Africa earlier this century. In the higher reaches of rainforest you will find the Antillean crested and the purple-throated hummingbird. The upper rainforest is also home to the endangered St Lucia parrot. Over the coast and the off-shore islands, you will come across tropicbirds and magnificent frigatebirds.

There are far fewer mammals, but there are many reptiles, from frogs to iguanas. One you will certainly hear is the tree frog, who peeps rhythmically at night, particularly after a rainstorm. Turtles also come to lay their eggs on St Lucian beaches between March and August. The National Trust (✆ 452 5008, 📠 453 2791) manages a number of St Lucia's Nature Reserves, which include the Maria and Fregate Islands on the east coast and the Pigeon Island National Landmark (as the name indicates, this is really a site of historical interest, but some of the plants are marked). There is a Marine Park in the Soufrière area which has been zoned into marine reserves and recreational areas, helping to protect the environment (preserving it for scuba divers among other things). Yachts need to buy a permit to anchor here. A camp-ground has been opened in Anse la Liberté near Canaries, with a local plant nursery and a nature interpretation centre as well as trails through the local area. Those with a particular interest in the natural life can contact the Forest and Lands Department (✆ 450 2231/453 2287), who can arrange knowledgeable guides for birders and plant or animal watchers.

Castries

If history were to be replayed as you cruised into Castries harbour, the hills around you would swarm with troops, the air hang heavy with the smell of gunpowder and the ground and the harbour be stained scarlet with blood. Castries was one of the most bitterly contested places in the whole of the Caribbean.

The town lies on the protected leeward coast of the island, at the head of an irregular and almost landlocked bay, framed by forested hills that rise in folds into the distance. The harbour mouth is guarded by Vigie Point (French for look-out), covered in yellow-brick barrack buildings and the graveyards of empire—you get a good view of them as you come in for the final wobbly descent into Vigie airport. The French have actually returned. They keep their embassy in one of these buildings.

Castries takes its name from the Maréchal de Castries, a French colonial minister, who was governor of the island in 1784. The name stuck, despite being rejected at the time of the French Revolution, when the town was known as *Félicité-ville*. Set out on a gridiron pattern, the centre of the town is mostly modern, concrete and functional. Near the market on Jeremie Street there is even an area of neo-brutalist housing estate imported from sixties Britain. But despite Castries's rather unfortunate habit of burning down (1796, 1812, 1927 and 1948), it has a few pockets of old creole architecture, mostly in the southeast corner of the town at the top end of Chaussee Road. Their balconies overhang the pavement on sturdy wooden stilts and the gingerbread patterns on the eaves here are more intricate than on any island in the Eastern Caribbean besides Trinidad. In all, the town supports about 60,000 people.

The centre of the town is **Derek Walcott Square**, recently renamed after he won the Nobel prize for literature (its previous name Columbus Square had long been controversial). In its centre is a magnificent saman tree which provides shade from the tropical sun. On the east side of the square, Laborie St, is the **Roman Catholic Cathedral**, which has an iron-work and wooden interior with yellow stained glass and a brightly painted, patterned roof and colourful murals in which many of the figures are depicted as Africans. Opposite the cathedral stands the library, an imposing colonial structure. Farther along Laborie Street you come to the small Constitution Park and the Court and Parliament buildings (both modern). This area, with William Peter Boulevard running off it, is the business and gravitational centre for limers and shoppers.

Another lively area of town is the **Market**, a couple of minutes' walk away on Jeremie Street, a magnificent old red iron market erected at the turn of the century. Recently renovated, it is now flanked by newer concrete buildings containing more markets and craft markets; the whole area is jumbled full of furniture, straw bags and sweetmeats and resounds to the chatter of buyers and the market ladies from the country, who sit watching over piles of eddoe, tannia, christophene and yam.

Morne Fortune (pronounced 'Fortunay' and supposedly meaning the Hill of Good Luck) looms above the town, and it is here that the fiercest battles took place in the 18th century. Nowadays the soldiers would be fighting their way through the scarlet and purple blooms of the bougainvillea in the private gardens as the road winds its way back and forth to the summit. The old imposing military hulks, barracks, stables and gun emplacements have been taken over by the modern-day establishment as official buildings. The La Toc Battery has been opened: a low 19th-century battery made of concrete with a couple of old cannon that point at the trees now that they have grown to obscure the view; worth a very quick look, and there is also a **walking trail** (*open 8.30am–3pm*). Close to the summit stands the tatty Fort Charlotte, which dates from the late 18th century, but not far off, most of the old colonial buildings now contain schools and a department of the University of the West Indies. There is a monument to the bravery of the 27th Inniskilling Regiment who actually made it all the way to the top in 1796. Also a monument to Sir Arthur Lewis, the first St Lucian Nobel Prize winner and first Chancellor of the UWI.

Nearby is Government House, the official residence of the Governor General, built of grey stones with white trimmings in the 1890s. It had something of a habit of killing governors. As Sir Algernon Aspinall relates in his *Pocket Guide to the West Indies*, one inhospitable Governor Farquharson was obliged to entertain a bishop; when it was time to retire he said, 'I suppose your lordship has heard of the insalubrity of this place; every room in the house has already witnessed the death of some Governor, but none of them has had the honour of killing a Bishop; so, my Lord, you have only to make your selection.' The Bishop departed immediately and Governor Farquharson died of fever in the house two years later.

The Morne dominates the town and from the top you get one of the finest views in the West Indies. To the north it commands Vigie airport and then along the coast to Pigeon Point. On clear days it is quite possible to see Martinique. The view is also spectacular to the south, where the Pitons are visible in the distance.

North from Castries to the Cap

As you head north out of town, you run along the harbour, passing the new government buildings on the right and the fish market with its colourful boats on the left. A side road leads left to the Institut Franco-St Lucien, a curious white pyramid, and then on to the Point Seraphine cruise ship dock and shopping complex.

Time was, not so long ago, when the cars had to be cleared off the road to allow planes to land at Vigie airport, which handles short-haul island-hopper flights. Now the airstrip runs alongside **Vigie Beach**, so if you want some last minutes of sun and sand before leaving, there are 2 miles of protected bay here. It is the site of many a forgotten invasion and the fortifications that opposed them, 18th-century strongholds that now lie buried under the bastions of the 20th-century Caribbean tourist hotels. The island opposite the Sandals Halcyon hotel is called Rat Island, a former nunnery, now deserted.

From the top end of Choc Bay a side road branches through the hills to the other side of the island where you will find the attractive half-moon bay of Grand Anse on the Atlantic coast. The family of the Empress Josephine had a sugar estate at Paix Bouche on the windward side of the island. Despite Martiniquan insistence to the contrary, the St Lucians claim that Josephine was born in St Lucia. At the **Marquis Estate** (✆ 452 3762) you will see a working plantation producing bananas and *copra* (dried coconut) and hear descriptions of old-time crops such as cocoa and coffee, and of course sugar. After the estate visit you can take a trip down the Marquis River to an Atlantic coast bay for a swim.

The main road north, which is being steadily developed with houses and shopping centres, emerges from the rolling hills on to **Rodney Bay**, named after the British admiral who made St Lucia his headquarters in the late 18th century. This is the location of Reduit beach and many of St Lucia's hotels and restaurants. In the bay the yachts and gin palaces lie at anchor in formation, just as Rodney's warships did 200 years ago.

Across the marina entrance stands the village of **Gros Islet**, famed for its parties on Friday nights when the few streets of simple, brightly painted clapboard houses seethe with dancers until the early hours. The town was proudly called *Révolution* when St Lucia was holding out at the time of the French Revolution. The 'islet' (Pigeon Island) from which the town takes its name is in fact no longer an island. It was joined to the mainland in the early seventies by an artificial causeway, part of a vastly expensive tourist development programme that foundered, leaving just a few abandoned foundations and a perfectly protected and stunning bay.

Pigeon Point, Pigeon Island that was, lies 1 mile across the bay, a barren outcrop with two peaks that the British fortified as soon as they took the island from the French in 1778. The stone ramparts and defences are still visible, 18th-century gun batteries, gun slides and the sunken 'musket redoubt' (a last ditch defence), 19th-century barracks and cookhouses. The most recent buildings are from an American World War II listening station. Since the earliest visitors came to St Lucia, Pigeon Island has been used as a vantage point to watch over Martinique, visible 20 miles away. Now the area is a National Park and there is a shop and a small Interpretation Centre (*adm*) in the recently restored officers' mess. Among the Amerindian artefacts, models of soldiers and pictorial descriptions of barrack life, there is a visual display of the Battle of the Saints in 1782, in which Rodney had his finest hour. A ferry runs a cross to Pigeon Point from Rodney Bay Marina several times a day.

At the northern tip of the island is the **Cap Estate**, an expensive residential area with smart villas and a golf course. Worth a visit in this area is the **gallery** of the St Lucian-born artist, Llewelyn Xavier (*©* 450 9155; *adm free, paintings from a few hundred dollars*). Go straight ahead at the second roundabout, past the house shaped like a banana, and it is a white building up on the left. Art on view includes work by locals Derek Walcott and Roy Lawaetz (as well as Xavier himself), Mr Canute Caliste from Carriacou and several Haitians, but the trip is worthwhile for the view alone, which takes in both the Atlantic coast and the Pitons.

South to Soufrière

The route to Soufrière from Castries follows a tortuous path above the leeward coast of the island, a series of switchbacks struggling up over the headlands and cruising down into the river valleys where fishing villages nestle among the palms. Alternatively, take a yacht and coast along the island for two hours and you will see the road straggle south against the backdrop of the St Lucian mountains, so often shrouded by passing rainstorms. Whichever route you take, the journey culminates in one of the most exciting views in the whole of the Caribbean, the twin peaks of the Pitons that soar from the sea's edge like vast tropical pyramids.

On land the journey starts at the summit of Morne Fortune, and drops into **Cul de Sac**, a wide valley once riffling with sugar cane and now carpeted with banana trees, passing the wire and security lights of the huge Hess oil bunkering facility. From here the road climbs a ridge and drops into another huge valley, at **Roseau**, also filled with bright green banana leaves that splay gracefully in an arch until their tips reach the ground. As you reach the valley floor you come to a side-road which leads to **Marigot Bay**, one of the most charming natural features in the Caribbean, a steep-sided harbour festooned with palm trees. It is now an idyllic hideaway with a cluster of low-key hotels and villas on the hillsides and bars around the waterfront. Yachts sit serenely on the calm of Hurricane Hole, an extremely safe anchorage. In 1778, Admiral Barrington is supposed to have eluded d'Estaing by bringing his fleet into the bay and camouflaging the ships with palm fronds. More recently, *Dr Doolittle* with Rex Harrison was filmed here. A small boat-taxi links one side to the other.

Farther down, just off the main road, you pass the **Barbay Distillery** (*©* 451 4315; *open weekdays; adm EC$10*), which can be visited. Set in a modern building, it shows the processes of fermentation and distillation that produce the local *Bounty* Rum in its various

the Pitons, St Lucia

white and red forms and *Titasse,* a coffee rum. The best view of the Roseau valley is from the heights just as you leave it to drive farther south.

The two fishing towns of **Anse la Raye**, where you will see a fine church, and **Canaries** lie on river mouths at the sea's edge. From here the road cuts deeper inland and then climbs into the rainforest, a profusion of majestic ferns, bamboos and grasses that sprout from the deep brown earth and ancient-looking lianas that hang from trees high above.

Finally the road clears another summit and, emerging from the dank rainforest you are faced with the twin points of the **Pitons** which stand out in the glare of the sun. The word 'Piton' means 'spike' and they are thought to be the sides of an eroded volcanic crater. They have long been a sailor's landmark and are spectacular when viewed from the sea, but the best view is from the leeward coast road because they have an identical shape and slide into dramatic place beside one another as you descend into Soufrière.

The town of **Soufrière** itself lies in a valley beneath the Petit Piton (2461ft). It is one of the oldest settlements in St Lucia, a thriving port in the mid-18th century, and takes its name from the volcanic vent nearby that emits sulphurous clouds. For a while in the 1790s it held the honoured republican name of *La Convention*, after the revolutionary tribunal in Paris. The town is quite tatty and obviously poor, but around the central Elizabeth Square there are some attractive old stone façades and wooden creole homes surviving from French times, their eaves a gingerbread filigree beneath corrugated iron roofs. Some of the traditional life persisits. On Saturday morning there is a market on the seafront and you may see cocoa beans drying in the sun on the pavement, before they are processed into cocoa sticks. The bay is extremely deep, dropping straight away as steeply as the Pitons rise above the surface. For those brave enough to swim in a fathomless place like this, the water has warm and cold patches, released by the volcano beneath the surface.

Inland from Soufrière, the road comes to the **Diamond Falls and Botanical Gardens** (*adm*), on the Soufrière Estate, where a path leads through tropical gardens into a cleft with a waterfall gushing into a small rockpool. The water descends 1000ft from the volcano above, where it leaves the ground at 106° Fahrenheit and has discoloured the river bed orange and gold with the volcanic mud. The water supposedly has similar properties to the water of Aix-les-Bains in France and is reputed to have considerable curative powers, 'efficacious in cases of rheumatism and kindred ills'. If you are happy to risk carbonate of magnesia and phosphate of lime then you can take the waters (brought down from higher up the mountain). Alternatively you can take a steamy bath in it. The **gardens** (*adm*) are pleasant to visit and you can expect to see typical Caribbean plants such as lobster claw and ginger lily, but also less usual ones like breadnut (a relative of the breadfruit) and a gri-gri palm with a hairy trunk. The old water-wheel was used to crush sugar-cane and limes.

The road to Diamond continues inland, climbing steadily into the St Lucia rainforest and losing itself in Fonds St Jacques, now a nature reserve, where among the wild orchids and the montane woodland you might catch a glimpse of the endangered St Lucia parrot among the flitting hummingbirds.

Travelling south from Soufrière back on the coast road, the road climbs for a couple of miles to **Morne Coubaril Estate** (✆ 459 7340; *adm, half-hour guided tour*), a restored and working plantation high in the mountains. Here you will see a glimpse of traditional life in 18th-century St Lucia including a plantation village with 'voltivier' roofs made of bamboo-like shingles on wattle and daub walls, and methods of processing tropical products, such as coconuts (used for oil, margarine and sun-tan lotion), cocoa (which is processed and dried here) and the local flour, from the vegetable manioc. Bar and restaurant for local food and juices.

Not far off are the **Sulphur Springs**, St Lucia's well-behaved *solfatara*. In the collapsed crater is a bubbling and steaming morass, 7 acres in size, devoid of plant-life, with grey mudpools that hiss and smell gently of stink-bomb. There was a vapour explosion at the Soufrière in 1766, but nothing too violent has happened since then. It is not expected to erupt because it constantly lets off steam. Paths are clearly marked and you are not advised to wander around on it because the mudpools have been known to move suddenly (one person was swallowed to the waist and ended up with third-degree burns). You may see a couple of rusty pipes sticking out of the ground, an attempt to tap the heat for power generation. As the tourist brochures say, the Soufrière is a 'drive-in' volcano. For the tourists who dare venture forth from the protection of their car, there are guides who will ply them with more Soufrière lore for a small fee.

From the mountain heights of the Pitons, the road steadily descends to the southern plains that once blew with sugar-cane, to Vieux Fort at the most southerly tip of the island. It passes through the fishing villages of **Choiseul**, with its black and white cemetery, and **Laborie**. Both are quiet and unaffected West Indian towns, full of clapboard houses on blocks, standing in neat yards in the shadow of breadfruit trees. Perhaps you will arrive on the day when the open-air butcher is at work, boiling up black puddings for passers-by. At Choiseul, the Arts and Crafts Development Centre displays and sells local handiwork including rocking chairs and carvings. There is a small restaurant if you want to stop for lunch.

Vieux Fort is named after a fortress, mentioned already by the island-hopping monk, Abbé Raynal, when he travelled the islands in the mid-17th century. St Lucia's second town, it is windswept and stands on an open bay, looking south towards St Vincent. It was here that the sugar industry was first set up in 1765, but now the town is quiet and the few streets seem empty. Hewanorra International Airport nearby was first built by the Americans during the Second World War as a refuelling point on their routes between the United States and Europe; now it receives long-haul flights from both directions.

Protruding into the rough water between the Atlantic and the Caribbean by Vieux Fort is the **Moule à Chique** peninsula, offering fine views towards St Vincent, a grey-green stain about 25 miles away to the south.

The **Maria Islands** lie off the Atlantic coast just out of Vieux Fort and are kept as a nature reserve. Those interested in discovering the delights of the *kouwès* snake (this is the only place on the globe where this species of grass snake lives), a lizard called *zandoli te* and the wheeling world of frigatebirds and brown noddies should contact the National Trust (© 452 5005). There is a small **museum** of natural life at the end of the Hewanorra runway opposite the islands (*open Wed–Sun, 9.30–5; adm*)

Vieux Fort to Castries—North along the Windward Coast

The Windward road winds along the rough Atlantic coast, over the spurs and the valleys thrown off by the central spine of mountains and passes through the plantations that provide St Lucia's food and export fruit. The centres are the towns of **Micoud** and **Dennery**. Between the two is the Fregate Island Nature Reserve. There is an observation trail where you can hope to see St Lucian orioles and tremblers and where frigatebirds nest on the islands in the summer months. At Dennery is one of the island's largest banana plantations, with acres of huge and bright green leaves unscrolling and become steadily shredded by the wind. From here the road cuts inland, over the **Barre de l'Isle** ridge, among the lianas and bushy ferns high up in the rainforest and then descends into Cul de Sac valley before climbing the back of Morne Fortune and dropping into Castries.

© *(1 758)–*   *Where to Stay*

The majority of St Lucia's hotels are on the beaches of the northern leeward coast, facing the calm Caribbean Sea and the sunset. There are plenty of humming hives of high-pressure luxury in the typical Caribbean beach resort mould, but St Lucia also has some charming smaller hotels offering classic Caribbean seclusion in dramatic settings, tucked away in the island's coves or in view of the Pitons. Many hotels follow an all-inclusive plan, including a number of more luxurious resorts, but there is still a good range of properties for the independent traveller. In recent years a number of small and individual hotels and guest houses, many in charming or traditional Caribbean settings, have opened up (in all price brackets) and so it is worth trying out more than one in the course of a week. There are plenty of villas on the island and accommodation in them can be arranged through outside operators or by the St Lucian company **Tropical Villas** (© 450 8240, ✉ 450 8089). Hotel bills (unless you are in an all-inclusive resort) are supplemented by a government tax of 8%, and most hotels also levy a 10% service charge.

luxury–very expensive

The white arches and orange roof tiles of the **Windjammer Landing Villas Beach Resort**, PO Box 1504 (© (758) 452 0913, ✉ 452 0907, UK © (0800) 373 742, US © (1 800) 743 9609, Canada © (800) 267 7600, *www.wlv-resort.com*) stand out starkly against the shades of green on Labrelotte Bay north of Castries. There are 114 extremely comfortable and elegant deluxe and superior rooms in varieties of one- to four-bedroom apartments and villas—bedrooms air-conditioned, living rooms fan-ventilated, all with maid service and some with their own plunge pool and sunning area. From the breezy central area laid with terracotta tiles you descend through the tropical gardens to a long and pretty curve of beach around which stand the four restaurants among the trees. Plenty of tennis and watersports by day, and in the evening you can dine by the swimming-pool (of which there are four).

Close by is a low-key and extremely comfortable smaller hotel, the **East Winds Inn**, PO Box 193 (✆ 452 8212, ✆ 452 9941, UK res ✆ (0171) 741 9511, US ✆ (212) 545 8437), which is set in a very attractive lawned garden of bamboo and mango trees running down to a beach with a good stretch of sand. There are 26 rooms in two different styles: stone and wooden cottages with gingerbread pointings and a small porch and screened windows, very comfortable inside with bamboo and rattan furniture and sunken showers made of stone; and breezy octagonal rondavelles with large porches, louvred windows and tall cane-backed chairs. There is a pool with a swim-up bar and a nice palm-thatch dining area close to the beach. Elegant and quiet ambience, all-inclusive plan with some dine-around options, no children in season.

If you prefer more of a resort style of hotel you can try the **Royal St Lucia Hotel**, PO Box 977 (✆ (758) 452 9999, ✆ 452 9639, UK res ✆ (0181) 741 5333, US ✆ (1 800) 255 5859), which holds massive pride of place right on Reduit Beach. It is large and has all the international standard trappings of the 20th century, from air-conditioning, cable television and king-sized beds down to the third telephone in the bathroom.

Near the northern tip of the island you will find **Le Sport**, PO Box 437 (✆ 450 8551, ✆ 450 0368, US ✆ (1 800) 544 2883, UK ✆ (0800) 590794), which devotes itself to a scheduled body-holiday for office-weary executives. As the name suggests, there are plenty of sports, both land and waterborne. And for less energetic rejuvenation, you can try the Moorish relaxation palace (algae bubble baths and seaweed wraps, loofa rubs, swiss needle showers and massage). Calorized cuisine or plain old chocolate indulgence. All-inclusive plan.

There is a clutch of excellent up-market hotels around **Soufrière**, set in some of the most dramatic surroundings in the Caribbean. **Anse Chastanet**, PO Box 7000 (✆ 459 7000, ✆ 459 7700, UK ✆ (0800) 894 057, US and Canada ✆ (1 800) 223 1108), is tucked into its own remote and attractive cove at the end of a steep and rickety road out of the town. There are 48 rooms in the resort, ranged on the steeply rising ground from the very pretty dark sand beach (12 rooms) and up beyond the main dining room and bar, where the rondavels and huge suites (some of them open-sided; showers with a view) take best advantage of their magnificent settings for the view, some overlooking the Pitons. All rooms are furnished in colourful French Caribbean 'madras' material and are fan-ventilated rather than air-conditioned. Friendly air, busy down on the beach where there is a beach bar and watersports, particularly scuba, but of course very peaceful in the privacy of the rooms. The resort has a conscious policy on detergents and uses mainly products from the local area, MAP, a variety of packages..

In its striking setting 1000 feet above the sea, perched on the shoulder of the Petit Piton and surrounded by greenery, the **Ladera Resort**, PO Box 255 (✆ 459 7323,

459 5156, US ✆ (1 800) 738 4752) is the ultimate in peace and tropical tranquillity. There is a variety of villas and one and two-bedroom suites in stone structures; open-fronted to take best advantage of the view and with a delightful intimacy with the tropical night, the breeze and the peep of the tree frogs. Very quiet and elegant ambience, old-time Caribbean feel with dark-stained wood and antique furniture, all rooms have private pools or plunge pools; room service. Dining with a view at the Dasheene Restaurant, for Caribbean and Californian cuisine.

Stonefield Estate (✆ 452 3483, ✆ 453 0394) has six villas of varying sizes scattered around the charming gardens of an old plantation estate just south of the town of Soufrière, in full view of the Petit Piton and a short walk from Malgretoute beach. They are furnished in the best West Indian traditions, with antiques, four-posters and mosquito nets, and they have louvred doors and windows, with fans to encourage the breeze. Utterly calm and charming, very low-key atmosphere, pool, no restaurant but each villa has a fully equipped kitchen.

moderate

The **Marigot Bay** area has a number of good places to stay, in this price range. Down on the waterfront, behind the screen of tall palm trees on the spit of land is the **Marigot Beach Club**, PO Box 101 (✆ 451 4974, ✆ 451 4973, US res ✆ (813) 530 5424), where a series of studios and villas (20 in all, comfortable with bright white décor and a kitchenette and porch, fan-ventilated) are ranged on the steep valley side amid the tropical bushes and trees. The central area is on the shoreline itself: a passable beach, watersports shop, pool and a brightly painted, pink and purple restaurant and bar with tables ranged on a deck around the outside. Easy air with yachtsmen and a passing crowd, stay and sail packages available. An excellent place to stay—small, intimate and impeccably clean and neat—is the **Sea Horse Inn**, PO Box 1825 (✆ 451 4436, ✆ 451 4872, *seahorse@candw.lc, www.seahorse-inn.com*), which is set in a former private house made of stone with stark white windows and balustrades. Now an upmarket bed and breakfast, it has a large central sitting area and dining room upstairs and eight comfortable rooms each with their own sitting area. Nice and breezy (no a/c, nor phones), very private, pool on a deck in the garden and a lovely view over the lagoon. Stay and sail packages. If you are happy to look after yourself, then there are villas dotted around the bay: contact **Oasis Marigot** (✆ 451 4185, ✆ 451 4608, UK ✆ (0800) 965015, US and Canada toll free ✆ 1 (800) 263 4202, *oasis@intlaurentides.qc.ca, www.oasismarigot.com*) who have large and comfortable one- and two-bedroom villas high on the hill above the Marigot Beach Club and elsewhere around the bay. The **Harmony Suites**, PO Box 155, in Castries (✆ 452 8756, ✆ 452 8677), are a group of apartment suites owned by a local Bristish family, set beside a white sandy bay, some with kitchenettes, all with excellent facilities including TV, restaurant, pool and beauty salon.

cheap

In the north of St Lucia, you can stay within a shout of **Reduit beach** without spending a fortune at the **Candyo Inn**, PO Box 386 (✆ 452 0712, ✆ 452 0774), which has 12 very neat and pretty rooms and suites decorated with white tiles, wicker furniture and floral fittings. It is set in a modern house with a small covered courtyard with plants and pool and bar in the garden at the back. Rooms have kitchenettes (there is a small food shop) and there is a restaurant, but there are lots of other restaurants all around of course; very friendly.

A small spot with a lot of style near Gros Islet is **Henry's La Panache** Guest House on Cas en Bas Road (✆ 450 0765, 🖅 450 0453). There are just eight simple rooms scattered on a hillside around a couple of charming and rustic Caribbean decks (tin roofs on wooden poles) in a garden where stone walkways meander through tropical profusion. Friendly and easy-going air, lots of information, particularly on natural history; hot water and showers in private bathrooms, fan ventilation, breakfast and snacks available by day, creole dinners sometimes. In Gros Islet itself there are rooms at the **Golden Apple** (✆ 450 8056); private baths, fan ventilation.

Tucked away, slightly remote in the residential Monchy district, so you would need a car (though buses do run the road below), is the **Country Inn** (✆ 452 8301). Three bedrooms and three apartments in a modern West Indian home, sitting area and kitchen facilities available, private baths, TVs, a/c and standing fans.

In **Castries** itself you might consider the gracious antiquity of the **Top o' the Morne Apartments** (✆ 452 3603, 453 1433; *moderate*), which are set in a former colonial administration building, a yellow brick structure with balconies running the full length front and back set at the top of Morne Fortune. The studios and one and two-bedroom apartments have big, breezy rooms, quite simply furnished with wooden floorboards, and a fantastic view of the town and harbour below from the balconies. Full kitchens and car hire available. Not far off is **Bon Appetit** (✆ 452 2757; *cheap*), very quiet rarefied air and a superb view, four simple double and single rooms with private showers and hot and cold water, central sitting area (cable TV) and nice dining room.

A cheap deal just out of town but on the bus routes to everywhere (also well placed for the airport) is the **Harbour Light Inn** (✆ 452 3506), which is set in a modern concrete structure without much charm; simple rooms with a choice of standing fans and a/c, private baths, sometimes a restaurant. The cheapest deal in town is **Lee's Guest House** (✆ 452 4285). Above **Soufrière** you can stay cheaply at **La Haut Plantation** (✆ 459 7008, 🖅 454 9463, *allainj.candw.com*). The name literally means 'up there' and it gives a good idea of the setting, way up above the town. Six large apartments with rattan furniture and a balcony or terrace, kitchenettes, restaurant with a view. There are also *cheap* rooms and apartments in the town at **The Still** (✆ 459 5175, 🖅 459 7301, but the rooms on the beach itself are *cheap to moderate*). There is some very simple accommodation in town at the **Home Hotel** (✆ 459 7318), share baths and cold water. There is a camp-site at **Anse La Liberte** near Canaries with cabins, cooking and washing facilities, as well as trails and an interpretation centre.

In the far south of the island you will find a charming garden setting and the atmosphere of the old West Indies at **Balenbouche Estate**, PO Box 489 (✆ 455 1244, 🖅 455 1342), a 200-year-old plantation house now restored. There are eight rooms in the old house and a bungalow, antique furniture and creaking floorboards (quite thin walls); quite simple, some share baths. Lots of good advice and a friendly atmosphere and endless speculation on the origin of the name. In Vieux Fort, perhaps as a stop on arrival at Hewanorra or just before leaving, you can find rooms at **Kimitrai** (✆ 454 6328).

St Lucia's French heritage extends into the food and the West Indian ingredients take on new life here in such creole dishes such as *soupe germou* (pumpkin and garlic soup) and *pouile dudon* (treacle and coconut chicken stew). As in any other of the islands, it is worth getting a spread of the vegetables, cooked in all the different ways—plantain boiled and fried, breadfruit, yam and christophene. Too many all-inclusive hotels in an island tends to spell the death knell for eating out and it seems that the restaurateurs in St Lucia have had quite a tough time as so many of the hotels have gone that way. Most large or hotel restaurants will accept credit cards; local ones will accept EC (Eastern Caribbean) dollars willingly and US dollars at a pinch. All bills are supplemented with an 8% government tax and most add 10%, or sometimes 15% for service as well. Categories are based on the price of a main course: *expensive*—EC$50 and above; *moderate*—EC$50–20; *cheap*—less than EC$20.

Castries and the North

expensive

The **Coal Pot** Restaurant (© 457 5566) has a charming setting on a wooden deck on the waterfront overlooking Vigie Cove on the outskirts of Castries (signs off the airport road). You dine on well prepared and presented French and creole cuisine in an open-sided, shingle roofed building with artwork on the walls. Their pepperpot has genuine Caribbean cassareep to flavour the pork and beef and there is a choice of sauces with your fish: creole, ginger, saffron dill or creamy mushroom. Intimate charming air and nice reception. High on a hillside in the Cap Estate you will find an attractive setting at the **Great House** restaurant (© 450 0450). It occupies the site of an old plantation house and has been rebuilt with some of the old West Indian charm. You enter through louvred doors and dine in the gracious mock-antique Caribbean interior or out on the veranda where vases overflow with greenery. Try snails in millefeuille with a balsamic vinegar sauce followed by roast kingfish in an orange and peppercorn crust or lamb noisettes in a rosemary and nutmeg sauce. Finish up with soursop ice cream in filo pastry. Set menu or *à la carte. Closed Mon.*

In the ever-busy **Rodney Bay** area you will always find a lively air at the **Charthouse** (© 450 8115), which is set on the waterfront in a timber-frame house hung with ferns and palms. You dine on house specialities of seafood and prime rib steaks or some hickory-smoked ribs. *Closed Sun.* If you think you might like an air-conditioned speakeasy with a feeling of mock-gangsterism, then try **Capone's** (© 450 0284) nearby, where the menu is Italian. Start with a Prohibition Punch, followed by chicken with spinach, cheese and red peppers. The bill comes in a violin case. If you cannot remember the code-word (Al sent me), then there is a pizzeria next door.

Close to the top of the Morne in Castries is **Bon Appetit** (© 452 2757), one of the most sympathetic spots on the island. There is a view as far as Martinique on a good night from the tiny dining room, which is candle-lit with madras tablecloths and is decorated with murals. The fare is international—seafood crêpe to start or heart of palm, followed by a choice of shrimp veal or filet of fish with fresh island vegetables. Remember to reserve a table in season. The well-known **San Antoine** (© 452 4660) has a certain old-time ambience, set in a 19th-century stone great house with tall arched windows. You begin with cocktails at the bar looking out through the trees, and then move through to the subdued, candle-lit dining room. The menu is French and international—*fruits de mer en papillote* or *chicken San Antoine,* a breast of chicken filled with crab, cream cheese and puréed spinach and wrapped in puff pastry.

Just outside Castries you will find **Jimmie's** (✆ 452 5142) just above the tiny working inlet, Vigie Cove, off the main harbour. It is as lively by day as in the evening: you sit on a floral deck just above the water or a terrace festooned with greenery. Simple lunches, more elaborate dinners: a seafood crêpe in white wine or local pot fish cooked in a broth, with lots of local fruit juices. Varied crowd; 'singers and speakers (of the House)', easy going and friendly.

moderate

You will find one of the most agreeable spots on the island at the **Snooty Agouti** (✆ 452 0321) in Gros Islet, where you sit at a palm-thatch bar upstairs in a wooden building and at tables by huge open windows. Trusty international fare collected from around the world and home-made in St Lucia: baked potatoes, pitta sandwiches, lasagnas, even rollmops and rice stuffed in a sea grape leaf served with brown soda bread; also chocolate puddings. Most importantly, the island's best coffee—lattes, mochas and cappuccinos, some iced, and blends from Tanzania, Panama, Sumatra— also cigars, from Cuba of course. Nice seating area, book exchange, Internet connection, sometimes jazz. Easy and friendly feel, open all day .

For a French creole meal you can try **La Creole** (✆ 452 0022), which is set in a modern house between Rodney Bay and Gros Islet. You dine on a breezy terrace upstairs decorated with fishing nets and unmade lobster pots: thick and spicy fish soup, Bel Helen salad (fritters, heart of palm, local vegetables and black pudding), fried sea egg, avocado *féroce,* octopus creole, a colombo or a shark *touffé.* No French Caribbean rum punches, unfortunately, but fun all the same. Another ever popular place for simple fare daytime and evening is **The Lime** (✆ 452 0761). Caribbean and international menu: accra fritters followed by filet of fish *bonne femme* in white wine and mushroom sauce, or omelettes and burgers.

In Vide Bouteille is **D's Restaurant** (✆ 453 7931), which has an excellent deal at lunch and dinner and so it sees a regular crowd. At dinner you dine by candlelight on a covered terrace with palm trees on the beach—chicken in coconut cream or mint and yoghurt, or lightly grilled fish. And on the main square in town is something of a St Lucian classic, **Rain** (✆ 451 3111). It is set in a magnificent town house, called the Floissac Mansion, dressed in a theme of green and white gingerbread, so you can take a moment on the balcony to watch the street go by before ordering. Simple meals by day, more adventurous international fare in the evenings: chicken breast in an oyster and plum sauce or grilled fresh catch.

cheap

A good place for an inexpensive meal in town is **Mel's Tavern** on Bridge St, a local bar set up a little like an English pub, with white walls and dark-stained wood. Lots of drinking and untypical fare for the Caribbean: toasties and home-made pies, even chip butties and egg banjos. It is best to get a table on the veranda over Bridge Street.

Kimlan's is another trusty favourite with the locals. Simple St Lucian fare, including excellent tropical juices, with bench seats on a balcony which give an excellent view of Derek Walcott Square. Rotis, chicken, fish or beef stew or curry with a volley of ground provisions. The **Angry Man Stall** is one worth stopping for on the way in or out of town (just off the John Compton Highway beyond the market, in a car park). You'll recognize it, a rastaman caravan, by the blue roof and the red, gold and green designs. Ital (rasta) food and juices: stewed veg in a cake or a *bellyfull dahl in de riddem* (another fried vegetable cake).

An excellent place for local food is **Laurel's Creole restaurant** on the road to the Windjammer Resort. It has a modern terrace hung with greenery and set with green plastic tables, where you will eat accras (fish batterballs) and hefty portions of local green fig and saltfish or creole fish. In **Gros Islet** there are some pizza places, **Key Largo** and burger bars.

very cheap

You will find endless snacks and pastries on offer in St Lucia, some of them fried on braziers in front of you. A *float* is a deep-fried dough cake and you will find variations such as codfish or corned beef fritters. Finish off with a coconut pattie or a delicious St Lucian fruit cake. In Castries there are also a number of takeaway vans where you can get a juice and a local meal in a polystyrene box in the daytime.

Heading South

If you are travelling around the island, there are some wonderful stopovers. On the route south make sure to stop in at **Marigot Bay** the idyllic cove on the west coast where small bars and restaurants sit on the waterfront surrounded by the greenery and steep slopes of the valley walls.

61° in the Shade (✆ 451 4111; *expensive–moderate*) has a charming setting, a small deck among the mangroves on the far shoreline (take the ferry over and then walk around to the right). You sit under blue parasols and a small tin roof with a view of the yachts; adventurous Caribbean and international fare, easy and lazy atmosphere. *Closed Tues.* Just along from the spit with all the palm trees is **Doolittle's** (✆ 451 4974) (*moderate*) where you can get international fare with a Caribbean accent; local fish and lobster with some Caribbean vegetables; bright pink and purple setting on a deck. Opposite you will find another easygoing spot on a deck on the waterfront, **Odin's** (*cheap*), and then high above the bay you will find **J-J's** (*cheap*), for trusty local fare, particularly popular on a Wednesday, when it's crab night (they cook up some crabs in a pot).

If you are exploring the **Soufrière** area you can try the hotels: **Dasheene** at Ladera Resort (*expensive*) has a magnificent setting, though you should reserve the best table or arrive early, and there is a large but nice setting on the sand at **Anse Chastanet**. **Mago Estate** (*expensive*) has a wonderful position, tables laid out beneath a huge rock in a cliff-face, overlooking the town and bay (at the end of a very rickety drive of the main road out of town). Very well prepared and presented French and creole food.

Farther up the hill you come to **La Haut Plantation** (*moderate*), which offers a nice mix of local and international fare; creole fish or lambi with local vegetables followed by banana, poppy seed or coconut cake; fantastic view across the valley. A restaurant with a difference is **Bang between the Pitons** (*expensive–moderate*), which as the name suggests sits on the waterfront between St Lucia's twin peaks. The setting is like a West Indian village and there are pretty clapboard houses and palm trees set around a yard where the tables sit under shelters. The menu is Caribbean, with sunshine soup (from pumpkin), followed by jerk (from Jamaica) and escoveitched fish. Access easiest by boat. In the town itself there is passable local food at **Jacquot Restaurant** and **Captain Hooks** (*cheap*). Near Vieux Fort look out for **Il Pirata** (*moderate*), an Italian restaurant in a waterfront setting at the end of the airport runway.

Bars and Nightlife

Most of the big hotels offer some entertainment, so you may see a few thighs singed under the limbo pole and hear Caribbean classics such as 'Yellowbird' and 'Scandal in the Family', but there are some more local entertainments too, in which you will find the locals making the best of Bounty Crystal, a local white rum, or Old Fort, and the award-winning *Piton, La Bière Sent Lisi.* Two good haunts in town are **Mel's**, where a lively crowd often gathers, and **Kimlan's. Spinnaker's Bar** has live music on Saturday evenings right on the road in Marissol and also offers food and jazz. **The Waves** on the waterfront in Choc Bay sometimes sees a lively crowd.

On the waterfront on Rodney Bay you will find the **Shamrock Bar**, frequented by white St Lucians and semi-permanent yachtsmen; darts, sports on the TV, pool and the occasional karaoke. Close by, the **Lime** is a popular gathering point at the weekends and particularly on Wednesday nights before the crowd moves on to **Splash**, the discotheque at the St Lucian Hotel. On Fridays the crowd gravitates around the **Late Lime Club** a discotheque, *adm exp* (women free Wed). The **Indies Nightclub** in Gros Islet was the in place at the time of writing:Wednesday is ladies' night and Friday is also popular. **Drive In** is a much more St Lucian affair in Grand Rivière, where you will hear local music and the heavy tones of Jamaican *dub* and *dancehall.*

But the best-known party in the island is the weekly *jump-up* on Friday nights at **Gros Islet**, where four or five clubs spill out on to the street, speakers turned into the road pumping out *soca, reggae* and the latest *zouk* from Martinique, visible just a few miles to the north. It has become a bit of a tourist event, but it is still quite fun. You can pick up grilled fish and chicken legs, cooked in braziers on the street and served with hot pepper sauce.

A less crowded variation on the theme is outside **J-J's** on the road that leads to Marigot Bay which sees all sorts of streetside activity on a Friday.

getting there

St Lucia has quite good air links. Flights from outside the Caribbean fly into Hewanorra International Airport near the south coast and 40 miles (over an hour's ride) south of Castries. If you are flying within the Caribbean, it is probably better to aim for Vigie Airport just outside the capital. There is a departure tax of EC$27.

By air from the UK: BWIA (© 454 5075) and British Airways (© 454 6172) both have twice-weekly flights. On days when no direct flights are operating, the best connections are via Barbados. Charter operators also offer seats from the UK (Caledonian and Britannia both © 454 8186), from France (Air Liberté, same phone no.), and from Italy.

By air from the USA: BWIA has a daily direct flight from Miami and New York, and American Airlines fly daily from New York (© 454 6717). Otherwise you can travel daily via American Airlines' hub in San Juan, Puerto Rico (served from all over the States) from where you can make the link on American Eagle. Air Canada (also © 454 8186) flies weekly from Montreal and Toronto.

By air from other Caribbean islands: There are links to most major islands nearby. LIAT (© 452 3051) flies to Barbados, north to Antigua and south to Trinidad and also Caracas. Air Martinique (© 454 6777) originates in Martinique and flies south to the Grenadines. If you wish to charter a plane try Helenair (© 758 452 7196) and Eagle Air Services (© 452 1900).

By sea: There are occasional **hydrofoil** connections to the island of Martinique and then beyond (more regularly) to Dominica and to Guadeloupe: contact *L'Express des Isles* (© 452 2211). Cruise ship passengers are well looked after at Point Seraphine in Castries, where there is a shopping mall to keep you occupied from the moment you leave the ship.

tourist information

UK: 421a Finchley Road, London N3 6HJ (© (0171) 431 4045, ● 437 7920).

USA: 9th Floor, 820 Second Avenue, New York, NY 10017 (© (212) 869 2950, ● 370 7867, toll free © 1 (800) 456 3984).

Canada: 4975 Dundas Street West, Suite 457 Etobicoke 'D', Islington, Ontario M9A 4X4 (© (416) 236 0936, ● (416) 236 0937, toll free © (1 800) 456 3984).

Germany: Postfach 2304, D–61293 Bad Homburg 1 (© (06172) 30 44 31, ● 30 50 72).

France: ANI, 53 rue François 1er, 7ième Etage, Paris 75008 (© 1 47 20 39 66).

In St Lucia itself write to the main Tourism Office in the **Point Seraphine Shopping Complex**, across the harbour from downtown Castries, where the cruise ships dock, PO Box 221 (© 452 4094, ● 453 1121). There are also helpful tourist information offices in Jeremie St in Castries, at **Vigie** airport (© 452 2596) and at **Hewanorra** airport in the south (© 454 6644). The Tourist Board puts out two publications—*Visions of St Lucia*, a glossy magazine with practical details and feature articles and the monthly broadsheet, *The Tropical Traveller*, for a more topical view. *The Voice* newspaper is published in Castries three times a week, on Tues, Thurs and Sat, with local news and events. Other local papers include *The Mirror*, published on Thursday, and the *Star, One Caribbean* and the *Crusader*, which are published at the weekend.

festivals

The St Lucians celebrate Independence on 22 February with official activities and their national day on 13 December with a round of sailing races, fêtes and *jump-ups*, but the highlight of the St Lucian cultural calendar is **Carnival**, a pre-Lenten blow-out of costumed street-parades led by bandwagons (artics stacked with speakers). Calypsonians and Kings and Queens of the Bands play to the crowds in the Marchand Stadium before they spill onto the streets, where the beat is so strong that even the buildings seem to rock in time with the dancers (in fact, parts of Castries are built on reclaimed land and they really do move).

There are a number of smaller festivals, many of them centred around music. An excellent **Jazz Festival**, with international musicians, is held in May (there is a broad selection of heavyweight jazz musicians and easy-listening artists, to suit everyone's tastes) and on 22 Nov the patron saint of music, St Cecilia, is remembered by island calypsonians and panmen. During the day musicians from outlying villages ride the roads playing from vans and then in the evening they collect for competitions. The **Rose** and the **Marguerite** (on 30 Aug and 17 Oct) are also musical celebrations, set around an imaginary court and its retinue, complete with finery and ceremonial garb and each with its flower cockade (a rose or a marigold). They stage a ball, and they are led by a chanterelle and a band (banjo, quattro, boom boom and drum). Well worth attending if you are on-island. The creole language (spoken by most St Lucians) is remembered on **Jounen Kweyol**, held on the weekend nearest 28 Oct. Culinary and musical blow-outs are staged. There is a billfishing competition in early Oct.

money

The official currency of St Lucia is the Eastern Caribbean dollar, which is fixed to the US dollar at EC$2.65 = US$1. US dollars are widely accepted in tourist areas, but generally the word *dollar* usually refers to the Eastern Caribbean dollar.

Banks: Open Mon–Fri, 8am–3pm, Fri 8–5.

Shops: Open weekdays 8.30–12.30 and 1.30–4, Sat 8–noon.

maps and books

One of the English-speaking Caribbean's most celebrated authors is St Lucian, the poet and playwright Derek Walcott, who won the Nobel Prize for Literature in 1992. His works, which often adapt worldwide themes to a Caribbean setting, include *Omeros*. Another St Lucian author is Garth St Omer, whose works include *The Lights on the Hill*. If you can track down a copy of *St Lucia, Tours and Tales*, by Harriet Durham and Florence Lewisohn, do so, because it gives a well-presented and amusing background to the island. And you might even find a copy of the *St Lucia Diary of Lt J. H. Caddy*, a military man who served time in the West Indies in the 1830s—a revealing description of his life riding out and dining out with occasional military manoeuvres during his stay in St Lucia in 1833–4, published by the St Lucia Archaeological and Historical Society. The Sunshine Bookshop in Gablewoods Mall has a good selection of foreign newspapers and books about the Caribbean and St Lucia.

watersports

Watersports are on offer in many of the hotels, but otherwise you can fix almost anything at Reduit Beach, including glass-bottom boat rides, waterskiing and parasailing, or a trip on a sunfish or a hobie cat. Contact the operators on the beach.

Windsurfing: Available at the main beaches through hotel watersports shops, but for experts the best winds are on the Atlantic coast: in the north (take the right turn just before Gros Islet town) you will find Windsurf Cas en Bas; and in the south of the island, near Hewanorra Airport, contact Island Windsurfing (© 450 454 7400) on Anse des Sables.

Day sails: For a day cruise of yo-ho-ho down to the Pitons, you can try the ever-popular catamarans *Endless Summer I* and *II* (© 450 8651). The 140ft square-rigged brigantine *Unicorn* (© 452 6811), which was used in the television series *Roots*, also makes the trip, as does the motor yacht *Vigie* (© 450 8232).

Sailing: All down its west coast, St Lucia is indented with coves that make protected harbours for yachts. There are three marinas on the island, and although they are functional now, each has its historical and romantic lore. In the north, Rodney Bay marina lies behind Reduit beach. In Vigie cove behind Point Seraphine is a smaller marina convenient for Castries and a few miles south of here is Marigot Bay. If you are crossing the Atlantic, the Atlantic Rally for Cruisers takes place annually in November/December each year and culminates in St Lucia. Contact World Cruising Ltd, PO Box 165, London WC1B 3XA (© (0171) 405 9905, ● 831 0161). St Lucia is also a great place to start a sailing holiday in the region. Many people charter a yacht here and then head down to the Grenadines.

The Moorings (© 451 4256), based in the idyllic setting of Marigot Bay, have a large fleet of bare boats and some crewed yachts too. You can also contact Sunsail Stevens Yachts (© 452 8648) in Rodney Bay, where there are also plenty of marina facilities.

Deep-sea fishing: Mako Watersports (© 452 0412) or Captain Mike's Watersports (© 452 7044) in Vigie Cove. Half-day US$400, full day US$800. There is a bill-fishing tournament in St Lucia each October.

Scuba diving: Excellent and well organized, with visibility up to 100ft and colourful coastal marine life. Instruction and equipment (including underwater cameras) are available through the large operators. Most of the diving takes place on the west coast; two popular areas are Anse Cochon and Anse Chastanet near Soufrière, the home of Scuba St Lucia (© 459 7755) based at Anse Chastanet, where the reefs start at 15ft below the surface. Also recommended is Buddies Scuba (© 452 5288) in Vigie and Dolphin Divers (© 452 9485), who operate out of Rodney Bay and Marigot Bay. A single-tank dive costs around US$45. Most hotels will provide **snorkelling** gear for a minimal fee if you wish to chase after an angelfish.

other sports

Golf: There is a 9-hole course in the Cap Estate near the northern tip of the island (© 450 8523). Clubs, carts and caddies are available for hire. There's even mini-golf in Gros Islet if that's your thing.

Tennis: Available at all the big hotels and most will let you play on their courts.

Riding: Hire of horses and riding instruction is available through Trim's Riding Stables (© 450 8273) on the Cassabar side, Country Saddles (© 452 1231) or North Point Riding Stables (© 452 8273) in the Cap Estate, about US$25 per hour. Rides will take you for a picnic and a canter along the beach in a secluded cove on the Atlantic coast

Hiking: A number of trails have been developed in the rainforest and walks can be arranged through the Forest and Lands Dept (© 450 2231).

Dominica

Dominica is practically all mountains and rainforest, a jumble of peaks and spurs so rugged and dramatic that the island has its own microclimate. Of all the islands that Columbus is supposed to have described to Ferdinand and Isabella of Spain by crumpling a piece of parchment and throwing it on to the table with a 'like this, your Majesties', Dominica is the one he would be most likely to recognize today. Wags claim that it has hardly changed since he was here five hundred years ago.

In its 29 miles by 16, Dominica has mountains over 4500ft, higher than anything on the British Isles. The water-laden winds of the Atlantic Ocean clamber up its slopes and then stack in huge clouds on the mountaintops, poised immobile before they ditch their load. The rainfall here is measured in tens of feet and romantics will tell you there is always a rainbow somewhere in the mist-veiled peaks of the island. The natural life is unparalleled and vegetation is explosive. A plot untended for 10 years will be 5ft under with trees as thick as your leg and a gardener's most useful tool is a machete. Dominica is overwhelmingly green.

Dominica (pronounced 'Domin-*eek*-er') is the least developed of the Windward Islands and for all the fertility, it is hard for the islanders to make a living. Many parts of the island are very poor and you will see more subsistence farmers working small plots cut out of the hillside than on the other islands. For years it was difficult enough to get to the island and relatively recently new roads have opened up parts that before could only be reached on horseback. Vans travel between the villages selling anything from tinned milk to Sunday dresses.

Apart from its wildlife, Dominica's most remarkable heritage is that it is home to the last surviving traces of the Carib race. To the Caribs, the island was *Waitukubuli* or 'tall is her body' and the wild terrain meant that it was the last island to be settled by Europeans. Once proud and warlike, the Caribs were left in peace on Dominica for a while, but ultimately they could not defend their homeland from the newcomers. There are no native Carib-speakers left, but their descendants are easily recognized in Dominica by their Amerindian features.

A quarter of the island's 75,000 or so population live in the capital Roseau, on the protected Caribbean coast. The island lies between two French islands, Guadeloupe to the north and Martinique to the south. The island was settled initially by the French, but then it went through the usual political confusion of the Caribbean islands, ending up in British hands. The official language has been English in Dominica for the last 180 years, but French *patois* can be heard all over the island and most of the population is Catholic.

In a part of the world renowned for its palm-fringed and dazzling white-sand beaches, Dominica is an odd man out. There is not a lot of tourism and most of the visitors that come are there for the diving and the natural life. The few beach resorts are set on dark sand and there are few restaurants and bars in the typical Caribbean mould. Visitors are expected to join in local life. Dominica is unpretentious and its beauty lies rather in its spectacular interior and its coral-clad, underwater slopes. It rightfully calls itself the *Nature Island of the Caribbean*. Five hundred years after Columbus crumpled his parchment, patches of Dominica are still 'unexplored jungle'.

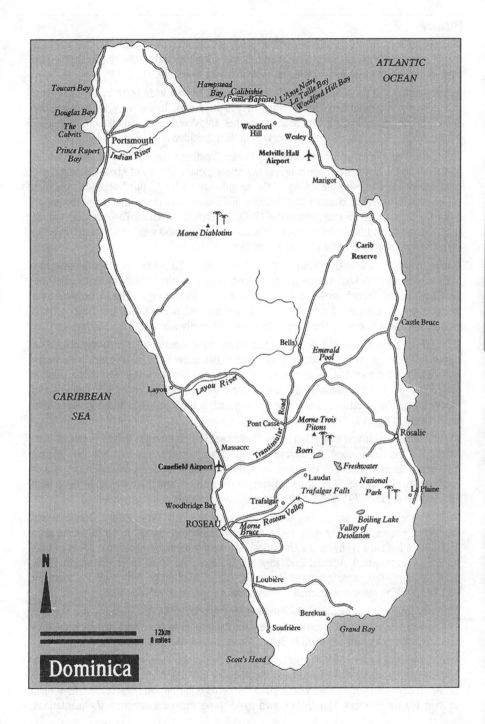

Dominica

History

Waitukubuli was christened on 3 November 1493, as Columbus made land after five weeks at sea on his second voyage to the New World. It was a Sunday, and to give thanks for the safe passage of his fleet the explorer called his new discovery Dominica.

As the heartland of the 'Cannibal Isles', Dominica was given a wide berth by the Spaniards, and only pirates, fishermen and foresters braved its coasts. In the very early years, the Spaniards considered making a harbour where their ships could refit and take on water after the Atlantic crossing, but they did not reckon on the opposition of the resident Indians.

The Caribs kept the Europeans at bay for 200 years. Dominica was officially neutral as late as 1748, left 'to the undisturbed possession of the native Indians' (Treaty of Aix-la-Chapelle), and a retreat for the Caribs squeezed out of the neighbouring islands. But Dominica's position between the two French colonies of Martinique and Guadeloupe meant that it was too important to be disregarded for long, and in the 1750s the French moved in. The campaign against the Caribs was so ruthless and thorough that there were just 400 survivors, who retreated to the windward coast where they would be left alone.

Dominica was caught in the crossfire of the European conflicts like the other Windwards, blockaded each time war was declared and encouraged to plant madly in times of peace. Traditionally, the French settlers planted coffee and the British sugar. The island was also a free port and for a while did a brisk trade as a slave market. In 1763, after the Treaty of Paris granted the island to Britain, the French lands were promptly sold to English planters.

Dominica's mountainous and fertile interior offered easy sanctuary for runaway plantation slaves, or 'maroons', who hid out in small communities in the hills. Initially they were happy with just their freedom, but, rallied by leaders with names such as Congo Ray, Jacko, Zombie and Jupiter, they soon began to steal cattle and torch estate buildings, encouraging other slaves to join them. The island militia was first sent out against them in 1785, flushing them out in the network of tracks in the hinterland.

As the French Revolution took effect in the Caribbean, French Royalists fled to Dominica from Martinique and Guadeloupe. Republican revolutionaries followed them clandestinely, offering freedom to the island slaves if they rose up against the planters (slaves on the French islands had been freed in 1794). They smuggled arms to the maroons and there was an invasion from Guadeloupe in June 1795, but the hills were cleaned out again and it was repulsed.

With the French in the ascendancy again in Europe in the early 19th century, Dominica was threatened once more, along with the other British Caribbean islands. In 1805, armed ships appeared in Roseau Bay, flying the Union Jack. At the last moment they tore it down and ran up the *tricolore* instead. Admiral La Grange was besieging the island for France and he blockaded Roseau. After chasing up and down the island, La Grange ransomed the town for £12,000, took all the slaves he could lay his hands on and sailed off to St Kitts.

Maroons were still hiding out in the hills and they rose up again in a guerrilla war between 1812 and 1815. Eventually crushed by Rangers, the leaders were hanged, but their memory remains in the peak near the town of Belles, Morne Nègres Marrons.

With Emancipation in 1834, Dominica became a refuge for French slaves from the neighbouring islands, where slavery had been reintroduced in 1802. Until 1848, when the French banned it once again, the slaves would make the perilous journey on homemade rafts at night in their bid for freedom. Dominica's own freed slaves moved away from the plantations, preferring to cut a plot of land out of the fertile interior, growing the produce they needed and selling the surplus at market. The new Dominicans were self-reliant and independent, with a spirit that would erupt at times—there were riots when the government demanded taxes for roads or even called a census.

Dominica is large and fertile, but the island was particularly poor. Some industries flourished, however, the most notable being Rose's, now part of the Cadbury Schweppes group, which provided lime juice for British ships. The drink became popular beyond the requirements for naval rations and in 1875 a factory was set up in Roseau to extract lime juice from the thousands of acres that were planted with the fruit. For a while, Dominica was by far the world's largest producer of limes and the fruit brought in about half of the country's export earnings. Since the Second World War this has declined and bananas have taken their place.

Despite spending most of its colonial life in the Leeward Isles, in federation with Antigua and Montserrat and islands further north, Dominica is much more similar to the Windward Islands and it became one of them in 1939. In 1951 the vote was given to all Dominicans over the age of 21 and the island became self-governing in 1967. In the ground-swell of the new political freedom, the Dominica Labour Party, led by Edward Le Blanc, rallied the new voters and was thrust to power. The seventies saw social unrest as demonstrations, racist attacks and strikes held the island to ransom and a state of emergency was declared more than once. The *Dreads*, called so because they wore their hair in dreadlocks, took to the hills, hiding out as the maroons had done 200 years before.

On 3 November 1978, 485 years to the day after the island was discovered by Columbus, Dominica took its independence from Britain. Then a few months later Hurricane David arrived—Roseau was literally flattened, there were 37 deaths and 80 per cent of the population were left homeless. The political unrest continued; an emergency government had to be installed, followed by two coup attempts and an invasion party which was arrested before it left the States.

Today Dominica is led by the Hon Edison C. James of the United Workers Party, which has 12 of the 21 seats in the Dominica Parliament. The Dominica Labour Party is in opposition with five seats and the Dominica Freedom Party (which was led for many years by Eugenia Charles, the Caribbean's first woman prime minister) has four seats. Elections are next due some time in the year 2000.

Writers and Artists

The writer **Jean Rhys** (1890–1979) came from Dominica. Her family owned an estate in Grand Bay and she was born in Roseau, but she left the island when she was 16 and moved to Europe. Many of her books include nostalgic memories of the Dominica of her childhood. Fame came with *Wide Sargasso Sea* (1966), some of which is set in the oppressive atmosphere of colonial Dominican society at the turn of the 19th century. Another Dominican authoress and politician, **Phyllis Shand Allfrey**, wrote the novel *The Orchid House*, also set on the island and screened by the BBC. The story of a private soldier's life is recorded in *Redcoats in the Caribbean* by James Aytoun, published by Blackburn Recreation Services Dept for the Cambridgeshire Regiment.

Dominica was very fortunate in the visit of the Italian painter, **Agostino Brunias**, who stayed on the island for many years in the late 18th century, recording the Dominican way of life and events. His paintings are extremely lively, giving a fascinating view of the lives of the free creoles, the plantations, vendors' stalls, dances and women washing clothes in the streams, much of which can still be seen in different forms today.

Getting Around

Public transport is mostly by Japanese van, with teenage minders leaning out of them to shout for passengers, and by unwieldy government bus. The major routes are all served, but remote towns have only infrequent services after noon and very few on Sundays (it is possible to get stranded in outlying areas, because the buses tend to go to Roseau in the morning and return in the early afternoon). However, **hitching** works quite well (you may be lucky enough to get a ride in one of the old Bedfords with the colourful wooden cages on the back). Though most would probably not take it, drivers might appreciate being offered a couple of dollars for the ride.

Buses travelling **south** go from the bottom end of King George V Street near the Old Market Square; for the **Roseau Valley** from the top end opposite the Police Headquarters. If you are heading **north**, buses leave from near the new Market building, next to the West Bridge. Sample bus prices, all set by the government, are: **Roseau** to Laudat—EC$3, Soufrière—$3, Canefield Airport—$1.50, Castle Bruce— $7, Portsmouth—$8.

Taxis also have fixed rates. **Roseau** to Canefield airport—EC$20, the southern hotels—EC$15, Papillote—EC$25 and **Canefield** to southern hotels—EC$40, Castaways—EC$40 and Portsmouth area—EC$110. The trip to Melville Hall airport is EC$140 per person, usually a minimum of two people (you will find that people hitch a ride on any car or minibus going). For an **island tour**, taxis can be hired for about EC$45 per hour.

Hire cars are available in Roseau from Avis (✆ 448 2481, ✉ 448 6681) at 4 High Street in town, Auto Rentals (✆ 448 2886, ✉ 448 0737), Bonus Car Rental (✆ 448 2650, ✉ 448 6050), Valley Rent a Car on Goodwill Road (✆ 448 3233, ✉ 448 6009), Wide Range Car, 81 Bath Road (✆ 448 2198, ✉ 448 3600). Hire costs around US$45 per day, jeeps US$55 and most companies will deliver to your hotel. You will need a local driver's licence, which can be obtained from the Traffic Department in Roseau, at the airport and at the car hire companies, price EC$30.

Beaches

Dominica has no white coral-sand beaches in the typical Caribbean mould and most beaches tend to be dark volcanic grey or jet black except in the far northeast, where there are some golden-sand beaches in the high-sided coves. Beach-bound tourists tend to head for Portsmouth, where there are some nice beach bars and some limited watersports, or the northeast where you will find good beaches (and a bar, the **Almond Beach Bar**, at Calibishie). There is a nice, lazy spot under a palm thatch roof at East Carib Dive, on the black sand of **Salisbury beach** at the rivermouth. Around Roseau, the waterfront is made up of fist-sized rocks that clatter as they race and recede with the waves.

Hampstead Bay, Calibishie (Pointe Baptiste) and **Woodford Hill Bay**: Dominica's best sand, quite remote in the northeast, but dramatic and overhung by cliffs, often with large waves (but also reefs offshore). Take a map or good advice about how to get there and all you need in the way of food and drink. Do not leave any valuables unattended in these areas. Other secluded coves to look out for are **Hampstead I** and **Billy Boo**.

Prince Rupert Bay, Portsmouth: The sand is black but passable in this area and there are good stretches of beach with some watersports and hotel bars to retreat to.

Mero: A good stretch of dark sand facing the sunset with a beach bar at the Castaways Hotel, some watersports.

Flora and Fauna

Much of Dominica is 100ft deep in tropical rainforest, undergrowth, overgrowth and canopy so thick that it is dark at midday. Trees vie with each other to grow tallest, stretching up to reach the sunlight, while lianas and creeping vines take an easier route, grappling the tree-trunks and using them to climb. In the branches sit orchids and ferns that explode in graceful curves. The forest gushes with water, it squawks and chirrups and is a botanist's utopia. With so many species in such good condition, Dominica has been called a living museum.

The Dominican forest has different zones, depending on elevation. At the lowest altitudes you will find cultivated patches, or the thick secondary forest that occurs when cultivated land is left fallow. Vines, ferns and many flowering trees and plants are found here. Above this, typical rainforest has a canopy at 100ft—huge tree trunks, some with buttressed roots, soar out of the forest floor, which is often relatively clear. Trees such as the gommier and the chataigner have bromeliads and orchids (and they in their turn insects and other animals) residing in their branches. The montane forest is smaller and many of the trees have aeriel roots. The sunlight does penetrate to the forest floor and so there is more ground growth including grasses and ferns. Finally, at the highest altitudes you will find elfin forest, stunted trees covered with mosses and lichens, plants which prefer the clouds and almost constant rain.

The **Morne Trois Pitons National Park**, a 17,000-acre reserve of rainforest in the centre of the island, is the Caribbean's oldest nature reserve and it contains many of the island's natural attractions. Perhaps the best dropping-off point is Laudat in the upper Roseau Valley (the Trafalgar Falls are just outside the park on the Trafalgar Road); from here it is possible to reach the Titou Gorge and the Freshwater Lake (not that interesting, can be reached by car) and Boeri Lake (an interesting walk to lake hemmed in by mountains). A very long day's walk will take you to the smelly and steaming Valley of Desolation and the boiling lake, high in the mountains (*see* 'The Roseau Valley', p.213 for more detail about the sights). On the northern edge of the park, off the transinsular road, are the Middleham Trails, leading to waterfalls lost in greenery—look out for, or keep you nose open for the Stinking Hole, where colonies of bats live. Just outside the Park is the Emerald Pool, a tame but popular cascade falling into a rockpool. Other visits to falls in the south include a walk up the Sari-sari River from La Plaine and the Victoria Falls above Delices. The Northern Forest Reserve is far larger and contains the island's highest peak, Morne Diablotin, and the parrot habitat, where you are most likely to see the island's two endangered parrots.

There are many marked **walking trails** in Dominica's parks. On paths the best footwear is a light pair of walking boots, but if you are walking up rivers you might opt for the local red, gold and green plastic sandals, nicknamed *toyotas* (because they hold the road well). Also remember a waterproof coat, a picnic and if you are out for a long day, take a jersey too. As with anywhere, you are advised to take little money and jewellery with you when you go off the beaten track in Dominica.

More information and help with trained guides can be found at the Division of Tourism (✆ 448 2351), the Division of Forestry office (✆ 448 2401 ext 3417), situated in the Botanical Gardens in Roseau and through Dominica Tours (✆ 448 2638). Otherwise you can go through Ken's Hinterland Adventure Tours (✆ 448 4850) and Antours, PO Box 428, Roseau (✆ 448 6460, ✉ 448 6780). Tour operators have a wide range of suggestions to add to those above.

Some 166 species of bird live in Dominica or migrate here with the tourists for the better weather during the winter season. Among the common bananaquits and bullfinches, the exotic flycatchers and fluorescent hummingbirds, Dominica has two endemic parrots. Both are endangered, and the sisserou is portrayed on the national flag. The sisserou, or imperial parrot, is one of the largest parrots in the world and has a purple breast and green wings. The smaller red-necked amazon or jacko is a little less scarce and might be seen racing by in a flash of scarlet. To have a hope of seeing the parrots (a trip can be arranged through one of the operators above) you may have to get up extremely early and hike into the hills to a special hide. Another bird almost unique to Dominica is the *siffleur montagne* or mountain whistler, which whistles its single melancholy note every few minutes in the rainforest.

As all over the Caribbean, fauna is much more limited. Agouti and a rare 3ft iguana scurry around the heights and manicou creep quietly; all around there is the constant susurration of island insects: you may see cockroaches wiggle antennae four inches long and there is a stick insect called *chouval bwa*. Out at night you may come across luminous flickering points that are fireflies and hear the blacksmith beetle, so large and monstrous that it clanks.

There are five species of snake, none of them poisonous. One of the rarest but most surprising is the shy boa constrictor, known as *tête chien* because of the shape of its head. Outside the Amazon basin it is found only in Dominica. It has been known to grow to 20ft long and as thick as a man's leg. There is an early story of a Dominican who was resting under a tree and woke up to find his leg inside one of these snakes up to the thigh. Friends helped him extricate himself, putting wedges in the snake's teeth and chopping it up into pieces to release him.

It might be possible (depending on the season) to arrange to catch crayfish and frogs, later served as mountain chicken. Hunting for frogs takes place at night, with the aid of burning torches that have a fatal attraction for the animals.

Whale watching is possible from Dominica in the season (November to March), when the whales come from up north to mate and calve in the calm, deep waters on the leeward coast of Dominica. Humpbacks, pilot whales, dolphins and particularly sperm whales, accompanied by their 20ft calves, have been known in the area. Tours are long and of course a sighting is not guaranteed, but they can be arranged through the Anchorage Dive Centre (✆ 448 2638, ✉ 448 5680) and Dive Dominica (✆ 448 2188, ✉ 448 6088).

Roseau, Dominica's capital, has 20,000 inhabitants, about a quarter of the population, and is the only sizeable town on the island. Framed by towering mountains on one side and looking out to an uninterrupted sea horizon on the other, the town stands at the mouth of the Roseau River and takes its name from the French word for the reeds that grew here, which the Caribs would use to poison the tips of their arrows. Lacking a proper harbour (that is in the Canefield area further north, where the drop off is less severe), it was never supposed to be the island's capital, but the intended site of Portsmouth was found to be unhealthy and so the administrators moved here in the late 18th century.

Roseau keeps many features of a traditional West Indian waterfront town. It was extensively rebuilt after Hurricane David in 1979, but it has not been redeveloped out of character and there are still many old creole houses in the town. Most modern building is now of concrete, but there have been recent plans to zone parts of the old town and so the colonial character of the town remains. Only the occasional satellite dish stands out among the shanties and the streets of traditional warehouses near the waterfront. With strong stone foundations and shuttered doorways that let through the breeze, the old storehouses and shops are topped with wooden upper storeys and steep roofs, many of them embellished with gingerbread fretwork. Some have balconies over the pavement, supported by sturdy wooden columns and giving welcome shelter in Roseau's regular tropical rainstorms. Although the town looks a little neglected, its roofs rusted and the buildings a bit run down, these attractive houses give Roseau a charming atmosphere.

Wherever you go in Dominica people seem to greet you, usually in French *patois*, but the liveliest spot in Roseau is the **market**, which can be found next to the river-mouth. There is a large covered area of tables, but the Dominicans mostly prefer to spread out their produce— guava, grapefruit, golden apple and ground provisions—on the ground in the open, with golf umbrellas to protect them from the sun and plastic sheeting at the ready for when it rains.

At the southern end of the **Bayfront,** which is gradually being redeveloped and is looking quite good at the moment, is the **Dominica Museum** (*open Mon–Fri 9–4, Sat 9–12;* adm), a very well laid out display of Dominican natural life—geological subduction zones, petrified wood and fossilized leaves—and then a look at the island's human heritage in displays of pre-Columbian axe-heads, pottery, a *coulevre* (for squeezing the poisonous juice from cassava) and a canoe. Plantation times are revealed in maps (showing just how developed the island was once), prints by Agostino Brunias, lime *equelles* for rinding the fruit, and town and country life in displays of Roseau's mulatto ascendancy and in household utensils used by subsistence farmers. Just behind the museum is the **Old Market Plaza**, a cobbled square which was formerly the market and once the site of Roseau's slave trading and public executions. There is a small tourist information desk on the square and a curious telephone-box like structure that was supposedly used in auctions.

Walking northwest on Castle Street and Virgin Lane, you come to the Catholic **Cathedral of the Assumption,** built in dark stone with Romanesque arches and completed in 1841. Even though the majority of Dominica's population was Catholic, the official Anglican government would grant no money for the building of the Cathedral. Summoned by a bell, the faithful would come out at night and carry stones from the Roseau river to the site. Once Roseau's main defence, **Fort Young** is now a hotel. It was erected in 1775 and visitors to the hotel will still see a few slim and elegant-looking cannons hanging around the foyer and courtyard.

Behind the town, at the foot of Morne Bruce, are the **Botanical Gardens**, which date from 1891. Landscaped with open lawns, they must be the only place of their kind that appear less fertile than the country surrounding them. There are 150 species, including traditional Caribbean plants such as allamanda and bougainvillea and some less well known: pompon rouge, or powder puff. Trees include cannonball, teak and pink poui, and a giant baobab tree that came down in 1979, when Hurricane David uprooted over half the garden's species, still lying on top of the yellow school bus that it crushed. It has even begun to flower again. A few of the plants are named, but it is really more of a park now; serious botanical visitors should go to the various gardens around the island. However, it is worth going to the aviary in the corner of the Gardens, where you can see some of Dominica's endangered parrots: the Jaco has a blue head and a green body with flashes of red and the Sisserou has a purple belly and green wings.

A path climbs **Morne Bruce** from the gardens, 500ft up through the creaking bamboo, to the crown-like Catholic memorial. The Morne takes its name from the 18th-century engineer who fortified it and it gives an excellent view across the town, covering the bay. Most of the buildings have fallen down now. Earlier this century the Morne was thought to be haunted: troops would be heard marching and supposedly a bugle sounded on dark nights.

The Roseau Valley

The extension of King George V Street leads out of the town and across a clattering wooden suspension bridge into the Roseau river valley—the bridge may seem high, but the Roseau river has been known to rise 20ft in as many hours—straight into the Dominican heartland. It is a fantastic area, a massive, steep-sided valley where the air hangs chill in the shaded corners and the road winds up though a tunnel of amazing vegetation which opens out periodically to reveal magnificent views. Some of Roseau's more prosperous citizens have retreated into the cooler heights of the valley, side by side with farmers who manage to terrace and cultivate the absurdly steep valley walls.

For a first-hand view of Dominica's extremes of vegetation you can go to the charming **D'Auchamps Gardens** (✆ 448 3346; *adm*) about halfway up the valley, where tropical flora (wild, domestic and medicinal) is revealed in all its rampant grandeur. A path leads through areas planted with plants from a traditional village garden, herb gardens and orchards, the rainforest and indigenous Dominican plants. You will learn about *mibi,* aerial roots and vines used for local weaving and the local thatch called *z'ailes mouche* or flies' wings, how oil comes from coconuts and flour from cassava. You can take a self-guided tour following a plant list for a small charge, but as always with botanical gardens, it is much more interesting if you can get a guided tour.

At the head of the valley, 5 miles up-river from Roseau, just beyond the village of Trafalgar, are the **Trafalgar Falls**, two spectacular cascades that tumble 90ft from the lip of a gorge, the water whipped into a maelstrom by upward winds, spattering down among titanic black boulders and orange iron-discoloured rocks. The vegetation is prodigious and provides pockets of quiet as you climb, before you emerge into the blanket of fine spray and white noise that fills the gorge, a deafening hiss and roar that drops into the pools of hot and cold water. The falls are smaller now that some of the water has been harnessed for hydroelectricity.

The Trafalgar Falls are easy to reach on a short outing from town and you can drive to within ten minutes of them. Take a swimming costume and gym shoes if you like clambering over rocks and consider getting a guide (*for perhaps EC$12*). You might need a jersey for your return because it can also get a bit cold and wet in the wind.

Twin pipes lead down from the falls, unfortunately giving it a bit of an industrial feel, carrying water to a hydroelectric generating station. They pass **Papillote Wilderness Retreat** (© 448 2287), where a small hotel is set in a charming 12-acre garden of truly Dominican profusion, with pathways and streams of rushing water spewed out by ornamental fish and iguanas. There are forests of white-leafed hibiscus, bromeliads and aroids, and orchids like butterflies, all sheltered by vast sprays of bamboo overhead (some plants are named). There is also a naturally heated mineral bath, for which the water comes from the springs higher up the mountain. This is a good place to stop for lunch on the veranda, and a swim in warm or cool water.

Morne Trois Pitons National Park

At the head of a side valley is the village of Laudat, the best dropping-off point for the 17,000-acre reserve. You can reach the **Freshwater Lake** by vehicle, a couple of miles beyond Laudat. The lake is at 2500ft and its history and mystery is really more attractive than its actual physical presence. In the early days of colonization, the lake was haunted variously by a vindictive mermaid who would lure travellers to drown them and, according to a writer called Oldmixon in 1708, by 'a vast monstrous Serpent, that had its Abode in the before-mentioned Bottom (an inaccessible Bottom in the high mountains). They affirm'd, there was in the Head of it a very sparkling Stone, like a Carbuncle of inestimable Price; that the Monster commonly veil'd that rich jewel with a thin moving skin, like that of a Man's Eyelid, and when it went to drink or sported itself in the deep Bottom, it fully discovered it, and the Rocks all about receiv'd a wonderful Lustre from the Fire issuing out of that precious Gem.'

A 40-minute walk beyond the Freshwater Lake, towards the Morne Trois Pitons, the island's second-highest peak, you come to the **Boeri Lake**, in the crater of an extinct volcano. The path climbs to 2800ft, passing over stream and through the thickest jungle. On days when the rainclouds are not obscuring them, the views carry down to the Atlantic coast, whole hillsides of green with barely a human structure in sight. Again the walk is really more interesting than the lake itself.

Dominica's volcanic heartland is the **Valley of Desolation**, appropriately named because very little will grow there—even Dominican vegetation is killed off by sulphur emissions. This foetid area, among the jumble of (almost) extinct volcanoes, four hours' walk away and over two mountains, is laid with titanic boulders and sulphurous cesspools of diabolic colours. The volcano beneath it all erupted last in 1880, showering Roseau with volcanic ash.

At its centre is the **Boiling Lake**, a seething and bubbling morass like an angry jacuzzi, constantly steaming at between 180 and 200°F, and fed by (occasionally poisonous) gases from underneath that make the whole lake rise by several feet. It has been known to measure about 70 yards across, but the level rises and falls. It has also been known to disappear down the plug-hole, re-emerging with a geyser spout and monumental rumbling.

South from Roseau

The road south from Roseau leads along the coast through the suburbs of Charlotteville and Castle Comfort, past a clutch of the island's hotels. In the 18th century a string of forts and batteries ran along the coast to the southern tip at Scotts Head. From Loubière, an impossibly steep road branches inland, climbing to the oddly named Snug Corner and over the summit, descending beneath the cliffs to the citrus orchards and banana plantations at **Bereuka** on Grand Bay, where fort ruins stand beneath the vast cliffs of the windward coast.

Eventually you come to the valley of **Soufrière**, one of the earliest areas of the island to be settled by the French. The town takes its name from the sulphur outlets farther up the valley, which flow into the river and provide heated water for bathing or washing clothes. It is a pleasant walk up the river among the 60ft bamboo trees that creak constantly and over to Grand Bay on the Atlantic side of the island, but if you feel like refreshing yourself with a drink, be careful, because you might scald your hand.

The southern point of the island is dominated by Scott's Head, a spit of land jutting into the Caribbean Sea. There is little left of Fort Cacharou that once dominated it, but it was attacked many times in the past. On one occasion Dominicans sympathetic to the French got the British soldiers drunk and spiked their guns with sand, enabling the French to overrun the fort with ease. The view from Scott's Head to Martinique, 20 miles south, and back along the leeward coast of Dominica, is stunning.

North from Roseau up the Leeward Coast

Despite being proposed in the 18th century, the road link from Roseau to Portsmouth, Dominica's second town in the north of the island, was one of the last to be completed, with some cuttings into the cliff-face over 50ft deep. The journey had to be made via the other side of the island or by boat until well into this century. The leeward coast is supposedly in the 'rain-shadow' of Dominica's central mountain range, meaning that it is dry. However, this description is judged by Dominican standards; it can still drench you without a moment's notice.

The road follows the coast, passing Woodbridge Bay, the cruise-ship dock and the deepwater port, where goods for the capital are unloaded. Just before the airport at Canefield is the **Old Mill Cultural Centre**, in the grounds of an old plantation estate. The gardens contain an aqueduct and water-wheel as well as less ancient steam-driven cane-crushing gear.

Just beyond Canefield you come to the settlement of **Massacre** (pronounced more as in French than as in English), the site of a sad episode that took place between two half-brothers, one half-Carib, the other European, in the early 1600s. Indian Warner was born in St Kitts, son of Governor Warner by a Carib woman, but had to flee when his father died and so he went to Dominica, becoming a Carib chief. The massacre took place when his brother Phillip was sent by the Governor of the Leeward Islands on a campaign to 'put down' the Caribs in 1674. Phillip and his troops are supposed to have feasted with the Caribs and he initiated the massacre by stabbing his brother. Beyond here you cross the **Layou River**, the island's longest. It flows broad and slow by the time it reaches the coast, but a road follows its tumultuous course inland for a while, where you will see spectacular scenery including cliffs.

Soon the leeward road passes beneath Dominica's highest peak, **Morne Diablotin** (4747ft), which takes its name from the black-capped petrel, supposedly a diabolically ugly bird that once lived on its slopes, prized by hunters in the 18th century. With webbed feet and black and white plumage, the diablotin was about the size of a duck and nested in the ground, flying down to the sea to fish at night. The morne itself can be climbed (*guide recommended*) in about three hours and the view is superb, though more often than not it is obscured by the clouds that hang on Dominica's mountains.

The coastal road continues to Dominica's second town of **Portsmouth**, crossing the **Indian River** just before the town. It is possible to arrange canoe trips up the river, where the banks are tangled with mangrove roots and the canopy is festooned with flying tropical overgrowth.

Portsmouth, another tired-looking town of 3000 inhabitants with dilapidated wooden buildings, stands at the head of Prince Rupert's Bay, sheltered in the north by the promontory of the Cabrits. The bay itself takes its name from the royalist prince who arrived in the West Indies in 1652 to find that Barbados and the Leeward Islands were in the hands of the Commonwealth. Two centuries ago the huge bay would see as many as 400 navy ships at anchor if a campaign was brewing.

On the northern side of the bay is a promontory, called the Cabrits (the name *cabrits* derives from the Spanish word for goat—animals left here as fresh meat for future arrivals low on stocks after the Atlantic crossing), where you will find the **Cabrits National Park**, two forested hills scattered with the fortifications of Fort Shirley and other batteries and military buildings. The fort, dating from the 1770s, has been restored to its fearsome brimstone glory after more than a hundred years of decay since it was abandoned in 1854 by the British. For an idea of the fort's former glory, take a look at the commandant's house with its cut-stone classical façade which is now being overtaken by massive tangled tree roots. The restoration received an award from American Express. Marked trails cover the promontory and there is a small museum (*adm free*).

From Portsmouth a side road leads north past the anchorages at Douglas Bay and Toucari Bay. It was from an estate just north of Toucari that John Mair and friends watched the Battle of the Saints in April 1782. They were breakfasting in the portico as the battle began (*see* Guadeloupe, pp.288–9).

The main road around the island leads inland from Portsmouth, winding into the hills, through violent Dominican fertility alternately soaked and shone upon at half-hourly intervals, and rejoining the north coast after 5 miles. In this area Dominica's best beaches can be found in the coves that look out towards the French islands of Marie Galante and the Saints. Beneath bright orange and muddy cliffs are beaches of large-grained golden sand, sometimes flecked with jet- black magnetic particles (*see* 'Beaches', pp.208–9).

The road continues to the villages of **Wesley** and **Marigot**, where unlike most Dominican villages English is spoken as the first tongue rather than French creole. They were settled by Antiguans and other Leeward Islanders who came as construction labourers and stayed when their work was finished.

The Transinsular Road to the East Coast

The grandly named Transinsular Road, formerly known by the even grander name of the Imperial Road, winds its laborious way into the Dominican highlands from Canefield airport. For years, journeys to the Atlantic coast had to be made by boat or on horseback along paths throttled by vegetation, but the Imperial Road commenced its journey to windward in 1909, setting off into the jungle, switch-backing gradually up thousands of feet and only emerging on the Atlantic coast in the late fifties.

It always seems to be raining somewhere up in Dominica's hinterland and you will certainly see a few rainbows among the peaks. The road also provides an excellent way to see some of Dominica's extraordinary fertility (you cut through the northern part of the Morne Trois Pitons National Park). Road signs are grappled with growth, lines of plants sit on telegraph wires, whole slopes are covered with elephant ears and creeping vines and there are fluorescent green ferns so large that they might fly away and waterfalls that descend from heights invisible from below in the spray.

The **Middleham Trails** lead off the main road and cross over the hills to the Roseau Valley at Laudat, via the Middleham Falls, stunning waterfalls 500ft in height. At Pont Casse there is a roundabout where the road splits three ways, left to the Layou Valley and back down to the Leeward Coast and right to Castle Bruce and the southeast corner of the island. The transinsular road continues straight on to the Atlantic coast just short of Marigot and Melville Hall airport. At **Belles** it is possible to join the higher reaches of the Layou River for a day-long hike and swim through flats and gulleys that emerge on the Layou road a couple of miles short of the west coast. Arrange a guide and take a pair of gym shoes and a swimming costume.

Back on the Castle Bruce road, a tamer walk through the jungle can be made at the **Emerald Pool**. Walkways are carefully marked out and lead down to the small pool, where a tiny cascade races into the warm and dank recess and roots like knotted fingers grapple rocks furred with moss. However, do not expect it to be isolated enough to go skinny-dipping.

The road passes beneath Dominica's second peak, **Morne Trois Pitons**, and then throws off another branch that leads to **Rosalie** and to **La Plaine**. Atlantic breakers pound the windward shore, where there are cliffs hundreds of feet high. Before the road was built, stores had to be winched up from the bays below. In Dominican creole, the Atlantic coast is known as *au vent*, literally 'in the wind', a reference to the trade winds.

Carib Territory

The Caribs retreated to the Atlantic coast of Dominica in the 18th century when Europeans took over the island. In the hundred years to 1750 their numbers had reduced from about 5000 to 400 and they knew their struggle was lost, so they took up a peaceful life as far as possible from the invaders.

The Carib Territory itself (then called the Carib Reserve) was not created until 1903, when Governor Hesketh Bell allotted some 3700 acres to the few hundred remaining Caribs. A hereditary chief was presented with a mace and an official sash and was referred to as 'King'. However, he was implicated in a smuggling racket in the thirties and the position went into abeyance until 1952, when the 'Chief' was reintroduced as an elected post within the local government system.

The Caribs have adopted a West Indian lifestyle, living in clapboard houses on stilts rather than their original *carbets* (pointed thatch huts) and they make a living in a similar way to other Dominicans. They do maintain some Carib traditions, such as building canoes, dug out from trees that they fell high up in the forest, and skilful weaving of rushes and reeds. They sell woven baskets (which fit inside one another like Russian dolls), mats and ornaments. One curious object is known as the *wife-leader*. It is a mesh of interwoven reeds that tightens when you put it over your finger and pull it, trapping you.

There are said to be no pure-bred Caribs left in the Territory, but the Carib features, which are like those of South American Indians, are immediately recognizable. Carib hair, dark and sleek and once the pride of their ancestors, is still much admired by Dominicans today (many of whom have tight African curls).

(1 767)– **Where to Stay**

Dominica's hotels are mainly small, family-run affairs, some of them set in the old-time buildings around the coast or hidden among the island's overbearing foliage (as you sit on the veranda you can practically see it grow). Few except the dive hotels have a resort feel, and there is usually no difficulty in finding a room. If you wish to hire a villa, contact the Tourist Board, but two excellent ones are mentioned below. The government levies a tax of 5% and most hotels charge service of another 10%.

expensive

The most charming place to stay on the island is at **Petit Coulibri Guest Cottages**, PO Box 331(*/* 446 3150, *www.wp.com\dolphin-soft\petit.htm*), which stand a thousand feet above the south coast looking out to Martinique; it is one of the Caribbean's gems. There is a remote and utterly peaceful air about the place, cut off from the rest of the island. Ranged on the hill beside the main house, along a stone walkway through the slender trees are four very large apartments built of stone with exposed stone interiors, tiles, louvres, solid wood staircases and a veranda which takes full advantage of the view; perfect for sitting and contemplating the changing patterns of sun and shade. Each unit is self-contained with a full kitchen, but meals (excellent) can be eaten on the veranda at the main house, where there is an excellent Caribbean library (also an art gallery, visits by appointment). The owners have a policy of low environmental impact (an organic garden and solar power for water and electricity). This is one for locking yourself away in undisturbed seclusion: getting to Petit Coulibri means negotiating one of the worst drives in the Caribbean, but it is emphatically worth the effort, because the place has unutterable charm; you probably won't want to leave anyway.

moderate

There is a small cluster of friendly and comfortable hotels on the coast a mile south of Roseau, all with a fine view west to the sea horizon. There is no beach here really, but smooth fist-size rocks that clatter and jangle as the waves move over them. The **Evergreen Hotel**, PO Box 309 (*© 448 3288, *® 448 6800) is low-key with small blocks of rooms around a courtyard and a pool and sundeck set on the seafront. There is a slightly rarefied atmosphere: the new rooms in the waterfront building are very comfortable, but the original house has charm too. Pool and terrace above the sea, where there is a chic glass-fronted dining room. Just 16 rooms, with air-conditioning, phones and cable TVs. The **Anchorage Hotel and Dive Centre**, PO Box 34 (*© 448 2638, *® 448 5680, *anchorage@mail.tod.dm*), has 32 rooms looking out to sea (go for the ones upstairs) and a block of standard rooms above the pool. There is a large and often lively terrace bar and dining room. Rooms a/c with phones and cable TV. If you are coming to Dominica specifically to dive, then you might choose the **Castle Comfort Diving Lodge** (*© 448 2188, *® 448 6088, *www.delphis.dm/dive.html*), where there is an active atmosphere as the daily dives go out followed by quiet and chat as divers relax after their exertions. 15 rooms altogether, four very comfortable ones in the block on the waterfront (wicker furniture and bright blue decor, with a balcony looking onto the sea). Friendly air, good diving packages.

Another option is to stay in Roseau itself. The most charming hotel is the **Sutton Place Hotel**, 25 Old St, PO Box 2333 (✆ 448 449 8700, ✉ 448 3045), where there are nine suites and rooms in an old three-storey stone town house which has been restored and refitted inside. It is small and intimate, with some four-posters and laquered furniture and floorboards as well as white tiles. Pretty dining room in yellow and red with chandeliers and a basement bar that you leave through the barrel hatch. Some rooms have kitchenettes, all have balconies, TVs, phones, a/c and fans.

The **Fort Young Hotel**, PO Box 519 (✆ 448 5000, ✉ 448 5006) stands above the waterfront in the town, its rooms set among the old battlements of the fort that guarded the town approaches for a couple of centuries. The attractive courtyard is still laid with flagstones and the pool and bar are lost in foliage within. 33 comfortable rooms and suites on the battlements, most with a sea view. The **Garraway Hotel**, (✆ 449 8800, ✉ 449 8807; *expensive–moderate*) is set in a glass-fronted building which stands tall on the Bayfront with a fantastic view of the sea horizon. It is modern and plush to international standards of comfort, with air-conditioning, deep carpets, king-sized beds and satellite television. It has 31 rooms and suites.

If you want to stay right on the sand, **Castaways**, PO Box 5 (✆ 449 6244, ✉ 449 6246, US toll free ✆ (1 888) 227 8292, *castaways@mail.tod.dm*) is Dominica's best beach hotel, set on black sand at Mero, a few miles north of Roseau. There is a large and attractive terrace with the bar and the Almond Tree restaurant, from which the wings run on either side, containing 27 rooms in all. There is a fantastic view of the sunset on the horizon through the flamboyant trees and palms and from the palm-thatch beach bar. Also a dive shop, though no pool. Rooms in an older Caribbean style with rattan mats and tiles, all with balconies, a/c, fans, phones and TVs.

The **Lauro Club** stands on a cliff above the sea, ten villas painted in bright colours, each with a view. They are comfortable inside with tiled floors and lots of wooden fittings including trellised doors and louvred windows. There is a restaurant and bar, but you can also cater for yourself in the villas. An easy-going spot can be found on the beach to the south of Portsmouth, at the **Picard Beach Cottage Resort**, PO Box 34 (✆ 445 5131, ✉ 445 5599, *picard_beach@tod.dm*), a collection of eight wooden cottages set in a pleasant tropical garden right on the beach. Each one has a small veranda. Very quiet and low-key.

Just south of here is the **Coconut Beach Hotel**, PO Box 37 (✆ 445 5393, ✉ 445 5693), which is set right on the brown sand beach and has a pleasant, quiet air. There are 22 units, apartments and bungalows, each with air-conditioning or a ceiling fan, all have kitchenettes. Very nice waterfront bar and restaurant (seafood speciality).

moderate–cheap

Dominica has some extremely fine **rainforest retreats**, with magnificent settings in the mountains that take the best advantage of the island's scenery, but which are a little untypical for the Caribbean. The rooms are often quite basic, though they usually have hot and cold water, and they are quite remote. In the heights of the Roseau Valley, near the village of Trafalgar, is the **Papillote Wilderness Retreat**, PO Box 67 (✆ 448 2287, ✉ 448 2285, *papillote@mail.tod.dm*; *cheap*) which is practically throttled by its 12 acres of tropical garden. There are six rooms and two units in a cottage which are quite private despite the daily turnover of visitors. The restaurant is on the garden terrace and serves local food.

The **Springfield Plantation Guest House**, PO Box 456 (✆ 449 1401, ✉ 449 2160, *springfield@tod.dm*, *cheap, some rooms moderate*) is even more remote, high up on the Transinsular Road. It is set in an old timber-frame estate house on 200 acres of former plantation grounds; all wooden floors and ceilings with exposed beams and a fantastic view down the valley. Two apartments and eight rooms, some with an antique air with louvres and four poster beds. Generally quiet, though there are students in residence sometimes because Springfield is also an educational centre.

The **Layou Valley Plaza**, PO Box 192 (✆ 449 6203, ✉ 448 5212) is hidden in the hills of the Dominican heartland and has a superb view over the uninterrupted greenery of the rainforest in the upper Layou valley looking towards Morne Trois Pitons. It is set in a modern villa with white walls and dark-stained wood and hanging greenery. Just six rooms, stylishly simple, and good home cooking (or you can cook for yourself).

Farther afield, on the edge of the Carib Territory, you will find a warm welcome at **Floral Gardens**, PO Box 192 (✆ 445 7636, ✉ 445 7333). Quite rustic and almost overrun with greenery as the name suggests, but an excellent riverside escape with 23 rooms and two suites, some on the river itself.

And there are also some villas for people who would be happy to look after themselves. If you would like stay in a classic, old-time West Indian timber-frame villa, **Pointe Baptiste**, c/o Mrs G. Edwards, Calibishie (✆ 445 7322) has one of the loveliest settings in the Caribbean. Set on the clifftops of the north coast, the main house has a tin roof and a huge balcony where you can settle and take in the islands of Marie Galante and Guadeloupe. There is a golden sand beach just below and the house with its creaky wooden floors and drawing room and library has an old-fashioned aura so rarely found anywhere nowadays. Housekeeper service, villa rates for six people in season which divide down to a very good *cheap* rate.

Close by, taking advantage of the beach are **Red Rock Haven Homes**, Pointe Baptiste's modern counterpart, PO Box 71 (✆ 448 2181, ✉ 448 5787). There are just three large and comfortable wooden cottages, each with a full kitchen and a fine view of the valley from the huge balconies. Housekeeper service for cooking if you want; one and two bedrooms.

D'Auchamps Cottages, PO Box 1889 (✆ 448 3346, *honychurchs @tod.dm*) are two small and pretty stone cottages set in the profusion of the Laudat Valley above Roseau, self-catering.

cheap–very cheap

In Roseau there is a number of small hotels and guest houses, including **Vena's** on Cork Street (✆ 448 3286), the birth-place of the Dominican novelist Jean Rhys, which offers simple rooms off a creaky corridor. A friendly and dependable haunt where chat and cheap rooms are available is the **Kent Anthony Guest House** in the middle of town on Marlborough Street (℗ 448 2730). Not far off, **Ma Bass Guest House** on Field's Lane (℗ 448 2999) also has rooms, some with private bathrooms. In the village of Laudat high in the Roseau Valley you will find some nice rooms at **Roxy's Mountain Lodge**, PO Box 265 (℗/📞 448 4845), where there are seven rooms in the original house and a new chalet. A good starting point for hiking in the National Park and a friendly, quiet air.

For accommodation in **Portsmouth**, there are six simple rooms at **Sango's Sea Lodge** (℗ 445 5211), in concrete and stone cottages, open-plan with fan ventilation, no phones or TVs, hot showers in a stone partition. In the town itself, the **Mango Beach Resort** (℗ 445 3099) is set in a modern block on the beach, fan-ventilated with TVs and phones or try **Douglas's Guest House** (℗ 445 5253), very simple. And in Calibishie you will find very simple rooms in a wooden house right on the beach at the **Veranda View Guest House** (℗ 445 8900), just two bedrooms with private bathrooms and mosquito nets on the beds.

℗ (1 767)–   *Eating Out*

Dominica is quiet and you will not find that many places to eat out at night outside the hotels. You will find good traditional Caribbean food, however: callaloo or pumpkin soup followed by fish or a curry goat sitting among prodigious quantities of local vegetables such as plantain, green fig and breadfruit. Dominica also has one or two specialities such as *mountain chicken* or *cwapaud* (in fact breaded frogs' legs), crayfish, crab-backs stuffed with land-crab meat and tiny fish in cakes called *tee-tee-ree*, fish-fry which are caught at the river-mouth in a sheet. There is a government tax of 3% added to all bills and most restaurants add a service charge of 10%. Categories are arranged according to the price of a main course: *expensive*—EC$50 and above; *moderate*—EC$20–50; *cheap*—less than EC$20.

For an evening out in old-Roseau elegance try **La Robe Creole** on Fort Street (℗ 448 2896; *expensive–moderate*), set in a stone town-house with a wooden floor and arched windows and doors. It is decorated with red and yellow chequered madras tablecloths and cushions on tall-backed wooden chairs—the waitresses also wear traditional madras costumes, from which the restaurant takes its name. Start with accras or crab-back and follow with steamed shrimp with creole sauce or mountain chicken in beer batter and coconut flakes (in season), followed by banana flambéed at your table. A mixed creole and international menu, often lively.

Two lively and less formal spots, both set in nice old creole town houses with their tables set out on a balcony above the street, are **Pearl's Cuisine**, on Castle St (℗ 448 8707) and **Callalou** on King George V Street (℗ 448 3386). Both offer regular Dominican fare, lambi or goat, chicken or fish, with ground provisions or coleslaw, followed by guava pie, both *moderate*. There are not that many restaurants open at night, so it is worth considering the hotel dining rooms: Fort Young in Roseau and Evergreen and the Anchorage in the Castle Comfort area, the last two with good waterfront settings. You will get the best in local fare at the **World of Food** (℗ 448 3286; *moderate*) at Vena's, where the open tin-roofed dining room gives onto a paved courtyard with a mango tree (you dine to the occasional thud and bump, bump, bump in season); full suppers of soup followed by chicken and fish and a volley of local vegetables and then ice cream. There are a few Chinese restaurants (with Dominican adaptions) around the town, try **Paiho** on Church Street: shark fin soup on an old Dominica balcony above the street.

There is a little more variety at lunchtime. **Guiyave** (*™* 448 2930) has a very attractive setting with a green and white balcony upstairs hung with plants overlooking Cork Street. A long menu with baked chicken with glazed spinach followed by local ice cream. The **Cartwheel Café** (*™* 448 5353) down on the Bayfront is also popular with island business people. It is set in a stone and wooden building with a few tables set among plants: sandwiches and salads or more substantial plates of chicken and pork. Roseau also has plenty of *snackettes*, usually teeming with schoolkids on their lunchtime break, where you can get a lunchtime pattie and a fruit juice—sorrel, soursop, lime and tamarind according to the season—followed by a coconut cake. Also the **Mousehole Snackette,** where you can grab a Cornish pastie or fish pie. Finally, don't forget **Al's**, with 12 different flavours of ice cream. *Open till 10pm.*

In Portsmouth you can try **Chez Danielle** (*™* 448 4116; *moderate*), which sits right on the dark sand in the town, with chairs under breadfruit trees. Mixed menu on a blackboard: French *steak au poivre* or a *brochette coq au vin:* Italian pizzas and creole dishes. An entertaining place to visit for lunch or dinner is **Sango's Sea Lodge** (*™* 445 5211; *moderate–cheap*), which sits on the waterfront just south of the town. The building itself is modern, but everything else is rustic. You sit at bench seats, sharing a whole meal presented on a banana leaf alongside rice and huge plantain chips organically grown in the garden: freshly caught grilled fish (the owner is a fisherman) sold by weight, or salad of squid. In town you can go to the **Mango Bar** and restaurant on Bay St in a brightly painted, tin-roofed building with open windows and doors. Chicken or fish, mountain chicken or crayfish.

Bars and Nightlife

Some of the hotels have happy hours, barbecues and a band in season—the Anchorage has an occasional steel band—but otherwise you will rely on Dominican entertainment—rum shops, discos and local fêtes, which are at their liveliest at the weekend. There are limitless rum shops on the island, where you will be welcome to try out a few of the Dominican rums: Red Cap, Soca rum, D Special and if you can find it some Mountain Dew. *Bois Bandé* (pronounced 'bawbandy'), a local concoction made from tree bark, has an interesting story which you might enjoy investigating. Recently the island has begun to brew its own beer, called *Kubuli.*

Many restaurants double as bars, but a nice bar to look out for on the bayfront is the **Club de Cave** which sees a young crowd late into the evening, in a dungeon-like, barrel-vaulted setting. **Wykie's** bar on Old Street is a favourite with island-execs and passers-through, a cosy creole town house all lined with bamboo. Discotheques include the **Warehouse** in Checkhall and **Mercury** in Pottersville near the bridge in town. There is a mix of music: Jamaican *reggae, soca* from down south and French Caribbean *zouk.*

getting there

By air: There are no direct flights to Dominica from outside the Caribbean and so you have to change, usually in Antigua, St Lucia, Barbados or St Maarten, or in the French islands of Martinique or Guadeloupe. LIAT (✆ 449 2421) has several flights each day, heading up or down the island chain from Antigua or Barbados; Cardinal Airlines (✆ 449 8922, ✆ 449 8923) fly north to St Maarten and south to Barbados and Air Guadeloupe (✆ 449 1060) flies from its home and on to Martinique. From **the States** you may want to fly via San Juan in Puerto Rico, from where American Eagle (✆ 448 0628) have daily flights. Cardinal Airlines will also charter aircraft. If you want to charter a helicopter, perhaps to take a sightseeing tour, contact Ranger Skyviews (✆ 449 2389, ✆ 449 2323).

There are two airports on Dominica: Melville Hall (code DOM) and Canefield (DCF). Melville Hall is inconveniently located on the eastern side of the island, 35 miles northeast of Roseau, so it is probably best to aim for Canefield if you can, which is on the west coast just north of the capital. There is a departure tax of EC$25 and a $5 airport security tax.

By sea: a couple of ferries touch Dominica on their way from Martinique to Guadeloupe (occasionally there are through schedules to St Lucia). The *Express des Iles* (contact Caribbean Express, ✆ 448 2181) touches the island five times a week, docking at the ferry terminal on the Bayfront in Roseau, and the Atlantika Car Ferry (✆ 448 6977) visits four times a week. Reserve a seat in season and during school holidays. The departure tax of EC$25 still applies.

tourist information

UK: 1 Collingham Gardens, London SW5 0HW (✆ (0171) 835 1937, ✆ (0171) 373 8743).

USA: Contact the Dominica Tourist Office, 10 East 21st St, Suite 600, New York, NY 10010 (✆ (212) 475 7542, ✆ 475 9728) or the Caribbean Tourism Association, 20 East 46th Street, New York, NY 10017 (✆ (212) 682 0435, ✆ 697 4258).

France: 12 rue de la Madrid, 75008 Paris, France (✆ 1 53 42 41 00, ✆ 1 43 67 32 85)

Canada (care of OECS): Suite 1050, 112 Kent St, Ottawa, Ontario K1P 5P2 (✆ (613) 236 8952, ✆ (613) 236 3042).

On the island itself, the main **Dominica National Development Corporation** can be reached at Box 293, Roseau, Dominica (✆ 448 2351/2045, ✆ 448 5840). For tourist **information** there is a kiosk at the Old Post Office on the waterfront in Roseau, at the nearby cruise ship berth and one at each of the airports: Canefield ✆ 449 1242; Melville Hall ✆ 445 0751. The tourist board publications include the small magazine *Discover Dominica* and the quarterly tourist paper *The Tropical Traveller.* Local newspapers include the *New Chronicle*, which is published on Fridays and *The Independent* and *Tropical Star*, which are published on Wednesday and Fridays.

The main hospital in Roseau is the **Princess Margaret Hospital** (✆ 448 2231). For emergency services, dial 999.

The **IDD code** for Dominica is ✆ (1 767) and this is followed by a seven-digit island number (these all begin with 44 and so are often only written with five digits). When you are on-island, dial the full seven digits. It is best to address **letters** to the Commonwealth of Dominica, because otherwise they often end up in the Dominican Republic. You are advised to be careful about **personal security** when in Dominica, particularly when on isolated beaches and remote roads in the countryside. Do not leave valuables unattended on the beach at any time.

festivals

Dominica maintains a traditional **Carnival** in the days before Lent (still called Masquerade from the French celebrations) with feasting and general revelling in the streets and bands of players dressed in fantastic costumes. Other celebrations are held around **Independence Day** (3 November), centring on folk arts, including music and dance as well as the traditional Caribbean *jump-up*. In **conte**, or story-telling, raconteurs compete with one another in telling humorous anecdotes of everyday life. **Jounen Kweyol**, a celebration of the creole language and customs, with cooking, radio and national costume, is celebrated on the last Friday in October. **Domfesta** is an annual festival of local arts, crafts and performing arts held in July and August. As in many Catholic Caribbean countries, some villages in Dominica celebrate their Saints' days with a Mass and then a party.

money

The currency of Dominica is the Eastern Caribbean Dollar which is fixed to the Greenback at EC$2.65 = US$1. Prices are often published in both dollar currencies, so it is worth knowing which currency you are dealing in.

Banks: Open weekdays 8–3, Fri 8–5.

Shops: Open weekdays 8–4, often with a stop for lunch; Sat 8–1.

watersports

With the exception of scuba diving, for which the island has a justifiably good reputation, watersports are not that developed in Dominica and you will be dependent on the hotels for small watersports such as kayaks, windsurfers and small sailing boats. Try the Anchorage Hotel (Dominica Tours ✆ 448 2638) or the Castaways at Mero. Sailing trips can also be booked through them. A general watersports operator is Nature Island Dive (✆ 449 8181, ✆ 449 8182) which offers kayaking and snorkelling around the southern area as well as hiking and mountain-biking in the mountainous interior.

Snorkelling: Equipment available through the dive shops and the hotels for non-divers. The best sites are off the north coast, for instance at Hodge's Bay and Douglas Bay, but also Soufrière Bay.

Deep-sea fishing: Contact Gamefishing Dominica on ✆ 448 7285.

Scuba diving: The island has an established reputation for its corals and fish, which are plentiful and in good condition for the Caribbean. Dives take place on the reefs along the leeward coast, mainly in the south near Scott's Head in Soufrière bay, where there is a Marine Park, and also in the Marine Park in Douglas Bay just north of the Cabrits. Brain corals, black corals and sponges are all on view on the walls and boulder-strewn drop-offs; also excellent fish-life, snake-eels, seahorses and squids with larger schools and a greater variety than elsewhere. Dominican oddities include hot and cold water springs under the surface (at Champagne in Soufrière Bay you will see and and feel the warm bubbling water, discoloured with sulphur and iron) and clear water beneath cloudy river outflows. There are also some wrecks.

Full instruction is available at most of the dive shops and most have some equipment like cameras for hire. If you will be diving a lot then it is worth enquiring about packages offered by the various hotels. Contact: Dive Dominica at the Castle Comfort Dive Lodge (© 448 2188, ● 448 6088, *dive@tod.dm*) and the Anchorage Dives (© 448 2638, ● 448 5680), both just south of Roseau and within a short ride of the southern area. Also Nature Island Dive above. The north of the island is also opening up and there are operations mid-way up the island in Mero: Dive Castaways (© 449 6244, ● 449 6246) and East Carib Dive (©/● 449 6575). There is also a dive shop in the Portsmouth area: the Cabrits Dive Centre (© 445 3010, ● 445 3011, *cabritsdive@tod.dm*), which has easy access to the sites in the Marine Park to the north of the Cabrits.

River-bathing: Perhaps preferable to sea-bathing is swimming in Dominica's **rivers**. There is plenty of flowing water on the island. So much, in fact, that they sell it to drier islands such as Antigua and St Maarten to the north. Waterfalls are also a good bet, because there is usually a pool beneath them. Some good places to swim are at the Trafalgar and Middleham Falls (*an hour's walk*), the Rosalie River on the east coast and the White River in La Plaine, whose source is the boiling lake. Otherwise, ask around. For a full day's outing you can float and clamber down the **Layou River**, starting at Belles in the rainforest on the transinsular road and working your way down through the Layou flats towards the west coast.

other sports

Sports on land (except for walking of course, *see* p.210 above) are relatively limited, though there are **tennis courts** at some of the hotels (Castaways, Reigate Hall) and there is even a **squash court** at the Anchorage Hotel. Nature Island Dive offer **mountain-biking** tours.

The French Caribbean

Midway down the chain of the Lesser Antilles are the islands of Martinique and Guadeloupe, the two large French outposts in the Caribbean. Together with the islands of St Barts and the French half of St Martin, which lie 150 miles to the north in the Leeward Islands, these two make up the French West Indies.

The familiar verve of the French is ever-present in these islands. Chic customers glide by shops filled with Christian Lacroix and Yves St Laurent, and lovers linger over a meal under coloured awnings while citizens play *boules* on the dusty town squares. There is a certain *coquetterie* in the dress and manner—on the *autoroutes* you will find yourself competing with Peugeots and Citroëns driven with a nonchalance both French and Caribbean (a fearsome combination). In Fort de France, the capital of Martinique, there is even a Parisian haste, a *je m'en foutisme* untypical of the laid-back Caribbean. The illusion of being in France—all the pleasure on the one hand and the frustrations on the other, of their style and infuriating obstructiveness—is only spiked by the unfamiliar bristle of coconut palms and the variety of skin tones among the faces.

But familiar Caribbean strains run through French islands too. The air pulses to the sound of the relentless French Caribbean rhythm, *zouk*. Away from the towns, the slopes are blanketed in typical Caribbean rainforest and the flatlands with sugar-cane or bananas sewn up in blue plastic bags. There the islanders walk at a relaxed and graceful pace, carrying the twin tools of the West Indies, the machete and the umbrella. You will sometimes still see *blanchisseuses* at work, their white washing spread all over the rocks at the riverside, keeping up a constant chatter of *créole*, the mix of French and African that has developed in the islands. The markets, under red corrugated-iron roofs, are typical Caribbean mayhem.

Although the smaller, more northerly islands of St Martin and St Barts are politically attached to Guadeloupe, it is really Martinique and Guadeloupe that are cultural sisters. These two have a stronger creole history and tradition; St Martin and St Barts have developed much more recently and in atmosphere they are really more like France in the tropics than French West Indian.

Politically, France has taken a radically different approach to its colonies from Britain. Instead of encouraging a gradual move to independence, France has embraced her Caribbean islands, taking them into the République and giving them the status of overseas *départements*, equal to that of Savoie or Lot-et-Garonne. Martinique and Guadeloupe are *régions* in their own right, with the extra powers and responsibilities brought by decentralization in 1985. They are administered by a *préfet* appointed by the French government. Their people vote in French elections and they each send three deputies and two senators to the National Assembly in Paris.

In standard of living alone, the contrast with neighbouring islands is striking, and it could never be maintained without direct support from Paris. Most French Antilleans appreciate the benefits and would not change their situation, except to gain the maximum self-government while under the French umbrella, but there are some who envy the other islands their autonomy. Independence movements have expressed themselves in graffiti campaigns and have occasionally erupted into violence, with bomb attacks.

But the official line is that life should be French, with all the benefits that brings. Milk costs the same as it does in the *métropole*, as continental France is called, and so does a car. There is National Service. Rumour has it that they even fly in croissants. To some Frenchmen the islands seem like an expensive burden, but then they are also a bridgehead in the Americas. Besides, most of the money sent here is used to buy French goods.

Due to the many American visitors, English is quite widely spoken in the French Antilles. However, it is much better if you can understand French if you are to deal with officialdom or if you want to go off the beaten track. In the villages on Martinique and Guadeloupe, and the islands off Guadeloupe, like Marie Galante and the Saints, you will hear creole or French and little else. Also, museums (and menus) are in French. The islands of St Martin and St Barts have a stronger French-speaking heritage and you will hear very little creole there.

French Caribbean History

The earliest French involvement in the Caribbean was as pirates and privateers in the 16th century. In fact it was a French pirate who had revealed to the whole of Europe what wealth the Spaniards were gaining in the New World. Off the Azores in 1523, Jean Fleury captured two Spanish ships which contained the riches of Montezuma's palace in Mexico, a prize worth millions.

Life 'beyond the line' was dangerous, because capture by the Spaniards meant certain death, but men like François le Clerc (known to the Spaniards as *pie de palo* because of his wooden leg) ran a fleet of ten ships and scoured the Caribbean Sea and the Bahamas for plunder. In 1553 he sacked nearly every major town, ransoming hundreds of thousands of pounds. Many of the buccaneers, who centred on the island of Tortuga off Hispaniola in the 17th century, were Frenchmen and eventually this led to the establishment of France's most successful colony in St Domingue, now Haiti.

It was on a privateering expedition in 1624 that the first French colony accidentally came into being. Pierre d'Esnambuc, after a fight with a Spanish galleon off the Cayman Islands, was forced to put in for repair at St Christopher, where the British had just established a colony. He made friends with the Governor Sir Thomas Warner and helped to protect him from the Caribs. Two years later he was back, and they settled the island together. From this 'Mother Colony of the West Indies' both nations looked farther afield. De Poincy, a Grand Cross and Bailiff of the Order of the Knights of Malta, whose name is remembered in the poinciana tree all over the Caribbean, directed the expeditions in the name of the *Compagnie des Iles d'Amerique*. Despite the opposition of the Caribs, the French boldly set out for the large Windward Islands of Martinique and Guadeloupe, planting settlements there in 1635.

In 1647, the age of *l'or blanc* began and sugar-cane, introduced by Dutch Protestants fleeing the Inquisition in Pernambuco, soon blanketed the islands. With a sharp eye for new technology, the French soon developed into the leading exporters of refined sugar to the voracious European markets. The industry required labour so slaves were brought over in their hundreds from Africa. Development went forward apace and in 1669, the seat of government was moved from St Kitts to Martinique, a shift that was to guarantee the island's predominance over the other French colonies into the 20th century. Most of the trade with mainland France was conducted through St Pierre on Martinique.

The 17th century was a time of expanding empires, and land was so valuable that they would snatch whatever they could get. Gradually, the French expanded their domain southwards, settling the swathe of islands from Guadeloupe to Grenada. French buccaneers settled on St Barts and the Virgin Islands and from Tortuga they moved into the western area of Hispaniola, which eventually became St Domingue (now Haiti).

By the 18th century, the French and British were at loggerheads in the Eastern Caribbean and they harried one another's colonies mercilessly. During the Seven Years' War, the British ripped through the islands and captured Martinique and Guadeloupe. It was considered so vital to retain a foothold in the Caribbean that at the Treaty of Paris in 1763, the French were prepared to relinquish all their claims to land in India, Louisiana and Canada (which simply had to be written off as *quelques arpents de neige*—a few tracts of snow). But with the British overstretched in the American War of Independence a few years later, the French in their turn whittled through the islands, reclaiming all their old colonies.

The French Revolution had profound effects in the islands. The traditions of *Egalité* and the Rights of Man had particular significance in the Caribbean because they could hardly tolerate slavery. The planters and officials shuddered at the ideas emanating from their capital: but each colony turned out differently. In Martinique the planters and royalists remained in the ascendancy: rather than lose everything they actually preferred to call in their old enemies, the English, to bolster the prosperous old regime. In Guadeloupe, however, the revolutionaries gained the upper hand. There was a reign of terror; the slaves were liberated, the planters put to death or exiled and the plantations, symbols of the *ancien régime*, were destroyed (there are no pre-revolutionary estate houses left in Guadeloupe). And the humanitarian ideas emanating from Paris proved to be the death of France's most prosperous colony, St Domingue. In 1794 it erupted in an armed rebellion by the slaves, a war of liberation that led to the founding of the world's first black republic, Haiti. Following the Napoleonic Wars, the other islands were returned to France and they have remained in her hands ever since.

Schoelcher and the Abolition of Slavery

The reintroduction of slavery in 1802 caused terrible disruption in Guadeloupe, where many of the former slaves preferred to die rather than lose their freedom. By 1834 slavery was abolished in the British colonies. Nearby St Lucia and Dominica were free, and so slaves on the French islands put out on rafts in a break for freedom.

Victor Schoelcher, the Father of Emancipation in the French Caribbean, was born in Paris in 1804 and entered the family firm of porcelain-makers. In 1829 he undertook a journey on behalf of the firm to Mexico, Cuba and the southern States. His business was not particularly successful, but having witnessed the depredations of slavery his life was changed for good. On his return to France he embarked on a career as a polemicist and pamphleteer, mobilizing the public imagination through his works. He continued for 15 years, but powerful lobbies opposed him, and it became clear that only a political reversal in France could affect the situation in the Caribbean colonies.

As it had been 60 years before, it was a revolution that overturned the law and in 1848 Schoelcher, the committed Republican, had his chance. On 27 April the law was passed abolishing slavery in the French colonies once and for all. Schoelcher was put in charge of dismantling it and he went to the Antilles. He was elected deputy of Guadeloupe.

After Emancipation, the French Antilles, like the British islands, were short of labour for the canefields as the freed slaves left the plantations to form their own villages. By 1870, some 80,000 East Indians, or *Z'indiens*, as they are known in creole, came to the islands as indentured labourers. Their faces are less visible nowadays, but you will still see Hindu temples dotted around the islands.

The French colonies in the Caribbean followed the vagaries of the various *empires* and *républiques* of French politics until 1946, when Martinique and Guadeloupe were elevated to the status of *départements* and later into *régions*. They are governed by an elected island assembly, the *Conseil Régional*, and a governor appointed in France.

Language and Culture

French colonization was always a more thorough-going affair than that of the British, and French culture can be seen to have penetrated all parts of French Caribbean life. The French Antilles have a deep pride in both French culture and their own creole version of it; there are understandable objections to the occasional accusations of being 'black Frenchmen' with no culture of their own.

It is often said how beautiful the people of Martinique and Guadeloupe are. The faces show a greater variety of colour than the British and Dutch Caribbean islands. Though the French islands always had a slightly higher proportion of whites, the old settlers were clearly also less prudish about taking an African mistress. The mix of racial strains is more thorough (though still not as thorough as in the Spanish islands) and it has created some striking faces.

And a hundred years ago the *doudous* (from *douce chérie*) of Martinique and Guadeloupe were as chic as their metropolitan counterparts. They presented themselves with characteristic Gallic flair (as they still do), bedecked in reams of brightly coloured cotton and yards of lace petticoat, with a *foulard* thrown over the shoulder. You can still see the chequered *madras* material in the two large islands. But the focal point of the impression was the

229

construction of the hat. This too was fashioned of bright silk material, often yellow and checked, and there was supposedly a code in its design:

Tête à un bout (one point): my heart is for the taking.
Tête à deux bouts: my heart is taken.
Tête à trois bouts: my heart is spoken for, but you can try your luck.

The French Antilles were one of the leading centres of *Négritude*, a French literary and philosophical movement of black consciousness that was born in the 1930s. Martiniquans Etienne Lero and Aimé Césaire, together with Léopold Senghor of Senegal, re-examined the position of the black man, formerly the slave, and his relation to the white man, the colonial master. Aimé Césaire became famous with his *Cahier d'un Retour au Pays Natal* in 1939 and a later play *La Tragédie du Roi Christophe*. He was also a leading light in Martiniquan politics and has only recently retired after nearly 50 years as mayor of Fort de France.

Creole is the mixed language that has developed in many parts of the French colonial world, and the Caribbean islands which have seen a French presence each have a version of their own. You will hear it spoken in Dominica, St Lucia and occasionally Grenada, which the French have owned at one time or other, and even as far away as Trinidad, taken there by French Royalists fleeing the *patriotes* in revolutionary times. The Eastern Caribbean creoles are not, however, mutually comprehensible with the *kweyol* of the Haitians, once also French subjects. There are creoles in French Guyana in South America and in Réunion, the two other French overseas Départements, and also in Mauritius. Curiously, the two smaller French islands, St Martin and St Barthélemy, have traditionally spoken English and latterly pure French. The creole language is a classic Caribbean melting pot, a pidgin formed by early settlers from different countries in order to communicate with each other and then steadily changed by the influx of African slaves, none of whom spoke a common language because they were purposely split up to destroy their traditions. French is clearly audible in creole and for tantalizing moments the stream will let you hold on to words and even phrases, but suddenly it will whiplash and escape your grasp, chasing off in a flurry of unaccustomed vowels and peculiar utterances. In the same way, in the rhythm and intonation, and in the sharp un-Gallic sounds, are distinct echoes and resonances of African languages. Sensibly, they seem to have got rid of the impossible-to-pronounce letters of French, 'u' and 'r', substituting 'oo' and 'w' instead.

But French is the official language of the islands, used in the schools and by the authorities, as well as on the menus, of course. It is mainly the country people who speak creole and as you must speak the official language to 'get on', people will actually bring up their children without using the language at all, speaking to them only in French. There is little written in the language because it has always had an oral tradition, particularly in song.

Most French Caribbean authors write in French and they have won plenty of French literary prizes over the years. Some to look out for are, from Martinique, Patrick Chamoiseau, winner of the Prix Goncourt with *Texaco* (also *Solibo Magnifique*, which is set in Fort de France), Aimé Césaire, Edouard Glissant, Joseph Zobel (*Rue Cases-Nègres*), Rafaël Confiant (*Eau de Café*, winner of the 1991 Prix Novembre), Daniel Boukman and Xavier Orville. Guadeloupean writers include Maryse Condé, whose finest book is probably *La Vie Scélérate*, Simone Schwarz-Bart (known for her *Ti Jean l'Horizon, Pluie et Vent sur Telumé Miracle* and *Un Plat de Porc aux Bananes Vertes*, with husband André), Max Jeanne, Daniel Maximin, Ernest Pépin and Gisèle Pineau, author of the prize-winning *La Grande Drive des Esprits*.

Martinique

Martinique has traditionally been the flagship of French culture in the Caribbean. It was the richest of the colonies and in the last century its social hub, St Pierre, the 'Paris of the Lesser Antilles', was renowned all over the Americas. Fashion followed Paris to the letter, and the great plays of the age were staged in the St Pierre Theatre.

Though the spirit of St Pierre died in 1902, when the city was destroyed in a cataclysmic volcanic explosion, Martinique is still that little bit more chic. The island is more developed than its *confrères*, and with 360,000 citizens, about a third of whom live in the capital Fort de France on the southeast coast, it is the most populous island in the Lesser Antilles after Trinidad. Martinique is a central link in the Eastern Caribbean island chain, lying between the Windward Islands of Dominica and St Lucia. It measures 48 miles by 19 at its widest point (75 by 30km) and with its curious skiing-glove shape, it has an area of 416 square miles (1080sq km). It seems larger because it is so highly developed. The north is dominated by the steep volcanic mountain of Mont Pelé (4656ft) and from there the land steadily falls away south to the central sugar plains of Lamentin and Fort de France, before rising again into the *mornes* (hills) of the southern peninsula. The island is of volcanic origin, except in the south, where age-old coral limestone formations have been pushed up out of the sea.

The French heritage constantly bombards the eyes, from the billboards to *boules* on the town square. The Martiniquans have a surprisingly faithful attachment to France, stronger than that of their compatriots in Guadeloupe, whom they consider a little wild and unpredictable. Despite subsidies from France that amount to a total of about 70 per cent of the island's GDP, Martinique receives a lot from tourism, which brings in approximately as much as the rest of Martinique's exports combined. In 1995 the island saw just short of a million stayover and cruise-ship tourists. The next principal earner is agriculture: one-third of the land is under cultivation and you will see banana plantations everywhere and sugar-cane, used for sugar and rum.

Most of the tourism in Martinique is concentrated around a few towns in the south of the island, and you can certainly have a good time there enjoying the best of the island's beaches and the restaurants in that area. But Martinique gives an excellent exposure to French Caribbean life, and its towns, rainforests and the remote east coast can be stimulating and satisfying to explore.

History

Martinique was discovered at the turn of the 15th century, on Columbus's first, second or fourth voyage, depending whose history you believe (it was actually his first landfall on his fourth voyage). Columbus apparently thought the island was inhabited by a tribe of Amazons because he was greeted only by women shouting *Madinina*. The Carib men must have been away raiding another island. Similarly, the origins of the name Martinique have been obscured by zealous historians. It may have been named for St Martin, but most think that the name derives from the Carib word *Madinina*, thought to mean 'the island of flowers'.

With or without menfolk, the island was left to the Caribs until 1635, when the Breton d'Esnambuc arrived from St Kitts with a hundred colonists and settled on the leeward coast near Le Carbet. They planted a cross and erected a fort, and after years of running battles with the Caribs they came to an arrangement in which the French lived on the Caribbean coastline and the Caribs on the Atlantic side.

Just as Barbados became the leading British island, so Martinique became the leading French colony in the 1650s. The islanders became fantastically rich growing sugar and shipping it out to Europe. They had an uneasy relationship with the French Crown: in 1717 the Governor tried to enforce the *exclusif* (a law stipulating that trade from Martinique must be made exclusively with France) and promptly found himself taken prisoner with his Intendant and simply sent back to France as an unwanted nuisance. A more conciliatory governor was sent out to replace him, one who was prepared to turn a blind eye to unofficial trading.

In the 18th century Martinique changed hands a number of times, like all the islands in the area, snatched by roving navies and swapped for other prizes at the end of each successive war. A new storm rose on the horizon as the ideas of the Revolution reverberated in the Caribbean. Martinique was divided along traditional lines; the townspeople, or *patriotes*, adopted the cockade and allied themselves with the revolutionaries, and the planters struck for the Royalists. Initially the *patriotes* took the island, rallied by the Revolutionary Lacrosse from St Lucia. General de Rochambeau and the Revolution came to the island in triumph; Fort Royal became République-ville. But within a year the planters had turned the tables and had contrived to get the British in, in order to restore the *ancien régime* and their prosperity. Martinique was relatively stable for the next 20 years under British rule and did not see the troubles that occurred in the other colonies of Guadeloupe and Saint Domingue.

In the first half of the 19th century, forces were mobilized against slavery in France, initially by Cyrille Bissette, a Martiniquan, and then by Victor Schoelcher (*see* pp.228–9). Slave riots took place in Le Carbet, St Pierre and in Grande Anse. With the coming of the Second Republic, the abolition of slavery in the French islands was proclaimed on 27 April 1848.

1902 was a momentous date for the colony because of the eruption of Mont Pelé, which completely destroyed St Pierre, then the commercial and cultural centre of the island. Fort de France took its place. In 1946, Martinique became a *département* with the same status and responsibilities as any other in *le métropole* and in 1985 it became a *région*.

Three Crowned Heads

In the 17th century, a Françoise d'Aubigné, the daughter of a colonial functionary, spent her childhood at the northern parish of Le Prêcheur, just as the colony was becoming prosperous. When she returned to Europe, she embarked on a course that would take her to the royal court of France. She became Madame de Maintenon and in 1684 she secretly married Louis XIV.

Martiniquan legend also relates a story of two young cousins, Yéyette and Aimée, who were walking one evening when they came across an old woman known in the area as a fortune-teller. They gave their palms to be examined and eventually she made her pronouncement: 'You', she said to the first, 'will be an Empress, and you', talking to Aimée, 'will be more than an Empress.' She walked off, refusing to respond to their pleas for more detail. Aimée Dubuc de Rivery was soon sent to a convent in France to complete her education and the incident was forgotten. But on her return journey to Martinique she was caught in a storm off the European coast and was taken captive by Barbary pirates. The Bey of Algiers sold the passengers of the ship as slaves, but kept Aimée because he was captivated by her beauty. Eventually he made a present of her to the Grand Turk in Constantinople. There, she penetrated the deepest secrets of the seraglio, to become the favourite of the Sultan, lover of his successor and finally the Sultana Validé, adoptive mother of Emperor Mahmoud II.

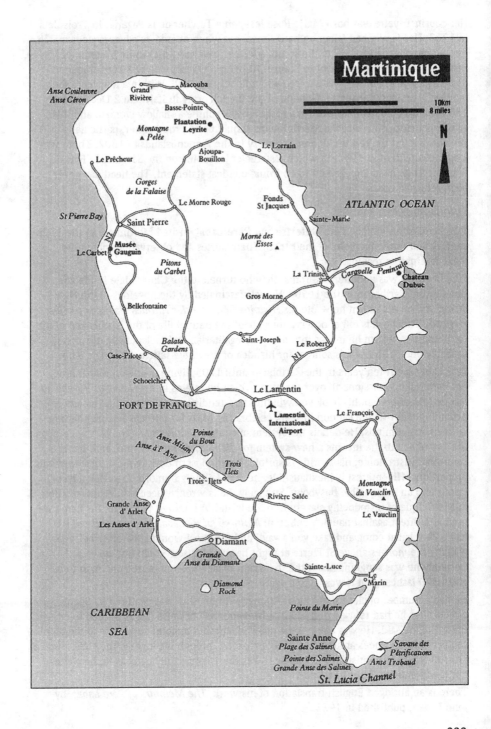

Martinique

10km
8 miles

N

Anse Couleuvre
Anse Céron

Grand
Rivière

Macouba

Basse-Pointe

Plantation
Leyrite

Montagne
▲ Pelée

Le Prêcheur

Ajoupa-
Bouillon

Le Lorrain

Gorges
de la Falaise

Le Morne Rouge

Fonds
St Jacques

ATLANTIC OCEAN

St Pierre Bay

Saint Pierre

Sainte-Marie

Musée
Gauguin

Le Carbet

Morné des
Esses

Pitons
du Carbet

La Trinité

Caravelle Peninsula

Château
Dubuc

Bellefontaine

Gros Morne

Balata
Gardens

Saint-Joseph

Le Robert

Case-Pilote

N1

Schoelcher

Le Lamentin

FORT DE FRANCE

Lamentin
International
Airport

Le François

Pointe
du Bout

Anse Mitan

Anse à l' Ane

Trois
Ilets

Trois-Ilets

Rivière Salée

Montagne
du Vauclin ▲

Grande Anse
d' Arlet

Les Anses d' Arlet

Le Vauclin

Diamant

Grande
Anse du Diamant

Sainte-Luce

Diamond
Rock

Le
Marin

CARIBBEAN

SEA

Pointe du Marin

Sainte Anne
Plage des Salines

Savane des
Pétrifications
Anse Trabaud

Pointe des Salines
Grande Anse des Salines

St. Lucia Channel

Her cousin Yéyette was born Marie-Rose Joséphine Tascher de la Pagerie, in Trois-Ilets in 1763. Her family had fallen on hard times, but when offered an advantageous match, her parents married her off to the son of a former governor, Alexandre Vicomte de Beauharnais, and she too went to France. At one stage Joséphine was condemned to death as a noble, but she was set free when Robespierre fell. Within a few years she married Napoleon Bonaparte, General of the French army in Italy. On 2 December 1804 she became his Empress. Many consider Joséphine a shallow woman, and it is somewhat surprising that the Martiniquans should be so proud of her, particularly as she was behind the reintroduction of slavery in the French islands in 1802. There was a curious incident in 1992, in which a statue of Joséphine on the Savanne in Fort de France had its head knocked off in an ironic political statement. The head has never been returned.

Two Dominican Monks

Two Dominican monks, **Père Dutertre** and **Père Labat**, visited Martinique in the 17th century and wrote memoirs of their trips. Their stories and observations about life make fascinating reading.

Père Dutertre was a soldier and romantic who turned to the Church late in life and came to the Caribbean in the 1650s. He was fascinated by the novelties of the New World and on his return he wrote his *Histoire Générale des Antilles Habitées par les Français*. The work is full of observations about the natural life of the islands and of the Carib Indians, whom he makes into naturally egalitarian and melancholic dreamers, probably one of Rousseau's sources for his idea of the *noble savage* 100 years later.

Père Labat spent ten years in the Caribbean until 1705, living mainly in Martinique, but undertaking missions all over the area, which he relates in his *Nouveau Voyage au Iles de l'Amérique*. In his book you will find him tending souls by spiritual means or defending them with a cannon instead, celebrating Mass for buccaneers and chatting with enemy admirals. He details the system of compensation among the buccaneers for the loss of a limb, he invents a new system for distilling sugar into rum, and, being a confirmed gastronome, his writing is sprinkled with descriptions of meals of sumptuous proportions. His interest is inexhaustible, he is unfailingly humorous, earthy, adventurous and an incorrigible busybody. Strangely, he is wrongly accused by folk tradition in Martinique of introducing slavery into the island. A hundred years ago, his name was used as a threat against naughty children: *Moin ké fai Pè Labatt vini pouend ou!* (I'll make Père Labat come and take you away!) and his ghost would apparently be seen walking the *mornes* above St Pierre at night because his soul could find no rest. Certainly he was sanguine about the treatment of slaves—he ordered one man to be given 300 lashes—but it was a cruel age.

He had a number of close shaves too. At one point his ship was captured by Spanish pirates after he had refused to fire the only cannonball because it was needed to crush the garlic, he said. He was about to be put to death, but a moment later he found all his captors on their knees around him. While rootling through his luggage they had found a cross of the Holy Inquisition. Of course it was there completely by chance, he claims, but it was enough to set him free.

There is an abridged English translation of his work, *The Memoirs of Père Labat*, by John Eaden, published in 1931.

Lafcadio Hearn

The traveller **Lafcadio Hearn** lived near St Pierre for two years in the late 1880s and he painted a series of tender pictures of Martiniquans and their lives: the *blanchisseuses* (launderesses) who rise at 4.30am when the local alarm clock, the *cabritt bois* (a cricket), stops chirruping, covering the rocks on the River Roxelane with the washing that they beat and scrub; the *porteuses* who carry supplies weighing up to 120lb on their heads, singing as they cross the mountain range in the heat of the day; a man infatuated by the *guiablesse* (a zombie), who leads him to his death when he tries to kiss her. It is all a bit romanticized, but his *Two Years in the West Indies* is a charming book and gives an unforgettable picture of Martinique before St Pierre was destroyed by Mont Pelé.

Getting Around

Public **buses** are a cheap way of travelling around the island and they depart from **le Parking**, on the waterfront at Fort de France, or from the main square in other towns. You will find both public buses, which follow a vague time schedule, and *taxis collectifs* (TCs), share-taxis (they can be a mini-bus or a car) that run a fixed route and depart when they are full. At the terminus, ask around and you will be directed to the first one headed in your direction. If you wish to get a bus from the airport into Fort de France (no buses run the route directly), you must cross the main road, beyond the car park in front of the terminal building, and flag down a *taxi collectif* on the other side.

Public buses are only allowed to stop at official stops, but you might be able to flag down a TC on the roadside if you are lucky. *Arrêt!*, shouted loud enough to be heard above the noise of the stereo system, is the word used to indicate that you want to get off. The buses run from 5am until about 7pm and the TCs a little longer. On Sundays and on public holidays the public transport system packs up in mid-afternoon and you can quite easily be left isolated. Some prices are: **Fort de France** to airport—Fr12; Trois Ilets—Fr22; St Pierre—Fr20; to St Anne—Fr35.

The tourist areas on the other side of Fort de France bay (Pointe du Bout, Anse Mitan, Anse à l'Ane) are best served by **ferry** (*vedette*). These leave from the waterfront next to the Savane, close to Fort St Louis, and keep up a regular schedule to Pointe du Bout from 6am until about midnight; 20-minute crossing.

Taxis are also readily available at the Parking downtown or the airport and can be ordered at any hotel. Taxi companies include Taxis Savane (✆ 60 62 73), Radio Taxis Service (✆ 63 10 10) and Radio Telephone Taxi (✆ 63 63 62). There is a stand in Le Marin (✆ 74 62 78). Some examples of fares are: from Lamentin airport to: city-centre—Fr90, Pointe du Bout—Fr170, St Anne—Fr290. Taxi-drivers are willing to take day tours (many of them speak English). If divided between four people, the price for a day's drive is reasonable value, but be sure to fix the price beforehand.

For maximum mobility, plenty of **hire cars** are available. In comparison with other islands nearby, Martinique's roads are good, though the islanders tend to drive with an abandon both French and Caribbean. Driving is on the right and your own licence is valid for the first 20 days, after which time an international driving licence is required. Maps are usually handed out by the hire companies. Found at the airport, in Fort de

France and in the tourist centres, the hire companies offer cars from about US$35–40 per day with taxes on top. Major credit cards are accepted as deposit. Companies (most of which have offices in town as well as at the airport) include: Avis (✆ 70 11 60, ✆ 63 47 19), Europcar in Fort de France (✆ 51 33 33, ✆ 51 22 44), Hertz (✆ 60 64 64, ✆ 51 46 26), Pop's Car (✆ 42 16 84, ✆ 42 16 85) and Tropicar (✆ 63 37 41, ✆ 58 44 22). You can rent scooters through Funny Rent Motorcycles (general ✆ 63 33 05), with outlets all over the island and Discount in Trois Islets and around the south (✆ 66 05 34).

Island tours are easy to organize in full- and half-day tours (usually taking in a meal as well). Three tour operators are: Caribtours, Pointe du Bout, Trois-Ilets (✆ 66 04 48), STT Voyages at 23 rue Blénac, Fort de France (✆ 71 68 12) and Madinina Tours, 89 rue Blénac (✆ 70 65 25). A helicopter can be chartered for excursions through Airway (✆ 51 57 03) and a sightseeing tour by plane through ACF Aviation (✆ 56 32 78). For a tour led by well-informed guides you can contact ZEMI (✆ 61 10 35).

Beaches

Martinique has beaches to suit every taste—busy strips with hotels and watersports and more isolated palm-fringed coves with fishing villages. Most lie on the protected Caribbean coast, but there are also quite a few hidden in the nooks and crannies of the Atlantic shore. The sand is best in the south; in the north it becomes dark and volcanic. Beaches are public in Martinique (though you may have to pay in some cases for access over private land) and although most hotels do not mind outsiders, one or two discourage them for the benefit of their guests. Most charge for the use of their facilities. The area south of Fort de France is very popular and many of the hotels are located on the beaches there (easily reached by ferry from the city). If you are in the north, your nearest beaches are likely to be in the lee of the Caravelle Peninsula, but only go on a calm and sunny day because otherwise the sea will be rough.

best beaches

Grande Anse des Salines: Martinique's best beach, a perfect curve of sand backed with palms trees right at the southern tip of the island. It gets crowded at the weekends, but can be fairly free during the week. There are often snack bars tucked under the palms and there is a restaurant, **Les Délices de la Mer**, at the far end of the sand, where you can retreat and soak up the scene over a creole platter.

Grande Terre beach: Just beyond the Grand Anse, it is more secluded and there are usually fewer people.

Anse Trabaud: A nice strip of sand, but a long drive through the back-country.

Baie des Anglais: A good strip of sand, also remote; *adm*.

Cap Chevalier: Busy at the weekend and popular with windsurfers because of the good winds. The sea is protected from the full force of the Atlantic by offshore reefs and there are plenty of snack stalls for a meal.

Pointe Macré: A quiet and remote but charming cove with steeply shelving sand.

Le Vauclin: Not good sand but popular windsurfing beach, active with beach bars.

Pointe du Marin: Back on the west coast, just out of St Anne, a very popular beach which attracts a crowd of nut-brown beach poseurs. All watersports are available here and there is a line of little cafés and restaurants above the beach where you can linger over an Orangina and a lobster salad.

Anse Caritan: Just south of St Anne, secluded.

Plage Corps du Garde: One of a number of passable spots between St Luce and Diamant, with facilities, and 2 miles (3km) of strand that is constantly washed with breakers, though beware because parts are marked as dangerous for swimming.

Les Anses d'Arlet: A trio of cracking dark sand coves with fishing villages along the southwestern tip of the island (the thumb of the skiing glove). Natural and undeveloped with hotels, except a few beach bars: **Bar Fredo** in Petite Anse d'Arlet, a hip spot with a sand floor where the chairlegs sink; **Ti Sable**, a more formal beach bar, is on the Grande Anse d'Arlet, as is **Cap Sud**.

Anse Noire: A steep-sided cove with black sand and beach, a popular day out from the town.

Anse à l'Ane: A 500-yard strip of brown sand between two huge headlands. You can find watersports equipment and it can be quite crowded.

Anse Mitan: In the developed area south of Fort de France and easily accessible from there by ferry, a passable strip of white sand with a host of hotels and bars to retire to if the sun becomes too hot.

Pointe du Bout: Man-made beaches crowded with high-pressure vacationers.

Caravelle Peninsula: A number of coves tucked in to the tortuous coast here, at Anse l'Etang and the Baie du Trésor; some facilities.

Le Baignoir de Joséphine: Waist-deep water and a silky-soft sand bottom, off Le Francois. Trips can be arranged to here and to the Fonds Blancs.

Flora and Fauna

Martinique has the best of both worlds, the verdant profusion in the mountainous rainforests and the open plains that now blow with sugar-cane and bananas, where cattle once were allowed to run wild in buccaneer-style farming. The rainforest is fantastic and well worth seeing, by walking (*see* 'Walking', p.260) or even simply by driving through it. There is an excellent road through the Pitons du Carbet and Finds St Denis where the ferns explode at the roadside. Just above Fort de France there is a display of tropical plants and trees at **Balata Gardens** just north of Fort de France. You will see tropical plants from around the world.

Island fauna is fairly typical for the Eastern Caribbean (including the *colibri* or humming bird, the manicou, an opossum like creature, and the *mygale* or trapdoor spider) but Martinique is unfortunate in suffering from a scourge that most of the Windwards lack—the *fer de lance* snake. Called *trigonocephalus* because of its triangular head, it grows up to 6ft long and has a pair of eyes that are supposed to glow orange in the night. It is curious that it came to be here in the first place, as its nearest relatives are somewhere in South America. In the times of fierce competition during the sugar years, snakes were sometimes surreptitiously introduced into the islands to make other planters' jobs more difficult, but the *fer de lance* has been here since before the Europeans arrived. Though the snake is extremely poisonous to humans, it poses little danger to visitors because it steers well clear of any inhabited locations. However, if you are rootling around in the undergrowth or stealing a stem of bananas, then watch out.

There is a system of **National Parks** in Martnique. At the far tip of the Caravelle Peninsula is the **Réserve Naturelle de la Caravelle**, where there are a number of habitats including dry forestland, savannah, cliffs and mangrove swamps. There are walking trails to explore them (✆ 47 18 00).

Fort de France

The capital of Martinique is set on a huge bay on the leeward side of the island, looking out on to the Caribbean Sea. Framed with hills of dark green rainforest, it was chosen, like all Caribbean capitals, for its harbour and strategic value. Now, transatlantic yachts lie in the bay, attracted more to the waterfront cafés than the protective walls of Fort St Louis.

Though it has been the administrative centre of Martinique since 1681, Fort de France was a dozy and unhealthy backwater until the beginning of this century, when the eruption of Mont Pelé destroyed the social and commercial capital of the island, the illustrious town of St Pierre, farther north. From just 10,000 inhabitants living in the gridiron streets between the Rivière Madame and the Rivière Monsieur, it has exploded to a city of over 100,000 people, spilling into suburbs along the coast and creeping steadily farther up into the surrounding hills. The people of Fort de France are known as the *Foyalais*, from a corruption of the town's 17th-century name, Fort Royal.

The original settlement grew up around the looming battlements of **Fort St Louis** (*guided tours Tues–Sat; adm exp*) on the promontory, which was first established in 1639. The fort is still in the hands of the Navy and though it is quiet now, it has been assaulted any number of times. In 1674, 160 men were faced by the Dutch Admiral de Ruyter, who arrived at the head of 48 ships and 3000 men. The French evacuated the fort pretty quickly and so the Dutchmen, lulled into a false sense of security, paused over some kegs of rum, only to find themselves harried by sober and determined Frenchmen. The Admiral cut his losses when a thousand of his men were killed and let the town be. There are guided tours of the fort, through the network of caverns, dungeons and ramparts, to hear the story of the invasion and see a museum in the Martignac Blockhouse (projected at the time of research) and the huge resident iguana. The fort juts into the sea, enclosing on one side the old *Carenage*, where ships would be 'careened'. Weights were tied to their masts and they were tipped up so that their hulls could be cleaned. Now it is the other side, the Baie des Flamands (flamingos), which is busier, where hundreds of yachts ride at anchor.

Across the road (the former moat) from Fort St Louis is the **Savane,** the large central park of Fort de France, which is towered over by lines of vast royal palms. Their solid grey trunks stand like marble columns, soaring to 100ft before they burst into curved fronds. In an alley on the northern side you will find a statue of Joséphine, the Martiniquan who became an Empress. Before she was 'beheaded', her face was turned towards her home in Trois Ilets, across Fort de France bay to the south. Two other memorials are dedicated to the war dead and to Belain d'Esnambuc, the explorer and founder of the colony, who stands scouring the horizon for land. The Savane, where the Martiniquans come in the evenings to 'promenade', is bordered by cafés and by the boulevard Alfassa waterfront, the site of all major events such as carnival and military parades.

Facing the Savane on the Rue de la Liberté is the **Musée d'Archéologie** (✆ 71 57 05; *open weekdays 9–1 and 2–5, Sat until noon; adm*), which deals with the Amerindian history of the island. The life of the Arawaks and Caribs, from their first arrival at the time of Christ to 1500, when the Spaniards appeared, is portrayed in a rich display of pottery and pictures. (It was closed during research but due to reopen during the life of this book.)

At the northwestern corner of the Savane is the **Bibliothéque Schoelcher**, a baroque iron agglomeration of arches, domes, fretwork and rivets, touched with russet and turquoise. The building was constructed by Henri Picq for the Exhibition of 1889 in Paris, at which the Eiffel Tower was the centrepiece, and then was dismantled and shipped out here to accommodate the library of Victor Schoelcher (*see* 'French Caribbean History', pp.228–9). It is a working library with over 200,000 documents and houses occasional exhibitions.

Within the confines of the ring road, the streets of Fort de France are narrower and the buildings taller than in most Caribbean towns, its pavements cluttered with Peugeots and Citroëns and the shop windows decked out with chic-looking mannequins. In true French form, the street names commemorate many of France's political and literary heroes.

The classical building to one side of the Bibliothèque is the **Préfecture**, the seat of the administrator, who is appointed by the Interior Minister in Paris. Other attractive buildings in the town include the Palais de Justice, which overlooks a small square with a statue of Schoelcher and the old hôtel de ville, now a theatre. On the place du Père Labat is the **Cathédrale St-Louis**, the sixth to be built on the site. This one dates from 1878, its predecessors having been destroyed by fire, hurricane and earthquake. It has beautiful stained-glass windows, an impressive organ and metalwork balustrades. Close by are the meat market, set in an old building, and the vegetable market, where you can get an excellent lunch.

On the banks of the Rivière Madame is the **Parc Floral**, a former exhibition ground with trees and modern sculptures (now unfortunately used as a car-park as well). There are artists' galleries and cafés in the former military barracks at the rear, where there is a **museum** devoted to island geology (*open Tues–Fri 9–12.30 and 2–5.30, Sat 9–1 and 3–5*). Outside is a series of markets dotted among the streets, with ranges of tables sheltering under huge gaudy parasols, selling anything from locks of straight black hair (to be plaited into tight African curls) to avocados. Worth a visit is the fish market on the western bank of the Rivière Madame, where women sell the fish caught and landed by the fishermen, from dawn until about 5pm.

The hills surrounding the capital are covered with houses, high-rise blocks and the '*instituts*' of a developed French *département*. As in the other islands, the Martiniquan *bons bourgeois* build their homes high on the hills for the fresher air and the commanding view. Across the Rivière Madame, the suburbs clamber up into the hills both inland and west along the coast, to Schoelcher. If you would like Fort de France's secrets to be revealed in a guided tour, contact **Azimut** (✆ 60 16 59), who offer historical, shopping and night-time tours.

South of Fort de France

The many coves and white-sand beaches make Martinique's southwest coastline the magnet for tourists. They centre around two areas, **Pointe du Bout**, near **Trois-Ilets**, within sight of Fort de France across the bay, and at **St Anne** at the southern tip of the island.

If you do not cross Fort de France bay by ferry, the main road skirts the bay, past the airport, and the D7 turns right at Rivière Salée. **La Maison de la Canne** (✆ 68 32 04; *open daily* *except Mon 9–5; adm*) is devoted to the history of sugar and rum and is set in a restored rum distillery. It has impressive models and sugar hardware on display.

Just before the town of Trois-Ilets another central piece of Martiniquan history is on view in **Le Musée de la Pagerie**, the childhood home of the Empress Joséphine (*© 68 34 55; open daily except Mon 9–5; adm*). Some of the sugar estate buildings have been restored and filled with the Empress's belongings, including portraits and some letters written to her by Napoleon. The setting, in a small valley of typical Martiniquan profusion, is idyllic. The **Parc des Floralies** nearby (*open Tues–Fri 8.30–5, Sat and Sun 9.30–1pm; adm*) is a working horticultural garden which can be visited to see Caribbean flora in all its extreme fertility.

Trois-Ilets is a small town set around a square above the sea which takes its name from the three small islands in the bay. It was in the 18th-century church that the future Empress was christened Marie-Rose Joséphine Tascher de la Pagerie in July 1763. Her mother, Rose-Claire du Verger de Sannois, is buried in the church. Just north of here is the tourist resort of **Pointe du Bout**, a conglomeration of hotels, cafés, restaurants and boutiques and a marina which has grown up on the point and on the white-sand beach of Anse Mitan.

The coastal road rises into cliffs as it turns south: the tourism evaporates and the land becomes drier and more windswept, where the shoreline is pitted with tiny coves with a profusion of coconut palms and small strips of sand. It is still quite natural and undeveloped and you will see fishermen's orange and green boats on the shoreline and their blue nets slung in the trees to dry. The road winds up over the cliffs and down into **Grande Anse d'Arlet**. It is a charming bay, less known than the beaches at Pointe du Bout, but popular with yachtsmen. Two miles (3km) farther on is another cove with the picturesque village of **Les Anses d'Arlet** between the headlands and then a third cove called the Petite Anse d'Arlet.

The best route to take from here follows the vagaries of the coastline and descends from the heights of Morne Larcher, past a brightly painted miniature wooden house at the roadside, once a monk's retreat, and along the flat into the town of Le Diamant, which is set on the magnificent sweep of the Grande Anse du Diamant and its 2-mile beach with brown sand and crashing breakers.

Diamond Rock

Off the Point, a mile from the shore, is the **Rocher du Diamant**, a pitted outcrop that rises sheer from the water to over 500ft. This rock, sometimes referred to as HMS *Diamond Rock*, witnessed one of the most curious of all episodes in the eternal struggles for empire between the French and British at the turn of the 18th century. The two nations were facing each other across the St Lucia Channel. From his look-out at Pigeon Island on St Lucia, Commodore Hood was stuck. All he could do was watch as the French ships dodged behind the Rock within the cover of their own guns, and sailed away unharmed. Hood decided to fortify the Rock.

Diamond Rock

For 18 months it stood as a British enclave within cannon-range of Martinique, denying the channel to French shipping. It was garrisoned by 120 men, who hoisted five cannon up on a rope from a ship, the HMS *Centaur*, 'like mice, hauling a little sausage' and built fortifications and outhouses. It became quite a community, with goats and rabbits and the Captain's dog and cat. Rope ladders were fixed to get from the upper battery to the shore and the mail and food were delivered in a communication bucket from the supply ship.

In May 1805 the French decided that they had had enough and they descended on the Rock in force. The two sides slugged it out for three days and two nights, until the British capitulated. When he eventually got back to Barbados the commander, Captain Maurice, was court-martialled for surrender, but then congratulated by Nelson for putting up such a good show. Ruins remain dating from the time the French sacked the Rock, but they are rarely visited and the crossing is often rough.

Heading further east, you will come to the **Trois Rivières Rum Distillery** (*open Mon–Fri 9–noon and 2.30–5; guided visits every 30 mins; free*), a working sugar and rum factory, where between February and July you can see the cane fed into the machines, cut to length, moved along a conveyor through three-stage crushers and the juice run down into a collecting vat while the bagasse is returned to fire the 100-year-old steam-engine. Hot and noisy, but interesting, and then you test the vintages—1986, 1982, 1980 and 1979. Two miles beyond the town of Rivière Pilote you will come to the modern sugar works and rum distillery at **La Mauny**. The huge works were built in 1984 and the whole process is explained on the tours, after which there is a free rum sampling and plenty to buy (*guided tours at 10am, 11, 12.30pm, 2, 4*). Back on the coast road at Anse Figuier is the **Martinique Eco-Museum** (*open daily exc Mon 9–5; adm*), which shows island life for the Caribs and Arawaks and then European and African colonists, up to 1950, with mock-ups of their houses and mannequins at work and play. Quite complicated and detailed, but lots of information (in French), including all the words derived from the Carib language: *alligator, avocat...*

On the dry **St Anne** peninsula you return to Martinique's tourist heartland. The town of Le Marin, where there is an attractive coral-rock church, is the centre of the sailing industry, as is demonstrated by all the yachts in the marinas, and farther around the bay is St Anne, a small but friendly town. Five miles (8km) farther on you come to the southern tip of the island at the **Pointe des Salines**, where the land is covered in cactus scrub. From the point St Lucia is clearly visible on a fine day, beyond the lighthouse on the Ilet Cabrits. It is named for its salt flats (or salt ponds depending on the season).

From Le Marin the road cuts across to the Atlantic coast through steadily expanding villages where the islanders are building their villas. **Le Vauclin** is the first major town, a cluster of nice old buildings around a church that sits on a hillside running down to the sea. There is an active fish-market. Inland is the Montagne du Vauclin, at 1640ft the highest in the south of Martinique. From the top, the panorama is fantastic, stretching as far as the Caravelle Peninsula in the north and to the southern tip of the island.

Headed north you come to **Le François**, where there are some more attractive old wooden houses, now steadily being swamped by new concrete suburbs. There is a classic French West Indian cemetery, with mausolea covered in black and white tiles, but the church looks as though it might be about to undergo a space-age transfiguration.

Habitation Clément (*open daily 9–6; adm*) is one of the finest colonial plantation houses in the whole Caribbean. On a hilltop sheltered by huge and ancient trees stands a house with a wooden interior and a tiled and louvred gallery, furnished with superb colonial antiques and old prints of French Caribbean life. There is a display of the process of rum, with exhibitions and films of coopering and the distillery which worked until 1978. Ageing and bottling still continue here, so the sweet smell of rum still hangs in the exquisite gardens, where there are 300 tropical species on view.

The road back to Fort de France passes through the Lamentin plains, the agricultural heartland of the island, which blow in green waves of bananas and sugar-cane.

N2–The Caribbean Coast, Fort de France to St Pierre

The road (N2) from today's capital to its spiritual ancestor, the once-august city of St Pierre, runs along the Caribbean coast, clinging to the headlands that cast out into the sea and sweeping down into the bays. The land is steep and rugged, with a covering of scrub that makes it look a bit like Corsica. North of Case-Pilote the dry cliffs at sea level give way to tropical rainforest in the foothills of the Pitons du Carbet, Martinique's second-highest peak.

Schoelcher, 3 miles (5km) from the centre of Fort de France, was a fishing village by the name of Case-Navire until 1899, when it was renamed in honour of the abolitionist shortly after his death. Now the *commune* of Schoelcher, creeping ever higher into the hills, takes the overspill from Fort de France. It has one of the colleges of the University of the French Antilles.

A number of small towns, each laid out in typical French Antillean style, with a town hall and church facing one another across the square, lie in the mouths of the valleys. Fishermen work from the black-sand beaches and you will see their blue nets spread out to be repaired. Their boats are painted bright colours to make them visible at sea and given lyrical evocative names such as *Regret de mon père* and *On revient toujours*.

Case-Pilote is named after a Carib chief who lived in this area and who welcomed the French when they settled, allowing Père du Tertre and the other Dominican missionaries to work among his people. Towards the end of his life he moved to Rivière-Pilote in the south of Martinique. **Le Carbet** takes its name from the rectangular thatched houses in which the Caribs lived. The town, which has a number of pretty wooden houses, fronts on to a coconut-lined beach on which Columbus is supposed to have landed during his visit. There is a small and lacklustre **zoo** in the town (*open daily 8–5; adm*), a series of animals from the Amazon in cages with not much to interest them: jaguars, ocelots, peccaris, sloths and capucin monkeys and a tapir who will wave his extraordinary proboscis at you as he investigates your smell. Not far inland is the small **Plantation Lajus**, home of Rhum J. Bally (*open weekdays 8–5, Sat shop only 9–12; adm*). The rum is not distilled here, but you will see it aged in vats and oak barrels, turning the fiery white '*rhum agricole*' into a mellow gold. The old creole house, built 1776, and the garden can also be visited.

In the hills above Anse Turin, sign-posted from the main road, is the **Musée Gauguin** (© 77 22 66; *open daily 9–5.30; adm*), commemorating the French artist, who lived on Martinique in 1887 before he moved on to Tahiti in the Pacific. There is a permanent exhibition of Gauguin's letters and sketches, and some of his paintings (in reproduction). Other traditional Martiniquan topics are covered as well, including the description of the checked *madras* head-dress and its codified intricacies by Lafcadio Hearn. Occasionally there is also an exhibition of work by local artists. Farther inland there is a butterfly farm, **La Vallée des Papillons** (*open daily 9.30–4.15; adm*) in the setting of another old estate house which is surprisingly interesting. In the artificially humid greenhouse you will see the fantastically coloured butterflies flying around drunkenly in the artificial forest of tropical plants, to points loaded with sugar solution. At the exit, butterfly species from around the world are on view in glass boxes and there are some remarkable foot-long insects from New Guinea. Plenty on sale, of course.

St Pierre

Until 1902, St Pierre was the cultural and commercial heart of Martinique and one of the prettiest towns in the Caribbean, considered the Paris of the Lesser Antilles. The red-roofed warehouses were stacked in lines on the hillside, overlooking the magnificent bay, where 30 ships might sit, delivering luxuries to the *Pierrotins* and loading the sugar loaves and rum puncheons that were the town's stock in trade.

The oldest town on the island, it grew up around the fine harbour, protected from the Atlantic tradewinds by Mont Pelé. Although the administrative centre soon moved to Fort Royal because of its superior strategic setting, the town thrived immediately from its beginnings in the 17th century.

The cobbled streets and the seafront promenade of 'Little Paris' were walked by the smartest Antillean ladies of the day, creole beauties with brown skin dressed in voluminous and brightly coloured skirts, parasols over their shoulders to keep off the sun. Cafés and cabarets did a grand trade on Saturdays as did the cathedral on Sunday. In 1902, the illustrious town of 26,000 inhabitants was the most modern in the area, with electricity and telephones, and connected from one end to the other by tram.

But for all the human endeavour, St Pierre was living beneath one of the Caribbean's most violent volcanos, the **Montagne Pelée** (the bald mountain). It had stayed silent for the first 200 years of the town's existence, until 1851 when it grumbled, blanketing the town with volcanic ash and creating a lake in its crater.

Towards the end of April 1902 the rumblings started again, this time accompanied by plumes of smoke that flashed with lightning. Four people from St Pierre climbed to the lip of the crater and found that the lake had disappeared and that it was now a cauldron of boiling mud, with an icing of ash racing over the surface in the wind. The rivers fed by it were poisoned by sulphur emissions and ran with dead fish.

On 5 May, the crater split open and an avalanche of mud and lava slid down the the mountain to the north of the town, engulfing a factory and killing 25 workers. Despite the ever-increasing plumes of smoke, still lit by lightning, the Governor came from Fort de France to urge the Pierrotins not to leave (there was an election at the time). News came that the Soufrière volcano on the island of St Vincent had blown and it was thought that this would relieve the pressure on Mont Pelé. Though about 1000 did choose to leave for Fort de France at dawn the next morning, the majority stayed put.

At a couple of minutes before eight on 8 May, Ascension Day, the mountainside itself split and gaped open as the eruption began. A shock wave hit the town at a speed of MACH 3 and this was followed by a pyroclastic flow; a cloud of poisonous gases burst out of the crater, thrown to a height of 300ft along with flames and molten lava which then swept down the mountainside at 250 miles an hour and engulfed the town. Only the north and south walls of houses remained standing as their interiors were swept out. With a temperature of 400°C, the cloud vapourized the town and then poured on down to the sea, turning it into a seething cauldron and setting the ships ablaze or capsizing them with a tidal wave.

Within two minutes 30,000 people were killed. They were knocked to the ground by the force of the *nuée ardente* and carbonized where they lay. Glasses wilted and pots and pans drooped in the heat. The city passed into complete darkness, pierced only by the light of burning houses. There was one survivor in the city itself. Auguste Cybaris had been thrown into a police cell the night before for being drunk. No doubt he woke with a start at eight the next morning, but the thick stone walls of his cell protected him from the heat and the grilled window kept out the fumes. He lived out his days until his death in 1955 with the Barnum Circus, appearing in a replica of his cell.

One ship also survived, the HMS *Roddam*, which was cut from its mooring by the tidal wave. Several of the crew were burned alive on deck by showers of molten lava and others died jumping overboard. The ghostly shell, heaped with grey volcanic ash, crawled into the harbour at Castries, St Lucia, later that day, its captain severely burned but still at the wheel.

The volcano continued to spit fire and lava over the next few months, but gradually calmed down. At the same time, there arose one of the most curious phenomena in the whole history of the Caribbean. In November of 1902, a glowing needle of solidified lava began to protrude from the crater. The plug steadily pushed upwards, until it reached a height of 800ft. After nine months it eventually collapsed.

After so many stories about the cataclysm at St Pierre and the talk of the ruins, it comes as a bit of a surprise to discover that people actually still live there. It is a busy country town. No doubt the inhabitants have faith in the team of boffins who live on the slopes of the mountain listening out for future rumbles. The cobbles of the old town can be seen protruding through the tarmac and the blackened walls and stairways still run down to the palm-lined promenade on the waterfront. The skeleton of the old theatre and the stone shells of the 18th-century warehouses have a slightly foreboding air, but the market and shops bustle happily around them. However, they still stand in the shadow of Mont Pelé, a monstrous and brooding colossus.

The **theatre**, with its double staircase, is a copy of the one in Bordeaux. Just nearby is the cell in which Cybaris spent the night after his drinking spree. Down on the waterfront there has been some restoration recently and you will see the newly repaired **Maison de la Bourse**, the old exchange, a tall and pretty creole building with overhanging balconies which are louvred and closed off. A traditional iron **market** building has also been put up and there is some trade in there; otherwise there are plenty of cafés along the waterfront. There is all the activity of the modern-day market farther along the waterfront. Across the Roxelane River to the north is the Quartier du Fort, the site of the first settlement on Martinique. The ruined fort near the seafront was erected by d'Esnambuc in 1635 when he arrived, planted a cross and claimed the island for France.

The **Musée Volcanique** (℡ 78 15 16; *open daily 9–5; adm*), established in 1932 by the American volcanologist Franck Perret, has an explanation of the volcanic eruption and exhibits including clocks that stopped at 8 am precisely and nails fused together in the heat of the *nuée ardente*. Guided tours do a circuit and release you to admire the view of the bay from the balcony. **Le Musée Historique de St Pierre**, on the rue Victor Hugo (℡ 79 74 32; *open daily 9.30–5; adm*), contains pictorial exhibits of life in St Pierre before the disaster in 1902. A little trolley train runs around the town with a commentary, if you can bear the embarrassment, four times daily during the week (© 55 50 92).

A commanding view of St Pierre Bay can also be had from the road that climbs past the cemetery. From here it continues into the rainforest in the foothills of the Morne des Cadets in Pitons du Carbet and to Fonds St Denis, an agricultural village perched on the mountainside over hairpin bends. This road was one of the early approaches from Fort de France to St Pierre through the plantations lands; called *La Trace*, it was cut out of the hills by the Jesuits in the 17th century. In the village of Morne Rouge you will find a third museum dedicated to the volcano and its disastrous effects on the town below, **La Maison du Volcan** (© 52 45 45; *opening times limited, so phone before visiting; adm*). You need to speak French to get the best of it. There are films and pictures of the town before the event and of the lava flow glowing as it flowed down the mountainside. The destructive power of the volcano was equivalent to a 100 megaton bomb.

North of St Pierre

As the road follows the coast north, skirting the slopes of Mont Pelé, you come to a less developed side of Martinique. **Le Prêcheur**, one of the first areas to be settled in the 17th century, was the childhood home of Françoise d'Aubigné, who would later become the Marquise de Maintenon. There are hot volcanic springs on the route up Mont Pelé. There is an excellent distillery to visit just outside the town, the **Distillerie Depaz**. Sign boards guide you through the process: cane cutters, huge aluminium vats for fermentation, still pots for distillation and warehouses which store the barrels. The estate house is stunning, but cannot be visited. Farther north along the coast you come to **Habitation Céron**, a distillery which originates from 1658, a charming series of buildings which follow a narrow valley engulfed in rainforest. As well as the old sugar estate buildings there is a '*gragerie*', or cassava mill, and a walk through the gardens where the plants are named (*adm*). Now it also works as a crayfish farm, for which it is famed.

Anse Ceron itself is a black-sand beach of unmanicured beauty. The coastal road does not run all around the island, but stops just beyond here. However, it is possible to walk from here through the forest to the village of Grand' Rivière. The 12-mile (20km) walk over the cliffs of St Martin takes about 6 hours, though you should allow longer in the rainy season when the going is harder.

St Pierre to the Atlantic Coast

The route to the Atlantic coast leaves St Pierre from the Quartier du Fort and cuts uphill into the botanical turmoil of the rainforest, climbing to **Morne Rouge** in the col between the Pitons du Carbet and Mont Pelé. The Maison du Volcan is set in a modern building in the town (*see* above). A hundred years ago this route was walked by the *porteuses*, with huge trays on their heads, laden with anything that needed to be carried to the Atlantic coast. It is a route steep enough to make a car strain, but these young women would carry up to 100lb for 15 hours a day with nothing but a drop of rum and some cake to keep them going.

Just beyond Morne Rouge is the dropping-off point for hikers headed to the summit of Mont Pelé. If you attempt this, it is advisable to take a guide. Also, as there are often clouds parked on the summit, take a waterproof jacket to keep off the wind and wet. There has been only one rumble from Mont Pelé since 1902, but if it starts to rain pumice stones, clear out quick.

Alternatively, the route passes over to the Atlantic coast, descending through the forest, where the road is overhung by vast sprouts of bamboo and 10ft tree ferns. **Ajoupa-Bouillon** is a pretty town laid out either side of the main road, which is lined with flowers and a red plant called '*roseau*'.

From here, two natural sites are worth visiting: the **Saut Babin**, a 40ft waterfall half an hour's walk southeast of the town, and the **Gorges de la Falaise** (*adm*). For the latter, you cut in from the road just above the town, going north on a path into the forest (about half an hour's walk, essential to ask for directions) and you will come to the river, which has carved a narrow bed for itself out of the volcanic rock. Take a swimming costume; it can be crowded. At **Les Ombrages** Botanical Gardens (*open 9–5; adm*) there is a botanic path through the rainforest, shaded by 100ft bamboo trees. The plants, from the rainforest and domestic gardens, are marked—*calathea ornata* (called musical paper) and *culotte du diable* (devil's trousers).

As the mountainside descends and turns into plains, so the rainforest gives way to cultivation: pineapples, bananas and fields of sugar-cane. In the 18th century, this area was completely covered with plantations, cane as far as the eye could see, broken periodically by a cluster of buildings: the estate house, outbuildings and a windmill.

Basse Pointe, on the coast, is the birthplace of the retired mayor of Fort de France, Aimé Césaire, and it has had a strong East Indian influence since the Indians came to Martinique in the last century as indentured labourers. There is a Hindu temple just outside the town. Inland is the **Plantation Leyritz** (✆ 78 53 92; *open 8–6; adm to the plantation gardens*), an old plantation house which has been restored as a hotel (with rooms in the slave quarters) and gardens. Machinery is scattered around the grounds and the old outhouses are fitted out as a restaurant. There is an odd exhibition of intricate dolls made from dried flowers.

The village of **Macouba**, named after the Carib word for fish, stands on cliffs at the northern tip of the island, looking out over the channel to Dominica. It was a prosperous settlement in the 17th century, when it derived its wealth from the cultivation of tobacco. The final stretch of road continues through wild country to **Grand' Rivière**, an isolated fishing village.

N3—Fort de France and the Pitons du Carbet

In the 17th century, the Jesuits cut a road through the mountainous interior of Martinique, linking the new administrative centre of Fort de France with the social and commercial hub at St Pierre overland. *La Trace* was initially just a track cut into the rainforest, used by horses and pedestrians, but in the 19th century it was enlarged by the army and then in the 20th century it was made into a major road. Today it makes a spectacular drive through some of the island's best scenery.

Across the Madame River, La Trace climbs through the prosperous suburb of Didier, favoured by the creole ascendancy for its commanding panorama, where spectacular villas perch above Fort de France in gardens of tropical flowers. As the town thins, the road winds into primeval rainforest, clinging to the hillside.

Suddenly a mirage arises before you, the **Sacré Cœur** from Montmartre, transported to Martinique... Erected in 1923 to give thanks for the lives of those who died in the First World War, it is not an exact replica, but its dome and spires stand brilliant white against the sparkling green of tropical rainforest and inside there is a warm glow from the stained-glass windows. There is a good view of Fort de France and the south of Martinique from the car park.

Soon La Trace becomes buried in the rainforest and the mountains loom either side. Six miles out of the capital, at the **Jardin de Balata** (© 64 48 73; *open daily 9–5; adm*), the botanical pandemonium is momentarily set into order. Two hundred species have been brought from tropical regions all over the world and cultivated in the garden, numbered so that you can put names to them: bananas, bamboos, orchids and endless palms. As you walk the paths you will see ferns like velvet, shrubs with flowers like little plastic animals or shaped like a fisherman's hat, and all around a plethora of palm trees. After a tropical shower the whole garden glints in the sunlight and the view opens out again as far as St Lucia. The gardens, an enjoyable tour even for uncommitted gardeners, give an idea of the absurd abundance of the Caribbean islands. The N3 then moves into the peaks and valleys of the Pitons du Carbet, running a contorted route as far as Deux Chous, where the old road descends into St Pierre and on to Morne Rouge.

N1—Fort de France to the Atlantic Coast

The N1 road leaves Fort de France heading east, past the airport at Lamentin, and into the central fertile plains, where much of Martinique's agriculture and industry is located. It emerges on the Atlantic coast at Le Robert, a fishing town on a wide bay.

La Trinité is the second-largest town on the island and an administrative centre for the northern Atlantic coast. The town is set on a sheltered bay and has an esplanade that teems with activity when the day's catch is brought in. In the hills above, the town of Morne des Esses is known for its weaving, techniques supposedly developed from its Carib heritage. The **Atelier de Vannerie**, the basket-weaving workshop, is devoted to the art (*open Mon–Sat 8.30–5.30; adm free*).

Beneath the town on the coast is the **Caravelle Peninsula**, a windswept outcrop that juts 7 miles into the Atlantic Ocean, which has recently been developed and has become something of a centre for tourism in Martinique. A number of hotels have been built there in recent years. The peninsula is hilly, with a shoreline of cliffs and small coves and rich orange earth. The last few square miles are a National Reserve and there is a small network of paths for walkers who wish to see the varied flora. You will also find the ruins of the **Chateau Dubuc** (*open Mon–Fri 8.30–12 and 2.30–5.30, Sun mornings only; adm to the museum*), the remaining walls of a 17th-century castle with a magnificent view. There is a small museum and an assortment of sugar-coppers, from which the estate derived some of its wealth—the rest was made in smuggling. The N4 leads from Trinité back to Fort de France, cutting through the hills via Gros Morne, the seat of government during the patriots' rebellion in 1790.

Continuing north along the coast, the N1 comes to Sainte Marie, with an attractive church built in Jesuit style. Just beyond the town is the **Musée du Rhum** at the St James distillery (© 75 30 02; *open weekdays 9–1 and 2–4.30, weekends 9–noon; adm free*). The old creole plantation house and the modern factory stand near one another, looking on to a garden full of sugar relics of all ages—crushing gear and steam engines. Inside the creole estate house is more sugar paraphernalia: rum barrels and boiling coppers, alongside a history of the sugar industry in Martinique. The informative tour is free and it culminates in a tasting-room, stacked to the ceiling with bottles of rum, which are available for purchase.

It is worth taking the detour a few miles inland to the **Musée de la Banane**, (© 69 45 52; *open Mon–Sat 9–5; adm*), which is set on a working banana plantation. There is an exhibition giving details of the history and culture (and agriculture) of the banana. There are botanical prints from two centuries ago and adverts from earlier this century, and you will learn odd facts (such as: in Indian legend it is a banana not an apple that 'Adam' gives to 'Eve'). A path leads you through the plantation, where you will see species such as *yamgambi, ice cream* and *bendetta*. During the week you can visit the packing house, where the banana 'bunches' are brought in, divided into 'hands', cleaned and then boxed.

L'Habitation Fonds St Jacques was once a thriving Dominican community and sugar plantation. It was run by Père Labat, who resided here in the 1690s, taking over a run-down plantation and turning it into the most prosperous on the island within two years. Some buildings have been restored and there is a small museum on the subject of sugar in the 18th century. The coastal road continues to wind through the plantations and along the shoreline to the town of Lorrain.

✆ *(596)–*

Where to Stay

Martinique is a surprise as regards its hotels. You might expect that there would be a string of luxurious and stylish enclaves of quiet and luxury in the island, but in fact there are only a couple (you have to go to St Barts for real luxury). The majority of hotels in the island are in the mid-range. You will, however, find the full range of settings, from the modern Caribbean dream on the beach to tiny *auberges* set in old gingerbread houses, hidden in the rainforest. Many of the best hotels are quite isolated, particularly from Fort de France, and with an island this size it is a good idea to have a car to get around (check with your hotel when making a booking because many of them have arrangements with the car hire companies). It is worth doing a bit of exploring and you may want to move from place to place. Rates quoted here are for a double room, though breakfast will often be included.

very expensive–expensive

By far the most original and most elegant hotel in Martinique is **Habitation Lagrange**, 97225 Le Marigot (✆ 53 60 60, ✉ 53 50 58). It is a little remote and isolated in the northeast, but that is part of its charm; if you are happy to be off the beaten track (at the end of a rather rickety riverside drive), it is an excellent place to stay. It is set in a beautifully restored sugar plantation house, turretted and wrapped around with a cast-iron balcony, dating from the end of the 17th century and which was restored in 1990 after being left derelict for many years. Downstairs the tall doorways are panelled with dark wood and the walls are painted with murals and hung with prints of the old West Indies. There are just 16 rooms in all, fitted with bright furnishings and creole antiques, wickerback and rocking chairs and murals and curious sculptures; the floors creak because they are wooden and the bathroms are old style with enamel and gold-lined taps. Very personable style and service, the only four-star hotel with French Caribbean chic.

If the beach is the most important feature, you can find international standards of comfort and service at the **Méridien** (✆ 66 00 00, ✉ 66 00 74) and the **Bakoua** (✆ 66 02 02, ✉ 66 00 41), which stand like factories on the man-made beaches of Trois Ilets.

There are plenty of friendly and comfortable small hotels scattered around the island. In the south of the island you will find a very pleasant small hotel in the **Manoir de Beauregard**, 97227 St Anne (✆ 76 73 40, 🖅 76 93 24), which is set around a charming and vaguely ecclesiastical-looking estate house which dates from the early years of the 18th century and has recently been restored after being gutted in a fire. The main house has black and white tiles and a grille metalwork entrance with heavy wooden furniture. The three rooms upstairs are decorated with antique furniture and four-poster beds. The others, making just 11 in all, are in a separate block across the garden, and are more modern. Quiet and pleasant atmosphere, swimming pool, air-conditioning in the rooms, beach not far off.

On the south coast, near the town of Le Diamant you will find a charming retreat, the **Relais Caraibes**, La Cherry, 97233 Le Diamant (✆ 76 44 65, 🖅 76 21 20), where 15 rooms (air-conditioning, no fans) are set in neat and pretty cottages in a profuse trop-ical garden. The main house is excellent, with its creole furniture and eastern rugs, set around a sunken garden; also the bar area and the open-sided dining room, which looks over the pool to a fantastic view of the sea down below. Each room is air-conditioned and has a terrace with a hammock, also TV and fridge. The Relais Caraibes is quite isolated, but you can hire a car there and guests can use the facilities of the Novotel Diamant on the beach a walk away down below.

The **Frégate Bleue**, 97240 Le François (✆ 54 54 66, 🖅 54 78 48), is an even smaller stopover, with just seven rooms in a private house. It is a '*Relais du Silence*' and it lives up to its quiet and peaceful name. A good feel with antique furniture and Persian carpets but also modern comforts (air-conditioning, television and telephones, pool and kitchenettes in the rooms, though there is now a dining room too). There is a distinct international air about the place and the owners, who live on the property, speak English. Again quite remote above the Atlantic coast, but within a shout of all the activity offshore.

The **Hotel Leyritz Plantation**, 97218 Basse-Pointe (✆ 78 53 92, 🖅 78 92 44), also has an isolated setting, in handsome gardens on cane- and banana-covered hillside in the northeast. The 18th-century plantation house has been rebuilt as a hotel and the slave quarters turned into the 50 hotel rooms (considerably improved since 200 years ago). The hotel can get a bit busy during the day, as a lot of visitors come by for lunch, but the early evening restores the plantation idyll.

moderate

Slightly isolated from the hurly-burly of the tourist resort, at the end of the beach at Anse Mitan is **Auberge de L'Anse Mitan** (✆ 66 01 12, 🖅 66 01 05; *cheap–moderate*), a retiring enclave of faded elegance. Built in the 1930s as a family home, it has an elegant foyer with wicker furniture set among the greenery and white tiles and a fine view over the bay to Fort de France. The 20 rooms and six studios are hung with prints, showing an older Martinique, but they have all the essentials of modern comfort, phones, air-conditioning and showers.

Another option in the middle of Anse Mitan is the friendly **Bonne Auberge**, 97229 Trois-Ilets (✆ 66 01 55, 🖅 66 04 50) and its restaurant Chez André, both festooned in greenery, with 32 comfortable and simple air-conditioned rooms in blocks. No pool, but the sea is a minute's walk away.

On the south coast there is a number of small hotels with an easy Caribbean feel. On the beach at Diamant is the **Hotel Diamant les Bains** (✆ 76 40 14, 76 27 00), with rooms in the hotel building and cabins scattered around the garden of palms and ginger-lily that run down to the sea. The rooms are pretty with white decor and bright colours (television, air-conditioning, fridge and telephone). The hotel is friendly and serves good local food on the terrace above the garden. Miles of brown sand beach to walk, and a pool.

The **Hotel Palm Beach**, 97223 Diamant (✆ 76 47 84, ✉ 76 26 98), sits right on the sand at the entrance to Diamant town. There are just eight rooms in a modern house, where guests gather in the central salon and outside on the terrace restaurant under the trees. Some nice furniture in the rooms, some with air-conditioning, also fans. Friendly reception and atmosphere.

The **Résidence La Margelle**, 97223 Le Diamant (✆/✉ 76 40 19), has just five rooms in an older-style Martiniquan house right on the seafront. It uses the best of its antique setting, with pretty wooden walls (some a little thin) and doors, louvred shutters and some gingerbread pointing—there is a nice sitting area looking out to sea with old furniture. Very quiet with antique comfort, hammocks in the garden and an easy atmosphere, good if you are travelling around the island.

Another off-beat and friendly spot is **La Petite Auberge**, 97228 St Luce (✆ 62 59 70, ✉ 62 42 99), which was built as a large, luxurious family home in the seventies and is now a small hotel. The lower floor is given over entirely to the restaurant and bar, where the dining room looks out over a pool to the sea; upstairs there are 12 quite simple rooms in a wooden upper storey, most of which have a small balcony. Beach not far off, lots of information about activities in the area, some entertainment.

On the grey sands of Grand Anse d'Arlet, a double room, simple but comfortable enough with air-conditioning, is available in the **Hotel Tamarind** (✆ 68 71 30), which sits on the waterfront in the middle of the small town. There are also villas to rent in this area.

There has been quite a lot of development on the Atlantic coast in recent years, in isolated parts of the rainforest, but particuarly also on the Caravelle Peninsula. The nicest is probably **Le Manguier** in Tartane, 97220 Trinité (✆ 58 48 95, ✉ 58 27 58), which stands on the hillside looking north over offshore islands. There are 16 studios, very comfortable though not huge, set in four modern buildings that take a little from the old Caribbean style (louvres, balconies and tin roofs) set in a steep garden of rampant greenery, also a pool with a view. Quiet and charming, There is no restaurant but rooms have kitchenettes and there are places to eat within walking distance.

La Caravelle, 97220 Tartane (✆ 58 07 32, ✉ 58 07 90), also sits on the side of a hill above Anse l'Etang, a nice beach. Up above you will find the main reception room, the pretty dining room and a terrace with a view; the 15 rooms are in a modern block below, quite simple, without TVs and air-conditioning, but perfectly acceptable.

In the town of Tartane itself is **Le Madras**, 97220 Tartane (✆ 58 33 95, ✉ 58 33 63), '*les pieds dans l'eau*' (literally 'feet in the water', meaning right on the beach). It has

13 neat, modern rooms on the first floor, each with fans, TVs and phones. Downstairs the large dining room has a good view of all the activity of the pier and the offshore island.

moderate–cheap

In Le Marin you will find the **Résidence La Girafe** (☎ 74 91 29, ✆ 74 90 51), seven studios and three apartments set in a modernized family house that dates from the 18th century. It is well situated in the middle of the town and overlooks the waterfront itself, but the courtyard at the back is quiet and the rooms are comfortable.

A cheaper option is the **Auberge du Marin,** 21 rue Osman Duquesnay (☎ 74 83 88), a friendly haunt on the spine of the hill. A young crowd filters through the simple rooms and central sitting area and dining room in a covered courtyard. Three rooms only, share baths.

cheap

Farther afield in the northeast there are some very nice and isolated stopovers. The nicest is **Auberge La Sikri,** 97214 Le Lorrain (☎ 53 81 00, ✆ 53 78 73), which is set high on the hillside of agricultural land above the town of Le Lorrain. There are eight rooms upstairs with private baths and hot and cold water (not a/c because there is no need) and a pleasant gathering point in the dining room and salon downstairs. Lots of advice about walking in the area.

The **Abri Auberge Verte,** 97216 Ajoupa Bouillon (☎ 53 33 94, ✆ 53 32 12), has 12 rooms in hillside cottages with louvres and terraces; a pool and an overlarge dining room with creole food. The management can arrange anything from hikes to cockfighting evenings.

On the west coast there is a number of places to stay if you are passing through. In Le Carbet you will find **Le Christophe Colomb,** 97221 Le Carbet (☎ 78 05 38, ✆ 78 06 42), which stands in a modern block just behind the black sand beach and its screen of palm trees. Four studios with kitchenettes and six rooms, but some share bathrooms and showers. Quite simple, but passable and clean; dining room; very calm and easy-going area.

At the roadside on the way into St Pierre there is a nice setting at **Le Grain d'Or** on Anse Turin (☎ 78 06 91). The attractive old wooden house has a pool and a terraced restaurant (*myriade d'accras, lambi citron*). Eight rooms. And in St Pierre itself you can stay at **La Nouvelle Vague,** 97290 St Pierre (☎ 74 83 88), with a waterfront restaurant on the terrace.

very cheap

There are not many very cheap places to stay on the island, but Martinique is linked to the **Association des Gîtes Ruraux**: their office is at 9 boulevard Général de Gaulle in Fort de France (☎ 73 67 92, ✆ 63 55 92) or by post at BP 1122, 97248 Fort de France Cedex. They have some 300 gîtes around the island, including flats and houses for rent by the week and by the month. Another budget alternative is **camping**. **Courbaril Camping** (☎ 68 32 30) has spaces in Anse à l'Ane, opposite Fort de France, for around US$5 per night, with chalets too. In St Anne, the **Camping Municipal** (☎ 76 72 79) has spaces and facilities just off the beach.

Martiniquan food has a traditional French flair and is considered by many to be the best in the Caribbean. Here, you can make your holiday almost entirely gastronomic, as there are cafés and open-air restaurants to linger in at every turn. You will find traditional *cuisine gastronomique*, but also its Caribbean or creole equivalent. Lovingly prepared, the dishes are often spiced and of course, it is all in the sauces.

Some creole dishes, many of them slightly more luxurious versions of usual Caribbean dishes, are: *crabe farci*, a very spicy stuffing of crabmeat in a crab-shell, traditionally served on Easter Monday; the avocado *féroce*, with a spicy fish filling; *blaff*, a way of cooking fish (the name is supposed to imitate the noise it makes when thrown into the water) with thyme, peppers, clove, parsley and onion; *accra*, seasoned cod or greens fried in batter; *écrevisses, soudons, oursins* and even *chatrous*, shrimps, clams, sea urchins and octopus. *Colombo* is the delicate French Caribbean version of curry goat or chicken and *z'habitants* is a local preparation of crayfish. *Touffé* is a method of cooking in a casserole, as is *fricassée*, another popular dish. *Boudins* are local spiced sausages. *Blanc manger* is a traditional pudding, a sort of coconut custard, made with milk, coconut, cinnamon, vanilla and nutmeg. Of course every good meal starts with an aperitif (*see* Bars and Nightlife, p.256) and it may be finished with a rum digestif too.

Many of the hotels have fine kitchens, but it would be a pity to miss out on one of the island's best-loved pastimes by not dining out as well. Fort de France has its share of restaurants, some in the heart of town, others overlooking the mêlée from verandas on high. France's other colonial interests are also represented in Martinique in Vietnamese and African restaurants. There are small restaurants to be found all over the island, so if you wish to join the Martiniquans in an afternoon's gastronomy, ask them when you come to a new town. Wandering and finding a restaurant is part of the fun, of course. Despite the local association with rum, there is certainly something of the traditional French homage for wine and it is imported in large quantities. Restaurants in Fort de France tend to be closed on Sundays, but in the tourist towns it may be another day of the week. A recent addition is pizzerias, which have appeared in all the main tourist towns.

The booklet *Ti Gourmet* lists many of Martinique's restaurants, with translations of the menus into English, recipes and useful facts including which are open on Sundays. Prices are for a main course at dinner time (excluding shrimp and lobster), divided as follows: *expensive*—above Fr100; *moderate*—Fr50–100; *cheap*—less than Fr50. Lunch is usually a little less expensive, but not much. Service, however, is *compris*.

In and Around Fort de France

expensive

There is a number of excellent restaurants in and around Fort de France. **La Fontane** (© 64 28 70) is high above the town in the area of La Fontane and serves some excellent creole fare. It is set in a charming and elegant old colonial house with a black and white tiled floor, louvred wooden walls. You dine outside by the small pool or inside among the antiques. The menu is creole: *yole de paupiette de de sarde à la citronelle* or *noisettes d'agneau aux cèpes, sauce mangue,* and the service very much French.

Closed Sun and Mon. **La Mouïna** (℗ 79 34 57) is also high above the town on the Route de la Redoute (No. 127) and it has a nice setting in a Martiniquan villa, where the dining room is set on the balcony above the garden. Smart and subdued, the menu is French and creole. A house speciality is the *assiette créole*, with stuffed crab, crayfish and boudin with local vegetables, followed by *l'île flottante* (meringues in *crème anglaise*). *Open for lunch and dinner, reserve; closed Sat lunch and Sun.*

moderate

Le Mareyeur (℗ 61 74 70) is a seafood restaurant just up off the main road to Schoelcher, heading north out of town. Quite a simple dining room with red and white chequered tablecloths, but the fish are exotic—*assiette des fruits de mer* (shrimps, cockles, mussels, crayfish and *bigornes)*, *beignets de requin* (shark fritters) and fish fricasséed, blaffed and paellaed. Some entertainment. *Closed Sat lunch and Sun.* There seems to be a string of good restaurants on the rue Victor Hugo, including an excellent creole restaurant at **Marie Sainte** (℗ 70 00 30). *Accras, beignets, fricassée de coq, morue case nègre* (from the novel) in a simple dining room. *Open for lunch and some evenings in the week;* closed Sun. **La Cave à Vin** (℗ 70 33 02) is set in a small pink dining room behind the wine shop of the name. It serves regional specialities from the metropole: *la véritable andouillette à la moutarde de Meaux* and a *filet de sole tropicale à la vanille Bourbon.*

cheap

Lina's Café (℗ 71 91 92), also on the rue Victor Hugo, stays open all day and specializes in sandwiches. An excellent option at lunchtime is to go to the vegetable market in the rue St Louis, where there are a number of **stalls** and **snackettes**, good for a sandwich or a platter. In the evenings a fun way to eat is to go to the caravans parked between the **Savane** and Fort St Louis. Communal tables are set out under large awnings, where you will sit among Martiniquan families on an evening out, everyone shouting above the sound of *zouk* music and the roar of rebellious gas stoves and generators. It stays open late, and you can get a brochette or a platter loaded with tropical meat and veg.

Anse Mitan and Pointe du Bout

moderate

The **Villa Créole** in Anse Mitan (℗ 66 05 53) has a candle-lit gingerbread veranda looking on to a profuse garden. Creative creole and French cuisine is accompanied by the serenading of the patron and others and then dancing. Try *filet d'agneau Bergerie* or *aiguillettes de lambi* à la Provencale. *Closed Sun and Mon lunch.* There is another friendly restaurant close by, **Chez André**, under the awnings at the Bonne Auberge Hotel. Veranda setting draped in flowers for *velouté de lambi* (cream of conch soup) and *accras de crevettes* (shrimp fritters).

On the road to Pointe du Bout there is a very nice dining room with a bamboo ceiling and plenty of greenery at **Au Poisson d'Or** (℗ 66 01 80). Créole fare—*soupe z'habitants* followed by *oursin frit* (in season) or a *côte de porc* with *christophines au gratin*—or simple veal chop with *frites*. *Closed Mon.* You can dine on a veranda with a view at **La Langouste** (℗ 66 04 99) by the ferry jetty. It has a fixed menu or *z'habitants* and *colombo de poulet* à la carte. There are pizzerias in the area where you can pick up a simple meal.

Over the headland in **Anse à l'Ane**, try **Le Nid Tropicale**, where there is a pretty yard fenced off from the beach. Creole fare—*daube de lambis* (conch) *à la crème de champignons*, or *filet de boeuf au ti-vieux. Closed Sun evening and Mon.* Close by is **Chez Jojo** (℗ 68 37 43), which has a simple beach setting and serves local food—*boudin de lambi* and *ananas* (pineapple) *flambé.*

Les Anses d'Arlet

It is well worth heading over to the **Anses d'Arlet** on the Caribbean coast, where you will find some fantastic settings along the waterfront in the dozy settlements. **L'Anse Noire**, on the black sand beach of the same name, has a lovely setting under palm trees and behind bamboo fences, an old tin roof held up by old wooden spars. Local food—fish, chicken and salads, *accras, brochettes.*

In the Grande Anse d'Arlet you will find a clutch of good places to retreat to from the overhead sun, particularly two beach bars. **Ti Sable** (℗ 68 62 44; *expensive*) serves grilled food and fresh fish landed by the local fishermen and a speciality creole and lobster buffet. Under palm-thatch parasols and a huge sea grape tree, in the yard of an old Caribbean beach house. *Open daytime and evening.* Next door is **Quai Sud** (℗ 68 66 90; *moderate*), where you can get a deep-fried camembert to go with seafood and fish.

Inland there is a good stopover, **Le Gommier des Caraibes** (℗ 68 62 79; *moderate*), set in a charming old Caribbean townhouse, the oldest in the area. The dining room, once a schoolroom, serves *harengs à l'huile* or a seafood salad, followed by a *colombo* or *crevettes à l'Armoricaine* (from Brittany). *Open for lunch and dinner.* In the next cove, the Petit Anse d'Arlets, there is a charming setting at **Chez Fredo**, where the chair-legs dig into the sand as you tuck into a grilled fish or a *brochette.*

The Southern Coast

In **Diamant** town, there is a string of nice restaurants on decks just above the waves, good stopovers if you are exploring for the day. Check out **Chez Lucie** (℗ 76 40 10; *moderate*) where you can start with *beignets de crevettes* and follow with a *fricassée*, a *blaff* or a speciality seafood dish.

There is also a nice setting at **Chez Christiane** (℗ 76 49 55; *moderate*), which serves creole fare in a nice old building in town, and but you might otherwise go for **Le Diam's** (*moderate–cheap*), a pleasant stop on the square, for simpler lunches or dinners.

Farther along the coast in **St Luce** you will also find a nice string of restaurants across from the waterfront where the fishing boats sit under the trees. You can get a nice meal at **Kaï Armande** (℗ 62 52 67; *moderate*), which serves local food and seafood, as well as some African specialities.

For such a large marina town, **Le Marin** is surprisingly short of restaurants. There is a café down in the marina and a beach bar not far off, **La Paillote,** with chairs and parasols under huge coconut palms. Otherwise you could try the small hotel, the Auberge du Marin (*see* 'Where to Stay').

In **St Anne** there is a charming dining room at **Poï et Virginie** (✆ 76 76 86; *expensive–moderate*). You dine on the waterfront (best seats right above the sea), set with wooden and wicker furniture, the walls lined with bamboo and hung with Haitian paintings. You might try the *plateau de fruits de mer* for two (*araignées, tourteaux, cigales, gambas, soudons, huîtres, langouste and palourdes*). Phone 24 hours in advance for this. Otherwise lobster-tail with mayonnaise. *Closed Mon, Tues lunch.*

Another smaller restaurant, in a hotel just along the seafront, is **La Dunette** (✆ 76 73 90; *moderate*), where you will find chicken *pipiri* (grilled and served with rice cooked in cinnamon and coconut) and a house speciality of *friture de volaille aux lambi envoutée de passion,* conch and chicken in a passion fruit sauce.

You might also try **Les Tamariniers** (✆ 76 75 62; *moderate–cheap*), in a pretty dining room hung with greenery next to the church, for novel creole cuisine including *blaffs* and *banane flambée.*

On **St Anne beach** itself there are plenty of places where you can be waylaid for a meal or perhaps just an orangina when the idea of tanning palls: **Les Filets Bleus** (*expensive–moderate*) has a palm garden with statues looking down onto the beach. Fine local fare—*court bouillon* or *civet de chatrou*. At **Le Touloulou** there is a lobster vivier where you can select your choice and you can follow with an *ananas flambé* or an ice cream from an endless choice of flavours. There are many crêperies and snackette wagons both down on the beach and in the town.

Behind the town, in among all the hotels and restaurants there is **Restaurant Frédéric** (✆ 76 95 84; *expensive*) with a charming setting (in a pretty, old-style Caribbean house with veranda all around where the tables stand) and a good creole and French menu: the house speciality is crayfish in sugar and rum with a saffron sauce. At the southern point of the island, at the end of Grande Anse des Salines, you will find **Aux Délices de la Mer** (✆ 76 97 36; *moderate*), which has a fantastic view of the bay and the hills beyond from its terrace. *Fricassée d'écrevisses* and *avocat aux crevettes*. There are also snackwagons on the bay here for a lunchtime snack.

On the **Atlantic coast** you will find some good places to eat scattered through the main towns. In **Le Francois** there is a fun spot called **Kai Nono** (✆ 54 32 76; *moderate*), and in Le Robert you can try **Aux Fruits de la Mer** Chez Fofor (✆ 65 10 33; *moderate*), which is upstairs above all the waterfront activity. Seafood specialities as the name suggests.

There are two attractive restaurants with good creole food in Trinité. The better is probably **Le Don de la Mer** (*moderate*), set on a pretty terrace above the sea: shrimp broth followed by fresh fish and by *banane flambée*; alternatively, try **L'Oasis** (*moderate–cheap*) for fricasséed crayfish and *christophine au gratin.*

One of the most renowned kitchens on the island, for its local cuisine, is at **Le Colibri** (✆ 61 91 95; *moderate*), in Morne des Esses. Clothilde Paladino has won prizes for her original variations on local recipes, including *tourte aux lambis* (conch pie), *écrevisses buisson* and *bisque, soufflé de christophene* and *flan au coco*. Family run with a West Indian welcome, good value too.

In **St Pierre** there is another waterfront view from the terrace at **La Vague de St Pierre** (✆ 78 19 54; *moderate*). Here you will be served with traditional French creole fare—fricassee and colombo and blaff, on a deck above the sea. An easy-going spot to aim for is **Le Mouillage** (✆ 78 15 09; *cheap*), at the entrance to the town. There is a fine view over the whole town and bay from **Le Fromager** (✆ 78 19 07; *expensive–moderate*). Pickled flying fish and *canard à l'ananas*—but watch out for bus tours. You get excellent value at the **Grain d'Or** (*cheap*) in Quartier Four just south of the town. Traditional Martiniquan fare. In **Le Precheur** you will find a couple of cool spots to linger overlooking the sea. Try **Le Relais Prechotain** (*moderate–cheap*), set in a colourful building on the waterfront.

In **Le Carbet** there are a couple of places worth stopping for (as well as taking time out on the beach to watch the sunset). Try **Le Trou Crabe** (✆ 78 04 34; *moderate*), which has a pretty setting right on the sand: *chatrou bonne femme* (octopus in a local sauce) and *poulet au coco* (chicken in coconut). A simpler spot is the rustic cabin and bar, **Chez les Pecheurs** (*cheap*), where you can get a very simple platter.

Bars and Nightlife

The traditional Martiniquan apéritif is the *ti punch*, which is prepared with the same ceremony as the local food. The sugar (or cane juice) is heaped in the glass and the lime is squeezed quickly and dropped in before the white rum is poured and stirred vigorously. In times past only the cane juice would have to be paid for in bars because the rum was so plentiful. Many restaurants also have fruit punches, made from fruits which have been steeped in rum, which are delicious. The local beer in Martinique is *Lorraine,* a passable brew. There is an infinity of local bistros, rum shops and supermarkets in Martinique.

There are plenty of bars in Fort de France and the busiest area is the Parking on the waterfront. The hip **Le Terminal** overlooks it from a balcony, where a mix of local executives and visitors loiter over absinthe cocktails or one of about 50 beers and rums until 2am. Also try **Le Cheyenne** nearby. The **Monte Carlo Club** on the boulevard Allègre has a cocktail bar with live jazz sometimes and the **Mayflower** on rue Ernest Déproge gets quite lively. The boulevard Allègre has a number of billiard halls, bars and slot machine arcades among the crêperies.

The many nightclubs and discotheques include the **Manhattan Club** on the rue François Arago for zouk music, **Negresco** and the New **Hippo** on boulevard Allègre. **Club Bitaco** is high in the hills of Ravine Vilaine (you have to follow the Route de Redoute off the bypass behind the downtown area) and in outlying towns you can try **Le Zipp Club** in le François and **Top 50** in Trinité. Any town staging a *fête patronale* will have public dances where you will be welcome to join in. For more local discotheques, of which there are many out in the sticks, you can ask around.

Some of the hotels have discotheques and they also stage folklore shows. Classical cultural events are staged in the Hôpital Civil on the road up towards Didier. You might also check CMAC (Centre Martiniquais d'Actions Culturelles), ✆ 61 76 76, and SERMAC (✆ 60 48 77) in the Parc Floral.

There are two **casinos** (*adm*) on the island, open from 9pm until 3am, one in the Méridien and the other in Schoelcher at La Batalière Hotel.

getting there

By air from Europe: Air France (© 55 33 33) has daily flights from Paris and weekly connections from other French cities including Lyon, Toulouse, Bordeaux and Nantes. These are supplemented by charters operated by Nouvelles Frontières (© 42 16 40), AOM (© 42 16 24), Corsair (© 42 16 41) and Air Liberté (© 42 18 34). There are no direct flights from other European countries; travellers can connect in Paris, or fly via Barbados, St Lucia or possibly Antigua.

By air from the USA: American Eagle (© 42 19 19) has regular services through its hub at San Juan, Puerto Rico. Air France also routes via Miami.

By air from other Caribbean islands: The island's carrier, Air Martinique (© 42 16 72), has hopper flights to Union Island, Mustique, St Vincent, Barbados and St Lucia, and Air Guadeloupe (© 42 16 72) flies north along the island chain, via Dominica and Antigua to St Martin. Air France flies to San Juan and Port au Prince in Haiti. LIAT (© 42 16 02) also serves islands to the north and south of Martinique, originating in Antigua and Trinidad. An airport security tax sometimes of Fr83 is payable by all passengers leaving Martinique (it seems to vary according to who's on the desk). **Charter** planes are available through Air Caraibes (© 51 17 27) and Antilles Aero Service (© 51 66 88).

By boat: There are two ferries which run hydrofoils between Martinique and Guadeloupe, touching Dominica *en route*: **Caribbean Express** at Terminal Inter Iles in Fort de France (© 63 12 11, ● 63 34 47), daily except Tues, also occasional sailings south to St Lucia; and **Madikera**, 108 rue Victor Hugo (© 91 60 87).

tourist information

France: 2, rue des Moulins, 75001 Paris (© 44 77 86 22, ● 49 26 03 63).

Sweden: PO Box 717 Fregativägen 14, S 181 07 Lidingo, Sweden (© 8 765 58 65, ● 8 765 93 60).

Canada: 1981 Ave MacGill College, Suite 480, Montreal PQH 3 A 2W9 (© (514) 844 8566, ● (514) 844 8901).

USA: 444 Madison Avenue, 16th Floor, New York, NY 10022 (© (212) 838 7800, ● (212) 838 7855, toll free © (1 800) 391 4909)

In other countries you should be able to get information through the various Maisons de la France. There is a Martinique website: *www.nyo.com/martinique.*

The main tourist office on the island is on the waterfront in Fort de France, at 2 rue Ernest Deproge, BP 520, 97206 Fort de France Cedex (© 596 63 79 60, ● 63 11 64), and is open weekdays 7.30–12.30 and 2.30–5.30, and Sat 8–noon. There is a tourist office in the airport at Lamentin (© 51 28 55) and another office, specifically for Fort de France, at 76 rue Lazare Carnot (© 60 27 73) in town. Around the island you will find some information offices in the various town halls, and of course you can also find plenty of information in the hotel foyers.

With its suitably sexy slogan, *Une Histoire d'Amour entre Ciel et Mer* (a love story between the sky and the sea), the Martinique Tourist Board puts out several publications, including *Choubouloute*, providing useful information such as watersports companies and ferry times and there is also a restaurant guide *Ti Gourmet*, to help you get to grips with the all-important island dining experience.

The **American Consulate** in Martinique is at 14 rue Blénac, Fort de France (✆ 63 13 03).

In the case of a medical **emergency**, contact the Hôpital Zobda Quitman (✆ 55 20 00) and if you need to contact the **police**, call 17. The **IDD code** for Martinique is ✆ (596), followed by a six-digit local number.

festivals

Bastille Day, 14 July, is celebrated in the Antilles as in France, but the major festival in the year is **Carnival**, which starts on the day after New Year's Day and continues with weekend processions until the beginning of Lent, when there are five solid days of dancing and street parades. On Lundi Gras they stage 'burlesque weddings' in transvestite costumes, Mardi Gras is the day of the red devils and Ash Wednesday sees black and white costumes and culminates in the burning of *Momo*, the Carnival spirit.

Many towns also celebrate their saint's day, in the **fête patronale**, with a round of races, competitions, outdoor dances and barbecued chicken legs. They take place mostly between July and January, and it is well worth checking the newspaper or Tourist Board to find out if one is going on. Towns also hold cultural festivals, with shows, parades and sailing races: Le Robert (April), Saint Pierre (May), Le Marin and Sainte Marie (both August). Another key date in the calendar is 22 May, which is the date of the Emancipation of the slaves in the French West Indies, remembered with general blow-outs.

In April, the **Martinique Food Show** brings together the island's best cooks and their dishes in competition with one another, and in July Fort de France stages a series of concerts and theatrical events at its **Cultural Festival**. November sees the annual sailing race to bring over the first case of Beaujolais Nouveau from the *métropole* and in December Martinique clubs and venues come alive with an International Jazz Festival or the World Crossroads of the Guitar, held in alternate years. There is a jazz festival in the last week in May, held at the Plantation Leyritz (✆ 78 94 67).

the Yoles Rondes

The *yoles rondes* are distinctive Martiniquan yawls with square sails and it has become popular to race them. They have huge square sails on a bamboo mast and are sailed by a crew of 11 or 12 men who clamber about on poles a good 6ft out above the water to make the best of the winds. They are often raced at the traditional Martiniquan *fêtes patronales*, but there is also a special eight-day regatta held around the island each July. There are many other regattas, with more regular yachts competing, centred on the sailing clubs at Le Marin (early June) and Fort de France (late June).

money

The currency of Martinique is the French franc, which exchanges roughly at US$1 = Fr5.5, though of course it floats on the open market. You will often find yourself offered a rate nearer Fr5 for the dollar, particularly in unofficial exchanges. US dollars are accepted in the larger hotels, but it is more convenient to carry francs for shops and restaurants. Major credit cards are also accepted in tourist areas and in Fort de France. Traveller's cheques in dollars or francs are accepted in many shops in town. Sometimes payment by credit card or by traveller's cheque will mean a discount on prices. **Service** is included (*compris*) in restaurant bills on the island.

Banks: Open for exchange on weekdays, 7.30–12 noon and 2.30–4. There is a bank in all the main towns.

Shops: Open weekdays 8.30–6, with a long break for lunch in the heat of the day (usually 12–2.30).

watersports

Windsurfing (*planche à voile*): A popular sport on Martinique, so you can hire equipment on all the major beaches, usually through the hotels. Advanced sailors should head for the Atlantic coast, around Vauclin for waves and Tartane on the Caravelle Peninsula for surf. You can hire boards at Cap Chevalier, Fun Alizé (© 74 71 58) on the busy Anse Michel beach and there are a number of operators at Pointe Faula outside Le François: try Le Club Nautique du Vauclin (© 74 50 83) and the Base de Plein Air et de Loisir (© 58 24 32) in Anse Spourtoune.

General watersports: Small watersports including waterskiing, jetskiing and kayaking can be arranged at the large resort areas on the Caribbean side. In St Anne contact Louis Petit (© 76 76 48) and in Tartane Sourtourne Location (© 58 56 67). For **kayak** trips you can contact Aventures Tropicales (© 64 58 49) in Cap Chevalier, Caraibes Coast Kayak (© 76 76 02) or Les Kayaks du Robert (© 65 33 89).

Day sails: Coasting the Caribbean shore of Martinique in a yacht is a fun day out and there are excursions from the tourist areas on the Caribbean coast and off the Atlantic side as well; some go as far as St Lucia for a weekend. Try the yachts *Raiatea* (© 66 07 24) in Trois-Ilets or Bambou Yachting (© 74 78 05) in Le Marin (go through the hotels for one in your area). And there are semi-submersible boats for a dry view of the corals: Aquascope Seadom Explorer at Pointe du Bout marina (© 68 36 09) and Aquascope Zemis in St Anne (© 76 83 71), reserve in advance. A particularly popular excursion is the trip to the Baignoir de Josephine and the Fonds Blancs, sandbars that rise to just below the surface near Le François (though it can be a bit crowded). You can go on an organized tour: contact Albert Mongin (© 54 70 23) or the Hotel la Riviera (© 54 68 54). It is also fun to take the day out to La Maison de l'Ilet Oscar (© 47 75 40) where there is a charming restaurant and some facilities.

Deep-sea fishing (*pêche au gros*): Can be arranged on *Little Maverick* (© 76 24 20) in Diamant or *Scheherazade* (© 66 08 34) in the Pointe du Bout Marina.

Diving (*la plongée*): Popular and well-organized and available in all the resorts. The best dive-sites for corals are around the southern edge of the island, off St Anne, around Diamond Rock and on the southwest coast around Les Anses d'Arlets (excellent for **snorkelling**), where you will find forests of seafans and sponges. There are many other reefs along the Caribbean coast, as well as some wrecks off St Pierre, sent to the bottom in 1902. Many of the big hotels have diving and teaching facilities (a medical certificate and insurance is necessary). A single tank dive coasts around Fr200. Planète Bleue (© 66 08 79) works from the Pointe du Bout marina, Sub Diamond Rock is on the south coast (© 70 10 65) and Histoire d'Eau in St Anne (© 76 92 98). In the north contact Carib Scuba Club (© 55 59 84) in Le Carbet just south of St Pierre.

Yachting: Martinique is a popular starting point for yachting holidays, many of which head down the island chain towards the Grenadines. There are marinas in Fort de France, Pointe du Bout and Le Marin and many of the big charter firms work from here offering skippered or bare boats. Contact The Moorings (© 74 75 39, ● 74 76 44) and Star Voyage, Port de Plaisance, 97290 Le Marin (© 74 70 92, ● 74 70 93), Stardust Marine (© 74 98 17, ● 74 88 12) and Sun Sail (© 74 77 61, ● 74 77 80), all in Le Marin.

other sports

Golf: There is one golf course on Martinique, the Golf de l'Impératrice Joséphine (© 68 32 81), just south of Trois-Ilets, an 18-hole Robert Trent Jones course, par 71. It gets booked up, but it is worth a try, green fee Fr270.

Riding: If you would like to see the rolling mornes or the beaches of southern Martinique on **horseback**, then there are several stables on the island. Try Ranch Jack above Anse à l'Ane (© 68 37 69), or La Cavale in the Diamant area (© 76 22 94) and in the area of the Rivière Salée south of Fort de France, the Centre Equestre de Thoraille (© 68 18 66).

Walking: Organized trips into the rainforest are arranged by Basalt (© 55 72 88), who arrange walks and Aventures Tropicales (© 64 58 49); both also arrange **canyoning** excursions. Also try Une Journée Verte in St Luce (© 62 54 23). You can also contact the Information Centre of the National Parks in Martinique (© 78 30 77).

Mountain biking: If you would like to explore the island by bike, contact V. T. Tilt in Anse Mitan in Trois-Ilets (© 66 01 01), Caraibe Safari (© 74 74 74) who work all over, and Loca'Raib (© 78 18 03) who are located in the north in St Pierre.

cockfights

Cockfighting can be seen in many islands in the French- and Spanish-speaking Caribbean. It is quite a spectacle and may well appear cruel to a visitor, but it is a sport followed avidly by the Martiniquans. The *pitt* is a circular ring banked steeply with seats, which on Sunday becomes a mêlée of gamesmen with fistfuls of notes, shouting to place their bets. All goes silent when the cocks are brought in by their owners, carefully prepared for months with alcohol to make their skin hard and groomed especially for the fight. The owners posture in the ring for a while, showing off their beasts to the crowd, testing the sharpness of the knives attached to their claws. Eventually the two cocks are released in the ring and all hell breaks loose: in the fury of the pit where the cocks lunge and lash, and in the stands, where men are standing and yelling, brandishing their fists. There are cock-pits in Morne Rouge, Ducos, Lamentin and Rivière Pilote.

the mongoose (mangouste) versus the snake

The mongoose was originally introduced to Martinique to reduce the snake population. Ironically, the animals promptly struck up a mutually beneficial arrangement in which the mongoose would avoid the snake by sleeping during the night and have a free run at the chickens (and other birds, some of which have become extinct as a result) in the daytime. As if in revenge, the islanders now wheel the two out against one another for sport.

Guadeloupe

The *Région* of Guadeloupe is made up of a number of islands scattered over 150 miles (240km) of the Lesser Antilles. Altogether they have an area of 658 square miles (1705sq km) and a population of around 410,000. Of the smaller islands, the Saints, La Désirade and Marie Galante lie close to Guadeloupe itself; St Martin (which shares an island with the Dutch Crown colony of Sint Maarten) and St Barts (St Barthélemy) lie to the north, amongst the Leeward Islands. Guadeloupe is by far the largest of the group and is shaped like a huge butterfly. Guadeloupe is in fact two islands, pushed together by geological movement, and each wing shows a different side of the Caribbean: in the west, Basse-Terre is mountainous and has the explosive luxuriance of the volcanic islands, its slopes covered with banana plantations and rainforest; the softer contours of Grande-Terre to the east have the coral reefs and white-sand beaches. Besides the exotic combination of French and West Indian elements, the large size of the island and the variety of countryside make Guadeloupe one of the most rewarding islands to visit.

The small town of Basse-Terre on the west coast of the island is the capital of Guadeloupe, but Pointe-à-Pitre on Grande-Terre has long been the commercial centre. Grande-Terre is more populous and industrialized, and its gently sloping *mornes* are covered in 12ft curtains of sugar-cane.

The island's economy has always been agricultural. Coffee gave way to sugar (and rum) and most recently to tropical fruits such as bananas. But as with so many Caribbean islands, tourism has grown here and become the primary industry most recently. Unemployment runs at around 30 per cent, but the standard of living is kept at a roughly similar level to that of mainland France and so Guadeloupe appears far more prosperous than other islands nearby.

There is an old saying of the French Caribbean which refers to *Les Grands Seigneurs de la Martinique et les Bons Gens de la Guadeloupe*. From the start Martinique was the senior, more prosperous island, the centre of French power in the area. The Martiniquans held political and commercial power over Guadeloupe and their business interests and influence continue today. But the Guadeloupeans have an independent cast of mind and they have always gone their own way. For the Guadeloupeans, the Martiniquans have too slavish an attachment to France. It is one thing to be 'Black Frenchmen', but if it has the effect of burying their own culture, then they will rebel against it.

Politically Guadeloupe has benefited from more autonomy in recent years, but it has also become more answerable for budget expenditure. France grants a huge amount of cash each year and the material benefits are clear to see, but there are some Guadeloupeans who would rather go it alone, without the protection of the Republic. The issue is an emotive one which erupts occasionally in violent campaigns, as it did in the late 1970s. Things have gone a little quieter of late because France basically rebuilt the island after the terrible destruction of Hurricane Hugo in 1989.

History

To the Caribs Guadeloupe was *Karukera*, thought to mean 'the island of beautiful waters'. Columbus was struck by the beauty of the waterfalls on the heights when he passed by on his second voyage in November 1493. He christened the island *Santa Maria de Guadalupe de Extremadura* but soon moved on. The 'Cannibal Isles' were dangerous country and, apart from one attempt by the Spaniards in 1525 to settle Guadeloupe so that their ships could take on water and refit here after the Atlantic crossing, the island was left well alone.

It was another hundred years before the next Europeans arrived in force. Led by de l'Olive and Duplessis, 600 French settlers disembarked in June 1635. They attacked the Caribs, driving them off the island within a few years to refuges in Dominica and St Vincent.

Guadeloupe was administered from Martinique. Not only did the Martiniquan Governor General have the ultimate say on affairs in Guadeloupe, but Martinique maintained a commercial hold. Trade to France had to be conducted through St Pierre, where the merchants would inevitably give a low price for Guadeloupean sugar, even after the extra costs of transportation. Revenge was sweet when four years under British rule (1759–63) turned out to be very prosperous ones for Guadeloupe because vast markets opened up to them in Britain and America.

During the French Revolution the Guadeloupean *patriotes* gained the upper hand, ousting the planters. They welcomed the revolutionary Victor Hugues and the new regime was installed. A guillotine was erected and 300 were beheaded. From his base on Guadeloupe, Victor Hugues rallied the slaves and liberal Frenchmen on all the Windward Islands with the promise of freedom, but within two years the rebellions were crushed and Hugues' position in Guadeloupe was unsure.

A momentous event took place on 16 Pluviôse of Year 2 (4 February 1794). Following the declaration of the Revolutionary Convention in Paris, the slaves in Guadeloupe were set free. However, a reactionary regime was installed at the beginning of the 19th century and slavery was re-established in July 1802. There were bloody riots, and many Africans preferred to commit suicide rather than submit to slavery once again. Finally in 1848 the slaves were freed once more, largely due to the efforts of Victor Schoelcher (*see* pp.228–9), who was subsequently elected deputy for Guadeloupe.

Guadeloupe was blockaded in the Second World War because it sided with the Vichy Government, but soon after the war Guadeloupe, like Martinique and French Guyana on the South American coast, became a French Overseas *Département*, with the same status as the mainland *départements*.

the travellers tree

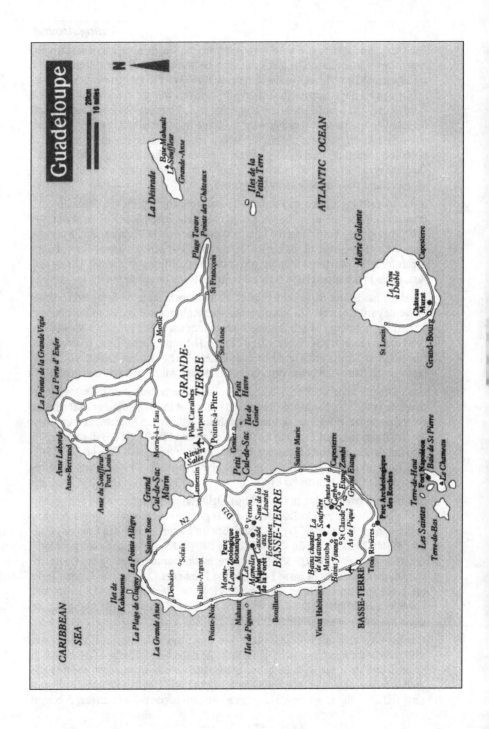

The public **bus** system is a good way to get around Guadeloupe and it reaches all major towns, eventually. The buses can often be heard before they are seen, as they are all equipped with extensive stereo systems. If you want to get on one, simply wave it down and if there is space the driver will stop. You will get to know the music of Guadeloupe, and your fellow passengers, quite well. There are bus-stops, but it is not necessary to use them unless you want to escape from the sun; to get off, you must either yell *Arrêt!*, or press the buzzer, which usually sounds like an air-raid siren. Buses leave when they have enough passengers and run from dawn until about 6pm. On Sundays and on public holidays the public transport system packs up in mid-afternoon and you can quite easily be stranded.

If you are catching a bus from Pointe-à-Pitre, your departure point will depend on the destination. The route along the south coast of Grande-Terre (Gosier—Fr8, St Anne—Fr10, St François—Fr15) is served from near the **Place de la Victoire**, on the eastern edge of La Darse, next to the ferries. To the northern part of Grande-Terre, buses depart from the **Mortenol Station**, across the dual carriageway from the Centre des Arts. Buses to the airport leave from the centre of town, on rue Peynier.

If you are headed for Basse-Terre (island), all buses leave from the Bergeverin Station on **Boulevard Chanzy**. Ask around for the correct bus; some go just to Lamentin or around the northern coast to Deshaies, others turn south and run down the eastern coast and on to Basse-Terre, the island capital. The trip to Basse-Terre takes around two hours and costs Fr25 (Fr30 to Trois-Rivières). The last bus in both directions between the two major towns departs at around 6pm. Miss it and you are stranded.

Guadeloupean **taxis** work on a fixed-rate basis and can be picked up in Pointe-à-Pitre (place de la Victoire, boulevard Chanzy and others), at the airport and at all the major hotels. Some taxi drivers speak some English and will give an impromptu tour. They are also happy to take a party out for the day at around Fr500 for a half-day and Fr800 for a full day (four people). Some numbers for taxis are: Radio-taxis CDL (✆ 20 74 74), SOS Taxis (✆ 35 42 18): at Place de la Victoire in town (✆ 83 99 99) and in Basse-Terre on the Cours Nolivos (✆ 81 79 70).

Sightseeing trips, taking in the principal sights on one or other island and usually with a lazy lunch-stop scheduled, can be arranged through the travel agents in town, or through any hotel lobby. Try La Guadeloupe sur Mesure, based in St François (✆ 85 54 08), Jet Tours (✆ 82 26 44), Trace des Iles (✆ 85 55 99) and Georges Marie Gabrielle Voyages (✆ 82 05 38). Sight-seeing by **helicopter**, zooming the Chutes de Carbet, the mountains of Basse-Terre and the Pointe des Chateaux on Grande-Terre are available from Héli-Inter Caraïbes (✆ 91 45 00) departing from Le Raizet and Caribbean Helicopters (✆ 88 76 98) in St François. Flights by light **plane** can be booked through Oceair (✆/▪ 93 25 50) at Le Raizet airport.

Car hire: Guadeloupe is a large island and to get the best of its great variety, you really need a car for at least some of the time. With the benefits of the EC, the roads in Guadeloupe are (usually) quite good, and Guadeloupean drivers push them to the limit. A foreign driving licence is valid for 20 days (a year's driving experience is necessary) and after that an international driving licence is needed. Avoid driving in central

Pointe-à-Pitre if humanly possible. Deposit is around US$300, unless you pay by credit card. Rates start at about US$45 per day. Some firms with offices at the airport are: Avis (℗ 21 13 54, ✆ 21 13 55), Europcar (℗ 21 13 52, ✆ 26 83 73), Karukera Car (℗ 21 13 79, ✆ 82 24 46), Pop's Car (℗ 83 39 73) and Tropic Car (℗ 91 84 37, ✆ 91 31 94). Motorbike rental is possible through Karib Rent (℗ 26 90 33) and Vespa Sun (℗ 91 30 36) in the city.

Beaches

For soft white sand brushed by palm trees and susurrating waves, go to the southern side of **Grande-Terre**. Some beaches become quite crowded because the area is fairly built up with hotels, but you can usually find a spot to yourself at the eastern end towards Pointe des Chateaux. Take a picnic with you because there are fewer beach bars there. Alternatively, there are the less typical beaches on the northwestern coast of **Basse-Terre**. The spurs and shoulders thrown off the mountains produce small protected coves between steep headlands and there is a string of excellent beaches with golden brown sand. This area is much less populous, but has some excellent beaches which have a wilder charm about them. Bathing topless is quite normal in Guadeloupe (though the West Indians themselves do not usually do it) and bathing nude is permitted in some places. All beaches are public and most hotels will allow you to use their facilities.

best beaches

Grande-Terre

Gosier: On the south coast of Grande-Terre, the built-up area with hotels and best avoided unless you wish to hire windsurfing equipment or go waterskiing. Opposite the town, a few hundred yards out to sea is a small island, the **Ilet de Gosier** (where people generally bathe nude). Trips to the island can be arranged from the waterfront or in the hotels in the area.

Petit Havre: And the other coves close to it are less populous and worth investigating.

Caravelle Beach: Heaped with blinding white sand, crowded and popular. At one end is Guadeloupe's Club Med, a factory of entertainment, patrolled by peak-capped security monitors—just don't overstep the line of the high-tide mark.

St Anne beach: Very popular, particularly at the weekends, with plenty of snackettes and some watersports.

Plage des Raisins Clairs: Just outside St François, busy with passable sand.

Pointe des Chateaux: The tapering spit of land towards the eastern tip of the island. Try **Anse à la Gourde** and the 1¼ miles (2km) of **la Plage des Salines,** where the

Atlantic waves barrel in. There is a nudist beach at **Plage Tarare**. On the south side there are some quiet spots among the trees along the roadside.

Le Moule: A reef-protected beach with some hotels and watersports and bars; also the **Plage de l'autre Bord** (literally the other side).

Northern Point: On the Atlantic side **La Porte d'Enfer** and two passable beaches on the northwestern coast, **Anse du Souffleur** at Port-Louis and the **Anse Laborde** just out of Anse-Bertrand.

Basse-Terre

La Plage de Cluny: Near La Pointe Allègre, **Tillette**, **La Perle**: all small coves with passable sand and palm trees, some with beach bars.

La Grande Anse: A huge bay backed with tall palms and stacked with golden sand, one of the most attractive beaches on the island, with restaurants.

Plage Caraibe: Golden sands and rocks, some facilities.

Malendure: Opposite Pigeon Island, very lively, despite the dark sand. Plenty of watersports and day trips.

beach bars

In Grande-Terre you will find bars and bistros along the popular beachfronts, to which you can retreat when the sun is at its height. St Anne and St François have a string of cafés along the waterfront where you can cast a critical eye at the windsurfers' technique over a beer or two. There are also snack bars along the road to the eastern tip at Pointe des Chateaux. You can have a good day out at the **Plage de l'Autre Bord** outside Le Moule, where there are beach bars and small huts for a local meal.

In easy-going Basse-Terre you will find beach bars spread out in the isolated bays. On the **Plage de Malendure** and on the mile-long strip of **Grand Anse** near Deshaies there are lots of sheds and snack-wagons under the palms. But the best of all is **Chez Françine** on the Plage de Cluny at the northwestern tip of the island. Françine has a wooden house and a covered terrace swallowed in banana and bougainvillea underneath the palms. There are deck chairs on the sand and soursop or coconut milk to accompany *accras* (codfish batterballs). Well worth stopping for.

Flora and Fauna

Guadeloupe is a geographical oddity because the butterfly's two wings are islands of completely different geological origin, separated by a small stretch of sea, the Rivière Salée. It is the meeting point of the two island chains that make up the Lesser Antilles—an inner chain of tall volcanic peaks that runs from Grenada up to Saba and the outer ring of coral islands from Marie Galante through Grande-Terre to St Martin and Anguilla.

Still odder are the names of the two islands: Basse-Terre and Grande-Terre. You might think that Grande-Terre would be the taller mountainous island, smothered in tropical rainforest, and that Basse-Terre would be lower. It is the other way around. There is a logical explanation, originating in now obscure sailing terminology. Basse-Terre is simply the 'lower ground' with regard to the prevailing wind. The pattern is repeated in the islands of the Saints, where Terre-de-Bas is downwind of Terre-de-Haut.

Guadeloupe can offer the best of Caribbean flora in its two halves. Grande-Terre's coast is lined with mangrove bushes and the white coral beaches for which the Caribbean is famous. And in Basse-Terre there is the spectacular beauty of the rainforest as well as the fascinating, if smelly, attraction of the Soufrière volcano.

The **Parc National** covers some 12,000 acres of the Basse-Terre mountains and they are as fertile as any in the Windwards. In the upper branches of the rainforest is another forest of hanging plants and explosive greenery—orchids and cycads, lianas grappling upwards to reach the sunlight and dropping aerial roots. Here you will see Guadeloupe's three humming-birds and the woodpecker, a *tapeur* in French, with a black stomach and back and a blue tinge to its wings, and perhaps a tiny *gobe-mouche* or Lesser Antillean peewee with an ochre-coloured breast. You might even see a Hercules beetle, a 6-inch monster that makes a metallic clanking noise. The stunted elfin woodland in the cloudy and windswept heights of the mountains has a whole new flora of dwarf palms and creepers. The headquarters of the National Park is in St Claude above Basse-Terre; Habitation Beausoleil, 97120 St Claude (✆ 80 24 25, ✆ 80 05 46).

Racing among the jumbled mountains are endless waterfalls that tumble into rockpools; ideal spots for a dip. There are lakes, hot springs, and in the south, the curiosity of the volcanic peak itself, where the ground steams constantly. The mountains are also crossed by a series of tracks, many of which make a good day's walk. Some leave from and return to **La Maison de la Forêt** on road D23, others are more adventurous and cross from one side of the island to the other (*see* 'Basse-Terre'). Guided tours can be arranged through the Organisation des Guides de Montagne de la Caraïbe (✆ 80 05 79) and Les Amis du Parc National (✆ 81 45 53).

There is little wildlife on Guadeloupe, but what there is can be seen in the zoo on **La Route de la Traversée** (D23) that cuts across the middle of the park. In the hills you might be lucky enough to see the *raton laveur*, the racoon, or an *agouti*, a little mammal like a guinea pig introduced by man into many of the islands.

On the lower land of Grande-Terre the flora and fauna are completely different and you will see egrets and endless doves in the rolling mornes, and sandpipers, snipe and yellowlegs (greater and lesser) around the mangrove swamps. On the coast there are pelicans and tropicbirds. You can find these, alongside a host of crabs and other crustaceans in the **Réserve Naturelle de Grand Cul de Sac Marin**, 650 acres of mangrove and swamp and 850 acres of marine park. There is also a marine reserve in the area of Pigeon Island on the west coast of Basse-Terre.

Grande-Terre

Pointe-à-Pitre

The town of Pointe-à-Pitre, the commercial capital of the island and major port, lies on the southern side of Grande-Terre, in the Petit Cul-de-Sac, the inlet formed as the two parts of the island have been pushed together. It has a population of 26,000 concentrated in the centre of the town, but 100,000 altogether including the suburbs along the coastline. The town first began to grow in the 1760s, during the British occupation of Guadeloupe, and supposedly takes its name from a Dutchman named Pieter, who had lived on the point near La Darse a century earlier.

Pointe-à-Pitre is hardly an attractive town, though some two-storey wooden buildings do give an inkling of its former mercantile pride. It has developed haphazardly, upset by earthquakes (1843), fires and hurricanes, the latest of which, Hurricane Hugo, cut through in 1989. In the centre, the old Pointe-à-Pitre has a similar charm to that of a French provincial town, with buildings with louvred windows and balconies close on one another and the smells of coffee and pâtisseries exuding on to the street below. Its tall buildings and narrow streets become very crowded during the day, with cars parked up on the pavement along their entire lengths. Beyond the Boulevard Chanzy, the newest *quartiers* have sprung up in a crop of ferro-concrete monstrosities from the fifties, proof against earthquake perhaps, but incredibly ugly. They have forced the traditional West Indian shacks farther out along the coast.

La Darse (meaning harbour) is still the heart of town-life. Markets appear on the wharves at dawn, as the ferries and the buses come and go, dropping people off for the day's work. Just above la Darse is the main square, **La Place de la Victoire**, whose name commemorates victory over the British by Victor Hugues and the revolutionary army in 1794. In his reign of terror, Victor Hugues erected the guillotine here, but now the square (partly given over to a car park, unfortunately) is more peaceful. It is planted with royal palms and mango trees (some sadly torn out by Hurricane Hugo), and is lined with cafés and a few nice old buildings, where the *Pointus* (the inhabitants of Pointe-à-Pitre) like to sit duing the day and take the evening air under the busts of famous Guadeloupeans. Behind the square, on the rue Alexandre Isaac, is the **Cathedral of St Peter and St Paul**, constructed in Empire style in 1807.

The main street, **rue Frébault**, with shops full of goods from mainland France, leads through the commercial heart of the town, down to **Le Marché de St Antoine**, an iron market with a red corrugated-iron roof. Guadeloupe may be one of the most developed islands in the area, but this is a truly Caribbean institution. It pulses from early morning, with the smell of fruits and spices, and offers anything from avocados to earrings for sale. Even for French speakers, the joking and haggling in creole is impossible to keep up with.

The **Musée Schoelcher** (*open weekdays 8.30–12 and 2–5.30, Sat until noon; adm*) is set in an impressive stone and stucco townhouse with a double staircase and metalwork balustrades (built in 1887) on the rue Peynier, outside which is a small sans-culottes statue of Victor Hugues the revolutionary. It contains some of the personal collections of the abolitionist, assembled in his 15-year struggle to outlaw slavery in the French colonies: pamphlets against the slave trade and a copy of the proclamation outlawing slavery, some prints comparing facial appearances (with some particularly unpleasant ones comparing negroes to animals) and some death masks, reflecting Schoelcher's interest in phrenology (with which he disagreed). Another leading light in Guadeloupe is celebrated in the **Musée St-John Perse** (*open weekdays 9–5, Sat mornings; adm*), set in an elaborate late 19th-century creole house on the rue Nozières. The poet and diplomat, Alexis Saint-Léger was born on the island of a long-standing family and was awarded the Nobel Prize for Literature in 1960. The story of his life is told upstairs and downstairs there are revolving exhibitions. The house itself looks a little odd, surrounded on all sides by louvres: it was supposed to have been shipped, in kit form, from Louisiana. A **guided tour** of Pointe-à-Pitre can be made, with explanations of the town's history and traditions, through Pointe-à-Pitre Tour, though there may have to be a minimum of four people (℗ 90 04 71).

The Southern Coast of Grande-Terre

Protected from the Atlantic weather by the rolling limestone '*Grands Fonds*', the southern coast of Grande-Terre has the mildest climate on the island and has become the centre for the tourist industry. The action of the waves on the coral shores has pushed up white-sand beaches, and on them the hotels have mushroomed. The main areas are Bas du Fort, just out of Pointe-à-Pitre to the southeast, and the towns of Gosier, St Anne and St François.

Leaving Pointe-à-Pitre on the road to Gosier (N4), you pass the buildings of the University and come to Bas du Fort, a busy area where there is a number of tourist apartment blocks and hotels around a marina, with restaurants and bars. Round the point is the Guadeloupe **Aquarium** (*open 9–7; adm exp*), which exhibits tropical fish from all over the world in the 20 or so tanks. You will see lion fish with fancy-dress tail and fins, fish that shine as though lit by ultra violet in a discotheque and a trapezoidal character called *lactophrys triqueter*, who will spit poison at you. It culminates in the walk-through shark tunnel. Commanding la Grande Baie, a little farther round and covering the approaches to Pointe-à-Pitre, is the **Fort Fleur d'Epée** (*open daily 9–6; adm free*). These coral-rock ramparts cut into the hillside were stormed and gallantly defended in the days of Empire but now it is really just a park within fortress walls and it is visited mainly by picnickers and lovers.

The town of **Gosier**, a centre of tourism on the island, spreads along the shore for several miles and the hotels have encrusted around the old town, cluttering the hillside down to the beaches and bringing with them a plethora of restaurants, bars and discotheques. The name Gosier derives from the *grand gosier*, or pelican, which can be seen all over the Lesser Antilles and occasionally fishes off the Ilet de Gosier, a couple of hundred yards off shore.

St Anne and **St François** are two other towns whose incomes have switched from fishing to sport fishing, though among the motorboats with huge fishing-rods sticking into the air you will still see *gommiers*, the brightly painted local fishing boats. Both towns still have a promenade, where fishermen's houses and restaurants mingle, looking across the sea towards Dominica.

Inland from the coast you come immediately into the *Grands Fonds,* a landscape of limestone that has eroded into many tightly clustered hillocks (it looks very regular from the air), which are tussocked with growth on top. For centuries they were carpeted with 10ft of sugar-cane and in the early years of the 18th century, St Anne was the commercial centre that catered for them, but by the end of the century it was already in decline, its prosperity destroyed by Guadeloupe's internal turmoil. On the dock at St François, where the yachts are moored, you will see flashes of local West Indian life as the ferry from the island of La Désirade puts in. Its inhabitants are mainly farmers and they bring their sheep, stuffed into sacks with just their heads sticking out, to sell in Guadeloupe.

Beyond St François, Grande-Terre tapers to a spike pointing out into the Atlantic Ocean and culminates in the cliffs of **Pointe des Châteaux**. The wind is strong off the ocean here and the waves have carved eerie shapes out of the rocks, including a blowhole that answers moments after a wave has disappeared under the lip of the rock. The landscape looks a little like Brittany, as though Guadeloupe had simply broken off the west coast of France and been transported 4000 miles west. From the cross on the point, high above the waves, it is possible to see La Désirade, a table-mountain with sweeping sides which emerges gracefully from the sea 6 miles (10km) away, and the uninhabited islands of Petite Terre. On the northern side of the peninsula is the **Plage de Tarare**, a nudist beach.

The N5 leads north from St François through the canefields and now residential land to **Le Moule**, on the Atlantic coast, where the waves come relentlessly barrelling in—suffering continuously from the Atlantic winds, the houses in the town were built with no doors facing east. Le Moule knew some prosperity as the principal port on Guadeloupe's eastern coast in the sugar years, and ships would edge in on the waves to the anchor ports still visible, but now it is poor and broken down. The town was wasted by Hurricane Hugo in 1989 and many of the buildings were destroyed. The **Musée Edgar Clerc** (*open 9–12.30 and 2–5.30, closed Wed pm; adm*) is devoted to pre-Columbian history with Arawak archaeological remains on view. There is also a distillery just outside the town, the **Distillerie Bellevue** (*open daily 9–5*), manufacturers of Damoiseau rums. The various processes of rum distillation are on view and of course the visit culminates in a free tasting.

Northern Grande-Terre

A number of roads lead back to Pointe-à-Pitre. Alternatively, you can continue into the northern area of Grande-Terre, where the land lies lower and in places is covered with mangrove swamp. It is fertile land, and everywhere you will see the cone-shaped shells of abandoned windmills, some still with their crushing gear discarded inside. In **Morne-à-l'Eau** is one of the best examples of the French West Indian chequerboard cemetery, with acres of black and white tiles on the mausolea. On the Festival of All Saints' there is a ceremony in which the whole graveyard is lit with2 candles. At **Port Louis**, there is a view over the Grand Cul-de-Sac Marin enclosed between the two halves of the island. Basse-Terre rises spectacularly, grey-green in the distance, topped with vast clouds.

On the northwestern coast of the island is **Anse Bertrand**, another town that saw its most prosperous times in the sugar heyday of the 18th century. The most northerly point on the island is **La Pointe de la Grande Vigie**, where the cliffs stand 250ft above sea level. On a clear day Antigua, 35 miles (56km) north, is visible from the point. Close by is **La Porte d'Enfer** (Hell's Gate), a massive fissure in the cliffs.

Basse-Terre

A coastal road circles Guadeloupe's mountainous volcanic wing and, through the middle of the island, La Traversée cuts a path up and over the rainforest to the Caribbean coast.

Leaving Pointe-à-Pitre, the N1 crosses to Basse-Terre over the **Rivière Salée**. Before the two parts of Guadeloupe were linked by bridge in 1906, the crossing was made by ferry. On one occasion, a party of Guadeloupeans were making for a ball in Pointe-à-Pitre, when they were swept out to sea. Garbed in evening dress, they drifted for five days before washing up on St Thomas in the Virgin Islands.

The main road (N1) to the town of **Basse-Terre** takes a left turn and travels down the eastern coast, beneath the towering mountainsides, before crossing over to the Caribbean coast near the southern tip. **Sainte-Marie** is thought to be the place where Columbus landed on his second voyage in 1493, meeting his first Caribs.

Capesterre takes its name from its position (*Capesterre* means windward in French, and the village is upwind of *Basse-Terre*). Outside the town, the **Plantation Grand Café** (*open weekdays 9–5, weekends in the winter season 9–12; adm*), a working banana plantation, is worth a visit. The tour includes an explanation of the process of cultivation, gathering and washing, sorting and boxing on a conveyor of hooks, a visit of the plantation house and, not to be missed, an alley with about 20 different species of banana and plantain from the world over: *Velutina* (from Assam), *Beccarrii* (Borneo) *Basjoo* (Japan). It is also worth making a visit to the **Distillerie Longueteau** just below here this area (*open daily 9–12, closed Sun; adm*), particularly during the harvest which lasts about six months from the end of January or early February. It is a distillery of *rhum agricole*, made from pure sugar-cane juice rather than molasses and you can see the whole process, from crushing in the vast and vicious-looking machines to fermentation and distillation in vats and the eventual products—a white rum and a gold rum. As you leave the town of Capesterre you pass along the **Allée Dumanoir**, a tunnel of magnificent royal palms. They stand like living grey columns (the telegraph wires were once simply nailed into them), soaring to 100ft, bursting with spiked fronds and tapering in a single 10ft spine.

Inland and uphill from St Sauveur, at the end of the **D4** road that winds up through the banana plantations into the rainforest, are the three **Chutes de Carbet**. Two of the falls cascade into rockpools from over 300ft. The middle one falls 350ft and can be reached on a well-marked path, and the lowest tumbles 65ft into a pool where you can take a dip after the short walk. From here the path leads on up into the rainforest, towards the summit of the Soufrière, a three-hour walk. It is these falls that Columbus mentions in his diary when he talks of 'a waterfall of considerable breadth, which fell from so high that it seemed to come from the sky'. Back down the hill, there are several lakes just off the road: the **Etang Zombi** and the **Grand Etang**. The **As de Pique**, a lake in the shape of an ace of spades, is beyond the serene Grand Etang.

The N1 coastal road continues to the village of **Trois-Rivières**. Down the hill and close to the harbour (where boats leave for the Islands of the Saints) is the **Parc Archéologique des Roches Gravées** (*open 8.30–5; adm*), where the main exhibit is a series of maniacal squiggles and outlandish faces on a rockface. They were carved by Arawak Indians before the Caribs bludgeoned their way on to the island in about AD 1000. The rock is set in a small botanical garden, in which plants are marked, including those used by the Arawaks. Another few miles brings you through a ravine to the Caribbean coast and down into Basse-Terre.

Basse-Terre

The town of Basse-Terre (14,000 inhabitants), the administrative capital of Guadeloupe, lies on the coast in the shadow of towering volcanic mountains. It is just 20 miles (33km) from Pointe-à-Pitre as the crow flies, but the journey takes about two hours by road because it twists and turns so laboriously over its 44-mile (70km) length. Some of the route is impossibly steep and windy, but take heart; lines painted on the road show that the Guadeloupeans actually compete in cycling races along here.

Founded by Houël in 1643, Basse-Terre is built on a hill and is much more attractive than the commercial city of Pointe-à-Pitre. It retains an antique feel that the other town has lost. Just above the port, stone houses with upper storeys of shingle-wood tiles and clapboard crowd over the narrow streets. The imposing official buildings, churches and town houses with wrought-iron balconies give it a gentrified air.

Behind the activity of the main streets, on the few areas of flat ground, there are two main squares: the **Jardin Pichon** and the **place du Champ d'Arbaud**, surrounded by the old buildings of Basse-Terre. Covering the harbour from the southern edge of town, **Fort Delgrès** is another lumbering colossus of a fortress with huge embrasures that now stand unemployed. It expanded steadily from its beginnings in about 1650, when Houël erected the first battlements and has also seen plenty of action. There are acres of ramparts and it is easy to imagine the roar of the cannon and the smell of cordite. There is a small **museum** in the fort (*open daily 9–5; adm free*), giving a good run-down of its history and of Basse-Terre.

Like any prosperous Caribbean port, the town has spread up the hill where the wealthier inhabitants take a cooler and loftier view of the proceedings in the city centre. The district of **St Claude**, strung out over the bends of a sinuous mountain road, contains some the most attractive houses on the island. A side road leads to the town of **Matouba**, which has a large East Indian population (who came here as indentured labourers in the last century). Just above the town is the Guadeloupe National Park, where there are a number of walking trails or 'traces'. The Trace Victor Hugues leads from Matouba up into the mountains and down towards Petit Bourg on the other coast. Other traces lead to La Maison de la Forêt or down to Petit Bourg. These are long and demanding walks, so you should be well equipped before setting out.

High in the rainforest is the **Maison du Volcan**, a museum (*open 10–6; adm free*). It is set in a garden festooned with greenery and tells of vulcanism in general and La Soufrière, which lurks just above it, in particular (including its eruption in 1976). Also close by are the **Bains Jaunes**, hot-water springs, and the **Chutes du Galion**, more waterfalls. The road leads farther up on to the slopes of the volcano itself, an extremely steep path, wide enough for one car, that stops 1000ft below the craters, at **Savane à Mulets**.

La Soufrière lives up to its name, as the summit is a morass of sulphurous fumaroles and solidified lava flows where plants are poisoned before they take root. It is still quite active, constantly letting off steam and occasionally rumbling and showering the neighbourhood with flakes of volcanic dust. It erupted in 1695 and in 1797. In 1837 the whole of Basse-Terre quaked but this was followed by 120 years of silence until 1956 and then considerable activity in the 1970s. There were dust and gas explosions, geysers appeared in lakes, and the rivers turned into mud and lava flows. At one point there were a thousand tremors a day and 70,000 people were evacuated from the southern end of Basse-Terre.

From Savane à Mulets, you can make the summit in under three hours, on a path that passes between boulders tossed out by the eruptions. At 4813ft (1467m), La Soufrière is the highest point in the Eastern Caribbean. When the clouds are not in attendance (though they make the whole climb that much more eerie), the view from the top is a cracker.

D23—La Traversée, Basse-Terre

La Traversée (D23) cuts across the middle of the island of Basse-Terre, climbing to the twin pyramids of the Mamelles (at 2500ft) through whole roadsides of ferns and banana plants and then descending in switchbacks to emerge on the Caribbean coast at Mahault. The road gives an excellent view of the rainforest in all its luxuriance, with occasional panoramic flashes between the trees.

At Vernou, a retreat where the wealthy have built their villas and set them in tropical gardens, is the **Saut de la Lézarde** (the lizard's leap), a waterfall and rockpool in a gulley at the foot of an impressive slope covered in banana trees. Higher in the rainforest, where it becomes dark because the canopy is so thick and grotesque mosses creep on the floor, is the **Cascade des Ecrevisses**, a tame fall where the Guadeloupeans like to go for a day out at the weekend.

La **Maison de la Forêt** (*open daily 10–5; adm free*) is a museum that describes Guadeloupe's natural life, from the *pâte calcaire* of Grande-Terre and early volcanic rumblings 15 million years ago to the flying cycads and bromeliads of today's tropical rainforest. It is well set out and explains the forest ecosystem, especially the effects of rain. It is a little technical and unfortunately only in French. There are a number of marked walks through the forest that start and finish at the museum.

The Traversée reaches its summit at the Mamelles, from where there is a spectacular view, and then begins to descend in hairpins to the coast. From the heights a number of paths lead off into the forest, some of them the old *traces* that were walked by the *porteuses* with huge loads on their heads. The **trace des crêtes** leads down to the Caribbean coast near Marigot and the **route Forestière de Grosse Montagne** leads back towards Pointe-à-Pitre. **Morne-à-Louis**, unfortunately scarred by its television transmitter, offers more views over the cumulus of peaks in mountainous Basse-Terre. Just down the hill from here is the **Parc Zoologique et Botanique** (*open 9–5, café; adm*), where a lacklustre series of cages among the creeping vines exhibits Guadeloupe's limited fauna (raccoon, mongoose, terrapins and iguanas) and unlimited flora, some of which is marked. La Traversée joins the N2 on the Côte-sous-le-Vent (the rain-shadow), the Caribbean coast, at Mahault.

N2—Around the Northern Tip of Basse-Terre

From the Rivière Salée the **N2** runs to the northern tip of the island and then down the length of the western coast. To begin with the land is blanketed with sugar-cane, but this changes as the road passes into the shadow of the mountains.

The **Domaine de Valombreuse** (*open 9–5; adm*) is a working garden laid out over 10 acres where you can see an overwhelming variety of tropical flora: spice gardens, orchids, exotic shrubs and flowering trees and a humid river ravine with tall trees and creepers. At the **Domaine de Séverin** you will see a working sugar-cane crusher, with a conveyor about 2ft wide driven by a water-wheel (it gives an idea of the labour intensity of this old industry). There is a small museum and shop next door, where you can buy the eventual product, rum. The **Musée du Rhum** (*open daily 9–5*), close by in Bellevue above Sainte Rose, continues the story. It gives a history of cane—sweet bamboo—from Persian times to its use in Europe in the sweet drinks of the 17th century and of course in rum. Plenty of rum paraphernalia—machetes, carts and copper boilers. Rum is on sale...

Pointe-Allègre is the northernmost tip of Basse-Terre and it was the spot chosen by the first settlers of Guadeloupe in June 1635. It was a shaky start, as they were constantly battling the Caribs. Eventually they decamped and headed for the southwestern coast at Basse-Terre.

Deshaies is an attractive fishing village that lies in a small bay, from which the road winds up and over to **Pointe-Noire**, a town dating from the 17th century. The **Maison du Bois** (*open 9.30–4.30; adm*) is a small museum just south of the town, with exhibits of traditional machinery, tools and furniture from the French Antilles, all in tropical woods. The secrets of boat-building, straining the poisonous juice from manioc to make cassava meal, and the styles of gingerbread woodwork on the eaves of Caribbean houses are displayed. It is worth a visit.

Another story of a natural product can be followed at the **Maison du Cacao** (*open daily 9–5; adm*) not far down the road. A series of boards in the main house and around the garden (where there are cocoa trees and other tropical crops) explains the history, culture and harvesting of cocoa and some of its beneficial properties: serotonin, which occurs naturally in the bean, is an anti-stress agent and there is an indecipherable anti-depressant in there too. At the end of the visit there is a tasting, of course, and plenty to buy, including locally processed cocoa in blocks. The **trace des contrabandiers** (smugglers' route) leads across the mountain range in the centre of the island from the Maison du Bois. A three-hour walk through the forest passes beneath Morne Jeanneton and will bring you into the hills above Lamentin.

At **Mahault**, La Traversée (D23) cuts across the island on the quickest route back to Pointe-à-Pitre. Alternatively, the N2 continues down the coast to Malendure, the popular beach and dropping-off point for the Pigeon marine reserve. Founded in 1636, **Vieux Habitants** was supposedly named by its early inhabitants, who moved here after serving out their indenture (a three-year contract in exchange for their passage to the island), to avoid confusion with those who still had time to serve. From here the road continues to Basse-Terre.

✆ (590)– Where to Stay

Guadeloupe caters for most tastes, with a few havens of discerning grandeur at the top of the range through the big beach hotels to smaller haunts that attract a crowd of independent travellers exploring the island. As on its sister-island Martinique, the majority of hotels are really in the mid-range, large humming resorts muscling in on the available beachfront space. However, the island is well worth exploring: if you are moving around, two very useful lists are those for the *relais créoles*, or inns, and the slightly cheaper *gîtes*. The former has no specific reservation system, but you can get a list of members from 12 rue F. Arago, Pointe-à-Pitre (✆ 82 17 42). The *gîtes* can be contacted through: AVMT, 12 Faubourg Alexandre Isaac, 97110 Point-à-Pitre (✆ 82 02 62, ✆ 82 56 65). Otherwise go through the Office du Tourisme, 5 square de la Banque, 97110 Pointe-à-Pitre (✆ 82 09 30, ✆ 83 89 22). Some of the nicer ones are mentioned below, but the list is not complete.

Bas du Fort and Gosier on Grande-Terre are the island's principal resort areas and they have lines of hotels along the seafront. Elsewhere on the southern coast, St Anne and St François each have a few beach resorts. After a week on the beach you might like to move to easy-going Basse-Terre, which has some fun *relais* and *gîtes* dotted around the countryside, lost in gardens of tropical luxuriance. In larger hotels they will probably speak English, but you will need some French if you step beyond the main tourist areas. Breakfast is usually included in the room rate. A service charge of 10% or 15% will be added to your hotel bill.

Grande-Terre

very expensive

Le Hamak, 97118 St François (✆ 88 59 99, ✆ 88 41 92), is the most elegant hotel on the island, an enclave of rarefied luxury tucked away on its own just out of the town. The 54 rooms are hidden in neatly laid out gardens of bougainvillea and crotons, each one with its own retreat behind a stucco wall. It is stately and quiet and lives up to its name—the patio of every room is slung with a hammock. The beach itself is man-made but it is passable. There is no pool, but there is a jacuzzi. The rooms are not huge but they are comfortable and well presented: a/c with coffee makers and fridges, TVs on demand. There is a fitness room and a beauty salon. Flights are possible straight in to St François airport nearby. If you like a more active resort-style hotel on the beach in equivalent luxury you can try the nearby annexe of the Méridien hotel, **La Cocoteraie**, PO Box 37, 97118 (✆ 88 79 81, 🖷 88 78 33). The 50 suites are in very modern-looking blocks ranged tightly around a huge pool, with dining room and pool bar on islands in the middle, decorated with huge Chinese vases. The rooms are extremely comfortable, decorated in strong colours: pink, blue and green: all have balconies. Watersports are available on the private beach and many other facilities in its sister hotel next door. Just outside the town of St François you will find a large but comfortable hotel, the **Plantation St Marthe**, 97118 St François (✆ 93 11 11, 🖷 88 72 47, US res ✆ (212) 673 3660, US website: *tmcauban@ix.netcom.com*). It stands out a mile because of its distinctive Louisiana style, with the metalwork balustrades on the huge balconies. Inside, the 96 rooms are extremely comfortable, with all conveniences. Large pool, plenty of sports facilities, shuttle to the beach and some entertainment. The **Auberge de la Vieille Tour**, Montauban (✆ 84 23 23 🖷 84 33 43), sits on a headland above the sea in Gosier and now has 150 rooms and 32 suites, which makes it large, but the setting is still good, overlooking attractive grounds that slope towards the hotel's own beach. It retains something of an old colonial air, in the plantation house and the subdued atmosphere of the two restaurants and bar, spiked only by the windsurfers down below and the boutique in the old windmill.

expensive

La Toubana, PO Box 63, 97180 St Anne (✆ 88 25 78, 🖷 88 25 57), is one of the most sympathetic hotels on the island. It stands high above a sandy cove, centred on a very attractive dining room with elegant metal furniture and a hilltop sitting area from where the view stretches out over the pool and to the islands and on to Dominica (or Club Med the other way) beyond. The rooms are scattered in 32 bungalows on the descending hillside, very comfortable with kitchenettes and surrounded by gardens. Some bungalows for four people, air-conditioned, TVs, tennis court. Easy-going local crowd, some entertainment in the evenings.

moderate

The **Relais du Moulin**, Chateaubrun, 97180 St Anne (✆ 88 23 96, 🖷 88 03 92), is also set around an old windmill. The 40 rooms, some with kitchenettes, are in bungalows and apartments scattered around charming tropical gardens, and have bright white modern decor. The inn has a family atmosphere, with tennis, riding and bicycle touring on offer: the hotel is 600 yards from the beach, but there is a pool. Another pleasantly unassuming *relais créole* is **Cap Sud Caraïbes**, route de la Plage, 97190 Gosier (✆ 85 96 02, 🖷 85 80 39), on the hill at Petit Havre in a residential area halfway between Gosier and St Anne. The 12 rooms are in a simply designed modern block which stands above a pool on the hillside a few minutes' walk from the Petit Havre beach. Private and friendly. There is a similar feel close by at **Le Petit Havre,** 97190 Gosier (✆ 8520 83, 🖷 85 20 43), where there are 11 quiet simple rooms.

There are two simple but pleasant hotels right on the beach in St Anne. The oddly named but stylish and friendly hotel **Mini Beach**, 97180 St Anne (✆ 88 21 13, 🖷 88 19 29), has a pleasant foyer with high-backed wicker chairs and a piano which guests have been known to play in the evenings. There are six comfortable rooms and three bungalows, nicely decorated with mosquito nets on the beds, some with a/c, some with fans, phones but not TVs. Beach and all the watersports close by. It is known for its dining room. A slightly less comfortable, but equally well-positioned retreat just along the beach is the **Auberge Le Grand Large** (✆ 85 48 28, ✆ 88 16 69), where there are simple rooms in the main house and in colourful bungalows set in a profuse tropical garden (some kitchenettes). **Village Caraïbes Carmelita's**, 97190 Gosier (✆ 84 28 28, ✆ 84 58 12), is another passable option close to the beach in St Felix, with 14 air-conditioned bungalows, some with kitchenettes, in a lawned garden with a pool.

cheap

A number of small and charming places are tucked into the back streets and corners of the towns of Gosier and St Anne. An excellent retreat set high on the hill in Gosier is **Les Flamboyants**, 97190 Gosier (✆ 84 14 11, ✆ 84 53 56), with a pool and open gardens out front, which overlook the Ilet de Gosier and Basse-Terre beyond—a moment of calm in the holiday hustle of the tourist town. The main house is an old villa, with an aquarium and fishing trophies, sharks and turtleshells on the wall. There are 20 studios and rooms, quite simple with air-conditioning; breakfast only served in the dining room. **La Formule Economique** (✆ 84 54 91) goes by an odd name but it has a lively atmosphere, in a villa tucked away at the back of the town. It is centred on a lively dining room on a balcony decorated with clocks, model ships and plenty of bottles of rum. There are just eight simple rooms. Also in Gosier, on the main road, the **Sodex Vacances Guest House** (✆ 84 10 25, ✆ 84 3949) has some very simple rooms and studios in a block overlooking a garden of Guadeloupean profusion.

If you need to be in Pointe-à-Pitre, you might try the space-age **Hotel Saint John**, 97110 (✆ 82 51 57, ✆ 82 52 61), in which the 44 rooms lurk in a profusion of arches and overhanging eaves. On the Place de la Victoire you can stay at **La Maison de Marie Galante** (✆ 83 87 83), set in a nice old town house; the **Karukera** (✆ 91 75 55), four rooms with private baths; and the **Victoria Palace** (✆ 83 12 15) with 15 rooms, some shared baths, some private.

Basse-Terre

On the island of Basse-Terre the hotels are a little bit more spread out—this half of Guadeloupe does not have so many of the picture-postcard beaches, but some of the hotels and inns have excellent settings above the water or hidden in the rainforest. Some hotels will have a car ready for you at the airport if you request it.

expensive

At the southern tip of the island, in **Trois-Rivières**, you will find a charming setting at **Le Jardin Malanga,** 97114 Trois-Rivières (✆ 92 67 57, ✆ 92 67 58). An old wooden estate house restored in colonial style sits on the hillside among the banana fields, over-looking the islands of the Saints to the south. There are 12 rooms with modern comforts (king-size beds, video mini-bar, phone, a/c) in the main house and three wooden 'cases' or wooden cottages. Excellent old-time atmosphere, with creole cuisine.

moderate

Just off la Traversée (D23) you will find a good stopover at **L'Auberge de la Distillerie**, 97170 Petit Bourg (✆ 94 25 91, ✆ 94 11 91, US res ✆ (1 800) 373 6246), which is set on a hillside looking back towards Grande-Terre. Next to the main house stands a large covered terrace with the dining room and salon for occasional entertainment. It is friendly and low-key. Named after tropical flowers, the 14 rooms are quite simple, but comfortable, and they have an air of old-time Guadeloupe, each with a balcony and a hammock giving onto a profuse garden, where thereis a small pool. Just down the hill is the quiet **Creol' Inn** (✆ 94 22 56, ✉ 94 07 54), where there is a small cluster of Guadeloupean 'cases' or wooden cottages (built in the style of the old-time Caribbean) with louvred doors and gingerbread trimmings set in a profuse tropical garden. The cases are self-contained with telephones, televisions and fans; each also has a veranda with a well-equipped kitchenette. Restarant and shop with food.

The area of **Grande Anse** in the northwest of the island has put in a recent bid as the place to be and there are a couple of excellent places to stay. One of the most charming hotels on the island can be found at **La Flûte Enchantée,** 97126 Deshaies (✆ 28 41 71, ✉ 28 54 43, *intermed@softel.fr, www.intel-media.fr.im-caraïbe*), which is hidden away in a tropical garden as thick as jungle. At the top of the garden stands the central house with its open sitting area where guests linger in the early evening before moving to the dining room which gives on to the lit pool. Beyond, the garden has paths (and a small railway) which lead down to the 12 fan-ventilated rooms situated in cottages; each has a terrace and a small kitchenette downstairs and bedroom upstairs. There is a charmed air about the place, which lives up to its romantic name. Not far off is another easy-going spot, the **Habitation Grande Anse**, 97126 Deshaies (✆ 28 45 36, ✉ 28 51 17, *hga@netguacom.fr, www.sicap.it/hga*), where there are 26 rooms in all, in a variety of rooms, studios with kitchenettes and apartments. The dining room, set on a creole veranda looking out on to a lawned garden, and the pool are down below and the rooms run in a tight stagger up the hill behind, modern and comfortable.

cheap

There are two other good options in the area of **Trois-Rivières.** You will find a friendly reception at **Chez Dampierre,** 97114 Trois-Rivières (✆/✉ 92 98 69), where 10 wooden and tin-roofed bungalows are set on a small area of hillside. They are quite small, but are passably comfortable and they are self-contained with kitchenettes. The other good option is the **Gîtes Checheti,** 97114 Trois-Rivières (✆ 92 96 40, ✉ 92 60 10), where there are three bungalows with rooms and studios set in nice gardens high above the town; quiet stopover. If you would prefer to be down on the seafront, within a couple of km of Grand Anse beach, then you can stay at **la Paillotte du Pêcheur** (✆ 92 94 98) where there are just a few apartments and a dining room.

In **Basse-Terre** itself is the **Gîte Le Houëlment**, 34 rue de la République (✆ 81 44 72), right at the foot of town. And there are simple rooms outside the town at **La Casa du Père Labat** (✆ 81 98 79; *cheap–very cheap*). Three very simple rooms, air-conditioning or fan, with a fine creole dining room.

Headed north you will find a charming spot at the **Gîte de Vanibel,** 97119 Vieux Habitants (✆ 98 40 79), which is set among the restored remains of a plantation high up in the hills. Self-catering apartments, made modern but retaining the stained wood, the louvres and the verandas of times past. Classic Caribbean gardens and some of the coffee plantation machinery still on view. Farther north you will find some waterfront hotels with a theme of sportfishing and diving. **Le Rocher de Malendure**, 97125 Bouillante (✆ 98 70 84, ✉ 98 89 92), has nine bungalows of which three sit on the *rocher* itself. There are simple rooms at **Iguana's Hotel,** 97125 Bouillante (✆ 98 91

91, ☎ 98 91 76), 10 rooms in a modern building at the roadside. Also try **La Grange Bel ô,** on the Chemin Poirier, 97132 (✆ 98 71 42, ☎ 98 96 79), where a charming creole house stands in a garden above the coast.

En route for Grande-Terre you will find an excellent stopover at **Le Duc'Ery,** 97170 Petit-Bourg (✆ 95 73 95, ☎ 95 32 94), a modern house with old creole overtones which stands high above an agricultural valley. Friendly reception, assistance with tours in the area, and good prices. There is a **camp-ground** on Basse-Terre at Deshaies—**Les Sables d'Or** (✆ 28 44 60).

✆ *(590)–*   ***Eating Out***

With its French roots, Guadeloupean cooking is excellent and the island will not disappoint those who wish to take part in a gastronomic steeplechase or just take some time out from the rigours of sitting on a beach. And many of the the the settings are excellent too, small cafés on the waterfront (St Anne and St François each have a string of them) and verandas on a hillside grappled by allamanda and slender fingers of bougainvillea, with the tremulous thunder of the rain on an iron roof.

The Guadeloupeans cook a full range of French food, but of course the island has a long tradition of creole food: fish and island meats like goat, spiced sauces, tropical vegetables and fruits. There are Guadeloupean versions of many dishes you will find in Martinique (their point of origin is usually contested) and they will be stamped with the island flavour. Snapper, *lambi* (conch) and *langouste* (lobster) are favourites, in a *blaff* (a way of boiling fish) or goat in a *colombo* (a French West Indian curry), served with flavoured rice and peas or local vegetables such as plantain or christophene and spiked with creole sauces. French wine is often drunk with a meal but, like their confrères in Martinique, the Guadeloupeans are slaves to the *petit ponch,* a rum-based apéritif that is small only in name, and the *ponch à fruits,* in which fruits are steeped in rum and sugar, giving it a sweet flavour.

There are literally hundreds of restaurants and cafés in Guadeloupe (at the last official count about 700), so the choice is limitless. There are Vietnamese and even Lebanese restaurants here. Most are fairly relaxed, but in the smarter ones men are sometimes required to wear a jacket. Eating out is not exactly cheap, but surprisingly the smartest restaurants are not drastically more expensive than the less smart ones. Categories are based on the price of a main course: *expensive*—Fr80 and above; *moderate*—Fr40–Fr80; and *cheap*—less than Fr40. Obviously many restaurants offer a *menu* for the day. You wll find them at Fr50 to Fr150. *Service* is, of course, *compris.*

Grande-Terre

expensive

An excellent French restaurant in a comfortable setting is **Côté Jardin** (✆ 90 91 28), which is tucked away behind the waterfront in the Bas du Fort marina. You sit inside in an air-conditioned dining room, at elegant white-laid tables in wicker chairs, some with huge peacock backs, with all the activity of the kitchen in view. Try *Gambas flambés du planteur passion* or *cuisse de canard confite* served with *pommes sautées paysanne* or, if you want to be extravagant, lobster, *émincé de langouste, sauce* *saffron*. Popular with business and political people for lunch, cool and elegant for dinner, excellent wine list. *Closed Sun*. You might also try **La Coupole** (✆ 90 97 34), which is positioned on the waterfront. It is a brasserie and so all its fish are out on display: oysters, local fish and of course *moules*, but also some meat and salad dishes. Pleasant dining room with a theme of wood and stained glass. **Le Dampierre** (✆ 84 53 19), which is set in a modern villa just off the main road at the eastern end of Gosier, is popular with local businessmen and families for its inventive creole fare.

High on the coast road between St François and **St Anne** (well signposted) you can find a charming gastronomic retreat, **Les Oiseaux** (✆ 88 56 92), a *restaurant frantillais* (i.e. the best in local ingredients cooked in French style). The dining room is set in a stone-walled room with wooden shutters looking on to a pleasant tropical garden: *lambis marinière*, with snails, cream and butter, or *requin au coco* (shark in coconut) or even a *fondu de poisson* which you cook yourself in maize and coconut oil. Not far off is **Le Flibustier** (✆ 88 23 36), which has a certain style—set on a hill like a pirate's look-out and decorated inside with the beams of a galleon. It's quite rumbustious: wine by the pitcher, chef with his hair tied back, who barbecues your meal and then presents it to you on a huge wooden platter. Naval battles and portraits of pirates on the walls. *Closed Mon, Sun evening*.

On the seafront in **St François** is the ever popular and lively **Le Vieux Port** (✆ 88 46 60), which sits in a tin-roofed wooden house on the esplanade just across from the sea. You sit among banana plants and wicker walls and the kitchen is open and on view: start with a *charlotte de boudin créole aux pommes* and then follow with a *croustillant de poissons au curry et à l'ananas*. Not far down the street, the rue de la République, you will find a string of charming spots '*aux pieds dans l'eau*' (literally: 'with feet in the water'). **Kotésit** (✆ 88 40 84) has a pretty set-up, with blue and white awnings on a wooden deck right on the small waves. French and creole fare: *vivaneau* (snapper) *et sa sauce, panaché de poisson poêlés* or lobster straight from the live tank. Not far off is **Le Zagaya**, which you will find stretching out over the water on a green and white deck, behind the streetfront facade of a pretty old creole house. Again lobster is a speciality, or start with a *salade de chèvre aux raisins* and then try *ouassous flambés* or *à la provençale*, followed by a *clafoutis aux fruits* to finish.

A sedate day out, lingering over a long lunchtime, can be enjoyed at **Le Château de Feuilles** (✆ 22 30 30), which is set in a charming creole villa and garden miles from anywhere in the north of Grande-Terre, near Campêche (well signposted). French and creole fare—*choucroute de poisson de papaye verte, charlotte au corossol* (mousse and cream) and a between-course swim if you feel like it, just beside the tables, followed up with one of 20 different varieties of fruit-flavoured rums. *Closed Mon, otherwise open daily for lunch, dinner Fri, Sat, ring to reserve.*

moderate

There are plenty of waterfront pizzerias and a few less expensive bistros in the **Bas du Fort marina**, where you can wander between video bars while you decide where to eat. **La Sirène** does a good crêpe. In **Gosier** you will find a good creole meal at **Mérou d'Or**, down at the waterfront opposite the Ilet de Gosier. Fresh fish—*blaffs* and *poissons en papillotte* in a typical French West Indian dining room with madras table-cloths. There are plenty of smaller cafés lining the main street.

In **St Anne** you will get an excellent creole meal at the small and friendly **Mini Beach** (℗ 88 21 13). In an open dining room to an occasional piano accompaniment, try *poisson grillé, sauce antillaise* or lobster (live from the vivier), followed by *fondant de chocolat.* In **St Francois** two popular spots, with a view of the windsurfers, are **Les Pieds dans l'Eau** and **Le Mareyeur.**

cheap

Recently a number of roadside pizzerias and *roulottes* (snackwagons) have put in an appearance all over Guadeloupe and they make a fast alternative to the traditional sit-down blow-out. An excellent place for a simple plate of chicken and chips is **Express Grill** on the main road outside Gosier. *Open daily until 1 or 2am.* You will find *grill-lades* in St Anne and St François. If you are feeling peckish late at night in **Pointe-à-Pitre**, there are snackwagons on the place de la Victoire. Afterwards you might like to grab an ice cream from the vendors with wooden buckets (they will explain how they work too).

Basse-Terre

Basse-Terre also has a number of good places to eat, dotted around the whole island, but particularly on the free and easy west coast around Malendure.

In **St Rose** you will find superb creole fare at **Chez Clara** (℗ 28 72 99; *expensive*) on the waterfront road. The dining room is on a very comfortable deck with a tin roof and you sit at wicker chairs. Clara herself presides, talking you through the menu on a chalkboard—fish and shellfish landed on the pier right across the road, a *feuilleté or a ragout de lambi* (conch) with a *gratin de fruit à pain* (breadfruit). Popular with the locals. *Closed Wed, Sun evening.* There are quite a few small fish restaurants along the front here which have *moderate* prices. You could also try **Chez Franko** or **Les Flamboyants,** both of which offer *blaffs* and *court-bouillons.* The **Domaine de Séverin** (℗ 28 34 54; *expensive*) is in an old plantation house on the northern slopes of the island on a sugar plantation. *Ecrevisses* (crayfish, from the pond on the estate) *en civet au vin rouge* or *feuilletté de lambi. Lunch daily except Mon, dinner Thurs–Sat.* And on the road around the northern tip of the island you will get a good local meal (with some French dishes too) at **La Nova** (℗ 28 40 74; *expensive*). It is set on a breezy, split-level terrace outside a modern local house. *Closed Tues.*

If you are on **Grand Anse**, you can catch a good lunch on the tropical terrace at **Le Karacoli** (*expensive;* you may find yourself dodging the twice-weekly tour buses). Creole food—*assiette belle négresse*, with all the fish and seafood you might want to try (*boudin, accras* and tropical *crudités)* followed by a *tartane do thon* or a *croustil-lant de lambi.* There are a number of snack bars on Grand Anse beach now during the day, so you can grab a meal from them.

In nearby **Deshaies** there are a number of bars and restaurants strung along the waterfront. The coolest is **Au Coin des Pêcheurs** (℗ 28 47 75; *expensive–moderate*), where you sit on a nice deck on the waterfront in the town. Local fare: *salade de pechê* or *fricassée de lambi* with *christophine au gratin.* **Le Mouillage** 'Les Pieds dans l'Eau' (℗ 28 41 12; *expensive*) is popular for creole cuisine; their speciality is *ouassous en sauce,* but you can get a *blaff de poisson et légumes* followed by *banane flambée.* **Le Madras** (℗ 28 40 87; *moderate*) is very local and offers creole fare inside a small, dark dining room set with madras tablecloths. *Boudin lambi* and stuffed crab backs. Lunch and dinner, set on a nice terrace.

Further south you come to **Le Rocher de Malendure** (✆ 98 70 84; *expensive–moderate*), where you dine on any one of a mulititude of different decks, looking through profuse tropical greenery to Pigeon Island. It is a fish restaurant—*escalope de marlin pané* or *ouassous en sauce*, even a fondue, but if you've been diving you might have the *assiette du plongeur* (sushi, Tahitian fish, smoked fish, *mousse de thazar...*); some meat dishes. **La Touna** (✆ 98 70 10; *expensive*), in the town of Bouillante, also serves fish and lobster on the waterfront, landed nearby. The cuisine is creole and French, seafood and fish, on a neat and pretty veranda. Some bar-trade with deep-sea fishermen dropping in to tell their war stories.

Caprice des Iles (✆ 81 74 97; *expensive*) offers a fine welcome and good French and creole cuisine in Baillif next to the castle at the corner, just before Basse-Terre, right next to the road but with a terrace on the waves. *Accras, boudin* and *vivaneau à la crème d'avocat*, followed by a *feuilleté de banane caramelisé*. There is a fun restaurant in St Claude, **Le Tamarinier** (✆ 80 06 67; *expensive–moderate*) where you will get the best in '*cuisine familiale et créole*'. And in Matouba, high above the town of Basse-Terre, there is a nice lunch-time stopover at **Chez Paul** (✆ 80 29 20; *moderate*). Accras followed by *féroce* with hot pepper or a fricassee with a spicy sauce and of course a volley of local vegetables. In the town itself you can get local fare at **Le Houëlment**.

Bars and Nightlife

Zouk is the current musical beat of the French Caribbean, another bustling rhythm with a double beat, often with echoes of West Africa. It can be heard on the buses and in the clubs, each as crowded as the other, along with just about all the other Caribbean beats. You get to know the songs as they are played over and over again: hear them again when you get home and you will start to twitch. Most clubs have a door charge of around US$10, which usually includes the price of a drink.

Outside the hundreds of bistros and bars you will find a few spots where hip chicks and lover-boys gather for an early evening drink. They are centred around the tourist areas. Among the many waterfront eateries at the Bas du Fort marina is **Le Jardin Brésilien**, a video bar with a list of cocktails as long as your arm. Perhaps try a balalaika or a samba depending on your mood. Live music and even fashion shows occasionally in season. There is a loud and lively bar called the **Zoo Rock Café**, which is all dressed up like a ship with square port holes and rigging; inside there is a black and white décor like zebra patterning. From here you can move on to **Π3.14**, a disco and pool bar, or **Velvet** right behind. Two other bar-discos are **Copacabana** and **Zenith**. Farther afield you can go for a dance at **La Cascade** (Tues–Sat) or **New Land** (weekends only), just off the main road to St Anne. A good place to enjoy a hilltop view and a cocktail is **La Toubana Hotel**, also outside St Anne. And in St François there are plenty of bars around the marina and good local discos at **L'Acapulco**, which is open at the weekends. There are casinos at **Caraïbe Club** in Gosier and in St François.

getting there

Like Martinique, the main airline of Guadeloupe is Air France (✆ 82 61 61). Air Guadeloupe (✆ 82 47 00) runs inter-island services from the airport at Pôle Caraïbes, a couple of miles from Pointe-à-Pitre.

By air from Europe: There are daily flights on Air France from Paris and depending on the season a weekly service from Marseille, Toulouse and Lyon. There are also charter flights on AOM (✆ 29 09 10), Air Liberté (✆ 26 61 31) and Nouvelles Frontières (✆ 90 36 36).

By air from North America: Air France serves Guadeloupe from Miami and connections from the USA can also be made via San Juan in Puerto Rico, the American Airlines hub in the Caribbean, served by American Eagle (✆ 87 70 40). From **Canada** there are flights from Montreal on Air Canada.

By air from other Caribbean islands: Martinique is linked to Guadeloupe on Air Guadeloupe, Air France and Air Martinique (✆ 21 13 42). If you are flying north to the smaller French islands of St Martin and St Barts, you can fly on Air St Barthélemy (✆ 27 71 90), Air Guadeloupe, Air St Martin (✆ 82 96 63), Air Caraïbes (✆ 82 12 25) and Winair (✆ 83 89 06), to Dutch St Maarten and beyond to San Juan. If you are flying to the English-speaking Caribbean, LIAT (✆ 21 13 93) has flights north to Antigua and beyond and south to Dominic. Charter aircraft tend to leave from Le Raizet, the old terminal.

By sea: Two companies run ferries between Guadeloupe and Martinique, touching Dominica *en route*, with occasional sailings as far as St Lucia: **Trans Antilles Express** (✆ 83 12 45, ● 83 72 27) at Quai Gatine in Pointe-à-Pitre and **Brudey Frères** (✆ 91 60 87, ● 82 15 62) at La Darse in central Pointe-à-Pitre.

tourist information

France: 43 rue des Tilleuls, 92100 Boulogne Billancourt (✆ 01 46 04 00 88, ● 01 46 04 74 03).

USA: 610 Fifth Avenue, New York, NY 10020 (✆ (212) 315 0726, ● (212) 247 6468).

Germany: Bethmannstraße 58, 6000 Frankfurt am Main 1 (✆ 69 28 33 15, ● 69 28 75 44).

On island, there are Tourist Information Offices in: **Pointe-à-Pitre**, Office Départementale, 5 square de la Banque, BP 422, 97110 Pointe-à-Pitre (✆ 82 09 30, ● 83 89 22) just off the place de la Victoire opposite la Darse and **St François**, on the avenue de l'Europe (✆ 88 48 74). On the westerly island of Basse-Terre, there are offices in the town **Basse-Terre** itself, in the Maison du Port (✆ 81 24 83, ● 81 18 10) and at **Bouillante**, opposite Pigeon Island (✆ 98 73 48). Office hours are 8–5 weekdays and 8–noon Sat. There is also a small information desk at the airport.

The Tourist Board produces a booklet called *Bonjour Guadeloupe*, full of useful facts like where to get your hair cut as well as advice on beaches and nightclubs. If you're on a gastronomic steeplechase, the pocket-sized *Ti Gourmet* has restaurant and other information and *Sentiers Gourmands* lists the finest creole restaurants on the archipelago.

To **dial** directly to Guadeloupe, the **IDD code** is ✆ (590), followed by six digits. On the island, the six digits suffice.

In a medical **emergency**, there is a casualty room at the main Pointe-à-Pitre **Hospital** at Abymes, emergency number ✆ 89 10 10. The **police** can be reached on ✆ 17.

Guadeloupe is generally lower-key than Martinique, but you may find that the Guadeloupeans are quite private. This is not to be confused with unfriendliness, because if you ask for assistance, even in faltering French, they will usually go out of their way to help you. A refreshing feature, in comparison to other islands, is an almost complete absence of hustlers, who can be trying elsewhere. Here, the state guarantees a certain standard of living and so there are very few of them.

festivals

Carnival gets going at the very beginning of the year and there are parades and competitions all over the island each weekend as Lent approaches. It all culminates in a three-day street party on *Lundi Gras, Mardi Gras* and *Mercredi des Cendres* (Ash Wednesday), when the spirit of *vaval* is burned for another year. The whole thing is taken very seriously and it is fun to follow on with the streams of dancers as they parade around, dressed as imps and bucca-neers, shuffling and dancing to the relentless beat of drum-driven French Caribbean music.

Formal celebrations include Bastille Day (14 July), Schoelcher Day (21 May) in commemoration of the abolition of slavery, musical Saint Cecilia's day (22 Nov) and each individual town's saint's day, the *fête patronale*. One of the Caribbean's most enjoyable spectacles is the **Fête des Cuisinières**, the cooks' festival, which takes place in August in Pointe-à-Pitre, in which island delicacies are dedicated and gastronomic parades take place before the customary over-indulgence in eating and dancing. Mid-July sees a festival of the Arts, Festag. On All Saints', the cemeteries are lit up with candles to the dead and people stay up all night in their honour.

money

The legal currency of Guadeloupe is of course the French franc, which exchanges at US$1 = Fr5.5 approx. US dollars and traveller's cheques are accepted in payment for hotel bills and generally on the tourist circuit. Credit cards are also widely accepted. However, if you go off the beaten track be sure to take francs. Hotels will change money, at a slightly inferior rate to the banks. In restaurants service is *compris*.

Banks: Open weekdays 8–noon and 2–4. Some banks open on Saturdays; try Crédit Agricole and Banque Nationale de Paris.

Shops: Similar hours to the banks in the morning. They also take 2 hours for lunch, but usually stay open until 6pm.

watersports

The best place to pursue watersports is on the sheltered southern coastline of Grande-Terre (where most of the hotels happen to be). Hotel watersports shops often have small sailing dinghies like sunfish and snorkelling gear for hire to non-guests. Basse-Terre has grown recently in popularity and the liveliest area there is Malendure, opposite Pigeon Island.

Windsurfing (*planche-à-voile*): Very popular in Guadeloupe. Equipment can be hired all along the southern coast of Grande-Terre, particularly in St François where advanced sailors collect on the Plage du Lagon, where you will see the sailboards beating back and forth on the sideshore winds; board hire through the Ecole de Voile (*©* 88 12 32) or UCPA (*©* 88 64 80). Over on the north side in Le Moule, an offshore reef causes waves; hire through Karukera Surf Club (*©* 23 10 93). It is sometimes possible to **surf** in this area.

Kayaks: Trips along the shoreline and in the mangroves can be arranged through Parfum d'Aventures in Grande-Terre (© 88 47 62) and Canoé-Kayac in Basse-Terre (© 98 69 24).

Day sails: Leisurely tours, rum punch in hand on a yacht or a glass-bottomed boat, are plentiful. Many go to the the islands in the Cul de Sac Marin and to the offshore islands, Marie Galante and the Saints, or to the remote and undeveloped island of Petite Terre. Try *Le Privilège* (© 93 65 84), *La Lambada* (© 24 33 60) from Vieux Bourg, *l'Aquarium* (© 90 92 38) and *Emeraude Guadeloupe* (© 80 16 09) out of Abymes. *Nautilus* (© 98 89 08) takes day cruises to the Ilet Pigeon from the Plage de Malendure. *King Papyrus* (© 90 92 98) leaves from the dock at Bas du Fort on daytime jaunts of tee-ree-ree and walking the plank and night-time sails where the mountains of Basse-Terre loom like Titans in the moonlight.

Yachting: If you want a proper sailing holiday, yachts can be chartered, bareboat or crewed, for a day, a week or more (for sailing trips to Marie Galante, the Saints and Dominica), from the companies in the Port de Plaisance marina in Bas du Fort, just outside Pointe-à-Pitre: Moorings (© 90 81 81, ● 90 84 87), Star Voyages Antilles (© 90 86 26, ● 90 85 73) and Star Dust (© 90 92 02). Other marinas are at St François, Deshaies and Rivière Sens near Basse-Terre.

Deep-sea fishing: Day and half-day tours in search of tuna and kingfish in the Caribbean Sea. Most popular on the west coast, where you can go out with Le Rocher de Malendure (© 98 70 84) in Malendure or Ricart's Fishing Club (© 98 74 29). In Grande-Terre you can contact Caraïbe Pêche (© 90 97 51) in the Bas du Fort marina.

Diving (*plongée sous-marine*): Also at its best on the west coast of Basse-Terre off Bouillante, where there is a marine reserve established by Jacques Cousteau around the Ilet de Pigeon. Contact Les Heures Saines (© 98 86 63, ● 98 77 76), who dive under PADI and NAUI as well as CMAS, the French system, in Malendure, Aux Aquanautes Antillais (© 98 87 30, ● 90 11 85) or Plaisir Plongée Caraïbe (© 98 82 43). Single-tank dives cost around Fr200 or US$40.

other sports

Hiking: On land, exploration of the National Park is best done on foot and there are two main drop-off points: **La Traversée**, the D23 road across the middle of the island and the foothills of **La Soufrière**. Guided walking trips can be arranged through the Organisation des Guides de Montagne de la Caraïbe, whose offices are at the Maison Forestière in Matouba (© 80 05 79). Other adventurous tours—canoeing and river-hiking and canyoning—can be arranged through Espace Loisirs, 97118 St François (© 88 71 93, ● 88 49 18), Parfum d'Aventure, 97180 St Anne (© 88 47 62, ● 88 47 91), Sports d'Av (© 32 58 41) and for personal treatment, Emeraude Guadeloupe, 97120 St Claude (© 81 98 28, ● 81 98 12). These companies also arrange tours by **mountain bike**, called VTT in French; otherwise contact Espace VTT (© 88 79 91).

Riding: On the beaches of Grande-Terre or for a day's picnic, possible through La Martingale (© 26 28 39) and le Cheval Vert (© 88 00 00). In the town of St Claude above Basse-Terre there is a stable, La Manade (© 81 52 21), from where you can ride into the rainforest.

Golf: On the edge of St François is the 18-hole Robert Trent Jones course (© 88 41 87).

'Quand bleuira sur l'horizon la Désirade'

Apollinaire

La Désirade takes its romantic name from the Spanish *deseata* (the desired one). In the 16th century the standard Atlantic crossing arrived at Guadeloupe and after four or five weeks at sea the sailors would be longing for land. La Désirade was often the island they saw first. Some feel that the real origin of the name is the word *descada*, meaning dry, which would be equally appropriate.

La Désirade lies about 6 miles (10km) off the Pointe des Châteaux, the easternmost tip of Grande-Terre. It is a table mountain, 8 miles by 1 (13 by 2km), with gracefully rising slopes topping 900ft above sea-level. It is windswept and covered in cactus scrub. The northern coast is a line of rugged cliff-faces, cut into strange shapes. The south of the island is protected from the wind and it is here that the 1600 inhabitants and most of the thousands of iguanas have chosen to live, spread along the coast from the main settlement of Grande-Anse. There is a track up to the highest point, the Grande Montagne, from the village of Grande-Anse.

La Désirade is dry and was settled only by a few poor white settlers at the beginning of this century. For many years it was a leper colony. Without the plantations there were no slaves and so the population of La Désirade remains predominantly white (also true on Terre de Haut in the Saints, but not so in Marie Galante). Today life is extremely simple and the economy of the island is mainly agricultural (sheep and small plots), or connected with the sea (fishing and boatbuilding). It is one of the least developed islands of the Caribbean—a reliable water supply was only introduced in 1991, by pipe from Guadeloupe. If you would like an utterly secluded escape, you can find it in La Désirade.

✆ *(590)–* ### Where to Stay

There are just a few **places to stay** on the island: **L'Oasis du Désert** (✆ 20 02 12), with eight air-conditioned rooms, in the Quartier du Désert, and **Le Mirage** (✆ 20 01 08) set on the beach, where there are seven rooms with fan ventilation and TVs, both quite simple and cheap. Camping is possible at Baie Mahault and people let out rooms in their houses. Full meal plans are available at the hotels but there are also some restaurants around the island, including **L'Esplanade** in Baie Mahault and the fish and creole restaurant **La Payotte** (✆ 20 01 94).

✆ *(590)–* ### Directory

You can reach La Désirade with Air Guadeloupe on scheduled flights (twice daily, reservations ✆ 82 47 00) or by ferry, leaving daily from the marina at St François. Yachts also take day trips from the marina.

When on the island, you can reach a **taxi** on ✆ 20 00 62 and hire a car or a bicycle through Location 2000 (✆ 20 02 78), who will also take you on an island tour. Alternatively you could **walk** the length of the island in a day. Look out for the ruined buildings of the leper colony near Baie Mahault and iguanas and agoutis. Reef-protected, golden-sand beaches are at Grande-Anse, Le Souffleur and at Baie-Mahault. Island tours and scuba diving can be arranged through Tony Dinane (✆ 20 02 93).

In contrast to La Désirade, Marie Galante has a more typical history for the Caribbean. The land was fertile enough to bear sugar and so in the 18th century it was covered with it down to the last square inch. Sweeps of cane blew in the breezes and every few hundred yards were the cone and sails of a sugar-mill. The cane still grows, but Marie Galante's hundred mills, which once stood proudly at nearly two for every square mile, are run down and are steadily being devoured by tropical undergrowth.

Shaped like a football, Marie Galante is a flat 59 square miles (158sq km) and looks similar to Grande-Terre, just 20 miles (32km) to the north.

The 20,000 inhabitants live on the protected areas of the coast, around the main settlement of Grand-Bourg. Sugar is still important to the economy (there are three remaining distilleries and Marie Galante rum is renowned) and there is some agriculture. The rum is the principal ingredient in the celebrations on Marie Galante, which are so popular with the people from Dominica that on public holidays they come streaming over in small boats to join the *fête*.

The island takes its name from Columbus's flagship, the caravelle *Santa Maria de Galante*, in which he led his second expedition to the New World in 1493. After coasting Dominica and failing to find a harbour, he saw Marie Galante and cruised north. For a while the island became a refuge for the Caribs fleeing the larger islands but in the age of empire it quickly became a strategic base, the first stop on an invasion attempt on Guadeloupe. The Dutch stripped the island systematically in 1676 and the British occupied it a number of times before it finally settled to France in 1815.

There are some very attractive beaches on the western coast of the island, to which the Guadeloupeans come for the weekend. The best are the palm-backed strand at **Vieux Fort** in the northwest and the beautifully calm **Petite Anse** near Capesterre in the southeast and, close by, **Plage de le Feuillère**, where you will find the **Fun Evasion** Mistral windsurfing school (✆ 97 35 21). Scuba diving is available through **Maison Poullet** (✆ 97 75 24).

Inland there are canefields and sugar-mills (*moulins*) on view—the **Moulin de Basse** and one at the **Château Murat**. In the Château, which has been restored to its 18th-century splendour, is the **Eco-Musée de Marie Galante** (*open 7.30–12.30 and 2.30–5.30, mornings only at the weekend; adm free*) dedicated to island traditions and of course the history of sugar. There are a number of sugar factories and rum distilleries: **Distillerie Poisson** in the west and **Distillerie Bielle**, inland at Rabi. North of here is a cave that goes by the name of **Le Trou à Diable** (the Devil's Hole), which goes quite deep underground. You should take a torch and the right footwear if you venture down it.

✆ (590)–   ***Where to Stay and Eat***

There are quite a few places to stay on Marie Galante, some of them are family run and fairly simple, all of them *cheap*. There are about 15 *gîtes* on the island, *see* 'Guadeloupe, Where to Stay', p.274 (✆ 97 64 33) or the Maison de Marie Galante in the main tourist office in Guadeloupe (✆ 97 10 41).

The **Auberge de l'Arbre à Pain**, (✆ 97 73 69) is on rue Dr Etzol in Grand-Bourg and there are seven air-conditioned rooms in a modern house. Near Capesterre, on Petite Anse beach is **Le Touloulou** (✆ 97 32 63, ✉ 97 33 59), bungalows set around a very pretty waterfront terrace restaurant. **Le Soleil Levant** (✆ 97 31 55, ✉ 97 41 65) is not far off the beach, with rooms and apartments; also **Hotel Hajo** (✆ 97 32 76) with just five rooms. In Saint Louis you will find **Le Salut** (✆ 97 10 26), with 15 rooms with fans or air-conditioning and the friendly *gîte* **Le Refuge** (✆/✉ 97 02 95) with a nice view from above the coast. **Au Village de Ménard** (✆ 97 77 02, ✉ 97 15 40) has seven modern and simple bungalows, set around a pool on a clifftop near St Louis, for those who are happy to look after themselves.

Each of the hotels has a dining room (Le Touloulou is good), but there are also plenty of places to eat out in Marie Galante. They are all pretty much in the *moderate* price category. You can find good creole and some Italian fare at **Maria Galanda** (✆ 97 50 56) in Grand Bourg. Two other excellent creole restaurants are **Espace Poirier** (✆ 97 77 05), in the middle of the town in a wooden house with tin roof and balcony surrounded by tropical plants—fish soup and seafood—and **Coté Plage** (✆ 97 76 25), in a wooden buidling above the sea just out of the town.

In Capesterre there is a charming spot at the **Bambou Club** (✆ 97 36 98), where you dine at chequered table-cloths in a tin-roofed dining room with bamboo walls and windows, just off Petite Anse beach. Creole fare: *Bébélé* soup and spiny lobster *à la bambou*. Not far off are two other charming spots: **La Braise Marine** (✆ 97 42 57) and **La Rose du Brésil** (✆ 97 47 39), both for creole fare. In St Louis **Chez Adé** has a pretty setting on a veranda with standing tropical plants. More creole fare: accras, *fricassée de lambi* followed by coconut ice cream. **A-Ka Pat** (✆ 97 05 74) is a very rustic affair right on the waterfront with a wooden terrace under a breadfruit tree. Fish and seafood specialities.

✆ *(590)–*   ***Directory***

There are regular **flights** (usually three a day) from Le Raizet on Air Guadeloupe (✆ 82 47 00) and also on Marie-Galante Aviation (✆ 97 77 02), who also charter out small planes as air-taxis, to Basses airport (✆ 97 82 21) in the south of the island. **Ferries** link Marie Galante to Pointe-à-Pitre several times a day: it's an hour's sail from La Darse in Place de la Victoire. Contact L'Express des Iles (✆ 83 12 45) or Brudey Frères (✆ 90 04 48). The journey brings you to Grand-Bourg or St Louis. A tour to the island can be arranged from Pointe-à-Pitre; ferries and yachts also make the crossing from St François.

Taxis can be contacted on ✆ 97 81 97 and there are **cars and scooters for hire** (best booked in advance) through Dingo Location (✆ 97 76 58), Magauto in Grand Bourg (✆ 97 98 75) or Eurodollar (✆ 97 06 02). It is quite possible to make a tour of the island in a day. Contact Max Savonnier (✆ 97 46 11) or El Rancho (✆ 97 81 60). There is a marina at St Louis.

A general **watersports** operator is Man Ballaou (✆ 97 75 24) in Grand Bourg, who will arrange windsurfing and kayaks as well as **scuba diving.** You can also try Pro Git Mag (✆ 97 97 86). These companies wil also set up excursions inland, including hiking and mountain-biking.

The Saints

The Saints are a collection of small islands that lie 7 miles (11km) south of Basse-Terre. They are volcanic, and rise sharply out of the water to nearly 1000ft, but they look tiny between the colossi of Basse-Terre and Dominica, the next Windward Island down the line. Stand on Le Chameau, the highest point on Terre-de-Haut, and you will feel as though you are on the lip of a swamped volcano crater; the islands make an almost perfectly round bowl.

Two of the islands are inhabited (3000 people in all) and their populations are curiously different. Terre-de-Bas was a plantation island and the people are mostly descended from the Africans taken there as slaves. Terre-de-Haut, on the other hand, was never planted and so there were never many slaves. Instead the islanders were descended mostly from white Frenchmen, originating from Brittany and Normandy—you can still see their blond hair and blue eyes. Their skin does not tan in the sun and it is clear that many of them are inbred. They are renowned fishermen, though, and before the age of baseball caps they would wear strange looking *salako* hats to protect themselves from the sun—white material stretched over a bamboo frame that sits close on the head like a small parasol. These 'coolie hats' are thought to have been brought by a Chinaman in the last century.

The Saints were supposedly named by Columbus in honour of All Saints' Day. They were settled and fortified in 1648 in order to defend the island of Guadeloupe. The ramparts can still be seen on the heights. Nowadays the islands are very peaceful and they have a charming, seductive atmosphere, so much so that there are more than 350,000 visitors each year.

The Battle of the Saints

To British historians, the Saints' most famous moment came in 1782, when the islands had a ringside view of the most decisive naval battle of the period, one which established British dominance in the Caribbean for the next 30 years.

The Battle of the Saints (La Bataille de la Dominique to the French) was fought on 12 April 1782. The British were beleaguered at the time, having recently lost the American War of Independence. De Grasse had successfully cut the British supply lines, and now he was turning to the British Caribbean colonies. His target was Jamaica, the richest British colony, and he was on his way to join the Spanish navy at Santo Domingo to attack it.

Leaving Martinique, de Grasse headed north. He was sighted by Rodney and the chase was on. For three days Rodney shadowed de Grasse without being able to commit him to a fight. Eventually they met off the Saints and the two lines, each of 30 ships, bore down on each other in slow motion in parallel and opposite directions, the French coming from the north. At eight in the morning the first broadside was fired. The fleets filed past one another, cannonading, until 11 o'clock when Sir Charles Douglas, with Rodney on the bridge of the *Formidable*, saw a gap in the French line, just a few ships behind de Grasse's flagship, the *Ville de Paris*. He steered for it and broke through the French line. The ships to his rear followed him through and in the manoeuvre they separated the French flagship from the bulk of the fleet. The French ships, so close together they made 'one object to fire at', were decimated. De Grasse stayed on his flagship, with 110 guns and 1300 sailors, throughout the conflict and when finally she was taken, he was one of only three men left uninjured. The whole scene had been clearly visible from Dominica and the Saints, and as darkness fell ships were seen burning into the night. Five of the French ships were taken and one sunk, and the rest of the tattered fleet headed for Cap Français under Admiral Bougainville and for Curaçao off the coast of South

America. When the two Admirals met, de Grasse is supposed to have said: 'You have fought me handsomely', and Rodney to have replied: 'I was glad of the opportunity'.

In the Second World War the islands saw no action. Fort Napoléon was used as a prison for those Guadeloupeans who disagreed with the decision to side with the Vichy regime.

The Islands

There is one main settlement on Terre-de-Haut, called Bourg, otherwise known as Le Village, which is set on a superb harbour. It has a silent, magical air. There are just four or five very attractive streets of creole houses, almost all of them with red tin roofs. Between the cafés on the waterfront you will see the fishermen who sit and chat over a game of dominoes. Terre-de-Haut is pretty touristy (it sees quite a lot of day-trippers from the mainland), but it handles it well and the island has a charming feel. The best **beach** is in Baie de Pont Pierre, but there is also good sand at Marigot Bay. On the south coast you will find seclusion at Anse du Figuier, named for the tree rather than the leaf, though even fig leafs are discarded at Anse Crawen. On land, all the 'sights' are within walking distance (eventually). The lumbering fortress on the hilltop, **Fort Napoléon** (*open 9–noon; adm*), is the island's principal sight. Completed in 1867, it commands the bay and has a magnificent view to Guadeloupe and down to Dominica. The fort has exhibitions of modern art and a museum of local history (including pictures of the Battle of the Saints) set in the vast, cool stone ramparts. Outside, among the cannon runners in the grass on the once formidable battlements, there is a botanical garden. There are a number of walks around the island Another peak worth climbing is La Bosse du Chameau (camel's hump) at the other end of the island, where the *tour modèle* dwarfs Fort Napoléon and gives a fine view from nearly 1000ft over the whole area.

You can visit **Ilet à Cabri** (Goat Island) where there is another fort, called Fort Joséphine. **Grand Ilet** is a protected sea-bird reserve and can be visited by prior arrangement. **Terre de Bas** has a number of ruined estate buildings inland and a couple of good beaches, including Grande Anse, the site of one of the island's two settlements and the Anse à Dos on the leeward coast.

Saint Jacques

The least known of all the Saints is the island of St Jacques. Christened *Santiago de los Vientos Alicios,* it was jokingly known as 'Jack of all Trades' to the English filibusters who plied their trade of 'cruize and plunder' from its shores. The only historian to mention it is a certain father Jerome Zancarol, who wrote that the food was good, the girls were beautiful and that the islanders' morals were the worst he had come across anywhere in the world. Apparently, sailors have heard the sound of violins on the 61st meridian, but the only record of the island's illustrious story is in *The Violins of St Jacques,* by Patrick Leigh Fermor.

ⓒ *(590)–* **Where to Stay**

Terre-de-Haut has the better places to stay and the most charming of these is the **Auberge des Petits Saints aux Anacardiers** (ⓒ 99 50 99, ⓐ 99 54 51; *moderate*), one of the red-roofed houses on the hills above town, with a terraced dining room and pool looking out over cracking views over the bay and on to the clouded Soufrière on Basse-Terre. Overflowing with antiques, eccentric air, Bengal tigers and little dogs accepted. There are 10 air-conditioned double rooms. The **Bois Joli Hotel** (ⓒ 99 50 38, ⓐ 99 55 05; *moderate*) is tucked away in its own garden at the other end of the island at Anse à Cointre. There are 21 rooms and eight bungalows scattered around a central house where there is a pool and pleasant deck above the sea. Back in Terre-de-Haut's beautiful main bay, beneath Fort Napoléon and beyond the house built like a boat that juts out into the water from a cliff, are two other small hotels, the **Kanaoa** (✆ 99 51 36, ✉ 99 55 04; *moderate*), which is set in attractive creole-style buildings with a waterfront dining terrace, and **Le Village Créole** (*moderate*) with 22 duplexes in a garden of croton and bougainvillea. There are also small guest houses and rooms for rent at good prices (✆ 99 53 83, ✉ 99 55 55; *moderate*). A few villas are available in Terre-de-Haut and some individual rooms can be hired in local houses. In Terre-de-Bas there are some rooms and one hotel, **Le Poisson Volant** (✆ 99 80 47), where there are simple rooms.

The hotels have some good dining rooms, but there is also a clutch of bistros and salad bars set on the waterfront in Bourg. At **El Dorado** (✆ 99 54 31), in a wooden house on the main square you dine on French and creole fare: home-smoked fish and grilled steak; or on pizza. **Le Mouillage** (✆ 99 50 57) is close to the wharf as you arrive and serves creole specialities including *boudin de poisson* (blood sausage from fish) or a conch *fricassée*. The **Centre Nautique des Saintes** (✆ 99 54 25) is right on the waterfront itself and serves grills and local dishes. Out of town you can get typical local food from **Le Triangle** in the western side of town: a charming wooden deck under palms looking over the sand. **La Paillotte** (✆ 99 50 77) in Marigot Bay has a very pretty setting under palm trees around a small gingerbread house. *Lunch only, Wed evenings for dinner and dancing.* In **Terre-de-Bas** there are a couple of very pretty creole restaurants, both on the Plage de Grande Anse, looking back towards Terre-de-Haut: **Chez Eugènette** (✆ 99 81 83), on a blue and white deck right on the sand, and **A la Belle Etoile** (✆ 99 83 69).

In town, there are a couple of waterfront bars including **Nilce's Bar**, where you sit under parasols or inside a pretty wooden creole house, and **Le Café de la Marine** and **Coconuts**. Some restaurants have a bar trade, and there is a night-club, **La Pompierre**, open at weekends.

✆ *(590)–* **Directory**

Getting to the Saints is easy. The islands are linked by many ferries from Pointe-à-Pitre (1 hour's sail) and from Trois-Rivières (20 minutes) on the southern coast of Basse-Terre. Terre-de-Haut has a magnificent harbour and it is a pleasure to see the peaks glide by as you arrive. There are airstrips on both islands and two daily flights from Pointe-à-Pitre to Terre-de-Haut (✆ 99 51 23), but if you do not like flying, beware, because the landing can be a bit hair-raising. There are several daily sailings from Bourg to Terre-de-Bas, often touching Bois-Joli. Terre-de-Bas has an airstrip suspended on a spit of land 100ft above the sea. There are no cars for rent (part of the charm on the island), but on Terre-de-Haut you can **hire a scooter** through ARS (✆ 99 52 63) or X-Becane Lognos (✆ 99 54 08).

Day sails are available through *Sea Lab* (✆ 99 56 10) and a general watersports operator is UCPA in Marigot, Terre-de-Haut (✆ 99 54 94).

Scuba diving is available through Espace Plongée (✆/✉ 99 51 84) and the Centre Nautique des Saintes (✆ 99 54 94).

Saint Martin

French Saint Martin shares an island with Sint Maarten, a member of the Netherlands Antilles (*see* p.394) and it is the smallest island in the world to be shared by two nations. The French half in the north is divided from the Dutch side by an imaginary line, marked only by an obelisk and a Bienvenue/Welkom sign.

Situated at the north of the Eastern Caribbean chain, Saint Martin looks across to British Anguilla and is about 20 square miles (53sq km) in area (the Dutch half is around 17 square miles/44sq km). From afar the island is attractive; its beaches glint yellow against the blue of the sea and inland the yellow-green scrubland rises majestically to hills of 1200ft. About 13 miles (21km) southeast is the other French island '*commune*' of St Barthélemy.

When you arrive, you will find that Saint Martin is crowded and built up. Everything is right here, though, for a trusty French break in the tropics, with windsurfers whistling across the bay and waterfront bistros ideal for lingering and watching a lunchtime fashion-show, even Parisian-trained hairstylists who will come to your hotel room. And in the gourmet restaurants, of which there are plenty, the food is served with customary French flair: a jaunty coquetry and at times a certain infuriating nonchalance.

Beyond the seaside screen of beach chairs and palm trees, you will still find a few pockets of real French West Indian life, with French Caribbean markets and manners. *Zouk*, the music of the French islands of Martinique and Guadeloupe, is heard most in the local clubs.

If anything, over the past few years, Saint Martin has become more French than it was, as large numbers of investors and immigrants from France have come to the island. They expect the place to be as French as possible, and so the *supermarchés* are full of French food and the cars are French. You will even see people playing games of *pétanque*. The population has rocketed with the tourist industry, now by far the largest income-generator. There is a certain French exclusivity in the language, but it is possible to get by in English.

The other major contributor is the French government. Saint Martin is a *commune* in the *Région* of Guadeloupe and it is administered by a *sous-préfet* appointed from Paris. The islanders vote members on to the *Conseil Général* that sits in Basse-Terre, Guadeloupe, and directly in the French elections.

History

Although the two communities on either side of Saint Martin avoided each other for most of their history (a road between the two was not built until earlier this century), it was not always possible: their pasts were occasionally linked and anyway quite similar. Saint Martin's history is included under Sint Maarten (*see* pp.396–7).

Getting Around

If you arrive at the airport on the Dutch side, the easiest way up to the French half is by taxi as hardly any **buses** run past the airport. Buses do run from Marigot down to Philipsburg and up to Grand Case with the occasional link on to Orléans. They leave from the rue de Hollande behind Marigot (fare to Philipsburg about US$1.50) from early in the morning for the workers and they run until about 10pm (not so late to outlying areas). **Hitchhiking** is the normal lottery; there are hundreds of cars but few seem to stop, so you may need a fair amount of patience.

Taxis, however, come two a penny (except in price) and are easily available at both airports and at the hotels. A taxi rank also works from the Marigot waterfront (✆ 87 56 54) and from Sandy Ground (✆ 87 08 08). Sample prices are: **Marigot** to Grand Case—US$8, east coast—US$15, Baie Longue—US$9, Juliana airport—US$8, Philipsburg—US$8.

A morning's **tour** of the island is easily arranged, though there is not much to see except views across Saint Martin to the surrounding islands. Shopping stops and time to pause in the bistros are built in to the tour. Hotel desks will fix one for you (safari buses will pick you up) or you can go through R. and J. Tours (✆ 87 56 20), Tropical Isle Tours (✆ 29 07 04) or St Martin Evasion (✆ 87 13 60). If you would like to take a tour by **helicopter**, Sint Maarten offers that too: Héli-inter Caraïbes (✆ 87 35 88).

For maximum mobility, to score a few duty-free bargains in Philipsburg or go out to dinner in the evenings, hire a car. There are plenty available at around US$45 per day with taxes, jeeps from about US$55. Any foreign licence is valid and driving is on the right. Hotels will arrange for cars to be delivered. The island's three towns do get congested, so leave plenty of time to get to the airport.

Some local firms as well as big international rental companies work from the Dutch side (*see* 'Sint Maarten', p.397) and Avis has an outlet in Marigot (✆ 87 50 60) and Hertz in Nettle Bay (✆ 87 76 69). Local French hire-companies include Sandyg (✆ 87 88 25) in Sandy Ground, Island Trans (✆ 87 91 32) in Marigot, Tropical Auto (✆ 87 94 81) in Marigot and Express Rent A Car (✆ 87 70 98). If you are fond of scams and are prepared to spend a couple of hours being given the hard sell about 'investment in vacationing' in a condominium complex, you can sometimes score a '$50 off your rental bill' voucher. And if you want a scooter or a bicycle, contact Location 2 Roues (✆ 87 20 59) at Galerie Commerciale in Baie Nettlé.

Beaches

There are excellent beaches on both sides of the island (*see also* 'Sint Maarten', pp.398–9). Those nearest the hotels are usually active and lively, but there are some more secluded ones too. Topless bathing is perfectly acceptable here and there are a few nude beaches (Baie de l'Orient is the only official one, but it has been known to happen at Baie Rouge and Baie Longue). Unlike the Dutch side, where hotels often have a shower room you can use, the beaches on the French side tend to be without changing facilities. On the larger beaches there are often concessionaires who will hire out snorkelling and windsurfing equipment. Some of the island's best beaches are on the eastern Atlantic coast, even though the sea is a little rougher there. You may see the word '*anse*' on the French side; it means cove and there are one or two delightful ones to visit. There has been some theft on beaches all over the island and so you are advised not leave belongings unattended.

best beaches

Baie Longue (Long Bay): A cracking mile of soft golden sand on the west of the French side, probably the best beach on the island. The best swimming is at the bottom end (near the Samanna Hotel). Take food and drinks.

Baie des Prunes (Plum Bay): Just around the corner, an afternoon suntrap, but with palms for shade, good snorkelling (but watch out for the rocks when swimming).

Baie Rouge: A fantastic stretch of golden sand with crystalline water that looks north toward Anguilla, liveliest at its eastern end. Huts have parasols, beach chairs and snorkelling gear for hire and drinks for sale. From the eastern end you can swim round to an idyllic smaller cove, **Crique Lune de Miel** (Honeymoon Cove).

Nettle Bay: The built-up strip to the north of Simpson Lagoon that runs into Marigot. The sand is all right and most watersports can be arranged here.

Anse des Pères (Friars' Bay), **Happy Bay:** Two small isolated coves between Marigot and Grand Case. Some watersports and a couple of beach bars on Friars' Bay.

Grand Case: Even the towns are on passable beaches in St Martin; a string of restaurants and bars sit above the water on this stretch of superb sand: sports equipment is available and there are plenty of places to retreat to at the height of the sun.

Anse Marcel: Recently been built up and so the valley is dominated by an infestation of mock-classical gingerbread, but the beach has brilliant white sand enclosed by enormous headlands. A short walk round the western point takes you to the tiny and secluded **Duck Beach.**

Baie de l'Orient: On the east coast as the name suggests, a stunning mile of fine white sand and clear blue water. It is very active at the northern end, with lines of beach chairs and sports on offer (even massage on the beach). There are some swimming areas and some reserved for motorized sports which are available here (even trips on a little sea-plane). Officially the southern end is a naturalist beach and so the odd nudie might wander by.

St Martin also has some off-shore islands in the northeast, where you can go for a day's excursion: the **Ilet Pinel**, not far offshore at French Cul de Sac (from where you can get a ferry) and **Ile Tintamarre**.

beach bars

There are a number of free and easy haunts above the waves in St Martin where you can linger over a beer after a dip. On Orient Bay you will find a whole string of bars, including **Coco Beach, Waikiki Beach, Bikini Beach, Kakao Beach** and **Kontiki Beach**, each with a range of coloured beach chairs out front and most with a covered terrace and tables scattered around a sandy garden; salads, grills and some creole dishes. At the top end is **Pedro's,** where there are beach facilities and a small snack bar.

In Grand Case you might look out for **Calmos Café,** where there are cable-barrels under parasols and golden palms on the sand. On the secluded Friars' Bay you will find **Kali's,** a hip spot run by a rastaman, where you might spend hours admiring the colours of the sea and the sunset to the tune of reggae and dub or just the susurration of the waves. Standard West Indian chicken and fish is served on the wooden deck above the sand. Full moon party. At the other end of the beach is the **Cranberry Café**, which sits on a nice wooden deck above the sand.

Marigot

Like its Dutch counterpart Philipsburg, Marigot has just a few streets, clustered between the sea and a salt-pond, but where the Dutch town looks inwards to its shops, Marigot looks out across the water. It is quite a nice small town, with active areas on two sides where you can sit and linger with just a few distractions between meals.

The old warehouses of the esplanade, **Boulevard de France**, are now fitted out with bistros and streetfront awnings and parasols and there is a new central area on the waterfront with some snack bars, a car park and the local market (*best Wed and Sat mornings*), where there are tourist stalls but also local produce (much of it shipped in from other islands) on sale. Behind, the few streets have recently been restored and you will see the old wrought-iron balustrades of the few town-houses and municipal buildings among the pastel-fronted shopping arcades. The marina **Port la Royale** is another lively area, lined on all sides with restaurants and bars. Some new roads have been built recently in an attempt to alleviate the inevitable problems of traffic.

The town, which takes its name from the swampy area of land that once existed in the corner of the bay (reclaimed long ago), first grew up in the 1680s, when the danger of raids that had forced the islanders inland to Orléans was passed. In the 1760s the fear revived; this time it was navies on the rampage rather than marauding boatloads of pirates, and so **Fort Louis** was constructed on the heights above the town, its outer walls using the contours and rock-formations already there and its inner citadel a separate building. It is neat and well kept and has a few cannon that look across the fine view of Anguilla, from where the old adversaries would nip over at the first sniff of war. The path to the fort leads past the church, with its fresco of a black Virgin in a Caribbean scene, the hospital and the Sous-préfecture, the residence of the island administrator.

Marigot architecture

Around the Island

The road west from the town leads from Marigot Bay and the Simpson Lagoon to Sandy Ground and is lined with hotels and local residences. On the left you will come to the excel-lent **Saint Martin Museum** (*open daily except Sun 9–1 and 3–7, English and French; adm exp*) with very detailed, if quite technical descriptions of the archaeological history of the island: the Archaic or Ciboney Indians, who left shaped shells and stone tools, the Huecoid Arawaks, who are remembered in their pottery and amulets, the Saladoid Arawaks, more intricate pottery with ghostly faces and lastly the Caribs, who left their *zemis,* stone interpretations of their gods. Also colonial artefacts: swords, musket balls and bottles; indigo, cotton and sugar. Finally the early 20th century is remembered in a series of old-time photographs of the island.

Leaving Marigot in the other direction you pass beneath the **Pic du Paradis**, the island's highest point, from where on a clear day there are fantastic views of islands as far away as Nevis (about 60 miles).

Grand Case is really a single shoreside street lined with old and new houses and festooned in tropical greenery, set on the wide sweep of the magnificent Grand Case bay. There is a friendly feel to the place as crowds of tourists come to its excellent restaurants and bars. But there is also something of a local West Indian life here and you might even see a cockfight in a pit at the western end of the village. Other spectator sports include watching the planes come in over the rooftops to land at the airstrip just behind the town. On Sundays there is often a *jump-up* on the beach, with a disco set up on the pier and braziers cooking chicken legs and soldier crabs in their shells.

Beyond here you come to the **Butterfly Farm** (*open daily, 9–4.30pm; adm exp*), which is worth a quick visit. There are 30 or so tropical species from around the world. To a background of suitable music you will see them through their two-week lifespan: from caterpillar and then chrysalis, like jade and electric blue earrings, through emergence, flight, feeding (on the over-ripe fruits left lying around), more tipsy flight, mating and then death. Species include the *owl* butterfly, the *zebra,* the *postman* and huge *monarchs.*

Orléans, or the French Quarter as it is sometimes called, is a collection of villas and one or two shops, which used to be the capital of the French half of the island in the early days.

✆ (590)– **Where to Stay**

Until recently it was the Dutch side that had the block resort hotels, thrown up by speculators as an investment, but they have arrived in Saint Martin too. However there are also a few more stylish places to stay dotted around the island, such as the French West Indian inns. Except in guest houses, the rates quoted usually include breakfast. A small government tax of 5% is added to your bill and service is 10% or 15%.

luxury

La Samanna, PO Box 4077, 97064 St Martin Cedex (✆ 87 64 00, ✆ 87 87 86, US ✆ (1 800) 854 2252), is an enclave of super-luxury set above the magnificent sweep of Long Bay in the west of the island. The main house, with its palm-thatched dining room with wicker chairs, stands on a bluff above the pool and sea, and the 80 extremely elegant and comfortable rooms, suites and villas are ranged right behind the sand, set in pretty tropical gardens. A theme of stark white and royal blue, the colour of the sea on a bright day, runs through the resort. Top-notch service and comfort and a simply superb sunset. Every comfort to give you the ultimate rest-cure (weights room, massage and beauty treatments, 24-hour room service). Certainly the most elegant place on the island to stay as well as the most expensive. The **Privilège**

Resort and Spa, Anse Marcel, 97150 (✆ 87 38 38, 📠 87 44 12, UK res ✆ (0800) 964470, US res ✆ (1 800) 874 8451) has a rarefied position high on the side of the hill in Anse Marcel in the north of the island. There are 37 rooms, some perched with a cracking view towards Anguilla, pleasant and comfortable, with bright Caribbean decor and all the necessities for a luxurious life (TV, VCR, radio, minibars). The hotel specializes in spa treatment with massages, shiatsu, lymphatic drainage, tonic cure, hydrojet, seaweed body mask, algotherapy, water jet steam room...and there is a sports centre: weights room, tennis, golf practice, squash, raquetball and shuttles down to the beach below. If you need a body-holiday there's plenty on offer here, and the atmosphere is quite brisk and efficient.

very expensive–expensive

In the cluster of hotels at the top of Orient Beach, the most comfortable is probably the **Esmeralda Resort**, PO Box 5141, 97071 St Martin (✆ 87 36 36, 📠 87 35 18), which has 51 units set in pretty terraced villas that echo the best of old Caribbean style with louvres, verandas and gently sloping roofs. The rooms, which look onto their own pool, have all you need in the way of 20th-century comfort with wicker furnishings, king-sized beds, TVs, phones, safes and kitchenettes. Sports on offer right on the sand, but a fine place to sit and relax on an old-time veranda.

Surrounded by all the activity of the marina at Oyster Pond, **Captain Oliver's**, 97150 St Martin (✆ 87 40 26, 📠 87 40 84), has an easy, nautical feel. There are 35 rooms, all brightly decorated with white tiles and pastel colours, with balconies overlooking the marina or the offshore islands towards St Barts. Kitchenettes in the rooms. Covered bar of dark wood with a pool one side and the harbour the other, where the boats dock. The hotel is not on the beach, but there is a large pool on the point and a boat taxi will take you across to Dawn Beach. Watersports and of course sailing (it is a Moorings hotel).

If you like a large and active resort there are two good options. Try the the **Nettle Bay Beach Club**, PO Box 4081 (✆ 87 68 68, 📠 87 21 51), where horseshoes of cottages and villas stand around pools on a windy waterfront and passable beach in Nettle Bay near Marigot. Comfortable suites and rooms, some with kitchenettes, decorated with tile floors and bamboo furniture; watersports available and tennis courts, some evening entertainment. Or you can try the Hotel **Mont Vernon**, BP 1174 Baie Orientale, 97062 St Martin (✆ 87 62 00, 📠 87 37 27, US office ✆ (212) 673 3660, *www.interknowledge.com/st-martin/mont-vernon*), a large three-star hotel which sits on a hillside above Orient beach. Lots of watersports and evening entertainment.

Another nice spot, with the advantage of being just above Orient Beach is the Hotel **La Plantation**, which has 49 rooms (16 suites and 33 studios) in styles that reflect old Caribbean architecture: wood-tiled roofs that reach over verandas with carved wooden balustrades and louvres (they can be closed off and air-conditioned or opened up to the breeze. Inside they are comfortable and modern, though with cable TV and phones. There are two restaurants.

In Grand Case, the hotel **Pavillon Beach**, PO Box 5133 (✆ 87 96 46, 📠 87 71 04), stands high above the sand. It is in a modern building which stands tall on the waterfront and has 17 compact studios and suites with kitchenettes, and a pretty terrace with balustrade from which to admire the sea.

Grand Case also has a number of smaller mid-range hotels and guest houses. Most do not have pools, but they are right above the waves. A stylish spot is the **Hévéa Hotel**, 163 boulevard de Grand Case (✆ 87 56 85, ✆ 87 83 88), which is set in and around a restored colonial house across the road from the beach and in more modern buildings behind. Some rooms have been redone in old West Indian style, with muslin bed-netting and dark wooden furniture. There is a nice dining area and a sitting area where the guests gather and read the books scattered around or chat in the early evening. **Chez Martine**, PO Box 637, Grand Case (✆ 87 51 59, ✆ 87 87 30), has just five large and comfortable air-conditioned rooms and one suite giving on to a large terrace in a house in Antillean style, carpeted and with some king-sized beds with wicker headboards. Quite private and quiet, and a nice restaurant on a terrace right above the waves. The **Grand Case Beach Motel** (✆ 87 87 75, ✆ 87 26 55) has just a few simple rooms in a concrete block right above the sand.

cheap

If you are happy to explore from a base that is quite isolated in the Quartier d'Orléans on the east coast, then you will find a friendly reception at **Gracie Mansion** (✆ 87 41 56). Set in a modern block at the roadside, the studios and suites are comfortable and breezy and overlook the sea to the offshore islands from a terrace. Some kitchenettes. In the backstreets of Marigot beneath Fort Louis you will find **Cigalon** (✆ 87 08 19). The rooms are a little enclosed but there is a nice terrace with vines growing over it from where you can watch town life go by. The **Rising Sun Inn** (✆ 87 33 52) has just 12 simple and air-conditioned rooms overlooking the lagoon near Orléans on the east coast. Also **Fleming's Corner** (✆ 87 70 25). There are also some cheapish places to stay on the Dutch side (*see* p.402).

✆ *(590)–* **Eating Out**

Eating out is something of a pastime in Saint Martin and there are some excellent restaurants on the island—offering both classical French cuisine and its creole counterpart. In fact between them, the two sides of the island have about 500 places to eat, so if you are one for a gastronomic steeplechase, there is plenty to occupy you here. Most of the restaurants serve basically French food which has been adapted to fit the climate: *'cuisine française aux parfums des îles'* as one restaurant expressed it neatly. Pretty well anything you would want to eat will be served here —duck, oysters, some venison— some of which don't really belong to the Caribbean. It is all imported daily from Miami. There is not really any need to dress up anywhere in the island except in the smartest hotels, but most restaurants would prefer you not to go in shorts during the evening. Prices are not cheap, but on the French side at least service is *compris*. Categories are arranged according to the price of a main course: *expensive*—US$20 and above; *moderate*—US$10–20; *cheap*—under US$10. For restaurants on the Dutch side, *see* pp.402–4.

expensive

Grand Case calls itself the 'gourmet capital of Saint Martin' and has a string of excellent restaurants. They all make the best of their settings on the waterfront—at night their lights shine out into the bay like a bar code—and so you will find yourself sitting at the edge of a terrace right above the waves. Most of them offer fundamentally French fare with a concession to the Caribbean in the lighter sauces and the mix of fruits and other spices. Perhaps the finest is the **Fish Pot** (✆ 87 50 88) which is set on a very elegant veranda with dark-stained wood and blue and white furnishings suspended above the beach, where birds twitter along in their own search for food while you dine. Start with sea scallop kebab in a coconut mango sauce or *soupe des poissons des Caraïbes* followed by a *filet de daurade coriphène* in a lemon and Jamaican pimento sauce or a *magret de canard*. You will also find an air of well-ordered calm at **Le Tastevin** (✆ 87 55 45), where you sit on a charming waterfront dining room among palm tree trunks and tropical foliage, with some alcoves reaching out towards the waves. Again French cuisine and some creative concessions to Caribbean flavours—*rosaie de St Jacques aux fruits de la passion* (scallops in a passion fruit sauce) and *médaillons de thon* (tuna) *sur un lit d'aubergine*. A third excellent option in the town is the **Rainbow** (✆ 87 55 80), which is a little more casual in style, and where the food is studiedly simple, but is equally as good. Here too you can also sit right above the water. You can start with a compendium of tastes in the *noix de St Jacques, terrine de saumon et crevettes, au beurre Nantais* followed by a *filet de vivanneau* (snapper) *au croustillant de parmesan d'oignons*.

In **Marigot**, there is an ever-popular dining room at **La Vie en Rose** (✆ 87 54 42), which has a commanding view over the waterfront square from the first-floor balcony with white and pink candy awnings. Innovative French cuisine is what they boast—try *les tournedos d'espadon et de thon aux cinq poivres* (sword-fish and tuna in five peppers) or *filet de vivaneau en croûte et sa crème de safran et caviar*. A rose for the lady at the end of dinner and an impressively large bill.

moderate

Just across from here is **La Maison sur le Port** (✆ 87 56 38), which serves French fare on a very pretty veranda with the lights of the Marigot waterfront ahead of you: duck in a passion-fruit sauce or a *filet de bœuf en brioche, sauce forestière*. Back in Grand Case **L'Escapade** (✆ 87 75 04) is a charming, family-run restaurant where you dine on the waterfront veranda attached to an old creole house. There are two cocktail rooms in the older part of the house and then you move above the water to dine on French and creole cuisine. Start with a lobster bisque and then try *mahi mahi* in a vanilla sauce or a *tartare de thon et sa mousseline de raifort* (raw tuna tartane with horseradish), followed by one of the many fruit ice creams. Not far off there is another charming setting at **l'Auberge Gourmande** (✆ 87 73 37), in a stone town house with louvred windows and doors opening on to the street. Friendly and intimate dining room for Caribbean and French fare: *millefeuille de mahi-mahi au beurre de citron et orange* (pastry-caked mahi mahi with orange and lemon butter sauce) or *poulet poche aux pommes at au cidre* (chicken breast in apples and cider).

There is a number of good restaurants serving **creole** food scattered around the island. One of the liveliest has the very original setting of an old wooden creole house: **Le Bistrot Nu** (✆ 87 97 09), which is hidden in an alley in the backstreets of Marigot (on the left as you leave Marigot to the north, opposite the school). Paysanne salad and provençale scallops, even a *boudin,* a creole blood sausage. It is fun, but it is small, so you have to be quite flexible about when you eat. *Open daily, 6.30–midnight, except Sun.*

In Sandy Ground the other side of Marigot you will find **Le Jardin Créole** (✆ 87 99 56) at the end of Eagle Road, in a waterfront setting of antique stone arches trained with greenery, flaming torches and waves lapping beneath you. Start with *petits boudins des Antilles* (creole sausage with nutmeg) and the best of Anguillan rock lobster in island thyme with a creole sauce or coraline butter. Just across the bridge you will find **Le Palmier** (✆ 87 50 71) on the terrace of a private house. Simple menu: *vivanneau sauce créole, lambi pané* (breaded lambi). *Closed Mon.*

Another good bet is **La Rhumerie** (✆ 87 56 98) in the valley of Colombier, which serves French and creole food on a small veranda in the countryside where you are surrounded by the encroaching jungle and the ringing of the tree frogs. You start with one of a volley of flavoured rums (in keeping with the name of the restaurant)— *maracudja* (passion fruit), *cajou* (cashew) and *quenette* (guinep). The tables are set with creole madras tablecloths, and you can get a good *boudin créole* followed by *blanquette pêcheur* or a *lambi à l'Antillaise. Dinner only, closed Thurs.*

Finally **Chez Yvette** (✆ 87 32 03) is hidden away in the Quartier d'Orléans, but serves excellent West Indian cuisine; lobster or conch stew or a seafood plate. *Closed Wed.* You can always get a pizza or a simple plate in the restaurants which line the waterfront in the Port Royale Marina in Marigot.

cheap

In Marigot you can eat quite cheaply in all the café/bars along the waterfront, where there are often evening grills. Grand Case has some pleasant places to eat for a (relatively) cheaper meal. At the **Cha Cha Cha** Caribbean Café there is a tapas garden with tables set around a sea almond tree and there is a cool beach-side setting at **Calmos Café**, where you eat under parasols and palm tees. But one of the best places to eat is at **Les Lolos**, where the food is cooked in front of you on flaming grills in the neat new building at the roadside: Jimbo Lolo, Chez Germaine, Cool Out Bar, Starzie's Place, Chez Cheryl and Talk of the Town. Grilled chicken, ribs, lobster, shrimp, stuffed crab, johnny cake, macaroni, plantain and rice and peas, take away or sit in at the easy-going waterfront bars. There are more 'Lolos' in Marigot at the roadside by the stadium on the road out to Grand Case.

Bars and Nightlife

In the old trading warehouses in downtown Marigot you will find a couple of cocktail bars patronized by hip chicks and cool dudes—the **Bar de la Mer** and **L'Arhawak,** right opposite one another, are always popular, often with live music. On the **Terrace des Naufrages** (shipwreck terrace) in Port Royale marina there are endless cafés where you can linger over an ice cream or a carafe of wine: **La Belle Epoque, Les Cocotiers** and **Le Bistrot des Arts.** In Nettle Bay, **Le Circus** is a video bar with a stray car in the dining room—pizzas and beer, rock music. Between Grand Case and the Baie de l'Orient is **Surf Club South,** which can get quite lively.

getting there

By air: Most flights arrive at Juliana airport on the Dutch side of the island (code SXM), which has excellent services and is the hub for the area. *See* 'Sint Maarten, Getting There', p.405, for details of flights into Juliana airport from Paris (Air France ✆ 29 02 02, and charters AOM, ✆ 29 25 25 and Air Liberté), Amsterdam (KLM), Italy (the charter airline Comitour), Miami and New York (American Airlines ✆ 87 70 40) and San Juan in Puerto Rico (their sister airline American Eagle), and connections to other Caribbean islands.

Espérance airport (code SFG) near Grand Case cannot take jet aircraft, but some hopper flights do put in here: Air St Martin (✆ 87 10 36), Air Guadeloupe (✆ 87 53 74) from Pointe-à-Pitre, Air St Barts (✆ 87 73 46, ✆ 27 67 03) and Air Caraïbes (✆ 87 84 80). The last two offer charter services as well. If you would like to charter a **helicopter** for a sightseeing trip or for a transfer to another island, contact Trans Hélico Caraibes (✆ 87 21 87) or Heli Inter (✆ 87 35 88).

By sea: There are daily **ferry** links to St Barts, on the Gustavia Express out of St Martin (✆ 27 77 24). There is also a ferry from Blowing Point, Anguilla to Marigot if you wish to go across for the day (20 min; US$20 return); departures about every half-hour. There is a departure tax of US$10.

tourist information

France: 96 rue de Rivoli, 75004 Paris (✆ 1 42 77 91 70, ✆ 1 44 59 22 75).

USA: 10 East 21st Street, Suite 600, New York, NY 10010 (✆ (900) 990 00 40, (212) 529 8484, ✆ (212) 460 8287).

Venezuela: Av Libertador Torre Maracaibo, Piso 11, Oficina F, Caracas (✆/✆ (582) 761 57 60).

There is a small tourist information office (✆ 87 57 23, ✆ 87 56 43, *sxmto@aol.com*, *www.interknowledge.com/st-martin*) on the waterfront in Marigot; open weekdays 8.30–1 and 2.30–5, Sat 8 to noon. If you think you might be spending time on the beach, remember to make a selection from the superabundance of tourist literature that litters the airport when you arrive. Of all the magazines, the most revealing and best informed is the joint publication *Discover*, which has some features alongside the normal tourist advice. *Reflets* is the official Tourist Board publication and there are a number of dining guides. *Radio St Martin* on FM 101.5 plays a good variety of Caribbean music.

To **telephone** Saint Martin from abroad, the **IDD code** is ✆ (590) followed by the six-digit local number. Within Saint Martin, dial just the six digits. Phoning from the French to the Dutch side, dial 3 and then the five-digit number, and from the Dutch to the French side dial 06 followed by the six digits. There are no coin-boxes on the French side and so you will need to buy a *télécarte* from the post office or the few newsagents that stock them.

In a medical **emergency**, there is a hospital in Marigot (✆ 87 87 67).

festivals

Carnival is celebrated at the beginning of Lent with street parades in Marigot and Grand Case on Mardi Gras and Mercredi des Cendres (on the Dutch side, Carnival is at Easter). In

May there is the **Saint Martin Food Festival** in which island crafts, recipes and drinks are displayed (and offered for tasting) to steel band and 'old-time' band music. The **Heineken Regatta** is held annually in March in both parts of the island. More official celebrations include **Bastille Day** (14 July), which sees fireworks, and **St Martin's Day** celebrated on 11 November with joint ceremonies with the Dutch side. Grand Case celebrates **Schoelcher Day** (21 July) with sailing races in traditional island vessels and a general blow-out.

money

The official currency of Saint Martin is the French franc (US$ = Fr5.5 approx). However, with so many visitors from America, the greenback is accepted everywhere. In local shops and eateries you may receive your change in francs and centimes. You will find that, unofficially, the exchange tends to be done at US$1=Fr5, which does not represent a good deal for the punter. Netherlands Antilles guilders or florins (the currency of the Dutch side) will not be accepted. Credit cards are widely accepted all over the island.

Banks: There are three banks in Marigot and they keep different hours, so you can usually find somewhere to change money during the day. Hotels are always willing to change money, but the rate will not be so good.

Shops: Hours as in France: weekdays 9–1 and 3–7. In Marigot you might try **Oro de Sol** for watches and **Cartier** for jewellery.

watersports

St Martin caters quite well for watersports around its beaches, around the hotels and particularly on Orient Beach, the liveliest on the island, where you can fix anything from beach volleyball and parasailing to a round-island guided tour by jet-ski (© 27 49 94). Most hotels have sailing dinghies for hire and they will usually lend to somebody from outside. General watersports operators in Nettle Bay include Blue Ocean International (© 87 89 73) and Kontiki Watersports (© 27 49 94).

Windsurfing: Very popular on the French side of the island and marginally cheaper there. You can get a board in Nettle Bay or Grand Case, but the winds are best on the east coast, where Baie de l'Embouchure is a good place to learn because of the gentler sea and onshore winds, and Orient Bay is the one to head for if you like speed sailing. Try Orient Watersports (© 87 40 75) and Windsurfing Club Nathalie Simon (© 87 48 16), who can help all standards of windsurfers.

Day sails: Lots of possibilities in St Martin, arranged through the hotel concessionaires or watersports shops. Some day cruises go to other islands like Anguilla—*Sea Hawk* (© 87 59 49) or *Elea* (© 27 34 93) and St Barts—MV *Voyager* (© 87 10 68).

Deep-sea fishing: Trips can be arranged (about US$700 for a full day) at the marinas. There are good fishing grounds off the Anguillan islands, where you can cast for bonito and spiked-back wahoo. Contact CSB (© 87 89 38) in Port la Royale Marina.

Snorkelling: There are excellent corals (do not pick any or use a spear-gun against the fish, as they are protected) in places off Saint Martin, particularly off the northeast of the island, where there is a reserve. The best beaches are Baie Rouge near the western point of the island and Green Cay opposite Orient Beach on the Atlantic side (also Ilet Pinel and Tintamarre). There are many glass-bottom boats and a large semi-submersible, **Seaworld Explorer** (departs from Grand Case, contact on the Dutch side, ✆ 24078).

Scuba diving: You will see the reefs patrolled by sergeant-major fish and grunts off the bay of Grandes Cayes on the shoreline and offshore round the islands in the northeast. Dives and instruction (PADI and NAUI) are available through Blue Ocean Dive Centre (✆ 87 89 73) at the Pirate Hotel in Marigot, Octoplus (✆ 87 20 62) in Grand Case and Scuba Fun Caraïbes (✆ 87 36 13) in Anse Marcel. A single-tank dive costs around US$45.

Yachting: There are three marinas where yachts can be hired for a day, a week or a month out on the water, perhaps on a trip to a neighbouring island. The biggest is Port de Lonvilliers in Anse Marcel, where you will find Stardust Marine (✆ 87 40 30, ✆ 87 40 31) with yachts and pleasure craft for hire, and Nautor's Swan Charter (✆ 87 35 48, ✆ 87 35 50). Sunsail (✆ 87 83 41, ✆ 87 11 61) are based at the Port Royale Marina on the lagoon in Marigot and the Moorings are at Captain Oliver's Marina on the east coast (✆ 87 35 26, ✆ 87 32 54).

St Barthélemy

St Barthélemy is one of the most chic, civilized and least-known parts of France. Here bronzed beauties cruise by on the beaches in just a nuance of a bathing costume and out in the bay the water whistles with windsurfers in red, white and blue. Dior, Chanel, Lacroix, jazz, restaurants to linger in, haute cuisine and Veuve Cliquot champagne. It is a chichi 20th-century playground, as only the French could conceive. Even the tourist brochures are stylish and sexy in St Barts.

Lying 15 miles (24km) southeast of Saint Martin in the north of the Lesser Antilles, St Barts is a crooked 6 miles by 3 or 4 (10 x 5km)—folds of volcanic lava and rubble that have been pushed up from beneath the ocean and sprouted a mantle of scrub. The fragmented coastline has some lovely coves, many of them culminating in perfect strands. There is an admirable neatness about the place and it is very attractive, as well as surprisingly rugged for an island of its size. St Barthélemy (pronounced 'San Bar-tailer-mee' in French) is the island's formal name, but it is hardly ever used. It is usually known as Saint Barth in French and St Barts in English. There are 6000 islanders.

Strangely, for much of the 19th century, St Barts belonged to Sweden and it was turned into a successful trading outpost. But they wave baguettes happily in the streets nowadays. Despite their interlude as Swedes, the St Barthéleminois are mostly descended from French settlers and you might see a traditional bonnet or hear a snatch of a strange French dialect in one of the original villages. The population has always been quite white because there were never many slaves.

As the tourist industry has steadily grown in the last 30 years, St Barts has taken on an overlay of the République—there is practically no recognizable West Indian culture outside the cultivated prettiness of the tropical gardens—and has turned from one of the quietest Caribbean

other sports

Hiking: A number of trails have been cut into the Saint Martin scrub, taking in the Mont des Accords and the Pic Paradis, which give cracking views of the islands and lowlands. The island's limited **flora** and **fauna** ranges from soldier crabs in their conical shells to the mournful white cattle egret on land and the yellowlegs who scurry around the mangrove swamps. Contact Action Nature (© 87 97 87) and Fun Raid Tour (© 87 59 24).

Paragliding: Contact the local Parapente Club (© 87 81 09).

Mountain-biking: This has recently grown up on the island and there are now trails cut all over the place. Contact Bike Power Cycle (© 87 13 74) or Frog Legs (© 87 87 05 11).

Riding: An early-morning dip on horseback can be arranged through Bayside Riding Club (© 87 36 64) near Orient Bay or OK Corral in Oyster Pond on (© 87 40 72).

Tennis: There are about 50 courts on the island, many of them lit for night-play. Contact any of the larger hotels.

Golf: There is a course on the Dutch side, at the Mullet Bay Resort (© 42081); green fees are very high, US$125 for the 18 holes, and residents of the hotel have preference in teeing off.

islands in the area into a trusted home-from-home for expatriate French. Like many Caribbean islands it was raffish and eccentric in the early years and there was no telling whom you might rub shoulders with in the bars. Nowadays it has less of the raw edge and a more professional, thoroughgoing attitude to tourism.

They do it with gusto and aplomb, though, and it is easy to have an excellent holiday in St Barts. There are excellent restaurants with huge wine cellars (some restaurateurs actually ship young in St Barts because it travels better), there are art galleries in the hotels foyers and fashion shows in the beach bars to amuse you over lunch. The island is a little *snob* at times, but people are on holiday, so it is generally friendly. It is the favoured haunt of a crowd of transient millionaires on their crusade against winter.

History

St Barts was not visited by Columbus, but later travellers called the island after his brother, Bartolomeo, who went with him to the New World. Like the rest of the Leewards it was given a wide berth by the Spanish colonists for their first hundred years because *Ouanalao*, as the Caribs knew the island, was dangerous cannibal country.

Settlers came in 1659, ekeing a living out of the scrubby, difficult ground with such crops as tobacco and indigo, but the main source of income for the next hundred years really lay in the island's position and in its well-protected coves. Smugglers and pirates, en route from South America to the Bahamas, would use the bays to repair their ships, and the islanders made a tidy profit by selling them the provisions they needed to refit.

The original St Barthians were Frenchmen from Normandy and Brittany. They had a few slaves, domestic ones only because there were no plantations. Even late in the 18th century there were still less than 1000 inhabitants on St Barts.

Then, on 1 July 1784, the St Barthians woke to find that their island was no longer owned by France, but that they were on lease to Sweden. The King of France had simply swapped it for a warehouse in Gothenburg and for trading rights in the Baltic, without even consulting them. St Barts was Sweden's only colony in the Caribbean and little remains of their influence except the old stone warehouses on the waterfront and a few street names in Gustavia, the capital. For the romantic story of how it all came about, *see* the history of Tobago (pp.109–10), King Gustav's original choice for his Caribbean base.

The Swedish reign benefited the islanders, however. King Gustav promptly declared the island a free port and before long St Barts was using the advantage of its position on the trade routes from Europe to the burgeoning United States and prospering as a market. While the other islands were held to ransom in the wars at the turn of the 18th century, St Barts continued to rake in the loot.

As soon as peace came to the Caribbean in the early 19th century and the seaborne trade waned, the island fell into a decline and the Swedish venture failed. The population, which had reached as high as 5000, began to tail off, particularly after the Swedish king emancipated the island's slaves in 1847. There was no land for the freed slaves to settle so they emigrated, mostly to the American Virgin Islands (there was another, later emigration to the USVI in the 1950s). In the end, King Oscar II put sovereignty to a referendum, and the islanders voted 351 to 1 to return to French rule. On 16 March 1878 St Barts was handed back to France.

Appended to Guadeloupe once again, the island's decline continued. When Guadeloupe was made an overseas Département of France in 1946, St Barts became one of its *communes*, under its financial control. St Barts has retained its duty-free status since Swedish days.

Today it is administered, along with nearby Saint Martin, by a *sous-préfet* appointed from Paris. The islanders vote members on to the Conseil Général and the Conseil Régional, which sit in Basse-Terre, Guadeloupe, and directly in the French elections. Like Saint Martin, St Barts receives some assistance from the French Government via Guadeloupe for roads and large municipal projects. Tourism is the big earner at the moment and the island maintains an exclusive and luxurious style.

Getting Around

Taxis are usually available at the airport during the day and on the main quay in Gustavia, though it is occasionally difficult to get one after dinner in the evening. You can also order them through a hotel or through the central number (✆ 27 66 31). Gustavia to the airport will set you back US$6. There is no bus service on St Barts, but hitching is a reasonably dependable way to get around the island.

Car hire: Recommended. It is fairly expensive, but of course it gives you much more flexibility. The island favourite is the Suzuki jeep (it used to be the mini-moke and its Volkswagen equivalent, the Gurgel, but they have mostly disappeared now), which can just about cope with St Barts' many steep hills. Some of the big international names operate out of the airport and many hotels keep cars for their guests. If you will want one during the high season, you should order it in advance. A foreign driving licence is valid, credit cards are accepted, driving is mostly on the right and many companies will deliver to your hotel. The minimum price in season is about US$35 a day plus taxes.

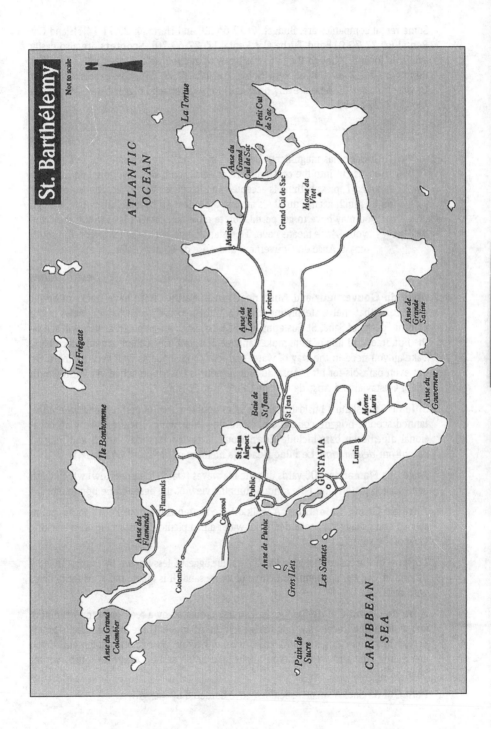

St. Barthélemy

Not to scale

Some rental companies are: Budget (✆ 27 66 30) and Hertz (✆ 27 71 14), Island Car Rental (✆ 27 70 01) and Turbe Car Rental (✆ 27 60 70). **Scooters** are also easily available for hire, though they are less likely to get you up the steep hills. Try Chez Béranger (✆ 27 89 00) or Rent Some Fun (✆ 27 70 59), the exclusive Harley Davidson dealer (if there are any on island) for scooters and bigger bikes, or St Barth Motos (✆ 27 67 89).

Beaches

St Barts has magnificent beaches, mounds of golden sand tucked away in coves cut into the coastline, protected on both sides by mountainous headlands. Topless bathing is accepted and happens everywhere, but surprisingly on a French island, nudity is against the rules. All beaches are public, though you may have to get permission to cross somebody's land (ask if they stop you). *Anse* means cove. The island's two best beaches are on the south coast: Anse du Gouverneur and Anse de Grande Saline.

best beaches

Anse du Gouverneur and **Anse de Grande Saline**: Both have stacks of bright white sand that shelve steeply into the sea in their own deep bays, with views of the volcanic peaks of Saba, St Eustatius and St Kitts. Both are popular, as you will see by the hundred-yard line of mini-mokes and jeeplets, but as yet there are no beach bars. Take all you need in the way of water and food, and shade as well because there are not even parasols for hire. Anse du Gouverneur is best approached via Lurin (south out of Gustavia) and Anse de Grande Saline from St Jean.

St Jean: The island's busiest beach; a calm double curve of perfect sand where the tanned scooter-brigade congregate, exercising their windsurfers or taking an occasional dip. Beach bars include **Eden Rock**, a pretty veranda retreat, and for real beachfront *dégustation*, **Le Filao Beach** (a member of '*Relais et Châteaux*').

Anse des Flamands: 600 yards of quite big waves (watch the undertow) which wash large scallop patterns into the sand; a stunning view of the deserted Ile Bonhomme.

Anse du Grand Colombier: A walk off the beaten track from Petit Morne, palm-shaded and usually very secluded (take water and a picnic). West facing, so a cracking view of the sunset.

Lorient: In the east of the island as the name suggests, less known by tourists than by fishermen, but has a magnificent curve of white sand. It is quiet, and good for families with children.

Anse du Grand Cul-de-Sac: A shallow bay protected by a reef; good for swimming and windsurfing (receives winds straight off the Atlantic). There are a couple of hotels here, where you can get a drink and a meal or borrow watersports equipment. If you are feeling chic and wealthy, you might take lunch at **Le Lafayette Club**, winter haunt of the stars.

Petit Cul de Sac: A smaller secluded cove bordered by mangrove.

Anse de Grand Galet: The closest beach to Gustavia (about 10 minutes' walk), where shells are washed up in piles of pink and orange on the soft light-brown sand. Beyond the town to the north is another suntrap beneath the hills, in the fishing village of **Corossol**. Just down from the nets and the boats there is a strip of beige sand so soft that you sink up to your shins and a cracking sunset view.

Gustavia

Only hints of a Swedish heritage remain in St Barts' capital after a hundred years and the recent tourist redevelopment. Almost all of the original Swedish town was destroyed by hurricane and a fire in 1850, and only a couple of houses remain in use (on the rue Sadi Carnot and the rue Jeanne d'Arc). But the streetnames: Vikingagatan, Hwarfsgatan, and Ostra- and Westra-Strandgatan on the harbour waterfront give an unusual impression for the Caribbean. The name Gustavia is taken from the enlightened despot King Gustav III who leased St Barts from France and gave the island the free-port status that enabled it to prosper.

Today the population of Gustavia is just a few hundred, a fraction of what it was 200 years ago when the harbour was filled with merchants and the warehouses were overflowing. Sailing craft are filling the harbour once again, though—the waterfront is given over almost entirely to marina space in season—as they cruise between the Virgin Islands and Antigua. And the port still maintains its mercantile tradition with chic-looking mannequins displaying Christian Lacroix and Gucci clothes at duty-free prices. But it is no longer Swedish in atmosphere: nowadays, with endless bistros, art galleries and police wearing *képis*, the ambience is distinctly French.

At the four points around the harbour stand the tired old fortresses that once guarded Gustavia. It is possible to visit Fort Gustave on the road out of town, from where there is a magnificent view of the harbour. Another remaining Swedish feature of Gustavia is the distinctive triangular-roofed clock-tower known as the Swedish belfry. It stands high above the town next to the **sous-préfecture** (formerly the island prison) and was originally built as a church-tower. The **English anchor** at the head of the harbour is about 200 years old, but it has only been in St Barts since 1981 when it was dragged here by mistake from St Thomas in the Virgin Islands. It was left on the quay and has just become part of the furniture.

Swedish Belfry

The **Municipal Museum** (*open Mon–Thurs 8–noon and 1.30–5.30, Fri 1.30–5, Sat 8–noon; adm*) can be found near the point of the bay, in the Wall House, an old Swedish warehouse that has been restored. On display you will see prints and pictures of old-time St Barts, alongside mock-ups of the traditional cottages and artefacts from island life (including a sling for lifting cows onto boats and a fishing boat). Also displays on the Swedish lineage of the island and some rushwork articles made of the *latanier* palm.

Around the Island

For an island with no peak over 1000ft, St Barts is extremely hilly and rough. There is little rain, not much cultivation, and the hills are infested with scrub, tall torch cactus and the distinctive St Barts palm tree, the *latanier*. For centuries the villagers were completely isolated from one another and would meet only in church after walking for hours along tortuous paths hacked out of the undergrowth. Nowadays the island is cut and crossed with impossibly steep and windy roads and the furthest reaches are occupied by holiday villas. In the narrow valleys you will see mournful white cattle egrets waiting for food while their companions graze.

You might catch snatches of a strange language in the country, the old speech of the islanders' Norman ancestors (the communities were so isolated that people living just 5 miles from one another spoke with a different accent). And you may just still see the womenfolk wearing their traditional frilled bonnets, or *calèches*—starched and prim white hats that keep the islanders' Norman skin protected from the sun. They are nicknamed *quichenottes*, supposedly a corruption of 'kiss-me-not', because it is rather difficult to get another face underneath them.

North of Gustavia the sea road cuts inland to St Barts' small industrial estate at **Public** and then emerges on the coast again at **Corossol**, a charming fishing village, where the houses clutter the slopes of a valley that opens on to the beach. In Corossol they wear the *calèche à platine*, with multiple hems, a frilly border and little chance of scoring a kiss. Farther up the coast in Colombier and in Flamands they traditionally wear the *calèche à batons*, strengthened with wooden slats. There is a private sea-shell collection on view in the town at the **Inter Oceans Museum** (© 27 62 97; *open daily 9–5; adm*), where you can see giant clams with wavy lips and some miniature creations of incredible intricacy.

All over this northern area you will see the *latanier* with its smooth trunk, a tangled confusion of stubs and then a series of fronds that grow like scratchy fans. When dried these leaves are very skilfully woven by the local women into hats, bags and table mats. Corossol is probably the best place to buy them.

East of Gustavia, **St Jean**, the site of the earliest settlement on the island, has become the centre of the tourist industry in St Barts—the old town has been swallowed by recent development and so when you arrive at the airport you are greeted by a neat collection of bistros and chichi boutiques.

As you go east the villas thin out on the hills and old St Barts begins to appear—dry-stone walls and distinctive houses with red roofs and sloping plastered walls. A few fishermen still work out of Lorient Bay. Boobies nest on the clifftops and in the mangroves you may see a pelican digesting a meal in the sun. The road rings the eastern end of the island, around St Barts highest peak, Morne de Vitet (about 930ft), emerging on the southern coast where there are magnificent views as far as Statia and St Kitts and then returning to the north coast at St Jean.

© (590)–

Where to Stay

St Barts has some extremely expensive and sumptuous hotels (none larger than about 60 rooms) in keeping with its exclusive image. You will find everything laid on to make sure that you have the most luxurious time, including life's essentials like art exhibitions in the foyers and on-call hairdressers. More seriously they are run to a very high standard and many are set in delightful tropical gardens. Most hotels have arrangements with car hire companies and will arrange a vehicle for you on request. Some hotels offer considerable reductions in summer packages. Service is usually charged at 10%.

There are also many **villas** to rent on the island. Contact Sibarth, PO Box 55 Gustavia, 97098 Cedex, St Barthélemy (✆ 27 62 38, ✉ 27 60 52); US PO Box 1461 Newport, Rhode Island 02840 (✆ (401) 849 8012, ✉ 847 6290, US toll free ✆ (1 800) 932 3222), UK freephone (✆ (0800) 898 318), France (✆ 05 90 16 20), Germany (✆ 01 30 81 57 30). Also: Ici et Là, Quai de la République, Gustavia (✆ 27 78 78, ✉ 27 78 28) and Saint Barth Immobilier, rue Auguste Nyman, Gustavia (✆ 27 82 94, ✉ 27 64 74).

luxury

Perhaps the most elegant and comfortable hotel on St Barts is in the southeast of the island: **Le Toiny** (✆ 27 88 88, ✉ 27 89 30; UK res (0800) 960 239, ✉ (0800) 968 152 (*Relais et Châteaux* in Paris); France ✆ 1 45 72 96 50, ✉ 1 45 72 96 69, US res c/o Wimco ✆ (1 800) 27 TOINY, ✉ (401) 847 6290). Just 12 one-bedroom and one three-bedroom villas make up the resort, which stands on the hillside, looking over the Anse de Toiny to St Kitts (there is no beach there, but each villa has a pool with a view to infinity). The villas are decorated in old colonial style—wooden parquet floors, mahogany furniture and four-poster beds, replicas from Martinique—but have all the 20th-century luxuries too, down to the two TVs hidden away in cupboards, video recorder, CD player, exercise bike and a shower in the open air. There are kitchenettes, but also room service and an excellent restaurant (the hotel is a member of the Relais et Châteaux chain). Car necessary.

The Hotel **Isle de France**, BP 612 (✆ 27 61 81, ✉ 27 86 83), also offers beach-front sumptuousness on the Baie des Flamands on the north coast. The mock-classical main house stands majestically above the sand, with 12 huge suites, all with sea view and marble floors, antique furniture and some private jacuzzis in outsize bathrooms. Across the road there are 17 slightly smaller but very comfortable rooms and suites in bungalows scattered around the *latanier* garden: also other facilities including the restaurant and sports room with resident trainer. Next door at the end of the beach is the well-hip and idiosyncratic **Taïwana** (✆ 27 65 01, ✉ 27 63 82; *absurdly expensive*). Difficult to recommend personally because guide-book writers (along with anyone else they do not like the look of) are unceremoniously booted out, but the place seems to have an easy exclusivity about it. If you stump up the loot, there's pretty well anything you might want; from helicopter transfer from Sint Maarten and champagne breakfasts to famous acquaintances in the next-door room (which now come in a serried rank of ochre, vermilion and royal blue stucco cottages), and of course privacy (from riff-raff).

The **Guanahani Hotel,** BP 609, 97098 St Barthélemy Cédex (✆ 27 66 60, ✉ 27 70 70, UK res ✆ (0800) 181 123, US res ✆ (1 800) 223 6800, ✉ (212) 758 7367) sits on land that gradually descends towards its own secluded beaches on the Anse de Grand Cul-de-Sac in the east of the island. There are 76 rooms in cottages, brightly painted and furnished with stylish lamps and fittings, each with their own terrace (some with sea view) and 13 with private pools. There is a beach bar, for a break from the endless diet of watersports down on the passable beach, and an à la carte dining room. Quite large, so it can be active (there is some entertainment at night), but you can also shut yourself away.

very expensive

The **Eden Rock** Hotel (✆ 27 72 94, ✆ 27 88 37, UK res (0800) 373 742, France ✆ 05 90 16 20, US toll free ✆ (1 800) 932 3222, ✆ (401) 849 8012) has a charming setting, its reception and dining room settled on top of the Eden Rock of its name, a lump that rises out of St Jean beach on the airport flight-path, and its rooms ranged around its flanks. There are six rooms on the Rock itself, perched right above the water's edge, and eight on the beach, all neatly decorated and extremely comfortable, with all modern comforts. A scene of rich red and green (reflecting the red tin roofs and Caribbean foliage perhaps) runs through the small resort, from the beach bar down below (where there are watersports) to the elegant dining room on the hilltop which is decorated with antiques. Close to all the action of St Jean, the hotel has a friendly and intimate air, carefully managed by its owner, a Yorkshireman. Look out for Hercule the iguana.

The **François Plantation** (✆ 27 80 22, ✆ 27 61 26, US toll free ✆ (1 800) 207 8071, *www.stbarths.com/franplant.html*) stands high on the hillside above Colombier, from where some of the 12 rooms have a magnificent view of the north coast from their private terrace. The estate house has an old-time Caribbean elegance; an antique drawing room and dining room with hefty antique furniture, where you will find classical French cuisine. The rooms stand in brightly painted hillside cottages, old Caribbean 'case' style built anew and set in superb tropical gardens, and they are furnished in dark-stained tropical wood. Quiet and reserved.

A hip spot, beautifully set in a garden of outrageous tropical profusion, is **La Banane**, in Quartier Lorient (✆ 27 68 25, ✆ 27 68 44). Just nine rooms, set in old creole wooden 'cases', all painted in vaguely complementary colours, gathered around a couple of pools with imitation rock waterfalls. Inside the rooms are studiedly eclectic in style, with antique furniture, colourful tiles and louvres on the windows. The bathrooms are excellent, part outdoor and overgrown with tropical flora. Share a shower with a banana plant. Very quiet and comfortable.

expensive

The Hotel **Emeraude Plage**, 97133 St Barts (✆ 27 64 78, ✆ 27 83 08), sits on the beach in the middle of St Jean, 30 rooms in quite tightly clustered bungalows running back from the sand itself in a garden of hibiscus. All rooms have a/c but can be opened up to get the breeze and they have phones and TVs, also a full kitchen. You can be self-contained if you want, but it is a friendly place: there is a central area with a library where guests meet, and it's a good option for families. The **St Barth Beach Hotel** (✆ 27 60 70, ✆ 27 75 57), sits right on the beach in Cul-de-Sac, 36 comfortable rooms in a modern two-storey block. Rooms are comfortable, air-conditioned with bright pastel fittings and there are plenty of watersports right outside.

The Hotel **Baie des Anges**, PO Box 162 (✆ 27 63 61, ✆ 27 83 44), has just ten rooms with kitchenettes on the superb sand of the Anse des Flammands. All modern comforts: a/c, fans, cable TV and video, quite quiet. An excellent option, tucked away in the south of the island in a prodigious garden, is the **Club des Salines,** BP 6 97075 Cedex (✆ 27 73 43, ✉ 27 64 65). It takes its name from the nearby beach, the Anse de Grande Saline. There are just six rooms scattered around the main house and pool, reached by wooden boardwalks through the greenery; they are set in tin-roofed houses with wooden walls and there is antique furniture, including four-posters with muslin nets, to go with the traditional architecture. There is no restaurant, but the rooms have kitchenettes. Extremely quiet, an excellent retreat.

moderate

L'Auberge Petite Anse, PO Box 117 (✆ 27 64 89, ✉ 27 83 09), stands on the clifftop at top the end of the Anse des Flamands, with rooms in the 16 bungalows. In Colombier you will find **Le P'tit Morne**, PO Box 14 (✆ 27 62 64, ✉ 27 84 63), where 14 apartments are in villas that stand high on a hillside overlooking the offshore islands to the north of St Barts. It is in a remote corner of the island and is quiet, but the rooms are fine and there is a pool. There are three cheaper places to stay: the **Sunset Hotel** (✆ 27 77 21, ✉ 27 81 59) in Gustavia has rooms with a/c, fridge, TV and phones and a very bright colour scheme. The **Hotel Normandie** (✆ 27 61 66, ✉ 27 98 83) is set back from the seafront in Lorient on a minor road and has seven rooms with a/c, TV and fridges and small restaurant, a small sitting room and pool. In Pointe Milou, in the area of Lorient you will find 10 rooms in bungalows at the improbably named **Les Igloos** (✆ 27 56 14, ✉ 27 82 72).

cheap

The **Nid d'Aigle** (✆ 27 75 20) is a guest house in Anse des Cayes, way up on the hillside on a extremely steep drive, just three rooms with a pool.

✆ *(590)–*   *Eating Out*

There are some excellent restaurants in St Barts, from pretty hotel dining rooms (these include Filao Beach in St Jean and le Gaïac at Le Toiny, which are both Relais et Châteaux and the dining rooms at François Plantation (La Route des Epices) and Eden Rock) to the waterfront bistros and converted hilltop homes. The cuisine is sometimes heavyweight classical French, but you will usually find concessions to the climate—lighter sauces and exotic ingredients—and even *nouvelle cuisine créole*. Just as in the métropole, eating and restaurants are a way of life, and you will find restaurateurs and a few randomly chosen guests and friends lingering over a bottle of wine long after the kitchen has closed. Dining out in St Barts is expensive, but it is worth remembering that service is *compris*. Many restaurants often set menus as well. Categories are arranged according to the price of a main course: *expensive*—Fr130 and above; *moderate*—Fr70–130; *cheap*—under Fr70.

expensive

Perhaps the most elegant setting with superb, top-notch fare is to be found at **Le Sapotillier** (✆ 27 60 28) in a stone house in the heart of Gustavia. You dine inside or in a vine-covered garden. The menu and the products are mainly French—*ravioli de foie gras* or a *fricassée de grenouilles, concassée de tomates, jus persillé* (frogs' legs fricassee with tomato and parsley sauce) or *a poulet de Bresse* (organically raised in France) *farci aux champignons et au foie gras* (stuffed with mushrooms and foie gras). Stylish, attentive service. **Au Port** (✆ 27 62 36) is another fine restaurant set in the centre of town. You dine upstairs in an old townhouse overlooking the quiet street, on French and creole fare and French recipes which have been créolized: *petit feuilleté de crabe, crème de mangue et papaye* (crab in puff pastry with a mango cream sauce and spicy papaya) or a *massale de cabri, gratin de banane* (goat cooked with curry with a banana gratin). Ever-popular, breezy and chic is **Chez Maya** (✆ 27 75 73), where you sit on a deck festooned with greenery or under a flamboyant tree right above the waterfront in Public, a short drive from town. A short but daily changing menu with fish and creole specialities, including chicken in *sauce chien*. If you are feeling extravagant, you might want to spend a few luxurious hours at the **Le Lafayette Club** (✆ 27 62 51), a beachfront restaurant in a charming setting on a deck overlooking Grand Cul-de-Sac. Grilled fish or marinated raw salmon or a beef fillet with roquefort sauce. Valet parking, fashion to keep you amused while you dine. *Winter season only, lunch only.*

moderate

Vincent Adam (✆ 27 93 22) has a menu at an excellent price (fixed, with six or seven choices) and a charming hillside position above an inland lagoon behind St Jean. You dine on the large gallery of an old Caribbean house, under parasols and full hanging plants. They make a virtue of unpretentious French cuisine—*suprême de volailleau vinaigre et à l'estragon* (chicken breast roasted with tarragon and vinegar)—with some concessions to the Caribbean—*filet de vivanneau en croûte, farci aux petits légumes* (snapper in puff pastry with vegetables)—followed by *crème brûlée*. There is a funny and friendly atmosphere in town at **Paradiso** (✆ 27 80 78), which is set in a pretty house with blue and yellow trelliswork and a terrace outside. French and creole: *ragoût de calamar à l'antillaise, macaroni frais* (creole-style squid stew with fresh macaroni) with daily specials. **La Mandala** (✆ 27 96 96) is worth a visit, at the very least for its fantastic view over the town. It also offers interesting fare: start the evening with *tapas* Caribbean style—*boulettes de lambi* (conch balls), *raviolis de crevettes* (small shrimp ravioli)—and then continue with more senior Caribbean and international dishes. **Inès Ghetto** (✆ 27 53 20, no reservations) has a charming setting in an old wooden Caribbean house which has been opened on one side to give onto a terrace, tropical garden and the open kitchen. A Bohemian feel, but distinctly Caribbean fare on the blackboard menu: *salade de crabe exotique* (with mango sauce) or the *assiette créole* with eight different Caribbean specialities. And not far off **Eddy's Restaurant** (✆ 27 54 17) is set among the original Swedish walls, a covered courtyard with greenery, hanging bamboo lamps and solid teak chairs. A mix of Caribbean and Thai flavours, *reggae* and *zouk* and a well-hip air.

On the far side of the harbour there is a number of bars that double up as restaurants. **L'Escale** (✆ 27 81 06) is ever-popular and offers simple fare presented by waiters who dance for you: pizzas and pastas in comfortable brown cane armchairs on a wooden deck on the bay, good for sitting and watching the activity of the bay. Nearby is **L'Entrepont** (✆ 27 90 60), an Italian restaurant set in a pretty tropical garden with tables under parasols scattered among sea almond trees and palms. Delicate carpaccios followed by pastas and Italian entrées: best pizza in town. Back in town there is a string of easy-going haunts with reliable fare. At **Côté Jardin** (✆ 27 70 47), just off rue Gambetta, you eat Italian and southern French food on a veranda, settled in canvas deck chairs.

Beyond the town there is a classic daytime setting near the Anse de Grande Saline, **Le Tamarin** (✆ 27 72 12), where you eat on a pretty tile and wooden terrace covered in greenery: meat and fish carpaccios with salad, fish speciality for the main course, grilled with a tamarind sauce. *Open Mon–Thurs evening.* And in the east, in Cul-de-Sac you will find **Le Rivage** (✆ 27 82 42), with a long menu of sandwiches and salads on a deck overlooking the sand. And for a thoroughly hip spot in Lorient, try the **Ti St Barth** (✆ 27 97 71), with yellow and blue hangings on a deck, exotic hammocks with a view: barbecued food, fritters with *sauce chien,* warm salads, local fish.

cheap

Chez Domi has a good and simple menu in its restaurant in town, which sits between the Ave Générale de Gaulle and Oskar II—with a steak and frites and some creole food with a *colombo* and a *court-bouillon du jour.* On the waterfront at the entrance to the town is **Le Repaire** (with its unlikely subtitle: *des rebelles et des émigrés*). A great spot for lingering over breakfast or a simple lunch. **Entre'Acte** in town also serves simple meals, sandwiches and some platters, as does **La Créole** in St Jean.

Bars and Nightlife

St Barts has a low-key attitude to entertainment (one tourism publication even warns that people looking for 'heavy action, glitter and gambling should be sent elsewhere'), but it is there in a few bars and piano lounges around Gustavia and the St Jean area. St Barts' famous names have been known to put in an appearance. In town the **Carl Gustaf Hotel** is a great place for a cocktail with a view and there is a superb spot just below here at **La Mandala**, where you sit on a terrace with Far Eastern furniture and huge cushions, sipping a sunset cocktail and taking tapas to the tune of jazz, rock and reggae. **Cups** is a sailing-theme bar set on a very pretty terrace around a swimming pool in St Jean, a gathering point for young visitors; also some food later on. There is sometimes jazz at **Le Patio** in St Jean and there is always a lively evening out at the dinner and show staged at the **El Sereno Beach** Hotel.

Hip chicks and tanned windsurfers collect in the garden at **Le Select** in the centre of town, an old mock-brick house. Lively, live music. If you prefer to watch than be watched, then you might retreat across the road to the balcony of the auspiciously-named **Bar de l'Oubli** (the bar of forgetting). Some of the restaurants strung around the waterfront of Gustavia double as bars before and after dining time. On the seaward arm of the bay is the **American Bar** at L'Escale: decor of all-American heroes—James Dean, Elvis and Marilyn Monroe—to go with American rock and a lively crowd late on. Upstairs there is a very lively spot at the **Jungle Café,** where the high-backed wicker chairs and profuse greenery give a feeling of jungle, with a view though, out onto the harbour and its absurdly large yachts and boats. A long list of jungly cocktails. St Barts' nightclubs include **Le Petit Club** (in town, next to Coté Jardin), **La Licorne,** a local disco in Lorient and **Feelings** in Lurin.

getting there

By air: St Barts cannot take international flights but it is well served from islands nearby, of which the most accessible is Sint Maarten (good connections); depending on your point of origin you might also head for Guadeloupe, Antigua or San Juan in Puerto Rico. Air St Barth (℗ 27 71 90) has about 10 flights a day to Juliana airport in Sint Maarten and also connects to Puerto Rico and Guadeloupe. Air Guadeloupe (℗ 27 61 90) flies from Saint Martin (Grand Case), Guadeloupe, Puerto Rico and as far as Santo Domingo in the Dominican Republic and Air St Thomas (℗ 27 71 76) flies from Puerto Rico and St Thomas. Winair (℗ 27 61 01 St Barts, 00 599 55 4210 Sint Maarten) makes the link to Juliana in Sint Maarten, as does Air Caraïbes (℗ 27 99 42) and St Barth Commuter (℗ 27 54 54, ◉ 27 54 58). You can charter a plane from these latter airlines, or go through Trans Caraïbe (℗ 27 93 36).

The airstrip on St Barts, situated on the improbably-named Plaine de la Tourmente(!), is one of the most 'sporting' in the Caribbean. The main problem is that at whichever end you make your approach, there is a hill just where you should be lining up. And so from one end passengers get a close inspection of some hillside forest and the roof of a hotel, and from the other they drop close enough to the road to read car-drivers' T-shirts. If you look over the pilot's shoulder, it may seem that he is going to miss the runway, but the small planes are so manoeuvrable that they can turn on a sixpence. The runway in St Barts closes at dusk, but you can usually make connections the same day from Europe and the USA. There is an airport tax of Fr30.

By sea: If this all sounds a bit much, there is a seaborne link from Saint Martin (both Marigot and Philipsburg) on the powerboats *St Barth Express* and the *Gustavia Express* (℗ 27 77 24) which make up to three crossings a day between them. If you just want a **day trip** to the island from Saint Martin, then there are plenty of yachts and launches that make an early start from Philipsburg. Try *Voyager I* and *II*. For a trip to one of the other islands, contact St Barth Voyages on rue Duquesne in Gustavia (℗ 27 79 79).

If an hour's bouncing the waves against the trade winds still sounds like too much, then there are **helicopters** available, Héli–Inter (℗ 27 71 14). Also *see* 'St Maarten', (p.397)

tourist information

Internationally publicity for St Barts is handled by Guadeloupe (*see* p.282) and the Maisons de France around the world. On island, the **Office du Tourisme** (℗ 27 87 27, ◉ 27 74 47) is on the Quai Général de Gaulle in Gustavia, open weekdays 8.30–12.30 and 2–5, Sat 9–12. An information bureau at the airport keeps the same hours. There is an annual glossy magazine *Tropical St Barth* with features about the island and some advice on sports, shopping and restaurants, and the annual *Ti Gourmet* gives hints about restaurants. The island has a web-page at: *www.st-barths.com*.

In a medical **emergency**, the Gustavia Hospital is on the seaward arm of the town, on the rue Jean Bart (℗ 27 60 00).

The **IDD code** for St Barts is 590 followed by a six-digit number. If you are calling within the island, dial just the six digits. There are no coin boxes on the island and to use a public phone you need a *télécarte*, bought in advance at the post office. If you do need to make a call, any hotel front desk will help out, for a price.

festivals

St Barts stages a number of traditional French and Caribbean events as well as get-togethers for interested sportsmen and wine-drinkers. **Carnaval** takes place around Mardi Gras, with dances at the weekend culminating on Ash Wednesday with the black and white parades and the burning of *Vaval*, the spirit of the French Caribbean carnival; on their **Saints' Days**, Gustavia (17 August), St Louis (25 August) and the eastern towns (27 and 28 August) come alive in trusted Caribbean style—*jump-ups* in the street. The feast day of **St Bartholomew** himself is celebrated (24 August) with fireworks and a regatta.

Mid-January sees the **St Barts Music Festival**, with performances of chamber music, dance music and jazz by top international musicians. April sees the **Festival Gastronomique,** the St Barts Food Festival, in which restaurateurs and wine-merchants from the major vineyards in France collaborate to create ten days of menus from around the regions of France (it is a French food festival, though some restaurant owners do produce creole dishes too), culminating in a party in Gustavia. There is also a **Film Festival** of Caribbean films held in late April. In mid-May in alternate years there are celebrations around the arrival of yachts from Lorient in France. In December, the St Barts Yacht Club organizes the **Route du Rosé**, a race for yachts of 65ft and above to bring a case of rosé wine from St Tropez, followed by the usual partying.

money

Generally speaking, St Barts is very expensive. Though the official currency is the French franc, the US dollar is accepted universally (US$1 = Fr5.5 approx). If you are one to watch exchange rates, then you might find that you can get a marginally better deal in francs than in dollars. Credit cards are accepted by all shops, restaurants and hotels. In restaurants, service is *compris* (remember this when signing checks). Hotels add a service charge of 10–15% to your bill.

Banks: Open on weekdays until mid-afternoon. BFC opposite the airport is open on Saturday mornings and Crédit Agricole in town has a hole-in-the-wall machine.

Shops: Open 8.30–noon and 2–5. St Barts has been allowed to keep its tax-free status from Swedish days and so you may find some (relative) bargains.

watersports

St Barts offers plenty in the way of watersports; the main centres are St Jean beach and the Anse du Grand Cul-de-Sac, but the hotels do have some equipment for hire, including snorkelling gear, windsurfing boards and small sailing boats.

Windsurfing: Try Windsurfing Water Play (✆ 27 71 22), a BIC centre in the Baie de St Jean; on the Anse du Grand Cul-de-Sac at the eastern end of the island, you will find **Wind Wave Power** (✆ 27 82 57) for a Mistral affiliated shop. It is a good place to learn because it is protected inshore but there are waves farther out.

Snorkelling: Try the reefs at Petite Anse beyond Anse des Flamands, Anse Maréchal and the Grand or Petit Cul-de-Sac. Organized snorkel and **kayak** trips are available through St Barth Adventures (✆ 27 50 79) and the companies below.

Scuba diving (*la plongée*): Also easily arranged on the offshore reefs and islands. Expect to see striped sergeant-major fish gliding by followed by grunts, and long-spined urchins lurking in among the seafans and staghorn coral. Reefs include the off-shore rocks of Les Saintes, Gros Ilets and Pain de Sucre. A one-tank dive costs from US$45. Contact the St Barth Diving Centre at Marine Service (℗ 27 70 34, ℗ 27 70 36) which is PADI certified, La Bulle (℗ 27 68 93, ℗ 27 62 25) or West Indies Dive (℗ 27 27 91 79, ℗ 27 91 80). Certification courses available. If you would like to look at the corals in the dry, then contact Aquascope at Marine Service.

Day sails: You can tour on a charming old 60ft schooner *Fabriano* (℗ 27 01 73) and on the catamaran *Ne me Quitte pas* (℗ 27 70 34) or the regular yacht *Outremer* through Nautica (℗ 27 56 50). **Motorboats** are available around the island, sometimes through your hotel; alternatively try St Barth Caraïbes Yachting (℗ 27 52 48) and **yachts** are also available for charter for a longer trip to other islands. Contact the companies above or Nautica.

Deep-sea fishing (*pêche à gros*): Casting for marlin and kingfish, six people for a half-day for about US$400. Contact Océan Must (℗ 27 62 25) or Marine Service above.

other sports

Tennis: There are courts at many of the hotels—Guanahani and the St Barth Beach Hotel—as well as the Sports Club of Colombier (℗ 27 61 07). There is even a squash court at the Isle de France hotel on Flammands beach.

Riding: If you would like to explore the island on **horseback**, contact Ranch des Flammands (℗ 27 80 72).

rocky coastline / Antigua

The Leeward Islands

The Leeward Islands lie in the north of the Lesser Antilles, the link in the arc between the Virgin Islands and the mountainous Windwards in the south. They stretch over 150 miles, scattered around the Dutch Windward Islands and the French islands of Saint Barthélemy and Saint Martin. It is an attractive area of the Caribbean, the horizon studded periodically with the shapes of islands that rise majestcially from the sea.

The Leewards lie in two lines. Montserrat and the twin islands of St Kitts and Nevis stand in the west, invariably capped in cloud, soaring from the water in a chain, the northern extension of the chain of the Windward Islands (*see* p.124). They have many of the features of the Windwards—rainfall, stunning, luxuriant vegetation and the same massive, majestic beauty. They are the peaks of a submarine mountain range, volcanic in origin, which until recently was thought to have quietened down, though the recent activity on Montserrat has shown that belief to be misfounded.

Antigua, Barbuda and Anguilla, on the other hand, are coral-based, and lie on the eastern lip of the Caribbean crust, pushed up as the Atlantic plate forces its way underneath. They lie lower in the sea than the westerly islands and their climates are milder, an advantage in the rainy season, when the other islands are often shrouded in cloud. Physically they are not that impressive, with a mantle of sparse and scrubby vegetation but between them these three islands boast the Caribbean's finest beaches.

The six islands were British colonies and a hundred years ago they were lumped together for administrative convenience as the Presidency of the Leeward Islands. Today, Anguilla and Montserrat remain British Crown Colonies or dependent territories, but since the early 1980s Antigua and Barbuda and then St Kitts and Nevis have gone their own way.

Antigua and Barbuda: Antigua

The graceful and welcoming contours of Antigua inspired Columbus to name the island in honour of a statue of the Virgin in Seville Cathedral, Santa Maria de la Antigua. Its rolling yellow-green hills and the sweeping curves of its bays are soft on the eye after the towering volcanic violence of the Windwards. Barbuda, Antigua's smaller sister island 30 miles to the north, is even gentler and more laid-back, never reaching above 130ft.

Antigua (pronounced more as in 'beleaguer' than in 'ambiguou(s)') has a population of 65,000 and is the largest of the Leeward Islands (108 square miles). For years it was the linchpin of British influence in the area—St John's was the seat of government and the principal military and naval fortifications were here. The island became fully independent from Britain in 1981 but it still maintains an important position in the British Caribbean, out of proportion to its size. It is the largest British island in the area and a hub for local transport (also it has an international test cricket ground).

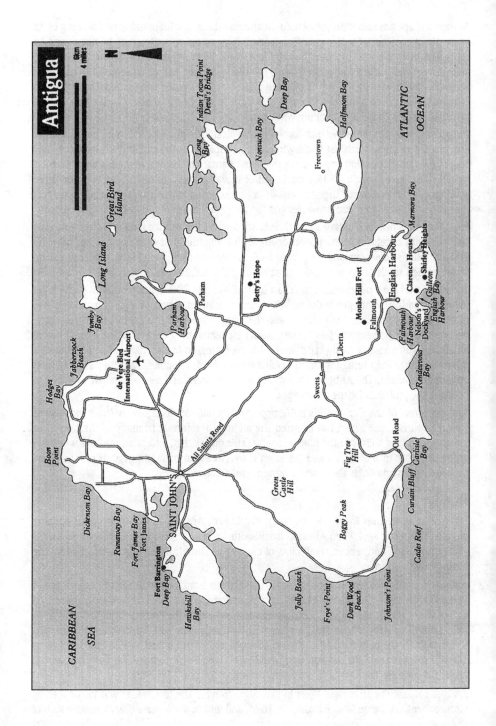

319

Antigua's shape has something of a confused amoeba about it, with pseudopodia heading off in every direction. These headlands enclose superb bays—used so successfully by navies and by smugglers over the centuries and now by more peaceable sailors. Except for one corner of ancient volcanic outflow in the southwest, the island is made entirely of limestone coral. The Atlantic coast, beaten by the waves over the millennia, looks pitted and scarred like a neolithic cake-mix, but on the protected shores of the Caribbean side the gentler wave-action on the reefs has pushed up miles of blinding white sand.

Antigua lies lower in the water than its southerly volcanic neighbours and its climate is gentler and drier. The same northeast trade winds blow in from the Atlantic, but Antigua does not collect the rain-clouds that linger above the Windwards. The early settlements were plagued by a lack of water and in 1731 a bucketful of it was reputed to have been sold for three shillings. This is not to say that Antigua does not experience tropical rainstorms, however: they can definitely catch you unawares and the proverbial bucketful will soak you in seconds.

For much of its history, Antigua's coastline bristled with forts and the land was covered to the last inch with canefields, dotted occasionally with a windmill and estate house. But now the 160 plantations have gone and their fields have turned into rolling scrubland, where the dilapidated conical shells of the windmills stand silent without their sails.

Today the land has a new regime; the coast is lined with the 20th-century bastions of the hotel industry, and inland Antigua is dotted with communications aerials. A high proportion of the island's income is derived from tourists and these are split roughly half and half between stay-overs and cruise passengers). Just as the colonial masters in their dockyards and barracks were an ambivalent presence in the 18th and 19th centuries, so the tourists are something of a mixed blessing. They bring the much-needed money for development, but they are a burden on island resources. The Antiguans are pretty cool, however, and they are mostly prepared to overlook the problems for the advantages.

Antigua is one of the Caribbean's more popular destinations. Recently, with an increase of package tourists, the island has adopted the all-inclusive format in many of the hotels, in which guests tend to stay in the hotel property. This means that, except on the days when the cruise ships put into St John's and the town is overrun with marauding bands of lobster-red shoppers, the island holds the tourist invasion remarkably well.

History

Like the other islands in the northeastern Caribbean, Antigua saw its first island-hoppers around 2000 years ago, when Arawaks from South America arrived in their canoes. For 1000 years they fished and tended small plots of cassava until their peace was interrupted by the intrusion of the Caribs.

Antigua's first permanent European settlement arrived from nearby St Kitts in the charge of Philip Warner in 1632. Like earlier settlers whose attempts had failed, they were plagued by a lack of water and by the Caribs, occasionally accompanied by the French, who nipped over on raids from the nearby Windwards. A war of attrition followed, with the colonists determined to exterminate the native Indians. Law No.88 in the old Antiguan Statute Book for 1693 reads *'An Act to encourage the destroying of the Indians and Taking their Periagoes (canoes)'*. It took its course. By 1805, the law was simply marked down as *'Obsolete'*.

Antigua became the archetypal West Indian sugar factory. The technology was introduced by Christopher Codrington from Barbados in 1674, and within a few years every available inch of land was covered with sugar-cane. The cultivation of sugar involved large workforces of slaves and this gave Antigua its present population of mainly African descent.

As the Caribbean empires flourished in the 18th century and the wars for territory heated up, the British chose Antigua as their main military and naval base in the Leeward Islands, creating a link between their other defences in Barbados to the south and in Jamaica in the Greater Antilles. The fortifications at Shirley Heights above English Harbour on the south coast proved so formidable that the French and Spanish navies simply avoided them.

In the 19th century the wars came to an end and the empires crystallized. The abolition movement managed to outlaw slavery in 1834, but the freed slaves had no choice but to continue working the plantations. There was no other source of employment. The slaves were free, but their situation hardly improved. As sugar declined in the late 19th century (the price of West Indian cane sugar could not compete with subsidized European beet sugar), Antigua waned and the island became another poor and quiet outcrop in the Caribbean backwater. It was not until this century that things began to pick up again. The latest empire to make itself felt is of course tourism, which Antigua has developed for the past 40 years.

A wartime agreement granting the United States bases on the island brought a large influx of Americans during the Second World War, and this put the island on the map. The agreements are still retained and the US Air Force and Navy still have bases in Antigua.

Antiguan politics have a similar heritage to those of other British islands. Trade unions sprang up all over the Caribbean in the thirties and the islanders rallied to them, first as a way to organize political power in the face of colonial rule and later to develop into the movement for self-determination and eventually Independence.

Vere Bird, a President of the Antigua Trades and Labour Union in the 1940s, became the leading light in Antiguan politics, becoming Chief Minister, and later Prime Minister under 'Associated Statehood' in 1967. He became the first leader of independent Antigua and Barbuda on 1 November 1981 and continued as Prime Minister until 1994, when his Antigua Labour Party was taken over by his son, the Hon. Lester Bird. They were re-elected with a majority of 11 out of 17 seats over the United Progressive Party led by the Hon. Baldwin Spencer. Elections are next due in March 1999. The Governor of Antigua is Sir James Carlisle.

Antigua Sailing

Antigua stages one the major regattas in the Caribbean sailing year. **Antigua Sailing Week**, or Race Week, is held at the end of the winter season, before all the yachts take off across the Atlantic to spend the summer in the Mediterranean. It attracts sailors from everywhere, and so for two weeks around the actual event the Antiguan waters are busy with craft of all sorts. There are five major races, each with a number of different classes, all followed by another fleet of sails along for the ride. Many of the races skirt the island and so Antigua's hills offer a fantastic view of the proceedings if you would prefer a land-based vantage-point. The races are of course a good enough excuse for what the Caribbean does best, which is to mix a rum punch and get everyone to 'jump-up' afterwards. There are plenty of silly races and wet T-shirt competitions for non-sailors and the week winds up with the Lord Nelson's Ball, a formal affair (for the Caribbean anyway) and prize-giving. For information, contact PO Box 406, St John's (✆ 462 0036, 📠 462 2627).

In the following week is the **Classic Yacht Regatta** which brings together yachts passed by the committee as of 'classic design', many of them fantastically beautiful with long-forgotten configurations of sails (three races). Contact the Classic Yacht Regatta (✆ 460 1093, 📠 460 1542).

Getting Around

The **bus service** in Antigua is scant. It tends to run early in the morning, bringing workers into town from the outlying areas, and it finishes around 6pm as they return home. Except to key areas, you will have difficulty finding public transport after dark or on Sundays. There is a fairly regular service (leaving either when the bus is full or when the urge takes the driver) between St John's and English Harbour in the south-east of the island. Getting back at night is a problem, though the All Saints'–St John's run continues until late. Other roads are run less frequently. No buses at all run either to the airport or to the northern tourist area, leaving you dependent on taxis, but a number of the hotels run buses for their workers, so you might be lucky enough to catch a ride with them.

The **East Bus Station**, on Independence Avenue on the outskirts of St John's, serves the north and east of the island. Opposite the St John's market is the **West Bus Station**, from which buses leave for villages in the southern part of the island. Travelling on the buses is cheap, and the longest fare across the island costs around EC$3. **Hitchhiking** around the island works adequately. To signal to both car and bus drivers, the traditional Caribbean sign is to point rapidly at the ground.

Good tourists, of course, go by **taxi**, and there is a superabundance of them in St John's and at the airport. They can also be ordered through all the hotels. The government fixes taxi rates and it is worth establishing the price (and currency) before setting off. The ride from the airport into St John's costs US$7, to Dickenson Bay US$11 and from St John's or the airport to Nelson's Dockyard about US$25. There are taxi stands: the 24-hour taxi service (✆ 462 5190) at the West Bus Station and the Reliable Taxi Service (✆ 462 1510). Many of the taxi-drivers are knowledgeable about Antiguan lore and so you will often get an impromptu tour if you wish, but any taxi-driver would be happy to take you on a more formal tour of the island, which will cover many of the island sights. A day's tour costs around US$60 and is easily fixed through any hotel foyer. Companies offering tours include: Coral Island Trading (✆ 460 5625), Wadadli Travel and Tours (✆ 462 2227) and Tropikelly Tours (✆ 461 0383), who offer among other tours off-road trips in four-wheel-drive vehicles to less-explored island sights.

Hiring a car is probably the best way to get around the island, and there are plenty of rental firms. Drivers must obtain a temporary permit, available from the rental company or the police on presentation of a valid driving licence and payment of US$20. If you are driving out into the country, take a reasonable map because there are few roadsigns. The roads were in a pretty awful state at the time of research, which makes the 40mph speed limit quite appropriate. Driving is mainly on the left, though there are recognized chicanes around the potholes. If you wish to go off the main roads it is advisable to get hold of a four-wheel-drive car, of which there are plenty for hire. The price of a day's hire starts at US$50 for a car and $55 for a jeep.

Car rental companies, which work out of St John's and often from the airport, include: Oakland Rent-a-Car (✆ 462 3021), National on All Saints' Road, St John's (✆ 462 0576), Dollar Rent-a-Car (✆ 462 0362), and Matthew's Car Rental, St John's (✆ 462 8803). You can rent a **bicycle** through Sun Cycles (✆ 461 0324), who deliver to your hotel. There is an off-road mountain-bike tour which takes in the northeastern part of the island (or anywhere that you specify): contact Cycle Crazy (✆ 462 9253).

Beaches

Between them, Antigua and Barbuda have some of the loveliest beaches in the Caribbean. Time was, not so long ago, that Antiguan families would simply move on if anyone was already on their favourite beach when they arrived for the Sunday picnic. Now they can be crowded, relatively— perhaps ten people scattered over a mile of isolated sand. In between the main beaches listed below are any number of small coves where you can be alone. Ask an Antiguan.

There is something for every taste on the island, and for once the tourist brochures' claims are correct: you can walk alone on a bay of silken sand, where coconut palms bend and brush the beach and the waves fizz around your toes, carving scallop shapes in the sand; or you can cut a windsurfing dash on crowded strands where the body-beautiful roam. In some places, though, mosquitoes dive-bomb you as you doze and the sandflies do bite, so you might have to evacuate in late afternoon. Take some repellent if you go off the beaten track. All beaches are public in Antigua, but the land behind them is sometimes owned by a hotel which may therefore restrict access. All-inclusive hotels may charge a day's fee for using the beach (which would include use of the sports equipment and facilities of the hotel).

best beaches

Dickenson Bay: The best bet for an active beach, on the west coast north of St John's, home to a clutch of hotels. Good sand and all the watersports and posing you will ever want; also plenty of watering holes to retire to.

Runaway Bay: The extension of the coast to the south of Dickenson Bay, a couple of hotels and some activity on excellent sand.

Fort James Bay: Further south again (closer to St John's), popular with the Antiguans at the weekend, but tends to be uncrowded in the week.

Hawksbill: One of a number of coves and bays south of St John's, many with hotels. The farthest from the hotel is a nudist beach. At **Jolly Beach** (also called Lignum vitae after the wood) you have to buy a daily pass.

Ffrye's Bay, Dark Wood Beach and **Crab's Hill Bay** (Johnson's Point): In the southwestern corner of the island, almost deserted strips of fantastic sand, best chance for being alone on superb sand, some bars but not many facilities.

Morris Bay and **Carlisle Bay:** They stand either side of the Curtain Bluff hotel in the southwest of the island; the waves splay in fans on the steep sand and there are reefs to explore.

Galleon Bay: A nice stretch of sand a water-taxi-ride from Nelson's Dockyard, inside English Harbour. Nearby **Falmouth Harbour** also has one or two good strips of sand.

East coast: The sea is a bit rougher here, but there are some protected spots in deep coves where nice sand washes up. Try **Half Moon Bay,** a lovely curve of sand, and **Long Bay.**

beach bars

There are good options on Antigua if you want to centre a trip to the beach around a bar. On Dickenson Bay there are some hotel bars, but a popular independent one is **Spinnakers**, where you can get a pleasant meal after sizzling in the sun. **Miller's** Beach Bar is on Runaway Bay, a neat series of parasols ranged behind a conch-shell-topped wall; facilities. It is quite large, so for something a little more secluded, you can head down further down the beach to Fort James, where there are a couple of bars. The **Candyland Bar** is really a shed with nice white trellises and a sandy floor; they serve chicken and macaroni, rice and peas or salad and of course a cold beer. Open at popular times. **Russell's** is actually inside Fort James and so is a little more formal. Great setting on a deck.

There is a number of great sunset-watching bars on the endless strands of the southwest: you will find the **Darkwood Beach Bar**, where a few parasols stand in front of a stretch of white trelliswork; some facilities. At Crab's Hill beach in the southwestern corner there is the small **Action Bar,** a tin-roofed shed where you can get a beer and a simple meal. At the southwestern tip there is **Turner's Rudder**, a beach bar and grill where you sit at upturned cable barrels on plastic chairs whose legs dig into the sand among palm trees. If you are headed out to the east coast for the day, then there is a passable bar at Half Moon Bay, **Harry's** Bar and Restaurant.

Flora and Fauna

Set in the yellow-green expanses of scrub, Antiguan gardens are splendid with the bright pinks and purples of hibiscus and bougainvillea. There is one pocket of lusher vegetation in a mainly dry island, **Fig Tree Hill** in the southwest, and here you will see slopes covered in elephant ears and of course fig trees (the local name for the banana). Flitting in its foliage you can find Antigua's two hummingbirds and several doves. On the plains you are bound to see the ever-present mournful cattle egret, standing sentinel by and sometimes on the back of the cattle that give it its name.

In the coastal ponds (there are many, behind the hotels on Dickenson Bay, in the creeks on the east coast and by Jolly Beach) you will see boobies, terns and sandpipers as well as the ubiquitous pelican. You can also visit the offshore islands, including **Great Bird Island**, which is particularly known as home to the red-billed tropicbird.

The **Nelson's Dockyard National Park**, which consists of about 15 square miles of the south of the island, is not a park in the sense of an area reserved for wildlife. In fact it is a centre for tourism, taking in bus-tours and considerable yachting activity. It claims to be 'an ever-evolving environment which preserves our history, culture and nature alongside today's needs'. There are some important natural areas in the area, however, including a wilderness area in Rendez-vous Bay. On the east coast, **Half Moon Bay** is also a Wildlife Reserve and can be toured. Tropikelly Tours (✆ 461 0383) can provide guides who are well informed about the natural life of the island.

Fortress-foraging

In the 18th century, Antigua's coastline bristled with forts and fortlets, many of which still exist, though they are mostly buried in 15ft of scrub. Aficionados and fort boffins will enjoy rootling around the ruins, and of course they still have the fantastic views for which they were built in the first place.

Fort James (early 18th century) and **Fort Barrington** guard the entrance to St John's harbour. Fort Barrington, on the south side, has a plaque commemorating William Burt, the Governor in whose tenure it was built. On it he signs himself *Imperator et Gubernator insularum Carib* (Emperor and Governor of the Leeward Islands). This Governor had some difficulties with the islanders, especially after drawing his sword at dinner and attacking some imaginary intruders supposedly lurking behind his chair.

Johnson Point Fort is at the southwestern corner of the island. Farther east, as you pass through Falmouth, **Monks Hill Fort** (as it is known to most Antiguans, though its name was officially Great George Fort) looms up on the hill. Built in the 17th century, it was a refuge for the women, children, slaves and cattle in case of attack by the French and their Carib allies. The track to the fort turns off the main road at the village of **Liberta**, and is only passable by four-wheel-drive vehicles. **Fort Berkeley**, a short walk beyond Nelson's Dockyard, was built in 1744 to guard the entrance to English Harbour. Its soldiers would haul up a chain boom if an invasion was threatened. Above Fort Berkeley the ground is crawling with earthworks and gun emplacements and on the other side of the harbour are the major fortifications of **Shirley Heights**. *The Old Forts of Antigua* by T. R. St Johnston gives a run-down of the fortifications which made the island the most fortified place for its size in the world.

St John's

Antigua's capital, St John's, stands on gently rising ground above a large bay. The central streets are laid out on a gridiron plan and although some are now being taken over by strips of concrete modernity, many of the older wood and stone buildings with overhanging balconies still remain among them, much as they were a century ago.

Over one-third of Antiguans live in or around St John's, and the town is showing the fruits of the island's prosperity with shops full of computers and clothes from all over the world. But a more traditional West Indian life can be seen just a few minutes' walk out of the centre of the town, where you will see the chaos of the market or fishermen making lobster pots and mending their nets.

Many visitors arrive in Antigua by the harbour, passing beneath the two defensive outposts at Fort Barrington and Fort James at the mouth of the bay. First steps ashore will lead into the air-conditioned environment of a duty-free shopping arcade, **Heritage Quay**, but the life of St John's is not far beyond.

Not far off, a stroll along the boardwalk, is **Redcliffe Quay**, an area of old St John's that has been restored. It is also a shopping complex (and altogether a more pleasant experience than Heritage Quay) and it is worth a detour for its cafés and restaurants even if you're not on the hunt for a bargain. There are old townhouses and warehouses with stone foundations and clapboard uppers, with brightly painted shutters and louvres. There's even a red British phone box to make you feel at home.

Towering above the town's activity from its stately position at the top of the rising ground are the twin grey towers of the **Cathedral of St John the Divine**. The octagonal structure was erected in 1845 after one of Antigua's relatively frequent earthquakes, and to prevent similar damage the interior has been completely lined with pine. The two life-size statues that stand at the gates of the cathedral, St John the Baptist and St John the Evangelist, were destined for French Dominica in the 18th century, but they were captured by a British warship and brought to Antigua.

The **Old Court House**, on the corner of Long Street and Market Street, dates from 1747, though it has been rebuilt a number of times, most recently after the earthquake in 1974. Now it is home to the **Museum of Antigua and Barbuda**, (*℗ 462 1469; open weekdays 8.30–4, Sat 10–2; adm free*), and it houses an exhibition of Amerindian Antigua (known to them as 'Wadadli'), with *zemies* from the 100 archaeological sites on the island, as well as colonial and more modern Antiguan memorabilia, including the cricket bat of Viv Richards (an Antiguan), used when he broke the world record for the fastest Test century.

Since Antigua began to host West Indian cricket Test Matches in 1981, the venue has been the stadium up above the cathedral. In 1736 this area was used as an execution ground following a slave rebellion. The ringleader Prince Klaas and four others were broken on the wheel (a punishment in which the victim was strapped to a cartwheel and his bones broken one by one), six were 'put out to dry' (hung in chains and starved) and 58 were burned at the stake. The Antiguans now enjoy watching the similar roastings meted out to visiting cricket teams. If there is a game on while you are in town, go to it. On Independence Avenue running south from here you will see the House of Parliament, a white modern building where the Antigua Parliament conducts its business, across an open pastureland to the left.

A walk back through downtown St John's will take you to the market, an enclave of traditional West Indian mayhem enclosed within walls, where the banter seems as much a part of the game as buying the local fruit and vegetables on display.

The Northern Coastline

The area north of St John's is the most developed in the island, both by the tourist industry, which has built hotels on the beaches at Runaway Bay and Dickenson Bay, and by prosperous Antiguans who have moved out of town to live in large villas set in hibiscus and bougainvillea gardens. At the eastern side of the northern coast is **Long Island**, a low island lying a few hundred yards offshore, once used for grazing cattle and sugar cultivation. Now home to an expensive hotel and villa complex, it was traditionally famed for exporting far more sugar than it could possibly produce, all illegally shipped in from Guadeloupe. Having sworn in seven hogsheads for export before the magistrate, the owner would promptly add the letters 'ty' and ship out that amount to eager British markets.

The main road passes the Vere Bird International Airport and beneath hills littered with windmill shells and modern communications aerials before returning to St John's.

East of St John's

Travelling due east from the capital on the Old Parham Road, you pass through lowlands that once were covered with canefields. A turn left leads to the old town of Parham, one of the first settlements and oldest harbours on the island. The few remaining old buildings are now surrounded by small clapboard houses set among the palm trees and more recent tourist development around the boatyard.

One of the oldest sugar plantations on the island, **Betty's Hope**, is off the main road to Indian Town Point on the east coast. The estate house is just foundations on the highest point now, but the twin cones of the sugar works and several outhouses have survived. One windmill has been restored with all its machinery and you can walk around the ruins of the boiling and curing house. In the visitor centre itself (*open Tues–Sat 10–4*) there is a small model of it as a working plantation and there are tools and descriptions of sugar planting, harvesting, crushing, boiling and curing and rum distilling and shipping.

The main road continues to the east coast, which has been buffeted and carved into limestone brittle over the millennia by the Atlantic's wave action. The coastline gives some cracking views of the jade and royal blue sea flecked with whitecaps. The much vaunted **Devil's Bridge** is a natural span cut out of the rock at Indian Town Point. On a rough day the area is spectacular as the full force of the ocean thrashes against the coral coastline, compressed and hissing as it bursts up through blowholes. Antigua's coastline has many indentations here, creating deep and well-protected bays, and just around the corner from all the spray are beaches tucked in the coves, as at Long Bay.

Just farther south, the village of **Freetown** was settled soon after Emancipation in 1834. The liberated slaves formed their own villages away from the plantations, often in remote areas such as this where they could settle on unused land.

St John's to English Harbour

If St John's was the administrative centre of the Leeward Islands, the British Navy maintained its rule of the Caribbean waves (often successfully) from the southeast of the island, at what is now English Harbour. The All Saints' road leads south out of St John's past the market through the centre of the island, rolling scrubland dotted occasionally with the cone of a windmill. **Liberta** is another small town created by the freed slaves. Eventually you run down to the south coast, and skirting the edge of the huge Falmouth Harbour, you come to **English Harbour**. The secluded inlet is now one of the prettiest and most picturesque spots in the Caribbean, but 200 years ago the West Indies was a hardship posting, and one visitor considered Antigua 'one of the most infernal places on the face of the globe'. On his first visit, the future Admiral Nelson thought of Antigua as a 'barbarous island' and the dockyard now bearing his name as a 'vile spot'.

Nelson's Dockyard

Set on a point deep in the tortuous recesses of English Harbour, Nelson's Dockyard (*adm*) is a conglomeration of restored stone warehouses, workshops and quarters that once made up an 18th-century naval station. Were it not for the flowery tropical shirts on the tourists and the gleaming white of the yacht hulls, you might imagine you could hear the whistles and drumrolls of an active barracks. The waters are still plied by sailing craft, and it is a sight to watch the yachts manoeuvring between the headlands and making for open water much as they did 200 years ago.

At the entrance to the dockyard, once guarded to deter intruders, you will be waylaid by the inevitable T-shirt sentry at the small shopping arcade. Once inside, the charm of the place takes over. The quarters, with gently sloping roofs that reach out and shade balconies, have all been repaired, as have the old sail-loft and workshops. Cannon and the odd anchor stand proud in mock menace and the boathouse pillars and sprays of tropical flowers give an air of groomed antiquity.

The dockyard was abandoned by the Navy in 1889 and fell into disrepair, but was restored by the Society of the Friends of English Harbour and reopened in 1961 as Nelson's Dockyard. Even if it has his name, Nelson himself certainly had no love for the place. He was based here for three years, as the young captain of HMS *Boreas*, between 1784 and 1787. He cruised the Leewards for much of the time, but during the hurricane season, when the French fleet was absent from the area, he spent time in the dockyard, jokingly threatening to hang himself.

He fell out with the islanders by enforcing the Navigation Act, which declared their profitable trade with American ships illegal (he had to stay on board his ship for eight weeks to avoid arrest when they took him to court). It was a pretty miserable time, though he found some solace in his marriage to Fanny Nesbit, a young widow from the nearby island of Nevis. He was happy to leave the Caribbean and did not return except briefly in 1805, hot on the tail of Villeneuve and the French fleet, in a chase of thousands of miles that culminated in the Battle of Trafalgar. Nelson's Dockyard is a bit of tourist trap, with hotels, bars and restaurants, and you can expect to see a few blistering-red package-holiday conscripts pressganged on to tour-bus lunches. However, with all the yachts, the place also retains a nautical air and there are always a few latterday sailors loitering on shore for a few days, looking for grog and a brawl like their predecessors in centuries past. There are excellent sign-boards illuminating the different buildings and how they were used.

In the attractive wooden building that was once the naval officers' house you will find the Nelson's Dockyard **Museum.** It covers the whole story of English Harbour, including the natural environment (from earthquakes to termites), the Arawaks and Caribs (with displays of their tools), the early Europeans (navigation instruments), and the people who lived in the dockyard (graffiti and tools such as blacksmiths' bellows and caulkers' tools). There are some small interactive models (e.g. to show how the capstans outside were used for careening)

On the opposite shore from the dockyard, **Clarence House** stands on the hill. This handsome Georgian Caribbean house, built of coral rock and with a large louvred veranda, was built in 1787 for Prince William Henry, later to be King William IV, who was in command of HMS *Pegasus* stationed at Antigua. He was a friend of Nelson and gave away Fanny Nesbit at their marriage. Clarence House is the official country residence of the Antiguan Governor General, though it was badly damaged in a hurricane and so is not occupied. It is due for restoration but no date has been set for its reopening.

Scattered all over the heights above English Harbour is the garrison of **Shirley Heights**, another extended family of barracks with arched walkways, batteries, cisterns and magazines. It was fortified in the 1780s by General Shirley, the Governor of the Leeward Islands from 1781 to 1791, in order to defend the harbour below. The fortifications had an uninterrupted view across to Guadeloupe, giving advanced warning of any impending French invasion, which means that the view is exhilarating. Once the fortress was constructed, the French never considered invading again, of course. The site was abandoned in 1856 and fell into ruin, but some buildings have been repaired. At the top of the hill you will find the **Dow's Hill Interpretation Centre** (*open daily 9–5; adm*) where a multi-media show takes you through a fairly simple display of Antigua's history, through American Indians, Columbus, European explorers and settlers, the plantation era and merchants, the triangle of trade and then naval years to modern Antigua and its carnival and Sailing Week. There is also a gift shop and a café with a view.

The Southwest

Many of Antigua's fine beaches are on the west coast south of St John's and these include Deep Bay, Hawksbill Beach and Darkwood Bay. Inland is **Green Castle Hill**, where there are some odd rock formations that have come to be known in tourist lore as the megaliths, imaginatively thought by some to have been used by the Caribs as a sort of shrine. The view is particularly good from the top of the hill.

The road emerges on the sea and skirts the coastline for several miles, in the lee of the Shekerley mountains, Antigua's biggest hills. The tallest among them is the 1319ft **Boggy Peak**, from which the view extends to Guadeloupe in the south and as far as St Kitts to the north on a clear day. It is also possible to see Barbuda, Antigua's sister island. To reach the peak you must take the steep road inland from Cades Bay on the south coast. The coastal road is a pleasant drive, through an undeveloped part of the island, where you can see fields of black pineapple, a small and succulent variety that Antigua exports.

At Carlisle Bay and the town of **Old Road** (from the old word 'roadstead' meaning harbour), the coastal road cuts inland into the island's lushest and most attractive area. At the village of Swetes, the road forks south towards English Harbour or north back towards St John's.

① *(1 268)–*   *Where to Stay*

Antigua has a few fine resort hotels tucked away in their own coves along its tortuous coastline. Many of them are extremely expensive retreats, ideal for the luxurious seclusion that the Caribbean does so well, and one or two sit in splendour in the historical setting of English Harbour. Antigua has also gone for the all-inclusive plan in a big way recently, in which you live in a compound where everything is paid for in advance and you do not need to use any money. Hotel rooms in Antigua are by no means cheap and the bill is then supplemented by a 8.5% government tax and usually by a 10% service charge (except in the all-inclusives).

luxury

Antigua's finest and most elegant hotel is **Curtain Bluff**, PO Box 288 (*①* 462 8400, *✉* 462 8409, US res *①* (212) 289 9888). It stands on a bluff on the south coast, above a superb double beach where the sand is carved into scallop patterns by the waves. Set in magnificent gardens, the hotel is stately and quiet, with 66 suites and rooms ranged on the small promontory overlooking the beach. There are many activities on offer within the all-inclusive price: fitness room, watersports including scuba, tennis courts, even a squash court and a fine dining room with an extremely long wine list; a jacket and tie are required for dinner. *Closed during the summer months.*

very expensive

If you would like to stay within the old English Harbour area, there are some good hotels which take advantage of the historic setting. The main house at the **Inn at English Harbour,** PO Box 187 (✆ 460 1014, ✆ 460 1603), stands on the hillside above the sailing activity of the harbour. There is a quiet and intimate air about the hotel, helped by the antique-looking stone buildings up top and their setting among charming tropical gardens. Down below there are 22 more modern rooms in blocks right on the beach, each of which have fridges and fan ventilation and a balcony or patio. Also watersports. In the evening a shuttle runs up to the main house where you take cocktails and then dinner on the dining terrace sheltered with date palms. **Galleon Beach** (✆ 460 1024, ✆ 460 1450, UK res ✆ (01453) 835801, US res ✆ (1 847) 699 7570) has a lovely setting just down from here, cottages and villas scattered in a sweep of open gardens that rise from the seafront in a bay framed by the lumbering slopes of Shirley Heights. There are 28 one- and two-bedroom cottages, beachfront and garden, quite simple but comfortable. In Nelson's Dockyard itself you will find a charming place to stay at the **Copper and Lumber Store,** PO Box 184 (✆ 460 1058, ✆ 460 1529), which has been historically reappointed in the old brick magnificence of one of the dockyard's finest buildings. Huge wooden supporting beams and slender balustrades run through the resort and there is a Georgian dining-room and quaint dungeon-like bar; rum puncheons in the courtyard, and 14 rooms and suites named after Nelson's ships...*Dreadnought, Victory.* It is well restored and attractive. There is no pool, but the beach is a short boat-ride away.

If you would prefer to be on the beach, then the best bet on Dickenson Bay is the **Siboney Beach Club,** PO Box 222 (✆ 462 0806, ✆ 462 3356, *siboney@candw.ag*). There are 12 very comfortable suites set in a three-storey block, each with a balcony looking out on to a fantastic tropical garden and pool. It has a lively thatch-roofed restaurant, looking over the beach through the palm trees, just a short walk down the sand from all the noise and activity of the beach bars and watersports. And for a more active beachfront resort-style of hotel you can try the **Hawksbill Beach Resort** (✆ 462 0301, ✆ 462 1515, *hawksbill@candw.ag*), which takes its name from the oddly shaped rock off one of its four beaches, looking like the bill of a hawksbill turtle rising from the water (alternatively a frog with a crown). From an old plantation house and windmill on a promontory, the 111 rooms are strung out along the waterfront in blocks and cottages. Quite large and lively, most watersports available, tennis, very comfortable rooms and some evening entertainment.

moderate

The **Admiral's Inn,** PO Box 713 (✆ 460 1027, ✆ 460 1534, UK res ✆ (01453) 835801 or ✆ (0181) 940 3399, US res ✆ (1 800) 223 5695) has a magnificent setting right on the harbourfront in Nelson's Dockyard, in the former engineers' office and store-rooms. The inn has beautiful worn bricks that were shipped out as ballast and dark wooden beams and floorboards. Fourteen rooms in all: some large ones on the first floor, others tucked away in the sail loft. Dining room on a deck out front among guinep and casuarina trees. No pool or beach, but the charming, historic atmosphere more than makes up for it. Not far off you will find their **Falmouth Harbour Beach Apartments**, PO Box 173 (same phones and fax), where there are 22 studio apartments with kitchens set on the harbourfront and on the hillside. Modern and well fitted, they each have balconies and verandas, some sports facilities and all the nautical activity and restaurants nearby. On the other side of the harbour you will find very good value at the **Catamaran Hotel**, PO Box 958 (✆ 460 1036, 📠 460 1506, US ✆ (1 800) 223 6510, Canada ✆ (1 800) 424 5500). It is set in a couple of modern blocks with mock-classical pillars and balustrades; 16 comfortable, fan-ventilated rooms in blocks on the waterfront, some kitchenettes, restaurant on the dock at the Catamaran marnina nearby, beach passable, a few watersports on offer.

In the northern end of the island, you will have a good reception at the **Sand Haven Hotel** (✆/📠 462 4491, UK res ✆ (0181) 948 3535), which sits in a modern brightly coloured block right on the mounded sand at the southern end of Runaway Bay. The 14 rooms are all quite simple, with fan ventilation and insect screens, no phones, but they offer good value for the beachfront. Another good spot, quite isolated in the north beyond the airport, is the **Lord Nelson Beach Hotel**, PO Box 155 (✆ 462 3094, 📠 462 0751). It sits on a breezy bay which is particularly good for windsurfing and so it attracts a young and friendly crowd. The hotel is family run and there is an easy air around the restaurant and bar. The 20 rooms are comfortable and good value; it would be advisable to have a car for some time at least.

cheap

Less expensive rooms can be found in St John's, at the **Spanish Main Inn** (✆ 462 0660) on Independence Avenue at the top of the grid section of town. It is set in an old timber-frame town house which has a fine old feel of antiquity, beamed and creaky-planked rooms, nice big open windows and a lively crowd hanging around in the bar downstairs (which has some live music). There are nine fan-ventilated rooms, all of which have private baths and showers and most a balcony that you can retreat to. Out of town you can try the **Vienna Inn** in Hodges Bay (✆/📠 462 1442), where there are six very simple rooms with private baths and some kitchens a couple of minutes' walk from the beach, and an Austrian restaurant to go with the name. Back in town, **Murphy's Place** (✆ 461 1183) on the All Saints' Road has four reasonably comfortable apartments with kitchens and a hearty Antiguan welcome.

Very cheap rooms can only be found in the south of town, beyond the market at the **Miami Hotel**, Market Street (✆ 462 0975), which will show you a different side of Antiguan life: private baths, nearly clean. There are some **guest houses** that can be contacted through the Tourist Board.

✆ (1 268)–

Eating Out

The food in Antigua is quite similar to that of other British West Indian islands: hotels tend to offer studiedly 'international' fare and local food has a good mix of fresh local fish and traditional Caribbean ground provisions. There are some exceptions, though, in a few hotel dining rooms and restaurants where you get good food in the best Caribbean settings. There is also good variety in the restaurants, with French, Italian and even Argentinian as well as West Indian. There are some lively local and tourist haunts, but Antigua has suffered recently because so many of the hotels have turned all-inclusive (their guests have paid for all their meals in advance and so they venture out to the restaurants less). Most of the good restaurants are in St John's, where they use the best of the old wooden timber-frame houses, or around the southeastern area of the island which can be quite lively because of the yachting fraternity. Restaurants add a service charge of 10% and there is a 7% sales tax on top too. Categories are arranged according to the price of a main course: *expensive*—EC$50 and above; *moderate*—EC$20–50; *cheap*—under EC$20.

Around St John's and the North

expensive

Julian's (✆ 462 4766) at the corner of Church St and Corn Alley has a charming dining room in a St John's house with tall shutters that open out onto the street and interior courtyard and fans whirring gently overhead. The cuisine is 'modern classical', with modern adaptions on classsical French techniques. Very comfortable atmosphere at candle-lit tables. *Closed Mon*. At **Chez Pascal** (✆ 462 3232) the service and the cuisine are trusty and traditionally French in style (even *escargots* are on offer), though Pascal, the chef, also uses the best of Caribbean ingredients: *crevette au safran* (saffron shrimps) followed by a *magret de canard* or a *filet de vivanneau grébloise* (snapper in capers and lime with a touch of cream). The restaurant, on a terrace with classical arches and balustrades around a lit pool, is now quite remote out on Galley Bay Hill (signed). The road is bumpy and then very steep, but it is well worth the effort. The **Bay House** restaurant (✆ 462 1223) also serves top-notch fare on the terrace at the Tradewinds Hotel on the hill in Dickenson Bay where you are surrounded by greenery and the peep of tree frogs. Plenty of fish dishes in exotic combinations.

There is a number of lively places around town. In the northern suburbs, tucked away on Gambel's Terrace off Fort Road you will find a friendly reception at **The Home** restaurant (✆ 461 7651), set in a villa with simple wooden chairs and tables. They serve 'Caribbean Haute Cuisine' (adapting international recipes to Caribbean ingredients) from a short menu and a long list of daily-changing specials on the blackboard: Arawak duck served in a pineapple rum or mango sauce, or sorrel-papaya sauce at Christmas-time, or chicken curaçao. In the middle of town you will find **Hemingway's** (✆ 462 2763) in one of St John's most charming wooden houses, white and green with a red tin roof, on Mary Street. Sit at the bench seats on the gingerbread veranda if you can. The specialities are creole food and seafood, and dishes comes neatly presented on large plates, their edges dusted with spices—start with a local pumpkin soup and follow with a Bajan flying fish. Lunches are simpler—burgers and salads.

moderate

O'Grady's Pub (✆ 462 5392) is another lively haunt in an attractive wooden St Johnian house where louvred doors open on to the veranda at the foot of Lower Nevis St. It is popular with expatriates and serves 'O'pub grub': shepherd's pie and fish and chips. Doubles as a bar. Close by is the ever-popular and lively **Pizzas in**

Paradise (✆ 462 2621), which makes the best of its setting in an old warehouse in Redcliffe Quay. Solidly international fare, pizzas particularly of course and often a musical accompaniment to your meal. You might also try the **Captain's Table** (✆ 462 9199), set in a charming old town house painted in outrageously bright colours, on Popeshead Street, for local and international specialities.

There is a number of smaller, local restaurants in St John's, good places to stop for lunch and to gather for a drink at the end of the day. The **Calypso Café** (✆ 462 1965) is on Upper Redcliffe Street and has tables scattered around a courtyard garden. Mostly local fare, curried chicken or flying fish in a beer batter, or a burger if you want it. *Closed Sun.* At **the Hub** (✆ 462 9442), which is also enclosed in its own court-yard, at the junction of Long Street and Soul Alley, there are tables set among tree-trunks on a red concrete floor. Easygoing and friendly. Local fare: simple lunches with sandwiches and platters for dinner including creole specialities such as roti or saltfish with *ducana* (sweet potato dumplings). You will find **Pari's Pizzas** up the hill and round the corner in Dickenson Bay. You can take out or eat in, seated in deck chairs on a covered red and green veranda with trelliswork and hanging plants.

If you want to eat more **cheaply** in town, there are a number of snack joints in the market area where you can grab a chicken or a pattie. In the evenings an American-style aluminium dispenser appears sometimes on the streets called the Pumpkin Runner for late-night snacks.

Around English Harbour

expensive

The smartest restaurant in the southeast is the **Southern Cross** (✆ 460 1797) at the marina on Falmouth Harbour, where you sit on a breezy deck high above the water on padded safari chairs, looking out over the ink-black water and the lights of all the yachts. The fare is fine Italian and international: *Spatzly* with beetroot and a gorgonzola sauce, grilled veal mignon with butter. Italian seems to be the flavour of the decade in the area: there are two other nice spots in the southeast. **Colombo's** (✆ 460 1452) is in Galleon Bay (the other side of English Harbour from Nelson's Dockyard), where you dine on an open-sided terrace with wicker lampshades. Also Italian and international fare. Some entertainment. Also worth making the detour for is **Alberto's** (✆ 460 3007), tucked away on its own in Willoughby Bay. It is set on a wooden deck with sloping tin roofs, trellises and lots of greenery. Steaks and some Italian dishes: veal *pizzaioli* or a ravioli of salmon and asparagus. Can get quite lively when people play the piano for fun. Popular on Fri and Sat.

moderate

There is a clutch of simpler but fun places to eat scattered around English and Falmouth Harbours, patronized by a lively crowd of itinerant yachtspeople. **Le Cap Horn** (✆ 460 1194) is set on a pretty veranda, with a mantle of greenery around the trellises. French and Argentinian fare, including huge *churrasco* steaks. There is a **pizzeria** next door: pizzas cooked on a wood fire.

The Mad Mongoose (✆ 463 7900) is a very lively spot, a bar and eatery, with some tables in a yard out front and others in an indoor dining room and bar (next to the pool table). Thoroughly international style: roast pork or panfried dolphin. Fun. *Closed*

Mon. **The Dock** is on a floating flat-bottomed deck, sticking out into the water as you would expect, in English Harbour, off the car-park. Cheery and American-style, with bench seats and stools around the bar and a menu offering all things to all tourists.. **Nations** is a much lower-key spot, a small shack behind a pink and white fence, with its own garden where some of the food is grown and a canvas roof under which you can eat. Chicken, conch or fish (the menu depends on what has been landed that afternoon) in a coconut sauce with rice and peas and fried plantain. Excellent rum punch. **Grace before Meals** is a shed selling burgers, rotis and hot dogs nearby.

Bars and Nightlife

There are some fun and lively bars which offer happy hours where you can take Antigua's not really very nice home-brewed lager, *Wadadli*, on a test run (plenty of others are available), particularly along Dickenson Bay, in town and around English Harbour. In Nelson's Dockyard itself there is a day-long view from the balcony at **Limey's Restaurant and Bar.** You might try

Antigua Directory

getting there

Antigua's Vere Cornwall Bird International Airport has excellent connections around the Caribbean and from Europe (about 8 hours) and North America. It is a hub for the north-eastern Caribbean. Departure tax of EC$35 (about US$15) is payable except by those who have spent less than 24 hours in the country.

By air from Europe: There are usually daily flights from Britain: British Airways from Gatwick (local ✆ 462 3219) and BWIA (✆ 462 0262) from Heathrow and Caledonian and Airtours (handled at the airport by Port Services, ✆ 462 2522). BWIA flies weekly from Frankfurt.

By air from North America: BWIA fly in non-stop from Miami every day and regularly from New York, and American Airlines (✆ 462 0950) have direct flights from JFK New York and easy connections via Miami and San Juan in Puerto Rico. Continental fly from Newark, New Jersey. Air Jamaica (✆ 462 0528) has also routed some flights from Jamaica to the States via Antigua. BWIA also fly from Toronto in Canada, as does Air Canada (✆ 462 1147).

By air from other Caribbean islands: Antigua is the headquarters of LIAT (✆ 462 3142), so the airline has more flights to and from this island than anywhere else. On LIAT and other carriers (Air Guadeloupe, Air St Kitts Nevis, handled by Port Services) there are daily direct flights or easy connections to all the islands between San Juan, Puerto Rico in the north and Trinidad and Barbados in the south. There are two daily flights to Barbuda. Another option is Carib Aviation (✆ 462 3147, 📠 462 3125), who offer an almost scheduled daily service across to Nevis and other British islands like Anguilla. Carib Aviation will charter aircraft as well, as do Norman Aviation (✆/📠 462 2445), Fly BVI and Tyden Air, which make the run up to the Virgin Islands, handled by Port Services. There are fairly regular flights to Jamaica on Air Jamaica. You can charter a **helicopter,** for sightseeing or for a transfer, from Caribbean Helicopters (✆ 460 5900).

By sea: There are no scheduled boat services to Antigua. You might persuade a freighter captain to let you aboard for the ride, but your best bet is to get a passage on a yacht, of which there are many based in English Harbour.

Twofers (two for one) at the **Main Brace**, the Copper and Lumber Store, on a Tuesday or a Friday. A popular place to move on to is **The Last Lemming,** downstairs at the Antigua Yacht Club in Falmouth (quite busy any night). The **Shirley Heights Lookout** high above English Harbour is something of an island institution. A good spot for a sunset drink, but particularly on a Sunday afternoon when a band plays in the sunset (starting at 3pm). It attracts a riotous crowd by the early evening.

In St John's you will find a lively haunt at **O'Grady's Pub** on Lower Nevis St, where there is a pool table area and a darts league, and sometimes entertainment. More loud music and wicked drinks at **Shooters Club**, on the High Street: pool table, dance floor and themed entertainment that changes nightly. Discotheques include **Ribbit**, in Green Bay, St John's and the **Safari Club** behind Pari's Pizza on the road up from Dickenson Bay. There is a circuit of shows that perform in the hotels: steel bands and the usual limbo dancers. There are a couple of **casinos** on the island, where there are slot machines and betting tables open until four in the morning: try the **King's Casino** at Heritage Quay in St John's.

© *(1 268)–*

tourist information

UK: 15 Thayer Street, London W1M 5LD (℡ (0171) 486 7073/6, 🖷 486 9970; enquiries can be sent on: *ronald@antiguahc.sonnet.co.uk*).

USA: 610 Fifth Avenue, Suite 311, **New York,** NY 10020 (℡ (212) 541 4117). Also at the Trade Missions: 121 SE 1st Street, Suite 1001, **Miami**, Florida (℡ (305) 381 6762) and 3400 International Drive NW, Suite 4M, **Washington** DC 20008 (℡ (202) 362 5122).

Canada: 60 St Clair Avenue East, Suite 305, Toronto, Ontario MT4 1N5 (℡ (416) 961 3085, 🖷 416 961 7218).

Italy: via Santa Maria alla Porta 9, 20123 Milan (℡ (02) 877983, 🖷 877983).

France: 43 Avenue de Friedland, 75008 Paris (℡ 1 53 75 15 71, 🖷 1 53 75 15 69).

Germany: Thomas Str 11, 61348 Bad Homburg (℡ (06172) 21504, 🖷 21513).

On Antigua itself, the main office is on Queen Elizabeth Highway just outside the gridiron area of St John's, PO Box 363 (℡ 462 0480/462 0029, 🖷 462 2483). There is also a desk at the airport. The tourist board publishes *Antigua and Barbuda Adventure*, a twice-yearly glossy with articles and lists of restaurants and boutiques, and the smaller guide *Life in Antigua*, with lists of restaurants and shops and articles of general interest about the island. There is a general website: *www.antigua-barbuda.com.* Information can also be found on *www.interknowledge.com/antigua-barbuda.*

In a medical **emergency**, there is a 24-hour casualty room at the St John's hospital, on Hospital Road (℡ 462 0251).

The **IDD code** for Antigua is ℡ (1 268) followed by a seven-figure local number. On-island, dial the seven digits.

Antigua has a number of **galleries** in which you will see the works of Caribbean painters as well as arts and crafts. **Seahorse Studios** are located in Redcliffe Quay and there you will find originals and reproduction prints and jewellery. **Harmony Hall** is difficult to find on the east coast at Brown's Bay, but there too you will find arts and craft from all over the

Caribbean (Harmony Hall has a sister property in Jamaica)—colourful work with calabashes and baskets. It is good for a daytime visit; there is a restaurant and a bar in the old windmill.

festivals

For 10 days or so in late July the **carnival** competitions wind up to the finals: Calypso King and Carnival Queen (Antigua also stages the Caribbean Queen competition which brings contestants from all over the area), steel bands (if you hear them practising, then just wander in) and junior competitions. The traditional *j'ouvert* (pronounced jouvay) takes place on the morning of the first Monday in August, and then the streets will pulse to the carnival parades until Tuesday evening. There is a **sports fishing tournament** in May and an annual **jazz festival** held over three days, usually in October. Obviously the **sailing regattas** mentioned above (*see* pp.321–2) are very lively occasions. There are other smaller events throughout the year which can be fun to attend, so it is worth asking around when you are on-island.

money

Antigua and Barbuda share their currency, the Eastern Caribbean dollar, with the other countries in the OECS (Organization of Eastern Caribbean States), from Anguilla in the north down to Grenada in the south. The EC$ is fixed to the US$, at a rate of about US$1 = EC$2.65. US dollars are accepted everywhere on the island, though change will sometimes be given in EC$. Credit cards are also widely accepted by hotels, restaurants and shops and as security for car hire. Though confusion rarely arises, it is a good rule to establish which currency you are dealing in.

Life in Antigua can be quite expensive. Not only do most necessities have to be imported, but the government imposes no income tax, preferring instead to raise taxes through sales of food and goods. Even in the markets, prices can be quite high.

Banks: Open weekdays 8am–2pm, Fri 8–2 and 3–5. Exchange can always be made at the larger hotels, but the rate will not be as good.

Shops: Usually open daily except Sundays, between 8.30am and 4 or 5pm, with an hour off between noon and 1pm. They will often stay open later when a cruise ship is in dock.

maps and books

Antigua was lucky in that the English wife of a planter, a Mrs Lanaghan, wrote of her life in the island in *Antigua and the Antiguans* in 1844, describing the island and the customs of its people (recently reprinted in two volumes). You may also find a copy of *To Shoot Hard Labour*, in which an Antiguan, Samuel Smith (1877–1982) tells stories going back to emancipation (his grandmother was a slave) and his working life. A modern Antiguan writer who now lives in the States is Jamaica Kincaid, author of *Annie John*, a disturbing book about a childhood on the island, and *A Small Island*.

There are also one or two informative booklets that describe the historic sights of the island. *The Romance of English Harbour* deals with Nelson's Dockyard and *Shirley Heights* by Charles Jane tells the story of Shirley Heights and its defence of the island. **First Editions** in the Woods Centre Mall behind St John's has a good selection of Caribbean books and you can also try the **Map Shop** in St Mary's Street in St John's. In English Harbour, try **Lord Jim's Locker** for nautical books, guides and novels.

watersports

Antigua is particularly good for sailing, but like the other coral islands it has some fine reefs, so snorkelling and diving are a pleasure. The best beach for general watersports is Dickenson Bay and here you can hire windsurfers and small sailing craft such as sunfish and hobie cats. Hotels on other beaches will usually have equipment available to their guests. A general watersports operator on Dickenson Bay is Sea Sports (℗ 462 3355).

Windsurfing: Many hotels have equipment, but intermediate and advanced windsurfers should go to Windsurfing Antigua (℗ 462 3094) at the Lord Nelson Beach Club in the northeast, where the winds are stronger. Other spots include Jabberwock Beach and Hodges Bay around the corner to the north.

Deep-sea fishing: Trips, casting for marlin and tuna, can be fixed up through some of the large hotels. Try *Shadowhawk* (℗ 462 0256) or *Missa Ferdie* (℗ 462 1440).

Day sails: For a rum-soaked afternoon of all-Caribbean tourist classics such as *Yellowbird* and walking the plank you can try *Jolly Roger* (℗ 462 2064), whose familiar red sails you will see off the coast, but there are lower-key trips which take in a picnic and some snorkelling on the offshore islands—Prickly Pear, Green Island and Bird Island. Try the catamarans *Kokomo* (℗ 462 7245) or Wadadli Cats (℗ 462 4792) and for a sunset or moonlit cruise *Sagitoo* (℗ 460 1244). A glass-bottom boat tour is available through Shorty's (℗ 462 6326), with schedules to offshore reefs and islands.

Yachting: A big activity on the island, with marinas around the traditional naval harbour sites of English Harbour and Falmouth Harbour on the south coast and at the Jolly Beach resort on the west coast. Yachts of all sizes can be hired, crewed or bareboats, for days, a week, or longer. Charter companies include Nicholson's Yacht Charters (℗ 462 6066, ◉ 460 1531) and Seagull Yachts (℗ 460 3049, ◉ 460 1767), both at English Harbour, and Sun Yacht Charters (℗ 463 2113, ◉ 463 2115, US toll free ℗ (1 800) 772 3500, Canada ℗ (207) 236 9611, *sunyacht@midcoast.com*).

Snorkelling: There are reefs on all sides of Antigua, which offer excellent marine life, including sergeant-majors, parrot fish and larger fish like rays and the occasional dolphin. Equipment can be borrowed from most hotels.

Scuba diving: Some good dive sites are: Cades Reef, a 2-mile protected reef off the south coast, and nearby Farley Bay and Rendezvous Bay, and Boon Point, the northernmost tip of Antigua. The reefs have also claimed quite a few ships over the years and so there are plenty of wrecks to dive. Diving can be arranged through Dive Antigua (℗ 462 3483) at Halcyon Cove on Dickenson Bay and Deep Bay Divers (℗ 463 8000) who work out of Redcliffe Quay in town. Dockyard Divers (℗ 464 8591) operate from Nelson's Dockyard and cover reefs and wrecks on the southern coast. Instruction is available at the above places; a one-tank dive costs around US$45.

other sports

Golf: There is one 18-hole course at the Cedar Valley Golf Club (℗ 462 0161) to the northeast of St John's, green fees US$35, and another at Jolly Harbour (℗ 464 9307).

Horse riding: A ride through Antigua's rolling dry hills or along the beaches can be arranged with the Spring Hill Riding Club near Falmouth (℗ 460 1333).

Barbuda

Barbuda's great attractions are its marine life and its beaches. Virtually undisturbed and visible very close to the surface, the reefs are forested with corals that move gently with the water and teem with fluorescent fish. The beaches are magnificent: the sand on Barbuda is supreme, the beaches are measured in miles and it is difficult not to be alone. There is so much sand that they even export it.

The island is 60 square miles of scrubland that barely clears the water, lying about 30 miles north of Antigua. It is made entirely of limestone coral deposits that have encrusted an outcrop on the same geological bank as Antigua. The Highlands, in the north of the island, struggle to top 130ft. The contours of *Dulcina*, as the island was known to the Spaniards, are even gentler than Antigua's and the pace of life considerably slower.

Caribs prevented early settlement of the island, but when they were wiped out, Christopher Codrington leased the whole island as a private estate, paying rent to the Crown of 'one fat sheep, if demanded'. It stayed within his family from 1674 until about 1870 and, because the soil was not fertile enough to support sugar-cane, it was used as a ranch for stock and work animals, a farm for provisions, a deer-park and eventually a cotton plantation. Many of the animals are still seen wandering about much as they always have, and the ubiquitous Caribbean goat gets everywhere. There are even rumours of Barbuda's having been used as a slave-farm, where the tallest and strongest slaves were encouraged to breed. Amateur anthropologists maintain that this is the reason for Barbuda's abnormally tall population.

In 1976 the 11-person Barbuda council was set up and the island was granted elected government (with just two appointed members). But, as in so many island partnerships, the Barbudians do still complain that they are neglected by the government in St John's. There are occasional words about the advantages of being independent of Antigua, but they are not very loud.

With just 1500 inhabitants, Barbuda is extremely quiet, and it is still surprisingly undeveloped as Caribbean islands go (petrol is hand-pumped here). The main activities are fishing and traditional West Indian subsistence agriculture with some building. 'Wrecking' was another source of income, as the reefs around Barbuda have been known to claim many ships in their time. There are reckoned to be around 200 shipwrecks off the island. Tourism amounts to two extremely expensive hotels, a small resort and local guest houses.

The few hundred Barbudians left on-island (many have emigrated but revisit their families often) have a tight-knit community, nearly all of them living in the only town (really a village), Codrington. The most common names (most people are called one of them) are Harris, Beazer, Thomas, Punter and Nedd. The islanders show a welcoming interest in visitors. One person claimed that on arrival at the airport not so long ago, he was greeted with the words: 'But nobody said you were coming...'

Beaches

 The **beaches** are of course superb. The best is probably the main south-coast beach which runs between Coco Point and River (the port area), but others include Low Bay by the lagoon on the western shore and Two Foot Bay and North Beach on the northern coastline.

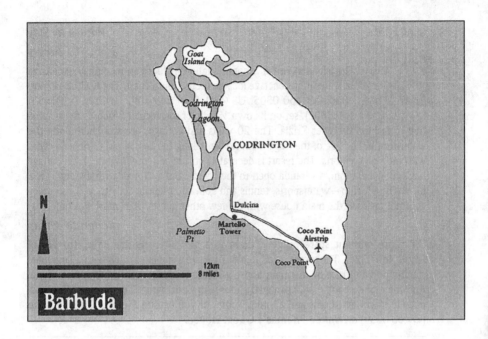

Barbuda

Around the Island

The **Codrington** family have left their name everywhere on the island: in the only settlement, just a few streets of concrete or clapboard houses and an airstrip, in the lagoon on which it sits, and in **Highland House**, their estate house that was built in 1750 but never really occupied. Its ruins, just walls, outhouses and a cistern steadily being reclaimed by the scrub, are visible a few miles north of the village. The island's other main sight is in marginally better condition. **River Fort** is a martello (round) tower with a skirting of walls that stands on the south coast, its gun turrets without cannon now, but still guarding the approach to the original docking area and harbour. For many years the island was a deer-park for the Codringtons and it is still possible to hunt them and to shoot duck.

For those with a more peaceable interest in wildlife, a visit to the **Codrington Lagoon** to see the thousands of frigate birds is very rewarding. You can take a boat out into the mangroves, where the birds, with their distinctive dark arrow shape with scissor tails, circle overhead to thousands of feet. The best time to go is between October and February—the mating and later the hatching season. You will see the males display, with their impossibly large gullets puffed up like vast red footballs so that their heads are forced skyward and their throats resonate with a clacking noise. The females cruise around and make their choice. From December their ungainly chicks start to hatch. To arrange the trip, ask around in town. There are **caves** in the northern part of the island, including **Dark Cave**, where a passage leads 100 yards underground. Coral reefs grow off nearly all Barbuda's coasts, waving forests of staghorn and elkhorn where angelfish, trumpetfish and wrasses flit, and they make extremely good snorkelling. The corals are so close to the surface that it is hardly necessary to dive, so divers have to look after themselves.

luxury

 The island's limited accommodation includes an incredibly expensive and luxurious enclave located on the south coast. The **K Club** (© 460 0300, ☎ 460 0305, US © (1 800) 648 4097, UK res © (01453) 835801), set on its own ½-mile of spectacular beach, is the inspiration of fashion designer Krizia. The 20 villas and cottages are stretched along the waterfront either side of the huge main house, taking the best of old Caribbean style, with modern comforts. The resort is decorated in jade and bright white. Each cottage has a huge bedroom, a veranda open to the breeze and a shower with a view. It is a luxury beach club—watersports, tennis and golf. After all the activity, you can enjoy gourmet meals in the main house with the few other guests. Stars most welcome.

moderate–cheap

For those without spare millions there is a small resort, the **Palmetto Hotel** (©/☎ 460 0326). The rooms stand in blocks above a sloping garden with a large pool standing on a terrace by the main house which is dressed up in old Caribbean style. And there are a couple of cheap guest houses in Codrington. The **Sunset View** just outside has a few rooms and a dining room, or you can try **Nedd's Guest House** (© 460 0059) or **Walter Thomas's Guest House**.

Barbuda (which has an unlikely but entirely appropriate airport code: BBQ) is 20 minutes north of Antigua **by plane** and **Codrington** is served by a return flight morning and afternoon by LIAT. Carib Aviation also have some flights during the week (© 460 0004 Barbuda, © 462 3147 Antigua). If you have booked with the Coco Point Lodge, you will arrive at their airstrip in the south. It might also be possible to catch a ride on one of the ships that makes the run with tinned food and essentials; ask around at the main dock in St John's.

There are just one or two **cars** available **for hire**. Bargain for them. Alternatively try to hitch a ride. Most drivers that pass will offer you a ride anyway, but with few cars headed anywhere you might want to go it can be a long wait. Because most of the food and other essentials of life are imported, Barbuda tends to be quite **expensive**. Bring things that you cannot live without. You are advised to change any EC$s that you will want in Antigua (it is good to have a few here, though US$s are widely accepted). If you would like a **tour of the island**, contact Barbuda Tour (© 462 0742) or talk to the knowledgeable Ivan Pereira a couple of days in advance (© 460 0258).

Redonda

The chain of Caribbean volcanoes passes by about 30 miles west of Antigua and among its peaks rises the tiny pimple of Redonda, so named because of its nearly round shape. It stands between Montserrat and Nevis, a circle of cliffs sparse on top, uninhabited except by birds. In its 1 mile by one-third of a mile, it reaches an impressive 970 feet.

For nearly 400 years after its discovery by Columbus it was ignored, but eventually in the 1860s somebody realized that centuries' worth of birdshit could be put to good use. Guano mining began, and at the height of production 30 years later the island produced 3–4000 tons of phosphate annually.

That the island should be worth something to somebody was enough to bring claims of sovereignty from all the powers in the area, and so before long Redonda was annexed by the British and attached to Antigua, capital of the Leeward Islands.

However, a rival royal bid was made by an Irishman who happened to sail past in 1865. One Matthew Shiel, himself of regal stock, he claimed, descended from the ancient Irish Kings of Tara, claimed the island and appointed himself king. He may have had right on his side: despite the presence of the superpowers of the age in the Caribbean for nigh on four centuries, none of them had actually made a formal claim to the island. The fact that the British 'annexed' Redonda gives credibility to the claim. In 1880 Matthew Dowdy Shiel abdicated in favour of his son, another Matthew Shiel, born in nearby Montserrat, when the boy reached the age of 15. At his coronation, Matthew Phipps Shiel took the title King Felipe I. Later he left for England, intending to train as a doctor but actually embarking on a literary career and eventually becoming a successful novelist. Thus the court of King Felipe was established there. It was a literary assembly whose courtiers included J. B. Priestley and Rebecca West.

Eventually the line passed to the poet John Gawsworth, self-styled King Juan I. In the kingdom's continuing prosperity in the middle of this century, an 'Intellectual Aristocracy' was established in commemoration of M.P. Shiel's literary achievements. Peers of the Redondan realm included other literary and not so literary luminaries as Dorothy L. Sayers, the publisher Victor Gollancz, Arthur Ransome, Dylan Thomas, Lawrence and Gerald Durrell, Diana Dors, Dirk Bogarde and Dylan Thomas. The Kingdom of Redonda was fêted and well known in its day. Matthew Phipps Schiel (1865–1947) was known for an overly florid and luxuriant prose style. A few of his books are still in print because there were revivals of interest in him in the 1920s and 1960s. His most famous work was *The Purple Cloud* (1901), an allegory in which the world is threatened with destruction. John Gawsworth's work has also been largely forgotten since his death in 1970.

This most illustrious of Caribbean lineages was thought to have gone into decline, but it has been traced to the county of Norfolk in England and it now apparently resides with the fifth King of Redonda, King Leo. He regards his reign as 'a trusteeship, to perpetuate and develop for posterity a charming and unique quirk of history... The realm is pledged to keep the memory and literary achievements of M.P. Shiel and John Gawsworth 'green' through its Intellectual Aristocracy...'

Oddly enough, the kingship of Redonda seems to have pricked the fancy of more than a few otherwise mature people and there have been a number of other claimants to the throne (Gawsworth admittedly left a trail of confusion in his intentions as to the inheritance of the title). As an 'incorporeal property' the title can be passed on by inheritance, given away or even sold, like an English manorial title. There was one story of another putative King of Redonda actually visited the island in 1979. Jon Wynne-Tyson (a literary executor of both M.P. Shiel and John Gawsworth as it happens) made a visit with a court historian and reaffirmed his suzerainty over the domain by planting his flag, blue, brown and green in colour and 'made from pairs of old royal pyjamas by Her Royal Highness, Jennifer Wynne-Tyson'.

Though Redonda is uninhabited now, there was once a post office there and it is possible to find Redonda stamps.

Montserrat

Montserrat, the most southerly of the Leewards, has a jumbled interior of rainforested mountains worthy of one of the Windward Isles to the south, but at 39 square miles (it is 11 miles by 7 miles at its widest point) its serried peaks are smaller, its slopes are gentler and island life is even slower. Like the Windwards, it also has a *soufrière*, a volcanic vent. This had been reckoned to be one of the Caribbean's less active volcanoes, but in June 1995 it started to erupt and it has held the island to ransom since then. The capital, Plymouth, has had to be abandoned and the population has been evacuated to the northern half of the island. Once Montserrat had 12,000 inhabitants; now there are reckoned to be about 5500.

Montserrat has always been a charming place. Without the typical Caribbean white beaches (its volcanic geology already saw to that, giving it dark sand instead), it never suffered a large beach-bound invasion, leaving the island tranquillity now lost to the rest of the West Indies. Instead it attracted a more stately visitor. It could be relied upon, and people actually retired there. In their present difficulties, crowded in temporary accommodation in the north of the island, just out of the shadow of the threatening colossus in the south, the islanders understandably show a little tension, but they have demonstrated remarkable resilience and they are still remarkably welcoming to outsiders.

Montserrat has a considerable, if distant, Irish heritage which, along with its luxuriant appearance, has led to its being called the 'Emerald Isle' of the Caribbean. Many of the place-names are clearly Irish, and although the islanders are obviously of African descent, at times it seems that you can hear an Irish lilt in their speech, momentary strains of brogue in the stream of West Indian. Whether this is imagined or not, Montserratian speech is one of the softest and most attractive of all variations in the English-speaking Caribbean. For all the Irish heritage (and there is a shamrock on one of the eaves of Government House), the island has been a British colony for most of its history. It is one of just five British Crown Colonies remaining in the Caribbean, administered by a Governor appointed from London in partnership with the island legislature.

Poor Montserrat. It is such a charming island and it deserves better than its recent run of terrible luck. The island was roundly trashed by Hurricane Hugo in 1989 and it was recovering and picking up again when the volcano started to rumble. There was a time when total evacuation from the island was considered, but this has been rejected for the moment. The worst of it is that this kind of volcano (as far as the volcanologists know) takes as long to calm down as it does to reach the height of its activity and so it seems that it will be causing trouble for years to come. It is honestly quite difficult to recommend going to Montserrat for the moment, though the north of the island is likely to remain safe. There's nothing to stop you— a few faithful regulars keep returning back as they always have—and a few others have visited out of curiosity. If you do go, you will be met with customary good cheer and courtesy.

History

Alliouagana (thought to mean 'land of the prickly bush') was deserted when Columbus passed on his second voyage. The Caribs were off raiding elsewhere. He paused long enough to name the island Santa Maria de Montserrate after the abbey near Barcelona in Spain and sailed for Hispaniola. Only pirates braved the Caribs' attention over the next 140 years.

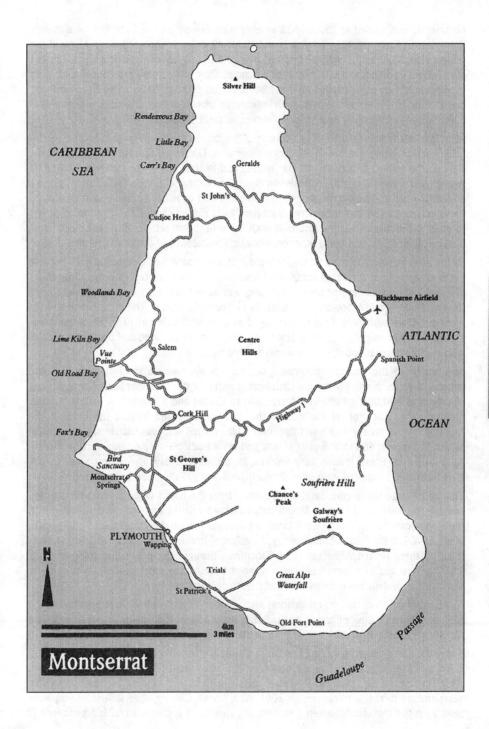

Montserrat

Montserrat was settled in about 1632 as a separate colony for the Catholics from mainly Protestant St Kitts, the then English island about 40 miles to the northwest. Many of the settlers were Irishmen, as was the first governor, and the island soon gained a reputation as a place where Catholics and the Irish were welcome. They came from Protestant Virginia, and the population was also swelled after the Battle of Drogheda in 1649, when Cromwell sent many of the Irish prisoners of war. Irish indentured labourers from the other islands would make their way here once their term was served on another island.

As with so many islands, the first half-century of colonization was a litany of hurricanes, earth-quakes and seaborne attacks. The raiders were French, Dutch and Spanish and, of course, the Caribs, who arrived in their thousands, burning and looting, killing the men and carrying off women and slaves. The Irish colonists had an understanding with their French co-religionists and often when the raids took place their property would be left alone. But relations between the Montserratian settlers themselves were hardly any more peaceful. Laws had to be passed to prevent them from hurling insults at each other in the street, 'English Dog, Scots Dog, Cavalier, Roundhead and many other opprobrious, scandalous and disgraceful terms'.

By the late 17th century the land was covered with sugar-cane well up into the hills. Because of the steep terrain, the cured sugar was loaded on to mules and casked only on the shore before shipping. Sugar meant slaves and a large number of Africans were brought in to work the canefields, giving Montserrat its mainly black population today. The occasional rebellions were put down ruthlessly. One was arranged for St Patrick's Day in 1768 when the slaves intended to take over Government House, but the plans were overheard by a slave-woman who told the planters and the rebels were captured and executed.

As sugar failed and Emancipation came, other crops were grown and Montserrat became famous for limes. It was the second Caribbean exporter of the fruit after Dominica and much of the crop, 180,000 gallons one year, went to Crosse and Blackwell in Britain. Cotton became an export crop at the end of the 19th century and formed the basis of the Montserratian economy well into this century. Like other Caribbean islanders, the Montser-ratians had moved on to small plots of land and were leading a simple agricultural existence. At the time of Emancipation they worked for sixpence a day, the lowest wage in the Caribbean and, a hundred years later, their situation was still the worst in the Leewards.

This pitiful state led to considerable emigration from the island when a better life seemed possible elsewhere, and so most Montserratians have a relative who left for the canefields in the Dominican Republic or to work in oil in Curaçao. The exodus culminated in the 1950s, when 5000 left for Britain. Subsequently, an influx of 'resident tourists', as they are known, many of them retired Americans and Canadians, brought the population back to about 12,000. Most recently there has been a wave of Dominicans and Guyanese, who came to work in the construction industry in the aftermath of Hurricane Hugo.

Montserrat had a late start on the political scene. Robert Griffith and William Bramble led the Montserratians in their efforts to obtain a fair wage and in their political aspirations. The Montserrat Labour Party took all five seats in the first elections in 1951 and again in 1955.

Today the island government, the Legislative Council, which has control over internal affairs, is led by Chief Minister Bertrand Osborne of the Movement for National Reconstruction, which has two of the seven Parliamentary seats. Elections to the Council are held every five years and are next due in November 2001. As a Crown Colony, ultimate executive power rests with the Governor, Queen Elizabeth II's appointed representative. Independence is mentioned less now in island politics, but anyway it would not be considered before Montserrat is economically independent.

Hurricane Hugo, which struck in 1989, caused terrible destruction to both human and natural life and in places the damage is still visible. There were 10 deaths. Not a single electricity pole was left standing and an estimated 95 per cent of houses were damaged. Apart from this upset, the standard of living in Montserrat had been rising steadily over the last 20 years and the island was very stable.

The Anatomy of a Volcano

Until recently Montserrat's *soufrière* was considered one of the less active in the Caribbean. Like the others it rumbled occasionally and let out the occasional spout of ash, as at the turn of the century, when activity all along the island chain culminated with the eruption of Mont Pelé in Martinique in 1902. However Montserrat was thought not to have erupted seriously for about 18–20,000 years and was therefore hoped to be on its way to extinction. It came back to life with a vengeance in July 1995.

There are two sorts of eruption in Montserrat: *phreatic,* in which steam and ash or sometimes gravel emerge in a grey cloud; and *pyroclastic*, when slides of superheated mud, gases and rubble make it over the lip of the crater walls and head off down the hillside. They run on a cushion of air at amazing speed, soundlessly, incinerating anything in their path. When they reach the sea they skitter and glide on the surface, steaming and fizzing. Rain brings further problems because it causes mud-flows: ash, rocks and general debris compound into sludge, which slides down the island's 'ghauts' (river ravines) without warning. Lastly, the islands nearby have been concerned that the activity could cause a tidal wave. In the heady moments of early rumour, word went about in Nevis that they might be hit by a 200ft wave (which would just about swamp the inhabited parts of the island). Ash, which is like fine concrete dust, is actually the pulverized residue of rock from inside the volcanic crater. On Montserrat, it has fallen to depths of several feet, smothering the south of the island completely, giving the houses a ghostly grey roof-cladding and turning the landscape into a moonscape, suffocating and killing the vegetation. Oddly enough, in smaller quantities it has exactly the opposite effect and it has made the grass on the Belham Valley golf course grow frantically. Like Saharan dust, volcanic ash gets absolutely everywhere, leaving a grey film on everything, even inside sealable containers in the kitchen. As you walk on it, it crumps and crunches with each pad of your feet and rises in little clouds, hanging in the air and getting into your hair and nose. And, like concrete, when it mixes with water it becomes hard. Ash has been known to blow down as far as Antigua.

The present activity began in late 1994, when increased earth tremors began to be felt. On 18 July 1995 the islanders heard a long low rumbling, apparently like a distant jet, accompanied by smells of sulphur and some falls of ash. The volcano was very much alive again. This continued for a couple of months until 21 August, which is remembered as 'Ash Monday' because of a major ash-fall that put Plymouth, the capital, in darkness in the middle of the day. A few days later the situation was regarded as serious enough to merit evacuating the people living in the south of the island. To add insult to injury, Hurricane Iris came along, ripping out the temporary accommodation.

Montserrat was lucky, though, that Hurricanes Luis and Marilyn did not hit the island full-on, but passed by farther north.

In October 1995 a 'dome' appeared in Castle Peak, a large extruding area of super-heated material that was constantly changing, building up and then collapsing, pushing up 'spikes' (*see* 'Martinique', pp.243–4), which then fell over. At night it glowed in places where rocks had rolled down and left the underside exposed for a while. In December 1995 the people were evacuated again for a couple of months. In April 1996 there was a third evacuation. Everyone was moved north of the Belham River Valley and crowded into the villages of the northwest. Businesses were run out of lorry-containers, the library became the prison, schools worked in morning and afternoon shifts; the main room at the Vue Pointe Hotel became chapel, courtroom and weekly disco.

Plymouth had to be abandoned. Lying on an open bay on the southwest coast, it was a classic small West Indian town, with old Georgian 'skirt and shirt' buildings—stone lower storeys with columns and arches and wooden upper storeys, topped with shaded balconies and red tin roofs. Once it had a population of 3500. Now it is entirely deserted, all its buildings covered in 2 feet of compacted grey dust. Those who have visited the town might remember a river course called Fort Ghaut in the south, just beyond the old island prison and before the collection of restaurants and bars in the old stone houses of Wapping. This gulley, normally 20 feet deep, is now completely full of ash, up to 2 feet below the level of the bridge. Government House, an attractive creole house built in the 19th century and the official residence of the Montserrat Governor, is ghostly and quiet, as though it were blanketed with grey snow.

People would return to clear the ash off their roofs from time to time and to keep their houses in order (in June 1997 20 people were killed when an eruption occurred suddenly and they were caught working their fields in the exclusion zone). Some factories remained open and the petrol station also continued to function. Now, though, it looks as though the south will be abandoned permanently as the island infrastructure has begun to be recentred in the north: a port has already been built in the north together with schools and housing. Many people were encouraged to relocate to Antigua, putting pressure on that island's health, housing and education services, and reducing the viability of the remaining community on Montserrat. At the time of writing there was considerable anger over the British government's financial offer to those who did wish to leave, and controversy over politicians' alleged overstating of the danger to the north and misinterpretation of the scientific data; yet in September 1997 the Montserratians requested permission to rename Plymouth Port Diana after the deceased British Princess of Wales.

Blarney

Of all the echoes you hear in West Indian English, the strongest in the speech of Montserrat is Irish. Some visitors have claimed that the Montserratians have the gift of the gab and a truly Irish wit. The West Indians have a pretty mean sense of humour anyway (just nip down to the market and catch the banter), but particularly after a few rum punches, you might just think that you are in Galway.

In the 17th century, there were about 1000 Irish families on the island, but since then, most of the original white settlers have left. However, their names certainly live on in black Montserratian families, such as Farrel, Daly and Ryan, as a quick look at the Montserrat telephone directory will show. The Irish harp is a national symbol and appears on the Montserratian stamps.

There is a nice story from the 19th century about an Irishman who arrived from Connaught to find himself addressed by a black man in Connaught brogue. He asked how long the man had been in Montserrat. 'Shure, yer honour, and three years it is that I've been here.' Flabbergasted, the Irishman replied, 'Glory be to God. And do ye turrn black in thot toime?' and got on the first ship back home (*The Pocket Guide to the West Indies*, Sir Algernon Aspinall, 1938).

Fans of Caribbean soca music will immediately recognize the name of (the Mighty) Arrow, who comes from Montserrat and whose calypso 'Hot Hot Hot!' made it to the top all over the world a few years ago.

Flora and Fauna

The confusion of soufrières or secondary craters and the mingling of mountains and hills make it like an enlarged picture of the moon.

Montserrat has the same botanic exuberance as the Windward Isles to the south—the thick dark earth cultivates a luxuriant flora: explosions of bamboo, mosses on the march, creepers grappling down below, and above orchids and airborne ferns. The national flower is the yellow *Heliconia caribaea*, known locally as lobster claw because of its odd shape, and the island tree is the hairy mango.

The national bird, the Montserrat oriole, is indigenous to the island. Its plumage is black and yellow and it can be found up in the mountains along with the purple-throated carib, one of Montserrat's three hummingbirds. Thrashers and bananaquits abound in the hibiscus and bougainvillea of the lower slopes and you might be lucky and see a chicken hawk hovering, spying out a meal. On the shoreline you can see waders such as the common gallinule and some species of heron, alongside cattle egrets, kingfishers and the odd booby or a tropicbird with its long tail feathers.

Montserrat's landborne wildlife is limited to agouti (very shy, guinea-pig-like rodents), lizards, 'mountain chickens' (frogs) and tree frogs, which make their shrill night-time call all over the Caribbean. You have a good chance of seeing iguana, a prehistoric-looking, tank-like lizard, at a daily feeding session; contact the Vue Pointe Hotel.

℗ (1 664)– **Where to Stay**

Just a couple of hotels have remained open on the island. There is a 7% government tax on hotel rooms and villas and usually a 10% service charge will be added to your hotel bill.

The **Vue Pointe Hotel**, PO Box 65 (℗ 491 5210, ℗ 491 4813, *vuepointe@candw. ag, www.mrat.com/vpl; moderate*), has ultimate easy old-time Caribbean grace and an attentive and welcoming air. The rooms are ranged regularly around the sloping, lawned garden in three small blocks and 28 very comfortable octagonal rondavels, with balconies, huge beds, and louvres and fans to coax the island breezes and keep you cool. The main house, with library and pool, stands high above the Caribbean coast. Vue Pointe is family run and has an excellent air of retreat, and a friendly crowd of regulars often gathers at the bar and restaurant. Beach bar down below and there are watersports on the bay. The other place to stay is at **Providence Estate House Bed and Breakfast**, St Peter's (✆ 491 6476, ✆ 491 8476, *harrisj@candw.ag; moderate–cheap*), which is set in fantastic gardens in the northwest of the island, a pink and white wooden house on a modern foundation which looks northwest towards Redonda and Nevis from a hillside setting of 600ft. The two rooms are furnished with antiques, but with televisions for those who want them. Breakfast on the balcony, a kitchenette for your use and dinner on request, very comfortable, pool: an excellent Caribbean retreat.

✆ *(1 664)–*   *Eating Out*

Montserrat's culinary tradition is mainly West Indian, based on the tropical vegetables and fruits that you will find on sale at the market, and the fish and animals that can be caught here. The island's Irish heritage is reckoned to reach as far as the food in **goat water**, a stew of goat meat with herbs, often served at ceremonies. Another local delicacy, only served on Dominica and Montserrat, is **mountain chicken**, which hops wild in the hills before it reaches your plate. In fact, it is not a chicken at all, but an outsize frog.

Most of the restaurants have either closed or relocated to the north of the island in the present troubles. The best place to eat is probably the dining room at the **Vue Pointe Hotel**, but **Ziggy's** (✆ 491 8282) is still there and the **Emerald Café** (✆ 491 3821) is now in St John's. **Nep Co Den** (now in Cork Hill) is still serving very fine rotis, but now has a competitor for the best on the island in **Del Pino**.

✆ *(1 664)–*   *Directory*

Blackburne airport has been closed since the eruption of the volcano. The only way to reach Montserrat is by sea from other Caribbean islands nearby. There are no tourist offices abroad, so to get information, you will need to contact the **Montserrat Tourist Office** in the island itself: Box 7, Montserrat (✆ 491 2230, ✆ 491 7430).The island newspaper is the *The Montserrat Reporter*, which was being published weekly.

If you are calling Montserrat, the **IDD code** is ✆ (1 664) followed by a seven-digit island number which begins 491. When on-island dial the full seven figures.

The currency of Montserrat is the Eastern Caribbean dollar (fixed to the US dollar at EC$2.65 = US$1) which is used on islands from Anguilla to Grenada. The US greenback is also widely accepted, but expect change in EC dollars.

Sports and activities can probably still be organized. **Watersports** including scuba can be arranged through Danny (✆ 491 5645) and Sea Wolf (✆ 491 7807). On land there are arranged **hikes**, or **mountain biking**: Island Bikes (✆ 491 5552), now in the northern hills. You are not permitted to go to the active volcanic area, but people have been known to do so. The Belham Valley **Golf** Club (✆ 491 5220), which has 18 holes playing to 11 greens, is still open.

St Kitts and Nevis

St Kitts and Nevis stand side by side in the arc of diminishing volcanic peaks in the Leeward Islands. Their concave slopes rise gracefully through shoreside flatlands to rainforested and often cloud-capped summits, fertile greens offset against the blues of the tropical sea and sky. They have strikingly beautiful views of one another, across the Narrows, a channel just two miles wide.

There is a strong and vibrant West Indian culture to these two islands, unlike on some others nearby, where life has been swamped by the international tourist industry. Unless you hide out in the tourist ghetto or lock yourself away in plantation splendour (St Kitts and Nevis have a stunning collection of plantation house hotels), you cannot help but notice the local life around you. Expect to be accosted in the street. You may be asked for money or given a slug of rum. Either way, the Kittitians (pronounced as in 'petition') and Nevisians (as in 'revision') will let you know their thoughts on life. Between them the islands have a population of 44,000, of whom about 9000 live on Nevis (many more Nevisians also live in St Kitts). Even with their slowly developing tourist industry, St Kitts and Nevis have faced difficult economic times and they are quite poor. Visit, though, and you will find two quite different Caribbean islands, both welcoming and laid-back in classic old-Caribbean style.

For all their differences, the two islands have lived fairly amicably together in their political unity, which was established when they took their Independence together from Britain in 1983, until fairly recently. Internal rivalry is of course very strong—every Kittitian has a relative on Nevis and vice versa—and the annual inter-island cricket match is a fiercely contested event. Recently though, there have been political rumblings on the smaller island and it seems that the Nevisians really are revisionist after all. In February 1997 the Concerned Citizens Movement was re-elected with Secession a stated part of their agenda and it seems that the two islands may well sever their formal political links during the life of this book (*see* p.351).

History

St Kitts was once known as the 'Mother Colony of the West Indies', because it was the first island in the Lesser Antilles to be settled permanently. Liamuiga, the Carib name for St Kitts, supposedly means 'fertile land' and it was the verdant growth that attracted European colonists in the early 17th century. Despite the hostility of the Carib Indians and risks from a local infestation of pirates, they came to plant tobacco.

The first settler was the Englishman Thomas Warner, who arrived in 1623. Next year he was joined by a French privateer, Pierre Belain d'Esnambuc, who called in to repair his ship after a fight with the Spaniards near the Cayman Islands. Welcomed by Warner, the Frenchman stayed for a while and then went to France to persuade settlers to return with him to St Kitts. The two men arranged to share the island and in 1627 divided it into three, with the French in the north and around Basseterre, and the English in the middle.

One of the main reasons that the French and English were happy to team up was that they needed to protect themselves against the Caribs, who were none too pleased about this intrusion into their islands. The battles began even in 1626, with the Caribs rallying in their canoes from other islands including Dominica and Guadeloupe, but the Europeans held their own. Steadily the Caribs were forced out and Liamuiga became St Kitts. The Spaniards were no more pleased at this intrusion into their backyard in the New World and in 1629 their fleet attacked the settlement. During the skirmish the colony was destroyed, but, as was to be the routine all over the islands, as soon as the invaders were gone the settlers filtered back and got on with their planting. The new settlers also started to look farther afield. Competition for empire was hotting up and English expeditions were sent to settle nearby islands. Nevis was one of the many 'Charibby Islands' made over arbitrarily to the Earl of Carlisle by Charles I in 1627 and the next year Oualie was promptly taken from the Caribs by the British. Montserrat and Antigua were settled in 1632. The French boldly took on the larger and more hostile Windwards to the south, heading for Martinique and Guadeloupe.

On St Kitts itself, the scene was set for the next 200 years—the French and British would be constantly at each other's throats. At one stage they managed to fall out on the basis that a tree had grown. A banyan marking the border in the north of the island had enlarged by putting out a few years' worth of aerial roots and the land enclosed by it just happened to include 250 French houses. War was just averted on that occasion, but St Kitts passed from one power to the other like a shuttlecock. Brimstone Hill was built and besieged. And as the navies whittled through the islands Nevis took a fair beating too. In 1706 the French swooped in, destroyed what they could (about £1 million's worth), and left with around 3000 slaves.

At the beginning of the 19th century, the British finally gained the upper hand in the endless series of wars and eventually both islands found themselves in the hands of the British, with whom they remained until Independence. Only a few hints of French influence remain in St Kitts today: a fleur-de-lys on the national coat of arms and, most notably, the name of the capital—Basseterre.

When the islanders were not being besieged, they were planting sugar-cane furiously. Nevis stuttered on its route to prosperity, but prosperous it became. At one stage a fleet of 20 ocean-going ships was devoted entirely to serving that island, sailing out with luxuries and manufactured goods such as tools and returning loaded with sugar-loaves. She was dubbed the 'Queen of the Caribbees'. The sugar industry also needed slaves and in the late 17th century Nevis had a slave market. Vast numbers of Africans were brought over. When the ships arrived in port, these frightened men and women would be oiled up before being made to parade through the streets singing, prior to being taken to auction.

With the 19th century, the West Indian sugar industry went into decline and the mansions into decay, though the planters kept up their balls and finery as long as they could. And after Emancipation in 1834, the 'apprenticeship' system soon broke down in 1838 and the slaves

Rum shop

were finally freed. On such small islands, many were forced to remain on the plantations, but eventually independent villages like Challengers on the leeward coast of St Kitts grew up.

The late 19th century was a lean period for all the Caribbean islands and St Kitts and Nevis slipped into obscurity. The sugar industry had more and more difficulty competing in the world market as Cuba and Santo Domingo gained the ascendancy. Today, apart from a small income from sugar, St Kitts–Nevis is dependent on a slowly expanding tourist industry.

Politics

St Kitts and Nevis are united in a constitutional Federation, in place since Independence from Britain in 1983. The two islands were originally shunted together in 1882, as the colonial authorities in London made one of their many political rationalizations, and they formed a part of the Presidency of the Leeward Islands. The island of Anguilla was appended to the Basseterre administration in 1871. The three islands followed much the same course as the other British colonies in the 20th century, led by the clamour for political change in Jamaica, Trinidad and Barbados in the 1930s. In 1951, the islanders were given the vote and the St Kitts and Nevis Labour Party, rallying the voices of people who had had no political say before, swept the board. 'Associated Statehood' in 1967 brought more internal self-government, but at this point Anguilla, which had felt neglected by the government in St Kitts, staged one of the world's lesser-known revolutions and made its claims for secession heard (*see* p.378). After a 15-year row, Anguilla eventually left the State of St Kitts–Nevis in 1982.

At Independence in September 1983, the Nevisians wanted to make sure they would not end up in the same position as Anguilla and so they renegotiated the settlement, inserting an 'escape clause' that allows them to secede from Federation with St Kitts if two-thirds of the Nevisians choose to do so. Nevis has its own five-member elected assembly to govern its own affairs. In the 11-member House of Assembly of St Kitts–Nevis, three of the seats are allotted to constituencies on Nevis and these can easily hold the balance of power. St Kitts–Nevis remains within the British Commonwealth. At the moment the country is headed by Prime Minister Denzell Douglas of the St Kitts and Nevis Labour Party which was elected in August 1996 with all but one of the seats in the House.

Flora and Fauna

The lower slopes of St Kitts are bright green with sugar-cane, but both islands have thick and fertile growth, starting as scrub and grassland at the shoreside and rising to rainforest, where you will find swathes of elephant ears, and gommier and Spanish oak trees whose upper branches dangle with lianas and explode with orchids and cycads. Close to the summits of the mountains the rainforest gives way to stunted elfin woodland. The wildlife in St Kitts and Nevis is relatively unspoilt.

Around the bright red flamboyant tree, poinciana (named after St Kitts' first French Captain General, de Poincy), and bougainvillea, you will see typical island birds such as the purple-throated carib and other hummingbirds, daring bananaquits and bullfinches. Offshore, you can see pelicans and the occasional frigate bird, and in the lowland thickets you may spot a warbler or a pearly-eyed thrasher. St Kitts' few deer have been forced to the north now that the road on the southeast peninsula has disturbed their peace, but they are shy. You are more likely to come across the green vervet monkey, introduced in the 17th century. About a foot high, it lives in the hills and travels in packs. You can tell when one is angry by the white line above its eyebrow which it wiggles at you furiously.

St Kitts and Nevis Directory

getting there

Robert Llewelyn Bradshaw airport, 2 miles from Basseterre on St Kitts, has no direct scheduled services from Europe or from the USA, so you will have to make a connection. Newcastle airport on Nevis can only take short hopper flights, but there are easy links both from Antigua and from St Kitts itself (by plane or by ferry, *see* below for connections between the two). There is a departure tax of EC$27 (US$10).

By air from the UK: The easiest connections from the UK and other European countries are via Antigua, from where hopper flights (theoretically) link up with British Airways and BWIA services from London. It is also possible to make same-day connections to the islands from Paris (Air France) or from Amsterdam (KLM) via Sint Maarten. There are direct charter services from the UK and Germany in season.

By air from the USA: The easiest connections from the USA are made via the American Airlines hub in San Juan, Puerto Rico, from where there are regular flights on American Eagle (✆ 465 2273), but of course you can make your way to Sint Maarten or Antigua and take a hopper flight from there. It is even possible via the Virgin Islands. Some charter airlines do fly in from the USA.

By air from other Caribbean islands: St Kitts is easily accessible by the hopper flights that pass up and down the island chain touching most of the islands between Antigua and San Juan, Puerto Rico. Most of them stop in Nevis too. Airlines with scheduled flights include LIAT (✆ 465 2286 St Kitts, ✆ 469 9333 Nevis). Winair (✆ 465 8010 St Kitts) flies in from Sint Maarten. If you need to charter an airplane, you can contact Carib Aviation (✆ 465 3055, ✆ 465 3168, Nevis ✆ 469 9295) which has nine-seater and five-seater planes, Air St Kitts–Nevis (✆ 465 8571, ✆ 469 9018, ✆ 469 9241 Nevis) or Nevis Express (✆ 469 9756, ✆ 469 9751).

Travel between theislands: LIAT flights operate half-a-dozen times a day, but are often fully booked. The local inter-island 'bus' service is really the ferry (usually twice daily both ways; no services Thurs and Sun; about 45 minutes; EC$20 return). Out of the winter season, you can sometimes get onto the Four Seasons ferryboat which leaves from their terminal on the waterfront in Basseterre, timings according to flights. The views are magnificent as the mountains shift slowly above you. Kenneth's Dive Centre runs a water-taxi

St Kitts

The familiar name St Kitts (from St Christopher) has been used by the Kittitians since the 18th century. It is not known how the island took the name of the travellers' saint (Christopher Columbus, who passed the island on his second voyage, did not call it this), but perhaps later explorers named it in his honour.

St Kitts is the larger of the two islands (68 square miles) and is shaped a bit like a paddle, set in the water so that the handle points southeast. The blade is covered in a ridge of volcanic mountains, tumbling steeply from the summits and then flattening out towards the sea. The slopes are traced with *ghauts*, or ravines, which look a bit like huge volcanic stretch-marks and give an idea of the upheaval that the mountains once underwent.

service for a minimum of four passengers (© 466 5320) and you can also contact Blue Water Safaris (© 465 9838).

tourist information

UK: 10 Kensington Court, London W8 5DL (© (0171) 376 0881, ● 937 6742).

Germany: Air Pass, Walter Kolb Str 9–11, 60594 Frankfurt (© (69) 9621640, ● 610637).

USA: 414 East 75th Street, New York, NY 10021 (© (212) 535 1234, ● 734 6511, toll free © (1 800) 562 6208).

Canada: 365 Bay St, Suite 806, Toronto, Ontario M5H 2V1 (© (416) 368 6707, ● 368 3934).

The St Kitts and Nevis Tourism Office has a website at: *www.interknowledge.com/stkitts-nevis* and an email address: *skbnev@ix.netcom.com*

The *Observer*, published weekly in Nevis, is the islands' unaffiliated newspaper. The others are *The Labour Spokesman,* which is published twice weekly by the ruling Labour Party, and *The Democrat,* the voice of the People's Action Movement, which is in opposition at present. Radio stations include the inimitable Radio ZIZ (pronounced as single letters more often than as the sleepy, soporific word that it spells) and Radio Paradise, a religious station with gospel music.

The **IDD code** for St Kitts and Nevis is © (1 869) followed by a seven-digit local number, beginning with 465 in St Kitts and with 469 in Nevis. Between the islands and on-island, dial the seven digits.

money

The currency of St Kitts and Nevis is the Eastern Caribbean dollar, which is shared with the other former British colonies in the area. It is fixed to the US$ at a rate of US$1 = EC$2.65. US dollars are accepted all over the island. Major credit cards are accepted in the tourist areas and it is a good idea to make sure which dollar currency you are dealing in.

Banks: Open Mon–Fri 8–3 (many remain open on Fridays until 5pm). The St Kitts and Nevis National Bank also opens on Saturday mornings, 8.30–11.30.

Shops: Open weekdays 8.30–noon and 1–4.

Like many islands in the Caribbean, St Kitts became immensely wealthy as a sugar factory in the 17th and 18th centuries (it was worth building the massive Brimstone Hill to defend it), but unlike most other islands, the slopes of St Kitts are still covered with canefields. The industry hardly pays its way—it was bought out by the government in 1975 and kept going because it employs a large number of islanders. Recently, however, cane-cutters have been brought in from Guyana and St Vincent.

In contrast to Nevis's quiet and almost comatose mature, there is a slightly raw air about St Kitts, more typical of the larger Caribbean islands. The majority of the Kittitians are charming, though, and will happily engage you in conversation. It is worth getting out to explore the northern areas of the island.

The ride from the airport into town is little more than a mile, but if you do not want to go by cab (EC$15), then it is a short walk over the sugar railway to the main road where a minibus will pick you up in a matter of minutes and take you to Basseterre for EC$1.

Buses, *Rude Boy, De Hunter, Big Blue* and *Sunbeam*, run the roads of St Kitts intermittently from 6.30am until about 8pm. Headed to the main part of the island (there are no buses to the southeast peninsula), they depart from the waterfront next to the Nevis Ferry Terminal in Basseterre, leaving when they are full or when the urge takes the driver. They do not generally circle the island, but run along either one coast road or the other, which means that you can be stranded in the northern canefields if you are on a round-island tour. If this happens, **hitch**, which is quite a good alternative anyway. Getting on to a bus is as easy as flagging it down on the roadside; to get off you must shout 'Driver, Stop!' The buses are inexpensive and EC$4 will get you to the north of the island.

Taxis are readily available. In Basseterre you will find them at the Circus and they can also be arranged through any of the hotels. Fares are fixed by the government. Some prices are **Robert Llewelyn Bradshaw airport** to: Basseterre—EC$15, Frigate Bay area—EC$27, Rawlins Plantation or Golden Lemon at the northern end of the island—EC$55; and from **Basseterre** to: Frigate Bay—EC$18, Brimstone Hill—EC$30, Rawlins Plantation or Golden Lemon—EC$50.

Most taxi-drivers will also be willing to take you on an **island tour**, which costs around EC$130 for three hours. Taxis can be ordered through the St Kitts Taxi Association (✆ 465 4253) and the Circus Taxi stand (✆ 465 3006).

Car hire gives the most mobility, particularly if you are staying in the north of the island, and a small car can be hired from about US$40 per day, or a jeep for slightly more. Before driving on St Kitts, you must purchase a local driving licence, obtainable on production of your own licence and EC$30 at the fire station in Cayon Street, Basseterre. Companies will collect you and smooth the process. Driving is mostly on the left, though there are recognized chicanes to avoid the numerous potholes in the country roads. Some hire firms are: Caines on Prince's Street, Basseterre (✆ 465 2366), Delisle Walwyn and Co. just off the Circus in Basseterre (✆ 465 8449), TDC Rentals (✆ 465 2991) and Sunshine Car Rentals (✆ 465 2193). You can hire a scooter through Easy Ride Moped Rentals (✆ 465 3429).

Organized island tours can be arranged through the taxi drivers or the travel agents in town: contact Sunshine Travel and Tours (✆ 465 2193) and Kantours (✆ 465 2098). Typically they take about 3½ hours at US$20 per hour, and they can be arranged to include a stop for lunch at one of the plantation houses (arrange this in advance) as well as island sights such as Brimstone Hill.

Greg's Safaris (✆ 465 4121) offer an interesting drive around the island, visiting areas otherwise inaccessible because they are on private land (*see also* under 'other sports', p.365).

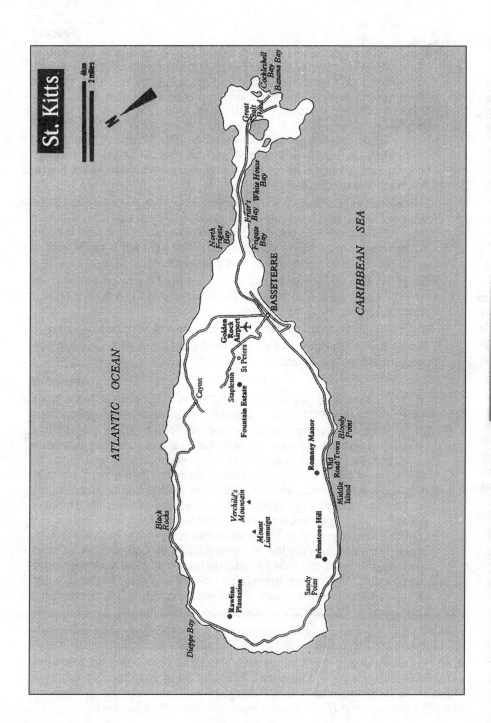

St. Kitts.

In the mountainous northern areas of St Kitts the beaches are mostly of black sand and there are not many beaches, but in the southern peninsula, which has been opened up by the peninsular road, the sand is golden brown and you will find a number of good strips of sand that are usually deserted.

best beaches

Frigate Bay (on the Caribbean side): Still the island's most popular beach, where you will find facilities for watersports, a bar and a couple of restaurants where you can get a meal. Its opposite number on the Atlantic side, **North Frigate Bay**, is pounded by ocean waves.

Friar's Bay: Over the headland going south from Frigate Bay, this is the nicest on the island and usually quiet and empty enough to feel secluded (though it has often been slated for development). On public holidays and when a cruise ship is in the bay there will be a cook-up and drinks on sale. Palm- and scrub-backed with a lagoon inland, it has magnificent views and superb mounded golden sand.

Sand Bank Bay: On the Atlantic side, with shallow water that rushes with wind and waves between huge headlands: no facilities and quite difficult to find, along a rickety sandy track leading left off the main road.

Major's Bay: Easier to find but not so nice, a thin strip of sand backed by a saltpond.

Banana Bay and **Cockleshell Bay:** Have development, now defunct, on their passable sand, and no shade or facilities.

beach bars

There is an excellent spot for chilling out on the beach at **Turtle Beach Bar** (✆ 469 9086) in the far south of the island, overlooking Nevis. There is good sand, shade on the seats and hammocks among the seagrape trees, and food on the covered deck of the bar itself: good snorkelling just offshore and other watersports such as kayaking, windsurfing and scuba-diving. It collects a lively crowd, particularly on Sundays when the Kittitians and expats make their way down here for the afternoon. Follow the south peninsular road past Great Salt Pond and then take a left. On Frigate Bay you will find the ever-popular **Monkey Beach Bar**, an octagonal wooden hut at the bottom of the beach where you can get a daytime drink between stints on the windsurfer or a sundowner. It is busiest on Fridays, when the crowds stay late. Just above the bar is the **Coconut Cafe**, on a deck overlooking the beach, and at the top end of the beach is the **New Anchorage** restaurant (✆ 465 8235), set in a modern villa just above the sand where you can get a salad or burger or a more substantial plate of West Indian food such as a curried conch or a stewed mutton. *Open all day in season.*

Basseterre

Basseterre, the small capital of St Kitts, has plenty of charm. It stands on the mile-wide sweep of a south-facing bay; a grid of streets lined with stone and wooden 'skirt and shirt' West Indian houses and sheltered by the magnificent green slopes of Monkey Hill and the South Range. It is home to about 17,000 Kittitians (about half the island's population).

The name Basseterre and its protected site have come down from the French, who first settled the area, but apart from this and the (not quite) gridiron layout of the town, nothing else French survives. The town was adopted by the British in 1727, in preference to their capital at Old Road. Today, the church towers, stone Georgian buildings and even the pointed iron railings speak of the island's 350-year association with Britain. Life itself is changing as the colonial memory recedes, but echoes remain in the uniforms of the police, Bedford trucks and the clock-chimes. Recent construction has given the town a little more of an upbeat air, but just behind the waterfront there are some tatty streets of fading buildings from the last century.

Visitors in the 19th century entered Basseterre through the arch of the **Treasury Building**, the domed colonial structure on the waterfront that housed the customs. Nowadays this is marooned inland by a huge new development, still in construction at the time of writing, with shops and cafés, cruise ship terminal, and marina. Behind it all, the old town still sits in gracious state, stone buildings with timber-frame upper storeys. The heart of the town is the **Circus**, where an elaborate green Victorian clock-tower stands beneath a ring of royal palms.

In the business streets behind the Circus, the government buildings can be found on Church Street and **St George's Anglican Church** on Cayon Street, built and rebuilt on the site of a French church of 1670. The formal centre of colonial Basseterre was Pall Mall Square, known since 1983 as **Independence Square**, where the goats mowing the lawn spike the imposing grandeur of the imperious Georgian houses and the **Roman Catholic Cathedral** with its impressive rose window and breezy interior with arched windows. Further east on the waterfront, you come quickly to the boats and drying nets in the fishermen's district. In the yards of beaten earth, small clapboard houses are shaded beneath a breadfruit tree or a palm. Just north of the new development is the main bus station and ferry terminal, which comes alive twice a day with the arrival of the *Caribe Queen* from Nevis. Traditional island sloops also dock here to collect anything from crates of drink to building materials before sailing off to Nevis. With a boom as wide as the mast is tall, they make a graceful sight plying between the islands.

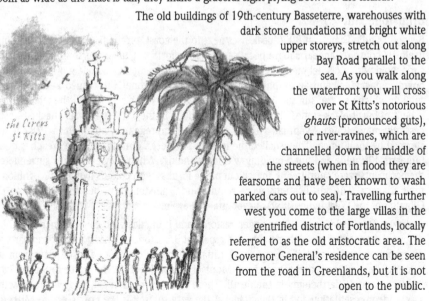

the Circus
St Kitts

The old buildings of 19th-century Basseterre, warehouses with dark stone foundations and bright white upper storeys, stretch out along Bay Road parallel to the sea. As you walk along the waterfront you will cross over St Kitts's notorious *ghauts* (pronounced guts), or river-ravines, which are channelled down the middle of the streets (when in flood they are fearsome and have been known to wash parked cars out to sea). Travelling further west you come to the large villas in the gentrified district of Fortlands, locally referred to as the old aristocratic area. The Governor General's residence can be seen from the road in Greenlands, but it is not open to the public.

Clockwise around the Island

A coastal road circles the island beneath the central mountain ranges, winding in and out of the ghauts, everywhere surrounded by canefields. Today the cane is crushed in one central factory, fed by a circular railway line around the island, but there were once 156 separate estates and the ruins of the old windmills and steam chimneys still stand proud behind curtains of bright green cane. Now that most of them are dilapidated, it is hard to imagine the atmosphere of a functioning plantation, but the rusting copper vats and the crushing gear still give a menacing air of industry and ceaseless human activity.

A couple of miles west of Basseterre, **Bloody Point** was the scene of an early massacre of the Caribs in 1626 when, in spite of their differences, the English and French teamed up. They were tipped off by a Carib woman that the Indians were preparing to attack and so the Europeans ambushed them, supposedly killing 2000. Strangely, the infant son of the Indian chief, Tegreman, was allowed to live and was brought up in the family of Ralph Merrifield in England. At **Old Road Town**, capital of the English part of the island in the 17th century, you can see one of the Indians' artistic memorials, their rock carvings: lozenge-bodied and anten-naed cartoon characters waving at you from the face of black volcanic rock. Just above the town is **Romney Manor** (*open Mon–Fri 8.30–4*), an old plantation house that is the home of **Caribelle Batik**. The old estate house burned down, but it has been partially rebuilt and the exhibits continue. The Indonesian process has been borrowed and has been turned to creating scenes with West Indian colour—anything from the fluorescent fish-life to the pastel nightlife.

A mile farther on is the town of **Middle Island**, where you will find the tomb of Sir Thomas Warner in a small green and white gazebo in the churchyard of St Thomas Parish Church, approached by an alley of palms. Warner was the pioneer British settler, who was knighted at Hampton Court by Charles I for his efforts. He first arrived in 1623 and died here in 1648, a 'noble and much lamented gent'. From St Kitts, he had settled Nevis, Antigua and Montserrat.

Brimstone Hill

Beyond Middle Island, an 800ft peak rises next to the coast, on the flank of Mount Liamuiga itself. Its contours appear square because a massive fortress sits on the summit—a 38-acre stronghold with a citadel presiding over bastions, miles of ramparts, parade grounds, barracks, powder magazines and an amphitheatrical cistern. Brimstone Hill, named because of the sulphur which you can still smell nearby, is a fitting name for this monster—the whole edifice is built of burnt black stone. The hill was first fortified in the 1690s and was attacked unsuc-cessfully many times. Eventually it was considered impregnable, but then in 1782 it was stormed by the French. They shelled the fortress for weeks until there were breaches in the ramparts 40ft wide and not a building was left standing. When they eventually surrendered, the occupants were permitted to march out of the fortress with colours flying in recognition of their bravery. The fortifications were rebuilt and Brimstone Hill became known as the Gibraltar of the West Indies. It was never attacked again.

Today much of Brimstone Hill has been restored and it bristles with cannon once more. But despite the odd whiff of sulphur the hellish aspect of Brimstone Hill has gone: the ramparts are overgrown with bougainvillea, and the Kittitians picnic in the grounds. The view from the summit is magnificent and ranges from Montserrat and Nevis in the south to Statia, Saba, St Martin and St Barthélemy in the north. There is an orientation centre downstairs with a short video presentation and in the citadel at the very summit is the **Fort George Museum** (*open daily 9.30–5.30, Thurs and Sun 2.30–5.30; adm*), displaying uniforms, maps and weapons alongside the history of St Kitts.

Sandy Point, a typical West Indian town where clapboard rum shops and the odd old stone building jostle new concrete structures, is the second-largest town on the island (population 7500). In the 17th century the Dutch were the great traders in the Caribbean and they kept warehouses at Sandy Point. A fire in 1663 cost them 65 warehouses full of tobacco. The island which lies 5 miles off the coast is Dutch St Eustatius. **Charles Fort,** another impressive military structure built in 1672, was the island's leper asylum. From here, the road runs through the canefields around the northern point of St Kitts, in the shadow of Mount Liamuiga.

Mount Liamuiga (pronounced 'Liar-mweagre') is the highest point on the island at 3792ft, and there is a crater lake just below the lip. The volcano, which was known for most of its history as Mount Misery, is (almost) inactive; it has been known to rumble very slightly once in a while. **Dieppe Bay** takes its name from the island's French heritage, which lasted until the early 18th century. The dilapidated stone and wooden buildings give an idea of the town's former prosperity as a sugar port. Returning down the Atlantic coast to Basseterre, the road passes the **Black Rocks**, volcanic extrusions that have blackened into weird black shapes since their eruption millions of years ago.

At Cayon a road cuts inland to Basseterre, running through the villages of Stapleton and St Peter's. Just beyond Stapleton is the Fountain Estate House, built on the site of **La Fontaine**, the residence of illustrious French Governor de Poincy in the 1640s. Not only was he Captain General, he was also Knight of Malta. He arrived with due pomp and circumstance and promptly erected himself a four-storey château in keeping with his station. The magnificent building was destroyed by an earthquake in 1689 and only the chapel and the steps remain.

The inland road rejoins the coast road as it approaches Basseterre, just by the central **Sugar Factory**. This monster is a proper factory, with conveyor belts feeding vast metal maws, banks of crushers that squeeze the very last drop of juice from the cane, and disgorge just a white pulp known as *bagasse*. All St Kitts' cane is brought in on the narrow-gauge railway track that runs around the northern part of the island. Among the modern equipment, vast brightly coloured baskets full of cane, you can see the discarded coal-fired engines of seasons past. It also has a distillery that makes the Kittitian rum, *CSR*. There are no regular tours, but it is usually possible to visit it during the cane-crushing season, between February and June, by asking at the gate.

South of Basseterre

Passing through the last of the canefields, and some of St Kitts' small industry (including the Headquarters of the Organization of Eastern Caribbean States's central bank), the road south from Basseterre climbs a ridge out of town and then descends into the tourist enclave of Frigate Bay, which is isolated from the local heart of St Kitts. In times past, Frigate Bay itself was the scene of early morning duels between slighted members of the St Kitts nobility, but now it tends to be clubs at dawn on the golf-course and a bit of jousting on jetskis.

In 1989 a road was constructed that opened up the south of the island beyond Frigate Bay and there are fine views along it as you head towards the south of the island. Plots of land have been sold, and large international hotel companies have begun to muscle in on the beaches, but little seems to have been built. From Frigate Bay, the road leads past the old salt ponds, common property in the days when the island was shared by the French and English, and comes to Cockleshell Bay and Banana Bay, where there are magnificent views of Nevis.

St Kitts (and Nevis) has far and away the finest collection of plantation house hotels in the Caribbean. Many are still surrounded by sugar cane as they were 200 years ago and they still retain the grace and hospitality of the era—they are small and are run in the style of a private house, with guests meeting informally for drinks before dinner. As former estate houses, most of these hotels are not on the beach, and so you might like to hire a car for mobility. Children are sometimes not encouraged. There are no really good beach hotels on St Kitts as yet, but the Frigate Bay area has some purpose-built shoreside condominium complexes. Hotels are supposed to be under construction on the southeast peninsula, but all seem to have fallen foul of Caribbean inertia somehow. St Kitts also has a number of villas for hire all over the island: details can be obtained from the Tourist Board, or _see_ **Travel**, p.8. A government tax of 7% is added to all hotel bills and most also add a 10% addition for service.

Plantation Houses

very expensive

Rawlins Plantation, PO Box 340, St Kitts (© 465 6221, @ 465 4954), has one of the Caribbean's supreme settings in the reworked buildings of a sugar estate on the slopes of Mt Liamuiga, looking north to Statia and Sint Maarten. There are just 10 very comfortable rooms scattered in wooden cottages and stone outbuildings (one in the windmill) among the tropical trees and hedges of the lawned estate gardens, each of them very private. When you feel like company you repair to the main house itself, with library and dining room, where among the stone walls, louvred shutters and antique furniture you take cocktails and then dinner on the veranda overlooking the swimming pool and grounds. A bewildering variety of tropical fruits for breakfast, followed by a buffet lunch (worth attending if you are not staying there, for the saltfish and funchi and the candied sweet potato) and then dinner of chicken and mango or lobster in puff pastry with a tarragon cream sauce. If this sounds over-indulgent then you can walk in the forests above the estate or knock a ball about on the grass tennis court. It is very expensive, but there is a reliably elegant atmosphere and there are few places like it anywhere in the Caribbean. Close by is the **Golden Lemon Inn** (© 465 7260, @ 465 4019, US res © (1 800) 633 7411), which is set in a 17th-century trading warehouse on the waterfront in Dieppe Bay. It is now meticulously restored and the old stone walls are more likely to echo with piano and singing accompaniment after dinner than the rumbling of rum barrels. There are 16 rooms, with wooden floorboards and louvred windows, gracefully furnished with antiques and with huge beds. But most charming are the 10 suites, which have been exquisitely decorated, each in a different style; tropical, oriental, Egyptian, and so on. The **White House**, PO Box 436 (© 465 8162, @ 465 8275), has an exquisite setting in the former colonial officers' mess. The site was chosen with discernment because it has magnificent views over the gradually descending country towards Basseterre. The drawing room and dining rooms are furnished to suit the period (perhaps a little more luxuriously than the original), with rugs, chaises longues and rosewood chairs. The bedrooms are also far more comfortable than any you might find in an old coach house. Very quiet and private, just 10 rooms. Pool in the gardens and other officer-like pursuits such as croquet and golf.

Ottley's Plantation Inn, PO Box 345 (✆ 465 7234, 📠 465 4760, US ✆ (1 800) 772 3039) is also set in magnificent grounds that fall gently down to the Atlantic from the slopes of the mountains. From the colonial grandeur of the enormous rooms and balconies (the great house has original stone foundations with restored timber upper stories) you look over restored stone outhouses and a superb lawn backed with royal palms to the Atlantic Ocean beyond. There are about 15 rooms and suites and again there is a private house atmosphere. MAP. The **Ocean Terrace Inn,** PO Box 65 (✆ 465 2754, 📠 465 1057, US ✆ (1 800) 524 0512, UK ✆ (0181) 367 5175), is close to town among the villas of Fortlands, but isolated from the relative hurly-burly in a walled garden that rambles across the hillside. The 54 rooms (air-conditioned with satellite television) make it sound large, but they are scattered around the main house and garden pool, where you can swim or take a jacuzzi and drink at the pool bar before dinner with a view of Nevis. The **Fairview Inn,** PO Box 212 (✆ 465 2472, 📠 465 1056), is set in a pretty Kittitian great house overlooking the Caribbean coast, with wooden floors and ceilings. It hasn't quite the style of the other inns of St Kitts, but prices itself accordingly. There are 23 rooms in stone cottages behind the great house, which has a busy and friendly bar.

Hotels, Self-catering and Guest Houses

The most modern and comfortable place to stay in Frigate Bay is **Horizons,** PO Box 521 (✆ 465 1627, US res ✆ (1 800) 699 1955), which is ranged in a series of pink and green villas on the rising ground high above Frigate Bay beach. It feels a little bit suburban, with two-storey apartments with their parking lots in gardens either side of the tarmac, but the 100 rooms (in one- to four-bed configurations) are extremely comfortable, with white tiles and bright Caribbean furnishings. There are 50 actual hotel rooms, all with magnificent views over the sea, and a restaurant, pool and bar. Packages available, including scuba and golf green fees. **Colony's Timothy Beach Resort,** PO Box 81 (✆ 465 8597, 📠 465 7723, US ✆ (1 800) 777 1700) is at the southern end of Frigate Bay. There are 60 plush and comfortable rooms and suites in blocks and a walkway of crotons and bougainvillea down to the pool and restaurant just above the beach. There are kitchenettes in some rooms. **Sun 'n' Sand Beach Resort,** PO Box 341 (✆ 465 8037, 📠 465 6745, US res ✆ (1 800) 223 6510) has a collection of cottages and studio apartments in a tropical garden around a pool and tennis courts, on the windy Atlantic coast.

Less expensive self-catering accommodation in Frigate Bay is available at the **Gateway Inn,** PO Box 64 (✆ 465 7155, 📠 465 9322, *www.ubnetwork.com/gateway/ index.html*). Within walking distance from the beach (oddly positioned at the top of the ridge), it has simple air-conditioned rooms with cable television, a little past their best, but a good price. If you are happy to be out of the way on the eastern Atlantic coast, then you might try the **Mule House** (✆/📠 466 8086). There are four self-catering apartments in a modern house, with balconies and comfortable furnishings. It is quiet and low-key but you will find yourself treated like family. Weekly rates.

There is a pleasant stopover in the very centre of town, right on the Circus with all the comforts for a businessman or a passing traveller: **Palms Hotel** (✆ 465 0800, ✆ 465 5889) is air-conditioned and carpeted, with cable television and video recorders.

cheap

There is a number of typically West Indian guest houses in Basseterre where you can find a simple but passable room. Try the **Glimbaro Guest House** on Cayon Street (✆ 465 2935, ✆ 465 9832), ten rooms, simple, functional, pink, some share baths, some private baths, restaurant downstairs. Probably the cheapest place in town at the moment is the **Harbour View Guest House** (✆ 466 6759), right on the waterfront in town. Purely functional, air-conditioned, modern and central. Also you might try the **On the Square** Guest House, which has pride of position on Independence Square (✆ 465 2485). Other options include the **Central Guest House** on the waterfront in town, very simple, with standing fans, and a lively local café, and the **Windsor Guest House** (✆ 465 2894; *very cheap*) on Cayon Street, with share baths.

✆ *(1 869)–* | *Eating Out*

The food in St Kitts is fairly typical of the British Caribbean: chicken, fish or goat, fried or in a stew, served with a tonnage of Caribbean vegetables. The more adventurous dining rooms will serve not only these, but also more exotic ingredients in tropical fruit sauces and some traditional European recipes. There is of course the rather less traditional burger to be found in the resort hotels, but it is well worth getting out to find a more Caribbean meal, either in the plantation houses, which serve excellent buffet lunches and set dinners, or in the side streets of Basseterre. Not many places accept credit cards. There is a government tax of 7% added to all bills and usually a 10% service charge as well. Categories are arranged according to the price of a main course: *expensive*—EC$40 and above; *moderate*—EC$20–40; *cheap*—under EC$20.

expensive

The finest evening's dining is at the **Georgian House** (✆ 465 4049) on Independence Square in town. You take a cocktail to start beneath the mango tree in the walled garden and then move inside the traditional town house with its wooden interior and polished herringbone wood floor. Dinner is candle-lit at tables with white linen and the atmosphere calm and comfortable. Start with a roasted red and yellow pepper soup and continue with a shrimp and sesame snapper, before finishing with a tropical fruit sorbet or white chocolate mousse cake. *Closed Sun and Mon.* At the **Patio** (✆ 465 8666) in Frigate Bay, you dine on the veranda or inside a private house where tables are lit by candle-lamps and you are served by waitresses in French creole madras costume. The menu is continental, with Caribbean adaptations. The restaurant has no licence to sell liquor, but wine and a small bar are complimentary. *Dinner only, by reservation, closed Sun.* **Fisherman's Wharf** (✆ 465 2754) has a waterside setting looking over Basseterre, on a wooden deck with bench seats. Seafood and grilled fare including barbecue shrimp, seafood kebabs and shark steak. Quite a lively atmosphere, on special nights and at weekends. **The New Anchorage** (✆ 465 8235) has a pleasant setting in the peach interior of a modern villa just off Frigate Bay beach.

Mixed international food and some West Indian specialities such as curried conch and stewed mutton; you can sit inside or out in the garden under parasols. *Lunch and dinner, breakfast in season.*

moderate

A popular spot in Basseterre, for a daytime drink or a cocktail at dusk, and light or fuller meals day long, is **Ballahoo** (✆ 465 4197), where you sit on a veranda right above the Circus in the centre of town. Quite a few tourists, but some locals too—chilli shrimps or Italian chicken breast. Very full menu all day and always a vegetarian dish. *Closed Sun.* **StoneWalls** (✆ 465 5248) sits in a charming Kittitian courtyard (of stone walls as the name suggests) on Princes St, with conch shell paths and profuse greenery. Grilled dishes with Cajun and Caribbean flavours, early evening bar. **Arlecchino** (✆ 465 9927) on Cayon St serves Italian food in a simple West Indian courtyard; pastas, pizzas and full platters. There is a very pretty restaurant set in an old stone and timber house (once the general's quarters) in the village of Old Road to the north of Basseterre: **Manhattan Gardens** (✆ 465 9121) serves simple burgers and West Indian dishes for lunch and mainly seafood for dinner.

cheap

Directly across the road on the waterfront is a Kittitian gem, the **Sprat Net**, which sits next to the stone walls of an old fort. Classic West Indian bar, easy atmosphere, grilled chicken, fish, rib or lobster, corn on the cob, johnny cakes. *Starts at sunset, Wed–Sun.* Back in town, **Chef's Place** (✆ 465 6167) on Church Street serves West Indian food to a local crowd. Delicious pumpkin or carrot soup, followed by turtle, saltfish and local fish. *Open for lunch and dinner.* There are plenty of local hide-outs in Basseterre where you can get traditional chicken or fish and tropical juice. Try **Victor's** (✆ 465 2518) in New Town, where you dine on mock-leather benches and plastic table-cloths in a modern pink town-house. Local juices to accompany Kittitian fare—plates of curry goat heaped with green fig and sweet potato. You can get an excellent takeaway pizza or a roti at the **Pizza Place** on Central Street in town. And if you would like a fry chicken to go, try **Gilly's** on Sandown Road or **Wendy's** on Cayon Street. On Fridays and Saturdays the Kittitians cook up chicken and fish on braziers at the streetside.

Bars and Nightlife

Much of the entertainment in St Kitts is centred around the hotels, whether it be singing along to Broadway tunes at the Golden Lemon or joining in the Jack Tar toga party. However, if you fancy a drink (perhaps a *Carib*, brewed under licence from Trinidad) with some Kittitians after work, **StoneWalls** gathers a crowd of professionals and **Bayembe** is the haunt of the students, lively in the early evening. There are plenty of rum shops around Basseterre: try **Five-Ways**, on the junction of five roads at the western end of Central Street, which collects a crowd of ministers and limers, and **Tiffin**, off Pond Road—turn at Uncle Jerry's corner. There are regular Sunday afternoon events, making a good day out, at the **Turtle Beach Bar** in the south and the **Monkey Beach Bar** on Frigate Bay, which is particularly busy on Friday nights. You can hear live music at the **Fisherman's Wharf** at the weekend. The **Lighthouse**, just out of town, has a clifftop bar with a view and an occasional discotheque at the weekends.

getting there

Details on getting to St Kitts are given on p.352.

tourist information

On St Kitts, the Department of Tourism can be found in Pelican Mall on Bay Road, PO Box 132, Basseterre (℗ 465 4040, ⬧ 465 8794). There is also a desk at Robert Llewelyn Bradshaw Airport. The Tourist Board puts out a glossy magazine, *The Traveller*, with essential information on restaurants and where to go shopping. As you drive around the island you will see signboards at places of historic interest.

festivals

The main event in the Kittitian calendar is **Carnival**, which takes place just before Christmas and lasts into New Year. It is a week of jump-ups, calypso and beauty queen shows and masquerades. Not many tourists attend, though plenty of Kittitians return to the island for the festivities and it is fun to watch the events in the stadium at Warner Park and around the streets of Basseterre. Grab a chicken leg and a Carib lager from one of the ladies fanning braziers at the edge of the park and join the crowd. There is a **Music Festival**, held each year over the last weekend in June, which features four days of local calypso music, reggae, an international band and gospel music. **Independence Day**, 19 September, is celebrated with traditional Caribbean feasting and festivities. **Tourism Week**, held in November, includes a food fair and seaborne activities like sailing races. There is also a fishing tournament in September (℗ 469 9690). There are other smaller events in the year, with more dancing in the streets of Basseterre: the Westbourne Ghaut **Block-out** (they block off the streets and have a party there with live bands) on the Queen's Birthday, **Easterama** at Sandy Point at Easter and **Village-arama** in St Johnston's, which sees fashion parades and the calypsonians sparring with one another in song.

shopping

There is a number of **art galleries** worth visiting in St Kitts. The **Spencer Cameron Gallery** (℗/⬧ 465 1617; open Mon–Fri 8.30–4, Sat 9–2.30) is set in a pretty colonial building on Independence Square. It exhibits some African but mostly Caribbean paintings, some painted by Kittitians and residents on the island, but also artists from elsewhere in the Caribbean, maps and limited edition prints of island scenes. On Fort Street in town you will find **Kate Design** with paintings and silks by Kate Spencer. Its sister gallery, the **Plantation Picture House** at Rawlins Plantation, can be visited on a lunch stop during a tour of the island.

watersports

The best place for watersports is **Frigate Bay**, in the hotel area south of Basseterre. Otherwise the beaches are fairly remote, except at the Turtle Beach Bar in the far south, where there are some facilities.

Windsurfing, small boat sailing and general watersports: Try Mr X Watersports (℗ 465 4995) and the Turtle Beach Bar (℗ 465 9086), *see* below. There are regattas during Tourism Week in November and occasional races to other islands.

Day sails: Scheduled catamaran cruises (trips to Nevis, sunset or daytime picnic and snorkelling extravaganzas) and charters can be fixed through Tropical Water Sports (© 465 4167) on *Celica III* and Leeward Islands Charters (© 465 7474) on the *Spirit of St Kitts* or *The Eagle.*

Deep-sea fishing: For steely-eyed shark-fishermen or women, can be arranged by day sail companies or on *Panda* (© 465 4438).

Scuba diving: A fair bit to offer, with submarine volcanic vents for explorations as well as the usual reefs, where if you are lucky you can see stingrays and even dolphins and whales. Much of the diving takes place off Nevis (a 10-minute run across the channel if you are in the south). Contact Pro Divers (© 465 3223, ● 465 0265), based at Horizon Villas above Frigate Bay and at Turtle Beach (© 465 9086), or Kenneth's Dive Centre (© 465 2670) on the Newtown Bay Road in Basseterre. Companies will provide instruction and referral training from courses back home. A single-tank dive costs around US$40 and operators have underwater photographic equipment.

Snorkelling: The best is in White House Bay off the south peninsular road, where there is a reef in 12 foot of water, and in the nearby areas of Ballast Bay and Shitten Bay, though these two can only be reached by boat. If you are driving around the north of the island, there is good snorkelling off Old Road Town on the leeward side of the island and Dieppe Bay on the northern coast. A glass-bottom boat, *Jazzie II* (© 465 3529), offers tours to the southeast peninsula.

other sports

Walking: On land there are well-organized tours around St Kitts, that make a close and informative inspection of plantation ruins (the conical windmills and tall square steam chimneys that you see from the road), and follow rivers up through the ever-encroaching undergrowth to hidden rockpools and waterfalls, high into the rainforest. Excellent walks are available through Greg's Safaris (© 465 4121). You will be told about island flora, fauna, folklore and medicinal plants as you climb through the St Kitts back-country, on walks that follow the old trails that once networked the island: one follows the route of the old English military road that linked the two sides of the island, another takes you up 3792ft to the top of St Kitts's highest peak, Mount Liamuiga, and down into its crater, 400ft down: or contact Kriss Tours (© 465 4042). There are full day and half-day hikes. Both companies provide drinks and snacks along the way.

Horse riding: A more leisurely look at St Kitts's plantation history may be had on horseback, riding around the island or simply cantering along the beach. This can be arranged through Trinity Stables (© 465 9603). It is planned (it is planned every year) to make it possible to ride on the sugar-cane train that circles the island through the canefields. Could be worth a try (© 465 8157).

Golf: There is a challenging and unforgiving (Atlantic winds, long fairways, plenty of water hazards) course at the 18-hole Royal St Kitts championship course in the Frigate Bay area (green fee around US$40). There is also a 9-hole course at Golden Rock. You might also consider going over to the course in Nevis (*see* p.376)

Nevis

At times it is the only cloud in the sky, but there is always a cloud on the summit of Nevis. Like all the tall volcanic Caribbean islands, Nevis blocks the path of the racing Atlantic winds which, as they rise and condense, stack in huge immobile cumulus clouds. This permanent white wreath supposedly reminded the Spanish travellers of the snow-capped peaks of home and so the island came to be called Nuestra Señora de las Nieves, Our Lady of the Snows. Gradually, the name has been shortened to Nevis (pronounced Nee-viss).

Nevis is almost circular (6 by 8 miles) and from the sea can look like a regular cone; deep green slopes rise in sweeping curves to the central Nevis Peak at 3232ft. About 9000 Nevisians live in settlements dotted all around the island.

For all its size, Nevis was the capital island in the Leewards for a time and the island was so illustrious that it was known as the 'Queen of the Caribbees'. Then, it had a population of 45,000, of whom 15,000 are said to have been white. Island society was so august and the estate houses so grand that ladies could walk down the stairs three abreast, panniered skirts and all. The 'old-time' elegance of the West Indies, which has been swallowed up pretty well everywhere in the Caribbean in the development of the last 30 years, is still just about visible in Nevis in the finely crafted bridges and dark stone walls that poke out of the ever-encroaching jungle. The plantation house hotels also retain the old grace and finery of centuries past and are some of the most exquisite hotels in the Caribbean.

A hundred years of association across the Narrows may have forged close relations with St Kitts, but it has not diminished Nevis's own traditions. The islanders have their own, five-person elected assembly (which meets just three or four times a year). Until now, when the Deputy Governor-General of St Kitts and Nevis is in residence you will always see two flags flying: one is for the Federation of St Kitts with Nevis and the other Nevis's own flag. Now they are considering severing links with the larger island.

Nevis is the smaller and quieter partner in the Federation with St Kitts, and the Nevisians go more placidly than their fellow-countrymen. In school, the children learn that there were no slave rebellions in the island's history which, if it were true, would probably make Nevis stand alone throughout the whole Caribbean. Certainly the Nevisians are extremely polite and they all have time to stop and talk to a stranger. But the island is changing as it gears up to the next century. Nevis has an unaccustomed buzz about it. People are building everywhere, their new houses creeping higher and higher up the hillsides, the number of cars has doubled in two years and there is even congestion in Charlestown. People actually seem to be in a hurry on what traditionally has been a comatose island. In just a few years the island has lost its innocence. And at the same time politics has taken a new turn (see below).

Even so, Nevis is still far less developed than most other Caribbean islands and it has oodles more charm than many other islands that pretend to be undiscovered.

Nevis and Politics

After simmering for years, the question of Nevis's Secession from the Federation of St Kitts-Nevis came to a head in 1996. It's a traditional Caribbean problem: the smaller partners in the convenient colonial administrative organizations have always felt put upon as the larger partner keeps the political power, usually by weight of population and therefore political mandate, and generally treats its own islanders better.

In Nevis's case, they felt they were disadvantaged by St Kitts' political control in decisions that should rightfully have been theirs. They were not getting their fair share of the importation taxes levied in the larger island (for goods that were then reshipped to Nevis) and their representations to aid agencies were being sidelined because they had to go via St Kitts. Their style of tourism is more upmarket than in St Kitts and they wanted to be allowed separate representation abroad. Their final grievance was that their growing offshore finance industry was being hampered: according to laws set in the St Kitts (and Nevis) Parliament, where Kittitians have a majority, of course, offshore companies were not allowed to invest in Nevis without first having representation in St Kitts, where of course they were being taxed. Outside investment was being discouraged and the Nevisians felt that they would have a better chance if they were able to do it alone. In a referendum in the seventies there was a resounding majority in favour of breaking the link with St Kitts. All but 12 people voted for Secession. Now that it looks more like a political reality, things have come rather more sharply into focus and suddenly it is a more daunting prospect. The debate has heated up. Besides the simple political issue, there are practical problems. St Kitts holds all the pension and social security money and this would have to be negotiated. The process now is that if a bill is passed in the Assembly with a two-thirds majority, the islanders can go to referendum. If that yields a yes vote, the Nevisians are permitted to secede, though the Federal Constitution does not lay out exact procedures to follow.

In 1996 the debate came to a head and the Nevisian politicians acted. A bill was put to the Nevis Assembly, then led by Vance Amory of the Concerned Citizens Movement with the

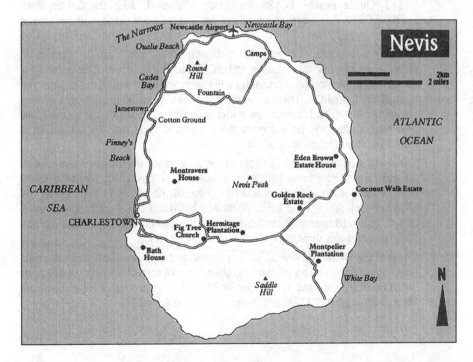

Nevis Reform Party in opposition. It looked as though it would be carried unanimously, but when it came to the second reading, in late 1996, two members, from the Nevis Reformation Party, did not attend the vote (despite the fact that the NRP and they themselves had been publicly in favour of Secession in the past) and so it was not carried. Their stated reason was that negotiations should be concluded with St Kitts before Secession was enacted, but rumours were rife of political shenanigans and gerrymandering. For their part, the government in St Kitts is not keen to let Nevis go and has stated that it will only negotiate when the refendum has produced a vote for Secession.

In February 1997, Vance Amory of the CCM called a snap election and was re-elected with the same balance of seats in the Assembly and the same NRP members in opposition. A bill leading to a referendum on Secession went through (on the nod); its second reading was set for October 1997. The general feeling on the island is that Secession will eventually go through.

Getting Around

There is an unscheduled but fairly regular **bus** service that sets off from Charlestown in both clockwise and anticlockwise directions (though not all the way round the island in one direction). Buses—*The Energizer, Captain* and *007*—leave from the town centre and run until 10pm (later on Saturdays), maximum fare possible is about EC$3. Hitchhiking works quite well in Nevis.

Taxis are available near the pier in Charlestown, at Newcastle airport, through the hotels or through the Nevis Taxi Drivers Association (✆ 469 1483) or the City Taxi Stand (✆ 469 5621). Some sample prices are **Charlestown** to: Pinney's Beach—EC$13, Oualie Beach—EC$25, Newcastle airport—EC$30, the Golden Rock Hotel—EC$30. Taxis can also be hired for a three-hour island tour for around EC$120.

You need a local licence if you wish to drive in Nevis, and it can be obtained on presentation of your own licence and EC$30 to the police in Charlestown (or Gingerland or Newcastle). Companies will collect you from your hotel and run you through the formalities. There is basically one road, about 20 miles long, that runs around the island, with one or two branches leading off it. Watch out for the goats, who seem to find the tastiest grass at the roadside. Cars get very booked up at Christmas, so you might want to arrange one in advance.

Car rental starts at around US$40 per day with insurance and 5% government tax on top and a jeep slightly more. Hire firms include: Avis (✆ 469 1240), Nevis Car Rental (✆ 469 9837) at the airport and Nisbett Car Rentals (✆ 469 9211 airport or ✆ 469 1913 in town), Striker's Car Rental (✆/📠 469 2654) and TDC Rentals (✆ 469 5690, 📠 469 1329). **Mopeds** are available for hire through Queen City Rentals (✆ 469 5389) and **bicycles** through Carlton Meades (✆ 469 5235).

Tours of the island (by vehicle) last 3 or 4 hours and they can take in lunch at a plantation house if you make a prior arrangement. You can contact a taxi driver direct, try Teach (✆ 569 1140) and T. Cee's (✆ 469 2911), or go through a travel agent: All Seasons Tours (✆ 469 1138) and Evelyn's Travel (✆ 469 5238).

Pinney's Beach: Nevis's stunning 3½-mile strand, which starts just north of Charlestown and is backed along almost its entire length by a confusion of palm trees, a cat's cradle of trunks and then a starburst of fronds. The golden brown sand shelves steeply into the sea and the scene is perfected by some cracking views of St Kitts. It is a good long walk and there is the occasional beach bar where you can stop to fortify yourself or linger over a sunset view. The Four Seasons Hotel sits smack in the middle and has brought large-scale watersports to the beach; windsurfing and small boat sailing can be arranged there.

Oualie Beach: Further round the coast to the north, more golden brown sand and a superb view across to St Kitts over the Narrows. A lively beach, with watersports shops and a bar at the hotel, and it sees a nice crowd.

Lovers' Lane beach: Excellent steeply shelved sand, no facilities and not much shade, but you are quite likely to be alone. It is quite difficult to find, along a rickety trail just after the hill

Newcastle Bay: More steep-sloping sand and quite big waves.

Indian Castle: On the eastern side of the island, below Gingerland, excellent sand and water, though no shelter or facilities.

beach bars

Pinney's Beach has a number of recommendable shoreside stopovers, ideal for lunchtime and a lazy afternoon on the beach. A clutch of them has gravitated around the Four Seasons: just outside the compound is the **Sunshine Bar**, a dead cool hang-out dressed up in red, gold and green, where you can grab a beer and listen to reggae all afternoon. Closer to town is **Grappy's,** a lean-to under the tall straight palms where they sometimes grill up. To the north of the Four Seasons, the **Beachcomber** is set in a converted villa: daytime snacks and seafood dishes, then drinks in the early evening followed by slightly finer fare. And just beyond here, the **Sand-dollar** is set back from the sand, but gathers a crowd from time to time. At the top end of the beach you will come to the **Mariner's Pub**, which serves excellent West Indian food on a rather functional deck with white plastic furniture—creole conch, rotis and catch of the day. Not far off is **Tequila Sheila's**, an open sided gazebo on the sand at the very top of the beach. They serve southwestern American food and grilled seafood at lunch and dinner. An excellent place to spend the day is at the **Oualie Beach Bar** farther around the coast, where there is often a lively crowd.

Charlestown

The island's capital and only town is Charlestown, a few streets of pretty old stone buildings with wooden balconies and gingerbread trimmings ranged along the Caribbean coast of the island. The town gravitates around the two small squares—Memorial or Independence Square and Walwyn Square—though they are actually more like triangles of grass because of the lie of the land. Here hucksters sell sweets and drinks, bus drivers wait for passengers and a small crowd of 'limers' passes the time of day. Named in 1671 after King Charles II, the town is home to 1500 Nevisians, who live mainly in a suburb of modern buildings that has grown up behind the original town. The occasional countryman still rides into town on his donkey, battling with the ever-increasing traffic.

Until recently Charlestown had a strong spirit of 'when the boat comes in'. Suddenly, twice a day, the customary atmosphere of sedation would switch to one of hectic activity with the arrival of the ferry from Basseterre. Supplies were brought in by boat and as the inter-island sloops or the ferry chugged into harbour, loaded to the gunwhales with crates of bottles and boxes of tins, the Nevisians raced to the pier. Business complete, the activity was eclipsed and Charlestown snapped back into its customary slumber.

Next to the ferry dock is the new waterfront, with a string of gazebos and a small tourist market, with shops in the restored cotton ginnery. Close by is the main Charlestown **Market**, at its busiest on Thursday and Saturday mornings, when the fruits and spices are heaped on the tables and lightning banter fills the air from soon after dawn. Back on the waterfront, the old stone warehouses that muscle in shoulder to shoulder have been redeveloped and now house cafés and restaurants among the modern businesses.

Alexander Hamilton

At the northern end of town, on a lane called Low Street, is **Alexander Hamilton House**, an attractive stone building set in a grassy garden. It was supposedly the birthplace and home for five years of the architect of the American Constitution, Alexander Hamilton, whose face you will see on the US$10 bill. The house was built in the 1700s and Hamilton was born there in 1757 of a Nevisian mother and a Scots father. When he was five, they moved to St Croix, from where Alexander eventually left to complete his education in the States. A patriot during the American Revolution, he was George Washington's aide-de-camp and was known as the 'Little Lion' because he was 5ft 7in tall and his blue eyes were said to turn black when he was angry. It was he who, having trained as a lawyer, first suggested the Federation of the American States in the form that was eventually adopted, and with its founding he became First Secretary to the American Treasury. He died in a duel with a political opponent, Aaron Burr, in 1804.

The building houses the **Museum of Nevis History** (*open weekdays 8–4, Saturday 10–1; small adm*) where there is an excellent chronological display of the island from Amerindian times to the present, with ghostly Arawak faces in pottery, pictures of 'old-time' Nevis with explanations of old island architecture, porcelain from the Bath Hotel, home crafts, and documents from the life of Alexander Hamilton himself. Upstairs, approached by a stairway from the grassy and tree-shaded courtyard, is the Nevis House of Assembly, where the five-man Nevis Parliament holds its four-yearly parliamentary sessions.

Headed in the other direction (east) out of town you will see the old **Bath Hotel**, a huge block of a building above the road to the right. It was constructed in 1778 in grand Nevisian style, complete with ballroom, balconies and accommodation for 50 guests. In Nevis's heyday people would come and stay here in order to take the spa waters, which come out of the ground at temperatures as high as 108°F. Supposedly they resemble those of Baden-Württemburg and were renowned for the treatment of rheumatism and gout. The waters were first mentioned by some visitors before Nevis was even settled. A captain John Smith, leader of the Jamestown settlers of Virginia, called here first in 1607. Some of his fellow travellers had been scalded by manchineel sap when they sheltered under the tree in the rain, but here they found 'a great poole, wherein bathing themselves they found much ease...they were well cured in two or three days.' The hotel was dilapidated for many years, although it has survived the earthquakes and hurricanes well. (At the time of writing it was fairly permanently occupied by the police.) The bath-house is no longer fully functioning either, though if you are scalded by a manchineel tree, you can still rush around here and take the waters from the stream.

Just behind here you will find **Government House**, built in 1909, the official Residence of the Deputy Governor-General of St Kitts and Nevis, which sits in lawned gardens on a hilltop that overlooks the town. Next door is the **Horatio Nelson Museum,** where the exhibit 'Nevis in the Time of Nelson' details Nelson's life and times in the West Indies. Nelson was based at English Harbour in Antigua on HMS *Boreas* in the 1780s, soon after American Independence and was unpopular with the West Indians because his job was to enforce the Navigation Laws (which banned their very profitable trade with countries other than Britain— they even sued him once and he had to stay on board his ship for eight weeks to avoid being locked up). However, eventually he found solace with the young widow Fanny Nisbet, whom he first met at Montpelier House. The bride was given away by Prince William Henry (later to become King William IV, who was based in Antigua at the time). There is an impressive collection of Nelson memorabilia, from letters, maquettes of ships and pottery from toby jugs made in his image to the porcelain used at his marriage feast.

Anticlockwise on the Island Road

Back on the main road, the town quickly thins into countryside with new concrete houses sitting behind their fences and old wooden homes on small plots of beaten earth scattered at the roadside. As you drive, you will come across age-old stand-pipes, delivering water as they have for the last hundred years, and impromptu roadside markets which switch sides at midday to take advantage of the shade.

The Nelson story continues briefly at **Fig Tree Church**, a small stone sanctuary in a tropical garden, which is where the marriage between the future Admiral and Fanny Nisbet took place. His signature can be seen in the register (a photocopy). The couple soon returned to England, but the marriage did not last and Nelson became involved with Lady Hamilton.

Fig Tree Church, Nevis

At Camps on the northern side of the island, you can follow the coast road to Oualie or take a road that leads into the forest and through the hills and emerges on the Caribbean coast at Cades Bay at the **Soufrière**. This is an active volcanic vent that first appeared with a hiss and a sulphurous stench when an earthquake struck in 1950. It is a bit lukewarm now, with just the odd trace of stink-bomb and some heated and barren patches of earth, but is a reminder that the underworld is not so far away in the Caribbean.

The main road returns to Charlestown along the Caribbean coast, skirting behind Pinneys Beach. You will come to the site of **Jamestown**, the first capital of Nevis, which slid into the sea during an earthquake in 1680. It is said that one man escaped the quake when the jail collapsed around him: 'Redlegs Greaves', a Scots gentleman pirate who retired to an estate on Nevis after a lifetime of freebooting, had been recognized by a former comrade in revelry and had been thrown in jail. Having been spared by the earthquake, he was eventually pardoned. From here the road winds through the manicured gardens and golf course of the Four Seasons Hotel and into town.

✆ *(1 869)–*   *Where to Stay*

Like St Kitts, Nevis has some extremely fine plantation hotels, where you can bask in 18th-century splendour just as the planters did 200 years ago. They are quiet and low-key and although most are not on the beach, the hotels usually run shuttle-buses. If being right on the sand is the most important thing, then there are also some nice beach hotels. Nevis is building steadily, some stylish hotels and some not so nice ones in modern concrete. A 7% government charge is added to all bills and most hotels also add 10% to your bill for service.

There is also a number of villas and cottages dotted around the island, for those who would prefer to be independent and perhaps do the round of the restaurants in the evening. Contact the Tourist Board or **Seashell Properties**, Main Street, Charlestown (✆ 809 469 1675, ✉ 469 1288, US toll free ✆ (1 800) 457 0444) or **Hart of Nevis** (✆ 469 3262, ✉ 469 2328), who have a number of houses and villas, most of them with pools, for rent.

very expensive–expensive

Montpelier Plantation Inn, PO Box 474 (✆ 469 3462, ✉ 469 2932, US ✆ (1 800) 223 9832, *www.stkitts-nevis.com/montpelier*), is a tropical island idyll of centuries past, where you will find a gracious old West Indian ambience, with a certain English style. There are 17 large rooms in cottages scattered around the grounds of a magnificent estate house, all linked by paths that wind among flamboyant trees and frangipani. The plantation is lost in the southern hills of Nevis, but there are shuttles to the beach and the hotel has a tennis court and a pool. The dining room, on a veranda off the main house, overlooks the lit gardense. Montpelier is quiet, luxurious and refined and it will not let you down. The **Hermitage Inn**, St John's Parish (✆ 469 3477, ✉ 469 2481, US ✆ (1 800) 742 4276), has a supreme setting on the southern-facing slopes of Nevis. The great house, a classic West Indian timber-frame building from the 1740s with louvred windows on stilts, stands surrounded by mango trees and other tropical greenery, and the 15 rooms are set in neat cottages with traditional shingle walls and tin roofs, wrapped in gingerbread woodwork and bougainvillea. The rooms have wooden interiors with four-poster beds and antiques and all have hammocks on their balconies from where you can savour the view. There is the easy-going air of a private house as guests gather for a rum punch and tannia fritters before an excellent dinner on the veranda. Some cottages have kitchens. **Nisbet Plantation Beach Club**, St James Parish (✆ 469 9325, ✉ 469 9864, US ✆ (1 800) 742 6008, *www.nisbetplanta-tion.com/, nisbetbc_caribsurf.com*), has the advantage among the plantation hotels of being set on the shore in 30 acres of lawned estate. There is a magnificent view from the great house to the seafront and passable beach (it is sometimes a little windy) down an alley of tall palms (lit at night) where the 38 rooms and suites are scattered in bungalows. During the day you can pass the time at the beach, pool and beach restaurant. In the evening you retreat to the great house, an exquisite setting for dinner. MAP. The **Golden Rock Plantation Inn**, PO Box 493 (✆ 469 3346, ✉ 469 2113, gdhobson_caribsurf.com), is a smaller and simpler plantation hotel set 1000ft up the mountain side and threatened with being swallowed up by its 96 acres of garden. You approach on a rickety, stone-lined drive up a steep hill to a small complex of old estate buildings converted into the hotel. Just 15 rooms, which stand in modern blocks behind the main house, some of them furnished with antiques or bamboo four-posters. The shell of the old windmill has been converted into a honeymooners' suite.

The **Four Seasons Resort**, PO Box 565, Charlestown (✆ 469 1111, ✉ 469 1112, US ✆ (1 800) 332 3442, Canada ✆ (1 800) 268 6282) sits on a superb stretch of Pinney's Beach. It is large, sumptuous, swish, brisk and without much character, but does a reliable beach-bound body-holiday—massage parlour, health centre, watersports and day cruises, tennis and golf, low-calorie meals and king-sized beds.

expensive–moderate

The **Oualie Beach** Hotel (✆ 469 9735, ✉ 469 9176) has a much more casual Caribbean style: a small, much more laid-back beach hotel just above the golden sand of Oualie beach, which sees a fun crowd during the day. There are 22 bright and breezy rooms in cottages with gingerbread trimmings and superb views of St Kitts, which you can gaze at from the screened verandas. Some rooms have mahogany four-poster beds with canopies. There is a lively bar and restaurant serving West Indian meals and plenty of watersports are available right outside on the beach. Secluded and comfortable, **Tequila Sheila's** (✆ 469 1633, ✉ 469 0129) stands at the very top of Pinney's Beach, with its 16 studios in staggered single-storey blocks just above the sea (sometimes there is sand). They are furnished with mahogany beds with muslin nets and decorated with Mexican tiles. They are fan ventilated and air-conditioned and each has a patio from which to watch the sunset.

moderate

Perched above Oualie Beach are the 11 **Hurricane Cove Bungalows** (✆/✉ 469 9462), which are ranged around the headland and have magnificent views out to sea. They are built simply of carefully finished wood, with muslin nets over the simple wooden beds, window shutters on stilts and a sitting area with huge windows to take advantage of the scenery. One- and two-bedroom units with full kitchens, some with private pools, but no restaurant.

cheap

There are simple self-catering apartments in town at **Meadville Cottages**, PO Box 66 (✆ 469 5235, ✉ 469 3388, UK ✆ (0181) 289 9685) on Craddock Road. Neat, clean and quite comfortable, with balconies to sit and relax on. Alternatively you can go for the **Seaspawn Guest House**, PO Box 233 (✆ 469 5239, ✉ 469 5706), on the edge of Charlestown with 18 clean and simple rooms each with a private bath. It is a good place from which to explore Nevis if your hotel is not the main point of the holiday. Close to the town centre is **Daniel's Deck** (✆ 469 5765), where there are no-nonsense rooms with private bathrooms at very cheap prices.

The finest food and the best settings are found on the verandas of the plantation house hotels (the Thursday night fish barbecue at Nisbet is well known and both Montpelier and the Hermitage have elegant dining rooms), but there is an increasing number of good restaurants outside the hotels in Nevis. Most restaurants add a 10% service charge to your bill. Categories are arranged according to the price of a main course: *expensive*—EC$50 and above; *moderate*—EC$20–50; *cheap*—under EC$20.

expensive

For an excellent and thoroughly original night out you can go to **Miss June's Cuisine** (⌀ 469 5330), which serves a compendium of West Indian and other dishes in a villa in the Jones Estate (unmarked, just off the main road, next to the two-hole Nevis Golf Club). You start with cocktails in the drawing room and move next door for a set menu of six or seven courses: soup, fish, a multiplicity of main dishes and vegetables on a buffet and then puddings, which Miss June talks you through (it can be as many as 30 dishes in all). Coming from Trinidad, she cooks plenty of spicy, Indian-inspired food, but also expect Asian, gourmet Caribbean and international fare. The menu varies nightly. She doesn't open every night (most likely on Mon, Wed and Fri) and you must make up a minimum party of eight—by reservation only, but well worth making the effort to get there. In town you will find that the best restaurant goes by the unlikely name of **Eddy's Restaurant** (⌀ 469 5958). It is set on Independence Square in a very attractive old town house, where you dine in the wooden interior on creaking floor-boards or on the veranda looking out on to the square. Daytime fritters and salads, rotis, night-time specials of soup followed by catch of the day, and dishes such as voodoo pasta. Some entertainment, bar attached.

moderate

Prinderella's (⌀ 469 1291) has a nice setting on Jones Bay and you can eat there to the wash of the breaking waves all day: chowder, salads and some more sophisticated

Nevis Directory

getting there

Details on getting to Nevis are given on p.352.

tourist information

The helpful **Bureau of Tourism** is on Main Street in Charlestown (⌀ 469 1042, ✆ 469 1066). There are also desks on the waterfront in Charlestown and at Newcastle Airport.

festivals

In Nevis, the island festival goes by the rather unwieldy name of **Culturama** (⌀ 469 5521). There are regular Caribbean carnival activities, so you can expect to see calypso and string band competitions and costumed masqueraders strutting through the streets of Charlestown. Culturama takes place in late July, coming to its climax on the first Monday in August. **Tourism Week** has displays of arts and crafts alongside horse-racing, a treasure hunt and music. If you are on-island at Easter, look out for the kite-flying competitions. In dishes, and in the evening chicken parmigiana or wahoo in Carib batter. Farther up the beach you can get a nice meal at **Tequila Sheila's** at the top end of Pinney's Beach. Flaming torches stand outside the open-sided gazebo and you can linger over grilled seafood or southwestern American fare. Among the beach bars, which also open up for the evenings, the **Mariner's Pub** is known for its local food—fry fish and chicken with rice and peas. Overlooking the yachts and the lights of St Kitts from the waterfront in town is **Unella's** (① 469 5574), a quiet haunt set upstairs on a stone-walled balcony and deck. Lunchtime salads, evening local fare, grilled fish served with capers and lemon or shrimp scampi sautéed in garlic. A nice daytime stop in town is the **Courtyard Café**, set in a courtyard behind an old town building where you eat on garden furniture beneath profuse greenery. Light daytime fare—saltfish patties, salads and burgers; more substantial meals in the evenings.

cheap

In Newcastle and well worth a stop for its local food is **Cla Cha Del**, from Claudia, Charles and Delroy (① 469 9640). But for the best in local food go to **Muriel's Cuisine** (① 469 5920) on Happy Hill in the back of town. Classic West Indian restaurant set in a modern house, with flowery plastic tablecloths and a daily varying menu of curries and stews and rotis, served with excellent johnny cakes. **Callaloo** in Charlestown has simple West Indian fare in an air-conditioned setting.

If you want to catch a sunset **drink** you can wander along to any of the bars along Pinney's Beach, but in town **Eddy's** often has a lively crowd in the early evening, particularly on Wednesday. There is something of a circuit of bars during the week: on Thursday people gravitate to the fish cook-out at **Nisbet Plantation** hotel; on Fridays the crowds make for **Sanddollar** after dinner and on Saturday they head down to **Tequila Sheila's**. The Caribbean night at the Hermitage is also popular. Some of the hotels lay on entertainment, perhaps a piano player or a steel band, but if you want to join in with Nevisians on their evening out you can try the local discotheque, **Club Trenim** on Government Road in Charlestown, which is liveliest at the weekends.

① (1 869)–

June there is a sailing regatta, with some races for local fishing craft, which makes a a colourful sight and in October there is a sportfishing competition.

shopping

There is a number of galleries worth visiting on Nevis. In Charlestown you will find the **Plantation Picture House**, which is set in a pretty white wooden house on the road heading east. On sale there are hand-painted silks and prints and some tropical tablemats by Kate Spencer from St Kitts.

On the road towards Pinney's Beach is the **Gallery of Nevis Art,** where you will find bright and colourful tropical work by Caribbean artists and expatriates. The **Eva Wilkin Gallery** (① 469 2242; open Mon–Fri 10–3 or call in advance) is set in the shell of an old windmill in Gingerland, to the east of Charlestown. Eva Wilkin lived and painted for many years in Nevis and some of her work is on view, alongside exhibitions of other painters. There is a shop downstairs.

watersports

There are just a few places where you can take part in watersports, on Pinney's Beach and at Oualie Beach. For waterskiing and small boat sailing, the calm waters of the west coast are ideal. General watersports equipment can be hired through the Four Seasons Hotel, where there are concessionaires, and at Oualie Beach, where you can arrange waterskiing or a sunfish or small boat through Nevis Water Sports (✆ 469 9518).

Windsurfing: Oualie beach is a good spot because inshore it is relatively protected, but further out, where the winds are concentrated by the Narrows, there are bumps and jumps. Further around the coast at Newcastle, the Atlantic winds make for more extreme sail-boarding; contact Windsurfing Nevis (✆ 469 9735, ✉ 469 9176), who offer instruction, 'guaranteed success', BIC and Mistral boards and Up and Tushingham sails.

Day sails: With snorkelling and a barbecue picnic, available through the catamaran *Caona* (✆ 469 9494). Sea Nevis (✆ 469 9239) arrange day sails and water taxis. You can always make your way over to the southeastern peninsula of St Kitts for a day (just a 10min ride).

Scuba-diving: Rental and instruction available through Scuba Safaris (✆ 469 9518, ✉ 469 9619) at Oualie Beach or at the Four Seasons Resort if you wish to go further and deeper, to explore caves and hot springs coming off Nevis's now dormant volcano.

Snorkelling: The best area is around Jones Bay, offshore at Prinderella's Restaurant.

other sports

Walking: There are some worthwhile hikes into the Nevisian jungle, which take a look at the island's more exotic flora and visit the old plantation estates. There are endless ruins on the island, and they make excellent foraging grounds for the walker/historian—the skeletons of mansions and boiling houses gape in their decay, cane-crushing rollers and boiling coppers are littered around long-overgrown gardens. There was once an Upper Round Road which ringed Nevis above the plantation estates, linking Zion, Rowlands and Hamilton. Some old estates worth seeking out are Montravers House, inland from Pinneys Beach, which was the finest on the island when Nevis was the Queen of the Caribbees (it even had a moat), and on the windward Atlantic coast, the Coconut Walk Estate ruins and the Eden Brown Estate House, famous for its ghost, the tortured bride who lost her husband in a duel with his best man on the very night of her wedding.

You are advised to take a guide when walking off into the country. Two companies have excellent guided walks: Eco-Tours (✆ 469 2091) who offer leisurely walks through the plantations, and Top to Bottom (✆ 469 9080), who take walks up into the rainforest, to Nevis Peak and to the old estates hidden in the Nevisian undergrowth, where you will learn the secrets of medicinal plants. The Nevis Historical and Conservation Society, which is based at Alexander Hamilton House (the museum in Charlestown), organizes a monthly hike and other events. (For a calendar of events, call them on ✆ 469 5786.)

Riding: A ride in the foothills of Nevis Peak or a canter through the surf can be arranged by the Hermitage Inn (✆ 469 3477) or Cane Gardens (✆ 469 5464, evenings). There is a Jockey Club in Nevis, with race meets about ten times a year, mainly on public holidays.

Golf: There is a very neat and well-kept 18-hole course designed by Robert Trent Jones II attached to the Four Seasons Hotel. People fly in from the islands around to play it, though it is extremely expensive and hotel guests have preference in teeing-off times.

Anguilla

Anguilla is a flat and barren island, 16 miles by 3 and mostly 15ft deep in scrub. Inland, the 'eel' (its name supposedly derives from eel in Spanish) is hardly an attractive island, but along its writhing coastline Anguilla has some of the Caribbean's most spectacular beaches—mounded with sumptuously soft and blinding white sand, set in an electric blue sea. On a coast 45 miles long, there are about 30 of them.

Anguilla is the most northerly of the British Leewards and it lies about 5 miles from the French part of St Martin, looking north and east into the Atlantic. Sombrero Rock, its dependency, is the northernmost point in the chain of the Lesser Antilles.

The 9000 or so Anguillians are pretty cool—for a small Caribbean island there is a remarkable air of independence and self-assurance. The island is quiet to the point of sedation and it seems that nothing could ruffle Anguilla's calm. But it is worth remembering that 20 years ago, when they wanted to secede from St Kitts and Nevis, they took to the scrub and staged a revolution. As with so many Caribbean islands, the Anguillians you meet here are only half the story, as there are probably more abroad than there are on the island itself. The island has never been able to offer its people a living and so traditionally they have travelled. The money they send home and the money generated by tourism over the last 15 years has made Anguilla quite prosperous.

As you travel around the island you will see the grey skeletons of partially built houses protruding from the scrub. You might think they were the results of recent hurricanes or the failed dreams of expatriates, paradise homes that have foundered on classic West Indian business inertia. But this is not the case at all, as most of them are owned by Anguillians abroad. In time-honoured tradition, the traveller returns when he has earned enough to buy a plot, then leaves again to earn more in order to build on it. Steel reinforcements are left sticking into the sky ready for the time that the family outgrows the house and they need a second storey (it's also a tax dodge). Among all the development, however, there are still people who lead fairly simple West Indian lives, in shingle and clapboard houses set in a small plot of beaten earth.

The Anguillians have been building steadily for the tourism industry as well as for themselves. The island has specialized in a brand of reliable low-key high luxury and has a string of extremely smart hotels, among the best in the Caribbean, though there are also some less expensive places to stay. There is also good variety in the restaurants—unexpectedly for a British Caribbean island it has become a place where you can expect to eat seriously—and a string of lively beach bars. For the moment the island has an easy air because it is not too crowded.

Apart from the impeccable beaches, it is the Anguillan people that make this barren islet a special place. As they greet you with the slightest wave and a soothing 'all right, all right', it is hard to imagine that there was ever a raised temper here, let alone a revolution.

History

In Amerindian times, Anguilla went by the name of Malliouhana and although it was probably christened Anguilla by a Spaniard, Spain herself ignored it because it offered no quick returns. The Spaniards' only fleeting interest in the island was in 1633 when the Dutch moved in. They promptly attacked it.

In 1650 some Englishmen, an assorted bunch of rovers and misfits, had a go at settling the island. They arrived to find that Anguilla was 'filled with alligators and other noxious animals, but the soil was good for raising tobacco and corn, and the cattle imported multiplied very fast'. Salt could also be harvested and this continued until quite recently.

Anguilla did not really turn out that well as a plantation island, perhaps because the settlers were more interested in other things; soon it was a 'nest of pirates and smugglers and outlaws, dangerous to every neighbouring island and a disgrace to the British name'. But the Anguillian settlers were themselves vulnerable to the usual raids and ransackings of the Caribs and other Europeans. The French defeated them and occupied the island and the Irish attacked a number of times, leaving settlers behind in their turn (you can just hear echoes of Irish in Anguillan English). The defenders had more success in the 18th century, though. In 1744 they repelled a large French force that landed at Rendezvous Bay. The story goes that when the Anguillians ran out of ammunition, they loaded up the weights from their fishing nets in order to keep up their fire.

The early settlers had made what they could of the barren land, renting it from the Crown for the price of 'a fat capon, a kid, or one ear of Indian corn on every feast day of St Michael the Angel'. Slaves were brought to the island, but the estates could not support them, so they were left to grow their own food or fish for four days a week. They were also encouraged to go abroad, using their skills as coopers (barrel-makers) or carpenters to earn a living.

They ventured as far afield as Trinidad and Puerto Rico, dealing in merchandise and practising a bit of smuggling. A tradition of boat-building grew up on the island. At one stage even the Governor was an 'honest old sloop man'. As they sailed, they would send home contributions from the money they earned abroad, 'remittances' that were the backbone of the economy.

Initially Anguilla had no governor and was administered by a notable on the island such as the doctor, who also acted as magistrate, but in 1825 the island was attached to St Kitts for administrative convenience. The Anguillians had very little in common with the people of this successful sugar colony founded on slave-labour, which in any case was about 60 miles away to the south. Occasionally they protested to the British Government, but without success. With little representation in the St Kitts House of Assembly, the Anguillians were treated as poor relations and they had to fight hard even to get their name added to the title of the country of St Kitts and Nevis in 1951.

The Revolution

In 1967, when all the British Caribbean colonies were given internal self-rule as 'Associated States' with Great Britain, with the option of Independence not far off, Anguilla suddenly found itself faced with the possibility of Independence in union with St Kitts and Nevis. The islanders promptly staged a revolution. On 30 May 1967, they rounded up the Kittitian policemen and shipped them out, refusing to recognize the authority of the Basseterre Government.

From the beginning the situation bemused outsiders, who wrote it up as 'the mouse that roared' and 'the eel that squealed', but they did not reckon with the determination of the Anguillians, who went as far as staging a tiny invasion (unsuccessful) of St Kitts to pre-empt attempts to take Anguilla by force. They held referenda and wrote their own constitution.

Disbelieving colonial officials were dispatched to persuade the Anguillians to rejoin St Kitts–Nevis, but the islanders were adamant. With political tension mounting in 1969,

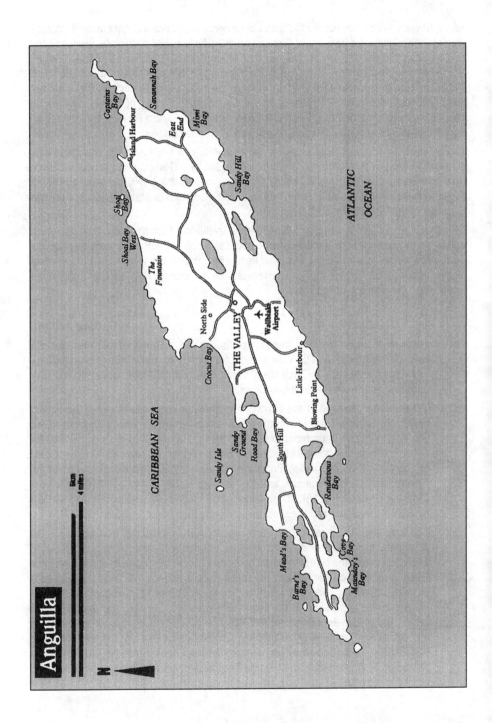

British troops were sent to occupy the island in an operation which was later dubbed Britain's 'Bay of Piglets' after the invasion of Cuba a few years before. Not a shot was fired, and the soldiers arrived to find themselves welcomed by people singing 'God Save the Queen'. When the troops were withdrawn, the London Metropolitan Police took over. All around them Caribbean countries were shaking off the colonial yoke, but Anguilla decided that it did not want Independence at all. It preferred to remain a Crown Colony of Britain. The whole episode is hilariously retold in Donald Westlake's *Under an English Heaven*, recently republished, available in Anguilla and complete with priceless photographs.

The political solution was long in coming, but eventually in 1982 Anguilla was granted its own constitution, with Ministerial Government headed by a Governor and ministers chosen from a seven-member House of Assembly. The Government is led by Chief Minister Hubert Hughes, leader of an AUP/ADP coalition formed after elections in March 1994. The current Governor of the island is Robert Harris.

Today some Anguillians depend on fishing for their livelihood, sailing to catch lobsters, which sell for a very good price and are flown out to hotels as far off as Puerto Rico each evening. But most work in the construction industry or in tourism, which has taken off since the early eighties. On an island where life has been precarious for so long, Anguilla is probably more prosperous now than it ever has been.

Getting Around

There is an almost mythical **bus** service in Anguilla, a couple of minivans that run from Blowing Point to The Valley, and occasionally on other roads, to an entirely unpredictable schedule. Catch them if you can. Hitchhiking is workable and may introduce you to some amusing islanders.

Taxis can be arranged at the airport or at Blowing Point and at any of the hotels. Drivers are happy to drop you for the day on a remote beach and then return to collect you. Most will give impromptu tours of the island, but organized tours cost US$40 for a couple of hours for two people. Contact: Frank Webster (✆ pager 497 2111 ext 256) or Harry's Taxi (✆ 497 4336). Prices for journeys are fixed (quite expensively) by the Government. Some examples are: the **airport** to Shoal Bay—US$10 (and from **Blowing Point**—US$15), The Valley—US$5 (US$10), Sandy Ground—US$8 (US$10), Covecastles and the southwestern end of the island—US$20 (US$17).

Car hire gives the most mobility and cars are readily available, from about US$35 plus taxes. A local licence must be obtained, but this is easily done on presentation of a valid licence to the company at the time of hire, or to the police in The Valley, price US$6. Driving is on the left and the speed limit is 30 mph (!). Traffic usually does proceed at a stately pace, but watch out for the couple of roundabouts and the odd hanging traffic light. Some of the many companies are: Connor's Car Rental (✆ 497 6894), Island Car Rentals on Airport Road (✆ 497 2723), Summer Car Rental (✆ 497 5278) and Tripple K (✆ 497 2934), some of which also hire out jeeps (at about US$50 plus taxes). **Scooters** can be hired through Boo's Cycle (✆ 497 2323) just above Sandy Ground and Sandy Island Enterprises (✆ 497 6395) in Road Bay who also have **bicycles**.

Anguilla's superb sand makes her beaches some of the best in the Caribbean. There are miles and miles of it, glaringly white and so thick and soft that it makes you stumble as you walk. Breakers clap and hiss as they race in a flurry of surf towards the palms and the seagrape. You will not find any crowded beaches on the island, though you can find watersports equipment at the hotels if you want action. There are miles of strand to walk in the cool of the early morning, and you can sizzle to your heart's content in the heat of the day. If beaches are your thing, Anguilla is close to paradise.

Anguilla lies at an angle close to the prevailing winds off the Atlantic and this means that with just a slight variation beaches can vary from one day to the next with regard to calmness, particularly at the eastern end of the island. Before setting out to somewhere remote, it is worth checking if the beach is calm. Two words of warning: beware of manchineel trees, which bear a poisonous apple and will blister you if you sit under them in the rain, and skinny-dipping, which is officially not allowed.

best beaches

Shoal Bay (on the northern shore): The island's most popular beach and also one of its finest, mounds of sand that are carved into scallop shapes by the meandering waves; you can walk for miles. There are one or two hotels and beach bars to retire to if the heat of the sun gets too much and there are reefs offshore for snorkelling. Fluffy beach towels and reliable snorkelling gear are for hire at Skyline Beach Rentals.

Little Bay: A tiny cove just to the east of town, cut out of the cliffs, so secluded that you must go by boat, unless you are prepared to clamber down the rockface (where there are ropes to assist you). No facilities; quite often day tours from St Martin.

Sandy Ground: A busy half-moon bay with a line of bars and restaurants right on the sand. It is a working bay, with ships unloading at the jetty and yachts at anchor, but the bars give it a good atmosphere. You can hire watersports equipment here.

Mead's Bay and **Barnes Bay**: Further west along the north shore, more blinding white sand with hotels standing on the clifftops above them and fantastic sunset views. Both have bars to retreat to in the hotels, and watersports equipment for hire. At the far **western end** of the island you will find a couple of tiny inlets with golden sand, enclosed by cliffs, which are perfect secluded suntraps.

Shoal Bay West: The most westerly bay on the south side of the island, a superb curve of sand where space-age villas cut the skyline and the swimming is impeccable.

Maunday's Bay: Another magnificent curved strip of sand on a protected cove, home to Cap Juluca, whose Moorish domes stick out of the tropical greenery.

Cove Bay, leading into **Rendezvous Bay**: A 2-mile stretch of superb sand; some hotels, but good for walking morning or evening; it's always easy to find an isolated spot with the hills of St Martin in view.

Mimi Bay and the wilder **Savannah Bay**: At the eastern end of the island, both quite windy and isolated, also walking beaches.

Captain's Bay: In the far northeast, a perfect and isolated cove, the ultimate secluded retreat.

Offshore islands: Anguilla's uninhabited cays—Deadman's Cay, Sombrero, Scrub and Little Scrub, Dog, Seal, Georgeous Scilly Cay and Prickly Pear Cay—may sound like a surreal shopping list, but there are some excellent stretches of sand on them and you can arrange to visit on a day trip. Ask at the watersports companies (*see* 'Anguilla Directory', p.390).

beach bars

There are some cool and easy beach bars around the island where you can find a fruit punch or a beer and a salad, or a full-blown meal, to fill a gap during the day's beach activity. Between the (relatively) more formal restaurants of Sandy Ground you will find **Johnno's** and **Tropical Penguin**, two lively bars with meals in the daytime which stay open on into the night. At Shoal Bay on the north coast there are some popular haunts to retreat to: **Uncle Ernie's,** a wooden lean-to which is festooned with photos of satisfied customers and has a grill permanently on the go, and **Madeariman Reef**, an open-sided bar looking over the sand from the trees.

Further east you come to Island Harbour, where the sleek Anguillian fishing boats lie at anchor in the bay. Offshore you will see **Gorgeous Scilly Cay**, which Eudoxie Wallace, Gorgeous to his friends, has landscaped with parasols, conch-shell walls and thatch shelters. Wave from the pier and they will come and pick you up for a day's 'liming' and snorkelling and a lobster lunch. Music a couple of times a week in season, even a helipad to make it easier for you. *Closed Mon.*

At the eastern limit of the (sandy) road on the south side of the island, there is a popular haunt at **Palm Grove** (✆ 497 4224) at Junks Hole on the windswept Savannah Bay. A wooden lean-to settled under the palms (a few of them without their fronds since Luis in 1995) on the bright white sand, some watersports and excellent grilled crayfish for lunch, popular on Sundays. Right at the other end of the island you will find an excellent beach bar on the superb sand of Shoal Bay West: the **Paradise Café.** Senior food for the beach, but a perfect setting on safari chairs on a simple deck, looking across to St Martin: stir-fry scallop salad, a prosciutto and shaved *pecorino* salad, or a home-speciality *bouillabaisse,* simmered in saffron.

Visible from Road Bay is **Sandy Island**, the archetypal paradise island, just a bar of sand with excellent snorkelling. Perhaps this is where the Lamb's Navy Rum girl lives. (Sandy Island was actually washed away during Hurricane Luis in 1995, but it has silted back again.) Day trips are arranged easily through **Sandy Island Enterprises** (✆ 497 6395). You can take a trip even farther afield, to **Prickly Pear Cay,** where there are a couple of bars: **Agatha's Place** and **Johnno's** to keep up your liquid balance while you snorkel and sunbathe.

The Valley (population about 800) is Anguilla's capital, though you should not think that this makes it a town; the density of houses is just slightly greater than elsewhere. Some official buildings and a few shops are bunched around a couple of hanging traffic lights. Blink and you will miss it.

Headed west from The Valley, the road moves into more open country very quickly, passing the airport and making towards the developed southwestern tip of the island. Anguilla's plantations were never very successful, but the **Wallblake House** is an attractive great house. Built in the late 18th century, it is set behind a white picket fence and has a cistern similar to those on the islands of Saba and Statia (Sint Eustatius) farther south. The house is private, but tours can be arranged through the Archaeological and Historical Society (✆ 497 2759). Driving west you come to a couple of roundabouts; at the second there is a side road down to **Sandy Ground**, a small village with some traditional Anguillan houses set on a thin spit of land between the sea and the last of the working salt pans. The pans are disused now, but the water still becomes curiously discoloured, lavender and grey, as the sun and wind continue to do their work. The road snakes further west, throwing off side-roads to **Blowing Point**, the departure point for boats to St Martin and to the hotels and isolated settlements.

Heading north and east from The Valley, you pass quickly into open country once again, which is dotted periodically with Anguilla's attractive old wooden houses and the half-built newer concrete ones. There are a couple of local settlements in this less developed area; one at **Island Harbour** on the north coast, from which many of Anguilla's fishermen set off. On the beach you will see the fishing boats, brightly painted so that they are more visible at sea, and built to a unique Anguillan design. In the main house of the Arawak Beach Resort there is a small display of Amerindian artefacts (plus some reproductions and some exhibits from modern-day Arawaks in Guyana)—*metape* strainers to get the poison juice out of cassava, pottery, cotton spindles and jewellery made of shells.

Anguilla's only historical sites can be found in this area. Just off the road close to Lower Shoal Bay, the **Fountain** (still closed under renovation) is contained within a National Park and has a number of Amerindian rock carvings around the island's only reliable source of water, cartoon faces which are each struck by the sun's rays in the course of the year. At **Sandy Hill Bay** are the remains of a 17th-century fort, now site of a police sub-station.

✆ *(1 264)–*   ***Where to Stay***

There is a good range of accommodation in Anguilla, from a couple of the Caribbean's most exquisite hotels through to the simplest guest houses, so the island can suit almost anybody's tastes. In between you will find some mid-range hotel accommodation; through the 'Inns of Anguilla' you can get a room at around US$100 a night in season. There are also many condominium complexes. Most of the hotels are set on one or other of Anguilla's pristine beaches. Hotel rooms can be booked in the UK through the **Anguilla Reservation Service** (✆ (0171) 937 7725, ✉ 938 4793), but you may prefer to buy a package from a tour operator at home.

A good alternative in Anguilla is to stay in a villa; there are many scattered around the island. Rental companies, who will often arrange a car for you, include **Anguilla**

Connection (✆ 497 4402, ✉ 497 4402) and **PREMS** (Property Real Estate Management Services), PO Box 256, The Valley (✆ 497 2596, ✉ 497 3309). Perhaps check them out while you are there in preparation for a return visit. The Government levies a room tax of 8% and most hotels charge service at 10%.

Hotels

luxury

The **Malliouhana Hotel**, PO Box 173 (✆ 497 6111, ✉ 497 6011, US toll free ✆ (1 800) 835 0796) is one of the Caribbean's finest, and it stands on the cliffs above the mile-long stretch of Mead's Bay Beach on Anguilla's northwestern coastline. Tall and slender arches and terracotta tiles on floor and roofs give a slightly Mediterranean impression, but the name Malliouhana is distinctly Caribbean, taken from the Indian word for the island. The 59 rooms, which include a few vast and spectacular suites, are luxuriously decorated, with paintings by the Haitian Jasmin Joseph and carvings from Indonesia, and many have balconies overlooking the bay and the sunset. Watersports include windsurfers, skiing and sunfish; there are tennis courts, two pools, a children's centre and a gym with a view. Also a superb restaurant on the cliff-tops, with French cuisine touched by the Caribbean, and a wine cellar of around 20,000 bottles and a luncheon bar above the beach. Extremely personable and dependably well run.

Cove Castles, PO Box 248 (✆ 497 6801, ✉ 497 6051, US ✆ (1 800) 348 4716, ✉ (310) 440 4220) is another haven of understated super-luxury, set on the magnificent curve of Shoal Bay West. The 32 rooms stand in 13 villas, strikingly white, with windswept geometrical faces, staring at a superb vista of St Martin. Inside they are spacious and elegant, with curved white walls, rattan furniture and each room has a view. Villas come with housekeepers and villa (room) service (they can personalize the menu if you want) and some watersports. Also a fine dining room.

Cap Juluca, PO Box 240 (✆ 497 6666, ✉ 497 6617, US ✆ (1 800) 323 0139) has its own inimitable style—white Moorish domes that rise out of Anguilla's superb southwestern sands, a surreal impression after a day in the Anguillan sun. The 98 rooms (suites in villas) are palatial, the tile floors covered by carpets from the east, and the bathrooms are no less than luxurious, jacuzzis in the sunlight. Plenty of watersports, a fitness centre, tennis courts and even croquet. Another extremely fine hotel, with a restaurant, Eclipse (from California), and a pool terrace restaurant for lunch.

very expensive–expensive

The **Cinnamon Reef Beach Club**, PO Box 141 (✆ 497 2727, ✉ 497 3727, *www.offshore.come.ai/cinnamon-reef/*), is set in the horseshoe cove of the isolated Little Harbour on Anguilla's southern coast. Villas and suites are set widely spaced in a tropical garden, in modern cottages splashed with bougainvillea and hibiscus, each with a hammock on the terrace, with stark white walls and some dark-stained louvres inside. With just 22 rooms, it has a friendly and lazy feel, a pleasant terrace and sitting area with a library overlooking the calm beach and bay and a large pool on a deck behind. The beach is not the best but always calm and swimmable and there are watersports and tennis; also an award-winning restaurant.

At the **Arawak Beach Resort**, PO Box 98 (✆ 497 4888, ✉ 487 4898), 14 rooms and suites stand in two-storey wooden buildings on a breezy cliff outside Island Harbour, decorated with Caribbean products: batique wall prints, Haitian carvings and Guyanese woodwork, sea grass matting, ghostly Amerindian faces on the lampshades and huge beds. The restaurant, Arietos, offers light, Arawak-inspired and vegetarian food.

La Sirena, PO Box 200 (✆ 497 6827, ✉ 497 6829, US toll free ✆ (1 800) 331 9358, UK ✆ (0800) 373 742), has a fine setting with white stucco buildings with Spanish tiles and woodwork balconies clustered around a pool and an explosive bougainvillea-garden at the western end of Mead's Bay. Twenty very comfortable rooms and an upbeat atmosphere for Anguilla with entertainment sometimes around the dining room and bar.

You might also try the **Fountain Beach Hotel** (✆ 497 3491, ✉ 497 3493), which is situated on the superb sand of Shoal Bay, just down from the busy area of the beach. There are 27 comfortable rooms and suites, decorated with bright white tiles and black wicker furniture from Haiti, some antiques; some with kitchens and balconies looking to the sea, others recently built with jacuzzi tubs in the living rooms. Very private and quiet, with pool, palm garden and an Italian and Caribbean restaurant.

moderate–cheap

The **Rendezvous Bay Hotel**, PO Box 31 (✆ 497 6549, ✉ 497 6026, US toll free ✆ (1 800) 274 4893), is a quiet resort in an older Caribbean beach-club mould. There is a central main house with dining room, games room and library where guests gather and mingle at meals. The rooms stand in two areas: an older block in a rocky garden and newer villas on the fantastic sand of Rendezvous Bay itself, each decorated with white tiles and wicker furniture. Very quiet and low-key. If you want to be close to the action of Sandy Ground you can try **Sydans Apartments** (✆ 497 3180, ✉ 497 5381), and for cheaper rooms you can go to The Valley: **Norman B's** (✆ 497 2242) near Crocus Bay has simple rooms, as does **Lloyd's** (✆ 497 2351).

Self-catering Villas

There is a good range of self-catering accommodation in Anguilla. Rooms and apartments tend to be set in a central building or clustered around a central garden; some will have a restaurant but all have kitchens. Some of the best in each category are as follows. The **Carimar Beach Club**, PO Box 327 (✆ 497 6881, ✉ 497 6071, US toll free ✆ (1 800) 235 8667, *www. carimar.com, carimar@candw.com.ai; very expensive*), has apartments (23 in all) in modern blocks either side of a pretty tropical garden, everywhere exploding with tropical growth, leading down to the superb sand of Mead's Bay. Bright white and modern decor with wicker furniture in large living rooms and patios, all modern comforts.

The **Frangipani Beach Club**, PO Box 1378 (✆ 497 6442, ✉ 497 6440, US toll free ✆ (1 800) 892 4564; *very expensive*), stands on the beachfront in Mead's Bay. The extremely comfortable and spacious rooms and suites are set in a mock Spanish palace, bright pink with curved red roof-tiles and balconies with classical balustrades. There are one- to three-bedroom apartments.

Shoal Bay Villas, PO Box 81 (✆ 497 2051, ✇ 497 3631, US toll free ✆ (1 800) 722 7045; *expensive*), has an excellent setting lost in the palms of Shoal Bay. There are just 13 individually decorated units standing around a pool, with all the activity of Shoal Bay nearby. There is a dining room, the palm-thatched Reefside Restaurant, which stands beneath the palms on the sand.

Blue Waters Beach Apartments, PO Box 69 (✆ 497 6292, ✇ 497 6982; *moderate*), are set on the other Shoal Bay at the eastern end of the island. Just seven one-bedroom and two two-bedroom apartments, at good rates. They stand in stark white buildings with stained-wood louvres, fan ventilation; a quiet resort with no watersports or central area, very private.

There are two less expensive villa hotels in Island Harbour in the northeast: **Harbour Villas** (✆ 497 4393, ✇ 497 4196, US res ✆ (206) 822 0589; *moderate*) are set back from the sea. Simple fan-ventilated bedrooms in five units, full kitchens and living area with wicker furniture and a balcony. **Harbour Lights**, PO Box 181 (✆ 497 4435), has just four rooms above the waves of Island Harbour. Quiet and simple but friendly.

✆ *(1 264)–*

Eating Out

There are plenty of restaurants dotted around Anguilla, many of them in charming shoreside settings. Some of the best food is to be found in the hotel dining rooms (try Malliouhana, Cove Castles and Cinnamon Reef; *all expensive*), but it is worth looking around. There are places where you can have a quiet and intimate evening for two and of course livelier restaurants as well. Obviously there is plenty of fish and seafood and it is definitely worth tasting crayfish and spiny lobster, caught in Anguillan waters (what remains after the rest has been shipped off to St Martin and San Juan). You will of course find local West Indian haunts where you can pick up a pattie or a chicken leg for lunch and trusted local fare for dinner.

Eating out is not cheap in Anguilla, but credit cards are accepted in the major restaurants if you don't want to think about it at the time. Categories are arranged according to the price of a main course: *expensive*—US$20 and above; *moderate*—US$10–20; *cheap*—under US$10.

expensive

Blanchards (✆ 497 6100, ✇ 497 6161) has top spot at the moment in Anguilla: you dine in a charming indoor dining room looking through large windows onto a flood-lit garden, just within earshot of the breaking waves of Mead's Bay. The cuisine gathers influences from around the world to make an eclectic and thoroughly satisfying mix: Cajun and American southwest, Thai and other Asian tastes, as well as some Caribbean flavours, on a daily-changing menu (with fresh food imported daily from Miami via St Maarten), all beautifully presented. Very elegant, reserve in advance (people fax down their reservations ahead of time), excellent wine list.

Hibernia (✆ 497 4290) is a small and intimate restaurant in Island Harbour in the northeast, well worth making the journey to get there. Here you dine on a prettily decorated terrace with a view on to a lit garden, with meticulously prepared dishes presented by the owners themselves. The cuisine is French with Caribbean ingredients, touched with a taste of Thailand—start with a combination of house-smoked fish (wahoo, kingfish, tuna and dolphin) and follow with duck breast from Périgord grilled and served with a lime grapefruit and orange sauce. *Closed Mon.*

In town, **Koalkeel** (✆ 497 2930) offers a 'Caribbean *dégustation*' menu, again with influences added from around the world, some of it cooked over a coal-kiln or outdoor oven: *ravioli de* (Anguillian) *crayfish* followed by a *feuilleté de snapper chinoise*, served in rice paper with Chinese vegetables and lemon soya sauce.

Cyril's Fish House (✆ 497 4488) sits across the road from the sea at Island Harbour in the northeast of the island. The tables are ranged on a charming deck which is decorated in a theme of blue and white, tablecloths and curtains, contained within wooden balustrades and trelliswork. As the name suggests, fish and seafood: angel hair pasta served with lobster meat *marinara* or grilled mahi-mahi on red onion marmalade.

Mango's (✆ 497 6479) has a good and pleasant setting on a terrace right on the sand on Barnes Bay. The veranda is open to the evening breeze and its 'new American' cuisine gives exotic variations on Caribbean food—seafood angel hair pasta and the house speciality of grilled jumbo shrimp, served in a curry of lime and coconut milk. Brisk and breezy. *Dinner only, closed Tues.*

Set on the beach in Sandy Ground, **Riviera** (✆ 497 2833) has a charming dining room set under palm trees. The menu is French, with Provençal specialities, and you will start with a *ti punch* and the oyster bar, and then follow with perhaps a crayfish bisque and *daurade grillé*, fillet of dorado served in a lime butter sauce. The style is light sauces and *nouvelle* presentation, with set menus and salads at lunchtime for a good break from the beach.

moderate

Arlo's (✆ 497 6810) is well known around the island for its pastas and pizzas. It is set in a modern house on a cliff overlooking Sandy Island. Tall safari chairs at the bar and tables on a terrace; pizzas and pastas *moderate*, other dishes, for instance *Leon's* (the chef's) snapper, *expensive*. There are a number of restaurants down in Sandy Ground, where you can grab a meal and then join the activity of the bars.

Just behind the beach itself is **Ripples** (✆ 497 3380), a dining room with window-shutters on stilts, brightly decorated in shades of pale blue and peach. Bench seats and tables, a lively buzz in the air most nights; Mexican, local and some English dishes: *quesadillas*, conch fritters and fish and chips.

The **Ship's Galley** (✆ 497 2040) has a pretty waterfront setting with white trelliswork hung with greenery and tropical flora. Lunchtime burgers and salads, dinner seafood speciality (fresh whelks) or a fillet of local catch in butter sauce.

cheap

A cheaper local meal can be found at the **Aquarium** in South Hill: seafood, stews, curries and local whelks on an upstairs veranda. There are other simple and local restaurants around town: try **Shalacks** on Hill St. You can get a roti or a fry chicken at the **Pepperpot** or in the **Roti Hut** at the end of the airstrip (with its accompanying drive-in ice-cream stop) and there are sometimes roadside fry-ups and vans selling chicken and fish.

Bars and Nightlife

The best bars are really the beach bars—there is a regular Sunday afternoon crowd at Shoal Bay—and the hotel bars. If you are feeling homesick for an English ale, then you will find Newcastle Brown (and Guinness) at **Roy's,** now on the beach (yes, it has grown up to their deck) in Crocus Bay. Pub-style, with darts, happy hour and a riotous bar; also fish and chips in an expanded menu. There is a nice spot on the cliff-top above Sandy Ground, right at the corner in the road, at **Rafé's:** a wooden and tin-roofed lean-to built with planks and driftwood with a few standing plants on the gravel floor. Chicken, ribs and kebabs with garlic bread, but also popular as a bar late on.

How do you decorate a sand-dune and turn it into a bar? By building a galleon on it. Bankie Banx, Anguilla's best-known singer-songwriter, has collected boats and driftwood from around the island and turned them into the **Dune Preserve,** a bar which

Anguilla Directory

getting there

The modest Wallblake airport in the centre of the island cannot take long-haul flights and so you must make a connection in the Caribbean, but it is usually possible to reach the island in the same day. Transit points are Antigua, Sint Maarten and San Juan in Puerto Rico. The journey by sea from Marigot, St Martin is perhaps a more charming way to arrive. There is a departure tax of US$10 (EC$26.50) if you are leaving by air, US$2 (EC$5) by sea.

By air from the UK: The easiest connections are made in Antigua, where LIAT (✆ 497 5000) links up with the regular British Airways and BWIA flights to ensure a relatively trouble-free onward journey. Also the charter airline Carib Avaiation (Antigua ✆ 462 3147), which flies so regularly that it has an almost scheduled service and quotes a seat-only price. An alternative is to take the BA flight to San Juan on Puerto Rico, and connect there on American Eagle (✆ 497 3131). From elsewhere in **Europe:** Air France, KLM and Lufthansa fly to Sint Maarten, from where it is an easy hop by plane or boat.

By air from the USA: The main gateways for Anguilla are San Juan, from where American Eagle has two flights a day and Sint Maarten, which is also well served from the States (*see* p.405).

By air from other Caribbean islands: Winair (Windward Island Airways, ✆ 497 2748) provides an air link from St Thomas and Sint Maarten. LIAT (✆ 497 5000) serves Anguilla from Antigua, San Juan and the Virgin Islands. Finally, the island's carrier, Air Anguilla (✆ 497 2643, ✆ 497 2982) has daily services from St Thomas and they will charter from San Juan or Antigua. You can also charter a small plane from Tyden Air (✆ 497 2719, ✆ 497 3079, US toll free ✆ (1 800) 842 0261).

By sea: Ferries link the port of Marigot in the French territory of St Martin with Blowing Point on the south of Anguilla. Services leave roughly every 30 minutes during the day and the crossing is 20 minutes. You will have to pay a departure tax from St Martin of US$10.

sits on a sand-dune at the western end of Rendezvous Bay (reached along a well-signed but very rough road). Multiple decks, upturned boats as roofs, wooden benches and barrels as tables, rigging strung with fairy-lights, even a galley (for simple fare at lunch and dinner) at the back, sometimes concerts from the man himself. Simply one of the coolest spots anywhere in the Caribbean.

Anguillan nightlife is quiet (the locals sometimes take the ferry over to St Martin for the nightclubs there, and there are also casinos in Dutch Sint Maarten if that's your thing) and so you are best advised to keep your ear to the ground to find out where the crowds are going. There is sometimes a barbecue or a band at one of the hotels: **La Sirena** has a weekly show by a troupe of dancers. It is definitely worth joining in the 'jump-ups' at **Johnno's** in Sandy Ground (usually Wed and Fri), which can get crowded and pretty wild. Sometimes the crowd moves on to the occasional jump-ups in **The Pump House**, not far down the road, tall stools and chairs set in the old salt factory building, or they head up the hill to **Rafé's**.

© (1 264)–

tourist information

UK: 3 Epirus Road, London SW6 7UJ (© (0171) 937 7725, 🕾 938 4739).

USA and Canada: Medhurst and Associates Inc, 1208 Washington Drive, Centerport, New York 11721 (© (516) 425 0900, 🕾 425 0903) and c/o Soleil International, World Trade Centre, Suite 250, San Francisco, California 94111 (© (415) 398 3231, 🕾 398 3669).

Germany: c/o Sergat Deutschland, Feldstrasse 26, D-64319 Pfungstadt (© (06157) 87816, 🕾 87719).

Italy: c/o B&DP srl, Piattari 2, 20122 Milano, Italy (© (02) 895 16917, 🕾 (02) 846 0841).

On-island, information and assistance can be obtained from the helpful office at the **Anguilla Department of Tourism** in the government buildings in The Valley, Anguilla, British West Indies (© 497 2759, 🕾 497 3091, www.candw.com.ai/-abtour), which is open 8–midday and 1–4pm. There are information booths at the airport and at Blowing Point.

If **telephoning** from outside the Caribbean, the **IDD code** for Anguilla is © (1 264), followed by 497 and then a four-figure island number. If calling within the island, dial only the last four digits.

In an **emergency**, there is a 24-hour surgery at the **Cottage Hospital** in The Valley (© 497 2551).

festivals

The main event in the Anguillan calendar is **Carnival**, which takes place in early August. It borrows a lot from other Caribbean carnivals, with floats and dancers 'jumping-up' as they cruise around town in troupes, all wearing themed costumes, and calypso competitions, where the Anguillians sing of island life and love. Held at the same time is **Race-week**, which is unique to Anguilla, the nation of seafarers and boat-builders. Traditional fishing boats are pitted against one another in races from bay to bay around the island. In May they celebrate Anguilla Day with a round-island boat race and in June the official birthday of the British Queen, with a fair and boat races.

money

The currency of Anguilla is the Eastern Caribbean dollar (fixed to the US dollar at a rate of about US$1 = EC$2.65). The US dollar, best carried in the smaller denominations, is perfectly acceptable, though you will occasionally receive your change in EC$. If you are on a tight budget, it is better to use EC$. Credit cards are accepted at the large and expensive hotels and in some shops.

Banking hours: Mon–Thurs 8–3, Fri 8–5.

Shops: Keep variable hours, though usually with a respectable lunch-break.

watersports

There's plenty of possibilities for an active beach and water-borne life in Anguilla's electric-blue sea. You are really dependent on the hotels, most of which have simple equipment (snorkelling gear, windsurfers and small sailboats); otherwise head down to Sandy Ground where you can arrange trips, though this is still pretty low-key by most island standards.

Day sails: The catamarans *Princess Soya* (℗ 497 3661) and *Chocolat* (℗ 497 3394) take day and sunset cruises for snorkelling and sunbathing. Some of these trips go to offshore islands, but you may want to make a special trip to Sandy Island, Scrub Island or Prickly Pear Cays: contact Sandy Island Enterprises (℗ 497 6395). You can also charter motor-boats to other islands nearby through many companies, including *Hoo Haa* (℗ 497 4040).

Snorkelling and scuba diving: There are some good coral reefs right offshore, including Little Bay (*see* 'Beaches' above) and Shoal (another name for reef) Bay—there is a marked snorkelling trail in Shoal Bay. Dive sites are to be found all around the island, particularly towards the western end, where reefs flash with butterflyfish and angelfish or a shimmering cloud of fry, and also on the offshore cays. There are also wrecks (some deliberately sunk), where you might see a jackfish or an octopus. Complete instruction and equipment hire are available through The Dive Shop (℗ 497 2020, ● 497 5125) in Sandy Ground and Anguillan Divers (℗ 497 4750). A single tank dive costs US$45 or $50, with equipment on top. If you would prefer not to get wet, contact Mike's Glass-Bottom Boat (℗ 497 4155) which takes reef tours and snorkelling trips.

Deep-sea fishing: For wahoo and tuna and sailfish, can be arranged through Sandy Island Enterprises. A half-day's sail with full tackle costs around US$350.

other sports

Tennis and horse-riding: There are courts at a number of the bigger hotels. If you want to gallop along the beach and through the scrubland you can contact El Rancho del Blues (℗ 497 6164).

The **Anguilla National Trust** organizes some visits to places of interest around the island from time to time: it is worth checking if anything is happening while you are on-island (℗ 497 5297).

traditional straw roofed hut with Kadushi cactus

The Dutch Caribbean

The Dutch Caribbean (Netherlands Antilles and Aruba) is made up of two groups of three islands, separated by about 500 miles of Caribbean Sea. The Dutch Windward Islands, Sint Maarten, Sint Eustatius and Saba (or the 3 S's in tourist jargon) are in the northeastern Caribbean, between the Virgin Islands and Antigua. Five hundred miles to their lee, off the coast of South America, are the trio of the Dutch Leeward Islands, Aruba (now autonomous), Bonaire and Curaçao (the ABC islands).

The Netherlands Antilles may be within the Dutch kingdom, but they are by no means a tropical version of Holland. The Dutch were never great colonizers and what influence they had has been creolized. In Curaçao curly gables will take you momentarily back to Amsterdam; everywhere roadsigns are in Dutch and post-boxes are painted Royal Dutch red; money is guilders and florins; the tastes and sounds of Holland percolate through.

But the reminders are fleeting: the gables may be there, but the *Landhuizen* (Dutch country homes) look odd painted orange and surrounded by miles of cactus; drivers here are much more akin to their fellow West Indians than the good burghers of the Netherlands and the guttural sounds of Dutch have a curious ring when thoroughly mixed with Spanish as in Papiamento *(see* p.426). Neither group of islands actually uses Dutch as a mother-tongue. The Dutch Windwards have been strongly influenced by the English-speaking islands around them and the Leewards are an enigmatic and exuberant mix of strains from all over the area—but they are distinctly West Indian.

Dutch Caribbean History

The Dutch first came to the Caribbean as traders in the early 17th century. Of the European nationalities beginning to protrude into the Spanish domain in the New World, only they had the fleets and so they acted as middle men for the new colonies that were springing up in the area. In an early piece of industrial espionage they introduced the cultivation of sugar to the islands of the Lesser Antilles; they provided the technology, the funding, the machinery and then shipped the produce back to eager markets in Europe.

The Dutch did not really colonize as much as occupy strategic ports in the New World, from which they could carry on their trading and attack the Spaniards. In the 1620s the Dutch West India Company took Sint Maarten because it was en route from Europe to their possessions in Brazil and later moved in on the nearby islands of Saba and Sint Eustatius as well. At the other end of the Caribbean they chose the ABC islands because there was salt there (on Bonaire), which they needed for their herring industry, and because Curaçao has one of the largest harbours in the world. At the beginning of the 18th century, the Dutch ports of Curaçao and Sint Eustatius were two of the three richest in the Caribbean (with Port Royal in Jamaica). Their warehouses were filled to bursting with goods; hundreds of ocean-going vessels would put in each year and off-load silks, slaves and gunpowder. Strictly speaking, trade with other colonies was illegal because they were under monopoly trading laws, but their goods were in demand and so they made a tidy profit smuggling, too.

Prizes so rich inevitably became targets and in the endless run of 18th-century wars the islands were at the mercy of the navies that chased each other around the Caribbean Sea. St Eustatius changed hands 22 times in all, its fortunes pilfered handsomely each time. But the wharves would fill up again almost as quickly, as trade with Venezuela and the North American colonies picked up.

The six islands eventually landed in Dutch hands for good in 1816 and then gradually, like the rest of the Caribbean, they were forgotten. The ports failed as world trading patterns changed and the islanders turned to planting: crops like cotton and cochineal, sisal (for rope) and aloe. Even these died with emancipation, which was declared by the Dutch in 1863.

It was not until the early 20th century that prosperity returned to some of the islands when oil was discovered in South America. Royal Dutch Shell and EXXON built refineries in Curaçao and Aruba in the 1920s and these two islands boomed, experiencing a wave of prosperity that only waned in the 1980s.

Since the sixties the Netherlands Antilles have joined the tourism race, particularly in Sint Maarten and Aruba, where hotels have sprung up on any available beach space. The islands have also resurrected the Dutch tradition of entrepôts (like the freeports of Curaçao and St Eustatius two hundred years ago) to encourage 20th-century traders. These seaborne shoppers arrive in port just as they always did, with a fistful of dollars to spend, only nowadays they are off-loaded by the thousand from cruise ships.

Politics

For years the name Curaçao was used to refer to all the Dutch possessions in the Caribbean and it is only really since the Second World War that the different islands have become known in their own right. In 1936 the Netherlands Antilles Staten (Parliament) was created and the colonies were made an integral part of the Kingdom of the Netherlands.

After the war (when Holland was occupied by Germany and the islands had to look after themselves), self-determination gradually moved into the political foreground. Autonomy, internal self-government, was granted in 1954, but unlike many Caribbean islands, the Dutch Caribbean has not actually taken the further steps towards Independence. With the exception of Surinam, which became independent in 1975, they have preferred to remain a part of the Kingdom of the Netherlands.

The administration was centred in Willemstad and as the Curaçaoans automatically had a majority in the Staten due to the size of their population, they tended to dominate the other islands. The Arubians particularly, with political aspirations of their own born of their oil wealth, resented the fact that decisions concerning their own internal affairs had to be passed in Curaçao. Eventually they struck out for their own self-government (see 'Aruba', 'Status Aparte', p.452) and they were granted Independence (still within the Kingdom of the Netherlands).

More recently Sint Maarten, also on a wave of prosperity because of its tourist industry, voiced similar requests, but these have been turned down by the Dutch Government. Now that Aruba has left the Netherlands Antilles, Curaçao returns 14 senators to the 22-member Staten, Bonaire three, Sint Maarten three and Saba and Sint Eustatius one each. The governor of each island is appointed by Queen Beatrix of the Netherlands on the advice of Parliament. Since 1986, each island has been responsible for its own decisions and its budget, once it has been allocated by the central government in Curaçao. Maria Liberia Peters, leader of the People's National Party, became prime minister of the five islands of the Netherland Antilles in a coalition government in 1988.

Sint Maarten/Saint Martin is the smallest island in the world to be shared by two nations. The southern half is one of the Netherlands Antilles, a part of the Kingdom of Holland, and the northern part is a *commune* of France (*see* 'Saint Martin', p.291). The distinct personalities of the two sides of the island are still just recognizable, though with the building mania of the last twenty years it has taken on a universal wash of concrete, and the feel of the island has changed irreparably.

Of Sint Maarten's 17 square miles, between four and five of them are under water in lagoons and salt ponds. Above the waterline, Sint Maarten is covered in yellow-green scrub, with startlingly steep hills that rise to around 1200ft. From the heights there are excellent views—Sint Maarten is surrounded by islands.

It is rather like a modern-day Babel—overdeveloped and confused. It has excellent beaches, dependable Caribbean sunshine and loose development laws. Together these are enough to have brought development corporations swooping in. They have built with abandon, throwing up resorts on any strip of sand they can find. Sint Maarten bulges with glittering casinos, shopping malls and fast-food joints; there are time-share sales and latterly a market in time-share re-sales. Hotels come in complexes here, and tourists by the jumbo-load.

Interestingly all the languages of Babel are there too. You will hear the drawl of a Texan vacationer alongside the clipped vowels of an Englishman on holiday; Dutch, French and Spanish fill the air. English-speaking West Indians have flooded in from down-island, Dominican girls sit and chat in upbeat Spanish, you will hear Haitian kreyol and the babble of Papiamento (*see* p.426), the extraordinary language from the Dutch Windward Islands. The island has a thoroughly international air, with lots of Latin music and other sounds from around the Caribbean.

Sint Maarten has also adopted Sint Eustatius's traditional role as the Dutch entrepôt in the Windwards. The streets of the capital, Philipsburg, are lined with air-conditioned boutiques, brimful with duty-free bargains. And cruise-liners disgorge still more tourists on one-day shopping extravaganzas. It is mercantile mayhem. The confusion is complete. But after centuries in the doldrums, the island is more prosperous now than it has ever been.

There were considerable problems in the aftermath of Hurricane Luis and Hurricane Marilyn, which brought a double hit (Luis caused the structural damage by tearing off roofs and then Marilyn dumped huge amounts of rain). Between them they destroyed 75% of homes on the island and an alarming 1200 yachts in the lagoon (sailors came from all around the area because of St Maarten's reputation as a hurricane harbour, but many were not properly anchored and so they smashed into one another; others were thrown up on to the land). There has been considerable building since then, with new roads and infrastructure projects.

So many tourists arriving each year cannot but have an effect on island life. If you style yourself a traveller, then Sint Maarten is really a place of curiosity, although the people who live there and on the islands nearby swear by it. You might take a look en route to another more peaceful island. But if you like a well-oiled vacation (often an impeccable package deal), with beaches, watersports, entertainment and a truly amazing variety of restaurants just a buggy-ride away, then Sint Maarten might be your place.

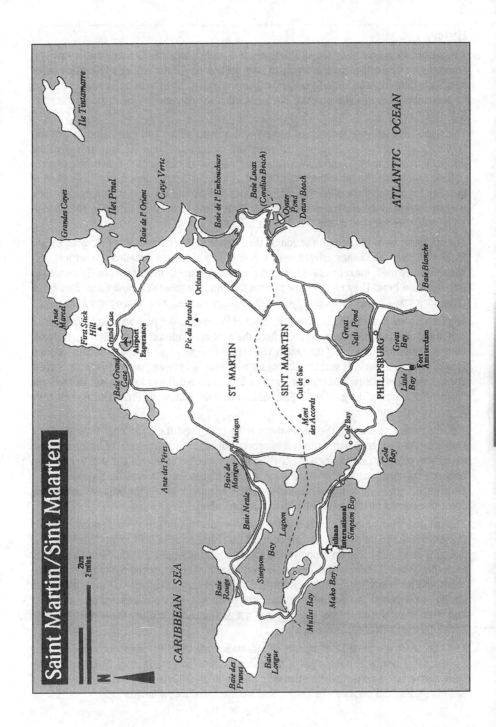

Saint Martin/Sint Maarten

N

2km
2 miles

CARIBBEAN SEA

ATLANTIC OCEAN

Île Tintamarre

Grandes Cayes

Îlet Pinel

Baie de l' Orient

Caye Verte

Baie de l' Embouchure

Baie Lucas
(Coralita Beach)

Oyster
Pond

Dawn Beach

Baie Blanche

Anse
Marcel

First Stick
Hill

Grand Case

Airport
Esperance

Pic du Paradis

Orléans

Baie Grand
Case

ST MARTIN

SINT MAARTEN

Cul de Sac

Great
Salt Pond

PHILIPSBURG

Great
Bay

Fort
Amsterdam

Little
Bay

Anse des Pères

Baie de
Marigot

Marigot

Mont
des Accords

Cole Bay

Cole
Bay

Baie Nettle

Lagoon

Simpson
Bay

Juliana
International
Simpson Bay

Mako Bay

Baie
Rouge

Mullet Bay

Baie des
Prunes

Baie
Longue

395

History

Though the PR moguls may swear otherwise, it is unclear whether Columbus ever saw Sint Maarten. He might have seen it on his second voyage, on 12 November 1493, as he sailed past Statia (Sint Eustatius) and Saba. He did name an island after the saint (St Martin's Day is 11 November), but this was probably Nevis. As other sailors came by, the name was fixed as Sint Maarten.

The Caribs and Arawaks continued to live here on and off for 140 years after his arrival. Settlement was difficult as there was no permanent water-supply, but the Spaniards were not initially interested in the island anyway, and only made occasional raids to take people to work in their gold-mines. To the Indians, Sint Maarten was Sualouiga, supposed to mean 'land of salt'. And it was the salt pans that attracted the first Europeans to Sint Maarten, as they ventured out from the original settlement in St Kitts. Some Frenchmen arrived in 1629 and in 1631 they were followed by the Dutch West India Company.

The Spaniards were spurred into action by the interest these countries were showing in Sint Maarten, and in 1633 they arrived with a fleet of fifty ships and expelled the settlers. But whatever they tried, the settlers kept creeping back and so the Spaniards eventually decided to put a garrison here. They fortified the point at the entrance to what is now Great Bay. By all accounts it was a miserable outpost, where the soldiers had rats for company and food.

The Dutch soon occupied Curaçao off the coast of Venezuela, but they were still looking for a port in the northern Caribbean, en route from their colonies in Brazil back to Europe. In 1644, Peter Stuyvesant, a director of the Dutch West India Company, led an attack on Sint Maarten to take the island back. It was in this engagement that Stuyvesant (later Governor of New York, then called Nieuw Amsterdam) was hit by a cannon-ball and lost his leg. In 1648 the Spaniards abandoned the garrison in Sint Maarten and the Dutch and French soon made their way back on to the island.

The agreement on sharing the island dates from 1648, and the traditional story tells of a Dutchman and a Frenchman setting off in opposite directions, with a bottle of liquor apiece to keep them going, walking around the coast until they met, whereupon a line was to be drawn between the two points. How the French got the bigger share is explained variously: the Dutchman's gin made him sluggish/he took time out under a tree/the wily, wine-drinking Frenchman sent a girl to waylay him (delete as applicable).

The sad drab truth of the matter is that the two sides decided that they would do well to stop skirmishing and so they signed a treaty on a hill that came to be called Mount Concordia. The salt pans remained common property and the two sides arranged that they would not fight each other even if their mother-countries went to war. This happened many times and the treaty was broken with the same regularity. The island changed hands 16 times, often with British involvement. The communities had little to do with each other except to march over and skirmish on the other side, and so it was not until the 20th century that a road was built to link the two halves of the island.

Sint Maarten saw some small prosperity as a plantation island, cultivating tobacco and growing provisions for nearby Sint Eustatius in the boom years of the 18th century. Sugar and cotton were also grown. Another industry that continued into the 20th century was the harvesting of salt from the inland ponds. At its height, Sint Maarten produced 4 million kg.

In 1848 the French emancipated their slaves in Saint Martin. Many of the Dutch slaves fled across the border, staying there until the Dutch declared emancipation in 1863. Gradually Sint Maarten's fortunes waned and it became poor and forgotten. Many of the islanders left in search of work elsewhere. And so it remained until about thirty years ago, when the tourist industry started to grow. In the 1950s, the population of the Dutch side dropped as low as 1500 but is has increased out of all proportion since then. (*See* also introduction to this chapter, p.392.)

Getting Around

A stream of **buses** links Philipsburg to Marigot and Grand Case. Only the occasional bus strays on to the airport road. The fares are US$1–2 depending on your destination. Buses are quite frequent until 10 or 11pm between Marigot and Philipsburg. They leave from Back Street in Philipsburg and in the country it is best to wait at recognized bus stops. **Hitchhikers** will find that a large proportion of the thousands of cars on Sint Maarten pass without stopping. If you are patient, it works all right.

Taxis are the government-approved, quite expensive, tourist-recommended method of travel and they wait in superabundance at Juliana airport and in town. They are not metered, but rates are fixed by the Tourist Board. Some sample prices are: **Juliana airport** to Philipsburg—US$10, Marigot—US$10, Grand Case—US$18–20. From **Philipsburg** to Marigot—US$10, Grand Case—US$18. In the unlikely case that you cannot flag one down, there is a taxi-stand just behind the court house in Philipsburg, and you can also arrange them through any hotel. There are despatch offices in town (✆ 22359) and at the airport (✆ 54317).

Tours of Sint Maarten are available, though there is not much to see apart from the views of the island and other islands. You will ride from shop to hilltop to restaurant in a little safari buggy. Tours can be arranged through any hotel desk (they will pick you up) or through Sint Maarten Sightseeing Tours (✆ 52646) or Island Reps Tours (✆ 52392), US$15 for about 3½ hours.

If you would like to tour by **helicopter**, Sint Maarten offers that too: Paradise Island Helicopters fly out of Juliana airport (✆ 54308, ✆ 54326).

If you want to test out the different beaches in the day and French restaurants at night, it is worth hiring a **rental car**, of which plenty are available from around US$35–40 per day or $45–50 for a jeep, plus insurance. Foreign driving licences are valid in Sint Maarten and driving is on the right-hand side of the road. Many hire companies are based just outside the airport, but companies will also deliver to the hotels. There are far too many cars on both sides of the island, even with the new roads that have been built since the hurricane, so expect traffic jams in the three small towns.

Some local as well as big international rental companies are: Opel Car Rental (✆ 53496), whose offices are just east of Juliana airport, Caribbean Auto Rentals (✆ 45211, ✆ 43155) on Union Road in Cole Bay, Avis (✆ 42316, toll free ✆ (1 800) 228 0668) in Cole Bay, Budget (✆ 54030) within walking distance of the airport building and Hertz (✆ 54314). **Motorbikes** and **scooters** are also available: there's even a Harley-Davidson motorbike rental shop in case you like the idea of cruising the Caribbean on a dream machine (✆ 42779).

If you are prepared to spend a couple of hours being given the hard sell about 'invest-ment in vacationing' in a condominium complex, then you can sometimes score a '$50 off your rental bill' voucher in one of the many promotional rags.

Sint Maarten is an ideal dropping-off point for four other islands, all of which are served by air and also by boat (on day trips in some cases). **Anguilla**, the enigmatic British Crown Colony, is just a 20-minute ferry ride out of Marigot, or you can go on *Santino*, 'the snorkeling luncheon party boat', and *Lambada* (both ✆ 42640). **St Barts**, perhaps the most chic piece of France anywhere, is 12 miles southeast of St Martin, reached aboard *Voyager 1* and *White Octopus* from Philipsburg or Marigot on the French side (both ✆ 24096) and occasionally *The Edge* (✆ 42640). Island Reps Tours (✆ 52392) arranges tours by plane to nearby islands with Winair.

The two other Dutch Windward Islands are easily reached: **Saba**, where pretty ginger-bread villages are clustered on sheer volcanic slopes, is an hour's sail away in the motorboat *The Edge*, above, and **Statia**, once the region's richest trading port (then known as the Golden Rock), is best reached by plane. Winair (✆ 42230) flies to these islands a couple of times a day from Juliana airport, return about US$60.

Beaches

The beaches all over the island are excellent (*see* Saint Martin in the French Caribbean section for the beaches on the French side, pp.292–3). In the irregular, indented coastline, wave action has ground down the coral and pushed up the grains in blinding-white mounds of sand on the shore. And with so many resorts and complexes, every conceivable activity is available on Sint Maarten. Modern-day knights joust on their jetskis, dipping and darting on the waves, inspected from above by para-sailors and by scuba divers from below. Screaming children can be stunned into rapt silence by being dragged around the bay on a high-speed sausage. Senior citizens ply the water sedately in pedalos. If you go over to the French side there are also one or two nude beaches and topless bathing is perfectly acceptable (this is becoming more common on the Dutch side). You will find facilities of some sort on all the beaches in Dutch Sint Maarten—some hotels have a shower room, for which they make a charge. A word of warning: there has been a certain amount of theft on the beaches and so you are advised not leave belongings unattended. The beaches took a bit of a beating during the hurricanes—in the turbulent seas the sand gets washed out and the rocks are exposed, but it gradually sifts its way back in and they were repairing them-selves at the time of writing.

best beaches

Cupecoy Beach: A series of suntraps close to the border with the French side at the western end of the island, all with a cracking view of the sunset. Coves with golden sand slope gently into the sea beneath 50ft cliffs. At the northern end of the beach nude bathing is permitted. For Sint Maarten Cupecoy is relatively secluded, though you are hardly likely to be alone.

Mullet Bay Beach: A classic stretch of Caribbean sand in the mile-long sweep of a gently curving bay; also Sint Maarten's busiest, with the thousands of guests of the nearby hotels, transported here by the buggy-load. All watersports are available and there are plenty of shaded retreats, palm-thatch umbrellas, where you can replace the fluids lost steaming in the sun.

Maho Bay: There is a sign here warning you that low-flying jumbos can ruin your bathing. Don't stand up when one's going over, they literally come that low. Hotels also hover above most of its length, making it another busy beach, buzzing with windsurfers and wetbikers. If the going gets too hot, you can always retreat to the terrace and watch the approach path of the incoming aeroplanes.

Simpson Bay: A fantastic, mile-long half-moon sweep just south of the airport, literally overrun with sand in places. Quiet for Sint Maarten, but popular with windsurfers. One or two of Sint Maarten's smaller easy-going hotels and guest houses are located here, so you can get a drink or lunch in the unpressurized environment of a beach club. Where other beaches lost their sand, Simpson Bay ended up with more than it knows what to do with.

Great Bay: Even Philipsburg itself has a reasonable strip of sand with a magnificent view on to Saba from just behind Front Street. Perhaps spare a moment to take a walk here before getting back into the shopping fray and exercising your credit card in another bout of impulse-buying.

Dawn Beach: A fine strip of sand on the Atlantic coast of the island. There are a couple of hotels here, but the crowds do not usually penetrate this far and so it is relatively quiet. The beach has a view of the dawn sun and of St Barts, but on a windy day the sea will be too rough for comfort.

beach bars

The busiest and best beach bars are really on the French side, on Orient Beach, but there are a couple of **beach bars** in Simpson Bay, on the strip near the bridge where all the watersports take place. **Indiana** develops St Maarten's habit of theme-parks with a pseudo-Indiana Jones creation, where wooden elephants appear to be wandering through the profuse tropical greenery, stalked by pith-helmeted waiters serving solidly international food: daytime soups, salads and sandwiches followed by ribs, steaks and racks of lamb. For something a little lower-key, you could try the funny little beach bar next door. On the remoter east coast you can stop off at **Mr Busby** on Dawn Beach, where there are parasols and sun loungers and a fearsome-sounding list of cocktails to keep you oiled in the sun.

Philipsburg

Philipsburg has just four streets, stretched out along the full length of a sand-bar that separates the Great Salt Pond from Great Bay. The Head of Town lies in the east and the Foot of Town in the west. Philipsburg is being rebuilt in concrete, but among the air-conditioned malls and modern office-blocks you will see a few old traditional gingerbread homes.

Front Street (Voor Straat) sells itself as the 'Shopping Centre of the Leewards' and the arcades and alleys (*steegjes*) manage successfully to delay most of the cruise-ship arrivals that come in safari-boats (the marine equivalent of the tourist bus), to Wathey Square, the little central square known locally as **de Ruyterplein**. Along almost its entire length Front Street is full of little arcades of theme-Caribbean architecture, everywhere hung with signs like: *Caution: Falling Prices!*, warbling and occasionally clunking as you pass the slot arcades, or ringing with bells like the shop Little Switzerland. It's so depressing that it's fun to taunt yourself. Of course there are some bargains to be had and there are one of two galleries with art that is probably worth seeking out. To round the experience off, you can go and taste guavaberry liqueur, in all its frighteningly bright concoctions in an aggressively brightly painted (but quite nice and old) wooden house. Back Street (Achter Straat), where the harvested salt was once stored in vast white stacks, has the administrative buildings and churches.

There is a **museum** at the Head of Town in the arcade nearest the pier (*open weekdays 10–4, Sat10–12; adm*), set upstairs in an old town house, where island archaeology and history are revealed in pottery shards, Spanish buttons and pipes, colonial maps (reprints of historical maps are for sale), china plates and recent marine recoveries.

Behind Philipsburg is the **Great Salt Pond**, its stone dividers still in place like little dykes, which was common to both nations in the 17th century, when salt was important for preserving meats that could not be frozen. Since the industry folded in 1949, land has been reclaimed to expand Philipsburg and part of it is used as the island rubbish tip.

Much of the local life has been squeezed out of Philipsburg, but you can still hear a lively medley of music and languages—the unaccustomed stream of not-quite-Spanish is Papiamento. Now people tend to live in the suburbs behind the salt pond, where you get an idea of Caribbean life in the raffle-ticket booths and the limers hanging around the superettes and rum shops.

On the back side of the Salt Pond you will find the small **Zoological and Botanical Gardens** (*open weekdays 9–5, weekends 10–6; adm*); there you will see Caribbean and South American animals including ocelot wildcats, capybara (like giant hamsters) and coatimundi (a large relative of the racoon) and grey-haired chacalacas (a riverside bird); there is a bat cave (including St Maarten's five native species), a 'terrarium' (not 'terror'ium, but you might wonder considering all the snakes and tarantulas) and a special hands-on area for kids; it's quite fun and impressive for a small zoo. The town continues up over the hill and down into the French side. There are some remoter areas down towards the coast.

Around the Island

The Sint Maarten countryside has little to offer. Much of it is as overgrown as the beaches, with houses rather than hotels. But the coast has superb views looking south to the other islands, grey stains on the horizon on a hazy day, but magnified and green if tropical rains have washed the sky. You can often see St Kitts about 45 miles away and Nevis is very occasionally visible from Cole Bay Hill. Beyond the immediate area of Philipsburg, the island has a fairly 'international' lifestyle which devotes itself to tourism, with hotels and condominium complexes and everywhere roadside restaurants and bars.

At the point on the western arm of Great Bay are the ruins of a fort built by the Spaniards in the 1630s. They demolished it when they abandoned the island and the remains were rebuilt by the Dutch and named **Fort Amsterdam.** The route to the French side of the island leads from Cole Bay. The border is marked by a small obelisk, but there are no formalities and unless you are looking out for it you will probably enter France without knowing.

Pretty much every available area of beach space in St Maarten is developed and so the coastline has an encrustation of resort-style hotels and condominium complexes. Unfortunately many of them were closed by the hurricanes and had not reopened by the time of publication (two years after the event). In recent months particularly, these hotels have been offering some amazing deals. Among them, however, you will find one or two small hotels with some character and charm, particularly in the Simpson Bay area. Many offer 'efficiencies' (self-catering apartments).

It is worth remembering that hotels usually add a 15% charge (sometimes 20%): 10% (15%) for service and the statutory government tax of 5%.

very expensive–expensive

If you want to stay in a resort hotel, you might try the **Oyster Pond Hotel**, PO Box 239 (✆ 22206, 🖷 25695, US ✆ (1 800) 231 8331), where the 200 rooms stand in a range of mock castles made of white stucco with views out towards St Barts (some also look over the main building, where there is a courtyard with white parasols. All the rooms are air-conditioned and have TVs, fans and some have fridges, and they are furnished with white wicker on terracotta tiles. It has enlarged recently, but retains its slightly rarefied atmosphere. There are watersports available if you want them, also tennis courts.

The **Divi Little Bay Beach Resort**, PO Box 61 (✆ 22333, 🖷 23911, US ✆ (1 800) 367 3484), is just outside Philipsburg on the western arm of Great Bay, overlooking Little Bay on the other side. The rooms stand in lines above the pool and in imitation-Spanish blocks on the point, where you will find suites of high luxury with balconies and jacuzzis. Facilities include watersports and diving, tennis and entertainment around the pool or in the discotheque.

Beyond the concrete infestation of Pelican Key is a small and pleasant resort: **La Vista**, PO Box 2086 (✆ 43005, 🖷 43010). It is not on the beach and it is quite a way from town, but it is self-contained and has a pool and terraces which look over the Caribbean Sea. There are 32 junior and penthouse suites decorated in high Caribbean pastel in very comfortable cottages, with kitchenettes and all other 20th-century conveniences.

Really the best side of St Maarten, for independent travellers at least, is to be found in its few small and easy-going hotels and guest houses on the beach; head for **Simpson Bay**, a fantastic south-facing beach. **Mary's Boon**, PO Box 2078, US address PO Box 523882 Miami FL 33125 (✆ 54235, 🖷 53403, US toll free ✆ (1 800) 696 8177, *marysboon@megatropic.com*), is a very low-key retreat with an old-time Caribbean ambience. Guests gather in the main house, where there is a small library and a charming bar and dining room on a balcony open to the waves and sumptuous sand. A colour theme of black and white runs through the decor of the rooms, which are linked to the main house by walkways through the garden of palm and flamboyant. There are 16 big rooms, with white walls and rattan wicker furniture, and they have been updated since the inn changed hands recently and have cable TV, a/c and phones. The air is still casual, though, and this makes an ideal retreat from the humdrum. Some watersports, pool.

Nearby, the pink **Residence la Chatelaine**, PO Box 2056 (✆ 54269, ✆ 53195), is also on Simpson Bay. There are 17 neat and plush one- and two-bedroom apartments set in blocks above the sand and surrounded by gardens of palm and sea-grape. All rooms are air-conditioned, and have kitchenettes; some four-poster beds.

moderate

Not far down the beach is another excellent retreat, the **Horny Toad** Guest House and Apartments, PO Box 3029, 2 Vlaun Dr (✆ 54323, ✆ 53316, US res ✆ (1 800) 417 9361 ext 3013), which has a variety of one-bedroom apartments in a building right on the beach and set in a pretty garden. Eight units, all with fully equipped kitchens (no hotel dining room) and private balconies with a view of Saba; very personable and friendly atmosphere from owner operators.

Almost invisible in the recent concrete explosion in town, there is a hotel which retains a certain old-time Caribbean style, the **Passanggrahan Royal Guest House**, PO Box 151 (✆ 23588, ✆ 22885, US and Canada toll free ✆ (1 800) 223 9815), on Front Street, formerly the government rest house. The reception area and restaurant are set in a charming green and white town house with gingerbread woodwork and louvred shutters, overlooking an overgrown palm garden. There is an old-fashioned air from the high-backed wicker chairs and the portraits, and the afternoon tea served in the garden. It is also right on the sand. Some of the 30 units are in the main house and one particularly fine suite above it, but a new modern block has been built to take the rest; no TVs, no phones. It is quite busy because of all the passers-by in the town. The mellow **Trade Winds Inn**, PO Box 3038 (✆ 54206, ✆ 54796), has 10 quite comfortable rooms in a modern block at the end of the beach. One- and two-bedroom suites with full kitchens and patios, pool on a deck right above the sea.

cheap–very cheap

If you don't mind being off the beach, then you can get a good deal and a perfectly comfortable room at the **Sea Breeze Hotel** in Cay Hill (✆ 26054, ✆ 26057), which has 30 rooms in a modern block just off the main road to Cole Bay outside town (it might be an idea to have a car). 30 rooms with phones, TVs, a/c and kitchenettes. The cheapest accommodation tends to be in Philipsburg. Simple rooms at **Jose's Guesthouse** (✆ 22231) on Back Street and at **Marcus Guesthouse** (✆ 22419) on Front Street. If you would prefer to be in Cole Bay, on the road to the French side, you can stay at **George's Guest House** (✆ 45363), where there are 11 rooms with private baths and fan ventilation.

✆ *(599 5)–*   ### Eating Out

Sint Maarten is as cosmopolitan in cuisine as it is in languages and so you will find a bewildering selection of restaurants—anything from Mexican to Vietnamese, supported by an endless range of burger and pizza joints. Dutch food is not widely available, although Dutch East Indian is (Javanese). There's even a sushi bar. Obviously the island is strongly influenced by the States (there are daily flights delivering fresh food) and you will find some cheery American-style eateries and some decks on the waterfront a bit reminiscent of Florida. The more upmarket restaurants are usually French or Italian. It is not necessary to cross to the French side of the island for good French cooking, though you should consider heading over to the excellent restaurants over on the French side. Reservations are advisable in season; all but the smallest restaurants accept credit cards. Generally speaking, eating out in Sint Maarten is expensive and you can expect a 10–15% service charge to be added to your bill. Categories are arranged according to the price of a main course: *expensive*—US$20 and above; *moderate*—US$10–20; *cheap*—under US$10.

expensive

The most elegant evening out is at **Spartaco** (✆ 45379), where you dine in a 200-year-old restored coral-rock house and on glass-fronted verandas which look out on to a tropical garden. The cuisine is Northern Italian—*gamberoni Spartaco*, grilled shrimp sautéed in tomato sauce with garlic and mustard, or *sovrana di pollo farcita mediterranea*, a breast of chicken stuffed with mozzarella, tomato and basil. Another calm and stylish dining room can be found at **Le Perroquet** (✆ 54339) on Airport Road, where you sit among wooden parrots and tropical greenery, with a view through louvred windows on stilts onto the lagoon. The menu is French with some concessions to the Caribbean: *canard croquant* in Grand Marnier sauce; and some oddities such as wild boar and alligator. Follow up with *fraise flambée*, a13th-century recipe which uses green peppercorn. There is a nice deck where you take cocktails beforehand and coffee afterwards; service brisk but friendly. *Closed Mon.*

There are some good restaurants just above the waves on the Philipsburg waterfront. You will find another very popular Italian restaurant near the foot of town, with a mural announcing its European heritage: **Da Livio** (✆ 22690), where you dine on a terrace right above the water. *Aragosta fra diavolo* (lobster in spicy red sauce) or the *manicotti della casa* (with ricotta cheese, spinach and tomato). Wines from the Venice area. *Closed Sun.*

The French restaurant **Antoine's** (✆ 22964) has a very pretty terrace setting with blue awnings above the waves. *Canard montmorency* in a brandy sauce or grouper in almonds, followed by profiteroles or a chocolate mousse. And if you would like a taste of the Dutch East Indies in the Dutch West Indies, try the **Wajang Doll** (✆ 22687) close by. The dining room is on a veranda behind a pretty wooden creole house. You'll discover it by the smells as you walk by—lemon grass, lime-leaf and galanka root. Distinctive Indonesian fare in *nasi goreng* and dragon-mouthed *sambals* and the *rijstafel*, which is made up of 14–19 separate dishes.

Lynette's (*expensive–moderate*) serves good West Indian fare in an air-conditioned upstairs dining room right at the end of the runway. Conch fritter or stuffed crab-backs creole followed by lobster crêpes with a white wine and mushroom sauce.

moderate

Sint Maarten also has plenty of easy-going restaurants with a nautical setting, on a deck in the marinas or above the lagoon. Ever-popular, the **Greenhouse** offers standard international fare; burgers, salads and steaks. If you would specifically like fish and seafood, try nearby at the **Seafood Galley**, with a pub-style interior and a seafood restaurant at the side. Start with the raw bar—oysters, clams and rock crab claws—followed by creole shrimp or soft-shelled crabs in creole butter. On Front Street you will find a lively lunchtime stop right on the sand at the **Boo Boo-Jam** restaurant: grills and salads, conch and seafood brochettes, some watersports if the urge to race off on a windsurfer strikes.

A place well worth pulling over for is the **Turtle Pier** quite close to the terminal on Airport Road, a deck sticking out on to the lagoon where there is often a lively crowd. Daytime salads and burgers, long seafood menu for the evenings, when there are specials: all-you-can-eat-bbq-ribs, Wed lobster night. There are a couple of very popular and lively cafés at the entrance to the Maho Bay complex, including **Chéri's Café**.

cheap

Cheaper meals can be found, particularly away from the tourist areas. Among the delis in Philipsburg, **Ric's Place**, a sports and video bar on Front Street, offers simple burgers and some Mexican fare: *nachos* and *tostadas*. On the road to French St Martin, you can stop off at **Bill's Texas BBQ Pit,** which serves an excellent take-away barbecue meal.

Bars and Nightlife

In town you will find a number of daytime cafés and bars along Front Street. **Ric's Place** is an American-style sports bar where you can keep up with the Stateside sports while enjoying unlimited refills of iced tea or the 'largest selection of beers on the island...' In Great Bay Marina you will find the **Greenhouse**, also pool tables on a breezy deck, some drinks specials and music in the evenings. On the main road in Simpson Bay, there are some no-nonsense bars: a busy bar-cum-discotheque is the **News Music Café**, a rock theme pub with black and white decor, neon signs, video screens and own-label drinks coolers; and next door the **Boathouse**, which is hung with rigging. You shouldn't miss it because there's a boat outside. Tucked away among all these places there is a smaller, easier spot called the **Soggy Dollar** which offers a good beer with a quiet crowd (and a laundry if you need it).

Turtle Pier, not far down from the airport, collects a good crowd of yachties around the bar (with some rusting hulks left by Hurricane Luis to admire), particularly at Happy Hour between 5 and 7. Music several times a week. In Maho Bay just up the road you will find the ever-lively **Chéri's Café**, usually crammed with tourists, all trying to be heard above the calypso music. Cheap drinks. For a quieter drink on a very pretty terrace, try **Paradise Café**, which is hidden away behind the Maho Bay area.

Some hotels have shows over dinner a couple of times a week. Discotheques include the **News Music Café** in Simpson Bay, **Chrysalis** in the Great Bay Beach Hotel and **Club Amnesia** at Maho Bay. You will also find some excellent bars and places to dance on the French side (*see* Saint Martin).

There are ten or twelve casinos in Dutch Sint Maarten, in the big hotels and along Front Street in town.

getting there

Most flights arrive at Princess Juliana airport which is something of an air crossroads for this area of the Caribbean. It is particularly busy on Sunday afternoons, when many organized tours change over. A departure tax of US$12 is payable except for destinations within the Dutch Caribbean.

By air from Europe: The French connections are the best. Air France (*℗* 54212) operates three times a week from Paris and there are charter airlines including Corse Air (*℗* 87 94 07, on the French side), AOM and Air Liberté from Paris and other French cities. There is also a weekly flight from Amsterdam on KLM (*℗* 52545).

By air from the USA: American Airlines (*℗* 52040) flies in direct from Miami and New York, and there are plenty of connections from other American cities through their hub San Juan, Puerto Rico. Continental (*℗* 53444) and ALM, the Dutch Caribbean carrier (*℗* 54240) also fly from New York. Also US Air (*℗* 54344) from Philadelphia and Baltimore, and Northwest (*℗* 54344). BWIA (*℗* 54646) touches the island as it breaks its journeys from further south in the Caribbean (eg. Trinidad, St Lucia and Barbados).

By air from other Caribbean islands: Sint Maarten is well served from around the Caribbean. Winair (*℗* 54237) is based in Sint Maarten and flies to all the nearby islands. LIAT (*℗* 54203) flies hopper schedules north and south along the island chain and touches most of the islands from Santo Domingo in the Dominican Republic down to Antigua and on further south. ALM flies daily to Curaçao, Aruba and Caracas, with occasional flights to San Juan, Santo Domingo and Port of Spain and Air Guadeloupe (*℗* 52032) and Air Martinique (*℗* 54212) fly to their respective home islands, as does Air St Barth (*℗* 53150) with plenty of flights each day (also *see* 'St Barts', p.314). There is a **ferry boat** from Marigot on the French side to Anguilla (20 minutes).

tourist information

There is no tourist office dealing specifically with the Dutch Caribbean in **Britain**. It is best to write to New York or to the islands themselves. In **Holland**, contact the Cabinet of the Minister Plenipotentiary of the Netherlands Antilles at Badhuisweg 175, NL 2597 JP, 's-Gravenhage, The Hague (*℗* 070 351 2811, ● 070 351 2722).

USA: 675 3rd Avenue, New York, NY 10017 (*℗* 212 953 2084, ● 953 2145, toll free *℗* (1 800) 786 2278) and at 1900 Summit Tower Blvd, Suite 600, Orlando FL 32810 (*℗* (407) 875 1111, ● 875 1115).

Canada: 243 Ellerslie Avenue, Willowdale, Ontario, M2N 1Y5 (*℗* (416) 223 3501, ● 223 6887) and 1682 Victoria Park Ave, , Scarborough, Ontario, M1R 1P7 (*℗* (416) 755 5247, ● 755 8697).

There is a website at *www.st-maarten.com* and you can email the tourism department on the island on *tourism@megatropic.com.*

On **Sint Maarten** itself the main tourist information office is in the Imperial Building, 23 Walter Nisbett's Road, overlooking the lagoon, (*℗* 22337, ● 24884) but there is also an information desk on the waterfront (just where the launches drop the cruise-ship passengers) and a booth at Juliana airport. Open weekdays 8–noon and 1–5. On the French side, there is a small tourist information office on the harbour in Marigot, open 9–12.30 and

2-5. There are also quite a few strategically placed information offices which encourage you to visit the time-share complexes as well as giving tourist information.

The Sint Maarten tourist industry is well organized; you will be bombarded with brochures and magazines. If you can find a copy, the magazine most worth reading goes by the name of *Discover*, and is produced in tandem by the tourist offices from both sides of the island.

To telephone Sint Maarten from abroad, dial **IDD code** ✆ (599 5) followed by the five-digit local number. Within Sint Maarten dial just the five digits, and from Saba or Sint Eustatius, dial 5 and then the five-figure number. Phoning from the Dutch to the French side, dial ✆ (00 590) and then the six-digit number; from the French to the Dutch side dial 3 followed by the five digits. There are no coin-boxes on the French side and so you will need to buy a *télécarte* from the post office or the few newsagents that stock them.

In the case of a medical **emergency**, the Sint Maarten Medical Centre is on Cay Hill (✆ 31127).

festivals

Carnival is held in April, with celebrations along traditional Caribbean carnival lines, including calypso singing and costumed parades through the streets of Philipsburg. Official holidays include Queen Juliana's birthday on 30 April (and you can always nip over to the French side on Bastille Day, 14 June) and Concordia Day (actually St Maarten's day) on 11 November, which is shared by both halves of the island. There are a few sporting events, including the annual Heineken Regatta, usually held in March, and some bike races and triathlons. The June Fest, also shared by both sides of the island, includes cultural events and general blow-outs.

money

The official currency on the Dutch side is the Netherlands Antilles florin/guilder, which is fixed to the US dollar (rate US$1 = NAFl 1.78), but you will only see this money if you are in a local supermarket or on a bus as all transactions in tourist hotels and restaurants on both sides of the island can be carried out in US dollars. Where there might be confusion, make sure which currency you are dealing in. NA florins are not accepted on the French side.

Credit cards are widely accepted on the Dutch side, as are traveller's cheques. Personal cheques are not accepted. You can change money at any of the hotel front-desks, but the rate will not be as good as at a bank, of which there are five or six in Philipsburg.

Banks: Open 8.30–3 on weekdays with an extra hour on Friday afternoons, 4–5.

Shops: Hours are 8–noon and 2–6, Mon–Sat, with hours extended to Sunday morning if there is a cruise ship in town.

shopping

All visitors are encouraged to go shopping as part of their vacation, and maps are even provided to ease your passage through the jungle of Philipsburg's four streets. Sint Maarten is a free port and so there is no duty—clearly there are plenty of good bargains for professional and casual shoppers, though the island hardly has the status that Sint Eustatius had two hundred years ago. For fashion you might try Ralph Lauren and Benetton, and for jewellery Carat. Little Switzerland has good crystal and porcelain, Delft Blue has Dutch chinaware and you can find souvenirs at the Shipwreck Shop.

Sint Maarten's well-oiled tourist machine offers the full range of watersports if you are looking for an active vacation. Most large hotels have snorkelling gear, windsurfers and small sailing craft on offer to their guests: more exotic sports like para-sailing and jet-skis are easily found on the busier beaches. If you are travelling independently and wish to hire sports equipment, you can use the hotels' rental companies. The main centres on the Dutch side are Pelican Watersports (© 42640) in the Pelican Resort in Simpson Bay and Westport Watersports (© 42557).

Windsurfing: Get gear at the places above, but advanced sailors will find the best winds on the French side, at Baie de l'Orient and Baie de l'Embouchure on the northeast coast.

Day sails: Excursions, anything from a snorkelling and picnic trip to an offshore island to sunset booze-cruises, are available all over Sint Maarten, in a variety of different styles of boats. The catamaran *Bluebeard* and the motorboat *Lady Mary* (both © 52898) departs daily for Anguilla, or you can go by motorboat on *Santino* (© 42640). The catamaran *Golden Eagle* (© 30068) has a number of different destinations through the week. If you wish to hire your own boat, however, for a day or a week or more, a number of the Caribbean's big charter operators have bases in Saint Martin (*see* p.302).

Deep-sea fishing: Trips can be arranged through *Zing* (© 52167) in Simpson Bay, Lee's (© 44233) or the major operators above. A half-day casting for tuna, tarpon and sailfish costs around US$400.

Scuba diving and **snorkelling:** If you would prefer to admire the marine life in more peaceable circumstances, Sint Maarten has some good offshore reefs for snorkelling. Try the rocks at the end of Little Bay and Simpson Bay, where you will see shoals of pink and yellow fish dip and dart. On the rockier east coast the reefs at Dawn Beach are good, but best of all are the small islands off the French side, Ilet Pinel and Ile Tintamarre (also called Flat Island). Deeper underwater off the eastm coast there are forests of coral, plied by angelfish and squirrelfish, and off the south coast is the wreck of the HMS *Proselyte*, cannons and anchor encrusted. A single tank dive costs around US$45. Contact the main concessionaires or go through Tradewinds Divers (© 75176) in Great Bay Marina in Philipsburg, Leeward Island Divers (© 43320) or Ocean Explorers (© 45252) in Simpson Bay.

other sports

Golf: The Mullet Bay Resort (© 52801) has an 18-hole course backing on to the lagoon. All equipment can be rented and there are pros to improve your game. Green fees outrageous at around US$110 in season for the 18 holes (includes cart). Residents of the hotel pay half-price and have preference in teeing off.

Tennis: There are about fifty courts on the island, many of them lit for night-play. Contact any of the larger hotels.

Riding: It is even possible to go for an early-morning dip on horseback through the Crazy Acres Riding Centre (© 45255).

Mountain biking: There are trails all over the island. For a guide, contact Tri Sport (© 54384). There was even tandem **skydiving** from 9000ft at the time of writing (© 75634).

Sint Eustatius

Sint Eustatius is a tiny island with a glorious and glittering past. In the 18th century it was so rich that it was known as the Golden Rock; its warehouses were brimful of silks, silver and guns from all over the world. At that time it was one of the most important places in the Caribbean, but the warehouses are gone and its fortune has waned. It was actually the first country in the world to recognize the United States, when Governor De Graaff saluted the merchantman *Andrew Doria* in 1776.

Statia to her friends, the island has an area of just 8 square miles and is situated close to St Kitts, about 30 miles south of Sint Maarten. Statia is of volcanic origin: hills in the north descend to a central plain, where the capital and only town, Oranjestad, stands on the leeward coast, and then rise again in the south to the Quill (1890ft), a perfectly shaped volcano, now extinct.

The population of Statia (pronounced stay-sher) is now about 2000, a fraction of the numbers who lived and traded here in the 18th century. It is extremely quiet. If you go, remember that the glittering tradition remains in only a few dilapidated red and yellow brick and stone walls. There is a small and limited amount of tourism. For now, Statia is the least developed island in the area, and she can only wait until the waves of Caribbean fortune favour her again.

History

Settled by the Dutch West India Company in 1636 after a failed attempt on St Croix in the Virgin Islands, Statia's beginnings were modest—small cultivations of tobacco and sugar. But the company had its eyes on trade. Only they had fleets large enough to supply the burgeoning West Indian colonies in the 17th century and over the next hundred years Oranjestad in Sint Eustatius, along with Willemstad in Dutch Curaçao, became the most important market in the New World.

It started with slaves, for whom there was ceaseless demand in the sugar-islands nearby. The Statian merchants were often paid in kind (hogsheads of sugar and puncheons of rum were accepted currency), so the warehouses filled up and Sint Eustatius became a massive entrepôt, presided over by merchants from Europe and the Americas. By 1750 the warehouses stretched all along the waterfront in Lower Town and as space ran out the merchants constructed dykes to reclaim land from the sea, so that they could build a second line of warehouses. Over the next forty years, these became so full that the doorways were blocked up and the goods were hauled in and out through holes in the roof.

Strictly speaking, almost all of the trade was illegal because of monopoly trading laws imposed by the other European nations (which demanded that the colonies should trade only with the mother country). This did not endear them to local colonial authorities. But the Dutch in Sint Eustatius recognized no trading laws and the sugar-manufacturers in the West Indies knew that they would get a better price and immediate payment if they sold their goods to the merchants in Sint Eustatius (rather than shipping them all the way home). Thus they were prepared to smuggle them there. In 1779 Statia grew around 500,000 pounds of sugar, but according to official records it managed to ship about 25 million pounds.

So prosperous an island was a valuable prize and altogether Statia changed hands a ridiculous 22 times, as the different navies vied for supremacy in the Caribbean. Despite a ring of about 15 forts, Statia was never properly defended.

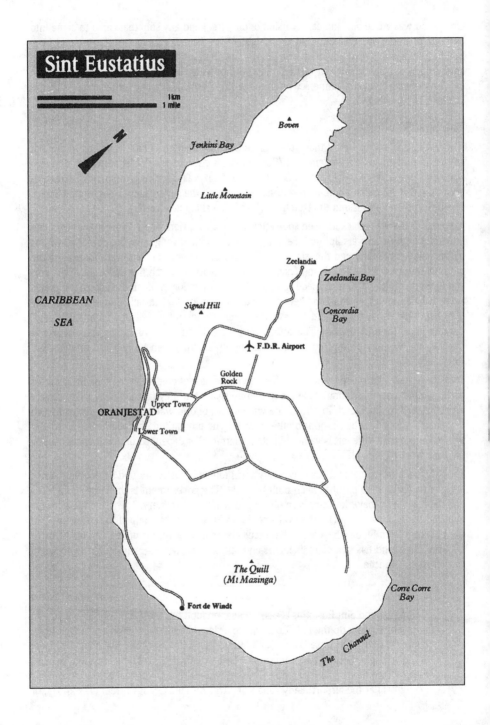

Sint Eustatius

1 km
1 mile

Boven

Jenkins Bay

Little Mountain

Zeelandia

Zeelandia Bay

CARIBBEAN

SEA

Signal Hill

Concordia
Bay

F.D.R. Airport

Golden
Rock

Upper Town
ORANJESTAD

Lower Town

The Quill
(Mt Mazinga)

Fort de Windt

Corre Corre
Bay

The Channel

Oranjestad was a free port (an early version of duty-free) and any ship that cared to come into harbour to trade was welcome. At the height of the island's prosperity there could be a hundred ships offshore at any time. The port became famous as an arms depot, with rifles and ammunition passing through in vast amounts. Gunpowder turned in a profit of over 100 per cent. American blockade-runners would dodge the British Navy and smuggle arms to the colonists in sugar-barrels.

The First Salute

It was with this trade in mind that Governor de Graaff saluted an unknown flag on a ship that arrived in harbour on 16 November 1776. It was the American colonist merchant ship, the *Andrew Doria*. Even if the gesture was not deliberate, it was certainly a momentous event, as it was the first time that a foreign power had recognized the sovereignty of the United States. The British were furious and the Dutch apologized, recalling de Graaff.

Maverick Statia was attacked again soon after de Graaff's action when Admiral Rodney sailed into harbour with 15 warships on 3 February 1781, seeking revenge. For the next few months he systematically plundered the island, confiscating all the goods in the warehouses and the personal fortunes of the Statian merchants. He even kept the Dutch flag flying above the port and lured in another 150 unsuspecting ships. When he auctioned off all the goods, the profits exceeded £3 million, of which he kept a sizeable proportion for himself. Understandably, the merchants did what they could to save their riches and stories tell of an unusually high number of deaths and funerals. The coffins were loaded with gold. As soon as he discovered the trickery, Rodney promptly had them all dug up again. When he had had enough, the British abandoned the island.

Statia never really recovered, and since then the island has suffered an ever-declining spiral. As trading foundered, the plantations were started up again, but they failed quickly when slavery was abolished by the Dutch in 1863. The warehouses on the waterfront were dismantled so that their bricks could be sold on to other islands. The population dropped as the prosperity waned. Those that were left became subsistence farmers, or depended on remittances sent by relatives working abroad.

Today Statia is very quiet and has only a very small tourist industry (around a hundred rooms), although a cruise ship pier has been built recently. The government is the largest employer and the only other major industry is an oil storage facility and refinery. The island has a listless and slightly tatty air, but a Dutch government and EC project has helped to restore some of the buildings from Statia's heyday. The present Lieutenant Governor of St Eustatius is Mr E. Locadia. The island has two commissioners and one senator, Mr A.K. van Putten, who sits in the Senate in Curaçao.

℗ (599 3)–   ***Getting Around***

Getting around Sint Eustatius is easy enough on foot, but there are also **taxis** if you do not want to walk up the hill. Taxis can be ordered at any hotel desk or through Rosie Lopes (℗ 82811) or Josse Daniel (℗ 82358). A guided tour of the island can be made, and if you spin it out to two hours it will cost around US$35. There are a few **cars** for hire, at around US$35 per day. Present your driving licence to the Avis desk (℗ 82421) at the airport, Lady Ama's Services on Fort Orange Street (℗ 82451), or

Rainbow Car Rental (✆ 82811). Scooters are available through Dive Statia (✆ 82435). Driving is on the right.

Beaches

There are only a couple of beaches in Statia and they do not have the white sand for which the Caribbean is known. Generally, the Atlantic side is unsafe for swimming because of the undertow.

best beaches

Smoke Alley Beach or **Oranje Beach**: Off the road down to Lower Town on the calm Caribbean side, with an excellent view of the sunset: popular among the Statians at the weekends. There is a beach bar, decorated with fishing nets and coloured lights, whcih sticks out into the sea.

Crooks Castle: Beyond Lower Town, another passable sunning and snorkelling spot.

Corre Corre Bay: On the Atlantic side of the island, a secluded cove. Skirt round the Quill to the southeast on Mountain Road and the path down to the bay is marked.

Concordia and Zeelandia Bay: Two miles of good walking and beach-combing on sand for flotsam cast ashore by the Atlantic.

Oranjestad

Statia's only settlement, tiny **Oranjestad**, has two parts, Upper and Lower Town, which are separated by a 100ft cliff. During Statia's supremacy as a trading port, goods were kept in the warehouses down below, between the cobbled street and the waterfront and many of the traders would live up above in Upper Town. Today the Statians still live up above, in new 'gingerbread' houses that have forced aside the dark-stone 18th-century foundations and barrel-vaulted graves, and in more modern concrete houses. The two halves are linked by an old stone walkway built in 1803. Down below, Lower Town has now fallen into almost complete dilapidation. Just a few buildings have been restored from the old ruins of red and yellow brick and some stone foundation walls are visible on the shoreline leading out into the water. The outer rim of houses has completely disappeared since the dyke was broken by a hurricane and the sea swept back in, but on a calm day it is just possible to see the base of the walls which run between Crooks Castle and Betty Bay, below the surface of the water.

The town takes its name from **Fort Oranje**, a fortress which rides high on the clifftop above the Lower Town. It was built by the Dutch in 1636 on the site of an earlier French fort. Even though the island was attacked so often, the fort saw little action. Some reports state that it is poised so precariously that it dared not fire its guns in case the whole structure slipped and fell off the cliff into the Lower Town. Fort Oranje has settled comfortably into its modern unwarlike role: of sitting and looking pretty. If you dare go close to the edge, it has an attractive view across Lower Town. Among its monuments, the most significant commemorates the firing of the salute to the *Andrew Doria* on 16 November 1776.

The **Sint Eustatius Museum** (*open weekdays 9–5, Sat, Sun 9–12; adm*) is located in Simon Doncker House just off the Wilheminaweg and central square. Admiral Rodney made it his headquarters when he ransacked the island in 1781. The exhibition has an Amerindian section with old Indian pottery and artefacts from the extensive archaeological programmes that have taken place in Statia; there are two very attractive period rooms, restored to the time of Statia's prosperity, including impressive antique furniture and a planter's tea service, and a more recent room, 'Granny Statia', exhibiting life on Statia within the last hundred years. Also on view are some small china pieces from the Nanking cargo (which was on order to the Dutch West India Company in Sint Eustatius when the Dutch East India Company ship that was carrying it sank in the South China Sea); they arrived two hundred years late, but they made it.

The Upper Town has some pretty and well-kept old houses made of stone and wood, but mostly it is a little tatty and goats, chickens and donkeys tend to have the run of the place. Statia's sizeable Jewish community, who suffered most of all during Rodney's ravages in 1781 (not only was all their money taken, but they were deported as well), is remembered in the ruins of the **Honen Dalim Synagogue**, on the little alley, Synagoogpad. On the Kerkweg, the **Dutch Reformed Church** tower, with a cemetery full of barrel-vaulted graves, has been restored and gives a fine view of the harbour.

South of Oranjestad is Statia's volcano, **the Quill**. It is perfectly shaped, with concave slopes rising to nearly 2000ft and a circular crater, from which it takes its name (*kuil* in Dutch means pit). Inside the crater, which is 900ft across and 550ft deep, is a moist and tangled rainforest, where the trees grow tall in their efforts to reach the sun and mosses infest their trunks. Some cultivation takes place in here. Its highest point is Mt Mazinga.

There are thought to have been about 19 forts dotted around Statia's barren coastline; a few are lost without trace. At **Fort de Windt** on the southern tip of the island, a couple of cannon look south over the superb view of St Kitts.

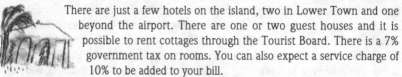

✆ *(599 3)–*   **Where to Stay**

There are just a few hotels on the island, two in Lower Town and one beyond the airport. There are one or two guest houses and it is possible to rent cottages through the Tourist Board. There is a 7% government tax on rooms. You can also expect a service charge of 10% to be added to your bill.

At the time of writing the **Old Gin House** was sadly closed and so there was not really anywhere to stay in real comfort. However, that is not to say you will not be comfortable and treated well at the other hotels and guest houses **La Maison sur la Plage**, PO Box 157 (✆ 82256, ✉ 82831; *moderate–cheap*), is a collection of cottages set beneath a hill above the isolated Zeelandia Bay, a 2-mile strip of brown sand dashed by Atlantic waves (swimming is not recommended because of the undertow). The main house has a bar looking out to the bay and the Quill volcano in the distance, and good dining on a trellis-work terrace with a rush-matting ceiling; guests gather before dinner for a drink and a game of backgammon. On a small island this is a secluded retreat, with good trails all around.

The **Golden Era Hotel**, PO Box 109 (✆ 82345, ✉ 82445; *moderate*), on the waterfront in Lower Town, is a modern construction that has none of the atmosphere of old-time Statia. There is a pool and bar down on the waterfront and a dining room which serves West Indian and international fare; rooms simple and passable. **Talk of the Town Hotel** (✆ 82236, ✉ 82640, US toll free ✆ (1 800) 223 9815; *moderate*) is situated in town and has 20 rooms, a few with kitchenettes, in the modern red-roofed main house and around the pool. Comfortable rooms, with air-conditioning, cable TV and phones.

You can get a simple room and good company at the **King's Well Inn** (✆/✉ 82538, US toll free ✆ (1 800) 692 4106; *cheap*) where there are nine rooms in a modern villa on the main road down to the Lower Town; there's a fantastic view if you get a room looking out to sea. The owners are friendly and so their terrace dining room attracts a crowd from all around.

You can also get a good price at the **Country Inn** (✆/✉ 82484; *cheap*), which has just six secluded apartments, set far away from the hustle of Oranjestad in Concordia, and at the **Airport View Apartments** (✆ 82299, ✉ 82517; *cheap*), which is just next to the airport. **Guest houses** include **Daniel's** (✆ 82358; *very cheap*) on Rose Mary Laan Road, and **Richardson's** (*very cheap*).

Eating Out and Nightlife

Statian food is generally international and West Indian and it tends to be quite simple. It is worth adding the hotel dining rooms into the equation. There is good fare to be found at **La Maison sur la Plage** and at **King's Well Inn** (*both moderate*) and there is a nice dining room at the **Talk of the Town** (*moderate*). Most of the restaurants also double as bars.

Restaurant categories below are arranged according to the price of a main course: *expensive*—US$15 and above; *moderate*—US$8–15; *cheap*—under US$8.

Of the independent restaurants, check out **L'Etoile** (✆ 82299; *moderate*), up the hill on Heilgerweg, which serves local fare. Start with a callaloo soup and follow with creole catch of the day. **The Stone Oven** (✆ 82543; *moderate*) on Faeschweg has wooden tables and bright tablecloths and serves fish and chicken. There is a nice café just next to the fort, the **Ocean View**, where you sit on a deck under canvas and a tree, with a view offshore: satay chicken, shrimp and steak dishes, pleasant atmosphere as professionals drop by for a bite for lunch or a drink on the way home.

If you feel like a Chinese meal or a roti, then go to **Sonny's Place** on Fort Oranje Straat, with a garden bar with trellises and a pool table inside. Down on the waterfront in the Lower Town you will find a nice spot at the **Blue Bead** bar and restaurant (blue beads were a form of currency two centuries ago), where you will be served steaks, chicken and fish platters as well as simpler salads.

Nightlife in Statia is limited to the hotels and the local bars, of which the best is **Kool Corner**, where the Statians can be found 'limin' at all hours: a wooden shed with coloured lights visible from outside and TV playing permanently. At **Franky's** on de Ruyterweg you can get simple meals—burgers and a fry fish or chicken—or simply have a beer when the band is playing. Make sure to finish off with one of Franky's ice-creams. There is a disco, **Largo Heights**, in the Mall.

getting there and around

Sint Eustatius is served several times a day by Winair (Windward Islands Airways) from Sint Maarten (local ✆ 82381), sometimes via Saba. There are also occasional flights to the island from St Kitts. On approach, the plane often circles the volcano, the Quill, so remember to look out of the window. There is a departure tax of US$5 for travel within the Dutch Caribbean and US$10 elsewhere. A couple of **charter** planes work in and out of the island: José Dormoy (✆ 82646) and Alvin Courtar (✆ 82218).

tourist information

There is no tourist office for St Eustatius in the UK, so you should write direct to the island or to **Holland**, at the Antillen Huis, Badhuisweg 173-5, 2597 SP 's-Gravenhagen (✆ 070 30 66111, ✆ 070 35 12722). In the **USA** you can contact them at PO Box 6322, Boca Raton, Fl 33427 - 6322 (✆ (561) 394 8580, ✆ 394 4294, toll free ✆ (1 800) 722 2394).

The main **Sint Eustatius Tourism Development Foundation** (✆/✆ 82433, *www.turq. com/statia*) is in Upper Town, close to the entrance of Fort Oranje. Hours are 8–noon and 1–5 on weekdays. There is also a desk at the airport, open for the scheduled flights.

In a medical **emergency**, contact the Princess Beatrix Hospital (✆ 82211) in Oranjestad. To telephone the island from abroad, dial **IDD code** ✆ (599 3), except from Saba and Sint Maarten where you dial ✆ (03), and then follow it with the five-digit Statian number. On-island, use the five digits only.

festivals

National holidays include **Statia Day** on 16 November, which remembers the event in 1776 when Statia saluted the young United States of America, and Coronation Day in memory of the crowning of Queen Beatrix of the Netherlands.

Carnival is the main event in the year and takes place for ten days from late July to early August. It is similar to other Caribbean carnivals, with a pyjama jump-up in the early morning at jouvert, a Carnival Queen and a calypso competition, culminating in the burning of Momo, the spirit of the Carnival.

Saba

Saba is impossibly steep, a mountainous pimple just 5 square miles in area, a central cone surrounded by little lieutenants. Standing about 30 miles to the south of Sint Maarten, the volcanic island of Saba is the final peak in the chain of volcanic islands that runs in an arc from Grenada in the far south.

Mount Scenery (2885ft), the island peak smothered in rainforest, is the highest point in the Kingdom of the Netherlands. Near the summit, Saba can seem like a tropical Gormenghast— clouds swirl through the dripping greenery and the gnarled branches of ancient trees are clad in creeping diabolic green mosses.

Besides the capital, The Bottom, there are three main villages on the island's slopes (Windwardside, St John's and Hell's Gate). They appear almost alpine with their stepped

money

The Netherlands Antilles florin (US$1 = NAFl 1.78) is the island currency, but US dollars are accepted everywhere alongside it. Credit cards are not that widely used. **Barclays Bank** (© 82392) is open on weekdays, 8.30–1, with an extra hour on Friday afternoons, 4–5.

maps and books

One or two books deal with Statia's famous past, including a good, if a little academic, history, *Sint Eustatius, A short history of the island and its monuments* by Ypie Attema.

watersports

These are limited in Statia. You might be able to borrow a windsurfer, but there are no small sailing boats for hire and there is no waterskiing.

Snorkelling: At Jenkins Bay in the north.

Scuba diving: Seems to be on the up at the moment. Advocates claim that there are the pristine corals and fish off nearby Saba and reefs that are clean and for the moment undived. There are some walls and pinnacles and some archaeological sites. About two hundred vessels are thought to have sunk off Statia, but the old wrecks themselves do not offer that much because the wood has invariably rotted away, leaving just a pile of ballast stones. After a storm, however, the sea still turns up the occasional 18th-century bottle, blue trading beads or a rare ducat. There are current attempts to create a marine park. There are three operators working in the island: Dive Statia (© 82435), Golden Rock Dive Centre (© 82964) and Blue Nature Watersports (© 82725).

other sports

Walking: The Tourist Board has marked about twelve trails around the island, of which the most popular is up the slopes of the extinct volcano, the Quill, and then down into its crater. The Statians have a tradition of land-crab-hunting by torchlight in the crater at night, which is a fun way to spend an evening. A guide can be provided by the Tourist Board for an outing to the crater; if you go at night, you are advised to take one. North of Oranjestad you might see coastal tropicbirds, distinctive with their long twin tail-feathers.

Tennis: There is a floodlit court at the Community Centre, in the southern area of town.

alleys, switchbacks and steep retaining walls (the base of one house perched on the roof of the one below) and their spectacular views: you are so high up that you can often see the curve in the horizon. There is a certain pastoral calm about the place as well.

Saba (pronounced as in sabre, the sword) is incredibly neat. Tidy gardens tamed from the tropical jungle nestle behind white wooden picket fences; fluorescent blooms stand out against the whitewashed clapboard walls of the houses with their horseshoe-shaped chimney-pots. Curiously, every single roof in Saba is painted red.

You have a good chance of getting a person's name right in Saba if you call them Mr or Mrs Hassell (about a quarter of the population are called Hassell). However, beware, because you might just come across a member of the two rival Saban dynasties, a Johnson or a Simmons. The population is just 1200 (mostly of British descent) and it is untypical in the Caribbean for being roughly half white and half black. With few plantations, most slaves on Saba were domestic servants and their numbers never exceeded those of the white population. Though the islanders all know each other, there are unspoken rules concerning skin colour (as there are in many Caribbean islands) and even today, there is little intermarriage between the races. And as with many small islands, much of the youth has left in search of work and adventure. The population appears to be mainly grandparents and infant grandchildren.

Relatively speaking there is a large population of expatriates, about 250, many of whom are students or teachers at the Saba Medical School. About three-quarters of the tourists who visit the island come for scuba diving, for which Saba has justifiably earned a good reputation recently.

Saba is quiet, calm, sedate and very stable. It is certainly not a place for a wild time, or for a beach-bound resort holiday (again it is untypical for the Caribbean in that there are simply no beaches there). However, if you are looking for a quiet Caribbean retreat with a gentle, old-time air, then Saba is a satisfying and very pleasant place to stay.

History

A stream of famous visitors passed by the island in the 16th century, among them Sir Walter Raleigh and Piet Heyn, the Dutch privateer, but most thought better of trying to land. Somebody must have done so, however, because in 1632 a shipwrecked crew of Englishmen found a plentiful supply of fruit on the trees but no inhabitants. (It was a tradition that sailors would plant food-bearing trees for just this sort of occasion.) The first permanent settlement of Saba was made by Dutchmen from nearby Sint Eustatius in about 1640, and they were joined by a succession of misfits, many of them English speakers. In 1665 an English pirate named Morgan paused to capture the island and he promptly deported everyone who wasn't English.

Saba was almost impregnable. There are few easy landing sites and the terrain is so precipitous that storming the island presented quite a problem. For their part, the Sabians supposedly defended themselves by man-made avalanches. They constructed platforms at the top of the ravines and loaded them with boulders, and on the approach of an enemy, they simply knocked out the supports. In 1689 the French had a go after successfully capturing Sint Eustatius, but decided in the end to leave the island alone. From then on, most changes of allegiance were by political arrangement. In 1816 the island was handed back to the Dutch for the last time.

The great Caribbean rover, Père Labat, dropped by in about 1700 and found that the islanders' principal trade was in boots and shoes. Even the parson was a cobbler. Labat bought six pairs. Since then Sabians have been in many trades. They had some success growing sugar in the fertile parts of the island. For this they brought in some Africans, whose descendants are still on the island. Slavery was relatively benign here compared with elsewhere in the Caribbean.

In the 19th century the Sabian men took to the sea and became renowned sailors. They were much in demand by the shipping lines and they captained ships sailing all over the Americas. (Give them a bit of encouragement and old Sabians will gladly tell you of the days when 'the boats were made of wood and the men were made of iron'.) The economy of the island was supported by the contributions that they sent back to their families. At home, with no men around, the Sabian women adopted lacemaking, or drawn-thread work, an industry that continues today.

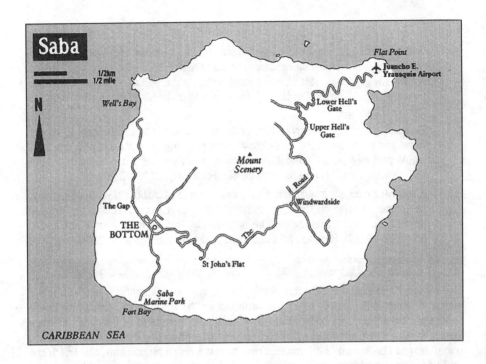

As shipping waned in the thirties, the oil industry boomed in Curaçao and Aruba, the Dutch Leeward Islands off the coast of Venezuela, and the menfolk rushed away to get work there. All these departures have reduced the population of Saba from around 2500 to its present level. Today the 'remittance money' sent home by Sabians abroad has dwindled but returns from tourism have increased. Other industries include the exporting of lobsters from local waters. Recently a University Medical School has been created and so there are quite a number of students during term time. Saba also receives grants from the Central Government of the Netherlands Antilles in Curaçao, to which they send one elected senator and two commissioners. It has an appointed Lieutenant Governor, presently Mr Sydney Sorton.

'The Road that Could Not Be Built'

Before the construction of The Road, anything from a bean to a grand piano had to be carried around on the pathways and so the Sabians decided that they needed a road. On seeking expert advice in the thirties, they were simply told that they shouldn't bother to try. But the Hassells and the Johnsons were made of sterner stuff than that and so Josephus Lambert Hassell, the architect of The Road, decided to take a correspondence course in civil engineering. In 1938 work began at Fort Bay, slowly winding its way uphill for the next five years to The Bottom. In 1947 the first car arrived and by 1951 it could be driven to Windwardside. The 19 miles of The Road cling to the mountainside, climbing to 1800ft as it winds from village to village, so you get some unexpected and stunning views as you drive around. To the builders' credit, The Road was repaired for the first time in the late 1980s.

With no buses, getting around Saba is really limited to **taxis**, and **hitching**, which works very well and will introduce you to the Sabians. There is only one road, so you can't really go wrong. It is usually enough to sit on the wall at the edge of town for someone to pick you up. The taxi-fare from one end of the island to the other comes to around US$15.

Taxi-drivers are willing to give a **tour of the island**, taking in the historical sights and views and a stop for lunch. They know about catching the last plane out, though it would probably not go without you anyway. A day's tour for two will cost around US$40, with a small charge for extra people. For a taxi, call (✆ 62281).

A few **hire cars** are available and they can be rented for about US$40–45 per day. Remember to drive on the right, and that Saba's only petrol station is in Fort Bay (✆ 63272), on the coast below The Bottom. Cars can be hired from B and D Car Rental (✆ 62212), Hardiana (✆ 62205) and Johnson's Car Rental (✆ 62469).

The Bottom, and On From There

The Bottom is the capital of Saba and despite its name it sits at an altitude of 850ft. It is a jumble of white walls, red roofs and green shutters set in neat little gardens, sitting in the bottom of a bowl (the name botte means 'bowl' in Dutch) thought to be the crater of Saba's extinct volcano. There are still some cobbled streets, laid with large stones. The evening shade comes early to The Bottom as it is towered over by vast forested escarpments. The Dutch and Saban flags fly alongside one another in front of the Lieutenant Governor's residence at the southern end of the town, a gingerbread house defended by a couple of fearsome cannon (at least four-ouncers).

Close by, down the hill and through the 'chicane' you come to **Fort Bay**. This is the island's main port and it has more than a little industrial quality about it, with a quarry, the electricity plant, the petrol station and the arm of the dock, which has stretched out into the sea since

windwardside village saba

1972. Before that, landing was a skilled technique which involved beaching the row-boat on one wave and scrambling out before the next one broke over you. At the other end of town, 520 steps lead down to **Ladder Bay**, the other main port, off the new road to Wells Bay. These steps have seen everything from shoes to the kitchen sink transported up and down them in their time. You might see a charcoal-burner's pit on the way down.

The Road passes by way of St John's to **Windwardside**, Saba's second settlement, which is scattered over the mountainside at around 2000ft and because of this occasionally disappears in the clouds. More white picket fences, barrel graves/cisterns and steep alleys. In one of the many neat houses, you will find the **Saba Museum** (*open on weekdays 10–3; adm a suggested donation of US$1*), dressed up as it was in its prime 150 years ago. It exhibits Saban memorabilia from Indian axe-heads to a Victorian mahogany four-poster bed with pineapple motifs. Outside the museum is a bust of 'El Libertador', Simon Bolivar, who recruited men here in 1816 for his struggle against the Spanish authorities in South America. There is a fantastic view across to Statia from the Lookout, just up the hill from Windwardside.

From Windwardside, The Road switchbacks its way through terraced cultivation to the alpine village of Hell's Gate (a curious adaptation of the original name of Zion's Hill), where each house seems to be held in place and prevented from tumbling down the hill by the one above. The church was constructed only in 1962. From here The Road makes its nineteen curves to get down to Flat Point, where the airstrip is situated.

Beaches

Saba has no 'beaches' as beaches are generally thought of in the Caribbean. However, a patch of migratory grey volcanic sand returns annually to the north coast of the island in the spring, staying over the summer until about November. This is at **Well's Bay**, at the end of the road from The Bottom. On a calm day, it makes a good picnic spot. The other place occasionally referred to as the 'beach' is the concrete ramp down into the water at Fort Bay, but you probably wouldn't want to sunbathe there at the moment because of the quarry. There is not much in the way of watersports otherwise but kayaks and sunset cruises around the island can be arranged through the three dive shops.

© (599 4)–   ### Where to Stay

There is a surprising number of places to stay on Saba. As well as a red roof, each has the cosy and friendly atmosphere for which the island is known. There are also about 20 villas (including Elsie's Cottage, Susanna's Cottage and Flossie's Cottage) for hire, some of them the charming wooden Saban cottages dotted around the island—more details of these can be obtained from the Tourist Board or through Saba Real Estate (©/❀ 62209). Many of the hotels offer diving packages in conjunction with the dive shops. There is a government hotel tax of 5% to be added to rooms and hotels also add a service charge of 10% or 15%.

expensive–moderate

The **Captain's Quarters** (© 62201, ❀ 62377, US © (212) 289 6031, ❀ 289 1931, *Rich_Holm@msn.com*), in Windwardside at the foot of the hill, has the best in old-time Saban charm. Twenty very comfortable rooms stand in small blocks; some in the charming central house which is decorated as the sea captain's home that it once was, with wooden floors, four-posters and louvred windows and a small library downstairs; others in more modern buildings. From the balconies you look over the pool and banana trees to the Caribbean Sea. The dining room is on a terrace beneath the main house and the bar is a popular gathering point. Perhaps the most luxurious resort on the island is **Willard's of Saba**, PO Box 515 (✆ 62498, ✆ 62482), which sits isolated above Booby Hill with a truly amazing setting looking south. There are just three rooms in the main house and two two-room bungalows perched on the hillside above the (heated) pool and hot tub with a view. Very modern and plush, bright white with bright pastel fittings, excellent restaurant; tennis court. The **Queen's Garden Resort,** PO Box 4 (✆ 63494, ✆ 63495, US toll free ✆ (1 800) 599 9407) is also set in modern buildings that stand high above The Bottom, on a hillside smothered in rain-forest, with views to the sea. There are 12 apartments (some studios) and three villas around the pool; all modern and comfortable and have cable TV, full kitchens and some have private jacuzzis. There is a restaurant in the hotel as well.

moderate–cheap

The **Cottage Club** (✆ 62386, ✆ 62476, www.turq.com/cottage-club/) sits on sloping ground in Windwardside, with a small assembly of cottages in island style, white shingle walls, gingerbread trimmings, green window frames and a red tin roof, that stand beneath the stone main house. Good interiors, large rooms with full kitchens and modern fittings (cable TV, fans, phones) each with a balcony from where you can watch the planes bell-flopping on to the runway fifteen hundred feet below. The **Gate House** (✆ 62416, ✆ 62415, US ✆ (708) 354 9641, http://members. aol.com/travelsaba/) is set in a classic Saban house (built recently in classic Saban style) with triple-pointed gables and shuttered windows in the village of Hell's Gate, set in fantastic greenery. Comfortable friendly atmosphere, brightly decorated rooms, some with kitchens, all with terraces; small pool. In Windwardside, looking southwest from the top of the ridge in town, is **Scout's Place** (✆ 62205, ✆ 62388), with 15 simple rooms, overlooking the attractive roofs and jungle-like greenery. There is a lively open-air bar, where the Sabians stop off on their way home from work and the dining room is presided over by Diana Medero. **Juliana's** (✆ 62269, ✆ 62389), also in Windwardside, has eleven private rooms, some with kitchenettes and some with their own balconies facing the Caribbean Sea. There is a dining room, Tropics Café, and a pool, all surrounded by white picket fences and gingerbread woodwork.

cheap–very cheap

In the Bottom, **Cranston's Antique Inn** (✆ 63203, ✆ 63469) is a former residence of the Lieutenant Governor and some Sabian sea captains. As the name implies, the inn basks in fading Saban glory, a pretty wooden creole house painted white with green shutters behind a picket fence. Some of the six rooms have four-poster beds, others share a bathroom; bar and pool down below. Nearby is the **Caribe Guest House** (✆/✆ 63259), where there are six rooms with private baths; although there is no restaurant, the kitchen is for the use of the guests. You can also find a cheap room at the **Mid-Town Apartments** (✆ 63394, ✆ 63263) nearby, very simple. The cheapest but by no means the least attractive place to stay on the island is at **El Momo**

Cottages, PO Box 519 (✆/● 62265), which clings to a steep hillside in Booby Hill above Windwardside. There is a small central area, a charming pool and a nice deck for sitting, or lying in the hammock. The five rooms are very simple (it's close to camping this), with outdoor basins (with a view) and a communal bathroom with sun-heated hot water for your shower. Breakfast and packed lunches available.

✆ (599 4)– Eating Out

You are likely to eat in the hotel dining rooms. Most serve a combination of local dishes—callaloo followed by fry chicken—alongside standard American fare of burgers and steaks. Try the **Captain's Quarters**, set on the veranda, **Willards of Saba** (by reservation only), **The Gate House** in Hell's Gate, **Tropics** at Juliana's and **Scout's Place**, set on the veranda, which can get quite lively. Many dining rooms and restaurants also double as bars. It is worth making a reservation at the hotel dining rooms in season. Categories are arranged according to the price of a main course: *expensive*—US$15 and above; *moderate*—US$8–15; *cheap*—under US$8.

Outside the hotels you will find good seafood and creole fare at **Brigadoon** (✆ 62380; *moderate*), which sits on a small terrace with fairy-lights and trellising in Windwardside. International and sea-food: fresh fish daily, creole shrimp, even a breast of duck. If you feel like a Chinese meal, try **Chinese 2** (✆ 62268; Chinese 1 has been superseded; *moderate*), set in a modern Saban house, where there is a huge selection of traditional Chinese dishes. And there is also an Italian restaurant, **Guido's Pizzeria** (✆ 62230; *moderate–cheap*), with pizzas and pastas, ravioli, even veal *parmigiani*, but also burgers. If you are feeling peckish in the daytime you can get a sandwich, soup or a pie from **Caribake,** near the tourism department.

Down in The Bottom you will get classic local cuisine at **Queenie's Serving Spoon** (✆ 63225; *moderate–cheap*)—pumpkin soup or callaloo, followed by a curry goat and a tropical fruit ice cream to finish. And **Lollipops** (✆ 63330; *moderate–cheap*) is another local bar and restaurant for classic West Indian fare; try fish or chicken with local vegetables—breadfruit, sweet potato and yam. For mid-morning refreshment you could try the **Kaffiehuis**, with coffee and other refreshments. Down by the harbour in Fort Bay you will find **In Two Deep**, where you can swap a few scuba war stories at a lacquered wood bar with stained-glass (plastic) scenes of underwater life. Sandwiches and salads. **Pop's** is a more local rum-shop nearby.

Bars and Nightlife

When Père Labat visited in 1701, he wrote: 'The settlers live as it were in a large club and frequently entertain each other.' It is pretty much the same today, except that they congregate in the bars dotted around the island, many of which are in the hotels and the restaurants. There are a few more local bars in The Bottom, including **Inner Circle,** which doubles as disco and snack bar. There is occasionally some entertainment in Scout's Place and if you want to go dancing, the **Mountain High Club** is open at the weekend at Guido's Pizzeria in Windwardside. You might try out Saba's own rum-based liqueur, which is steeped in cinnamon, cloves, brown sugar and fennel seeds, actually quite a smooth and tasty concoction.

getting there

The only scheduled flights that go to Saba are the five or so each day on Winair (℗ 62255). They originate in Sint Maarten and sometimes touch down at Sint Eustatius. You can also get to Saba by the power-yacht *The Edge* (℗ 42640), which departs three times a week from Pelican Marina in Sint Maarten.

There are a number of organized **tours** on offer from Sint Maarten, both by sea and by air, which come for a day's sightseeing. *Voyager* (St Maarten ℗ 24096). There is a departure tax of US$2 if you are travelling to Sint Eustatius or to Sint Maarten and US$5 for elsewhere.

Flying into Saba is a novel experience. Juancho E. Yrausquin airport is on Flat Point—named so because it is one of the only flat places on the island (even if there is a 130ft cliff at either end). At 1312ft, this strip is one of the shortest in the world (this includes most aircraft carriers), and as you look at it from the air, it seems impossible that anything could land on it. But be reassured, the STOL Twin Otters can land on a sixpence and they usually take only half the runway. There are a number of photographs on the walls of the airport illustrating some past events, including a 'spectacular prang' in 1971.

tourist information

The **Saba Tourist Office** (℗ 62231, 🖷 62350, *www.turq.com/saba*) is in Windwardside, on the road down to the Bottom. The staff are helpful and are in the office on weekdays, 8–noon and 1–5. They will also send information abroad. There are occasional art tours on the island.

In the **USA** you can contact them at PO Box 6322, Boca Raton, Fl 33427-6322 (℗ (407) 394 8580, 🖷 394 8588, toll free ℗ (1 800) SABA DWI (722 2394)) and in **Holland** some information can be obtained from the Antillen Huis, Badhuisweg 173-5, 2597 JP 's-Gravenhagen (℗ 070 351 2811, 🖷 070 351 2722).

Not so many years ago, isolated Saba had only a weekly mail service, but now communications are rather easier. To **telephone** the island from abroad, dial ℗ (599 4) and then the five-digit Saban number. If phoning within the island, dial the last five digits only. In case of a medical **emergency**, contact the M. A. Edwards Medical Centre (℗ 63288) in The Bottom.

festivals

Saba's **Summer Festival** runs for a week in July, following traditional Caribbean carnival lines with calypso shows, a festival parade in the streets and the usual jump-ups in the evenings.

money

The currency of Saba is the Netherlands florin (US$1 = NAFl 1.78), but US dollars are accepted everywhere. Barclays Bank operates in Windwardside, 8.30am to 1.30pm on weekdays. Places accustomed to tourists, for instance hotels and dive-shops, will accept credit cards. Others will not.

watersports

Scuba diving: Saba does have a name as a **diving** destination. The island's slopes descend as steeply beneath the water as above and the coral growth there is as lush as the flora on land. There is a great variety in a small area, with caves, particularly pinnacles and lava flows and good visibility, often as much as 100ft. The fish life is abundant, big and not too shy and the small marine life is excellent. Expect patrols of sergeant majors (striped and very aggressive) and soldierfish to dart around the coral forests and sponges; you might also see a turtle or a migrating humpback whale or even a formation of flying gurnards.

The **Saba Marine Park** was established in 1987 to protect the marine life, and has placed mooring sites in the seabed (the coastline is so rough that all dives are made from boats). They can be contacted at PO Box 18, The Bottom (© 63295, ● 63435). Spearfishing is illegal, as is the removal of any coral.

There are three dive operators on the island: Saba Deep, which works from Fort Bay (© 63347, ● 62389), Sea Saba (© 62246, ● 62377), in Windwardside and Saba Reef Divers (©/● 62541). Saba has a four-person decompression chamber. A one-tank dive costs around US$45.

other sports

Walking: All over the island you will see the stone walls of old-time Saba, when the villages of the island were linked in a network of stepped pathways (before the arrival of cars in 1947). People would walk or ride a donkey to get around. Any older Sabian will tell you about the morning rush-hour (a crowded ¾hr walk) over the hills from Windwardside to The Bottom, and how the islanders used to arrive at parties in their walking boots. A few of the ingenious old paths remain and they make good walking trails. A favourite walk is up to Saba's summit, **Mount Scenery**, best when the peak is not engulfed in cloud. A sign on the road at the start (past the tourist office) forewarns you that there are 1064 steps. It is hot work and a good 1½-hour hike, though you can miss the first bit out by taking the upper road. Cable and Wireless (who operate the radio mast on the summit and have to climb the hill quite often) have the right idea, and they have erected a shelter on the way up. The flora is fairly typical of the steep volcanic islands, with whole hillsides of elephant ears on the lower slopes and an ever-thickening rainforest with its profuse growth that eventually gives way to elfin woodland. Gnarled trees are covered with mosses that creep, tangles of lianas hang suspended and cycads and bromeliads explode from their perches in the trees. Perhaps you will see a trembler or a garnet-throated hummingbird in the upper woodland.

There are a number of trails in the northern part of the island, between Well's Bay and Hell's Gate, where there are a couple of abandoned villages. In these remoter areas you will see sea-birds rising on the updraught as the winds rise on the island slopes. You may come across terns and brown noddies as well as tropicbirds and Saba's national bird (it appears on the island crest), Audubon's shearwater, locally known as a *Wedrego*. Further details of walks on the island are available from the tourist office in Windwardside or through James Johnson (© work 63281, home 63307), who will talk you through the nature and history of the island as you go.

The Dutch Leeward Islands: Curaçao, Bonaire and Aruba

Each of the ABC Islands is long and thin, poised irregularly a few miles off the coast of South America. You can see the mountains of Venezuela from them on a clear day and yet the islands not are geologically connected to the continent. They are made up of packed lava and ashes pushed up from the sea floor over the millennia. As the sea has risen and receded around them, generations of coral have left reefs on their slopes, lining their coastlines with a stone like a sort of limestone brittle, locally called *klips*.

Low-lying, the Caribbean winds race over them, hardly pausing to form clouds and rain as they do elsewhere, and so these islands have none of the lushness and exuberant fertility of other West Indian islands (rainfall here is just 20 inches annually as opposed to 300-odd inches in the Windwards). Instead they are semi-arid and look something like Arizona—parched flatlands covered with about 10 foot of thorny scrub and the occasional candelabra cactus standing around in an exclamatory pose. The rolling scrubland of all three islands is known in Papiamento as *cunucu*. The average temperature is 82°F, but the Passatwinden (Dutch for the trade winds) take the edge off the heat. Sucked inevitably towards the equator, they are sometimes almost strong enough to lean against standing up, particularly in the early months of the year when they are at their height. Like the Sirocco and the Föhn they actually send people a bit dotty, so you will know what's up when drivers seem psychotic in February. Another curious effect they have is on a native tree called the divi-divi; its branches become a gnarled and knotted brush pointing southwest, resembling a woman bent at the waist in a gale, her shawl and thigh-length hair swept away on the wind.

One of the most striking things about the ABC islands is the colours. The buildings here do not have the pastel wash of most Caribbean islands, nor the primary glare of Haiti, but a strong and distinctive colour scheme all of their own—ochre, orange and russet brown, with the occasional dark green and even vermilion. It was in 1817 that the Governor, Vice-Admiral Kikkert, whose eyes were supposedly suffering from the combination of the white-washed walls and the Caribbean sun, decreed that no building should be painted white. The orange *dakpannen* (Dutch roof-tiles) and the curious colours of the walls soak up the sunshine. You will see Portakabins and mausolea imitating the colour scheme and even the Curaçao national bird, the *trupial*, is conveniently a shade of gold and orange.

With South America so close, Latin life runs strong through the islands. You will hear salsa and merengue on the buses, and some Latin features are visible in the Dutch and African faces. Spanish is clearly audible in the language and the islanders dress and often hold themselves with Latin poise. And there is some competition between the islands. When Aruba took its Independence in 1986, the Curaçaoans threatened to take a shotgun to the Aruban bird on the Autonomy Monument in Willemstad. In return the Arubians will tell you Curaçaoan waters are shark-infested. They both dismiss the Bonaireans, who apparently sing their Papiamento.

Dutch Leeward History

A succession of Indian tribes lived on the three islands before Columbus discovered the New World. For the last three hundred years it was the Caiquetios, who came under a *cacique*, or chieftain, from the mainland. They had a peaceful enough life, fishing and trading in their *piraguas*, hollowed-out canoes, and chewing chicle leaves (from the tree that provides the substance for chewing-gum), which they kept in bowls slung around their necks.

But things were to change with the arrival of the Europeans. The first came in 1498 as they explored the coast of South America—Alonso de Ojeda, one of Columbus's lieutenants, and Amerigo Vespucci, the Florentine explorer whose name was later mistakenly given to the whole continent of America. Vespucci called Curaçao the 'Land of the Giants' because the Indians were so large. Old prints show diminutive conquistadors clad in helmets and clutching pikes meeting vast Indians with clubs and bows and arrows.

The islands offered nothing to the Spaniards in their search for Eldorado and the Fountain of Youth, so all three were marked down as *islas inutilas* (useless) and passed over. Indieros, red slave traders who dealt in Indians from the South American continent, used the islands as a base and they shipped off those who lived there to work in the gold-mines in Hispaniola. Those they left behind were encouraged to chase off any other Europeans showing an interest in the island.

In 1527 the Spaniards did make a settlement of Curaçao and bred cattle there. Jack Hawkins, the English pirate, visited the island in 1565 and described it as 'one great cattle ranch'. He saw a hundred oxen butchered in one day. The hides were stripped for curing and their tongues cut out to be eaten. The rest of the carcass was thrown into the sea.

Isla inutila or not, Curaçao proved a perfect base from which the Dutch could harry the Spaniards in the Indies in the early 17th century. The Dutch West India Company descended on it in 1634 and in a fairly typical invasion for the time, they chased the 20 Spanish settlers around the island for three weeks until, exhausted, they surrendered. To protect the rear approaches of Curaçao they put garrisons on Bonaire and Aruba in 1636. The Spaniards, intent on keeping other Europeans out of their empire in the New World, decided to sack Bonaire in 1642, but they arrived to find that, as usual, the Dutch had fled. They pillaged and burned the settlement for a week and then left, so before long the Dutch came back at their leisure.

In 1638 the governor of Curaçao was Peter Stuyvesant, perhaps best known nowadays for being on the front of a cigarette packet. Later he would become the Director General of all the Dutch possessions in the New World, which he administered from Nieuw Amsterdam, now New York. He set the island on course for its great prosperity and by the 1650s it was flourishing. Merchants flooded in and the Dutch fleets fed the trade.

The driving force behind the success of Curaçao was traffic in humans to work the burgeoning Caribbean sugar-plantations. Red Indians were replaced by black Africans, and the infamous slave trade was under way. On arrival after four to six weeks on the horrific 'Middle Passage', the slaves would be rubbed down with oil and paraded through the streets singing before being auctioned. Buyers came to Curaçao from all over the Caribbean, and at its height in the 18th century about two-fifths of all slaves brought to the Americas came via Curaçao.

Meanwhile Aruba and Bonaire were kept as farms to supply the senior colony of Curaçao. They were left unsettled, except by ranchers and a few government farmers who scratched the infertile soil together to grow maize. Aruba was particularly known for its horses, which were sold on plantations in the Caribbean and in South America. Paardenbaai (Horses' Bay), the original harbour off Willemstad, is where they were traditionally loaded and landed. Bonaire was more of a cattle ranch. Boca Slagbaai in the northwest is where the animals were slaughtered just before being shipped to Curaçao. Its main commodity, though, was salt (in the days before refrigeration it was essential for Dutch trading ventures between Europe and the New World). The harvesting took place in the shallow ponds in the south of the island and the industry has continued on and off until today.

Curaçao became a valuable prize and its fortunes waxed and waned on the winds blowing from Europe—wars put the island under blockade, but brought untold riches in the supply of arms and gunpowder. The British invaded twice during the Napoleonic Wars, once capturing Curaçao while everybody was out celebrating the New Year, but by 1816 the islands were back in Dutch hands.

Connections with South America were strong and the islands, particularly Aruba, just 15 miles from the mainland, were often a political refuge. 'El Libertador', Simon Bolivar, came here after the collapse of the First Republic in 1812. As late as 1927 the Curaçaoans found themselves invaded by the Venezuelan rebel leader, Rafael Simon Urbina, who stormed Fort Amsterdam and stole all the weapons before departing with the Governor as a hostage. Two Curaçaoans buried in the Panteon Nacional in Caracas for their part in the Venezuelan War of Independence are Luis Brion and Manuel Carlos Piar.

Then decline began and even trade failed. Successive governors tried different schemes to keep the islands afloat financially, including the cultivation of aloe, now used in cosmetics, cochineal dye and sisal for rope. The salt industry was continued in Bonaire and in 1825 gold was discovered in Aruba. Bonaire was so poor after the slaves were emancipated in 1863 that in their despair, the government put it up for sale. The islanders reached their lowest point at the end of the 19th century and many went abroad to look for work, sending money back to keep their families at home. They went off to the (then) Dutch colony of Surinam or joined the streams of West Indians who dug the Panama Canal.

'The Ditch', as the canal was known, immediately reaffirmed Curaçao's status as a port, but it was the discovery of oil in Venezuela that would change Curaçao and Aruba so dramatically and secure the two islands' prosperity for the 20th century. Their Dutch heritage meant a stable political climate and their steep shores allowed the approach of ocean-going tankers which could not get to the South American coast. Crude oil was shipped in shallow-bottomed boats from Venezuela, refined and then shipped on in ocean-going tankers. Royal Dutch Shell moved into Curaçao in 1915 and built a refinery, and in 1924 the Lago Oil and Transport Company, a subsidiary of Standard Oil of New Jersey (EXXON), came to Aruba. Workers flooded into the islands to join the boom, from the Dutch Windwards and Surinam and from the English colonies. The populations rocketed, each multiplying by five times. The refineries directly employed as much as 15 per cent of the population of both islands.

The islanders talk in apocalyptic terms about 'Automation', which slashed the workforce in the fifties and sixties. The ageing plants were dealt another blow in the early 1980s when OPEC agreements forced up the price of crude oil and the industry foundered. The two giant oil companies have sold up and moved out, and now the refineries work at massively reduced capacity. The islands depend now mainly on tourism.

Papiamento

Of all the creole languages that have developed in the Caribbean, the most enigmatic is Papiamento, spoken only in the Dutch Leewards. Its heritage is thought of as almost mystical: a blend of strains from Spain, Portugal, Holland, England and France, from Africa and even from local Indian languages.

The language developed as a pidgin in the 17th century as the port of Curaçao grew. Into the mix of Dutch traders and African slaves came Portuguese-speaking Jews from Brazil and other South Americans who spoke Spanish. In the 18th century, Papiamento (the word means 'babble' and is supposedly closely related to the word for parliament) crystallized as the language of the three islands. It took on a life of its own, with expressions to reflect local existence: *'Pampuna no sa pari calbas'*, 'the pumpkin plant bears no calabash' (a Caribbean way of saying 'like father like son'), and *'Un macacu ta subi palu di sumpinja un biahe so'*, 'a monkey climbs a cactus only once' ('once bitten, twice shy'). From Curaçao the language spread to Aruba and Bonaire, where it has now developed different accents.

Unlike other Caribbean islands, where the creoles are usually treated with a certain ambivalence, Papiamento is spoken by islanders across the social spectrum. It is used in the home, in church and in newspapers. Dutch may be the official language, but Papiamento is now also used in schools.

Listening to Papiamento can give an impression that you are hearing a stream of Spanish; words will seem to offer meaning, but then the impression will dissolve as the unlikely guttural sounds of Portuguese and pursed Dutch noises jump out at you. Papiamento is a good language to get worked up in and no doubt you will hear the islanders do just that.

Curaçao

Traditionally Curaçao has always been the heart of Dutch influence in the Caribbean; the powerhouse of their trading ventures and the administrative centre of the Dutch Caribbean. Even its name is fancifully thought to come from the Portuguese word for heart, *corazon*.

Curaçao is oddly shaped, a bit like a rebellious bow-tie, and at 38 miles by 9, it is the largest of the Netherlands Antilles. It is hardly an attractive island. Like its neighbours it is low and scrubby, covered in *cunucu*, with cacti that strike theatrical poses. Its shores are cut with inlets that make perfect harbours.

With 145,000 islanders, Curaçao is heavily populated. Centuries of business as a trading port have brought racial strains from all over the world, giving it a very mixed population. Like Aruba, it experienced boom years earlier this century when Shell built a vast refinery and bunkering station on the island. The money poured in and the population rocketed, from 33,000 in 1915 to 145,000 in 1975. Jokers claimed that the Curaçaoans liked to change their clothes twice a day and their car every three months in those days, but it all changed when 'Automation' cut the refinery workforce from 18,500 to 4000.

In the early eighties things got even worse with the oil-crash and the world economic recession. The price of oil plummeted and sales decreased, and eventually Shell sold the refinery and left in 1985. The volume of trade passing through the port (still one of the largest in the world) has rallied after the problems in Panama, as did off-shore finance, another important sector. The government of Curaçao is trying to increase tourism and this is now the island's second industry.

Its economy may be depressed, but that does not mean that the island itself is, for that would be to underestimate the Curaçaoans. A few may have left the island to find a better life elsewhere, but most have an irrepressible Caribbean spirit and a conviction that the future will see them right.

For details on Curaçao's history, *see* p.424.

Curaçao Liqueur

On a still day, the tangy smell of orange peel drying in the sun used to hang on the Curaçao air. It was the skins of the laraha orange, which were being made into **Senior Curaçao** of Curaçao liqueur, original namesake of the more famous **Bols**. These green Valencia oranges, which grow normally elsewhere, grow small and bitter in the barren earth of Curaçao (the tree features on the national coat of arms) and you can see the distilling process at the **Curaçao Liqueur Distillery** (© 461 3526; *open Mon–Fri, 8–noon and 1–5; adm free; samples on offer, plenty of opportunity to buy*) in the hall of the Landhuis Chobolobo on the outskirts of Willemstad. It is a small operation, just four or five vats. Distinctive round bottles with slim tall necks are corked and labelled by hand. The original orange liqueur is best, but there are three other flavours on offer. If you catch a whiff of something pungently sweet, then it is Curaçao's current smell, the refining crude, that hangs on the air around the oil refinery.

Getting Around

There is a public **bus system** in Curaçao and the important routes are run roughly every half an hour. NAFl 1.50 will get you around town and NAFl 2.50 will take you up to Westpunt, as far as you can go. It is important to stand at the bus-stops to ensure that you will be picked up. There are two terminals in Willemstad: the main one in Punda, behind the round market, which serves the east end of the island and the harbour area, and one at Riffort, just over the pontoon bridge, which serves the hotel area, the airport and the west beyond.

You will also see **share-taxis**, like South American *colectivos*, running the town routes. Again, it is best to wait at a bus-stop, but sometimes they will stop if you flag them down. NAFl 1.50 for a ride (US90c). Private minibuses will drop you off where you want to go, in an order that seems best to the driver; the further you go, the more you pay, up to about three florins.

Taxis are not metered so it is worth fixing the price before setting out. They can be found at any of the hotels and through the main despatch office (© 869 0752). Some sample prices are: **Punda** to: the airport—US$11, Curaçao Caribbean Hotel area—US$11, Underwater Park area—US$11. **Airport** to Otrobanda—US$11, Curaçao Caribbean—US$11, Princess Beach—US$15. If you wish to take an island tour by taxi, the going rate is about US$25–30 per hour. You can arrange a bus-tour of the island through Taber Tours (© 737 6637) or Daltino Tours (© 461 4888), at about US$45 for a three-hour trip.

If you want the mobility to reach the Westpunt under your own steam, plenty of **rental cars** are available. Foreign and international licences are valid, and prices start at around US$35 per day. Driving is on the right, and where there are no road signs, traffic from the right has priority. If you do intend to hire a car, then look out for discount vouchers in the tourist magazines. Rental companies include some of the international names, Avis (© 868 1163) and National (© 869 4433). Local firms, which offer better basic rates, include Caribe Rentals (© 461 3089) and Star Rent-A-Car, where you can find a jeep (© 462 7111). Some companies will deliver for you. If you want to rent a **bicycle**, try Easy Going cycle rental (© 869 5056).

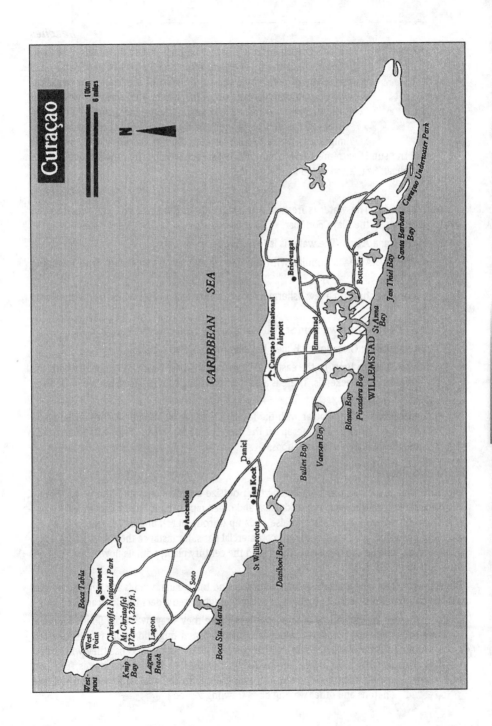

Curaçao

1 10km
0 miles

N

CARIBBEAN   SEA

West Point
Boca Tabla
● Savonet
Christoffel National Park
Mt Christoffel
372m. (1,239 ft.)
West Point
Knip Bay
Lagun Beach
Lagoon
Soto
● Ascension
Boca Sta. Maria
● Jan Kock
Daniel
St Willibrordus
Daaibooi Bay
Bullen Bay
Vaersen Bay
Blauw Bay
Piscadera Bay
Curaçao International Airport
● Brievengat
Emmastad
WILLEMSTAD
St Anna Bay
Bottelier
Jan Thiel Bay
Santa Barbara Bay
Curaçao Underwater Park

429

Curaçao's coastline is not great for beaches and so the hotels have been known to build them. They are often small strips of hard sand on a substructure of coral rock, but in the west of the island you will find secluded sun-traps cut into the *klips* where the water is warm and shallow. Some beaches have changing rooms and a small shop selling drinks, but if you go farther afield remember to take a picnic. You might also take a parasol because the beaches are usually shadeless and the sun is extremely hot. The north coast, battered by the onward swell of the Caribbean Sea, is too rough for swimming.

best beaches

Westpunt: The water is fresh and translucent. In the heat, you can retire to the clifftops and the Playa Forti bar.

Playa Casa Abao: The water is jade in colour.

Knip Bay: A beach popular with the Curaçaoans at the weekend, with changing facilities.

Lagun Beach: With a few fishermen's huts, a tiny secluded cove just below the Bahia Inn.

Daai Booi Bay: Down from St Willibrordus, is a small cove enclosed in cliffs.

Vaersen Bay: Close to the Bullen Bay oil terminal, also secluded.

Santa Barbara Bay: To the east of Willemstad, the best beach, very popular with the Curaçaoans at weekends. There is a bar and changing rooms. There is a fee of US$4 to park a car.

Caracasbaai: Also popular with the locals. There are also some beaches on uninhabited Klein Curaçao, an outcrop off the east end of the island. Trips can be arranged through the big watersports shops.

Flora and Fauna

The three islands have similar flora among their outsize boulders and sand dunes. The blanket of scrub is broken by prickly pear and organ pipe cactus, locally known as *kadushi* (it is used for fencing and also ends up in soup here), and by several species of plant that were cultivated on a commercial basis, for instance the spiky and fleshy-leaved aloe and the agave, also called the century plant, with its flowering 30ft stem.

There are very few land animals, just a few lizards and the iguana, who is shy because he also ends up in a traditional dish. You might be lucky enough to see a deer on Curaçao.

However there is a large variety of birds, partly because they stray over from South America, but also because the islands are a stopover for the winter migration from North America. Among the usual bananaquits (which you will no doubt see because they will have a go at your sugar-bowl), there are yellow orioles, hawks and doves, the odd hummingbird and even burrowing owls. In the coastal ponds you will see herons and other wading birds trawling for food.

Willemstad has been a trading port for centuries. **Punda** at the harbour mouth, a Dutch port transported to the tropics, dates from the 18th century, and in the recesses of the harbour is the Schottegat, Punda's 20th-century equivalent, all factories and container wharves. Willemstad is still one of the busiest harbours in the world—so many ships use the channel that the hotel at the harbour entrance has had to take out marine insurance just in case.

The **Handelskade**, overlooking the St Anna Baai, is one of the Caribbean's most impressive and unlikely sights—an apparition of Amsterdam in the Caribbean sun, a line of tall coloured buildings with curly gables and orange roof-tiles. Two hundred years ago the waterfront at Punda (which takes its name from the point on which it sits) buzzed with ocean-going ships, offloading their cargoes for storage in these warehouses. Walled against a land-attack and built unusually tall because of the confined space, Punda's narrow alleys gathered around **Fort Amsterdam** at the beginning of the 18th century as the big Dutch trading houses sent their agents to Curaçao.

Willemstad's mercantile tradition is continued today and picturesquely precious Punda is still bulging with goods on sale, now displayed in air-conditioned comfort for the benefit of the less hardy seagoers who arrive by cruise-ship rather than by clipper.

Another amusing and surprising feature of Punda is the **Koningin Emmabrug** (the Queen Emma Bridge), which links it to **Otrobanda**. It stands on 15 or so pontoons, which buck and sway with the swell of the sea, making it impossible to walk in a straight line (people jerk in unison as they cross, like a crowd of choreographed drunkards).

The first pontoon bridge was erected in 1888 by Leonard B. Smith, and was free to people without shoes. It is free to everybody today and so there is no need to take off your shoes as the toll-dodgers used to. But you may arrive at the shore to find that it has disappeared (there is an engine attached to the end pontoon). This is because the bridge has to open to let in the ships arriving in Willemstad harbour. While the Queen Emma Bridge is closed, a ferry (free to people with or without shoes) makes the crossing from about halfway down the Handelskade. It announces its departure with a siren.

On Sha Caprileskade, around the corner from the ferry terminal, is the **floating market**, where a line of Venezuelan sloops berth diagonally against the quay, shaded by vast awnings attached to their masts. Snapper and flying fish, stacks of melon and finger rolls of miniature bananas are piled on monumental slab tables on the wharf. The produce is mostly grown in Venezuela and is shipped to Curaçao overnight in time for the early morning market. The supply seems never-ending and if you ask for something not on display, the trader will rootle around on board ship and find it. Prices are very good here, but if you care to bargain, a couple of extra tangerines might be thrown into your bundle.

The original centre of the town is **Fort Amsterdam**, built by the Dutch immediately they arrived in 1634. It is now the seat of the Government of the Netherlands Antilles and also houses the Governor's Residence. There is a small museum (*adm*) of religious artefacts in **Fort Church**, which still has a British cannonball buried in its outside wall from an attack in 1804.

On Columbusstraat is the **Mikve Israel Synagogue**, the oldest in the Americas. Modelled on the synagogue in Amsterdam, it was built in 1732 by the large community of Jews that had taken refuge in Curaçao a century earlier. The floor around the mahogany altar is sprinkled

facades in Willemstad

with white sand in memory of the journey through the desert and two of the four chandeliers date from 1707 and 1709. In the courtyard is the **Jewish Historical Museum** (*open weekdays 9–11.45 and 2.30–5; adm to the museum*), where a 250 year-old *mikvah* (a ceremonial bath) and circumcision instruments are on display. The **Beth Haim Cemetery** (House of the Living), also the oldest in the Americas, dates from 1659 and is on the inner harbour, just outside Willemstad to the northwest.

As Punda expanded (the town walls were demolished in 1861), the wealthy Curaçaoan traders built their Dutch colonial town-houses away from the trading centre, in areas like Scharloo and Pietermaai along the coast. The **Bolivar Museum** (*open weekdays, irregular hours*), on Penstraat, has antiques and some memorabilia from the South American Wars of Independence led by Bolivar in the early part of the last century; it is set in an odd octagonal building, where his family took refuge in one of his two stays in exile on the island.

The traders also crossed over St Anna Baai to **Otrobanda** (literally 'the other side'). The area is run-down and ramshackle now, but its 18th-century Dutch rococo architecture and elaborate gables give an idea of Curaçao's former grandeur. Today it is very much residential and also sees the seamier side of Curaçao life.

A classic Curaçaoan building with raised balconies and twin pointed roofs, the old sailors' hospital on Van Leeuwenhoekstraat, has been converted into the **Curaçao Museum** (*open 9–noon and 2–5, Sun 10–4, closed Sat; adm*). Inside there are artefacts from the chicle-chewing Caiquetios, early Delft Blue china, a merchant's tablet advertising a tobacco shop, a revolving exhibition of island painters and a typical Curaçaoan kitchen, painted with red and white spots (supposedly it makes flies dizzy, but more likely it is superstition).

On the sea as you leave Otrobanda is the Curaçao **desalination plant**, which produces around 1.6 billion gallons of water from seawater annually. Time was when the oil tankers used to bring water as ballast and the Curaçaoans complained that it tasted of oil, but now the desalinated water is pure enough to brew Curaçao's Amstel beer. On the waterfront here, leading past the fishing huts, the Curaçaoans take the air in the early evening.

Fort Nassau, on the hill behind Punda, is no longer a fort, but still has the commanding view over the harbour and its approaches for which it was originally built. Behind, it looks over Emmastad, the most modern extension of the capital, where you will find the container wharves and dry docks. Around the edge are the suburbs, with supermarkets, cinemas and fast-food joints, where the majority of Curaçao's 145,000 population live, in neat fenced gardens with a satellite dish and two cars.

The fort also has one of the best views of the **Refinery** and on a still day you will recognize the pungent smell that hangs on the water (a cross between pitch and petrol). This monolithic assembly of silver chimneys and silos was once the largest refinery in the world, but has been run down since Shell sold the plant to the Curaçaoan Government in 1985. Recently it has been reactivated by Isla NV, owned by Petroleos de Venezuela.

On Fokker Weg you will see the futuristic **Autonomy Monument**, a sculpture of six birds commemorating the self-determination of the Netherlands Antilles in 1954. Aruba's bird remains despite its political separation in 'status aparte' in 1986 (*see* p.452). And on Rijkseenheid Boulevard is the **Amstel Brewery**, the only one in the world that uses distilled seawater. Amstel, whose familiar red and white bottle tops you will see all over the Caribbean, started to brew under licence here in 1960 and today they produce 3 million gallons of lager annually. In a walk among the copper vats you will see the malt, germinated barley sent out from Holland, mixed with Curaçao water, fermented to make 'wort', and then matured. You can follow this with a visit to the bar.

Curaçao *Cunucu*

Curaçao's 15ft-high *cunucu* is dotted occasionally with the orange roofs and white gables of the *landhuizen*, Dutch colonial plantation houses. Driving through the scrub, you will also see the original slave houses, with angled walls and shaggy maize-thatch roofs surrounded by cactus fences. Unlike other islands, where many slaves moved to the towns after emancipation, many more remained on the land in Curaçao, scratching a living from the earth. Hummingbirds and mockingbirds live in the scrub and along the northern coast you might be lucky enough to see an osprey.

A number of the *landhuizen* can be visited. Perhaps the best is the **Landhuis Brievengat** (✆ 767 8344; *open Mon–Fri, 9–noon and 3–5; adm*), once an aloe and cochineal plantation that has been restored to show life in the early 18th century when the house was built. Brievengat is just north of Willemstad, close to the sports stadium. Every Friday evening there is a public dance (*entry NAFl 10*) and one Sunday each month there is a day jamboree with music and folk dancing.

Other *landhuizen* worth visiting include **Jan Kock** (✆ 884 8087; *irregular opening times, telephone beforehand*), and **Ascension**, restored and still used by the Dutch Navy (*open first Sunday of each month from 10am onwards*). The 17th-century **Chobolobo Landhuis** on the outskirts of Willemstad is the home of the Curaçao Liqueur Distillery, well worth a visit (*see* p.428).

Driving west from Otrobanda the coast road passes the main hotel strip and Bullenbaai oil terminal, where the storage tanks rise and fall as they are filled or emptied into the ocean-going tankers. On the road to the airport, opposite the Hotel Holland you will find the **Hato Caves** (*open 10–5, tours on the hour; adm*), where there are hourly tours that guide you through the geology of the island and explain the life and religion of the Indians, whose petroglyphs you will see on the rockfaces. Near Ascension you will find the **Country House Museum** (*open daily 9–4; adm*), a mud and thatch house of the type built by the former slaves when they were freed in the last century.

At the northwestern tip of the island you will find the **Christoffel National Park**, 4500 acres of nature reserve on the slopes of Curaçao's highest hill, Mt Christoffel (1239ft). The park is laced with trails, for walkers and for vehicles, clearly marked and with displays of the semi-arid flora of the Dutch Leeward Islands, including the divi-divi and agave. Iguanas, like neolithic lizards, scuttle about and you might even see a Curaçao deer, a flitting orange troupial or an inquisitive-looking barn owl with a heart-shaped face peering at you. Some paths lead to the summit of Mt Christoffel, from where it is possible to see the mountains of Venezuela on a clear day. The entrance to the park is at the Savonet Landhuis (*itself not open to the public*), where there is a **museum** of Curaçaoan geology and natural history, with exhibits of Caiquetio Indian life (✆ 464 0363; *open Mon–Sat 8–4, Sun 6–3; adm*).

Passing **Boca Tabla**, a cave that can be entered from the landward side and which reverberates and echoes each time a wave crashes into the cave-mouth, the road leads to the sedate village of West Point and the *kadushi* cliffs at the western tip of the island.

East of Willemstad is the **Curaçao Seaquarium** (*open all days 10–10, until midnight Fri and Sat; adm*) where you can see the underwater world indigenous to Curaçao in a normal state of gravity— anything from an anemone or a panting shark with a beady eye to corals like a hundred pink molar teeth. You can take a glass-bottom boat out to the reef from the Seaquarium and in the shop you might pick up a Dutch onion skin or a continental squat (bottles).

✆ *(599 9)–*   ***Where to Stay***

Curaçao does not have that many hotels. There are some major resort complexes set on the coastline, with international standards of comfort, but you will find also a few smaller, lower-key spots inland. If you are travelling through you can find cheap places to stay in Curaçao, in the same hotels as the higglers and traffickers (travelling salesmen and women), who come in their droves to buy wares and take them off home to sell them. Curaçao gets pretty hot in summer and so it is worth paying extra for a fan or air-conditioning. There are many apartments for hire, starting at about US$200 for a week's rent; contact the tourist board. There is a 7% government tax on all rooms and most hotels charge 12% for service.

moderate

The **Avila Beach Hotel** (✆ 461 4377, ✉ 461 1493) on Penstraat is still the most charming hotel in Curaçao. It has 90 rooms in all, some in a plush block, others in the original antique building (that was the invading British Governor's residence in 1812), but it retains its rarefied and sophisticated air. A mixed crowd, some younger and some seasoned travellers, congregates on the two beaches and at the schooner bar. Perhaps the most sympathetic of Curaçao's large and humming factory-style hotels is the **Princess Beach Resort and Casino** (✆ 736 7888, ✉ 461 4131), east of Willemstad. The 341 rooms and suites are strung out along the waterfront in blocks above a beach that is not that exciting. Nightly entertainment, boutiques, beauty salon, pool bar.

The **Lion's Dive Hotel and Marina** (✆ 461 8100, ✉ 461 8200), just above the Seaquarium, is a statement in pastel pink and lime green, bananas, bougainvillea and balconies. Rooms are quite small, but comfortable. The hotel is home to **Rumours**, one of Curaçao's best bars, and it attracts a young and lively crowd, who dive by day and booze by night. At the lower end of the price range, the **Coral Cliff Resort and Casino** (✆ 864 1610, ✉ 864 1781) is a smaller hotel, with just 35 rooms, which sits on the coast, west of town. The rooms are modern and air-conditioned with cable television and they stand on the hillside above the sea, relaxed and isolated from the bustle of the town hotels. Watersports and scuba. The **Hotel Holland**, F. D. Rooseveltweg 524 (✆ 868 8044, ✉ 868 8114) near the airport, has 40 very comfortable rooms and has introduced a dive shop. A bit isolated from town, but a friendly hotel with a casino.

Beyond here, on the road to West Point you will find a small hotel set in an old country house, the **Landhuis Daniel** (✆/✉ 864 8400). Just 10 rooms, with pool and watersports, small and friendly. At the western end of the island at Westpunt you will find the small **Jaanchie's Apartments** (✆ 864 0126), within easy reach of the island's best beaches. It is very simple and has a popular open-air restaurant which will serve you island delicacies like cactus soup and iguana stew. The six or so rooms are simple, but the asking price is good and you can bargain from there. There are plenty of hotels at the bottom end of the range in Willemstad, of which the best is probably the **Pension La Creole**, in the Saliña area of the town. **Hotel Stelaris** on de Rouilleweg (✆ 462 5740), overlooking the St Anna Baai from the Otrobanda side, is a reasonably secure alternative. If you want full exposure to the intrigues of Curaçao life, try the **Park Hotel** on Frederickstraat in Otrobanda (✆ 462 3112, ✉ 462 5933). All these budget hotels serve meals.

✆ (599 9)–

Eating Out

There is a surprising number of good restaurants in Curaçao, both in regard to their cuisine and to their atmosphere, and so it is well worth venturing out of the hotels to find them. With its tangled heritage, the island has food from all over the world (perhaps most surprisingly from Indonesia, from the Dutch West Indian–Dutch East Indian trading connection). Most restaurants add a service charge of 10% to their bills. Price categories are arranged according to the charge for a main dish: *expensive*—US$18 and above; *moderate*—US$10–18; *cheap*—US$10 and below.

expensive

De Taveerne (✆ 737 0669) in the Saliña area is set in an old octagonal Curaçaoan *landhuis*, Groot Davelaar; candle-lit and furnished with antiques, a very comfortable surrounding for lunch or dinner. Catch of the day creole and outsize steaks. A number of Curaçao's restaurants are located in forts: there is an excellent setting and superb cuisine to go with it at **Fort Nassau** (✆ 461 3086). You take your cocktails on the battery, where there is a cannon's eye view of Willemstad, and then move through for new world cuisine—seared shrimp in pepper vodka or the day's catch in tropical fruit chutney on a bed of beans and pancake—surrounded by the old battlements. **Bistro le Clochard** (✆ 462 5666) is in the Riffort at the mouth of the St Anna Baai, where cocktails are accompanied by the hull of an occasional passing freighter. French and Swiss cuisine by candle-light in the fort's cavernous jail and the old barrel-vaulted cistern—shrimp *provençal* and *rösti* in white wine and mushrooms. Take a constitutional on the battlements. *Closed Sun.*

If you want to eat Dutch in the Kingdom of the Netherlands, try **'T Kokkeltje** (✆ 868 8044) in the Hotel Holland, with its windy view of the airport runway. There may not be the cockles from which it takes its name, but mussels are imported weekly in the months with a letter 'r' in and served with white wine and lemon. One or two clogs and a Delft Blauw beer dispenser, but not Dutch stodge. Try *sliptong in loombooter gebakken* or *haring* in season.

And for a taste of the Dutch East Indies in the Dutch West Indies you can try **Surabaya** (✆ 461 7388) under the arches of the Waterfort. *Rijstafel* and *pangsit* pancakes, closed Sun. Another option is the new restaurant **Le Jardin** (✆ 465 6091) located at Pietermaai 16. Here you can savour international cuisine in a renovated old building.

moderate

Fort Waakzamhied has a cracking position, around the battlements of another fort, where you sit on a breezy terrace and watch the lights of Otrobanda. All meals are grilled on the barbecue and accompanied by salads and chips. There is a nice informal atmosphere and often a crowd of Curaçaoans. Two local restaurants definitely worth visiting are: **Chez Susenne** (✆ 868 8545), where Susenne herself cooks Curaçaoan dishes, while her hip sons preside over the dining room; *balchi piska* (fishballs), *masbangoe* (sardines) and *snijboonchi* (stringbean soup); and the **Golden Star** (✆ 465 4795) on Socrates Straat, a classic West Indian restaurant, air-conditioned with plastic tablecloths, fake roses and excellent local food. Try *carni stoba* (meat stew) or *stoba de carco* (conch and vegetable in a strong creole sauce). *Open until 1am, closed Sun.*

Particularly popular with the Curaçaoans is the cheery, American-style **Cactus Club** (✆ 737 1600), difficult to find at 6 van Staverenweg. International standard burgers and shakes, but always crowded. At the western end of the island at the Christoffel Park you will find good local food at the **Oasis** Restaurant—goat stew with *funchi* or seafood. You might also try **Playa Forti** on the clifftops, with a cracking sunset view.

One of the best places to eat on the island, a lively local spot for lunch Curaçao-style is the **Marshe** just next to the monstrous circular new market in Punda. You eat at communal slab-top tables alongside bus drivers and local business people and drink out of frosted glasses, while the food is cooked over charcoal stoves around the edge of the building. It is some of the island's best food because it is cooked in this way, though if you are obsessive about hygiene this place might not be for you. Exotic *sopi* (soups) of local fish and traditional *juwana* (iguana) are available and to follow you can try a good Caribbean 'rice and peas' dish or another Curaçaoan favourite like *stoba*, meat stew made with papaya, or *komkomber* (cucumber) or even *snijboonchi* (if you dare). Other dishes include *giambo with funchi* (cactus fruit and maize meal) and

Curaçao Directory

getting there

Curaçao has extremely good air connections, from Europe, the US, South America and points around the Caribbean, to its airport at Hato, 7 miles (11km) north of Willemstad. Other possibilities include a boat from Venezuela, though this is recommended only for the traveller with plenty of time to spare. An airport tax of US$12.50 is payable upon leaving Curaçao, US$6 to the Dutch Caribbean.

By air from Europe: The most convenient service is on the Dutch airline KLM (local ✆ 465 2747), which has daily services non-stop from Amsterdam. There are connections from most major airports in Europe. An alternative is to travel via Miami (*see* below).

toetoe (pronounced tutu), more maize meal with beans, bacon, sugar and all topped with melted cheese. The meal is served from steaming silver vats and is washed down with a sticky red drink like strawberry Ribena. Lunch is served Mon–Fri and is cheap.

If you are still feeling peckish after a night out on the town, you can grab a snack at a **truck di pan** (literally a bread-truck), which can be found all over the island. You choose between a pan *galina* (chicken), pan *steak* or *porchop*, hacked in half, doused in hot pepper sauce and served up in a bread roll.

Bars and Nightlife

Rum Runners is a popular bar dressed up in high fluorescence and cocktail paraphernalia on the waterfront above the St Annabaai channel, so you can watch the cruise ships and freighters as you sip a bahama mama or a piña colada. Out of town to the east is another very popular bar, **Rumours**, set on a terrace above the sea at the Lion's Dive hotel. In Spanish Water you might try the **Terrace à la Mer**. In Salinja you can try **Crocodile Dundee**, always lively late on, happy hour 9–10.

For a cocktail and a view try the terrace at **Fort Waakzamheid** in Otrobanda, and if you would like a drink in plantation estate surroundings, visit the **Tinashi bar** at the **Landhuis Brievengat**, open weekdays until 6pm. On the last Sunday of the month they hold open house with a folkloric show; the Brievengat also has an excellent discotheque a couple of times a week, where the Curaçaoans like to shuffle and sway to loud bands playing merengue, soca and salsa. Dance lessons on Thursday, open on Friday from 10pm until the early hours. Another good weekend venue, popular with the locals, is at Playa Canoa, a fishing bay on the north coast, where they dance on Sunday afternoons.

Most of the regular **nightclubs** are in Saliña on what is known as Hanchi macacu ('monkey's parade' in Papiamento). The most lively place in the area is **Club LA** (L'Aristocrat) on van Lindbergweg. Raised platform for a big band, but all styles of music (live Fri, Sat, when it is packed). Cover charge. Close by is **Façade**, which is a little more sophisticated. **The Pub** is an American-style bar with loud rock music, Blondie to Doble R. **Le Mirage** out near the airport is a government brothel. There are ten **casinos** in Curaçao, all of them located within the hotels. Most are open from 2pm until 5am.

© (599 9)–

By air from North America: There are many flights each week from Miami to Curaçao on the national airline ALM (© 869 5533), American Airlines (© 869 5707), United Airlines (© 869 5533) and Air Aruba (© 868 3777). This is the best stopover point from the USA and Canada, although there are also direct and connecting flights from New York and Atlanta.

By air from Latin America: Curaçao is well connected to the South American mainland. There are regular services from Caracas and Maracaibo in Venezuela, Bogotá in Colombia and other Central American countries. There are also links to Paramaribo in Surinam and Georgetown, Guyana.

By air from other Caribbean islands: There are numerous flights linking Curaçao with Aruba and Bonaire; there are more services at weekends, but these tend to be the most heavily booked. The Dutch Windwards are served by a daily flight to Sint Maarten. For the rest of the Caribbean, the options are Port of Spain in Trinidad (twice weekly), Kingston in Jamaica (twice weekly), the Haitian capital Port au Prince (daily), Santo Domingo in the Dominican Republic (three a week) and Havana in Cuba (twice a week).

tourist information

There is no Curaçao Tourism Development Bureau office in the **UK**, so it is best to write to the USA or Curaçao itself.

Holland: Vasteland 82–84, 3011 BP Rotterdam, Postbus 23227, 3001 KE Rotterdam (✆ 414 2639, ✇ 413 6834).

USA: 475 Park Avenue South, Suite 2000, New York, NY 10016 (✆ (212) 683 7660, ✇ 683 9337, ✆ US (800) 3-CURACAO); and 330 Biscayne Bouevard, Suite 808, Miami, FL 33132 (✆ (305) 374 5811, ✇ 374 6741.

Germany: Arnulfstraße 44, D-8000 München 2 (✆ 089 598 490, ✇ 089 592 391).

On island there is a helpful office at the airport in addition to the main office at 19 Pietermaai, PO Box 3266 Willemstad (✆ 461 6000, ✇ 461 2305). The Tourism Bureau issues a yellow pamphlet called *Curaçao Holiday* with listings of current events.

In a medical **emergency**, there is a 24-hour room at St Elizabeth's Hospital (✆ 462 4900). The **police** can be reached on ✆ 114. The **IDD code** to call Curaçao is ✆ (599 9), followed by a seven-figure island number. On-island use just the seven digits.

festivals

They do not really need an excuse for a party in Curaçao—Friday night is enough anyway. The whole island gets down at **Carnival**, the big event of the Curaçaoan calendar. Weekends see *tumba* street parades and the main festivities are held in the last few days in the run-up to Lent, including more costume masquerades, all-night jump-ups and the burning of Rey Momo, the spirit of carnival. There are a number of **music festivals** across the year— salsa (August) and an annual Jazz Festival held in October/November. There is even an Oktoberfest (untypically in October). The Curaçao Sailing Regatta is held each year in April, based at the Seaquarium.

money

The currency of Curaçao is the Netherlands Antilles florin or guilder (NAFl), which is fixed to the US dollar at a rate of US$1 = NAFl 1.78. However, the US greenback is widely accepted all over the island and you might not even see florins except in change. US$ traveller's cheques and major international credit cards are accepted in all the hotels and any but the most offbeat restaurants and guest houses.

Banks: Open 8.30–noon and 1.30–3.30, Mon–Fri. There is an exchange at the airport open all day Sunday. You can change dollars and cash cheques with the hotel cashiers.

shopping

Hours are 8–12 noon and 2–6. Just as they did 200 years ago, traders will stay open longer if a large ship has come into town (though it tends to be cruise-ships now rather than merchantmen filled to the gunwales with porcelain and silks). Most shops will close for a couple of hours at lunch.

If you are looking to score a few duty-free purchases, then Curaçao is a good bet because it has some of the Caribbean's best shops—some visits may even be billed as a 'shopping experience' anyway. A large proportion of the wares are mass-produced tourist rubbish (twee clogs and windmills made in Dutch Delft Blue china), but, because Curaçao is such a massive trading-port, it is surprising what can turn up. A couple of shops worth considering are **Penha** (the distinctive building on the waterfront) for perfumes and chic clothes. You can find European fashion at **NafNaf** and Italian shoes at **Manhattan**. US residents returning home can take in up to $600 of duty-free goods.

watersports

Watersports centre around the seafront hotels, but if you are staying inland and want to take out a windsurfer or a small sailing boat or go waterskiing, you can usually hire equipment from them (ring and check before arriving). Try Piscadera Watersports (© 462 5000) at the Curaçao Caribbean Hotel or Dive Curaçao and Watersports (© 736 7888) at the Princess Beach Hotel. The Spanish Water lagoon to the east of Willemstad is another popular place for watersports.

Sailing: If you want a **day's sail** or a sunset cruise, you can join the yacht *Insulinde*, which stops for a picnic on Port Marie beach (© 660 1340) or the *Vira Cocha* (© 676 0030), a reconditioned Norwegian-style rescue boat. Taber Tours (© 737 6637) runs day-trips and picnics or a sunset tour.

Fishing: The Curaçao Yacht Club arranges the 'Blue Marlin Tournament', a yearly fishing tournament in March or April, and they will also fix up **deep-sea fishing** trips on the high seas casting for marlin and bonito, at around US$350 for a half-day with tackle. Alternatively Piscadera Watersports (*see* above) will also take you out.

Scuba diving: Curaçao's underwater world is excellent and the government have set aside 12 miles of reef and coastline on the southeastern shore of the island as the protected Curaçao Underwater Park. Visibility is often up to 100ft and the coral reefs, stacked with staghorn and gorgonians, teem with wrasses and snappers, while lobsters and the odd languid turtle cruise around. Wreck dives include the *SS Oranje Nassau* and the 'car wreck'—a barge of cars that went down in a storm. Most hotels can lay on watersports and some run dive-boats down to the Underwater Park. Outside the big hotels mentioned above, operators include **Sammy's Scuba Centre** at Boca St Michel (© 868 4414) and the Lion's Dive Hotel (© 461 1644) which collects a friendly crowd.

Snorkelling: You will find excellent corals within a breath of the surface in many of the bays along the south coast, Knip Bay, Vaersen Bay and Blauw Bay for example. In the Underwater Park a snorkelling trail has been created, between the Seaquarium and Jan Thiel beach, but you must go by boat to reach it. A glass-bottom boat operates out of the Seaquarium (© 461 6666).

other sports

Tennis: Most of the big hotels have courts and you can usually book them as an outsider.

Golf: You can play at the Curaçao Golf and Squash Club (© 737 3590) in Emmastad behind the harbour, where the 18 holes share 10 oiled sand greens.

Riding: If you wish to take a day out in the *cunucu*, riding on horseback, contact the Rancho Ashari at Groot Piscadera (© 868 6254).

Bonaire

The underwater life of Bonaire is supreme. Miles of spectacular corals line its shores and the warm water teems with tropical fish, flashes of pastel and fluorescent colours—a Diver's Paradise. So says every car numberplate on the island, anyway. Shameless PR perhaps, but the island has managed its reefs well and it has a justified reputation as one of the world's top diving destinations.

Bonaire is the second largest of the Netherlands Antilles (a crooked 24 miles long by 5) and it lies 30 miles east of Curaçao, 40 from South America. It is mostly low and parched scrubland, with salt-ponds in the south and rolling land that rises to the 784ft peak of Mt Brandaris in the northwest. The name Bonaire is supposedly derived from the local Indian *bo-nah*, meaning low country; the Netherlanders would have felt at home when they arrived in 1626.

Bonaire has a population of about 15,000 and it is fairly quiet and secluded, unlike its brash neighbours in the Dutch Leewards. There are just two small settlements, Kralendijk the capital on the leeward coast and Rincon in the north. And the Bonaireans are quiet too. They think of the Curaçaoans as wild and spendthrift, whereas they consider themselves more measured and careful. Before the days of bank loans, the Bonaireans had a system called the *samm* in which they would club together, pooling a sum of money every month, which they would each receive in rotation, enabling them to buy an animal or building materials for a house.

Bonaire has never seen the extreme wealth of Curaçao and Aruba, but for the moment it is probably more prosperous than it has ever been. The traditional salt industry has been revived, automated to bring it into the 20th century, and the island earns some money from radio transmitting stations, Radio Nederland Wereldomroep (the Dutch World Service), and the religious broadcasting station, Trans World Radio. The biggest income earner is tourism, which sees a trusty crowd of tourists (over 65,000 each year), about half of whom come for the diving.

Bonaire is changing fast. Outsiders are flooding in and investment, once so difficult to come by, is now clearly visible. Hotels have sprung up and the islanders are building houses for themselves too. The old feeling that time forgot the island has pretty well evaporated, but it is still possible to escape here for a rest-cure. And it is still pretty quiet after dark. Most visitors are in bed by about 10pm, building up their strength for another day underwater. For details on Bonaire's history, *see* p.424.

Getting Around

There is a sort of bus service in Bonaire—minibuses run sporadically from the centre of Kralendijk up to Rincon. No buses run south past the airport. Hitch-hiking around the island is relatively easy. **Taxis** meet the flights and can be ordered through hotels or from the central depot (*©* 8100). They are unmetered, with fixed prices for each run. Prices increase by 25 per cent between 8pm and midnight, and by 50 per cent from midnight until 6am. Some sample prices are: **airport** to Kralendijk—US$8, and to Habitat Hotel—US$10. If you wish to take a tour of the island, any taxi driver will oblige; the rate is around US$35 for half a day (which is about all you need).

You will be most mobile in your own vehicle and there are plenty available for **hire** on the island. A licence from an EC country, the States or Canada is valid and prices range from around US$35 a day for a small car, plus insurance. Driving is on the right. Rental firms include: At the airport, AB Car Rental (*©* 8980, *©* 5034), Hertz

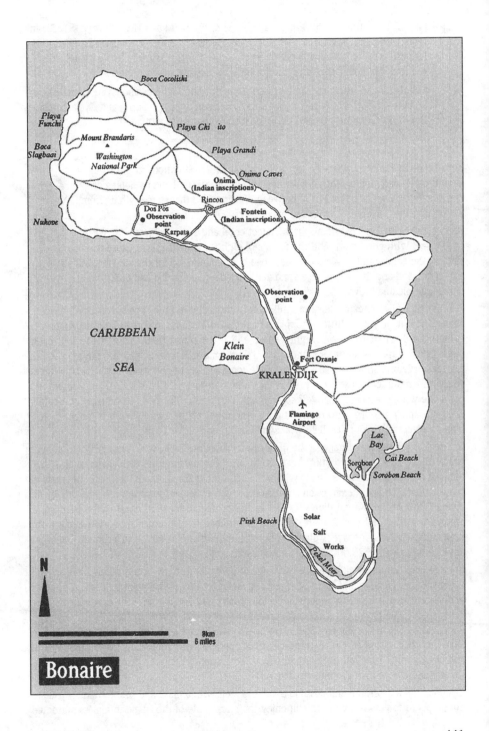

Boca Cocolishi

Playa
Funchi

Playa Chi ito

Boca
Slagbaai

Mount Brandaris ▲

Playa Grandi

Washington
National Park

Onima Caves

Onima
(Indian inscriptions)

Rincon

Dos Pos
Observation
point

Fontein
(Indian inscriptions)

Nukove

Karpata

CARIBBEAN

Observation
point

SEA

Klein
Bonaire

Fort Oranje

KRALENDIJK

Flamingo
Airport

Lac
Bay

Cai Beach

Sorobon

Sorobon Beach

Pink Beach

Solar

Salt

Works

Pekel Meer

N

8km
6 miles

Bonaire

(✆ 7221), Sunray (✆ 5230), Total (✆ 8313), Budget (✆ 8315), Avis (✆ 5182). In town, Avis, J.A. Abraham Blvd (✆ 5795), Budget, Kaya L.D. Geharts 22 (✆ 8300), Island Car Rental, Amboina 66 (✆ 5111; *open 24hrs*), Trupial Car Rental (✆ 8487). A number of hotels also have cars for hire, so check at the front desk.

Scooters and bicycles can be hired from Hot Shot Scooter and Cycle Rental, Kaya Bonaire 4 (✆ 7166), Avanti Rentals, Kaya Herman Pop 2 (✆ 5661) and Cycle Bonaire, Kaya L.D. Gerharts 11D (✆ 7558), next to Cultimara supermarket.

Diving

Bonaire, often ranked among the top few scuba-diving destinations in the world, is famous particularly for its range of incomparably colourful coral and its sloping drop-offs (not vertical walls, but slopes of between 45° and 60°) that start anything from 20 to 100 yards offshore. Visibility is dependably 100ft, often more.

Brain corals with jigsawed hemispheres, sheet coral and star coral jostle for space on the reef with gorgonians and the forests of elkhorn and staghorn. Close to the surface, the corals tend to grow bunched together, reaching up for the sunlight, but as you descend and the reds, oranges and yellows fade, you find flat and bulky corals of blue, purple and brown.

Fish life glides by beneath the surface, dipping and darting in little shoals; peacock flounders change colour at you, a little school of needlefish will come and poke at you. Angelfish coloured a deep rich blue or bright yellow and black purse their lips and the four-eyed butterflyfish wink. Look out for seahorses and Christmas tree worms, and you might even see a green turtle or a shovel-nosed lobster. While some fish grunt and swim away, crabs witness you with a fixed look of shock, eyes out on stalks and upturned in quizzical amazement. At night the whole seascape changes: some corals close down for bed but orange tube corals wake up and transform into orange tubes. Nocturnal brittlestars light up if touched, and tarpons attracted by your flashlight will swim up and nose at you.

The reefs on Bonaire are managed by the **Bonaire Marine Park**, which has jurisdiction over nearly the whole of the coastline to a depth of 200ft and imposes strict laws against the removal or killing of any marine life within the area. It has placed mooring sites in the reefs to protect them. The park charges an admission fee (*US$10, valid for one year*), payable by all divers. Most of the 80-odd dive-sites are on the protected leeward coast of the island and around the islet of Klein Bonaire, none more than a few minutes' boat-ride away from Kralendijk. There is one wreck dive, the hulk of the *Hilma Hooker*, a ganja-runner that went down after its load of 25,000lbs of resin was confiscated.

Bonaire is extremely well organized to cater to divers and many of the hotels have special dive-packages. Nearly all of them offer resort courses for those who want to learn. A number of dive-centres also cater to underwater photography and you can hire the cameras and vast lighting equipment from Captain Don's Habitat Dive Shop (✆ 8290), the Sand Dollar Dive and Photo (✆ 5252) in the Bonaire Beach Hotel, and the Flamingo Beach Hotel (✆ 8285). The Dive Inn (✆ 8761, ✉ 8513) is an independent operator with good rates for equipment hire and instruction. Once you have arranged your equipment, it is quite possible to take off in a car and chose your own shoreline to dive off.

If you are not a diver, it is still possible to see the reefs with a mask and snorkel. And if you are not prepared to get wet, you can still enjoy the marine life of the island in a glass-bottomed boat; contact Bonaire Dream (© 4514). Most of the hotels stage **slide shows** of the coral reefs (*Capt Don's: Mon–Thurs; Sand Dollar: Sun and Tues*).

Snorkelling

Many of Bonaire's reefs are close enough to the shoreline to be reached with a mask and snorkel and you will see crowds of tropical fish loitering close in, too. As with diving, watch for fire corals—many colours, but always white fringes—which will give you a nasty sting. Equipment can be hired for the day from the dive shops.

If you take a tour to the north of the island, try **Playa Funchi**, for leaf corals and fire corals, and also in the Washington Park, **Boca Slaagbaai** where you will see tiger grouper and white-spotted filefish among mountainous star corals and cannon (from a film set). At **Nukove** nearby you can see redlip blenny and yellow pencil corals among the elkhorns. **South of Kralendijk** you can cast off the waterfront and be right among the reefs. Try **Punt Vierkant** just beyond the airport for the gorgonians and giant brain corals and the **Witte Pan** area by Pink Beach, where you will see staghorns patrolled by barracuda and octopuses.

Beaches

The beaches in Bonaire are all right. One or two places have mounds of soft pink and white sand, but most are a hard strip of sand in a cove cut out of the limestone cliffs of former coral reefs. Unless you go to a hotel beach, usually small strips on the inner leeward coast, do not expect 'facilities', and remember to take food and drink. You are quite likely to be alone on the beaches in Bonaire; however, nudity is officially frowned on outside the area of **Sorobon** on the east coast.

best beaches

Pink Beach: The best beach on the island, south of Kralendijk, along the side of the salt flats. Its name comes from the colour given by the corals that grow in the area (it is pink when wet and it dries to white).

Bachelor's Beach: On the road back to town, a short drop off the *klips* into the warm water and sandy floor.

Cai Beach: On Lac Bay on the opposite windward coast, where the mangroves grow in flying tangles, this is protected from the Atlantic waves and is popular with the locals at weekends.

Sorobon Beach: On the other side of the bay, has mounds of soft sand in a small half-moon-shaped cove. Calls itself 'clothes-optional'. It is private and charges *US$15 adm.*

Playa Funchi, **Boca Slaagbaai** and **Playa Frans**: In the north of the island, worth the detour for the snorkelling and some sand, though there is little shelter from the sun. Take anything you will need in the way of a picnic as there are no shops in the area. On the route back to town, stop off at the 1000 Steps.

Finally there are some unfrequented sandy beaches on **Klein Bonaire**. Any hotel will run you out and collect you later on (if they forget, it is just a 20-minute swim back to Kralendijk).

Flora and Fauna

Among Bonaire's 190 or so species of birds (boobies and pelicans, bananaquits, sand-pipers and oystercatchers), the king is certainly the pink flamingo. There are thought to be about 15,000 on the island, one of only a few colonies in the western hemisphere.

Flamingos are shy birds and quite easily disturbed (by humans at least, though they seem to have got used to aeroplanes), so the Bonaireans are understandably reticent about revealing the exact location of the two nesting sites on the island. However, you can fix up a guided visit through Bonaire Sightseeing Tours (✆ 8300 or 8778; ✆ 8118 or 8865), usually to the southern colony near the salt pans in the morning and the northern colony by Goto Meer in the afternoon. If you have binoculars or a telephoto lens, take them because you will not be allowed too near, particularly while they are breeding in the early part of the year.

Flamingos nest on little round mounds of mud about a foot high, on which is poised a single large egg. When either parent is not occupied with incubation, you will see them standing around in groups, legs bent forward at the knee, passing the time of day. To feed they have to visit the salt-water lakes dotted around the island, where they advance in ranks, heads moving left and right underwater as they trawl for food. It is a little water shrimp that they find there that gives them their striking pink colour.

Bonaire has little in the way of landborne animals, apart from wild donkeys and goats, who nibble at everything in sight, but you will see plenty of lizards and the occasional example of its prehistoric antecedent, the iguana.

Kralendijk

Bonaire's small capital, Kralendijk (pronounced as in marlinspike), lies on the protected inner coastline of the island, looking across to the uninhabited coral football, Klein Bonaire. It has a few neat streets of russet and ochre Dutch Antillean buildings, gardens filled with banana and palm trees, and is patrolled by lazy dogs and lizards. To the 1500 inhabitants, the town is known familiarly as 'Playa' (Papiamento for beach), really a bit of an exaggeration because there is only a measly strip of hard sand here. Kralendijk (meaning coral dike) is a rather more appropriate name because the shore-line is mostly a coral-limestone wall.

The town has always been a backwater and there was not even a pier until this century. Before that, ships would tie up to a cannon sticking out of the ground. Today the waterfront comes alive when the boats from Curaçao dock, but the main centre is on Breedestraat, which has recently come out in a profusion of duty-free stores and a shopping mall.

Fort Oranje surveys the scene as it has since the middle of the last century, its cannon covering the bay. Close by is the **fish-market**, a mock-classical temple dressed in pink, which looks slightly out of place for the Caribbean, until it too comes alive in the afternoon, selling the morning's catch of fish and imported vegetables.

The **Instituto Folklore Bonaire**, Kaya J.C. v/d Ree (✆ 8868; *open weekdays 8–noon, 1–5; adm free*), the local museum, has exhibits of chicle-chewing Caiquetio Indian life before the Spaniards came and musical traditions of the later Bonaireans.

The **Bonaire Art Gallery**, Kaya L.D. Gerharts 10 (✆ 7120, ✆ 7121), specializes in 'Contemporary Art of the Caribe and the World'. Ninety per cent of the art is local, with international exhibits by the likes of Hundertwasser, Appel, Marcel and Fini. There are also two work studios, an etching press, and art supplies for sale. The strict environmental laws prohibiting the use of any object found in the sea has resulted in a thriving culture of 'drift-wood art'.

Around the Island

Headed south out of Kralendijk the road skirts a lagoon and rejoins the coast at the airport, passing the antennae of Trans World Radio. The countryside is flat, desolate and wet. The southern toe of the island is just a rim of land separating Bonaire's salt-pans from the sea.

Salt

Each salt-pond in Bonaire, dammed off with low mud walls, has a different colour—the faintest pink or lavender and then grey—before it turns to the bright white of the mature salt. You will see the harvested crop in huge blinding-white mountains, stacked by a conveyor belt and a vast double-armed crane.

Seawater, the sun and constant winds are the essential ingredients for the salt industry. In Bonaire the process takes about eighteen months from the moment the seawater is introduced into the Pekelmeer (pickle lake). By opening and closing locks it is passed through condensers where it becomes brine and then to crystallizers where the salt forms over the course of a year in depths of about 8 inches. It is washed and stacked before export.

Slaves were brought in to work the salt pans. It was gruelling work and their existence was miserable. Their families lived 15 miles away in the north of the island and they were allowed home for one day a week. The industry collapsed soon after emancipation in 1863 because it was unviable without forced labour. It was precarious at the best of times (too much rain would ruin the crop) and it lay dormant for a hundred years before being revived in the sixties by the Antilles International Salt Company NV. The salt produced on Bonaire's 9000-acre 'farm' is used for industrial purposes.

Continuing around the coastline, you will see two small communities of **slave huts**, built in about 1850 in traditional Leeward Islands style, with square-topped gables and palm thatch. These two-man shelters were constructed in accordance with the slaves' wishes in preference to a single dormitory. There are also a number of obelisks, originally painted blue, orange, white and red, which were used to guide ships to the correct part of the coast. The road leads round the southern tip of the island and up the east coast, past Sorobon and back to Kralendijk.

Two roads lead north out of Kralendijk, one following the leeward coast past the hotels and the second cutting inland through the *cunucu* to the opposite coast. As the settlers crept in to the island in the early 1800s, they settled the area north of Kralendijk, and you will see human order imposed on the scrub—tall cacti trained to make hedges around the simple old Dutch Antillean houses of baked mud and maize thatch.

Before reaching the village of Rincon, a road leads out towards the coast and to the caves of **Onima** and **Fontein**, where there are Caiquetio inscriptions on the roofs of the caverns. Using the red dye for which the island was known early on by the Europeans, the Indians scrawled their diabolic squiggles and cartoon faces on the dark orange rock. **Rincon** was settled early, its inland site giving the inhabitants a chance to escape marauding raiders, and it is now a sleepy Bonairean village dressed in Dutch Antillean orange.

The **Washington Slagbaai National Park** (*open 8–5; adm adults US$5, children US$1*) preserves 22 square miles of northwestern Bonaire, home to some of the island's 100 or so species of bird and the occasional iguana, though these are shy because they fear the cooking pot. Traditional Bonairean crop plants are also there: aloe, divi-divi, sisal and agave, a small explosion of cactus leaves at ground-level with a stalk up to 30ft in height. A number of trails are marked around the park, for drivers and for walkers, including a path to the summit of Mount Brandaris. Slagbaai, a cove on the western tip of the island, means 'slaughter bay', and was where animals were killed before being shipped out to Curaçao. (Bonaire was used by the Curaçaoans as a ranch for a couple of centuries.)

Heading back down the leeward coast, the view is upset by the BOPEC oil terminal, the Radio Nederland antennae and the desalination plant. The road soon reaches the hotel strip and comes into Kralendijk.

✆ *(599 7)–*   *Where to Stay*

Bonaire's hotels are mostly ranged along the protected leeward coast of the island, many of them in a cluster north of Kralendijk. They are all new and few have much charm, but divers (who make up 60 per cent of tourists) do not care, generally, as they are there for the marine life. When diving is at issue, the atmosphere tends to be brisk and business-like, but with regard to anything else it is typically Caribbean and very low-key. There is a room tax of US$4.50 per person per night and most hotels will charge 10–15% for service.

Bonaire also has a number of villas for rent. Contact the local tourist office at Kaya Simon Bolivar 12, Kralendijk (✆ 8322 or 8649, ✉ 8408) for an extensive list. They can also provide you with a useful map, with a good street plan of Kralendijk, the best birdwatching spots, and dive and snorkelling sites.

expensive

Bonaire's top hotel is the **Harbour Village Beach Resort**, Kaya Gobernador N. Debrot 72, Playa Lechi (✆ 7500, ✉ 7507, US ✆ (1 800) 424 0004), modern Caribbean luxury in a theme of Antillean orange and green. The 70 rooms and suites are ranged in villas around the central pool and bars, and each has a view of the marina or the hotel's fine beach. Watersports on offer. The **Sand Dollar Beach Club**, Kaya Gobernador N. Debrot 79, Playa Lechi (✆ 8738, ✉ 8760), a mile or so north of Kralendijk, has a feel of cool modernity, where fully furnished self-catering apartments are clustered overlooking the garden to the sea. The dive operation is on the seafront, the pool and tennis courts behind. The Green Parrot restaurant is lively, situated on the rocks above the sea, with burgers and some better dishes. Studios and one- to three-bedroom condos.

Captain Don's Habitat, Kaya Gobernador N. Debrot 85 (✆ 8290, ✉ 8240, US ✆ (1 800) 327 6709) has luxury suites, villas and cottages, and a pool. There are now 60 rooms in the sandy garden of cactus, palm and aloe, but the Habitat has kept the friendly feel of a diving inn. There is a small beach, but the gravitational pull is of course towards the diving pier. Some other watersports and entertainment a couple of nights in the week. Most stays are sold as diving packages. The **Sunset Beach Hotel**, Kaya Gobernador N. Debrot (✆ 8291, ✉ 8118) has 145 rooms, all rather plain, but with air conditioning, coffee makers and fridges. Few rooms have sea views; extensive grounds with two tennis courts and a small pool. Also in this area is the **Lions Dive Hotel Bonaire**, Kaya Gobernador N. Debrot 91 (℡ 5800, ✆ 5850).

The **Divi Flamingo Beach Resort**, J.A. Abraham Blvd 40 (℡ 8285, ✆ 8238) has more of a resort feel: it stands astride the promenade at the southern limits of Kralendijk. It is a hive of activity, relatively speaking, with two dive shops, a casino, a couple of pools, 145 rooms and the Chibi Chibi restaurant, which has a charming setting on stilts above the floodlit sea (reserve early if you want a waterfront table). It is Bonaire's first hotel and the regime has softened a bit since it was used as the island prisoner-of-war camp. The **Plaza Resort Bonaire**, J.A. Abraham Blvd 80 (℡ 2500, ✆ 7133) has 198 rooms, in what is aspiring to be a five-star resort. Next door is **Port Bonaire** (℡ 2500, ✆ 7133), a 64-room, waterfront condo resort, which shares the Plaza Resort facilities.

A short walk north from the town centre you will find **Club Nautico Bonaire**, Kaya Jan N.E. Craane 24 (℡ 5800, ✆ 5850) with 24 rooms, suites and penthouses with balconies and full facilities. The **Lac Bay Resort**, Kaminda Sorobon 64 (℡ 8198, ✆ 5686), is on the windward coast of the island, in a protected nature area. Here, too, you will find the **Sorobon Beach Resort**, Sorobon 10 (℡ 8738, ✆ 8760), Bonaire's 'naturist' resort. 30 rooms are available in simple chalets with self-catering facilities, but no air conditioning. There is a private, 'clothes optional' beach and a small, family-style restaurant and bar. Daily shuttle service into Kralendijk.

moderate

The **Carib Inn**, J.A. Abraham Blvd 46 (℡ 8819, ✆ 5295), is still an original dive inn, with just a few rooms on the waterfront in the south of Kralendijk. Very low-key, no restaurant or bar, but most rooms and suites have kitchenettes. If you want to get away from the main strip you can try the **Bonaire Caribbean Club**, PO Box 323 (℡ 7901, ✆ 7900), lost in the Bonaire *cunucu*. Just 20 rooms, some with kitchenettes, scattered around a garden.

At the north end of Playa Lechi you will find the **Black Durgon Inn** and **Black Durgon's Pilot Fish**, Kaya Gobernador N. Debrot 145 (℡ 5736, ✆ 8846), an 8-bedroom inn, with 1-bed apartments and a 2–3-bed villa, with air conditioning and cable TV, in a relaxed setting with views of Klein Bonaire. **Sunset Inn**, Kaya L.D. Gerharts 22 (℡ 8291, ✆ 8118) has seven basic rooms within walking distance of the restaurants and shops. Other places you could try include **The Great Escape**, E.E.G. Blvd 97 (℡/✆ 7488), **Cyndanny Lodge**, Kaya Inglatera 12 (℡ 5516, ✆ 5517), **Avanti Bungalows**, Punt Vierkant 9 (℡ 8405, ✆ 8605), or the **Sitting Coconut**, Kaya Grandi 60 (℡ 7620, ✆ 7520).

cheap

There is a profusion of rooms on offer in guest houses. In town the **Leeward Inn**, Kaya Grandi 60 (℡ 5516, ✆ 5517), offers reliable and clean rooms, at cheap prices, as does the **Hotel Rochaline**, Kaya Grandi 7 (℡ 8286, ✆ 8258). The **Blue Iguana**, Kaya Prinses Marie 6 (℡/✆ 6855), does bed and breakfast, within walking distance of the waterfront and shops. In Rincon you can get a very cheap room at the **Rose Inn**, Kaya Guayaba 4 (℡/✆ 6420, ✆ 6455).

There is a clutch of surprising restaurants on tiny Bonaire. Generally the menus are international, particularly in the hotels, but you will find some good local restaurants. None is particularly cheap. Categories are arranged according to the price of a main dish: *expensive*—US$15 and above; *moderate*—between US$8 and $15; *cheap*—US$8 and below. Service is charged at 10%.

expensive

In the middle of town, there is an easy atmosphere at **Rendez-vous**, Kaya L.D. Gerharts 3 (© 8454). Here you can eat on a streetfront veranda or just inside in an air-conditioned dining room. Some local dishes—*keshi yena* (chicken, vegetables and raisins, covered in gouda cheese) and some international, with exotic mixes of Caribbean ingredients in traditional dishes—chicken apricot and mango melba. Leave your lighter as a memento of your visit if you like. *Closed Sun.* At **Richard's**, Abraham Blvd 60 (© 5263), you dine on a breezy Bonaire terrace overlooking the waterfront in the south of town. Tasty home-made soups and specialities in seafood and local fish. The bar attracts a crowd of locals. *Closed lunchtime.* At the **Beefeater**, Kaya Grandi 12 (© 7776), you dine inside in the redecorated rooms of an old Bonaire town house and its very pretty courtyard. You can expect the steaks of the title, but also more exotic seafood and fish including garlic-flavoured shrimps, also vegetarian dishes, followed by an array of fruit ice creams. To the north of town near the hotels, **Den Laman**, Kaya Gobernador Debrot 77 (© 8955) specializes in seafood and you dine in a glass-fronted dining room decorated with fishing gear on lightly grilled snapper and kingfish. *Closed Tues.* At the Divi Flamingo Resort on J.A. Abraham Blvd is the **Chibi Chibi** (© 8285). This is a delightful restaurant on stilts above floodlit water, so you can observe the aquatic life as you dine. Another waterfront eatery is the **Zeesicht**, Kaya K. Craane 12 (© 8434), which serves breakfast, lunch and dinner, with a varied menu including good conch sandwiches and Indonesian dishes. The service can sometimes be slow. The **Mona Lisa Bar and Restaurant**, Kaya Grandi 15 (© 8718) is a colourful, lively place with a mix of Dutch, French and Indonesian cuisine; bar snacks are available until late. *Closed Sat and Sun.*

Bonaire Directory

getting there

Bonaire has quite good air connections for so small an island. You can also fly via Aruba or Curaçao, which are well served and have endless connections to Bonaire. There are also many flights from Caracas in Venezuela. The Flamingo Airport Bonaire is located at Plaza Medardo Thielman (© 5600, ● 8608). There is a departure tax of US$10 (international and Aruba), or US$5.75 (within Netherland Antilles).

By air from Europe: KLM has two weekly flights direct from Amsterdam, and also via Curaçao and Caracas.

By air from the USA: ALM offers flights from Miami (daily) and Atlanta (Sat and Sun). Air Aruba flies from Newark (Thurs–Mon), and also from Tampa and Miami.

In town, there is an Italian restaurant, **Otello**, on the Kaya Prinses Marie (✆ 4449) (*open daily 6–11*) and a good Chinese and Indonesian restaurant at the **China Garden**, Kaya Grandi 47 (✆ 8480). **'T Ankertje**, Kaya C.E.B. Hellmund 17 (✆ 5216), at the southern end of the waterfront promenade, serves simple Caribbean dishes alongside sandwiches and burgers, for a good price. *Closed Sat and Sun.* In the Sand Dollar Beach Club you will find the **Green Parrot** (✆ 5454), located on a hotel pier, you can enjoy the lively atmosphere, burgers and barbeques surrounded by water and with a great view of the sunset. **Mi Poron**, Kaya Caracas 1 (✆ 5199), one block from the Roman Catholic Church, serves reasonably cheap, authentic creole and vegetarian dishes. *Closed Mon.* For a cheap pizza, try **Cozzoli's Pizza**, Harbourside Shopping Mall and also in Rincon (✆ 5195), or try the **Sandwich Factory**, Kaya Prinses Marie (✆ 7369), an American-style deli serving sandwiches and pizza. *Closed Fri–Sun.* There are also snack joints in town for simple grilled chicken and there is a **refreskeria** on Kaya Simon Bolivar.

Bars and Nightlife

The hippest (and only) bar on the island is **Karel's**, which is perched over the sea in the centre of town—seats tightly packed around the cocktail counter with the waves washing back and forth beneath you, with live music and dancing (Fri and Sat). The owner runs the **Zeezicht** restaurant opposite, so you can always stumble over for a meal. The Bonaireans have their own favourite bars within the restaurants, where you will meet them as you take a drink before your meal.

If you want to dance, you could try the **Fantasy Disco**, Kaya L.D. Gerharts 11 (✆ 7345), or if you'd rather not exert yourself, head for the new **Bonaire Twin Cinema** on Kaya Prinses Marie (✆ 2400 or 0960 7371). Alternatively, if you fancy a flutter, check out one of the **casinos**, either at the Plaza Resort or the Divi Flamingo Beach Hotel—the only barefoot casino in the Caribbean.

Most of the hotels offer nightly entertainment: check the schedule of 'Bonaire's Weekly Happenings' at Tourism Corporation Bonaire, Kaya Lib. Simon Bolivar 12, for more details.

✆ (599 7)–

By air from other Caribbean islands: ALM has connections to Aruba, Curaçao, San Juan, Santo Domingo (and also to Surinam). Air Aruba has daily flights to and from Aruba via Curaçao.

tourist information

There is no tourist office specific to Bonaire in **Britain**, but you can get information in **Holland** through Interreps BV, Visseringlaan 24, 2288 ER Rijswick, The Netherlands (✆ 70 395 4444, ✆ 70 336 8333). In the **USA**, the Bonaire Tourism Corporation is at Adams Unlimited, Rockefeller Plaza, Suite 900, New York, NY 10020 (✆ (212) 956 5911/00, ✆ 956 5913) or Cline Group Advertising, Dallas Air Park, 6340 Beech St, Plano, Texas 75093 (✆ (972) 267 6700, ✆ 267 6770). In **Venezuela** contact Organizacion Ebor CA,

Bonaire Directory

Torre Capriles, Piso 2, Oficina 202, Plaza Venezuela, Apartado 52031, Sabana Grande, Caracas (✆ 0602 793 5669, ☎ 781 7445).

On **Bonaire**, Tourism Corporation and Information office (✆ 8322, ☎ 8408; *www.Bonaire.org, TCB@Bonairenet.com*) is at 12 Kaya Simon Bolivar, a little inland in Kralendijk.

In a **medical emergency**, there is a hospital in Kralendijk (✆ 8900). Good news for divers: the island has its own decompression chamber.

For **police**, call ✆ 8000/113, or go to Kaya L. Simon Bolivar 4.

To telephone Bonaire from abroad, the **IDD code** is ✆ (599 7) followed by the four-digit island number. If phoning within the island, dial the last four digits only.

festivals

The Bonaireans get out into the streets in costume at **Carnival** time (Mardi Gras) in February and at Easter, when there is a sort of harvest festival. The 24 and 29 June see local festivities and 6 September is Bonaire's **National Day**, when there is a general jump-up around the island, particularly in Rincon. There is a five-day **Annual Sailing Regatta** in the second week of October, **fishing tournaments** during the year and **windsurfing competitions** in January and September.

money

Officially Bonaire's currency is the Netherlands Antilles florin or guilder (NAFl), which is fixed to the US dollar at a rate of US$1 = NAFl 1.78. However, you may not even see this currency because the greenback is perfectly acceptable for all transactions. In local shops you may receive change in florins. Restaurants and hire shops in Bonaire are prepared to accept most credit cards and the hotels take traveller's cheques.

Banks: Open 8.30–noon and 2–4.

Shops: Open about 8–noon and 2–6.

watersports

Apart from the diving, many of the hotels on Bonaire offer a few sports including **windsurfing, waterskiing** and small sailing boats. Even if you are not staying there, it is easy to arrange at the hotel front desk.

Aruba

Aruba lies within sight of South America, just 15 miles north of the Paraguana peninsula in Venezuela. It is 20 miles long by 6 wide; with a rainfall of about 17 inches a year (less even than Bonaire and Curaçao); its low-lying land and few hillocks are parched and scrubby with cactus, dotted only occasionally by diabolic boulders and divi-divi trees. The island's name is supposed to derive from the native Indian words for shell, 'ora' and island, 'oubao'.

Like Curaçao, Aruba saw an explosion of prosperity earlier this century with the arrival of the oil industry. EXXON built the then largest refinery in the world on the island in 1929, and the population exploded from 8700 to 60,000 by 1972. For centuries a poor backwater, Aruba changed completely, and from nothing became very prosperous. Today the population is about 90,000.

Windsurfing: Waist-deep water and constant onshore winds can be found on Lac Bay, home of 'Jibe City' (© 0960 7363/7264). Bonaire Windsurf Place (© 5279 or 0960 7495), Plaza Resort Bonaire (© 2500), and The Castle (© 8196, ● 5686) also hire out boards and sails suitable for both beginners and the more experienced, including children. Kayaks can also be hired by the hour from these places, and also from the Sand Dollar Beach Club (© 8738) and the Sunset Beach Hotel (© 5300).

Deep-sea fishing: Trips are easily arranged at the Harbour Village Marina or through your hotel. Piscatur (© 8774) will take out four fishermen in a 30ft diesel boat, for US$275 half-day, US$425 full day, or in a 15ft skiff for two people, US$125 half day, US$225 full day. This includes tackle and bait, catch cooked on board. Also Slam Dunk (© 5271) offers the same rates for a 30ft boat but for six people. A tournament is held each spring.

Sailing: For a charter, contact the *Oscarina* (© 8290), a 42ft cutter, for a day's picnic or a sunset cruise. Trips are also available in a **glass-bottomed boat**, which sails out from the Harbour Village Marina; tickets are sold in all hotels (daily, 2 and 4pm; adults US$15, under 12s US$7.50). A sailing regatta is held annually in October, five days of racing around the island. On land there is a nightly jump-up on the main square in Kralendijk.

other sports

Tennis: There are a number of tennis courts, in town (free) and at the following hotels (a fee for non-guests): Sunset Beach Hotel (open 8–10.30, 3.30–9), Sand Dollar Beach Club (open 9–9), Divi Flamingo Beach Resort (open 8am–10pm), Harbour Village, and Plaza Resort Bonaire. Many of them are equipped with floodlights for night games. Professional instruction is also available.

Horse-riding: Can be arranged through Kunuku Waharama (© 2500 or © 0960 7462); half-hour and hourly rides available, as well as carriage rides for the more sedate.

Mountain biking: Call Cycle Bonaire (© 7558).

If you want to **work out,** head for Joe's Fitness Centre (© 2842), Body Work Sport School (© 4184/5234), or Harbour Village health spa (© 7500).

But in recent years the oil industry has foundered and so the islanders have thrown themselves with gusto into the latest Caribbean industry, tourism. The island has a façade of overwhelming modernity, and has geared itself up to the arrival of over half a million tourists a year. It has opted for tourism on a grand scale—pristine and well packaged, in huge air-conditioned blocks, with glitzy floor-shows and in-house doctors. They do it pretty well. The new hotels in the high-rise strip are impressive and very comfortable. It is crowded and a little sanitized, but it is well organized and so you get a good body-holiday in Aruba. And the Arubians themselves are probably more gracious about the invasion of tourists than any other Caribbean islanders.

It is possible to spend a week on the island without meeting an Arubian, but this would be a pity because they are a spirited bunch. In 1986, after fifty years of political wrangling, they achieved something which most Caribbean islands only ever dream of: they defied the colonial administration and won consent to go it alone as an autonomous country, with 'Status Aparte'.

So close to Venezuela, Aruba has a strong South American heritage. Aruban Papiamento is more Spanish than that of the other two islands, and it is also clear in the faces. Aruba's tangled racial heritage has more South American Indian than African because there were never really any slaves on the island.

Every car that cruises by in Aruba proclaims 'One Happy Island' from its numberplate. So it may seem, now that the island has its freedom to guide its own affairs as an autonomous country, but the future is not without its difficulties: the island is overwhelmingly dependent on tourism. However, beyond the tourism superstructure you will find a lively mix of West Indians of Dutch, Spanish and British heritage, steadily crystallizing into a nation and struggling to carve out a path for themselves.

Status Aparte

Aruba is an autonomous country within the Kingdom of the Netherlands and since 1986 it has no longer been a member of the Netherlands Antilles. Traditionally Curaçao maintained a dominance over its partners and this was particularly resented by the Arubians, who had earned their own wealth from oil, but found that their money had to pass through the coffers in Curaçao before it was allocated back to them. Parliamentary decisions affecting only Aruba had to be passed in the Staten (Netherlands Antilles Parliament) in Willemstad, where the Curaçaoans commanded a majority. The result was that the Arubians depended on the Curaçaoans for everything down to the last typewriter. In the end they pushed for autonomy. The movement began in the forties as 'Separacion', steered by the charismatic politician Gilberto François Croes, known as Betico, and after endless lobbying, the Dutch Government agreed to their wishes and granted Aruba 'Status Aparte'.

On 1 January 1986, Aruba raised its own flag and became autonomous, though still within the Kingdom of the Netherlands, with its own currency and elected Parliament, finally separate from Curaçao. They were due to take full Independence in 1996, but they have seen the difficulties that the other islands in the Caribbean have had and so these plans have been shelved indefinitely. The Kingdom of the Netherlands still has responsibility for defence and foreign affairs. Aruba's Socialist Democratic system is currently led by Prime Minister Henny Eman of the Aruba's People's Party (AVP). His government holds the majority in Parliament through a coalition government established in 1994 with Glenbert Croes (the current Minister of Transportation and Communication), who heads the Aruba Liberal Organization (OLA). Aruba's former Prime Minister Nelson Oduber, of the People's Electoral Movement (MEP), heads the opposition government. Elections are scheduled to take place in 1998.

Getting Around

There is quite an efficient **bus service** in Aruba, linking Oranjestad to the southeast of the island and also running west and then north along the hotel strip (fare US$1). Buses also run from the airport into town (if you are booked into one of the larger hotels, then you may find that there is a pre-paid bus waiting for you anyway). Buses run to an official schedule and the drivers almost stick to it. Roughly speaking, there is one an hour (or two on a major route) up until early evening. Minibuses also run local routes, price NAFl 2.

Taxis are available at the airport, in town and at all the hotels, or they can be fixed through the central depot at the Alhambra Bazaar (✆ 822 116). They can be quite

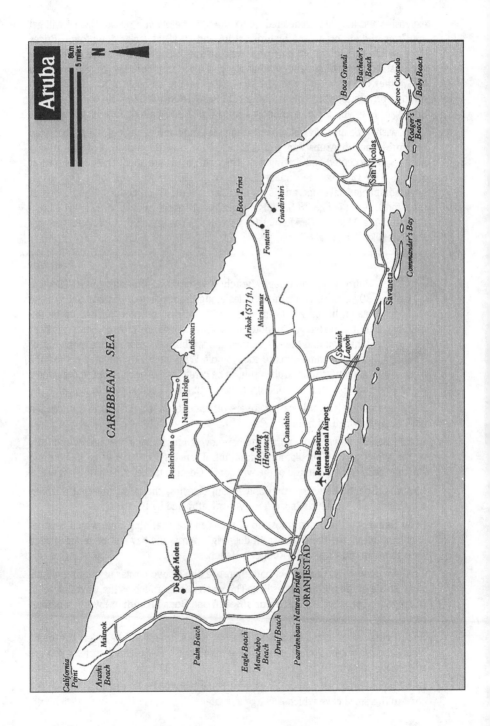

Aruba

8km
5 miles
N

CARIBBEAN SEA

California Point
Arashi Beach
Malmok
Palm Beach
Eagle Beach
Manchebo Beach
Druif Beach
Paardenbaai Natural Bridge
ORANJESTAD
De Olde Molen
Bushiribana
Natural Bridge
Andicouri
Arikok (577 ft.)
Miralamar
Hooiberg (Haystack)
Canashito
Reina Beatrix International Airport
Spanish Lagoon
Boca Prins
Fontein
Guadirikiri
San Nicolas
Savaneta
Commander's Bay
Boca Grandi
Bachelor's Beach
Seroe Colorado
Rodger's Beach
Baby Beach

453

expensive and they are unmetered, so fix the price before you set off. US$14 will get you from the airport to the high-rise strip, and US$8 as far as downtown. Prices increase after midnight. Taxi-drivers, who all speak English, are quite well versed about island history/lore and will happily give an island tour. The charge is around US$30 per cab for an hour on the road. Island tours by bus can also be fixed up through private tour bus companies; try De Palm Tours (✆ 824 400) on L. G. Smith Boulevard in town, or Aruba Friendly Tours (✆ 823 230), also in Oranjestad.

If you wish to be more flexible about seeing the island and dining out, there are plenty of **rental cars** in Aruba and you can pick one up at the airport. Foreign driving licences are accepted and driving is on the right; roads are good. Daily rates start at around US$35 for the smallest car, with insurance on top. The usual large companies have operations on the island, with an office in town and one at the airport: Avis (✆ 828 787), Budget (✆ 828 600) and National (✆ 821 967). Local firms include Marco's Car Rental (✆ 865 889). You can hire a **bicycle** through Pablito's Bike Rental (✆ 878 655).

Beaches

Palm Beach and **Eagle Beach**: Two of the Caribbean's finest. They are 30yds deep and run for miles along the protected western coast of the island, heaps and heaps of sand like talcum powder, pushed up by the bluest of water. At the hotel strips they do become crowded, but it is here that you find the windsurfers and wetbikes for more active moments, or shade and a drink to cool you off. With the winds you may not feel the (very) strong Aruban sun, so be careful when you are out in the middle of the day. Eagle Beach is not officially topless, but it has been known to happen.

Elsewhere on the leeward coast there are other coves, not unknown to tourists, but not usually crowded with them.

Arashi Beach: Towards the northern tip, renowned for its romantic sunsets and calm waters, which make it popular for windsurfing. There is good underwater life here and you may even catch a glimpse of the wreck of a German tanker sunk in the last war.

Malmok Beach: Between Palm and Arashi beaches, the latest hot spot for both professional and amateur windsurfers, who are attracted by the flat water.

Baby Beach: At the easternmost tip of the island, a charming cove which is palm-lined and quiet. The water is just 4ft deep right across the bay and there are shaded areas to retreat to. Close by is **Rodger's Beach**.

On the windward coast north of here there are one or two coves cut out of the limestone brittle of the northern coastline. The water can be rough as the waves barrel in off the Caribbean Sea, but **Bachelor's Beach** and **Boca Grandi** are worth a detour, particularly for windsurfers.

Boca Prins: Also on the Caribbean coast, a tiny strip of sand between two cliffs, where the waves are rough enough to deter all but a few diehard surfers; you are advised not to swim here.

Dos Playa: If you enjoy swimming whilst being buffeted by waves, head just up the coast to this small cove which is marginally safer.

There are one or two islands off the south coast also mounded with sand. The most popular is **De Palm Reef Island** (you can get a ferry from Balashi—$3 crossing), though it is worth checking with the skipper for other beaches that might be less crowded that day.

Oranjestad

Named in 1824 after the Dutch royal family, Oranjestad (pronounced *Oran-yeh-stat*, population around 17,000) sits on Aruba's principal harbour Paardenbaai (Horses' Bay) in the southwestern corner of the island. Today, cruise ships arrive to deliver tourists in their thousands, but two hundred years ago, when the island was really just a ranch, it was horses, which were simply driven off the side of the deck and left to swim for land. (As a tourist you can expect a gentler arrival.)

The oldest building on the island, **Fort Zoutman**, stands sentinel above the bay, where fleets of yachts glint at the quay's edge. Built in 1796, Fort Zoutman saw action only once, when the British invaded in 1799, and now it houses the **Museo Arubano** (✆ 826 099; *open Mon–Fri 9–12 and 1–4; adm*), where island history is illustrated with Indian artefacts and scenes from Dutch colonial days. At J.E. Irausquinplein 2A you will find the **Museo Archeologico** (✆ 828 979; *open weekdays 8–noon and 1.30–4.30; adm free*), which delves deeper into Aruban Indian life with displays of Caiquetio tools and a couple of 2000-year-old skeletons, found buried in vast clay pots and under turtle shells.

Today, Oranjestad's front-line defences are glitzy duty-free shopping arcades in mock Dutch colonial buildings. Behind this pastel façade, plied by droves of tourists, is a more natural Oranjestad, much of it built in the boom period of the thirties, where Aruban homes and bars open on to the street. The old town-houses have angled tile roofs with dormer windows and tall louvred doors that encourage a breeze through the rooms.

The town has an impressive collection of coins from all over the world in the **Museo Numismatico**, behind the police station at 7 Zuidstraat (✆ 828 831; *open weekdays 7.30–noon and 1–4.30*)—30,000 pieces of money of all shapes and sizes from 400 countries across the world, from ancient Byzantium, through sunken treasure to Aruba's own currency, introduced in 1986. It is also possible to see a private collection of shells (700 species down to 1mm in length) owned by the De Man family, 18 Morgenster Street (✆ 824 246; *by appointment only*) in the outskirts of the town.

Around the Island

As you fly in to land on Aruba, the island looks impossibly small, with just a few folds in the scrubland, but it can take a surprisingly long time to get around it. If you venture further than the beach you will see farmsteads decorated with magical symbols—circus-like decorations of stars, kiss-curls and lozenges—surrounded by cactus fences. Just a few of these simple old Aruban dwellings remain, clay houses with roofs of cactus wood and dried grass, built after Emancipation in 1863.

Travelling west along the coast from Oranjestad town centre you come to Aruba's commercial wharf and the industrial estates, and then you immediately emerge into hotel territory at Eagle Beach. As the road swings north you will see an unexpected sight: a genuine scarlet Dutch windmill from Friesland. Built in 1804, **De Olde Molen** was transported and reassembled here as a tourist attraction in 1961. Unfortunately the Aruban winds turned out to be so strong that they were forced to take off the sails. It is now a restaurant.

Close by is the **Bubali Pond**, once a salt-pan, but now an official birdlife reserve protected from development by the government. It provides a refuge for the island's birds, many of whom fly in at sunset to roost there for the night. Apart from the usual pelicans and frigate birds who sit poised on rocks or in the bushes, you can see turnstones and sandpipers strutting around searching for food in the water.

East of the capital, heading towards the northern coastline, you pass through Ayo, where the *cunucu* is interrupted by an assembly of oddly shaped boulders, granite rocks the size of buildings. At **Balashi** and **Bushiribana** you can see the ruins of the gold mines and the smelting works. Gold was discovered in Aruba in 1825 and the island experienced something of a gold rush, which lasted until 1913 (another explanation for Aruba's name is 'Ora uba', meaning 'gold was found here'). Many birds feed on the fruit of the organ cactus (they look like pipes) and hanging in the trees you may see the little bag nest of the oriole. Grassquits and orange troupials flit around the scrubby vegetation. At **Andicouri** the coastline has been carved into a **natural bridge**, a 30-yard span of coral wall, by the Caribbean waves.

Southeast of Oranjestad, the road passes the airport and beneath the **Hooiberg** (meaning haystack), a local landmark (with steps in it which make its 541ft even easier to climb), on to Frenchman's Pass, an impressive gulley on an island so flat and to Spanish Lagoon, and then to the island's industrial area and the site of the distillation plant.

San Nicolas, Aruba's second town, has a population of 15,000. It grew up around the gates of the Lago oil refinery that opened here in 1929, and quickly became bigger than Oranjestad itself. So many of the workers came from the British Caribbean islands that the streets of wooden shanties looked like a town in Trinidad. You will hear English spoken in the streets.

North of San Nicolas you will come across caves with Amerindian hieroglyphs on the roof at **Guadirikiri** and **Fontein**. Some of these exploding squiggles and schematic faces are thought to be genuine, but others were more likely drawn by a European film-crew that was here about ten years ago. Inscriptions (genuine) can also be found on rocks at **Arikok** on the route back to Oranjestad.

Ⓒ *(297)–*   *Where to Stay*

Aruba's hotels have gravitated around two main areas. The strip at Palm Beach is affectionately known as the 'high-rise hotels' and it is easy to see why. It looks a bit like Miami Beach, a mile's worth of skyscrapers humming above ant-like vacationers. Activity is intense—casinos, Vegas-style shows and serried ranks of jet-skis. The newest additions are very large and impressive. Slightly lower-key, but on an equally good beach (Eagle Beach) are the 'lower-rise hotels', where some less imposing structures lurk among the ferro-concrete monsters. If conferences are your thing, then they do those too. For villas and apartments, of which there are plenty, you can contact the Tourist Board. All hotels charge a 6% government room tax and 11% service charge on top of their bills.

expensive–very expensive

In the high-rise strip, the **Hyatt Regency** (✆ 861234 or 861682, ✆ 821682, US ✆ (1 800) 233 1234) stands tall with 360 luxurious rooms and suites. You glide up to an atrium set with pillars, dark-stained beams and wrought-iron chandeliers, passing into a palm garden with split-level pools, waterfalls, waterslide, a restaurant in mock ruins and finally to the beach. All the requisites for a body-holiday—tennis, water-sports, massage and aerobics, cable television etc.

The **Americana Aruba Beach Resort** (✆ 864 500, ✆ 863 191, US ✆ (1 800) 223 1588), just along Palm Beach, is also dressed in the strong pastel shades of today's Caribbean. Again a good feel, with international standards of service. It has 420 rooms, three restaurants, watersports, swim-up bar, casino and a nightly show. On Druif Beach around the southwestern point of the island, in the area of the 'low-rise hotels', is the **Divi Aruba Beach Resort** (✆ 823 300, ✆ 834 002, US ✆ (1 800) 367 3484), which has 200 rooms in blocks strung along the seafront and partially hidden in a tropical garden. There is a more relaxed air about this place, but it too offers high Caribbean luxury—all the sports and a couple of restaurants, and bar by the pool. All-inclusive plan only. A new addition is the **Aruba Marriott Resort** (✆ 869 000, ✆ 860 649), a plush resort that opened in 1995, with more than 400 oversized ocean-front guestrooms, 100ft² balconies, casual and formal dining, casino, a free-form swimming pool with swim-up bar, health spa, meeting and banquet facilities, water-sports, and a spectacular beach.

moderate

Around the point are the low-rise hotels, which have a rather more relaxed feel than their high-rise counterparts. On the point of the vast Eagle Beach is the twin hotel combination of **Manchebo Beach Resort** (✆ 823444, ✆ 832446, US ✆ (1 800) 223 1108) and **Bucuti Beach Hotel** (✆ 831100, ✆ 825271, *intl233@mail.Setarnet.aw*). The 'Bucuti Wing' is pastel and plush, a counterpoint to the Manchebo Beach Hotel, which has 70 rooms and retains something of a beach-club feel. You dine in a concrete galleon half-submerged in the sand of Eagle Beach. **Talk of the Town**, PO Box 564 Oranjestad (✆ 823 380, ✆ 833 208, US ✆ (1 800) 223 1108), is in the outskirts of town on the road to the airport, a sympathetic businessman's stopover. The 63 rooms are set around the pool and palm courtyard. It is low-key and away from the main beach area (it has its own small strip across the road). The hotel takes its name from its restaurant, considered to be one of the best on the island.

cheap

A small hotel off the traditional Aruban tourist track is the **Vistalmar**, Bucutiweg 28, Oranjestad (✆ 828 579, ✆ 847 739), with rooms set in a villa on the seafront, kitchens, maid-service and watersports. Other reasonably priced rooms, usually with kitchens, include **Coconut Apartments**, Noord 31 (✆ 866 288, ✆ 865 433), near the high-rise strip. Not far from the downtown area you will find **Cactus Apartments**, Matadera 5, Noord (✆ 822 903, ✆ 820 433); **Palm Beach Apartments**, Palm Beach 39 (✆ 867 786, ✆ 861 885); **Boardwalk Vacation**, Bakval 20, Noord (✆ 866 654); and **Blue Village**, Cunucu Abao 37 (✆ 878 618).

As befits the mix of Aruba's population, there are restaurants of almost any nationality in Aruba—Argentinian, Chinese, German, Japanese—as well as almost any style—grill, gourmet, seafood, bistros, pizza huts. And of course do not forget Aruban food itself, for dishes such as *sopito* (fish chowder with coconut), *calco stoba* (conch stew) and *keshi yena* (spiced chicken covered with Dutch cheese). Many restaurants are set in old Aruban town and country houses. Portions are usually large and most restaurants add a 15% service charge to your bill. Categories are arranged according to the price of a main dish: *expensive*—US$25 and above; *moderate*—between US$15 and $25; *cheap*—US$15 and below.

expensive

The place to linger over the best meal on the island is outside on the terrace at **Papiamento** (℗ 864 544) at Washington 61, in Noord. The plantation house is one of the oldest in Aruba and you can eat French and Caribbean specialities here, presented in clay pots (which you break with a hammer), or on a marble slab, which sizzles at your table. The seafood combination is superb (lobster, shrimp, crab, scallop and others on a bed of home-made noodles), or you can try local catch, home-smoked by the owner, Eduardo Ellis, a man with a compelling chuckle.

Chez Mathilde, at Havenstraat 23 in town (℗ 834 968), is set in an Aruban town-house. The menu is French, tournedos and thermidor served in candlelit intimacy, complemented by an extensive wine-list. *Dinner only.*

moderate

There are a number of restaurants serving Aruban food, of which the nicest is **Gasparito**, at Gasparito 3 (℗ 867 044), quite close to the high-rise strip. It is set in a pretty Aruban house—tiled floors, white-washed walls and *dakpannen*; all over the walls inside you will see Aruban paintings as the dining room doubles as a gallery. You might try the *combo* (fish cake, *kari kari* and chicken stew) or shrimp *en coco* (in coconut milk and brandy), followed by *banana na forno* (banana baked in cinnamon syrup). *Open for lunch and dinner.*

Not far off is **The New Old Cunucu House**, 150 Palm Beach (℗ 861 666), where you can eat outside on the terrace or in another Aruban homestead. The menu is a bit more international, but you can have the house veal escalope in white wine cream sauce or pan-fried, brandy-flamed conch. **La Paloma**, at Noord 39 (℗ 874 611), also behind the high-rise strip, is a bright and breezy Italian restaurant serving northern Italian fare and seafood. *Linguine scampi marinara* or Caribbean shrimps; local crowd at the bar. If you would like the best of Aruban seafood, then try **Driftwood** at 12 Klipstraat in town (℗ 832 515): *kreeft* (lobster), *carco* (conch) and *masbangoe* (sardines). More local restaurants can be found heading east from Oranjestad.

An excellent spot is **Mi Cushina** at Irausquin Blvd 228 (℗ 872 222): *kreeft stobá* or *hasá* (lobster stewed or baked) or *bestia chiquito stoba* (stewed lamb). *Open for lunch and dinner except Thurs.*

A seafood restaurant with a difference is the **Nueva Marina Pirata** (✆ 827 372), a barge in the mangroves of Spanish Lagoon. Grilled catch of the day in spicy creole sauce and some Aruban dishes—*casuela de mariscos*. Or you might try **Brisas del Mar** (✆ 847 718) at Savaneta 222A, a small seafood restaurant also on the waterfront, with views of the departing freighters.

At the *refresquerias*, a cross between a bar and a bakery, where you can sit out on the pavement with a beer, you can get *pan bati*, a sort of flat johnny cake and *rotis*, pastry envelopes stuffed with meat that originate from Trinidad. If you are peckish and see a vision of a white truck coming at you out of the night, then stop it—it will be a snack unit, the mobile equivalent of a *refresqueria*.

Bars and Nightlife

 Aruba's well-oiled tourism machine has a whole smorgasbord of entertainment laid on with Carnival shows and cabaret extravaganzas, or join-in limbo shows and congas to steel bands. There are even Country and Western evenings for the homesick. Details available through the hotels.

There are now 11 casinos on the island, but the best has to be the Alhambra Bazaar, where if your luck is out, at least you can be sure of getting something for your money in the all-night shopping arcade.

Outside the hotels are some fun bars: in Oranjestad you will find both locals and visitors at the **The Wine Cellar** on Klipstraat—not in fact a cellar, but a classic cocktail bar, walls decorated with atmospheric shots of other capital cities. Live music by house band Jemm (Fri, Sat). You might also try **Jimmy's Place**, a popular pub a little further down the boulevard, features cold beers and traditonal Dutch melted cheese sandwiches. On Main Street in San Nicolas, **Charlie's** is something of an institution— for fifty years it was a drinking man's bar, but now the second generation of Charlies has allowed women in. The ceiling is festooned with anything from car numberplates to favourite videos. **Cheer's Café**, located at the Port of Call Mall, is also a popular local hang-out. It is particularly packed on Tuesdays (ladies night), with its mix of both Latin American music and rock.

The rock and house music at **Whiskey's Roadhouse Café**, on L. G. Blvd, across from the high-rise hotels, attracts a young crowd. For more typical island music, try the **Kokoa Bar**, on the beach in front of the Aruba Palm Beach Resort, where you can enjoy a drink with a great view of the setting sun. Other options include **Joey's Drive-in Bar**, or any one of the hundreds of rum shops.

Since **Club Visage** burned down in 1995, the most popular dance club is the **Cobalt Club** at the Royal Plaza Mall, which appeals to a wide range of ages and musical tastes (ladies night on Wed). If you prefer a more exclusive atmosphere, try **Desire's Nightclub**, in the Seaport Village in downtown Oranjestad. Other discotheques include **Reflections**, for old-time, sixties music. **Chesterfield** nightclub in San Nicolas opens on Fridays.

getting there

By air: Aruba is very well connected by air with many flights from the USA as well as from Europe and South America. Queen Beatrix airport is a couple of miles from the main town of Oranjestad. A tax of US$20.00 (Passenger Facility Charge) is payable upon departure. This is usually now included in the price of most airline tickets, but you are advised to check.

By air from Europe: KLM has several non-stop flights each week to Amsterdam, from where there are easy connections all over Europe. Alternatively you can go via Curaçao, which has connections to other cities in Europe.

By air from the USA: Aruba has very good links from the US: Air Aruba and American Airlines have several daily links to Miami and New York; there are other scheduled flights to Atlanta, Baltimore, Houston, Orlando.

By air from other Caribbean islands: There are countless links to nearby Curaçao (Air Aruba and ALM), and some direct flights to Bonaire. Further afield there are links to San Juan on American Airlines and Santo Domingo in the Dominican Republic (Curaçao also has excellent connections around the Caribbean). **South America** is very well served and there are flights to Maracaibo, Valencia and Caracas in Venezuela, Bogotá in Colombia as well as San José in Costa Rica, Quito in Ecuador and Lima in Peru.

tourist information

There is no yourist office for Aruba in the UK:

Germany: Postfach 1204, D-64333 Seeheim (℗ 6257 962 961, 🖷 6257 962 919).

Holland: Schimmelpennicklaan 1, 2517 JN Den Haag, The Netherlands (℗ 70 356 6220, 🖷 70 360 4877).

USA: 1000 Harbour Boulevard, Weehawken, NJ 07087 (℗ (201) 330 0800, 🖷 330 8757); Greater Miami Office, 1 Financial Plaza, Suite 136, **Ft Lauderdale**, Florida 33394 (℗ 954 767 6477, 🖷 767 0432); 199 14th Street NE, Suite 1506, **Atlanta**, GA 30309–3686 (℗ (404) 892 7822, 🖷 873 2193). There is a general freephone number, ℗ (1 800) TO ARUBA.

Canada: 86 Bloor Street West, Suite 204, Toronto, Ontario M5S 1M5 (℗ (416) 975 1950, 🖷 975 1947).

There are several offices in South American countries, including **Venezuela:** Torre C, Piso 8, Oficina C–805, Chuao, Caracas, Venezuela (℗ (0603) 959 9166, 🖷 (0602) 959 6346).

On Aruba itself, contact the **Aruba Tourism Authority** at PO Box 1019, 172 L.G. Smith Boulevard, Oranjestad (℗ 823 777, 🖷 834 702; *www.arubatourism.com*). There is a small but helpful office in the airport and one in the cruise-ship docking terminal.

In a medical **emergency,** there is a casualty room at the Dr Horacio Oduber Hospital on L. G. Smith Boulevard (℗ 874 300). However, before phoning for an ambulance (℗ 115), check with the hotel front desk because there could be a house-doctor on call.

The **IDD code** for Aruba is ℗ (297), followed by a six-digit Aruban number. If you are telephoning within the island then just dial the last six digits. (Local numbers used to be five digits only, but were changed in early 1997 to include the prefix 8).

festivals

The major event in the Aruban calendar is **Carnival**, which is held in the run-up to Lent. Starting with the Lighting Parade, there is a kiddies' romp, and then musicians' competitions, and it all culminates eventually in the Old Mask Parade on the Sunday before Lent along the waterfront in Oranjestad, to music so loud that the streets seem to vibrate.

At New Year the Arubians have a tradition of open house, in which choirs and troupes of singers go from home to home singing *dandes*, songs like a melodic version of medieval Gregorian chants. In June there is an annual jazz and Latin music festival with big name performers from outside.

money

With 'Status Aparte' in 1986, Aruba adopted a currency of its own, the Aruban florin (AFl), which, like many Caribbean islands, they fixed to the US dollar (at a rate of US$1 = AFl 1.77). However, with their economy so closely geared to American visitors, they also accept US dollars in nearly all transactions (though you will need Aruban coins for pay telephones, etc.). Credit cards are accepted in any but the smallest restaurants, and traveller's cheques are accepted in the hotels. Service charges in Aruba are usually 15%. The Netherlands Antilles guilder (the currency of nearby Curaçao and Bonaire) is not accepted in Aruba.

Banks: Open 8–4 weekdays. You will get a slightly better exchange rate at the bank than at a hotel cash-desk.

Shops: Open 8–noon and 2.30–6pm, longer if there are cruise ships in. In case you are held up on the beach during the day, you can always go out and exercise your credit card with a bit of night-time shopping at the Alhambra Bazaar, where shops stay open until midnight.

watersports

Aruba has the whole range of opportunities for watersports, from waterskiing to fleets of wetbikes. The principal centre is Palm Beach, but hotels usually have equipment available for their guests. There are three large sporting outfits that operate from town and can be contacted through desks in the hotels: Pelican Watersports (© 831 228), De Palm Watersports (© 824 545) and Red Sail Sports at Palm Beach (© 861 603). Waterskiing, motorboat hire and parasailing are easily arranged on the high-rise hotel strip at Palm Beach. If you want to tame a jet-ski, you will find a little daytime colony of them at the top of Eagle Beach. You can even arrange to go **sailcarting** if you don't fancy getting wet: contact Aruba Sailcart, Bushiri 23 (© 835 133).

Windsurfing: The classic place to windsurf is off the upper end of the west coast, just beyond the high-rise strip, where the winds get a clean run across the island. Close in it is a good spot for beginners because the water is flat and shallow and farther out the winds build up. Instruction is easily available.

Intermediate and advanced sailboarders can sail waves at Boca Grandi (easiest because it has a sandy bottom), beyond the northwest point, and along the southern coast where there are sideshore winds. Some hire companies will allow you to take their boards to these places. Try Vela Aruba, the Mistral operators, at the top end of Palm Beach, Sailboard Vacation, L. G. Smith

Blvd 462 (© 862 527) in front of Malmok Beach, or Roger's Windsurf Place (© 861 918) at Malmok. A windsurfing tournament, the Hi-Winds Pro Am, is held each year in June.

Sailing: Most hotels have small sailing boats on hand, but if you would prefer to take a day's cruise on a larger yacht, this is also possible through the companies above or through individual operators: *Tattoo* (© 828 919), *Wave Dancer* (© 825 520) or *Mi Dushi* (© 828 919). Trips will vary from a sunset cruise on a trimaran with full boozatorium and on-board steel band to a full-blooded day's sail on the Trades.

Fishing: Deep-sea fishermen can go out in search of sailfish, bonito and kingfish in the waters around Aruba. Six fishermen can hire a boat for around US$350 for a half day, US$500 for a full day. Yachts include Capt Eduardo Pinzon's *G-String* (© 931 1409), Capt Kenneth Pichardo's *Kenny's Toy* (© 825 088) and Capt Bobby Croes' *Bobby C.* (© 832 556). The Deep Sea Fishing Tournament is held each year in October through the Aruba Nautical Club (© 853 022).

Scuba diving: A reef runs all along the protected leeward coast of Aruba, giving miles of diving, often with 100ft visibility, for scuba-diving enthusiasts. The best marine life is on the south coast between Spanish Lagoon and Commandeur's Bay, where there is a number of offshore islands. Coral has also begun to encrust Aruba's two wrecks: the *Antilia*, a German freighter that was scuttled off Malmok, and the *Pedernales*, an oil transporter also sunk in the Second World War by a submarine.

Instruction is available through many of the hotels, starting in the swimming pool and venturing out on to the reefs. Dives cost around US$50 each for a one tank dive, and can be arranged through the hotel or through the major sports shops. Contact Aruba Pro-Dive (© 825 520), Native Divers (© 864 763), Red Sail Sports (© 861 603) or Pelican (© 831 228).

Snorkelling: There are reefs along the south coast at Arashi and Palm Beach and farther afield at Baby Beach in the southeastern area of the island. Trips can be arranged through the big operators. If you would prefer not to get wet, you can try a glass-bottom boat through the major operators above. There is also an Atlantis Submarine at the Seaport Village Marina in town (© 836 090).

other sports

Golf: There are two golf courses: the 18-hole Tierra del Sol course, home to the Aruba Aces Championship, a senior PGA tour event, and the 9-hole Aruba Golf Club course with oiled sand 'greens', currently being renovated and not in the best state of repair.

Tennis: Can be fixed up through any number of hotels.

Riding: If you want to ride the cactus plains of the *cunucu*, then horses are available through Rancho El Paso (© 873 310), at Washington 44. El Paso offers one-hour rides through the countryside and 2-hour rides to the beach. There are two new ranches which operate on the windward side of the island, Rancho del Campo in Sombre 22E (© 850 290) and Rancho Diamari in Diamari (© 860 239). Both offer 2½-hour rides to and from the natural pool. They use the small sturdy breed known locally as 'Paseo'; rides cost about US$20 per hour.

The Virgin Islands

The Virgin Islands must have been a nightmare for the early cartographer—more than a hundred islands scattered over 1000 square miles; forested volcanic colossi that soar from the water and tiny cays that barely make it above the surf. One smudge and he was finished. To sail among them is a glorious sight, as stunning as it was 500 years ago when Columbus himself passed through. He was so awestruck by their beauty that he compared them to St Ursula and her 11,000 virgins—a name which has remained ever since.

The Virgin Islands lie at the eastern extremity of the Greater Antilles, 50 miles east of Puerto Rico. Eighty miles to their east, across the Anegada Passage, are the Leeward Islands, which run south from Anguilla and Sint Maarten. The Virgin Islands are nearly all of volcanic origin (now completely inactive) and so they rise steeply out of the water to as much as 1000ft within a few hundred yards of the coastline. From their summits the views over the islands are superb. The island peaks run in two main lines, facing each other across Sir Francis Drake Passage.

Politically the islands fall into two groups, both of them possessions—in the west are the United States Virgin Islands, an unincorporated Territory of the USA, and to their east lie the smaller British Virgin Islands, one of Britain's five Crown Colonies in the Caribbean. The USVI has a much larger population (about 120,000 compared with the BVI's 18,000). However, many more BVIers have moved to the USVI to live and work. The population of both groups is mainly of African origin, descended from former slaves but, besides the Virgin Islanders themselves, there are large communities of Puerto Ricans and West Indians from down-island, as well as expatriate communities of mainland Americans and some British.

The United States Virgin Islands are more developed than their British counterparts. In St Thomas, life is upbeat and clearly American—you will see the big cruising cars and drive-through banks and fast-food joints, and see 10-year-olds wearing outsize sneakers with an infestation of untied laces chatting about HBO satellite TV. St Croix, the largest of the Virgin Islands, is a little less developed than St Thomas and has a more pastoral air. St John is almost entirely given over to the National Park and so in places its slopes rise in uninterrupted green from the shoreline to the summits. Cruz Bay is the one small pocket of real development and it has a quiet but undoubted charm.

Life in the BVI is even gentler and slower still (the USVIers like to take a break there) but, encouraged by the government, things have been moving on apace recently. Because so much of the tourism in the BVI takes place on the water, it is generally less visible there, but Tortola particularly has seen rapid growth. In parts of the BVI you can still just see some trace of an older West Indies—wooden houses, cows loose on their tethers and the occasional person riding a donkey—but as with the USVI this is steadily disappearing.

The Virgin Islands

80km
48 miles

Anegada
(UK)

Tortola

Virgin
Gorda

UK
US

Puerto
Rico

Culebra(PR)

Virgin Passage

Saint
Thomas

Saint
John

UK
US

Vieques (PR)

N

Saint Croix
(US)

Traces of the British, who have all but withdrawn from this tropical colony, remain only in the scarlet pillar boxes and telephone boxes and the peaked caps of the customs officials.

In the past there has been talk of the two groups of islands forging closer political links, with the BVI attaching themselves in some way to the USVI to gain from the investment that tourism has brought to the economy. However, having seen how recent development has changed things next door, the majority of BVIers are happy to remain unconnected. Many BVIers, or 'belongers' as they are known, already work in the USVI and take their money back home to the BVI to build a home for their retirement.

Most people who come to the Virgin Islands will spend time on the water: on a ferry, belly-flopping on to the sea as their seaplane comes in to land, in snorkelling gear, or cruising in a yacht between secluded coves and waterfront beach bars. The cartographer's nightmare is a sailor's paradise.

The British Virgin Islands

The British Virgin Islands—50 or so reefs, rocks and raging volcanic towers—are sprinkled across the sea to the northeast of the USVI. They run in two lines about 3 miles apart, enclosing the Sir Francis Drake Channel. The bays make magnificent anchorages, as good now as when Columbus passed by, and later when pirates caroused and careened their ships here. The British Virgin Islands are some of the best sailing grounds in the world, and on land their coves hide some great places on which to be marooned (particularly in five-star luxury).

Tortola is changing as the tourism industry develops and there is an increasingly upbeat air in the island. Construction has recently broken the green continuity of the hillside scrub as the islanders build themselves larger homes and outsiders build vacation villas. Cruise ships have been permitted to put in to Tortola for a few years now. Virgin Gorda on the other hand is only gradually being developed and so life still moves at a dozier, more typical Caribbean pace there. The other islands are pretty well undeveloped.

There are about 18,000 inhabitants in the BVI, most of whom live on Tortola. However, for generations they have been travelling to the American Virgin Islands and there is probably a larger number than this living there. They benefit from their special status and from having the dollar as their currency, but they talk fearfully of how the USVI have been overdeveloped and of the crime level there. In the BVI the policemen carry truncheons rather than guns. Some islanders claim that the very word 'British' adds a stability of sorts.

In times past the BVI have looked east to the Leeward Islands and they still do in some matters such as sport, carnival and music, which is mostly calypso. However, most BVIers admit that American influence will inevitably increase and the old British ways recede. There is continual American investment and most consumer goods originate in the USA anyway. Basketball is a popular sport with the youth (as it is all over the Caribbean) and it is probably a matter of time before softball overtakes cricket in popularity.

Over 200,000 tourists visit the BVI each year, of which the majority come for the sailing. The BVI have angled their tourism cleverly at the upper end of the market, setting themselves up as a sophisticated Caribbean playground. They do it pretty well. The BVI are pretty expensive, but they are mostly easy-going and there is a lower hustle factor than elsewhere in the islands, even if the Belongers can be a little unforthcoming sometimes. You can get a very good tropical break in the BVI and for a price you can get luxurious seclusion on a tropical island resort.

History

History and legend are closely intertwined in the Virgin Islands—the coves and bays that make such perfect quiet and secluded anchorages were also ideal as pirate hangouts and so the two have become confused. As late as 1792, when the British had officially been in control for over a hundred years, Tortola was still described as a 'pirates' den'. The islands' most important industry, smuggling, was never recorded anyway.

When Columbus first arrived here in the late 15th century, the Virgin Islands were seeing waves of the belligerent Carib Indians from down-island passing through, stopping by before they raided Arawak Borinquen (now Puerto Rico) in the quest for enemies to barbecue. The fact that the Spaniards settled Puerto Rico made no difference; they were still a good target and were just as tasty. But the Spaniards turned out to be more of a match than the Arawaks and in 1555 they bore down on the Caribs in the Virgin Islands and wiped them out.

Soon after the Caribs were eliminated another threat began appearing in the Virgin Islands—pirates. They used the bays to anchor and climbed the heights to watch for a sail to appear on the horizon. Jack Hawkins and Sir Francis Drake passed through, the latter giving his name to the channel through which he escaped in 1585 after raiding the Spanish *flota* with the riches of Mexico aboard. There are endless legends of buried treasure in the BVI.

The first permanent settlers on the islands were Dutch buccaneers and cattle ranchers, who arrived on Tortola in 1648. They barbecued beef rather than human limbs and sold the smoked meat to passing ships. In 1672 they were ousted by English buccaneers and the eastern Virgin Islands were taken over by England. Despite the official status, the smuggling continued as the buccaneers became settled.

Although the islands are not particularly fertile, they were able to grow cotton and experienced some prosperity at the height of the sugar era during the 18th century. Slaves were brought here and the steep hillsides were terraced and planted with cotton and cane. Quakers who came to the islands had a hand in freeing some of the slaves (they thought slavery immoral and rallied against it) and the plantations folded quickly, even before emancipation in 1838. As they failed, so the white population left. In 1805 the population was about 10,500 (9000 slaves) and a century later there were 5000, of whom two were white. The remaining islanders became subsistence farmers on the land abandoned by the white settlers. This has only changed in the last few years with the advent of the tourist industry.

Early on the British Virgin Islands were governed by an elected council, but in 1867 this was abolished and the islands were simply appended to the Leeward Island Federation as a 'Presidency'. The British Virgin Islands are still a Crown Colony of Britain and are nominally administered by a Governor appointed in London, but since the Second World War they have steadily taken on internal self-government. There is a 12-member elected council with a ministerial system. The Chief Minister is the Hon. Ralph T. O'Neal of the Virgin Islands Party and the opposition leader is Conrad Maduro of the United Party.

Lying so close to their American counterparts, the British Virgin Islands have often considered political union with the USVI. In the fifties, as the other British Caribbean countries were trying to move together in the West Indies Federation, the British Virgins turned away and seemed to be on the point of making the link. There were even rumours in the 1960s that the British Government had offered to sell the islands to the United States. But no union was formed and most of the islanders now feel that it was the right decision.

The biggest foreign exchange earner is tourism: of the 200,000 or more visitors each year, there are 80,000 cruise ship arrivals and of the rest 60 per cent come for the sailing. Other industries include construction (the scars of quarrying and building plots are visible in the hillsides), some light manufacturing and an expanding offshore finance sector.

✆ *(1 284 49)–*   ### Getting Around

With so many islands, travelling by boat is a good way to get around and the Virgin Islands are also well served by ferries. The main terminals are at West End and Road Town on Tortola, Beef Island (near the airport) and at the Valley and North Sound in Virgin Gorda. There are five or six sailings each day between Road Town and the Valley, on Speedy's (✆ 55240) and Smith's (✆ 44430). If you want to go to Virgin Gorda (the Valley or the North Sound) from the airport, the North Sound Express (✆ 52271) meets flights in Beef Island, making about four trips a day. The boats are sleek and fun to ride as they skim across the water with a sonorous rumble. There are some scheduled flights between the islands, on Gorda Aero Services (✆ 52271, same as the North Sound Express) between Tortola and Virgin Gorda and Anegada.

There are three or four daily sailings from West End to Jost van Dyke on the Jost van Dyke Ferry Service (✆ 42997). Peter Island is served by the Peter Island boat, which departs from the CSY marina in Road Town; about eight crossings a day. There are no actual ferries to Anegada, so if you want to visit by sea your best bet is to take one of the many day sailing cruises. Up-to-the-minute ferry schedules can be found in the BVI *Welcome* tourist magazine. An alternative way of travelling in the Virgin Islands is to go to the marinas and talk somebody into taking you on their yacht.

Sailing and Charters

Cruising Sir Francis Drake Channel is one of the finest experiences the Caribbean can offer. The islands lie like sleeping animals around you, set between a fantastic blue sea and sky; close at hand small cays move with you as you cruise and on the horizon the volcanic colossi do not budge. You can moor in coves where headlands enclose a horseshoe of white sand and a few palms and where the water is so clear that the boat seems to be suspended in the air. When it gets too hot on board, swim to the beach and collapse there. At sunset there is nothing better to do than to watch for the Green Flash, as the sun vanishes below the seaward horizon.

The Virgin Islands offer some of the best sailing in the world—the waters are safe and sheltered by the large islands, but there are constant breezes. Anchorages are good, the distances between them are short and the sailing itself is relatively easy (with the exception of Anegada, there are few reefs) and so the area is ideal for bareboat chartering. The industry is well developed and companies have chase boats and vehicles. The BVI also have an excellent string of beach bars and restaurants which make for a lively bar-hopping holiday if you prefer.

The charter companies have yachts of all sizes available for hire, from simple 30-footers for two to luxury motor-cruisers with on-board Renoirs, jetskis and clay-pigeon traps. Crewed yachts come with a skipper and a cook, but there are plenty of bareboats for those who would prefer to look after themselves. Yachts usually have snorkelling equipment, but as you go up the scale there will be video recorders, windsurfers and often diving gear. Prices start at around US$100 per day per person and for extreme luxury expect to shell out around $400 (though really the sky is the limit). Hire is considerably cheaper in the summer months (as much as 40 per cent off) and you will find the channel and coves a little less crowded then.

Charter Companies and Marinas in the BVI

The two largest **bareboat** charter operators are **The Moorings** and **Sunsail**, both in Tortola. The Moorings are based at Wickham's Cay II in Road Town, PO Box 139 (✆ 42331, ✉ 42226, US ✆ (1 800) 535 7289). Sunsail are based at Soper's Hole at the West End (✆ 54740, ✉ 54301, UK ✆ (01705) 219345, US ✆ (1 800) 327 2276, *www.sunsail.com*). **Footloose** Sailing Charters (✆ 40528, ✉ 40529), based at Nanny Cay, take on some of the Moorings boats once they have left the Moorings fleet. Other operators include **North South Yacht Vacations** at Nanny Cay, PO Box 281, Tortola (✆ 40096, ✉ 57543, US ✆ (1 800) 387 4964, *www.inforamp.net/~norsouth; 75403.1127@compuserve.com*) who offer some of the best prices in the BVI on their fleet of crewed and bareboats.

Companies give a briefing before you set out and will provision your yacht on request. Most have skippers who will help you out for a couple of days and then leave you to get on with it. The Moorings and Sunsail have other outlets elsewhere in the Eastern Caribbean and so you can sail to other islands down the chain if you wish.

The BVI also has a large number of more traditional **crewed** yachts for hire. Many of these are owner-operated and so they can give a more personal touch. They can pick you up wherever you want (at the airport for instance). Unlike the bareboats, which can be ordered directly from the charter company, to book a crewed yacht you should contact a yachting broker in your country; details are available through the tourist boards (*see* also p.9). For charter companies based in St Thomas, *see* p.505.

There are many **marinas** in the BVI where you can take on all the provisions and services you will need. In **Tortola**, there are marinas in Road Town, Wickhams Cay I, which is closest to town, and Wickhams Cay II, Nanny Cay and Soper's Hole Marina at West End. Other, smaller marinas are scattered along the southern shore towards the eastern end of the island. In **Virgin Gorda** you can go to the Virgin Gorda Yacht Harbour (✆ 55555) and the Bitter End Yacht Club in the North Sound.

Tortola and Beef Island

Tortola (the Turtle Dove) is the largest of the British Virgins (21 square miles), and set in a huge bay on its south coast is the BVI capital, Road Town. The island is irregularly shaped, long and thin, 10 miles by 3, but the roads are so wiggly that it takes 45 minutes to get from one end to the other and it is so mountainous that you cannot cross over from one side to the other without ascending to about 1200ft. Mount Sage, whose upper slopes are covered with such lush and explosive greenery that it is almost rainforest, is the highest point in all the Virgins (1716ft). It is worth exploring the heights, if only for the magnificent views of the other islands. About 13,000 of the 18,000 population live on Tortola.

Tortola has become noticeably busier recently and there has been construction all over the island. For a while there was a rather unsettling, island-wide colour-scheme of obscure colours such as lavender, fuchsia and magenta, but thankfully this seems to have faded now. The island seems to have ridden the recession and then the hurricane damage quite well and now that they have built a cruise-ship dock, Tortola beetles with an endless stream of safari buses on island tours. Even so, the islanders are pretty easy-going and with the exception of a few sports cars and construction lorries, life still proceeds at a fairly gentle pace.

Getting Around

There is a rudimentary **bus service** that runs along the south coast of Tortola, emanating from Road Town (fares $1–3, timings unpredictable). Catch it if you can find it. Hitchhiking is possible and about as haphazard as anywhere else. The most reliable method of travel is by **taxi** and these are easily found in town and the airport/ferry terminals. Fix the price beforehand. Rates are pretty high, about US$14 from **Road Town** to West End, Cane Garden Bay or Beef Island. You can order one through the BVI Taxi Association (✆ 42322), the Waterfront Taxi Stand (✆ 43456) or Soper's Hole Taxi (✆ 54665). Drivers would be happy to take you on an island tour; price around US$45 for up to four people; otherwise you can contact Nature's Secret Adventure Company (✆ 52722) or Travel Plan Tours (✆ 42872). You can always sightsee by plane with FLY BVI (✆/✉ 51747), who make a run down Tortola to Soper's Hole and then along the small island chain up to Necker Island, price $50 per person.

Maximum flexibility comes with your own **hire car**, but at a price (from about $45 per day plus taxes in winter, less in summer). If you wish to drive, you must obtain a BVI temporary driving licence (from the car rental agency or traffic department on production of $10 and a valid licence from elsewhere). There is often a hefty deposit (credit cards OK). Driving is mostly on the left and the speed limit is supposedly 40mph in the country and 20mph in town. Watch out for speed bumps in the settlements and traffic jams in Road Town at the beginning and end of the working day (9am and 4.30pm). Rental firms include Avis (✆ 43322, ✉ 44218), Caribbean Car Rental (✆ 42698, ✉ 42420) in town, Island Suzuki near Nanny Cay (✆ 43666), who hire out jeeps, and National (✆ 43197, ✉ 44085) at Duffs Bottom.

Beaches

Tortola's best beaches are along the north coast, secluded and protected by the massive volcanic shoulders that lumber down from the mountainous heights. If there is a busy beach then it will be there. On the south coast the sand is not so good, but you will have winds for windsurfing and sailing in the channel.

best beaches

Cane Garden Bay: The most popular beach on the island, on the north shore of the island over the incredibly steep hill over from Road Town. The sand is good and behind it sits a string of beach bars and a couple of small hotels, from where there is a cracking view of Jost van Dyke. You can hire watersports equipment here, through Baby Bull Watersports—snorkelling gear, windsurfers and small sailing boats—when frying in coconut oil loses its appeal.

Apple Bay and **Carrot Bay**: Two small coves with passable sand to the west of Cane Garden Bay. You can surf here when the waves are up.

Long Bay: Over the hill, worth a visit for the sand; there's a restaurant to retreat to at the Long Bay Hotel.

Smuggler's Cove (officially Lower Belmont Bay): Really the prettiest and best beach on the island, beyond Long Bay at the western tip of the island on the north shore. It is a perfect curve of palm-backed sand, one of the most secluded on the island; good snorkelling.

Brewer's Bay: Off the incredibly steep road in the other direction from Cane Garden Bay (over to town), reached by jeep-trail; it is secluded and has a campsite.

Trunk Bay, **Josiah's Bay**, **Lambert Long Bay** and **Elizabeth Beach**: Further east along the north shore, they have excellent sand, but you should beware the under-current in the latter two.

Long Bay: There is another Long Bay on Tortola, or at least on Beef Island just close to the airport (turn just before the airstrip itself). Looking across to Great and Little Camanoe, this Long Bay arches in a stunning half-mile strip of soft white sand and shelves gently into calm translucent sea. The snorkelling on the Camanoes and Scrub Island is excellent.

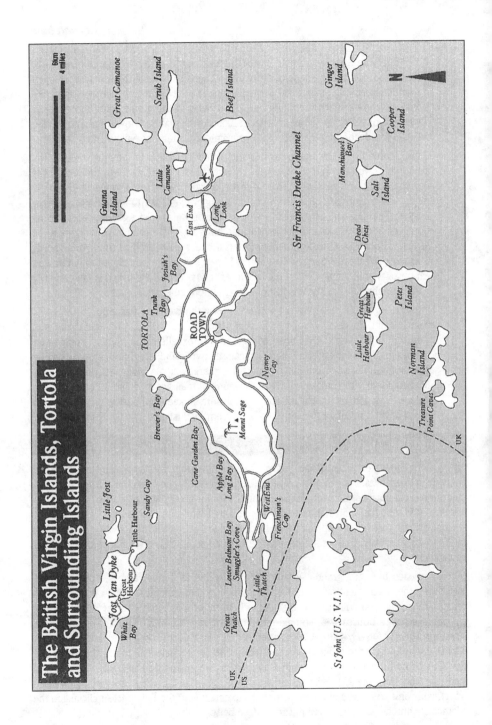

The British Virgin Islands, Tortola and Surrounding Islands

6km
4 miles

N

Great Camanoe

Scrub Island

Beef Island

Ginger Island

Cooper Island

Manchioneel Bay

Salt Island

Guana Island

Little Camanoe

East End

Long Look

Sir Francis Drake Channel

Dead Chest

Josiah's Bay

Trunk Bay

TORTOLA

ROAD TOWN

Peter Island

Great Harbour

Little Harbour

Brewer's Bay

Nanny Cay

Mount Sage

Norman Island

Cane Garden Bay

Apple Bay
Long Bay

West End

Frenchman's Cay

Treasure Point Caves

UK

Little Jost

Sandy Cay

Jost Van Dyke
Great Harbour

Little Harbour

White Bay

Great Thatch

Lower Belmont Bay
Smuggler's Cove

Little Thatch

St John (U.S. V.I.)

UK
US

471

The BVI have some classic beach bars, of which Tortola's best is **Bomba's Surfside Shack** on Apple Bay at the west end on the north shore. True to its name it is a shack, made of driftwood (Bomba's is one of the few places which benefits from the hurricanes in recent years; the flotsam merely becomes an extension). It's a great spot for chilling out, particularly at the monthly full moon party, which is famous for its jars of unusual drinks additives. Who knows, perhaps you too will feel like decorating the walls with your knickers after a heavy evening's liming.

Cane Garden Bay is lined with bars standing almost shoulder to shoulder, right on the sand, where you can retreat for a beer and a chicken or fish platter in the heat of the day and watch the yachts run over to Jost van Dyke. Some are also worth visiting at night, when there are often live bands and big crowds. **Quito's Gazebo** gets very busy on Tuesdays and at weekend evenings, but they also offer a good spot for chilling out by day, with drinks and snacks. You can have a game of darts to go with your Red Stripe at **Paradise Club**, or follow more Caribbean pursuits (just the Red Stripe) at **Stanley's Welcome Bar** and **Rhymers**. **Myett's** is an octagonal gazebo where you eat upstairs with a fine view of the beach. At the far end of the beach is the curiously named bright blue bar **De Wedding**, which is more quiet and isolated.

There are a couple of stopovers on Brewer's Bay: the **Bamboo Bar** hides in a forest of palms behind the curve of soft brown sand. If you are in Trellis Bay on Beef Island, you can stop for a snack at **De Loose Mongoose**, an excellent and friendly stopover on the beach. If you look offshore here you can see two island blips in the bay: the further one (sometimes quite difficult to spot as it merges into a bigger island behind) is **Marina Cay,** which makes a nice day out on its small beach. It has a Pusser's Bar to slake a thirst and get a meal and some watersports to keep you busy when you're tired of sizzling in the sun: a free ferry runs over from Beef Island.

Around the Island

Strung along the water's edge, **Road Town** takes its name from the bay on which it sits, Road Harbour (a 'road' was an open anchorage in the 17th century) and it is the centre of government and most business activity for the islands. It is not a very attractive town altogether. Much of it is modern, built haphazardly on reclaimed land and there is a semi-permanent stream of traffic running on the coast-road through town. The seaborne activity still continues in the town, however, in the marinas and the ferry dock and this gives the place a pleasant nautical air.

If you approach by sea, a grandiose building, with a line of slender arches, dominates the waterfront, the government offices or Central Administration Complex. Not far inland, on the original shoreline, you will find Main Street, where there is a clutch of older BVI buildings, clapboard wooden houses with shingle tiles, most of which contain shops. The **BVI Folk Museum** (*open Mon–Fri 9.30–4.30*) is worth a quick look. It is set in a pretty blue and white timber-frame house with wooden shutters and contains a small exhibition of natural and marine life and human history in Amerindian pottery and plantation artefacts. There is also some crockery from the RMS *Rhone*, which sank off Salt Island in 1867. Continuing on Main Street, you come to a string of island institutions to detain you: the Episcopal Anglican and the Methodist churches and the island prison wedged between them.

Just off Main Street farther inland, the small J.R. O'Neal **Botanic Gardens** (*open Mon–Sat 9.30–5.30, Sun noon–5*) give an excellent exposure to the diverse tropical flora of the Caribbean. Around a short alley of royal palms are laid out cactus gardens, a lily pond and a fern house and of course endless tropical flowers. There are some medicinal plants, and occasional benches to rest the feet. A charming place to stop for a moment.

Roads lead out of the town in both directions along the wiggly coastline, passing Tortola's other small settlements in the many bays, West End and Long Look (in the east), where many 'belongers' have returned to build their homes. If you want to get to Cane Garden Bay (a popular north-coast beach), you must head inland and up. The **ridge road** runs along the backbone of Tortola and gives some superb views of the other islands.

Sage Mountain National Park, which contains the highest point in the Virgin Islands, is a small area of (almost) rainforest, where tall and slender trees soar and hanging vines drop to the ground and where the ferns and philodendrons quiver on the breeze. Since the 1960s, the park has been allowed to grow naturally and the vegetation, which has some lusher growth like that on the bigger Windward Islands, is thought to be similar to the island's original growth, before the land was cleared for planting. A number of trails have been cut through the forest and there are some lookouts, from which the views are superb.

Back down on the coast road, heading west from Road Town you come to Sea Cow's Bay and Baugher's Bay, and the road eventually wiggles into **Frenchman's Cay** at the western end of the island. Once this was a favoured pirate hideout—it was easily defended and had good lookouts. Nowadays there is still a working boatyard, a very busy marina and a collection of pretty pastel boutiques and bars and the **West End**, the ferry terminal for the USVI and Jost van Dyke.

Heading east from town you pass the large H. Lavity Stout Community College in Paraquita Bay and then come to the settlement at East End. Over on the north coast you will find an old plantation estate house and the ruined walls of other estate buildings which saw prosperity as a sugar factory in the 18th century and then again as a rum distillery in the age of Prohibition in the States, when the rum would be smuggled to thirsty illicit drinkers. Back on the southern shore, the main road eventually reaches a toll bridge over to **Beef Island**, the site of the airport. The island takes its name from its former use as a cattle ranch by buccaneers, but now all there is to see are a few goats and guest houses, private villas and the occasional 48-seater plane pitching and reeling as it comes in to land—NB the nonchalant sign at the roadside: '*Beware low-flying aircraft*'.

Great Camanoe and **Scrub Island** also lie off the northeast tip of the island and they have a few private homes. To visit them, take a boat from Beef Island. **Guana Island** is private and is devoted to a hotel, a classic island retreat (*see* below). It is kept quite private. **Marina Cay** however, also with a hotel out in Trellis Bay, can be visited for the day.

✆ (1 284 49)–   **Where to Stay**

Tortola has only a few nice hotels (the BVI's smartest hotels are mostly on Virgin Gorda or on their own island) and not all of them are on or even near beaches—many are quite functional stopovers which are used as a base by sailors. There are very few cheap places to stay anywhere in the BVI (with the exception of the many campsites). For some reason, most of the hotel rooms in Tortola seem to have kitchenettes. It is worth enquiring about weekend and other packages. With so little to choose from, it is definitely worth considering taking a villa on Tortola; there is a good variety in a broad range of standards. Villas can be arranged through BVI Club US and UK and **Rockview Holiday Homes** (✆ 42550, US ✆ (1 800) 782 4304). A government tax of 7% will be added to all bills.

luxury–expensive

Guana Island, PO Box 32 (✆ 42354, ⊚ 52900, US ✆ (1 800) 624 8262), offers some of the best in Virgin Islands' luxury and seclusion, on a private island of 850 acres just north of Beef Island. Tennis, watersports—windsurfing, sailing, fishing trips and seven beaches—and even croquet are there, but the club is most special for its gracious atmosphere amid superb hillside settings. Each of the simple but elegant and comfortable rooms—almost Mediterranean in style it seems, with white stucco and coloured shutters—has a terrace and an expanse of view in its isolated setting. From solitude in the rooms, you can venture to the company of the main house (relative company anyway because there is a maximum of 30 guests), with dining room and of course library, or to the beach for the watersports. Afternoon tea, honour bar and a friendly dining room on a veranda with a view—pure luxury.

The **Sugar Mill**, PO Box 425 (✆ 54355, ⊚ 54696, US ✆ (1 800) 462 8834), is charming and has an intimate atmosphere. The central area is set in restored stone estate buildings surrounded by luxurious tropical greenery in Little Apple Bay. The 22 rooms (one two-bedroom apartment) are modern, white and bright and very comfortable, ranged on the hill behind, each with a wonderful view of Jost van Dyke from the balcony, over the pool and seaside beach deck and restaurant (for lighter, daytime meals). The hotel is renowned for its dining room: you take cocktails in the gazebo of tall arches and then move to the setting of antique stone walls in the old boiling house, to the tune of water falling into copper kettles (*see* below).

At the **Long Bay Beach Resort**, PO Box 433 (✆ 54252, US ✆ (1 800) 729 9599, *res@longbay@idestin.com*), the 105 rooms (cabanas, studios and villas in a variety of configurations) are scattered around Long Bay, a picturesque cove in the west of the island. They stand in the seagrape just behind the excellent sandy beach and on the steep hillside behind, each very comfortable with bright decor and all mod cons (full kitchens in some cases). Breakfast terrace by the pool, dinner in the elegant Tropical Garden dining room in the main house on the hillside. The hotel is now quite large and had a faintly chaotic West Indian feel about it. Position relative to the beach determines the price of the rooms.

expensive–moderate

The **Frenchman's Cay Resort Hotel**, PO Box 1054, West End (✆ 54844, ⊚ 54056, US ✆ (1 800) 235 4077, Canada ✆ (1 800) 463 0199, *www.frenchmans.com*; *fmchotel@caribsurf.com*), has a small number of one- and two-bedroom villas (full kitchens and living rooms) standing on a hillside with views along Sir Francis Drake Channel to islands from St John to Peter Island. Hammocks in the garden around the octagonal main house, where there is a restaurant; small stony beach with snorkelling, tennis. Quiet, but within a shout of the West End bars. If you want a comfortable spot in Road Town, you might try **Treasure Isle Hotel**, PO Box 68 (✆ 42501, ⊚ 42507, US ✆ (1 800) 437 7880), which stands above the marinas on the hillside, with a pool and a restaurant, the Lime and Mango, on a pretty deck. Just 40 rooms and three suites, typical Caribbean comfort with television and air-conditioning. For something a little more isolated, you might try **Marina Cay**, c/o Pusser's PO Box 626, Road Town (direct ✆ 42174, ✉ 44775), which is set on a tiny blip (no more than 100 by 200 yards) offshore at the eastern end of the island. There is a secluded and intimate air most of the time because there are just four rooms and two two-bedroom villas tucked away around the island. However, you can expect some activity with passing yachts and other visitors who come to enjoy the beach and the few watersports, including scuba. Fantastic view from the sunset bar on the heights.

moderate

There is an excellent and friendly guest house in Trellis Bay, the **Beef Island Guest House**, PO Box 494 (✆ 52303, ✉ 51611). Just four rooms set in a house, around a central living area that is open to guests (with video and paperback library). Right on the beach, a fun spot with seclusion or activity (e.g. windsurfing) just a short walk away. Rate includes breakfast at the rustic beach bar, De Loose Mongoose, next door. The **Sea Breeze Hotel** (✆ 51560, ✉ 51792) has just a few rooms at good rates in the Sea Breeze marina on the south side of the island not far from the airport at Beef Island. The rooms are perfectly comfortable, set in a block just back from the waterfront itself, though there is a fairly businesslike feel because it is a working marina.

cheap

The **Cane Garden Bay Beach Hotel**, better known as Rhymer's, PO Box 570 (✆ 54639, ✉ 54820, *www.bviguide.com/rhymers.html*), sits right on the beach, painted in faintly alarming shades of pink and lemon yellow. There are 21 rooms, all with air-conditioning and televisions and kitchen equipment, quite simple, in the centre of the action. It is worth asking around in Cane Garden Bay and then bargaining. Just beyond Government House in town there are cheap and simple rooms at the **Sea View Hotel**, PO Box 59 (✆ 42483, ✉ 44952). There is a **camp-ground** in Brewer's Bay on the north coast, with showers, loos and a concessionary shop hidden among the seagrape and palms; fixed sites and bare sites, also very cheap.

✆ (1 284 49)–   **Eating Out**

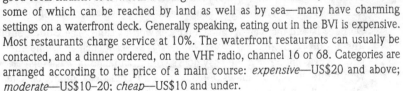

Most restaurants and hotel dining rooms in Tortola are 'international' in style, though there are one or two other nationalities represented besides West Indian fare, which features in some good local haunts. It is worth bearing in mind all the beach bars, some of which can be reached by land as well as by sea—many have charming settings on a waterfront deck. Generally speaking, eating out in the BVI is expensive. Most restaurants charge service at 10%. The waterfront restaurants can usually be contacted, and a dinner ordered, on the VHF radio, channel 16 or 68. Categories are arranged according to the price of a main course: *expensive*—US$20 and above; *moderate*—US$10–20; *cheap*—US$10 and under.

expensive

The most elegant restaurant in Tortola is **Brandywine Bay** (✆ 52301), which has an excellent setting in an open tropical house on a headland east of Road Town, towards Beef Island. Start with a cocktail on the terrace and move to the stone-built dining room hanging with greenery. The menu is international with a taste of Florentine fare, often grilled and then served with artistic attention to detail: home-made mozzarella and *pomodori* or beef *carpaccio* flavoured with lime and olives, *bistecca alla fiorentina* and nightly changing pasta specials; long wine list including Italian. It is well worth getting to the dining room at the **Sugar Mill** (✆ 54355; *expensive–moderate*), which has a set Caribbean and international menu which revolves fortnightly and combines classical ideas and techniques with Caribbean fruits and spices in an innovative and satisfying way: smoked conch terrine or Caribbean sweet potato soup with gingered shrimp to start, followed by fresh fish with sun-dried tomatoes and a herb vinaigrette or tropical game hen with orange-curry butter. In Road Town the **Captain's Table** (✆ 43885) has a very pleasant air, its dining room overlooking the yachts of the Inner Harbour marina from a terrace festooned with greenery and with outhanging awnings. There is a nightly-changing French and international menu—sautéed scallops in mango vinaigrette or a rack of lamb in rosemary sauce, also a live lobster speciality, followed by crêpes suzette.

moderate

Next door is the **Hungry Sailor**, which serves simpler meals in a pretty garden setting under palm thatch at **Pusser's Outpost** (✆ 44199). You will find a stylized old-time nautical feel, stained wood and wicker chairs with maquettes of sailing ships and figureheads, set to 20th-century comfort, where the international menu includes tenderloin in flaky pastry and the Pusser's Fisherman's Platter. Another cheery spot is **Pegleg Landing** in Nanny Cay, which sits on a deck supported by criss-cross stilts as the name hints. There is a cracking view down-island to go with your beer and snack (potato skins and wings) or more substantial platters. The best in West Indian food can be found at **C & F Bar and Restaurant** (✆ 44941) just out of Road Town in Purcell Estate. Classic setting on a covered terrace with red concrete floor, plastic tablecloths, fake roses, fishabilia on the walls and waiters watching the telly. Delicious shrimp in lemon butter and a tonnage of ground provisions. Go east from town, left at the roundabout, left again and it's at the next turning right.

Alternatively you might try **Mrs Scatliffe's** restaurant (✆ 54556), set on the tin-roofed veranda of her home in Carrot Bay on the north side, where you will be fed a set menu of fine West Indian fare: callaloo or breadfruit soup with home-made bread, pot-roast pork or chicken and coconut, and superb ice creams; sometimes a scratch-band, or just the cooks singing in the kitchen while they work; remember to reserve. **The Apple** restaurant (✆ 54337) is situated in Little Apple Bay and is also popular for local fare; seafood speciality including whelks and conch as well as fish.

On **Beef Island** there are a couple of places worth visiting. The **Conch Shell Point Restaurant** (✆ 52285; *expensive–moderate*) serves French and some international fare on the point beyond the ferry docks. You sit at tables in waist-high alcoves, set with white linen and candles, looking out into Trellis Bay, dining on a marinated salmon and conch starter followed by swordfish in a mango sauce or chicken breast with shrimp in herbs and butter. For a lively evening out you can catch a ferry to the **Last Resort** (✆ 52520) on Bellamy Cay just offshore—open veranda with barrel chairs and a donkey that likes to stick her head through a doorway to be fed. Hot buffet dinner: pumpkin soup followed by chicken in curry and honey (or roast beef and Yorkshire pudding). Always entertainment: it's particularly noted for a show in which the owner takes the mickey out of life, the universe and yachtsmen, but there's also music and comedy.

cheap

In town the café **Capricio di Mare** has true Italian style for a bit of loitering over a cappuccino opposite the ferry pier. Daytime salads and sandwiches. If you are feeling a little home-sick for the NBA or for Guinness on tap, the **Virgin Queen**, upstairs just near the roundabout in town, has a television constantly going and English pub food. The **Midtown** restaurant on Main Street has plastic tablecloths in an air-conditioned dining room setting with classic West Indian fare—curry goat and fry fish.

Finally you might try the **Roti Palace** close by, on Abbott Road in town, for a roti—a spicy envelope of bread with chicken or beef. And if you would like a late-night goat-water or a chicken leg you can take away at **Nito's,** in a grounded bus at the roundabout in town.

Bars and Nightlife

 There is always a lively drinking crowd out in Tortola—yachties and newcomers alike. There are plenty of tourist bars, with the pretty mock-nautical setting of the Pusser's Pubs, but there are also classic West Indian rum-shacks too. An event not to be missed if you are on island at the full moon is Bomba's full moon party where the drinkers spill out on to the road from **Bomba's Bar** in Apple Bay—known for its mushroom-based drinks additives.The national drink of the BVI (for the tourists anyway) is the Painkiller, usually mixed with local Pusser's Rum—cream of coconut, orange juice, pineapple juice and rum, topped with nutmeg, but there are endless other exotic cocktails. You could always try some guavaberry liqueur, from St Maarten, which is reported to make you 'frisky, happy and loving'. Most bars have a happy hour to catch you early.

In town an ever-popular haunt is the **Pusser's Store and Pub**, just across from the ferry terminal, where the nauticalia of model ships and shields and the dark-stained wood and brass give it the feel of a British naval-theme pub—you even get your drink in a glass pint-mug. Also try the **Virgin Queen**, an upstairs bar next to the roundabout where you can get American light beers, but also Beamish and Boddingtons. A more traditionally Caribbean waterfront bar is the **Paradise Pub**, on the road to West End, which is set around a covered courtyard; darts and rowdy drinking games, dancing at the weekends.

The **West End** has some good bars—**Pusser's Landing** on Frenchman's Cay is bright pink and ever-popular, and across the bay, garish in even more outrageous lavender and fuchsia is the **Jolly Roger**, which has seen some riotous excesses in its time, along the lines of its name. And the **beach bars** in Apple Bay and Cane Garden Bay are of course lively; **Quito's Gazebo** and **Myett's** have live music a couple of times a week. Finally, if you want a cocktail and a fantastic view you can go to **Skyworld.**

Jost van Dyke

The little island of Jost van Dyke lies about 4 miles off Tortola's West End. It is a perfect place to be marooned; there is a sleepy, very Caribbean air and it is less developed than the other islands. There is hardly anything there—just a couple of square miles of scrub, idyllic beaches and bars to retreat to and about 120 inhabitants, who cluster around the two main settlements of Great Harbour and Little Harbour at the east end of the island. A dirt track leads between the two, but there are hardly any vehicles. The island has only received electricity and telephones recently and some of the traditional West Indian life remains here—cattle and goats wander around, dragging their tethers and you might see a charcoal bonfire smoking away. There is nothing to see above the waterline. Industry includes a little sand-mining and building. And yet Jost van Dyke, supposedly named after a Dutch pirate, used to be cultivated from shoreline to hilltops (highest 1070ft), terraced to grow cotton and sugar-cane. In those days this barren outcrop was quite prosperous. It is also the birthplace of two famous men.

Dr John Lettsom was born to a Quaker planter family in 1744 and eventually became the founder of the London (later British) Medical Society and the Royal Humane Society. He is remembered for his efforts in the rhyme:

> *I, John Lettsom,*
> *blisters, bleeds and sweats 'em*
> *If, after that, they please to die*
> *I, John Lettsom.*

His fellow Quaker, born on the island in 1759, was William Thornton, another medical doctor, who campaigned against slavery in the islands. He became a US citizen and won the competition to design the Capitol in Washington, later serving as the first superintendent of the US Patent Office.

Beaches

There are two fantastic bays on the south coast: **Great Harbour** and **White Bay**, where the snorkelling is particularly good. And off the east end of the island there are other superb strips of sand. **Sandy Cay** is a blip with a fine beach and good snorkelling and **Sandy Spit**, off Green Cay, is the archetypal sandy spit with nothing but a few palm trees and luscious, foot-deep sand. There is a small watersports shop, **Wendell's**, in Great Bay.

Where to Stay

© *(1 284 49)–*

There are few places to stay on Jost van Dyke. The **Sandcastle**, Suite 237, Red Hook Plaza, St Thomas, USVI 00802 (USVI © (809) 775 5262, ✆ 775 3590, direct © (809) 496 0496; *expensive–very expensive*), is a Caribbean dream, with four breezy cottages lost in a garden of palm trees on White Bay, a stunning white-sand cove with absurdly blue water. Very secluded and low-key—hammocks, watersports if you want them, an honour bar and a library to keep you busy. The occasional crowd of yachtsmen drops in for dinner by candle-light (there is no electricity); the dining room serves fine continental fare with Cajun seasoning. Rooms quite simple, but there are few settings like it. **Rudy's Mariner Inn**, Great Harbour (© 59282 or (809) 775 3558; *moderate*) has just five rooms with kitchenettes; simple. Over in Little Harbour you can get a *cheap* room at **Harris's Place** (✆ 59566, ✆ 59296). You can also find a tent or cabin to stay in at the **White Bay Campground** (✆ 59312 or 59358).

✆ *(1 284 49)–* | **Eating Out and Bars**

All the restaurants in Jost van Dyke double as bars and some of them have entertainment and a barbecue in the week. If you arrive mid-afternoon, you may have to wake up the barman. Alternatively come up on the radio, channels 16 or 68. You can have a candlelit dinner above the surf at the **Sandcastle** (reserve on channel 16 by 4pm; *expensive*)—black bean soup followed by Cajun blackened fresh local fish in a pineapple raisin chutney and vegetables done to a turn. If you are stopping by for a drink, try **Gertrude's** oversized bar next door.

Great Harbour is really one long string of beach bars where you can also get a meal. The large and pre-fab **Club Paradise** (*moderate*) will fix you a soup and a salad or a fish, along with a game of darts. **Ali Baba's** is a covered terrace on the sand with an attractive wooden bar. At the eastern end of the bay, beyond **Happy Laurry's** (also worth a stop) is **Foxy's** (reserve on channel 16 or ✆ 59258), a riotous place with multiple decks under rush and tin roofing on the waterfront. Endless business cards, nautical flags and the odd hammock under the palms. Foxy himself will occasionally sing to you over the barbecue and in season he has live music a couple of times a week, but the highlight of the year is the New Year's Eve party, which attracts as many as 2500 people from 300 yachts. All the bars along the waterfront have bands and so there is drinking and jumping-up until near dawn. Also very popular is Foxy's wooden boat regatta in August or September.

There is also a number of bars in Little Harbour: **Abe's by the Sea**, a covered terrace on the waterfront festooned with fishnets and fan coral, has plenty of happy punters to judge by the photographs they leave. West Indian fare and fish, some specials. At **Sidney's Peace and Love**, which is decorated in a serious shade of yellow, they leave their T-shirts as a memento instead; local fare. Close by is the purple and pink **Harris's**, a sandy terrace with drinks and simple meals.

Virgin Gorda

Virgin Gorda lies within sight of Tortola across Sir Francis Drake Channel, and when you get there Road Town seems almost like an uncaring metropolis. Life proceeds at an even more sedate pace and you will find that the people all greet each other. Come to that, they may all know each other anyway, because there are only 1500 of them. There is a charming and slow life West Indian life here, with some older wooden houses in among the newer encrustations of concrete. Most of the hotels don't have locks on the room doors on Virgin Gorda, for good reason.

Virgin Gorda was the 'fat Virgin' according to the Spaniards, because they thought its shape from the south was like a pregnant woman reclining. For a while Virgin Gorda was the capital island among the British Virgins, but in 1741 Tortola took over. The island is 8 square miles in area and, like Tortola, it is long and irregularly shaped, rising from plains in the south to

1370ft at Gorda Peak in the north. Generally speaking, the island is furred with scrub and cactus, inhabited by lizards and geckos. Supposedly there is also a very rare 5ft iguana that lives in the hills. Birds include warblers and the usual cattle egrets on the plains and you may find that the odd cheeky bananaquit takes a fancy to your lunch.

Getting There and Around

You can fly in to Virgin Gorda, on charters from San Juan or the USVI, on GAS (Gorda Aero Services, ✆ 52271), or Carib Air (✆ 51905). Otherwise fly to Beef Island and take a ferry transfer (*see* p.488).

There is nothing like a bus service on Virgin Gorda, but hitching is no problem. Taxis will let you hop in on someone else's fare and will ask for a few dollars for the ride. There are **hire-cars** and jeeps available (for regulations and prices see under Tortola). Contact Mahogany Car Rentals (✆ 55469, ✆ 55072) or Andy's (✆ 55511, ✆ 55162), both in the Valley and both quite expensive. Taxis can be found through both these operators and hotels often have cars available for their guests too.

Beaches

In the whiplashes and switchbacks of Virgin Gorda's coastline are some classic Caribbean coves crowned with coral sand. Virgin Gorda also has a fine collection of beach bars. The most popular beaches are in the southwest, a series of coves collectively called the Baths. If you are not coming by sea, then they are reached by a series of lovely paths that descend through greenery and boulders, meandering over roots that are out looking for water. Once you have reached the shoreline the sand is so soft that you will sink in up to your ankles. You can swim among the boulders as the waves break over you. In season the more popular beaches can be crowded, but it is usually possible to find a solitary spot. Watersports have to be arranged through the hotels, though snorkelling gear can be hired at the Baths.

best beaches

The Baths (in sequence heading south: Trunk Bay, Little Trunk Bay, the Baths, Spring Bay, also known as the Crawl, and Devil's Bay): They can be reached on marked paths through the scrub, leading off from **Mad Dog Bar**, a wooden house with a veranda on the hilltop, where you can get a hot dog or a sandwich. There is another more formal restaurant on the hilltop which tends to attract day trippers, **Top of the Baths.** Down on the beach itself, shaded by vast rocks is the **Poor Man's Bar**, a shack with some benches where you can get a beer and a snack.

Little Savannah Bay, **Savannah Bay**, **Pond Bay** and **Maho Bay**: Isolated coves on the west coast as you head north out of town, under the broad sweeping arc of the towering volcanic hills. A few villas and places to get a drink and something to eat, but generally pretty quiet.

Leverick Bay: A lively spot with a bar and some watersports equipment—you can windsurf over to the beaches on Mosquito Island, where there are some good strips of sand to collapse on to. You will find a classic beach bar on Prickly Pear Island. The **Sandbox** is a long wooden shack with lots of watersports—jet skis and glass-bottom boat tours—and loungers for a bit of sizzling and time out from the snorkelling.

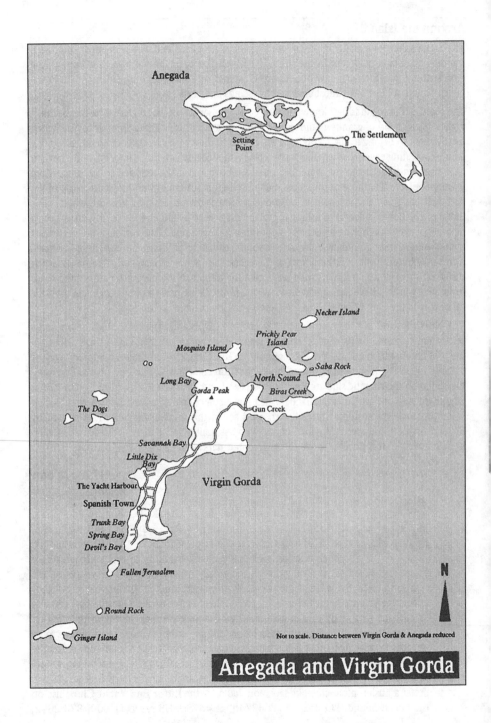

Anegada

Setting
Point

The Settlement

Necker Island

Prickly Pear
Island

Mosquito Island

North Sound

Saba Rock

Oo

Long Bay

Gorda Peak

Biras Creek

The Dogs

Gun Creek

Savannah Bay

Little Dix
Bay

The Yacht Harbour

Virgin Gorda

Spanish Town

Trunk Bay
Spring Bay
Devil's Bay

Fallen Jerusalem

N

Round Rock

Ginger Island

Not to scale. Distance between Virgin Gorda & Anegada reduced

Anegada and Virgin Gorda

Around the Island

The island splits quite neatly into two, with settlements at each end, barely connected through the hilly scrubland between. In the south is Spanish Town, or the Valley as it is known, the closest thing to a town; its few houses are clustered on rolling ground. In the north is the North Sound, a huge bay almost enclosed by islands and reefs.

The south of the island is best known for the curious assembly of vast rocks called **the Baths**, a giant's playground of granite boulders along the western shore. These smooth rocks, which hardly seem to belong in the Caribbean, are buried to their necks in sand and jumbled on one another, creating caverns where the waves crash and race and you can clamber about. They are as impressive underneath the water's surface as above and make for good snorkelling. More granite boulders like those at the Baths make up **Fallen Jerusalem** off the south coast of the island. It has this name because it looks like a ruined town crumbling into the water. (The island is a National Park and so fishing is prohibited, as is collecting the corals. You are asked to be careful when anchoring a yacht or swimming near the reef.) The remains of a very early copper mine can be found close by on the southeastern tip of Virgin Gorda. There is a small number of hotels in the southern area of the island, but plenty of bars and restaurants which thrive off the yachting traffic. A road leads past the airport to the northern part of the island; from here you will have a magnificent view down the Sir Francis Drake Passage and then the other way to the North Sound. Trails to Gorda Peak are marked off this road.

The **North Sound** is a huge protected bay encircled by islands and reefs, with hotels and a settlement clustered on its edges. The road leads left down to Leverick Bay, a tourist development of hotels and villas, and goes straight on to **Gun Creek**, a local town scattered over the hillside. Opposite them are the Bitter End Yacht Club and Biras Creek, two hotels. Enclosing the sound on the Atlantic side are Prickly Pear Island and tiny Saba Rock and Mosquito Island. Slightly further out are Eustatia Island, which has just a couple of private houses, and Necker Island, a small green lump rimmed with sand set in the translucent blue. It is owned by Richard Branson, founder of Virgin Records, who has built a house there and a couple of villas in Balinese style. It is private (above the high-water mark), but can be hired (*see* p.483).

      ✆ *(1 284 49)–* **Where to Stay**

luxury–expensive

In the northern peninsula, **Biras Creek**, PO Box 54 (✆ 43555, ▤ 43557, UK res ✆ (0800) 894 057, US ✆ (1 800) 223 1108, ▤ (310) 440 4220), is one of the Caribbean's finest hotels and has been offering high-grade, low-key luxury to returning guests for years. The 32 suites are strung out on the breezy Atlantic waterfront, where you are sent to sleep by the wash of the waves (it may seem loud on the first night, but they encourage you not to move for at least a couple of nights because most people come to love it) and in a sandy garden behind. The restaurant is set above the main house on the heights—guests gather for drinks before dinner, and then move to the dining room terrace, from which there is a superb view across the North Sound and out to the Atlantic, where the moon glints on the sea's surface. Biras Creek has a elegant and rarefied air of well-manicured Caribbean luxury and will not let you down. If you prefer a busier, more club-like feel, you could try the **Bitter End Yacht Club**, also on the North Sound, PO Box 46 (✆ 42746, ▤ 44756, US res ✆ (1 800) 872 2392,

☏ (312) 944 2860). Bitter End sells itself as a yacht club and resort, and there is a nautical feel in the dark-stained wood and brass and pewter tableware in the dining room, as well as the constant waterborne activity. And a sense of desert-island seclusion within a shout of civilization can be found in their luxurious, mock-rustic cabins on the hillside. A couple of restaurants and entertainment in season, hammocks everywhere but you should spend at least some time on the water.

A stay on **Necker Island** (☏ 42757, ✉ 44396, UK ☏ (0171) 727 8000, ✉, US ☏ (1 800) 557 4255, *www.virgin.com/ultimate/ultimate.html*) seems like the ultimate Caribbean dream for some. It has to be hired as an entire island (there are prices for up to 10 and up to 20 guests), though there are 'celebration weeks', in which couples can join a mix. The island has beds for 20 guests in the main house and the two smaller Balinese cottages (Bali Hi and Bali Lo). The open-sided main house, with its magnificent hilltop setting and views as far as Tortola, is the nerve-centre of the island. It has a snooker table and excellent sitting area with books and boardgames, video recorders and CD players, hammocks and an exercise room. Pool, tennis courts and all meals included at the huge dining-room table. A statue waves you welcome and goodbye.

In the southern half of the island, **Little Dix Bay**, PO Box 70 (☏ 55555, ✉ 55661, US ☏ (1 800) 223 7637), is a grand and luxurious resort set on a magnificent half-moon curve of sand backed with palms and seagrape. It is quite large (102 rooms), but it is well spread out in tropical gardens. The main dining room is under the distinctive double-pointed shingle roofs and around the central sugar mill. Watersports and tennis accompany Caribbean island tranquillity.

There are some **self-catering apartments** worth a look if you are happy to be isolated and to look after yourself: **Mango Bay Resort**, PO Box 1062 (☏ 55672, ✉ 55674, *mangobay@caribsurf.com*, *www. travelnx.com/mango bay*, US toll free ☏ (1 800) 451 3356) is on Mahoe Bay, just a few one- and two-bedroom villas, quite spacious but a little past their best, lost in profuse greenery on a nice beach. Another nice option, a little farther down the track in Mountain Trunk Bay, are **Diamond Beach Villas** (☏ 55452, ✉ 55875, *diamondvg@aol.com*, US ☏ (1 800) 871 3551, Canada ☏ (1 800) 487 1839), which are set in the hillside above a charming beach; very pleasant bedrooms and sitting rooms (with a balcony with a view, of course) set in one and two-room self-catering apartments with tropical gardens all around.

moderate

The **Leverick Bay Resort**, PO Box 63 (☏ 57421, ✉ 57367, US ☏ (1 800) 848 7081, Canada ☏ (1 800) 463 9396), offers the least expensive deal in the northern hemisphere. The 16 rooms stand on the hillside above the bay, each alarmingly brightly decorated with a/c and TV and full kitchen as well as a cracking view from the balcony. Very comfortable, though, and some activity around. They also handle a number of one- to five-bedroomed villas in the area. At the southern end of the island, **Guavaberry Spring Bay**, PO Box 20 (☏ 55227, ✉ 55287), is a surprising retreat: hexagonal chalets on stilts, swallowed in explosions of tropical plants and the rocks of the Baths. There are 21 rooms in one-bedroom and two-bedroom chalets, with full kitchens and all simply furnished, but with nice West Indian louvres and screens, with fans to whip up the breeze. Very peaceful and secluded, a short walk from the best of the beaches. In the Valley you can find simple but pleasant rooms in the **Ocean View**

Hotel (✆ 55230), right behind the marina in town, a modern block surrounded by trees. There is a charming smaller property, more in the style of a West Indian inn, where you are welcomed by the owners themselves, at the **Olde Yard Inn**, PO Box 26 (✆ 55544, ✆ 55986, *oldeyard@caribsurf.com*, US ✆ (1 800) 633 7411, *www.travelxn.com/oldyard*), just off the road to the north of the island. The 14 rooms, fan-ventilated (some air-conditioned if you want) overlook a charming garden, where there is a pool, jacuzzi, a library and video room and an excellent restaurant. They have won awards for their environmental policy.

cheap

You will find cheap accommodation at the **Taddy Bay** (✆ 55618) in the Valley, just two bedrooms with a kitchen for you to use.

✆ *(1 284 49)–*   **Eating Out**

In the north of the island, there are really only hotel dining rooms for eating out in the evening, though by day you can always get a snack at the beach bars—try Saba Rock and Prickly Pear Island. Categories are arranged according to the price of a main course: *expensive*—US$20 and above; *moderate*—US$10–20; *cheap*—less than US$10.

Biras Creek Hotel (*see* above) has a magnificent setting high on the hill; *haute cuisine* and a superb wine list, and a five-course dinner for a fixed price. If you are in Leverick Bay you might try the **Pusser's Restaurant** (*moderate*), bright pink and purple gingerbread with a mock-nautical ambience, plush armchairs and painkillers; local fish and international dishes. **Saba Rock,** a tiny lump which protrudes from the water near the Bitter End Yacht Club, was for a long time the classic bar from paradise; rumbustious, faintly riotous and given to impromptu jam sessions when people grabbed the intruments and played. At the time of writing is was being redeveloped and was nothing more than a flattened lump with a yellow JCB beetling around on top.

In the southern half of the island you can find a good meal at **Chez Bamboo** (✆ 55963; *expensive*). There is a brightly coloured courtyard setting with trellises and hanging plants and the fare is seafood with some French dishes. There's a charming Italian restaurant in the isolated recesses of Maho Bay (more easily reached by yacht than by car really), **Giorgio's Table** (✆ 55684; *expensive–moderate*) with a lovely view of the islands from a shorefront deck. Pizzas and pastas for lunch and more substantial fare at dinner from a short menu including *filetto ai funghi porcini* and daily specials. The **Top of the Baths** (✆ 55497; *expensive–moderate*) is a bit touristy but it does offer trusty international fare with an excellent view down to Tortola, on a terrace with a pool and shell-backed metal chairs: lunchtime fritters of the day or a salad; dinner a grilled lamb loin with mint pesto sauce from a long menu à la carte. If you feel a little regimented you can always try the Mad Dog Bar next door for a snack.

Be sure not to miss **Thelma's Hideout** (✆ 55646; *cheap–moderate*), which is set in a fairy-lit West Indian yard with trees and hanging plants just off the road to Little Dix Bay. Local fare: doved pork, baked chicken and curry goat; ring to reserve a table, and a dish. Another simple spot in town is **Anything Goes** (*moderate*), which is set on a concrete-floored and tin-roofed courtyard with a fence: grilled kingfish and local veg or burgers. The **Crab Hole** (*cheap*) is also an amusing local stopover, for a stew chicken or fish, on a simple deck with ongoing pool and dominoes in the backstreets of the Valley. The shopping centre at the marina is a gathering point and the **Bath and Turtle** (✆ 55239; *cheap*) can get quite lively. Pub food, *pâtisserie* and lending library. There are quite a few snackettes along the roadsides in Virgin Gorda: heading south out of town try **Dixie's** for a chicken or fish and an ice cream, or **Leroy's** for a local plate and juices.

Some of the restaurants in town will double as bars. Alternatively, try **De Goose,** set on a small patio under a tin roof hung with flags. Music nightly. There is a full moon party held each month on Savannah Bay.

Islands in the Chain

Heading southwest along the line of amoebic islets and cays on the southern side of Sir Francis Drake Channel, you pass Fallen Jerusalem, a national park made of similar boulders to those at the Baths and then Round Rock. Next in line, Ginger Island is uninhabited, but there is a small settlement set on the popular protected anchorage of Manchineel Bay in **Cooper Island.** Set in the palm-backed bay, there are just a few cottages, a boutique, a dive-shop, Underwater Safaris, for guided dives and tank refills (the island also has quite good snorkelling), and of course the beach bar itself, which offers daytime and evening meals—conch fritters and chicken roti and sautéed shrimp in butter and white wine, some barbecues. It depends on the crowd, but it can get very lively. The **Cooper Island Beach Club** (✆ 43721, VHF channel 16, *info@cooper-island.com, www.cooper-island.com,* US ✆ (1 800) 542 4624, ✉ (413) 863 3662) has rooms that are pretty, comfortable and *moderate* in price.

Next in the line is **Salt Island**, another 200 acres of scrubland that enclose a salt pond. Once the population of this island was as high as 100, mostly involved in the collection of salt, which they would sell to passing ships (the rent of the island is still set at one sack of salt a year payable to the Queen of England, but it is apparently not often demanded any more). Today the population is not usually more than about four or five, though building is just beginning on the sandy seafront at 'The Settlement'.

Nowadays, most people come to Salt Island to visit one of the Caribbean's finest wrecks, the shell of the 310ft RMS *Rhone*, which lies on her side in two bits in depths from 30 to 80ft, her ribs scattered higgledy-piggledy. Snorkellers can enjoy the shallower end, playing in the exhaled bubbles of the divers below, an eerie experience. The area around the wreck is a Marine National Park and so the usual rules apply.

Peter Island, which lies about 5 miles across the channel from Road Town harbour, is almost entirely devoted to an extremely luxurious hotel. The only other inhabitant lives in a small wooden house across the bay. The **Peter Island Resort**, PO Box 211 (✆ 42561, ✉ 42313, US ✆ (1 800) 346 4451; *luxury–very expensive*), was undergoing a major refurbishment at the time of writing; it has 50 rooms in all (also one excellent villa on the hilltop), of which the most elegant and comfortable are on the beach on Deadman's Bay (the redecorated rooms on the marina may rank with them now). There are two dining rooms, a drawing room with newspapers on hand-held sticks, and low-key entertainment each night in season. And there are good uncluttered beaches on the island (Deadman's Bay, where the waves break in scallop shell shapes, is charming, and White Bay is reclusive and isolated), watersports and bicycles to get around on. If you would like to go over for dinner, or for a day out on the beach (you can use the resort's facilities), the ferry sails about six times a day from the CSY marina on the eastern side of Road Town harbour.

Just off Peter Island is a cay called **Dead Chest**, a small scrub-covered lump that calls to mind the pirates who used these anchorages before today's sailors arrived. Blackbeard is supposed to have left 15 of his more rebellious sidekicks here with just a cutlass and a cask of rum. The pirates did not survive long, but the island was immortalized in the sea-shanty:

> *Fifteen men on a dead man's chest*
> *Yo ho ho and a bottle of rum.*
> *Drink and the Devil have done the rest*
> *Yo ho ho and a bottle of rum.*

The last BVI island in the chain, next to the US Virgin Island of St John, is **Norman Island**, which also features in pirate lore. Treasure has supposedly been found here. Ruins remain from past settlement, but Norman Island is home only to a few goats and seabirds today and the island's only industry is apparently smuggling. The snorkelling at the Indians and at Treasure Point caves, where there are caverns partly submerged in water, is excellent. Offshore, in the protected anchorage of the Bight, you will find one of the Caribbean's most unlikely, but sometimes most lively bars, the **William Thornton**, or the Willy T. as it is familiarly known by the crowd of latterday pirates and tourists who turn up for the evening. Built as a Baltic trader in 1915, it now has a restaurant (reserve on channel 16; *moderate*) where the hatch-covers are the tables and your legs dangle in the cargo hold serving international fare such as conch fritters, teriyaki chicken, shrimp creole, and a bar which is famous for body-shots (a variation on the theme of a tequila shot). Well worth a look if there is a crowd in.

Anegada

Anegada lies out on its own about 15 miles north of the main group of the British Virgins, visible only from the mountaintops of Tortola and Virgin Gorda. It is unlike the other islands because it is not of volcanic origin. Rather it is a coral cap that just makes it above sea level (there is nothing over 28ft), rimmed with reefs and about 14 miles of beach. Anegada means 'the drowned one' in Spanish, a fitting name because it is full of lagoons and marshes and is occasionally further soaked by passing tidal waves.

British Virgin Islands Directory

getting there

By air: The BVI are still relatively remote and you will have to make a connection to get there (the biggest aircraft that can land in the BVI is a 49-seater). The main hub in the area is San Juan in Puerto Rico and plenty of airlines make the onward connections, though if travelling from Europe you might consider changing in Antigua or St Maarten. Alternatively you can charter a small plane. The main airstrip in the BVI is Beef Island at the eastern end of Tortola, but there are also smaller strips in Virgin Gorda and Anegada. There is a departure tax of $10 if you are leaving by air and $5 if you are departing on a boat or a ferry.

By air from the UK: British Airways has a couple of flights a week to San Juan, arriving early enough to make the connection the same day. There are also charter flights. It is perhaps preferable to fly via Antigua, where LIAT usually connects with BA and BWIA flights from the UK and Europe.

At 15 square miles, Anegada is the second largest of the British islands. It is arid and scrubby and supports little life other than goats and donkeys. However, there is an ancient colony of about 400 20lb, 5ft iguanas. Once these animals lived all over the Virgin Islands, but they featured heavily in a local stew and so they are now endangered. Moves have been made to protect them by taking some to Guana Island off Tortola.

Only about 250 people live on Anegada, centred around **The Settlement,** and traditionally the islanders have depended on the sea for a living. When they were not away pirating or smuggling they fished, or looted the ships that were wrecked on the reefs.

Anegada's underwater life is superb. The coral reefs are endless forests of seafans, barrel-sponges and gorgonians, abounding with fish—parrotfish, squirrelfish and thin trumpetfish hanging upright in the water. There are an estimated 300 wrecks on Horseshoe Reef which make for good exploring. According to some estimates, there is a billion dollars of treasure on Anegada's reefs. Scuba diving and other watersports, including bonefishing and deep-sea-fishing trips, can be arranged through the Anegada Reef Hotel.

☎ *(1 284 49)–*   *Where to Stay and Eat*

The island's only hotel, the **Anegada Reef Hotel** (☎ 58002, ✉ 59362; *expensive*), is small and low-key in the best lazy Caribbean style, with just 10 oceanfront and six garden rooms (air-conditioned) among the casuarina pines on the island's protected southwestern shore. The restaurant prepares an excellent lobster as well as other seafood and fish on the beach barbecue; some jeeps for hire. At **Neptune's Treasure** (☎/✉ 59430; *moderate*) there are four rooms each with private bath and a porch in a modern building, with an honour bar; some tents available (*very cheap*). Tents are also available at **Mac's Place Camping** (☎ 58020, VHF channel 16) in Central Loblolly Bay, where a tent is *cheap* and a bare site less than US$10.

Loblolly Bay beach on the north shore has excellent sand and makes a great day out. There are a couple of beach bars to retire to for a grilled fish and a beer, the **Big Bamboo** and **Flash of Beauty.** In town you can eat at **Del's** Restaurant and Bar—shrimp or cracked conch; *all moderate*. On the north side you can try the **Cow Wreck** Beach Bar and Grill looking out onto the Atlantic waves.

© (1 284 49)–

By air from the USA: Connecting flights can be arranged via San Juan, Puerto Rico (e.g. American Airlines and Delta from Atlanta) and through the USVI (*see* pp.492–3).

By air from other Caribbean islands: There are flights to Tortola from Puerto Rico on American Eagle (local ☎ 51122), LIAT (☎ 52577), who also fly to Antigua, St Kitts and Sint Maarten, to which Winair (☎ 51711) also makes the link. Local airlines include GAS (Gorda Aero Services, ☎ 52271), and Air St Thomas (☎ 55935), which flies in from the USVI. Carib Air (☎ 51905) have scheduled flights from the USVI and the smaller Puerto Rican islands of Vieques and Culebra. Services to Virgin Gorda are more limited, though there are direct links from San Juan and St Thomas on Air St Thomas and the USVI on GAS. Planes can be chartered through GAS and Fly BVI (☎ 51747).

Ferries between the USVI and the BVI: There are plenty of ferries from **St Thomas**, USVI to **Tortola** in the BVI. Most depart from the Charlotte Amalie waterfront, touching West End on Tortola and then continuing to Road Town. The crossing takes just over an hour with customs. Companies include Native Son Inc (✆ 54617) and Smith's Ferry Services (✆ 44495). Speedy's (✆ 55240) runs a service three times a week from **St Thomas** to **Virgin Gorda**, a two-hour ride through Sir Francis Drake Channel, return fare about $40. **St John** also has links to West End on Tortola, usually four a day on Inter-Island Boat Services (✆ 54166) and an occasional sailing to Jost van Dyke and Virgin Gorda.

tourist information

UK: 110 St Martin's Lane, London WC2N 4DY (✆ (0171) 240 4259, ✆ (0171) 240 4270, *charlie.hampton@fcb.co.uk*).

USA: 370 Lexington Avenue, Suite 511, New York, NY 10017 (✆ (212) 696 0400, toll free ✆ (1 800) 835 8530), or 1804 Union Street, San Francisco, CA 94123 (✆ (415) 775 0344, toll free ✆ (1 800) 232 7770).

Germany: Wallstraße 56, D-40878 Düsseldorf/Ratingen (✆ (02102) 71 11 83).

In the **BVI** itself, the main tourist board is in the Social Security building in Road Town on Tortola, PO Box 134, Road Town (✆ 43134, ✆ 43866, *bvitourb@caribsurf.com*). The Virgin Gorda Tourist Board is in the Virgin Gorda Yacht Harbour (✆ 55181). The Tourist Board put out the quarterly *Welcome Tourist Guide*, in which you will find plenty of useful information about current events and the latest investment opportunities. There are two weekly newspapers published in the islands, *The Beacon* and *The Island Sun*. The tourist paper, the *Limin' Times* gives an up-to-the-minute breakdown of boozing opportunities.

The *Welcome Tourist Guide* has been put on-line and so you can access some information direct from the screen at Internet site *www.bviwelcome.com* or email them on *iponline@caribsurf.com*. Their Electronic Beach Bar is a general chat forum in which you can swap stories and opinions.

In a medical **emergency**, dial 999 or contact the Peebles Hospital in Road Town, Tortola (✆ 43497). On Virgin Gorda there are clinics in Spanish Town (✆ 55337) and at North Sound (✆ 57310).

The **IDD code** for the BVI is (1 284 49) followed by five digits. On-island, people always say a number as five digits, but when you call you must dial seven figures, using the prefix 49.

money

The currency of the BVI is the US dollar (adopted in 1967). You will find that major credit cards are very widely accepted in the hotels, restaurants and shops.

Banks: Mon–Thurs 9–3, Fri 9–5.

Shops: Generally keep hours of Mon–Sat 9–5.

festivals

The highlight of the BVI calendar is **carnival**, which builds up in July and culminates in early August. There are bands and calypso competitions at the Carnival Village in Road Town, Tortola, and then the carnival bands parade through the town. Go if you get the chance.

Easter sees kite-flying competitions for the kids. Many **regattas** are staged each year by the BVI Yacht Club (℗ 43286): the main event is the three days of the Spring Regatta in April, but there are also pursuit races and an Anegada race. Another fun event is the HIHO (Hook in, Hold on) Windsurfing Challenge held in June or July (℗ 40339). Scratch and Funchi bands (banjo, washboard, bathtub (bass) and sometimes ukelele and flute) play at Christmas time. Definitely worth a look are the huge party at New Year at Foxy's in Jost van Dyke and Foxy's Wooden Boat Regatta, held in May.

watersports

There are plenty of opportunities for watersports fanatics around the BVI. In fact, not to spend some time on the water is really to miss the point. For general beach-bound watersports (kayaks, windsurfers and small sailing boats) the best beach is probably Cane Garden Bay on Tortola, where you can talk to Baby Bull Watersports.

Tortola and Beef Island

Windsurfing: Equipment and lessons can be found at Boardsailing BVI, who have operations at Nanny Cay (℗ 40420), also kayaks, and Trellis Bay (℗ 52447, ● 51626) in the northeast, where the onshore winds are funnelled between the islands into the bay, which itself remains calm. BIC, Mistral and Fanatic equipment; hire $20 per hour, $55 per day.

Sailing: Obviously the islands are best known for their sailing. If you would like to test out the Virgin Islands winds and waters, but would rather not take out a 50ft yacht, many of the hotels have small sailing boats. Also you can get instruction at the Offshore Sailing School (℗/● 45119), on a five-day land-based course at the Prospect Reef hotel or a six-day live-aboard course.

Day sails: And if you're not sure you want to do the actual sailing bit, there are plenty of options for half-day or full-day trips and sunset extravaganzas; these include trips to an offshore island with picnic and snorkelling stops, usually across the channel to Norman Island or Virgin Gorda, but occasionally a full day out to Anegada. Contact the catamarans *Kuralu* (℗ 54381) or *Patouche*, a 48ft catamaran (℗ 46300). Also *Ppalu* (℗ 57500) and *White Squall II* (℗ 42564), a traditional schooner.

Scuba diving: There are some good reefs in the BVI, where staghorn and elkhorn stand tall by sponges and seafans and patrols of sergeant majors and triggerfish follow wrasses, grunts and groupers. Spiked sea urchins and spiny lobster lurk in the crevices and depths. For all the islands that soar to 1000ft from the sandy bed there are also plenty of coral-clad pinnacles that do not quite make the surface, and these make good diving grounds. The most popular sites are the **Indians** near Norman Island, **Blonde Rock** and **Painted Walls** between Dead Chest and Salt Island and Alice in Winderland to the south of Ginger Island. Also the **Dogs** off Virgin Gorda.

There is also a number of wreck dives in the islands, among them the RMS *Rhone* which is widely reckoned to be the best wreck dive in the western hemisphere. A Royal Mail ship that sank off Salt Island in a hurricane in 1867, the 310ft *Rhone* lies in depths from 30ft down to 90ft. Other wreck-dive sites include the *Chikuzen*, a ship in 70ft of water, 6 miles north of Beef Island. Further north of here, Anegada is the only coral-based island in the group and it has the richest marine life of all. There is a park fee of $1 to dive.

Dive companies include Underwater Safaris (© 43235, ● 45322, *undsaf@caribsurf. com*, US toll free © (1 800) 537 7032) at the Moorings in town, Baskin in the Sun, (© 45854, ● 45853, *Baskindive@aol.com*) at the Moorings in town, Blue Water Divers (© 42847, © 40198, *bwdbvi@caribsurf.com*) at Nanny Cay Marina. A single tank dive costs $55, two tanks $80. All companies will provide instruction and referral training if you have completed part of your training back at home.

Sport-fishing: Also good within a short distance of the BVI, so if you wish to cruise after wahoo, marlin and kingfish, contact *Blue Marlin* (© 59837) or the M/V *Whopper* at the Prospect Reef Resort (© 43311), around $650 for a full day, including tackle and bait.

Virgin Gorda

The island divides neatly into two halves: if you are staying around the North Sound all the sports are available through the various hotels. Leverick Bay has some sports including parasailing and windsurfing (also a spa for the less physically active) and Prickly Pear Cay has some motorized sports. In the south of the island there is slightly less on offer, but you can fix up some sports in the marina.

Windsurfing and **small boat sailing** (hire and lessons): This can be fixed up through the Bitter End Yacht Club on North Sound and at Leverick Bay. Other hotels will also have equipment. There are also Boston whalers for hire for the day from many places.

Day sails: Contact *Misty Isle* (© 55643) in the main marina in the Valley, and in the North Sound you can call the Bitter End or Biras Creek (© 43555).

Scuba diving: There is plenty on offer within a short boat ride from Virgin Gorda including Dog Island, Ginger Island and the Invisibles and some ships which have sunk intentionally or unintentionally. Contact Dive BVI in their shops at the Yacht Harbour near Spanish Town (© 55513) and in Leverick Bay (© 57328). Diving is quite expensive in Virgin Gorda.

Deep-sea fishing: This can be fixed up through the hotels.

other sports

Tennis: There are courts in many of the hotels on Tortola and Virgin Gorda and at the Tortola Tennis Club in Road Town.

Riding: If you would like to explore Tortola on horseback, contact Shadows Stables (© 42262), based in the Ridge Road near Skyworld, who will take you through the rainforest on Sage Mountain or down to Cane Garden Bay. On Virgin Gorda, Little Dix Bay Resort keeps some horses, if you want to explore by riding or to gallop through the surf.

Biking: If you would like to explore Tortola by mountain bike, then you can contact Last Stop Sports (© 40564, ● 40593) at Nanny Cay, who take excellent guided trips around the island. They offer a hiking/biking option in which you walk up to the rainforest on one of Tortola's old 'donkey trails' and then cycle back down to the coast on the backroads and tracks.

The United States Virgin Islands

The US Virgin Islands consist of three main islands and around 70 cays, most of which are too small to be inhabited. The largest of all the Virgin Islands is St Croix (84 square miles), which lies on its own, 40 miles south of the main group. St Thomas (33 sq m) is the next largest, and the islands' capital, Charlotte Amalie, is situated on its southern shore. Four miles east of St Thomas you will find the third main island in the group, St John (just 16 sq m).

The islands were bought by the USA in 1917. For 250 years before that they were Denmark's only colony in the Caribbean. Echoes of the Danes remain in the pretty waterfront towns with their warehouses and narrow stepped alleys (still with names like Raadet's Gade and Gamle Gade) and the now ruined plantation windmills out in the country. Danish was never really spoken here so the language has gone, but it seems strange that in a part of America they should still drive on the left. Each car that cruises by announces 'American Paradise' on its numberplate. And as somebody thrusts a rum punch into your hand as soon as you arrive at the airport, in the tropical heat, while strains of calypso fill the air, you might imagine that you are in paradise after all. It is certainly truly American in style—everywhere there are yellow hanging traffic lights, burger joints and cheery waitresses in shorts. You can have a good time here, but the paradise façade hides most of the same problems that affect the other Caribbean islands. The tourist invasion is relentless. It is big business (the USVI receive well over a million and a half visitors each year), the islands are almost completely dependent on it.

The US Virgins (with the exception of St John, where building has been purposely held back) are among the most developed islands in the Caribbean. Hotels and condominiums cover the hillsides and there can be as many as ten cruise ships in Charlotte Amalie harbour at one time. This is tourism at its most advanced—with stateside entertainment shipped in, carefully packaged 'vacationer's investment opportunities' and lots of reductions on car hire, restaurants, even watersports (particularly because the islands are still recovering from the effects of Hurricane Marilyn a couple of years after the event). There is considerable variety within the islands and it is worth making the effort to visit another island from your chosen one.

The United States Virgin Islands, particularly St Thomas, are too developed for some tastes (St John is the exception and still has genuine small-island charm), but they remain very popular, mainly with American visitors. The setting is wonderful—the towns are as pretty as any in the West Indies and, of course, the sea, sand and sailing are impeccable.

History

At the time that Columbus arrived in the Caribbean in 1492, the Virgin Islands were seeing the first waves of attacks on the Greater Antilles by the Carib Indians. These belligerent island-hoppers, who decorated themselves with red warpaint and feathers, had come up all the way from South America over the previous centuries and had squeezed out the Arawaks as far as the Leewards. They would pass through the Virgin Islands in their vast war canoes on raids from down-island, make a lightning attack and steal a few women, and then paddle back again. The Spaniards battled successfully with them over the next century, trying to keep them away from Puerto Rico. But as the first scourge receded another arrived. Pirates began to infest the islands, taking refuge there after their raids on Spanish shipping and settlements.

In the 1620s adventurers started to arrive and to plant crops—the Dutch and English and French settled in St Croix—and buccaneers took over the smaller islands, letting cattle roam and then killing it and selling the cured meat to to passing sailors (Beef Island in the British Virgin Islands takes its name from this). These islands became stopping-off points for ships travelling up and down the island chain and for those that had just crossed the Atlantic. The Virgin Islands became known as markets and goods would be brought here for distribution all over the Caribbean. Pirates would also offload their loot here, and then spend time ashore, revelling and waiting for another expedition.

The Danes moved in to St Thomas in 1665 and allowed the trading to continue. Business was so successful that by the end of the 17th century the British Admiral Benbow described St Thomas as 'a receptacle for thieves' (as seen from an English official perspective at least). In 1724 the island was declared a freeport and it was soon on its way to being the richest port of its day. The Danes claimed St John in 1684 (though they did not settle it until 1717) and they bought St Croix from the French in 1733 for 750,000 francs. Both these islands were soon covered with sugar-cane. The Danish islands' neutral status sheltered them from the worst effects of the wars between Spain, France and Britain. In wartime they were entrepôts and a haven against the marauding freebooters (hired by the warring nations to harry enemy and neutral shipping) and in peace they were the headquarters of the smuggling trade in the area. Slave auctions also brought in huge revenue. In the War of American Independence they shipped arms to the colonists. British objections to the trade led to two occupations in the Napoleonic Wars (1801 and 1807), but the islands were handed back to Denmark in 1815.

The Danes were the first to abolish the slave trade, in 1792, but slavery itself was not abolished until much later. In 1848 the Danish King Frederik VIII issued an edict that all slaves would be emancipated in 1859, but on hearing this the slaves revolted. When the Governor-General Peter von Scholten, a man with a mulatto mistress himself, faced the crowd on St Croix to make the announcement, he realized that he was unwilling to impose the law and simply announced that he was freeing them then and there. The slaves remained free and the Governor was tried for dereliction of duty, but was eventually acquitted. At about this time the islands went into financial decline: sugar failed in St Croix and St John as it did in most of the

USVI Directory

getting there

The USVI have international airports on the two largest islands, St Thomas and St Croix and these have excellent connections with the States. There is no airstrip in St John.

By air from the UK: There are no direct services from the UK or Europe to the USVI, but British Airways (✆ (1 800) 247 9297) have twice-weekly flights from London Gatwick to San Juan, Puerto Rico, and a number of charter airlines also fly the route. Connections are easy from here. There are more daily connections through Miami on American Airlines, so this might be a better option. Lufthansa (✆ 1 800 645 3880) fly to San Juan from **Frankfurt**, Maatinair from **Amsterdam** and Iberia (✆ 1 800 772 4642) from **Madrid**.

By air from the USA: St Thomas and St Croix are served by numerous airlines including American Airlines (✆ (1 800) 474 4884), who have direct services from Miami, New York and Raleigh/Durham; Delta (✆ (1 800) 241 4141, ✆ 776 1011) from Atlanta and Orlando; US Air (✆ 1 800 622 1015) from Baltimore and Philadelphia; and USVI Prestige Airlines (✆ 1 800 299 8784). Many services stop first at St Thomas then continue to St Croix. From other points in the USA, passengers can either make a connection at one of those cities or fly to San Juan in Puerto Rico, from where there are endless connections.

West Indies, and trading in St Thomas fell off too. Eventually the islands became a burden to the Danish government and so they began to look for a way of getting rid of them.

The United States first showed interest in the islands in 1866, but at that stage the Virgin Islanders themselves vetoed the transfer. The subject came up again when the Americans were concerned about German naval movements in the Caribbean in the First World War. This time the islanders voted for secession to the United States and the Americans bought the islands for $25 million. Early on the islands were administered purely as a naval base because of their strategic position, but in 1927 the islanders were granted citizenship of the USA and in 1931 the islands were placed in civil jurisdiction.

Initially the Governor was appointed by the President in consultation with the elected Senate of the USVI, but this was changed in 1970 and since then the Governor has been chosen by the Virgin Islanders themselves in elections held every four years. Since 1972 they have sent a delegate to the House of Representatives, though he has no vote and so has more of a lobbying role. Though the islanders are US citizens they do not vote in national elections. Unlike Puerto Rico, which is part of the federal banking system, taxes paid in the USVI stay within the islands. The current Governor is Roy Schneider, with elections scheduled in late 1998.

In 1931 the American President, Herbert Hoover, described the US Virgin Islands as 'an orphanage, a poor house' and, soon after, the Virgin Islands Company was established to improve the infrastructure. The production of sugar was centralized and industry was stimulated through tax incentives. In 1966 a huge oil refinery was established on St Croix by the Hess Oil Company. Other industries in operation today include the production of rum, some light manufacture and the assembly of parts from outside the islands.

The USVI have one of the highest per capita incomes in the Caribbean. By far the largest income-generator today is the tourism industry, which had topped nearly two million visitors when Hurricane Marilyn struck in September 1995. Visitor arrivals declined and many long-term residents left the islands for good. There were some difficulties in the following seasons, but the islands are building in confidence once again.

✆ (1 340)–

By air from other Caribbean islands: San Juan, which is a hub for the area, has numerous shuttle services into and beyond the USVI, both St Thomas and St Croix: Carib Air (✆ (1 800) 981 0212), American Eagle (✆ (1 800) 474 4884), Air St Thomas (✆ 776 2722). Going east and south, there are also direct links to Anguilla, Sint Maarten, St Kitts and Antigua: LIAT (✆ 774 2313), Air Anguilla (✆ 776 5789). Bohlke International Airways (✆ (1 340) 778 9177, ✉ (1 340) 772 5932) offers a charter service around the islands.

getting between the islands

There are countless island-hoppers that link St Thomas and St Croix, but the most original way to make the link is by seaplane. The service can be a little sporadic but it has been going strongly recently. These beasts (known as the 'Goose' and the 'Mallard' on island) bounce over the waves as they struggle to get airborne and once in the air they thrum like an outsize tuning fork; they are fun to ride. The terminal in St Croix is in downtown Christiansted and in St Thomas it is next to the Havensight Mall in Charlotte Amalie. Contact Seaborne Aviation (✆ 777 4491). If you would prefer not declare your body weight (needed for correct balancing of the seaplanes), then you might try Air St Thomas (✆ 776 2722, US ✆ (1 800) 522 3084) or GAS (Gorda Aero Services).

United States Virgin Islands Directory

USVI Ferries: The link between St Thomas and St John is made by boat. Ferries depart from Red Hook at the eastern end of St Thomas every hour on the hour, 8am–midnight daily, with sailings as early as 6.30am, Mon–Fri, and arrive at Cruz Bay in St John. Crossings the other way start earlier, running 6am–11pm. The crossing takes 20 mins, price $3. There is no reason to book as the ferries rarely reach their capacity. There is also a 30-min ferry from Charlotte Amalie to Cruz Bay, departing six times a day, a 45-minute ride, daily, fare $7.

There are ferries from St Thomas to St Croix at the moment, usually two runs each way each day, taking around an hour. They depart from the waterfront in St Thomas, from the Edward Wilmott Blyden IV terminal, and from Gallows Bay just outside Christiansted in St Croix: contact Virgin Hydrofoil Services (✆ 776 7417) and Fast Ferries in St Croix (✆ 773 3278).

Yacht hire and marinas: The Virgin Islands Charteryacht League, Yacht Haven, St Thomas, USVI 00802 (✆ 774 3944, ✆ 776 4468), has a large number of **crewed yachts** on their books, as has the Charter Yacht Owners' Association in Frenchtown (✆ 777 9690, ✆ 777 9750, US toll free ✆ (1 800) 944 2962, *www.usvi.net/vimi/cyoa/*). For **bareboats** you can contact a number of companies, including Caribbean Yacht Charters (✆ 775 6003) in the lagoon at Compass Point and Island Yachts (✆ 775 6666) at the American Yacht Harbour at Red Hook. If you want to hire a gin palace you can contact Virgin Island Poweryachts (✆ 776 1510). It is also worth talking to your respective tourist board or yacht broking companies in your own country. In St Thomas there are **marinas** at Flagship (at the Yacht Haven), the Sub Base, French Town and there are three in the lagoon at Red Hook. There are two annual charterboat shows in November and May each year in Charlotte Amalie harbour in St Thomas. In St John there is a marina in Coral Bay and in St Croix there is a number of marinas including Green Cay, Gallows Bay and Salt River. For day sailing cruises, *see* the watersports sections for individual islands.

tourist information

UK: 2 Cinnamon Row, Plantation Wharf, York Place, London SW11 3TW (✆ (0171) 978 5262, ✆ 924 3171), **Germany:** Hertzogspital Str 5, D-80331 Munich (✆ (089) 23 66 210, ✆ 26 04 009); **Denmark:** Park Allée 5, DK-8000, Arhus C (✆ (86) 181933, ✆ 180660) and **Italy:** Via Gherardini 2, 20145 Milano (✆ (02) 3310 5841, ✆ 3310 5827).

St Thomas

The life of St Thomas has traditionally centred around the island's magnificent harbour—a steep-sided bowl partly closed by islands—which has attracted shipping from the earliest days. The lines of 18th-century trading warehouses in Charlotte Amalie are just as busy today as they have ever been, and the harbour teems with yachts, motorboats and cruise ships.

St Thomas is one of the most developed islands in the whole Caribbean. About 50,000 people live on its 33 square miles, most of them in the extended suburb of Charlotte Amalie, the capital town in the USVI. Buildings have sprung up everywhere—villas, hotels and vacation condominiums—and there is even a rush hour. Only in the west end of the island, beyond the airport, is it less built up. In such a crowded place there is some tension (some of it racial) and it occasionally spills over into violence.

USA: 1270 Avenue of the Americas, Suite 2108, **New York**, NY 10020 (© (212) 332 2222, ✆ 332 2223); 3460 Wilshire Boulevard, Suite 412, **Los Angeles**, CA 90010 (© (213) 739 0138, ✆ 739 2005); 2655 Le Jeune Road, Suite 907, Coral Gables, **Miami**, FL 33134 (© (305) 442 7200, ✆ 445 9044); 444 North Capital St, Syite 298, **Washington**, DC 20001 (© (202) 624 3590, ✆ 624 3594). There is a freephone no. (© (1 800) 372 USVI).

Canada: 245 Britannia Rd E., Missassauga, Toronto L4Z 2Y7 (© (416) 233 1414, ✆ 233 9367).

The Head Office of the **USVI Division of Tourism** is at PO Box 6400, Charlotte Amalie, St Thomas 00804 (© 774 8784, ✆ 774 4390). Local tourist information offices are mentioned in the separate island sections. The tourist board has a website at: *www.usvi.net.*

The **IDD code** for the USVI is © (1 340), followed by a seven-figure number on the island. If you call within or between the islands, dial just the seven figures.

money

The currency of the US Virgin Islands (and the BVI for that matter) is the US dollar. Credit cards are accepted in hotels and all but the smallest shops and restaurants. Tipping is the same as in mainland USA, 10–15%.

Banks: Open Mon–Thurs 9–2.30, Fri 9–2.30 and 3.30–5.

Shops: Open 9–5 every day exc Sun, though they will often open up for the cruise ship trade.

maps and books

One of the best books to come out of the Caribbean is Herman Wouk's *Don't Stop the Carnival,* which tells the story of a statesider who comes down to the islands and sets up as a hotelier. In an unending litany of comic woe, every conceivable disaster befalls him in a book that is excruciatingly funny and ruthlessly tense (very unlike later books by Wouk). Budding hotel managers would be advised to read this book; the hoteliers themselves swear by it. It is rather difficult to look them in the eye after reading it. The **Dockside Bookshop** at Havensight Mall in St Thomas has an excellent selection of Caribbean books.

But overdeveloped as it is, the island is attractive to many for its good hotels and upbeat tempo. Top entertainment acts come down to perform in the island hotels, maintaining St Thomas's tradition as the 'nightclub of the Virgin Islands', and, of course, if you want to join the fray, St Thomas has some of the best shopping in the Caribbean.

Getting Around

There is a **bus** service around St Thomas, run by VITRAN and designed primarily for the islanders themselves. Services are reasonably frequent from the outskirts of Charlotte Amalie (along the waterfront and out through the suburbs) to Red Hook and then along the Smith Bay road and west out to Bordeaux, running until about 8pm. No standees, maximum fare $1, *'exact change only, please'.* A very small percentage of cars will stop for a hitchhiker on St Thomas, and on an island with thousands and thousands of them it can be a pretty depressing wait.

Taxis are everywhere and work to fixed rates (displayed in some hotels; the taxis themselves are unmetered). All the same it's best to make sure of the fare in advance. You might find that other passengers hop in along the way, which is accepted practice. There are single rates, but for two people the trip from **Charlotte Amalie** to the airport costs around $8, to Magen's Bay—$8, Coki Beach—$10 and to Red Hook—$10. If you don't see one on the street, taxi-drivers can always be found through the hotel lobbies. Virgin Islands Taxi Radio Dispatch is on ✆ 774 7457 and the VI Taxi Association is on ✆ 774 4550. Drivers will happily take you on a tour of the island—about $30 per hour for two people with extras paying $12. However, this can be arranged more cheaply if you are prepared to go by safari bus.

Car hire is the best way of getting about if you are travelling around the island a lot. Cars are easily available for upwards of $40 per day with insurance on top, but the roads become extremely congested in town, so leave plenty of time. A valid driving licence is enough. The many firms (at the airport and in town) include: ABC Auto and Jeep Rentals (✆ 776 1222), Dependable Car Rental (✆ 7754 2253, toll free ✆ (1 800) 522 3076), E–Z Car Rentals (✆ 775 6255, ✆ 775 7870, toll free ✆ (1 800) 524 2027), Island Car Rentals (✆ 774 3333, ✆ 776 5644) and Paradise Car Rentals (✆ 775 7282). **Scooters** are also available, with a hefty deposit ($200), for around $25 per day from Paradise Scooter Rental (✆ 775 2724). Remember that in the US Virgin Islands you must drive on the left.

You can take an airborne **sightseeing** trip on a seaplane through Seaborne Aviation (✆ 777 4491): they take off and land in the harbour and then zoom the islands, running as far north as Necker Island in the chain of the BVIs.

Beaches

All beaches are public in the USVI and there are one or two places with changing facilities. Topless and nude bathing is frowned upon. You are advised to keep an eye on belongings left on the beach while you swim.

best beaches

Magens Bay: The island's best-known and most popular beach, a superb, mile-long strip of extremely fine sand and coconut palms protected by a huge arm thrusting out into the Atlantic Ocean. It is on the north coast of the island and to get there you have to go over the central mountain range, which gives a fantastic view. Gets crowded at weekends. There are changing facilities, beach bars and restaurants, and snorkelling equipment for hire. Adm 50c, parking $1. There are one or two tiny strips of sand along the arms of Magen's Bay where you can sometimes be alone: **Community Bay,** on the northern arm near the point and **Paradise Beach** opposite here on the south side (approach by a side-road off the Hull Bay road).

Hull Bay, Stumpy Bay: Isolated coves west of Magen's Bay, sometimes big breakers for surfing.

Mandal Bay: East of Magen's Bay, quite secluded with good snorkelling, though the surf can get up.

Brewer's Beach and **Lindbergh Beach:** On the south side of the island either side of the airport and relatively free of crowds. The latter has hotels nearby where you can get a drink and a windsurfer.

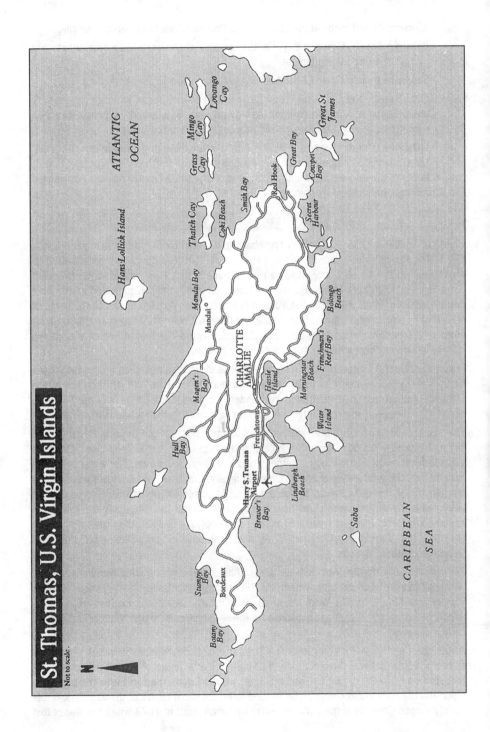

St. Thomas, U.S. Virgin Islands

Not to scale.

N

ATLANTIC OCEAN

Hans Lollick Island

Locango Cay

Mingo Cay

Great St James

Grass Cay

Great Bay

Cowpet Bay

Thatch Cay

Smith Bay

Red Hook

Coki Beach

Secret Harbour

Mandal Bay

Bolongo Beach

Mandal

CHARLOTTE AMALIE

Frenchman's Reef/Bay

Mogen's Bay

Morningstar Beach

Hassle Island

Hull Bay

Water Island

Frenchtown

Harry S. Truman Airport

Lindbergh Beach

Brewer's Bay

Saba

Stumpy Bay

Bordeaux

Botany Bay

CARIBBEAN SEA

497

Morning Star Beach: At the Frenchman's Reef Hotel, east of Charlotte Amalie.

Bolongo Beach, Cowpet Bay: On the southern shore; each has a hotel where you can hire watersports equipment.

Sapphire Beach: On the Atlantic-facing east side, good for the snorkelling.

Coki Beach: Next to Coral World (not working at the time of writing), can get very busy. There is some snorkelling and diving, but it is mainly a people beach—sunbathing, hair-braiding, jetskis and loitering by the snackwagons.

Offshore Islands: For real seclusion, it is worth considering a trip to one of the offshore islands. Recommended are Hans Lollick to the north of St Thomas, Great St James to the east and Saba and Buck Island off the south coast. Trips can be arranged through the watersports operators.

Charlotte Amalie

Charlotte Amalie is a classically pretty Caribbean town—red roofs and bursts of palm fronds that scatter the hillsides around a bay and steep alleys that lead down to the harbour. The warehouses on the waterfront are doing a roaring trade as they have on and off for over 300 years. Even in 1700 Père Labat, the roving Dominican monk and self-confessed gastronome from Martinique, found silks from India and gold-embroidered Arabian muslin cloth. It was all off-loaded by pirates who stopped in port to spend their loot before heading seawards again for more 'cruize and plunder'. The infamous Blackbeard, Edward Teach from Bristol, was known to have hidden out here when he was not on the high seas.

Encouraged by the Danes, the trade became a little more regularized and at its height the harbour would see as many as 1300 vessels in a year. In the late 18th century, the future architect of the American Constitution, Alexander Hamilton (on the reverse of the $10 bill), decided the town was so rich that 'gold moved through the streets in wheel-barrows'.

The seaborne arrivals continue—marauding characters pour off the ships, with fists full of dollars to spend—but nowadays they race past the rum shops and load up into little safari buses instead, ready to go shopping in the network of alleys downtown. The wares still come from all over the world; they are just shipped in legally, that is all. It is fascinating mercantile mayhem and it gets quite frantic, so you are advised to avoid Charlotte Amalie on a busy day (when as many as ten cruise ships have been known to call in). Originally the town was known as Tap Hus (roughly translated as the rum shop), but in 1730 the Danes renamed it after the wife of their King Christian V. As well as the name, many Danish buildings also remain in Charlotte Amalie.

The heartland of Charlotte Amalie is the alleys of brick and plaster trading warehouses, some of them from the 18th century, which are still buzzing with trade: Palm Passage, Drake's Passage and King Christian Walk. As in all West Indian islands, the main **market** in the middle of the town sells fruit and vegetables to the St Thomians who dare venture that far into town.

At the other end of Main Street (formerly Drinningens Gade, where you can find a yellow arched building that was the birthplace of Camille Pissarro, father of French Impressionism) there is a small cluster of monumental buildings around **Emancipation Park**; the huge post office and the once grand Grand Hotel (it used to be the social centre of the island, now it is mainly shops). Close by is the dark red **Fort Christian**, built in 1672 when the Danes first arrived, which stands on the waterfront guarding the bay. In its time it has been the Governor's house, the garrison and recently the prison, police station and courts. It is now home to the **Virgin Islands Museum** (*open Mon–Fri 9–noon and 1–5; adm free*) and the underground cells have displays of the simple island existence of the Arawaks and the planters' and traders' sumptuous life when St Thomas was in its prime. Over the road is the island **Legislature**, formerly the Danish barracks, a grand structure from the 1870s that is dressed up in lime-green, where the 15 US Virgin Island Senators do their business. You can listen in on a session in the gallery if you want (*open 8–5*).

On the hillside behind above the park, aloof from all the trading activity on the waterfront, is **Government House** (*open during working hours, 8–5; adm free*), a three-storey building with pretty wrought-iron balconies that was built in 1867 for the Danish colonial council and is now the official residence of the islands' Governor. Only the wooden-floored and formal entrance lobby can be visited, but you can see the names of the early Danish governors and their American counterparts and some Royal Danish porcelain, including the writing set with which Governor van Scholten signed the proclamation for the abolition of slavery.

Climbing the **99 Steps** to the top of Government Hill you come to what is known as **Blackbeard's Tower**, an extremely fine lookout, where the pirate was supposed to have lived around 1700. He was an extremely violent man, who would occasionally shoot one of his sidekicks to keep the others on their guard and he liked to adopt an especially demonic appearance when going into battle by burning fuses in his hair. He was eventually killed in a shoot-out with the British navy in 1718. On Crystal Gade you will find the **St Thomas Synagogue**, which dates from 1833, with a sand floor, local mahogany benches and Ark.

On the western outskirts of the town you come to **Frenchtown**, the original settling point of a group of immigrants from the island of St Barthélemy in the Leewards, who first came over in 1852. Their descendants form a distinct community on the island (there have been more recent influxes of immigrants too): some remain in Frenchtown and work as fishermen, others have become very influential and own some of the most valuable land on the north side.

At the opposite end of town is the Yacht Haven, St Thomas's main yachting marina, and close by is the West India Company Dock, where you will find the **Havensight Mall**, another agglomeration of tourist shops in long warehouses. If the hustle gets too much, you might take a ride up the hill, in a bubble-car ski-lift of all things, to **Paradise Point**, another shopping centre, for a fine sunset view and and excellent banana daiquiri. You can arrange a personalized tour of Charlotte Amalie, conducted by a guide with a special knowledge of its history, on ✆ 771 2346.

Around the Island

The island of St Thomas is highly developed all around. The hills above Charlotte Amalie are covered with homes to their summits and wherever you go on the island you are not far from a residential area. Near the top of the central range is **Drake's Seat**, the vantage point supposedly used by Sir Francis Drake in his privateering days in the 1580s. Where the old English sailor had henchmen to scour the magnificent view across to the BVI for ships, today's visitors will find T-shirt vendors. At the actual summit is Mountain Top, where there is another cracking view of the north coast, complete with shopping centre for when the view palls.

Worth a visit in this area is the **Estate St Peter Greathouse Botanical Gardens** (℗ 774 4999), where you can see countless examples of tropical plants, from the many different Caribbean floral regions—cacti, water-plants, tropical crops (including 20 species of bananas) and flowering trees, ornamental flowers like heliconia, Indian head ginger and an orchid jungle; 300 species in all alongside a small aviary, a nature trail and iguana and monkey habitats. The great house has been modernized and is surrounded by decks and lookouts, from where there is an excellent view of Magens Bay.

The southeast of the island is built up with condominiums and vacation homes that take advantage of the beaches in that area. **Coral World** was closed at the time of publication but was due to reopen during the lifetime of the book. (It is a small underwater world complex at Coki Beach in the east of the island, with good displays—a walk-in observatory 20ft underwater and a predator tank where sharks and tarpons patrol.) The west end is the least developed area of St Thomas and is mainly residential.

℗ *(1 340)*–   ### Where to Stay

St Thomas has its share of large and expensive luxury beach resorts, mainly scattered along the south and east coasts of the island, but it also has a surprising collection of excellent small hotels in Charlotte Amalie, many of them set in charming antique townhouses on the hillside with a view of the town below. Many hotels offer packages if you contact them in advance, but it is made easy for you if you arrive without a booking because there is a hotel booking booth with direct phone lines at the airport. Villas are also available all around the island, many of them on the slightly less developed north side: contact **McLaughlin Anderson Villas**, 100 Blackbeard's Hill, VI 00802 (℗ 776 0635, ● 777 4737, toll free ℗ (1 800) 537 6246) or **Calypso Realty**, PO Box 12178, VI 00801-5178 (℗ 774 1620, ● 774 1634, ℗ (1 800) 747 4858). The government adds a 8% room tax to all bills and most places charge 10% for service.

Beach Hotels

luxury–very expensive

The most elegant and luxurious place to stay in St Thomas is the **Ritz-Carlton**, Great Bay, USVI 00302 (℗ 775 3333, ● 775 4444, US res toll free ℗ (1 800) 241 3333). The balustrades and pediments of a mock Italian renaissance palace painted in tones of peach look a little odd amid the permanent blooms of bougainvillea and the luxuriant Caribbean sky, but the amphitheatrical setting of the rooms, standing in blocks above a superb bay, is magnificent. Watersports around the pool and beach, rarefied atmosphere in the main house and dining rooms, very plush, with shops. The **Marriot's Morning Star Beach Resort**, PO Box 7100, St Thomas 00801 (℗ 776 8500, ● 776 3054, US ℗ (1 800) 524 2000), also has a secluded feel, just outside Charlotte Amalie. It has 96 extremely comfortable rooms, set in blocks along a good beach where there is a pool, with modern facilities such as cable TV and some attractive older Caribbean features such as balconies and louvred shutters, all dressed in buttery yellow and bright blue. If you like a large and active beach resort try the **Stouffer Grand Beach Resort**, PO Box 8267, St Thomas 00801 (℗ 775 1510, ● 775 2185,

US res ✆ (1 800) HOTELS 1, UK ✆ (0800) 181737), at the eastern end of the island. About 300 rooms, air-conditioned and all amenities, all the watersports, fitness centre, beauty salon, kids' programme. At the **Point Pleasant Resort**, 6600 Estate Smith Bay (✆ 775 7200, ✉ 776 5694, toll free ✆ (1 800) 524 2300) there are 134 extremely comfortable suites in villas ranged on a steep hillside with wonderful gardens and wooden decks that give a superb view of the isalnds to the east. Each has a large and breezy main room.

expensive

A smaller, very private retreat, with personal service, is **Pavilions and Pools**, 6400 Estate Smith Bay, St Thomas 00802 (✆ 775 6110, ✉ 775 6110 ext 215, US res ✆ (1 800) 524 2001), where there are 25 large, recently restored units on the forested hillside either side of a small central area. Each has a view through glass windows to a private deck with a personal pool and all are air-conditioned with kitchenettes, cable TV, VCR and phones and have showers with garden greenery. Trails down to Lindquist Beach, all the activity of Sapphire Beach nearby; good idea to have a car.

moderate

Set in a profuse tropical garden and looking out on to a very pleasant curve of sand on Lindberg Beach, quite close to the airport, is the **Island Beachcomber Hotel**, PO Box 30579, St Thomas 00803 (✆ 774 5250, ✉ 762 5615, US ✆ (1 800) 982 9898). It is lower-key than most of St Thomas's beach hotels. The 50 rooms are in simple two-storey blocks over looking the beachside bar. Some watersports. Another *cheaper* option can be found at the **Bolongo Beach Resort,** 7150 Bolongo, St Thomas 00802 (✆ 775 1800, ✉ 775 3208, toll free ✆ (1 800) 524 4746), not in the main part of the resort, but in the annexe behind where there are simple rooms. A variety of packages on offer (most guests are all-inclusive), but you can use the hotel facilities or just use the rooms as a base. An excellent and very informal spot, overlooking Hassel Island from just beyond Frenchtown, is the **Admiral's Inn** (✆ 774 1376, ✉ 774 8010, US ✆ (1 800) 544 0493, *admirals@admirals.com, www.admirals.com/*). It is set around an old holiday villa (where the dining room is) and the rooms and pool stand above it on the hillside, painted in a faintly alarming medley of canary yellows, pinks and sky blues. Good atmosphere from travellers who chat to one another over breakfast. Just above the beach in Estate Nazareth at the southeastern corner of the island is the **Sea Horse Cottages**, PO Box 2312-1306, St Thomas 00803 (✆ 775 9231). There are 16 units in one- and two-bedroom configurations, in cottages and a small block, each with kitchenette, set in a pleasant tropical garden that descends the hill to the coast. Pool, small beach and snorkelling a breath off the coast. Very relaxed atmosphere.

Town House Hotels

If you would like to experience some of St Thomas's antique charm, Charlotte Amalie itself has some sophisticated and tranquil retreats. The **Hotel 1829**, PO Box 1567, St Thomas 00804 (✆ 776 1829, ✉ 776 4313, US ✆ (1 800) 524 2002; *very expensive–moderate*), on Government Hill, has an excellent old-time island ambience. The original stone and brick of the town house is exposed in places and there are patterned tiles and Tiffany stained glass. There are 14 suites and rooms, some huge, with a magnificent setting overlooking the town and harbour (in the time-honoured tradition of traders), others tucked away at the back looking over the courtyard where there is a pool. Often a lively atmosphere in the cavernous backgammon bar and on the balcony restaurant (renowned around the island). The **Galleon House**, PO Box 6577, St Thomas 00804 (✆/✉ 774 6952, US ✆ (1 800) 524 2052; *moderate–cheap*), is not far off and has cracking views of the red roofs of Charlotte Amalie. There are 14 comfortable rooms, a pool and (best of all) a central dining terrace where a friendly crowd gathers to read or listen to the wind-up piano—anything from the 'Blue Danube', through ragtime to James Bond theme tunes. The **Villa Santana,** USVI 00802 (✆/✉ 776 1311; *moderate*), stands among the many private villas and homes of Denmark Hill and its seven rooms have plenty of charm, set in stone and wooden buildings from the last century. The rooms are smartly decorated, with lacquered wooden furniture. There is a pool, but otherwise the facilities are limited: very quiet, best for independent travellers who will be out exploring. The **Danish Chalet Inn,** PO Box 4319 (✆ 774 5764, ✉ 777 4886, US res toll free ✆ (1 800) 635 1531; *moderate–cheap*), is a home away from home, where there are 10 rooms with plenty of modern comforts (a/c, TV, VCR, phone) in a private house high up overlooking the town; some share baths. Friendly atmosphere. The **Heritage Manor Inn**, PO Box 90, St Thomas 00804 (✆ 774 3003, ✉ 776 9585, US res ✆ (1 800) 828 0757), is at 1A Snegle Gade in town, a pretty pink façade with cast-iron balustrades and white stucco. Just eight rooms, with fans, air-conditioning and shared kitchen, small pool at the back cut in the stone of the old oven, some shared baths.

The **Miller Manor**, PO Box 1570 (✆ 774 1535, ✉ 771 598; *cheap*), with the faded elegance of a town house and a fantastic view of the bay, has 24 passable rooms. Higher up the hill, perched 500 feet above the harbour you will find a very good deal at the **Island View** Guest House, PO Box 1903, USVI 00803 (✆ 774 4270, ✉ 774 6167, US res toll free ✆ (1 800) 524 2023, *islandview@worldnet.att.net*, *www.st-thomas.com/islandviewguesthouse*; *cheap*), where there are 15 rooms with comfortable furnishings and a variety of shared and private bathrooms. At a pinch, if you are down to your last few dollars, go to the marina and ask a yacht owner if you can sleep in a berth on board while the yacht is not on charter; some owners are prepared to allow this in exchange for a few hours' work.

✆ *(1 340)–*   **Eating Out**

As a developed island, St Thomas has a grander variety of restaurants than others, and so you can eat anything from 'contemporary exotic' and even 'passionate' cuisine through to good local rice 'n' peas. Many menus are solidly American—burgers and steaks—but everything can be imported, so you will find fine French fare as well as Caribbean seafood and fish. Categories are arranged according to the price of a main dish (excluding lobster and steak): *expensive*—US$20 and above; *moderate*—between US$10 and $20; *cheap*—US$10 and below. A 10% or 15% service charge will be added to your bill, for your convenience... *'Tipping* is not a city in China...'

expensive

Some of the best local food can be found in Frenchtown, just outside Charlotte Amalie. Here you will find a charming restaurant at **Craig and Sally's** (✆ 777 9949), where there is an easy air supported by quiet opera and classical music. It is set indoors, but has trelliswork walls and murals of Caribbean scenes. An eclectic menu with tastes drawn from around the world, presented with artistic flair—a grilled salmon fillet with spicy cilantro and a fresh papaya sauce. Award-winning wine list, with bottles stacked against the walls. On Back Street you will find the ever-popular **Virgilio's** (✆ 776 4920), which serves classic Italian dishes in a small, but brisk and busy dining room hung with pictures and stained-plastic windows. Eggplant *parmigiana*, followed with pastas and meat and vegetarian dishes. There is an extensive wine-list and it is worth going just for the cappuccino, to which is added a secret recipe of eleven ingredients including Galliano, Bailey's and Kahlua. **Hervé's** (✆ 777 9703) has a very pleasant veranda setting on Government Hill, where you can dine on cuisine that is 'classical French' and 'contemporary American'. Black chairs and red and white tablecloths on a terrace dining room overlooking the lights of town to go with black sesame-crusted tuna in a ginger-raspberry sauce or grilled lamb chops stuffed with spinach and served with Montrachet and pine nuts on a chilled pear purée. Just up from here, the dining room at the **Hotel 1829** is well thought of around the island and has a very pleasant setting for excellent international fare. The **Chart House** (✆ 774 4262) at Villa Olga has a charming setting among the old stonework and wood and metal balconies of the old villa itself. International fare and cheery American-style service: Caribbean lobster and Alaskan king crab, pastas and salads.

moderate

Back in Frenchtown, **Alexander's Café** (✆ 776 4211) serves Austrian and Central European food in plush, black and white air-conditioned comfort decorated with Alpine scenes—wursts, Nürnberger Rostbraten and schnitzels. *Lunch and dinner, closed Sun.* **Alex's Bar and Grill** next door serves simpler meals to music and the television; grilled honey-mustard shrimp and club sandwiches, lively crowd at the bar. Close by is a typically Caribbean waterfront bar and restaurant, **Hook, Line and Sinker** (✆ 776 9708) where you sit at bench seats on a wooden deck looking out into the marina. Simple fare, burgers, fried fish and steaks. Behind Frenchtown on Crown Bay you will find a charming setting on the waterfront at **June's Seaside Saloon.** Very pretty white wooden deck and a choice from a long Caribbean and international menu.

For something a little more West Indian try **Cuzzins** (✆ 777 4711) on Back Street in town, an air-conditioned lounge with brick walls, popular for local food—curried and stewed meats (chicken, conch, mutton and goat) accompanied by bewildering local vegetables. In all the mayhem of the downtown alleys you will find a very nice cool and air-conditioned stopping point for a lunch or an afternoon, at **Gladys' Café** (✆ 774 6604), in the chichi setting of the old warehouses of the Royal Dane Mall: pasta primavera with sautéed conch, lots of sandwiches and vegetarian dishes. Then you can stumble out as the sun goes down and head for **Cafesito,** which uses the best of its position on the streetfront looking out into the harbour. Courtyard with parasols and trelliswork for tapas and pitchers of sangria and more substantial Mediterranean dishes.

Beyond Charlotte Amalie you will find good fare and an easy-going atmosphere at the ever-popular **Blue Marlin** (✆ 775 6350), where you dine on a tin-roofed, double-level deck looking out onto the lagoon. Excellent fish and seafood: try shrimp and linguini with a Thai-spiced lemongrass broth and roasted peppers and follow with sea scallops or sea bass. There is usually a lively, young crowd at the **East Coast** restaurant (✆ 775 1919) in Red Hook, which is set in a wooden building with a terrace out front. Start off in the sports bar and then move through for lots of fresh fish or shrimp scampi or conch *parmigiani*. **Eunice's Terrace** (✆ 775 3975) offers a trusty West Indian meal on a terrace hung with greenery close to the Renaissance Grand Beach Resort: start with conch fritters and follow with boiled fish or escoveitch. Even more remote, on the north side of the island you will find a good restaurant at **Ferrari's Ristorante** (✆ 774 6800), which is usually frequented by the locals. Here you will get Italian food, lots of linguini, on a balcony with a superb view.

cheap

On the waterfront in town is **Percy's Bus Stop**, a London bus, a No.12, somehow re-routed on its journey to Piccadilly Circus; red tablecloths and a single decorative flower, simple West Indian fare, stew chicken or conch. Finally, if you do not want to spend too much and don't mind dining out of a polystyrene box on your knees, then you can get an excellent batter chicken or ribs swimming in barbecue sauce, set in a lump of coleslaw, at **Bill's Texas Pit BBQ**, strategically placed snackwagons on the waterfront in downtown Charlotte Amalie.

Bars and Nightlife

 An excellent bar to start the evening with in Frenchtown (whether you'll eat nearby or not) is the **Epernay Champagne Bar**, where hip chicks and executives gather after work for sushi and goat cheese. Close by, **Alexander's Bar** is also a lively gathering point. Otherwise you might try one of the small town hotels—**Blackbeard's** or **1829**, where the bars some-times have piano players.

Downtown there are lively bars at **Rosie O'Grady's** and down on the waterfront at the **Green House**, ever-cheery, ever-lively, every night a happy hour. You could even try the **Hard Rock Café** (much in the style of other Hard Rocks around the world), if that's your thing. You can catch a game of pool or air-hockey with a few locals at **Wet Willie's** at the eastern end of town. There are also bars in the Sub Base area: **Tickles** is a yachties' hangout, so it gets quite lively. Try **Barnacle Bill's** (the outsize lobster on the roof was blown off in the hurricane, but you should spot it by the noise of a band playing or by the sounds of talent-night on a Monday). In Red Hook there is a cracking bar, a shed in a parking lot (at Red Hook Plaza), **Duffy's Love Shack**. Bamboo rattan interior, tables out on the tarmac, lots of exotic cocktailsand Jimmy Buffet music; and the theme to *2001* if you order a *Love Shack Volcano*. All quite fun, some food, dancing later on; on Wednesday ladies drink free. The bar at **East Coast** can be fun and there is often a rumbustious white crowd at the **Warehouse**—'*A Poor Man's Bar; No pets; No dirtbags*'; pool, pinball, loud rock music and a load of beer.

The **jazz** has just begun to reappear after the Hurricane (check the papers and tourist magazines). And if you want to go dancing, there are places open, usually at week-ends. **Sib's Mountain Bar** gathers a young crowd at weekends and you might try **Havana's** at the West End close to the airport. After you've gone at it too much on Friday and Saturday you can join the crowd of other sybarites recovering on Sapphire Beach on Sunday afternoon.

For general information about the US Virgin Islands, see USVI Directory, pp.492–5.

tourist information

While on island you can get tourist information at the **airport**, at **Emancipation Square** in Charlotte Amalie and at the **West India Company dock**, where the cruise ships let off their passengers. There is a plethora of tourist material and the island produces a bright yellow brochure, *St Thomas This Week*, with advice on beaches, watersports and other essentials like shopping and investment in real estate.

In a medical **emergency**, contact the St Thomas Hospital and Community Health Centre (© 776 8311). The bigger hotels sometimes have a doctor on call. You are advised to be careful with regard to **personal security** after dark in Charlotte Amalie.

shopping

St Thomas (particularly) and the other Virgin Islands offer some of the Caribbean's finest hunting grounds for shoppers. As you step off the cruise ship, the dockside warehouses are ranged in front of you and there is literally no manufactured accessory you cannot find. In St Thomas prices will occasionally be marked at about 60 per cent of their stateside price. American citizens are encouraged to spend with special tax concessions when they return home—their duty-free limit is doubled from $400 worth of goods to $800, with yet more concessions on drink (USVI rum).

There are two main shopping areas on St Thomas, the **Havensight Mall**, by the West India cruise ship dock, where three lines of air-conditioned glass-fronted boutiques jostle for business, and **downtown** Charlotte Amalie, which has been involved with trade for over 300 years and is really an outsize emporium. It is a network of alleyways and streets with everything on sale from Swiss watches and jewellery from the world over to Chanel perfumes and the *chic*-est French modes. There is a small mall at Mountain Top, so you can shop with a view if you want. It is known for arts and crafts, as is Tillett Gardens. The new mall at Paradise Point (just a cable-car ride above Havensight Mall) has an artisan's gallery.

You can try La Romana for Italian clothes, A. H. Riise or Little Switzerland for jewellery purchases and Tropicana for perfumes. Gucci have just one shop for leather clothes and you can try Louis Vuitton for leather goods as well.

watersports

The hotels have windsurfers and small sailing craft available if you wish to sail around the bay in a hobie cat or a sunfish and snorkelling gear for exploring underwater. If life is more fun on a wetbike, again try the big hotels, particularly around the eastern end of the island, where the liveliest beaches are Lime Tree Beach, Coki Beach and Sapphire Beach. You can even arrange parasailing in the comfort of a flying deck-chair and complete with stereo.

Windsurfing: Can be fixed up at the hotel beaches on the south shore and on the eastern sides where the winds are the best, for example at Point Pleasant Resort (© 775 7200) where they have *BIC* equipment. Any major hotel will have equipment, but for the best winds, try Bluebeards Beach and Sapphire Beach, where **kayaks** are also available.

Day sails: For snorkelling and a picnic on an offshore cay or an isolated bay, try the catamarans *Daydreamer* and *Coconut* (© 775 2584). For a bit more old-time Caribbean authenticity you can sail to an offshore cay on a traditional gaff-rigged boat, the *Jolly Rover* (© 775 6500).

Deep-sea fishing: Is good off St Thomas and is easily arranged. Wahoo, skipjack, sailfish, tuna and white and blue marlin cruise the depths around the islands and there is something to catch at all times of the year. Contact *Marlin Prince* (© 779 5939) and *Fish Hawk* (© 775 9058) among the sleek chrome machines at Red Hook, or *Prowler* (© 779 2515). Powerboats can be rented through See and Ski (© 775 6265) and Nauti Nymph (© 775 5066).

Snorkelling: The Virgin Islands are surrounded by reefs and St Thomas has some excellent reefs where you can hang around in a school of triggerfish or linger among the seafans. Coki Beach is often busy and other spots include Sapphire Beach, Secret Harbour, Great Bay and Botany Bay. Offshore islands with good reefs include Hans Lollick to the north and Lovango Cay, Mingo Cay and Grass Cay off the east coast. You can take a **kayak** tour with a difference, an educational tour through the mangroves and lagoons, where you will see ducks, rays and tarpon and learn about the importance of the mangrove swamp; Virgin Islands Ecotours (© 777 2155).

Scuba diving: There's also plenty on offer to divers around St Thomas. The crystalline water often has visibility up to 100ft, and the Virgin Island outcrops, forested above the surface, are covered in coral below. Simple dive-sites off the south coast include Cow and Calf and the shelves of St James Island, Water Island and Flat Cay near the airport, and more advanced sites are the tunnels at Thatch Cay and the spine of Sail Rock off the west coast. They also go to the RMS *Rhone* off Salt Cay in the BVI.

Once again, the hotels usually lay on equipment and often they can give instruction, but there are outside dive operators if you are travelling independently. Try the Chris Sawyer Diving Centre (© 777 7804, ● 775 9495) and Coki Beach Divers (© 775 4220, toll free © (1 800) 474 *COKI*) at Coki Beach in the east and Underwater Safaris (© 774 1350). Dives cost from about $50 for a single tank dive. There is a decompression chamber on the island (© 776 2686).

If you would prefer not to get wet, you can try Atlantis Submarine (© 776 5650), which provides excursions under the waves for a close inspection of the submarine underworld. It leaves from the Havensight Mall, near the cruise-ship dock for reservations, price around $50.

other sports

Golf: The 18-hole Mahogany Run Course (© 777 6006) is on the northern side of the island, east of Magen's Bay. Green fees about $45. Watch out for the Devil's Triangle, holes 13, 14 and 15, the middle one of which has you driving over the sea.

Tennis: There are limitless courts on the island and a game is best fixed through a hotel. Guests usually play for free but visitors will be charged a fee.

Mountain biking: Island Bike Adventures (© 776 7127) offer a tour on the north side of the island that runs down from the heights to Magens Bay.

St John

First appearances are enough to reveal that St John is altogether different from St Thomas. Unlike its larger neighbour, where houses line the hillsides to their very summits, St John is mostly green and forested. As you make the short crossing over the Pillsbury Sound to the island, the pressurized tempo of St Thomas will evaporate and St John will welcome you with a nonchalant calm.

Since 1956 St John has taken a different path from the other Virgin Islands. Laurence Rockefeller and his Jackson Hole Preserve Corporation granted about half of the island to the National Parks. That part of St John has remained undeveloped since then and so much of the land is now undisturbed forest. The National Park has opened up the forests with walking trails and holds seminars on the natural life of the island. The development that there is is really only in two clusters, around Cruz Bay in the west and Coral Bay in the east.

St John still has a unique atmosphere; there is an easy small-island charm with the upbeat activity of a seafront holiday resort. And yet all the comforts of modern America are within a whisper (or a short trip by car ferry to St Thomas). The islanders joke that St John is really a part of the BVI and in some ways it feels more similar to them than to St Thomas. There is a close-knit community, with its large proportion of expatriates, and generally they welcome the tourists and the yearly invasion of 'snowbirds' (migrant winter residents) graciously.

The capital, Cruz Bay, has just a few streets which are centred on the harbour and clamber up the hillside above the bay. The waterfront has a feel of a modern Caribbean playground—neat and tidy with little complexes of shops and restaurants and day-trippers shifted around in safari buses—but there are lots of bars which come alive at night and over the hill there is a robust local community. On the eastern shores, over the uninterrupted stretches of green, you will find the only other settlement, Coral Bay, where there is another small community, hillsides of private villas and some cool and easy waterfront haunts. It is not hard to imagine how life was 50 years ago when the islanders travelled everywhere by donkey on small trails cut out of the forest. All may be quiet today, but once St John was as much a hive of plantation activity as the rest of the Caribbean islands. Two hundred years ago the slopes were cut with terraces for the sugar-cane. In 1733 St John saw one of the Caribbean's most successful slave rebellions, in which the Africans revolted and held out for over nine months, successfully beating off attempts by Danish and British troops to put them down. When they were eventually defeated by French soldiers brought in from Martinique, many preferred to commit suicide by jumping off the cliffs at Mary's Point rather than allow themselves to be returned to slavery. Just a few plantation ruins remain, throttled by the jungle.

As on all the islands, the vast majority of St John's income derives from tourism. Over half a million tourists visit the island each year, the majority on day trips from the cruise ships in St Thomas. Things are developing on the island too. Outside the National Park, ever more villas and private homes spring up on the available private land (though building was slowed a little by Hurricane Marilyn in 1995).

Today's population of 4500 is less than that in the island's plantation heyday. Nowadays the island is tranquil, favoured by a few writers and recluses and by campers (St John goes out of its way to provide a nature-based holiday for those who want it and the campsites are often booked up well in advance). The desperation suffered by the rebellious slaves seems as far away as the mercantile mayhem of St Thomas.

There is no **bus service** in St John and so if you do not want to pay for a taxi, you will have to hitch a ride, which is not that easy, or walk. If you can persuade a taxi driver to take you, **taxi** rates, for two people, are as follows: **Cruz Bay** to Trunk Bay—$7.50, Cinnamon Bay—$8, Annaberg—$12.50, Coral Bay —$12.50. You may find that somebody hops on to your ride and shares the price. A two-hour tour of the island by taxi will cost $30.

Cars are available for hire, though when you are out driving you should watch for safari buses and water delivery trucks on the steep bends. Jeeps are popular here and daily rates start at around $50. Companies include Delbert Hill Jeep and Auto (✆ 776 6637), Avis (✆ 776 6374), St John Car Rental (✆ 776 6103) and Spencer's Jeep Rentals (✆ 776 6628), all of them in Cruz Bay. Remember to drive on the left.

Beaches

St John has some magnificent beaches. Between the forested fingers of the coastline, the water in the coves is crystalline and on a sunny day it will glow in the richest shades of turquoise. The most accessible beaches are located along the switchback meanderings of the northern coast. They are distinctly more secluded than the beaches on St Thomas, but this does not prevent crowds building up on the more popular ones, particularly if a cruise ship crowd is in.

best beaches

Trunk Bay: St John's answer to Magen's Bay, mounds of blinding white sand backed by palm trees. There are changing rooms, a snack bar, a hire shop, lifeguards and a snorkelling trail through the corals, where you will be surrounded by parrotfish and tangs.

Cinnamon Bay: East of Trunk Bay, rimmed with the softest sand and has a snack bar and changing rooms attached to the Cinnamon Bay campsite.

Maho Bay: Next cove along, excellent sand, and the cove connected to it, **Francis Bay**, has good snorkelling. Both bays have a superb view out over the other islands.

Gimbey or **Jumby Bay**: Heading back to Cruz Bay from Trunk Bay, a small and charming strip of sand (quite difficult to find, down wooden steps), secluded and completely without facilities: nearby is another couple of thin strips of sand in **Hawksnest Bay,** where you can usually be alone.

Caneel Bay: The hotel has a number of small beaches within the grounds, though access is sometimes restricted because it is over the hotel's private land.

Salt Pond Bay and **Lameshur Bay**: Off the beaten track on the south coast, where there are few people, calm water and good sand. Take a picnic and drinks if you plan to stay for the day.

Off-shore cays: Include Henley Cay (out from Caneel Bay) and Lovango Cay (farther out), both worth the visit for their sands. Off Leinster Bay in the north is Waterlemon Cay, a short ride out of Francis Bay, where the snorkelling is good.

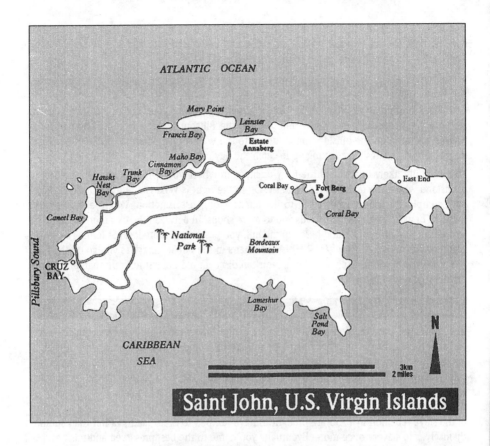

Saint John, U.S. Virgin Islands

St John National Park

The 13,000 acres of the St John National Park are managed from the office in Cruz Bay, where you can get information, along with films and maps, at the Visitors' Centre, opposite Mongoose Junction. The park is cut and crossed with about 20 **walking trails**, and many species of plants in the forest are marked. Some 5600 acres of the National Park are offshore, covering reefs and marine life.

A number of activities are arranged: some from the National Park Office in Cruz Bay (the bird walk), some from the Cinnamon Bay Campground (✆ 776 6330, the Reef Bay hike) and others which are self guided (the snorkel trail in Trunk Bay, Annaberg, the petroglyph trail). The guides are well versed in island flora, fauna and history.

The walks and snorkelling tours cover all the terrain of St John, from the mangroves on the shoreline at Leinster Bay, where you may see gallinules and a mangrove cuckoo among the leafy sprouts, and into the lusher vegetation on the upper mountainsides. On the offshore islands you can see frigatebirds and the usual boobies and pelicans. A popular hike leads from

Centerline Road in the middle of the island over to Reef Bay, from where they arrange a trip back by boat to save you the walk. Day hikes may include picnics and snorkelling breaks. There are also evening slide shows in the camp grounds.

Cruz Bay

Cruz Bay, the miniature capital of St John, is a typically cheery West Indian waterfront town set on a west-coast bay just a few miles across the Pillsbury Sound from St Thomas. The houses scattered on the hillside tumble down to the waterfront, where a couple of pint-size pastel-painted arcades have sprung up to catch the day-trippers.

You are quite likely to arrive at the ferry dock, from where you will walk straight out into a bandstand where the taxi drivers like to sit. Off to the right is Wharfside Village, a small shopping complex; a little further away to the left is Mongoose Junction, where a very pretty network of walkways and stairs leads you to more shops. In between the two there is a cluster of restaurants and bars. Behind here, up the hill, you pass into a more local St John. The small island **museum** (*open Mon–Fri 9–5*) is downstairs in the public library as you go up the hill. Alongside the St Johnian schoolchildren, you can discover old-time St John through prints and the descriptions of their slave revolt in 1733.

Around the Island

In its plantation days the slopes of St John were completely covered in sugar-cane, but since the early 19th century the land has been left, and so the island is now carpeted with 50ft-high jungle. Just a few mill ruins poke out from beneath the overgrowth. To drive along the north coast, follow the bay past Mongoose Junction, where the road starts to switchback, clambering up the slopes and sweeping down into the successive bays. On each headland there is a view of the other Virgins. At Mary Point is a ravine called Minna Neger Ghut, where the last survivors of the slave rebellion in 1733 are thought to have jumped to their deaths rather than submit themselves to slavery once more. Eventually you come to the best-preserved and most accessible of the estate ruins at **Estate Annaberg** (*open in daylight hours, no guides; adm free*), a former sugar plantation with displays showing the process and describing the buildings.

Centreline Road carves a path into the forested hills, wiggling over the impossibly steep slopes and passing beneath Bordeaux Mountain, St John's highest peak. From **Coral Bay Overlook** there is a superb view of the islands to the northeast, looking along Sir Francis Drake Passage towards Virgin Gorda about 20 miles away. From here the road descends towards St John's only other settlement at Coral Bay, a light smattering of houses around the harbour (though increasing madly at the moment) with an easy-going atmosphere in the waterfront bars and restaurants. Coral Bay was the first area settled by the Danes and Fort Berg, the dilapidated fort on the point, dates from 1717, the year they arrived. Beyond the town, roads lead both south around the coast and to the eastern tip; these areas are mainly residential.

© (1 340)–   **Where to Stay**

There is a small selection of hotels on St John, mostly concentrated around Cruz Bay. Another option is to consider taking a villa, of which there are plenty on the island (*see* p.512). There are also a couple of campsites, if you want to see the National Park from close up. Government tax of 8% is levied on all hotel bills.

Caneel Bay, PO Box 720, St John 00831 (✆ 776 6111, ✉ 693 8280, US res ✆ (1 800) 928 8889, ✉ (212) 758 6640, *www.rosewood-hotels.com*), is set on the magnificent sweep of Caneel Bay, with rooms ranged along the waterfront overlooking Pillsbury Sound and St Thomas. Set amid lawned expanses and superb manicured gardens, the restored stone estate buildings lend the hotel an elegant and stately air, but there is also plenty of activity for those who want it in the way of watersports. It has been upgraded recently to cope with the demands of modern travellers, with weights room and tennis pro, and the next generation as well with a children's centre. However all the traditional sybaritic pleasures are available too in the excellent restaurants and beauty treatments. The **Gallows Point Suite Resort**, PO Box 58 (✆ 776 6434, ✉ 776 6520, US ✆ (1 800) 323 7229, *www.gallowspoint-resort.com*), is a collection of suites set in striking modern buildings on the clifftop just out of Cruz Bay (a walk or a drive from the beach), surrounded by fine greenery. The suites are individually decorated, but they are quite spacious, very comfortable and their balconies have a fine view of the other islands. Pool and swimming area down below. They have kitchenettes, but there is a central restaurant for dinner.

moderate–cheap

Just beyond here you will find a really charming spot, set in a sandy garden with trees, statues and occasional hammocks, at the **Frank Bay Bed and Breakfast** (✆/✉ 693 8617, US toll free ✆ (1 800) 561 7290). Just three guest rooms in a family house, brightly painted with mosquito nets hanging over beds with batique spreads (two share baths): you start the day with breakfast on the veranda chatting to other guests. Nice and secluded, but a short walk from town. There is a number of less formal hotels in Cruz Bay itself. The **Raintree-Inn**, PO Box 566, St John 00831 (✆/✉ 776 7449, US res ✆ (1 800) 666 7449), is a busy spot in the heart of Cruz Bay's tiny downtown. Nice wooden verandas, around which there are eight air-conditioned rooms, three apartments and the Fish Trap restaurant, itself set on a pretty wooden deck hung with greenery. The **Cruz Inn**, PO Box 556 (✆ 693 8688, ✉ 776 7449, US ✆ (1 800) 666 7688), takes a rather more aloof view from the hillside over a bay behind town. Friendly with quite simple rooms, some share baths, cheap to moderate. Cheaper rooms can be found in the modern, lime-green and pink blocks of the **Inn at Tamarind Court**, PO Box 350, St John 00831 (✆ 776 6378, ✉ 776 6722, US res ✆ (1 800) 221 1637). The 20 rooms in modern concrete blocks are simple but adequate with bright decor and some with air-conditioning. There is a charming courtyard bar and restaurant where you sit in the shade of a huge tamarind tree, as the name suggests. Some studios and some well-priced single rooms.

St John has a number of **campgrounds** on its forested shores. The camping is by no means that 'rustic'; you live in permanent 'tents' (raised floors with walls and netting at either end or wooden cabins with mosquito screens) connected by a lacework of paths and wooden walkways to the central area, washrooms, concessionary shops and beaches. Hikes, watersports and even environmental lectures. These resorts do get booked up well in advance, so you'll need to reserve early for the winter season. Try **Maho Bay Camps**, PO Box 310, St John 00830 (✆ 776 6226, ✉ 776 6504, US res ✆ (1 800) 392 9004) in Maho Bay, where the most comfortable rooms are separated off as the **Harmony Resort** (✆ 776 6240), though it still benefits from the same facilities. The setting is charming; there are breezy and comfortable cottages ranged on the hillside, carefully hidden among the profuse greenery and linked by wooden walkways. Kitchenettes and balconies, watersports down below. In the next bay is the **Cinnamon Bay Campground**, PO Box 720 (✆ 776 6330, ✉ 776 6458, US res ✆ (1 800) 539 9998), at sea level in the forest. Cottages and tents and simple cooking facilities, and a restaurant too. On the south coast there is a sister resort to Harmony at the **Concordia Eco-Tents** (✆ 693 5855, ✉ and res as above), multi-level tents with kitchens and private shower-rooms, set in drier vegetation with a fantastic view over the east end of St John and the BVI. Finally there are *cheap* rates at the **Hansen Bay** Camp Ground (✆ 693 5033 or inquire at Vie's Snack Shack) on the wiggly peninsula beyond Coral Bay. Isolated and quiet.

St John is also an ideal place in which to hire a **villa**, if you are happy to look after yourself. Windspree Vacation Home Rentals, 6-2-1A Estate Carolina, St John 00830 (✆/✉ 693 5423), has a number of villas in different configurations of rooms in the Coral Bay area and St John Properties, PO Box 700, St John 00831 (✆ 693 8485, ✉ 776 6192, toll free ✆ (1 800) 283 1746) and Cruz Bay Realty, PO Box 66 (✆ 693 8808, ✉ 693 9812, US toll free ✆ (1 800) 569 2417), have villas and apartments around the island. Prices range from $100 to $400 per day for a single-bedroom villa.

✆ (1 340)– **Eating Out**

St John has quite a good variety of places to eat for a small island (perhaps worth investigating on an evening out from St Thomas). As well as the more formal dining rooms of the big hotels, you will find lively restaurants in Cruz Bay and some easy-going haunts around Coral Bay in the east. The larger restaurants will accept credit cards. Service charge runs at 10–15%. Categories are arranged according to the price of a main dish: *expensive*— US$20 and above; *moderate*—between US$10 and $20; *cheap*—US$10 and below.

expensive

Asolare (✆ 779 4747) has top position for cuisine and particularly for its setting: you dine at wicker-backed chairs on a screened veranda made of stone high above Cruz Bay, with a fantastic view across to St Thomas. The fare is Thai-Asian cuisine and a few continental dishes: *Namtok* salad (rare beef tenderloin with roasted rice crumbs in lemongrass, coriander and mint) or a Peking roasted quail in a sweet and sour Asian slaw. The **Château Bordeaux** (✆ 776 6611) has an equally spectacular setting, overlooking the east coast from an almost alpine deck in the central mountains. You dine at pretty tables with lace tablecloths and mock silver cutlery, on international cuisine. To start, spicy grilled shrimp in a Thai curry marinade with Jamaican jerk couscous or baby wild greens with goat's cheese tossed in a raspberry walnut vinaigrette.

moderate

In Cruz Bay is a charming and very lively restaurant where you will find excellent food, **Morgan's Mango** (✆ 693 8141), a white, pink and turquoise terrace with wooden floorboards, torchlit and with a friendly tree growing through it. The food is Argentinian and new Caribbean in style, so as well as a 14oz steak with *chimi-churri* sauce, you can expect Cuban citrus chicken and spicy voodoo snapper. There is a long cocktail menu for before dinner, and in season it is worth reserving. The **Paradiso** restaurant (✆ 776 8806; *expensive–moderate*) is in the Mongoose Junction II shopping centre in a pretty dining room with a hardwood floor. Italian fare. **Café Roma** (✆ 776 6524) also serves Italian food in a pretty air-conditioned dining room upstairs on Main Street in Cruz Bay, with a mural of an Italian scene: Venetian shrimp in lemon and garlic and a multiplicity of pastas and pizzas. It is well worth stopping in at **La Tapa** right in the middle of town. Here you will get cocktails and *tapas*: *brochettas,* home-made *mozzarella di bufala* and *pâté maison*, in a charming old local house with open doors and a small patio out front.

There are some fun places to get a meal at the other end of the island, around **Coral Bay**. **Shipwreck Landing** (✆ 776 8640) has a mixed menu; you eat on a wooden deck overhung by palms and sprays of bougainvillea and a tin roof, right across from the sea. Chicken teriyaki or Mexicali, lime butter mahi-mahi or burgers and sandwiches, also daily pasta and fish specials. Close by is **Miss Lucy's** restaurant, dressed up in pink right on the waterfront, which also serves a good Caribbean fish.

cheap

You can get a good meal at the **Lime Inn** where they serve wholesome American and Caribbean fare—burgers and chicken or fish, and at **Local Culinery,** where you can get a plate of heavyweight Caribbean fare. There's even a deli in Mongoose Junction. Finally, to round off an evening, drop in to the **Garden of Luscious Licks** on Main Street, where you will find health foods and ice creams. Fresh salads, good veggieburgers, freshly squeezed juices, brownie bars and peace pops. 'Positive vibes—and hugs—the kind of hangout place that nourishes the body and the soul!', if you like that sort of thing. They say that **Miss Vie**, beyond Coral Bay, makes the very finest conch fritters, but she'll also cook up a mean West Indian supper. Very rustic and fun.

Bars and Nightlife

St John can get surprisingly lively and at the weekend you will find Cruz Bay buzzing past midnight. Some of the bars put on bands. Start off at La Tapa and Woody's Seafood Saloon, both in the middle of town, for an early evening drink and then move on to explore. Wharfside Village, the downtown mall, is the busiest area: the **Pusser's Pub** is done up in the brass and polished wood of mock nauticalia—there is an oyster bar up top in the Crow's Nest. **Larry's Landing** is all about beer, television and pool: *'No one under 18, No pets allowed'* and on Kongens Gade you will find **Grumpy's almost by the Sea**—'where hurricanes and hangovers make the only difference, 2000 miles away from self-importance'—an upstairs deck where you sit under parasols and the branches of a tree, good for a beer and a bit of amateur philosophy if you're up to it. Just above here is a fun spot, **Crash Landing,** where they have managed to turn a barren cliffside into a bar—a multi-level maze of boardwalks, bricks and stone, trees and fairy-lights, brightly coloured cocktails, bench seats and bar stools, statues and flaming torches, even mini-golf, but most easily recognized by the crashed toy plane. The **Lime Inn**, fairy-lit and brightly coloured, can be quite lively and has a band a couple of times a week. In **Coral Bay** try **Don Carlos** for a lively drinking crowd and **Skinny Legs** for television and beer. **Sea Breeze** sees a rumbustious crowd from time to time.

For general information about the US Virgin Islands, see 'USVI Directory', pp.492–5.

getting there

It is one of the pleasures of St John that it can really only be reached by boat. Ferries can be caught from downtown Charlotte Amalie (about six times a day on Transportation Services, ✆ 776 6282) and from Red Hook in East End (hourly on Transportation Services). You can also visit from Tortola in the BVI (three or four sailings a day on Inter-Island Ferries, ✆ 776 6597, departing West End terminal) and there are even ferries from Jost van Dyke (a couple each day on Inter-Island Ferries).

tourist information

There is a tourist information office in Cruz Bay (✆ 776 6450), PO Box 200, USVI 00830, opposite the ferry dock; and the National Park Service has a visitors' centre in Cruz Bay opposite Mongoose Junction (✆ 776 6201; open 8–4.30), for an orientation video, bookshop and other information. For more information you can write to Virgin Islands National Park, PO Box 7789, St Thomas VI 00801.

In a *medical emergency*, contact the DeCastro Clinic in Cruz Bay (✆ 776 6252).

watersports

Watersports are mainly handled by the hotels but there are a few outside operators. They will fix up windsurfing, kayaking and snorkelling gear (*see* 'Beaches' for the best sites). General watersports operators include St John Watersports (✆ 776 6256) and Cinnamon Bay Watersports (✆ 776 6330) in Cinnamon Bay (good for windsurfing and kayaking). At the other end of the island, contact Coral Bay Watersports (✆ 776 6850).

Day sails: The catamaran *Jolly Mon* (✆ 776 6239) takes a ride around the island with snorkelling stops. A day's sail can also be fixed up through *Serenity* (✆ 776 6922) and for a motor yacht, contact the M/Y *Cinnamon Bay* (✆ 776 6462). And if you want a more traditional sailing yacht, complete with on-board loony dog, try the *Spree* (✆ 771 3734). Powerboats can be hired through Ocean Runner (✆ 693 8809).

Deep-sea fishing: Can be arranged on *Gone Ketchin'* (✆ 776 7709) or the watersports companies.

Scuba diving: At the east end of the island. Favourite dive-sites include the reefs and cays to the north of the island, Eagle Shoal to the south, Ten Fathom Pinnacle and even the steamship *Rhone* off Salt Cay in the British Virgin Islands. Contact the companies above, or if you're at the east end, ring Coral Bay Watersports (✆ 776 6850). **Snorkelling** is particularly good in Haulover Bay, Leinster Bay and on Waterlemon Cay. In Salt Pond Bay you may be lucky and see a turtle in the sea grass. In Trunk Bay you can even take a guided underwater swim with air pumped from the surface: contact Snuba (✆ 693 4220)

other sports

Tennis: There are courts in the hotels as well as four public courts in Cruz Bay.

Riding: Pony Express (✆ 776 6494) will take you on guided tours through the island's blanket of forest and to hidden coves where you can ride along the sand.

St Croix

St Croix (pronounced St Croy) is the largest of the Virgin Islands. Unlike the hillier islands of St Thomas and St John, St Croix has stretches of flat and fertile land between its hills and so it has traditionally been agricultural. Once, its 84 square miles were divided up into about 100 sugar plantations. But now agriculture is in decline and has been overtaken by tourism as the main industry and source of revenue.

But tourism is not as intensive in St Croix and you can still find deserted beaches on the island. The streets of Christiansted simply do not have the pressure-cooker effect of Charlotte Amalie. Things are more low-key here, but you will find some surprisingly good places to stay and eat, also some with genuine Caribbean character, particularly around the towns. The island's name is French (a straight translation of Columbus's original name for it, Santa Cruz), but this is one of the few legacies of the short French ownership in the 17th century. The island was bought by the Danes in 1733 after they had established themselves in St Thomas.

From time to time, St Croix has been the senior island of the three US Virgin Islands, because of its successful plantation economy and because it had the largest population (presently about 55,000). The Governor resided here in the 19th century and it was in Frederiksted on St Croix that he declared that the slaves should be freed in 1848. Earlier this century the island's importance declined with the failure of agriculture, while St Thomas became an important naval base and then boomed with the tourist industry. Only recently have the Cruzians started to catch up with their neighbours.

St Croix has a mixed community—as well as the original Cruzians, who are mainly of African descent, a large number of Puerto Ricans have made their way on to the island over the last hundred years, escaping the poverty of the larger island. There are also many 'down-islanders' and there is even a small community of Danes, the strongest remnant of the colonial legacy. It is not very strong, but one commentator claimed that a week among the Cruzians was like a tropical version of a tortured Ibsen play! Generally the Cruzians are polite and quite reserved.

It is not entirely a happy community, though, as shown by the looting and racial problems that followed Hurricane Hugo's incredible destructiveness in 1989, when 90 per cent of the Cruzians were left homeless (some claim that the island has still not completely recovered). About 20 per cent of the population moved off the island after the hurricane and some have returned since. On a lighter note, there is little love lost between the St Thomians and the Cruzians, who consider St Thomas over-developed and rather stressful.

Christiansted, the capital, and Frederiksted (once the more important town because of its better harbour) are traditional West Indian waterfront towns, where the arched walkways can transport you back to the days of clippers and ocean-going trading ships and wharves heaving with tea-chests. They have been well restored and they have undoubted Caribbean charm.

Getting Around

A system of local VITRAN **buses** runs between the two main towns, price $1, but these are supplemented by share-taxis which run the same routes, leaving when they are full or the driver has the urge. You can pick them up at the supermarkets. They tend not to stray off the main routes, so if you want to get to the east end of the island or off the beaten track (around the rainforest area) you will have to hitchhike, which does not work brilliantly, or take a **taxi**. These can be found at the hotels, at the airport and on King Street in Christiansted or by Fort Frederik in Frederiksted. Rates are set by the government and cabs are not metered, so it is sensible to check the price beforehand. Typical fares: from **Christiansted** to the airport—$10, Frederiksted—$20, north coast—$16. Taxi operators are St Croix Taxi Association (✆ 778 1088) at the airport, Antilles Taxi Service (✆ 773 5020) in Christiansted and Combine Taxi and Tours (✆ 772 2828) in Frederiksted.

Taxi drivers will willingly take you on an island tour—many are well informed—for about $30 per hour. Tours can also be made in tourist safari buses (about $20), if you can bear the embarrassment. Contact St Croix Safari Tours (✆ 773 6700), departure about 10am from Christiansted. Alternatively try a bit of aerial sight-seeing with St Croix Aviation (✆ 778 0090) or by helicopter, Crucian Helicopters (✆ 690 4356) for a fully narrated tour around the coast of the island.

Hire cars are readily available, but come at a price, starting at $45 or $50 a day (you can sometimes find reduced offers in the promotional literature). Most companies will deliver the car to you. The roads in St Croix are quite good, certainly when compared with elsewhere in the Caribbean. Hire firms include the big international companies, which have an office at the airport and town: Avis (✆ 778 9355, toll free ✆ (1 800) 331 1084), Budget (✆ 773 9636, worldwide ✆ (1 800) 527 0700) and Hertz (✆ 778 1402), and local firms such as Olympic Ace Rent-A-Car (✆ 773 2208, ✆ 773 6870) in the Caravelle Arcade in Christiansted. Remember to drive on the left.

Beaches

There are some excellent beaches in St Croix. The main ones have some development, but there are many charming and isolated coves tucked in between them. If you want to find a secluded spot to yourself, it is worth asking around or simply taking side-roads and tracks down to the sea. The snorkelling is good and many reefs are close to shore. All beaches are public, though if you want to use a hotel's deck chairs or changing facilities, you may well be charged (up to $5). All the watersports are available on the island.

best beaches

Buck Island: St Croix's best beach is actually on an offshore island, a couple of miles from the coast at the east end. The Buck Island underwater life is particularly good—there is an enormous reef of seafans, and antlers of staghorns teem with angelfish in shimmering yellow, blue and green. A snorkelling trail guides you through all this. The island is a National Park. Many boats make the tour out there, about an hour's sail, for the day or half a day (about $25 for a half- day, $40 a full day).

Protestant Cay: The closest beach to downtown Christiansted is on the small island a couple of minutes' swim off the waterfront, or an expensive $3 ferry ride. Watersports equipment is available here.

Beauregard Bay: Site of the Buccaneer Hotel, to the east of town, a small, palm-backed strand, where there are chairs and facilities ($4 fee) as well as a beach bar.

Shoy Beach: A perfect half-moon curve of luscious sand. There are no facilities and you have to find your way down through the trees, but it is a superb, quiet suntrap.

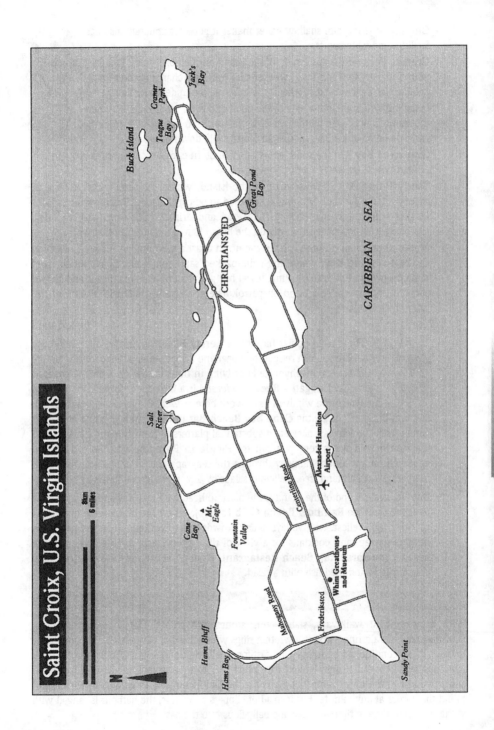

Saint Croix, U.S. Virgin Islands

N

8km
6 miles

Hams Bluff

Hams Bay

Cane Bay

Mt. Eagle

Fountain Valley

Mahogany Road

Centerline Road

Frederiksted

Whim Greathouse and Museum

Sandy Point

Salt River

Alexander Hamilton Airport

CHRISTIANSTED

Buck Island

Teague Bay

Cramer Park

Jack's Bay

Great Pond Bay

CARIBBEAN SEA

Chenay Bay: Its calm shallow water makes it good for children; also has facilities and watersports.

Cramer Park (at the eastern tip of the island on the north side): Popular with Cruzians so it fills up at weekends. There is a changing room, but take drinks, a picnic and snorkelling gear to see the underwater life.

Isaac's Bay: On the other side of the point and even more isolated, where the snorkelling is even better. The best way to get to this beach is from the eastern end of Jack's Bay, though you must walk down there.

Grapetree Bay: On the south shore at the eastern end, a secluded strip of sand where the waves get up sometimes.

Sandy Point: At the western tip of the island, where the sand comes ashore in mounds; quite isolated, and you are advised to be careful about locking your car and leaving belongings unattended. Take food and drinks. In season (May to July), leatherback turtles make their way up the beach here at night to lay their eggs.

North shore: Cut into the cliffs of the north coast are a number of coves, of which the best is **Cane Bay**, where the palm-backed sand comes and goes, but the reef remains, giving superb snorkelling. Jewel fish glint among the coral heads and striped sergeant majors cruise around on patrol. There is also a good strip of sand at the Carambola Hotel.

beach bars

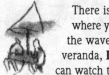

There is a popular haunt at **Chenay Beach**, a simple, open-sided bar where you can retreat for a beer and a snack after a sailboard trip taming the waves or rehydrate after lying in the sun. Set on a pretty, covered veranda, **Duggan's Reef** (*moderate*) is a little more formal, though you can watch the windsurfers at work here as well. Burgers, salads and island-fare. On the north coast, the **Cane Bay Beach Bar** has a charming setting on a deck across from the waves; snacks and substantial platters of fresh fish and steaks. For a meal on a wild waterfront you can try **Picnic in Paradise** (✆ 778 1212). You approach on a wooden walkway through the seagrape and sit on a waterfront deck shaded by a sea almond tree. Delicious salads by day, more formal meals by night.

But the western end of the island is the place to head for a lazy day and a sunset view over the sea. The **Rainbow Beach Club** (*cheap*), set on the best stretch of sand, is probably the liveliest, with volleyball and crowds at the weekend. It serves salads and burgers (cheap) and cocktails for a view of the Green Flash. A little higher up the beach is the **Sprat Hall Beach Restaurant,** where you can get local fare including conch fritters and fried fish with a salad.

Christiansted

With its waterfront walkways, slab paving stones and arched Danish storage houses, Christiansted is an alluring harbour town that rings with echoes of another age. The inevitable invasion of air-conditioned boutiques and fast-food halls that makes it a 20th-century trading town has been kept out of sight—neon signs must not protrude beyond the original façades—and so you have the impression that a colonial official in serge with gold epaulettes might round the corner at any minute. But instead of clippers at anchor, the harbour is ranged with yachts and from time to time the seaplane belly-flops into the bay.

The town was laid out by the Danes when they arrived in 1733 and is named in honour of King Christian VI. It is protected by a large barrier reef, on which the waves break a few hundred yards out from the shore. Any potential invading force would have had to negotiate the reef and then face unformidable **Fort Christiansvaern** (*open weekdays 8–5 weekends 9–5; adm*—this also admits you to the Steeple Building across the way). Nobody did and so the yellow fort never saw action, but it is pleasant to visit (it seems that the walls were used mainly to lock the soldiers in at night rather than keep invaders out). It was started in 1733, with stones brought from Denmark as ballast, and since 1878, when it was abandoned by the military, it has functioned variously as a police station and courthouse.

The fort's guns have a good view over **Protestant Cay**, an island-hotel just a few minutes' swim out to sea. It takes its name from the French era when only Catholics could be buried on the mainland, and so Protestants were buried here. It is mostly referred to as the Hotel on the Cay, and is supposed to be the setting for Herman Wouk's classic novel about the nightmarish life of a Caribbean hotelier, *Don't Stop the Carnival* (*see* p.495).

Back on the mainland, newly arrived captains would first check in to the **Old Danish Customs House** before unloading. It was built in the 1750s, and the staircase, a suitably imposing entrance for the captains, was added later. The National Park Services have their offices here. Next stop was the **Old Scale House** (weighing scales still in place), built in 1856, where they would measure their cargo.

Beyond the **Old Danish West India and Guinea Company Warehouse**, which the company used as its headquarters from 1749 (now the post office), is the **Steeple Building**, a Lutheran church constructed in 1735 (the steeple itself was added in 1794). Today it houses the **National Park Museum** (*open Mon–Fri 9–4; adm includes fort*), where you can see exhibits of Indian calabashes, maps of Danish St Croix and diagrams of rum production.

On King Street (Kongens Tvaergade), you will find **Government House**, with its arched veranda and red pillar boxes. It is two private homes set around a garden, joined together when Governor van Scholten bought them in 1830s. The staircase at the entrance leads to the main hall, now redecorated with chandeliers and mirrors like those under which the islanders danced a hundred years ago (the Danes took the originals with them when they left in 1917, but gave some others back to the islands in 1966). Today the buildings house the court and government offices.

In the Caravelle Arcade in the centre of town you will find the **St Croix Aquarium and Marine Education Centre** (✆ 773 8995; *adm*), which is well worth a visit. There is a series of small aquaria, which are brought alive by Lonnie Kaczmarsky, who will tell you stories of the dentist shrimp (which cleans the teeth of other fish without them eating him), sponge crabs which disguise themselves with sponges and then eat them if they cannot find a meal, and the importance of mangrove swamps where so many fish start their lives. He takes guided snorkelling tours. There is a Discovery room for children.

Those looking to score a few duty-free bargains will find the main shopping streets just behind the waterfront around King Street and King's Alley, in the old trading houses. Another echo of the old West Indies (from before the age of the supermarket) can still be seen in the covered **market** (*weekdays and Saturdays*), which has been there in one form or other since 1735. A few Cruzians have stalls selling ground provisions to other islanders.

Around the Island

St Croix's 84 square miles were once divided into about a hundred sugar plantations and the windmills once used to crush the cane (without sails and growing steadily more dilapidated) seem to be on every hilltop. From them there are splendid views across the island and often as far north as the other Virgin Islands, grey stains on the horizon 40 miles to the north.

Travelling west from Christiansted on the north shore road you pass **Salt River**, a mangrove bay where Columbus put in for water in 1493, and then you follow the grassy slopes of the coastline. Eventually you come to Cane Bay, where the road twists and drops into small coves forested with palm trees that are cut into the northern cliffs. The views are spectacular. Finally the road turns inland past Fountain Valley to the Centerline Road. All over the island you see the ruins of plantation buildings poking out of the undergrowth.

The **Centerline Road** runs west from Christiansted to the town of Frederiksted, mostly in a direct straight line in the centre of the island. As it leaves Christiansted it passes close to St Croix's small industrial area, where you will find the Hess Oil Refinery on the south coast, now running at a reduced capacity, and the aluminium plant. The road eventually passes the Alexander Hamilton airport. (Alexander Hamilton came to St Croix from Nevis as a boy and grew up in Christiansted before leaving for North America in the 1760s.)

Across the road you approach the **St George Village Botanical Gardens** (*open daily, guided tours, 9–4; adm*) through an alley of royal palm trees and emerge into 16-acres of neatly tended gardens that was a plantation estate and before that an Arawak village. Some buildings around the great house have been restored and on the various trails you will find many Caribbean favourites marked: the bulbous sandbox tree (the pods of this spiky-barked tree were used to hold sand that was then sprinkled on ink to stop it smudging), the kapok tree with spikes on its trunk, the autograph tree (you can write on its leaves), the St Croix agave and the dildo cactus, named for its shape. There is an orchid house and a collection of all the plants in St Croix that are endangered.

Sugar-cane was the source of St Croix's wealth for many years and the crop blanketed the land as late as 1966. It is gone now, but the distillation of rum has continued, with imported molasses, at the **Cruzian Rum Distillery** (*© 772 0799; open 9–11.30 and 1–4.15, adm free*), just off Centerline Road to the south. A half-hour guided tour will lead you among the vats of distilling molasses, where the smell will have you teetering on the walkways. Some rum is bottled here for sale in the USVI, but most is exported. Tours finish with a snifter in the bar.

A couple of miles farther along the road is the **Estate Whim Plantation Museum** (*open Mon–Sat 10–4; adm exp*), which will cast you back to the days of plantation splendour, when planter Mr McEvoy lived in this oval house with the air of a church, surrounded by a small moat. It has been restored and refitted with period furniture, the huge bedroom at one end with a four-poster and a planter's chair with extended arms and the sumptuous dining room at the other. In the dungeon-like outhouses you can see the tools of all the island artisans— cooper (barrel-maker), logger, wheelwright, joiner and blacksmith—also a history of slavery and field work.

Frederiksted

St Croix's second town is Frederiksted, set on the west coast, 17 miles west of Christiansted. Founded in 1751, Frederiksted has always been important because it has a better harbour than

Christiansted, and large ships were able to dock there. Nowadays the traffic is mostly cruise ships, but even a hundred years ago liners were passing by; in 1887 Lafcadio Hearn stopped off in the town *en route* for Martinique, describing it in his *Two Years in the West Indies.* To him it had 'the appearance of a beautiful Spanish town, with its Romanesque piazzas, churches, many-arched buildings peeping through breaks in a line of mahogany, bread-fruit, mango, tamarind and palm trees'. The town, much of which was rebuilt after it was burned in a riot in 1878, was well known for its elaborate West Indian gingerbread architecture.

The pretty arches are still along the waterfront, but the feel of the Spanish town has gone. Frederiksted has its own life separate from the east end of the island (it is a popular day out for the locals on Sundays) and it has been developing recently with a series of new malls and restaurants. There are many very pretty buildings and there have been efforts recently to restore them.

As usual, the harbour is watched over by a fortress, **Fort Frederik**, now run down. Named after the Danish King Frederik V, it was constructed in 1752 to encourage the settlement of the town (it was also a refuge in times of trouble). It was it was here that Governor van Scholten made his announcement that he was abolishing slavery in the Danish islands in 1848, against the orders of his king. It also had a curious role in that it was the first fort to recognize, unofficially, the young nation of the United States on 25 October 1776. The glory of the official recognition went to St Eustatius, a dozy island now but a very important port at that time, about three weeks later (*see* p.410). There are exhibitions of hurricanes and of the transfer of the Virgin Islands to the USA (with a photocopy of the US$25 million cheque). Opposite the cruise ship pier close by is the **Old Customs House**, where the duty would be paid on the incoming and outgoing cargo. From here, Strand Gade runs past a line of old stone warehouses with arched walkways above the pavement.

The Rainforest

A mile out of Frederiksted, towards the north coast of the island, is St Croix's miniature 'rainforest'. It does not receive enough rain to be a real rainforest, but the vegetation is different from the rest of the island and as you drive along **Mahogany Road**, the creepers and lianas will reach down to grapple with you. Orchids perch and ferns explode in the upper branches, just beneath the 100ft canopy, and you may see a hummingbird flit by. There is a number of roads leading from the top of West End Road into the forest (many are unpaved and so it's best to go by jeep), and there are endless footpaths if you wish to walk. In the forest you will find **St Croix LEAP** (from Life Experience Achievement Programme), which has a wood mill and craft shop selling products made from local timber.

The East

The eastern end of St Croix is drier and less lush than the west. It is becoming steadily built up with housing estates and holiday condominium complexes and there are some fun restaurants and beach bars. The beaches are worth a visit (some busy, others secluded), but otherwise all you will see among the windmill cones and the modern villas are a few goats and the dildo cactus. Point Udall is the easternmost point in the United States (unless you include the Aleutian Islands in Alaska).

Like St Thomas, St Croix has a good variety of hotels. For those who want a beachfront resort there are plenty to choose from, but there is also a good selection of smaller inns, both on the beach and also with antique (and mock-antique) charm, set in the older Danish buildings. The **Small Inns of St Croix** has a number of charming places on its books (✆ (1 888) INN USVI). There are few cheap places to stay in St Croix. **Villa Rental** can be arranged through Island Villas, 6 Company St, Christiansted (✆ 773 8821, ✉ 773 8823, US ✆ (1 800) 626 4512) or CPMI (Caribbean Property Management and Investments), PO Box 26160, Gallows Bay (✆ 778 8782, ✉ 773 2150, US ✆ (1 800) 496 7379). USVI government tax of 8% is levied on all hotel bills.

luxury–expensive

The **Buccaneer Hotel**, PO Box 25200 (✆ 773 2100, ✉ 778 8215, US ✆ (1 800) 255 3881), just outside Christiansted, is set in 300 acres of rolling grounds that descend to a string of private beaches and is the most elegant hotel on the island. It is large, with 150 rooms around the central estate house of coral rock, but elegant and comfortable in an older Caribbean style. The **Cormorant Beach Club**, 4126 La Grande Princesse (✆ 778 8920, ✉ 778 9218, US ✆ (1 800) 548 4460), is a smaller retreat (just 38 double rooms) with modern Caribbean island comfort set on the beach to the north of Christiansted. It has everything for the luxurious escape—sumptuous high-pastel rooms with their own balconies and a view of the ocean, afternoon tea and no telephones. And when you feel like emerging from your seclusion, there are watersports on the windy beach right outside and for the evenings a charming restaurant looking out through the palms.

A comfortable beach hotel on a quiet beach is the **Chenay Bay Beach Resort**, PO Box 24600, St Croix 00824 (✆/✉ 773 2918, US ✆ (1 800) 548 4457). There are 50 prettily decorated rooms in quite simple cottages set in a horseshoe around a grassy garden above a small, calm beach. Air-conditioning, television, telephone, kitchenettes and balconies.

Right on the beach west of town you will find a charming small resort, the **Hibiscus Beach Hotel,** 4131 La Grande Princesse, USVI 00820-4441 (✆ 773 4042, ✉ 773 7668, US toll free ✆ (1 800) 442 0121), a small assembly of two-storey blocks with pretty gingerbread trimmings that stand among the palm trees. There are 37 very prettily decorated rooms with all mod cons and comforts (cable TV, phones and air-conditioning), each with a balcony or terrace. Very nice atmosphere, particularly when you're dozing in a hammock hung between the palm trees.

expensive–moderate

At the other end of the island you will find an extremely fine setting at the **Sprat Hall Plantation**, PO Box 695 (✆/✉ 772 0305, US ✆ (1 800) 843 3584), a couple of miles north of Frederiksted. The estate house, in which three rooms are decorated with period furniture, including four-posters, dates from the late 1600s. Sprat Hall stands in open grounds just in from the coast, where there is a private beach and bar. Small but friendly, just 12 rooms and suites, some with kitchens, but a fine antique dining room with home Caribbean cooking. And on the north shore you will find a small clutch of friendly and secluded places to stay around Cane Bay. **The Waves at Cane Bay**, PO Box 1749 Kingshill, USVI 00851 (✆ 778 1805, US toll free (1 800) 545 0603), has 11 large rooms in two blocks and a villa standing right on the (now, after the hurricane) rocky waterfront. Comfortable self-contained accommodation with all you need to look after yourself (kitchens and a screened porch with a view), but a very friendly atmosphere downstairs.

Close by is the **Cane Bay Reef Club,** 1407 Kingshill, USVI 00851 (✆/✉ 778 2966, US toll free ✆ (1 800) 253 8534), which has nine suites in a modern block on the waterfront. It is brightly decorated, with full kitchens and balconies looking out onto the waves that crash on the volcanic shoreline. Again a very low-key and friendly air, a good escape. Just outside Frederiksted, the **Seaview Farm Inn,** 180 Two Brothers, USVI 00840 (✆ 772 5367, US toll free ✆ (1 800) 792 5060), has eight suites set in spacious gardens around a large open deck, pool bar and a grill restaurant. The rooms are nicely decorated with Mexican tiles with a screened porch and living room.

moderate–cheap

Set in a very attractive private house on the hill above Christiansted **Hilty House**, PO Box 26077, St Croix, USVI 00824 (✆/✉ 773 2594), has just four rooms and two cottages. It is very elegant and stylish (with echoes of the seventies when it was restored), with a quiet air and a gracious welcome and personal attention. Pool and sunning deck if you want to relax; otherwise it's a good idea to have a car. Bed and breakfast. There is also a number of small hotels and inns set in the old buildings of Christiansted. The **Pink Fancy**, at 27 Prince Street, a little way from the centre of town (✆ 773 8460, ✉ 773 6448, US ✆ (1 800) 524 2045), is set in an old town house with arched brick foundations and a clapboard upper storey, louvred windows and shutters. As the name suggests, it is painted pink, but the 13 rooms are decorated with brazil wood in keeping with the antique style. They have all the modern comforts you need though, including kitchens: the hotel serves breakfast, but has no restaurant.

The **Danish Manor Hotel**, 2 Company Street (✆ 773 1377, ✉ 773 1913, US ✆ (1 800) 524 2069, *www.danishmanor.com*), has a nice courtyard with exposed brick and stone and 34 rooms that give onto the pool and explosive greenery. Friendly atmosphere, lively restaurant. There are not many cheap places to stay in St Croix. In town you can try the **Cactus Inn** (✆ 692 9331) on King St where there are simple rooms with a/c, cable TVs and private bathrooms.

At the other end of the island there is a number of good places to stay in Frederiksted. **On the Beach Resort,** PO Box 1908 (✆ 772 1205, ✉ 772 1757, US toll free ✆ (1 800) 524 2018) has 20 units in a concrete block that stands above the beach and some suites in newer villas around a pool in a garden. Some kitchens, strong gay clientele. In the town itself you will find a very quiet and charming spot in a restored townhouse (thought to be a former Lutheran parsonage dating from the early 1800s) at the **Prince Street Inn**, 402 Prince St, USVI 00840 (✆/✉ 772 9550, US toll free ✆ (1 800) 771 9550). There's a delightful ambience about the place, as soon as you walk through the metal gates into the stepped garden and into the wooden interior of the old house. The rooms, which all have kitchens, are quite simple but the prices are excellent.

Christiansted

Where some islands have a bit of a shortage of good restaurants, that is not a problem in St Thomas and St Croix where there are plenty, many set in the pretty town houses and warehouses along the waterfront in Christiansted. If you are staying at the eastern end of the island it's worth making the effort to get to Frederiksted, perhaps for an early evening cocktail at one of the beach bars and then dinner. Restaurants accept credit cards and most charge service at 10%. Categories are arranged according to the price of a main dish: *expensive*—US$20 and above; *moderate*—US$10–$20; *cheap*—US$10 and below.

expensive

The **Top Hat** restaurant (℗ 773 2346) on Company Street is run by Danes and retains some Danish elements in its menu. There is a lively bar where you can linger among photographs of happy diners wearing a top hat before moving in to the wooden-walled dining room with its tray roof and network of supporting beams. Home-made sausages followed by *frikadeller* (crisp, roasted meatballs) with red cabbage and mashed potato, or Copenhagen steak.

The most charming setting for dinner in the town is at **Indies** (℗ 692 9440), where you sit under a colourful tin roof in a courtyard surrounded by standing plants. There's a daily changing good-value menu which always has some fresh fish and uses the best of island spices: soups and salads followed by grilled wahoo with fresh mango tomato chutney and filled plantains. Hip air and excellent fare.

Picnic in Paradise (℗ 778 1212) has a charming setting on a waterfront deck and an airy dining room, on the north shore near the Carambola Hotel. Quite innovative international cuisine with a seafood medley in puff pastry and pastas.

moderate

At **Tivoli Gardens** (℗ 773 6782) you eat on a breezy veranda surrounded by white trellis work and hung with greenery. Try chicken Tivolese, in tomato sour-cream sauce, or *crevettes à la Chinoise* in sugared soy sauce. **Kim's** restaurant (℗ 773 3377) is a small and charming spot behind a façade of Danish arches at 45 King St, with a white interior and orange decor and painted flowers. Topnotch local food, daily soup specials and some international dishes, friendly service. Great ice creams.

The curiously named **Anabelle's Tea Room** (℗ 773 3990) uses the best of its setting in a courtyard, where you dine under parasols and trees. Spanish, Cuban and general West Indian fare. The **Bombay Club** (℗ 773 1838) is a popular spot around town at lunch and for dinner, set in the air-conditioned vaults of an old townhouse: international fare including *fajitas,* ribs, burgers and sandwiches, or *linguini zingaro* (with prosciutto, garlic, basil and lemon). **Luncheria** (℗ 773 4247) is set in a pretty courtyard on Company Street in town. Mexican food; *enchiladas, burritos* and *tostadas.*

There are some fun places beyond the town, too: **Duggan's Reef** (℗ 773 9800) is very popular with the locals and so it is a fun place for a meal out. It has a cracking setting on a breezy terrace overlooking the shore to Buck Island; dinner served nightly, with international fare including lobster pasta and chicken teriyaki. Not far off, there is an international style snack-bar at **Cheeseburgers in Paradise**, which is set in a pretty tin-roofed shack by the roadside heading east from town. Excellent cheeseburgers, sandwiches and salads, popular with a local white crowd. And on the north shore there is another fun spot at **Off the Wall** (✆ 778 2227), an easy waterfront bar under palm thatch dressed up in purple, yellow and green. The fare is simple, with burgers and local grilled fish.

cheap

For something a little more local, try **Harvey's** (✆ 773 3433) on Company Street, which has a classic West Indian setting, complete with plastic tablecloths and foldaway chairs. No written menu—chat with Sarah through the stable door into the kitchen. Try callaloo followed by conch in butter sauce, or chicken or goat (curried or stewed). It comes with a tonnage of ground provisions—sweet potato, plantain and yam. Another option is **Junie's**, near the Seventh-Day Adventist church and the Hess oil refinery. Plastic table-cloths, huge anthuriums and loud music; stew fish, chicken or curried shrimp with another tonnage of ground provisions.

For the best roti and take-away chicken, try **Singh's Fast Food** restaurant at the top end of King Street by the Anglican Church in town, and for Mexican fare go to **Margarita's** Tex Mex, where there are a few seats outside and an air-conditioned dining room with Mexican hats and chilli pepper lights.

Frederiksted

St Croix's second town has a different feel and it is worth investigating the bars and restaurants, perhaps after a day on the beach. **Le St Tropez** (✆ 772 3000; *moderate*) stands in the centre of town on King Street, its open-sided dining room built of brick, stone and wood, and palms outside in the courtyard garden. The cuisine is French—even *cuisses de grenouille persillées* (frogs' legs) as a starter, followed by *magret de canard aux baies roses*. Charming and intimate feel.

The **Café du Soleil** (✆ 772 5400; *moderate*) has a very attractive setting with pink decor and trelliswork on an upstairs deck, looking through lit trees to the sea. The menu is French and international. Start with a *panache* of seafood in saffron broth, with leeks and tomatoes; follow with chicken breast in a marsala or tricolor salsa. *Closed Thurs.*

The **Blue Moon** (✆ 772 2222) is set in the interior of an old trading house on Strand Gade on the bay front. A daily changing menu with local seafood and international dishes. There is piano and jazz entertainment sometimes, to go with the pictures of musicians on the walls.

Pier 69 is ever popular, a courtyard with parasols and a bar-boat set inside, with music at the weekends. For something a little more West Indian try **Motown** (✆ 772 9882; *cheap*), in one of the old warehouses on Strand Gade; excellent West Indian fare: shrimp or conch in butter sauce, curried or stewed goat. There is even a deli, **Turtles,** down on the waterfront heading south out of town.

Many of the restaurants listed above and the beach bars double as bars for an evening drink. There are some fun bars on the waterfront in Christiansted, where the yachties crawl ashore for a beer, others are hidden away in the arches (you will have to look quite carefully as you are stumbling around town). You can start an evening at **Stixx Hurricane Bar** or the bar at the Comanche Hotel, which is mellow, and good for an early evening drink listening to the piano player, or head off to the **Company Street Pub,** which can get pretty wild and noisy. **Cocktails** on Kongens Gade is another loud and lively video bar with a raucous crowd—an American-style sports bar with a weekend karaoke session.

There are plenty of bars to detain you in Frederiksted: **Pier 69** is a cheery haunt for a daytime stopover and **The Saloon** is an air-co sports bar with wooden tables and a

St Croix Directory

For general information about the US Virgin Islands, see 'USVI Directory', pp.492–5.

getting there

For international flights, *see* p.492. There are endless links to St Thomas, some on the international airlines which make a stop at both the main islands when they fly down, but also on smaller planes: Vieques Air Link (✆ 778 9858), American Eagle (toll free ✆ (1 800) 474 4884). In addition, a number of hopper airlines fly into St Croix from both directions along the island chain, from Puerto Rico and down to Sint Maarten and Antigua: Air Anguilla (✆ 778 1880), LIAT (✆ 774 2313). A charter jet can be hired through Bohlke International Airways (✆ 778 9177, ✉ 772 5932).

There are also good options for travelling by sea at the moment: contact Virgin Hydrofoil Services (✆ 776 7417) and Fast Ferries (✆ 773 3278). And you can even travel by seaplane: contact Seaborne Aviation (✆ 773 0103), who have about ten crossings a day. For more details, *see* p.493.

tourist information

The main St Croix Tourist Board is on Queen Cross St in the market square in Christiansted, PO Box 4538, Virgin Islands 00822 (✆ 773 0495, ✉ 773 0495). Tourist arrivals can also check details with the information office at Alexander Hamilton airport and in Frederiksted on the pier (✆ 772 0357). St Croix produces a pink island guide, *St Croix This Week*, with details of current events and helpful hints on the watersports and shops and even how to invest in a dream vacation or local real estate. You will find some informative signboards scattered around Christiansted and flyers advertising watersports and restaurants pop up everywhere you go. There are plenty of American newspapers available on the island, but St Croix's very own satirical rag, *Island Melee*, will lock you into island scandal and lots of nonsense besides.

In a **medical** emergency, go to the St Croix Hospital and Community Health Centre in Christiansted (✆ 778 6311). **Ambulance** ✆ 922, **police** ✆ 915.

pool table. On King Street **Lost Dog** is set in a stone warehouse; there are video games and a juke box, and T-shirts and a surf board on the wall; lots of beer.

The beach bars north of **Frederiksted** are ideal for a cocktail while you watch the sunset and they are particularly popular on Sundays, when the crowds come west for the afternoon. On the way home they stop off at **Mt Pellier Domino Club**, a rum shop hidden away in the rainforest. The big feature of the bar is the drinking pig: you hand the pig a can and it cracks it, slurps it and spits the can out again (they don't give it real beer of course; non-alcoholic beer only, please). It's only a second-generation drinking pig. You can see the grave of the original pig, Buster, at the bar.

A number of the hotels stage steel-band shows and live music, particularly jazz: ask around. If you are in need of a discotheque, there are a couple on the island: **Two plus Two** on the Northside Road just west of town, and **Lizards**, mainly at the weekends.

© (1 340)–

watersports

Most watersports can be arranged through the hotel and independent operators around the island—wetbikes are for hire if you want to scoot around among the yachts at anchor and waterskiing is also easily arranged. If you wish to go parasailing, you can get airborne in Christiansted practically without wetting your feet. A general operator is St Croix Water Sports Centre (© 773 7060) at the Hotel on the Cay.

Windsurfing: The best winds are at the eastern end, off Chenay Bay and Teague Bay. Contact the watersports operators or go through the hotels, who also have small sailing boats, sunfish and hobie cats.

Day sails: There are plenty of organized cruises which are quite fun (many go to Buck Island). You can try Mile Mark Charters (© 773 2628), who arrange trips out of Christiansted, Captain Big Beard's Adventure Tours on the catamaran *Renegade* and the *Buck Island Flyer* (© 773 7977) or Llewelyn's Charters (773 9027) for a trimaran trip. *Diva* (© 778 4675) takes more personalized trips with a maximum of six.

Deep-sea fishing: This is quite well organized in St Croix, with fleets of sleek cruisers in which to ply the deep for 6ft marlin, sailfish and wahoo. A full day costs around $600; a half-day from $400. Try *Ruffian* (© 773 6011), which leaves from Gallows Bay, and Lisa Ann Charters (© 773 3712) at Green Cay Marina.

Scuba diving: The island is almost completely ringed by barrier reefs and there are endless dive-sites, some of which drop off just a few hundred yards offshore. It is particularly good for its soft-coral life. There is a wall off the north coast between Christiansted and Hams Bay in the west: the Salt River drop-off starts in 20ft of water, dropping to thousands, as with the Cane Bay drop-off (from 35ft). Frederiksted has good corals and offshore at Buck Island is another popular spot. The best **snorkelling** areas are listed under 'Beaches', p.516. Buck Island has underwater guided trails for snorkellers.

Many of the hotels offer dive-packages and it is also easy to fix up lessons if you wish to learn. A single-tank dive costs from $50. Outside operators include V.I. Divers (℗ 773 6045, ✆ 773 2859, toll free ℗ (1 800) 544 5911, *vidivers@aol.com* and *71307.2505 @compuserve.com*) or Dive Experience (℗ 773 3307, ✆ 773 7030, toll free ℗ (1 800) 235 9047) in Christiansted, the Cane Bay Dive Shop (℗ 773 9913, ✆ 778 5442) on the north shore and in Frederiksted, and Cruzan Divers (℗ 772 3701, toll free ℗ (1 800) 352 0107) also in Frederiksted.

other sports

Golf: There are two 18-hole courses on the island, the Carambola (℗ 778 5638) on the northern shore and at the Buccaneer Hotel, east of Christiansted (℗ 773 2100). Green fees $40-50. The Reef is a 9-hole course in the eastern Teague Bay area (℗ 773 8844), green fee comparable.

Horse riding: Can be fixed up through Paul and Jill's Equestrian Stable at Sprat Hall Estate in Frederiksted (℗ 772 2880), for a ride through the diminutive rainforest or around old-time St Croix, the land of the windmills.

Tennis: There are courts in practically every hotel on the island: some have a tennis professional who can give lessons.

Mountain biking: Can be fixed through St Croix Bike and Tours (℗ 772 2343), who offer a variety of tours: a coastal historic tour running through Frederiksted and the west coast, looking at the history and the natural life; and a tropical rainforest tour. They have some single-track rides through the rainforest.

Hiking: The St Croix Environmental Association (℗ 773 1989) leads a number of guided hikes in the Salt River National Park, the rainforest and at the East End. For walking tours of Christiansted and Frederiksted, contact Take-a-Hike (℗ 778 6997).

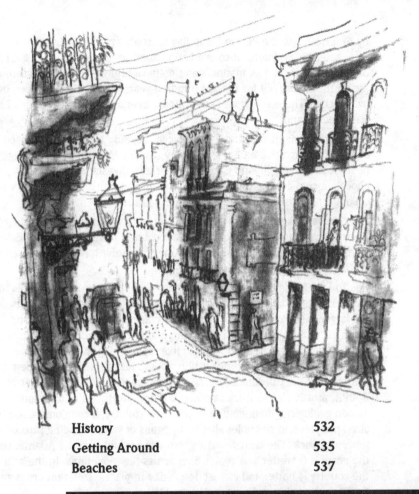

Puerto Rico

By American law the Puerto Rican flag must always fly side by side with the Stars and Stripes. Puerto Rico is a Latin American island and so certain themes—music, dance, manners and political pride—run strongly through life on the island, but for the last hundred years Puerto Rico has been owned by the USA. The result is an extraordinary overlay of America on this Latin Caribbean island.

The duality runs throughout Puerto Rican life. Side by side you will see air-conditioned high-rise buildings and tiny wooden West Indian shacks, pristine neon-lit shops and chaotic Caribbean markets, dog-stands and *kioskos*, chocolate-chip cookies and *chicharrón* with spicy sauce. The currency is the US dollar, but it is often referred to as the *peso*.

Even the languages exist in tandem. Traditional Spanish is the tongue of the Puerto Rican Parliament and of the poor country man, but much of daily life takes place in English. Business-like American order has been imposed on the Latin Caribbean chaos.

Puerto Rico is the smallest and most easterly of the four major islands in the Greater Antilles and it lies about 1000 miles southeast of Miami, between the larger island of Hispaniola and the archipelago of the Virgin Islands. It is oblong in shape, about 100 miles from end to end by about 35 from north to south. It seems much larger though; like many of the mountainous Caribbean islands, the interior is very rough. Just a thin band of coastal plain runs around the Cordillera Central, a cumulus of peaks that rise to over 4000ft, mostly clad in thick rainforest. In the northwest of the island there is an odd geological phenomenon in the karst country, a conglomeration of hill-sized pimples and sinkholes shaped by aeons of water dripping through the limestone rock. The climate varies across the island—on the Atlantic coast in the north it is wetter and cooler than across the mountains. In the southwest the country is hotter and almost desert-like in places. Different crops and fruits, such as aloe and pineapple, grow there.

There are about 3½ million Puerto Ricans on the island (3352 square miles), of whom about one-third live in and around San Juan, the capital, which lies towards the eastern end of the north coast. The islanders have a mixed ancestry, a blend of the early Spaniards and the original Arawak Indians (some towns in the centre of the island have distinctly Amerindian names) and then Africans. Over the centuries, migrants from all over Europe and the Caribbean have added to the mix, followed in this century by the Americans. Puerto Rico has a population noticeably whiter than the other Latin Caribbean islands.

Traditionally Puerto Rico has had a rural economy, but that has changed over the last fifty years as the island has been encouraged to develop an industrial base. American firms have invested in Puerto Rico and, whilst this has brought huge opportunities for work, unemployment is still running at 20 per cent. Notwithstanding this, Puerto Rico has one of the highest standards

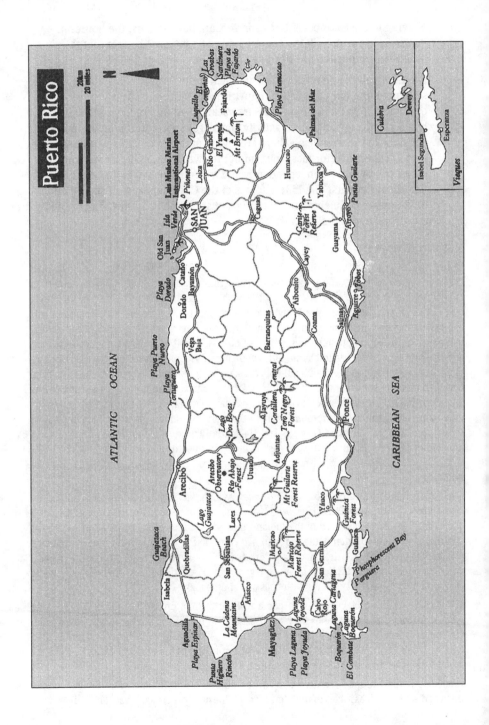

of living in the Caribbean. Unlike most Caribbean islands, the houses in Puerto Rico are all built in concrete now. The material benefits of the American connection are clear.

Even with all the pharmaceutical and manufacturing concerns, tourism is still one of the most important industries on Puerto Rico. It is very well organized. If you like a high-pressure vacation—a mugged-by-sunshine holiday with day-long beach activity and Vegas-style entertainment to keep you busy in the evenings—there are plenty of places on offer. But Puerto Rico is big enough for mass tourism not to swamp local life. Those who prefer to travel more independently and adventurously will find some superb Caribbean retreats. The hilltop towns of the Cordillera and off-shore islands of Vieques and Culebra are charming and show the Spanish Caribbean at its most rural and laid-back.

Suggested Itinerary

In two weeks, you can spend time in San Juan, where there are some excellent new small hotels and guest houses that use the best of their settings in old San Juan buildings, and then take off to tour the coast, as well as one of the offshore islands. You might even fit in a quick visit to the Virgin Islands. You are likely to arrive in San Juan, where there are some fun bars and restaurants and many museums. From here head east, to the eastern beaches and natural parks such as the El Yunque rainforest and Las Cabezas. A visit to either Vieques or Culebra is a must. Both have small-island charm, but if you choose Vieques, make sure to visit the phosphorescent bay. Back on the mainland, Ponce is a pretty town and is worth a quick look; from here head for the southwest coast, to Boquerón or perhaps Cabo Rojo, both seaside towns where the Puerto Ricans themselves take their holidays. From here it is a short ride up into the mountains, along the *ruta panoramica*, where there are two superb *paradors* hidden away in the rainforest—the Hacienda Gripiñas and Hacienda Juanita. It is worth tailoring your trip around any festivals in the countryside. Ask at the tourist board.

History

The native Tainos called Puerto Rico *Borinquen*, which was supposed to mean 'Land of the Noble Lord'. These Arawak Indians, who had come up from South America along the island chain, were the most advanced of the Indian tribes who had lived on the island (the Archaics and the Igneris were hunter-gatherers who had come to the island as fishermen). Their skin was copper-coloured and they had long dark hair. They lived in thatched huts in villages, around a ceremonial area called a *bateye*, a few of which can still be seen on the island, where they would dance and play games with balls and shuttlecocks.

Columbus was the first European to come to Puerto Rico, on 19 November 1493, as he worked his way along the islands back to Hispaniola on his second voyage to the New World. He named it San Juan Bautista (St John the Baptist). Travelling with him was a man called Juan Ponce de León, who was to return as the first governor of the island in 1508. In 1511 the island was given the name of Puerto Rico (Rich Port).

Immediately the European settlers arrived, the 30,000 Taino Indians were divided among them and set to work as slaves in the hunt for gold. Inevitably there was war. The Indians were soon defeated and retreated to the hills or fled the island. Ponce de León himself set off on his quest for the Fountain of Youth. He died in Havana of wounds received while exploring Florida and his body was returned to Puerto Rico. Eventually it was placed in San Juan Cathedral.

By the late 1500s the mines were exhausted and the few remaining Spaniards made a hard living out of cultivating sugar, cotton, ginger and indigo. They suffered the usual natural scourges of the Caribbean, including disease and hurricanes. They also were visited periodically by the canoe-borne Caribs from down-island, who would make lightning raids (5000 attacked them in 1525). And then another human scourge put in an appearance in the middle of the 16th century: pirates. These men arrived with gold in mind, too—Spanish gold—or, if they could not find that, any loot they could lay their hands on.

Puerto Rico was a strategic port and the pirates infested its waters, trying to capture Spain's Central American riches as they were shipped back to Europe. Funded from Mexico, San Juan was fortified in defence against them. Perhaps the most famous pirate to attack the island was Sir Francis Drake. He made it into the harbour past the guns of El Morro and set the Spanish ships alight, but was bombarded in his turn—legend says he was forced to retire when a cannon-ball tore through his cabin, mortally wounding Jack Hawkins. The Dutch had a crack in 1625 and burned the town as they were forced out.

Meanwhile the island was neglected by Spain, and the islanders took to smuggling. Officially the Puerto Ricans could trade with no ships except those from Spain—but at one stage not a single Spanish ship called for seven years, so they carried on brisk illegal trade in tobacco, ginger and cattle with other Caribbean islands. At one stage, Puerto Rico was nearly given to Britain in exchange for Gibraltar.

It was not until 1765 that the Spanish king sent an envoy to develop the island. Alejandro O'Reilly advised that sugar should become the main agricultural crop as in the other Caribbean islands and the trading laws be amended, and Spaniards should be encouraged to settle here. Within a few years the ships of the new American Republic were doing a brisk legal trade.

As the 19th century progressed, the political scene became more important. The Puerto Ricans were granted citizenship of Spain in 1809 during the Napoleonic Wars and rights were accorded with a more liberal Spanish constitution in 1812. Steadily a Puerto Rican island identity crystallized and the struggle for autonomy began, encouraged by the wars of independence in South America. Spain started to clamp down in 1825, and sent over a series of ruthless military governors, later called the 'Little Caesars'. One governor even banned goatee beards because they were emotive of revolution. In 1856, the reformer Betances was exiled for his anti-colonial views. Encouraged by the revolution in the Dominican Republic in 1862, he and other exiles plotted revolution in Puerto Rico and Cuba.

On 23 September 1868 their first uprising came in the town of Lares in the northwest of the island and the Republic of Puerto Rico was declared. But the colonial authorities responded quickly, crushing the revolt at San Sebastian. It is remembered as the *Grito de Lares* (the cry of Lares) and became symbolic of the struggle for independence. On 22 March 1873, slavery was abolished in Puerto Rico.

Politically the Puerto Ricans divided into two camps: the autonomists, who wanted independence, and the conservatives who wished to remain connected with Spain, but with increased self-government. Their hope was that a new Republican government in Spain would grant them autonomy without a war. Their wish was granted and on 28 November 1897 the Puerto Ricans were finally allowed to govern themselves. They elected their own Lower House and half the Senate. The Governor was appointed from Spain, but his powers were restricted.

But it was not to last for long. Within nine months the Americans had invaded as part of the Spanish-American War. The campaign lasted 17 days. In December of that year, after four hundred years as colonial masters, the Spaniards handed Puerto Rico to the Americans at the Treaty of Paris. Initially the Puerto Ricans were hopeful that American intervention and severance from Spain would improve their political status, but it steadily became clear that the USA wanted to keep the island and would impose its political will. The Jones Act of 1917 granted the Puerto Ricans American citizenship and an elected bicameral legislature, but still the key administrative posts were appointed from the US government. Political struggle was by no means dormant for long. There were attacks on the government and in 1937 19 people were killed at an *Independentista* rally when police fired on the crowd.

On 5 August 1947 Harry Truman signed the bill that created the Commonwealth of Puerto Rico, ratified by the islanders themselves in 1952. As in the USA, the government is divided into executive, judicial and legislative branches. There are two houses of parliament, a 51-member House of Representatives and a 27-member Senate. The Governor is elected for four-year terms in line with the elections on the mainland.

The island does not pay taxes to the Federal Bank in the same way as a State of the Union and consequently has no representation in Congress. The elected Resident Commissioner, Carlos Romero Barceló, has observer status—more of a lobbying role. The island also receives financial support in grants for public works, the universities and food stamps ('pan' cheques).

Today the politics of Puerto Rico are dominated by the status of the island with regard to the USA and there are two main possibilities (the desire for independence has faded into insignificance). The majority of the voters swing between maintaining the Commonwealth status and becoming the fifty-first State of the Union.

The governing party is the New Progressive Party, led by Governor Pedro Rosillo, which advocates progress towards statehood. Elections are next due in 2001.

Latin Heritage and the American Legacy

In places, Puerto Rico can seem exactly like America itself. Kids wear jeans, sneakers and T-shirts and cruise around in large gas-guzzlers, spending their evenings in drive-in cinemas and fast-food joints. Buses cost a quarter, exact fare only please. The billboards scream at you: 'Buy Buick!' and 'Drink Bud!'; it's just that the models have Puerto Rican faces.

For all the superficial change, beyond the coconut suntan oil on Condado beach and the glass-fronted skyscrapers of Santurce and the coastal factories, once you are out into the country, Puerto Rico becomes far more like the other Caribbean islands, and stateside USA seems to belong to another age. In the country towns the islanders pass the time of day chatting on the plaza, surveyed calmly by the local church, or wait patiently to sell their fruits at a roadside stall. And in the evenings they promenade and take the night air.

And for all the changes that America has brought, the Latin heritage also rings clear in modern Puerto Rican life. Besuited executives wilt as soon as they emerge from their air-conditioned offices, so many islanders prefer to wear the *guayabera*, a square-tailed, pleated long shirt. Cotton *guayaberas* are worn instead of a suit; pineapple-fibre is for more formal evening occasions. You will certainly hear the bustling and compulsive rhythms of *salsa* blaring in the street and the macho poise and swagger is all too evident. The country is strongly Catholic—there are convents, monasteries and even one or two shrines where the Virgin Mary has appeared to the faithful. The Caribbean-wide desire for a jump-up expresses itself in the week-long *fiestas patronales*, in which each town celebrates its saint's day.

There have been changes, however, in traditional island life. The role of the family, traditionally an extended collection of uncles, aunts and grandparents, has taken a turn for the nuclear and romantic old gents lament the demise of the serenade, impossible now that she lives on the thirteenth floor.

Another issue that has changed with the American presence is the feeling of being Puerto Rican. Perhaps more than any other American minority, the Puerto Ricans are Puerto Rican first and American second. In the last century there was a strong desire for independence on the island, but this was killed with the uninvited arrival of the American army. The island was forcibly made a Commonwealth of the United States. The issues still remain—streets and plazas are still named after the *Independentistas* of the 19th century and many Puerto Ricans are voluble in political discussion—but with the easing of the relationship with the USA and the material benefits that the association has brought, the desire for independence has faded and it is hardly a practical solution now. In a recent vote, the Independentistas polled just three per cent.

As citizens of the USA, the Puerto Ricans can move to the mainland if they want to (Puerto Rico is a crowded island and emigration acts as a pressure valve). There are large communities of Puerto Ricans all over the States, particularly in New York, where there are supposed to be more Puerto Ricans than in San Juan. Many of these 'Neoyorkinos' as they are known maintain close links with their island.

For their part, the Americans have pumped huge amounts of money into the island, in health care, food stamps, unemployment benefit and tax concessions. The island is strategically important and they maintain huge military bases there. Puerto Rico has some of the best schools in the Caribbean.

Getting Around

There is an extensive network of **públicos** (Ford vans, marked with P or PD), that run to and from the central plaza in each town. Travelling like this works, though it can take a while, because you may have to take successive *públicos* from one town to the next (their beat is not usually longer than two or three towns). The system is typically West Indian and services are quite frequent, but do not work to any recognizable schedule; *públicos* leave when they are full or when the urge takes the driver. You can flag them down on the roadside to let you on or shout to get off. Service is more limited at the weekend. Travelling in them is fun because there is the latest *salsa* music to sing along to and you will get to know your fellow passengers fairly well. Destinations are marked on the windscreen. The *público* terminals in San Juan for journeys around the island are at the **Luis Muñoz Marin International Airport** and at the Plaza del Mercado (at the end of metropolitan bus routes 1 and 2) in **Río Piedras**. The metropolitan area of **San Juan** is served by air-conditioned buses known locally as **guaguas** (pronounced wahwah). From Old San Juan (Plaza Colón and the harbour area) you can get to Bayamón, Cataño, Country Club and Río Piedras (close to the Plaza del Mercado *público* terminal). The fare is 25c, exact change only. Wait at the yellow posts (*paradas*). *Guaguas* do not run very often (about every 20–30 minutes), but they go on until around 10pm. There are some recently privatized routes around the city, with smaller and faster buses, price 50c. **Línea** services, in vans like *públicos*, will drop you off where you want to go in the order that seems best to the driver. If your feet get tired within Old San Juan itself, you might consider using the little safari buses (free) that run a circular route around the area. A word of warning: if you want to get to and from the airport by bus, the *guagua* drivers will sometimes not let you aboard with luggage, so basically you are forced to go by taxi.

Taxis are readily available at the airport, at all the hotels and in areas like the dock in Old San Juan. Cabs are metered according to a fixed scale set by the government: the arm is supposed to be up when you board and then lowered as you set off. Special 'Tourist Taxis' charge set rates along popular routes. The rates are usually displayed on the outside of the door. A cab from the airport to Old San Juan costs around $16, Condado—$12 and Isla Verde—$8. Taxi drivers will happily take you on a longer tour at around $20 per hour.

Island **tours** can be arranged to the principal sights—a day's excursion to El Yunque and Luquillo or over to Ponce, for instance—through VIP Coach and Tours (✆ 783 6096) and the Tour Co-op of Puerto Rico (✆ 253 1448). Most companies will pick you up and deliver you to your hotel.

Car-hire is really the best way to see the island for the independent traveller and there is a limitless supply of them in Condado and Isla Verde. Although you can get a good price out of season, prices are high over the winter. Most companies will deliver and pick up rental cars for you. Driving is on the right and, although speed limits are indicated in miles per hour, distances are in kilometres. US licences are valid for three months. UK licences are valid, as are international licences. If you wish to travel around the island, in the Cordillera or around the less populous south coast, it is essential to have a good map and these can usually be provided by the hire company. Road signs are not brilliant, but the roads themselves are good. Small cars start at around $50 per day inclusive of insurance in the winter, mileage unlimited.

Hire companies include the big international names: Avis (✆ (800) 874 3556), Budget (✆ 791 3685), Charlie (✆ 728 2418) and National (✆ 791 1805). Other island companies are: Afro on Ponce de León (✆ 724 3720), L & M on Ashford Avenue (✆ 725 8307) and Target on Baldorioty Avenue in Santurce (✆ 728 1447).

Ferries operate within San Juan harbour. *Aqua Expresso* links San Juan to Hato Rey and Cataño, every half-hour, 6am–9pm ($1). From **Fajardo** on the east coast you can reach the off-shore islands of **Vieques** (*weekdays twice daily, 9.30am and 4.30pm, weekends three times daily, fare $3, crossing 1 hour, ferry originates in Vieques*) and **Culebra** (*weekdays once a day at 4pm, returning next morning at 7am, with additional sailings at the weekend, fare $2.50, crossing 1¼hrs*). Ferries are rarely full, but you can reserve on ✆ 863 0852.

There are small **airstrips** dotted around Puerto Rico. Flights can be caught from Isla Grande airport in Condado or from San Juan International airport to: Ponce, Mayagüez, Palmas del Mar, Fajardo and the offshore islands of Vieques and Culebra.

Puerto Rico's hundreds of miles of coastline have a great variety of beaches—from protected coves on the southwestern shore where the snorkelling is excellent to the busy, people-packed, golden sand strands in San Juan and the surfing beaches at the northwestern tip of the island. Perhaps the best beaches, though, are on the offshore islands of Vieques and Culebra, where the sand is white and undeveloped and the reefs are good. Going to the beach is a popular day out at the weekend among the Puerto Ricans and the government has developed some of the more popular spots with *balnearios.* These 13 public beaches have changing rooms with lockers, lifeguards, a car park and usually a small restaurant. *Open Tues–Sun 9–5; adm usually a dollar parking and 50c entrance.* Some also have sites where you can pitch or hire a tent for a minimal fee.

best beaches

The Eastern End of the Island

Condado and Isla Verde: The bays around San Juan are the busiest on the island. These two famous strips are crowded and highly developed, backed by high-rise hotels that make them look a bit like Miami beach. All the watersports are on offer here (from parasailing to sail-boat trips), through the hotels or the independent operators, and there are plenty of restaurants for a bit of time out from the sunning and swimming. The beach is always busy around Condado beneath the high-rise complexes; further east, the Ocean Park area is popular with a gay crowd. Bus T1 passes Isla Verde. Beyond the skyscrapers there is a collection of *kioskos,* semi-permanent lorries selling cooked fish and batter-fried vegetables.

Piñones: Heading east the action evaporates and the skyscrapers turn to palm trees in this remoter area, where the Atlantic waves barrel in on to golden-red sand. **The Reef** restaurant stands on the rocky point, a hang-out by day and night, often with live music; beyond here there are plenty of smaller restaurants, including *El pulpo loco* (the loopy octopus) for a simple meal, and *kioskos,* for a crabstick or a fried codfish batter in a seagrape leaf with a chilled coconut to drink.

Luquillo: Some 30 miles out of San Jua is one of the island's most popular beaches, another stunning 1-mile-long half-moon bay backed with forests of palm trees. This *balneario* becomes very crowded at the weekend as the San Juañeros pour out of town in search of sun and sand. There are some watersports, including windsurfers and more *kioskos,* in a line of pre-fab concrete buildings at the roadside, selling anything from coconut water to a full meal. The lobster *tacos* at kiosk Juan Y Fela are superb.

Las Croabas: Also on the eastern coast; the old and new, fishing shacks and villas, are side by side on the shore.

Seven Seas Beach: Quite popular and there are good strips of sand on the offshore cays; Palominos is reached from the El Conquistador resort and Icacos can be reached from the marina in Fajardo. Take what you need in the way of a picnic to the latter.

Playa Humacao and Punta Santiago, fabout 15 miles (24km) south of Fajardo: Two more deserted strips of sand that suddenly explode with activity at the weekend.

Palmas del Mar, 5 miles (8km) further south: A huge development where you can find watersports for all the family.

Punta Guilarte: A *balneario* near Arroyo. Generally, the south coast towards Ponce does not have the sand and the reefs of the northeast, but in the mangroves and the seafront towns you will find small coves where you will often be alone.

The Southwest, Ponce up to Mayagüez

There is just one rather disappointing cove at Parguera before you reach the western coast, where you will find many of the island's most glorious beaches and the best view of the sunset and the Green Flash.

Boquerón: This magnificent curve is one of the best known on the island—ever popular at the weekend and less crowded during the week. Backed by a forest of palms, the 3 miles of sand gently slope away into the warm limpid water where the laziest of waves play.

El Combate: Towards the southwestern tip of the island, another beach idyll lined with fishermen's shacks on the shore and their boats in the jade-coloured water. A perfect view of the sunset. You can also find deserted suntraps around the *salinas*, the salt flats, in this area.

Playa Buye: A small beach to the west of Cabo Rojo, overlooking the bay of Puerto Real where more fishing boats lie at anchor. North of here the seafront is developed between Playa Joyuda and Playa Laguna, so you can hire a windsurfer or bask on the thin beach before retreating inside for another piña colada.

North of Mayagüez the coastline becomes rougher where the cliffs of the Cordillera and the Atlantic waves meet. There are a few passable stretches of sand in the area (there is a *balneario* at Añasco), but **Punta Higüero** and **Rincón** are most popular with surfers and windsurfers. The biggest breakers can be found along Route 413, near El Faro. There are a number of surf shops in the area.

Playa Espinar, close to Aguadilla: Half a mile of white sand and water good for lively bathing.

The North Coast back to San Juan

The north coast of Puerto Rico is pounded by the Atlantic waves and so it can get pretty dramatic, but the miles of sand are protected by reefs in places which create good swimming beaches. Protruding through the sand you will see the limestone base of old coral reefs, like a sort of stone peanut brittle.

Jobos: Close to Isabela, a stretch of sand between the cliffs, where you can escape the crowds. Take water and a picnic. There is a *balneario* among the palms at Guajacata just outside Quebradillas.

Dorado: Several beaches encrusted with hotels, good places to get hold of watersports equipment if you want to pause for an afternoon in an island tour.

Playa Sardinera: A popular strip with a *balneario* and *kioskos*, where you can stop for a chat and buy a drink to stave off a thirst in the height of the sun.

Flora and Fauna

Puerto Rico has the full variety of Caribbean wildlife, from the coral reefs that skirt the island and the coastal mangrove swamps to rainforest at 4000ft. In El Yunque and the rough mountains of the Cordillera you will see trees that soar and explode into canopy at 100ft, tangled with lianas and creeping vines, montane forests of extraordinarily lush ferns and palms, and on the upper slopes stunted elfin forest where mosses fur the prehistoric-looking tree bark.

In the heights you might see the Puerto Rican parrot, recently close to extinction but now flourishing, lizard cuckoos, warblers and screech owls—and hummingbirds, tiny delicate creatures with a metabolic rate so high that they must fly all day to keep up their intake of nectar. In the lower mountains, among Puerto Rico's man-made inland lakes, you will see kestrels and hawks on the hunt, cruising on the spirals of rising air and casting a drilling eye over the undergrowth, and in the flatlands the cattle egret standing around, dumbstruck and mournful.

There are mangrove swamps all around the coastline, where you will see crabs with their eyes out on stalks, surprised to see you perhaps. These monstrously tangled waterways are refuge to hundreds of different birds, including the exotic green-backed heron and the purple gallinule. You might also see a mockingbird or a whistling duck. On the offshore islands you will come across boobies, solitary pelicans and maybe even a red-billed tropicbird with an 18-inch tail.

Puerto Rico has the usual roll-call of Caribbean reptiles including lizards and iguanas, but the one the islanders think most fondly of is the coquí, an indigenous tree frog who you will hear singing every evening. *Eleutherodactylus portoricensis* is about 1 inch long with smooth and almost transparent skin, and he disappears into moist and cool hideouts during the day. His local name derives from his dual peep, sung loudest after rain—an immediately recognizable 'co-quí co-quí co-quí!'

There are twenty Forest Reserves (*see* pp.544, 549, 551), of which the best known (also one of the closest to San Juan) is **El Yunque**. Other mountain parks a little more off the beaten track are: the **Carite Forest Reserve**, in the Cayey mountains south of Caguas, the **Toro Negro Forest**, just east of Adjuntas in the centre of the island (this park contains the mountain Cerro de Punta, Puerto Rico's highest peak) and **Río Abajo Forest**, in the karst country south of Arecibo. If you would prefer somewhere less hilly, you could try the coastal mangrove

pelicans

swamps, for instance at **Guánica Forest**, on the south coast to the west of Ponce, which has extensive bird-life, or **Piñones Forest**, just a stone's throw out of San Juan to the east.

There is usually a ranger's hut in the parks, where you might get information to help you get the best out of the natural life. Their services are free of charge. They also publish information (usually) in both Spanish and in English. For more information, contact the Natural Resources Department, PO Box 5887, San Juan 00906 (✆ 724 3724). Information on El Yunque can be obtained on ✆ 888 1880 or ✆ 766 5335. Tour operators specializing in nature and adventure travel include **Tropix Wellness Tours** (✆ 268 2173, @ 268 5882) and **Fondo de Mejoramiento** (✆ 759 8366).

San Juan

The capital of Puerto Rico captures best the duality of this American-Caribbean island. Side by side here you will see charming Spanish colonial town houses and modern glass-fronted offices, West Indian shanties and massive air-conditioned tourist hotels.

Since it was founded in 1520, San Juan has expanded from a little collection of shacks huddled together for protection near the point at El Morro into a massive metropolis. It crept along the peninsula and over to the mainland and then splurged around the lagoons and beaches into suburbs, eventually becoming a city of over a million. It has its own university, a huge international airport, and is the top financial centre of the whole Caribbean area.

The seven blocks of **Old San Juan**, which have recently been restored to their original state as an 18th-century Spanish colonial city, are one of the most charming spots in the Caribbean. Among the steep and narrow alleys, you will see the old gas lanterns and cast-iron balconies and louvred windows. The houses are painted in pastel blue and yellow, cut with white door-frames and window sills.

The whole of Old San Juan is surrounded by massive defensive walls 30ft thick and studded with lumbering fortresses. *Garitas*, little stone sentry-boxes perched above the sea, run around the town. The streets are laid with adequines, cobblestones of a rich blue-grey colour that were brought out as ballast in the ocean-going ships. They speak of the days when the island was the 'Rich Port' of its name and San Juan a very wealthy harbour town. At its less crowded moments the colonial city has such an aura of history that you might expect to see a bearded merchant or a cleric in flowing vestments swish past.

Despite its slightly tourist-precious air, Old San Juan is fun because it is also a living city, with banks and bookshops, business-people and domino players, and when there are not too many cruise-trippers around, it has real charm. After dark the islanders promenade, and the bars and restaurants come alive as crowds of young Puerto Ricans loiter around the night-clubs. One of the most special things about the

defensive walls around San Juan

town are the inner courtyards: they are usually surrounded by arches and the internal steps are decorated with beautiful patterned tiles. Unfortunately they are mostly behind closed doors; some museums and restaurants are set around courtyards and these are worth a look, but if you see an open door it is well worth the risk of peeking inside.

On the western point of the peninsula is **San Felipe del Morro** (*morro* means headland), a fortress and a half (✆ 729 6960; *open daily 9–5, a small historical museum and video shows for the studious visitor; adm, children free*). Its walls, 20ft thick, rise from the sea to a height of 140ft, and inside it contains a network of tunnels, dungeons and bastions on six levels. On the uppermost level, the cannon were placed on runners so that they could get a better angle of fire. Construction began in 1540 and it was not completed until 1783. Sir Francis Drake was one of the first to attack it in 1595, and it was last shelled by the Americans in 1898.

One of the few buildings older than El Morro is the crenellated **Casa Blanca** (✆ 724 4102; *open Tues–Sun 9–noon and 1–4.30*), built in 1521 as the Ponce de León family home, which it remained for the next 250 years. It was eventually restored as a museum of island life in the early colonial days, with old wooden furniture including a throne, and arms, not all original, but pleasant enough to view. Another is **La Fortaleza** (✆ 721 7000; *hourly tours in English and Spanish, 9–4; adm free*), which overlooks San Juan bay from the top of the city walls. This mansion (the 'fortress' that was originally built here in 1532 as a defence against Carib Indians has long been swallowed up by plaster walls) is the official residence of the Governor of Puerto Rico. It sells itself as the 'oldest executive mansion still used as such in the Western Hemisphere', but for all the tourist twaddle it is a pleasant visit to see the corridors of power and ceremonial rooms. Both have good gardens.

Another pillar of the Spanish establishment was **San Juan Cathedral** on Calle Cristo (✆ 722 0861; *open daily 8.30–4*), a grand Spanish colonial church dressed in beige with white stucco and topped with three red and white cupolas. It was begun in 1521, but the first thatch-roofed building had to be rebuilt after a hurricane. There is a marble tomb containing the remains of Ponce de León himself, brought here in 1913.

When León's remains were originally returned to Puerto Rico he was buried in his family chapel, the **San José Church** on the Plaza San José, a little north of the Cathedral (*open Mon–Sat, 8.30–4*). The chapel is of medieval design, its domes supported by coral rock walls and Romanesque arches, and laid with ochre tiles. In the centre of the plaza, where young San Juañeros like to loiter at night, stands a statue of Ponce de León, built from cannon captured during an unsuccessful attack on San Juan by the British in 1797. Behind here is the old **Dominican Convent**, where two cool floors of arched cloisters surround an inner courtyard. Built in 1523 by Dominican friars, it has offered sanctuary to besieged citizens and pious besiegers (the Earl of Cumberland in 1598) and until 1966 it was the headquarters of the US Army Antilles Command. Now once again it has a more peaceful mission as home to exhibits of modern art (eventually intended to become the San Juan Museum of Fine Art). Next to the convent on Calle San Sebastian is the **Pablo Casals Museum** (✆ 723 9185; *open Tues–Sat, 9.30–5.30; adm free*), dedicated to the cellist who came live in Puerto Rico in 1957—as well as hearing recordings of his concerts, you will see his favourite cellos. Close by is the **Plaza del Quinto Centenario**, an open square dedicated to the last five centuries of Puerto Rican culture. The striking and controversial totem pole at its centre, the **Totema Tellurica**, represents a soil core of Puerto Rican history. Just beyond here is the vast and surprisingly attractive **Cuartel de Ballajá**, a former military barracks now brightly restored to a more peaceful mission, as the home of the **Museum of the Americas** (✆ 724 5052; *open Tues–Fri 10–4, weekends 11–5*), which illustrates American culture over the centuries, and mounts other revolving exhibitions. A short walk away, at the corner of Norzagay and MacArthur is the **San Juan Museum of Art and History** (✆ 724 1875; *open Tues–Sun 8–4; recommended donation $1*), where there are exhibitions of Puerto Rican art and an audiovisual presentation (*11 am*) of the history of San Juan. Concerts are also staged here in the courtyard.

Back in the heart of town is the **Plaza de Armas**, once the parade ground and now an open piazza with fountains and bandstands, department stores, cafés and department stores. Originally it was larger, to accommodate military manoeuvres, but it became San Juan's central square. On the northern side is the **Alcaldía** (City Hall), a copy of the City Hall in Madrid. Started in 1609 and completed in 1789, it has an attractive staircase and coral rock arches and was the nucleus of San Juan social life; now it contains a tourist information desk, a gallery and offices. Calle Luna has the oldest recorded whorehouses in the Americas.

Just south of here on Calle Cristo are two more museums set in San Juan's charming 18th-century town-houses: the **Centro Nacional de Artes Populares y Artesenías**, with exhibits of island crafts (✆ 722 0621; *open Mon–Sat 9–5; adm free*), and the **Casa del Libro** (✆ 723 0354; *open Tues–Sat 11–4.30*) with exhibits of the art of printing and bookbinding, and a library of books, including some from the 15th century. The small shop is a treasure trove of unusual souvenirs, such as prints made with 15-century woodblocks.

Across the way you will find the tiny, ornate **Capilla del Cristo**, where behind a grille a silver altar commemorates the apparently miraculous survival of a rider who supposedly plunged off the cliff on a round-the-city horse-race. You get a good view over the harbour and the city beyond from **Parque de las Palomas** (pigeon park, with special nesting holes), but do not go too close to the edge or you could end up in **La Princesa** prison, 50ft below. It is no longer a jail, but is used by the Tourism Company.

If you walk down the hill beneath the city walls you come to the dock in San Juan Bay, where the vast and gleaming cruise ships tie up before they each off-load their thousand-odd passengers. Behind the Customs building and coast guard station on the headland is **El Arsenal** (✆ 724 5949; *open Wed–Sun 9–4.30; adm free*), the old Spanish naval base, where more revolving art exhibitions are staged in the three galleries.

Back up top, Calle Fortaleza is full of shops and bars (one claims, erroneously, that the piña colada was invented there) and runs the full length of Old San Juan from La Fortaleza itself to **Plaza Colón** (Columbus Square), where a statue commemorates the explorer, at the entrance to the colonial city.

Just above the Plaza Colón, the eastern extent of Old San Juan is guarded by another fortress, **El Fuerte Castillo de San Cristóbal** (✆ 729 6960; *open daily 9–5, tours in Spanish and English; adm*), a vast and lumbering affair worthy of its counterpart on the western point of the peninsula. Completed in 1678, it is a classic piece of 17th-century military architecture, with five bastions, each of which had to be captured before the main keep could be taken. Its 27 acres are a maze of ramparts, tunnels and arches, bristling with cannon, overlooking the Atlantic approaches to the island.

Just outside the northern city walls beneath San Cristóbal, you will see another side of Puerto Rico. The rundown area of **La Perla**, with its wooden shacks and forests of television aerials, is an alter-ego to neat and tidy Old San Juan. You are advised to be careful if you go there.

As you travel farther east you come to a more modern Puerto Rico in the white, pillared and domed **Capitol**, the seat of the island legislature (Senate and House of Representatives) (*②721 6040; open on weekdays, guided tours by appointment*). Started in 1925, the Capitol contains the Puerto Rican Constitution in an urn. Inside the elaborate dome, friezes depict Puerto Rican history.

San Juan Suburbs

Soon after you pass the Capitol the hotels and the expressways begin to appear and you cross from the peninsula on to the mainland. On the Atlantic waterfront is the high-rise **Condado** strip, where a range of humming factory hotels jostle for beach space, and fast-food joints and designer shops muscle in on Ashford Avenue beneath them. A few miles farther along the coast, through the continuing suburbs you come to Ocean Park and Isla Verde, lines of luxury hotels and high-rise condominiums set on excellent beaches. These two strips are developed to bursting point, and you can expect canned music, cable television and Vegas-style entertainment.

Across the Condado Lagoon, where the windsurfers fly back and forth, you come to the business/residential districts of **Miramar**, and **Santurce**, with the grand, walled homes of San Juan's wealthy. Among the industrial estates on the shores of the San José lagoon are the shanty towns where the poorest San Juañeros live.

Following Highway 1 south out of Santurce you come to **Hato Rey**, the business capital of Puerto Rico. On the **Golden Mile** you will see the glass-fronted head-offices of the corporations and banks that operate on the island. Nearby is the suburb of **Río Piedras**, home of the **University of Puerto Rico**, its faculty buildings scattered around the distinctive clock-tower. In the **University Museum** (*② 763 4408; entrance on Avenue Ponce de León; open Mon–Sat, hours vary, and weekends 8–3.30; adm free*) there are exhibitions of contemporary sculptures and paintings from Puerto Rico and Latin America.

South of here at the bus terminal is the **Plaza del Mercado**, San Juan's biggest market, where the island produce, tropical fruit and vegetables, is shipped in from the country and stacked in colourful piles on the tables and where the Puerto Ricans haggle.

Further on to the south are the **Botanical Gardens** (*② 798 8191; open Tues–Sun, 9–6; adm free*), 200 acres that are peaceful and green after the mayhem of the city. Among the walks and waterways is an endless variety of palm (from the tall spiked royal palm to the scratchy sable), 60ft bamboos, an orchid garden and everywhere Puerto Rican lovers. The entrance is on the south side of the intersection of Route 1 and Route 847 (hard to spot).

West of Hato Rey, a 75c ride on the ferry across the bay from Old San Juan brings you to the suburb of **Cataño** and the vast **Bacardi Rum Plant**, on Route 888 (*② 795 1500; open Mon–Sat, 9.30–3.30; adm free*), where you can whizz around the outsize stills in trolley buses, zip through the museum and then claim a free daiquiri. On Route 2 travelling towards Bayamón are the ruins of **Caparra**, the island's oldest settlement, founded in 1508 by Ponce de León, but only used for ten years before the pioneers decamped for Old San Juan. A small museum, the **Museum of the Conquest and Colonization of Puerto Rico** (*② 781 4795; open Tues–Sat 9–4; adm free*), has about as many excavated artefacts on view as there are words in its title.

Driving east on the north coastal route 187 beyond Isla Verde you come to the area of Piñones, where there is a forest reserve in the mangroves and you can hope to see herons (green-backed and tricoloured), pelicans digesting a meal and crabs holding their arms across their bodies as though they were broken. Boats can be fixed up at the Cangrejos Marina on the Laguna Torrecilla. From here you pass palm-backed sand beaches and mangrove for 6 miles (10km) before turning inland and eventually coming to **Loíza**. The area has a strong African influence and is best known for its church, Iglesia San Patricio, built in 1645, and its saint's day festival, dedicated to Santiago Apostol (from 25 July, *see* 'festivals', p.566).

El Yunque Rainforest

Luquillo, 35 miles (56km) outside the capital, is best known for its beach, a mile-long strip backed with more palm trees, which is very popular with the San Juañeros at the weekends. Visible from the beach is the **Sierra de Luquillo**, a 3000ft mountain range with a mantle of rainforest, where the Atlantic winds stack in vast rainclouds and then go at it hammer and tongs, dropping as much as 200 inches of rain a year (around a hundred billion gallons of water). **El Yunque** (the Anvil) is a spectacular rainforest, where the air fizzes with mist and rain among 100ft trees, and exotic birdlife (60 species) flits among the perfectly formed ferns, scratchy sierra palms and the tabanuco trees, which seeps a sap smelling like Vicks (*see* 'Flora and Fauna', p.539). The rainforest is home to the Puerto Rican parrot, and if the squawking was not enough, the forest also rings with the dual tone of millions of tiny tree frogs (*coquís*).

El Yunque is a popular place to visit and you can get information at the **Sierra Palm Visitor Center** on route 191. A number of concrete trails have been laid in the forest to give you a close-up view of the intricate beauty of the individual plants—tiny orchids the size of a cent coin—and panoramic views as far as the coast. The trails, which are well maintained, start from Route 191 or 186, and include **El Yunque**, **Mt Britton** and the relatively easy 8 miles of **El Toro**, also known as the Tradewinds. Take a pair of training shoes (or better) for the slippery rocks, and waterproofs if you do not want to get too wet. There are two waterfalls worth the detour, **La Coca Falls**, not far into the park and **La Mina Falls**, which are more remote (approach from the Palo Colorado Recreation Site). The locals drink the water, but it is better to take your own, to be absolutely safe.

Back down below the mountains, Route 3 continues from Luquillo Beach to **Fajardo** at the northeastern tip of the island, a sleepy town around a typical paved plaza. On the coast a few miles away (Playa de Fajardo) you will still see the town's traditional side—fishermen from the fleet of small boats selling their catch on the beach—but the bay between here and Las Croabas has also become a major tourist centre, with three marinas and ranges of villas perched on the hills above. You can hire boats to reach the tiny offshore cays where the snorkelling and diving are excellent. La Playa is also the ferry terminal for the islands of **Vieques** and **Culebra**.

At the northeastern tip of the island is **Las Cabezas de San Juan Nature Park**. (℗ 722 5882, weekends ℗ 860 2560; *open at weekends only, unless you can claim to be a group; call to reserve; adm*), with the central visitors' centre set in an old lighthouse, El Faro (the park also goes by this name). It is quite tame; you are guided along forest paths and boardwalks that give you a close-up view of the mangroves. There is also a phosphorescent lake in the park which is well worth a visit (*see* 'Vieques', p.563).

Turning south, the road passes Roosevelt Roads, a vast US Naval Base, **Playa de Humacao** and Humacao itself (turn off on Route 30 for a trip back through the mountains to **Caguas** and eventually San Juan) before it disappears south into the cane-covered hills to **Yabucoa** and the south coast. Arroyo, Guayama and Aguirre are sleepy and charming rural and waterfront towns where the old wooden buildings around the plaza have been encrusted with concrete suburbs. At Salinas, Route 3 meets Route 1, which continues to the city of Ponce.

From San Juan to Ponce

Two freeways (tollway Route 52 and untolled Route 1) carve a way up into the mountains south of San Juan *en route* for the Caribbean coast and 15 miles (24km) out of the capital they meet at **Caguas**. Named after an old Amerindian chief, the city is set in the massive foothills of the Cordillera Central. From here Route 172 switchbacks up into the mountains to be swallowed by tunnels of bamboos and ferns. Both the main roads cross the Panoramic Route near **Cayey**, where the land is dotted with small private tobacco plantations and drying sheds, and then descend to the south coast, from where they head west towards Ponce.

Back up in the hills on Route 153 is the town of **Coamo**, established in 1579, the third oldest on the island. The old church and the town houses of its former splendour can still be seen set around the classic plaza. There is a small **museum** in the inner courtyard of one of the houses on the plaza, with a display of family life a hundred years ago, but Coama is best known for its **thermal springs** just south of the town. They were used by the Arawaks and are thought to have been visited by Ponce de León in his search for the Fountain of Youth. They became popular as a resort in the 19th century but fell into disrepair, and have recently been rebuilt as a *parador*, with the spring water brought to the pool at 110°C.

Ponce

Ponce (pronounced *Pon-tsé*, with pursed Spanish vowels) is Puerto Rico's second city and it is situated across the Cordillera on the southern coast of the island. Founded in the late 17th century, Ponce may take its name from the first governor of the island, Ponce de León, but perhaps instead from his great-grandson (presently the source of raging academic controversy). The city may be only an hour and a bit's drive from the capital nowadays, but 50 years ago the journey of 70 miles was daunting; the 200,000 Ponceños have always been cut off from the capital. They have a proud tradition (and an idiom of speech) all of their own and they refer to their city as *la Perla del Sur* (the Pearl of the South).

As you come to the outskirts on the freeway you pass the old clapboard shanties alongside new residential villas, and a plethora of sports stadia and drive-in fast-food joints, eventually coming to the centre of the town, where the old plastered and wooden buildings are embellished like wedding cakes with streetfront pillars with recessed balconies, and intricate latticeworks of wood and iron. The centre of the city is looking very attractive at the moment because a number of streets have recently been restored.

Plaza Central

The heart of the city is the old Plaza Central, where the Ponceños gather by day in the shade of the neatly trimmed fig trees and promenade in the evenings. It is guarded on one side by the Cathedral of Our Lady of Guadeloupe, a 17th-century Spanish creole church (designed by

Puerto Rican architects who had studied in Spain) with classical pillars and devotional statues, topped with rounded silver towers. The Casa Armstrong Poventud, a restored neo-classical town-house from the turn of the century, is home to the **Ponce Institute of Culture** (✆ 844 8240; *open Mon–Fri, 8–noon and 1–4*) which offers some tourist information and has a small display of antique furniture. More comprehensive tourist information is available from the offices of the **Puerto Rico Tourism Company** on the first floor of Las Delicias Shopping Mall across the square (✆ 840 5695; *open Mon–Sat 8–5*).

Also on the plaza is Ponce's most famous sight, the **Parque de Bombas** (*adm free*), a striking red and black wooden structure with towers and arched windows, which was built in 1882 for an agricultural fair held on the plaza. There is old fire-fighting equipment on display, including hand-pulled tanks, in which the water preesure was built up by the movement of rushing to the scene of a fire. Discover why the heroes of Polvorin were court-martialled. The **Ponce Museum of History** (✆ 844 7071; *open Mon, Wed–Fri 10–5, Sat, Sun 10–6; adm $3*) is set in two attractive houses that have been joined together on Calle Isabel. The story of Ponce is told in Amerindian artefacts and its literary, commercial and agricultural prowess are illustrated in documents and pictures. .

The renowned **Ponce Museum of Art** (✆ *848 0511; open daily 10–5; adm $3*) on Avenue Las Americas has over 1000 paintings and 400 sculptures on view (among them the best collection of European art in the Caribbean). The Puerto Rican artists exhibited include Jose Campeche (1751–1809) and Francisco Oller (1833–1917), along with Latin-Americans Murillo and Rivera, and Reubens, Velasquez and Gainsborough.

Around the Plaza

As in many Puerto Rican coastal towns, the plaza is a few miles from the coast. On the shore-line itself is Playa de Ponce, a collection of old brick warehouses and more modern storage areas. The La Guancha Boardwalk is a popular gathering place with pairs of lovers and families in the evenings and weekends. From here you can sometimes get a ferry to mile-long Caja de Muertos, a rough and rocky protrusion a few miles offshore, so named for its coffin-like shape (the ferry was not functioning at the time of going to press). For current information phone ✆ 721 5495. It is a popular destination for a day out with the locals, for its beaches, reefs and guided nature walks through the island's dry terrain.

Like many West Indians, the wealthy Ponceño traders built their mansions on the hill above the town. The hillside community is called **El Vigia** (the lookout) because they would watch for merchant ships approaching the harbour, and no doubt any other interlopers who appeared. The outsize cross that dominates the town has replaced a wooden one that guided the ships to the right part of the coast. The **Castillo Serailles** (✆ 259 1774; *open Tues–Thurs 9.30–4.30; Fri–Sun 10–5; adm $3*) is probably the most sumptuous of these mansions and now open to the public. It was built in 1933 as a family home (on the proceeds of the local rum, *Don Q*), in Spanish revival style (which has Moorish influences) in a grand hillside garden. A lovely indoor courtyard leads to a wood-panelled living room and library and an extraordinary medieval dining-room. Downstairs in the kitchen are the original fridges, stoves and massive sinks.

Behind the town is the **Tibes Indian Ceremonial Center** (✆ 840 2255; *open Tues–Sun 9–4; adm $2*), an Amerindian site discovered in 1974. An Arawak village of thatched *bohíos* has been reconstructed; as have some *bateyes*, stone-lined ceremonial grounds used for sports (using a shuttlecock or a ball), dancing and inhaling hallucinogens (cajoba seeds). Among the skeletons unearthed by the archaeologists were decorated ceramic pots, axe-heads and *zemies* (ceremonial idols).

The **Hacienda Buena Vista** (about 7 miles (11km) north out of Ponce on Route 10; ✆ 722 5882, ✆ 284 7020 weekends; *open Fri–Sun; they do not accept casual callers, so reserve; adm $5*) is a restored coffee and corn plantation from the late 19th century, a time when Puerto Rico produced some of the most famous coffee in the world, drunk in coffee-houses as far afield as Paris and Vienna. You can see original machinery restored and working: pulping, fermenting, rinsing, drying and husking the coffee berries. The whole complex is driven by a network of waterways—collected from a waterfall at the top and channelled for 200 yards to the estate, where it is sluiced off to run the different machines (waterwheels, crushers and turbines). Not a pint of the water is wasted as it is all channelled back to a waterslide where it is frothed up and dropped into a communal bath, the 19th century's answer to the jacuzzi. Among the exhibits at the estate house museum are a dripstone (to provide cool and clean drinking water) and stencils that were used to mark up the bags of coffee beans.

Ponce to Mayagüez on Route 2

The southwest coast of Puerto Rico is the driest part of the island, but inland the mountains manage to support coffee (now almost gone) and the traditional Caribbean crop, sugar-cane. Route 2 follows the southern coastline, in the shadow of the vast Cordillera (past small fishing villages where the houses stand on stilts at the water's edge and vendors sell oysters at the streetside), and then cuts inland into the hills and the Spanish colonial hill towns.

Guánica sits on the waterfront among the cactus and mangrove forest. The beaches are placid nowadays, but they saw action in July 1898 when a force of 16,000 American troops landed there and began a 17-day campaign (called a picnic by one journalist) that culminated in the surrender of Puerto Rico to America. Just south of here is the **Guánica Forest Reserve**, where ornithologists will have a field day, so to speak, among the rocky scrubland. The 1600 acres have been designated a 'World Biosphere Reserve' by UNESCO and are part of the US National Forest network. The reserve is home to about half of the species to be found on Puerto Rico. Among the knotted guayacan trees (*lignum vitae*, a wood so hard it was used to replace metal propeller shafts and ball-bearings) you will see bullfinches, hummingbirds and possibly even the guabairo or whippoorwill, a bird that was thought to be extinct for 80 years, but which was found on the reserve in the 50s. There are trails in the park and rangers to help you on your way. A popular day's trip off the south coast is to **Guilligan island**, for the reefs and the iguanas.

Farther along Route 116 is the resort town of **Parguera**, which has sprung up around an old fishing village. It is a lively holiday spot, popular among the Puerto Ricans themselves, who have built cabins on stilts above the water, and there are many cafés and small places to stay. Just west of Parguera, among the coastal mangrove swamps, is a well-known phosphorescent bay, though reports say that it has lost much of its luminescence (there is an excellent bay on Vieques).

San Germán

San Germán is the oldest settlement on Puerto Rico after San Juan and one of the island's most charming Spanish colonial towns. It had to be moved a number of times to be safe from the Caribs and pirates in the 16th century but it settled here in the foothills of the Cordillera in 1573. Today the town has 30,000 inhabitants and a university.

The central streets of old San Gerrmán remain intact, running parallel and enclosing a series of paved plazas lined with trees, above which the old white colonial buildings stand proudly in the sun and the town houses from the coffee era display their elaborate gabling. The **Porta Coeli Church** (meaning 'Heaven's Gate'; *open Wed–Sun 9–noon and 1–4*) was built in 1606 by Dominican friars, and is one of the few examples of Spanish baroque architecture in the Caribbean. Recently restored, it stands above the Parque de Santo Domingo, an old market-place, and is approached by brick steps. Inside the wooden beams and ceiling are thought to be original, though the balcony is not. Statues and paintings from the 19th century are on view. It is really more of a museum of religious art than a working church, as Mass is celebrated only three times a year.

The Southwest

The remote Cabo Rojo district in the southwestern corner of the island is the driest area of Puerto Rico and has long been known as a vacationers' spot because of the beaches. Puerto Real on the coast was once the principal harbour for merchandise offloaded for this part of the island and it is still an important fishing area. The seaside villages in this area have an easy, holiday air and you will find stalls selling clams and oysters at the roadside.

Boquerón is just such a place. It is well known for its **balneario** (many say it is the best beach on the island) but less known for the **Boquerón Nature Reserve**, which includes two swamp areas, the Laguna Boquerón and the Laguna Cartagena. Boardwalks run through the mangrove, where you can expect to see plenty of birds sporting spiked haircuts and glaring plumage—including ducks, herons, pelicans and the purple gallinule. At the southwestern tip of the island, where there are sandy salt pans once used by Ponce de León, is the Cabo Rojo lighthouse, built on the 100ft clifftops by the Spaniards a century ago. This area was a favourite pirate haunt in the 17th century, used by the Spaniard Roberto Cofresi.

North of Boquerón you pass the other resort town of **Playa Joyuda**, which is stretched along the seafront in a long string of restaurants and villas. There is a good beach just out of the town, which continues into Punta Arenas. Offshore is a tiny island, **Isla de Ratone**, nothing more than a beach and a few casuarina pines. It can be visited by arranging a boat in the town. Inland, Laguna Joyada is designated as a wildlife reserve. Continuing north you come to Puerto Rico's third town of Mayagüez.

San Juan to Mayagüez

The north coast, running west from San Juan, is the most developed area of the island. Routes 2 and 22 eventually emerge from the sprawl of suburban San Juan and cruise the 80 miles to the northwestern corner at Rincón, bypassing resorts, towns and factories. They follow the coastal plain, 5 miles broad, in the shadow of the mountains—minor roads labour tortuously up into these forested peaks of 1500ft, known as karst country, where the rainwater has carved a landscape of sharp pinnacles and caverns out of the limestone rock.

Bayamón has been all but swallowed up by the ever-encroaching San Juan, but it seems that modernity has already arrived anyway in the form of shopping malls and the Alcaldía, a massive space-age construction of glass and yellow beams that seemingly hovers above the road. One of the island's finest artists, Francisco Oller (1883–1917), came from here. His work is on show at the **Museo Francisco Oller** in the old Alcaldía (*open Tues–Sat, 9–4*), along with Arawak figurines.

The beaches around **Dorado** have been developed as a tourist resort—the ¼mile waterslide at Cerromar being the next most appealing feature after the sand—though the town itself retains something of the sedated feel it had before the tourists arrived. Farther down the coast, by 15 miles (24km), Vega Baja is set among fertile grounds that once riffled with sugar-cane.

Arecibo, set on a bay 50 miles west of San Juan, was founded in the late 16th century and is now home to about 80,000 people. It was named after an Arawak Indian chief, Aracibo, whose tribe used a cave, the **Cueva del Indio**, a few miles west of the town, for their ceremonies. There are petroglyphs visible on the cave walls. Arecibo is one of the industrial centres of Puerto Rico—pharmaceutical companies established themselves here during 'Operation Bootstrap', the American investment programme, in the 1940s.

In the mountains 15 miles (24km) south of the town is the **Arecibo Observatory** (✆ 878 2612; *open Tues–Fri 2–3, Sun 1–4.30; adm free*), the largest radio telescope in the world—a 20-acre dish that fits neatly into a karst sinkhole 1300ft across, the sort of place where James Bond might hang out. Radar and radio waves bounce off the dish and are collected by the huge triangular measuring gear slung 600ft above the bowl, and then analysed by the batteries of computers in the buildings nearby. The observatory, run by Cornell University, was responsible for discovering the first pulsars and quasars.

Route 10 leads across the island to Ponce via Utuado and Adjuntas, the heartland of the *jíbaro*, the self-reliant Puerto Rican farmer who cuts a living out of the mountains and cultivates the fertile ground of the rainforest. About 8 miles (13km) west of Utuado is the **Caguana Indian Ceremonial Park** and museum (✆ 894 7325; *open Wed–Sun, 9–4.30, museum open Sat and Sun 10–4; adm free*), towered over by mountain peaks. The stone-lined playing fields (called *bateyes*) were built about 800 years ago by the Arawaks for their ballgames and religious ceremonies. It is a bit sad and empty because the activity is long gone, but the gardens are pleasant enough to walk in.

For a close up of the **karst country**, a sea of forested cones, take the minor roads south and west of Arecibo to the forest reserves of **Río Abajo** on Route 621, where you will see the forest at its richest and may come across a Puerto Rican parrot (you can also get a boat trip on **Lago Dos Bocas** from nearby) and to **Lago Guajataca**, on Route 446 to the west.

The karst cones are mirrored below ground by a series of sinkholes and caverns. The limestone base of this area has been eroded over the millennia by acidic water, and all the dripping has created stalactites, stalagmites and caves. Rivers emerge momentarily in the base of a sinkhole and then disappear again underground. It is one of the largest cave-systems in the Americas.

The **River Camuy Cave Park** (✆ 763 0568; *open Tues–Sun 8–4; adm $10*), on Route 129, puts all of this on view in a regimented way, with bilingual lectures followed by a trip in a little trolley bus and then a walk, strictly monitored to keep you on the concrete path (you are asked not to touch anything because human oils quickly destroy aeons of work on the limestone by dripping water). You wind down the overgrown walls of a sinkhole into the depths of the karst to a cavern 170ft high where mighty and bulbous stalactites continue to drip and stalagfruitcakes of goo below rise to meet them at a speed of about an inch per million years. You will see the 'witch', complete with a drip on the end of her nose, and you will even discover the secret of curving stalactites. The underground Rio Camuy can be seen crashing through the base of the Tres Pueblos sinkhole. You may have to wait up to an hour for a place on a tour. The **Cueva de Camuy** (✆ 898 2723; *open daily 9–5, adm*) is a different venture on Route 486, where there are go-carts and horses to keep you amused as well as the cave.

The town of **Lares**, perched on the hillside at the southern edge of karst country, has a special place in the Puerto Rican soul. The *Grito de Lares* (the cry of Lares), a revolt which many feel was the first expression of Puerto Rican national consciousness, took place here in 1868. When liberals such as Betances were expelled from the island in 1867 by the Spaniards, from their exile they tried to raise the Puerto Ricans. Their plans were rumbled, but they captured Lares and declared the Republic of Puerto Rico. Their first crack at independence was short-lived, because they were defeated the next day when they advanced on the nearby town of San Sebastian. The 'cry' is celebrated every year by *Independentistas* on 24 September. An obelisk in the town square commemorates the heroes of the revolt.

Back on the coast, Route 2 hits the west coast at Aguadilla, spread along the seafront. Christopher Columbus is supposed to have landed between here and Añasco on his second voyage in 1493. The controversy over exactly where continues, each town claiming the honour. The waves can get up in this area and **Rincón**, backed by the massive foothills of La Cadena mountains, is a popular surfing spot. The world championships were held here in 1968 and 1988.

Fifteen miles south of here is **Mayagüez** (pronounced Majjawezz), Puerto Rico's third town, an industrial centre and important port. Rebuilt after an earthquake in 1917, Mayagüez now has a population of around 100,000 and is dotted with modern blocks, but it still pulses around the traditional square, the Plaza Colón, where Columbus and the classical Alcaldía (Town Hall) face one another through the trees. In the outskirts you will see the factories that process over 50 per cent of the tuna fish eaten in the USA.

The gardens of the **Tropical Agricultural Research Station** (✆ 831 3435; *open Mon–Fri 7–4; adm free*) are attached to the University of Puerto Rico and are sited on a former planta-tion in the north of the town, on Route 65. Tropical plants from all over the world are neatly set out. Check out the smells of the leaves—cinnamon, citrus and clove—and oddities such as the cannonball tree (with fruit like wooden cannon balls and yet the most ephemeral flowers that die at dusk), the Panama canoe tree and pink torch ginger.

At **Mayagüez Zoo** (✆ 834 8110; *open Wed–Sun, 9–4; adm*) a little north of town on Route 108, the animals' compounds are laid out in a garden of tropical exuberance. As well as Bengal tigers and the Andean condor, you can see the outsize rat called a capybara.

La Ruta Panorámica—West to East

The Panoramic Route follows a tortuous path along the chain of mountains in the Cordillera Central, running for a hundred miles (as the crow flies, though he might have some difficulty over these mountains). Starting at Mayagüez the road climbs quickly into the hills, often touching heights of 3000ft and passing close to the island's highest peak, the Cerro de Punta. It crosses the main San Juan–Ponce road near Cayey and then descends to Yabucoa on the southeastern coast. The vistas are quite spectacular; with just a small turn in the road whole new valleys and views of the coast can open up. There are also some strategically placed lookout towers. Some days you will find yourself in the clouds at this height, but whatever the weather the flora is as exuberant and stunning as the views. The road will often be swallowed up in a tunnel of foliage: strangled mahogany, bamboos, sierra palms, mango trees, coffee plants and 30ft tree ferns of luminescent green, as powerful a colour as the night-time glow of the fireflies. The Ruta Panorámica is marked (though the route numbers vary along the way) and it takes a couple of days at least to cover the ground at leisure. You could take far longer over it, stopping at the mountain *paradors*.

From Mayagüez the road climbs into traditional coffee country around the town of Maricao. The **Maricao** and (a little further east) **Mt Guilarte Forest Reserves** are two of the lesser known and less developed reserves on the island, but there are trails that will lead you among the mahogany, tabanuco and trumpet trees of the forest (ask around because many are unmarked and you may decide to take a guide). Woodpeckers, cuckoos and hawks as well as the more delicate hummingbirds live in the luxuriant trees. In the ponds of the **Maricao Fish Hatchery** (© 838 3710; *open weekdays 7.30–noon and 1–4, weekends 8.30–4; adm free; tours by appointment*) set in tropical gardens off Route 120, they raise around 25,000 fish each year for the lakes around Puerto Rico.

At Adjuntas the Ruta Panorámica joins the main Ponce to Arecibo road for 5 miles (8km) before turning east to the **Toro Negro Forest Reserve**, where a path leads from the road up Cerro de Punta, at 4390ft the highest peak on the island. On a clear day you can see for 50 or 60 miles, beyond the coasts of the island. Unfortunately you will find that you are not alone up there, because there are some communications antennae on the peak. Many rivers rise in this area and there are plenty of waterfalls and rock pools beneath them in which to swim. Try the Inabón river, which thrashes out a ravine for itself heading south from the reserve. The Dona Juana Falls in the **Dona Juana Recreation Centre** are 200ft high. Most of the trails in the forest are unmarked and so you should ask directions.

Thirty-five miles (56km) farther on you come to the towns of **Aibonito**, the highest town on the island, and **Barranquitas**, birthplace of the 19th-century Puerto Rican leader Luís Muñoz Rivera. The **San Cristóbal canyon** is a spectacular river ravine that runs between the two towns. Its sides are almost sheer and in places they plummet for 500ft, but they are still infested with tropical growth. There are two easy descents (though you will have to ask because they are not marked). From Aibonito go north on Route 725 and after three miles descend on a path to a 10ft waterfall on a rocky face. Outside Barranquitas on Route 156 you can climb down into the other end of the ravine among the riotous mosses and greenery.

Not far after crossing the main San Juan–Ponce Expressway (Route 52) you come to the **Carite Forest Reserve**, a 6000-acre reserve in the Sierra de Cayey, where 50 species of birds live, including hummingbirds and the Puerto Rican tanager. There are waterfalls and a small pool called Charco Azul about 10 yards across where the water is a strong blue colour. Just next to the reserve, high on Route 134 you will find a friendly mountain stopover and retreat at **Las Casas de la Selva**. The estate is on 1000 acres of former coffee and banana plantation which has now been replanted with mahogany and teak in a sustainable forestation project. There are organized walks on old mule trails to rock pools, with guides to explain bird life and medicinal uses of plants, a library in which to chill out, and some simple rooms. Ring in advance (© 721 3148, @ 724 0870). From here the road descends to the southwestern coast at Yabucoa and returns to the tourist world at Palmas del Mar.

Puerto Rico has something to suit every taste. It is well known for the large glitzy casino hotels along the coast in San Juan, but behind these you will find smaller, more personable inns. There is a range of small hotels and guest houses set in San Juan's charming old buildings to suit most budgets. And away from the city there are some unexpected gems (particularly the luxurious Horned Dorset Primavera on the west coast), both in the resort towns on the seafront and also in the mountains where some of the charming *paradors* use the best of the old Puerto Rican plantation estate settings. If you are travelling around the island it is useful to have the comprehensive list of hotels in *Qué Pasa*, the tourist brochure. A government tax of 7% is applied to all hotel bills (9% in hotels with a casino) and service charge is 10–15%. All except the smallest hotels accept credit cards.

San Juan

very expensive–expensive

The most elegant place to stay in Old San Juan is the **Casa San José**, 159 Calle San José, Puerto Rico 00901 (© 723 1212, ✆ 723 7620; US res © (1 800) 223 6510), an old San Juañero town house which has been restored to its old colonial glory, with chequerboard tile floors and exposed beams, pretty stairway tiles and an interior courtyard with three stories of wooden balustrades. And it has been decorated with antique furniture, with chandeliers and Oriental carpets in the large drawing room, lending it an exquisite air of calm. Four suites and six rooms, with sumptuous four-poster beds. Breakfast and afternoon tea, but no formal restaurant.

expensive–moderate

Another charming retreat, set around the interior courtyards of three Old San Juan houses is the **Gallery Inn**, 204 Calle Norzagaray, Puerto Rico 00901 (© 722 1808, ✆ 724 7360), so called because it is a working artists' studio. Ten comfortable rooms and suites around five brick-laid courtyards, everywhere with sculptures and profuse with greenery, all linked by a network of stairways. You may enjoy the buzz of artists at work, or you can lock yourself away in the isolation of your suite. (There are special 'Portrait Packages' in which your room is free if you commission a bust.) Outsiders are permitted to view the gallery area. A larger, more formal hotel in the old city is the **Gran Hotel El Convento**, PO Box 1048, 100 Calle Cristo (© 723 9020, ✆ 721 2877), near the cathedral. The former 17th-century Carmelite convent has been completely refitted but retains an atmospheric air with old beams and chequerboard tile floors, and the arched balconies above the courtyard and pool. The dining room is in the old chapel and the rooms are more comfortable than the former occupants' cells.

cheap

Also set in a colonial San Juan town house is the **Caleta**, Caleta de las Monjas 11 (© 721 5264, ✆ 724 0870), which has cheerfully furnished self-catering apartments. Just off the Plaza de Armas in the centre of Old San Juan you will find a very cheap place to rest your head at the **Hotel Central** (© 722 2751 and © 721 9667), more of a travelling businessman's rather than a tourist hotel. Simple fan-ventilated rooms with share or private bathrooms, café downstairs.

Condado and Isla Verde

very expensive–expensive

For a large hotel with all the glitz, try the **Hotel Condado Beach** on the Condado strip, PO Box 41226 (✆ 721 6090, ✉ 724 7222, US ✆ (1 800) 468 2822), a pink colossus on the waterfront. In the swish foyer with arches, palms and vaulted ceilings you will see pictures of the Vanderbilt family, whose holiday home it was (before expansion). It has something of the manicured sophistication of those years. No casino, but plenty nearby. The Vanderbilt Club within the hotel caters for business people. In Isla Verde the **El San Juan Hotel and Casino**, PO Box 2872 (✆ 791 1000, ✉ 253 0178, USA ✆ (1 800) 468 2818) has a similar humming quality as it towers above the beach. Pith-helmeted guards greet you as you pass into the massive elaborate foyer of dark-stained wood, imitation gas-lamps and chandeliers. Huge lounging area and pool outside with swim-up bar, and then the superb sand. The rooms are high-luxury, down to the third telephone in the bathroom. Ten restaurants, bars, clubs and casino on the premises.

moderate–cheap

Behind these monumental blocks on the seafront you will find smaller, more personal (and better priced) hotels and guest houses in Condado, Ocean Park and Isla Verde. The **Hostería del Mar**, 1 Tapia St, Ocean Park, Puerto Rico 00911 (✆ 727 3302, ✉ 268 0772) has 17 rooms in a block set behind a charming beachfront restaurant with louvred windows on sticks. Rooms comfortable, with wicker furniture, TVs, mostly air-conditioned but some fan-ventilated (some with balconies, some with kitchenettes). Sunning deck upstairs and watersports right outside.

Not far down the excellent strip of sand is **Numero Uno on the Beach** at 1 Calle Santa Ana, Ocean Park, Puerto Rico 00911 (✆/✉ 726 5010), a friendly guest house set in an old family villa. There are just eight rooms with private baths, air-conditioning and fans, and a library and TV room. All meals served on the deck next to the pool, where the guests meet at 7pm for a drink before dinner. Mixed crowd. **Tres Palmas**, 2212 Park Blvd, Puerto Rico 00913 (✆ 727 4617, ✉ 727 5434), has eight rooms and three simple apartments in a Spanish revival-style villa across the road from the sea. Airco, TV and fridge, quite simple. A good place to stay if you want to be on the beach in Isla Verde without spending a fortune is **Casa de Playa Beach Hotel** at 86 Ave Isla Verde, Puerto Rico 00979 (✆ 728 9779, ✉ 727 1334, USA ✆ (1 800) 829 3636). Twenty comfortable rooms with air-conditioning, phones and cable TV, flowery decor and wooden furniture; outside a restaurant and beachfront bar behind the palms.

cheap

Across the way are two cheaper guest houses: the **Green Isle Inn** at 36 Calle Uno (✆ 726 4330, ✉ 268 2415), with 17 rooms and its sister property the **Casa Mathieson Inn**, 14 Calle Uno (✆ 726 8662). Finally you can also try the **El Canario Inn**, 1317 Ashford Ave (✆ 722 3861, ✉ 722 0391, US 800 533 2649), a charming little hotel with just 25 rooms and a lush garden courtyard, offering excellent value for money. In Miramar, the **Hotel Toro** (✆ 725 5150) has very simple rooms for hire at even lower rates.

East of San Juan

expensive

There is a number of fine places to stay scattered around the eastern part of the island. If you are one for a large resort, with golf, beach-bound watersports, tennis, horseback riding, a multiplicity of restaurants and even an outdoor movie theatre all in the one complex, then go for **Palmas del Mar**, PO Box 2020, Humacao, Puerto Rico 00792 (✆ 852 6000, ✉ 852 6320). Country club atmosphere, with rooms, suites, villas or apartments linked by shuttles. Another large resort, with similar style and standards, is **El Conquistador Resort and Country Club**, PO Box 50053, San Juan, Puerto Rico 00902 (✆ 863 1000, ✉ 863 6500, US ✆ (1 800) 468 8365). Set on the hillside above the northeastern tip of the island with rooms and apartments set all around, the main house is spectacularly decorated with murals. There's an offshore island with beach. The **Río Grande Plantation**, PO Box 6526, Loíza Santurce, Puerto Rico 00914 (✆ 887 2779, ✉ 888 3239) has good-value rooms in different styles on 40 acres of old plantation in the foothills of the El Yunque rainforest, on a river-bend. Sumptuous suites with kitchenettes and cable TV, pleasant gardens. Some weddings and events, but a good place from which to explore.

moderate

Not far off is **Le Petit Chalet**, PO Box 182, Río Grande, Puerto Rico 00745 (✆ 887 5802, ✉ 887 7926), a very pleasant villa retreat in a backdrop of overwhelming greenery. There is a low-key but very personable atmosphere in the house—you can walk in the hills or sit and relax looking through the arches to Luquillo on the coast. Delicately prepared *nouvelle cuisine*.

moderate–cheap

In Luquillo itself there are comfortable rooms at the **Parador Martorell**, 6a Ocean Drive (✆ 889 2710, ✉ 889 4520). Just 11 rooms, with air-conditioning and TV, a small library and a downstairs patio. In the Las Croabas area is the *parador* **La Familia**, PO Box 21399, Puerto Rico 00738 (✆ 863 1193, ✉ 860 5345), where there are 35 air-conditioned rooms, a pool and sundeck, beaches and watersports not far off. No restaurant, but plenty of places around. Almost opposite is the pink **Aguiar** Guest House (✆ 863 4511), with four rooms, some kitchenettes.

cheap

Just outside **Fajardo** there is a good stopover, the **Fajardo Inn**, PO Box 4309, Puerto Real, Puerto Rico 00740 (✆ 863 5195, ✉ 860 5063), a small and comfortable bed and breakfast with nine rooms (clean and air-conditioned with TVs) and long, shady colonial verandas. Personal service. Nearby, at **Anchor's Inn**, Route 987 (✆ 863 7200) the rooms are simple but comfortable and the restaurant, though tourist, serves excellent *criolle* cuisine.

Ponce

If you require standard international comfort and service then you can select the **Ponce Hilton** (✆ 259 7676, ✉ 259 7618; *expensive*), but for a little more Caribbean style and charm, try the **Hotel Meliá**, PO Box 1431 (✆ 842 0260, ✉ 841 3602; *moderate*), situated in the historic area in the centre of Ponce. It keeps some of the old-time feel of the town in the period foyer and courtyard, though the comfortable rooms are modern. It has managed to poach one of the best chefs on the island from the Hilton. He now runs his own restaurant, **Marks**, attached to the hotel. The **Hotel Belgica** (✆ 844 3255; *cheap*) is across the main square at 122 Villa, in a large town-house with wrought-iron balconies. As the name suggests, the **Colonial Guest House** on Calle Marince has been restored to offer the best in old-time Puerto Rican ambience (✆ 841 7138; *cheap*). It is set in a very nice town house with an inner courtyard, furnished with an eclectic assembly of clocks, furniture and modern paintings. The least expensive place to stay in town is the **Hotel Colville** on Avenida Muñez Riviera at the corner of Las Américas (✆ 843 1935; *cheap*), with simple rooms. Call before 10pm or you'll end up at the **Hotel Eden**, a drive-in knocking-shop way out of town; about $25 for a garage, a large double bed and mirrors all over the walls. Along the coast, just outside Ponce, is **Hotel Las Curachas**, Carretera No 2 (✆ 841 0620; *moderate–cheap*). Built right on the water, with wooden walkways running out to sea, it has a quiet, somewhat mysterious atmosphere—like a hotel from a Graham Greene novel.

There is a *parador* off the San Juan–Ponce road: **Baños de Coamo** (✆ 825 2186, ✆ 825 4739; *cheap*), just off Route 153. The *baños* are the hot springs that attracted so elegant a crowd in the last century. They have lost most of their refinement now, the rooms are sparse and functional, but there are still one or two fine buildings around the courtyard and the dining room has been restored nearly to its former elegance. Not a bad stop if you are travelling through.

The Southwestern Corner

In the southwestern corner of the island you will find a number of seaside resort towns with small and friendly hotels. These are popular with the Puerto Ricans at the weekends and in the holidays (prices tend to rise for the summer months rather than in the winter season). A pleasant beachfront hotel around Guánica is the **Copamarina Beach Resort**, PO Box 805, Guánica, Puerto Rico 00653 (✆ 821 0505, ✆ 821 0070, USA ✆ (1 800) 468 4553; *moderate*), where there are 69 rooms in quite attractive, red-roofed blocks laid out around a lawned garden of palms. There is a fresh-water pool, tennis courts and watersports available on the reasonable beach right out front, or the better public beach nearby. **Jack's** Guest House in Caña Gorda (✆ 821 2738; *very cheap*), on the road back inland has very simple, fan-ventilated rooms for hire. In the centre of **San Germán**, off Highway 2, is the **Parador Oasis**, PO Box 144, PR 00683 (✆ 892 1175, ✆ 892 1175; *cheap*). It is set in an old town house, with colonial foyer furnished with ornate woodwork and wicker-backed rocking chairs. The dining room overlooks the pool, as do some of the 50 rooms. Another agreeable stopover for the setting and the friendly crowd.

On the south coast the nicest place to stay is in the *parador* **Villa Parguera**, PO Box 273, PR 00667 (✆ 899 3975/7777, ✆ 899 6040; *moderate*), which overlooks the lagoon and the mangrove islands where the holiday houses stand on stilts. The 63 rooms stand in two-storey blocks with balconies giving on to a palm garden and the pool. There is no beach, but you can find sand just a boat-ride away. Not far along the waterfront is the **Posada Porlamar**, PO Box 405, PR 00667 (✆ 899 4015, ✆ 899 5558; *cheap*), also a *parador*, which is slightly simpler, but has air-conditioned, comfortable rooms in a cabin. There is no restaurant, but the 18 rooms have kitchenettes. There is a number of **guest houses** in the streets behind the waterfront, of which the most comfortable is probably the **Parguera** Guest House (✆ 899 3993; *cheap*) opposite the Porlamar with double rooms with private bath and air-conditioning. **Hilda's** guest house, Calle 2 (✆ 899 4055; *cheap*), is set in a modern villa—two apartments built with all mod cons; also **Pargomar** (✆ 899 4065; *cheap*), three simple, air-conditioned rooms. On Calle Principal there are rooms at the **Flamboyan** (✆ 899 3524), kitchen facilities, private bath, air-conditioning.

Boquerón has a similar seaside feel about it, and excellent sunset views from the superb beach, which is just a short walk from the town. The best place by far to stay is **Wildflowers**, 113 Calle Manoz Rivera (✆ 851 1793; *moderate*). The American couple who own it used to be auctioneers and have decorated the spacious, high-ceilinged rooms with antiques. From the kitchen come superb homemade cakes and mouthwatering Cape Cod cuisine. **Parador Boquemar**, PO Box 133, PR 00622 (✆ 851 2158, ✆ 851 7600; *cheap*), is a modern block in the centre of the town. The 63 air-conditioned rooms are fitted out with TVs and fridges and balconies that overlook the pool. At **Casitas de Cristina**, PO Box 150, Boquerón, Puerto Rico 00622 (✆ 254 2801; *cheap*), on Avenue José de Diego in the centre of town, there are four simple and adequate apartments and two studios. There are plenty of **villas and houses** for rent in the area (✆ 851 4751). If you want peace and isolation, head for **Bahia Salinas Beach Hotel**, PO Box 1329, Cabo Rojo, PR 00623 (✆ 254 1212, ✆ 254 1212), all on its own on the salt flats near the Cabo Rojo Lighthouse. All rooms have two verandas looking out to sea, from which to view spectacular sunsets.

On the other side of Cabo Rojo, between Playa Joyuda and Playa Laguna you wil find a string of hotels and restaurants. The most comfortable is **Perichi's**, a *parador*, PO Box 16310, PR 00623 (✆ 851 3131, ✆ 851 0560; *cheap*). The service is personal and friendly and there is a popular restaurant downstairs. 22 rooms with balconies and a pool. There are rooms at **Tony's** (✆ 851 2500, ✆ 851 0445; *cheap*); pool, simple accommodation and a seafood restaurant. In Punta Arenas you can try the **Costa del Sol** Hotel (✆ 851 5196; *cheap*), where the 11 rooms are decorated simply and have air-conditioning and TVs.

The Northwest

There are not many hotels in the northwest of the island, and those that exist are a bit disappointing. The exception is the **Horned Dorset Primavera**, PO Box 1132, Rincón, Puerto Rico 00677 (✆ 809 823 4030, ✆ 823 5580; *very expensive–expensive*), one of the most elegant hotels on the island. The 24 suites, most of which stand on the seafront in Spanish revival-style buildings, are furnished with tile floors, brass fittings, louvred windows and doors, and four-poster beds. The bathrooms are laid with marble and each suite has a balcony with a view onto the garden or to the sea horizon. The main house has the grace and finery of the old Spanish colonial days. Above, approached by the 'embracing' staircase, is the restaurant, one of the best on the island, with chequerboard floor, wrought-iron lamps and candles. Downstairs are the classical balustrades of the terrace, just above the waves, together with the rarefied air of a country house in the drawing room and library, where Proust and the *New*

Yorker magazine will keep you busy. Quite isolated, but ideal if you're happy to lock yourself away. One of the Caribbean's few *Relais et Châteaux*.

North of Mayagüez you will find a passable beach hotel in the *parador* **Villa Antonio**, PO Box 68, Rincón, Puerto Rico 00677 (✆ 823 2645, 🖷 823 3380; *moderate–cheap*), just south of Rincón. The hotel itself is modern and air-conditioned and the cottages and apartments are comfortable if a little uninspiring, but they give right onto a fine brown-sand beach. In Rincón itself is the **Lazy Parrot Inn**, PO Box 430, Rincón, 00677 (✆ 823 5654, 🖷 823 0224; *cheap*), with seven rooms each with TV, refrigerator and bath, and its own art gallery selling local crafts. In Quebradillas on the north shore you will find the *parador* **Vistamar** (✆ 895 2065, 🖷 895 2294; *cheap*), a modern block on a hilltop off Route 113, with comfortable rooms.

Inland you will find two of the island's finest *paradors*, lost in the mountains and the rainforest. Near Maricao on Route 105 is **La Hacienda Juanita**, PO Box 777, Maricao, Puerto Rico 00606 (✆ 838 2550, 🖷 838 2551, US ✆ (1 800) 443 0266; *cheap*), set in the original estate house of a coffee plantation. Very much a mountain and forest escape—no TV or phones; 21 rooms, some with antique furniture and others simpler, set in the estate buildings around the main house, where there is a superb veranda for your meals and chairs swinging from the ceiling for ruminating in afterwards. The hotel is still family-run and the restaurant produces some excellent home cooking—a really good spot to relish local cuisine. Quite low-key, with real isolation; about thirty species of birds to spot, some trails. The **Hacienda Gripiñas**, PO Box 387, PR 0064 (✆ 828 1718, 🖷 828 1719; *cheap*) is one of the loveliest spots on the island. The inn is set in a charming wooden West Indian house, formerly the estate house of a coffee plantation, built in 1853. There is a superb veranda over-looking the explosive tropical flora where you can take an early-evening cocktail in time-honoured Caribbean style. The 19 rooms are in the main house and an extension—many have the gracious atmosphere of the planters' days. It is high in the mountains and so it can get quite cold at night (the pool is freezing in the winter). A few valleys away in **Utuado** is the **Casa Grande**, PO Box 616 Utuado, PR 00761 (✆/🖷 894 3939; *cheap*), a third *parador*, also set on a former coffee plantation. The main house stands on the hillside with the wooden cabins on stilts containing the 18 rooms strung out beneath it. Lost in the rainforest, the inn is private and quiet, another good weekend retreat from the city or the high-pressure tourism race.

✆ *(1 787)–*   **Eating Out**

Puerto Rico, and particularly its capital San Juan (which is both a large city and the centre of the tourist industry), has a grand variety of places in which to eat out, with endless styles—Spanish, Chinese, seafood and *nouvelle*—and as many settings—sophisticated dining rooms, waterfront fish restaurants, milk bars and local *fondas*. The hotels tend to have international and continental menus and of course, as Puerto Rico is a part of America, there are endless burger bars. You will find the service slightly snappier than in much of the Caribbean. Restaurants accept credit cards and service runs at 10–15%. Categories are arranged according to the price of a main course: *expensive*—$25 and above; *moderate*—$15–25; *cheap*—$15 and below.

It would be a pity to ignore Puerto Rican food itself; which can be quite heavy; the Puerto Ricans are hearty eaters. Main course is often a thick soup or a stew, such as *asopao*, which is made with pork, chicken or seafood. You also get a mound of rice in *arroz con pollo* (chicken or another meat with rice cooked in coconut). To accompany it you will have *mofongo*, battered spiced plantain, or *arroz con habichuelos*, rice and beans (*cristianos y morros* are white and black beans). *Lechón asao*, roast suckling pig, is a popular dish, and otherwise seafood and goat meat are often used. The Tourism Company has a system of recommended local restaurants around the country called *Mesones Gastronómicos*, at which you will find reliably prepared Puerto Rican cuisine.

Snacks are also very popular in Puerto Rico and you will see *kioskos* at the roadside all over the island (there is a string of them at the roadside in Luquillo). They sell a bewildering variety of snacks—seafood appears in crab-sticks, or deep-fried crab with yucca which is then presented to you in a sea-grape leaf, and you will find lobster and chicken tacos. *Alcapurrias* are meat or crab fritters and traditional Caribbean codfish also comes frittered as *bacalao*. *Pinchos* are kebabs of chicken, pork or shark, served with a thick tomato sauce and a lump of bread. *Chicharrón* are pieces of fried pork rind like outsize pork scratchings. Sweet potato and banana are often fried too. Cheese is often used to best advantage. Try a *sorullo*, a sugared cheese roly-poly. *Picadillos* are meat patties and *empanadas* and *pasteles* are made with fried cassava dough inlaid with meat or raisins and beans. A locally brewed (light) beer is *Medalla*. It is always worth seeking out locally grown Puerto Rican coffee, which a hundred years ago was exported all over the world.

San Juan and the Suburbs

The capital has the greatest concentration of restaurants and bars, many of them in the old buildings of the colonial area, which are pleasant surroundings.

expensive

The two top places to dine in San Juan are in Condado. **Ramiro's**, at 1106 Magdalena (℗ 721 9049), offers 'creative cuisine'—Spanish and international fare delivered in neat *nouvelle* form in an elegant, carpeted dining room with wooden panelling, candles and mock-antique chairs. Calm and subdued as you tuck into lobster in anisette and cilantrillo sauce, or buffalo, lamb and venison in a three-pepper sauce. Close by, **Don Pepe** (℗ 723 1082), is set in a mock classical mansion on Calle Luisa with marble tile floors, chandeliers and conspicuous antique furniture. Cool, bright and brisk, international cuisine: duck *à la Vigarrade* or a *paella* speciality, *marinera* or *Valencia*. In Old San Juan itself there is a small and attractive dining room at **La Chaumière** (℗ 722 3330), 367 Calle Tetuán. French cuisine, style and service.

moderate

Al Dente (℗ 723 7303) is set in a very pleasant dining room of arches, white walls and mannequins on Recinto Sur in Old San Juan. The fare is Italian, including pumpkin *linguini* in basil and olive oil followed by *pollo alla Contandina*, chicken sautéed in white wine. There is a clutch of lively and good restaurants among the bars on Calle San Sebastian (*see* below). **Amadeus** (℗ 722 8635) is a relaxed retreat, with an arty crowd. Try the fried dumplings with guava sauce or chicken breast stuffed with *escargots*, mushrooms and parsley. And nearby **El Patio de Sam** (℗ 723 1149) is another haunt popular with the locals, set in an attractive town house. It attracts a fun crowd, particularly at the weekends, and serves good food—lobster tail broiled or scampied, or fillet of flounder parmesan. Just down the hill, on Calle St Cristo is **La Ostra Casa**, a bar in the courtyard of a 16-century house that once belonged to the Spanish viceroy. The friendly owner serves snacks and light meals, and occasionally bursts into song. A restaurant with a very pleasant setting for an evening out is the **Bistro Gambaro** (✆ 724 4592), on Calle Fortaleza, in the centre of the city. You dine inside or within the walled courtyard of an Old San Juan house, with good jazz in the background. There is a set menu of pasta, fish, meat or chicken (for example, served with a sweet and sour sauce and a mandarin glaze), followed by banana mousse in puff pastry. Also on Calle Fortaleza is **The Parrot Club** (✆ 725 7370), at present the trendiest spot in Old San Juan. Sip exotic cocktails at the bar, then have a squid sandwich or chicken casserole. **La Mallorquina**, on Calle San Justo (✆ 722 3261), has been something of an institution in the city since it was built in 1848. It has seen generations of San Juañeros deep in political discussion over a meal (the broken vase in the corner is witness to a flared temper apparently). Nowadays the visitors tend to be tourists and the service a little brisk, but you get a good local meal in historic surroundings. The house speciality is *asopao,* or you might try various seafoods cooked in wine. Restaurant **Galleria** (✆ 725 1092) on Calle San Justo serves good Italian food in a somewhat precious atmosphere with pale green furnishings, live piano music and chichi locals.

In the **Condado** area there is an excellent restaurant for local cuisine, **Ajilli Mojilli** (✆ 725 9195), which is popular for its food, but has an edgily trendy atmosphere. *Mofongo* filled with shrimp or seafood, or chicken breast in an orange, lemon and almond sauce. The dining room, which is attached to the Condado Lagoon Hotel, is air-conditioned and modern and a little characterless, and the service can be somewhat disdainful. One of the most entertaining restaurants on the island is **La Casita Blanca**, a brightened-up version of a Puerto Rican *fonda,* set in the *barrio* (the ghetto). You feel that you have come into someone's home when you arrive—you sit either outside in the courtyard, under the guinep trees, or indoors on foldaway chairs at tables with bright plastic table cloths. The waiters wear neckerchiefs and the place is generally hip. Appetizers —codfish or sugary corn fritters—arrive in a banana leaf and you eat them with *mariada,* a local mix of wine, rum, mavi and fruit juices. Follow up with goat stew or fish dishes and finish with coffee and their own additive (with rum and cinnamon). Well worth a visit for its novel atmosphere and some of the best local food. **Che's** (✆ 726 7202) is a popular Argentinian restaurant set in a large dining room on Calle Coaba in Isla Verde: *churrasco* and *parillada Argentina.* And if you want a fast Mexican meal in cheery pink and green surroundings, then **Mona's** (✆ 728 0140) on Calle María Moczo in Ocean Park is the place to go. Rock music and the best *fajitas* in town.

cheap

There are plenty of cafés in Old San Juan where you can rest your feet after a morning's walking around. **Casa Papyrus** (✆ 724 6555), on Calle Tetuan, doubles as a book and CD shop and has good vegetarian food and delicious home-made lemonade. A great find is **La Bombonera** on Calle San Francisco. It is a popular gathering point, particularly after Mass on Sundays. Past the pastries section at the entrance you can sit at the long bar on round stools or at the bench tables along the walls. Busy, and full of waiters in red coats storming around tending to singles reading the paper, doting lovers and noisy families. Try local dishes or an omelette, with superb lemonade served in crushed ice. Also try **Café Berlin** (✆ 722 5205) on the Plaza Colón, part art gallery, part vegetarian café (plus some meat dishes); plenty of pastries and freshly squeezed juices. You might also stop at **Butterfly People** (✆ 723 2432) on Calle Fortaleza; after inspecting the butterfly designs you can grab a salad or a grilled platter in a courtyard hung with greenery. There is even a Hard Rock Café, set around a charming San Juañero courtyard, if that's your thing.

There are a couple of *Metropol* restaurants (in the Hotel Pierre, Condado and Isla Verde) which serve mainly Cuban food—*congri tamali*, arrowroot-flavoured pork with rice and beans or chicken *Viñales*, after a town in the west of Cuba, baked in wine. **Dunbars'** is a lively bar and restaurant where you can get wings, a salad or a sandwich while watching the sport on TV.

Around the Island

You will find good local *fondas* everywhere in the country, though they will not usually provide gourmet dining. However, the Tourist Board sponsors a list of restaurants called the *Mesones Gastronomicos* which are located throughout the island. There are about 40 of them and they are listed in *Qué Pasa.*

In Fajardo, you will find two good restaurants: **Rosa's** Sea Food (✆ 863 0213) is in an ugly concrete house, but serves good local food—shrimp, crayfish as well as steak or BBQ chicken Rosa style. Don't be put off by the touristy atmosphere of **Anchor's Inn** (✆ 863 7200), on the road to Las Croabas; seafood is excellent (especially the fish soup) and the *mofongo* (mashed plantain with pork, lobster or chicken, served in traditional wooden goblets) is hard to beat.

Ponce has a few good dining rooms—in the Playa area south of the town you will find **El Ancla** (✆ 840 2450), where you can eat seafood, including the house speciality, red snapper stuffed with lobster. *Open daily, main dish $15.* Near the main city square is one of Puerto Rico's top restaurants. In 1996, award-winning chef Mark French left a job at the nearby Hilton to start up on his own. At **Mark's** (✆ 284 6275), local cuisine takes on a gourmet air (try fried plantain *tostones* with caviar and cream cheese as a starter). Meals are pricey (*around $30 for a main course*), and it's a good idea to book, as the restaurant fills up with foodies from across the island.

Along the coast heading west is **Pito's** (✆ 841 4977), a waterfront restaurant which collects a lively crowd at weekends, when they tuck into seafood and Spanish fare. You can eat under parasols on a deck above the Caribbean Sea. Try shrimp in white wine sauce with linguini, *$17.* Not far off is **Las Marguaritas** café (✆ 841 6617) where you can have a fresh fillet of local fish in Cajun spices or butter sauce for $15. Both have live music occasionally.

If you're beginning to tire of Puerto Rican food, head to Boqueron, where in the kitchen of **Wildflowers** guest house (✆ 851 1793) Tom Smith cooks up a storm—delicious dishes featuring healthy ingredients and creamy sauces, and at low prices too. North of here in Playa Joyuda there is a good restaurant at **Perichi's** (✆ 851

3131), a seaside *meson gastronomico* with good lobster specialities. A little further along the same road, **Tony's** (✆ 851 2500) has the reputation for serving the best fish and seafood on the island, though the service is brusque. *Main courses around $15.* **El Bohío** (✆ 851 2755) also stands on the waterfront and serves local food and seafood for *$15–$20 a main course.*

A little inland, near Maricao, **Hacienda Juanita** (✆ 838 2500) is a romantic old coffee plantation homestead, now a family-run hotel. Here you'll find really top-notch local cooking—the sort of home-made fare that doesn't make it to the menus of touristy establishments. The Sunday buffet lunch on the long, wooden verandahs has become a local institution. For gourmet meals, undoubtedly the best place to go is the restaurant at the **Horned Dorset Primavera Hotel** in Rincón (✆ 823 4030), which combines chic, heady luxury and laid-back charm. Menus change frequently, but you may encounter chilled leak soup, duck confit with grilled vegetables or a tangy lemon pie. The **Lazy Parrot Inn** in Rincón (✆ 823 5654) has a tasty selection of grilled and barbecued dishes for under $15.

Bars and Nightlife

Old San Juan's bars may be frequented by cruise-ship tourists by day, but they are more local at night when the San Juañeros venture outside to take the evening air in a promenade (or its car-borne equivalent, in which they cruise around, stereo blaring). One of the most charming spots is the cocktail bar **La Violeta**, at the top end of Calle Fortaleza. Here you are cast back in time in an old colonial drawing room with rocking chairs, wicker armchairs and family photographs above the piano. There's a nice crowd, at the bar or hidden away in the private rooms off the courtyard. For a beer and a game of pool, go round the corner to the **Small World Bar**.

The liveliest street in Old San Juan (one long traffic jam in the late evening) is Calle San Sebastian, where there are cocktail bars alongside more raucous drinking and dancing bars. **El Quinqué** sees an arty crowd, sometimes jazz; and **Hijos de Borinquen** is traditionally a revolutionary bar (as shown by the graffiti). You might also try **Aqui se Puede**. At the top end of Calle San Sebastian, on the Plaza San José, a lively crowd gathers around **Los Balcones de Nono**, with latterday pirates serving at the bar, and at **Nono's**, where you are watched closely by a bull's head while you drink. Round the corner is another fun drinking dungeon, **El Batey**, where the walls are smothered with caricatures and graffiti, or stripped down to the bare brick.

One of the best bars in the city is on Calle Loíza in the Santurce area, **Shannan's Pub**, an Irish theme bar with a very lively crowd at the weekend—videos, sleek chicks in black and cool guys. A new and even trendier Irish bar has opened on Ashford Avenue: at **Houlihan's** you can get authentic draught stout. Close by is the **Apple Jazz Club**. **Peggy Sue** on Roberto H. Todd is more of a dancing club and back in old San Juan you will find **Lazer Disco**, brick and glass decor UV-lit, with salsa, merengue and rap. The larger hotels in Condado and Isla Verde have discotheques, sometimes cabarets. The **Black Angus**, on Calle Fernandez Juncos, is one of the best-known brothels in the world.

Ponce is pretty quiet at night, but some bars are worth a detour; try **Paradise Café** on Calle Major, with live music at weekends, and **Café El Paseo** on the Paseo Arias with a piano bar. **Café 149**, also on Paseo Arias, is a pool bar and drinker's hangout.

Vieques, Culebra and Mona

There are a number of islands and plenty of tiny cays off the coasts of Puerto Rico. To the east lie **Vieques** and **Culebra**, midway between Puerto Rico and the Virgin Islands, to which they are geologically related. You can fly or take the ferry from Fajardo. **Mona** stands out on its own, 50 miles off the west coast, halfway between Puerto Rico and the Dominican Republic. These islands are remote and it is helpful to speak Spanish in order to get the best out of them.

Vieques

Vieques (pronounced 'Byekess') lies 7 miles from the eastern shore of Puerto Rico and is 25 by 5 miles, larger than Culebra. With 9000 inhabitants and about as many horses, it is a good example of a small Spanish Caribbean island, easy-going and well worth a visit. Its connection with the military has meant that it has remained relatively undeveloped—there is an easy, unexpected tranquillity when the island is not being invaded. As for beaches, Vieques has some of Puerto Rico's best. On a coastline of 60 miles, there are about 40 of them.

The town (and ferry arrival point) is **Isabel Segunda**, on the north coast. On the plaza is a bust of Simon Bolivar, El Libertador, who came to the island in 1816. Overlooking the town is a fort, built in 1843 and restored to its intended original state. Now a museum.

The only other settlement is **Esperanza** on the south coast, a string of villas, guest houses and restaurants along the Malecón, where the Viequenses can be found liming and taking the evening air. The pier was connected to a railway and was the loading point for the island's sugar crop, but the bay is used mainly by fishermen and sunbathers now. The quay at Mosquito on the northwest coast was built in the Second World War as a port for the British Navy. From the Punta Mula Lighthouse the views are spectacular.

Sun Bay, often written Sombe, just east of Esperanza, is the best known of the island's beaches and has public facilities. You can hire watersports equipment here and in Esperanza. Other beaches, many of which have taken on the colours of military-speak, are in Camp Garcia. Enter by the gate on Route 997 and you will come to a sign to **Red Beach**—roads lead off this to **Barracuda** and **Garcia** beaches—and then half a mile beyond here you will come to a turning leading to the best beach on the island, **Secret** or **Hidden Beach**. Farther on is a cracking bay called **Blue Beach**. Finally, in the far northwest of the island is another good beach, **Green Bay**, which is approached by the airport road.

A trip to **Mosquito Bay**, one of Vieques' three phosphorescent bays, is one of the most extraordinary sights in the Caribbean. The bio-luminescence arises from a chemical reaction in microscopic protozoa living in the water, which glow when they are moved. They shine in weird bright green whorls and clouds as you move through the water, or as you kick and splash. You will see fish dart away ahead of you (huge mantas are known to glide by too) and if you flick the water with your canoe paddle you can set off a bright green arc of spray. Launch trips can be arranged (the motor makes an impressive trail), but it is best to go by canoe, which can be arranged through the Esperanza Hotel.

There are many daily **flights** from San Juan (both the international airport and Isla Grande), St Thomas and Fajardo (from where the flight is good value). Contact Vieques Air Link (✆ 722 3736 in San Juan and ✆ 741 8211 on the island). The **ferry** ride from Fajardo is also very good value at just a few dollars. *Públicos* will take you around the island, or contact Island Car Rentals (✆ 741 1666), or Sammy's Car Rental in Esperanza (✆ 740 0106). There is a helpful **tourist office** on the northern side of the plaza in Isabel Segunda (✆ 741 5000). **Snorkelling** is best off Esperanza and there are reefs in Hidden Bay and Blue Bay. **Scuba** diving can be fixed up through **Vieques Divers** (✆ 741 8600). Trips around the island on **horseback** can be fixed up through Casa del Francés, a small hotel in Esperanza with an inimitable style and a manager to match.

✆ *(1 787)–*   ### Where To Stay and Eating Out

There are only small hotels, with personal service and an easy-going atmosphere, along with well-stocked libraries. If you wish to hire a villa, contact **Vieques Villa Rentals,** Calle Gladiolas 494, Esperanza, Puerto Rico 00705 (✆ 741 8888). Government tax on hotel rooms is levied at 7% and service is usually 10%.

moderate

La Casa del Francés, PO Box 458, PR 00765 (✆ 809 741 3751, ✉ 741 2330), just outside Esperanza, is a charming retreat in the best West Indian tradition, run by a latterday Hemingway. It is set in a classic Caribbean great house with an inner courtyard and terraces smothered in greenery. There are just 12 rooms and a fine dining room. **Water's Edge**, PO Box 1374, North Shore, Vieques, PR 00765 (✆ 741 1128, ✉ 741 0690), is just what it says, with eight rooms looking out over a sandy beach.

cheap

Just above **Isabel Segunda** is a friendly guest house, the **Crow's Nest**, PO Box 1521 (✆ 741 0033, ✉ 741 1294), with 8 self-catering rooms around a modern villa. There is a pool, a bar with a view, and an excellent moderately priced seafood restaurant. Also in a modern house above town, overlooking the fort and Culebra, is **Sea Gate Guest House**, PO Box 747 (✆ 741 4661), patrolled by dogs, of which the owner has 20.

There are a number of guest houses in Esperanza, including **Tradewinds** (✆ 741 8666); and you will find **Christina's Restaurant** (*moderate*) and the **Posada Vistamar** (✆ 741 8716; *moderate*). **Tito's** (no phone), a couple of streets behind the main drag, is a cheaper option.

In Esperanza there is a string of bars and restaurants from which to watch the sunset. Try **Bananas**, a busy joint set on a terrace on the street front, with steaks or shrimp for $12; or **El Quenepo**, a simple spot where you can get an octopus, conch or snail salad. **El Gringo Loco** is fun—a wooden deck bar in the mangroves.

Culebra

Seven miles by four, Culebra rises lazily from the water in a range of low scrubby hills, surrounded by its satellites, a host of rocks and cays. Around them stretches a series of spectacular coral reefs. Life is peaceful for the 2000 Culebrans, many of whom live around the only settlement of **Dewey** (locally known as Puebla), just a few ramshackle houses and the odd grocery shop in a bight on the south shore. Not much seems to happen here: just a few fishermen working from the bays, and once-domestic animals wandering around the scrub, much as it was two or three centuries ago when the pirates would drop by. There is a sleepy atmosphere; it's a tropical island idyll, Spanish style. Information and assistance can be obtained from the Tourist Office in the Alcaldía (Town Hall) in Dewey. The town does come alive once a year, during the *fiesta patronal* on 17 July.

Seeking out the **wildlife** can be rewarding. Four species of sea turtle come to the beaches to nest—they crawl up the sand at night, dig a hole with their back flippers in which they lay their eggs, and then scoop the sand back over them before disappearing back into the sea. You might have to stay up most of the night, but if you get a chance to see the giant leatherback laying its eggs between April and July, it is well worth it. The best beaches are Resaca and Brava; you might wish to go with a guide.

In the flatlands around the coast and the mangrove swamps you might come across such characters as the sandwich tern or the black-and-white sooty tern, the red-billed tropicbird or red-footed booby. Culebra has an extensive wildlife refuge, which includes all its offshore rocks. Inland you may see a large iguana, a sort of 4ft armoured lizard.

There are some spectacular beaches on Culebra, particularly on the north shore. The best known of these is **Flamenco Beach**, a cracking strip of bright white sand. Other beaches worth visiting are **Resaca** and **Zoni** on the east coast. You might also consider a trip over to one of Culebra's 23 satellites—Pirate's Cay in Ensenada Honda, Culebrita, Luis Peña. Fix it up through a fisherman and remember to arm yourself with a picnic and snorkelling gear.

A few **watersports** (windsurfing, sailing and snorkelling) can be arranged through the hotel and through the small shops in the town. **Diving** among the excellent coral reefs, where deep blue angelfish glide and groupers pout, can be fixed up through the Culebra Underwater Diving Association (✆ 742 3839) or at the Culebra Dive Shop (✆ 742 3555).

Posada la Hamaca (✆ 742 3516; *cheap*), one of the *paradors*, has nine comfortable rooms. **Villa Fulladoza** (✆ 742 3576; *cheap*), is an apartment complex backing on to the marina.

Mona

Mona Island is the remotest of them all—50 miles from Puerto Rico and further from civilization; an oval 25 square miles surrounded by coral reefs which make excellent diving. Mona is administered by the Department of Natural Resources (✆ 722 1726 on Puerto Rico) as a reserve and is deserted now except for passing fishermen and the lighthouse keeper. There are a few animals, descended from the stock once farmed here but now running wild. The only way to get here is by plane or by persuading a launch owner in Mayagüez to take you. Carry everything you need (including water), because there is not so much as a grocery store on the island.

getting there

By air from Europe: British Airways run two flights a week from Gatwick to Luis Muñoz Marin airport in San Juan. Lufthansa fly from Frankfurt and Iberia from Madrid. Another alternative is to make a connection in Miami. KLM fly twice weekly from Amsterdam.

By air from the USA: Puerto Rico is a domestic destination for US airlines and an American Airlines hub: American Airlines, American Eagle, US Air, Eastern and Delta all run frequent flights from Miami and many other US cities (including Atlanta, Baltimore, Boston, Dallas and Orlando).

By air from other Caribbean islands: San Juan is very well served from the Caribbean and South America by: BWIA (from Trinidad, Antigua, Jamaica and Barbados); ALM (from Sint Maarten and Curaçao); Air France (from Guadeloupe and Martinique). Hopper airlines include LIAT (© 791 3838), whose flights to and from the Eastern Caribbean terminate here—direct services to the Virgin Islands, Anguilla, St Kitts, Antigua and beyond—and many other smaller airlines such as Air St Thomas (© 791 4898, US © (1 800) 522 3084) and Sunaire Express (US © (1 800) 595 9501). Puerto Rico has the same entry requirements as the US.

tourist information

The **Commonwealth of Puerto Rico Tourism Company** can be contacted at:

Spain: Calle Serrano 1, 2 izquierda, 28001 Madrid (© (341) 431 2128, ● 557 5260).

France: 5 bis, rue du Louvre, 75001 Paris (© 1 44 77 88 00, ● 1 42 60 05 45).

Germany: FVA Puerto Rico, c/o Discover the World Marketing, Eifelstrasse 14a, 60529 Frankfurt, © 4 69 350047, ● 49 69 350040.

Italy: Piazza Castello 11, 20121 Milano, © 02 72 00 26 86, ● 02 72 02 23 06.

USA: the Puerto Rican Tourism Co is at 575 Fifth Avenue, 23rd Floor, **New York**, NY 10017, © (1 212) 599 6262, ● 818 1866, toll free © (1 800) 223 6530.

Canada: 41–43 Colbourne Street, Suite 301, Toronto, Ontario M5E 1E3, © (416) 368 2680/2689/3147, toll free © (1 800) 667 0394.

On **Puerto Rico** itself, you can write to the Head Office at La Princessa, Box 4431, Old San Juan Station, San Juan, PR 00905–4431 (© 721 2400 and 722 1709, ● 722 5208). The island is dotted with information offices, which you will find at the International Airport (© 791 1014), next to the Condado Plaza Hotel in Condado (© 723 3135) and in the Alcaldía in town. There is also a very helpful office, *la casita*, near Pier 1 on the cruise-ship dock in Old San Juan (© 722 1709). Outside the capital, each major town has an information bureau in the Alcaldía, the Town Hall, on the main plaza, open weekdays. In Ponce go to the Casa Armstrong-Poventud off the central square (© 840 5695). Open 8–noon and 1–4.30. You can get information about the **Paradores** at 301 Calle San Justo, Old San Juan 00905 (© 721 2400 and 721 2884, US © (1 800) 443 0266).

The Tourism Company publishes a quarterly guide, *Qué Pasa*, with listings of current events as well as the hotels and restaurants. English is widely spoken in the tourist areas of Puerto Rico, but if you venture off the beaten track into the country you will find it very useful to speak Spanish. It is also worth requesting an English-speaking guide in some places if you need one. If you are driving and want to listen to the latest *salsa* music, tune in to Sal Sol on 98.5 FM or Z93 on 93.7 FM.

In a medical **emergency** you can contact the 24-hour emergency rooms at Ashford Memorial Community Hospital at 1451 Ashford Avenue (✆ 721 2160) or the San Juan Health Centre, 200 De Diego Avenue (✆ 725 0202). Ambulances can be reached on ✆ 343 2550. You are advised to have extensive medical cover, because charges for treatment in Puerto Rico are high. If you wish to contact the **police**, the general emergency number is ✆ 911; the central number is ✆ 343 2020.

The **IDD code** for Puerto Rico is ✆ (1 787), which is followed by a seven-digit island number. There is an international telephone exchange on Baldorioty de Castro in Miramar. Alternatively, most hotels will put calls through for you for a price.

festivals

Every town in Puerto Rico celebrates its saint's day in a week-long blow-out of Masses, feasts, candle processions with statues, masked street parades and music centred on the plaza. These are fun to attend, and you will certainly be included in the activities if you are around. The daytime parades are a riotous procession of *veijantes* (masked figures) and diabolos dancing in ghoulish, brightly coloured costumes, and everywhere the streets are alive with impromptu *kioskos* and games: a favourite is a crank-up merry-go-round where you bet on tin horses.

Main Towns and *Festas Patronales*

2 Feb	Mayagüez, a very spectacular celebration in honour of *La Virgen de la Candelaria.*
19 March	Lares, *San Jose*
1 May	Arecibo, *San Felipe Apostol*
13 June	Barranquitas, *San Antonio de Padua*
17 July	Culebra, *La Virgen del Carmen*
25 July	Loíza, *Santiago,* one of the best known on the island
25 July	Fajardo, *Santiago*
21 Aug	Adjuntas, *San Joaquin and Santa Ana*
3 Sept	Jayuya, *Nuestra Señora de la Montserrate*
29 Sept	Utuado, *San Miguel Arcangel*
29 Sept	Cabo Rojo
7 Oct	Yauco, *Nuestra Señora del Rosario*
4 Nov	Aguadilla
8 Dec	Humacao
16 Dec	Ponce, *Nuestra Señora de Guadelupe*

At **Christmas** Puerto Rican towns are strung end to end with fairy lights and coloured tinsel, often with a life-size nativity scene in people's front gardens, but the most spectacular and riotous event over the Christmas period is the **Festival of the Innocents**, which takes place in the small town of Hatillo, near Arecibo, on 28 December. Groups of men (mainly) dress in suits of brightly coloured ruff-like material, wearing ghostly masks and spend the day driving around the country on decorated floats. In the afternoon they converge on the town square, where they bounce their vehicles from side to side until they nearly tip over. Well worth a visit for a riot of colourful excess. Another very popular event, held in January, is the Fiesta de la Calle de San Sebastian, in which the street is crammed with costumed people dancing and generally making whoopee. There are many more formal events and festivals, including classical concerts, theatre and even ballet performances.

money

The currency of Puerto Rico is the US dollar, but it is often known as the peso. Quarters are called pesetas and cents centavos. Traveller's cheques and credit cards are widely accepted in the tourist areas, but out in the country you will need to pay in cash. Small notes are useful for this as well as for tipping (the usual dollar or 10–15%).

Shoppers will find endless hunting grounds in Puerto Rico and with no sales tax it is quite good sport. Individual shops and even malls are often found in the big hotels, but they are thickest on the ground in Old San Juan.

Banks: Open weekdays 8.30–2.30 and Saturdays 9.45–noon.

Shops: Open Mon–Sat 9–6 and will accept credit cards quite happily.

watersports

Watersports depend mainly on the hotels and their concessionaires. All sports, **waterskiing**, **parasailing**, outings in small **sailing craft, pedalos** or **jetskis** are easily arranged in the major tourist areas of Condado and Isla Verde, and in the major resorts of Dorado (20 miles west of San Juan) and Palmas del Mar in the southeast. If you travel further afield sports become less available, though you will find operators on most of the popular beaches at the weekends.

Windsurfing: Popular all over the island (particularly in Condado lagoon, try San Juan Water Sports, ⊘ 725 8122) and rental equipment is easily found.

Surfing: Popular in the northwest, around Aguadilla, Añasco and Rincón, where the wind and waves often provide high sport. Hire is around $20 per hour for a board and instruction is available through all the main beaches.

Sailing: There are endless excursions, usually out of the marinas in Fajardo (they normally offer transfers from hotels in San Juan), which will take you for a day's sailing and snorkelling, with a stop on an isolated beach for a picnic. In San Juan contact Caribe Aquatic Adventures (⊘ 729 2929 ext 240, ⊘ 765 7444 eves) and Castillo Watersports (⊘ 791 6195) for a ride on the catamaran *Barefoot III*, and in Fajardo Captain Jack's Catamaran (⊘ 863 1905) and Captain Jayne's Sailing Charters (⊘ 791 5174). In other towns ask at the hotels or see the tourist literature. If you are sailing, there are marinas around Fajardo.

Deep-sea fishing: The northern shore of Puerto Rico drops away to 6000ft within a couple of miles, and there are some extremely fine waters. Cast for white and blue marlin, wahoo and sailfish and perhaps you could improve on one of Puerto Rico's many world records. You can set off from the Club Náutico in San Juan, with Benitez Deep Sea Fishing, Fernández Juncos Avenue (⊘ 721 7335) or Southern Witch in Miramar (⊘ 731 9252). If you are on the west coast you can contact Western Tourist Services (⊘ 834 4008) in Mayagüez. A boat for six people costs around $650 for a full day's sail.

Snorkelling and **diving:** Fajardo and its islands also have the best of the reefs and sand-bars. The reefs teem with schools of grunts and solitary graceful angelfish and butterflyfish. Most hotels will fix it up for you, or contact Caribbean Divers (© 722 7393) in Fajardo, or in San Juan Caribbean School of Aquatics in La Concha Hotel in Condado (© 728 6606), and Mundo Submarino (© 791 5764), Isla Verde. The southwest has a number of dive shops; contact Parguera Fishing Charters in Lajas (© 899 4698) and Boquerón Dive Shop (© 851 2155).

other sports

Golf: There are 16 courses in Puerto Rico, some of them attached to the big hotels. On the outskirts of San Juan is the Luis Ortiz course (© 786 3859). There are two 18-hole courses in Río Grande just east of the capital, the Berwind Country Club (© 876 3056) and Club Westin Rio Mar (© 888 8815). These courses are open to the public at varying times, so it is best to ring before arriving. At the Dorado resort area there is a number of courses (© 796 1234) and also at the Conquistador resort (© 863 1000) and the Palmas del Mar development, which has an 18-hole course (© 852 6000). In the northwest try Punta Borinquen (© 890 2987) in Aguadilla.

Tennis: Courts proliferate around the tourist hotels, though it may be difficult to get a court in winter. If the hotel you are staying in does not have one, they can arrange it elsewhere. You can also play at San Juan Central Park, off Route 2 (© 722 1646).

Hiking: There are endless possibilities in the mountainous interior of the island. Most national parks have trails. You can struggle up switchback paths in the mountains, taking a quick dip in the waterfalls, or stalk pelicans and tropicbirds in the mangrove swamps. The parks are coordinated by the Natural Resources Department, PO Box 5887, San Juan 00906 (© 724 3724). For details of companies that arrange nature and adventure tours, *see* 'Flora and Fauna', p.540.

Riding: You might prefer to ride through the mountains or to gallop through the breakers. Around Luquillo you can go to Hacienda Carabalí (© 889 5820) and in the southeast of the island you can go to the large centre at Palmas del Mar (© 852 6000).

Pot-holing: Puerto Rico's underground rivers have carved out some extremely impressive cave systems in the limestone rock. There are tame, trolley-borne tours on offer, but if you are a spelunker, then you might want to check out the lesser-known caverns in an inde-pendent party: contact the Puerto Rico Speleological Society, PO Box 31074, 65th Infantry Station, Rio Piedras, Puerto Rico 00929.

Baseball: The favourite spectator sport in Puerto Rico, as in the other Latin Caribbean islands of Cuba and the Dominican Republic. The season runs over the winter months here, from October to April, and some Puerto Rican sportsmen in the major leagues return here to play. There are stadia in San Juan, Santurce, Caguas, Ponce, Mayagüez and Arecibo. You are quite likely to see softball being played as well.

Cockfighting: Another very popular sport in the Latin Caribbean islands. There is an organized and rather plush *gallera* in Isla Verde, at the Club Gallístico (© 791 1557; *open Sat 1–7, adm*), but if you go to a *gallera* in a country town, you will see all the frenzied passion of a local tournament, where pride as well as money ride on the result. The sport is cruel and often ends with one of the birds being killed. Usually Sat and Sun afternoons.

herding Zebus

The Dominican Republic

Hispaniola is the second-largest island in the Caribbean (after Cuba) and it is shared by two countries, each with a surprisingly different heritage. In the east is the Spanish-speaking Dominican Republic, a bustling Latin American island. In the western third of the island is the press of Haiti, a country unlike anywhere else in the world. Here there are echoes of France, but also reverberations of Africa that are the strongest of any Caribbean country.

The Dominican Republic is one of the poorest countries in the Caribbean, but a quick walk down to the Avenida del Puerto beneath the colonial city in Santo Domingo, where the Dominicans take the evening air, will show you that it is also one of the liveliest. The country is large, and so beyond the coastal encrustation of beach resorts tourism is barely visible. Here you will find a charming Latin people and, particularly if you speak Spanish, a country that is very rewarding to travel.

The Dominican Republic is the second-largest country in the Caribbean, 18,750 square miles or about the same size as Scotland. It is cut by three main mountain ranges running west to east. In the middle is the massive Cordillera Central, where you will find the Caribbean's highest mountain, Pico Duarte (10,417ft). In the north the rainfall is high and there are extremely fertile plains, everywhere planted with neat lines of fruit or swathes of sugar-cane. Just 100 miles away, the southwest of the country is so arid that it is desert.

The capital, Santo Domingo, is situated on the south coast and is the oldest city in the Americas. Around two million of the total population of almost 8 million live in the shanties of greater Santo Domingo. Despite this increasing urban population, the majority of Dominicans still lead a rural life in small towns or in *bohío* shacks out in the country, where they make a living through sugar, tobacco, cocoa and coffee or small agricultural concerns. The country also has large reserves of ferronickel bauxite, as well as some gold and silver. The biggest sector of the Dominican economy nowadays is tourism, but despite its one million annual visitors, the Dominican Republic has not been swamped by the industry. It is possible to combine a tourist's beach-based holiday with travel to the towns of the interior to discover the flamboyant style of Dominican life.

The Dominican heritage is both Latin and Caribbean. The men are macho here; they will strike up a matador's pose as a woman walks by, or maybe just grab her and dance in the road. After dark the tree-lined streets come alive as people take the evening air and the portable stereos strike up with the latest sounds of *merengue*, the national rhythm.

A look at the faces will show what a vibrant and thorough mix the Dominicans are. In colour they range from white (about 15 per cent) to pure African (about 15 per cent), but the majority of the Dominicans are some-where in between, often with clearly visible Arawak Indian features. There is not much overt colour prejudice, but it is clearly a social advantage to have

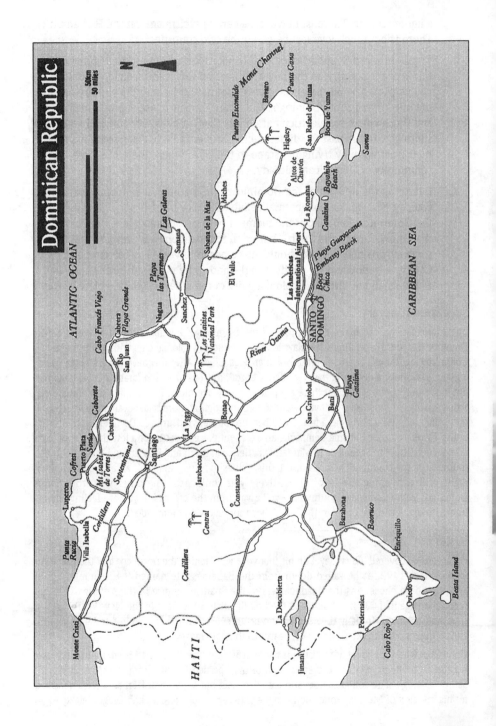

Dominican Republic

ATLANTIC OCEAN

CARIBBEAN SEA

50km
50 miles

N

Mona Channel

Puerto Escondido
Bavaro
Punta Cana
Higüey
San Rafael de Yuma
Boca de Yuma
Altos de Chavón
Suana
La Romana
Catalina
Bayahibe Beach
Las Galeras
Miches
Sabana de la Mar
Samaná
El Valle
Playa Guayacanes
Embassy Beach
Las Américas
International Airport
Boca Chica
Playa las Terrenas
Nagua
Sánchez
Los Haitises
National Park
River Ozama
SANTO
DOMINGO
Cabrera
Playa Grande
Cabo Francés Viejo
Río
San Juan
Cabarete
Sosúa
Puerto Plata
Cofresi
Cabarete
Bonao
San Cristóbal
Baní
Playa Catalina
Luperón
Mt Isabel
de Torres
Septentrional
Santiago
La Vega
Jarabacoa
Cordillera
Central
Constanza
Punta
Rucia
Villa Isabella
Cordillera
Barahona
Baoruco
Enriquillo
Beata Island
Monte Cristi
HAITI
Jimaní
La Descubierta
Pedernales
Oviedo
Cabo Rojo

a lighter colour. There is, however, a certain racism against the Haitians. There is not much love lost between the two countries.

The Dominican Republic is extremely poor (one recent estimate puts two-thirds of the country on the poverty line) and this is immediately visible if you venture beyond the enclave of the tourist hotels into the country or into the outskirts of Santo Domingo. The island infrastructure is pretty inefficient and those who have electricity are often plagued by power cuts and water shortages. In the past the dissatisfaction has erupted in riots; some express their frustration by trying to escape to the USA, where there is a large community of Dominicans already.

But for all the difficulties the Dominicans have a natural exuberance and the country has considerable natural beauty. Package tourists get a good deal in the Dominican Republic at the moment (it is considerably less expensive than most Caribbean islands), but as an independent traveller you will find some surprisingly cool hang-outs in the beach towns—Las Terrenas and Cabarete (renowned for windsurfing)—and some mountain retreats, as well as the small but attractive colonial glory of the oldest city of the New World.

Suggested Itinerary

In two weeks you can make a good tour of the Dominican Republic. If you arrive in Santo Domingo it is worth spending a few days looking around the colonial city, with an outing to the Columbus Lighthouse or a day on the beach at Boca Chica. After this head for the north coast: on your way make a detour in the Cordillera Central, to Constanza and Jarabacoa. Santiago has not much to recommend it, but there are places to stay overnight. Puerto Plata and particularly Sosua are lively tourist resorts; if you want something slightly more relaxed, then move straight on to Cabarete (which still has a fun crowd because of the windsurfing). Do not miss the resort of Las Terrenas on the Samaná Peninsula, an excellent place to settle for a few days. From here take the ferry over to Sabana de la Mar (an experience in itself) and look around the agricultural southeast of the country. There are also tourist hotels to retreat to in this area if you feel like a night of luxury along the way. Alternatively you could head the other way from Santo Domingo, to the desert-like southwest, well away from the crowds. If you are feeling adventurous, take a few days' break in Haiti, which is thoroughly recommended.

History

Columbus discovered 'Quisqueya' on his first voyage, reaching the north coast of the island on 5 December 1492, as he sailed down from the Bahamas. He named it Hispaniola, 'Little Spain', and he chose it as the headquarters of the Spanish Empire in the Americas. On his second voyage in 1493 he established the first Spanish settlement in the New World with a thousand colonists. Initially they settled the north coast, but the site proved to be unhealthy and so they moved to the south coast, nearer to the gold mines.

Columbus was not a great administrator and in 1502 he was recalled to Spain in disgrace, but his son Don Diego oversaw the expansion of the Spanish Empire from the glorious city of Santo Domingo. The conquistadors and colonizers set out from here: Hernán Cortés departed for his invasion of Mexico, Ponce de León went to settle Puerto Rico, and Diego Velázquez to

Cuba. But as the gold in Hispaniola dried up and the mines of Colombia and Peru were discovered, Santo Domingo gradually lost its lustre. It remained the official capital, but the colonists simply moved on and eventually the island was eclipsed, ignored by Spain.

Buccaneers moved into the remote northwestern part of Hispaniola in the late 1500s (*see* **Haiti**, 'History', p.610), managing to hang on despite repeated attempts to root them out by the Spaniards. Finally, at the Treaty of Ryswick in 1697, the Spaniards acknowledged their presence and ceded the western third of the island to France. Over the next hundred years Saint Domingue, as the French part of the island was known, became the archetypal West Indian sugar factory, the richest colony in the world. In the east, Santo Domingo languished.

But it was the fall of the French colony that was to stir the torpor of Santo Domingo. In 1793 Saint Domingue was involved in a civil war as the slaves rose up in rebellion. The Spaniards stepped in on the side of Toussaint and the slaves, but then soon found themselves without an ally as Toussaint switched sides to the French. In 1801 he invaded Santo Domingo and the whole of Hispaniola was in his hands.

In 1809, with the help of the British, the Spaniards forced the Haitians out of the eastern part of the island and the colony was restored to Spanish colonial rule. But, following the lead of other colonies on the South American mainland, the creole Dominicans started an independence movement to drive out the colonists. In 1821 they succeeded and the eastern part of the island became independent. It was not to last. In 1822 the Haitians, under General Boyer, occupied the new country, unifying the whole island under the name of Haiti. Some of the Dominicans welcomed him (slavery was abolished), but the occupation fostered a spirit of Dominican nationality and an underground independence organization, *La Trinitaria*, was formed, led by Duarte, Sánchez and Mella. In 1843 Boyer was ousted from power in Haiti in a coup, and then on 27 February 1844 the Dominican rebels took their chance, storming the Ozama fortress and freeing the Dominican Republic once again.

Since independence, Dominican politics have swung between a state of ineffective liberal democracy and the extreme of repressive dictatorship. During the latter periods, dictatorial rule was maintained by terror tactics—many died in office at the hands of assassins. In the chaos, the USA has decided to step in to maintain order more than once.

The Trinitaria found themselves ousted from power almost immediately in 1844 and for the next forty-five years the power swung between two self-appointed generals, Buenaventura Báez and Pedro Santana. Santana even invited the Spaniards back in to administer the country in 1861, but the colonizers were forced out in a violent campaign, culminating in the Restoration of 16 August 1865.

The Americans also were beginning to show an interest. In the 1870s, the US Senate failed to pass a bill for the annexation of the country by just one vote. By 1907, having reneged on its foreign debts, the bankrupt Dominican Republic was placed in the receivership of the USA. In 1916, after an invasion of Haiti the previous year, the Americans occupied the country, staying for the next eight years. A few Dominicans resisted the occupation, but others welcomed the stability it would bring after years of turbulent internal politics. The Americans brought many improvements in island infrastructure—roads, schools, sanitation and public health, but there was a brooding political resentment at the military rule and eventually in 1924 the Marines left.

Within a few years another despot was in control. Rafael Leonidas Trujillo, the Army chief of staff, had himself elected in a rigged ballot in 1930. His thirty repressive years in power are still remembered with horror and bitterness. It is true that he turned the economy round to begin with, but the price was ruthless dictatorship. The country became his personal fiefdom, a police state. Trujillo himself was responsible for the disappearance of thousands of people. He renamed Santo Domingo Ciudad Trujillo in his own honour, and helped himself to a personal fortune estimated at one billion dollars. Finally, in 1961, he was assassinated and the country was plunged into chaos. Fearful of another Cuba, the Americans took it upon themselves to invade again in 1965.

Next year Joaquín Balaguer, once a moderate associate of Trujillo, was overwhelmingly elected President in what seemed like a vote for peace. He was re-elected twice, but was ousted in the elections of 1978 (only after he returned ballot boxes that had been stolen, under pressure from the USA). He was elected once again in 1994, taking his sixth Presidency at the age of 86. As in many Caribbean islands, politics is a source of considerable dispute and sometimes erupts into violence in the streets, so it is best to avoid the cities in the run-up to election time once every four years. The last election was on May 16th, 1996, when a young Dominican intellectual, Dr Leonel Fernandez Reina, was elected President of the Dominican Republic.

The economy of the Dominican Republic is based on the export of nickel, bauxite and gold and agricultural products including sugar, coffee, tobacco and cocoa and some fruit. The other major sector is tourism, which has been the principal industry and primary foreign income earner since 1984 with around 1,932,227 visitors annually, followed by the export and the free zones industries.

Merengue

Dancing is something of a way of life in the Dominican Republic—they take music with them everywhere on noisy portable stereos and you will see even two-year-olds moving to a beat, developing their sense of rhythm. The buses are like mobile discotheques and it is not unusual to find that the passengers sing along. The national sound is merengue, a typically Latin beat, relentless, bustling and compulsive.

Most popular merengue is produced on modern instruments now, but you will certainly still see the traditional three-piece band of the *perico ripiao*, made up of a drum, an accordion and a *güira* (a cheese grater scratched with a metal stick or a soul comb) and sometimes a *bajo* (a sit-on bass-box with metal teeth that the player thrums). Another sound to make a hit recently is *bachata*, a slower and more melodic rhythm, though still an excellent one to dance to (the leading performers are Antony Santos, Raulin Rodriguez, Joe Veras, Luis Vargas and Luis Seguras among others).

An annual **Merengue Festival** is held in Santo Domingo in the third week of July. There are three main stages for the bands on the Malecón, but the radio stations and the drinks companies set up their own stalls there too. It is one of the year's liveliest events, a week's blowout of dancing, drinking and local food in the capital. If you cannot make that, there are endless discotheques, even in the smallest Dominican towns. After an evening's promenading around the town square the locals end up there. Friday, Saturday and particularly Sunday nights are most popular. Leading merengue singers are Juan Luis Guerra y 440, famed for his classic songs, Sergio Vargas, Fernando Villalona and, most popular for their (incredibly fast) dance music, Rokabanda, Coco Band and La Banda Gorda.

Amber

The Dominican Republic possesses one of the world's largest reserves of amber, a semi-precious gem. It is not a stone, but petrified sap from trees that grew on the island 50 million years ago. It has been known as a 'touchstone' in the past because of its static qualities. The word electricity derives from the Greek for amber, *elektron*.

The featherweight gem varies from an almost transparent variety that has undergone the least chemical reaction, through the familiar yellow and amber colour to a deep red (the price increases with the depth of colour). Value is increased further by wisps of blue smoke within it, gases that were caught as the sap formed in the old rainforests millions of years ago. Most exquisite (and most expensive) are pieces in which leaves and insects have been caught.

There are three main mining areas in the Republic, the largest being at Cotui in the Cibao, in the mountains just south of Puerto Plata on the north coast and at El Valle close to Santo Domingo.

Several museums exhibit amber, including **Joyas Criollas** at the Plaza Criolla and the **Amber Museum** in Santo Domingo and in Puerto Plata (*see* p.587). There are pieces for sale in these places as well as in any tourist shop you might go into. It is possible to visit the amber mines, though you will have to do much of the organizing yourself. Start off at the museums. It is illegal to export unpolished amber from the Dominican Republic.

Larimar

Larimar, or Dominican turquoise, is unique to the Dominican Republic. It is a very hard, semi-precious stone, slightly lighter in colour than other turquoise and it is mined in the southwestern corner of the country. You will find examples of jewellery made from larimar in all the tourist shops and markets.

Some Advice

To get the best out of the Dominican Republic, it is essential to speak at least some Spanish. English is enough in the tourist areas, but if you go off the beaten track you will find few people who understand it.

It is a good idea to lock your bags when you send them into the aeroplane hold. Once beyond the airport, you are unlikely to encounter any trouble. However, you will definitely come across hustlers, particularly in downtown Santo Domingo. They are persistent and quite persuasive, and have a whole inventory of drugs and services on offer. Most of them are also tricksters. If you want to be sure of a guide's reliability, go through the tourist office. You will not be hustled that much beyond the tourist towns, though you may find yourself surrounded by a crowd of inquisitive kids. A stock of pencils or small presents to give away would help.

Unfortunately travellers who venture out and about are at the mercy of unscrupulous traders and so you will find yourself outrageously overcharged for snacks, drinks and bus-fares. It is of course haphazard, but this practice has become quite widespread over the last few years as tourism on the island has increased.

There are quite often power cuts in the Dominican Republic, though the situation improved dramatically in 1993 (cynics say in the run-up to the 1994 presidential election). Take a torch or candles. Spare batteries are easily available. Remember that the water supply will probably be cut off too. Tourist hotels usually have their own generating system. Mosquito coils are available and make life a bit more comfortable. You may consider using a mosquito net (available in Santo Domingo). It is a good idea to have a room with a fan in the summer months because the nights can be hot.

Do not drink unpurified tap water. It is quite easy to get hold of purified water in the main towns (most cheap hotels have it), but off the beaten track you will have to stock up. Drinks bought on the street are dodgy because they will not be made from purified water. Key words are *filtrada* and *purificada*.

Women travellers may find themselves the centre of some macho attention, usually verbal but occasionally tactile. You are advised not to make long journeys alone or to go to the downtown areas alone at night. All white foreigners are *gringos* to some of the Dominicans, and so you may find that you get some odd reactions. If someone moves away on the bus, or shouts *SIDA* at you, they probably think you have AIDS.

The authorities take a very hard line with drugs and suspects are liable to find themselves in an unpleasant Dominican jail for a few weeks before they think about a trial (they have no system of bail here either). There are fewer drugs in the Dominican Republic than in most other Caribbean countries.

In the remoter tourist areas you may find yourself stopped by the road police for no apparent reason: they will check around your car or bike until they find something wrong with it. The going rate for an easy time is a few pesos (it increases around Christmas time). If you wish to make a moral stand, prepare for an argument.

Prostitution is pretty big in the Dominican Republic (there is a considerable trade in sex tourism) and so single men particularly will find themselves approached by *aviones*, as they are known (often with some pretty surprising tactile introductory lines). The country is very poor and so it is inexpensive. Apart from all the weird and wonderful strains of clap you could catch, the island is fizzing with HIV.

Getting Around

The Dominican Republic has an extensive transport system, on which you can reach almost anywhere from Santo Domingo within the day. At the top end of the range you will get the pleasure of your own seat in an air-conditioned bus with Bruce Lee videos to keep you amused. Lower down the scale, buses are a bit ramshackle and you will get to know your fellow passengers pretty well: they tend to be fairly crowded. The back row of the bus, the source of all gossip, is known as *la cocina* (the kitchen).

Within **Santo Domingo** (and other towns), the quickest method of transport is the crowded *públicos*, or share taxis. These are private cars, which run along the main drags, picking up and setting down passengers as required. Fares are 2 pesos or 4 pesos, depending on the distance. You can also take the big yellow public buses that run fixed routes for 2.50 pesos, but it can be a long wait as there are no schedules.

The cities of the Dominican Republic are linked by **coach service**, with as many as five daily runs to the north coast by each company. Most routes originate in Santo

Domingo, so be prepared to change or to stay overnight there. Coaches leave according to a schedule from a terminus, or the main plaza in a smaller town. There is a system of reservations, but this is not all that reliable. To be sure of a seat, you must be in the queue about an hour before departure.

Terrabus (sic) has the smartest and most comfortable buses, with on-board snacks and videos. They work from the Plaza Criolla in Santo Domingo (✆ 541 2080). Other companies include Caribe Tours, which depart from Avenida 27 de Febrero (corner Leopoldo Navarro), not far northwest of the colonial city (✆ 221 4422), or from Avenida Estrella Sadhala in Santiago and from Calle 12 de Julio in Puerto Plata. Metro Buses (✆ 566 7126/29) leave from the corner of Avenida Winston Churchill and Hatuey in Santo Domingo (Puerto Plata ✆ 586 6161/6062). Apolo can be contacted on ✆ 537 0000 in Santo Domingo. In Santiago and Puerto Plata buses terminate in the suburbs.

Guaguas are privately operated minibuses which run between the towns, picking up passengers in the villages on the way. These are the loudest, most crowded and best fun of all, particularly if you join in when they sing along to the latest merengue and salsa on the stereo. You will see the best side of Dominican life here, cooped up with the shopping and the chickens. *Guaguas* run local routes and tend to leave when all the seats and any room in the aisles have been filled, starting about 6am and running until dusk and beyond. Out in the country just hail them down; in town go to the plaza. In **Santo Domingo**, buses headed west depart from the Parque Independencia, but most leave from Parque Enriquillo at the intersection of Avenida Duarte and Calle Caracas, north of the colonial city. Listen out as they drive around the square shouting for passengers. You can catch a bus from here to the **airport**. Fares are low: Santo Domingo to Boca Chica costs RD$12, Santiago RD$55 and Higuey RD$60.

One problem with *guaguas* can be the drivers, many of whom drive as fast as their engines will take them and some of whom have been known to drink. Take your chances. Another problem, thankfully restricted to the tourist areas of the north coast, is an almost constitutional habit of overcharging foreigners (in places as much as five times what the locals pay for the same trip). If this annoys you, all you can do is find out what the going rate is before getting to the bus stop and stick to your guns. Alternatively, practise swearing and cursing in Spanish.

Between the smaller towns the local *guagua* will often be a pick-up truck, brimful of Dominicans and their produce and animals. **Hitching** works adequately around the Dominican Republic, though you might be expected to sub the driver. Women passengers will often be offered the front seat. This is merely politeness rather than a way to get to know you better.

Taxis are available in the tourist areas and at the airports. They are expensive in comparison with local transport. They are unmetered, so be sure to arrange the price beforehand (rates are fixed in hotels, but you can bargain if you want). The going rate for a trip from Las Américas international airport to downtown Santo Domingo (about 18 miles) is about US$20 (RD$250). Taxi firms include Aero Taxi (✆ 685 1212) and Taxi Anacaona (✆ 530 4800). There is quite a motorbike culture in the Dominican Republic and you can catch a *motoconcho*, a motorbike taxi, for just a few pesos. Fix the price before setting off.

Organized **tours** will take you to all the recognized sights and beaches as well as for night-time excursions around Santo Domingo. Hotel front desks can arrange them for you (and you will be picked up there), or you can go to the tour companies direct. In Santo Domingo contact Metro Tours in Avenida Winston Churchill (✆ 544 4580), Prieto Tours, Avenida Francia 125 (✆ 685 0102), Emotion Tours, 76 Independencia Ave (✆ 682 4487), or Landscape Tours, 220 Roberto Pastoriza Ave (✆ 565 2514). Prieto Tours also work out of Puerto Plata (✆ 586 3988), as do Apolo Tours (✆ 586 5329/6610), who will take you up the mountain, by cable car. Tropical Tours work from La Romana, Casa de Campo nearby (✆ 556 3636). You can take a tour of the River Ozama, departing beneath the Alcázar, on the Ferry Centenario (✆ 682 1546).

In such a large country it is convenient to have the freedom of travelling by **hire car**, but these come only at a price. Your licence is valid for 90 days. Driving in the Dominican Republic is mainly on the right and is quite an experience. In town it is chaotic, with cars and buses nosing for position and generally ignoring the unspoken rules that govern driving elsewhere. On the country roads it can be downright dangerous as all the same manoeuvres are performed at high speed. The main roads are quite good, but in remoter areas the surfaces will often be quite rough. Leave plenty of time if you are going off the beaten track. There are not that many petrol stations in the remoter areas of the country. All in all you might prefer to go by bus.

Insurance is not usually comprehensive and some companies will expect you to pay the first US$500 of a claim against you. Rates start at US$50 per day for a small car. You will have to leave a hefty deposit. Hire firms in Santo Domingo include Budget on John F. Kennedy (✆ 562 6812), Hertz, Avenida Independencia (✆ 221 5333), Nelly on Avenida Winston Churchill (✆ 567 1015/16) and Thrifty on Jose Maria Heredia (✆ 686 0133). In Puerto Plata, try Budget on Avenida L. Ginebra (✆ 586 4433). Budget and National also have offices at the airport. In La Romana contact Honda (✆ 556 3835) and Nelly (✆ 556 2156), both on Avenida Santa Rosa.

You can easily hire a **motorcycle** or a moped in the tourist areas. If you get one, be extremely careful to lock it up, and put it behind closed doors at night. In the remoter areas, away from the most dangerous traffic, motorbike is probably the best method of travel. However, do not take any risks with larger vehicles. Drive defensively and be ready to get off the road if the situation requires. Hire costs from at least US$30 a day.

Finally, it is possible to travel in the Republic by **air** as there are a number of airstrips around the country capable of taking small aircraft; in Santo Domingo's western suburbs is Herrera airport (✆ 567 3900) and there are strips in Santiago, Puerto Plata, Cabo Rojo, La Romana (for Casa de Campo) Punta Cana, Barahona and Samaná at Las Terrenas and Portillo. There are no scheduled internal flights, but you can charter small aircraft through Bavaro Sun Flight (✆ 685 8101, ✆ 686 4309), Caribair on Avenida Luperón (✆ 542 6688) and Air Santo Domingo on 27 De Febrero Ave (✆ 683 8020).

There are miles and miles of beach in the Dominican Republic, many of them developed with hotels or condominiums and with every conceivable watersport on offer, but in remoter areas you will find seemingly endless stretches of sand that are completely deserted. Beaches with hotels tend to be well kept and sprayed to get rid of sandflies, but off the beaten track, remember to take insect repellent. You are advised to watch your possessions closely on the beaches.

North Coast

Punta Rucia: In the remote area between the Haitian border and Puerto Plata you will find a secluded bay, close to Columbus's La Isabella. There are hotels in the area.

Luperón: Better known, set on a wide bay with excellent golden sand and palm trees with a hotel to retreat to in the heat of the midday sun.

Cofresi: A mile-long strand and a single hotel, relatively untainted despite being so close to Puerto Plata.

Playa Dorada: Heading east from Puerto Plata, the beaches and hotels really start. The beach in the town itself is disappointing, but 3 miles to the east, you will find a superb strand; active and busy with all the watersports. Officially the hotels each have their strip of beachfront on the 2 miles of sand and palms. You can negotiate with the concessionaires for a windsurfer or a waterskiing trip.

Sosúa: A crescent curve of mounded white sand brushed by more palms. It is a very busy beach and inevitably you will be accosted to buy a wood carving, a T-shirt or any number of other exotic services. There are bars around the whole length of the beach. Watersports are available. There are other smaller coves with fantastic sand and less of a crowd close by.

Cabarete: Nine miles farther down the coast, this is best known for its winter-season winds, which blow off the Atlantic with such force that they held the 1987 world windsurfing championships here. It is a very laid-back and friendly town strung along miles of excellent, light-coloured sand, where you can hire a sailboard.

Try **Playa Grande** close to Cabrera, and **Playa la Preciosa** and the secluded beach at the headland of **Cabo Francés Viejo:** These beaches stretch along the coast right down to the eastern tip of the island, many of them picture-postcard Caribbean— white sand and palms and ridiculously blue sea. Many face on to the Atlantic and so the waves are big and the undertow is strong.

Samaná Peninsula: There are some good beaches here, though not many near to the town itself. The best are on the northern shore, where they run seemingly endlessly east and west from Playa Las Terrenas (do not swim off the town centre itself because of the sewage). Watersports are available at the hotels. It is well worth exploring because you will find superb, deserted strands. You can find transport in Sánchez.

Puerto Escondido: On Samaná Bay itself you can go to the beach in the town (over the hill to the southwest and behind the Baha Beach Resort). Otherwise head for **Cayo Levantado**, off the southern shore, 6 miles east of Samaná—take a boat from the quay (*RD$50 return*), or from the beach opposite the island.

Las Galeras: Buses run to this beach on Baha del Rincón at the northeastern tip of the peninsula. The beach is OK, and there are places to get a drink or a meal.

East of Santo Domingo

Boca Chica: About 20 miles east of Santo Domingo, this is the busiest of all the beaches, particularly at the weekends when Dominicans stream out of the capital. It is noisy, with hundreds of portable stereos blaring out the latest merengue.

Embassy Beach: In the area of Juan Dolio you will find palms and snackbars and a smaller crowd here where the waves roar in between two arms of coral-rock and the gentler **Playa Guayacanes**. Or you can find your way down to **Playa Real**, a quieter spot where there is a hotel and restaurant to retreat to.

Bayahibe Beach: There is a beach in Casa de Campo, Playa Minitas, but it is surrounded by private land and so entrance is restricted (it is man-made anyway and gets quite crowded). All watersports are available. Preferable is this wilder and remoter strip of stunning white sand lapped with gentle waves and fringed with palms and with a small fish restaurant for a drink when the going gets too hot.

Playa Catalina: A fantastic beach on an uninhabited island offshore opposite La Romana. Trips (*expensive*) can be arranged from the front desk at Casa de Campo, otherwise hire a boat to run you across, but take a picnic.

The beaches run in an almost continuous stretch from south of **Punta Cana**, the island's most easterly point, up to **Miches**. An occasional hotel breaks the isolation, but access to the beach is often reserved for guests only. The waves can be quite big as they come straight in off the Atlantic, so be careful when you swim, but if you want untouched sands to walk, you will find 20 miles of them here.

West of Santo Domingo there are few beaches. The coastline is mostly rocky until the Barahona peninsula, where the white sands resume. Here you will find beaches at Paraiso, Los Patos and San Rafael.

Flora and Fauna

The Dominican Republic has rainforests, lowlands, deserts and coastal swamplands (and, at Lago Enriquillo, land more than a hundred feet below sea level). On the barren or 'bald' plains near the summits of the Caribbean's highest peaks, the vegetation is stunted, 'dwarf forest' of ferns and grasses, but this soon descends into pines and into the dripping, tangled rainforest. Among the buttressed mahogany trees, infested with lianas and creeping vines, you will see rufous-throated solitaires, the greater Antillean elaenia and the Hispaniolan parrot, the green cotorra. Lower down you will also come across the Hispaniolan woodpecker, a noisy character, and plenty of hummingbirds, including the Hispaniolan emerald and the tiny zumbadorcito, one of the most minute birds in the world.

In the coastal areas you will find many of the Caribbean's most elegant birds, including ibises, herons and flamingos and the magnificent frigate-bird, as well as terns, todies—red and green plumage and a long, straight bill—and turnstones.

Trees include lignum vitae, or tree of life, and satinwood, with a grain so fine that it is used in veneers. The coconut palms are endless and the towns are decorated with ceiba, or kapok, and many species of flowering tree like the flaming poinciana, the flamboyant. There has been considerable deforestation in the Dominican Republic as people have gone higher into the hills to chop wood for burning and for cultivation. Efforts have been made to improve the situation.

Island fauna is more limited, though there is a variety of reptiles, from tiny lizards that crawl around upside down on the ceiling, through iguanas to crocodiles. You might come across the odd vast spider, the size of a man's outstretched hand—a tarantula.

There are five main **nationalparks** in the Dominican Republic (two in the Cordillera Central, Isla Cabritos on Lago Enriquillo, Los Haitises on Samaná Bay and Parque Nacional del Este) and you will need permission to visit them. This can sometimes be obtained from the park office at the gates, but it is best to make sure by visiting the main office in Santo Domingo; Departamento de Ecoturismo, 359 Avenida Independencia, esquina Cervantes (✆ 221 5340, ✆ 685 1316; *open 8–3, permits RD$75, daily rate for a guide RD$100*). If you do go off on your own, stock up on food and water because it is often difficult to find provisions in the remoter areas. For more details on the National Parks, *see* under separate entries in the following text.

Santo Domingo

The capital of the Dominican Republic, Santo Domingo (called La Capital) is the oldest city in the New World. In the early 1500s it was the seat of the Viceroys of the Americas, replete with fittingly glorious coral-stone palaces and among them the earliest cathedral, university and hospital in the New World (the oldest surviving building dates from 1503). From here the conquistadors departed on their expeditions to conquer the mainland and to settle the other islands. But the glory was eclipsed within a couple of generations as the riches of the Spanish Main were revealed and the administrators moved there. In 1562 much of the town was destroyed in an earthquake and by 1586, when Sir Francis Drake had taken a share (25,000 ducats to be precise), it was in ruins and it never really recovered.

Today, though the colonial city has been restored and the streets retain some of their former splendour, there is little that is glorious about Santo Domingo outside this immediate area. It is a working city of about two million people—the streets teem with lottery ticket vendors, fruit sellers and the endless traffic. Away from the city centre are prosperous-looking villas set in tree-lined boulevards running down to the seafront, the lively Malecón. Behind this screen of prosperity, in the ever-expanding shanties are some of the Caribbean's poorest slums.

The Colonial City

The centrepiece of the colonial city is the **Alcázar de Colón** (*open daily except Tues, 9–6; adm*), a two-storey, coral-stone palace with recessed arches, for sixty years the seat of the Spanish Crown in the Caribbean. It was constructed in 1510 by Don Diego Columbus, son of the discoverer, during his tenure as Viceroy, reputedly without the use of a single nail (doors and windows turned on pivots sunk into the walls). It was restored in 1957 with stone from the original quarry and period 16th- and 17th-century pieces, including outsize earthenware water-carriers and pint-size chairs. It is a nice place in which to pass the time of day, beneath the gargoyles and 17th-century tapestries and among such viceregal paraphernalia as the leather- and velvet-covered travelling trunks.

La Atarazana is opposite the Alcázar and runs down to the river beneath the square. In the 16th-century the eight buildings housed the royal armoury, the customs house and the official warehouses of old Santo Domingo; they have a similar role today inasmuch as they are stuffed with duty-free goods shipped in for sale. In the last building you will find the **Museum of Marine Archaeology** (*open 9–5; adm*), with relics from wrecks that have foundered on the island's coasts—the *Guadeloupe, Tolosa* and *Concepción.* Also discover about life on board ship in the 17th century, including why the poop deck is so called. You will find idyllic court-yards in which to rest in the Atarazana when you are gorged with buying and strolling the historic streets, museums and art galleries, and there are also a couple of fun bars opposite the Alcázar (though Wendy's has put in a worrying appearance).

The oldest surviving building in the Americas, the **Casa del Cordón** (*adm free*), is just up the hill from the Alcázar, on the corner of Calle Emiliano Tejera and Calle Isabel la Católica. Built in 1503, it is named after the cord of the Franciscan order that is carved in stone above the lintel. Today it is the Banco Popular, but they permit tours during working hours.

South of the Alcázar, by the **Calle de Las Damas** (where the court ladies would take the evening air in colonial times), you come to the **Capilla de Nuestra Señora de los Remedios**, a recently restored 16th-century chapel. Opposite is the **Museo de las Casas Reales** (*open daily except Mon, 9–6; adm*), formerly the palace of the Governors and Captains General, with some of the finest exhibits of the Spanish colonial heritage in the Americas, including handblown glass, armour and weapons. Also there are reconstructions of Columbus's voyages and his ships the *Niña,* the *Pinta* and the *Santa María.*

Across Calle las Mercedes is the monumental **Panteón Nacional**, with an eternal flame to the heroes of the Republic, including the assassins of Trujillo. The building dates from 1714 and was a Jesuit monastery. The Calle de las Damas continues south, lined with attractive old palaces, until it reaches the old fortress of the colonial city, the **Fortaleza Ozama** on the banks of the river (*open daily except Mon, 9–6; adm free*). Its heart is the Torre del Homenaje (the Tower of Homage), a minor colossus with walls 4ft thick, where for centuries prisoners were held. Nearby there is a good art gallery and café in which to sit, located in an alley, the **Plaza Toledo**, which is named after the wife of Bartholomew Columbus. You can see the works of Dominican painters—Alberto Ulloa, Freddy Javier and Martos García. Off the Calle de las Damas is the **Casa de Bastidas**, which has a pleasant courtyard in which to recover from the fray of Santo Domingo.

Not far off is **Parque Colón** (Columbus Square), where a statue of the explorer stands pointing to the horizon surrounded by arched walkways and coral-stone town buildings. On the south side is the **Catedral de Santa María la Menor** (*open Mon–Sat 9–6; adm free*), the first cathedral in the New World, which was built between 1523 and 1540. It is an attractive conglomeration of styles, with friezes and statues and gracefully curved roofs of rusty dark rock, though it is not particularly magnificent. Its grandeur lies in its status as the Catedral Primada de América (the senior cathedral in the Americas). Sir Francis Drake had no fitting respect for it in 1586, and used it as a place to hole up during his raid, chipping off the nose and hand of Bishop Bastidas's statue in a fit of anger.

It is also one of the many resting places of Columbus (other claims are from Seville and Cuba). For a while he lay in a huge marble tomb, supposedly brought here by his daughter-in-law in 1544, many years after he died. His next journey was in 1796, when the whole of Hispaniola was ceded to France—he was moved to the cathedral in Havana so that he would remain in Spanish soil—and then in 1898 he was supposedly taken back to Seville. However, in 1877 Padre Francisco Billini discovered a small crypt containing some ashes. He declared them the ashes of Columbus. Now he has been moved (or may not have been according to whose version of history you credit) a few miles east to El Faro, the huge lighthouse dedicated in 1992. There are many other things to see in the cathedral, including a huge mahogany throne and gold and silver ware from across the centuries. Diagonally opposite is the **Palacio de Borgella**, built during the Haitian occupation of 1822–44, and seat of the Dominican Congress until 1947 when it moved to the Palacio Nacional.

The main street of old Santo Domingo is **El Conde**, which leads west from the Parque Colón towards the Parque Independencia. Around the gridiron of streets of the colonial city you will find endless other ruins and monuments, some of them modern, but many which will cast your mind back to the glorious days of the 16th century. Now in ruins, the **Hospital Iglesia di San Nicolás de Barí** was the first hospital in the New World; also dating from 1510 is the **Convento de los Dominicos**, which once housed the first university founded here in 1538. On Calle Padre Billini you will find the **Convento de Santa Clara**, a refuge for the Clarissa Sisters, dating from 1522, and the **Museum of the Dominican Family** (*open daily 9–6; adm*), with exhibits of the good life in the 19th century. In the Puerta de la Misericordia you will find the old refuge of the city dwellers during hurricanes, and the spot where Mella initiated the revolt against Haitian occupation in 1844.

El Conde itself is a lively pedestrian precinct, usually teeming with people out promenading, sitting in the cafés and browsing the shops, which are among the city's best. At its western limit is the **Parque Independencia**, a major terminus for local transport and the official centre of the country (from where all distances are measured; there is even a bar called Kilometro Zero). On the square itself, behind the crumbled city wall and one of the old city gates, the **Puerto del Conde**, is a mausoleum constructed in 1976. Inside you will see an eternal flame and a monument to the 1844 Independence leaders, Duarte, Mella and Sánchez.

The Modern City

The modern city of Santo Domingo lies north and west of the Parque Independencia, leading off in broad streets lined with trees where the villas stand back from the endless parade of motorbikes and the red and blue share-taxis. **The Malecón** (the sea promenade, officially called Avenida George Washington) has an avenue of *palma cana* on the seafront, and is one of the liveliest spots in town. The road has recently been extended to the east, running beneath the walls of the colonial city and along the Ozama River. The whole strip comes alive at dusk when the Dominicans take the evening air, walking up and down past the hundreds of portable stereos blaring out merengue. Unfortunately many people seem to take the air in Toyota convertibles and so it becomes one big traffic jam, but it is fun to be a part of. The Malecón is particularly lively during carnival and the merengue festival (*see* p.574), when the parades go by.

Another scene of Dominican mayhem is the **Mercado Modelo**, to the north of the colonial city on Avenida Mella (another major shopping street). It is one of the main Santo Domingo markets and so you will find anything on sale from plantains and root vegetables to T-shirts and arts and crafts.

The **Plaza de Cultura**, on the Avenida César Nicolás Penson, is the site of a number of museums. The **Museum of the Dominican Man** has excellent exhibits from Taino life and more recent Dominican lives like those of the cane-cutters and modern carnival players. The **Museo Nacional de Historia y Geographica** (*open daily except Mon, 10–5; adm*) has more Arawak Indian exhibits and also Trujillo memorabilia. You will also find the **Galería de Arte Moderno**, the **Teatro Nacional** (the National Theatre and home of the Symphony Orchestra) and the **Bibliothéca Nacional** (National Library).

The **Palacio Nacional** (✆ 686 4771; *adm free, by appointment only*), on Calle Dr Delgado just to the northwest of Parque Independencia, is an imposing mock-classical edifice of rose-coloured marble that might come from 17th-century Europe. In fact it was built in the 1940s and for a while it was the home of the Congress of the Dominican Republic. It is quite closely guarded, but is open to visitors by guided tour.

In the northwest of town you will find a quiet retreat from the mayhem of Santo Domingo, the kempt botanic violence of **Jardín Botánico Nacional** (*open 9–5; adm*), at the top end of Avenida Sir Winston Churchill. More than 200 species of palm are on display and there is also a Japanese garden and an orchid pavilion. Train and boat rides are available with screaming Dominicans. To the northeast of here is the **Parque Zoológico** (*open daily 10–6; adm*), where in the 10 acres of landscaped gardens above the river you will find dromedaries roaming, more miniature train rides and a vast aviary.

Across the River Ozama is the immense **Faro a Colón** (the Columbus lighthouse), a monumental construction in the shape of a cross that was dedicated in the discoverer's honour during the 500th anniversary celebrations in 1992. It contains a number of museums and libraries and a lighthouse with an 80-mile radius and a laser that can throw a cross up into the Santo Domingo sky. Columbus's remains made what is possibly his final journey when his ashes were brought to a chapel in the lighthouse.

The idea of a lighthouse was first mooted in the last century, but this particular design was submitted for a 1929 competition by a student of architecture from Manchester, J. Gleave. Construction was undertaken by Trujillo but was abandoned until it was taken up again by Balaguer in 1987. It is vast, and will give a fine view over Santo Domingo.

A little farther out along the coast is the **Parque de los Tres Ojos** (the three 'eyes', four in fact), limestone sinkholes with pools. In the caves there are some impressive stalactite and stalagmite formations. From here the Avenida de las Américas, lined with the flags of all the American nations, leads along the south coast to Boca Chica and the airport.

The road from Santo Domingo to Santiago and the north coast runs beneath the Cordillera Central, the Republic's largest mountain range and then into the fertile Cibao valley before rising again into the hills of the Cordillera Septentrional on the north coast. From the road you will see huge plantations of citrus pineapple and banana alongside cattle pastures and the plots of the subsistence farmers cut into the deep brown earth, with their small thatched *bohíos* right by the side of the road.

The town of **Bonao**, halfway to Santiago, has recently been transformed by the discovery of mineral deposits (nickel and bauxite) and the arrival of the mining industry, an overlay of modernity on the traditional town centre.

The road is good to **Constanza**, home to a small community of Japanese, brought here by Trujillo, a small and lazy town which stands among the pineforests at 2000ft. A short distance off the main road is **Jarabacoa**, a friendly town with a population of about 40,000.The temperature is cooler than on the coast and so these valleys have become the favoured retreat of the Dominican wealthy. At this height they cultivate different crops, including tomatoes, onion and garlic, apples, peaches and even strawberries, many of which are flown out to the USA and even Europe.

Two waterfalls (*saltos*) can be visited from here: **Jimenoa**, a 70ft cascade into a rockpool about 4 miles through the plantations and about 10 minutes' walk along an irrigation canal, and **Bayguate**, about 6 miles from the town. There is a popular picnic, dancing and general gathering place at the junction of the two rivers at the bottom of town. There is occasionally frost up here and so a swim in the water is pretty invigorating. Out of Constanza you can visit the **Aguas Blancas**, a run of two waterfalls a few miles south of the town.

Jarabacoa is also the dropping-off point for an ascent of **Pico Duarte**, at 10,416ft the island's highest peak, lost in the Bermúdez and Ramírez National Parks. The mountain has only recently been called after Duarte, the Independence hero. Before that it had a spell as Pico Trujillo after the dictator, but for most of its history it was known as Pico la Pelona (the bald mountain) because of the barren plains near the top. A bust of Duarte has been placed at the summit. The usual route passes Monabao and La Ciénaga, via Casa Tabalone, through the changing vegetation of palms and tangled rainforest to pines and ferns and diabolic dwarf growth. It is possible to hike, without the use of mountaineering gear, but you need to be reasonably fit. Take food for four days and warm clothing for the evenings (there are wooden cabins en route). Arrange a permit (*RD$75*) and a guide (*RD$125 a day*) and make sure to inform the National Park staff at La Ciénaga that you are going.

A number of wealthy towns draw their prosperity from the fertile Cibao Valley, the breadbasket of the Republic that sits between the two Cordilleras. The people are renowned for their pride and the area is referred to jokingly by Dominicans from elsewhere as the 'Republic of Cibao'. As you descend into the Cibao valley you come to **La Vega**. For a spectacular view, climb to the top of the Santo Cerro (just north of the town). Nearby are the ruins of Columbus's original settlement of Vega Real (Royal Valley), which was abandoned for the present site after an earthquake.

Santiago (population 500,000) is the Dominican Republic's second city and quite a change from the mayhem of the capital. The romantic sounding, 'St James of the thirty noblemen' is set on the banks of a river gorge, inland where it was less vulnerable to attack, and it has a stately and confident air. There are some grand town-houses from the last century, when Cibao agriculture was the engine of the Dominican economy. The city is generally bypassed by tourists, but a traveller may enjoy the pace of life here after the capital, before rejoining the fray on the north coast. You will not be pestered by hustlers in Santiago.

A striking and rather ugly 200ft obelisk stands above the town, commemorating the heroes of the Restoration of 1844, when the Dominican Republic forced out the Haitian occupation (it was originally built by Trujillo in honour of himself). There is a fantastic view from the top. The **Museo del Tabaco**, on Calle 30 de Marzo, tells the tale of tobacco, historically, as used by the Taino Indians (who thought the plant magical), pirates, slaves and smugglers, and from cultivation to cigars. In the town centre the **Museo de Arte Folklórico**, set in an elegant old town-house, exhibits local arts and crafts as well as the '*lechones*', the mischievous imps of the Santiago carnival. Ruins fans will enjoy the old colonial ruins at Jacagua in the north of the city.

As you head northwest along the Cibao from Santiago towards the Haitian border, the land becomes steadily drier. The town of Monte Cristi is known as '*Estamos muriendo de sed*' (we die of thirst), because it is so windswept and desert-like.

The North Shore to the Amber Coast

The 150 miles of coastline from Monte Cristi to the Samaná peninsula contain the bulk of the island's tourist industry. You will come across vast factory hotels in complexes, but in other places you will find palms and beaches as far as the eye can see, offset with the glorious blue of the reef-protected sea. There has been considerable building all along the coast and this is set to continue. Northeast of Monte Cristi (the northwesterly point of the country), beyond the cacti and the salt pans, is the **Parque Nacional El Morro**, on a point (*el morro*) that sticks into the sea like a pimple, where you will find an undeveloped reserve that has extensive birdlife, including oystercatchers, ruddy turnstones, plovers and seabirds like noddies and terns. Cayo Cabrito just offshore takes its name from the goats that were left there to graze (there are many places around the Caribbean called *cabrit*, which means goat).

The coastline is remote from the road for several miles as you head east (you can get to the stunning beach at Punta Rucia), but you can turn north to **Luperón**, a fishing village, where the country starts to get a bit greener. Close by are the remains (archaeological only now) of Columbus's first settlement, La Isabella. Just before Puerto Plata is **Cofresi**, named after a buccaneer (he got about a bit, there is another town named after him on the west coast of Puerto Rico; *see* 'Beaches', p.579.)

Puerto Plata

The 'Silver Port', founded at the beginning of the 16th century, lies on the Atlantic coast in the shadow of the Cordillera Septentrional. At the western end of the Malecón (so long that it never becomes busy, though people do collect at the eastern end), you will find the **Fortaleza de San Felipe** (*open daily except Thurs 9–noon and 3–5; adm*), a lumbering brute that was built in 1577 to defend the town from pirates. They managed to take the place over eventually and so Spain sacked it in 1605. Puerto Plata now has a faded charm in its many elaborate wooden gingerbread houses and Spanish plazas. Tourists are well known here, but they have not swamped the local life. Playa Dorada, a few miles through the canefields to the east of Puerto Plata, is the main tourist area. It is a gaggle of modern hotels all collected together in a little complex.

The **Amber Museum**, 61 Calle Duarte (✆ 586 2848; *open Mon–Sat, 9–5; adm*), has a series of exhibits about the origins and mining of amber, with pieces containing prehistoric creepy-crawlies on show, in an elegant old town-house. There is a sales room with amber jewellery on sale.. At the **Brugal Rum Distillery**, on the Avenida Colón (*open Mon–Fri 9–noon and 2–5*), a tour will take you through the Republic's second industry (for years the backbone of the economy), from cane-cutting to rum punch, with samples to taste if you have not already had enough from the fumes. One of the stranger sights in the Caribbean is a cable-car (*teleférico*) that runs from behind the town to the summit of **Mt Isabel de Torres** (2600ft), from where the view is magnificent, when it is not in cloud. There are botanical gardens and a restaurant at the top. *Working daily except Wed (summer season restricted), 8–5.*

East to Samaná

The town of Sosúa splits into two halves: **El Batey**, the tourist area in the east with restaurants shoulder to shoulder and buzzing nightlife, where you might notice a residual European influence from an influx of German Jews who settled here to escape persecution in the 1930s; and the more Dominican part, **Los Charamícos**, across the glorious half-mile bay in the west.

Soon after Sosúa you come to **Cabarete**, a resort town strung along the coastal road just by a huge bay. It is renowned for windsurfing, and so it attracts a fun, active crowd who spend the day on the waves and the evenings in the beach bars and restaurants. Hotels are springing up here as the crowds discover it. At Cabarete the endless beaches begin, all of them undeveloped. The coastal road leads through the local towns of Río San Juan and Cabrera down to the town of Nagua, towards the Samaná peninsula. This is an extremely poor area of the country, as you can see by the houses, which are made of wattle and daub (mud and wood) and with the stems of palm fronds.

The Samaná Peninsula

North and slightly east of Santo Domingo, the Samaná Peninsula is one of the most beautiful parts of the island. Its mountainsides are cut by swathes of light green coconut palm and deep green pine trees, and the small clapboard *bohíos* of the Dominicans are painted in pastel washes of pink or purple. In Samaná Bay you will see the fishermen standing in their flat-bottomed boats and casting their fishing nets. There are spectacular beaches on both sides of the peninsula, though not in the town itself, some of which can only be reached by boat.

Columbus appeared in the bay in 1493, but was met by such a volley of arrows from the local inhabitants (probably Caribs from down-island on a raid against the Tainos) that he named it 'Golfo de las Flechas'. The original town of Samaná was populated by escaped American slaves who came to the free island of Haiti in the early 19th century. There are Protestant churches in the area (in a strongly Catholic country) and it is just possible still to hear the locals speaking old American English.

Today Samaná is an ugly concrete infestation along a four-lane seafront boulevard (the old wooden houses were destroyed in the name of tourism development) that was destined to be big but never took off. The odd-looking aqueduct in the bay was supposed to lead to a hotel on the offshore island, but that too was never built. However, if there is no charm in the town, the people make it extremely lively and great fun. The Báhia de Samaná is the winter home of up to three thousand humpback whales, who come here to mate and to give birth at the Silver Bank in January and February. Trips taking several hours can be arranged in town, for a minimum number of people (*expensive*). You will see babies piggy-backing and the adults making whale-style whoopee, splashing their tails or jumping clean out of the water. There have been problems recently with the noise of the engines interrupting the whales' highly sensitive hearing (letting sharks come in and steal the young) and so some boats will not go too close.

In the hills above Samaná (on the road to Las Terrenas), you can visit the **Río Limón Waterfall**, which falls 160ft in a number of chutes. **Las Terrenas** itself lies on the north coast of the peninsula and is a very low-key resort town with an easy air and some small and hip places to stay, on what are some of the country's best beaches. Barely any package tourists make it over there, so it is the best resort on the island for the independent traveller. There is not much to do, but there are watersports and it is a great place for hanging out.

To the south and west of Sanchez is **Los Haitises National Park**, an area of karst limestone and coastal mangrove swamps. It includes also a number of small offshore cays inhabited by hawks, pelicans, noddies and roseate terns. Deeper in the swamps you will see the ungainly jacana, with overlong toes that help it walk over water-lilies, and herons and ibises. You can arrange a trip from Samaná.

East of Santo Domingo

Headed east from Santo Domingo on the Avenida de las Américas, you first come to **Boca Chica**, just past the airport, a good beach that becomes very crowded and noisy at the weekends as the Dominicans escape in droves from the capital. At **La Caleta** you can see an Arawak burial site. Passing by San Pedro de Macoris you come to **La Romana**, still a sugar town and cattle grazing area, but now famed for the vast (and very expensive) resort a few miles to its east, Casa de Campo, where there is a whole host of hotels, villas, golf courses and polo pitches. In this area you will still meet English-speaking West Indians whose parents came from down-island to work in the sugar industry earlier this century.

Set high on a river-bend, **Altos de Chavón** is a Spanish medieval clifftop town built of rusty coral rock, everywhere festooned with bougainvillea and sprays of hibiscus, and inhabited by a colony of artists. Its heart is the **Iglesia St Stanislaus**, and all around are aged cobbled alleys and streets. There is even an amphitheatre, where Frank Sinatra and Julio Iglesias have sung in recent years. And yet, there is something slightly wrong about Altos de Chavón. Somehow there is an unruly Gothic air to the medieval idyll—it is slightly overdone, very neat and really rather twee. It comes as no surprise to find that it was all designed in 1978 and that Frank Sinatra actually inaugurated the amphitheatre. There is a free bus service from Casa de Campo, and it's worth a look if only for the novelty, some good restaurants and the fantastic view over the Chavón river valley.

About 20 miles (32km) northeast of La Romana, lost in the cattle and sugar-cane flats of the southeast, is the genuine 16th-century town of **Higüey**. A charming church lies at its centre, the **Basílica de Nuestra Señora de la Merced**, supposedly erected on the site of a battle in which the early Spaniards fended off the Caribs. It had long been a place of pilgrimage and then in the 1950s the massive new church was built. The monumental **Basílica de Nuestra Señora de Altagracia** (the patron saint of the Dominican Republic) is built of concrete and shaped like a 200ft pair of hands held in prayer. The town has certainly seen tourists—they pass through in busloads—but it has an easy, parochial air. Pilgrims arrive on 21 January and 16 August.

Beyond Higüey the countryside becomes wilder and you will see the *campesinos* riding around on their horses and palm-thatch *bohíos*. Many of the roads turn to dirt tracks. Heading south, on a metalled road, you will come to the small town of **San Rafael de Yuma**, where you will find the restored house of Ponce de León, who lived here for three years before he went to settle Puerto Rico in 1508 and then travelled on to Florida. The road reaches the coast at **Boca de Yuma**, a quiet fishing village.

On the western road, past several caves, is the **National Park of the East**, which contains much of the V-shaped point of land and the island of Saona off the southern shore. The western entrance to the park is at Bayahibe, not far from La Romana. Paths do cross the park, but you will need to find a guide. On the south coast is Catalinta Bay, a phosphorescent bay where the water glows in green luminescent whorls as you drag your fingers through it. In the park you may see lizard cuckoos and orioles and on the coast oystercatchers and other seabirds like pelicans and magnificent frigatebirds.

If you head northeast of Higüey you reach the coast at **Bavaro**, where the beaches begin, continuing almost uninterrupted for the 30 miles (50km) from here to Laguna Nisibón. They are spectacular and developed only with the occasional huge hotel complex. They are bordered along their whole length by palms and seagrape and are excellent for walking, though you should be careful of swimming because of the Atlantic currents. Beyond Miches you enter wild farming country and eventually come to the sleepy town of Sabana de la Mar, from where you can get a ferry across to the Samaná peninsula.

West of Santo Domingo

The southwestern corner of the Dominican Republic is the remotest area and in places it is barren and desert-like, though this means that the sun is more reliable than on the north coast, of course. Not much organized tourism happens in the region (though there are recent developments in Barahona) and so you get a good view of local Dominican life. As you get closer to the frontier with Haiti you can expect army activity to increase: you will be stopped and may be subject to searches.

Taking the Carreta Sanchez out of Santo Domingo you come to **San Cristóbal**, most infamous for being the birthplace of Trujillo. During his life he built it up with a grandeur that befitted his status as dictator—see the plaza and the ornate church and his mausoleum (although he is not buried there; his remains were taken to France). **Casa las Coabas**, his family home, overlooks the town from a hill. It is now in disrepair, but it is due for restoration. Also being restored is the **Castillo del Cerro**, another of Trujillo's palaces, a monstrous over-elaborate affair on a nearby summit. It too is being restored and you can visit for a small fee. Also worth a visit are caves at El Pomier.

Passing through endless canefields you come to the prosperous town of Baní, birthplace of Máximo Gómez, a hero of the Cuban Independence movement, and eventually to Barahona, an industrial but nonetheless sleepy town. The countryside in this area turns to barren hills covered with organ-pipe cactus trained into fences and prickly pear. From here, one road runs south into the V-shaped Barahona peninsula, passing through poor fishing villages like Enriquillo and Oviedo, with excellent beaches, before heading north to the town of Pedernales on the Haitian border. It was from the Baoruco mountains that Enriquillo led his guerrilla campaign against the Spaniards in the 1520s.

The **Jaragua National Park** lies in the southwestern tip of the island, 500 square miles of cactus plains, sea and discoloured limestone shoreline. You will see pelicans and terns on the coastline. The park is remote. Go by jeep and take plenty to eat and particularly to drink if you are going off the beaten track. **Beata Island** off the southern tip of the island has excellent birdlife too.

From Barahona a road inland leads towards Jimaní on the Haitian border. The town is close to the **Lago Enriquillo**, a saltwater lake that lies 140ft below sea level. **Isla Cabritos** (Goat Island, after the livestock left to forage there) is a national park in the centre of the lake. The 5-mile-long island is dry and scrubby but supports a wide variety of wildlife, including alligators and iguanas. Among the birds that live on the island are flamingos, clapper rails and roseate spoonbills. You can usually get permission to go to the lake at the park office in **La Descubierta**, a hot and desolate town (you should also request permission in the National Parks Office in Santo Domingo before you set off). If you make the trip, make sure to stock up on food and drink, which is not that easily found in the remote areas beyond Barahona. About half a mile before La Descubierta there are Arawak petroglyphs carved on a cliffside. In the town is a *balneario*, a freshwater swimming pool.

✆ *(1 809)–*   ***Where to Stay***

The Dominican Republic has a full range of hotels—large, self-contained resorts of international standard luxury set on glorious sand, through to the smaller, more personal beach clubs; and in the mountains, small, hillside retreats. If you are travelling the island you will probably spend some time in the capital, Santo Domingo, where you will find restored colonial palaces as well as good guest houses. The Dominican Republic offers well-priced package tours at the moment and with a bit of shopping around, independent travellers will find some very good prices in the off-beat tourist resorts. In the larger tourist hotels you can pay with credit cards and traveller's cheques, but in more local hotels you will have to pay in pesos. A government tax of 8% is added to all bills and service is usually charged at 10% or 15%.

Santo Domingo

expensive

The hotels in Santo Domingo are not near to the beaches, but if you want high Caribbean comfort in glitzy pink right in the city, try the Ramada Renaissance **Jaragua** Resort on the Malecón, 367 Avenida George Washington (✆ 221 2222, ✆ 686 0528, US ✆ (1 800) 223 9815). Multiple restaurants (one low-cal), casino, club, tennis courts and 300 rooms in high pastel decor with cable television. A slightly more Dominican version of this international standard fare can be found at the **Santo**

Domingo Hotel, farther along the Malecón (✆ 221 1511, 🖶 535 4050, US ✆ (1 800) 223 6620). The hotel was decorated by the Dominican designer Oscar de la Renta and there are echoes of another era in the arches, dark-stained louvres and palms in the courtyard. It is very much a modern hotel though, with the 215 rooms all in one block and with a special floor devoted to business travellers. It is low-key; they serve afternoon tea and there is no discotheque or casino. Two restaurants and a swimming pool.

moderate

Across the road you will find its sister hotel, the **Hispaniola**, PO Box 2112 (✆ 221 7111, 🖶 535 4050), which is slightly more upbeat. The Hispaniola is also a modern town hotel with 165 rooms in a block, but it has a nice feel. Bar, casino and CNN to keep you in touch.

moderate–cheap

If you would prefer the old-style surroundings of the **colonial city**, where you can stay in a restored *palacio*, there are a couple of comfortable options. The best known is the **Hostal Nicolás de Ovando** (✆ 687 3101, 🖶 688 5170; *temporarily closed*) on the Calle de las Damas in the oldest part of town. It is set in the house of a 16th-century governor—from the days when Santo Domingo was a gracious viceregal capital. The rooms are set around three charming tiled courtyards, each surrounded by colonnades. Within, the hallways are inlaid with dark mahogany beams and hung with tapestries and paintings on exhibit. There are 45 rooms, some dressed up in colonial grandeur (rooms at the rear above the new Avenida del Puerto are quite noisy). A smaller and quieter, but equally gracious palace is the **Hostal Nicolás Nader** (not to be confused) on the Calle Luperón (✆ 687 6674). Another charming retreat from the bustle of the town, set around an interior courtyard, with arches and mahogany beams. Just 10 rooms, furnished in dark colonial style but with air-conditioning. No restaurant, but a lively bar, and a parrot. **Hotel David's**, 308 Calle Arzobispo Nouel (✆ 685 9121, 🖶 688 8065), is not set in such an old house, but has the grace of an old town house in the colonial city nonetheless. There are just nine rooms with air-conditioning and cable television, and hot and cold water. The central sitting area (also on a streetfront balcony) has a tile floor and comfortable furniture and a grand-father clock. Restaurant. Just outside the colonial zone, **La Casona Dorada**, just off Avenida Independencia (✆ 221 3535, 🖶 221 3622), is set in a restored colonial villa from the last century, now redecorated to plush modern comfort. There are 10 air-conditioned rooms with modern wooden furniture, and a palm-courtyard with a pool at the front.

very cheap

There are plenty of **guest houses** around the town, many of which offer a single rate. At 62 Calle Danae you will find **Hotel La Residence** (✆ 682 4178) with clean and comfortable rooms; no restaurant, but there is one next door. Close by, at 26 Calle Danae is **La Gran Mansion Guest House** (✆ 682 2033), eleven simple rooms with private baths, cafeteria. There are yet cheaper places to overnight around the Parque Independencia. Try the hotel training school, the **Hotel Bolívar** at 62 Avenida Bolívar (✆ 685 2200), with all mod cons—cable television, air-conditioning and excellent service; or two highly recommended spots in the centre of town, the **Hotel Aida** on Calle Espaillat (✆ 685 7692) and the **Independencia** on Calle Arzobispo Nouel, equina Estrelleta (✆ 686 1663).

The Central Mountains

There are not many places to stay in the central mountains, but in Constanza you will find the **Hotel Nueva Suizza** (✆ 539 2233; *cheap*). There are 60 simple rooms with superb views. Also **Mi Cabaña** (✆ 539 2472; *very cheap*). In Jarabacoa you can stay at the small and friendly **River Resort** (✆ 574 2918; *very cheap*), concrete but comfortable cabins with kitchens and a pool set among the pines on the edge of town. No restaurant, but you can order food. In the middle of town, the **Hotel Pinal Dorado** (✆ 574 2820; *very cheap*) has a charming courtyard restaurant filled with flowers, opposite a modern block with rooms. People speak highly of the **Bella Vista Hotel** (*cheap*), a collection of wooden cabins high on the hillside out of town.

Santiago

The smartest hotel in Santiago is **El Gran Almirante**, slightly out of town on the Avenida Estrella Sadhalá (✆ 580 1992, ✉ 241 1492; *moderate–cheap*). It is modern and comfortable, air-conditioned with a good restaurant and a café, pool, cable television, massage parlour and executive floor. Good service, but a bit characterless. **Camino Real** is right in the centre of the town on one of the main shopping streets at 34 Calle del Sol (✆ 581 7000, ✉ 582 4566; *cheap*). Also modern in style, but there is a fine view of the town from the top-floor dining room. There are 71 rooms. The **Hotel Mercedes**, 18 Calle 30 de Marzo (✆ 583 1171, ✉ 583 8464; *very cheap*), has a bit more style. It is set in an old town house with a large tiled foyer with pillars and wicker furniture. Rooms are pretty simple (though with air-conditioning and phones), some with stained-glass windows and balconies. If you want somewhere even cheaper to stay there is a clutch of small and very simple hotels around the Plaza Valero.

The North Coast

West of Puerto Plata there are few hotels. However, at **Punta Rucia** you will find the small and friendly **Orquideria del Sol** (✆ 583 2825; *moderate–cheap*), which overlooks the beach through a garden of orchids, as the name suggests.

In the town of **Puerto Plata** the most sympathetic place to stay is the small **Hostal Jimessón**, at 41 John F. Kennedy (✆ 586 5131, ✉ 586 6312; *cheap*), where you enter from the street into a 19th-century foyer—wood-panelled and tiled, with rocking chairs, antique mirrors and a collection of clocks and gramophones. Beyond here the 22 rooms are modern, but well kept and comfortable. The **Latin Quarter** hotel on the Malecón, esquina Carolina (✆ 586 2588, ✉ 586 8646; *cheap*) has standard rooms and restaurant and bar. There are plenty of *very cheap* places to lay your head; try the **Hotel Atlántico** at 24 Calle 12 de Julio with simple and clean fan-ventilated rooms or a family house at the **Hotel Alfa** at 20 Calle Padre Castellanos (✆ 586 2684). Fan ventilation, private bath if you want, simple and friendly. You can also stay very cheaply at **Long Beach** at the end of the Malecón, which is quite active.

Playa Dorada itself is set on a fantastic beach. If you are happy in a large complex, the resort has excellent facilities—all the watersports, sports on land, restaurants, clubs and casinos. The **Caribbean Village** (✆ 320 1111, ✉ 320 7135; *expensive*) is very comfortable. There are over 300 rooms and suites in villas; all air-conditioned with cable television and large balconies. Tennis on the resort and golf right next door; the beach is a short walk away. All inclusive rate. The **Victoria Resort**, PO Box 22 (✆ 412 2525, ✉ 412 2526; *moderate–cheap*), also has a certain style. The main house stands above the lake and swimming pool, finished with Spanish colonial trimmings and classical motifs. In spirit the hotel is more 20th century, with high pastel decoration in the rooms and wicker furniture. All the sports; dining on the breezy terrace to the sound of a band. If you would like to stay on the beach itself you can try the **Playa Naco** Golf and Tennis Resort (✆ 320 6226, ✉ 320 6225; *moderate*), where there is a variety of one- and two-bedroom apartments, or the suites at the **Dorado Naco** resort (✆ 320 2019, ✉ 320 3608; *moderate*). Both are large timeshare hotels, but you can use the facilities of either; five restaurants, nine bars, all modern Caribbean comforts, including a good stretch of beach with all the watersports.

A few miles along the coast you come to **Sosúa**, which has one or two resort hotels, but preferable are the small and friendly retreats that are dotted around the town (in El Batey). The best place to stay is the **Tropix Hotel** (✆ 571 2291; *cheap*), which you will find a couple of minutes' walk across the main road. There are just 10 rooms, in blocks overlooking the pool behind the main house, set in a cool garden. There is a communal kitchen, with a daily menu on offer if you do not want to cook and outside is the *barita*, an honour bar in a breezy clapboard house under the fishtail palms. Laid back and well away from the hustle of the town, a charming place to stay. There are other cool and easy places around town. Try **JJ's Auberge** in the heart of town at 8 Calle Dr Rosen (✆ 571 2569, ✉ 571 2865; *very cheap*)—'tranquil accomodations in midst of Sosúa hub-bub'. Just six simple rooms around a charming courtyard with pool, palms and a rubber tree. Air-conditioning and fans, no restaurant, but breakfast available. Slightly busier, but a fine cliff-top retreat nonetheless is **Charlie's Cabañas** (✆ 571 2670, ✉ 571 3586; *cheap*). There are 28 rooms in cabañas, concrete and quite simple, but with balconies or verandas. Also a good restaurant and bar on the rocky waterfront, a walk to the beach. Alternatively try **Pension Anneliese**, Calle Dr Rosen (✆/✉ 571 2208; *very cheap*), 10 comfortable rooms in one large house, with a bar and pool in the garden. Finally you will get a good deal at **Sosúa Ocean Front Guest House** (✆ 571 2284; *very cheap*), private apartments with kitchenettes.

Cabarete has a number of laid-back hotels in the easy-going spirit of the town. At the top end of the range, the nicest is **Casa Laguna** (✆ 571 0725, ✉ 571 0704; *moderate*), just across the road from the beach. The 48 airy studios stand in blocks around the tropical garden and pool and they are spacious and breezy, with louvred windows and their own balconies. You will find very comfortable villas at the **Nanny Estate** (✆ 571 0744, ✉ 571 0655; *moderate–cheap*), a couple of miles outside the town. The apartments are ranged shoulder to shoulder, looking diagonally through the palm garden to the sea. Each one has two huge bedrooms and a roof terrace where you can trap the sun for bronzing. Pool, watersports and a good restaurant. Right on the main beach in town is the **Cabarete Beach Resort** (✆ 571 0755, ✉ 571 0831; *moderate–cheap*), where there are 28 rooms with private bathrooms and fans or air-conditioning, beachfront deck restaurant, half-pension plan only. There is an excellent place to stay on the quiet outskirts of town to the east, the **Ocean Breeze** (✆ 571

0656, ☏ 571 0657, USA ✆ (1 800) 524 7610; *cheap*). Just eight comfortable and modern rooms, with a couple of apartments, each with a balcony above a garden and pool. Very calm, bed and breakfast package. You can stay very cheaply at **Casa María** in a holiday villa on the streetside. Five very simple fan-ventilated rooms, breakfast available.

The Samaná Peninsula

The best beaches of the peninsula are on the Atlantic coast and so the place to head for is **Las Terrenas** (best approached from Sanchéz), where there are some cool and low-key haunts in which to pass your time. The best fun is the **Hotel Tropic Banana** (✆ 240 6110, ☏ 240 6112; *cheap*), which has held hip sway over the town for about 20 years. There are about 30 rooms scattered in small blocks around a palm garden and pool, but the heart of the hotel is the main house, where the hip chicks and pig-tailed windsurfers loiter listening to a local band in the afternoon and evening. Comfortable rooms furnished in rattan, with a veranda for taking it easy after action on the beach or in the bar. Bed and breakfast. Just a little way out of town there is another charming place to stay at **Isla Bonita** (*temporarily closed*) (in Santo Domingo, ✆ 562 6209, ☏ 562 4648, or Las Terrenas ☏ 240 6070; *cheap*), two villas side by side in a sandy garden that overlooks a superb beach. Very low-key, fan-ventilated with muslin nets on the veranda, hot and cold water, watersports nearby and an Italian restaurant. Just nine rooms. You might also try **Las Cayenas Hotel** (✆ 240 6080, ☏ 240 6070; *cheap*), set in an old plantation-style house nearby. Some stylish rooms upstairs, a nice restaurant on a deck and a friendly, quiet air. Not far away is the **Hacienda** (✆ 240 6066, ☏ 240 6070; *cheap*), just four rooms in a private house in the lovely setting of a covered terrace and a tropical garden. Very friendly. You can stay cheaply in the town at **Finchen** (*very cheap*), or the simple, functional **Hotel Dinny** (✆ 240 6113; *very cheap*). There are a couple of places to stay on the superb beach of the Playa Bonita area just out of town: the **Hotel Acaya** (✆ 240 6161, ☏ 240 6166; *cheap*), with an attractive palm-thatch bar in a tropical garden, 16 rooms, some watersports; and the **Atlantis Colonial Palace** (✆ 240 6111, ☏ 240 6101; *cheap*), with rooms in a curious house with gothic columns, arches and balustrades. Quiet but pleasant.

On the south side of the Samaná peninsula you will find an unfeasibly smart and elegant retreat in the **Hotel Gran Bahía**, PO Box 2024, Santo Domingo (✆ 538 3111, ☏ 538 2764, US res ✆ (1 800) 221 4542; *expensive–moderate*), a few miles east of the town itself, opposite Cayo Levantado. The hotel is an extraordinary compendium of turrets, triangular eaves, awnings and balconies, all trimmed with very pretty white gingerbread and balustrades. In the great house is a foyer with a fountain and tiled floor, upstairs the rooms are extremely attractive. Small beach, but trips to Cayo Levantado are available. A gracious air of the old-time Caribbean. At the northeastern tip of the peninsula you will find the small and comfortable **Moorea Beach Hotel** (✆ 538 4105, ☏ 538 2545; *moderate*), which overlooks the sand at Las Galeras. Also try comfortable **Hotel Nilca**, next to Codetel. There are not many hotels in the town of Samaná itself, but you can find a comfortable room at the **Tropical Lodge Hotel** (✆ 538 2480; *cheap*) just outside the town, good restaurant. There are simpler rooms at **Cotubanama** (✆ 538 2557; *very cheap*), just up from the Malecón. Clean and comfortable, if simple, private baths and a good French restaurant.

East of Santo Domingo

The beaches begin to appear, and the hotels with them, beyond the airport. **Boca Chica** is active day and night, and it is very popular with the Dominicans themselves. **The Hamaca Beach Resort**, PO Box 2973, Santo Domingo (✆ 523 4611, ✉ 523 6767), is a comfortable hotel set on a good strip of sand. Rooms in blocks, but all the requisites for a 20th-century break. Alternatively try the **Don Juan Beach Resort** (✆ 687 9157, ✉ 688 5271; *moderate*). As the name suggests, life centres around the beach and night-time activity. The 124 rooms are in a block above the pool within spitting distance of the sand, where there is every watersport imaginable, and entertainment. Quite a few package tourists but a lively hotel. There are plenty of **guest houses**, many of them a bit sultry, along the strip, but you will find 10 clean and comfortable rooms at the friendly **Don Paco Guest House** (✆ 523 4816; *very cheap*) at 6 Calle Duarte. You can also find rooms at **El Cheverón** (✆ 523 4333; *very cheap*), simple. Or if you would prefer to rent an apartment, contact **Caribe Sol** on Calle Rafael (✆ 523 4010, ✉ 523 4140).

Heading east, just beyond La Romana you will find **Casa de Campo** (✆ 523 3333, ✉ 523 8548; *luxury*), the Dominican Republic's leading resort. It is set on a huge estate with 900 rooms and villas, in landscaped grounds with golf courses (there are three), tennis courts (14), and set on cliffs overlooking the sea. The rooms are luxurious, designed by Dominican designer Oscar de la Renta. Buses shuttle the length and breadth of the complex, racing you from villa suburb to the beach and from the massage clinic to the hilltop restaurants at Altos de Chavón. There are also rooms at the **Posada Inn** in Altos de Chavón (same contacts as Casa de Campo; *moderate*), a small hotel (just 10 rooms) where there is a pool and rooms with a superb view of the river valley below. High luxury and a faintly Gothic twist on medieval Spain.

A few miles along the southern coastline at Bayahibe you will find the **Club Dominicus** (✆ 562 6000, ✉ 221 6806; *moderate–cheap*), which is isolated from the rest of the island in both space—on its own beach away from the crowds—and time—it has an air of the pre-Columbian Caribbean in the mock-rustic *bohío* thatch cabañas, each with a hammock. A large resort, but a good retreat.

The far northeastern coastline is dotted with an occasional but usually huge hotel complex. The best is probably the **Bavaro Beach Resort**, PO Box 1 Higüey (✆ 686 5773, ✉ 682 5771; *expensive–moderate*), really four hotels rolled into one, set on a magnificent mile-long sweep of impeccable sand backed along its entire length by palm trees. All the watersports; pools, golf and plenty of evening entertainment. You will have a good, active beach holiday here even if you do not see much of Dominican life.

Other hotels include: **Hoteles Riu Palace**, Naiboa, Taino (✆ 221 2290, ✉ 685 9537); **Bavaro Fiesta Palace** (✆ 562 8222, ✉ 562 8998); **Melia Bavaro** (✆ 552 0840, ✉ 552 0604).

West of Santo Domingo

There are few hotels to the west of Santo Domingo, but a few miles beyond the town of Barahona try the **Barahona Beach Club**, where there is a complex of suites and apartments with watersports, riding and tennis. The **Hotel Guayocura** is in the town itself, a small and simple hotel. There are guest houses in all towns.

Eating Out

Like dancing, eating is a favourite pastime in the Dominican Republic and the islanders savour it as they dine out with their families in the evenings. The food is heavy by most standards and many of the meals are centred around a meat stew with a salad. Starters are *sopa* (soup), or *chicharrones*, crispy pork rind or chicken pieces that are served with a spicy dip. *Sancocho* is a thick stew made with seven or more different meats and vegetables including yucca, plantain and potato, steeped in herbs, and other favourites include *mondongo*, a stew made with tripe, *mofongo*, plantain mashed with spices and garlic, and *mangú*, boiled plantain flattened with meat or egg. *Locrio* is similar to paella, rice and meat or possibly seafood, which is good in the Dominican Republic. Finally, for a filling local meal, try *arroz con pollo* (chicken and rice) with fried plantains at the side. The Republic grows its own coffee in the northern mountains, which is really quite good. During the day it is drunk as espresso, in tiny plastic cups. *Arepa* is a sweet cake served with the main course.

The Dominicans make the best of their fruits, which grow in profusion in the island and end up in ice creams and in drinks served in the small bars open on to the street. *Jugos* are drinks made from fresh fruit, water, sugar and crushed ice—extremely refreshing. *Bastidas* are a milkshake version of the drink, the best of their kind in the Caribbean. *China* or *naranja* (orange) is exceptionally good; other fruits include *chinola* (passion fruit), *lechosa* (papaya), and *zapote* (melon).

The Dominicans brew a number of beers; Presidente is an excellent light-coloured lager beer and Quisqueya is a slightly darker brew. Rums are white, the traditional tipple and mixing drink, *dorado* (gold) and *añejo*, aged in the barrel, which is drunk as a liqueur.

Restaurants

There are literally thousands of restaurants, cafés, local bars and ice-cream halls in the Dominican Republic. Part of the pleasure is simply to wander until you find one you like the look of. As you walk, you get the idea that entertainment is probably the country's biggest industry. Santo Domingo has an extraordinary variety of restaurants in both style—gourmet, seafood, Italian, Argentinian—and setting—in the old colonial palaces of the Alcázar, modern villas and in open-fronted cafés along the Malecón. In restaurants outside the hotels, if you do not pay by credit card, you must pay in Dominican pesos. Categories are arranged according to the price of a main dish: *expensive*—RD$100 and above; *moderate*—between RD$100 and $150; *cheap*—RD$100 and below.

Santo Domingo

expensive

In the capital, the top gourmet restaurant is **Cantabrico** (© 687 5101), set in a formal, air-conditioned dining room with paintings and stained wood skirtings on Calle Independencia. The cuisine is international with a long seafood menu; try a crayfish brochette or sea bass *à l'orange*. Ever popular and filled with a lively crowd, Vesuvio (© 221 3333) sits right on the Malecón. Glass-fronted and modern, the dining room is decorated with colourful friezes of tropical fruits and fish. You start with a cocktail about the size of a swimming pool and set about the huge menu of Italian and international food—stuffed queen conch cannelloni with pink bechamel sauce or *veal scalopina au poivre vert*. Not far off is the renowned **Don Pepe** (✆ 689 7612), also set in a converted suburban villa, on Calle Santiago at the corner with Calle Pasteur. It is a bit stuffy and formal, presided over by major-domos in tuxedos, but it serves good Spanish fare—suckling pig and variations on the vast crabs that are on view as you come in through the door. There is also a good wine cellar.

moderate

At the opposite end of the scale, full of the joys of life and with a riotously informal air, is **El Conuco** (✆ 686 0129) at Calle Casimro de Moya 152. 'Conuco' means 'country' and the theme is current throughout the restaurant, as is obvious immediately you walk under the rustic thatch roof and palm supports. Huge pestles and mortars, pitchforks, loofahs, lechones and fishtraps adorn the walls, between the *cibaeño campesino* (farmer's sayings) on wooden plaques. And the menu is farmers' food, dressed up a little for the capital—all the tripe dishes you can imagine and some a little less of an adventure, for example *chicharrones de pollo* (deep-fried chicken) or *filete de rez, con longos*. A fun place. When the waiters have had enough, they turn the music up, grab their instruments and dance for you. **El Mesón de Castilla** (✆ 688 4319) on Calle Dr Baez is a more subdued but easy-going restaurant with a dining room decorated with tiles and beams. The menu is Spanish and international— try the *paella gran mesón* in cream or brandy.

In the colonial city there are plenty of stopping points for when you tire of the sight-seeing. Just off the Cathedral Square, at the very foot of El Conde you come to a paved alleyway set with tables and chairs that have spilled out of restaurants. La Cocina has a pretty setting in a mock-colonial brick and wood house with arches and ragged plaster walls. *Comida criolla gourmet—filete de res a la mostacta con alcachofas rellenas* (beef steak with mustard and stuffed artichokes), or pork filet with tamarind sauce. Next door is **Che Bandoneon**, which also makes the best of an old restored town-house with a pretty interior courtyard. The menu is French and Argentinian, with steaks galore including *filete a la parrilla a las tres pimentas*, pastas and *crêpes de la passion*, with a *bandoneon* (accordion) and guitar accompaniment. A pleasant place to sit and eat for an evening. Not far off is the **Mesón Bari**, a lively joint at the corner of Calle Salome Ureña. It is the favourite gathering point of Santo Domingo's writers and artists on a Friday night, so the diet is as much philosophy, gossip and beer as it is creole food; *lambi guisado* and *bistek empanado*. There are limitless restaurants along the Malecón. If you would like a simple meal with a spectator sport thrown in, then try the **Barra Uno**, where you can watch the waiters taking food to the tables on the other side of the road, dodging the traffic. A few dishes have gone end-up, but they haven't lost a waiter in nearly thirty years. A seafood restaurant in a garden setting, very popular with the Dominicans, is **Captain Crusty** on Avenida Tiradentes, quite far to the northwest of the city. A good lunchtime stop, in the shade of a flamboyant tree. Fish and seafood menu—shrimp *ceviche* or *crêpe* or a St Peter fillet of fish (breaded). Also, *para los alergicos*—chicken. If you want to wander, take in a drink or two and then decide where to eat, you can try all the restaurants in a line at the

Atarazana, opposite the Alcázar de Colón—perhaps the **Mesón de Jamón**, or is it Muséo de Jamón, with so many haunches hanging from the ceiling.

cheap

And back in the very centre of the town, just south of the Parque Independencia, is another favourite local restaurant, where you linger over your meal and the staff stand around chatting to one another most of the time: the **Independencia** has some of the best in local food, *asopao, salcocho* and *ensaladas*.

There are three good **vegetarian** restaurants in Santo Domingo. On Calle Luperón you will find the **Bethel**, the most health-conscious of the three. **Ananda's** on Calle Casimiro de Moya and **Ojas** on Calle Gazcue both serve a huge variety of tropical vegetables and fruits in Dominican sauces.

very cheap

One of the best Dominican meals, a takeaway, can be found at **De Nosotros Empanadas**, just down Avenida Independencia at the corner with Dr Delgado. Superb patties—chicken, shrimp and even lobster in creamy sauces—and a soft drink to accompany them. You can also find very local meals at one of hundreds of **pensións** around the city. They are family kitchens that open up to all-comers. Your average plate of rice 'n' beans is also known as the *bandero nacional* (national flag) because it is an unofficial national dish. Finally, you might consider a snack on Vicini B (leading down to the obelisk on the Malecón), where you sit in a rocking chair as they cook your *chimichurri* (a spicy sausage burger).

Santo Domingo Bars

Just as there are hundreds of restaurants in Santo Domingo, the bars seem to go on forever. Once again, set off until you find one you like the look of. Popular with the locals for a daytime stop are **Kilometro Zero** (all official distances in the country are measured from the square) and the other bars on the Parque Independencia. Following El Conde down to the colonial city you will find lots of bars and *heladerías* (ice-cream bars). Look out for the **Café Colonial** and the **Polo Ground**, where the walls are covered in baseball memorabilia. There is an excellent (if a little touristy) clutch of café-style bars in the Atarazana, overlooking the Columbus palace: **Drake's Pub**, with its brick and plaster walls and huge wooden bar, is always a lively option and next door is the marginally quieter **Café Montesinos**. Both are set in the restored surroundings of the oldest part of town. Popular with the Dominican youth are the **Café Atlántico** at the corner of Avenida Mexico and Abraham Lincoln, and the **Exquesito**, on Avenida Tiradentes, a cheese and wine/Seven Up/beer bar that collects a lively crowd early on in the evening. If you feel like watching the Dominicans at it, dancing the merengue (and maybe having a go yourself), the popular **discotheques** include **Neon 2002** at the Hispaniola Hotel and on the Malecón **Vertigo** and **Bella Blu**, all glass, pillars and palms, which attract a slightly older crowd. On Calle Abraham Lincoln there is a popular club called **Guacara Taina**. Discotheques usually have a cover charge of RD$75–150. If you simply want to hang out with the Dominicans to loud music, then it is simple enough to wander down to the Avenida del Puerto, which warms up at about 10 and buzzes till 2am.

Restaurants Around the Island

In **Jarabacoa**, you will find an easy-going restaurant on the Parque Central, **Don Luis** (*moderate–cheap*), where you eat on a breezy terrace with white wicker furniture; rice and beans or pizzas. There is local fare at **La Basilia** on Calle Colón (*moderate–cheap*). The most elegant restaurant in **Santiago** is **El Café** (✆ 971 4466; *expensive*), just off Calle 5, near esquina Texas. The cuisine is French and international—almond sea bass in a sauce of almond, lemon, parsley and butter, whisky lobster and some unlikely and exotic meats. The candle-lit dining room is subdued, presided over by tuxedoed waiters, with some piano entertainment. You can also try **Pez Dorado** (✆ 582 4071/2518; *expensive*) on Calle del Sol at the Parque Colón. Seafood and fish mainly, with a few oriental dishes, in a plush, air-conditioned dining room with wicker furniture. Shrimps *chofan* (cooked in flavoured rice), sea bass in a white wine sauce or sweet and sour grouper. People also speak highly of the **Camp David** restaurant (*expensive*), which is set high on the hillside outside the city with a superb view over the whole valley. International fare. There are a number of fun **bars** in Santiago, among them the stylish **Francifol** on Calle del Sol, with a wooden and tiled floor and soft American music or bossa nova—popular with a young crowd late on—and **Pops**, an American-style bar on the Avenida 27 de Febrero, out near the Gran Almirante, behind the Supermercado Modelo.

Puerto Plata

In **Puerto Plata** the top restaurant is **De Armando** (✆ 586 3418; *expensive*), on Calle Separación in the centre of town. It is set in an old wooden house which has been refitted and enclosed with glass to make it air-conditioned. You still take cocktails on the veranda, though, in an inside gazebo. The decor is pink and luxurious and the fare international. Try *cordero al vino*, lamb cooked in a wine sauce, or sea bass with shrimps and clams. Some entertainment with a *perico ripiao* (string) band. **Ristorante Valther** (✆ 586 2329; *expensive–moderate*) has a superb tropical setting in a lovely open-sided creole house lost in explosive Caribbean overgrowth, on Calle Hermanas Mirabal. You sit out under the banyan tree with the frogs singing all around you and then move on to the veranda for *camarones al gusto* (cooked to order) or pasta. **Roma II** (*moderate*) is a restaurant and pizzeria in an air-conditioned dining room. Italian fare: pizzas and pastas or *pulpo a la vinagreta*, octopus in a vinaigrette sauce. The **Taberna Restauranto Costa Brava** (*moderate*), just off the Plaza Central, serves Spanish and local fare in a pretty wooden house with open shutter doors. Down on the Malecón is a popular bar and restaurant, **Willy's Sports Centre** (*moderate*); local fare, *chofan mixto*, different meats and fish buried in rice, or lemon chicken. **Uncle Dick's** is a fun bar and restaurant set in a clapboard house in the centre of town. A hip crowd crawls out of the woodwork and gathers here, not all of them for the exchange library in the corner of the bar by the look of it. Quite lively. There is a television-bar **Castilla** on Calle José del Carmen Ariza. You can find a good Dominican snack at the stalls in the alleyway opposite the stadium at the eastern edge of town.

Sosúa

In Sosúa you will find an Italian restaurant with a charming setting on the clifftops at **La Puntilla de Pierfiorgio** (*expensive*), where iron garden chairs and tables sit on terraces around a gingerbread house. Specialities include *tagliatelli 'la puntilla*, prepared with parmesan and cream, or you might go for cannelloni beef in bechamel sauce. The **Caribbean** restaurant (*moderate*) is set in a glass-fronted dining room with pretty tables laid with white tablecloths and flowers. Good Caribbean fare—pork fillet exotica, cooked in pineapple, banana and curry or simple barbecue chicken.

Pavillon (*expensive*) has a good setting, a mock Arawak cabana with *bohío* thatch and pillars inlaid with pebbles and walls of coral rock. Simple menu, steaks and seafood, a lively crowd, with parrots and greenery. There is often a **vegetarian** menu at **Tropix Hotel** (ring and ask on ✆ 571 2291; *moderate*), just over the main road. Good poolside setting and friendly crowd. You can find cheap Italian food at **Mama Mia's** on Calle Dr Rosen. Calle Pedro Clisante has a string of cafés and bars.

The **Atlántico** restaurant (*expensive–moderate*) is famous for its seafood. It has an excellent position on the **Charramícos** side of the town, with a lovely view of the palms and activity of Sosúa Beach. It is set on its own veranda, with rafters and wooden seats and tables. The menu will vary according to the catch of the day, but there is often sea bass in an orange sauce or paella, the house speciality. Up in the town, **La Beto** is another good restaurant serving French cuisine; you sit under awnings on a streetfront veranda. You will find good Dominican food at **Deportiva**— shrimp, conch and local juices and at **Café Central**, near the entrance to the town.

There is a string of **beach bars** on the main Sosúa beach, any of which is good as a daytime hangout. For a cocktail at sunset it is well worth heading for **Charlie's** bar on the cliffs at the bottom of Calle Dr Rosen. Many of the restaurants above have bars but you will find a string of popular haunts on the main street: **Treetops** is a thatched upstairs deck hung with flags, music all day, happy hour 5–9.30pm. Also worth a stop is **PJ's Shack**. **La Roca** is set in a nice old building at the top end of the street. **Moby Dick's** is the town discotheque.

Cabarete

Cabarete has a surprising clutch of beach bars and restaurants where you might easily find yourself lingering, escaping the sun during the day and over a meal in the evenings—there is even a **Crêperie du Pirate** if that sounds like your style. At **La Louisianne** (*expensive–moderate*) you dine on a stone-floored, breezy terrace under palm-thatch, right on the beach. French cuisine—grilled red snapper almondine and sautéed sea scallops on pilau rice. As the name suggests, **La Casa del Pescador** (*expensive–moderate*) has fish and seafood on offer, also under palm-thatch and with a great view of the breakers offshore. Shrimps in garlic butter followed by lightly grilled fish and a *banane flambée*.

A very popular restaurant for local food is **Leandro's** (*moderate*), an open dining room with a thatch roof just off the road. Good for a rice 'n' peas, *chicharrones de pollo* or *chivo grisado* (goat stew). A hip spot is **Las Brisas** (*moderate*), which also overlooks the beach from a breezy seaside terrace with palm thatch and a stereo playing the latest rock and merengue. It attracts a windsurfing crowd (as the name would suggest), so it is quite fun. A salad and a beer by day, barbecue or kebabs in the evening.

Samaná

In **Las Terrenas** on the Samaná Peninsula there are some surprising and excellent restaurants too. You arrive at **Jikaco** (*expensive*) along a pathway flanked by huge crotons and birds of paradise and lit with flaming torches. The dining room is open to the still air and is a pleasant enough place to spend the time drinking anyway. But it is well worth eating; the menu is French and Basque—*calamare à l'encre* or *crabes farcis* followed by *poulet basquaise* or *filet de poisson grillé*. The most formal restaurant in the town (and that is not saying much) is **Chez Paco** (*expensive–moderate*), farther along the waterfront. After a drink in one of the rocking chairs at the beachfront bar, you retreat to the subdued, candle-lit dining room. The menu is varied, using the best of local ingredients and the house speciality is the *terrine de mariscos*.

A superb Caribbean beach setting can be found at **La Salsa**, in a cosy, palm-thatched deck right on the seafront. Low coloured lights and a French menu—*poulet à l'ananas* to go with Celia Cruz, Neil Young, Kassav, John Lee Hooker and the gentle wash of the waves. A bar from paradise. **El Tiburin** is set in another classic waterfront deck; salads and omelettes and some fish specialities. **Isla Bonita** has an Italian kitchen serving five or six pastas a night as well as the day's catch and if you want a cheap local meal, go to the **Hotel Dinny**. If you simply want to drink, try any of the restaurants. In the daytime there is often a small crowd at the **Coco Loco** beach bar.

You will probably pass through the town of **Samaná** itself, where there are some good cafés overlooking the Malecón. The nicest is **L'Hacienda** (*expensive*), on a side street just behind the Café de Paris, which has something of a hacienda feel in the open room, the curved arches and tiles, but uses the best of the Caribbean in the decor of brightly coloured chairs. The food, all prepared on a grill that sits on the streetfront, is steaks, in a rum or wine sauce, and kebabs, touched with home-made sauces, all to music from around the Latin world, merengue, flamenco, sals. At **le Boucanier** (*moderate*) you sit on a brightly lit terrace above the water with the fishing boats around you and views of the bay. *Pollo à la curry* or *filet de mérou provençale*. There is a string of bars and cafés on the other side of the Malecón, an ideal stop if you are waiting for, or have just got off the bus to the capital. There is even one that calls itself **Samaná Sam's**. At the **Café de Paris** (*moderate*) you can get salads and crêpes all day, or just loiter with the rest of them over endless drinks.

The cheapest place to eat is the cavernous double pyramid on the hilltop behind the town, the **Restaurant China** (*cheap*), where there is a huge menu including pastas and omelettes as well as traditional Chinese dishes and some novel ones made with Caribbean ingredients. There are a number of discotheques in the town, which gets quite lively at the weekends. In the resort area of **Las Galeras** there is a nice restaurant at **Jardín Tropical** serving French and international fare.

East of Santo Domingo

At Boca Chica you will find a long string of snack bars and beach restaurants specializing in fish and seafood. The veranda at the **Casa del Mar** (*moderate*) is slightly removed from the hurly-burly of the beach activity and you can get a plate of seafood or a steak.

There are a number of restaurants in the Altos de Chavón village above Casa de Campo. The smartest is probably the **Casa del Río**: from which in the evening you get a superb view of the river, floodlit below. All very atmospheric and mock-medieval, with rather nouvelle dishes to go with it. Caribbean lobster roasted and baked in vanilla

Dominican Republic Directory

getting there

The main airport is at Santo Domingo, about 18 miles east of the city itself (internal flights leave from Herrera airport in the west of the city). Most of the charter flights to the tourist resorts of the north coast will fly into Puerto Plata or Punta Cana in the east of the country. The national carrier is Dominicana.

By air from Europe: There are almost daily flights to Santo Domingo from Madrid (Iberia or Dominicana), where connections can be made from the major cities in Europe. Air France has four flights a week from Paris and there are weekly flights from Lisbon and Amsterdam.

By air from the USA: There are daily direct links to Santo Domingo, Puerto Plata, La Romana and Punta Cana from Miami, New York, and New Jersey (Dominicana, TWA and American Airlines), with connecting flights from other cities in the USA. Other cities with direct links are Boston, Raleigh/Durham and Tampa.

By air from other Caribbean islands: There are many daily flights to Santo Domingo from San Juan (American Airlines and Dominicana) and from Curaçao on most days (ALM or Aeropostal), also Aruba. Occasional services link the city to Sint Maarten, Martinique and Guadeloupe, Port au Prince in Haiti next door, Kingston and Montego Bay in Jamaica, and Santiago in the east of Cuba. There are also plenty of links to **South America**, including Caracas, Lima, Bogotá and Chile.

There are direct flights to **Puerto Plata** from Miami and New York, and also from San Juan (daily service by American Airlines). There is also a link to Grand Turk and Providenciales in the Turks and Caicos Islands. Santiago is served twice daily from San Juan and La Romana is served daily from San Juan too, mainly for guests at Casa de Campo.

Entry regulations: Visitors from Denmark, Finland, Greece, Iceland, Israel, Liechtenstein, Norway, Japan, Argentina, Ecuador, Peru among others can enter the Dominican Republic on a valid passport and can stay for 90 days without a visa. Citizens of Belgium, Canada, France, Holland, Jamaica, Portugal, the USA, Germany, Spain, Canada, Switzerland, Netherlands, Italy, Poland, Portugal, France, Monaco, Mexico, Surinam, Britain and its dependencies must purchase a **tourist card** on arrival. This costs US$10 and is valid for 60 days (it can be renewed twice at no further cost). You must surrender it when you leave. There is a departure tax in the Dominican Republic of US$10. The authorities insist that foreigners pay it in US dollars.

tourist information

USA: 1501 Broadway, Suite 410, **New York**, NY 10036 (✆ (212) 575 4966, ✆ 575 5448), toll free ✆ (1 888) 374 6361; 2355 Salzedo Street, Suite 305, Coral Gables, **Florida** 33134 (✆ (305) 444 4592, ✆ 444 4845). US toll free ✆ (1 800) 752 1151); 561 West Diversey Building, Suite 214, **Chicago**, IL 60614 164 (✆ (773) 529 1336/37, ✆ 529 1338) toll free ✆ (1 888) 303 1336).

and vinegar or lamb loin in orange marmalade and pastry. Then take a constitutional walk on the battlements. If you are on for something simpler and rather less expensive, you can try the **Café del Sol** (*moderate*) where you can get a pizza or a salad. **Papa Jack's** is a fun bar, with a drinking crowd downstairs and a gallery upstairs.

© (1 809)–

Canada: 2980, Rue Crescent, Montreal, Quebec, H3G 2B8 (© (514) 499 1918, ● 499 1393).

Spain: Juan Hurtado de Mendoza, 13 Apto 305, 28036 Madrid (© 1 350 9483, ● 1 350 6579)

Germany: Hochstraße 17, 60313 Frankfurt (© 49 69 9139 7878, ● 49 69 283430).

France: 11, Rue Boudreau, Paris 75009 (© 1 43 12 91 91, ● 1 43 12 91 93).

Belgium: Ave Louise 160 A, Louizalaan, Bruxelles 1050 (© 2 646 0840, ● 2 640 9561).

Italy: Piazza Castello 25, 20121 Milano (© 39 2 805 7781, ● 39 2 865 861).

United Kingdom: 1 Hay Hill, Berkeley Square, London W1X 7LF (© (0171) 495 4322, ● 491 8689).

The main tourist information centre in the Republic is on the Avenida Mexico (at the corner with Avenida 30 de Marzo) in **Santo Domingo** (© 221 4660, ● 221 4660/682 3806), where you will find helpful staff. There is a helpful kiosk at the airport and also at Long Beach, **Puerto Plata** (© 586 5000/ 3676); in **Santiago** (© 582 5885); in **Jarabacoa** (© 574 6189); in **La Romana** (© 550 6992); in **Higüey** (© 554 2672); in **Samaná** (© 538 2332); in **Barahona** (© 524 3650); in **Boca Chica** (© 523 5106); in **Santo Domingo's** colonial zone (© 682 0185 ext. 1321). Open 8–3.

Most **museums** are captioned in both Spanish and English and generally admission is about RD$10. In certain places men are not allowed to enter in shorts as a mask of respect (at the cathedral, however, there is usually somebody on hand to lend you a pair of track-suit bottoms for a few pesos).

The Dominican Republic's leading **newspaper** is the Spanish daily *Listin Diario*. English-language papers include *Hispaniola Business*, the *Santo Domingo News* and *Touring* which include plenty of tourist information and listings of current events. American newspapers and magazines make their way down after a few days and are available in the Santo Domingo bookshops.

In an **emergency** you can contact the **police** (Politur) in Santo Domingo on © 221 4660 ext 285/286/287 or Puerto Plata on © 586 2331. Few police speak English and so if the problem is not urgent it might be best to contact the tourist authorities/hotel.

In a **medical** emergency, there are 24-hour casualty rooms available in **Santo Domingo**, Clínica Abreu, on Avenida Independencia (© 688 4411) or Clínica Gomez Patiño, Avenida Independencia 701 (© 685 9131), and in **Puerto Plata**, Grupo Medico Dr Bournigal (© 586 2342). A general emergency number is 711.

International and local calls can usually be arranged by hotel receptionists, but you may find it easier to go to the Codetel or TRICOM offices, open daily 8am–10pm or midnight, depending on the size of the town. The **IDD** code for the Dominican Republic is ✆ (1 809). Dialling into the country is far easier than dialling out.

Britain has an embassy in the Dominican Republic at Avenida 27 de Febrero No. 233, Edif. Corominas Pepin, 7mo, Piso, Santo Domingo (✆ 472 7111, ✉ 472 7574). The **US Embassy** is at César Nicolás Penson in central Santo Domingo (✆ 221 2171, ✉ 566 8013); the **Canadian Embassy** is at 30 Máximo Gómez, Santo Domingo (✆ 685 1136, ✉ 682 2691).

festivals

As befits a Catholic country, many of the Dominican festivals are based on church celebrations. However, as well as religious processions, the Dominicans make sure to get a week or so's dancing out of a festival. Apart from the major dates in the Christian festival calendar—New Year's Day, 21 January (Our Lady of Altagracia, patron saint of the Dominican people), when Dominicans visit their families in the country, **Carnival** (celebrated over the weekend nearest to 27 February), Good Friday and Christmas Day—Dominicans also remember Independence Day (27 February) with carnival parades and Restoration Day (16 August), when the Dominicans finally became free from Spain in 1865.

Each town also celebrates the day of its patron saint (with an associated blow-out) in its *fiesta patronal*. These start with a Mass in the early morning and continue with street games, horse races and sports such as running and shinning up a waxed pole (*palo encebao*), even bull-fighting, and later dancing. In remoter areas the celebrations can have a strong trace of Dominican *santería*, similar to Haitian voodoo, in which drums produce such a relentless rhythm that the dancers go into trance. Another big festival, also drum and music based, is the **Fiesta de Palo**, in which the *novena* is celebrated over the nine days that run up to the Fiesta de la Sanctissima Cruz on 3 May.

Major *fiestas patronales*:

13 June	—	*San Antonio* in Sosúa
29 June	—	*San Pedro Apostol,* San Pedro de Macoris
5 June	—	*San Felipe,* Puerto Plata
22 July	—	*Santiago Apostol,* Santiago
25 July	—	*San Cristóbal,* San Cristóbal
15 Aug	—	*Nuestra Señora de Antigua,* La Vega
24 Sept	—	*Nuestra Señora de las Mercedes,* Constanza
4 Oct	—	*Nuestra Señora del Rosario,* Barahona
24 Oct	—	*San Rafael,* Boca Chica
4 Dec	—	*Santa Barbara,* Samaná

A list of the upcoming *fiestas patronales* can usually be winkled out of the tourist offices. It is worth attending if you hear of one happening.

money

The currency of the Dominican Republic is the peso (RD$), divided into 100 centavos. At present it stands at US$1 = RD$14.02 (about RD$20 = £1) and this rate makes travel quite cheap in the Republic. Most banks have exchange facilities for dollars into pesos. The authorities are strict about changing pesos back into dollars and it is not that easy (it is theoretically possible, up to a small amount, at the airports or at the Banco de Reservas in Santo Domingo, on presentation of a recent exchange receipt, and your and passport).

You are quite likely to be accosted in the street by someone whispering furtively, 'dollars, dollars, I change 100 for 1500', and flicking through a wad of notes. The best advice is to say no: their rate is not that much better than the official one and you always run the risk of their sleight of hand and quick turn of speed.

Credit cards are widely accepted by hotels, tourist restaurants, travel agents and the car hire firms. Outside these areas you will be given a blank look if you flash your plastic at somebody. Take pesos in small denominations.

Banks: Open weekdays, 8.30–3.30, with an extra stint on Saturday morning for foreign exchange, 8–noon.

Shops: Open am and pm, with a long siesta over lunchtime, Mon–Sat, 8.30–noon and 2.30–6.30. Government offices open weekdays 7.30–2.30. Dominicans will usually expect you to bargain, not only in the markets. You can also buy duty-free goods in US$ inside the free zones, some of which are at Las Atarazanas in the colonial district of Santo Domingo, Centro de Los Héroes and the airport. Goods must be bought a couple of days in advance; they will be given to you once you are past the ticket barrier at the airport.

maps and books

The Dominican Republic's most famous book is *Enriquillo*, by Manuel de J. Galvan, which tells the story of the Taino nobleman who took to the hills and waged a guerrilla war against the Spaniards in the 1520s. He is something of a national hero. Sumner Welles's *Naboth's Vineyard* gives an excellent view of the country in the 1920s. It was republished by Arno Press in 1972. Samuel Hazard wrote an enlightening account of the island in *Santo Domingo Past and Present with a Glance at Hayti*, published in 1873. There are some factual errors, but it is interesting reading because it was written at a time when the Dominicans were considering joining the United States.

watersports

Watersports gravitate around the tourist centres. The larger hotels usually have them on offer (anything from parasailing to banana boat rides), but as an outsider you may not be allowed into the hotel compound. If you are travelling independently, the best bet is to go to more off-beat areas like Sosúa, Cabarete and Las Terrenas. Boca Chica, the favourite with the Dominicans themselves, has most sports on offer too.

Windsurfing: Extremely good in the Dominican Republic. You can pick up a board in most places on the north and east coasts, but all standards of windsurfers can enjoy Cabarete, a few miles east of Sosúa, where the hotels are devoted to windsurfing. The winds run across the bay, slightly onshore and several hundred yards out there is a reef where you can sail waves. Winds are at their highest in the early part of the year. Mistral, BIC, Fanatic and F2 boards are available here. You might also enjoy taking a kayak out on to the waves. **Surfers** will find big waves at this time off Playa Grande near Rio San Juan and at Macao.

Sailing: For small **sailing craft**, two-person hobie cats and sunfish, you will depend on the hotels, but if you wish to charter a larger **yacht**, you can go to the marinas at Boca Chica, the Sailing Club of Santo Domingo (Club Nautico de Santo Domingo) (✆ 685 4940) at La Romana and at Boca de Yuma in the far southeast. **Deep-sea fishing** trips, on the hunt for magnificent 10ft marlin in the Mona Channel, can also be arranged from Boca de Yuma, which holds a fishing tournament each year in June. Alternatively try Club Andres in Boca Chica (✆ 685 4940) or the quay in Samaná. In Puerto Plata contact ✆ 586 1121. The fishing is also good off the north coast in the region of Monte Cristi, where they hold a couple of yearly competitions.

Scuba diving: Not that developed in the Dominican Republic and your best bet is the hotels, some of which run instruction courses for beginners. There are reefs off all sides of the coast, many of which can be reached by snorkellers. Diving reefs include Catalina Island and Bayahibe near La Romana, and there are wrecks on the reefs off Monte Cristi and near Miches. There is a marine park near the airport at La Caleta (make arrangements in Boca Chica) and other good areas include Las Terrenas. Try Dominican Adventure Dive Center in the capital, Abraham Lincoln Avenida 960 (✆ 565 9771). Another useful contact in Santo Domingo is Mundo Submarino (✆ 566 0430), who arrange trips for trained divers and sailing and snorkelling excursions. There is a general watersports operator in Puerto Plata, for diving and deep-sea fishing (✆ 586 1121). In Sosúa contact Northern Coast Watersports (✆ 571 1028), in Samaná try Samaná Tourist Services (✆ 538 2332) and in Las Terrenas, the Tropical Diving Centre (✆ 240 6110).

other sports

Polo: The Dominican Republic must be one of the only places in the world where you can hire polo ponies (at Casa de Campo).

Riding: Possible in a number of resorts throughout the island.

Golf: There are three courses at Casa de Campo in the east, two in Santo Domingo, the Country Club and Cayacoa, and two near Puerto Plata (9 holes at Castambar).

Tennis: Courts are everywhere. Once again, go to a nearby hotel.

Walking: Walkers will not find anything organized, except occasionally by the National Parks Service (*see* 'Flora and Fauna' p.581). However, if you are prepared to rough it a bit, the parks can provide excellent hiking.

Baseball: The Republic's national sport (if you don't include dancing); some of the Dominicans play in the national leagues in the States, returning home to winter in the warmth, where they keep their eye in with the local teams. There are stadia in Santo Domingo, Santiago, Puerto Plata, La Romana and San Francisco de Macoris.

Cockfighting: Another very popular spectator sport, particularly in the country areas (*see* 'Martinique' p.260). The Gallera Santo Domingo is about 7 miles from the city.

Wrestling: Last but not least, if you get a chance to see a Dominican wrestling match, go to it because it is a great spectacle. The fervour is extraordinary, and is matched only by the suspension of disbelief.

Ruins of Sans Souci near Milot

Haiti

The rhythms and reverberations of Africa echo more strongly in Haiti than in any other Caribbean country—in the speech and the faces, in the sheer effervescence of its people, and in the spiritual world and the relentless beat of African drums. Haiti, which staged the Caribbean's only successful slave rebellion, fighting for its independence in 1804, is the oldest black republic in the world.

Haiti was originally an Arawak name for the island and supposedly meant 'mountainous land' (a good guess at translation, if nothing else because the island has three vast mountainous ranges). Haiti has the western third of the island of Hispaniola. Like its neighbour it has the same rainforested mountains and fertile valleys, as well as areas that are practically desert. It is about 10,700 square miles.

If Santo Domingo has a pastel wash, Haiti is a land of primary colours, where scarlet, yellow and overpowering blue dominate life, on windowframes and doors, on the buses and in the 'naïve' art. There are around 7½ million Haitians and they are almost entirely of African origin, descended from slaves brought to the French colony of Saint Domingue. They speak *kreyol*, a language in which French and African strains are clearly audible. Officially the Haitians do not distinguish between white and black, but skin colour has long been a point of controversy in Haiti, enough to cause massacres and political violence.

There is grinding poverty—Haiti is the poorest country in the western hemisphere. As in many Caribbean countries, the people are poorly dressed, but here they are also poorly fed. You will see fifty children clamouring at the only standpipe for miles around, collecting water which they take home balanced on their heads in vast plastic buckets. Out in the country they go to church if they can afford shoes. In Haiti, shoe-shine boys are grown men, not children.

Politics has also been hard on the Haitians. Over the last two centuries they have seen endless internal strife as a succession of corrupt dictators jockeyed for position and then administered with a brutal disregard for their population's pitiable situation. Despite a desire for stability among the people themselves, it seems a forlorn hope that the situation should improve radically in the near future. On the international scene, Haiti has been embattled from the beginning, shunned as a stronghold of black magic and most recently a stronghold for AIDS. They were blacklisted by the USA until the USA freed her own slaves.

For all this, though, the Haitians maintain an undefiable optimism and they are certainly not resigned in their poverty. The country has an irrepressible spirit, and they escape their drab physical existence in many ways. The most notorious is the religious cult of *voodoo* (*see* p.613), but the islanders also express themselves in vibrant traditions of naïve art and a lively street

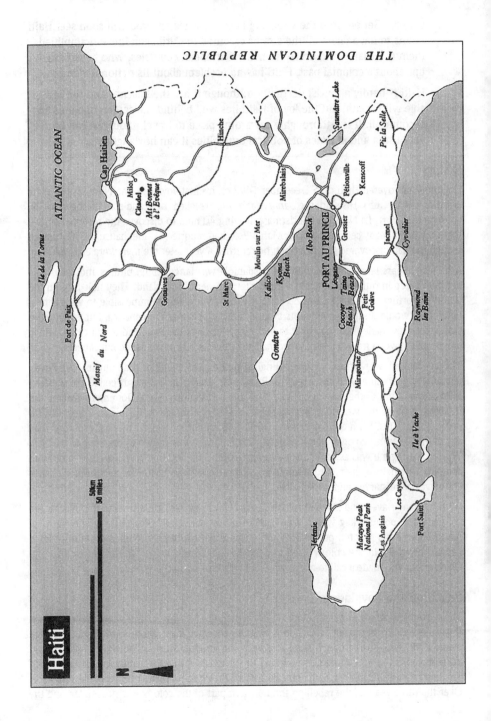

Haiti

culture. Get out into the streets of Port-au-Prince and you will soon see. Haiti seems to have taken all the strains essential to Caribbean life and amplified them to a blare. And unlike so many Caribbean countries, who have hang-ups about a colonial past, Haiti has no problem about its national identity.

Haiti is hardly a tourist destination, though it has the beaches and the reliable winter sun, but the joy of Haiti lies well behind the screen of palms and coconut oil. It is a thoroughly rewarding place to travel, though it can be very tiring and at times of political difficulties it can be dangerous.

History

Columbus discovered Haiti on 5 December 1492 on his first voyage to the New World, as he sailed east from Cuba. His ship, the *Santa Maria*, was wrecked there and so with the wood he constructed a fort, La Navidad (Christmas), leaving 40 men to discover the reserves of gold that they had already seen and which Marco Polo had reported as 'inexhaustible' (Columbus thought he had discovered Japan). When he returned a year later the men were all dead.

A hundred years later, as the colony of Hispaniola was languishing, pirates and sea-rovers began to creep into the inaccessible northwestern corner of the island. They holed up on the island of Tortuga, fortifying themselves so that they were almost impossible to winkle out. Often they would disappear on jaunts around the Caribbean as mercenaries, but when there was peace they made their way over to the remote areas of the mainland to kill cattle, which they smoked over a frame called a *boucan*. They came to be known as the buccaneers.

The buccaneers were mostly French (English pirates had a similar hide-out in Port Royal, Jamaica) and eventually, at the Treaty of Ryswick in 1697, the Spaniards ceded the western third of the island to the French crown. Over the next century, Saint Domingue became the richest colony in the world, supplying sugar, coffee and indigo to France in a fleet of 700 ocean-going ships. With annual exports worth $40 million, it was far more prosperous than any of the American colonies and its capital, Cap Français, was known as the Paris of the New World. The regime was as brutal as it was successful. The 500,000 slaves were treated with abominable cruelty—the planters would flog them close to death for the most minor offence and slaves were starved and buried alive.

With so many slaves, and internal rivalries between the whites, mulattos and free blacks, the colony was a powder keg which was sparked off by the French Revolution. The National Assembly in Paris granted political rights to the mulattos, but the whites would not let it happen in reality in the colony itself and so the rebellions started. The mulattos Ogé and Chavannes, who made a call to arms, were publicly broken on the wheel.

Rebellion and Revolution

These events were overtaken in August 1791, when the first major black rebellion took place. It was initiated by Boukman, a voodoo *houngan*, who gave instructions to torch the northern plains with the call of a conch shell and with the voodoo drums. The slaves pillaged and burned, subjecting the white slave-owners to the tortures they had undergone themselves. The few who escaped fled to Cap Français and left the country, many settling in eastern Cuba. Over the three years of the rebellion the northern part of the colony was devastated and the lines were drawn for civil war between the blacks in the north and the mulatto-dominated south. The French colonial authorities were powerless to intervene.

The rebel leader in the north was the remarkable Toussaint L'Ouverture (called so either because of an opening he created in a battle or for the gap between his teeth) who sided with the French Republicans after they abolished slavery in 1793. Toussaint had educated himself with the sanction of his white master (whom Toussaint helped to escape during the 1791 rebellion) and he entered the rebel army as a herb doctor. His skill as a military man, supposedly learned from a book about Alexander's campaigns, soon became clear, and by 1796 he was the undisputed leader of the former slaves in the north. He then showed his brilliant colours as a politician and he administered his country humanely, ending the massacres and managing to restore some of Saint Domingue's former prosperity. He was the unofficial governor of a colony that was independent from France in all but name.

But when he tried to introduce a constitution that allowed the country autonomy and appointed him governor for life, it was too much for Napoleon, who wished to re-establish his power in the Americas. In 1801 Bonaparte despatched an army of 34,000 men, led by his own brother-in-law Leclerc, with instructions to subdue the slave armies and to retake the colony for France. It was an unsuccessful campaign and Leclerc's soldiers died like flies from disease (in all over 100,000 European soldiers died trying to take Haiti back, a huge number in those days). Leclerc treated with Toussaint and, during a dinner to discuss the affairs of the colony, had him seized and deported to France. Toussaint's final words on departure from Saint Domingue were, 'In overthrowing me, they have cut down in Saint Domingue the trunk of the tree of black liberty. It will shoot up again through the roots, for they are numerous and deep.' Toussaint was held in a castle in the Jura mountains, ill-fed and without warmth. His letters to Napoleon went unanswered and within a year he was dead.

The blacks did not revolt immediately, but they buried their arms rather than turn them in. In May 1802, the Convention in Paris reintroduced slavery and the blacks rose up against the French once more. More whites were massacred and the French army, decimated by disease and guerrilla war, evacuated. On 1 January 1804 Jean Jacques Dessalines tore the white strip out of the *tricolore*, and proclaimed the independent black Republic of Haiti in the northern half of the island.

Dessalines was a tyrant, but he started to rebuild the economy, forcing the former slaves back to their plantations. Ever fearful of an attack by the French to retake the colony, he maintained a large army, introducing into Haitian society a traditional power which continues even today. But soon he became unpopular, particularly with the mulattos, and he was assassinated in 1806.

His death led to civil war again between the mulatto south, under General Pétion, and the north, which adopted the negro Henry Christophe as its leader. As leader of Haiti, Christophe, a megalomaniac and an immense man in size and energy, wished to show that the first black republic was as capable as any European power. He had himself crowned king (Dessalines had made himself an emperor in imitation of Napoleon) and he built a magnificent palace worthy of any European kingdom at Sans Souci near Cap Haïtien in the north of the island (his court still sounds faintly comical to European ears as it included the Counts of Limonade and Marmelade). Nearby, his citadel is one of the most extraordinary feats of engineering in the world. But his reign was also tyrannical and in 1820, as armies closed in on him, he committed suicide by shooting himself with a silver bullet. He was buried in the citadel. After his death, the two sides of the country were united again, under the southern General Boyer.

Boyer treated with France, who finally accepted Haitian Independence at the price of 150 million French francs as compensation (later reduced to 60 million). He also invaded Santo Domingo which had just won Independence from Spain.

In the 72 years between Boyer's flight in 1843 and 1915, Haiti saw 22 heads of state, most of whom left office by violent means. Some tried to improve the infrastructure of the country, but the aspirations of the early leaders foundered with a succession of corrupt and self-seeking dictators. Rivalry continued between the whites and the mulatto élite and the blacks, who dominated the army, flaring up from time to time in politically motivated massacres. In the fields, the Haitian peasants suffered a continuing poverty, scraping barely enough food from the soil to survive.

In 1915, after the dismemberment of President Guillaume Sam, the Americans invaded the country, concerned with the influence of the German community in the country at the time of the First World War. There followed 19 years of heavy-handed administration. It brought considerable development in roads, sanitation and in schools, but the Haitians opposed it with a nationalist movement which erupted increasingly in violence. Eventually Haiti was flourishing in 1930 and they wanted independence again. In 1934 the Marines left.

The mulatto élite had come to prominence again during the American occupation and it was not long before internal political troubles started along the traditional lines. Coloureds found their way into the positions of power. They also led campaigns against voodoo. Until the accession of François Duvalier in 1957, and since the deposition of his son in 1986, Haiti has suffered the political turmoil it has always faced.

The Duvaliers

The Duvalier regime was another brutal chapter in Haitian history, in which the country was hijacked by a ruthless despot who then arranged to hand over power to his son. It was characterized by repression, particularly through 'Papa Doc's' private militia, the notorious *tontons macoutes* (the name means 'uncle knapsack' and comes from a character in Haitian folklore who carries off children in the middle of the night). Father and son amassed vast personal fortunes from the Haitian national coffers.

François Duvalier, a doctor and union leader and a member of Haiti's emerging black middle class, was elected president at the age of 50 in 1957. For the first few years in his 14-year rule Papa Doc terrorized the country, consolidating power and rooting out potential rivals in the army, the church and the mulatto élite. He was a shrewd manipulator and ensured that there was no organized resistance to his regime. He was also a practising vodunist—his loa was *Baron Samedi*, the guardian of cemeteries and a harbinger of death. Thousands of Haitians died in his regime. In 1964 he had the constitution changed so that he could be elected president for life, which he remained until his death in 1971.

As his son, Jean Claude, then 19 years old, took over there was initially some political liberalization and there was foreign investment as the regime became less isolationist. But the status quo was maintained by the usual terror tactics and once again, the poorest Haitians benefited little. Haiti was the poorest country in the western hemisphere. Many Haitians took their chance and tried to get illegally into the USA. Corruption ran rife. In the face of the poverty, 'Baby Doc' lavished an estimated US$7 million dollars of national money on his wedding in 1980.

In the early eighties he cracked down on any liberalization and the new political parties were banned. Riots broke out as the regime began to founder in 1984 and by late 1985 the country was in open revolt. Eventually, in what was known as *Operation Deschoukay*, the regime collapsed on 6 February 1986 and 'Baby Doc' fled the country for France. The country lurched from one ineffectual government and political crisis to the next until Jean-Bertrand Aristide, a religious priest, was elected in a landslide victory in December 1990. He introduced radical changes, but his government soon foundered on the inertia of military and neo-Duvalierist power and eventually he was deposed in a coup, led by certain sections of the army. The coup provoked international condemnation, and resulted in the imposition of an embargo by the Organization of American States. Other nations suspended aid and froze government assets.

After many attempts, Aristide was finally able to return in late 1994, sponsored by the USA, to serve the rest of his term of office. This was facilitated by US military back-up and later by UN troops. On his return to power, Aristide began to downscale the role of the army and police force within Haiti, which ultimately resulted in the breakdown of law and order. Presidential elections were held in December 1995: in spite of the low turn-out, René Préval, one of Aristide's aides, won a landslide victory. He was inaugurated in February 1996. Rony Smarth was appointed prime minister, but has since resigned; his successor has yet to be appointed.

In the country itself, the Haitians continue to suffer political turmoil. There seems to be a general will among the people for internal stability, but for the moment, with endless suspicions of corruption and involvement in drug-trafficking at the highest levels and the unpredictable activities of the rival security forces and traditional political power-blocs, it is impossible to say what will be the outcome. The future is by no means bright. Many Haitians are still trying to escape to the USA.

The economy is in a mess: inflation is running out of control and three-quarters of the population of Haiti is reckoned to be on the breadline. The majority are subsistence farmers, but many work in the coffee industry. The low wages make a certain amount of industry possible, including the manufacture of some electronic goods, shoes and base-balls. The usual Caribbean mainstay, tourism, has fallen off because of the political problems. For the same reason, mineral resources remain untouched. The literacy rate in Haiti is 48 per cent.

Voodoo

Voodoo is an essential part of Haitian life, but one that is little understood outside the country—with sensationalized stories of frenzied drumming, dancing and sacrificial black magic ceremonies, it is one of the sources of the country's mystery and its bad PR.

Voodoo (*vodun* in Haitian kreyol) is a religion (a system of beliefs at least), in which the spiritual world is inhabited by *loas* (pronounced 'lwa'), spirits who can have a direct effect on human life. There is no

Voodoo sacrifice

overall voodoo theology, complete creed of beliefs or order of service, and the spirits will be different in different parts of the country. The saying has it that 90 per cent of Haitians are Catholic, but 99 per cent of them believe in voodoo.

Voodoo started on the slave plantations as a form of celebration, in which some of the spirits from Africa were invoked, but over the years many have taken on noticeably Catholic characteristics; other new spirits were discovered in Haiti. Good and evil are not so clear cut as in the monotheistic religions. Spirits can be angry or content and will bring happiness and good luck if treated well, but they can also be vengeful. Over the years it has been used as a political weapon and denied as quackery and superstitious nonsense. However, voodoo runs very deep in Haitian society. It is one of the strongest expressions of the Haitian spirit, in defiance of their poverty.

The principal loas are *Papa Legba*, the guardian of doors, gates, roads and crossroads, who acts as a sort of go-between for the believers and their other loas. *Erzulie* is a female loa and resembles the Virgin Mary, though she does not perform any specific function. *Damballa*, on the other hand, is the spirit of water and so he can send rain enough to provide for the crops, but when angry he will cause destruction in floods. Others include *Papa Zaca*, the father of agriculture, *Ogun*, the spirit of war and the well-known top-hatted *Baron Samedi*, who watches over cemeteries, and spirits who control the livelihoods of fishermen, hunters or tradesmen, such as *Aewé*, the spirit of the sea and fishermen. Christian deities are acknowledged, but they are far more remote than these spirits, except Erzulie of course. Each spirit has its favourite colour, often white or grey, but sometimes red, and animals that are sacrificed to them must be of that colour.

The voodoo ceremony itself takes place in a *hounfort*, a building with an altar and an area of beaten earth where the dancing takes place. It begins with a ritual very similar to Catholic liturgy, but then the drumming strikes up (on drums of different sizes, carved out of mahogany, with a skin stretched over the top and held taut with vast pegs) and the dancing begins. A loa will reveal him or herself to the *houngan* (the nearest thing to a priest) and the particular rhythms of that loa will be played. A *véver*, a patterned symbol, is drawn on the ground with cornmeal or with ash to appease the specific loa. Eventually, if the conditions are right, the loa may come and 'mount' a dancer, who will then go into a trance, sometimes screaming and flailing around, often intoning predictions. The first loa to mount a person becomes their guardian angel for life.

There is another side to Haitian spiritual life, connected to voodoo, in which magic can be used in curing an illness or warding off evil spirits or to change the course of events. An illness might be the act of a loa, and so the sick person would seek the advice of the houngan or perhaps a *bocor* (a sorcerer), to find out why it is. Some cures will resemble old wives' brews, other have more sinister ritual. The sorcerer has a powerful hold over his devotees, but the final arbiter is his success. Docteurs Feuilles, practitioners of traditional medicine, use local plants for their cures.

One of the most sensational aspects of Haitian life is that of *zombies*, of which evidence exists, and which make fascinating and ghoulish stories. Supposedly a person is fed a potion which makes their metabolic rate drop so low that they appear to be dead. After they are buried, the administrator of the poison will then dig them up, restoring them to full physical capacity, but keeping their mind in limbo. The zombie is then transported to the other end of the country and used as a slave.

Voodoo ceremonies take place according to a calendar and to celebrate special events. You will hear the drumming blow on the still night air, and if you are driving around at these times you may well see streams of people heading for the local *hounfort*. It is very difficult for a white stranger to attend a local voodoo ceremony. Unless your contacts are very good, the best you can really hope for are the various shows that admit foreigners. These are impressive sights nonetheless, though it is difficult to tell how authentic they are. For an interesting read, try *The Serpent and the Rainbow* by Wade Davis (Simon & Schuster Ltd), an anthropologist who investigated the story of zombies.

Taptaps

Taptaps are the brightly decorated buses that you see barging their way through the traffic in Port-au-Prince or chasing from one town to the next, loaded to the gunwales. They take their name from the old lorries, whose engines would labour over the hills with a *tap-tap-tap*, but now they can be anything from a Mitsubishi van with a cage on the back to a vast 7-ton Mack lorry with multiple horns and flashing lights.

The decorations on the cage are all-important and make the buses look a bit like old circus or gypsy caravans. The basic wooden frame on the back is often red, but it is carved in graceful sweeps, with curves and cresting waves. It is embellished with stars and diamonds in red, gold and green, kisscurls and unwinding squiggles. Along each side you will see a kreyol maxim, often religious, lit by a stream of coloured flashing bulbs: *'Pran courage fre la Tribilation'*, *'A Koua Bon'* (*'Béni Soit L'Eternel Nissan'* looks a bit odd). There is often a biblical scene painted on the bonnet.

Clearly there are more normal-looking buses around, but these coloured ones are very popular and are a sort of Haitian street art. You can get a large lorry on longer journeys (as a foreigner you might be offered the front seat; take it because it gets pretty crowded

tap-tap being loaded

in the back), but within the towns there are smaller versions on the back of pick-ups, cages with whirligig fans on the front, coloured plastic windows and loud *compas* music on the stereo, making the whole thing like a mobile discotheque. Be careful walking through the traffic in Port-au-Prince, otherwise you might look up and receive a final sacrament as you are run over by a bus screaming *'Dieu Te Bénisse!'*

Haitian Art

Another of Haiti's most vibrant traditions is that of 'naïve' art. It is unique, and uses a simple, almost childlike style, usually without the use of perspective, and invariably using very bright primary colours. As well as on canvas, it appears all over the island— in churches, on the taptaps and in a profusion of murals in the wake of *Operation Deschoukay*, the ousting of the Duvaliers, and for the recent election. Catholicism, the loas of the voodoo world and rural Haitian life are typical themes in Haitian painting.

Haitian naïve painting became known outside the country when the American teacher De Witt Peters came to Haiti in the early forties. The form had been frowned on initially by the Haitian élite, who tended to look to French culture for their inspiration, but Peters recognized the extraordinary flavour of the primitivists and helped the artists to develop their skills by setting up the Centre d'Art, which provided materials for the painters and sponsored them. The school produced the likes of Philomé Obin, Hector Hyppolite, a voodoo houngan, Bazile, Dufont, Benoit and later Lafortune Félix. Sculptors were also encouraged and Liautaud, Brierre and Jasmin Joseph became famous.

There are many places to view and to buy Haitian art. It can literally be bought by the yard and you will even be approached in the street by people clutching their latest masterpiece, but the galleries, both downtown and in Pétionville, contain the best (and most expensive) works. You can buy at the renowned **Centre d'Art** (✆ 22 2018) in the Musée d'Art Haïtien on the Champ de Mars. In Pétionville there is a selection of galleries, including the **Mapou Galerie** at 8 rue Panaméricaine (✆ 57 6430), and the **Galerie Nader** at 48 rue Grégoire (✆ 57 5602), both of which have a good selection.

Selden Rodman has written a number of histories of Haitian art. He described the growth of the primitive school in *Haiti: The Black Republic* (published 1954) and later wrote *The Miracle of Haitian Art* (published 1974). His most recent book, published in 1988, is *Where Art is Joy. Haitian Art: the first forty years*.

There is also a strong tradition of arts and crafts on the island, and if you go to the Marché de Fer, you will be inundated with offers of gaudy religious paintings, mahogany work and ghostly faces in shawls made of leather. The best place to go for ironwork and for metal sculptures is an alleyway which leads off avenue John Brown as you leave Port-au-Prince for Pétionville.

Some Advice

Because of the political unrest, there is very little tourism in Haiti at the moment. There are hardly even any hustlers any more. However, it is a fascinating country in which to travel, even allowing for the fact that it is quite hard work.

A white traveller in Haiti will soon become familiar with the word *blanc* (white), which the islanders will say at every turn. It is not a racist insult: although it means white, all foreigners in Haiti are referred to as *blanc*, even black visitors. It is a cross between an exclamation and a greeting to a stranger (if a Haitian wants to insult you he will do it with a babble of incomprehensible expletives in Haitian kreyol). There is no reason to feel threatened by the word *blanc*, but it may not be a request for you to stop and talk. You are quite likely to be shouted at in the street, but this is not always with malicious intent: it is often a humorous quip in the Haitian street-theatre (though it can still be a little disconcerting to find that the whole road collapses in raucous laughter).

Dollar, on the other hand, is definitely a request for money, and you sometimes get the idea that this is the first word that a Haitian child learns. White travellers, who must have money to have got to Haiti in the first place and are therefore all assumed to be rich, will find themselves surrounded by crowds of kids requesting a dollar, or five. The best advice is not to give in to their demands, even though they are quite persistent. It is important to distinguish between the hustlers who nobble you at the gates of your hotel and in downtown Port-au-Prince (making a reasonable living out of it), and the genuinely poor countryman to whose life the donation of a dollar would make an appreciable difference.

When they are out and about, Haitian **hustlers** are far and away the best in the Caribbean (to be fair they are also the poorest). They will pester you relentlessly if you are alone. And they are pretty sophisticated: suddenly they will be there and they will stick to you like a limpet. Some of them are good guides, others are just small-time dealers. It can be extremely tiring being alone in Haiti, as you spend all day explaining that you wish to be alone, and so it may be easiest to come to an arrangement with one guide just to keep the others away. Offer a daily rate (perhaps US$15–25) and pay for meals that you eat together.

As in any city you are advised to be aware when in Port-au-Prince (watch your pockets in public places). Violence in Haiti tends to be political, and surfaces at election time and in regular *coups d'état*. Consider getting out of town then, though trouble is not generally directed at foreigners. Women do not usually suffer sexual harassment in Haiti. There is a problem with venereal diseases, most notably with HIV. When visiting Haiti you should take a preventative medicine against **malaria**.

You are advised not to drink the **water** in Haiti, or to buy the iced drinks off the streets, sold from the tricycles with a box of concentrates on the front. Stick to soft drinks and coconuts. Purified water (*Culligan* is an accepted term for purified water) is easily available in the shops. The electrical supply in Haiti is hopeless. Expect it to be off for most of the day and to come on at any time between 6 and 8pm.

Lastly, **photography** is something of a problem in Haiti. It can be quite entertaining as all the Haitians dive for cover at the sight of a camera. If you look too determined, they will remonstrate with you and tell of their soul being stolen. The odd Haitian has been known to sell his soul for a few dollars—take your choice. If you go ahead without paying, expect to be screamed at and cursed in kreyol and for the whole street to collapse in giggles again.

Getting Around

Around Port-au-Prince you can take *camionettes*, like small taptaps, which run specific routes through the town, picking up and setting down where you please. They do not have a schedule, but they are frequent, starting at dawn and running until dusk (only infrequently on the important routes after dusk). A ride costs 2 gourdes.

Otherwise take a *publique*, recognizable by the red cloth tied to the rear-view mirror. These pick up any passenger and the driver decides who to let off first. If you want to get up to Pétionville, flag down a *publique* on **avenue John Brown**, which leads out of the Place du Marron Inconnu or catch it earlier down by the Marché de Fer.

Taptaps run the length and breadth of the country. If you are on a long journey, you may find it more comfortable to ride in one of the more regular buses, though these can be crowded enough. Once again, they leave when they are full (ask around for the next one to leave). Jacmel and Cap Haïtien are quite well served, other towns have only a couple of services a day. Get to the bus stop early. If you are going to a beach, ask the driver to drop you off. Buses going **south** and **west** leave from behind the customs building, towards the waterfront from the Marché de Fer. If you are going **north**, you leave from the top of Boulevard Jean Jacques Dessalines. Fares are generally pretty cheap. Hitchhiking in Haiti is not really recommended.

Taxis are available at the airport and at major hotels and restaurants. They are not always in the best condition, but usually get you home. They are unmetered and rates are officially set by the government, so you should establish the price (don't forget to bargain) and make sure of the currency before you set off on the journey.

Taxi-drivers would be happy to take you on a **tour** for about US$15 per hour, though not all speak English. You will probably get the runaround, and be taken only to the galleries where the driver gets a commission on your purchase, but be firm if there is a place you particularly want to visit. The Association des Chauffeurs Guide, 18 Blvd Harry Truman, can be contacted on ✆ 22 0330, or Nick's Taxis on ✆ 57 7777.

Car hire is another option, but not one to be taken lightly because it comes with its hazards. Driving in town is chaotic, and on the country roads it can be pretty dangerous as larger vehicles have little sympathy for cars. Officially driving is on the right. Drivers can use a licence from home for the first three months. It is best to use the large international firms (Avis, ✆ 46 2696; Budget, ✆ 46 0554; Hertz, ✆ 46 0700). Most of them have offices at the airport and in town. Weekly rentals will bring the price down. Cars are available at around US$40–45 per day, plus insurance, through the hotels and at the airport..

You might be able to hitch a ride on the graceful old boats that ply between the ports taking produce.

Beaches

Haiti has a full range of beaches, from strips of idyllic white sand to secluded coves which you can only reach by row-boat, and with the political trouble they have become generally deserted. The more popular beaches, if they are owned by a hotel or have been developed by a cruise ship company, will charge an entrance fee. You will find most water-sports available here. You can also go further afield and discover fishing villages on idyllic half-moon coves. Remember to take all you need: picnic, mosquito repellant, water and snorkelling gear.

Guilou, near Gressier, and **Taino**: The nearest beaches to Port-au-Prince are to the south, off the route to Miragoâne. These are both well served with watersports huts and snack shops.

Sun Beach: Near to Guilou and Taino.

Cocoyer Beach, close to Petit Goâve: Very attractive and slightly more isolated.

Jacmel Beach: On the south coast, this beach is not very attractive (it has dark sand), but not far east are **Raymond les Bains** and **Cyradier**, where the sand is whiter. There are no facilities here.

Les Cayes: The best beaches are on **Ile à Vache** (again, take provisions, though the island is inhabited), and around **Port Salut** to the west, where there are some cracking strips of white sand brushed by palms.

Jérémie: An area which also has some superb coves that can only be reached by hiring a boat.

Ibo Beach on Cacique Island (30 mins ride, 5 mins by boat; adm). **Kyona Beach** (50 mins from Port-au-Prince; adm): Both developed with watersports and crowded at the weekends. Close by are **Kalico** and **Ouanga**, a little lower-key.

Moulin sur Mer: Here you will find restored plantation ruins and an aqueduct.

Amani-y Beach, just south of St Marc: The most attractive beach in this area, palm-backed and with a splendid view of the sunset.

Rival: With its colonial ruins, a few minutes' walk from the Cap.

Cormier: This fishing village 5 miles to the west of Rival is the most popular in the area.

Coco Beach: Has been developed by a cruise-line company (*adm*).

Flora and Fauna

The 'mountainous land' of Haiti is extremely fertile, particularly in the well-watered heights of the northern and southern massifs, each of which has developed unique flora. The nearest park to Port-au-Prince is in the hills above Kenscoff; **Morne la Visite** lies between Furcy and Seguin and in the lush montane forests you will find parrots and parakeets and the Hispaniolan hummingbird. Similar vegetation and birdlife can be found at the western end of the peninsula, at the remote **Macaya Peak National Park**. Take everything you will need if you go exploring here.

At **Saumâtre Lake** near the Dominican border you will see crocodiles and extensive birdlife including flamingos and jacanas with rebellious toes and an embarrassing splurge on their faces. Across the cactus plains in the centre of the island where the hawks and hummingbirds hover, the Massif du Nord has more rich red earth and precipitous slopes which can be treacherous after rain. There is considerable deforestation in Haiti as the islanders chop down trees for burning. If you go out into the country you will see the charcoal pits in which the Haitians prepare their fuel.

There is little organized about the national parks in Haiti, though there is sometimes a ranger's hut available. Take all you need in the way of food and water and a four-wheel-drive car. You should get permission in Port-au-Prince before you visit the parks, through ISPAN (Institut pour la Sauvegarde du Patrimoine National), PO Box 2484, 86 avenue John Brown in Port-au-Prince (© 22 5286).

Port-au-Prince

The capital of Haiti is tucked deep into the southeastern corner of Haiti's huge bay and is backed by the mountains of the southern peninsula. It was founded in 1749, and became capital of the new republic in 1806. Today it has a population of 1.8 million.

The small commercial area downtown is set out in a gridiron of unattractive streets, scattered at intervals with old-time churches, gingerbread mansions, a few glass-fronted structures and large classical official buildings. The human activity is immeasurable—vendors stand three deep on the pavement and there is a constant rush of traffic—and the street theatre is ever-present. Clustered around the town centre are the *cités*, the poorest shanties you will see in the Caribbean, where the stoves light up long before dawn as families prepare their cassava bread. On the hill, aloof from the bustle of Port-au-Prince, is the capital's prosperous alter-ego, Pétionville. Here, villas sit in stately calm behind 10ft walls and wrought-iron gates.

The heart of the town is around the imposing **Palais National** downtown, a vast white pile with classical columns and cupolas, the former home of President Duvalier and the seat of the government. Built in 1918, it is guarded and is not accessible to the public. It looks across the square to the statue of the **Marron Inconnu** (the unknown maroon soldier), a runaway slave with a machete who is blowing into a conch horn, raising the slaves to rebellion.

Just east of the Palais National is the **Place des Héros de l'Indépendence**, or Champ de Mars, an open park where other national heroes are commemorated—Toussaint L'Ouverture, Jean-Jacques Dessalines, Christophe and Pétion. The bunker-like **Musée National** (*open Mon–Fri 10–2 or 3.30; adm*) is also on the square and contains national treasures like the pistol with which Christophe shot himself and the *cloche de la liberté*, rung by

Toussaint himself at Ennery. The crown of Emperor Faustin I is on display and there is even an ancient 13ft anchor, supposedly from Columbus's *Santa María*, which was wrecked off the island in 1492.

Close by is the **Musée d'Art Haïtien du College St Pierre** (℗ 22 2510; *open weekdays 9.30–1.30, Sat till 12.30; adm free*) in which many of the country's finest works of art are displayed. De Witt Peters' Centre d'Art was moved here. The exhibitions change, but there are often paintings by Hector Hippolyte, Sénèque and Philome Obin.

You will find other permanent exhibits of Haitian art in the Episcopalian **Cathédrale de la Sainte-Trinité**, where the apse was painted by Obin, Benoit, Bazile and Leveque. Scenes from the birth of Christ to the Crucifixion are represented in the bright colours of the naïve school.

The main thoroughfare in Port-au-Prince is the **Boulevard Jean-Jacques Dessalines**, a little closer to the waterfront, where the vendors line the street. Each person has their beat and in the covered walkways in front of the buildings you will find music vendors with elaborately arranged stacks of cassettes, tables of sweets and cigarettes, watchmenders and moneychangers fanning a wad of notes. Trade becomes more hectic as you approach the **Marché de Fer,** where the vendors stand three-deep, women standing in line, their arms slung with towels and a huge basket of soap and flannels on their heads, or seated in front of rebellious piles of tropical fruits. The Marché de Fer (the ironmarket) itself is magnificent and seems to cover whole acres with its iron columns and huge riveted arches. Its corrugated tin roofs are painted red as those on all Caribbean markets are. Erected by President Hyppolite in 1889, it looks slightly odd with its minarets—originally the Marché de Fer was intended for India. But around it, the human endeavour is uniquely Haitian. Expect to be accosted to buy at every turn—most of what you are offered will not be much good, but who knows, you could pick up a bargain in there.

The **Oloffson Hotel** at the head of the rue Capois is something of an institution around the city, and a good place to retreat to for an afternoon drink or a rum punch in the evening. The hotel and the rum punch were made famous by Graham Greene, who used the setting for his novel, *The Comedians*, about life in Haiti under Papa Doc. You may still meet the man on whom he modelled the journalist Petit Pierre (Aubelin Jolicoeur). The hotel also attracts a transient crowd of journalists and researchers, so there is often good company there. There are plenty of pictures to buy on the walls and the occasional show of Haitian dancing. It's worth a visit for the building itself, which is a gingerbread masterpiece.

Around Port-au-Prince

Removed from all of the activity of downtown Port-au-Prince, on the cooler heights of the mountainside, **Pétionville** is stately. The large hotels and fine restaurants have a magnificent view of the town and the bay beyond from 1500ft. The buildings are grand, but there is not much to see here. There is a beautiful forested valley, where the lianas creep and the trees block out the sun—leave the town on the rue Borno.

The **Barbancourt Rum Distillery** (℗ 55 7303; *free tasting, bottles from US$5*) is on the road to Kenscoff, set in a mock Teutonic castle. The family has been distilling rum on the island since 1765. You are invited to sit on the veranda, surrounded by vast rum puncheons and cane-crushing gear, tasting their 19 varieties of flavoured rums—hibiscus, apricot, coffee, mango, coconut.

Ten miles beyond Pétionville, and 3000ft higher up into the cultivated slopes, you come to **Kenscoff**, another retreat with an excellent climate (take a jersey if you stay there) and more superb views. The fruit and vegetable market held every Friday seems to go on for ever. There is a handicraft centre and a café at the nearby Baptist Mission, the Mountain Maid, which sells excellent woodwork at good prices (*open 8–5*). Fort boffins will enjoy the ruins of Fort Jacques and Fort Alexander, with their thousands of cannonballs. Beyond Furcy is the Morne La Visite National Park and east of there is Haiti's highest mountain, Pic la Selle.

Gonâve Island lies in the bay off the capital, with mountains that rise to 2500ft and superb coral reefs. It is 30 miles long and skirted with mangrove swamps, where you can come across herons, clapper rails, roseate spoonbills and the occasional flamingo.

Around the Island

Travelling 2½ hours in a taptap will get you over to **Jacmel** on the south coast of the island. A few magnificent old gingerbread town-houses remain from its glorious days as a coffee port at the turn of the century, but its trade was cut off by Duvalier in the fifties and it has decayed. Founded in 1698, it is more accessible now since a good road has been built. You will find the usual Haitian press, particularly around the ironmarket. In the hills west of the town is the **Bassin Bleu**, a triple waterfall where each cascade drops into a rockpool. You will be told the legend of a goddess who combs her hair with a golden comb but vanishes with the approach of humans. You are advised to take a guide (you would be lucky to get away without one) and they will encourage you to go by horse.

On the northern side of the peninsula, where the rugged landscape has a rare physical beauty, you pass through **Léogane**, supposedly the city of the Arawak Queen Anacoana who ruled at the time of the Spaniards' arrival, and then climb into hills of banana and coffee plantations before descending into **Miragoâne**. Off the road to Les Cayes is a lake where birdwatchers can spot many of the great Caribbean shorebirds—magnificent frigatebirds, blue herons, white ibises and ungainly purple gallinules with overlong toes.

The tarmac road crosses over the mountains, passing the *cailles,* the wattle and daub shacks of the small Haitian farmers, and then skirts the south coast and comes to **Les Cayes**, situated on a large fertile agricultural plain. Vache Island sits in the bay about 30 minutes from the town. You can hire a motorboat to get there for the day.

From Les Cayes the increasingly rough road crosses back over to the north coast towards the town of **Jérémie**, where the old colonial-style buildings stand in faded grandeur, its coffee wealth now diminished. The town was the home of the father of Alexandre Dumas, the author.

North of Port-au-Prince

The main road to the north and Cap Haïtien runs along the coast as far as the town of St Marc, from where it descends into the Artibonite Valley, flooded in places to create ricefields, but dry enough in others for cacti to line the hills. At **Gonaïves**, just under a hundred miles from the capital, Dessalines proclaimed Independence in 1804. From here, the main road climbs to over 2000ft into the extraordinarily lush hills of the Massif du Nord.

There are two waterfalls inland north of Port-au-Prince. Closest to the city is the **Ville Bonheur** waterfall, southwest of Mireblais (also the scene of a very popular pilgrimage for the Haitian Catholics and *vodunistes* each year on 16 July, in memory of an appearance of the Virgin Mary). The '*saut d'eau*' is made up of several streams that cascade 100ft on to rocks in a maelstrom of spray. More remote from the capital is the **Bassin Zim**, close to the town of Hinche, where two cascades tumble 100ft out of the thickest rainforest.

The **Cap**, as Haiti's second city is known, lies on the north coast about 150 miles from Port-au-Prince. In French colonial days, Cap Haïtien was the island's capital (called Cap Français), a city so illustrious that it was known as the 'Paris of the Antilles' (as was St Pierre in Martinique later on). Some of the grand buildings remain, but most were destroyed in the slave rebellions in the 1790s. Isolated from Port-au-Prince, it always had an independent attitude, but this was too much for Papa Doc Duvalier who cut it off and let it fall into decay. Today it has a population of around 100,000.

Close by is the town of **Milot**, from where Christophe ruled his northern kingdom. His magnificent palace, the **Sans Souci**, was built in 1813 above the town, and was supposed to rival Versailles. It was partly destroyed in an earthquake in 1842 and the marble floors of the galleries are gone, but the design of the palace can be seen in the surviving walls and the last of the yellow plaster remains in places.

But Christophe's most lasting monument stands at the top of a mountain, 3000ft above the town. The **Citadelle** (*open till 5pm; adm includes Sans Souci*) broods like a vast colossus on the peak of Mt Bonnet à l'Evêque, a tropical Gormenghast. It is a two-hour walk in the heat of the Caribbean sun to get there, and yet every stone that was used to build it was carried up between 1804 and 1817. The whole population of the north was involved, about 200,000 people, of whom an estimated 20,000 died. Their megalomaniac leader Christophe just mixed their blood into the mortar. When it was completed, he was supposed to have impressed visiting dignitaries with the loyalty of his troops by marching them into the abyss. The walls are more than 100ft high and 30ft thick in places, arrowslits (for cannon) were 4 feet wide, there were 365 cannons, weighing 5 tons each, and 250,000 cannonballs—10,000 soldiers could hold out here for a year. The Citadelle is so vast that it makes the mountain on which it squats look square from 20 miles. From Milot you can walk the 4–5 miles and 3000ft, or you can take a horse. If you have a car, you can drive to within half a mile. **Bois Cayman**, also near the town, is reputedly where the slaves would meet at the time of their rebellions two hundred years ago.

If you explore the northwestern peninsula, one of the least touched parts of Haiti, you will find no restaurants or guest houses. Stock up with food and drink in Gonaïves or Port de Paix and take extra fuel as there are no petrol stations between the two towns. Roads (tracks) are rough, particularly after rains, and many of the villages are linked to the road by footpath. It is possible to visit **Ile de la Tortue**, the old stronghold of the buccaneers. Life is very basic there too.

© (509)–   ***Where to Stay***

There are a few hotels and guest houses in the centre of Port-au-Prince. Most of the best hotels are off the road leading to Pétionville or in Pétionville itself. There are not many traditional Caribbean beach hotels in Haiti, but you will find some wonderful creole town houses. Few visitors mean that prices are fairly low at the moment. An energy tax is often levied and service is usually charged at 10%.

Port-au-Prince and Pétionville

El Rancho, PO Box 71, rue José de San Martin, just off the Panaméricaine, (✆ 57 2080/4, ● 57 4134; *moderate*), 3 miles from the city centre, perches on the hillside above the plain, with a terrace for tea and dinner overlooking the swimming pools and dip and sip bar. The hotel has a touch of colonial Spain in the arches and orange roof-tiles and some rooms are sumptuously decorated, with massive mahogany furniture and local works of art. It has recently been renovated. Also tennis courts and a masseur, casino and dancing (Fri).

Close by is the **Montana Hotel**, PO Box 523, rue Cardozo, (✆ 57 1920/1, ● 57 6137; *moderate–cheap, all taxes included*), with just 24 rooms set around a modern town-house with spectacular views over the city and the bay beyond. Glorious swimming pool and a tennis court and gardens.

A particularly nice hotel in Pétionville is the **Villa Créole**, PO Box 126 (✆ 57 1570/1, ● 57 4935; *moderate*), another elegant retreat just beyond *El Rancho*. You are luxuriously cocooned from Haitian life on the balcony—large poolside veranda and restaurant, tennis courts and comfortable rooms, recently upgraded.

On the Place St Pierre, in the centre of town, you will find the **Hotel Kinam** (✆ 57 6525/4557, ● 57 4410; *moderate–cheap*), which has excellent prices. It is set in an old town house that has been restored, and the rooms, neat with white tiles and wicker furniture, have been added behind in mock-gingerbread blocks on two sides of the swimming-pool. There is also a good restaurant. The menu is French and creole (or a *menu léger* if you want it)—*poulet djon-djon* or *cabrit boucane* (grilled goat) in *sauce 'ti malice*.

The **Hotel Oloffson**, PO Box 260 (✆ 23 4000/4101, ● 23 0919; *moderate–cheap*) is on the rue Capois not far from the Port-au-Prince city centre. It is one of the Caribbean's classic hotels, a magnificent gingerbread town-house, tin-roofed and turreted and dripping in the most luxurious fretwork. It was made famous by Graham Greene as the setting for *The Comedians*. The bar and balconies, which overlook the gardens above the town, collect an interesting crowd and serve excellent rum punch. Rooms in the main house are decorated with antiques and there are more modern rooms in a block behind. The owner has a band, who make a fair amount of noise when they are practising.

In the town centre, on the eastern side of the Place des Héros is the **Plaza Holiday Inn**, (✆ 23 9800/9773, ● 22 0766; *cheap*), blocks set around a pool in a garden festooned with tropical plants. It is mainly used by businessmen. Close by is the **Hotel Park** (✆ 22 4406), with clean and simple rooms.

The **Visa Lodge Hotel** (✆ 49 1202/3/4 or 46 2662) is also popular with businessmen; in an industrial area near the airport, it has its own pool and restaurant.

On the road up to Pétionville you might try **La Griffone,** 21 rue Jean Baptiste (*✆* 45 4095; *very cheap*) in the foothills, and in Pétionville itself is the **Marabou,** 72 rue Stephen Archer (*✆* 57 1934; *very cheap*), with just 15 rooms. The **Villa Kalawes,** 99 rue Grégoire (*✆* 57 0817; *cheap–very cheap*), is just out of the town on the road to Kenscoff, and in Kenscoff itself is the **Florville** (*✆* 45 2092 in town; *very cheap*). The cheapest rooms can be found in the downtown area of the city, though many are not that salubrious.

South of Port-au-Prince

In **Jacmel** you will find more of Haiti's spectacular creole town houses now acting as hotels and guest houses, including the **Manoir Alexandre** (*✆* 88 2511; *very cheap*) on the hill, surrounded by palms.

La Jacmelienne sur Plage, PO Box 916 (*✆* 88 3451; *cheap*) is a beach hotel set on the black sand bay of Jacmel, soulless because of the lack of visitors during the week; pool, double rooms. Also try **Guy's Guest House** (*✆* 88 3241).

Farther afield in Les Cayes is the **Concorde** (*very cheap*) and in Jérémie there are two small hotels, the **Trois Dumas,** where the author Dumas was born, set in a hillside garden with a view of the town, and the **Pension Fraenkel,** with simple and very cheap rooms.

North of Port-au-Prince

On the coast to the north of the capital there are a number of hotels in an area called the Côte des Arcadins, where Haitians take a break at the weekend, at either the hotels or their villas. The smartest is the **Moulin sur Mer** (*✆* 23 5700/05, *✉* 23 5720; *✆* 22 1918, *✉* 22 7652 in Port-au-Prince; *moderate*) which is set in the grassy expanse of a former plantation on the coast. The estate house, which has five rooms with antique furniture, dates from the 1750s. (There is also a private museum there, which is worth a visit, and a mule-driven mill for crushing sugar-cane.) Another 40 rooms are set in gingerbread blocks painted in red and white running down to the waterfront, all with a/c, fans and screened balconies, with tile floors and large wooden double beds. There is a nice restaurant with classical columns on the shaded beach, with a fantastic view of the Ile de Gonâve.

The **Wahoo Bay Beach** (*✆* 23 2950/53, *✉* 22 5332; *cheap*) is an active resort, also set right on the excellent beach, where there are sports laid on for the guests. 24 reasonably comfortable rooms, with a/c or fans, and wicker furniture.

Kaliko (*✆* 20 8040, *✉* 46 2592 in Port-au-Prince; *cheap*) is another nice small resort, where there are 41 rooms set in rondavels on gradually descending ground on a forested hillside above the beach. There are two rooms per rondavel, and the decor is white with murals on the walls. There is a charming beach club atmosphere (though it is not usually full, of course), with the pool and restaurant just above the sand, among the casuarina pines and palm trees.

Lastly you might try **Ouanga Bay** (*✆* 23 6000; *very cheap*) where there are 25 rooms in a single block on the waterfront. Quiet, with some sports.

If you stop over in Gonaïves on the trip north to the Cap, there are a couple of guest houses, including **Chez Elias** (✆ 74 0318; *cheap*), and just outside the town, **Chez Frantz** (✆ 74 0348; *cheap*).

In **Cap Haïtien** the best hotel is the **Mont Joli**, PO Box 12 (✆ 62 0300/26, 🖷 62 2266; *moderate*), a chic Haitian stopover on the hilltop above the town, where the terraces overlook the town and bay. There are 54 rooms and a swimming pool.

In the gridiron of streets down below you will find an oasis of calm at the **Roi Christophe**, PO Box 34 (✆ 62 0414/0514; *moderate*), which is set in a charming old colonial mansion with faded rustic gentility, with tall doors and nice wicker furniture on black and white floor tiles. There is a pool and an interior courtyard with shaded gardens around the hotel. There is a number of guest houses in the town, cheap, simple and mostly clean. Try **A à Z**, an old colonial town-house on the main square across from the cathedral and the **Pension Colon** on the waterfront.

About 5 miles west of the Cap the **Cormier Plage Hotel**, PO Box 70 (✆ 62 1000; *moderate–cheap*), has 30 rooms which are scattered along the seafront, shaded by a screen of trees. The hotel restaurant is good, especially for locally caught seafood.

✆ *(509)–* **Eating Out**

Though the colonial connection was severed almost two centuries ago, the Haitians maintain a sympathetic link with the French in their treatment of food, and Haitian creole cooking is excellent. They use the fish and the seafood of the Caribbean and cover them with strong creole sauces—lobster and lambi swim in thick and spicy oil and the traditional Caribbean chicken comes crisp and flavoured with lime or coconut. The French

Haiti Directory

getting there

The main airport (✆ 46 0642 or 46 4105) is 13km from the capital Port-au-Prince, on the north side of Delmas. A taxi into town costs US$15–20; a cheaper alternative is to take a *taptap*. Some flights and charters fly into **Cap Haïtien** on the north coast. There are two points of entry on the Haitian border with the Dominican Republic, at Jimani in the south and at Ouanaminthe in the north. There is a departure tax of US$25, usually payable in dollars, and a 10 gourdes security tax, payable in local currency.

By air from Europe: Air France (✆ 22 1700, 46 2085/6) has a weekly flight from Paris (Thurs). From other cities in Europe you will need to change planes, which is most convenient in Miami.

By air from the USA and Canada: Direct links to Haiti can be made from Miami; with flights on American Airlines, Haiti Trans Air, Hanair and Halisa Air. American Airlines expatriate community make sure that there is plenty of traditional French cuisine too, and you will even be offered snails and frogs' legs. Haiti's fertile hills produce all the Caribbean vegetables, including plantain and breadfruit, which are served at all creole tables, and fruits, from pineapple to papaya, which make their way into the delicious ice creams and sorbets. Even in the few small places in downtown Port-au-Prince the food is good—you will find traditional Caribbean cook-ups with rice 'n' peas or *tassot* (dried and grilled chicken or pork)—as are the barbecued roadside snacks, though these are best left alone for the first few days unless you think that your stomach is up to it. The local beer, *Prestige*, is quite drinkable. Prices are mostly listed in Haitian dollars (H$). Categories are arranged according to the price of a main dish: *expensive*—US$15 and above; *moderate*—between US$8 and $15; *cheap*—US$8 and below.

The smartest restaurants around the capital are in Pétionville. **Chez Gérard**, 17 rue Pinchinat, near Place St Pierre, (✆ 57 1949; *expensive*) is set in its own profuse tropical garden. You start at the bar in large leather armchairs, and then move on to tables set out on terraces beneath columns and arches, for French and creole fare—poached red snapper or duck in green pepper sauce followed by chocolate marquise. *Closed Sun.* At **Les Cascades**, 73 rue Clerveaux (✆ 57 0724; *moderate*), you take cocktails upstairs before descending to the level of the waterfalls and the tropical greenery to dine. The menu is French with a lot of seafood; you can try scallops topped with shrimp or veal in a creamy ginger sauce. *Closed Sun.* You might also try **La Souvenence**, 8 rue Gabart (✆ 57 7688; *expensive*), gourmet French dishes. **Bolero**, 18 rue Louverture, between Grégoire and Lamarre (✆ 57 1929), serves pasta and pizza. **Le Coin des Artistes**, 59 rue Panaméricaine (✆ 57 2400), offers seafood, as does **La Voile**, 32 rue Rigaud (✆ 57 4561). There are very few restaurants in downtown Port-au-Prince.

✆ (509)–

(✆ 22 4300, 23 1314/6, 49 0312) offer two flights daily from New York and Miami. Halisa Air (✆ 23 4001, 49 2871/72) flies from Miami (Mon–Fri). Air Canada (✆ 46 0441/2) flies once a week from Montreal.

By air from Central America: Copa (✆ 23 2326/27) offers flights from Panama City (Sun, Wed).

By air from other Caribbean islands: Many links have been cut since the recent troubles, but ALM (✆ 22 0900, ✆ 46 1090) flies from Curaçao (Mon, Tues, Fri) and Air France makes the link from Martinique and Guadeloupe a couple of times a week. Air Guadeloupe has weekly flights from Pointe-à-Pitre (Sun), Santo Domingo (Tues) and San Juan ((Wed). **Cap Haïtien** on the north coast is linked nearly each day to the Turks and Caicos Islands and directly to Miami on charter flights.

tourist information

There is not much tourism in Haiti at the moment and there are no tourist boards around the world. You might get some information by contacting the embassies. In **France**, the Ambassade d'Haiti is at 10 rue Théodule Ribot, 75017 Paris (✆ 47 63 47 78).

In Haiti itself, contact the **Secrétairerie d'Etat au Tourisme**, 8 rue Légitime, Port-au-Prince (✆ 23 5631 or 23 2143, ✆ 23 5359), or **Maison du Tourisme**, 35 rue Capois et rue Magny, Port-au-Prince (✆ 22 8659, ✆ 228896). However, you will also find that travel agents and hotel managers are quite well informed. There are many missionaries in Haiti and in remote areas they can be helpful.

In a **medical** emergency, contact the Hôpital Canapé Vert, rue Canapé Vert, Port-au-Prince (✆ 45 1052/3/0984). If you are having problems, most hotels have an English-speaking doctor on call.

Emergency phone numbers: For **police**, call ✆ 114. For an **ambulance**, call ✆ 118.

The **IDD code** for Haiti is ✆ (509), followed by a six-figure national number. Just the six digits should be dialled within Haiti. The **US Embassy** is near the waterfront in Port-au-Prince on Harry Truman Boulevard (✆ 22 0354) and the **British Consulate** is at the Hotel Montana, PO Box 1302, Port-au-Prince (✆ 57 3969, ✆ 57 4048). The **Dominican Consulate** is at the Hotel El Rancho, 121 rue Panamericaine, Pétionville (✆ 57 1208).

Strangely, the official **language** in Haiti is French. You will find that in the towns French is enough to get by, but in the country it is not that widely understood. English is understood in the tourist hotels, and Spanish is useful, as many Haitians are fluent in the language. Around 90 per cent of the Haitians communicate in *kreyol*, an extraordinary mix of French and African that has grown into a new language. Of all the French creoles in the Caribbean (there are others in the French Antilles), this is the hardest baked and it is certainly not easily comprehensible even with French. You will see expressions written in kreyol on the taptaps and daubed on the walls. There is a different spelling system from the official French, but if you read it out loud you can sometimes hear the French meaning.

tour companies

Agence Citadelle, ✆ 23 5900 or 22 5900, Place du Marron Inconnu
Chatelain Tour, ✆ 23 2962
Continental Tour, ✆ 23 0611
Southerland Tour, ✆ 23 1600
Sans Souci, ✆ 45 6980
Continental Travel Service, ✆ 22 1752 or 23 0611

festivals

Carnival is the principal festival in the Haitian calendar and celebrations take place each Sunday starting on Epiphany (6 January) and culminating on Mardi Gras just before Lent. Costumed dancers fill the streets, all strutting in time to *ra-ra bands* and following the bandwagons (articulated lorries stacked with speakers).

The Haitian Independence Day is 1 January, also known as *Jou d'Ian*, on which wreaths are laid at the statue of the Marron Inconnu in Port-au-Prince. Each town and village has its *fête patronale*, in honour of their patron saint. For forthcoming celebrations, ask around.

money

The official currency of Haiti is the *gourde*. The currency was introduced by King Christophe at the beginning of the last century, when he supposedly made the gourde or calabash (a large fruit with a hard exterior that can be used as a bowl) into the currency, slowly introducing notes to replace them. The name remains. The exchange rate used to be fixed at 5 gourdes to the US dollar, and although this is no longer the case, five gourdes is still referred to for ease as a *'dollar haïtien'* (H$). If you go off the beaten track, you should get hold of some gourdes.

At present, the rate is US$1 = 16.25 gourdes (or US$1 = H$3.25), although obviously this is subject to fluctuation. You should bring either US dollars or French francs with you; other currencies such as sterling can be changed, but at a very poor rate.

The US dollar is not really legal currency beyond the tourist hotels and restaurants, which can accept traveller's cheques and credit card bills in dollars. You will be approached in the streets by characters flicking a wad of notes. Dealing on the street is not illegal but is not recommended: you are advised to be cautious and discreet. However, businesses that deal in foreign goods do need hard currency to buy in their products, so they have been known to buy dollars at a preferential rate. Carry around plenty of small change. **Banking** hours are weekdays 9–1. **Government offices** keep hours of 8–noon and 1–4.

maps and books

Haiti has quite a literary tradition of its own and has inspired plenty of books by writers from other countries. One of the country's earliest literary sons was Alexandre Dumas, author of *The Three Musketeers* and *The Count of Monte Cristo*. The Cuban Alejo Carpentier wrote a magical representation of life under Christophe, including the building of the Citadelle, in *A Kingdom of this World*.

In the 1930s the Haitians re-evaluated their culture and their African heritage much as other Caribbean writers did. Perhaps the best novel from this period was about Haitian peasant life, called *Les Gouverneurs de la Rosée*, by Jacques Roumain. It was published posthumously in 1944 (Heinemann put out a translation under the name *Masters of the Dew*). Other works by Roumain include *La Montagne Ensorcelée*. Another excellent author of the period was Jacques Stephen Alexis, who wrote a number of novels including *Compère Général Soleil, Romancero aux Etoiles* and *L'Espace d'un Cillement*. More modern, *The Beast of the Haitian Hills*, by the brothers Philippe and Pierre Marcalin, tells a fatal tale of peasant and voodoo life.

The Trinidadian historian C. L. R. James treated the subject of the Haitian revolution in *The Black Jacobins*, an angry and extremely powerful book that was first published in 1938. *From Dessalines to Duvalier* by David Nicholls is an excellent history of Haiti for those who would enjoy a detailed account of the country since the rebellion and Independence.

Many books look at the sensational side of Haitian life and mystery, of which the most famous is probably *The Magic Island* by W. B. Seabrook, published in 1929. An authoritative and scholarly view can be found in Alfred Métraux's *Le Vaudou Haïtien*. The American anthropologist Zora Neale Hurston's work *Tell my Horse* describes a visit to Haiti earlier this century and tells some stories of voodoo. A more recent and frightening tale of a scientist's explorations into the supernatural is told in Wade Davis's *The Serpent and the Rainbow*.

Graham Greene's novel, *The Comedians*, describes the oppressive life under 'Papa Doc' Duvalier in the sixties. The inspiration for the hotel is the Oloffsen in the southeast of town. This book was once banned in the country. Brian Moore's *Another Life* tells a story similar to that of Aristide in fictional form. Two recent travel books are *Best Nightmare on Earth*, by Herbert Gold (Grafton 1991) and *Bonjour Blanc* by Ian Thomson (Hutchinson 1992).

Audubon, the great bird artist who was the inspiration for all the Audubon birding societies, was from Haiti.

watersports

Haiti is not very well organized for sports, but it is possible to find some watersports, windsurfing and sailing, through the beach hotels. Try the beach hotels north of the capital particularly at Ibo and Kyona beach. There is a marina at Ibo beach where you can fix up a deep-sea fishing trip.

Diving: There is a superb coral reef at Sand Cay out in Port-au-Prince harbour (it is also good for snorkelling). The other main reefs are on the island of Gonâve in the bay, a half-hour boat trip from the hotels. Labadie on the north coast has good snorkelling.

other sports

On land there are few sports on offer.

Tennis: Courts can be fixed up through the hotels.

If you have the stomach for a **cockfight** after Sunday lunch then you can go to a *Guaguère* and watch the frenzy of the audience and the two poor battling cocks.

Miniature football: In the Haitian streets you will also see an entertaining version of this game, played with five a side and a goal 2ft high. It is very skilful and fun to watch.

Havana Cathedral

Cuba

To call Cuba an enigma is an understatement. The region's largest island takes everything Caribbean to the logical conclusion, from perfect beaches and fine scenery to rich culture and cuisine. Yet politically it is like nowhere else on earth, let alone the Caribbean: the last relic of state socialism, a communist outpost moored 90 miles south of Key West, Florida.

Presiding over 11 million people is a seemingly invincible leader. Fidel Castro—variously described as *el lider maximo, el comandante, el jefe,* or simply *El*—came to power on the first day of 1959 after a three-year struggle with an archetypal Latin dictator, Fulgencio Batista. Castro shows no sign of loosening his grip on the country as the century draws to a close. Cuba's geo-political status, as ideological thorn in the side of nine US presidents and hence off-limits to American tourists, means it differs from all the other Antilles. A few US visitors circumvent the tight economic embargo, but the absence of large numbers of Americans means the social character of the place is very different from that of its neighbours.

From a Caribbean perspective, Cuba looks like an alligator, a large and threat-ening predatory beast that might switch its tail and lunge at the smaller creatures in its wake. So it might when it comes to Caribbean tourism. When Cuba finally opens up to American visitors it could draw at a stroke many of the tourists upon whom the smaller islands depend. But look again at the map and you will see that Florida is poised above Cuba like a great incisor about to close on the Yucatan Peninsula, perhaps catching Cuba by the tail. As far as the United States are concerned, Cuba looks like a wriggling tiddler.

Times are slowly changing in Cuba in response to the dire state of the economy, but communism, Cuban-style, is still everywhere in the island—in the rhetoric of the seemingly invincible leader, Fidel Castro, in the hideous post-revolutionary buildings, in the sinister state bureaucracy, and in the queueing that is a way of life. Yet beneath this communist overlay the typical themes of the Hispanic Caribbean ring through, in the beaches and palms, in the relentless *salsa* music and the easy-going, multi-racial population.

At 750 miles from east to west and averaging around 60 miles in width, Cuba is about as large as all the other Caribbean islands put together. Its 44,000 square miles make it about the same size as England or Pennsylvania. It lies at the mouth of the Gulf of Mexico in the northwest of the Caribbean, just south of the Tropic of Capricorn. Cuba is as beautiful as anywhere in the Caribbean. It has three magnificent mountain ranges—in the west, the Sierra de los Organos; the Sierra Escambray in the centre; and the Sierra Maestra in the southeast. In between, the undulating plains are immensely fertile. Seeds seem to explode in the rich red-brown earth, growing into the swathes of sugar-cane and the tobacco for which Cuba is celebrated. And wrapped around the island are some of the best beaches in the world.

Of Cuba's 11 million people, one-fifth live in and around Havana, the capital, in the northwest of the island. As in the other former Spanish Caribbean

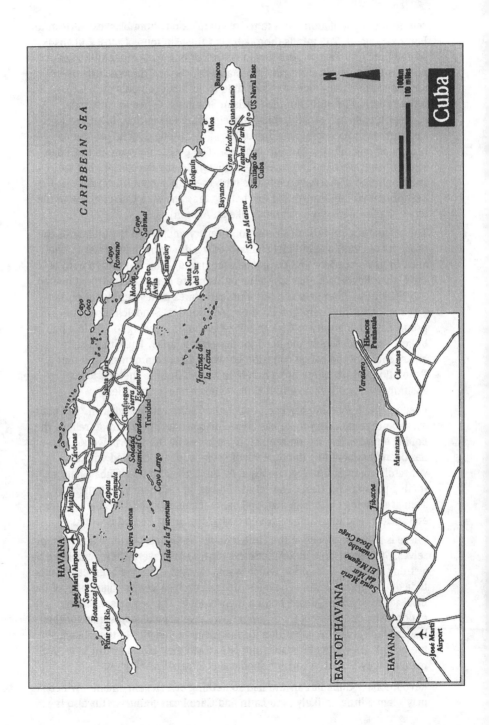

colonies, the population has a range of complexions from blackest African to European blond. The mix is thorough, and the skin tone of most Cubans is somewhere in between. Although a certain draining of colour still takes place as you move to more privileged areas of society, there is little overt racial discrimination: one of the notable social achievements of the Revolution has been to diminish racism. Standards of health care and education have increased dramatically since the Revolution, too. Even after the cataclysmic economic decline of the early nineties, social provisions remain among the best in Latin America. The position of women in Cuban society may have been improved considerably by the Revolution, but the Latin tradition of *machismo* remains with the Cuban men (they joke that the best thing that the Spanish did for them is the *mulatta,* a Cuban girl with the looks of a Spaniard, who can move like an African).

The art and the rhetoric of Revolution is everywhere—on the billboards the thoughts of Lenin and of Fidel stand side by side. Cubans still refer to one another as *compañero* and *compañera* (comrade). Che Guevara, a hero of the Cuban Revolution, has lost none of its lustre here. Dot-matrixed now, this 'Knight without flaw and without fear' stares benevolently out on the Cubans, exhorting them to fulfil their social duties. Schoolchildren still promise eternal loyalty to Che and the Revolution, vowing to 'die in a hail of bullets like Che' should the need for martyrdom arise. The Cuban state makes much of the handy collusion between Che, communism and the Revolution, which blurs into a non-holy trinity. But the rhetoric looks absurdly overwrought now that Cuba stands alone in its beliefs.

Even so, the leadership has been reluctant to soften state socialism. The liberalization that has taken place has been timed astutely by Castro to relieve the boiling tensions in a nation brought to its knees by the superpowers. Cuba has been hammered by the removal of Soviet support, coupled with a vengeful economic embargo imposed by the United States—Cuba's natural trading partner. Yet Castro has let the brakes off sufficiently with measures such as allowing Cubans to own dollars, to maintain stability in the economy and society, and tourism has shored up the regime as he said it would.

There is an ambivalence to the United States on the part of the Cubans themselves. State-sponsored anti-American propaganda is everywhere, amplified by a strong streak of Latin pride which wants to stand up to the overbearing attitude of the United States. The main effect of each successive tightening of the blockade is to unite Cubans behind their regime. The people are solidly nationalistic and many of them, even now, have a genuine affection for their leader who carved out a position for the island in defiance of the 'colossus in the north'. They would certainly not like to see their island return to its pre-revolutionary state as a corrupt unofficial colony of Washington.

Revolutionary Cuba has always had something of a siege mentality, which may seem a little unlikely for a Latin and Caribbean country. This also is partly sloganeering, but comes not without some good reason: the failed Bay of Pigs action of 1961 is merely the most notable example of US action against Cuba. There have been plenty of other attacks on the country's leader, and some on its industry too. The army and police, instruments of state security, have frightening power. Yet the average visitor will be blissfully unaware of political tensions. Even in their hardship the Cubans have an explosive vitality that filters into everyday life. All foreigners can expect to be treated with kindness, respect and genuine interest—though hustling has begun and instances of robbery and muggings have increased.

Music is a national pursuit, and you will hear the compulsive rhythms of *rumba*, *son* and *salsa*, blasting out of ancient Soviet loudspeakers, or played by impromptu bands at the street corner and in the bandstands in town squares. Four centuries of Spanish heritage also ring clear in Cuban life. In the old colonial town centres you will find *plazas* overlooked by beautiful churches and old houses with wrought-iron balconies. Old Havana is both stunning and decrepit—a square mile of colonial palaces and colonnaded streets.

Of course, it is possible to have a typical Caribbean sun, sea and sand holiday here. Though it is firmly at the primitive end of the Caribbean tourism league, Cuba has the resorts and beaches, 10-mile strips in places with idyllic offshore cays—but for the traveller who wants to explore beyond the coconut oil and jet-skis, there is a stimulating and increasingly vibrant island waiting just beyond the beach. As the island climbs back towards its rightful place as *de facto* Caribbean supremo, there could not be a better time to visit Cuba.

Suggested Itinerary

If you have just a couple of weeks in Cuba, the best way to divide your time is to begin with a few days in Havana, enjoying the colonial city and the newly opened array of hotels, bars and restaurants—some old, pre-revolutionary favourites are being rapidly restored. If you have a strong interest in tobacco you could head for the plantations and cigar factories west of the capital in Pinar del Río, making sure to take the coastal road one way. Otherwise, go east. Take the rickety old 'Hershey' train through the canefields to Matanzas and on to the superb if touristy beach at Varadero, Cuba's best place for watersports and sophisticated nightlife. Then start wending south, calling in at the old port of Cárdenas, a typically drowsy provincial town just a few miles from the flashy resort area, and the Indian village reconstructed in the swamp of Guamá—one of the best areas for wildlife anywhere in the Caribbean. Just south, the beach resort of Playa Larga is scattered with memorials to the repelling of the Bay of Pigs invasion.

Moving east along the coast, the scenery becomes more dramatic as you pass the city of Cienfuegos en route to the jewel in Cuba's colonial crown—Trinidad, at the foot of the Sierra Escambray mountains.

If time allows, continue through a string of handsome cities—Sancti Spíritus, Camagüey, Holguín—to the heartland of the Revolution, Santiago de Cuba and the Sierra Maestra mountains where Fidel and Che established a power base. The best is yet to come as you move east to Guantánamo, past the chunk of Cuban territory in the possession of the US Navy, and to the port of Baracoa—the first town to be established in Cuba, and the last call for most visitors.

History

Columbus landed in Cuba on his first voyage to the New World, touching the eastern end of the island on 27 October 1492 as he sailed south from his first landfall in the Bahamas. Confidently he sent off emissaries to find the Imperial court of Japan (he presumed he had discovered the East Indies), but all they found were fifty Arawak huts. He explored the south coast on his second voyage in 1494, but he never accepted that Cuba was an island. It was first circumnavigated in 1508 by Sebastian de Ocampo, whose son Diego sent Spanish settlers from Santo Domingo in 1511. The *conquistador* Diego de Velázquez arrived with 300 men, to be met by the Arawak chief Hatuey, originally from Hispaniola, who roused the Indians into resistance. Hatuey besieged the Spaniards in their fort for three months, but was betrayed and captured. He was offered salvation if he became a Christian, but preferred not to go to heaven, fearing that it was full of Spaniards. Hatuey's name lives on in Cuba as the country's first revolutionary and on the country's leading beer. His people were wiped out within fifty years; just a few Amerindian features can be seen in the faces in the Baracoa region in the extreme east. Velázquez founded seven *villas,* or fortified towns, ranged mostly along the southern shore of the island from Baracoa to Batabanó—the original site of the capital, Havana.

Cuba was eventually to become one of the jewels in the Spanish Crown, but initial development was slow. Without the precious metals found elsewhere in the Spanish colonies, the settlers could do little besides growing tobacco and curing hides. They were also constantly at the mercy of pirate raids. Sir Francis Drake besieged Havana in 1586 and failed, but the likes of Henry Morgan and Montbars the Exterminator held whole towns to ransom. Their main target, though, was the yearly *flota,* the fleet that transported the combined riches of Central and South America back to Spain. It would assemble in Havana harbour and so steadily the town grew in importance, becoming capital in 1589. In 1628, Piet Heyn, at the head of the Dutch West India fleet, captured the entire *flota* and its treasure worth millions within 100 miles of Havana.

Havana became one of the three richest and finest Spanish colonial cities, alongside Mexico City and Lima. Spain officially maintained a monopoly of the trade and the merchants became incredibly wealthy—their magnificent houses are still to be seen. Away from the city, the country languished, involved mainly in small agriculture, and making a bit on the side through smuggling. It was not until a British invasion in 1762 that the island was opened up to traders of all nations. The economy boomed.

The British introduced sugar, a crop that was to change the face of the island to this day (Cuba is still one of the world's largest exporters of sugar). At the end of the 18th century, when the rule of law in France's richest colony, Saint Domingue (now Haiti), collapsed, Cuba became the main sugar island in the West Indies. Slaves had to be brought in their thousands to cultivate the cane and over the next hundred years Cuba developed into one of the most brutal slave regimes. The unfortunate Africans were worked for as much as 19 hours per day, seven days a week. One in ten died each year, and as many as a quarter would be ill at any time. Despite the abolition of slavery in most other Caribbean islands by 1848, slavery continued in the Spanish colonies until 1886. The industry was run on mutual fear, with the call 'Remember Haiti!', as a reminder of what would happen in a slave rebellion. The Torre de Iznaga, a slave watchtower near Trinidad, was the tallest building on the island when it was built in 1820.

After the Independence of the South American republics and Mexico at the beginning of the 19th century, Cuba was the last remaining 'Jewel in the Spanish Crown'. There was anti-colonial unrest and an Independence movement began to crystallize, calling for the abolition of slavery. The Cubans rebelled in 1868, led by the landowner Carlos Manuel de Céspedes. Now celebrated in a thousand street names, Céspedes freed his slaves as a gesture and then armed them. There followed ten bitter years of war against the Spanish authorities. Céspedes died in 1874, but his movement was carried on by men such as Antonio Maceo and Máximo Gómez, whose vast statue stands on the Malecón in Havana. After 200,000 people had died, a truce was drawn up in 1878, but within two years the Cubans had rebelled again under Calixto García, and this time were brutally crushed.

The Spanish sent 250,000 troops to control the population of one million, but fighting broke out again in 1895. This insurrection was inspired by José Martí, a respected author and journalist. Martí was killed in an ambush before he had fired a shot, but he is still considered the hero of Cuban Independence (revered by communists and anti-communists alike) and you will see his bust in every town on the island. The whole country rose up against the colonial authorities and by 1897 the rebels had forced the Spaniards to concede autonomy, but they were set to fight for complete Independence. In 1898, however, the Americans intervened, officially because their warship, the USS *Maine,* was blown up in Havana harbour (by whom, it was never discovered). With Roosevelt at their head, the Americans defeated the last of the Spanish troops. They would not even allow the Cuban rebels the pleasure of accepting the Spanish surrender. In 1899, in the Treaty of Paris, the Americans took possession of Cuba and Puerto Rico in the Caribbean, and the other Spanish territories of Guam and the Philippines. At the eleventh hour of a long and bitter struggle, independence had been denied at the last minute.

The Americans installed the government, piled in money in investments and reserved the right to intervene again in Cuban affairs 'to preserve its Independence'. As José Martí himself had warned when he spoke of 'historical fatalism', the Americans were in control and it would now be impossible to be independent of their influence. Cuba became a colony in all but name.

For the next thirty years the Cuban Republic was headed by corrupt and ineffectual leaders before it degenerated into dictatorship and gangsterism in the thirties. General Gerardo Machado, elected in a landslide vote in 1924, was ousted in 1933. Eventually the infamous Fulgencio Batista, who had been in the background for twenty years, seized power in a military coup in 1952 and tightened his ruthless and brutal grip on the country. Though the economy had grown considerably over the previous few years and some Cubans lived in style in Havana, the lot of the average Cuban was pitiful. Unemployment was around 50 per cent and nearly a quarter suffered from malnutrition.

The Revolution

The starting date of the Revolution, as it is officially chronicled, was 26 July 1953. A bespectacled lawyer, Fidel Castro, led an attack by 130 young men and women upon the highly fortified Moncada garrison in Santiago. Militarily the assault was an abject failure and most of the rebels were rounded up and tortured or killed. But at his subsequent trial, Castro was to make his mark with a five-hour indictment of the Cuban system that has become known as the 'History will Absolve Me' speech. He was sentenced to fifteen years in jail, but his revolt had caught the imagination of the Cuban people. After twenty months he was released and went into exile in Mexico, from where he launched the revolutionary 26 July Movement (M-26-7), which devoted itself to the overthrow of the Batista regime. It was here that they were joined by Ernesto 'Che' Guevara, an Argentine doctor.

In October 1956, 82 rebels sailed to Cuba in the small yacht *Granma*, now on display outside the Museum of the Revolution in Havana. They barely made land, and lost most of their equipment in the process. Within a month they had been ambushed by Batista's troops. Only a dozen of them were left to make their way through the Sierra Maestra, the mountains in the southeast of the island. Crucially, two of the survivors were Guevara and Castro. They began to pick off military outposts and build support. Steadily their numbers swelled. Supported by underground movements in the cities, who in turn were rallied to general strikes by the guerrilla radio station, *Radio Rebelde*, the insurrection gained ground all over Cuba. In May 1958, Batista put 10,000 men into the Sierra Maestra to defeat the rebels, still numbering only 300, but the assault failed and many of the soldiers went over to the guerrillas. The morale of the Batista regime was broken. As the Revolution spread west, government troops refused to fight. It was only a matter of time before the regime collapsed. In the early hours of 1 January 1959, Batista fled the country. Castro accepted the surrender of the Moncada garrison that he had stormed so unsuccessfully five years earlier, and on 8 January the 31-year-old lawyer entered the capital in triumph.

The M-26-7 movement assumed control of the country. The new government began sweeping educational and agricultural reforms. A huge literacy campaign was introduced, in which students left their schools to live and work in the country for a year, cutting illiteracy to four per cent, the lowest in Latin America. The casinos and brothels for which Havana had become so famous were closed down. There were immediate agricultural reforms and the maximum private landholding became 1000 acres. This was followed by further nationalization of foreign banks and other businesses. These moves understandably alienated the USA, whose interests in Cuba amounted to close on one billion dollars.

The USA reacted by sponsoring the Bay of Pigs invasion attempt by Cuban exiles. Castro oversaw the defence personally and defeated it with ease. The Cubans rallied behind him. And so began the US trade embargo which has gradually tightened ever since. (Now, besides prohibiting direct trade between the two countries, Washington operates draconian controls against companies in other nations that deal with Cuba.)

Forced to look elsewhere for oil and for much of its basic supplies, Cuba turned east. There was little evidence of initial communist inclination on the part of Fidel Castro; his actions were proclaimed to be nationalist and anti-imperialist. But two days after the Bay of Pigs attack, he proclaimed the Revolution to be a socialist one. Later in the year, as the press was muzzled and promised elections were shelved, he said that he was a Marxist-Leninist and would be until the day he died. Opposition and the other groups who had worked independently of him for change in Cuba were shunted aside and silenced. Soviet aid and trade began to replace the US connection, much to Washington's concern.

In October 1962 the situation flared up again with the Cuban missile crisis. Reconnaissance photography revealed that the Soviet Union had begun to ship nuclear missiles to the island, which was a priceless strategic outpost in the western hemisphere. Kennedy sent out the US Navy to intercept the shipment and threatened war unless they were removed. Without consulting Castro, the two superpowers eventually agreed that the missiles would be withdrawn by the Soviet Union if the USA did not invade the island. At one stage, the possibility of 'exchanging' West Berlin for Cuba was discussed between Washington and Moscow.

When communism failed to deliver the optimistic early dreams of the Revolution, intentions for rapid industrialization had to be revised. Sugar remained the island's economic base and it became clear that the 'moral incentives' of working for the state alone were not enough to encourage the Cubans into high productivity. The state became dependent on an extremely favourable trade deal with the USSR, whereby sugar was sold to the Eastern Bloc at inflated prices and oil shipped to Cuba at an artificially low rate. This ultimately amounted to a subsidy of ten dollars per person per day.

The social revolution could now get under way. Sufficient food was made available at minimal prices and education was made available to all. The improvement in health care was something of a miracle: Cuba eradicated the diseases of poverty that had afflicted much of the population under Batista. Microbrigades were sent out to provide housing for the rapidly expanding population (it has doubled since 1959). There are people in Cuba who still live in thatched *bohío* huts, but only by choice. However, since the money from the Soviet Union ran dry on 1 January 1992 living standards have steadily worsened.

As the Revolution becomes middle-aged, Cuba is still under the authoritarian control of the Communist Party, headed by the Central Committee and ultimately the Politburo. Fidel is president of both. At grassroots level, the primacy of the party is maintained by the CDRs (Committees for the Defence of the Revolution), which monitor every aspect of Cuban life, from cleaning up the streets to providing marital advice and informing on black marketeers.

Theoretically there is elective power through the National Assembly of People's Power, but the ideological leader of the country is the Communist Party. There have been many accusations of human rights abuses against Cuba, though the number that the government admits to is low by Latin American standards. However, there are definitely restrictions on personal freedoms such as travel and political activity, which is closely monitored.

The economy is still not efficiently run. With the exception of the tobacco farms, it is mostly state-controlled, though there are now a number of joint ventures with companies from abroad and many of the farms have now passed into cooperative control. Cuba was one of the world's largest sugar producers, but the harvest has fallen dramatically over the last few years. The hard-currency debt is thought to be about US$10 billion. Shortages reached a desperate level in 1994—queues longer than ever, fuel rationed to the point of non-existence, nothing remotely desirable in the shops for local people. The transport systems more or less collapsed. Yet Cuba has now turned the corner, and largely thanks to tourism is now enjoying economic growth. In 1996, for example, World Tourism Organization figures show the island at the top of the Caribbean league for growth, with a 25 per cent rise on the previous year. Much of this comprises low-margin mass-market packages, and of course tourism is a notoriously fickle industry and one which in the past the Cubans have considered trivial and demeaning. It has imposed severe strains on society. Yet it is helping the country to recover from apparent economical calamity.

Politically Cuba has shown little inclination to move with the changes in the post-communist world. There has been no talk of the Communist Party relinquishing ultimate control. But economic liberalization means that everyone is an entrepreneur now. The vitality that seems so naturally Cuban is returning to the island.

Fidel Castro

The world's longest-serving political leader, Dr Fidel Castro Ruz has ruled Cuba since his M-26-7 Movement swept the Batista regime out of the country as the year 1959 dawned. Even after four decades of what has been a turbulent, repressive regime, this charismatic leader still commands the admiration and respect of many. Increasingly, it must be said, these are people outside rather than inside the country; his political stamina and consummate skills are envied by other leaders, who line up to meet him at international events. Within Cuba, his achievements in welfare are becoming less and less significant amongst a young population eager for increased freedom and economic opportunity. But all Cubans recognize that he has carved out a path of Cuban self-respect and independence, in defiance of José Martí's 'historical fatalism' (the inescapable dominance of the USA). To them he is known, affectionately or otherwise, as *Fidel*.

Just across the Florida Straits, of course, he is despised by many of the Cubans in exile. Many Americans also regard him as a harbinger of the communist scourge and would therefore like to see him toppled. The CIA is known to have made several inept attempts on his life using exploding cigars and *femmes fatales*. He uses each attempt to vilify the over-bearing attitude of the 'colossus in the north'.

Fidel still appears in his battle fatigues and cap when he addresses his people, but they have the lustrous sheen of good quality material nowadays. The five-hour speeches and rapturous applause from half a million people have also gone, but he remains an impressive speaker, who will hold forth eloquently and persuasively without notes. The main topic of political conversation throughout the 1990s is who could possibly succeed him (current betting is on power devolving to a triumvirate of young politicians), but for most Cubans—many of whom have never known any other leader—life without Fidel is a difficult concept.

Cigars

It is an ironic twist that the world's most accomplished capitalists prefer cigars made in one of the last vestiges of communism. Despite the years of economic privation, cigars made in Havana and elsewhere in Cuba are still the world's finest. The tobacco plant cannot be mass-cultivated like sugar; it is best tended by an individual farmer, and many of the Cuban tobacco plantations are still in private hands. West of Havana, you will see the tobacco fields and the distinctive *vegas* (drying sheds)—clapboard buildings with shaggy thatch or more modern aluminium roofs—where the leaves are hung over bamboo spars to dry. Then they are baled up according to age and the position on the plant in which they grew and sent off to the factories.

In the factory itself, the cigar-maker stretches out the leaves and cuts the youngest one to size and holds it in his (or, since the Revolution, her) open hand, placing two slightly older leaves with stronger flavour on top. Offcuts and tobacco shavings are then packed in the centre and the cigar is hand-rolled. It gets its shape between boards in a vice, pressed for 20 minutes, turned and pressed again. On removal it is cut at one end for length and then the outer cover, the tenderest leaf of all, is rolled around the exterior (this leaf is slit down the middle and the cigars are rolled alternately left and right). The mouthpiece is sealed with a touch of glue, the labels slipped on and the cigar is sent off to be packed, between thin layers of cedar wood to keep them dry, or in a palm leaf if they are for local consumption. The cigar makers are kept amused and informed by a *lector*, who reads to them from the newspaper as they work. In some factories, their day is also enlivened by visits from tourists.

Monte Cristo, H. Upmann, Romeo y Julietta and Davidoff are among the most celebrated cigars in the world. You can see them being packed in the factories around the island (especially in Pinar del Río). Visits are arranged most easily through Cubatur, for a few dollars. You will have difficulty talking your way into a factory, but you can try.

What happens to the cigars after manufacture is an interesting topic. As a foreigner, you will be constantly assailed by people—mostly youths—whispering that they can sell you cigars. You will be assured that their brother/cousin/friend works in the factory, and can supply cigars at far below the official price. If you show interest, you will be led to a home and shown the goods. Although this is unlikely to be a dangerous move, it is not a sensible way to buy cigars. There is a flourishing black-market trade in second-rate cigars and first-rate boxes and labels. You may be told that the box seal will be broken for you, but that you will then have to buy the contents. Even if the cigars are genuine, the contents are likely to have deteriorated, having been kept in warm conditions rather than in a humidor. And if you try to take cigars out of the country, you could find that they are confiscated if you are unable to produce an official receipt.

The problem with buying legally, from hard-currency stores, is that service is poor and the choice is often absurdly limited. You might as well wait until you are in the duty-free shop at Havana or Varadero airport where, although prices are no different, the range of cigars and care taken of them is about as good as you will find anywhere in Cuba itself.

Note that despite the flourishing black market in Cuban cigars all over the United States, it is illegal to import them to the US.

Music

Within an hour of arriving in Cuba you will discover how central music is to Cuban life. Where most Caribbean islands have a rhythm of their own, Cuba has several, most notably *salsa*. Cuban *salsa* is distinctly Latin, but it is different from the *salsa* of Puerto Rico, which has been influenced by the Neoyorkeñans (Puerto Ricans living in New York). *Salsa* grew out of *son*, with a guitar and a *guiro* (washboard) and heavy drum backing. Other Cuban rhythms include *rumba*, *danzón* and *cha-cha-cha*. All of these are preferable to the endless renditions of *Guantanamera* (the girl from Guantánamo), which you hear bashed out relentlessly and often tunelessly in tourist spots all over the island. This is an example of yet another style, the *guajira*.

Every Cuban town has a music scene that appeals to the whole age-range of population. This may just be a few old gents bashing out tunes in the town square, or it may be within a *casa de la trova*—literally 'house of the troubadours', in practice a state-sponsored hall where bands play and rum is consumed, both with considerable gusto.

At carnival time—Havana's reappeared in 1997, after several years when it was cancelled for economic reasons—look out for the wind-up organs that play old *son* rhythms. Cuban jazz is also excellent, and you might just catch groups such as *Irakere* while you are in town. There is an awful lot of Western pop tosh, too, but fortunately the real Cuban thing shines through.

Cabaret

There are cabarets all over the island, many of them in the tourist hotels, but the most spectacular of them all is definitely the *Tropicana*. Set in the outskirts of the capital, it has changed surprisingly little since Havana was at its sleaziest in the fifties. It is a show of hundreds of dancing girls (and a few men), who appear on catwalks, on trapezes, descending out of trees...

Voluptuous matriarchs act as 'commères', singing and spurring on their cohorts of thrusting beauties to feats of dancing and athletic daring. In unison thirty of them strut around the stage high-kicking, skirts flailing, head-dresses quivering and cascading, thighs up to their ribs, scrunching up their noses at moments of high exertion. A familiar *salsa* pulse drives them on, backed by relentless African drums. It is a celebration of bodies as only the Latin Americans know how.

Eighty US dollars will get two people to and from your hotel, a ringside view of the action and a couple of drinks—that's probably cheaper than it was in the 1950s.

Coping with Cuba

Outside the established tourist network, life in Cuba can be wearing. A fearsome bureaucracy hampers an overloaded system. If your time is short, Cuba can be infuriating, particularly when it comes to travel. From the end of July into August and over the Christmas period, when the Cubans themselves like to go on holiday, things are yet more hectic. You will find that you are in competition with them for the scarce resources.

You will need a fair amount of patience and it is a good idea to take plenty of books to Cuba, to while away time spent in queues. They will be gratefully received when you have finished reading them (English is the Cuban's second language in school). Altogether it may be easier to be a package tourist.

Meal times can be frustrating in the last bastion of state-socialist catering; sometimes, the simplest plate of food can take an hour to arrive. But in the course of a few years, the amount of restaurants has rocketed with the arrival of *paladares*—private restaurants that can serve some exceptional food (but also many dismal dishes). In towns and cities, it is easy to pick up snacks and drinks along the street. The new markets in each town have a good range of fruit and vegetables, and are supplemented out in the country by roadside vendors.

Queueing is something of a way of life in Cuba. Sometimes you have to queue to buy a ticket and then queue to collect your purchase. The Cubans themselves are inured to the practice and simply wait patiently (it can be three or four hours in a state-run restaurant sometimes). Dollars are the answer to avoiding this. If you have to queue, check that you are at the back by asking *último?* or, if you are addressing a woman, *última?* (it means 'last') and then take your place.

Hustling has started up in Cuba and you can now expect to be accosted around the tourist areas much as you would elsewhere in the Caribbean. You will be offered a variety of services or simply asked for money. Hustlers can be very persistent, but clearly it is better not to give in. **Begging** is also on the increase.

Cuba remains reasonably safe, though the economic decline combined with the rise in tourism means that foreigners are becoming targets for robberies more frequently. Be careful after dark in Havana, and anywhere that is crowded with tourists.

Women should have no problem in Cuba other than the occasional over-attentive local—harassment can be verbal, but is rarely physical. Plenty of Cuban men see foreign women as a potential ticket out of the country (Cuban women regard foreign men in the same way), so you may receive a proposal as well as a proposition. A 'wedding ring' can be a convenient defence against a persistent man.

Lastly, the Cubans place restrictions on **photography**. In particular, be careful not to take pictures in the presence of uniformed personnel or around industrial or military installations—this includes happy snaps of Cuban sugar factories and any old forts with aerials sticking out of them. The Cubans say that the security apparatus is still in place, so if you do not want to end up in a pickle like Wormold in *Our Man in Havana*, do not get caught making detailed plans of the inside of a Cuban Hoover. These restrictions may seem absurd, but the regime has keen memories of US attempts to wreck the sugar industry and destabilize the island.

Getting Around

If you like your transportation to have a good deal of planning , then perhaps you should select a different destination. Travelling around the island is one of the main problems—or joys—of a visit to Cuba. Much transport infrastructure crumbled with the economic collapse of the early 1990s, and although services are improving you can still expect to find problems booking seats or arriving at approximately the right hour (or day). Because Cuba is such a large island, this can be stressful in the extreme if you have a tight schedule. And unlike elsewhere in the Caribbean, playing the irate foreigner with officials will not work here.

If nothing else, though, transport is cheap and convivial. At the bottom of the transportational hierarchy is the **hitchhiker**—Cuba is the only place on earth where this practice is regulated by the state. Each town has an official hitching point, where travellers register their destination with an official in curious yellow trousers who wields a clipboard. Any state or private vehicle that passes is required to stop (tourists are not). He or she then instructs the driver to fill up the vehicle with hitchers, who pay a few pesos—usually less than the equivalent bus fare—for the ride. For women, Cuba is one country where hitchhiking is more or less guaranteed to be safe.

Next up is the **passenger truck**, plying a fixed route and offering the chance to stand up in the back for about the same as the bus fare. You may elect to do this simply because of the shortage of **buses**, known locally as *guaguas* (pronounced 'wawa'). These run long-distance (Interprovincial), between the towns within a province (Intermunicipal). The two terminals are often in different places. Interprovincial services (usually large and decrepit ex-Mexican buses) or link the major cities of Cuba. It is pretty well impossible to get a seat on these services because the few seats are understandably reserved for the Cubans themselves. In theory there are frequent direct services between the larger towns and cities, but it is unlikely that you would find a seat on one of these. If you want to try it, the Interprovincial terminal in **Havana** is near the Plaza de la Revolución, on the Avenida Rancho Boyeros (✆ 70 9401).

Intermunicipal *guaguas* link the towns within a province, for a fare of a couple of pesos. These buses tend to be rattly old European models, donated by communities in

France and Spain when they have reached the end of their natural lives. They are uncomfortable and crowded, but they are one of the best exposures to Cuban life. With luck, you might just get a seat.

To guarantee a seat, and often a speedy journey, seek out a *colectívo* (a long-distance share-taxi). These take up the overspill of the national bus network. The average *colectívo* is a grand old Cadillac or Pontiac built some time before 1959 and lovingly preserved. They usually park outside the intermunicipal bus station and depart when they are full, or when the urge takes the driver. Ask around for your destination; they travel as far afield as 100 miles. Prices are roughly three times the fare by bus. You can also rent the entire car and persuade the driver to take you further afield, as an unofficial taxi, at a price.

Tourists are encouraged to travel on **organized bus tours** and it is possible to see many of the main sights within a day's drive of Havana or Varadero if you are prepared to go on a 'day trip', e.g. Trinidad or Pinar del Río. Regular tours are booked through the Cubatur offices in the hotel foyers. Travellers can also buy a transfer only ticket on these organized bus tours. These are wildly expensive (by Cuban standards), but comfortable. It is possible to make the same tours independently by taking a taxi, if you can get a good rate, and then split it between four people. Negotiate with a *colectívo* driver, or indeed anyone who owns any sort of car.

Cuba's **rail** network is pretty impressive, at least in theory. Lines run the length of the country, with branches to the north and south. Travelling by train can give another good introduction to Cuban society as well as offering a relatively flexible method of travel. Seats on trains are more easily accessible by foreigners than buses; you are supposed to buy tickets through the hard-currency organization **Ferrotur**, though for short journeys this is not worth the time, trouble or money. Long-distance services such as Havana–Santiago must be booked through the official channels—expect the trip to cost around forty dollars, and to take anything up to sixteen hours.

Most long-distance services arrive at and depart from Havana's Central railway station, on the southern edge of the colonial city. Foreigners buy tickets in dollars from the Ferrotur ticket office at the far end of the platforms on the north side of the station. Matanzas is served four or five times daily from the station at Casablanca, across the water from the colonial city.

Car rental in Cuba gives independence of travel, but it is expensive. Cuban driving is fairly typical of the Caribbean and so you are advised to keep your eye on the road, rather than the landscape. The main highway is the *autopista*, running from Pinár del Rio in the west, past Havana and along to Santa Clara, where it dissolves into the older *Carratera Central* which straggles down to Santiago and beyond. Road surfaces are dreadful, signposting is poor and lighting nonexistent. Other motor vehicles are rare on Cuban roads, but in their stead you find a motley selection of pedestrians, cyclists, farm machinery and animals.

You could get lucky and rent a car on the spur of the moment, but advance booking is preferable. It is possible to book one before you fly and pick it up at Havana airport. Your home driving licence is valid.

The main **hire firm** in Cuba is Havanautos, which has offices in all the major tourist hotels and the airports, but competition has increased significantly over the past few years with companies such as Transautos undercutting Havanautos. Prices begin at US$40 per day for the smallest, cheapest Mexican-built Nissan. Insurance adds $5-$10 per day on top.

The old coupon system for buying fuel has vanished, and you now fill up at any of the growing number of **Cupet** service stations.

For long journeys, **flying** is an appealing alternative. Fares are low by international standards, such as $80 for the Havana–Santiago hop of over 500 miles, though frequent delays and cancellations make flying an unpredictable experience.

Urban transport offers the most telling insights into the state of the Cuban economy. The principle form of mass transit in Havana and some other cities is the **'Camel'**, an enormous humped vehicle hauled by a gruff old tractor unit. The flat fare for these is 20 centavos, i.e. less than one US cent. These are supplemented by local *guaguas* on fixed routes (fare 20 or 40 centavos, exact change only), and some smaller and more expensive microbuses (fare around one peso). In smaller towns, the only form of transport may comprise a horse towing a carriage crowded with passengers and their possessions. The usual flat fare is one peso.

The other form of motorized urban transport, of course, is the **taxi**—of which there are three basic types. Official *turist taxis* are available in all the tourist areas, and charge fares in dollars—a 3-mile journey will costs around $5. **Local taxis** are popularly known as *los incapturables*, because demand for these 'peso taxis' far exceeds demand; foreigners can expect priority in return for paying in dollars. These two official kinds of taxi are supplemented by almost anyone who owns a motor vehicle of any kind. You can flag down any car and request a ride, and more often than not the driver will be prepared to reach a mutually agreeable price. The same technique applies if you want to rent a car for a day.

In the 1990s, Cuba has become a nation of **cyclists**. More than a million Chinese bicycles have been imported, and these are ridden recklessly all around the island. You can rent them in tourist areas, but serious cyclists should bring their own machines.

Beaches (Clockwise from Havana)

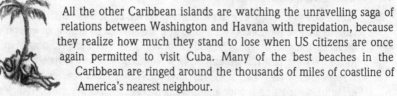

All the other Caribbean islands are watching the unravelling saga of relations between Washington and Havana with trepidation, because they realize how much they stand to lose when US citizens are once again permitted to visit Cuba. Many of the best beaches in the Caribbean are ringed around the thousands of miles of coastline of America's nearest neighbour.

Cuba is relatively flat, at least when compared to other Caribbean islands, and the 1200 or so offshore cays have produced coastlines that slope gently into the sea, the softest sand and superb coral reefs. Around fifty of the beaches (*playas*) have facilities and hotels for the thousands of Cubans who pour out of the cities in trucks at weekends. Others have been developed with tourist hotels, and kitted out with watersports facilities. Yet you do not need to stray too far from the beaten track to find idyllic strands, tucked between the 'dark teeth' of the coral coastline and the shoreline mangrove swamps.

The law declares all beaches in Cuba to be public, though many local people complain that they are not allowed to use the best beaches such as the one at Varadero, the island's premier resort. Topless bathing is not allowed in theory, but is widely practised by tourists.

best beaches

Playas del Este: The closest of the beaches to Havana which are strung out over 20 miles of the northern coastline of Havana province.

El Mégano and the busier **Santa María del Mar**: Good strips of crystalline sand.

Boca Ciega and **Guanabo**: Farther east on the Vía Blanca, the northern coastal freeway, these are the most developed beaches.

Jibacoa: Idyllic bays where the snorkelling is particularly good.

Puerto Esperanza: The mountainous area to the west of Havana has fewer beaches, though there are some attractive bays that are enclosed by lumbering headlands.

Varadero: At 12 almost-uninterrupted miles, one of the longest beaches in the Caribbean—a supreme strand, as much as 40 yards wide and mounded for most of its length with satin-smooth granules of sand that trickle through your toes. It is built up but very popular, mostly with foreigners—it offers all the watersports, evening fun in the bars and discotheques. Varadero is about 100 miles from Havana and 20 from Matanzas. Many visitors fly straight in to Varadero airport and out again after a week or two, blissfully content with the beach and unaware of the rest of Cuba.

La Panchita and **Playa Juan Francisco**: The northern coastline of Villa Clara province is not developed and it is off the beaten track anyway, but among the mangrove swamps you will find small beaches with fishing villages and offshore there are more idyllic sands on the cays.

La Tinaja and the oddly named **XI Festival** beach on the **Punta de San Juan**: North of the remote town of Morón in Ciego de Avila province.

Cayo Coco (with an airstrip), **Cayo Guillermo** and **Cayo Paredón Grande**: In contrast, the islands of the Archipiélago de Camagüey have been chosen for development and so it is easier to get out on to their superb sands and coral reefs. Cayo Coco was the target of a feeble attack by anti-Castro Cuban exiles from Florida, but no impact was made upon the high-grade resort. Farther east are **Cayo Guajaba** and then **Cayo Sabinal**, which can be reached by the day from Santa Lucía.

Santa Lucía: Another 10 miles of idyllic, palm-backed sand with 20 miles of brilliant off-shore coral reefs—good for snorkellers as well as divers. The area is built up, with a marina and hotels with watersports. Of all the resorts in Cuba, this is the most isolated from real Cuban life and culture.

Guardalavaca: As you head east from Santa Lucia the beaches are undeveloped and do not have facilities, so take food and water.

Don Lino: Here you will find a small cove with a hotel where you can get refreshments and windsurfing or snorkelling gear. The reefs continue to the eastern tip of the island. For swimming, try **Playa Corinthia**, a few miles west of Moa. Beyond here there is no discernible beach to **Baracoa**, the place where Columbus first landed.

Yateritas: Round the eastern tip of the island, also popular with the locals.

Punta Berracos, **Daiquirí** (where the drink of the same name was invented a century ago) and at **Siboney** beach: Beaches with facilities as you approach Santiago de Cuba from the east.

There are fewer beaches on the protected southern shore of the island. Much of the shoreline is mangrove swamp, impenetrable forest of the sort that the cruiser Granma encountered when it came ashore in 1956 (near Las Coloradas). If you are dying for a beach in Camagüey, instead of going north, you might try going south through the hill and cattle country to **Santa Cruz del Sur**, where there is an attractive beach and offshore cays and reefs.

La Boca and **Ancón**: Close to Trinidad, each with hotels nearby.

Rancho Luna: Near the mouth of Cienfuegos Bay.

Playa Girón and **Playa Larga**: Backed with sea-grape and palms and shelving very gently into the water.

Cayo Ernst Thálmann: Offshore; you will find more sun-bleached sand and water the colour of aquamarine.

Island Beaches off the South Coast

There are two main archipelagos off the south coast of Cuba, with hundreds of islands, cays and sandbars. In the Batabanó Gulf south of Havana you will find a string of islands stretched between the Isla de la Juventud and Cayo Largo. On the former there are beaches on the south coast, at **Playa Larga** and **Punta del Este**. A series of subsurface reefs and sandbars that just break the waves run east, past the undeveloped Cayo Avalos and Cayo Rosario to **Cayo Largo**, another island that has been developed as a tourist resort. This island is nearly all beach and the water is stunningly blue, and so you can go to any bit of 15 miles of sand between **Playa Sirena** in the southwest and **Playa Tortuga** in the northeast.

Archipiélago de los Jardines de la Reina (the Gardens of the Queen): Another 100-mile string of islands and barrier reefs teeming with tropical fish, off the province of Ciego de Avila.

Isla de la Juventud (Isle of Youth): With so many good beaches to choose from on the mainland, you would not go here merely to sunbathe. But there are many good diving opportunities on Cuba's largest offshore island; *see* p.659.

Flora and Fauna

Cuba, like many of the Caribbean islands, is extremely beautiful and it has a grand variety of flora, varying from thick mountain forest through the extraordinarily fertile plains where sugar-cane (*guarapo*) and tobacco sprout from the rich brown earth, to the dry cactus flats and the coastal mangrove swamps that are home to endless birds and reptiles. Cubans maintain, probably correctly, that the island has the richest flora and fauna in the Caribbean. Of the 60 species of palm, the royal palm is the most magnificent—100ft tall, with an explosive bush and a topmost spike—and it is the national tree. Other palms include the *barrigona*, rather rudely called the *palma puta* because it looks pregnant (Cuban *macho* men will also point out tiny grasses like legs that close up at the touch and make jokes about their women), the traveller's tree that opens like a fan and the stunted fossil palm, recently almost extinct.

Cuban forests were once an excellent source of hardwoods, including mahogany, teak and ebony, of which some still grow. There are many flowering trees, such as the African tulip tree and the flamboyant which explodes into scarlet bloom in the summer. There is one that grows lots of wooden pineapples on its branches.

Real pineapples grow on spiky plants at ground level and are one of the many Cuban fruit crops, some of which are exported. You will also see huge citrus orchards of orange, lemon, lime and grapefruit and more exotic fruits such as soursop, mango and guava. Such produce can now be found freely on sale at markets all over the island.

The white mariposa, the butterfly flower, is Cuba's national flower.

Cuba has a greater variety of animals than the other Caribbean islands, including a range of reptiles from 12ft crocodiles (you can see them in the Zapata peninsula, where they are farmed for their meat), tank-like iguanas, endless lizards and geckos, down to the tiny almiqui, a shrew-like reptile found only in Cuba. There are 14 species of snake, but none of them is poisonous. Rodents include the agouti and the jutia. There is the odd wild boar, introduced by the Spanish as meat in buccaneer days. In the coastal waters there are five species of turtle and the occasional endangered manatee or sea cow.

Insects include nearly 200 species of butterfly and hand-sized tarantulas which will give you a bit of a fright.

The zunzuncito hummingbird is the world's smallest bird, and one of Cuba's 380 local and migratory species. In the forests you will find solitaires, owls and parrots, and on the plains there are hawks and the mournful cattle egrets that keep a daytime vigil with the grazing cattle. Vultures gather in small and ominous groups by the roadside. The Cuban trogon, with its green, red, white and blue colouring, is the national bird. Around the shoreline you will see single pelicans diving and magnificent frigatebirds soaring, looking for other birds to prey on; in the swamps there are herons that stand around on one leg waiting to strike for food, and flocks of flamingos that strut in unison.

Havana

Cuba's capital, La Habana, lies on the northern shore of the island, towards the western end, about 90 miles across the Gulf Stream from Key West in the USA. Its population of just over two million makes it the largest city in the Caribbean. The city was founded in 1514 as San Cristobal de la Habana, but diametrically across the island at present-day Batabanó; after five years it shifted to a magnificent natural harbour on the north coast. Its importance grew as it became the principal port for the Spanish Main. Ships put in here, their last stop before the Atlantic crossing back to Europe. By 1558, the small collection of coral-stone buildings and palm thatch *bohíos* had become the capital of Cuba.

Heading west from the harbour along the Malecón (the Embankment, or sea wall) you will see the history of the city mapped out before you, from the stunning colonnaded courtyards of 16th-century *palacios* in Old Havana, past the stately 19th-century colonial edifices of Habana Central and the vast and luxurious Art Deco palaces thrown up in the thirties and forties in Vedado, to the imposing ferro-concrete monstrosities that followed the Revolution.

The city seems steeped in decay. Initially the Revolution set about correcting the economic imbalance between Havana and the rest of Cuba, which meant putting a higher priority on developing the country than on maintaining the capital. The state discouraged farmers from moving into shanty towns as they have on the outskirts of most other Caribbean capitals—and there has been no money available in recent years to keep up the repairs.

Old Havana

Habana Vieja is by far the most beautiful town in the Caribbean, a view shared by Unesco, which designated Old Havana as a city of world heritage. It is a square mile of glorious colonial palaces ranged in lines along narrow alleys and around handsome plazas. Behind the grey façades of coral rock, embellished with wrought-iron balustrades and stained-glass windows, you will discover idyllic interior courtyards, forested in greenery and overlooked by cloistered walkways. On the cobbled streets and in the colonnades you can almost imagine the merchants of the 17th century clattering past in their carriages. You can wander for days.

Much of the old city is in distressing disrepair. The stucco and plasterwork has crumbled and in places whole façades are shored up with timber spars and scaffolding. Gradually restoration is taking place, mostly with help from European organizations.

A few sections remain of the old city wall. This was started in 1633 to keep out the plague of pirates and freebooters who were roving the islands at that time, but it was not completed until over a century later in 1767. You may hear a cannon fired at 9pm each day, which once warned the citizens to get within the city walls. To protect themselves from sea attack, they slung a chain across the entrance of the harbour.

The oldest part of Havana is the **Plaza de Armas**, where the city's first Mass was said in November 1519, in the shade of an old ceiba (silk cotton) tree and where the neoclassical

Templete has stood since 1754; at present this elegant shrine is under repair, but is due to reopen in 1998. Murals by the French artist Vermay commemorate the event. From here you can see the tiny Giraldilla, Havana's symbol, a statue of a woman holding a cross, who stands atop the tower of the **Castillo de la Fuerza Museum** (*open daily 9–6; adm*). Constructed between 1538 and 1542, la Fuerza is Cuba's oldest surviving fortress. As a tourist attraction, though, it is challenged—the dollar admission charge takes you around a selection of uninteresting rooms which double as dismal art galleries.

At the centre of the Plaza de Armas, surrounded by the royal palms of Cuba, stands a statue of Carlos Manuel de Céspedes, the father of Cuban Independence and hero of the 1868 War of Independence. But his old adversaries still dominate the square around him in the massive **Palacio de los Capitanes Generales**, the seat of the Spanish colonial government. Today this huge palace, which was built between 1772 and 1776, is home to the **Museo de la Ciudad** (the museum of Havana City; *open daily 9.30–6*), dedicated to the history of Cuba. On view are the splendour of colonial days and mementoes of 20th-century Cuban triumphs as well as archaeological and folklore collections. A statue of Columbus stands in the cloistered courtyard. The colonnaded **Palacio del Segundo Cabo**, which stands next to the museum and was built in the same period, is occupied by the Ministry of Culture, but you are permitted to go into the inner courtyard. There are one or two cafés on the square.

A number of other gracious old *palacios* look on to the square and on to the nearby Calle Obispo, including the **Méson de la Flota**, the **Palacio Intendencia**—now the Letras Cubanas Publishing House—and **La Casa del Agua**, where you can get stone-filtered water in metal beakers for 5 centavos. There is also the old university bell, an old pharmacy and herb shop, dressed up as it would have been in the last century, and the **Casa de Las Infusiones**, where you can stop for a vanilla or lemon tea. The **Casa de la Obrapia** (*open Tues–Sat 10.30–4.30, Sun 9–1; closed Mon*) is set in a 17th-century town house with a delightful courtyard and has an exhibition of 18th-century and 19th-century furniture. Downstairs there is a room devoted to Cuban journalist Alejo Carpentier.

On the Calle Oficios, which runs south from the Plaza de Armas, you will find the old **Monte Piedad** (the pawn shop), now the **Museo Numismático**, with Cuban notes and coins on display. A much more intriguing place is the **Museo de Automobile** (*open daily, 9–6*), with some of Cuba's stately old motor cars on view. These include a 1902 Cadillac, Al Capone's 1924 Packard and the lime-green Chevrolet saloon driven (apparently ineptly) by Che Guevara.

The **Plaza de la Catedral**, just northwest of the Plaza de Armas, is another cobbled square enclosed by stunning colonial balconies and colonnades. At its head stands the baroque cathedral itself, originally built by the Jesuits in 1704, with towers of different size. Though it is dedicated to the Virgin Mary, it is usually known as the Columbus Cathedral—the bones of Christopher Columbus were reputed to have spent some years here between 1796 and 1898, brought from Santo Domingo and then taken to Seville. The rest of the square was built in the first half of the 18th century. Directly opposite the Cathedral is the **Museo de Arte Colonial** (*open Tues–Sat 10am–5pm, Sun 10am–1pm; closed Mon*), where there are exhibits of 19th-century furniture and carving. Check out the washstand. In the square you will see a shocked-looking face built into one of the walls. It is in fact a postbox, Cuba's oldest.

The old city is studded with colonial masterpieces: churches, seminaries and convents and old family *palacios*. A third stunning square in Old Havana is the **Plaza Vieja**, to the south of the Plaza de Armas. Look out for the Palacio de la Artesanía on Avenida Tacón, the Palacio del

Arzobispo de la Habana on Calle Chacón, the old Convento de Santa Clara on Calle Sol, now restored, and the nearby Iglesia de Nuestra Señora de la Merced.

Most of the Revolutionary monuments and museums are on the open street between Calles Zulueta and Montserrate, parallel to the Prado—a boulevard with raised gardens and wrought-iron street lamps where Cuban gents congregate to read the paper and foreigners inevitably get nobbled by the hustlers. As you walk south from the Máximo Gómez statue at the harbour mouth, you come first to a tank that was involved in the Bay of Pigs battle, and then the former **Palacio Presidencial**, where Batista only just escaped an attack by 40 students in March 1957 by hiding in a lift. The palace has been turned into the **Muséo de la Revolución** (*open Tues–Sat 10–5, Sun 10–1*), and on its three floors it gives a detailed history of Cuba from the arrival of the Spaniards to the Revolution and beyond, covering moments such as the conquistadors, Eduardo Chíbas's suicide as he addressed the nation on the radio, and conflicts such as the Bay of Pigs. It is a striking collection and gives a good insight to the machinations of the regime. Outside, the cabin cruiser *Granma* sits behind a glass screen.

The modern building next in line is the **Museo Nacional de Bellas Artes** (*open Wed–Sun 9–5*), the National Art Museum, with Cuban rooms and works foreign artists including Goya, Velazquez, Rubens and Turner. At the top of the slope is the most imposing building in Havana—the **Capitolio**, an imposing edifice in the style of the US Capitol in Washington. It was built by the Henderson Corporation in the thirties to house the old Cuban House of Assembly. After being closed for years, it is now open to tourists and constitutes one of the most remarkable sights in the city. While much of Cuba went hungry, no expense was spared to construct this vast marble confection. A 24-carat diamond is embedded in the floor at the centre, marking the spot from which all distances are measured.

From here you can continue south towards Havana's grand old Central railway station. Across the road is the **Casa Natal de José Martí** (*open 9–5 Tues–Sat, 9am–1pm Sun; closed Mon*), where Cuba's independence hero was born. It traces his perambulations in exile (including a visit to Britain in 1894) and gives a strong impression of the man whose image is everywhere .

The western side of the Parque Martí, and the Capitolio, marks the transition to Central Havana, which dates from the last century. This is where you will find most of the capital's shopping streets. It is not a comfortable area in which to stay after dark.

Vedado

As you travel west from Central Havana, you pass through run-down residential streets, but soon these open out into **Vedado** district. Built in the thirties and forties, the huge Art Deco palaces and villas are a reminder of just how luxurious and rich Havana was at that time. The best view of all is from the top of the **Havana Libre Hotel**.

The central street is Calle 23, better known as **La Rampa**, which runs from the Malecón up towards the Columbus Cemetery. At the foot of La Rampa are all the airline offices. As you ascend, you find the **Coppelia** ice-cream parlour on your right and the **Havana Libre Hotel**—formerly the Hilton—on your left.

In the southern area of Vedado, between the Avenidas Rancho Boyeres and Céspedes, you will find the the vast open space of the **Plaza de la Revolución**, dominated by a New Age statue of José Martí and a 380ft obelisk, a masterpiece of supremely ugly concrete architecture. The ground floor is taken up by an exhibition of Revolutionary glories, while the lift to the top yields spectacular views across the Caribbean's largest city.

The square comes into its own when hundreds of thousands collect there to hear Fidel speak, usually at the New Year celebrations. Beyond here are the headquarters of the Cuban Communist Party, not open to the public.

The **Cementério Cristóbal Colón** is a vast acreage of imposing mausolea and marble statuary set around an octagonal chapel. Among the graves of the martyred revolutionaries there are areas dedicated to the particular professions. It was in a speech outside the Columbus Cemetery that Castro declared the Revolution a socialist one in 1961—commemorated with a relief which bears one of only two three-dimensional images of Fidel anywhere on the island.

The best new attraction in Havana is the **Model of the City**, at Calle 28 between Avenidas 1 and 3 in the western district of Miramar (*open Mon–Fri 9.30–5.30*). An extraordinarily detailed wooden model gives you an excellent overview; it is colour-coded by date, so you can trace the development of the city

Across the harbour mouth from Old Havana (a 10-centavo ferry ride) you come to Casablanca, where you can climb to the 56ft statue of Christ. Making your way around to the distinctive Morro lighthouse is tricky because much of the intervening land is occupied by the military; you may find it easier to get one of the many buses that run through the tunnel beneath the mouth of Havana harbour. The Morro itself is dominated by a lumbering fortress that guarded the harbour approaches. Beyond here you come to the suburb of **Cojímar**, the setting of Hemingway's *The Old Man and the Sea*. It was a fishing village, but now most of the fishermen have moved to more comfortable houses—it is only just possible to imagine a marlin's huge tail and backbone discarded on the beach. A bust commemorates the writer. The hero of *The Old Man and the Sea* is said to reside in Cojímar, and any local will point you in the direction of Gregorio Fuentes. He looks remarkably well considering he claims to be nearly 100 years old. Visitors are invited to pay a few dollars to meet him.

Altogether more interesting is Hemingway's house, **La Vigía** (*open Mon, Wed and Sat, 9–4, Sun 9am–12 noon, only on days when it is not raining, because of worries about tourists churning up the turf*), where the writer ('Ernesto' to the Cubans) lived in the forties and fifties, in the suburb of San Francisco de Paula, southeast of Havana. It is maintained exactly as he left it in 1960. The walls are lined with hunting trophies and you can see his typewriter at chest height (he wrote barefoot standing up) and the sad record of his decreasing weight in the bathroom (he was dying from cirrhosis and eventually shot himself in 1961 in the USA). Because of thefts by souvenir collectors, visitors are now restricted to looking in through the windows and doors. The small estate stands on a cliff and has an excellent view looking north from the garden—La Vigía means lookout.

The Hemingway Marina, five miles west of the capital, is Hemingway's only in name and in his love of sport fishing. It is a modern tourist complex and marina.

South of Havana itself is the **Parque Lenin**, just outside the Havana ringroad, a huge area of parkland with lakes, an amusement park, art galleries, a spiral aquarium, and a massive, blinding-white bust of Lenin himself. There are also stables to hire horses, a diminutive train to ride, and in the evening you may like to visit the drive-in cinema (*Autokine*), if you can get hold of a car. There is a railway terminal in the park, reached from Central Station.

The park gets busy at the weekends, when the Habañeros pour out of the city. Close by to the south are some **Botanical Gardens**, with an effusion of Caribbean flora and **Expocuba**, a series of pavilions that illustrate the country's successes in industry and social progress.

West of Havana

The province of **Pinar del Río** occupies the western tip of Cuba, and with the Sierra de los Organos (which seems to collect rainclouds) along its northern shore, it is both beautiful and fertile. It is here that Cuba's finest tobacco is grown. Among the royal palms and the karst limestone outcrops, the hills are smothered in bright green plantations and dotted with aluminium and shaggy-roofed *vegas*, the tobacco drying houses. If you drive out to the west of the island, make sure to travel on the northern coastal route between Cabañas and La Esperanza, either outbound or on your return—much slower, but much more scenic than the *autopista.*

In the hills north of San Cristóbal are the botanical gardens of **Soroa**, with a walkway through Cuba's explosive vegetation. The garden, which covers a hillside, was built by a Spaniard in memory of his daughter who had died in childbirth. Besides 'mother-in-law's tongue' and the 'elephant's foot' tree from Mexico there is an **orquidareo** (*open 8.30–12 noon and 1.30–4pm for a guided tour, best in November and December*), where most of the island's 250 varieties of orchid (including the extraordinary 'Queen's shoe') are on view. There is a waterfall nearby.

The city of **Pinar del Río**, 110 miles from Havana, was once nicknamed Cinderella because it was so poor. Subsequently, it has grown on the back of the tobacco industry. You can visit any number of cigar factories, or the **Museo del Tabaco**, in the west of the town, on Calle Ajete, where there is an illustration of the industry from seed to cigar. Some of the many other museums include the **Museo Provincial de Historia** on Calle José Martí (*open Tues–Sat 9–4, Sun 9am–1pm*), with displays of Cuban life from the local Indians onwards.

North of Pinar del Río, the valley of Viñales has an extraordinary geographical phenomenon in its karst mountain outcrops, once the supports of a vast plain which collapsed through water erosion millions of years ago. (Called *mogotes* in Cuba, they look similar to the Burren in western Ireland and the 'haystack mountains' of South China.) The verandah of the Motel las Jazmines presents one of Cuba's most attractive views, where these vast neolithic fruit cakes soar from the lush tobacco fields. The *mogotes* are laced with cave-systems where the *Guanahatabeyes*—cave-dwelling Indians who were Cuba's earliest inhabitants—lived and where you can take boat trips. West of Pinar del Río the mountains subside and the province becomes more Cinderella-like.

East of Havana

Beyond the beaches of Playas del Este to the east of Havana and past the drilling heads of Cuba's oil industry, you come to the city of Matanzas, set on a deep bay about 60 miles from the capital. You can also make the journey by the 'Hershey Railway' (so-called because it was built by the American chocolate company), which departs four times each day from Casablanca station in Havana. This is the only electric railway line in Cuba, and also one of the most scenic rides—much of it through startling gone-to-seed sugar plantations.

Matanzas, which takes its name from a massacre (perhaps of Spaniards, but more likely of bloodstock), was founded in 1690. The city did not really develop until the 19th century, when it became immensely wealthy through the sugar industry. It became a Cuban leader in matters cultural and it is full of grand old buildings from the period, including the **cathedral**

and others ranged around the **Parque Central** and the **Teatro Sauto**, built in 1863. It is a gentler town after the bustle of the capital.

The **Museo Farmacéutico** (pharmaceutical museum; *open Mon–Sat 10–6, Sun 10–1*) is near the Parque Central and has an original display of old wives' remedies and medicinal plants. Nearer the waterfront, you will find the provincial museum in the **Palacio de Junco** (*open Tues–Sun 10–5; closed Mon*), a beautiful mansion built by a sugar planter in the last century, which recounts Matanzas' history and its connection with sugar.

Matanzas is the gateway to **Varadero**, Cuba's premier resort—basically a 12-mile-long beach known as the Hicacos Peninsula, itself is as large as many Caribbean islands. Varadero devotes itself to sun, sea and sand vacations, with watersports by day and exotic cabaret and clubs to keep you satisfied in the evenings. The town, which consists mainly of high-rise and beach-front blocks interspersed with pretty coral rock houses and wooden villas from pre-revolutionary days, is strung out along the peninsula for about eighty blocks. The best-known house is some way beyond the main resort: the Du Pont family vacation home, a Spanish-revival villa, now a restaurant, but with some rooms left as they were when it was first built. There is a bar on the rooftop with an impressive view of the area. **Parque Josoné** is a modest sort of pleasure garden, usually frequented by tourists, with restaurants and cafés.

The town of **Cárdenas**, not far south of Varadero, is a backwater of a port where very little ever happens—and it remains largely untouched by the tourist race. Its sleepy nature gives a good idea of rural Cuba. It is known, rather grandly, as the 'City of Flags' because the Cuban flag was first raised here in 1850, in a failed insurrection. It was also the birthplace of José Echevarría, a militant student leader who was killed by the Batista regime in March 1957. A **museum** of Cárdenas commercial and revolutionary tradition has been created in his home on the street now named after him (*open Tues–Sun, 9.30–noon and 1–6; closed Sun afternoons*).

As you travel south from the provincial capital you pass through the endless canefields, the source of Matanzas' wealth, and across the drowsy agricultural heartland of Cuba. On the southern seaboard of Matanzas province is the swamp of the Zapata Peninsula, the largest expanse of wilderness in Cuba and probably the Caribbean. There is a great deal of wildlife, particularly birds. The set-piece tourist attraction is **Guamá** Indian village, a resort built of palm-thatch *bohíos* and decorated with sculptures by Rita Longa. You approach it from the highway on a long, leisurely boat ride. Nearby is a **crocodile farm**, best visited at feeding time in the early evening. Note, however, that the biggest concentration of mosquitoes in Cuba regards the nightly arrival of visitors as a feeding frenzy—wear plenty of repellent.

Just south, on the coast itself, is the place renowned among the Cubans for being the site of the 'First major defeat of Imperialism in Latin America'—the **Bay of Pigs**. Fidel himself returned to the battlefield in April 1961 in order to repel the landing by Cuban exiles, despatched by the USA. It is a proud piece of post-Revolutionary history, with memorial stones along the route to those who died. In the resort of Playa Girón, the main attraction is a **museum** devoted to the repulsing of the invasion force. You cannot miss the British Sea Fury fighter at the entrance (*open Tues–Sat 9–5*).

The city of **Cienfuegos** is 40 miles east of Playa Girón. It is set on an almost landlocked bight on the south coast of the island. Cienfuegos is an industrial and port town, with a population of 100,000 and a large naval base. It is also the venue for the biggest nuclear power installation in Cuba, begun but never finished by Soviet scientists. The city centre has some elaborate old Spanish colonial buildings, including the **cathedral** with its octagonal cupola and the **Tomas Terry theatre** on the attractive and open square of the Parque Martí. The waterfront Prado is uninspiring, but it leads south to the extraordinary folly of **Valle Palace**, a zany conglomeration of the styles of the three religions of Christianity, Judaism and Islam.

A further 50 miles east of Cienfuegos, along a spectacular coastal road that winds over the headlands thrown off by the peaks of the Sierra Escambray, you come to the extraordinary and charming town of **Trinidad**. The 20th century appears to have bypassed the place, one of the original seven Spanish *villas*, making it prime tourism territory. Trinidad has been restored entirely to its early 19th-century glory—cobbled streets, Spanish colonial town-houses, wrought-iron street lamps, cannon at the street corners with muzzles buried in the ground to stop the carriage wheels clipping the walls. Two hundred years ago Trinidad was one of Cuba's richest trading ports and its fleets would sail as far afield as Brazil and the Baltic. Today the streets may be festooned with telephone wires, but the narrow streets still have a pleasant and antique feeling, overlooked by wrought-iron balconies and pastel plaster façades. The cannon still do a useful job too, defending the stonework from wayward lorry wheels. Along with Old Havana, Trinidad is on Unesco's world heritage list.

The town is one of Cuba's oldest and was founded by Diego Velásquez in 1514. In 1518 Hernán Cortés embarked on his conquest of Mexico from a house on the beautiful central square, the Plaza Martí. The site is now occupied by the **Museo de Archeológia Guamauhaya**, which has a lacklustre display of pre-Columbian Indian life, including burial pots. Set in a pretty townhouse diagonally opposite is the **Museo de Arquitectura de Trinidad**, which illustrates the development of Trinidad's buildings and their embellishments in pictures, including the pineapples that appear all over the town. Look out for the ingenious 18th-century steambath and the toilets with a communicating door between men's and women's; and see which side you can lock it from. The **Museo Romántico** is also on the square, a classically beautiful colonial palace set around a courtyard, stuffed with elaborate furniture and with marvellous views from the upstairs windows. It seems obligatory for all newly married couples in the province of Sancti Spíritus to pose for photographs here. The **Museo de la Lucha Contra Bandidos** tells the story of the struggle against counter-revolutionaries. *All museums above open Tues–Sat 9–12 noon, 2–5, Sun 9–1; closed Mon.*

The **Torre de Iznaga** is a reminder of Trinidad's other career as a centre of sugar. This folly stands a few miles out of the town on the road to Sancti Spíritus, the provincial capital. It was actually an observation tower for plantation overseers to watch the slaves.

Above Trinidad, straddling the three provinces of Villa Clara, Cienfuegos and Sancti Spíritus are the mountains of **Sierra Escambray**, Cuba's central mountain range, where immensely fertile peaks and valleys reach 3000ft in places. The northern slopes are covered in tobacco plantations and their shaggy drying-houses. The highest summit is Pico San Juan (3800ft) just northwest of Trinidad on the south coast. A trip to **Topes de Collantes** is a good day out from Trinidad—the views are magnificent. The **Soledad** botanical gardens are east of Cienfuegos and you will see 60 sorts of palm among the 2000 species of plant in the pleasant parkland. Look out for the 'pineapple tree'.

In the centre of the island, directly north of Trinidad is the city of **Santa Clara**, capital of Villa Clara province. The city has a population of 200,000 and is the home of one of Cuba's four universities. It is quite industrialized, but still supports a tradition of agriculture, with sugarcane flats interspersed with fields of maize, beans and yuca (cassava) as well as ranches of cattle—no doubt you will come across the *vaqueros* sitting on their huge saddles, driving the herds along the local roads.

Santa Clara is also central to the triumph of the Revolution, a role emphasized in 1997 when the remains of Che Guevara were re-buried at a huge mausoleum on the edge of the city. The choice of Santa Clara as location for the revolutionary's final resting place was natural: it was here, in December 1958, that he commanded the decisive victory against Batista's troops. The location of the battle is now one of Cuba's oddest museums is the **Tren Blindado**, an armoured troop train that stands derailed at the site where it was stormed by the revolution-aries. The exhibits are set inside the old wagons, which still sport their old military colours. The wagons are *open Tues–Sun 9–12 noon and 3–6, closed Sun pm and Mon*, but you can wander around the site at any time.

Northeast of Santa Clara, one of Cuba's most atmospheric old towns is peacefully off the tourist circuit. **Remedios** was the old provincial capital until a terrible fire in 1692, and has preserved much of its 17th-century architecture. The main square is dreamily beautiful, domi-nated by the handsome Parroquia de San Juan Bautista de Remedios.

The province of **Ciego de Avila** is mainly agricultural, with more sugar-cane flats and pineapple plantations. Its capital, the city of Ciego de Avila, is quiet and lacklustre, and is only really only visited because it happens to lie on the main east-west road and railway line. A more pleasant place to visit goes by the unlikely name of **Morón**, with the atmosphere of a 19th-century country town. If you wish to fix up a shooting trip, you can do so on the Laguna de Leche and in the swamps north of the town. It is now the gateway to the massive Cayo Coco development on one of Cuba's largest offshore islands. A 20-mile-long causeway leads north from Morón to Cayo Coco, with links extending to neighbouring islands. The develop-ment of the resort, which took place in the early 1990s during severe economic stringency, was personally overseen by Fidel Castro. The resort has proved to be a success, particularly with European visitors, though it feels very isolated from the rest of the country.

The city and province of **Camagüey** comprise altogether a better prospect. The city of Camagüey, originally called Puerto Principe, was one of Cuba's earliest settlements, estab-lished on the coast in 1514, but moved inland to save it from pirate raids. Today it is Cuba's third largest city and it sits on the plain among the canefields and cattle ranches. It boasts many old Spanish colonial buildings, among them the **Teatro Principal**, **La Soledad** church and the 18th-century **Palace of Justice**. The large earthenware pots which you can see all around the city were used for storing and keeping water cool, and have become the symbol of the province.

There are two museums bearing the name of Ignacio Agramonte, a hero of the Cuban War of Independence who was born in Camagüey. The **Museo Ignacio Agramonte**, which is the provincial museum, is set in a magnificent building on the Avenida de los Mártires and depicts local history and the many moves the town has made. The **Museo Casa Natal de Ignacio Agramonte** (*open Mon and Wed–Sat 10–6*) gives a more personal view of the rebel leader's life and achievements in the charming house where he was born.

Holguín and **Granma** provinces straddle the island as it widens towards the southeastern tip. They consist mainly of agricultural plains, rising into the foothills of the Sierra Maestra on the south coast. **Holguín**, a small colonial town with three main squares surrounded by an infes-tation of concrete, is scattered in the lee of a large hill, the Loma de la Cruz, from where the views are magnificent. The **Museo de Ciencias Carlos de la Torre** (*open Tues–Sat, 9–6,*

Sun 8–12 noon) is set in a fine colonial house on Calle Maceo and has displays of Cuban animals from crustaceans to mammals, including an exhibit of the rare manatee.

Beyond the town are the beaches and resorts around Guardalavaca on the north coast. **Gibara** lays claim to be Columbus's landfall on the island in 1492, when he thought he had discovered Japan. In **Banes**, ten miles inland from Guardalavaca, there is the excellent **Museo Indocubano** (*open Tues–Sat 10–5, Sun 9–12 noon*), with an extensive collection of Siboney and Taíno artefacts, including their illustrated pottery and descriptions of their ceremonies.

The capital of Granma province is **Bayamo**, one of Cuba's oldest towns, founded by Diego Velázquez in 1513. The Church of San Salvador is one of the oldest buildings in Cuba. The town was also the home of Céspedes, who initiated the Cuban War of Independence here in 1868 by freeing his slaves and arming them against the Spaniards. He is remembered in the Parque Céspedes and the **Museo Casa Natal de Carlos Manuel de Céspedes**, a colonial house on Calle Maceo, which tells of his life and struggle (*open Tues–Sat 12 noon–7, Sun 9–1*). The **Museo Nico Lopez** (*open Tues–Sun, 8–6*) tells the story of the Bayamo people who staged a rebellion in 1953 to coincide with the Moncada garrison attack. The province is named after the boat in which the revolutionaries sailed from Mexico. Las Coloradas has a concrete memorial to the landing.

Santiago de Cuba

In Oriente province, 60 miles east of Bayamo, is Cuba's second city, Santiago de Cuba. The town sits on the edge of a massive harbour, where the Sierra Maestra mountains tumble down to the south coast. It has a special place in the panoply of modern Cuba as the spiritual home of the Independence movement and of the Revolution. Independence heroes such as Céspedes and José Martí are buried in the city. The Moncada Barracks, where Castro made his first attack in 1953, have become a shrine to the Revolution. Castro returns to speak here often, usually in the summer celebrations around 26 July each year.

Santiago de Cuba is the third oldest city on the island. It was founded in 1513 by Diego Velázquez, and for forty years it was the colony's capital. Some buildings survive from the earliest period (among them is the oldest building on the island, Velásquez's palace), but the town's charming atmosphere comes from all the 19th-century town-houses, with their wrought-iron balconies and shuttered windows, that line the steep streets and stepped alleyways. You will find it an excellent city to wander in, more compact and less overwhelming than Havana.

Santiago has a complex heritage as refugees have fled here in floods from every conflict in the islands nearby. A strong French heritage dates from the influx of 30,000 planters who fled Saint Domingue at the time of the Haitian Revolution in 1791. In addition, there is a substantial community from elsewhere in the Caribbean—particularly from Jamaica, due south of Santiago. The city centre is **Céspedes Square**, set on the hill a few hundred yards above the harbour. It is one of the finest squares anywhere in the Hispanic world. On its southwest corner is the house of Diego Velásquez, built in around 1514. Recently restored, it is a charming house with balconies set around inner courtyards. It is now home to the **Museo de Ambiente Historico Cubano** (*open Mon–Sat 9–5, Sun 9–1*). On the south side is the **Cathedral**, first built on this site in 1524, though the imposing edifice has been enlarged since then.

To the east of the square, past the famous Santiago Casa de la Trova (one of the best in Cuba) is the **Bacardi Museum** on Pío Rosado (*open Mon 3–7, Tues–Sat 9–8.30, Sun 9–1*), a splendid 19th-century mansion built by the founder of the rum dynasty. It is now Cuba's closest equivalent to the Victoria and Albert Museum in London, and houses a fine collection of 19th century artefacts and art. The national hero **José Martí** is buried in a vast concrete mausoleum in the Santa Efigenia cemetery to the west of the town.

As the spiritual home of the Revolution Santiago has plenty of museums dedicated to the armed struggle in the 1950s. The most famous is of course the **Moncada Barracks**, restored (with all its bullet-holes) as it was after the attack on 26 July 1953. Like many of Batista's barracks, it has been turned into a school, but there is a small and interesting museum on the assault (*open Mon–Sat 9–5*) off the Avenida de los Libertadores. Close by in the **Parque Historico**, site of the hospital where Castro was tried following the attack, and where he delivered his five-hour speech asserting 'history will absolve me'.

Farther out of town to the south is the lumbering **Morro** fortress, rising several hundred feet above the sea, built on the point at the harbour mouth in 1643. Inside is the **Museo de la Piratería** (*open Tues–Sat 9–6*), where exhibits of pistols, cutlasses and maps illustrate Caribbean piracy, including an assault on the Morro itself by Henry Morgan in 1662. There are supreme views along the south coast and into the mountains above the town. On the road east out of the town, towards the south-coast beaches, is **Siboney farm**—yet another museum on the assault on the Moncada Barracks. It was from here that Castro's rebels set out to storm the garrison. The route into the town is dotted with memorials to the dead.

Soon after, you come to one of Cuba's most curious parks as outsize pterodactyls and brontosauri in concrete appear around you in the 'Dinosaur Park' or the **Valle de la Prehistoria** (*adm free*). North of here is the nature park of **Gran Piedra**, set around the 4000ft mountain of the same name, where you can walk among the explosive vegetation of the Sierra Maestra. The area gets crowded at weekends, when the Santiagueros pour out of the city to get here. On a clear day you can see the Blue Mountains of Jamaica 80 miles to the south.

The remote and thinly populated province of Guantánamo runs from Santiago to the eastern tip of the island. The capital, also called Guantánamo, is not an attractive town and is probably best known as the hometown of the woman celebrated in the song 'Guantanamera'. It is also the site of a political oddity in the US naval base, 45 square miles of America in the socialist state of Cuba. It was leased by the USA in 1902 and the Americans pay a handsome $2000 each year for the pleasure. You are not allowed near it, but can get a view from the hills above.

The road continues along the south coast and then cuts into the mountains to the north coast and the city of **Baracoa**. Despite its somnolent ambience, this port with 60,000 inhabitants is perhaps the most alluring town in the whole of Cuba. Established in 1510, it is certainly Cuba's oldest Spanish colonial town. It is steeped in history, and is surrounded by fine scenery—including the magnificent plateau of El Yunque, the table mountain which dominates every view of the town. In the central square, where the locals gather to play dominoes, is a statue of Cuba's first rebel, the Indian Hatuey. The town is guarded by a series of forts, of which one, **Matachín**, has been turned into a museum of Baracoa history (*open Tues–Sat 9–5, Sun 9–1*).

Isla de la Juventud

Sixty miles south of the mainland, in the bay made by the alligator's tail (in the west of Cuba), is the flat **Isle of Youth**. Discovered in 1494 by Columbus, it was a pirate haunt for several hundred years. Until 1978 it was known as the Isle of Pines, but the government changed the name to one felt to be more socialistically uplifting. The main town is the lively **Nueva Gerona**, in the north of the island. Good roads run to the southwest and southeast coast where there are good beaches, but much of the country in the south is swampland. There are regular flights to the island from Havana, costing as little as $20 each way; you could alternatively travel by hydrofoil (two hours) or ferry (six hours) from Surgideno de Batabanó, south of Havana.Today the Isla de la Juventud has a population of about 70,000 and it has a youthful atmosphere to go with its name—students come to take courses here, many of them from African countries. It has a slightly remote and a distinctly relaxed feel after the mainland. Surrounded by reefs, it has excellent diving and the fishing, one of the islanders' main occupations, is good too.

Easily the most intriguing tourist attraction is the **Presidio Modelo** (*open Tues–Sat, 9am–5pm, Sun 9am–1pm*), the former high-security prison with its five round cell-blocks, where Castro and his fellow rebels did a stint after the Moncada garrison attack. Most of the prison has been converted into a school, but part has been preserved as it was when Castro was imprisoned here. There are caves to explore in the east of the island.

Cayo Largo, at the other end of the archipelago, has been developed exclusively as a tourist resort. If you want to spend a few days uninterrupted in the relentless pursuit of beach lounging and watersports, this place is as good as any in Cuba—except for the interruptions caused by numerous charter flights carrying day-trippers from the mainland. If you feel the need for greater isolation, you can go even further afield and be even more remote in the nearby cays of **Cayo Rico** and **Cayo Pájaros**.

© (53)–   ***Where to Stay***

Whether you are travelling independently or as part of a package, the accommodation picture in Cuba is better than it has been for decades. The sheer magnificence of a building like the Hotel Nacional at the foot of La Rampa in Havana gives an idea of the opulence and splendour (their decadence aside) of the hotels of Cuba in the forties and fifties. The exterior remains, in decay, but the hotel has a very different atmosphere now. You would do better to select one of the newly restored hotels in the old part of town, or indeed to choose to spend much less by staying with a family.

Beyond the capital, rooming with a family becomes all the more appealing because the regular tourist hotels are distinctly unappetizing—awkwardly located, shabby and with questionable facilties. A number of hotels in resort areas have recently been built in joint ventures with foreign companies, bringing styles and fittings to which westerners are more accustomed. Throughout the island, though, tourist hotel rooms are usually air-conditioned with private bath. In Havana, most will have a television showing American films and possibly providing access to CNN.

Foreigners are encouraged to use the 'dollar hotels', aimed squarely at tourists, rather than the more homely 'peso hotels' (at which you will still have to pay in hard currency). Hotels vary in price and in standard, with many in Havana (where there is a decent range of standards), and in the main beach centres, and usually a couple in each major provincial town.

If you are moving around, you can try to get Reception at your current hotel to book the next night, but in several lengthy visits to Cuba the researcher for this section has only once failed to find a hotel room on demand (on that occasion, the hotel receptionist provided her spare room for the night). Finding a room is most difficult in the Cuban summer holiday season (July and August) and over the winter (December, January and February). Unusually for the Caribbean, single travellers can expect a reduction of about a third on the double-room rate. It is also possible to **camp** while travelling around the island and many towns have well-equipped campsites where you can stay for a couple of dollars, tent and facilities included.

Havana

In the past few years several old colonial buildings have been converted into stylish hotels in and around Old Havana, making this area the obvious choice for travellers on any budget. Best of all in terms of location and comfort is the **Hotel Santa Isabel** (*expensive*), right on the Plaza de Armas at the heart of the old city. Much of the fabric of the originial Palacio de los Condes de Santaventa, complete with an ancient iron elevator, has been retained, but the Hotel Santa Isabel boasts modern facilities in its 30-odd rooms, plus a cool and restful bar that offers a handy retreat from the heat of the day. Pricey, but worth it. Just along Calle Obispo, at the corner of Mercandares, the newly refurbished **Hotel Ambos Mundos** (*expensive–moderate*) has been comprehensively gutted and refitted since Hemingway stayed here in the 1930s, though the connection is being assiduously milked. A third good choice in the immediate vicinity is the **Hostal Valencia**, at 53 Calle Officios (✆ 62 3801; *moderate–cheap*). It is set in an old colonial palace with a courtyard surrounded by two stories of balconies with lamps and balustrades. It has 11 rooms and suites, named after the provinces of Spain, some decorated in older style with louvres and tiled floors. Cafeteria only. Good feel of peace in the city.

The other big concentration of attractive hotels is on the edge of colonial Havana. The **Plaza Hotel** (✆ 62 2006, ✉ 63 9620; *moderate*) has a breezy tiled foyer with echoes of grander colonial days, decorated with palm trees and hints of art deco in the stained glass. The rooms are large and comfortable and there are two restaurants (one à la carte) and two bars. Just east is the **Hotel Sevilla** (✆ 33 8560; *moderate*), a 1920s building that has been tastefully refurbished. The foyer is decorated in elegant Spanish style with Moorish touches, in marble and mosaics. Quite simple rooms, 188 in all, tiled with wooden furniture, all air-conditioned with telephones, a television and fridge. Nine floors with a huge restaurant with a view at the top, giving excellent views of the city. The pool is large and attractive, even though it sits just a few yards from the busy Prado. The **Hotel Inglaterra** (✆ 62 7072, ✉ 62 6715; *moderate*), standing next to the Teatro Nacional in the heart of town, is set in an ornate and grand old building on the Parque Central. Some of the large rooms have balconies overlooking the street, the restaurant is good and the bar downstairs is a popular gathering point for travellers. Budget travellers congregate at the ever-reliable **Hotel Caribbean**

(© 62 2071; *cheap–very cheap*), on the Prado down towards the Malecón. Once you actually find the place (it is unmarked from the outside, but is just north of the corner of Calle Colón), it proves a friendly and comfortable base for the independent traveller, with clean rooms, some of them looking out on to the Prado itself.

In Central Havana, the obvious choice is the **Hotel Deauville**, just off the Malecón (© 62 8052; *moderate–cheap*), with 148 rooms and a swimming pool and restaurant.

The **Hotel Nacional** in Vedado (© 78920, ✆ 335054; *expensive–moderate*) is set one of Havana's most sumptuous and magnificent neo-colonial buildings. The foyer is very elegant with colonnades and old Cuban tiles and fine old lifts, set on an attractive courtyard with palm trees. It has 483 rooms, all with mini-bars, telephones and televisions and some antique decor. Quite smart and comfortable, executive floors with business facilities. Not far off are the large, imposing hotel blocks that were erected in the decades before the Revolution in the district of Vedado.

The former Havana Hilton, taken over by the revolutionaries, is now the **Havana Libre** (© 30 5011, ✆ 32 8722; *expensive–moderate*), which stands tall at the top of La Rampa. There is a fantastic view of the city, over Old Havana and the harbour, from the Turquino bar on the top floor. Entertainment is provided. Similar in style, a huge and imposing block, is the **Capri Hotel** (© 32 0511, ✆ 33 3009; *moderate*), across La Rampa, pool and cabaret. Cheaper alternatives, but without any charm, include the **Colina**, on Calle L. (© 32 3535; *cheap*) and the **St John's**, on Calle O. (© 32 9531; *cheap*).

The most comfortable place to stay in the **Vedado** district is the **Hotel Victoria** (© 32 6531; *moderate*) on Calle 19 and M. Close to the commercial centre of the town, this is probably the best hotel for business travellers—business facilities available, also a pool. Farther into the Vedado district, a taxi ride or a long walk from the centre of the town, the **Hotel Presidente**, on Calle Calzada (© 32 7521, ✆ 32 3577; *moderate*) has a certain style, with awnings on the outside and a foyer with marble floors, chandeliers and huge vases. Even the rooms have a grander feel than elsewhere, though they are not that large. There is a good bar on the top floor and a swimming pool. On the coast is the **Havana Riviera** (© 30 5051; *moderate*), a tall, ugly block on the Malecón with a similar feel to the Havana Libre, with pool and cabaret.

West of Havana

In the city of **Pinar del Río** to the west of Havana, the **Hotel Pinar del Río** (© 5071; *moderate*) is a textbook example of the accommodation in almost all the provincial capitals: a 136-room hotel with a swimming pool and nightclub, on the edge of town, utterly devoid of character and seemingly based on a (flawed) design imported direct from Bulgaria. But at least the price is reasonable.

In the area of **Viñales** to the north the **Motel Los Jazmines** (© 3 3404; *moderate*) has a superb view of the valley from up above. There are about 70 rooms and a pool and a good restaurant upstairs. On the other side of the town is the 18-room **Motel La Ermita** (© 9 3204, ✆ 9 3294; *moderate*), also with a pool and a good view from the hillside. On the way back to Havana, in the hills of Soroa, you can stay at the **Villa Soroa** (© 2122; *cheap*). It has a pool, but it is sometimes difficult to get a room.

East of Havana

In the **Playas del Este** you can find beach hotels, though they tend to be full of package tourists and they become very booked up at the weekends when the Habañeros escape from the capital. In Santa María del Mar the best is probably the 20-room **Hotel Atlántico** on the Avenida de las Terrazas (℗ 2551; *moderate*), where the local Intur office is situated (they can help find you a room) or the cheaper **Villa las Brisas**, further west and a little inland on Calle 11 (℗ 2469; *cheap*).

There are numerous hotels in Varadero and of course many of those are set on the magnificent beach. Most are large, but they are well spaced and the layout gives a relaxed feel with large pools and tropical gardens between the buildings and the beach. There are some smaller hotels set back from the shore for those who do not require beachfront space.

At the top of the range are the newest joint-venture developments towards the far end of the peninsula, such as the vast **Hotel Melia Las Américas** (℗ 66221, ✆ 66161; *expensive*). It has over 400 rooms ranged around a cool and pleasant central area with fountains and greenery, and all the modern conveniences down to the video and mini-bar. There is a large pool and palm-thatch restaurant just above the beach. If you are not on a package holiday it is often difficult to get a room. Next along, the **Sol Palmeras** (℗ 66110, ✆ 66353; *expensive*) has rooms as well as a number of bungalows set around the lawned gardens above the beach. All the watersports to keep you occupied by day, quieter in the evenings. If you're one for an all-inclusive holiday, the Jamaican organization SuperClubs has a property on a good strip of sand, **SuperClub Varadero** (℗ 66180, ✆ 33 7005; *expensive*). There are 270 rooms and suites altogether, all with balconies. A reliable diet of daytime and evening activities, watersports, jacuzzis, aerobics, piano bar, pasta restaurant and discotheque.

A mid-range resort hotel in the more densely packed southwest of the peninsula is the **Club Tropical**, on Avenida Primera at Calle 22 (℗ 66 3915; *moderate–cheap*). There are 142 rooms in all, but staff are quite friendly, some entertainment in the evenings and right in town. Perhaps preferable are the **Villas Punta Blanca** (℗ 66 3916; *moderate–cheap*). Rooms are in small blocks and in 30 luxury holiday villas from before the Revolution that are stretched along the beach. Also a central area with pool and watersports, some evening entertainment. There are cheaper options in the centre of town. The **Hotel Pullman**, a little inland on Avenida Primera at Calle 49 (℗ 66 2575; *cheap*) is friendly and has just 15 rooms. The **Dos Mares**, Avenida Primera at Calle 53 (℗ 66 2702; *cheap*) has some small but comfortable rooms. Close to the bridge from the mainland, the **Villa Sotavento**, Avenida Primera at Calle 12 (*cheap*), is part of a large hotel, but offers some well-priced rooms.

There are three hotels on the **Zapata Peninsula**, of which the most distinctive is undoubtedly the **Villa Turística Guamá** (℗ 2979; *cheap*), on the Laguna de Tesoro, a reproduction of an Arawak village, complete with thatch-roof *bohíos* on stilts and wooden walkways over the lagoon. It is a little isolated, but has a pool and of course a nearby crocodile farm for your amusement; be warned that the mosquitoes are even more voracious than the crocodiles. Less comfortable is the **Villa Turística Playa Larga** (℗ 7219). On the southern coast is the **Villa Turística Playa Girón** (℗ 4110; *cheap*), with 190 rooms in concrete *cabañas*, one of which has been left, collapsed, since it was shelled in the abortive 1962 Bay of Pigs invasion. Good swimming-pool, some entertainment.

Along the coast at **Cienfuegos**, the most comfortable hotel is the **Jagua** (✆ 6362, ✉ 33 5056; *cheap*), in the south of the town: 140 rooms with a good pool. The **Pasacaballo** (✆ 096212) on the heights above the harbour mouth has a pool and a good view, but is 15 miles south of the town; the **Rancho Luna**, 10 miles out of Cienfuegos on the same road (✆ 048120, ✉ 33 5057) has cabins on a good beach. In Trinidad, the **Las Cuevas Motel** (✆ 2324; *cheap*) sits on the hill above the town, and on the nearby beaches are the large **Hotel Ancón** (✆ 4011) and the **Costa Sur** (✆ 6100), about 6 miles out of the town.

In **Ciego de Avila** there are a couple of dollar hotels, including the large **Hotel Ciego de Avila** (✆ 28013; *cheap*) in the north of the town, with pool, a bar and a night club, and the **Hotel Santiago Habana** (✆ 25703; *very cheap*) on the Calle Honorato del Castillo in the centre of the town. The **Hotel Morón** (*moderate–cheap*), a mile south of the town of that name, is a standard four-storey concrete monstrosity. On Cayo Coco, prices and standards rise rapidly. Of the new hotels the best is the **Hotel Cayo Coco** (✆ 33 5388; *expensive*), a large and rambling development of pseudo-colonial cottages at the end of the causeway from the mainland. The catering facilities are excellent—thankfully, given the distance from the nearest mainland alternatives.

At **Camagüey** there are a couple of dollar hotels, of which the larger is the **Hotel Camagüey** (✆ 71970; *cheap*), 2 miles east of town on the Carretera Central, with 110 rooms, pool and a cabaret. You might also try the **Villa Marguan** on the edge of town (✆ 72160; *cheap*), 35 rooms, with entertainment. Beach resorts at Santa Lucía on the north coast include the 220-room **Hotel Mayanabo** (✆ 48184), with a pool, bars and watersports, and the apartments of the **Villa Tararaco** (✆ 48222).

In the area of **Holguín**, the **Pernik** (✆ 481011, ✉ 4141; *moderate*), large (200 rooms), but with a good pool, restaurant and friendly atmosphere, is where the locals gather. Otherwise try the cheaper **Motel El Bosque** (✆ 481012; *very cheap*) on Avenida Jorge Dimitrov, with 70 cabins and a pool. Southeast of Holguín by five miles is the **Hotel Mirador de Mayabe** (✆ 422160; *cheap*), with 24 rooms and a cracking view of the valley; pool and nightclub. In the resort area to the northeast of Holguín, the 220-room **Hotel Guardalavaca** (✆ 30145; *cheap*) is set on the stunning Guardalavaca beach, with plenty of watersports, and the smaller **Don Lino Beach Hotel** (✆ 20433; *cheap*) has good *cabañas* and watersports.

In **Bayamo** in Granma Province you might stay at the **Motel El Yarey** (✆ 66613), just off the highway near Jiguaní—fourteen rooms dressed up as country dwellings.

Santiago de Cuba

If location is important, then the only address in town is the newly restored **Casa Granda** on the west side of Parque Céspedes (✆ 86035; *expensive–moderate*). The building is an attractive old *palacio* with a busy atmosphere. Its 55 rooms have increased in price, but if you are on a tight budget and decide to treat yourself just once during your trip then this is the place to do it.

The flashiest hotel is the startlingly modern **Hotel Santiago de Cuba** on Avenida de las Américas (✆ 42612, ✉ 41756; *expensive*). Decorated in the three colours of the

Cuban flag, it is the tallest building on the island outside the capital, with 290 rooms and good business facilities. The irritating thing about it is the distance from the centre of town—about two miles. The hotel opposite, the **Las Américas Hotel** (✆ 42011; *moderate–cheap*) with 64 rooms, has the same problem, but it has a pool and entertainment. Half a mile further out of town, the **Motel San Juan** (*cheap*) has only recently changed its name from the Leningrado. The new name is better suited to this villa in a leafy suburb on the edge of town. There are 32 simple rooms. High on the hill is the **Rancho Club** (✆ 33202; *cheap*), to be avoided if you do not have a car, despite the good views, because of the difficulties of getting into town.

If you are catching a flight you might consider going to the **Hotel del Balcón del Caribe** (✆ 91011; *cheap*), near the Morro fortress on the point. It has a pool, but is inconveniently far out of town if you plan to use it as a base from which to visit Santiago. If you want a beach hotel you can try the **Hotel Bucanero** (✆ 7126), set on a small cove cut into the coastline, with watersports and a swim-up bar, or the **Hotel Sol** with tennis courts and other tourist facilities.

Guantánamo has the absolutely standard **Hotel Guantánamo** (✆ 32 6105; *cheap*), a mile or two north of the city centre—and a second much more intriguing choice 12 miles south. The **Hotel Caimanera** (*moderate*), poking into Guantánamo Bay, seems to be more an exercise in propaganda than a commercial venture; it rarely attracts significant numbers of visitors, yet it is a smart new place within sight of the US naval base that occupies the territory to the south.

In **Baracoa**, the renovated **Hotel El Castillo** (✆ 42103; *moderate–cheap*) has two dozen rooms ranged around a decent pool, and its high location gives good views over the town and mountains. On the seafront, the **Rusa** (*cheap*) is named after a Russian woman who lived there.

Isla de Juventud

Hotel Colony (✆ 98181; *moderate–cheap*), on a superb beach in the southwest of the island, about 25 miles from Nueva Gerona, with 77 rooms looking over the sea, pool, bars, nightclub and watersports. You might also try the **Villa Isla** on the road out of Nueva Gerona towards Santa Fe (✆ 23290; *cheap*). There are 20 rooms, and a swimming-pool. **Rancho el Tesoro** (✆ 24081; *cheap*) is a little farther out of town, 39 air-conditioned rooms. Cayo Largo has a number of beach hotels with pools, bars and endless watersports, reserved entirely for tourists; try the **Hotel Isla del Sur** (✆ 794215, ✆ 332108; *moderate*), which has 59 comfortable and air-conditioned rooms with satellite TV and a pool just above the beach, moderate. The **Villa Capricho** (✆ 513033, ✆ 332108; *moderate–cheap*) has 60 rooms in cabanas with thatched roofs and a hammock outside; it's simple and rustic inside, but right on the cracking beach.

✆ *(53)*—   ***Eating Out***

The last few years have seen Cuba rescued from its status as gastronomic wasteland and transformed to a place where the potential from the land and sea is beginning to be realized. Not only are there many more places to eat—many of them serve decent meals at reasonable prices. The two dynamics that have been responsible for this happy state of affairs are products of the rise in tourism. Foreign investors have pushed up standards of dining in the big hotels, which has forced other places to improve. The other force is the creation of *paladares*—small, privately run restaurants offering good home-cooked food (and, it must be said, some poor home-cooked food in places). Faced with increased competition on two fronts, state restaurants were obliged to pull their gastronomic socks up.

This happy state of affairs applies in Havana, Varadero and other places where tourists congregate. Elsewhere, the menu is not quite so appetizing: at the hotel restaurants in outlying areas, it can be a frustrating wait for even the simplest meal. The menu too is often frustrating, because you will find that many of the dishes are not available.

The Cubans like to start their meals with fresh fruit—it gets the gastric juices working, they say, though supply is somewhat erratic. In Cuban cooking, outside the finest criollo restaurants, the standard meal comprises chicken, rice and beans, perhaps with one or two tropical veg. Sometimes pork is substituted for chicken. This diet gets quite heavy on the stomach (especially if you try crocodile meat, a speciality at Guamá). Only in the top Havana restaurants will you find menus employing seafood and fish with more adventurous sauces. Vegetarians are not likely to enjoy a terribly happy time, since the concept of voluntarily not eating meat is not an easy one for the average Cuban to grasp.

Coffee—referred to jokingly as 'American' if you go for English-style dishwater—is usually drunk by Cubans as espresso, available in bars on the street. The *Coppelia* is the local ice-cream parlour, usually marked by a queue.

To find a *paladar*, ask locals such as taxi-drivers for recommendations; but follow up offers on the street with circumspection.

The 'official' restaurants described below are arranged according to the price of a main dish: *expensive*—US$15 and above; *moderate*—between US$8 and $15; *cheap*—US$8 and below. Service is not charged officially, but tipping is becoming the norm.

A good way to start any evening in Havana is a cocktail in the **Turquino Bar** on the top floor of the Habana Libre Hotel. It gives a fantastic view of the city as the sun goes down. In **Old Havana**, the top address is the **Floridita** on the corner on Montserrate and Obispo (*expensive*), a low-lit salon hung with velvet curtains and trimmed with chrome. Ernest Hemingway's chair is roped off in a corner—the writer used to kick off each evening with a daiquiri or several here. El Floridita specializes in fish, seafood— try the giant Hemingway plate of lobster, shrimp and fish in garlic sauce—and of course, daiquiris, as drunk by Hemingway himself. A better alternative is the nearby **Restaurant Hanoi** (*cheap*), where the menu has nothing to do with Vietnam. Standard Cuban dishes of rice, beans and fish are served in pleasant surroundings.

Another famed spot on the Hemingway trail is the **Bodeguita del Medio**, on Calle Empredado (*moderate*), where he downed post-prandial *mojitos*. Customers are encouraged to sign their names on the wall, as drunken writers have since the 1940s. Ask about the chair (the upside-down one on the ceiling). Hearty creole food, *pierna de puerco asado rollo* or cooked *en su jugo*. For the setting alone, go to the **El Patio** restaurant on the Plaza de la Catedral (*expensive*), with a view across the cobbled square from beneath the arches and stained-glass windows; *langosta enchilado* and *lonjas de pavo al jugo*, sliced roast turkey. There is a café downstairs on the patio itself. A simple Italian restaurant, the **Don Giovanni** (*cheap*), is set in restored colonial rooms on Calle Tacon. There are other bars and restaurants around the Plaza de Armas.

In **Vedado** there is a number of restaurants outside the hotels. The best, certainly for the view anyway, is **La Torre** (*moderate*) in the edificio Fosca on Calle 35, with reliable Cuban and international fare. And in **Miramar**, the best restaurant is **La Cecilia** on 5th Avenida between 110 and 112 (*expensive*), which offers international fare, good food and service. On the waterfront just over the bridge from Vedado on the Malecón is **1830** (*moderate*), which is set in a small and attractive palacio with tables inside and out, Cuban and international fare, service average. Across the harbour in the Morro Castle (beneath the Havana lighthouse) you will find a couple of good restaurants: **La Divina Pastora** (*expensive*), which has a fantastic view over the Malecón and the buildings of Havana, specializes in seafood such as *camarrones al ajillo* (shrimp in garlic), while **Los Doces Aposteles** (*moderate*) offers Cuban cuisine.

At the Hemingway Marina in the west of Havana there is a place predictably called **Papa's**, which serves Cuban and international fare including seafood. The walls are decorated with murals of the undersea world. At the adjacent **Fiesta**, there are Spanish and Cuban dishes as well as international meals. There is a good club at the marina if you wish to go dancing. At **Cojimar**, to the east of Havana, is the **La Terraza** restaurant, which has fish and seafood on offer.

In the **Pinar del Río** area you are still mostly limited to the hotels, but a stroll around the city centre could reveal some new alternatives.

Varadero offers perhaps even more choice and value than Havana. Competition between hotels and restaurants has cut prices and raised standards. If money is no object, begin an evening at the **Mirador Bar** at the top of the **Las Americas** restaurant, a beautifully tiled and breezy terrace approached by a tiny stairway. Downstairs in the restaurant (*expensive*) you dine on antique chairs in magnificent surroundings—rum shrimp or Dakota chicken marinated in apple and lemon, while the waves thunder below. If you prefer to spend a little less and be more at the centre of things, you could try the **Parque Josoné**—a walled park on the east of the main strip, with statues among the palms and a lake where you can take out a boat. There are three restaurants: **El Retiro** (*moderate*), set in an old family house with the paintings still

Cuba Directory

getting there

By air from the UK: Until 1991 there were no direct flights between London and Havana. Then an occasional charter using a clapped-out Ilyushin 62 began operating from Stansted. Now Cubana, the national airline, flies three DC-10s per week between Gatwick and Havana. These are supplemented by frequent charter services to Varadero and other resort airports.

By air from Europe: Cubana also flies to Havana from Paris, Berlin, Frankfurt and Madrid. Iberia flies from Madrid, while LTU of Germany has a regular service from Düsseldorf. Aeroflot flights from Moscow to Havana can be joined in Shannon in Ireland.

hanging, and international fare; **Dante's** (*moderate*), an Italian restaurant serving some of the tastiest pizzas in Cuba; and **La Campagna** (*moderate*), set in an old house on the hill, where you will find creole food. Not far off on Avenida Playa at Calle 40 is **El Bodegon Criollo** (*moderate*), in a breezy coral-rock house. This is an offshoot of Havana's **Bodeguita del Medio**, complete with graffiti all over the walls. Local fare as the name suggests—*bistec de cerdo grille* and *picadillo a la criollo*. The greatest concentration of choice is close to the bridge from the mainland. **Mi Casita**, on Avenida Playa between Calle 11 and 12 (*moderate*), is a pretty spot, set in a coral-rock villa with paintings and antique furniture. Set international menu of fish, lobster or chicken. Not far off is **Las Brasas** (*moderate–cheap*), which serves creole fare—*lonjas de cerdo al jugo*, roast pork chops in a natural sauce, or *pollo en salsa*.

Bars and snack-bars have proliferated all over town, but most of the club action is in the west. Nightclubs include the **Cueva del Pirata**, where the entry charge covers a cabaret and dancing, **Tuxpan** in the hotel, and **Kastillito**, between Calle 49 and 50. There is a cabaret at the **Hotel Internacional**.

In **Cienfuegos**, go to the **1819**, in an old town-house on the Prado, for Cuban food or the nearby **Mandarín** for Chinese and local dishes. The **Covadonga** on Calle 37 specializes in paellas and seafood. The choice of places to eat in **Trinidad** has rocketed in the past few years. Try the **Trinidad** on Calle Maceo for international fare and **El Mesón del Regidor** on Calle Simón Bolívar, where you will find creole and Spanish food.

As you head farther east you will become more and more dependent on the hotels, but in **Holguín** you can try **El Quinqué** and **El Ranchón Criollo**, both of which serve creole food.

In **Santiago**, there are sister restaurants to the Havana restaurants **La Cecilia** and **Tocororo**, both of which serve international food (*expensive–moderate*). For seafood try **El Cayo** and **Los Corales** (*both moderate*) and if you want Cuban creole food, try **La Casa de Rolando**. In **Baracoa**, the best alternative to the average restaurant at **El Castillo** is one of the expanding number of *paladares*.

On **Cayo Largo** you will be dependent on hotel dining rooms or outdoor barbecues, but on the **Isla de Juventud** the possibilities are slightly better. In **Nueva Gerona** the fun restaurant is **El Avión**, where meals are served in the fuselage of an old airliner.

© (53)–

By air from the USA: Once upon a time, Miami–Havana was the world's busiest international air route. Since 1996, when President Clinton suspended the remaining air link, there have been no direct flights at all. You have to fly via a third country, usually the Bahamas, Jamaica or Mexico.

Before buying a ticket to Cuba, note that most US citizens are still prevented, by Treasury Department regulations, from visiting the island except in specified personal or professional circumstance. Non-US visitors intending to travel from the US must obtain a Tourist Card in advance, which most agencies specializing in travel to Cuba can obtain easily.

By air from Canada: There is a weekly scheduled flight from Montreal on Cubana, and there are many charter flights from both Montreal and Toronto to Havana and Varadero.

By air from other Caribbean islands: The most frequent links from Havana are with Kingston, Jamaica and Nassau, Bahamas. In addition there are charters linking Havana and Varadero with the Caymans, Santo Domingo and Montego Bay. There are some services from the Dominican Republic to Santiago. Services to Latin American countries include flights to Cancún, Mérida and Mexico City; Caracas; San José; Bogotá; Buenos Aires; and Lima.

tourist information

Promotion of Cuba abroad is patchy, with a scattering of official tourist offices; elsewhere, you must rely upon the Cuban Consulate. In the **UK**, contact the Cuban Consulate, in the same building as the Cuban Embassy at 167 High Holborn, London WC1V 6PA (✆ (0171) 240 2248, ✆ 240 6656).

There are Cuban tourist offices in **Canada**: 55 Queen Street East, Suite 705, Toronto, Ontario, M5C 1R5 (✆ (416) 362 0700, ✆ 362 6799), and 440 Boulevard René Lévesque Ouest, Montreal H2Z 1V7 (✆ (514) 857 8004, ✆ 875 8006); **France**, 280 Boulevard Raspael, 75014 Paris (✆ 1 45 38 90 10); **Germany**, Steinweg 2, D 6000 Frankfurt am Main 1 (✆ 069 288 322); **Italy**, Via General Fara 30, terzo piano, 20124 Milano (✆ 66 9814 63167); and **Spain**, Paseo de la Habana 28, 28036 Madrid (✆ 411 3097).

On the island itself, **Cubatur** operates information desks in tourist hotels, but these serve mainly to sell tickets on organized excursions. Your best source of information is almost always going to be local people.

Cuban **newspapers** are of the *Pravda* school of journalism—neither interesting nor enlightening. *Granma*, the official government paper (named after the boat in which Fidel arrived in Cuba from Mexico), is published daily. There is not much hard international news. Its English-language sibling is *Granma International*, which trills the triumphs of communism. Other local journals include *Trabajadores* (Workers), the trade union paper, and *Juventud Rebelde* (Rebel Youth).

Foreign news magazines, sold in some hotels, are the most reliable source of printed news.

Cuba's **medical services** are good, and minor treatment will routinely be given free to foreigners at local clinics. If you are given a prescription, you may have a difficult time finding a pharmacy with the required drugs in stock. For extensive medical attention in Havana, the main clinic for foreign patients is the **Cira García Clinic**, on Avenida 20 in Vedado (✆ 26811). Treatment here is quite expensive and payment is due in dollars.

The **IDD telephone code** for Cuba is ✆ (53), but only certain numbers can be dialled direct. Mostly these are numbers beginning 33 or 66—which connects to a modern, digital network that operates in isolation from the rattly old Cuban telephone system that has been barely touched since the Revolution. This 'normal' network is chaotic—try, try again. There are a few old payphones (taking 5 or 20 centavo coins), but these rarely work. Tourist hotels often have card-operated Etecsa telephones, for which they sell phonecards. This is a cheaper way of calling abroad ($4 per minute to Europe) than the normal operator-assisted rate of $6 or $7 from hotels. If you plan to have a long conversation with someone abroad, get them to call you straight back—hotel front desks are used to this and do not seem to mind at all.

The **British** Embassy in Cuba is a handsome villa at 708 Calle 34 in Miramar, Havana (© 33 1771). The **Canadian** Embassy is at 518 Calle 30 in Miramar (© 33 2516) and the **German** Embassy is at 313 Calle 28, also in Miramar (© 33 2539). Because it has no diplomatic relations with Cuba, the **United States** has no Embassy in Havana. Instead, it officially has merely a US-interest section of the **Swiss** Embassy. In practice, a huge building that is the US Embassy in all but name is at the eastern end of the Calzada in Vedado, overlooking the Malecón (© 33 3551). You are most likely to notice the building when you are told to walk on the other side of the road.

festivals

Much to the relief of the Habañeros, the annual carnival returned to the capital in 1997. After several years of suspension because of economic privation, it has returned bigger and brighter than ever before.

Traditionally, **Carnaval**— the brightest and liveliest event in the Cuban year—was held around the holiest date in the revolutionary calendar, 26 July. This was not to commemorate Fidel's first strike against the Moncada garrison—rather, his attack in 1953 was carried out under cover of Carnaval. The end of July was chosen to mark the completion of the sugar harvest.. This still holds in various places outside the capital, and it is possible to hear Fidel speak during this time (usually in Santiago). However, in **Havana** the celebrations are now spread across three weekends each Feb or March. In **Varadero**, there is a winter carnival staged for the tourists, during the second week in February. Go to it if you are around.

The New Year also coincides with the **Anniversary of the Victory of the Revolution** and at that time Fidel often appears to a crowd of hundreds of thousands in the Plaza de la Revolucion in Havana. Other public holidays tend to commemorate revolutionary and historical moments, including the birthday of José Martí (28 January), the Bay of Pigs Victory (19 April), the death of Che Guevara (8 October) and the landing of the *Granma* (2 December). The city of Havana has more festivities on 14–16 November, with some carnival-like celebrations. The capital also stages a festival of the classical arts in November and a Latin American film festival each year in December.

money

The currency of Cuba is the **peso** (symbol $), divided into 100 centavos. Officially, the exchange rate is set at the (ludicrously inflated) rate of US$1 = 1 peso. Some hotel desks continue to maintain this fiction, thereby fleecing holidaymakers, but *casas de cambio* in towns and cities will change cash dollars for pesos at the rate of 20 pesos to one dollar. It used to be the case that foreigners could rarely pay for anything in pesos, but since a realistic dollar exchange rate was established it is now possible to buy almost anything with pesos. You may also appreciate the currency for its aesthetics, too—the three-peso note bears a strong image of Che Guevara, as does the coin of the same value.

US dollars, however, remain the main currency for visitors to Cuba. In many businesses—hotels, restaurants and taxis, etc—it is assumed that you will pay in dollars. You may receive change in a third, tourist currency, 'convertible pesos'. You are encouraged to think of these as souvenirs, but most sensible travellers exchange them for real dollars at the airport.

Tipping used to be discouraged, but it is becoming more common. A gratuity will be readily accepted, but since US citizens do not visit Cuba in significant numbers there is not yet a tradition of adding 15 per cent to every bill.

Because of US-imposed restrictions, you should not take American Express traveller's cheques to Cuba nor attempt to use a credit card issued in the USA. Other brands are normally accepted.

Changing traveller's cheques into dollars is most easily done at hotels, though you may pay a charge of four per cent. On dollar traveller's cheques that are issued by a US bank, you are asked not to indicate where the cheque was cashed. Most credit cards and travellers cheques are accepted in payment for hotel bills, restaurants and other tourist activities. You can draw money on non-US Visa and MasterCard credit cards at several hotels, again in exchange for a percentage fee.

Visitors to Cuba are encouraged to spend, spend, spend. Many hard-currency shops are stocked with imported goods. There are some good **duty-free** deals when you compare the prices with those at home (e.g. rum, whisky, Caribbean rums and musical hardware), but mostly the contents are tourist souvenirs of varying degrees of tackiness. The best buy, of course, is cigars (*see* p.640).

There is little of interest in the local shops except for those keen to snap up bargain-priced Cuban music on vinyl. Cuban clothes are hardly in the vanguard of fashion. Bookshops (*librerías*) occasionally turn up Cuban classics.

maps and books

There are many histories of Cuba written in English, of which the most monumental is *Cuba, or The Pursuit of Freedom*, by Hugh Thomas. This ends with the Revolution, but there are plenty of other books with which to pick up the threads. One of the most readable is Peter Marshall's *Cuba Libre—Breaking the Chains? Fidel—a Critical Portrait* by Tad Szulc gives a very detailed and well-researched account of the Cuban leader, and is an informative and easy read. The other great revolutionary figure, Che Guevara, was the subject of several biographies in 1997, the 30th anniversary of his death. At the head of the field is *Che Guevara: A Revolutionary Life* by Jon Lee Anderson, a massive and finely researched work.

One of the most celebrated Cuban writers is Nicolas Guillén, author of among others *Patria o Muerte*. Alejo Carpentier was a Cuban journalist and writer, author of *El Reino de este Mundo* (*A Kingdom of this World*), about the Haitian revolution, and other works that have influenced Latin American authors. Ernest Hemingway lived for twenty years on the island and is remembered for his Nobel Prize-winning *The Old Man and the Sea*, which gives the most poignant picture of a poor fisherman's life in fifties Cuba. *Our Man in Havana* is another classic by Graham Greene, in which the vacuum-cleaner salesman Wormold gets in a pickle as his ring of fictional agents starts to take on a disturbing life of its own. It was first published in 1958, shortly after which the story of Cuba started to become stranger than fiction.

The cartographic void that existed in Cuba for three decades after the Revolution is now being filled, and reasonable maps of the island and its cities are available in hotels, petrol stations and hard currency shops.

watersports

Availability of watersports is patchy. Equipment may be of a poor quality or nonexistent—small sailing craft are difficult to find because many of them sailed off one-way to Florida in the 1994 exodus. For the best selection, go to the Playas del Este, Varadero, Cayo Coco, Playa Santa Lucía and the offshore islands. Waterskiing is popular in Cuba and is easy to arrange.

Yacht tours: These are limited, but available through the Hemingway Marina, west of Havana (at Calle 248, Santa Fe) and at Varadero. Out on Cayo Largo, you can take a boat trip to Cayo Avalos or Cayo Rosario, for snorkelling and a picnic.

Deep-sea fishing: Popular in Cuba, and you can take a launch out into the Gulf Stream and cast for blue, white or black marlin, yellowfin tuna, sailfish or wahoo. Again, try the Hemingway Marina. The other principal resorts also have boats equipped for offshore fishing and for deep-sea trips, including the Playas del Este, Varadero, Playa Santa Lucía, Guardalavaca, Santiago de Cuba and on the Isla de la Juventud. Sailing is cheap compared with most Caribbean islands. You can reckon on US$250 to charter a boat for the whole day, but do not expect the same standards as you might find around, say, the US Virgin Islands.

Scuba diving: Divers will find some superb reefs off Cuba. Whole forests of black coral, sponges and gorgonians fur the submarine walls and the sloping drop-offs, and in the shallow sandy bottoms between the islands schools of tropical fish dip and dart in unison, while single angelfish float and lobsters and crabs scuttle. On the north coast, dives can be arranged at the tourist resorts and instruction is available. On the protected south coast there are stunning underwater landscapes in the cays of the two archipelagos—between the Isla de la Juventud (go to the Colony Hotel) and Cayo Largo there are supreme reefs with crystalline water, good also for snorkelling, and the cays of the Jardines de la Reina are yet more beautiful and remote. Underwater photographic equipment is also on hand at the bigger dive shops.

other sports

Tennis: Courts are attached to most of the larger hotels and in the resort areas. Inland fishing and hunting (for anything from quail and snipe to wild boar and even an alligator if you so desire) is possible in season. Book through Cubatur; the resorts will provide guides, boats and weapons.

Hiking: This is not an organized activity in Cuba, which is either a boon—no crowds or over-hiked trails—or a pain, if you like to have good map and a fair idea of where you are going. The Sierra Maestra in the southeast of the island is the best territory for getting good and lost.

Riding: It is possible to set up horseback outings along the beach or into the hills in many of the resorts; it is popular with the Cubans and so there are plenty of stables.

Spectator sports: In Cuba these are mostly free. In relation to its population, Cuba is the most successful sporting nation at the Olympics. It is well worth taking time out to watch a Cuban game of **baseball**—there are stadia all over the island. In the back streets you will see a scaled-down version of baseball played by children in which they are not allowed to run, which is quite fun to join in. You will also see games of dominoes being played quickly and demonstratively in the town squares (dominoes is a popular game all over the Caribbean).

Jamaica

Everyone has an image of Jamaica: the island idyll of palms and beaches, a hedonist's paradise of rum, reefers and reggae rhythm, a land of plantation houses and fantastically beautiful tropical gardens: Jamaica is all these things. Although often considered to be a little threatening, Jamaica is among the liveliest of all the islands, its allure the strongest of all the former British Caribbean islands.

Jamaica lies in the western Caribbean to the south of Cuba and, at 4411 square miles (about half the size of Wales), it is the third largest of the Greater Antilles. Physically the island is spectacular. The coastline rises immediately into mountains, and within a few hundred yards of the sea you can be at 1000ft (some two-fifths of the island is above this height). It is so mountainous that parts of the Blue Mountains and the Cockpit Country, a moonscape of forested limestone hillocks, are barely accessible. And Jamaica is immensely fertile, particularly in the east and along the north coast, where you could almost expect a pencil to take root.

On a map Jamaica may look as though it languishes like a turtle, but nothing could be further from the truth when it comes to the Jamaicans themselves. Between 2½ and 3 million Jamaicans live on the island (probably more than this number live elsewhere in the world). The streets are something of a theatre as the Jamaicans shout and quip with one another. Markets, from downtown Kingston to the three or four people selling fruit at the roadside in the country, are mayhem. The Jamaicans do not suffer authority or formality gladly (queuing died soon after the British left) and they are very forward; some stop you to give advice or to say hello, others to hustle you.

You are very likely to be accosted in the main tourist areas—Jamaica has always been exuberant and at times slightly rough, but the reports that call it unsafe are ill-founded, as long as you take advice and use as much care as you would in any poor country. One solution to the problem is never to leave the compound of your hotel, but this is to miss out on the best of Jamaica, which you will find in the local villages beyond the resorts. Occasionally the fervour spills over into violence, but this is rarely directed against foreigners. Avoid Kingston at election time when political tensions are at their highest.

Jamaica became independent from Britain on 6 August 1962, but the echoes of three centuries of British colonial rule still ring through. Churches and Georgian great houses were constructed by the planters in the style of buildings at home, and clocks chime as they do in Britain. Jamaica has moved on since Independence, but many British institutions remain in creolized form, including the Westminster model of democracy and the belts, peaked caps and serge trousers of uniformed policemen.

And yet things are never quite as they seem; a very strong African element underpins the British façade. Jamaican marching bands may wear scarlet tunics with trimmings of gold braid, but their movements are not the clipped and

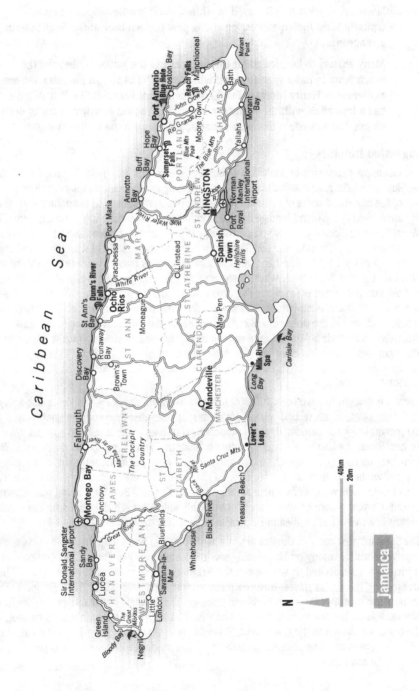

formal procession of the British, they have a rhythmic swagger that is Jamaican. Cricket is still played in whites, but it has developed its own, typically West Indian expression and is now thrown back at the English with a vengeance.

Many visitors to Jamaica go for the sun, sea and the ganja, but beyond the beach Jamaica has a special appeal which over the centuries has attracted men as diverse as Henry Morgan, Errol Flynn and Noel Coward. The British have had a love affair with the island for centuries. Tropical paradise or tricky destination, Jamaica offers the most romantic liaison with the Caribbean.

Suggested Itinerary

You can make a good tour of Jamaica in a couple of weeks; this will give you some time in the well-known tourist resorts as well as a look at something more Jamaican, the magnificent interior of the island and some of the inland activities such as river-bathing and rafting. Whether you arrive in Kingston or in Montego Bay, you can follow the coastline. Stay a few days either in Montego Bay or Ocho Rios, until you get the urge to look beyond the beaches and bars. Go east to Port Antonio, a charming and laid-back town in the far east, the lushest and most strikingly fertile area of the island. From here, you can make your way over to the southern side of the island via the Blue Mountains, where there are now inns and guest houses in all price ranges, and then drop down into Kingston. The capital will also show you the Jamaicans' Jamaica— check out the markets downtown and make a ferry trip over to Port Royal. From here you should head west to the sleepy towns of Treasure Beach and Black River, where the Jamaicans themselves take their holidays. Leave enough time for Negril, which is a tourist town with a difference—great for a few days' 'hanging out' waiting for the sunset and the flight home.

History

There are thought to have been 100,000 Arawaks living on Jamaica when Columbus arrived on 5 May 1494, on his second voyage. He went to investigate reports of gold on *Xamayca*, as the Indians knew the island and which supposedly translates as the land of 'Wood and Water'. To him it was the 'fairest isle that eyes ever beheld; the land seems to touch the sky...' But there was no gold and so he left. It was another nine years before he returned, on his fourth voyage, washed up here after exploration of the Central American coast, this time unintentionally. His ships were worm-eaten and they sank off St Ann's Bay; the admiral was stranded there for a year before he was rescued (two of his sailors braved the high seas and hostile Indians in a canoe and paddled to Hispaniola, from where they fetched him).

The Spaniards first came to Jamaica to settle in 1510 and to begin with they used the island to supply the senior colony on Hispaniola (now the Dominican Republic). Colonization was a failure, but it succeeded in wiping out the Arawak Indians within a hundred years. They worked the Indians as slaves, tortured them to death and even killed them for sport. The Indians also died like flies from European diseases. The Spaniards' first settlement, Sevilla la Nueva, was on the north coast, near St Ann's Bay, but it proved to be an unhealthy spot, so the town was moved to the south coast. St Jago de la Vega (now Spanish Town) became their principal settlement. The colonists planted crops, but their main occupation was farming pigs for their fat and hides.

The colony was neglected in favour of Havana and the settlements on the mainland coast and faced regular attack by pirates in which hard-won wealth could disappear overnight. Jamaica languished for 150 years until the British arrived in 1655. Little remains of Spain's influence now, apart from a few names, but in the hills, the *cimarróns*, later known as the maroons (slaves armed and set free by the Spaniards to attack the British), were to have an effect on Jamaican life until the 19th century.

On capturing the island in the heartland of the Spanish Indies, the English immediately fortified Port Royal, which soon became a base for the *buccaneers*, who would come here to repair their ships and sell their loot. In time of peace these 'brethren of the coast' could not be officially sanctioned because they trod too fine a line between freebooting and piracy, but when the islands were at war, they were an invaluable fighting force. Port Royal, the richest and most decadent town of its age, received its come-uppance in 1692 when it was destroyed in an earthquake (*see* p.691).

Pirates continued to plague the coasts of the island, though, until about 1720, and the likes of Charles Vane, Blackbeard (a natty dresser who would go into battle with lit fuses in his hair), 'Calico' Jack Rackham (supposedly called so because of his penchant for calico underclothes) and his women pirates Anne Bonney and Mary Read, would use the bays along the coast to drink captured rum and to refit their ships before setting off again on the high sea.

But at the same time, Jamaica was growing into Britain's wealthiest colony in the West Indies. The island became a massive sugar factory and for a while Jamaica was the largest sugar producer in the world. The planters and merchants at any rate enjoyed immense wealth and they built their great houses on the estates and town houses in the capital. The whole venture depended on a massive workforce, made up of slaves from Africa, shipped in to the market in Kingston. The slaves were subjected to brutal treatment in what was a cruel age and the estates were run on the basis of mutual fear. The planters maintained their law with a rod of iron and with a liberal use of the whip, while always living in the fear that the slaves would rebel, which from time to time they did.

Some slaves ran away to the mountains and joined the communities of maroons, hunting pigs and planting a few crops, and occasionally descending from the hills at night to attack the plantations, torching the fields and stealing cattle. They settled in townships in the Cockpit Country and in the mountains of the east and became expert at defending themselves from the raiding parties sent out against them. They fought a guerrilla war and would disguise themselves with jungle foliage, ambushing the routes through the hills and then filtering away into the forest. Led by men such as Cudjoe, Accompong and Cuffee (and the woman maroon Nanny, one of Jamaica's national heroes), they eventually forced the government to sue for peace, and in 1739 the maroons were granted an area of land to themselves, in what is now Trelawny parish, where they would be left undisturbed. In return they promised to cease hostilities against the plantations and to hunt and return runaway slaves. A treaty was also made with the maroon leader Quao in the Blue Mountains in the east.

The maroons were quiet for half a century, but the slaves themselves revolted. Tacky's Rebellion took place in 1760 as a band of Coromantee slaves broke into a fort and stole arms and ammunition, attacked a few plantations and then took to the hills. Tacky was killed by one of the maroons who had been called out against them, and his followers committed suicide rather than surrender, but revolts broke out all over the island and it was months before the old order was reimposed.

In 1795, when the French Revolution had an explosive effect on the French colony of Saint Domingue, and the slaves took over the country in open revolt, a second maroon war broke out in Jamaica. This time 300 of them held out against 4500 trained troops and militia, once again waging a guerrilla war against the government and torching estates. Tracker dogs were brought from Cuba to find them and the maroons knew their time was up. Under the terms of the treaty they should have been allowed to settle elsewhere on the island, but the majority were deported to Nova Scotia and then eventually shipped to Sierra Leone.

At the end of the 18th century the abolitionist movement, led by men like William Wilberforce, was born in Britain, and despite the objections of the West Indian planters, the slave trade from Africa was banned in 1808. Slave laws were passed in Britain but the planters refused to institute them. Unrest continued on the island, and Jamaica erupted in another massive revolt in 1831. It was led by Sam 'Daddy' Sharpe, who has since become another of Jamaica's national heroes. He was hanged for his action, but it was enough for Parliament in London to force the Emancipation Act for all the West Indian islands in 1834. There was a period of 'apprenticeship' for four years, in which the slaves were tied to the plantations, but in 1838 the slaves were set free unconditionally.

They left the estates and took plots of land where they could find them and turned to subsistence agriculture. With the help of Baptists, Methodists and other missionaries, who had sided with the slaves against the planters, they formed free villages. For their part, the planters fared badly, despite waves of immigrant workers (East Indians mainly, but also some voluntary Africans), and steadily the sugar industry, now competing with islands which still had slavery, steadily declined.

The pressure for political change came soon after the slaves were freed. Their cause was adopted by men like the mulatto lawyer George William Gordon and the preacher, Paul Bogle. Matters came to a head under Governor Eyre and in 1865 there was a rebellion in Morant Bay in the southeast of the island, led by Bogle. The riot was put down brutally. The blame for it was laid at Gordon's door and he was hanged. Bogle was hunted down and he was tried in Morant Bay, where he was sentenced and hanged in the arch of the Court House where his rebellion had taken place. Statues of him stand at the Court House today and in National Heroes Park. Eyre was recalled and dismissed from the colonial service, but his last act was to get the Jamaican Assembly to vote for its own demise and give power to the Colonial Office in London. In 1872 the capital was removed from Spanish Town to Kingston.

In the 20th century, as the original plantocracy declined, more black and mulatto Jamaicans began to be elected to the local assemblies and to enter the civil service. Changes were particularly influenced by another Jamaican national hero, Marcus Mosiah Garvey.

Garvey was born in St Ann's Bay in 1887 and as a young man he travelled around the Americas. Seeing the desperate poverty in which blacks were living everywhere, he resolved to unite the African race to better their situation in the white-ruled world. In 1914 he founded the Universal Negro Improvement Association, which by the 1920s had become an international movement, with offices all over the Americas, in African countries, and even as far off as Australia. They were all linked with the newspaper, the *Negro World*. The UNIA ran successful businesses and banks and a shipping line, the Black Star Line (after the White Star Line), in competition with the whites. There was even an aim to go 'back to Africa', to create a model state in which the blacks could be proud.

Garvey became a champion of the blacks everywhere because he brought them pride and self-respect in a way that had never been possible under colonial rule, but he was generally disliked by the white establishment and in 1922 he served a jail-term in the States for supposed fraud. He returned to Jamaica in 1927 and set out aims for a political party in 1929. In 1935 he moved his offices to London. Though his movement was eclipsed after his death in London in 1940, his remains were flown back in triumph to Jamaica in 1964. He was proclaimed the country's first national hero soon afterwards.

Pressure for political change grew ever stronger in the 1930s, in the wake of the Depression. There were riots all over the Caribbean in 1938 and soon after this, the Jamaican trade unions and then political parties were born. The two leaders who emerged were the flamboyant Alexander Bustamante, later leader of the Jamaica Labour Party (JLP) and Norman Manley of the People's National Party (PNP). In 1944 adult suffrage for all Jamaicans was introduced, the first in the Caribbean, and in 1957 cabinet government and full internal autonomy were granted. In a referendum put to them by Bustamante in 1961, the Jamaicans decided not to remain in the West Indies Federation, and within the year they had taken Independence, the first British Caribbean island to do so, on 6 August 1962.

After Independence, politics continued to be dominated by these two men, who also later became Jamaican national heroes. The Jamaican Parliament, set up following the Westminster model, is made up of a 60-member House of Representatives, elected every five years, and a smaller Senate, to which members are appointed on the advice of the Prime Minister and leader of the opposition. The country remains within the Commonwealth and the Queen is represented by the Governor General, at present Sir Howard Cooke. The judicial system is based on British law and the highest court of appeal is the Privy Council in London.

Until recently, the PNP, now led by P. J. Patterson, and the JLP still dominated Jamaican politics. In early 1996 a third party, the National Democratic Movement, was formed. Led by Bruce Golding who came from the JLP, it has held its own with about 15% of the vote. Elections in Jamaica tend to be somewhat traumatic, despite efforts to calm them in recent years and they are always hard, if not entirely honourably, fought. The 1980 election was extremely bloody (500 people died) and it returned the JLP, led then and still by Edward Seaga, with a massive majority. He followed monetarist policies that reversed the decade of left-inclined government from the PNP under Michael Manley (son of Norman Manley). In 1989, Michael Manley was re-elected on a less radical ticket than before and then the PNP was re-elected in 1993 with P. J. Patterson at its head. Elections are due some time before March 1998.

The Economy

There are three important sectors of the Jamaican economy: the mining and export of bauxite and its derivative, alumina which makes aluminium; tourism, which is the largest earner of foreign exchange—in 1993 Jamaica had over a million and a half tourists, with an earning of around US$1000 million; and agriculture, which is the largest employer at around 35 per cent of the workforce (about half of Jamaica's population lives in rural areas) and contributes about 10 per cent of GDP. Export crops include sugar, bananas, coffee and cocoa. The best known unofficial export earner in Jamaica is, of course, marijuana, and at one stage this was thought to top all others.

Rastafari and Revival

Jamaica has a mind-boggling proliferation of religions—Anglicans, Presbyterians, Congregationalists, Methodists and Moravians, Baptists and Seventh Day Adventists, as well as Islam, Judaism and lesser known faiths such as the Bah'ai. Many of them were introduced by missionaries in colonial times, others adapted by the slaves from their African beliefs, but perhaps the best known outside the country is the Rastafari religion. It is known for its dreadlocks and reggae music and also for its connection with ganja (there are many opportunist pseudo-rastas around the tourist areas in Jamaica), but it is less appreciated for the quiet and peaceful ideals that its true adherents follow, in fear of Jah (God).

Rastafari was born in the thirties at the time of the crowning of Haile Selassi as King of Ethiopia, after the Ethiopian War. They consider Haile Selassi *Ras* (prince) *Tafari* (to be feared), the King of Kings, Lord of Lords, the Conquering Lion of Judah. Haile Selassie died in 1975, but is still revered by the rastas, who do not believe that he is dead. The rastas consider themselves brought to 'Babylon' by the white man (they think of themselves as one of the lost tribes of Israel), and their aim is eventual return to Africa.

There are different rasta sects, but as a rule genuine rastas are gentle people who follow their avowed beliefs of 'peace and love'. They are vegetarians, and many are herbalists living in the mountains; some are teetotal and do not smoke tobacco. They do regard ganja as sacred and the 'chalice' (pipe), as it is known, is supposed to bring wisdom.

There are a number of semi-religious sects in Jamaica, part Christian, part animist, with a view of the spirit world not dissimilar to the voodoo of Haiti. The best known are *Pukumina* (also written *pocomania*), and *Revival Zion*, which believe in the Holy Trinity, but also invoke spirits from the worlds beyond direct human experience. *Kumina* is more purely African and its adherents also invoke spirits, particularly those of ancestors. These sects are particularly strong in the countryside and some involve ceremonies with drumming and dancing to drums, with the eventual possession of one of the participants by the spirits. Quite a lot of Jamaicans believe in *deads* and *duppies* (the ghosts of people who have died, but who are not at peace), some of whom remain in conflict with the living over issues dating from their lifetime. *Obeah* is another system of beliefs in which individuals are able to affect the outcome of their lives with the use of spells and specially prepared potions.

Jamaican Music—Ska, Reggae and Dancehall

Visitors joke that the Jamaicans switch the roll of their gait as they walk down the street, passing each successive shop and its stereo system. This is not far from the truth, as music is played everywhere, constantly, and almost always at high volume. Buses are like mobile discotheques, usually audible before they come into view, and out in the country you can see a stack of speakers higher than the bar that has the stereo. Like so much Caribbean music, Jamaican songs have a strong element of comment and satire and singers will often address topical issues in their lyrics.

Mento was a lively dance rhythm and it lasted for many years in the early part of this century. Bands played accoustic guitars, a ukelele, a fiddle and a boomer box (a sit-on box with metal teeth) and their lyrics were often jokingly rude about life and love. In the early sixties, with the arrival of the electric sound system, Jamaican music began to evolve very quickly: mento was overtaken by *ska*, a riotous and often compulsive beat, and after a few years this developed into the slow and heavy drum and bass rhythms of *rocksteady* and *rub-a-dub*. Like the steel pans of Trinidad, these sounds came from the yards of downtown Kingston and were disapproved of initially by the authorities, but they are an elemental expression of Jamaica and unique in their inventiveness.

Reggae, which speeded up rocksteady again and introduced the *chaka-chaka* lilt to the rhythm, developed in the late 60s as singers like Jimmy Cliff and Bob Marley and the Wailers began to have their success on the island. It was not until around the time of his death in May 1981 that Bob Marley and more generally reggae gained international fame. Other leading reggae groups and singers include Toots and the Maytals, Burning Spear, Third World, Black Uhuru, Peter Tosh and Gregory Isaacs. And abroad, among the large expatriate Jamaican community in Britain, reggae groups, including Steel Pulse and Aswad, flourished.

The mid-eighties and early nineties were dominated by another rhythm, *dancehall*, a compulsive and monotonous rap grafted on to a hard reggae beat. Its rhythm makes it danceable, but like all Jamaican music it is the lyrics, often rude or controversial, that make it so popular. Dancehall addressed the issues of the day, anything from sex to corruption (a fair dose of the former, which are known as slack songs), although they are nigh incomprehensible unless you can understand *patois*. There are singers (who tend to be slower and more melodic) and DJs, who rap their lyrics to a number of established rhythms (cherry-o, satta, taxi). Leading DJs include Shabba Ranks, Buju Banton, Cocoa Tea, Mad Cobra and a singer-DJ duo called Chakademus and Pliers. Singers include Tony Rebel, who often addresses cultural issues, and Beresford Hammond, who is big on love ballads. Recently the scene has begun to change again. Through the efforts of Irie FM, culture reggae has undergone a revival and Jamaica is beginning to sound a little more as it did in the seventies. Many of the heavyweight DJs have softened up their lyrics. The biggest singers on the island at the moment are Luciano and Anthony B. At the time of writing the popular rhythms were pepper-seed and kettle drum.

The two central dates of the Jamaican music calendar are the annual **Reggae Sumfest**, which takes place in August in Montego Bay, and **Reggae Sunsplash**, now held in February. Reggae Sumfest is a six-day bonanza of reggae, featuring individual singers, dancehall and big bands. It is a fun event, more like a day at the races than a concert in the European style, with games being played at the rumshops and stalls that line the back of the concert area. Reggae artists from all over the world come to it and they each play a set of a couple of songs, so you see about twenty performers in a night. It usually gets started at about 10pm and goes on until dawn, and beyond. Sunsplash follows much the same pattern.

You get a good idea of Jamaican music from just wandering around the streets of Kingston, but to see it Jamaican-style, you have to get out into the concerts and clubs; ask around, but your best bet is probably in Kingston or Negril. You may find a world-famous band playing to a crowd of just a few hundred. (The tourist hotels often play calypso, which comes from Trinidad and Barbados at the other end of the Caribbean anyway.) During the day you can listen to non-stop reggae on Irie FM (105.5 or 107.7). Any club or record shop will sell you cassettes of the latest tunes.

Jerk

Jerk is a special Jamaican way of barbecuing seasoned meats slowly over a wood fire set in the ground. The technique was supposedly developed by the maroons, runaways who lived in the mountains in the 18th century, who would cure meat for sale. Traditionally they would kill early in the week and cook it in an underground oven for a couple of days before taking it to market on Friday or Saturday. Nowadays the fresh meat is seasoned with a marinade (of as many as twenty spices including peppers, scallions, pimento and ginger) and then it is cooked over a pit on slats of green pimento wood, which itself increases the flavour. Meat is 'jerked' all over the island now, but the home of jerk is Boston Bay, beneath the John Crow Mountains in Portland parish in the east, where the maroons lived. There are a number of shacks at the roadside, where they start to cook early in the morning—don't arrive after about 4pm or it will all be gone.

Jerk Centres are among the best local Jamaican restaurants. Despite their name, they are not for the socially ungainly, but a place where you order jerk (pork, chicken, 'spear ribs', sausage, fish and even lobster), which you eat with a special sauce and with a festival, a sweet and heavy roll. As you order, the cook will suddenly pull out a machete before you and proceed to chop the food into bite-size pieces and throw it on to a piece of paper. You will then be asked if you want hot pepper sauce. Jerk seasoning is already pretty spicy, so try one tiny dash on a corner of the meal on your first time out, because Jamaican hot pepper sauce has a vicious and searing scourge and a habit of affecting everything edible for miles around.

Getting Around

The Jamaicans have been complaining bitterly about their **bus** system (minibuses and larger) recently as, particularly in Kingston, it has become very slow, crowded and hot. However, it is possible to get almost anywhere in Jamaica on a bus, eventually, and it will give you excellent exposure to Jamaican life. Buses are fairly noisy (if not because of the people, then because of the relentless pulse on the stereo) and if you are sitting, you may find that a 'standee' will hand you their bag to hold. Check the fare as you get on, though you may not actually hand over the money until later in the journey. In the country, flag buses down from the side of the road with a frantic wave. You will also find that share taxis, often referred to as *Ladas*, (known familiarly as the 'Life and Death Association' and 'robot' taxis because they are driven by automatons), run the same routes for the same fare.

There are a number of terminals in **Kingston**, including the Parade (downtown), Half Way Tree, Cross Roads, Barbican and Papine. If in doubt about which bus to take, ask a fellow passenger, or one of the lads with dollar notes folded around their fingers (and then expect to be hustled aboard). In town the buses will stop only at official stops. *Fare J$6–12; they run until 10pm.* There is a bus service (roughly every half hour) from the airport to the Parade, downtown. Buses to towns on the north coast leave from downtown Kingston, west along Beckford Street from the Parade. For Spanish Town and Mandeville go to the station at Half Way Tree. The different rest stops *en route* from the capital are known for their different snacks. At Old Harbour (going west) there is fry fish and bammy; at Melrose Hill (near Mandeville) the popular meal is roast yam and salt fish; at Fates Pen (towards Ocho Rios) you will find a variety of snacks and at Friendship Gap the popular snack is fry chicken.

In **Montego Bay**, north coast and Kingston buses leave from the terminal at Barnett St and local taxis from below Sam Sharpe Square, at the junction of Market St and Strand St. Buses for Negril leave from Creek Street. In **Negril**, buses leave from near the roundabout at the southern end of the beach, over the bridge from the crafts market; in **Ocho Rios** from the roundabout that leads up to Fern Gully and to Kingston, buses headed east to Port Maria leave from near the clocktower; and in **Port Antonio** on the foreshore road behind the Bank of Nova Scotia. In **Mandeville** they leave from beneath the church on the main square. **Hitchhiking** in Jamaica is usually a bit slow, but is worth chancing if you're on for an adventure. To signal to a driver, point repeatedly and rapidly at the ground and shout.

Taxis are readily available in Jamaica, through any hotel lobby if you cannot find one yourself, which is pretty unlikely around the tourist areas. Steel yourself to run the gauntlet of drivers touting for business as you emerge from the airport. The Tourist Board sets a standard fare, posted in JUTA taxis and quoted in both US and Jamaican dollars. With the others, bargain. Taxis are not usually metered in Jamaica and so you are advised to settle the fare before you set off. All licensed taxis have the red PPV plates. Some restaurants will send a car to pick you up and return you to your hotel if you request. There are **taxi stands** at the following numbers: Montego Bay (✆ 952 0521), Ocho Rios (✆ 974 2971), Port Antonio (✆ 993 2684) and Negril (✆ 957 3227).

Many of the taxi drivers make good **tour guides** if you wish to take a ride to the local sights or up into the hills. Any hotel lobby will find a driver for you and the price is reasonable when divided between four.

You can **fly** to a number of towns on the island. There are regular scheduled flights between Kingston (Tinson Pen airport) and Montego Bay and the other tourist areas. Contact Air Jamaica Express who have offices in Montego Bay (✆ 952 5401), Kingston (✆ 923 8680), Negril (✆ 957 4251) and Port Antonio (✆ 993 2405). You can take a sight-seeing flight over the Cockpit Country from the Sangster airport in Montego Bay and in Ocho Rios you can even go sightseeing by helicopter: call Helitours (✆ 974 2265/1108) a couple of days in advance.

Car hire: the Jamaicans joke that you buy the car each time you hire one because it's so expensive. However, if you can afford it, it is well worth having one to explore the mountain roads and the successive headlands and bays along the coastline. There are plenty of hire cars available, but it is still a good idea to arrange it a few days ahead in season.

The Jamaicans are pretty awful drivers and the roads are notorious for being pot-holed. Avoid driving in downtown Kingston except for sport. The traffic is generally chaotic and the Jamaicans perform some remarkable manoeuvres in their constant hurry. Driving on the high roads is correspondingly more dangerous, as all the same manoeuvres are performed at high speed. The country is not that well signposted, so take a good map (easily available from the hire companies and the Tourist Board). Driving happens, mainly, on the left. Finally, watch out for goats and cows.

A driving licence from home is acceptable, minimum age 25. Take a credit card for the hefty deposit. There are many hire companies, with a variety of different contracts—read yours. The Jamaica U-Drive Association represents a number of car-hire companies with a standard code of business and rates. You can get their list at the Tourist Board offices. Reckon on rental of at least US$60 plus charges for the smallest car for a single day with reductions for a week's hire. There are other smaller, local enterprises which offer lower rates. Remember that car rental companies will deliver to you, though if you are in another town there may be a delivery charge.

All the big hire companies have offices at the **Montego Bay** airport: Avis (© 952 4543, ✆ 979 1067), Budget (©/✆ 952 3838), Hertz (© 979 0438. ✆ 979 0439), and Island (©/✆ 952 5771, toll free © (1 800) 892 4581). Also Caribbean Car Rentals (©/✆ 952 0664). In **Negril** there are a couple of firms at the airstrip or you could try the Rite Rate Rent a Car (© 957 4267) and for cars and jeeps, Tanka's Car Rental (© 957 4488). In **Ocho Rios** contact Island Car Rentals (© 974 2334) Paramount (© 994 2357) or Caribbean (© 974 2178), and in **Port Antonio** try Eastern Rent a Car (© 993 3624) or Don's (© 993 2241). The big firms are represented in **Kingston**, at the Norman Manley airport and in town, Bargain (tel 968 3617, ✆ 929 4998), Island (© 926 8861, ✆ 926 6987, US toll free © (1 800) 892 4581) and at the airport (© 924 8075); also Garmack Car Rentals (© 978 0278, ✆ 978 0970).

For the very brave and for pot-hole dodgers, there are **mopeds** and **motorbikes** for hire in all the tourist areas. Drive defensively, and be prepared to get off the road in a hurry. Make sure to get hold of a helmet somehow. They are quite expensive, at around US$30 a day for a motorbike and $12 for a bicycle. In **Mo Bay** try Montego Bike Rentals on Gloucester Avenue (© 952 4984); in **Negril** Dependable Bike Rental (© 957 4764) on the beach, and in **Ocho Rios** at Abe's (© 974 1008).

Jamaica is very well served with organized **tours**—there is endless information in the hotel lobbies. These take in many of the sights mentioned in the text and are an easy way to get around for those without transport. Tour companies operating out of the tourist towns include, in **Montego Bay**: Glamour Tours (© 979 8207), Forsythe's (© 952 0394) and Caribic Vacations (© 953 9895); in **Negril** try JUTA (© 957 9197); and in **Ocho Rios** Blue Danube Tours (© 974 2031) and The Touring Society of Jamaica (© 975 7158). In **Port Antonio** you will also find JUTA (© 993 2684). You could try a downhill bicycling tour which is fun and a good way to see the Jamaican countryside: Blue Mountain Tours (© 974 7075) start at nearly 6000ft in the Blue Mountains in rainforests and run for 17 miles down to a waterfall. In Kingston, try Galaxy (© 925 1492) and Sunventure Tours (© 960 6685).

Many of these tours are a little tame, but if you want to look at Jamaica in more depth there are organizations who are able to tailor-make tours for you. SENSE, PO Box 216, Kingston 7 (© 702 0314) can arrange tours as varied as a river-canoeing trip, bird-watching tours, an architectural tour or even a jam session in a Trenchtown yard. You can also contact the Touring Society of Jamaica (©/✆ 975 7158), who have a number of tours including a great house and gingerbread tour and an art tour.

Some Advice

Particularly as a new arrival, you will be accosted by taxi-drivers, higglers (street vendors), hustlers and the occasional Rent-a-dread on the street in Kingston and around the beaches in the main tourist areas, and you will be asked to buy goods and then offered a whole inventory of services. Until you get a tan or learn to 'give them the eye', they can be quite persistent.

While travelling in Jamaica, take the same precautions you would in the cities of any foreign country, and be wary. Do not flash a full wallet around or hang an arm with a bracelet out of a bus window. You are advised not to walk around downtown Kingston alone after dark. If you wish to go to an area you think might be dodgy, you can always get a Jamaican to go with you.

The Jamaican authorities strongly disapprove of illegal **drugs** and they nobble offenders from time to time (there are quite a few foreigners serving time in Jamaica for drug possession). In practice, you will be offered almost anything by the beach hustlers, from a single spliff to a hunnerd-weight of cullyweed, along with other drugs, including cocaine and crack, dropped in en route from South America. Buying and consuming proscribed drugs is against the law and the risks are obvious.

Beaches

There are innumerable excellent beaches on Jamaica, from the seemingly endless strand at Negril with its fantastic view of the sunset, to the tight bays in the east where the mountains tumble into the sea around you. There are secluded beaches where you will be alone and there are active beaches with all the watersports to keep you busy.

Though all beaches are officially public below the high water mark (you can swim in from the open sea), many Jamaican beaches are effectively private because there is limited access over land. This guarantees some privacy on your hotel beach, but it limits exploration of the beaches around the island. Some hotels allow people from outside to use their facilities for a small fee. There are, of course, public beaches in Jamaica which are usually lively. The Jamaicans are far too modest (in public, about their bodies at any rate) to go nude on the beach, but several of the resorts do have designated nude beaches.

best beaches

Montego Bay: The popular public beaches are Doctor's Cave beach and Cornwall Beach (well known for its beach parties), both popular with the locals, lively and usually crowded, changing facilities, *small adm*. There are bars where you can get a drink to cool you off and watersports can be arranged there. At the end of Kent Avenue, beneath the airport run-in, is a small strip of sand, Dead End Beach and beyond the airport there is another passable public beach, Tropical Beach. At Rose Hall, ten miles to the east of the town, there is a beach club where you can spend the day chilling out in the hammocks and testing out the kayaks and sunfish, adm expensive. There is a charming ebach bar, the Time and Place, on the coast just down from the Trelawney Beach Hotel; swimming not brilliant, but a brilliant stopover by day. At Silver Sands near the town of Duncans there is a private villa complex where you are usually allowed in to the beach to swim; bar, changing facilities, *adm*.

Negril: An almost uninterrupted 5 miles of golden sand running north from the roundabout at the centre of the town (south of here it is nearly all 'ironshore' cliffs). It is good to walk, or if that seems too energetic, there are hip places to loiter and wait for the Green Flash at sunset. There are beach concessionaires who will arrange most watersports. North of here, there is another wide curve of sand in Bloody Bay, steadily being developed and beyond here you will find other tiny inlets with lovely sand.

Ocho Rios: The main beach is UDC beach right in the middle of town, a magnificent curve of white sand where you can try out all the watersports: jetskis, small sailing boats. West of the town there is a good strip of sand with a bar at the foot of Dunn's River Falls and a very nice strip of sand at Mammee Bay, with snack bar. Headed farther west you will come to an undeveloped strip of sand at Salem and then the hotel beaches at Runaway Bay. There is a public beach, Puerto Seco, in Discovery Bay.

Headed east from the centre of Ocho Rios town there are some small and pretty coves cut into the cliffs: Shaw Park Beach and the beach at Sans Souci if you can gain access. In Oracabessa to the east of Ocho Rios you will find a hip spot called James Bond Beach (called so because Ian Fleming's house, Goldeneye, is not far off), where there is a small beach bar and facilities. This is not to be confused with the place sometimes called James Bond beach just out of Ocho Rios to the west, where there are some security problems. Beyond Oracabessa the beaches peter out.

Port Antonio: In the town itself you can go to Navy Island off the bay, Errol Flynn's old haunt, where there is an attractive strip of sand with shallow water. Call up and catch the ferry over from the market in town, for a small charge. Jamaica Reef Beach overlooks the island from Titchfield Hill. East of Port Antonio, Frenchman's Cove, is the island's most charming: headlands hanging with greenery contain a small cove of sand and palms. San San beach, a hotel beach with facilities, is officially reserved for hotel guests, but you are permitted into Dragon Bay beach, which has some facilities. There is a beach bar at the Blue Hole and you will find the very lively Winnifred Beach at Fairy Hill—lots of bars and activity at weekends.

Boston Bay: Big waves whipped by the trade winds roll in from the east and surfers get out and do their stuff occasionally. There is a good strip of sand at the head of the bay and of course you can grab a jerk chicken or pork for lunch. Further along the dramatic northeastern coastline you come to Long Bay, where there is a fishing village and a lovely deserted stretch of sand. There are no watersports here, of course, just coconut palms and sand. The beaches along the southeastern coastline tend to be brown sand and the water a little muddy, but there is a passable stretch of sand at Lyssons Beach.

Kingston: The local favourite beaches are Fort Clarence, where there is an admission charge, so many Jamaicans prefer to go to Hellshire, where the mounded sand is backed with endless wooden snack huts—check out the curious-looking beach chairs made of driftwood. Some people go just for the fish or lobster and bammy, which is cooked to your order. These beaches are quite hard to reach (buses from the parade). There are dark-sand beaches on the Palisadoes peninsula, but an excellent day out isto catch a ferry over to Port Royal and then hire a boat to take you over to Lime Cay, where the snorkelling is excellent, or Maiden Cay, which is no more than a sand bar.

West of Kingston: The few beaches along the south coast are all remote (completely untouched by the lobster-pink scourge of tourists on the north coast) and you should take snorkelling gear, towels and drinks, and pick up a picnic in town if you are headed down here.

Treasure Beach: This small resort area has brown sand but two good beaches in Frenchman's Bay and Great Bay and there are facilities and bars in the hotels. Not far off, Alligator Pond, the fishing village in Manchester Parish, has a reasonable strip of sand. Bluefields Bay is a very natural stretch of shallow water with trees lining the shore.

inland bathing and river-rafting

Some of the best bathing in Jamaica is in the river rockpools beneath the waterfalls. Some rivers disappear in the limestone caverns and flow underground, emerging in a pool. If you go off the beaten track, ask around, because the locals will know where the best spots are. It is better not to swim after rain because the mud will have been stirred up.

Somerset Falls at Hope Bay (near Port Antonio) are a little tame, *adm.* Preferable, though difficult to get to, are **Reach Falls**, inland from Manchioneal, 20 miles beyond Port Antonio, a series of pools, a stunning waterfall and a cave, *adm free.* If you go into the John Crow Mountains to Ginger House south of Port Antonio, there is a cascade and rockpool called **Jupiter.** At Upton above Ocho Rios (ask around), you will find good swimming and rapids at **Spanish Bridge. Irie Beach** is a lovely daytime stopover high in the hills above Ocho Rios, where the White River runs through a gulley, cool green water sluicing over rocks and into pools; sunbathing, bar and snacks, adm. The **YS Falls** in St Elizabeth Parish are an extremely impressive series of seven falls with rockpools and a spacious garden: quite a lot of tourists, but supremely beautiful; you ride to them by trolley bus through fantastic Jamaican countryside, *adm exp.* There are also some superb falls off the beaten track at **Maggotty** and at the **Black River Gorge** near Apple Valley.

Flora and Fauna

From its wet and mountainous northeast corner, where the jumble of the John Crow Mountains and Blue Mountains soars to thousands of feet, Jamaica's stunningly beautiful countryside descends through dwarf and montane forest, where mahogany and mahoe trees are grappled by creeping vines, lianas and ferns; through hilltop coffee and spice plantations, where you will see overgrown telephone wires and fences, headed west through the immensely fertile banana and yam plots in the rich red earth of the Central Mountain range, and so down on to the sugar flats that ring the coast in the west. Jamaica has an amazing variety of geography. In the south and southwest of the island, the rainfall is low (by Jamaican standards), and you will find savanna and scrub country. But then there are also huge areas of swampland covered with mangroves.

If you are not accustomed to the tropics, the plant-life is almost bewildering. The national tree of Jamaica is the mahoe and the national flower, which also grows on a tree, is the lignum vitae (the wood of life). There are endless palms, from the magnificent royal palm, which grows to over 100ft, to the typical seafront coco palms that lean out over the beach into the sunset. Jamaica has many botanical gardens, some of them left to decline into riotous growth, but most worth visiting even for botanical novitiates (they are excellent for escaping the hustle and bustle of the towns for a while). They were set up in order to encourage Jamaica's agricultural development as most of the food crops were brought in to the island, from the breadfruit shipped by Bligh to the mango from the south seas. The Jamaicans all keep flowering gardens too, so you will constantly see bougainvillea and hibiscus reaching out into the road. Even the traditional farmer's hedge, made with quick-stick (called so because it takes from just a cutting placed in the ground), comes out in a riot of lavender blooms.

With the extraordinary variety of terrain and vegetation comes an equal diversity of bird life, with over 250 species seen during the year—25 of these are endemic and about half are migratory. In the heights you may hear the mournful solitaire, or see the Jamaican eleania or the Blue Mountain vireo and a handful of warblers. In the lower mountains are hosts of grackles and grassquits, the Jamaican euphonia and woodpecker and two rare parrots, yellow-billed and black-billed. The Jamaican nightingale sings at dawn and sunset. You will also see hummingbirds, including the Jamaican national bird, the doctorbird, or red-billed streamertail, whose forked tail is about twice as long as its emerald green body. The smallest bird on the island is the tiny vervain or bee hummingbird. The Jamaican tody, called robin redbreast, is odd because it lays its eggs at the end of a 2ft underground tunnel. Among the lilies and aerial roots of the mangroves in the morasses are gallinules and green-backed herons, and whistling ducks. Offshore you may see sooty and noddy terns.

The animal life is not so varied, though there are many reptiles, ranging from the crocodiles of the Black River swamp and the Jamaican boa (rarely seen), which grows up to 15ft in length, to the tiny geckos that find their way all over the walls and the ceiling. The snoring frog is the second-largest tree frog in the world and there are many other varieties to be heard chirruping at different altitudes. The iguana was thought to be near extinction, but some have been sighted in the Hellshire Hills up to 7ft long. The few rodents include jutia, but this is rare. Manatees, lumbering great walrus-like creatures without tusks, are occasionally sighted in Milk River on the south coast and turtles come to the island. Some terrapins live in the rivers.

Kingston

Jamaica's capital, a sprawling city of nearly one million people on the south coast, is the hub of the Jamaicans' Jamaica. It is the political, cultural and business centre of the island and it buzzes with the most vibrant and vigorous of Jamaican life. Downtown on the Parade the press is incessant as the busmen shout and the higglers tout their wares; goats wander oblivious and the traffic bobs and weaves; everywhere is the deafening rap of dancehall; an occasional policeman in dark serge trousers and a peaked cap tries to keep order. All the extremes of Jamaican life are there: the poor urban shanties, the markets in the downtown area, the grand old institutions in the few remaining Victorian buildings close by, the gleaming air-conditioned offices of New Kingston and the fortified villas that take a cool view of it all from the Kingston mountainsides.

The city owes its birth to the death of Port Royal in the earthquake of 1692 (see p.691). The new city was originally laid out on a gridiron pattern and within a few years it was the commercial and social centre of the island. Hundreds of ships would put in to Kingston's magnificent harbour and the city grew as the traders built themselves magnificent wooden town-houses to match the splendour of the estate houses in the country. Kingston became the capital of the island in 1872. Another earthquake struck in 1907, killing 800, and much of the old town was destroyed—stone and brick buildings by the quake itself, wooden ones by the fires from escaping gas. Modern Kingston is not an attractive city as far as its buildings are concerned.

The waterfront, the heart of the town until earlier this century, is quiet now that the big passenger liners and the freight ships no longer call. The docks are in decay and a few characters 'lime' on the Boulevard. Just off the waterfront is the **Victoria Crafts Market**, where the Kingstonians sell their tourist souvenirs, straw hats and wooden carvings, and among them one or two finer pieces. The **National Gallery** at the foot of Orange Street (© 922 1561; open Mon–Fri 10–5; small adm) is well worth a look. There is a very impressive display of Intuitive paintings as well as wood carvings by Mallica 'Capo' Reynolds and work by the sculptress Edna Manley.

King Street, one of Kingston's main shopping streets, leads from the waterfront up to the Parade, from where the **Market** spills out into the road. This is the heartland of the downtown area and it is mercantile mayhem. Outside the shops of King Street, watchmenders, clothes vendors and sweet and cigarette salesmen tout their wares from countless stalls and from blankets laid out on the pavement. This is *ben dung* plaza at its best—the higglers generally prefer to lay their wares out on the ground than use tables and so you literally have to 'ben dung'. Periodically the higglers are cleared off the street and told to go back into the market buildings, but they always come back because they prefer it here and trade is better.

Bex juice seller

The **Parade**, called so because the colonial soldiers would parade here, is officially called William Grant Park. It is the terminal for Kingston's bus system—yet more chaos. The hawkers tout iced drinks from their handcarts with a shout of *Bag-juice!, Box-drink!* and the busmen practically kidnap you to put you on their bus (your intended destination seems only a secondary consideration). The small square, a park shaded by trees where more limers hang out among the statues of famous Jamaicans, is overlooked by the **Ward Theatre** on the north side, a wedding-cake affair which was built after the 1907 earthquake.

East of the downtown area, which has become run down since many of the businesses moved to New Kingston in the 1960s, you will find a few of the attractive timber-frame buildings with which Kingston was originally built. **Headquarters House** was the seat of Parliament earlier this century. Once used by the military (hence the name), it was actually built in the 18th century by a merchant, Thomas Hibbert. Next door is the modern **Gordon House**, the present seat of the Jamaican Parliament, where the representatives and senators do their business. Further east, on South Camp Road, is the Sabina Park cricket stadium, where the international tests are played. To the west of the Parade are some of Kingston's poorest shanty towns, including Trench Town, immortalized by Bob Marley. It would be unwise to go there without a guide.

Back on Duke Street, you pass the Gleaner Building and come to **National Heroes Park** (✆ 922 0620; *open Mon–Sat 8.30–4; adm free*), which was dedicated following Independence in 1962. There are monuments to Paul Bogle and George William Gordon, champions of the poor in the last century, and to Nanny the Maroon and Sam Sharpe. The graves of Marcus Mosiah Garvey, founder of the UNIA, and the fathers of modern Jamaican politics, Norman Manley and Alexander Bustamante, are also there. Simon Bolívar, *El Libertador*, the hero of South American independence, who stayed in exile in Jamaica, is remembered here as well. On East Street is the **Institute of Jamaica**, which has a natural history museum.

The buses run up Slipe Road from the Parade towards **New Kingston**, the commercial centre of the modern capital. Knutsford Boulevard is the principal street, with the shops and banks. On Hope Road is the classical **Devon House** (*gardens open daytime and evenings until 10pm, Devon House open Tues–Sat 9.30–4.30; adm to the tour of the house*), set in gardens of palms and flowering trees. This huge wooden house with louvred balconies, parquet flooring throughout and very attractive palm-patterned silk wallpaper was built in 1881 for a Jamaican merchant and it has been restored as a museum, furnished with period antiques. It's quite touristy as well as popular with the Jamaicans themselves, but worth a look, particularly for the patties and ice creams on sale in the stables.

In a large area of parkland just up from here are **Jamaica House**, built in the 1960s as the residence of the Prime Minister, now just his office, and **Kings House**, the official residence of the Jamaican Governor General. You can visit the grounds. The red, green and black house at 56 Hope Road is the old **Tuff Gong** recording studio, where Bob Marley lived and recorded. It is now the **Bob Marley Museum** (*open Mon–Sat, 9.30–4.30, Wed, Sat afternoons only; adm*); you can see his golden and platinum disks and album covers, press clippings and the 'Shot Room' where an attempt was made on his life. The tour culminates with twenty minutes of your favourite track on the video. At the top of Old Hope Road are the **Hope Botanical Gardens** (*open daily 8.30–dusk; adm free, tip guides*) which were established in 1881. The vast lawns are lined with royal palms, and bougainvillaea explodes in colourful blooms. The 150 acres are a good retreat from the humdrum of downtown Kingston, as well as a favoured spot for Jamaican limers, picnickers and lovers. Guides are available to point out the many plants such as bottle brush and pimento (which goes into jerk seasoning). **Hope Zoo** has a few lacklustre exhibits including Jamaican crocodiles and American owls and parrots. At the top end of Hope Road is the Mona Campus of the **University of the West Indies** on an old sugar estate between the hills, where the old aqueducts and some stone buildings are still visible.

There is a lively art scene in Jamaica and in Kingston there are a number of good **galleries**. Try the Contemporary Art Centre at 1 Liguanea Avenue, Kingston 6; the Mutual Life Gallery in the Mutual Life building in Oxford Road; the Frame Centre Gallery in Tangerine Place; and the Bolivar Bookshop and Gallery, 1A Grove Road.

Port Royal

At the tip of the Palisadoes Peninsula, past the Royal Jamaica Yacht Club and the Norman Manley airport, is the settlement of Port Royal. The peninsula almost encloses the bay, making the harbour one of the best in the Caribbean. The British fortified it immediately they arrived in 1655. Very soon it became a haunt for the buccaneers, who had been driven out of the island of Tortuga off Hispaniola. These men were possessed in their hatred of the Spaniards, the dominant power in the region, and were useful as an unofficial army for the governor.

They brought back vast piles of loot from their attacks on Caribbean shipping and land raids on Cuba, Hispaniola and the Spanish Main. Port Royal was the sorting station for it all and it quickly became the richest town in the area. Grog by the shipload, silks from the east, chests of jewels and gold and silver were auctioned off by the returning buccaneers, who then gambled and drank and generally made whoopee until the money ran out and they had to go off again to find more. It became a commercial centre where the inhabitants wore the latest fashions from London and artisans including ivory-turners, pewterers and potters gathered around the trade. The town was also full of pimps and prostitutes and at its height in the 1680s there was one ale-house to every ten inhabitants. In the opinion of one man, 'this place has been one of the lewdest in the Christian world, a sink of all filthiness and a mere sodom'.

When it came, a few minutes before noon on 7 June 1692, the earthquake seemed like divine retribution, as 2000 people died in three minutes. Fort Charles sank three feet, whole streets of the 'Gilded Hades' slid into the sea, fissures opened in the ground and a tidal wave threw a ship into the middle of the town. Some continued drinking and others started to loot the shops and cut the gold off the dead. Another 2000 were dead of disease in a few days. One Lewis Galdy had quite a story to tell, after being swallowed up by the earth and then thrown out again into the sea as another shock came. His tomb, with his story on the stone, is in the graveyard of St Peter's Church. Next to it is the simple grave of three children who died in the earthquake in 1692 but whose bodies were preserved under a falling wall. They were discovered by marine archaeologists and were buried in 1992.

The merchants rebuilt their town, but in 1703 a fire destroyed it again and the last of the inhabitants moved off to Kingston. The area remained a naval base, where Horatio Nelson served at the time of the American War of Independence. **Fort Charles** was his base and you can still visit it today, with its castellated ramparts and cannon and a fantastic view of the Kingston mountains. It is dozy and quiet and has been left high and dry due to sedimentation (once ships could tie up to its walls, but it is now inland). There is a small **Maritime Museum** in the fort (*open daily 10–1 and 2–5*) with descriptions of Port Royal in its heyday and some artefacts recovered during excavations of the town.

Beyond the fort is the **Giddy House**, once a Royal Artillery store, which lurched to its present position in the earthquake of 1907. The old naval hospital building, an early cast-iron section building built in 1818, was badly damaged in Hurricane Gilbert and the **Museum of Historical Archaeology** that it contained had to be closed. Presently there is an ambitious plan to create a park in Port Royal which will restore some of the old buildings and the old naval dockyard: there are even plans for an underwater viewing walkway to look at the submerged buildings.

A visit to Port Royal is a good day out from Kingston. Although the town is in fact quite run down, it provides a welcome respite from the hustle of Kingston. The ferry to Port Royal leaves Pier 2 on the Kingston waterfront about 6 times a day, fare J$1. After the few sights and a meal of fried fish and bammy, you can take a trip to one of the offshore cays or across to Port Henderson.

Into the Blue Mountains

The Blue Mountains rise behind Kingston as steeply as theatre curtain and as soon as you leave the town you will be surrounded by countryside, winding up into the mountains. The A3 or Junction road goes via Half Way Tree and Constant Spring and then up to Castleton and over to the north coast at Annotto Bay. Set either side of the road at **Castleton** are some botanical gardens that date from 1869, set in 39 acres in the dramatic, incredibly fertile (and pretty wet) Wag River valley. The plants are marked and there are guides who will explain the 35 palms among the 60ft explosions of bamboo and point out the lair of the trap-door spider (sealed watertight and lined with silk).

The main entrance to the Blue Mountains is from Papine at the top of Old Hope Road, along the magnificent cleft of the Hope River valley. If you take the left fork just after the Blue Mountain Inn the road winds gradually up to Irish Town, a typically laid-back and charming village and then to Newcastle, one of the barracks of the Jamaican Defence Force, its buildings stacked top to toe down the hillside. The road leads over the parade ground and when they are parading the traffic is held up. Just above here, beyond the Gap Café, you come to the Hardwar Gap which leads to the northern side of the Blue Mountains. Here you will find Hollywell Park Ranger Station, where you can get information about the **Blue Mountain National Park**. From the town of Section you can reach the remote Cinchona Gardens, started in 1868 to grow cinchona from which quinine was extracted, now a peaceful retreat with rhododendrons, lilies and orchids, or take the road down to Buff Bay.

Back down below, the right fork leads to Gordon Town and Guava Ridge, where you will find Sangster's 'Old Jamaica' liqueur factory at World's End. The air hangs with the creamy and exotic smells of the concoctions to be mixed into the rums. There is a shop on the premises. At **Mavis Bank** (*tours daily*) is one of Jamaica's coffee factories, which is well worth a visit, best during picking time between September and February. Blue Mountain Coffee is reckoned by some to be the best in the world and it retails at four or five times the amount of any other pure arabica coffee on the market. You will see the 'cherry berries' come in from the field, thrown into water to remove the 'floaters', and then pulped and sweated for a few days. Once they have been dried, by laying them out onto concrete barbecues, they are husked and 'rested' for a few weeks as 'dry parchment' and then hulled of another layer of skin. Finally they are sized and packed in barrels and bags or sometimes roasted and ground. The **Blue Mountain Peak** itself is Jamaica's highest (7402ft) and the ascent can be made in seven hours from Abbey Green. The mountains are often lost in cloud and mist in the day and so to get the best chance of a clear view you should aim to reach the peak soon after dawn, when you might be able to see as far as Cuba and Haiti. On the way down you will pass through elfin growth, stunted grasses, knee-high trees and lichens, and then into montane woodland, still swirling in cloud, where the ferns and orchids sit in the upper branches and trees reach tall to catch the sunlight. (*For a tour, see 'Walking' in the Jamaica Directory, p.732.*)

Clockwise from Kingston

West of Kingston by 12 miles, across sugar flats and swamps, is **Spanish Town,** the capital of Jamaica for over three centuries until 1872, except for a brief interlude (1755–8) when the Kingston merchants managed to force through a bill moving the capital there. The town has a few traits of its former glory and magnificence—a cluster of old-time stone and timber buildings around a square of elegant and monumental colonial edifices—but it has mushroomed recently with suburbs, mostly modern villas. It is worth a quick look as you are driving through.

Santiago de la Vega was laid out by the Spaniards when they moved here from the north coast in 1523, but there is nothing left of the original *plaza* in the central square of Spanish Town. The Georgian architecture and the iron railings around the park give the square a distinctly British feel and it was the social hub of Jamaica during colonial times. The **Rodney Memorial**, sculpted by John Bacon, commemorates Admiral George Rodney following his victory at the Battle of the Saints off Guadeloupe in 1782 (widely reckoned to have saved Jamaica from invasion). Opposite is the **Court House**, which was burned down in the 1980s and is no more than a facade now. On the east side of the square, the colonnaded building with wooden upper storeys and a balcony is the former **House of Assembly**, where Jamaica's elected representatives met until the British Commonwealth Office took over government of the island in 1866. Now it houses the Parish Council Offices. Opposite it stands **King's House**, built in 1762, which was the official residence of the island's governor. The proclamation of the Abolition of Slavery was read from the building, but it was was burned down to its façade in 1925. In the overgrown courtyards there is a lacklustre series of exhibits at the Jamaican People's Museum of Craft and Technology: examples of architectural techniques and old-time household utensils.

Look out for the **Cathedral Church of St James**, head of the diocese of Jamaica, on Barrett Street. It was built in 1714 on the site of an original Spanish church, but there are commemorative tablets from the earliest English settlers to Jamaica. Beyond this rarefied square with its colonial echoes, Spanish Town is a busy Jamaican town, partly industrialized, partly fading timber businesses and homes.

Past the massive ruins of 17th-century Colbeck Castle near Old Harbour you come to the town of **May Pen**. There are many Pens in Jamaica; the name refers to a farmstead where animals were kept. At Toll Gate you can take the turning to the south coast, along the meandering Milk River with its pastures and canefields, past a village called Rest, eventually coming to the **Milk River Spa** (✆ 925 9544), where the highest levels of natural radioactivity in the world occur in the water—about fifty times the radioactive levels of Baden-Baden. The water comes out of the ground at 120°F and the spa is popular for its supposed healing powers. Not far from here, the town of **Racecourse** has a large East Indian population, who stage very colourful festivals at Divali and Hosay.

Mandeville, the capital of Manchester Parish, is set in mountainous uplands at 2000ft, which gives it a cooler climate than the rest of Jamaica. In British days Mandeville was a hill station, to which the colonial authorities and the planters would retreat in the heat of the summer (in those days nobody lay on the beach because the heat was thought to be degenerative). It was even laid out like a village green, with the Georgian court house and the parish church standing opposite one another across the open square. Nowadays they stand rather oddly aloof among all the chaos of the Jamaican market and the taxi-men touting for business. The area around the town calls itself the feeding tree (the Jamaican equivalent of the breadbasket) and you will see the neatly tended lines of green crops offsetting the orange of the rich Jamaican earth—there are also endless stalls at the roadside selling cashews and strings or bags of whatever fruits are in season. In the 1950s the area suddenly became the centre of the Jamaican bauxite industry, but the town still has a stately air and many Jamaicans have returned from abroad and built themselves retirement homes here.

There is a number of unlikely-sounding but entertaining things to do around Mandeville. **Mrs Stephenson's garden** (*adm*), on the northern outskirts of the town, is interesting to visit, even for those who are novices, botanically speaking. She has 50 species of orchids as well as such flowers as the ortanique (a cross-fertilized citrus fruit), the stag-horn fern and pig-tailed anthurium. Not far off at Shooter's Hill, in the shadow of the huge bauxite plant, you will find the **Pickapeppa Sauce Factory** (© 962 2928, *visit by arrangement*), the source of the pungent concoction that the Jamaicans dash liberally on their food. The **ALCAN aluminium factory** is also an interesting experience: you see the rich red Jamaican earth conveyed (3½ miles on a conveyor belt), slurried with caustic soda, pressure cooked in liquid digesters until it becomes sodium aluminate, passed over with succulents, purified and heated to become alumina trihydrate and finally heated in a kiln, ending up as a white powder, aluminium oxide. (If this all sounds a bit much, you see it on film anyway.) Finally **Marshall's Pen** is a charming and peaceful spot, a classic 200-year-old Jamaican great house set in gentle hills, once a coffee plantation and now a farm for Jamaican red poll cattle. Bird-watching tours and private visits to the house, which is still lived in, are available if you arrange it in advance (contact through the Astra Hotel).

Following the main road west out of Mandeville you descend to the plains of St Elizabeth at Spur Tree. The views are fantastic, as they are on the south coast at **Lover's Leap**, a 1600ft drop sheer into the sea from the Santa Cruz mountains. The story goes that two slave lovers were chased here by an ardent planter who fancied the girl, and they jumped to their death rather than be split up. On the road to Black River is **Bamboo Avenue**, one of Jamaica's best known sights. It is certainly impressive, a three-mile tunnel of bamboo, still mostly complete, which creaks constantly in the breeze. At Middle Quarter you will find vendors at the roadside selling bags of 'swims' (shrimps cooked in pepper sauce).

Black River itself is a faded and rundown Jamaican town on the south coast, but one which was clearly prosperous at the turn of the century as there are magnificent gingerbread houses decaying on the waterfront. It made its wealth through exporting dyes—indigo and logwood, which were used in jeans. You can take boat-trips into one of Jamaica's two swamps called the Great Morass (the other being in Negril). Tendrils hang like curtains from the extended families of mangrove trees and great blue herons and jacanas or purple gallinules creep and strut around. You may also see a crocodile flop into the water and cruise lazily away, or pose for a photograph. These crocs are tame enough to be moved around in the water for the best shot. There are three or four daily tours, starting by the bridge in town; contact South Coast Safaris (© 965 2513) or St Elizabeth Safari (© 965 2374). A few miles down the coast to the east is **Treasure Beach,** a lovely, laid-back seaside town stretched along a series of passable beaches. It is only gradually developing with tourism and has a charming feel when compared to the resort towns on the north coast. The Jamaicans themselves like to go on holiday there.

The coastal road continues through drowsy towns and plains in the shadow of huge forested mountains, to Bluefields, from where Henry Morgan set off to sack Panama in 1670, and then to **Savanna-la-Mar**. The town of Sav-la-Mar, as it is known, is run-down and tatty. Once it was a thriving port, exporting sugar from Frome, but its position on the coast has not always been a blessing as it is scourged by storms—in 1912, a schooner ended up in the main street.

Twenty miles further on you come to the western tip of the island and the resort town of **Negril**, which stretches north and south along 7 miles of spectacular beach and 4 of ironshore cliffs. The town's well-known hippy history is all but over now that the big players of Jamaican tourism have muscled in on the beachfront space (it has even been gentrified to the point of having a golf course), but it still has a laid-back and easy-going air.

Negril was a pirate haunt, and the crews of corsairs would lie in wait for ships en route from the Spanish Main to Havana. 'Calico' Jack Rackham and his disguised women companions Anne Bonney and Mary Read were captured here in 1720, while on a rum blow-out. They were taken off to Spanish Town and found guilty of piracy, robbery and felony. Rackham was executed and then 'hung out to dry' (in an iron frame) on Rackham Cay off Port Royal, but the two women, who were renowned for being just as fierce as their male counterparts, pleaded pregnancy and were jailed.

The town remained a backwater until a road was built in 1959 and hippies began to wash up here. They rented space on the floor in the local houses and enjoyed the magic mushroom omelettes, the weed, the palm-backed beach and the sunsets. Hanging out is still the main pastime here, on the beach by day and the bars by night (some quite good bands play in the music parks in Negril). There are not really any sights in Negril, unless you wish to go to the top of the lighthouse at the southern end of the West End Road (south from the roundabout), though you can visit the Great Morass, a vast swamp behind the Norman Manley Boulevard, where there are herons and other waders among the mangroves. Bloody Bay, off the road to Montego Bay, takes its name from the whales that were beached and cut up here, or possibly from pirate battles of centuries past.

The road northeast to Montego Bay follows the magnificent coastline, skirting the bays and clambering over lumbering headlands to **Lucea**, the capital of Hanover Parish, which is set on a wide harbour overlooked by cliffs. The clock on the court house in the town was sent here by mistake (it was supposed to have been sent to St Lucia), but the residents kept it and built a special tower, complete with cupola that resembles a German helmet, donated by a German plantation owner. There is a small but worthwhile museum in the town, the **Hanover Museum** (*open Mon–Fri; adm*) in the former workhouse and police station, with displays of historical artefacts of the area since Arawak times—a zemi, an Arawak canoe, coins (quotties, gills, bobs and bits), an orange rinder, a floor brush made from a coconut and a coconut oil lamp called a kitchen bitch.

The North Coast

The north coast of Jamaica is legendary as a tourist destination, the favoured haunt of Britons such as Winston Churchill and Noel Coward and royal families from all over. The villas of the rich and famous have dotted the hillsides since the thirties and although Port Antonio is quiet now, it was so popular at the turn of the century that it boasted a 400-bedroom hotel there. People would come on packages on the banana boats for the winter season. Today's tourists fly into Montego Bay by the jumbo-load; it is the main airport for the north of the island.

Montego Bay

Situated in the northwest of the island, Montego Bay, or **Mo Bay**, as it is usually known, is Jamaica's second city. Mo Bay is also Jamaica's tourist heartland; its coastline has become encrusted with humming factory-like hotels for miles and the beaches are awash with lobster-red trippers sizzling in coconut oil. Rude-boys joust on their jetskis and higglers apply their

high-pressure selling techniques from the roadside. Downtown it is mayhem as the goats and boys pushing handcarts compete for road space and relentless horns and shouts of *Bag-juice!* interrupt the pulse of dancehall music. Old-time Montego Bay looks on from its Georgian stone buildings and timber houses as it has done for two centuries.

The bay was first named by Columbus for its favourable winds, the 'Golfo de Buen Tiempo', but when the Spaniards settled the area it came to be called 'manteca' after the butter or pig fat that was its trade. Development was slow because of the maroons in the mountains, but in the 18th century there was big business in sugar ('Monk' Lewis thought it the prettiest town in Jamaica), and then in bananas in the 19th century. The latest boom, tourism, began in 1906 with the opening of Doctor's Cave Beach.

The centre of the town itself is **Sam Sharpe Square**, still occasionally called Charles Square as it was originally known. Sam Sharpe, now a Jamaican national hero, was hanged here, near where his statue stands. His 1831 rebellion went far further than his intended sit-down strike—plantations were torched and riots continued for months—but it speeded the eventual end of slavery. In one corner of the square is the **Cage**, once used as a lock-up for slaves out after curfew at 3pm and drunks or sailors in the town after their curfew at 6pm.

The St James Parish Church is behind the square, an imposing structure straight out of England with arched windows and a mahogany interior, which was first erected in 1778. Montego Bay's town **market** (as opposed to the craft market) is on Fustic Street, down at the end of Railway Lane, and it is well worth a visit to see the traditional way of buying ground provisions West Indian style. Headed north from the downtown area you come to the main tourist drag on Gloucester Avenue, a mile-long strip of all-day cafés, mid-range package hotels and tourist shops. Modern Mo Bay has spread all over the hills that are the backdrop to the old town and along the coastlines for several miles east and west. The surrounding countryside is dotted with the remnants of 18th-century Jamaica in the plantations and their great houses, some of them restored or turned into hotels. Many of the places mentioned below can be visited on the endless tours arranged from Montego Bay.

South of Montego Bay

Just out of Montego Bay to the south are the **Barnett Estates** (*open daily; adm*), an estate house which can be visited and a working plantation. The great house, with a stone base and wooden upper floors and balconies, dates from the 18th century and has been restored to show the life of a Jamaican planter two centuries ago. Furniture includes original antique chairs with the family crest and silver platters and goblets, and four-posters with pineapple headboards. The kitchen is in an outhouse (against the threat of fire) and you will be told of the use of herbs in traditional medicine. The visit to the plantation is by trolley bus: as you pass through mango and coconut walks (cultivated today), and taste the milk and flesh of a coconut, you will hear the story of sugar-cane and its harvest.

The **Rockland Bird Feeding Station** (*©* 952 2009; *open daily 2.30–5; adm*) in Anchovy, three miles south of Reading, is open to the public in the afternoon, when a stream of Jamaica's colourful birdlife heads in for feeding—hummingbirds including the vervain, the Jamaican mango and the doctor bird. You might even get one to sit on your finger while it feeds (*see* 'Flora and Fauna', p.688). You can also see warblers, tanagers and the yellow and black Jamaican oriole on the short walks in the forest.

Belvedere Plantation is off the road to Savanna-la-Mar. You approach the old estate buildings through citrus, pineapple and banana plantations. You will see a riverside garden with plants such as puss-tail, anato, which provides red food dye (and lipstick of a sort) and, no relation, shame-a-lady. The great house is in ruins, but a post-emancipation village (*adm*) has been created with traditional village skills on view—weaving, blacksmithing, a herbalist's garden and a small crusher where you can get a drink of cane-juice. High in the hills as the name would suggest, **Croydon in the Mountains** (*open Mon–Fri; adm*) is a working plantation off the road to Cambridge. After a tour of the grounds, where you can see a number of exotic fruits including strains of pineapple: bullhead, natty, cowboy, Natal Queen and smooth Cayenne, you can see how coffee is grown and harvested (pulping, fermenting, drying, hulling, selecting, roasting and eventually grinding and brewing).

The road follows the railway and the valley of the Great River to Cambridge, high in the absurdly fertile Jamaican mountains. **Seaford Town** is the home of the descendants of German families who arrived in 1835. The community has become inbred and many have emigrated, but the blond features and blue eyes of the 200 or so that remain are clearly visible, even if they hold themselves more like Jamaicans when they dance. Passing the village of Magotty the road and railway come to **Appleton Sugar Estate** (*adm and rum-tasting on offer in the reception area*), set in swathes of cane that make Jamaica's most famous rum. During working hours there is a tour of the distillery, which produces 10 million litres of rum each year in the column stills and the oak barrels of the cool storage house. You might be lucky and get a tour of the sugar factory itself, where the canes are crushed on conveyors and the liquid is boiled and then granulated in a centrifuge. Not far off are **YS Falls** (*open daily; adm exp*), some of Jamaica's most beautiful waterfalls. You ride to them in a tractor-drawn jitney, which is a bit embarrassing, but you can concentrate on the spectacular scenery, open fields like parkland with isolated trees where Jamaican red poll cattle graze the luxurious grass. There are bars at the reception area and at the falls themselves, where you can swim.

North of this area is the **Cockpit Country**, a weird landscape of shaggy hillocks like 300ft haystacks. They were carved into their regular, egg-box shape by water action as it fell on the limestone plateau. Even today the Cockpit country is very remote country: two centuries ago it was the maroon heartland, and in the south is the infamous area known by soldiers as the 'land of the look-behind'—it was so treacherous that they would apparently ride back to back on their horses. The maroons held out here (*see* 'History', p.677), in settlements where the villages of Accompong, Maroon Town and Quick Step are today, descending to attack the plantations at night. The maroons, who still have some autonomy and self-government, celebrate their treaty with the British each year on 7th January in Accompong.

East from Montego Bay

Rose Hall Great House (*℗ 953 2323; open daily 9–6; adm exp*) is Jamaica's most famous great house, an imposing Georgian mansion that stands on the hillside 10 miles east of Montego Bay. Built in the 1770s, Rose Hall has been restored to its former splendour as the most illustrious manor on the island, with mahogany floors and panelling, chandeliers and period antiques and some very attractive silk wallpaper painted with tropical birds and palm trees. But Rose Hall is most famous for the legend of its mistress Annie Palmer, who came here in 1820. A renowned beauty, feared as a black magician, she is supposed to have got through three husbands (by poisoning, by stabbing and then pouring boiling oil into his ears, and by strangling) and innumerable lovers, including slaves, whom she simply killed when she was bored with them. She was 4ft 11 and murdered in her bed. There is a bar and restaurant downstairs in the barrel-vaulted cellar, with photographs taken by visitors in which mysterious faces appear. There is apparently no evidence for the legend, but an amusing version was written up by H. G. de Lisser in his *White Witch of Rose Hall*.

Another magnificent plantations great house, **Greenwood** (*open daily, 9–6; adm*), sits high on the hillside 4 miles farther on, also comanding a magnificent view over the coastline. Built in the late 1700s, it was a home for many years of the Barrett family from which the poet Elizabeth Barrett Browning was descended and it is still lived in. On view are musical instruments, including wind-up organs and an excellent polyphon, the old carriages and portraits and the Barrett family library. The view from the veranda is so broad that you can see the curvature of the earth.

The sugar factory and rum distillery at **Hampden** is well worth a visit in the cane-cutting season between January and July. You will see the cane lifted on huge gantries and dumped into vast metal maws where it is washed and separated and then beaten and cut to length by treadlers. Four mills squeeze out the last drop of juice (leaving the pulp or 'bagasse', which is so dry that it can be used to fire the steam turbine). The juice is sluiced to be clarified at high temperature in white plastered vats, then evaporated in vacuum pans and eventually crystallied into sugar granules in a centrifuge. The by-product, molasses, is used for rum, which you can also see being made: first it is fermented in bubbling, oily black vats and then distilled a number of times, through low wines and high wines, until it is condensed into clear white rum (85–90 per cent vol). Hampden factory produces about 160,000 tonnes of sugar each year and roughly a million litres of alcohol, much of which is used in manufacturing chocolates. It is also possible to visit the estate house, which straddles the border of St James Parish and Trelawny.

Back on the coastal road, on the fringes of a mangrove swamp, the **Jamaica Safari Village** makes for a slightly odd experience. It is really a small zoo, with snakes, a lioness and some birds, but it is best known for its crocodiles, which lurk in the mangroves with a huge diabolic and toothy smiles. This was the film location for James Bond's lucky escape from a sticky marooning in *Live and Let Die,* when he used crocodiles as stepping stones. Unfortunately the stuntman, Ross Kananga (who owned the farm), did not fare so well on an earlier take of the shot: he fell in and had to have 193 stitches.

Just down the road is the town of **Falmouth**, capital of Trelawny parish and site of some of the finest Georgian architecture on the island. The town was founded in 1790 and for a time was the busiest port on the north coast, but the sugar trade declined and the town faded with it.

Nowadays Falmouth is a fairly ordinary Jamaican town, best known for its 'flea-market' on Wednesdays, in which goods are brought from abroad for distribution to shops all over the western part of the island.

The main road passes St Peter's, the parish church (supposedly a direct copy of the church in Falmouth in Cornwall in England) and then heads through the centre of the town, turning at the red-tin-roofed market building and a large roundabout, a tank which was once the town's water supply. From here you can glimpse the older area of town, well worth a look, where some of the original Georgian buildings are still standing, with verandas supported on stilts, reaching out over the pavement, and timber-frame upper storeys on stonework bases. Some have recently been restored. Look out for the huge court house, and Market Street, with the post office and the Methodist manse. On the point the fort is tired and dilapidated, its barracks now a school. Just east of Falmouth is a phosphorescent lagoon at **Rock**. You can arrange a trip from the deck restaurant, Glistening Waters: it is best seen on a moonless night when there has been no rain (the outflow of the Martha Brae dissipates the microscopic protozoa which emit light when stirred).

Good Hope Great House (*adm free, but you'll have to buy lunch or dinner*) is one of the most beautiful on the island, recently restored with original antique furniture—four posters, commodes, huge glass hurricane lamps—and a wild orange wood floor throughout. It is difficult to get to, along rickety country roads, but it has a stunning view across the Trelawny countryside from its vantage point on a small hilltop. South of here there are some caves at Windsor where, conducted by torchlight, you will see rock formations in the shape of a hand and of Moses. If you're in luck, the guide might even play a tune for you on the stalactites.

For the next 20 miles the main road to Ocho Rios and Kingston runs inland and then skirts the coastline, which is lined with endless snack bars, fruit stalls and rum shops, until it comes to Discovery Bay. This is named after Columbus's arrival here in 1494 (so the history runs, though some dispute the point of landing). He is commemorated in **Columbus Park** (*adm free*), a small museum/park with a few artefacts at the roadside. At first it seems a little unadventurous but in fact it is worth a good look because it gives an excellent overview of Jamaican agricultural and industrial history. **Runaway Bay** takes its name from another moment in Jamaican history, when the last Spaniards gathered in 1655 before making a break for Cuba 90 miles to the north. The seven miles of the **Runaway Caves** (*open 9–5*) have been used by other runaways—slaves and pirates—and latterly by disco-goers. They are firmly on the tourist trail (yet more carvings for sale), but merit a visit for a swim in the Green Grotto and to see the extraordinary and alarmingly long, snake-like, thigh-thick fig-tree roots which have made their way down into the caves in search of water.

Inland, beyond the stunningly fertile areas of the Orange Valley, **Brown's Town** has a cut stone and wood church, which stands opposite a classic Caribbean iron market, to which the local farmers bring their produce from the hills around. At Nine Mile, seemingly lost in the Jamaican interior, you will find the **Bob Marley Mausoleum** (*adm, no cameras*), on a hillside in the town of his birth, now behind a huge chain-link fence and barbed wire. The mausoleum itself is made of grey marble and is adorned with gifts and dedications sent to the singer. You'll be hustled like mad and told all sorts of tall stories.

Back on the coast, you pass between the site of Nueva Sevilla, the first Spanish settlement of 1510 (where a few remains are still visible), and **Seville Great House**, which stands high on the hill; built in 1750, the original wattle and daub walls still exist beneath the plaster. It houses an exhibit called Maima-Seville, commemorating the many influences that have contributed to Jamaica today (Arawak Indian, European and African) with a video presentation. A little farther on is the town of **St Ann's Bay**, capital of the parish of St Ann. It is the birthplace of Marcus Garvey, the Jamaican national hero and founder of the UNIA (*see* 'History', p.678) and he is remembered with a statue in front of the town library. Seven miles farther along the coast you come to the resort town of Ocho Rios, announced by a small fortress (don't bother to investigate, it contains the local sewage plant) and the enormous bauxite shipping station just before the town.

Ocho Rios

Ocho Rios, or 'Ochee' as it is often known, is Jamaica's second tourist town, about 70 miles over the hill from Kingston and the same from Montego Bay. It is another businesslike tourist town that was created in the sixties from a tiny fishing village on a magnificent beach. It is a little ugly and has developed completely without plan, but it is business as usual as two or three cruise ships call in some days and the tourists come in droves. Ocho Rios has some of the island's best beaches and a couple of Jamaica's smartest hotels as well as a string of high-pressure fun-factory resorts. The name, which looks as though it might come from 'eight rivers' in the vicinity, is more likely a corruption of Las Chorreras, meaning waterfalls or spouts, of which there were many coming off the hills that rise immediately behind the town. Ocho Rios has no real centre, apart from the clocktower—it is scattered along the coastline for several miles. Such unashamed tourism and lack of heritage makes it feel a little soulless at times, but of course that doesn't mean you don't get a good holiday there.

Dunn's River Falls (*open daily, 8–5; start at the bottom and buy another carving at the top; adm*) is probably Jamaica's most famous sight, a series of waterfalls that tumble 600ft from top to bottom. It is a bit of a rigmarole as you have to join a conga of other tourists, holding hands and clearly dicing with death as you edge gingerly up among the relentless two- and three-foot cascades, but it is a quite beautiful and surprising feature and if you take it all with a pinch of salt it can be quite fun.

The road to Kingston leads south out of town from the roundabout up into the mountains towards Moneague. As it climbs, the road passes through **Fern Gully**, an absurdly fertile chasm three miles long where the vegetation makes a tunnel over the road and only angled shafts of sunlight penetrate to the gulley floor. Creepers and lianas tangle and many of Jamaica's 500 varieties of fern explode in the upper branches of the trees. Until a few years ago the gulley was alive with fireflies at night, but now the petrol fumes have killed them off. There is a number of gardens on the hills above Ocho Rios. **Coyaba River Garden and Museum** (*adm*) is set in a cleft shaded by huge cedar trees. You take a guided tour among the waterfalls and streams, where you will see *impatiens* (or Busy Lizzie), Poor Man's Orchid (on the cloven-leafed bauhinia tree) and many palms such as the *makali* palm, with fronds shaped like fans. The museum gives a quick view of St Ann's Parish since Arawak times—old maps, quaint colonial pictures and more recent island life.

The **Shaw Park Botanical Gardens** are also laid out on a hillside, where two rivers run down into multi-layered lily ponds. Here you will see a stunning range of ornamental tropical plants including heliconias, ginger lilies and red shrimp plants.

Heading east from Ocho Rios, over the White River (good swimming if you follow it up on the backroads, including Irie Beach, *see* p.687), you come to the **Prospect Plantation** (*open daily 10.30–3.30; adm*). There are three daily tours of its grounds, where many of Jamaica's plantation crops are set out on view, including cassava, banana, coffee and of course sugar-cane. See how unripe ackee was used for soap in old-time Jamaica. Horseback rides are available into the mountains. Close by is **Harmony Hall**, a very pretty, turreted estate house from the 19th century which has been restored with gingerbread fretwork and tray ceilings. Now it houses a gallery and craft shop; upstairs there are paintings by artists who have worked in the island and by the the Jamaican 'Intuitives'; there are displays of crafts from around the Caribbean; also temporary exhibitions and regular craft fairs. Downstairs there are clothes and books for sale and a café and bar.

On the hill above the town of Port Maria is Noël Coward's house **Firefly** (*adm exp; video and tour*), chosen with customary discernment because from its 1000ft vantage point it has perhaps the finest view in the whole of the Caribbean. The view takes in the Blue Mountains to the south and the northern coastline where the successive headlands outreach one another into the Caribbean Sea. Coward lived here for the last 23 years of his life until he died in 1973 (the same site was chosen by Henry Morgan three hundred years before him: his old kitchen is still standing and now contains a café and gift shop, with Noël Coward paintings transferred onto t-shirts and baseball caps of all unlikely things). Noël Coward is buried in the garden under a simple marble tablet. The house has been restored as he left it, with his musical scores, records, crockery as used by the Queen Mum on a visit and some paintings still on view. Author Ian Fleming, creator of the character James Bond, lived on the coast nearby from 1946 until his death in 1964, in a house called **Goldeneye**. The name James Bond itself was borrowed from the cover of one of Jamaica's other renowned birdwatchers, an ornithologist this time, the author of *The Birds of the West Indies*.

Following the coastal road farther east you come to **Port Maria**, the capital of St Mary parish, which sits on a stunning bay, but has little to recommend it. The island in the bay, Cabarita Island, is named after the Spanish word for goat: animals were let loose here so that sailors would have a supply of fresh meat in the early days of Caribbean exploration. Some way inland on a rickety road is **Sun Valley Plantation** (© 995 3075; *three tours each weekday, 9, 11, 3; adm*), a working banana plantation. A tour takes you through the cycle of a banana (*best on Tues and Wed, when they are reaping*) and tells of other tropical plants including ackee and nutmeg.

The poor and remote east of the island begins beyond the town. It remains undeveloped because there are few beaches before Port Antonio, and so you will see a more natural Jamaican life as you drive through. The main road heads inland into the hills, re-emerging at Annotto Bay from where it heads into Portland parish and Port Antonio, following the magni-ficent coastline beneath the massive and beautiful foothills of the Blue Mountains. One of the main roads to Kingston turns south from here. If you take it, it is well worth stopping at the botanical gardens at Castleton. Buff Bay (in name only) is now a faded parish town, with its old buildings in decay, and Hope Bay is a small fishing village best known for the Somerset Falls just above the town: there are falls, pools and a swimmable channel (*open 10–5; adm*). Soon afterwards the road crosses the **Rio Grande**, Jamaica's largest river, and best known for river-rafting since Errol Flynn joined the banana growers who shipped their fruit downriver on bamboo rafts.

Port Antonio is the capital of Portland parish. Both the town and its parish are charming and spectacular, among the most beautiful places on the island. The town's heyday is clearly past, for the moment at least, as the grand old buildings show in their distressed decay, but its setting, on the point between two bays and with vast and fertile mountains behind it, makes Port Antonio incomparable. Once it was described as the 'most exquisite port on earth'.

Port Antonio was a Spanish settlement, and although it was laid out in 1723, it remained a sedate coastal town until the late 1880s, when it became the centre of the banana trade and exploded into prosperity. By the turn of the century it was the most important town on the north coast. Tourists poured in from the USA and the place was so popular that there was a 400-room hotel, three storeys high with verandas on all sides, an Italian orchestra to play at mealtimes and a massive ballroom. In the winter season it was patronized by the likes of Rudyard Kipling. As the banana trade failed in the thirties, so did the hotel and with it the tourist trade in Port Antonio. The town received a fillip in the fifties with the arrival of the film star Errol Flynn. He bought Navy Island in the West Harbour and the glamour returned with his parties, to which guests like Bette Davis and Ginger Rogers came.

The most attractive area of the town, where you will find the classic Caribbean timber-frame houses with gingerbread fretwork and wrought-iron filigree, are on the point between the two bays, or 'Titchfield Hill'. The remains of Fort St George, a few embrasures and some mean-looking cannon on rollers, have been turned into a school. The centre of the town itself is the clocktower at the head of West Street, and not far from here you will find Musgrave market, always worth a visit, but particularly active on Thursdays and Saturdays. The view from the Bonnie View Hotel is superb. Port Antonio is still the main shipping port for bananas and you will see the huge Jamaica Producers banana boats in harbour a couple of times a week.

Above Port Antonio, between the Blue Mountains and the John Crow Mountains, is the maroon settlement of Moore Town. In the 18th century, the Windward maroons occupied this area and they are supposed to have lived in Nanny Town, beneath the Blue Mountain Peak. They were forced out of the town by the British in 1730, but in 1739 they signed a treaty allowing them to live in peace. Legends grew up around the place and around their leader Nanny, who was supposed to have supernatural powers. Locals say that the spirits of the maroons still inhabit the area. Nanny became a national heroine of Jamaica in 1975. It is possible to visit the town, but it is worth remembering that it is much like any other remote Jamaican town nowadays. **Bump Grave**, opposite the school, is supposed to contain the remains of Nanny. Close by there are some waterfalls: **Nanny Falls**, a short distance from the town, and **Jupiter Falls**, lost in the densest greenery, and a rockpool where you can swim. Ask around for directions. **Nonsuch Caves** (*open daily, 9–5; adm*) are made up of nine chambers in Athenry Gardens up in the hills behind Port Antonio—walkways and lighting to let you see the stalactites and stalagmites (shapes include a woman with a basket on her head, organ pipes and an owl). The gardens have a magnificent view of the town from above.

Back on the coast the main road leads east out of Port Antonio, passing through small villages and some of Jamaica's expensive villas until you reach the **Blue Hole**, a limestone sinkhole with patches of hot and cold water fringed with palm trees and coloured a beautiful shade of royal blue. There is a bar and restaurant (*adm free if you go to the restaurant*). Beyond Boston

Bay, home of jerk (*see* p.682), the road follows the rugged southeast coast to **Reach Falls** (*adm*), a couple of miles up into the hills and well worth a visit, as the river cascades 25ft into a rockpool.

From here you pass into the parish of St Thomas and to the tip of the island. Inland is the town of **Bath**, Jamaica's favourite resort two centuries ago because of the hot and cold springs, and home to the second-oldest botanical gardens in the western hemisphere (now dilapidated). At the Bath Fountain Hotel (✆ 982 2132) you can have a dip in the waters, which are supposed to have curative properties.

On the south coast, **Morant Bay** is the capital of the parish and the site of the famous 1865 rebellion, after which over 400 people were executed, including Paul Bogle and George William Gordon, who were hanged outside the town hall. The road follows the coast from Morant Bay through Yallahs and on to the capital.

✆ (1 876)–   *Where to Stay*

Jamaica has a superb, wide-ranging selection of hotels, which use the best of the island's dramatic coastline and interior. Some are extremely expensive and luxurious, but there is something for everyone in Jamaica. You will find secluded mountain retreats, plantation houses and classic laid-back beachfront spots tucked in between the larger resorts—excellent stops if you are travelling the island. Jamaica is also the Caribbean leader in all-inclusive hotels (*see* p.37) and these offer a full range too, with à la carte dining and champagne in the jacuzzi through to the activity-led fun-factories of times past. Chances are your hotel will be booked in a package, but you can also reserve direct, or book through the **Jamaica Reservation Service**, 1320 South Dixie Highway, Suite 1180, Coral Gables, FL 33146 (✆ USA toll free ✆ (1 800) JAMAICA and in Canada ✆ (1 800) 432 7559). A number of companies will help with booking smaller and more remote hotels, or will arrange an itinerary for you around the island. Contact Caribbean Travel and Tours Ltd, 12 Worthington Terrace, Kingston 5, (✆ 960 3598), or in Mandeville Countrystyle, PO Box 60 Mandeville, Manchester Parish (✆ 962 3725, ✆ 962 1461). Most hotel rates are quoted in US dollars—you can pay with credit cards and traveller's cheques in all hotels. A General Consumption Tax of 15% is levied on all purchases and hotel bills. Some hotels also charge 10% for service.

Villa Rental: Individual villa rental, with anything from a studio to seven bedrooms on offer, can be arranged through JAVA, the Jamaica Association of Villas and Apartments, based in Ocho Rios, PO Box 298, Pineapple Place (✆ 974 2508, ✆ 974 2967). They can be contacted in the USA at 1501 West Fullerton Avenue, Chicago, IL 60614.

Kingston

The most charming and comfortable hotel in Kingston at the moment is the **Terra Nova Hotel**, 17 Waterloo Road, Kingston 10 (✆ 926 9334, ✆ 929 4933, US and Canada res ✆ (1 800) 742 4276; *expensive*). It is a 1924 mansion fronted with classical balustrades and white and yellow awnings, set in an expanse of gardens: inside chandeliers hang above the heavy décor and formal wooden furniture and flooring. In this rarefied atmosphere, away from the hustle of town, you are cosseted by staff in black and white formal dress, complete with cummerbunds. There are just 21 rooms in the main house and a newer block, a pool and grill. And the Edwardian elegance of the dining room is the setting for one of Kingston's best formal restaurants for classic international cuisine.

The **Hotel Four Seasons**, 18 Ruthven Road (© 929 7655, ● 929 5964, US and Canada res © (1 800) 742 4276; *moderate*) is also an Edwardian town house with additions. The hotel is quite large, with 79 rooms, some decorated in bright, modern Caribbean style. The interior of the dining room, with its panelled walls and dark, sumptuously thick carpets, is a little unlikely for the Caribbean; you can also eat out on the breezy veranda. There's no pool, but the front desk will arrange for you to go to one. If you are in Kingston on business you might prefer one of the two larger high-rise hotels at the bottom of Knutsford Boulevard: the **Jamaica Pegasus** (©/● 929 5855; *moderate*), and the **Wyndham Hotel** (© 926 5430, ● 929 7439; *moderate*). They both offer international standards of accommodation and business facilities, and a brisk and busy atmosphere, but little Jamaican character. The **Indies Hotel**, 5 Holborn Road (© 926 2952, ● 926 2879; *moderate*) has just 15 rooms in blocks behind a small town house with a pretty foyer with wooden floor and tray ceiling. The rooms, each one with TV, air-conditioning and phones, lead off a peaceful courtyard festooned with golden palm and colourful crotons. They are comfortable though quite basic. All meals are available in the restaurant. Some *inexpensive* rooms.

Next door to the Indies Hotel is **Holborn Manor Guest House** (© 926 0296; *cheap*), a popular stopping-off point in town for younger travellers. There are 10 fairly basic but clean rooms with private baths, now gentrified to the point of having telephones and some televisions. There is a friendly atmosphere; home-cooked breakfast is included. The **Central Court Hotel** (© 929 1026; *cheap*) at the junction of Lady Musgrave Road and Old Hope Road has simple rooms at very cheap prices.

Rooms with a View and into the Blue Mountains

Within a shout of town (a short ferry ride across the harbour) is **Morgan's Harbour Hotel** (© 967 8075/967 8030, ● 967 8073; *expensive*), which is built into the old colonial brickwork of Naval Dockyard, a short walk to the east of the town itself. There are 40 air-conditioned and fan-ventilated rooms, decorated with Jamaican wood furniture and set in a shaded, sandy garden with a pool and seafront bar—some rooms have superb views over Kingston and to the hills beyond. There is a marina and some watersports. The hotel is within a shout of the international airport; convenient if you need to take an early flight or have arrived late.

Close to Kingston, and yet distinctly removed from the bustle of the city is **Ivor Guest House**, Skyline Drive, Jack's Hill (© 702 0510, ● 702 0380; *moderate*). There is a magnificent view from the terrace and garden—make your way up there at cocktail time, when the lights from the town are spectacular. Ivor is a small and elegant colonial house offering the sort of gracious hospitality that sits comfortably with the wooden floors, door-frames and the antiques. There are just three bedrooms: two in the old house itself with four-poster beds, and another in a self-contained cottage. Lunch, afternoon tea, cocktails and dinner are all served.

Maya Lodge, PO Box 216 (✆ 702 0314; *cheap*), near Ivor Guest House, just above Kingston, is lost in the deepest Jamaican fertility at the end of a rickety lane, with 6 cabins, hostel space for 10 and tent sites stretched around a curving hillside from a modern main house. It is a friendly place; guests meet on the thatched veranda which seems almost threatened by the ever-encroaching greenery. Endless information is available on Jamaican wildlife and walking. It gets quite cold on winter evenings, so take a jersey. The menu offers local Jamaican food, strong on vegetarian dishes. Facilities are very basic.

Higher up into the Blue Mountains you will find the **Pine Grove Hotel**, c/o 62 Duke Street (✆ 977 8009, ✆ 977 8001; *cheap*), with 14 rooms scattered on the hillside beneath the central house, where there is a restaurant and bar. Yet higher in the mountains, on an old coffee plantation at 4000ft is **Whitfield Hall Hostel**, contact 8 Armon Crescent, Kingston 6 (✆ 927 0986; *cheap*), another retreat lost in the grandeur of the Jamaican peaks. It's very remote (you need a four-wheel drive to get there, which can be arranged with the number above); meals can be prepared on request, but you can take your own food. No electricity: lighting is by gas lamps. It is a favourite drop-off point for those climbing the Blue Mountain Peak. Not far off is **Wildflower Lodge** (✆ 926 5874, 929 5394; *cheap*), which also has beds and provides meals on request. Make sure you book with these last two.

Above Red Light on the road to Newcastle, below the 17 mile post, is a small and pleasant place to stay, the **Mount Edge Bed and Breakfast** (✆ 0991 4292; *cheap*). There are just two rooms, one with a magnificent view right from the pillow, in a stone and wooden house. It offers hot and cold water, use of kitchen (or meals can be prepared), and is very calm and quiet.

Just beyond Irish Town on the Irish Town road, scattered over the summit and flanks of a 3100ft hill among the camelback ridges and outrageous greenery of the Blue Mountains, you will find the cottages of **Strawberry Hill** (✆ 944 8400, ✆ 944 8408, UK res ✆ (0800) 614 790, US ✆ (1 800) *OUT POST*; *luxury*). The area of Strawberry Hill once belonged to Horace Walpole, gothic novelist and son of the British Prime Minister, and is named after his estate in London. The hotel, built when the old Great House was destroyed during Hurricane Gilbert in 1988, has been designed in the best romantic old-colonial Jamaican style: the clinker-laid wooden cottages have white louvred windows, tray ceilings, shingle roofs, wooden floors and furniture, and some four-poster beds, with some novel modern touches, including Jamaican dancing scenes and even illustrations from Madonna's *SEX* book in one cottage—and the comforts are modern. There are just 18 rooms (studios up to four-bedroom cottages, some with kitchens), one with facilities for the handicapped. Everywhere there are balconies with stunning views from which you can watch the clouds track through the banana leaves. Well worth a visit.

Clockwise from Kingston

There is nowhere good to stay in Spanish Town, so you are advised to stay in Kingston. There are rooms on the south coast at the **Milk River Mineral Baths** (✆ 987 6544/995 4099; *cheap*). The building is a genuine old Jamaican red-tin-roofed affair with gingerbread pickings, louvres, screens and cooling vents; the 20 rooms are authentically decorated and very comfortable, with TVs, phones, fans and Bibles in each. The baths downstairs are free while you are staying at the hotel. It sees mainly a Jamaican crowd who come to take the spa waters, so it is an amusing place.

In Mandeville the most comfortable place to stay is the **Mandeville Hotel**, PO Box 78, 4 Hotel Street (*Ø* 962 2460, *Ø* 962 0700; *moderate*) which is set in its own enclave just off the town square. The building is modern but the hotel has an unhurried air about it. There are 60 well-decorated rooms (some of them suites) with TVs, phones and fans, with a bar, the Manchester Arms, downstairs and a pool in the pleasant gardens. The **Astra Hotel**, PO Box 60 (*Ø* 962 3265, *Ø* 962 1461; *cheap*), is a friendly, family-run hotel just outside the town centre, on Ward Avenue. It has 40 comfortable, clean rooms upstairs in the villa and in modern blocks behind; it's also a good source of information about the area. In the town of Christiana, in the hills to the north of Mandeville, you will find a nice retreat in the **Hotel Villa Bella**, PO Box 473 (*Ø*/*Ø* 964 2243; *moderate*). The style of the décor harks back to the fifties; the building is modern, but there is a gracious air of times past in the drawing room and on the veranda, where an old sign says: 'ring twice for ice water, three times for the maid'. There are well-kept, comfortable rooms upstairs.

There is a number of guest houses in the area around Mandeville: some of the villas are built with 6 bedrooms (for the families of the returning residents), which are let out when they are not there. Try **Kariba Kariba** at 39 New Green Road (*Ø* 962 3039; *cheap*) where there are five rooms and suites with bathrooms and a restaurant.

The area to the west of Mandeville, running from Treasure Beach up to Black River and on to Bluefields, has some charming small, typically Jamaican guest houses and some inns off the beaten track. The **Treasure Beach Hotel**, PO Box 5 (*Ø* 965 2305, *Ø* 965 2544; *expensive*) is a traditional beachfront resort hotel, with a relaxed atmosphere. There are 36 modern and very comfortable rooms in small blocks ranged along a palm-dotted hillside around a large main block with dining room and bar. They look over the pool and garden and a stretch of brown-sand beach. **Sunset Resort Villa**, Calabash Bay PA (*Ø* 965 0143, *Ø* 965 0555, US res *Ø* (1 801) 487 8127; *expensive*) is set in a modern villa on the clifftop above Calabash Bay. There are 12 rooms, all with private patios, air-conditioning and satellite TV, and a couple with kitchens (but there is also a restaurant serving international cuisine). Palm-thatch gazebos offer the finest view of the sunset. Some *moderate* rooms.

The most stylish place to stay in the area is **Jake's**, Treasure Beach PA (*Ø*/*Ø* 965 0552, UK res *Ø* (0171) 431 4045, US *Ø* (1 800) *OUT POST; moderate*), a hip retreat on the cliffs of Treasure Beach, with a superb view across the sea to the sunset. Jake's is quite rustic, with adobe buildings marooned in a sea of tall wild grass, but its colours give it plenty of style. The cottages are painted rich red and mauve, turquoise and tangerine. There are just seven rooms, with muslin nets and fans (anyone who insists on air-conditioning would not be right for this place), and solar-heated water. Behind the tin-roofed gingerbread terrace, with its bar and sitting area, is a scattering of parasols and upturned cable-barrels to eat on; Jamaican fare is adapted a little for the European palate. And just above the sea is a meandering, tile-studded swimming pool with Adirondack chairs strategically positioned for watching the waves. There is a small beach. You will probably need to book in advance in the winter season. The

Golden Sands Motel (✆/✉ 965 0167; *cheap*) is an ugly concrete construction on the golden-brown sand of Frenchman's Bay. There are three buildings in fact, with 20 simply decorated rooms, some with private kitchens. Cold water is laid on and so, if there are enough people, is a restaurant; it's excellent value with a funny transient crowd. Near the Golden Sands Motel is the **Four M's Cottage** on the beach (✆ 965 0131, ✉ 965 2697, restaurant and kitchens; *cheap*). There are villas for hire in this area and you are often able to find rooms in people's houses by walking around the town and asking: **Ital Rest** has two rooms, and camping space available. There is one place to stay in the area of Alligator Pond, **SeaRiv**, on the road to the Kaiser port (✆ 962 7265). The building is a modern concrete villa which, if you don't mind the isolation, makes a passable stopover, with reasonable rooms at a good price. Fans and phones, no TVs, and a nice section of dark-sand beach, usually all to yourself.

In Black River itself, a characterful colonial Jamaican house is **Waterloo Guest House** (✆ 965 2278; *cheap*) where there are five fan-ventilated rooms in the rickety main house and 16 with air-conditioning and televisions in a new block behind. It has a swimming-pool. Just to the north of the town you will find the **Ashton Ocean View Great House and Hotel**, PO Box 104 Luana (✆/✉ 965 2036; *cheap*). It is set in an old estate house which commands a magnificent view over the countryside around. It has been modernized, and painted oddly in white and turquoise, but shades of the old plantation style return in the lacquered wooden floor, the rugs, the wooden interior walls and louvred day-rooms. There are 24 rooms, 11 of these in the tin-roofed main building, which has less atmosphere. Rooms have fans and air-conditioning, phones and TV.

There are some excellent villas in the Bluefields area (try Mullion Cove and Bluefields Bay Villas), but if you are passing through there is an excellent guest house at **Natanias's** (✆/✉ 963 5342, US toll free ✆ (1 800) 330 2332; *cheap*) just up from Whitehouse. There are 16 rooms in a modern wooden house with huge walkaround balconies, rooms with wooden furnishing and louvred windows. Good central area and a small secluded beach; very quiet, but friendly. **Shafston Estate Great House**, Bluefields PO (✆ 0997 5076; *cheap*) has a superb setting high on the hills above the town (village) of Bluefields at the end of an impossibly rickety road. There are 10 extremely basic rooms, with shared bathrooms with cold water only, but the place has the unforgettable aura of an old Jamaican estate house and a veranda from which you can admire a hazy horizon that stretches from Whitehouse to Savanna-la-Mar. Not everyone's cup of tea, it's firmly on the backpacker circuit; all inc. **Lochiel Guest House** (✆ 955 9344; *cheap*) is also set in an old Jamaican estate house just outside the town of Savanna-la-Mar. There are 12 fan-ventilated rooms; some, in the main house, have lumbering old furniture and wooden interiors and others, in a block behind, are a bit more modern. Some rooms share bathrooms but there is hot and cold water. Breakfast is included.

Negril

Long renowned for its pleasure-seeking and sensual way of life, Negril has excellent and easy-going places to stay, on both sides of town (the beach and the cliffs). The laid-back style has also been updated and repackaged for the nineties man and woman, in some very expensive all-inclusive hotels.

The best of the traditional 'resort' hotels in Negril is **Swept Away**, PO Box 77 (⚟ 957 4040, 🖅 957 4060, UK res ⚟ (0181) 367 5175, US and Canada ⚟ (1 800) 545 7937), where there are 134 rooms in villas that stand in profuse tropical gardens of palms (coconut palms, Japanese fan palms, sago and date palms, travellers' trees) right on the beach. Each room has a large veranda and is furnished and louvred with stained wood, with cool terracotta tiles on the floor; there are fans and air-conditioning, but no TVs. You can enjoy the full range of body-beautiful activities, from aerobics in the sports complex to beauty treatments in the salon with a spa. There are watersports on the beach and evening entertainment. Heterosexual couples only.

Grand Lido, PO Box 88 (⚟ 957 4010, 🖅 957 4317, UK res ⚟ (01749) 677200, US ⚟ (1 800) 859 *SUPER*) has taken the all-inclusive concept upmarket, packaging sheer luxury, with 24-hour room service and champagne at the flick of a finger. It still has the brisk air and the constant activity and entertainment of the all-inclusive and it is quite a large resort, with 200 rooms set on excellent beaches; as always with Superclubs, there is a nudist area (well tucked away). The grounds are lovely and the rooms very comfortable: all have TVs, fan-ventilation and air-conditioning; many have an excellent view of the magnificent sweep of Bloody Bay. There is plenty to keep you busy: a beauty parlour, watersports and jacuzzis, nine bars, a games room, a library and afternoon tea. Jackets are required in one of the *à la carte* restaurants (but they can lend you one if you forgot yours).

very expensive

The most original of the all-inclusive hotels at the top end of the beach is **Hedonism II**, PO Box 25 (⚟ 957 4201, 🖅 957 4289, UK res ⚟ (01749) 677200, US ⚟ (1 800) 859 *SUPER*). It calls itself the naughtiest club in town and has been offering an adult playground now for over 15 years, with the slogan 'Be Wicked for a Week!' The resort allows couples and groups, but encourages singles in an endless catalogue of hedonistic activities: bar open 19 hours a day, nudes and prudes beaches, watersports, diving, trapeze and juggling instruction, wet T-shirt competitions, body-painting lessons (yours or somebody else's), singalong piano bar, drink and dance till you drop (or find a partner), mirrors on the bedroom ceiling, breakfast served until late—and then it all begins again. There is an à la carte restaurant for the evening. You may be put in a room with a stranger if you arrive as a single. It's pricey but a riot for a weekend or a couple of days during a trip around the island.

expensive

The best of the more traditional (non all-inclusive, non-resort) hotels on the beach side of town is the unusual **Negril Cabins** Resort, PO Box 118 (⚟ 957 4350, 🖅 957 4381), 50 African-looking cabins on stilts set in superb lawns and tropical gardens. There is a meandering pool with a swim-up bar and an easygoing atmosphere about the central areas. The rooms, some louvred and fan-ventilated, others with air-conditioning and TV, all have a balcony and makes a very comfortable retreat. There's tennis and a fitness centre, and the beach is just 5 minutes' walk away.

But the most stylish of the small hotels in Negril are really the ones on the cliffs, where you will find palm-thatched wooden cabins with louvres and ceiling fans, set in charming and abundant jungle-like gardens, with magnificent views over the cliffs to the sea. **Tensing Pen Village**, PO Box 13 (① 957 4417, ⊛ 957 0161, US res ① (216) 546 9000), has 12 very quiet and secluded rooms, in stone and wooden cottages or cabins, on paths that meander through wonderful greenery of sea grape and bougainvillea, right on the cliff edge. Rooms are fan-ventilated with ice-chests, four-posters and louvred French windows giving on to a balcony; no TVs. Tensing Pen was opened in 1975, and takes its name from Sherpa Tensing, the first man to climb Everest. The charming central house, under a huge fig tree, has a library, sitting area and a small kitchen.

Catch a Falling Star, PO Box 22 (① 957 0390), is a similar hideaway on the cliffs, a few one- and two-bedroom cottages linked by stone-lined, sandy paths in a garden of crotons and sea grape and flamboyant trees. There are hammocks on the cool verandas and a jacuzzi in the garden; rooms are louvred and screened. It's comfortable and peaceful, set around a central house and small gym. Breakfast (no other meals) is served right on the spectacular cliffs.

moderate

Banana Shout, PO Box 4 (① 957 4007), back on the cliffs, also has real charm—rooms overlook the sea or the tropical profusion of a garden, where hummingbirds flit around the lily ponds. There are 10 rooms in villas and cottages, with dark wooden furniture, screens and louvres, decorated with Haitian art. All rooms are fan ventilated and have kitchens (there is no restaurant, though breakfast can be ordered). Simply walk down the steps cut in the cliffs for a swim. The 12 villas and two studios of the **Rock House**, PO Box 24 (①/⊛ 957 4373), in a garden setting on the cliffs, have a wonderfully relaxed atmosphere. Accommodation is very comfortable with four-posters and muslin netting, outdoor showers with hot and cold water, and a slightly surreal pool-bar down on the cliffs.

cheap

Just south of Negril Lighthouse there are cabins, cottages and tent sites at **Lighthouse Park** (① 957 4490); the tent sites are very cheap. **Addis Kokeb**, PO Box 78, Somerset Avenue (① 957 4485), is a guest house on the cliffs, in its own stony garden with trees and cactus and aloe plants. There are a couple of simple cottages, and communal rooms that serve as a gathering point in the wooden main house, with kitchen and library. Some rooms share baths. You can also try **Errol's On the Beach** (① 957 3312), where there are eight simple rooms in small clapboard houses, with fans or air-conditioning; there's a restaurant and bar. There are a number of places where you can stay cheaply on the beach.

The very simple double rooms at **Roots Bamboo** (① 957 4479) have private baths and porches, giving on to the lush beachside garden. There's not much atmosphere, but it has a restaurant and bar, and some very cheap tent sites. And you can find comfortable rooms at a small spot with the unlikely name of **Perseverance Resort** (① 957 4333). They're basic but clean, with some private baths and some fans. Other similar accommodation is available through **Ms Gloria** (① 957 4741), who has just a few plain rooms on the beach, and **B.T.'s Resort** (① 947 4744), across the road from the beach, which offers basic rooms in cabins.

The North Coast—Montego Bay

Montego Bay is the leading resort area in Jamaica and you will find the town itself studded with huge tower blocks of hotel rooms. Farther afield, tucked away in their own coves, are some of the Caribbean's most luxurious resorts.

luxury

Round Hill Hotel and Villas, PO Box 64, Montego Bay (✆ 952 5150–5, 🖨 952 2505, UK res ✆ (0171) 730 7144, US ✆ (1 800) 424 5500) is the smartest and most sophisticated resort on the island. The pineapple of traditional West Indian welcome is the leitmotif of the hotel's décor. Round Hill lies 8 miles to the west of Montego Bay and has 27 villas set in hillside gardens; the pool, the blocks, each containing the 36 private rooms, the central foyer and the dining room are ranged around an amphi-theatrical slope, with the private bay below them, where there is a private beach protected by an offshore reef. Recently redesigned by Ralph Lauren, the décor uses traditional Jamaican styles, with white louvred screens and latticework offsetting the dark blue and dark green colours of the awnings. Round Hill is elegant but also relaxing, managed by staff who have been here for years. Watersports and a number of other activities are available if the library palls.

Another enclave of low-key, high luxury lies a few miles further west at the **Tryall Golf, Tennis and Beach Club**, PO Box 1206, Montego Bay (✆ 956 5660, 🖨 956 5673, US and Canada res ✆ (1 800) 336 4571). The great house, an elegant conglom-eration of buildings with overhanging eaves, terraces and balustrades, set around the stone shell of an old plantation house, stands on the crest of a hill amid palm trees, with the golf course and the sea stretching before it. There are 47 very comfortable rooms and 55 villas ranged on the hills behind (these are self-contained, with pools, gardeners and maid service, but you can use the facilities of the hotel). Scuba and other watersports are available if you are feeling active, including tennis and golf; otherwise laze around over lunch and afternoon tea on the veranda.

The **Half Moon Golf, Tennis and Beach Club**, PO Box 80, Montego Bay (✆ 953 2211, 🖨 953 1731, US res ✆ (1 800) 237 3237, European representative Windotel ✆ (0171) 730 7144), lies 8 miles east of Montego Bay. It is a sumptuous resort, set in manicured gardens and buildings of old colonial grandeur, giving on to a lovely half-moon curve of beach. A motif of neo-classical black and white runs through the resort, from the atrium of the great house to the chequerboard floors and classical columns of many of the rooms. Half Moon is a large hotel (and it does get quite full): there are 340 rooms in all, with 39 swimming-pools, 13 tennis courts and four squash courts, a chil-drens' entertainment centre, and plenty of watersports (jetskis excluded) with stables and, across the road, a golf course. The rooms are set in low blocks attached to the main house; there are also huge suites on the seafront, and villas around the grounds.

very expensive

A smaller beach resort in a more contemporary Caribbean style, with tall blocks standing over a pool above the beach and the broad expanse of sea, is **Coyaba Resort and Club**, Little River PO (✆ 953 9150, 🖨 953 2244). There are 50 very comfortable rooms, with terracotta tiles and mock antique furniture; each has a balcony. There is a personable and intimate air about the interior of the hotel. Life centres on the beach, however, where there is a bar and a deck stretching out into the shallow water towards a reef. Dining takes place in the pretty, vine-covered restaurant or above the beach itself. There's a fitness centre and watersports; all-inclusive packages available.

expensive

Good Hope, PO Box 50, Falmouth (✆/✉ 954 3289, UK res ✆ (0800) 614 790, US ✆ (1 800) *OUT POST*) is set in a restored 18th-century estate house overlooking a fantastic stretch of Trelawny countryside, a patchwork of rich red-brown earth and orchards, against a backdrop of the Cockpit Country. Built of stone and wood, with huge windows and breezy louvres, the house has original antique furniture, planters' chairs, vast glass hurricane lamps, four-poster beds and commodes, all on the original floor of wild orange wood. There are only 10 bedrooms, scattered around the main house, the garden buildings and stables, and so Good Hope never seems full. There is a pool and tennis court, and you can take a ride on horseback through the valley beneath the house—or you can simply watch from the drawing room or the veranda as the view alters constantly with the changing light of the day. Ideal for the lazy life among old Jamaican plantation elegance. The **Reading Reef Club**, PO Box 225, Reading Post Office (✆ 952 5909, ✉ 952 7217, US res ✆ (1 800) 223 6510) sits on the waterfront across the bay a little out of the town, and is quiet and well off the beaten tourist trail. There are just 28 rooms in three villa-style blocks set in an attractive garden of traveller's palms and heliconia, and the resort stands around a pool on a pleasant if slightly pebbly beach. The rooms are brightly decorated and furnished with wicker; all have ceiling fans as well as air-conditioning and some have balconies looking out on to the sea. There are some suites. The friendly bar has a wonderful view and, above it, the restaurant serves fine international and Caribbean food, including curried lobster and catch of the day as well as pastas. There is a dive shop on the premises and snorkelling right offshore.

For a more usual all-inclusive holiday in a busy beach hotel, offering a diet of constant activity and entertainment, and mostly buffet food, you can try either of the two Sandals resorts in Montego Bay, of which the better is probably **Sandals Royal Caribbean**.

moderate

Montego Bay and its surrounding area has a number of smaller hotels which still have a certain style. They are ideal for more independent travellers who want a stopover on arrival in Jamaica or are passing through while touring the island.

The **Relax Villa** Resort, 26 Hobbs Ave, White Sands Beach PO (✆/✉ 952 7218, US and Canada res ✆ (1 800) 742 4276) is close to the airport, in a couple of modern blocks set in the tropical gardens of a hillside estate. It's friendly and well run, with large rooms and (one-, two- and three-bedroom) apartments, all of them comfortably decorated in bright white and pastel colours, with balconies, air-conditioning and fans, TVs, etc. The beaches are not within walking distance, but easy to get to by car or taxi. Pick-up from the airport is offered and car-hire is available at a reasonable price here. It's a good place to start your holiday. **Orange River Ranch**, PO Box 822, Montego Bay (✆ 979 3294) is set in 989 acres of fertile Jamaican countryside just south of Montego Bay. The hotel is on a remote and quiet hillside (though tours visit occasionally); its central house has a wraparound veranda hung with flowering vines, and a white picket fence. Set in a modern block behind, the 24 rooms are slightly small but pretty and comfortable and many have an excellent view of the Orange River valley; fans, phones and a small veranda. Facilities include a pool, riding stables, and a shuttle service to the beach. Very peaceful, a good escape.

cheap

The **Ramparts Inn Hotel** at 5 Ramparts Close (℡ 979 5258) has a homely feel, set in an attractive hilltop house and garden with a view over the town and the expanse of Montego Bay. There are just 10 rooms, all air-conditioned, some with a view. The central areas include a pool on a deck, a bar and a TV room; there is a complimentary beach shuttle. The restaurant serves breakfast and lunch. There are also plenty of guest houses in Montego Bay, quite a few of them in the area close to the airport (some will pick you up when you arrive). Perhaps the friendliest stopover in the area is the **Ocean View Guest House** (℡ 952 2147), which is on Sunset Boulevard, just above the airport. There are 12 rooms, some air-conditioned and some with fan ventilation. Inexpensive meals are cooked to order and served in the busy central area (where there's a TV and some books), or under parasols on the veranda at the front. There is no pool, but a washroom you can use if you've been to the beach before flying out late in the day.

Alternatively you might try the **Ridgeway Guest House** just up the hill from the airport roundabout (℡ 952 2709, ✆ 940 0636), where there are rooms and self-contained apartments with fans and air-conditioning, and meals cooked to order. Further up the hill, on Leader Avenue off Queen's Drive, you will get a good rate at **Leader Guest Apartments** (℡ 952 0361), where there are 21 rooms in a no-nonsense block. The rooms have baths, hot and cold water, some balconies but there are no meals (nor kitchenettes, though it's OK to bring food into the rooms). The **Coral Cliff Hotel**, PO Box 253 (℡ 952 4130, ✆ 952 6532), on Gloucester Avenue, has a traditional Jamaican charm and enjoys a lively crowd of repeat visitors. It has the air of a grand old villa from colonial times, with a large breezy balcony above the street and tropical gardens punctuated by vast royal palms. The interior is charming and homely, with wooden floors and airy corridors. There are 21 rooms in older Caribbean style (with stained wooden walls and dark-stained furniture) and above them a pool and 10 rooms in the newer block; the library area has chess and backgammon.

Outside Montego Bay

In **Runaway Bay** (most of the way to Ocho Rios) you will find a resort devoted especially to children at **FDR** (Franklyn D. Resort), PO Box 201 (℡ 973 3067, ✆ 973 3071; *very expensive*), a 'giant step for kid kind'. The package is all-inclusive here, but the activity is centred mainly around taking the children off your hands. A 'girl Friday' puts them through their paces at finger painting, tiny tots' computer programming, kiddies disco technique or simply runs them around until they tire out so that you can busy yourself with more important things like windsurfing and sitting at the pool bar. She also cooks and babysits for you. It has 67 modern, high-pastel suites. The **Eaton Hall Beach Hotel and Villas**, PO Box 112 (℡ 973 3503, ✆ 973 2432, US and Canada res ℡ (1 800) JAMAICA; *very expensive*) has an Edwardian atmosphere a little unexpected in the tropics; the main house has dark floors and beams, and even a fireplace in the foyer. It sits on low cliffs, with its 52 rooms and 5 villas ranged to either side in two-storey blocks. The pool and bar stand above the waves, and there is a diminutive but inviting beach (some watersports available), cut into the cliffs. Rooms are comfortable, with four-posters and wooden floors. The package is all-inclusive, but the pace is relaxed. **Portside Resort and Villas**, PO Box 42, Discovery Bay (✆ 973 2007, ✉ 973 2720; *moderate*) is a small and concentrated cluster of pointy-topped villas in the town overlooking Discovery Bay. They vary in size from one bedroom to five; you can cater for yourself or use the central hotel facilities. The central dining room is right on the waterfront and the resort has its own beach, next to the main Puerto Seco beach. Cooks are available. The **Runaway HEART Club**, PO Box 98, Runaway Bay (✆ 973 2671, ✉ 973 2693; *moderate*) in a stately house surrounded by extensive, well-tended gardens a short way in from the coast, has the feel of old Jamaica. There are just 20 comfortable rooms with balconies, air-conditioning and phones, but no TVs. A shuttle takes you to the beach. The service is energetic and enthusiastic if a little raw, as most of the staff are drawn from the hotel training school next door. It is a quiet and fun place to stay.

The **Salem Resort** (✆ 973 4256, ✉ 973 5017; *cheap*) has a slightly unfortunate position right on the road in Salem, east of Runaway Bay, but offers comfortable rooms with TVs and balconies in a modern block at reasonable prices; meals are available. The **Villa la Rose**, Runaway Bay (✆ 973 3216; *cheap*) offers outstanding value and a friendly reception. It is set in a modern house and the nine rooms are carpeted and simply decorated. There are ceiling fans and hot and cold water. You can cook for yourself or eat out nearby.

Ocho Rios

Ocho Rios has put in a late bid as Jamaica's leading tourist centre (it used to be a sleepy fishing village, but it has a string of good beaches) and there are some excellent hotels in the town, and a string of restaurants, bars and clubs to keep everyone occupied in the evening.

all inclusives

Ciboney, PO Box 728 (✆ 974 1027, ✉ 974 5838; *very expensive–expensive*), is an all-inclusive resort with a certain elegant style. There are 250 rooms in suites, set on the hillside above a huge mock-colonial plantation house. There are tennis courts and squash courts, a spa for manicures, pedicures and water-jet treatment etc. and if you are feeling hot you can always take a dip in one of the resort's 90 swimming-pools. A regular shuttle takes you to the beach, where there are watersports. Plenty of restaurants, including one with light menus (five courses for just 1000 calories). Another hillside enclave, all but hidden in an explosively fertile Jamaican garden, is the **Sans Souci Lido**, PO Box 103 (✆ 974 2353, ✉ 974 2544; *very expensive*), a more modern version of Jamaican luxury. It lies 4 miles beyond the town centre and the 70 rooms with balconies stand on the hillside above the hotel spa, with its pool and work-out area, around the point from the beach, where most watersports are available. In a rather different style is **Couples**, PO Box 330 (✆ 974 4271, ✉ 974 4439; *expensive*), another resort to the east of the town, where you will find an action-packed regime of daytime watersports and other essential activities like massage and pool volleyball. Everything happens in pairs here, from the swimming-pool loungers to the cocktails (the bar is open all day of course). Breakfast and lunch are buffets, but dinner is *à deux*, à la carte. You must arrive in a man-woman couple.

Not far away, the **Boscobel Beach**, PO Box 63 (✆ 974 3331, ✆ 975 3270; *very expensive*), is also all-inclusive in plan, but it caters specifically for families with children. They will be taken off your hands at all moments and put through their paces in arts and crafts and given lessons in Jamaican *patois* while you follow the more urgent pursuits of tanning and windsurfing. There are 200 rooms in the complex, which is set on a cracking beach.

very expensive

The **Jamaica Inn**, PO Box 1 (✆ 974 2514, ✆ 974 2449, US res ✆ (1 800) 243 9240), 2 miles from the centre of the town, is one of Jamaica's most elegant hotels. Its setting is magnificent, enclosed in its own pretty bay, with a fantastic stretch of sand between small headlands. The old white and Wedgwood-blue estate house has a gracious colonial air, echoed in the old plantation style of the columns and balustrades, and louvred doors and fantail coolers above them. Each impeccably decorated room looks out on to the sea from an external living room on its own colonnaded balcony. There is a pool and some watersports (kayaks and sunfish) if you are feeling active, or the library and Scrabble if the desire should pass. Just 45 rooms and a certain formality (a jacket and tie are required in the winter season) but friendly: the staff recognize guests who return year after year.

expensive

Ocho Rios also has a number of smaller, more moderately priced properties, which are used by the package companies but which still have a certain individuality and style. The **Shaw Park Beach Hotel**, PO Box 17 (✆ 974 2552, ✆ 974 5042, UK res ✆ (0171) 581 4094) centres on an Edwardian-style villa, with wooden panelling and solid furniture, that stands above a protected cove with an excellent beach, where a number of watersports (glass-bottomed boat trips, windsurfing, sunfish and scuba) are available. Its 118 rooms and suites are comfortable and modern and all have a balcony or terrace with a view across the sea, air-conditioning and phones; most have TVs. The waterfront terrace provides a lovely setting for dinner; there's evening entertainment and Ocho Rios town is not too far off.

moderate

The **Hibiscus Lodge Hotel**, PO Box 52 (✆ 974 2676, ✆ 974 1874) stands in very pretty gardens on the clifftops in town. The pool, some of the rooms, the dining room and bar (where the chairs are slung from the ceiling) are all set on stepped terraces on the cliffside itself, shaded by tropical greenery and a huge almond tree (from which the restaurant takes its name). It is within walking distance of the centre of town, but it is quite private and has a friendly atmosphere and charming setting. There is snorkelling down below in the daytime, and some entertainment in the evenings. Rooms are comfortable if not luxurious. Another good option in the middle range and excellent value for money is the small **Ocean Sands Resort**, 14 James Avenue (✆/✆ 974 2605). The hotel is in a simple modern block above its own small strip of sand and shallow water out to the reef, and it has a friendly, quite homey atmosphere. There are 28 pretty pastel-decorated rooms, all with tiled floors, telephones and air-conditioning or a fan (some with balconies), overlooking the pool and the restaurant which sit above the sea on a deck. Some evening entertainment. In the centre of town itself you will find a small number of slightly cheaper rooms at **Pier View Apartments**, PO Box 134 (℗ 974 2607, ℗ 974 1384), a short walk from the Ocho Rios Bay Beach. The rooms are cheaper than the suites and they are set in two modern blocks above a crammed garden. All have TVs, air-conditioning and fans and most have balconies; some suites have kitchens. No pool or dining room, but all the restaurants are close by. Some *inexpensive* rooms.

cheap

James Avenue, at the lower end of the market, is a good area to find accommodation. Across the road from Ocean Sands is the **Marine View Hotel**, 9 James Avenue (℗ 974 5753, ℗ 974 6953). The building is uncompromisingly concrete, with pink, white and grey décor; but the large tiled rooms are available at good rates (the cheapest are the ones with ceiling fans). There is a pool and a restaurant where you can get all meals. Just up from the White River on the main road is the **Hummingbird Haven**, PO Box 95 (℗ 974 5188, ℗ 974 5202), a garden retreat set in 6 acres of forested hillside, just up from the beach. There are a few simple cabins and endless tent-sites. A restaurant is nearby but there are also limited cooking facilities available; it's a friendly stopover for independent travellers.

As you head **east of Oracabessa** and then south towards Port Maria you will find a small hotel popular with independent travellers, the **Caribbean Pearl**, PO Box 127 Port Maria (℗ 994 2672, ℗ 994 2043). The hotel is set in a modern house on the hillside which has a pool on a terrace out front and an excellent view of the broad sweep of the sea. The eight spacious rooms have tiled floors and nets on the beds, and wooden and wicker furniture. It's quite a sociable place, with a communal area for the TV and other gatherings. Packages include breakfast and dinner. Not far off, perched on the hillside, is **Blue Harbour**, PO Box 50, Port Maria (℗ 994 2262, US res ℗ (505) 586 1244), where accommodation is sometimes available when the whole place has not been block-booked. This is where the guests of Noël Coward used to stay—he lived here himself until he moved up to Firefly, on the hilltop above. Blue Harbour's 12 comfortable rooms have wonderful views over the bays and coastline.

In the hills above Ocho Rios, tucked away off the main road south from the town, is **Murphy Hill** guest house (℗ 922 0440). It nestles under a large and ugly antenna and the rooms are not brilliant, but there is a pool and the view is superb; ring to reserve and make sure to order your meals.

Another spot where you will find very basic accommodation (cabins and tent-space) and a serene atmosphere is **Goshen Wilderness Resort**, lost in the country to the south of Ocho Rios (signed off the White River Road). Very cheap rooms and camping space are available to the east of Oracabessa, in Port Maria, at **Mike's Sea Lawn Coral Beach**, which offers simple rooms with cold water only, and meals to order. There's some snorkelling down on the reef.

Port Antonio

The **Trident Villas and Hotel**, just east of the town, is one of the most sumptuous spots on the island, PO Box 119 (℗ 993 2602, ℗ 993 2590, UK res Windotel ℗ (0171) 730 7144, US res ℗ 404 237 4608; *very expensive*). There are 12 rooms and 14 cottages set neatly in luxuriantly lawned gardens of palms and pine hedges with roaming peacocks and doves, all on a dramatic ledge of pitted volcanic cliffs. The rooms are exquisitely decorated—tiled, with stained-wood panelling and solid furniture in the black and white colour scheme that runs throughout the resort. Ventilation is mainly by fan and sea breeze here, though there is air-conditioning, and each room has its own veranda. There is a charming and very private beach in its own protected inlet, and some sports, including windsurfing, dinghy sailing, scuba and tennis; there's some *luxury* accommodation, particularly the magnificent Imperial Suite.

The **Hotel Mocking Bird Hill**, PO Box 254 (℗ 993 7267, ℗ 993 7133; *expensive*) stands high on the hillside a few miles to the east of Port Antonio, and has a magnificent view, nearly 180 degrees wide. The stark concrete of the villa belies the relaxed air, and eco-friendly philosophy of the place. The 10 rooms, with locally made bamboo furniture, pretty floral decorations, balconies and hammocks, are set in 6 acres of forest crisscrossed by paths and scattered with benches. The dining room is on a very attractive balcony and offers exceptional home-made fare: jams, mayonnaise and breads, including rye, sunflower, coconut, even cheese breads, baked in their own solar oven. And inventive Jamaican dishes are served with vegetables from Mocking Bird Hill's own organic garden. It is an extremely peaceful spot and you will be looked after well.

Goblin Hill Villas at San San (℗ 925 8108, ℗ 925 6240; res 11 East Avenue, Kingston 10, ℗ 925 8108, ℗ 925 6248, US res ℗ (1 800) 472 1148; *expensive*), has 28 one- and two-bedroom villas in a 12-acre hilltop setting of charming gardens. Goblin Hill is run more as a villa resort than as a hotel and so there is no central restaurant. The villas have maid service and all meals can be provided, though there are full kitchens if you want to look after yourself. The rooms are comfortable and fan ventilated, on a split level or on two floors, all with patios and many with fantastic views, with air-conditioning in the bedrooms and king-size beds. There are no TVs in the villas, but there is a central TV room. Quite a few families come to the resort so there is a children's play area and some activity programmes. There is a charming bar, where you sit on fan-backed wicker chairs, on a stepped deck that twines around a huge fig tree.

If you would prefer to be on the beach itself, **Dragon Bay**, PO Box 176, Port Antonio (℗ 993 3281, ℗ 993 3284; *expensive*), is set on a very pretty cove. There are 30 rooms, mostly in one- to four-bedroom villa combinations, athough some rooms alone are available, and they stand on a hillside just above the central pool and restaurant. They are furnished with bamboo in a bright white colour scheme, with fans in the main rooms, and air-conditioning in the bedrooms; some have kitchenettes. The beach is pretty and quite busy; watersports are available there including scuba and small sailing boats. There are two restaurants: a thatch-roofed bar on the beach that serves breakfast and lunch, and a more formal dining room on a terrace for dinner. The **Fern Hill Club**, PO Box 26 (℗ 993 3222, ℗ 993 2257; *expensive*) has 31 rooms and suites in villas high on the hill above San San farther east of the town. The appearance is striking—white-painted villas with sharply pointed shingle roofs stand out starkly against the greenery of the beautifully forested hillside. The brightly decorated rooms have TVs, fans and air-conditioning, plus some jacuzzis, two pools and tennis courts; the beach down below (reached by shuttle) offers watersports. The central great house, with a restaurant serving international and Jamaican fare, has a magnificent view of the coastline and mountains around. Friendly but rather quiet.

Across the channel on Titchfield Hill you will find several smaller hotels and guest houses, some of them set in the classic old Jamaican town houses from the turn of the century, built with shingle tiles and cast-iron balconies. **De Montevin Lodge**, PO Box 85 (✆ 993 2604; *moderate*), has 15 rooms in the three storeys of the red-painted brick house; a couple have their own cast-iron filigree balconies. The wooden stairs and door surrounds and large number of pictures of the British Royal Family, create a Jamaican home atmosphere. Rooms have fan ventilation; all meals are available.

Not far away from De Montevin Lodge is **Ivanhoe's** on Queen Street (✆/✆ 993 3043; *moderate–cheap*), where the 15 rooms are in a modern extension, with plush décor, ceiling fans and hot and cold water, attached to a traditional wooden Jamaican house; all meals are available.

To the east of Port Antonio you will find a very small and simple guest house, **Draper San** (✆ 993 7118; *moderate–cheap*), which sits in a pretty garden plot on the roadside in Drapers village, within earshot of the waves in the bay below. It's friendly, with just six rooms, a sitting area and kitchen; Italian food is cooked to order.

The **Holiday Home** (✆ 993 2882; *moderate–cheap*) is set in another traditional wooden house on King Street and has nine rooms and a nice balcony where meals are served. The walls are a bit thin; there are some private baths, with cold water only.

A few miles to the west of town, **Rio Vista Resort and Villas**, PO Box 4, St Margaret's Bay (✆ 993 2244; *moderate–cheap*) have just a few one- and two-bedroom cottages, with magnificent views over the Rio Grande river valley or over the sea. The rooms are brightly decorated in white and they are fan-ventilated; with satellite TV and maid service.

Heading east from Port Antonio you come to **Boston Bay**, where villas with rooms to rent are steadily springing up, and then to **Long Bay**, which has become quite a popular stopover on the 'backpack' circuit. Rooms in private houses are available there, though most are not registered with the Tourist Board. There were no telephones in Long Bay at the time of writing, but you can try **The Chalet** and **Coconut Isles**, both in modern buildings just above the beach. **Blue Heaven Resort**, messages via Port Antonio (✆ 993 9847; *cheap*), offers extremely basic rooms in bamboo cottages on a nice creek.

A number of guest houses and small hotels are opening up along the southern coast of St Thomas, all signed on the roadside as you head east of Morant Bay. In the town itself, the **Morant Villas** (✆ 982 2422; *cheap*) is officially recommended, but the **Golden Shore Beach Hotel** on Windward Drive, PO Box 8 Lyssons, St Thomas (✆ 982 9657; *cheap*) has a bit more style for excellent value. It is on a lovely beach, quiet but with the occasional weekend crowd. The rooms are fairly basic but clean, some with air-conditioning, some fans; all rooms have private baths, but some have only cold water. You sleep to the wash of the waves. There is a bar under the palms, with meals available (order by 6pm).

© (1 876)– **Eating Out**

Once the staple diet of the plantation slaves, ackee and saltfish is now a Jamaican national dish. Ackee is the yellow fruit of the ackee tree from Africa, which cooks and tastes like scrambled egg, and salt fish is salted cod, originally imported as food for the slaves. Other classic Jamaican dishes include curry goat, callaloo and rice 'n' peas, cooked in coconut milk. Good use is made of the Caribbean vegetables—pepperpot is a thick soup based on okra; popular traditional vegetables are breadfruit and plantain and the many roots such as yam and eddoe. Fruits—soursop, sweetsop, coconut, mango, pawpaw and pineapple—are served at breakfast, as midday thirst-quenchers and in the ice-creams at dinner. Many restaurants will offer you Jamaica's own Blue Mountain coffee, considered by many to be the best in the world. It rounds off a dinner well.

In hotel dining rooms you are likely to come across international-style fare (with the occasional Jamaican buffet), but some are becoming more adventurous, and there is a greater variety on offer within the hotels now. You have to go outside the hotels or go local to get good Jamaican food. Jerk centres (*see* p.682) are well worth the visit, and an excellent lunchtime snack is a patty and a soft drink, rounded off with plantain tart or a coconut cake. A proliferation of snack bars and restaurants has opened up along the roadside over the last few years and so there are plenty of stopovers for lunch. Some restaurants and the occasional hotel dining room require a jacket and occasionally a tie for dinner. Credit cards can be used in the larger restaurants. There is a General Consumption Tax of 12½% and many restaurants also charge service.

Categories are arranged according to the price of a main dish: *expensive*—J$300 and above; *moderate*—between J$150 and $300; *cheap*—J$100 and below.

Kingston and Surrounding Area

expensive

There are a couple of smart restaurants just outside the town, easily reached by car or taxi. The **Blue Mountain Inn** (© 927 1700) is the most formal and smartest restaurant around Kingston. It sits in a vast cleft in the mountains, on the road to Gordon Town. The interior is dressed up as a drawing room, carpeted in red with black beams and white walls, and there's a magnificent view of the river from here and from the vine-covered terrace, where you can take coffee to the rush of the river water. The menu is international: start with an ackee quiche and follow with lobster bathed in mint and ginger sauce. Jackets are required.

Another very nice spot is **Ivor Guest House** (*see* p.704). There is a nightly changing, four-course set dinner, with three or four choices of main courses. Dishes are mainly international, but they make good use of local ingredients, so you might start with smoked marlin with cream cheese and capers, and follow with a fillet of sea snapper brushed with eskellion, scotch bonnet and spice butter, then top it off with a tropical fruit ice cream.

Guilt Trip (℡ 977 5130) is laid-back and open late, on a terrace with latticework walls and a wooden roof hung with greenery, overlooking a lawn and fountain. The fare is international with a distinctly Jamaican twist: try the pimento-stuffed chicken breast or roasted snapper fillet in a passion-fruit cream. And the desserts are magnificent; there is also a bakery on the premises which specializes in cakes, so afternoon tea is particularly popular here. It's difficult to find, and there is no sign: head up Hope Road, turn left (onto Barbican Road) at Matilda's Corner (at Liguanea Plaza). Just a few hundred yards on, down over the bridge, look for the sign for the Orchid Patch on the right; it's in there somewhere.

Another fashionable spot with a lively atmosphere and very fine food is the **Crossings New World Café** (℡ 978 3547) right next to the petrol station on Old Hope Road where it meets Mountains View Avenue. Menus come in record sleeves and the décor in the dining room upstairs is hip; there are bars downstairs. Exclusively Jamaican ingredients are used in international recipes: lots of pasta and seafood; cho-cho bisque with dill and red pea salad; and conch is a speciality. Serves brunch and dinner.

The **Devonshire** at Devon House is more formal; you dine on verandas overlooking an inner courtyard with a small forest of greenery and a lily pond. Try the roast sucking-pig and Island coconut lobster; lots of steaks if you want them. At **El Dorado** at the Terra Nova Hotel (℡ 926 9334), on Waterloo Road, in the colonial setting of a neoclassical villa built at the turn of the century, you dine on lobster tail flamed with brandy and grilled chicken with guava sauce.

moderate

Something of the Port Royal of the 1680s still exists in the old brick warehouse building of the **Grog Shoppe** at Devon House—the guests behave rather better now, though. There is an easy mix of visitors and some locals here. After you have tucked into a list of exotic and colourful cocktails (their names taken from some sensational moments in Jamaica's history, including Devon Duppy and the White Witch), you will be served local Jamaican callaloo and hot pot, as well as Blue Mountain burgers and steaks. It's a pleasant spot with tables inside under a ship's figurehead or a fairy-lit mango tree. *Open all day and into the evening.*

Heather's in Haining Road has tables set on a terrace beneath a mango tree. It's popular with expats, who cluster here for a drink and sometimes a plate of food after work: a long menu includes seafood and fish specialities, cottage pie and burgers, and even bangers and mash. The **Café Central**, in a small concrete garden with tables under the trees around the gazebo bar, is a more easygoing spot, which sees a mix of Jamaicans and expatriates. The café's courtyard is tucked away at the very end of Central Avenue (off Constant Spring Road). There is a general menu that features stir-fries and sandwiches, but also some tasty cheese dishes including melted cheese sandwiches. *Open for lunch and dinner, Mon–Sat; closed Sun.* The **Hot Pot** is a much more Jamaican affair, set in a courtyard under umbrellas. It serves trusty if odd-sounding Jamaican food in large portions—anything from gungo soup or beef balls to the less worrisome steam fish and fricassee chicken, with a tonnage of rice 'n' peas.

At lunchtime you might try **The Pantry** on Dumfries Road for Jamaican fare: soup and a plate of fried rice or a sandwich. In the evening they serve mackerel rundown, chicken in sweet potato or an ackee pizza. Close by, the **Indies Pub** draws a crowd after work and at lunchtime, when it is popular with New Kingston business people. Simple chicken and fish with chips, or a pizza. Just down Holborn Road you can get a good Jamaican 'roti' from the **Mango Tree Café** in a bamboo- and tin-walled concrete yard. Fast-food joints are popular and some of the malls stay open late as people loiter while they eat; try those at Liguanea Mall on Hope Road.

There are a few exclusively **vegetarian** restaurants around Kingston—though a number of places offer a vegetarian dish on their menus. The **Eden Restaurant**, on Eastwood Park Road, just above Half Way Tree, offers lunch and dinner until 8pm. *Closed Sat—they are Seventh-Day Adventists.* You can also get good vegetarian fare among the botanical pandemonium of Jack's Hill (above the city in the mountains) at **Maya Lodge** (✆ 927 2097, *see* p.705).

cheap

There are several jerk centres in town. The most popular is the **Chelsea Jerk Centre** on Chelsea Avenue in New Kingston, where you can buy chicken or pork doused in hot pepper sauce. *Closed Sun.* Alternatively try **Peppers** on Upper Waterloo Road. On weekday evenings you can always get a barbecued half-chicken from one of the women cooking on upturned braziers at the roadside, and patties are available around town.

Mandeville

In Mandeville, the **Hungry Hut** is a good spot for local fare, curry goat and a stewed chicken with ground provisions, as is the **Grove Court**, opposite the Court House on the Square, both *moderate–cheap*. At the **Angel Food Health Restaurant** in Mandeville Plaza there are vegetarian dishes and natural juices.

Negril

Negril has literally hundreds of restaurants and snack bars along its roadsides. There is no really smart and formal restaurant (except the à la carte restaurants in the all-inclusives—but to go there just for a meal, you would have to buy an evening pass, for two), but there are many beach bars which serve drinks and snacks by day and then turn into lively bars and restaurants by night. A few of the restaurants offer a pick-up service.

moderate

Kuyaba (✆ 957 4318) is on a meandering wooden deck right on the sand of Negril beach, under a pointed thatch roof. The name means 'heaven' in the Arawak Indian language and, with its candle-light and serene seaside ambience, it's about as close as Negril's got. It serves simple fare by day and then in the evening more adventurous cuisine—snapper stuffed with orange and shrimp in a coconut sauce. Take advantage of the free pick-up service. The restaurant **Red Snapper** (✆ 957 0100) has several different dining areas, 20 feet above the sea on the cliffs. Start with a cocktail served in a pineapple, while being serenaded by a mento band or a drummer. The kitchen is on view as they grill—a long menu including seafood (some home-smoked) and vege-tarian dishes. Crab legs in garlic are followed by conch, or snapper curried in a coconut sauce. The **Hungry Lion** (✆ 957 4482), set in a forested tropical courtyard across the road from the cliffs, is a charming and original restaurant, with bright yellow walls and sprays of bougainvillea, benches and tables under a tin roof, and a fountain. Exotic natural foods and juices are a speciality—eggplant parmesan followed by lobster in lemon butter or kingfish in coconut milk—served by hip waiters. It is quite small and popular, so it fills up quickly; get there early. *Dinner only.*

At the far end of town, beyond the lighthouse you will come across the **Lighthouse Inn** (Ⓓ 957 4052), which sits on a deck beneath trees garlanded with fairy lights. Enjoy the conch or any number of fish steaks, pepper shrimp and other Caribbean combinations including ginger chicken; free pick-up service. Another restaurant with great Caribbean style, in a wooden building among the trunks of royal palms, is **Paradise Yard Café**, about half a mile inland from the roundabout, on the road to Savanna-la-Mar. You sit at benches and tables on open terraces, in a proper yard of beaten earth, eating foreign and authentic Jamaican food—enchiladas, jambalaya, callaloo alfredo and fricassee, or the speciality, rasta pasta: red (tomatoes), gold (ackee) and green (green peppers).

cheap

Two restaurants that are praised for their specialities are **Cosmo's**, where you are supposed to get the best conch in the town, and **Erica's** (quite a long way down on the cliffs), where you are assured the finest lobster in town (served, among other ways, in butter, lime and garlic). And for an excellent local meal, you should try the **Three Sisters** restaurant, in an old wooden house that looks a bit like a church about half a mile inland on the Sav road. Real Jamaican dishes (oxtail, brown stew chicken, tripe beans and peppered steak) are presented at tables with bright tablecloths and plastic roses, and served with a tonnage of ground provisions; also juices. *Closed in the evening.* There are a couple of places which specialize in chicken: at **Chicken Lavish** (they also serve steam fish and curried or sweet and sour chicken), close to the centre of town, you can dine on the covered terrace enclosed by a white picket fence, or order a takeaway; and at the bottom of the West End Road you will find the inimitable **Roy and Felix (Serious Chicken)**, which is set in a colourful bamboo and thatch construction at the corner of Summerset Road.

Montego Bay

Montego Bay has a good selection of restaurants, in and outside the hotels, some of them in very elegant surroundings. Eating out is pretty expensive though, so you may want to go local some of the time.

expensive

The finest restaurant around, for the cuisine and for the setting, is **Norma's** (Ⓓ 979 2745), a few miles east of Montego Bay in Reading (signed from the road). You dine in the open air on a wooden deck beneath a huge sea almond tree, with the water washing quietly over the rocks beneath you, and the lights of Montego Bay sparkling on the hillside opposite. Norma uses the best of fresh local ingredients in some unlikely but satisfying combinations—the crisp flesh of an otaheite apple sits well in the rich body of a pumpkin soup; as main courses snapper is marinaded in lemon, lime and ugli fruit, capers and herbs and then grilled, chicken breast layered with cream cheese; desserts include a white chocolate and pear cheesecake with a lacing of rum. The menu changes nightly; it's open at lunchtime, but ideal for a lingering dinner for two. *Closed Mon.*

The **Town House**, Church Street (*✆* 952 2660), is set in an elegant Georgian mansion (variously a manse, masonic lodge, warehouse, hotel, synagogue and residence of the governor's mistress), overlooking the parish church. The dining rooms are in the brick-laid cellar (where the walls are covered with paintings, which you can buy if the desire should strike) and upstairs, with some tables looking over the street. The menu is international with some Jamaican flavours: red snapper is served as a papillotte, cooked in a cheese, wine and lobster sauce, and Jamaican chicken curry is served with breadfruit, ackee and plantain.

moderate

The **Houseboat** (*✆* 952 5817) is a fondue restaurant, an unlikely concept for the Caribbean, but an original one and actually quite fun. The houseboat itself sits on the lagoon in the Freeport area and you ride across to it on a small hand-drawn ferry floating on oil barrels. There are three courses, all of them fondues: cheese sauce and wine to begin with, into which you dip Jamaican hard-dough bread; then the meats and vegetables—steak, chicken, shrimp and plantain—with Béarnaise, spicy tomato and teriyaki sauces and mango chutney; and finally a chocolate fondue, made of local Jamaican chocolate, into which you dip fresh Caribbean fruits. Take a constitutional on the upper deck and admire the lights of the Bogue Hills.

Marguerite's has a superb setting on the waterfront at the heart of the Gloucester Avenue strip. It is both a smart restaurant on a seafront deck, which serves international fare with a Caribbean twist, and a bar-grill, with a waterslide off the roof to cool you down when the drinking in the sun becomes too much. A lively spot for a daytime or early evening drink.

Just down the road you will find an ever-popular spot for a trusty Jamaican meal (and some more regular international fare): **The Pelican**. It is set in a modern and aggressively air-conditioned room, with quick service, 'Please Wait to be Seated', but it pulls a lively crowd of Jamaicans and tourists and you can get a curry goat or a brown stew with rice cooked in coconut milk.

cheap

If you want to go a little more local try lunch at **Smokey Joe's** downtown, in a dingy dining room in a little alley off St James's Street. Delicious pumpkin soup is followed by curry goat and rice 'n' peas or a fish platter and a Red Stripe.

There are plenty of stalls around the downtown area for a lunchtime pattie and an ice cream. Finally, the **Pork Pit**, back on Gloucester Avenue, opposite Walter Fletcher beach, is a classic among jerk centres and something of an institution around Montego Bay. It serves excellent jerk—chicken and pork, some 'spear ribs' and sausage—which is hacked to pieces before you, tossed into a basket and thrust through the small window. You eat at picnic tables, mitigating the effect of their electrifying jerk sauce with a festival roll, yam or sweet potato. Also on offer are some Jamaican standards: steam fish and rice 'n' peas. There are endless bars which double as simple eateries along Gloucester Road, offering burgers, salads and sandwiches, usually with music, sometimes a live band. Many of these restaurants stay open all day.

On the **north coast** between Mo Bay and Ocho Rios there are plenty of small and local restaurants, good stopovers for a beer and a chicken or fish. At the village of **Rock** on the coast you can get a tasty conch and a beer at **Glistening Waters** (© 954 3229; *moderate*), where you sit on a breezy wooden deck at the waterfront surrounded by deep-sea fishing boats. It serves a good conch as a starter and then wholesome Jamaican food: chicken or fish with a heap of coleslaw and coconut-flavoured rice. There is a lively crowd of Jamaicans at the weekend, and you can see the phosphorescence in the bay from here. The restaurant has a boat in which you can take a tour of the lagoon.There is a charming bar and restaurant, **The Time and Place**, just down from the Trelawny Beach Hotel (*moderate–cheap*). Thatch-covered bamboo shacks with a sandy floor and festooned with greenery, right on the waves. Burgers, seafood and fries.

Ocho Rios

Ocho Rios has only a few good restaurants outside the hotels.

The most pleasant, for its setting high above the lights of Ocho Rios in a charming old 1860s house, is **Evita's** (© 974 2333; *expensive*), which you enter through an arbour of four-poster bedposts. You can dine outside on a vine-hung veranda, or in the attractive wooden interior with its stained-wood floor and louvres. The fare is Italian, including dishes from a classic fettucine Alfredo to a Fra Diavolo, but there are also some Caribbean–Italian combinations—pasta *escovicha* and lasagne *rastafari*. Perhaps the best known restaurant in town is **The Ruins** (© 974 2442; *expensive*), on da Costa Drive. It gets very crowded, so it's hardly one for a romantic meal *à deux*, but it has a delightful setting: wicker chairs and tables on a deck by a floodlit waterfall beneath huge fig trees, with the sounds of the water and the occasional serenade. The fare is partly international (*coq au vin*, lamb chops in mint sauce) and otherwise Chinese (including the chef's special dish of lotus lily lobster).

The **Almond Tree** restaurant, at the lower end of *expensive*, also has a very sympathetic setting at the Hibiscus Lodge Hotel, on the main street of Ocho Rios. You dine on a terrace high above the sea, with gingerbread fretwork surrounded by greenery and a huge almond tree. Pumpkin soup is followed by snapper or kingfish in coconut and then a volley of tropical fruit ice creams.

Many of the bars in the town double up as restaurants and so you can take a drink and look at the menu before you decide whether to eat. A bar with a reliable kitchen goes by the odd-sounding name of **Bibirips** (*moderate*). This tin-roofed TV-bar has a balustraded seating area on the clifftop just behind a car park; the menu is plain and wholesome Jamaican food. You might think that it was just another over-imaginative T-shirt, but in fact there really is a **Hard Rock Café** (*moderate*) in Ocho Rios. It offers simple fare, such as grilled fish and shrimp fettucine, and a long list of cocktails, which you can take around the waterfall, or sip while making use of the pool table.

For something a little more Jamaican you can try one of the two jerk centres. The **Double V** (*moderate*) is very touristy and lunch comes complete with MC accompaniment, loud music and embarrassing dancing competitions. A much more low-key spot, also popular with the locals after work, is the **Ocho Rios Jerk Centre** near the 'roundabout' to Kingston (*moderate*). There are also plenty of more authentic Jamaican restaurants, all-day diners and bars around the town: **Parkway** Restaurant, on Main Street (*moderate*), is a true West Indian dining room, air-conditioned, with the television playing and tables set with plastic table-mats. Enjoy the Jamaican chicken or a fried rice and shrimp followed by banana cake. In a similar vein is the **Lobster Pot** just down the road (*moderate*). A rather tired interior displays some interesting decorative touches that include plastic roses in curious vases made of heat-stretched Red Stripe bottles, the occasional lobster hanging in a fishing net and a whole picket fence. It serves outstanding Jamaican food: brown stew fish, fricassee chicken and creole shrimps, presented to you with a tonnage of rice 'n' peas and coleslaw. On weekend evenings people sell cooked chicken at the roadside in Ocho Rios.

Port Antonio

There are few places in which to eat in **Port Antonio**. If you want to dine out you will have to go to the hotels.

Trident Villas (*expensive*) serves a six-course candle-lit set dinner of very fine West Indian and continental fare in a subdued and elegant setting. The dining room at the Hotel Mockingbird Hill, **Mille Fleurs** (Ⓒ 993 7267; *expensive*), set on a charming veranda, offers innovative cuisine using the best of the exotic Jamaican fruits and vegetables: carpaccio of tropical fruits or ackee soufflé followed by a soup (combinations such as tomato and sweet potato) and then an ital rundown or chicken in June plum sauce. The three-course menu has a choice for each course (and always includes a vegetarian dish). There is an Italian restaurant (and part-time lingerie shop) in the middle of town, above the War Memorial square, the **Trattoria Romagna** (*moderate*). Its simple and cavernous dining room has a veranda overlooking the activity of the street, where you can enjoy seafood, pasta and pizzas. *Open every day, lunch and dinner.* **Huntress Marina** (*moderate*) serves fish and chicken dinners on a rickety palm-thatch deck that overlooks the harbour.

Numerous cheap local restaurants in Port Antonio will fix you an excellent rice 'n' peas, a curry goat or an escoveitched fish. **Daddy D's** is a popular local diner; brightly painted, with plastic tablecloths and flowers. **Tri-Me** is another excellent stopover for a stew fish or fry chicken. *Closes early.* If you want an ice cream, try **Cream World** on Harbour Street in town. You can pick up a barbecued chicken leg from the people cooking on braziers on the roadside in town, but if you suddenly feel like a jerk (pork or chicken jerk, that is) you can try **Stop Brap Jerk** on the eastern harbour, where there is a concrete deck under the almond tree, and a fine view.

A few miles east of Port Antonio you come to **Boston Bay**, home of jerk. There are three or four centres on either side of the road—**Sufferer's Jerk Centre**, **Mickey's**, **Shaggy's**, and a little down the road, **Fuzzy's**. You sit on open-air terraces amid the barbecues. Chicken and pork, occasionally other meats, are chopped (hacked to bits) to order and served with a festival roll and a beer to wash it all down.

Bars and Nightlife

Entertainment in the hotels is varied—in some places it owes nothing to Jamaica, and is as packaged as the holiday that gets you there (wet T-shirt competitions, pot-belly contests, fire-eating, and limbo competitions that nobody wins because they all fall over backwards). However, there are some quite good combos who will serenade you at dinnertime. There are good discotheques in some of the larger and more sophisticated hotels, and there is often a lively crowd at the all-inclusives if you can get in for the evening.

The clubs are fun and worth a visit to see the Jamaicans themselves at play, though you should be slightly wary in some areas of Montego Bay and Kingston about going in alone. You can always get a Jamaican to go with you. There are plenty of venues for concerts around the island—keep an eye on the papers because sometimes world-famous reggae bands will play a gig in a small club. And there are limitless bars around the island, from the hillside setting of plantation house restaurants or a local rumshop to the cliffs and beachside bars of Negril, where the crowds gather to watch the sunset with almost religious adoration.

The national brew of Jamaica is Red Stripe beer, though you will also find many imported beers. Appleton is the best-known rum—the smoothest is Appleton Gold, but the most popular among the Jamaicans is Appleton Overproof, a white rum which is also known as John Crow Batty because of its fearsome strength.

A great place to start any evening in Kingston is at **Ivor Lodge** in Jack's Hill. It has a fantastic view across the city from the veranda, as far as Port Royal in the distance. Good for a rum punch in old Jamaican surroundings. Back down in the thick of the town there are plenty of haunts, part bar, part restaurant and sometimes part café too, frequented by Kingstonians. **Heather's** on Haining Road is ever popular; close by, **Carlos Café** on Belmont Road gathers a lively crowd of drinkers and diners under its awnings and umbrellas. You might also join the preppy drinkers at **Peppers** on Waterloo Road, or try **Chaser's Café**, on Barbican Road, where an animated bunch hang out drinking and generally make whoopee. A hip crowd gathers to chill out at the **Crossings Café**. You could try the jazz evening on the last Wednesday in the month, downstairs in the Mutual Life building on Oxford Road—you'll hear anything from Third World to soca jazz. The **Countryside Club** on Eastwood Park Road is a popular venue for late-night drinking and dancing. Discotheques include the **Asylum** nightclub on Knutsford Boulevard and **Mirage** at the Sovereign Centre on Hope Road.

Negril has a multitude of bars and clubs along its 10 miles or so of seafront. Besides the beach bars there are plenty of spots on the cliffs where you can spend the day chilling out until the great highlight of the day, watching the sunset. Traditionally **Rick's** is the popular venue for this pursuit—worth trying once though it does involve buying drinks with tokens and it can get pretty packed, because tourists are bussed in for the event, and you might feel compelled to jump 40ft into the water below. If you want something a little less crowded, try the **LTU Pub** a couple of hundred yards further on; still lively at times, but with fewer lobster-red tourists and more locals.

Another popular daytime hangout is the **Pickled Parrot**, perched on the cliff, a shingle-roofed gazebo and platforms on the cliff-edge with the waves crashing beneath; it offers drinks and simple meals all day long, satellite TV, swings and a waterslide.

The sunset's just as good from the beach. Try **Alfred's Ocean Palace**, which can get particularly lively and **De Buss**, last resting place of a pink and green double decker that washed up here, perhaps in the sixties, and is now decrepit to the point of collapse; there is a bar with occasional live music and a jerk centre.

Negril is known for its music—ask around, or consult the papers or the posters nailed to the telegraph poles, to find out who's playing. The main reggae parks are **Central Park** and **MX3**.

In **Montego Bay** things are a bit more upbeat—the major gathering joint is along Gloucester Avenue. **Walter's** is probably the liveliest place, a garden bar with television (you can keep up with the NFL at most bars in the area), popular with locals and tourists; you can sit inside or in the open air under parasols. **Hemingway's Pub**, just above it, is another busy watering hole; the air-conditioned lounge-bar has leather benches, stained wood and brass. **Marguerite's** is a much frequented bar right on the waterfront in town (*see* p.722). Nearby, **Tino's Reggae Café** is an easy outdoor haunt on the street, recognizable by the ever-present throb of heavy reggae bass-lines. **Pier One**, near the centre of the downtown area, is a very lively bar, particularly on Fridays, when it will often double as a dance venue.

Ocho Rios is similarly upbeat and so outside the hotels, where there are plenty of shows, you will find a string of bars and clubs. A couple of places popular with the Jamaicans are **Bibirips** (*see* p.723) and **The Mug**, which is west of the town near St Ann's Bay. It attracts a fun crowd, particularly on a Wednesday. In the centre of town you will find **Bill's Place** on Main Street, an easygoing upstairs bar with a loud crowd, or you can head for the trusty **Little Pub**, where you can often hear loud rock music and there are shows in the evening. Two other spots are popular with the locals after work: try the **Ocho Rios Jerk Centre** (*see* p.723) or a rasta spot called the **Jungle** near White River. You are advised to be careful in this area. The hotels offer plenty of entertainment, and many also have discotheques. Outside you will also find a string of bars and clubs.

If you want to try out a Jamaican club, head for the **Acropolis** (pronounced Acro-Palace) on Main Street, the **Limelight** at Burger King plaza, or best of all the **Roof Club** on St James's Avenue, an open-air lounge and roof top terrace where you will hear the latest sounds on the Jamaican scene, as well as some more traditional reggae. For something a little more sultry, a dose of Jamaican go-go dancing, you can try the **Wicky-Wacky Club**. There are occasional concerts at the **White River Reggae Park**.

Port Antonio is much more mellow, but there are some good bars—you can catch a drink at the **Rafter's Rest**, at the bottom of the Rio Grande. Two good restaurant bars in town are the **Admiralty Club** on Navy Island, where you can get a cocktail above the water and the **Huntress Marina**. If you want to go dancing, try **Lexus** on West St, **Blue Jay's Club**, which is a little sultry or, best of all, the **Roof Club** on West Street, a wild and hip spot which is well worth checking out.

getting there

The main airport for tourist arrivals in Jamaica is the Sangster Airport in **Montego Bay**, recently refitted, which serves the resort towns of Negril, Montego Bay, Runaway Bay and Ocho Rios. If you are travelling on to Port Antonio or to Kingston itself you should fly to the Norman Manley airport just outside Kingston. Long haul scheduled flights often make a stop at both airports. The national carrier is Air Jamaica UK. You need an onward or return ticket to get into the country and there is a departure tax of J$400.

By air from Europe: Direct flights to Jamaica from Europe include British Airways (℗ (0345) 222111) from London, three times a week, Air Jamaica UK (℗ (0181) 570 7999) and a weekly Martinair service from Amsterdam. There is also a weekly Aeroflot service from Moscow, via Shannon in Ireland to Kingston. If flight timings are not convenient, flying via Miami is a serious option. There are also plenty of **charter** flights from Holland, Switzerland, Italy and also from Britain, some of which offer flight-only tickets.

By air from the USA: There are direct scheduled flights to Montego Bay (and often to Kingston) on either Air Jamaica or American Airlines from Atlanta (daily), Baltimore (daily), Dallas (daily), Houston (daily), Los Angeles (daily), Miami (plenty each day), New York (several flights daily, also on Continental), Orlando (weekly), Philadelphia (daily), Raleigh Durham (weekly) and Tampa (daily, also on Northwest Airlines).

By air from Canada: There is a daily scheduled service on either Air Jamaica or Air Canada from Toronto to Kingston, sometimes stopping at Montego Bay, and a multitude of charter flights.

By air from other Caribbean islands: Air Jamaica has recently made Montego Bay its Caribbean hub, with connections to Antigua, Barbados, St Lucia, the Turks and Caicos and Nassau. There are flights most days from Grand Cayman on either Air Jamaica or Cayman Airways; two weekly flights to Nassau in the Bahamas and two to Havana in Cuba on Cubana (there are also charter flights from Montego Bay to Cuba). There are links with Santo Domingo (twice weekly, on Trans Jamaica Airways), Sint Maarten, Antigua and Barbados (all twice a week on BWIA), Port of Spain in Trinidad (almost daily on BWIA) and Curaçao (twice a week on ALM). Most connections from South America are made in Miami, from where there are plenty of flights each day, but there are direct links to Kingston from Peru, Panama and Colombia.

tourist information

UK: 1–2 Prince Consort Road, London SW7 4BZ (℗ (0171) 224 0505, ✆ 224 0551).

Germany: Falkstraße 72–74, 6000 Frankfurt 90 (℗ 069 70 74 065, ✆ 069 70 10 07).

France: 32 rue de Pont Thierry, 4th floor, 75008 Paris (℗ 1 45 61 90 58, ✆ 1 42 25 66 40).

Italy: c/o Sergat Italia, Piazza dei Cenci 7A, 00186 Rome (℗ 06 686 9112).

USA: 801 Second Avenue, 20th Floor, **New York**, NY 10017 (℗ (212) 688 7650, ✆ 856 9730). There are also offices in **Chicago:** 500 North Michigan Avenue, Suite 1030, Chicago Illinois 60611 (℗ (312) 527 1296, ✆ 527 1472); **Los Angeles:** 3440 Wilshire

Boulevard, Suite 1207, Los Angeles, CA 90010 (℗ (213) 384 1123, ● 384 1780); and **Miami**: 1320 South Dixie Highway, Suite 1100, Coral Gable, Florida 33146 (℗ (305) 665 0557, ● 666 7239).

Canada: 1 Eglington Avenue East, Suite 616 Toronto, Ontario M4P 3A1 (℗ (416) 482 7850, ● 482 1730).

In **Jamaica** itself there are offices in Kingston: the Tourism Centre in New Kingston, at 2 St Lucia Avenue, PO Box 360, Kingston 5 (℗ 929 9200, ● 929 9375), and at the airport (℗ 924 8024). In Montego Bay the office is in the north of the town, near Cornwall Beach, PO Box 67 (℗ 952 4425) and another in Sangster airport (℗ 952 2462). In Negril the office is in Adrija Plaza (℗ 957 4243) in Ocho Rios at the Ocean Village Shopping Centre close to Turtle Beach (℗ 974 2570) and in Port Antonio at the City Centre Plaza (℗ 993 3051) and on the High Street in Black River (℗ 965 2074). You will also find a number of small octagonal tourist information booths around the main towns, with helpful staff.

The principal Jamaican newspaper is the *Daily Gleaner*, released in the morning. The same company, a formidable Jamaican institution, puts out *The Star* in the afternoon, daily except Sundays. Other papers include *The Sunday Herald*, and *The Observer*, also published daily. The Jamaican tourist publications are quite good, with current events as well as advice on shopping opportunities.

In a medical **emergency**, you may find that there is a doctor on call to the larger hotels. If not, contact the University Hospital in **Kingston**, Mona Campus in the east (℗ 927 1620), the Cornwall Regional Hospital in **Montego Bay**, in Mt Salem behind the main town (℗ 952 5100); and in **Port Antonio** the General Hospital on Naylor's Hill (℗ 993 2646).

The **IDD code** for Jamaica is ℗ (1 876), followed by a seven-digit number. On-island, you should prefix a one if you are dialling long-distance; for local calls dial the seven digits.

The British High Commission is at 26 Trafalgar Road, Kingston 10, in New Kingston (℗ 926 9050). The American Embassy is in the Jamaica Mutual Life Centre building, 2 Oxford Road (℗ 929 4850) and the Canadian High Commission is at 30 Knutsford Boulevard (℗ 926 1500–7), both in New Kingston.

festivals

The annual Jamaican Independence celebrations take place on August 6 with parades and marching bands in the National Stadium in Kingston. It's all a bit staid but quite fun. At about this time, as well as at Christmas and at Easter, you will find many concerts staged, many by big name Jamaican musicians. The biggest music festivals of the year, though, are the Reggae Sumfest Festival now held in Kingston in August, and Reggae Sunsplash in February, gatherings for rastas and reggae fans from all over the world. In April there is a carnival week with celebrations all over the island, but particularly in Kingston. You might wish to visit the Maroon Festival held at Accompong in January. The National Dance Theatre Company stages performances twice a year that are well worth attending. The Jamaica Tourist Board publishes a twice-yearly list of forthcoming festivals and events giving exact dates.

money

The currency of Jamaica is the Jamaican dollar (J$), which fluctuates on the international exchange. At present it exchanges at a rate of about US$1 = J$35 or sterling about £1 = J$54. Tourist activities tend to be linked with the US dollar, which is also accepted as legal tender on the island. Hotel and hire bills can be paid with a credit card or traveller's cheques, as can shopping bills in the tourist areas and in the shops in Kingston. It is often better to use Jamaican dollars in restaurants and bars because you will usually be offered a very unfavourable rate of exchange. The going rate for tipping is 10–15%.

You will certainly need some Jamaican dollars for getting about on the buses and for a patty and a skyjuice at the roadside. There are foreign exchange desks in most hotels, at airports and in many banks. Occasionally you will be offered a black market rate on the streets. This is usually about 10% better than the bank rate and invariably quicker, but it is illegal and comes with attendant risks. Keep your exchange receipts if you want to change Jamaican dollars back into another currency on departure.

Banks are open Mon–Thurs 9–2 and Fri 9–4.

Shops: Hours are weekdays 8–4, and Sat 8–1, but if you are looking to score duty-free bargains you will find that hours in hotel boutiques and in-bond warehouses are extended.

maps and books

Two early travelogues of Jamaica are Lady Nugent's *Journal of Residence in Jamaica 1801–3* and Matthew 'Monk' Lewis's *Journal of a West Indian Proprietor*, written in 1834 and published after his death at sea on his return from the West Indies.

Andrew Salkey's *A Quality of Violence* looks into the life of a Jamaican village during a drought at the turn of the century. Roger Mais also wrote books about Jamaican country life. His best-known book is *The Hills are Joyful Together*. Also look out for V. S. Reid. John Hearne's excellent short book *Voices under the Window* gives a very colourful idea of the mercurial nature of the Jamaicans in the frenzy of the crowd.

There is some good contemporary literature coming out of Jamaica, including *Bake Face*, short stories by Opal Adisa Palmer, and collections by Olive Senior, *Summer Lightning* and *The Arrival of the Snake Woman*; also *Mint Tea* by Christine Craig. Anthony Winkler has written three excellent books which cut straight to the heart of 20th-century Jamaican life: *The Painted Canoe*, *The Lunatic* and most recently *The Great Yacht Race*. Jamaican poets include Lorna Goodison and Mervyn Morris. A good magazine of current Jamaican culture is the *Jamaica Journal*, which is available in big bookstores.

Herbert G. de Lisser has put some of Jamaica's traditional tales into novels in *Morgan's Daughter*, *The White Witch of Rose Hall* and *Psyche*. If you can track down a copy of *How to Speak Jamaican* by Ken Maxwell, read it. *Jamaica Labrish* will give you a chance to read some of Louise Bennett's hysterical machine-gun poetry at a gentler pace, and the *How to be Jamaican Handbook* takes a chuckling look at all aspects of Jamaican life and love, from the north coast hustler to the ICI (a higgler for the nineties).

watersports

Watersports are laid on by all the beach hotels in Jamaica, either in-house or through beach concessionaires. If watersports are important to you, you should check carefully before you select a particular hotel. Independent travellers can sometimes hire equipment at a hotel, but usually they will have to go to the watersports shops on the larger public beaches. The full range of watersports is on offer in Jamaica, from a ride in a stately pedalo or on a trusty wetbike to a high-speed ride on an inflated sausage or an evening cruise to catch the sunset.

Windsurfing: Available all over the island, but connoisseurs say the best beach for the sport is Burwood Beach, a public beach beyond Trelawny Beach just outside Falmouth. Small sailing boats are available through the general operators, as is **waterskiing**. In Montego Bay the best beach for watersports is Cornwall Beach, but some are also available at Doctor's Cave beach. General operators in Montego Bay include Seaworld (℗ 953 2180) and Resort Divers and Watersports (℗ 952 4285). Negril Beach is probably the best on the island for watersports, everything is available: try Blue Whale (℗ 957 3792) or Aqua Nova (℗ 957 4323). In Ocho Rios you can also get a jetski or a ride strung beneath a **parasailer** from UDC Beach at Garfield (℗ 975 4420) and Resort Divers (℗ 974 5338). In Port Antonio you can contact Lady G'Diver at Dragon Beach (℗ 993 8751).

Yachting: Day and half-day trips, usually taking in some snorkelling and a picnic stop, are available through the hotels in the major resort areas. In Mo Bay try *Calico,* which departs daily from Pier 1 (℗ 952 5860) and in Ocho Rios try *Red Stripe Cruising* (℗ 974 2446), or *Wild Oats* (℗ 975 4153). There are lots of silly, mock-piratical excursions also on offer, so if you are in the mood for an afternoon of rum-soaked fun and tee-ree-ree, you can fix these through any hotel. For a day, sunset or disco cruise out of Montego Bay, contact *Jamaica Queen IV* (℗ 953 3992) and in Ocho Rios try the Pirate Ship Cruise (℗ 974 2323) or *Heave Ho* (℗ 974 5367). In Port Antonio, you can arrange a day's sailing and snorkelling (℗ 993 9044). The Montego Bay Yacht Club holds the Miami to Mo Bay Yacht Race in February, and the Royal Jamaican Yacht Club on the Palisadoes peninsula outside Kingston holds a regatta in August. Keen sailors will find themselves taken on as crew during the friendly weekend regattas.

Deep-sea fishing: Possible in all the resorts, but reckoned to be at its best off Port Antonio in the east. There is an annual fishing tournament for all fish held there in March and there are marlin fishing tournaments held in Montego Bay and Discovery Bay in September and early October, before all the fishermen return to Port Antonio for the year's major event in mid-October (℗ 993 3209). Other fish inhabiting the waters off the Jamaican north shore are kingfish and sailfish with a fin like a sail, as well as wahoo and tuna. In Ocho Rios contact *Free Spirit* (℗ 974 5338); in Port Antonio *Semper Fi* (℗ 997 7926) and in Negril try *Striker* and *Neptune* (℗ 957 4401).

Scuba diving: Jamaica is surrounded by offshore reefs, furred with sponges and corals, where tropical fish play and barracuda stalk their lunch. The reefs are supposed not to be in the best condition because they have been stripped for their corals, but some are now protected and there are still enough around the north coast resorts to keep divers occupied. The major operators of the Jamaica Association of Diver Operators work under PADI specifications—you must show your certification—and most can provide instruction. Some smaller operators do not. Underwater photographic equipment is for hire at the bigger rental companies. A two-tank dive costs around US$55. Most companies offer free pick-up from your hotel. Glass-bottom boats are available on most beaches too for a trip to a nearby reef.

Dive operators around **Montego Bay** include Poseidon Divers on Gloucester Ave (✆ 952 3624, ✆ 952 3079) and Reef Keeper Divers (✆ 979 0102, ✆ 979 0101) at Walter Fletcher Beach. In **Negril** operators are Dolphin Divers (✆ 957 4944) with three locations and the Negril Scuba Centre at the Negril Beach Club (✆ 957 4425). **Ocho Rios** has many outfits including Resort Divers (✆ 974 5338) and Sea and Dive Jamaica (✆ 974 5762). In **Port Antonio** try Lady G'Diver (✆ 993 3281) and in **Kingston** contact Morgan's Harbour Hotel in Port Royal (✆ 924 8140).

River-rafting: Another classic tourist activity (but nonetheless good fun). It takes place on several rivers: the Martha Brae near Falmouth (✆ 952 0889) and the Great River at Lethe (✆ 912 0020) near Montego Bay, the White River (✆ 974 2527) just out of Ocho Rios and, best of all, the Rio Grande near Port Antonio, winding up at Rafter's Rest (✆ 993 5778), adm exp. Wear a bathing suit because when you have finished your rum punch you'll be expected to dive in. Some companies offer torch-lit night-time cruises.

other sports

Tennis: There are courts at most of the hotels and if not the sport can easily be arranged through a front desk.

Golf: There are many golf courses in Jamaica. The best around Montego Bay are Half Moon (✆ 953 2211/2560), at the hotel east of the town; luxuriant and well-kept, green fees expensive, and Tryall (✆ 956 5681), set out on the coast beneath the Tryall resort about 15 miles west. Also Ironshore (✆ 953 2800) and the Wyndham Rose Hall course (✆ 953 2650) to the east. The Negril Hills Golf Club (✆ 957 4638) is outside the town on the road towards Savannah-la-Mar. In Runaway Bay there is a course attached to the Super Clubs Breezes hotel (✆ 973 2561), and just the other side of Ocho Rios there is the Sandals Golf Club at Upton, (✆ 975 0181). There are two clubs near Kingston: the Caymanas Golf and Country Club (✆ 922 3386) and Constant Springs Golf Club (✆ 924 1610), and one in Mandeville, the oldest in the Caribbean supposedly, with 18 tees that play to nine greens (✆ 962 2403).

Riding: If you wish to go horse-riding, for anything from a beach canter at dawn to a day-long trek through the plantations in the Jamaican highlands, there are stables in all the main towns. Riding out costs roughly J$250 per hour. You are advised to call a couple of hours before arriving to book the horses. In Montego Bay, try the Half Moon Hotel Stables (✆ 953 2286), Oasis Riding Stable at Rose Hall (✆ 953 3013) and the Good Hope Estate in Falmouth (✆ 954 3289). **Polo** is quite big in Jamaica, and you can even hire polo ponies at Chukka Cove Farm (✆ 972 2506) near Ocho Rios, or get a refresher course if you haven't hit a nearside forehand for a while. There is good riding out from Chukka Cove. In Port Antonio rides into the mountain foothills are available through the Bonnie View Hotel

(© 993 2752). If a nag seems a bit much, you can take a **cycling** tour of the Blue Mountains from Ocho Rios instead. It sounds like quite hard work, but this is a specifically downhill tour (*see* p.684).

Walking: Walkers are not really that well served for a country as magnificent as Jamaica but there are some good new places opening up. The country offers a huge variety, in the scrubby bush of the Hellshire Hills, around the Cockpit Country southeast of Montego Bay and on the trails of the Blue Mountains in the east. The Blue Mountain Peak is usually climbed very early in the morning, so that you are at the 7402ft summit at dawn, with the best chance of seeing Haiti and the Sierra Maestra in Cuba. However there are many other trails in the Blue Mountains. In Port Antonio contact Valley Hikes (©/⊛ 993 2543, © 999 7529) who have guided hikes into the Rio Grande Valley. In the Blue Mountains you can contact SENSE Adventures at PO Box 216, Kingston 7 (© 702 0314) and the Forestry Dept, 173 Constant Spring Road (© 924 2667) for information and a few ideas. Also contact the guest houses and small hotels in the Blue Mountains themselves. If you do go, you should wear ankle-length boots and take a woolly jersey because it gets cold in the mountains. Also take a waterproof, because somehow it always seems to rain.

Spectator sports: These include **cricket**, which is something of a national preoccupation. You will see it played in the streets (join in), yards, country roads, on the beaches and in Kingston at Sabina Park (well worth going to a match if there is one on). The only time when the radios stop playing dancehall music is for the cricket commentary. Even the hustlers are magnanimous if the West Indies are winning. **Horse racing** is popular in Jamaica and you will find details of coming meetings in the local press. The main stadium, to the west of Kingston, is Caymanas Park.

Cayman Islands & Turks & Caicos

The Cayman Islands

The tiny Cayman Islands are well known internationally as an offshore banking centre, the official home to massive corporations, but they are equally celebrated among diving fiends as having some of the finest coral grounds in the Caribbean. Successfully managed, the two industries have combined to make the Cayman Islands the most prosperous islands in the Caribbean for their size.

The three Cayman Islands lie in the western Caribbean, northwest of Jamaica and south of Miami and Cuba. They are the coral-encrusted summits of a submarine mountain range (around them the slopes descend to the Bartlett Deep and the Cayman Trough, at 3500 fathoms the deepest water in the Caribbean). The islands are in two groups, separated by 89 miles of sea. In the south is Grand Cayman, where the capital George Town is situated. Its two partners are to the northeast: Cayman Brac and Little Cayman are just 5 miles apart.

No point on the Caymans rises to more than 140ft, and so they do not have the rainfall and the luxurious greenery of other Caribbean islands. They are covered mainly in a tangle of scrubby forest and mangrove swamps, with superb beaches along some of the coasts. There is not much wildlife on land, just the ubiquitous Caribbean goat and a few indigenous iguanas (though there are endemic parrots on Grand Cayman and Cayman Brac). Turtles still visit the islands, but the marine crocodile, from which the name *cayman* comes, is no longer seen. Venture beneath the waterline, though, and the marine life is amazing. The Cayman Islands have a stunning variety of corals, sponges and tropical fish in excellent, clean water.

There are about 24,000 Caymanians in a current population of 32,000 and they are some of the most approachable people in the Caribbean. Most live in the towns of Grand Cayman; Cayman Brac has a population of about 1300 and Little Cayman just 70. About half the islanders have a mix of African and European blood—you will recognize the familiar orange-red of the Caymanian hair. Caymanian English is easy to understand—if you hear a different *patois*, it is probably Jamaican. Unlike other Caribbean islands there is no hustling and very little crime in Cayman (as it is usually referred to). The islands are strongly influenced by the USA—home-delivery pizzas, gas-guzzling cars, satellite television, cheery American restaurants and the occasional desperate-looking person power-walking their way along the West Bay Road in the midday heat. In places Grand Cayman looks as though it is in danger of becoming an outsized shopping precinct.

The Cayman Islands package is very slick. The islands are hardly cheap, but what they offer they do well. It's ideal for high-pressure nineties executives who want comfort on call and a by-the-hour, percentage return on their leisure time (if you begin to feel out of touch you can always hire a cellular phone and call the broker). You can even take an extra-curricular course in the advantages of offshore banking in the Caymans. However, Seven-Mile beach in Grand Cayman is an ideal vacation destination and elsewhere on the islands you can still experience a slow and gentle pace of life ideal for a break from the humdrum.

History

As Columbus passed Cayman Brac on his fourth voyage in 1503, he saw 'two very small and low islands, full of tortoises, as was the sea all about' and it was the animals that gave their name to the islands. Columbus called them the *Tortugas* after the turtles, but a while later they became known as *los lagartos* (from alligators); eventually the name *Caymanas* stuck, taken from the crocodiles and iguanas seen there. The first reference to Grand Cayman was by Portuguese sailors, who called it Cayo Manos when they passed in 1526.

Initially, Little Cayman became a stopover for its reliable supply of fresh water and the easily available food, the iguanas and turtles (the latter will stay alive for weeks if laid on their backs). The islands were convenient hide-outs for pirates. It was not until the invasion of nearby Jamaica in 1655 that the islands were settled. Supposedly two soldiers by the name of Walter and Bowden came to Grand Cayman (their names are still evident in the Caymanian names Watler and Bodden). In 1670 the Spaniards gave up Jamaica and the Caymans to Britain at the Treaty of Madrid. This did not make the islanders any safer, though, as they were still harassed by the Spaniards and roving bands of pirates who still put in occasionally. The settlers farmed cotton and turtles (as many as forty turtling ships would set out from Kingston in the season) and they became wreckers—taking what they could find from the ships that foundered on Cayman's treacherous reefs. The wrecks are still happening, though salvage laws are stricter now.

In 1802 the population on Grand Cayman had climbed to 933, of whom just over half were slaves until Emancipation in 1834. Cayman Brac and Little Cayman were only settled permanently in 1833. By the turn of the century, there were 5000 Caymanians, and without employment on the islands the men went to sea to make a living. They were renowned for their seamanship and were in particular demand by National Bulk Carriers of New York.

For three centuries the Cayman Islands were administered as a part of Jamaica, but on 4 June 1960, as the Jamaicans prepared for Independence, the Caymanians seceded, preferring instead to become a Crown Colony directly dependent on the UK. Today the Cayman Islands are administered by the representative of Queen Elizabeth, Governor John Owen MBE, who presides over the eight-strong Executive Council. The Governor is in charge of defence, foreign affairs, police and internal security. Elections to the 18-member Legislative Assembly take place every four years and are next due in 2000.

Alongside tourism, the central pillar of the Cayman economy is offshore finance, and among the reams of tourist bumf (Cayman seems to produce more than anywhere else in all the Caribbean) you will find brochures on how to invest in the islands. They are basically tax free (though visitors will find themselves paying a 10 per cent government tax on their hotel room) and the handling of money is made as easy as possible (no direct taxation, laws of confidentiality, absence of exchange controls, teams of lawyers and accountants to handle it all, good communications). The islands are famous for it and they have attracted over 500 banks and 30,000 companies to register there. Hardly any even have an office; they are simply a plaque on the wall.

Getting Around

A **bus** service emanates from town, departing from behind the Court House on the main square and running until dusk. Green-striped minibuses run along the main Seven Mile Beach strip to West Bay in the north, where most of the Caymanians live, and yellow-striped buses serve the eastern end of the island. There are stops along the route, but hail them madly anyway. Except on the 7-mile strip, **hitchhiking** is quite a reliable way to get around. Elsewhere on the island, and on Cayman Brac, you will find that the Caymanians sometimes stop without even being flagged down.

There is an abundance of **taxis** in Grand Cayman: if there is not one to hand, just wander into the foyer of the nearest hotel. Fares are fixed by the government: **airport** to George Town—US$10, mid-way up Seven Mile Beach—US$14, West Bay (top of Seven Mile Beach)—US$22.50, Spanish Cove—US$27, Bodden Town—US$27, East End and North Side—US$50, Water Cay—US$60.

Taxi-drivers would be happy to take you on an island **tour**, with up to five people in the cab. Reckon on an hourly rate of US$30. Tours are also available by bus. Contact Evco Tours (✆ 949 2118), Majestic Tours (✆ 949 7773) or Tropicana Tours (✆ 949 0944). If you would like to take an airborne tour of the island, contact Cayman Helicopters (✆ 949 4400).

Cars are readily available for hire. Driving is on the left. Everything in the Caymans proceeds at a stately pace, the driving included, which is something of a relief after other Caribbean islands. There are so many cars on Grand Cayman that turning right can actually be a bit of a problem because it takes so long for a gap to appear in the traffic. You need a local driving licence (issued by the hire firm, price US$6) and a credit card or cheque deposit. Better rates for a week's hire. Rates start at US$30 for the smallest car, with charges on top. Contact Cico Avis (✆ 949 2468, ✇ 949 7127, ✆ (1 800) 228 0668), Andy's Rent a Car (✆ 949 8111, ✇ 949 8385), Coconut Car Rentals, with good rates (✆ 949 4037, ✇ 949 7786, ✆ (1 800) 262 6687) or Dollar (✆ 949 4790, ✇ 949 8484). You can get a jeep through Soto's 4X4 Jeep Rentals, (✆ 945 2424, ✇ 945 2425).

Scooters and motorbikes are widely available and are a very good way of getting around. Rates around US$25–30 per day, driving licence required. Contact Cayman Cycle Rentals (✆ 947 4021) or Soto's Scooters (✆ 947 4652). **Bicycles** are available through the same companies for about US$12–15 per day (the only hill on the Cayman Islands is at the east of Cayman Brac).

Diving

Scuba-diving in the Cayman Islands is some of the best in the Caribbean. Cayman is known particularly for its 'walls': the islands are surrounded by a few miles of sand and reefs and then suddenly the sea bed drops almost sheer to 20,000ft. Visibility is superb in the Caymans, often as far as 150ft.

There are caverns, pinnacles and underwater ravines, all of them encrusted with a vast array of corals, sponges and gorgonians: corals like tufts of shaggy white wool, thin tube sponges and vast barrel sponges, the jigsaw patterns of purple seafans standing against the tide, and deep down the fingers of the black corals. Single damselfish pout and shimmering schools of bar jacks and blue tangs dip and dart in unison in your exhaled bubbles. Camouflaged crabs eye you with suspicion from their hide, and little red and white banded coral shrimps tangle their spindly feet and antennae. Tiny, shy seahorses lunge to find the cover of the coral; starfish flip as they move. At Stingray City in the North Sound, you can cavort with tame rays five feet across; at Tarpon Alley you will see tarpon and grey reef sharks.

There are reefs on all sides of Grand Cayman, but most popular is the **North Wall** off the north shore. Cayman Brac is less well known than Grand Cayman, but if anything the diving is even better there. The main sites are around the **West End**. In Little Cayman, when the weather is good and the channel is not too rough, the diving is better still at **Jackson Bay** and **Bloody Bay** on the north shore. The wall here starts at 18ft below sea level. There are plenty of wrecks off the Caymans, the best known being the *Balboa* off George Town.

The Cayman Islands have strict laws for the protection of their reefs and fish, and there is zoning to encourage regeneration of fish and coral life. Spearfishing and setting traps are prohibited; there are strict rules about anchoring. You are not allowed to take any corals or sponges, dead or alive. However, many of the diving outfits have underwater photography equipment for E6 slide photographs and video, so you can keep them on film at least. If you happen across any buried treasure, then you'll have to work out an agreement with the Cayman government, because all wrecks and hoards officially belong to the Crown.

The first outing is often at 8am in Grand Cayman; there are so many operators that there is often a race for the good dive-sites. Dive shops usually offer a two-dive outing each morning, which costs from US$60 and a single-tank dive in the afternoon, at about US$45. Night dives cost around US$50. If you need equipment that is charged on top. Divers should have a 'C' card or take a resort course (about US$75), available with most dive shops. There is a decompression chamber on the island (✆ 949 4324).

There are about 40 dive outfits on the islands—some even specialize in older-guy instructors or blonde-waif instructresses for your maximum diving pleasure. Instruction is available in a number of different languages. Two large and established operators in **Grand Cayman** are Fisheye on Seven Mile Beach (✆ 945 4209, ✉ 945 4208, *www.fisheye.com*) and Bob Soto's Diving Ltd (✆ 949 2022, ✉ 949 8731, US toll free ✆ (1 800) BOB SOTO), which has recently won an award for marine conservation. Large operators have all the facilities, but they take out large groups of divers, sometimes on double-decker dive boats. However, these crowds are usually broken down into groups of eight or ten, each with a dive-leader. If you would prefer a more personalized trip on a smaller boat, you might want to go with one of the smaller operators, who also have the advantage of a certain flexibility—they may well be able to visit a particular dive-site for you. Try Divers Down (✆/✉ 945 1611), on the West Bay Road, Dive Tech/Turtle Reef Divers (✆ 949 1700, ✉ 949 1701), in the West Bay area, next to the turtle farm, and Dive 'n' Stuff (✆ 949 6033, ✉ 945 9207), on the outskirts of George Town. The Cayman Marine Lab (✆ 916 0849, ✉ 945 5586) is run by a trained marine biologist who gives a lecture each day in between the dives. Two friendly operators set in slightly out-of-the-way hotels are Sunset Divers (✆ 949 7111, ✉ 949 7101, US toll free ✆ (1 800) 854 4767), south of George Town, and the Cayman Diving Lodge at the East End (✆ 947 7555, ✉ 947 7560).

The scuba diving in **Cayman Brac** is even better than that in Grand Cayman—divers' groups have taken to leaving painted driftwood signs to record their trip and general satisfaction. There are three dive operators on the island, all in the southwest, in or near the hotels: Dive Tiara (✆ 948 1553), Brac Aquatics (✆ 948 1429), and Reef Divers, based at the Brac Reef Beach Resort (✆ 948 1323).

The diving on **Little Cayman** is the best in the Cayman Islands. There are a number of dive operators on the island, each attached to accommodation. Contact the Southern Cross Club (✆ 948 1099), the Little Cayman Beach Resort (✆ 948 1033), which has a photographic centre, or Paradise Villas (✆ 948 0001).

For those who do not dive, but who would like to see the colourful reefs, there is always the Atlantis Submarine (☏ 949 7700, US toll free ☏ (1 800) 887 8571). The submarine leaves from South Church Street, just down from the museum and trips are quite expensive, starting at about US$55, but the guides are informative and knowledgeable. On some trips, divers outside the sub talk to you through headsets and describe the marine life—find out how groupers cope with the boredom of middle age. You get a deeper tour in the three-man submersibles of Research Submersibles (☏ 949 8296, ✉ 949 8574). They dive the wall down to 800ft; you visit the odd wreck or hang between huge barrel sponges and turtles, with lamps to illuminate the corals as the sunlight fades. Price about US$300 per person.

Beaches

The Caymanians ask you not to wander around the town in your bathing costume; nudity and toplessness are illegal but, if you are determined, you may find somewhere right off the beaten track to strip off.

best beaches

Seven Mile Beach: The centre of the island's tourism, home to the majority of the hotels, watersports and diving operations, its gently shelving sands extend from just north of George Town up the west coast to West Bay. It is marginally less crowded at the northern end, though even here it almost entirely built up. Signs on the road indicate paths down to the beach between the hotels. Facing west, Seven Mile Beach has one of the finest views of the sunset anywhere, with a good chance of seeing the Green Flash.

Smiths Cove: A favourite with the Caymanians, a small cove a mile or so south of town.

Spott's: Not far east of George Town, a passable public beach, with mounded, steeply sloping sand, sunshades and hammocks.

East End (Heritage Beach or **Pirate's Beach):** Isolated suntraps hidden behind bushes of sea grape at the end of sandy tracks.

Rum Point: Set among casuarina pines that roar on the breeze looking out on to the North Sound, water that's clear and shallow for a hundred yards offshore, now quite smart and expensive, with a restaurant, a bar and a snack bar as well as a watersports shop. You can reach Rum Point on a ferry from the Hyatt Hotel.

Water Cay: A small beach, also with a bar, Kaibo—palms, simple fare, hammocks and picnic tables, and a view over the sand on to the lagoon.

Grand Cayman and George Town

The Cayman Islands' capital is on a broad bay in the southwest of Grand Cayman. The nucleus is almost entirely a modern town, with streets of smart glass-fronted offices and air-conditioned shopping malls, but there are a number of very pretty timber buildings from old-time Cayman dotted around. Nothing remains of the 'Hogstyes' that gave the town its original name, before it was called after King George III at the beginning of the 19th century. The remains of the town's original defence, Fort George, just a few waist-high walls, lie on the shore just north of the cruise ship terminal and main dock. Close by is the Emslie Memorial Church, built in the 1920s on the site of an earlier church.

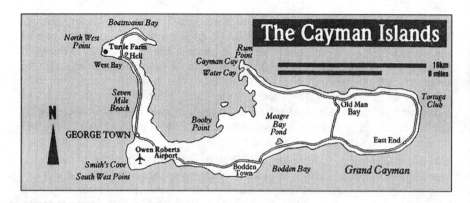

Inland you come to the main square, a small park with lawns and trees surrounded by a cluster of official buildings. A statue of James Manoah Bodden, Cayman's first national hero, stands in the park. Perhaps the prettiest building is the public library, which stands on the eastern side of the square; across from here is yet another shop.

Back on the waterfront, just down from the cruise ship dock, the **Cayman Islands National Museum** (*open Mon–Fri 9.30–5.30, Sat 10–4*) is set in the Old Courts Building, one of the island's finest traditional buildings. Built some time in the middle of the last century, with a solid lower storey and a wooden upper, it has served variously as post office, jail and library as well as the court house. The excellent museum has various displays showing the natural history and cultural heritage of the islands: geological exhibits include unique Cayman stones; there are displays of seafaring life; fragments of wattle and daub structures; tiny coins called quotties; also an audio-visual presentation.

Leaving the town centre you soon arrive in the suburbs, modern concrete houses enclosed within chain-link fences, with satellite dishes sitting in the garden. Scattered among them are a few older houses, invariably neat, with wraparound verandas where bench seats hang from the ceiling on chains, set in yards full of pretty blooms surrounded by white picket fences.

West Bay Road runs north straight out of the town, tracking behind the tourist development on **Seven Mile Beach**, to the old settlement of **West Bay**. Seven Mile Beach is not actually seven miles long (more like 5½). Either side of the road there are shopping malls, restaurants and bars dotted among the endless hotels and condominium complexes. Many of the Caymanians themselves live in West Bay—their ancestors moved to this area when they were emancipated in the 1830s. It is jokingly referred to as the 'Republic of West Bay'. **Hell** is a small moonscape surrounded by mangrove and the occasional frangipani. It looks like petrified cake-mix, a series of grey pinnacles whipped up by some diabolic chef. In fact it is limestone 'cliff-rock' that has been eroded unevenly (through former wave action), leaving a pitted and scarred stony mess. It is called Hell because the sharp points appear like the flames of hell turned to stone. You can send a postcard from the postbox, which will be stamped 'Hell'.

At the northwestern point you will come to the **Turtle Farm** (*open daily 8.30–5; adm*), a farm and research station that breeds the green sea turtles. You can see almost the whole life-cycle of the turtle in the farm. They start as eggs, white and very slightly larger than ping-pong balls; these hatch after about 60 days of incubation in a heated room. Hatchlings are transferred through the series of tanks as they increase in size, about a foot across at one year, 80lbs in weight by the time they are five years old. They can grow as large as 6–7ft long and reach 200–600lbs. A small percentage of the turtles are released into the wild each year, but most only make it into soup. They are butchered at four or five years old. Unfortunately it is not possible to see the most interesting part of the turtle's life cycle, the very beginning, when the female turtles crawl up on to the beach to lay their eggs; it usually happens at night and so all you see are their tractor-like tracks in the sand next morning. Females each lay an average of five times between May and October. The sex of turtle hatchlings depends on the temperature in the nest—a particularly hot spring will bring more females and a cold one more males.

Other rarer and endangered turtles, including loggerheads, hawksbills and ridleys, are also on view in the farm and there is a small menagerie of iguanas and alligators. In the café an excellent series of displays illustrates Cayman history and the use of turtleshell across the ages. It was used as far back as Roman times; from the Renaissance it was used in Europe as decorative inlay on furniture and in combs, fans and brushes. It was even thought to ward off disease and so made into linings for bathtubs.

In the eastern part of George Town is a small wildlife park, **Cardinal D's Park** (*adm*). There is a walkway past a lagoon and through some gardens where you will see indigenous Cayman birds and animals as well as some from overseas: emus, American wild turkeys, toucans, parrots, macaws and the Cayman blue iguana. Great for children—buy a bag of feed and the ducks, turtles and fish race over.

If you head out of George Town to the east you come to **Bodden Town**, the island's only other town, and the first capital. Out in the country you will see the cattle grazing and their constant companions, the cattle egrets. A road loops around the shoreline at the east end of the island and among the scrub you may see the rare Cayman iguana. Along the southern shore, look out for the blow-holes cut into the ironshore, which blow like a whale with each incoming wave.

In the heart of the Cayman scrub, off the road linking the north and south shores, you will find the **Elizabeth II Botanic Park** (*adm*). There is a visitors' centre, from which lead a number of walks. A mile-long trail cuts through the Cayman bush (Cactus County, Bull Thatch Bend and Epiphyte Woodland), where you will see iguana habitat, water holes with buttonwood trees, and plants (with informative labels) such as agave and 'duppy bush', so called because its leaves shimmer in the moonlight, and Cayman's various epiphytes and orchids.

© (1 345)–   *Where to Stay*

The majority of the hotels are along the 5 miles of Seven Mile Beach to the north of George Town; they range from simple but quite expensive guest houses to the height of luxury. Many offer diving packages. There is very little cheap accommodation in Cayman so you might prefer to stay in a self-catering or 'efficiency' apartment, in one of the many condominium complexes (these have some common facilities such as watersports and a pool, but no restaurant or bar). There are also plenty of villas for rent: contact **Cayman Villas**, PO Box 681 (© 947 4144, ◎ 949 7471, US toll free © (1 800) 235 5888), or you can book through your nearest Department of Tourism reservations office. All hotels add a government tax of 10% and usually a service charge of 10% and hotel room rates are usually listed in US$.

The **Hyatt Regency Hotel** on West Bay Road (PO Box 1588, ✆ 949 1234, ✆ 949 8528, US toll free ✆ (1 800) 223 1234) is the most luxurious place to stay on the island. It is large (236 rooms), modern and very neat, decorated in plush Caribbean pastel, with echoes of the colonial era in its mock-classical columns and tall Georgian-style windows. The atmosphere is quite up-beat, with a dip and sip bar, watersports across the road on the beach and low-calorie *cuisine naturelle* in one of the four restaurants. You can stay in similar extravagance but right on the sand at an excellent part of the beach, in the **Westin Casuarina Resort** (✆ 945 3800, ✆ 949 5825, US res ✆ (1 800) WESTIN 1). It has 343 rooms ranged on five floors, north and south wings dressed in mock-classical airs and graces (including a cloistered walkway to the restaurants), pointed in a shade of light blue that matches the Caymanian sea. There is an attractive pool, surrounded by profuse greenery, above the beach where all the watersports are on offer. Rooms, cool and carpeted, have all the requisites for luxury—TVs, air-conditioning and fans, coffee-makers and mini-bars; most have balconies. The nicest of the big, factory-style hotels right on the beach is the **Holiday Inn**, PO Box 904 (✆ 947 4444, ✆ 947 4213, US toll free ✆ (1 800) 421 9999). The four storeys of rooms stand above a central pool area with palms and palm-thatch parasols, from where it is a short hop to the sea and the watersports. Lively in the evenings.

very expensive–expensive

Unlike the pastel palaces, the **Beach Club Colony**, PO Box 903 (✆ 949 8100, ✆ 947 5167, US toll free ✆ (1 800) 482 DIVE) has a low-key, more West Indian atmosphere, with that classic Caribbean beach-club feel. The 41 rooms look down from balconies or give straight on to the sands of Seven Mile Beach; in the middle stands the central house, with the restaurant and bar set on an attractive, breezy brick-pillared terrace. Rooms are comfortable but not sybaritic, with telephone, air-conditioning and TV.

Condominium complexes vary much less in price than the hotels; the eminently comfortable **Lacovia Condominiums**, PO Box 1998 (✆ 949 7599, ✆ 949 0172) occupy an excellent spot on Seven Mile Beach. On offer are 45 apartments in a variety of configurations up to three-bedroomed suites. At **Villas of the Galleon**, PO Box 1797 (✆ 945 4433, ✆ 945 4705) there are 74 units, all pleasantly decorated in white and bright pastel, right on the beach; or you could try **Victoria House**, PO Box 636, (✆ 945 4233, ✆ 945 5328), smaller, just 25 rooms, but with a friendly atmosphere.

moderate

There is a number of small, relaxed dive resorts on the island. The **Sunset House Hotel**, PO Box 479 (✆ 949 7111, ✆ 949 7101, US toll free ✆ (1 800) 854 4767) is a short distance south of George Town and very popular in the early evening, as the name would suggest. Its blocks of rooms, the pool and restaurant and a palm-thatch bar fringe the ironshore coastline and the reefs begin close by. All 59 comfy rooms have telephones and air-conditioning, some fans.

If you are happy in the isolated southeast of the island you can try the **Cayman Diving Lodge**, PO Box 11 (✆ 947 7555, ✆ 947 7560), with just 17 rooms and a very easygoing atmosphere, just above the beach. Plenty of sports facilities are available at an all-inclusive rate.

Of the few reasonably priced places to stay, the best is **Erma Eldemire's Guest House**, PO Box 482 (℗ 949 5569, ℗ 949 6987), also south of town, where there are three apartments (with kitchens) and nine simple double rooms; there's a common kitchen for breakfast, a sitting area and a veranda. **Adam's Guest House** on Melmac Avenue, south of George Town, PO Box 312 (℗ 949 2512, ℗ 949 0919) is set in a private house. There are three rooms, an 'efficiency' studio and a two-bedroom apartment. In West Bay, close to Morgan's Harbour, is **Whitehaven Inn Guest House**, PO Box 30424 (℗ 949 1064, ℗ 947 4980), just five rooms, with dark-stained wooden furniture. Rooms have fans and air-conditioning, some share baths; bed and breakfast is included. It's a little isolated (a good walk from the beach and the bus route) so you may need some sort of transport. Inexpensive apartments (similar to a condominium) can be found at **Calypso Cove Apartments** (℗/℗ 949 3730).

℗ (1 345)–   ***Eating Out***

As Grand Cayman has developed over the last 20 years, so too has a wide range of restaurants—from successful local ventures serving West Indian food, and tiny local Caymanian restaurants in the back streets of George Town, to gourmet establishments with celebrity chefs from the USA, imported dial-a-pizza parlours and burger joints. There are also restaurants specializing in Italian, French, Mexican and Chinese food. Much of the hotel food is imported, but there is generally good local seafood: spiny lobster, conch or turtle (farmed on Grand Cayman). Make sure you reserve tables in winter, when there will be a waiting list of up to three days in the more popular restaurants. Restaurant bills are quite steep in the Caymans and most restaurants except the smaller local ones add a 15% service charge on top. Prices are usually quoted in Cayman dollars. The price categories used here are: *expensive*—CI$20 and above; *moderate*—CI$12–CI$20; *cheap*—CI$12 and below.

expensive

A number of restaurants vie for the top spot in Cayman at the moment: **The Grand Old House** (℗ 949 9333) is in a charming old gingerbread town house on the shoreline south of town. Tables are ranged on the two-tier screened veranda and on the waterfront itself, where they are are hung with fairy lights. Chef Tell Erhardt of US television fame is the inspiration here. The menu is international with some variations on traditional Caribbean themes—citrus-crusted Atlantic salmon on a bed of wilted spinach or sautéed fresh snapper with shallots, mushrooms and a Chardonnay *beurre blanc* are followed by heavyweight puddings. There is a long wine list of good quality. *Closed Sun.* **Ristorante Pappagallo** (℗ 949 1119) has a spectacular setting on a lagoon in West Bay north of Seven Mile Beach, though the pointed thatch roof is more reminiscent of the South Pacific than the Caribbean. As dusk falls, the mangroves around the lake are lit up—a good setting for a cocktail before you move to the veranda or the air-conditioned dining room to eat. The restaurant specializes in northern Italian cuisine, with good Caribbean seafood.

Hemingway's (℗ 949 1234), at the Hyatt Regency, is another spot for an elegant and intimate meal out, where you dine in a formal dining room or out on the terrace through the French windows. The menu is international; *cuisine naturelle* dishes include poached salmon with Sicilian beans. **Lantana's**, at the Caribbean Club on West Bay Road, a little to the south of Hemingway's, serves New American and Caribbean cuisine in a simple and brightly decorated a/c dining room. **Smuggler's Cove** (✆ 949 6003), set on the waterfront in town, has tables on a terrace under the sea grape trees. The **Wharf Restaurant** (✆ 949 2231), on the rocky waterfront, is large and ever popular, its tables scattered between the brightly lit terraces and the covered veranda. Enjoy the Caribbean and international fare, and the tarpon feeding at nine each evening (though the fish seem happy to swim for you at any time).

If you are driving out of town for the day and would like to linger over a gastronomic treat rather than a light bite, two places are highly recommended: **Rum Point** (contact through the Hyatt on ✆ 949 1234) is all dressed up with brightly painted fish on the walls, starfish chairbacks and outrageously bright tablecloths. At **The Lighthouse** (✆ 947 2047), you dine on a wooden terrace to the roar of the waves breaking on the reef. There is a long wine list to go with the Italian and seafood menu. Cheaper alternatives include the nearby **Reef Point**, a local lunch-stop and **The Edge** at Bodden Town.

moderate

Ottmar's, in the Grand Pavilion Hotel (✆ 947 5656), takes its name from its prize-winning chef. The indoor dining area is elegant and plush, with neat table-cloths and candles. The menu features French techniques adapted to Caribbean and American food. Chapultepec is an Aztec-influenced dish of the fish mahi-mahi, or you can plump for red snapper caprice, with banana chutney and fresh mango slices.

The **Whitehall Bay Restaurant** (✆ 949 8670) perches on a gingerbread deck on the waterfront, with abundant greenery and bright pink décor. It offers the best in simple island fare as well as a few salads—local pepperpot, coconut shrimp, and cracked conch, seasoned and deep-fried. The **Crows Nest** (✆ 949 9366), just inland from the coast south of George Town, enjoys an equally attractive setting and easygoing atmosphere. You dine on a screened veranda painted in a riot of pinks, oranges and blues, lush with greenery and lit by torches. It serves Caribbean fare and seafood: try the fiery coconut shrimps followed by jerk turkey salad or peppered dolphin with a strawberry sauce. At the **Almond Tree** (✆ 949 2893), you sit under the eponymous tree (and breadfruit and guinep trees) in a mock-rustic setting evocative of the South Seas, and dine on Caribbean and international fare.

cheap

If you're feeling homesick for a cheery American diner, there are plenty of places to go. **Eats** is a traditional American diner in the Cayman Falls Plaza, quite a good place for breakfast or for burgers and pizzas. And there is always the **Texas Lone Star**, serving Tex-Mex food, just outside the entrance to the Hyatt.

Other breakfast haunts where you can sit all day pondering the excesses (alcoholic and probably financial) of the night before include the **Hog Sty Café** in town, which has a brightly painted terrace on the waterfront: burgers, sandwiches and pub grub. For something a little more Caribbean, you can try **Coralita's**, in the centre of town. They offer some of the best basic island fare—fritters and callaloo followed by conch burger or chicken and chips liberally dashed with hot pepper sauce (beware).

Finally, if you feel like a late-night jerk, you can go to the **Breadfruit Tree Garden Café**, set in a pretty garden or **Champion House II**, both offering simple West Indian fare in the backstreets of George Town.

Bars and Nightlife

Cayman has recently begun to brew its own beer, Stingray, which is quite dark and bitter for a Caribbean brew, not really what you would expect and probably best avoided. However, lighter beers are available—all the American ones and Red Stripe from Jamaica and Carib from Trinidad. The big Caymanian cocktail at the moment is the Mudslide, made with vodka, Kahlua and Bailey's Irish Cream, if you think you can bear it. There are plenty of bars around the island, some of which have superb waterfront settings. Those on the cliffs to the south of the town tend to be popular with the locals for sundowners after work: try the **Sunset Bar** (at the Sunset House Hotel), with plenty of palm thatch on a walled terrace and an expat crowd; just out of town, sit under parasols on the waterfront terrace of **Paradise Cove**—it can be quite lively at sunset, when there is a happy hour, which attracts a nice mix of locals and tourists. It also has a sandy platform just off the road for a bit of daytime lounging in the sun. Or you could investigate the **Blue Parrot**, south of the Sunset Bar. **Durty Reid's** is an all-American bar in the eastern outskirts of town, with big-screen TV and walls covered with pictures of the US Marines. In Bodden Town you will find **The Edge**, a slightly dark and dingy bar-discotheque with a pool table and juke-box and a terrace over the waterfront. On the north coast on the road to Rum Point is **Apollo 11**, a bar set in a large shed; look out for the huge bar stools, cut from whole tree trunks.

Many of the simpler restaurants in town double as bars and so you can linger as you eat or hop from one to the next as you decide whether to eat. Close to the Hyatt is the **Texas Lone Star**, which can get pretty rowdy in the evening. It is set in a wooden cabin, its walls covered in T-shirts (left by satisfied customers no doubt). Televisions hang from the roof, visible from all angles and playing continuously, so you can catch up on the NFL.

Legendz, in the Cayman Falls Mall, is a themed bar which honours such 20th-century heroes as James Dean, Marilyn Monroe, Elvis and Jimi Hendrix—their portraits appear on the walls fighting the fluorescent décor and slender metal furniture for your attention.

You'll have a good night out at the **Holiday Inn**, where there is a comedy club, Coconuts, with artists brought in from abroad. Afterwards you can head outside to the bar on the beach, where you can drink and dance to the resident singer, Barefoot Man, and his band (actually quite fun, and particularly recommended because for once there is no cover charge). There is jazz on Wednesdays at **Casablanca**, a bar-restaurant chequered in black and white, with fifties film stars all over the walls, where you drink Guinness and Victoria bitter, and food is served till midnight; popular with expats. **The Links** at Safehaven also has a jazz happy hour on Fridays.

There are three main nightclubs: **The Planet 'Niteclub and Sports Bar'** is a big and busy air-conditioned club, where a good mix of young Caymanians, expats and tourists gather. Fluorescent strips and flags surround the central bar, with a dancefloor for the discotheque and band music on one side, and a pool hall on the other; TVs faithfully play the sport above. The music changes nightly, from Caribbean sounds (Wed) to BPM (beats per minute) and high-energy dance music; there's a cover charge. **Sharkey's** is a large video dancefloor with disco lights and a bar topped by a huge, fairy-lit model shark. Big nights are: Monday (disco); Friday (80s); Saturday (90s). You can avoid the weekend cover charge by drinking early at the **Liquid Lounge** next door; admire the fishy pictures up on screen.

There is something of a circuit when it comes to the bars and clubs in Cayman. This changes from time to time, but at the time of writing the early evening bars were **Deckers**, the **Lone Star** and **Legendz**. Then you moved on to: **Sharkeys** (Mon); **Rumheads** (Tues); jazz at **Casablanca** (Wed); **The Planet** (Thurs); and **Shakeys** again (Fri and Sat). On Sundays Grand Cayman is dead.

Cayman Brac

Ask a 'Bracker' and you'll be told that success has gone to their heads in Grand Cayman. Cayman Brac, they say, still has the easygoing tranquillity that Grand Cayman had 20 years ago, before there were any hotels along Seven Mile Beach. It is true that Cayman Brac is far quieter and calmer: there are just a couple of hotels and a few villas and none of the buzz or the endless traffic of Cayman.

Cayman Brac is 12 miles long and about a mile wide. It takes its name from its cliff (Brac means cliff in Gaelic), a central core of limestone that extends along the middle of the island. The island rises gradually from the west, achieving a vertiginous 140ft in the northeast, the highest point in the Cayman Islands. There are a number of caves in the limestone, none that exciting. The island is scrub- and cactus-covered, but can be surprisingly lush in the wet season.

Getting Around

Hire cars are available through Brac Hertz (℡ 948 1515) Avis (℡ 948 2847), and at Four D's Car Rental (℡ 948 1599). **Scooters** and **bicycles** can be hired through B&S Motor Venture (℡ 948 1646), close to the hotels in the southwest of the island. The bus stop signs are for school buses and not for adults. If you stick out your thumb, the few cars that pass will probably pick you up.

Beaches

There are no great **beaches** in Cayman Brac. Most of the shoreline is rocky and the only place where there is any sand at all is in the southwest where the hotels are. There is a small public beach, however, just east of the hotels, with mounded sand and swimming protected by the offshore reef. For the limited **watersports**, you are dependent on the hotels.

Around the Island

A road runs along the coastline, on the stretches of low-lying land either side of the raised central 'brac'. The main settlements are at the eastern end, around the airport, and at Stake Bay, where you will find the island administrative buildings and the small **Cayman Brac Museum** (*open daily 9–12 and 2–4, Sun pm only*). This has two rooms of artefacts gathered from around the island, from domestic items such as garden tools and 'yobbas' (water storage

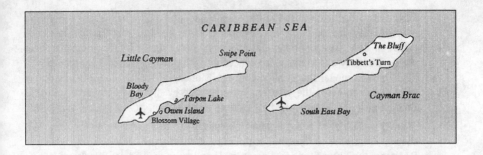

CARIBBEAN SEA

Little Cayman   Snipe Point   The Bluff   Tibbett's Turn

Bloody Bay   Tarpon Lake   Cayman Brac

Owen Island   South East Bay

Blossom Village

bowls) to ancient-looking communications paraphernalia and an early ice-making machine driven by kerosene. Other exhibits tell the romantic story of Brac's connection with the sea.

On the brac itself (reached on the central island road) you can take a walk in the **Cayman Brac Parrot Reserve**, on a path cut into the central bush with annotated trees and plants: mango, hemlock and liquorice, and the 'dildo' cactus, covered in spikes. If you are lucky you might disturb a pair of Brac parrots, which will fly away twittering and screeching. Following the track beyond here to the eastern end of the island, past thatch palms and agave (originally used for making rope) and a few small plots of farmed land, you come to the top of the brac. There are lighthouses (old and new) and, curiously, two Portaloos, at the time of writing anyway.

The island's carnival, **Bracchanal**, is held at Mardi Gras (Shrove Tuesday) each year and involves street parades and dancing.

✆ (1 345–)   **Where to Stay**

There are two main hotels on the island, on the southwestern shore, both specialists in diving (packages available), and each with a busy beach-resort atmosphere. The **Divi Tiara Beach Hotel** (✆ 948 1553, ✉ 948 1316, US toll free ✆ (1 800) 367 3484; *expensive–moderate*) has 59 rooms in blocks ranged behind the seafront. There is an attractive bar area on a deck under the trees just above the excellent powder-soft sand where hammocks hang among the palms. Facilities include tennis courts, a pool, jacuzzis, watersports and snorkelling. Not far off is the slightly smaller (40 rooms) and quieter **Brac Reef Beach Resort**, PO Box 56 (✆ 948 7323, US ✉ (813) 323 8827, US toll free ✆ (1 800) 327 3835; *moderate*). Modern, comfortable rooms, with fans, TVs and air-conditioning, are set in blocks that overlook a sandy garden with a tangle of sea grape trees. There is a reasonable beach and some sports—including diving, of course. Other options for accommodation include the condominiums at the **Brac Caribbean Beach Village** (✆ 948 2265, ✉ 948 2206, US toll free ✆ (1 800) 791 7911; *expensive*), and several houses to rent at **La Esperanza**, PO Box 28 (✆ 948 0531, ✉ 948 0525; *moderate*), in Stake Bay on the north shore.

Eating Out

In the southwestern corner of the island, near the hotels, you can find delicious international fare, moderately priced, in the congenial surroundings of a neat and pretty dining room at the **Coral Isle Club**.

Outside the hotels and condominiums there are a couple of easygoing restaurants with a genuine West Indian feel about them, serving home-cooked Caribbean food. Near the turning to West End, **Aunt Sha's Kitchen** is a local eatery; the dining room is on a terrace dressed in pink, and the constant roar of breakers provides the soundtrack to your meal. Fried kingfish and curried chicken are served with coleslaw or rice 'n' peas. On the north coast you will get an equally good West Indian meal at **La Esperanza**: fish, chicken or shrimp followed by a key lime pie. In West Bay you can try **Edd's Place**, for local and international fare, or the **G&M Diner**. For a daytime sandwich or salad, check out **Angie's Ice-Cream and Subs**, close by. There's even a drive-through take-out of all things in Cayman Brac, **Blackie's Seaview** at Tibbett's Turn on the north coast, but it is not often open.

Little Cayman

Five miles west of Cayman Brac is Little Cayman, dozier, more isolated and less developed even than the Brac. It is just 10 miles long, about a mile wide and makes it to a massive 40ft in elevation. The scrub- and mangrove-covered land is relieved by salt-ponds and inland lagoons. At its height, when the island was frequented as a source of fresh water, the population reached 400, but nowadays it is inhabited by just 70 or so, most of whom are involved with the tourism business. The place is barely developed—electricity reached the island only in 1990; there is only one policeman, one petrol pump and one bank, open only for a few hours a week. The population of birds is far greater than that of humans and around the ponds on the south coast you will find boobies, ducks and stilts, and flights of magnificent piratical frigatebirds, which puff out their huge red gullets when courting. There are around 2000 iguanas on the island, but unfortunately they have a potentially fatal habit of sunning themselves on the road.

The **beaches** around the hotels in the southwest are passable, though there is quite a lot of turtle grass just offshore. There is good sand on Owen Island and a reasonable beach at Point of Sands at the east end of the island looking out to Cayman Brac.

Getting Around

Hire cars are available through McLaughlin Jeeps (✆ 948 1000), and Paradise Villas, ✆ 948 0001, both of which are within walking distance of the airstrip. All of the hotels seem to have **bicycles** available, and these are quite adequate if you are going to stick to the southwestern corner of the island, where all the hotels are.

Around the Island

The only area in Little Cayman that can be described as a settlement is in the southwest, the cluster of houses that make up the 'Village', as it is usually known. Officially it is called **South Town**, but this does not imply another town on the island as there is none. Elsewhere, there is just the occasional house or hotel dotted along the shoreline, mainly on the south coast of the island. The grass airstrip is close to the town. It is quite entertaining watching the flights come in and go out. The plane has to cross the main (only) road to get to the terminal building and it is kick-started out of a wheelbarrow.

A road (tarmacked in places, but mostly dirt trail) rings the island just in from the coast. As you head east from the Village you pass between the hotels on the shoreline and the Booby Pond inland, a lagoon fringed with mangrove where boobies and frigatebirds roost and nest. At the western end there is a house with a veranda from which you can view the birds through a telescope. Farther up on the south coast you come to Tarpon Lake, where a boardwalk leads out into the lagoon. On the north coast is Bloody Bay: some say it was so called because of the blood on the beach after a conflict between the British and Spaniards but the beach may also have gained its name from whalers who came here to butcher their catch.

Where to Stay

© (1 345–)

The most stylish place to stay on Little Cayman is the **Southern Cross Club** (© 948 1099, ☏ 948 1098, US toll free © (1 800) 899 2582; *very expensive*), which stands on a sandy stretch of shoreline on the other side of town, nearly opposite Owen Island. There are just 10 spacious rooms, furnished in breezy and bright Caribbean fabrics and louvred for fan-ventilation (there is also air-conditioning), set in double bungalows scattered loosely around the garden. There is a central clubhouse with a freshwater pool and sunning deck. The plan includes all meals.

Pirate's Point, (© 948 1010, ☏ 948 1011, US toll free © (1 800) 327 8777; *expensive*) occupies its own small stretch of beach to the west of the Village. Ten rooms are set in cottages (only four of them air-conditioned) in a garden overgrown with sea grape trees, palms and casuarina pines. You will be well looked after in the dining room. Meals are part of the all-inclusive package; some diving and fishing packages are available. If you'd like a busier, resort-style hotel, then try the **Little Cayman Beach Resort** (© 948 1033, US ☏ (812) 323 8827, US toll free © (1 800) 327 3835; *expensive*), situated on a private stretch of beach just down from the Village. The 32 rooms stand in two-storey blocks either side of the central garden and sitting area. There's a pool and an open-air bar, with steps down on to the passable beach. Rooms are large and comfortable, with air-conditioning, fans and TVs—all the modern comforts. There are the usual sports including diving and fishing, kayaks and sea cycles and a tennis court. There are also eight suites attached to the hotel. **Paradise Villas**, PO Box 30 (© 948 0001, ☏ 948 0002; *expensive–moderate*), on the seafront just close to the airstrip in the Village, are 12 villas built in pink and white wood, with balconies overlooking the sea. The smallish rooms are furnished in pastel tones and have fans and air-conditioning. There's a freshwater pool and watersports. If you would prefer to stay in an apartment, contact the **Conch Club Town Houses** (© as the Little Cayman Beach Resort), or **Blossom Villas** (© 948 1000, ☏ 948 1001; *both expensive*).

Eating Out

Each of the hotels has its own dining room and most of them offer a meals-inclusive package. You can also get them to make you a picnic if you are going to take off for the day. The **Hungry Iguana** at Paradise Villas is a gathering place for Little Cayman residents. The main room is part American diner and part bar, with bench seats on one side and a long high bar on the other, serving Caribbean and American lunches and dinners, burgers and salads, fresh catch lightly grilled or blackened, some pizzas, and occasional barbecues under the trees above the beach. There is another dining room at the restaurant, where you can eat gourmet meals flambéed at your table.

getting there

By air: Most flights go into Grand Cayman (from where local connecting flights can usually be taken on the same day to Cayman Brac or Little Cayman). The national carrier is Cayman Airways, Grand Cayman (✆ 949 2311), in Cayman Brac (✆ 948 3235), also USA and Canada toll free (✆ (1 800) 422 9626), UK res ✆ (0171) 491 7771). There is a departure tax of CI$10 (US$12.50).

By air from Europe: British Airways (✆ as Cayman airways) have a twice-weekly service direct from London Gatwick. Otherwise you can connect in Miami.

By air from the USA: The main centre for flights to the Cayman Islands is Miami, from where five or six flights originate each day (Cayman Airways, American Airlines, United Airlines and Northwest). Other direct links, some of them stopping at Miami, include Atlanta, Baltimore, Charlotte, Chicago, Houston, Memphis, Orlando, Seattle and Tampa.

By air from other Caribbean islands: There are five flights a week to Kingston, Jamaica, on Air Jamaica or on Cayman Airways, sometimes stopping in Montego Bay.

Getting between the islands: Island Air (✆ 949 0241) flies twice daily between Grand Cayman and Cayman Brac (✆ 948 1656), touching Little Cayman (✆ 948 0021) en route. Cayman Airways also have a flight to Cayman Brac most days.

tourist information

UK: the Cayman Islands Department of Tourism, 6 Arlington St, London SW1A 1RE (✆ (0171) 491 7771, ✆ 409 7773).

Germany: Marketing Services International, Johanna-Melberweg 12, D-60599, Frankfurt am Main (✆ (069) 60 320 94, ✆ 62 92 64).

Italy: G & A Martinengo, Via Fratelli, Ruffini 9, 20123 Milano (✆ (02) 4801 2068).

USA: There are many offices. In **New York**, write to 420 Lexington Avenue, Suite 2733, New York, NY 10170 (✆ (212) 682 5582, ✆ 986 5123); in **Los Angeles**, 3440 Wilshire Boulevard, Suite 1202, Los Angeles, CA 90010 (✆ (213) 738 1968, ✆ 738 1829); **Chicago**, 9525 W. Bryn Mawr, Suite 160, Rosemont, Ill 60018 (✆ (847) 678 6446, ✆ 678 6675); and **Miami**, 6100 Blue Lagoon Drive, Suite 150, Miami FLA 33126 (✆ (305) 266 2300, ✆ 267 2932).

Canada: Contact Earl B. Smith Travel Marketing Consultants, 234 Eglington Avenue East, Suite 306, Toronto, Ontario, Canada M4P 1K5 (✆ (416) 485 1550, ✆ 485 7578).

Japan: International Travel Produce Inc. Kawase Building 4th Floor, 14-1,2 Chome Tsukui, Chuo-ku, Tokyo 104 (✆ 03 3546 1754, ✆ 03 3545 8756).

On island, you can write to the Cayman Islands Department of Tourism at PO Box 67, The Pavilion, Cricket Square, George Town, Grand Cayman, British West Indies (✆ 949 0623, ✆ 949 4053). There is an information desk at the airport and at the cruise ship terminal when a ship is in town.There is no actual website devoted to tourism, but some tourist information can be found on *www.caymans.com*

Tourist magazines include *Key to Cayman* yearly, *Destination Cayman*, *What's Hot in Cayman* (a monthly) and the Cayman Airways in-flight mag, *Horizons*. The local newspaper is the *Caymanian Compass*, published on weekdays with a weekend section on Fris.

In a medical **emergency** the Caymanians are able to care for you well at the hospital on Hospital Road in George Town (☏ 949 8600), but first try the front desk at your hotel as there may well be a doctor on call. The emergency telephone number for the ambulance is 555 and for the police 911.

The **IDD code** for the Caymans is ☏ (1 345) followed by a seven-digit number. On-island, dial all seven figures.

festivals

The big event in the Caymanian calendar is **Pirates Week** (☏ 949 5078) in October, a swashbuckling affair of fake eye-patches and tee-ree-ree. Choreographed invasions amuse the tourists, but the evenings are enjoyed by tourists and locals alike in the bar.

There is also a carnival, **Batabano,** held over a weekend in March or April each year, in which the islanders and visitors dress in theme costume and shuffle-step through the streets of George Town. **Million Dollar Month** (June) is a month-long fishing competition, in which you might just hook the US$25,000 prize money for catching the largest blue marlin of the competition, ☏ 949 5587. There are a couple of other **fishing tournaments** over the year. **Aviation Week** in June sees any number of aircraft arriving from Miami. There is also a **windsurfing competition** (January) and a couple of **regattas** (one in Oct).

money

The currency of the Cayman Islands is the Cayman Islands dollar, which is fixed to the USA dollar at a rate of CI$1 = US$1.25. It comes as a bit of a surprise to find that the greenback is worth just 80 Cayman cents, but business is booming in the Caymans. US dollars are also valid and are accepted everywhere anyway, so you might not even see the local money. Prices are often quoted in both currencies. If prices are quoted in Cayman dollars, multiply by one and a quarter to get the equivalent US dollar price. All major credit cards are accepted around the islands, in the hotels, restaurants and shops, as are traveller's cheques. Tipping runs at 10–15%, usually added to your bill by the restaurants and hotels.

Banks: Open Mon–Thurs 9–2.30 and Fri 9–1 and 2.30–4.30. A couple of banks in town open on Saturday mornings.

Shops: Open 9–5 and usually closed on Sundays. There is plenty of duty-free shopping.

watersports

You can to fix up anything from nitrox night-diving to a ride on a bouncy banana, from a pedalo to a jet-ski. The best area is Seven Mile Beach in Cayman. For diving, *see* p.736.

Snorkelling: Excellent in all three islands. In Grand Cayman, there are reefs off the south coast and in the northeast, though you should be careful of the currents here. Some of the best snorkelling is at Cemetery Beach at the northern end of Seven Mile Beach, Eden Rock and Devil's Grotto south of George Town and at Soto's Reef. On Cayman Brac, there is excellent snorkelling opposite the old Buccaneer Inn, close to the airport, and west of there towards Stake Bay. On Little Cayman, snorkel off the north shore in Jackson's Bay, directly opposite the road that crosses the island.

Windsurfing (and small sailing boats): Can be hired at many of the hotels and watersports shops along Seven Mile Beach. The best winds, though, are out at the East End, where you will find Cayman Windsurf at Morritt's Tortuga Club (© 947 7492). General operators include Sailboards Caribbean (© 949 1068), which has a MISTRAL concessionary and Don Foster's Watersports (© 945 5132).

Day sails: Very popular, can also be arranged through the watersports shops and the many small boat operators. Typically they include snorkelling and lunch or a sunset cruise, and some of them make a visit to Stingray City (*see* below). Catamarans include *Cockatoo* (© 949 7884), based at Parrots Landing and Fantasea Tours' *Don't Even Ask* (© 949 2182). You can get an afternoon of rum-soaked fun and tee-ree-ree on the mock-pirate boat *Jolly Roger* (© 949 5577). The (nearly) tall ship *Nancy* (© 949 8988), a wooden schooner (top sail gaff-rigged), offers slightly less raucous daytime and sunset trips. Most companies offer transport from your hotel.

A trip to **Stingray City** is the ultimate in tourist junkets, but entertaining nonetheless. In fact there are two stingray cities: both are sandy sections of sea bed in the North Sound— one lies in 15 feet of water and the other rises to within 3 feet of the surface. The stingrays were first attracted here when fishermen came to clean their catch and threw the fish innards into the water. Now they know they will be offered food and so they are friendly to humans. Stand in the water and you will see the grey shadows cruise by on the bottom of the sea, first circling and then touching you; some pass between your legs, or flare their wings against you as they sniff for food. The guides lift them out of the water to show you their mouths, or to wear one as a hat. Trips can be arranged with any of the general watersports operators, or through one of the local (and cheaper) companies in Coconut Plaza. For some reason they are all called Ebanks, but you can choose from: Captain Marvin (© 947 4590), Frank's (© 947 5491) or C+G (© 947 4049), from US$25 per person.

Deep-sea fishing: Casting for tuna and wahoo or 6ft marlin is another popular day out on the high seas, and the Caymans have a host of sleek vessels. Rates are US$600–1000 for a full day for six people, US$350–400 for a half-day. Try Bayside Watersports © 949 3200 and Black Princess Charters, © 949 3821. Also try Cayman Sunset, © 949 3666, in Morgan's Harbour. The fishing off Little Cayman is excellent, as is the bone-fishing in the shallow flats; contact the hotels.

land sports

Tennis: There are plenty of courts around the island.

Golf: There are a couple of courses on Grand Cayman. With such low-lying, sandy land, you might expect a links course, and this can be played at Safehaven on the West Bay Road; 18 holes and par 71, © 949 5988. The course at the Hyatt Regency Hotel (© 949 8020), can be played as a 9-hole full-length course or an 18-hole course with par-3 holes (using the same fairways and greens; played on alternate days of the week). You can also play a third course, designed for the short-hitting Cayman ball. Book well in advance. There is even mini-golf—on West Bay Road, by the Hyatt Hotel.

Hiking: The Cayman Islands National Trust arranges a number of **walking** tours around the island: George Town, West Bay and Bodden Town. They also have a guided tour of the bush in the middle of the island, the Mastic Trail (© 949 0121). If you would like to take a **horseback ride** along the beach, contact Nicki's Beach Rides (© 947 5839), mobile (© 916 3530; *expensive*).

The Turks and Caicos Islands

The Turks and Caicos Islands stick out like a spur at the southeastern tip of the Bahamian archipelago. Almost unknown for centuries, over the last few years they have become very popular with divers for their pristine corals and extensive fish life. There is also a steadily increasing trade in traditional Caribbean tourism. Like the Bahamas, the islands are set in shallows, but here the skies are so clear and the sea is so intensely turquoise that it all appears almost surreal.

The TCI are eight main islands and a host of tiny cays situated about 575 miles southeast of Miami and 100 north of Haiti, with a total land area of about 166 square miles. They stand in two separate groups, both scrub-covered limestone outcrops that rise no more than 250ft and in many places are close enough to sea level to be mangrove swamp and salt ponds.

On the Caicos Bank in the west are the Caicos Islands, of which the best known and most developed is Providenciales. The name Caicos is supposed to derive from the Spanish for 'cays' (*cayos*). Twenty-two miles farther east, across the 7000ft depth of the Columbus Passage, are the Turks Islands—Grand Turk and Salt Cay—the cap of an outcrop that broke away from the main Bahamian archipelago millions of years ago. The 'Turks' in the name is supposed to come from the red dome of the Turk's head cactus, which looks a bit like a fez. Not far east of Grand Turk, the sea floor drops sheer into the the Atlantic Ocean.

The two groups of islands are historically distinct. The Caicos islands were settled by Loyalists at the time of the American Revolution, who came to cut cotton plantations, while the Turks Islands, where more visible old-time architecture remains, were settled by Bermudian salt rakers. The bulk of the country's population of 14,000 are of African descent, the descendants of slaves brought by the salt rakers and planters. The population on Providenciales has been supplemented by expatriates from Britain, North America, Europe and Hispaniola. The native islanders are quiet, private and reserved, but friendly when you get to know them. Although the official language is English (with a Caribbean lilt), you will hear other accents and languages spoken, including strains of French-sounding Creole from the large Haitian population.

The Turks and Caicos Islands are one of five remaining British Crown Colonies in the Caribbean. You still occasionally see the British imperial regalia paraded in the guise of the Royal Turks & Caicos Islands Police Force. But as the islands develop (particularly Providenciales), the influence of the USA rings ever louder. The cars are left-hand drive (although driving is still on the left side of the road), American cable television is standard fare, and almost everything is imported from Miami. The islands' economy rests on two principal industries: tourism and offshore finance. Annual tourist arrivals just broke the 100,000 mark in 1996, while the TCI's status as an international tax haven is steadily growing, supported by the Financial Services Commission and a sterling cadre of financial professionals.

Until recently, the Turks and Caicos Islands were never really that well known. For a hundred years, an igloo appeared on the national flag because a colonial flagmaker, who presumed that they were near the Arctic, reputedly mistook their symbol, a pile of salt, for an igloo and kindly added a door. But their isolation is an attraction for some and those who do visit, to enjoy the islands' magnificent beaches and superb diving, often return. For the moment, most of the Turks and Caicos Islands still retain the tranquil feel of the British West Indies as they were forty years ago. But there are signs everywhere, especially on Providenciales, proclaiming future development, so this may not be the case for long.

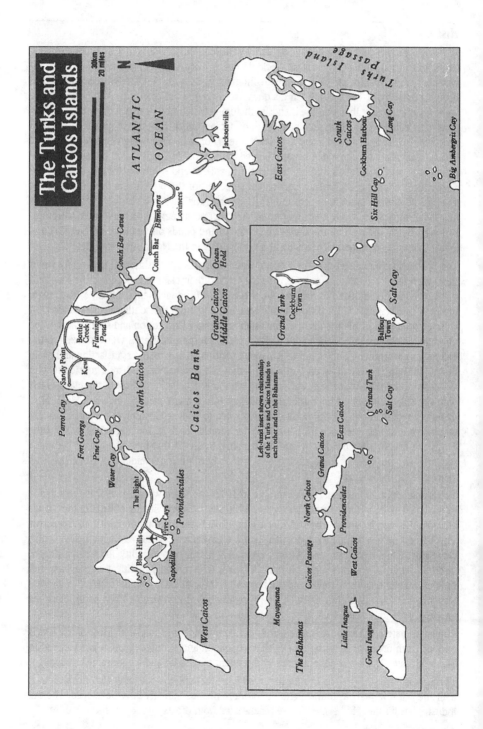

The Turks and Caicos Islands

30km
20 miles

N

ATLANTIC

OCEAN

Turks Island Passage

Conch Bar Caves

Bottle Creek
Flamingo Pond

Sandy Point

Kew

Parrot Cay

Fort George

Pine Cay

Water Cay

The Bight

Blue Hills

Five Cays

Sapodilla

Providenciales

West Caicos

North Caicos

Caicos Bank

Conch Bar

Bambarra

Lorimers

Ocean Hold

Grand Caicos
Middle Caicos

Jacksonville

East Caicos

South Caicos

Cockburn Harbour

Six Hill Cay

Long Cay

Big Ambergris Cay

Left-hand inset shows relationship of the Turks and Caicos Islands to each other and to the Bahamas.

The Bahamas

Mayaguana

Caicos Passage

Little Inagua

Great Inagua

West Caicos

Providenciales

North Caicos

Grand Caicos

East Caicos

Grand Turk

Salt Cay

Grand Turk

Cockburn Town

Salt Cay

Balfour Town

History

A theory which is enjoying growing popularity with some historians is that Columbus actually made his original landfall in the New World on Grand Turk, rather than on San Salvador. If it was not Columbus himself, then the next contender was Ponce de Léon, who is supposed to have dropped by in 1512, while on his quest for the Fountain of Youth. At any rate, there were Arawak Indians living on the islands at the time of Columbus's arrival (the oldest archaeological site in the Bahamian archipelago lies on Grand Turk) and their thousands of years of peace were destroyed within a few decades by the Europeans. They were within easy reach of Hispaniola and so were rounded up and shipped out to work in Spanish gold mines. The population gone, the islands had nothing to offer the Spaniards and so they were left alone for the next couple of centuries. It was a convenient stopover for the buccaneers from the island of Tortuga off Hispaniola to the south, and so pirates used the bays to careen their vessels and to lie in wait for shipping, but it was not until 1678 that permanent settlers returned. Over the summer, Bermudians came to rake salt from the inland ponds on Grand Turk, Salt Cay and South Caicos, a commodity in demand as a preservative in the North American states.

The Spaniards complained that the settlers would drop the salt business all too readily when there were ships around to plunder, and so they staked their claim and occupied the islands in the 1710s. France invaded during the American War of Independence but the islands were returned to Britain by 1783. Following the war, Loyalists from the southern states of the USA were granted land in the islands and they established sea island cotton and sisal estates in the uninhabited Caicos Islands. In 1799, both groups of prosperous islands were annexed to the Bahamian government. Subjection to Bahamian control caused great dissatisfaction and eventually in 1848 the islands were granted internal self-government led by a president who answered to Jamaica. But the estates and the salt industry failed and most of the planters left (you can still see ruins poking out of the undergrowth in many places), and so in 1873, after many years of financial difficulty, the islanders voted to annexe themselves to Jamaica, under whose control they remained until 1959. When Jamaica took its Independence in 1962 the Turks and Caicos were handed over to the Bahamas again. At that time, the islands became a separate Crown Colony and, after the Bahamas became independent, a Governor was appointed for the islands.

The islands became internally self-governing in 1976 and there were plans for independence in the late 1970s, but these were shelved in 1980. As a Crown Colony of Britain, the islands are administered by a Governor, the Hon John P. Kelly, in conjunction with an Executive Council (partly elected, partly appointed) and a 13-member Legislative Council. The British Governor, Chief Secretary and Attorney General retain responsibility for foreign affairs, internal security, defence and offshore finance. The primary political parties are the Progressive National Party (PNP) and the People's Democratic Movement (PDM). The present leader is Chief Minister Hon. Derek Taylor, representing the governing PDM party. Elections are held every four years, with the next scheduled in early 1999.

The legal system is based on the centuries-old common law of England. Most of the law is derived from ordinances passed in Legislative Council and statutes specifically extended to TCI by Britain. The law is administered by a resident magistrate and a non-resident judge.

The islands have struggled financially in the 20th century and the economy has only picked up over the last few years as tourism and the offshore finance industry have developed. The salt industry has finished, but some income is generated from the export of conch and lobster.

Getting between the islands: As with most buses in the West Indies, you will find that the islanders say 'good morning' when they board the small planes which link the chain of islands from Providenciales to North Caicos, Middle Caicos, South Caicos and Grand Turk. (Occasional services go to Pine Cay and Salt Cay.) Scheduled daily flights are offered by SkyKing and Turks and Caicos Airways (✆ 946 4255), with chartered services available from Inter-Island Airways and Provo Air Charter (✆ 946 5040). If you cannot get a seat, ask around; you may well find that someone is chartering a plane and wants other passengers to share the cost.

There is no scheduled **bus service** (except for the schoolkids on Providenciales) and so you must either walk, hitch (usual lottery, but quite dependable) or take a **taxi**, which works on fixed rates and is expensive. Island tours are available on Providenciales through the Provo Taxi Association (✆ 946 5481) or Island's Choice Taxi Service (✆ 941 0409). **Day trips by boat** to nearby cays and islands are offered by J. & B. Tours (✆ 946 5047, *jbtours@caribsurf.com*, *www.nobis.com/jbtours*) and Silver Deep (✆ 946 5612), while Majestic Tours (✆ 946 4999) combines air flights to the other islands with guided ground tours.

Cars and scooters are available for hire on the major islands. Rates start at US$35 per day for a small car. Remember to drive on the left. In Provo, contact Provo Rent-A-Car (✆ 946 4404), Tropical Auto Rentals (✆ 946 5300), Turks & Caicos National Car Rental (✆ 946 4701), Budget Rent-A-Car (✆ 946 4079) or Rent-A-Buggy (✆ 946 4158). Provo Fun Cycles and Autos (✆ 946 5868, *naseem@caribsurf.com*) rents jeeps, motorcycles, scooters and bicycles, as does Scooter Bob's (✆ 946 4684) and Sunrise Auto Rental (✆ 946 4705).

On Grand Turk, car rentals are available from Tropical Auto Rental (✆ 946 1000) or Dutchie's (✆ 946 2244). On the other islands, ask at the hotels or airport. A licence from home is valid, but a government tax of $10 is levied on all cars hired and $5 on motorbikes.

Beaches

For their soft ivory sand, lack of crowds and backdrop of extraordinarily powerful blue sea, the Turks and Caicos beaches reign supreme. In fact, along the vast majority of the islands' estimated 200 miles of pristine beach, often only accessible by boat, there is complete isolation.

best beaches

North coast of Providenciales: The barrier reef lining the coast breaks the incoming surf to create calm, crystal-clear water. Although hotels and proposed condominium developments dot the uninterrupted 12-mile stretch, they still number less than a dozen, with plenty of peaceful, pristine sand for long strolls.

Malcolm Roads: On the island's northwest shore. Accessible with a four-wheel-drive vehicle via a trek through hills and bush, the spectacular two-mile beach and excellent snorkelling are worth the trip. Tiki huts provide shade and an interesting picnic spot.

Far eastern shores: Secluded beaches with small cliffs and stone jetties, accessible by various roads and paths in the Leeward community.

Sapodilla Bay Beach and **Taylor Bay Beach**: Towards South Dock, an anchorage for visiting yachts, and both sporting warm, shallow waters and an escape from the resort 'crowd'.

Erebus Beach (at the mouth of Turtle Cove Pond), **Smith's Reef** and the **White House Beach** (off Penn's Road in the Bight): The most accessible snorkelling.

Little Water Cay: Rare and endangered Turks and Caicos rock iguanas waddle down to meet your boat and there is an interpretative nature trail. Plenty of opportunity for beachcombing on vast stretches of sugar-white sand.

Pine Cay: Offers a simply stunning 2 miles of silky sand that shelves gradually into the shallows. The Meridian Club (✆ 946 5128) is a private resort on the island where you can get lunch if they are not too full and if you contact them in advance.

Parrot Cay: Also fringed with white coral sand and washed by the azure sea, a former favourite of pirates. A lavish resort and villa project is being finalized.

North Caicos: Miles and miles of wild sand beach, much of it protected from the Atlantic swell by offshore islands and reefs.

Mudjin Harbour: On Middle Caicos, the most photographed area of the country, the harbour envelops breathtaking views of coastal bluffs, caves and cove-enclosed beaches. There is a nature trail along the cliffs and a vacation community is being built overlooking the beach.

The northern side of South Caicos: Minutes from the airstrip there are idyllic curves where the waves clap and hiss—vast stretches of utterly uninhabited beach (take a picnic and snorkelling gear if you wander off there for the day).

Grand Turk: The entire leeward shore is edged by one long beach. The most popular picnic and party spot is at **Governor's Beach** which runs south from Cockburn Town. There is food and drink at the nearby Arawak Inn & Beach Club (✆ 946 2277, ✆ 946 2279, *www.4arawak.com*).

Pillory Beach: a wide stretch near the Guanahani Beach Resort, where Columbus is thought to have landed, which has a small beach bar. There are hotels dotted along the central shore where you can get drinks and watersports gear, but there are miles of sand to walk—this is also a good spot to see the Green Flash at sundown.

Salt Cay: Jagged ironshore embraces sandy coves on the eastern side while a gorgeous white beach edges the entire northern shore.

The Islands

Grand Turk (about 6 miles by 1) is the seat of government (population 3800) and site of the nation's capital at **Cockburn Town**, situated on the sheltered leeward coast. Overlooking the waterfront are some classic, Bermudian-style West Indian buildings, timber-framed houses with louvred windows and gingerbread verandas (some of which have been turned into attractive inns). Among them are the official government buildings, guarded by a couple of cannons. In one of the restored buildings at Guinep House you will find the **Turks and Caicos National Museum** (✆ 946 2160). There are displays of natural history and human heritage—Taino Indian, Spanish, African and Bermudian, but the major exhibit is a display of what is thought to be the oldest shipwreck in the Americas, a caravel which sank on Molasses

Reef perhaps as early as 1513; there is also archaeological and historical research going on, and artefact conservation facilities. A shop offers a wide selection of books, maps, postcards and island handicrafts.

Behind the waterfront are the old salinas (salt flats) and the residential districts of the island, which, despite the satellite dishes, retain an old-time Caribbean feel. Many buildings have walled courtyards meant to keep wandering donkeys from dining on the foliage. The attractive island church and its graveyard are in the middle of the town pond. A 140+-year-old lighthouse awaits restoration at the northern tip of the island. Beyond Government House (called Waterloo because it was built in 1815) is a former US airbase to which the astronaut John Glenn was welcomed back to land after the first voyage into space. At the southern tip of the island is where some historians believe that Columbus made his first landfall in 1492.

Seven miles to the southwest of Grand Turk is 3½ square-mile **Salt Cay** (another of the original salt-raking settlements). The industry is defunct, but the sun still does its work and you will see the blinding-white expanses of sea salt on the island, studded by old windmills. There are just 300 islanders, centred around Balfour Town, a peaceful, tidy, idyllic village. Pastel homes and pretty walled gardens line the streets. In the past, whaling helped support the economy and humpback whales are frequently spotted off the west coast during migration.

The **Caicos Islands** were traditionally the more agricultural of the two groups. They had a few prosperous plantation years in the late 1700s, boasted a sisal plantation in the 1900s and produced a variety of fruits and vegetables, especially in fertile North Caicos. **South Caicos** (population 1220) was once the centre of commercial activity, for the collection of salt and its fine natural harbour. It was also the first island to have a commercial airstrip. Now, it retains a slow, old-time atmosphere, but continues to be the centre of the islands' fishing industry, with conch and lobster available on the bank to its west, and excellent bonefishing.

East Caicos is uninhabited, save a few roaming donkeys and cattle, but once was the site of a large sisal plantation complete with railroad and turn-of-the-century cattle farm. However, changes are in the offing as the government is proposing to sell much of this land for development of a cruise ship port. There is a supreme beach (17 miles long) on the north coast.

Middle or Grand Caicos is the largest island, and the least inhabited (population 270) in the towns of Conch Bar, Bambarra and Lorimers. Conch Bar is the largest settlement and home to the island's airstrip. Nearby, you'll find Village Cave with its network of tunnels and caverns. It boasts four species of bat and was once mined for guano, which was exported and made into fertilizer. Tours are available, ask at the airport. There are a number of pre-Columbian archaeological sites, including a Lucayan Indian ball court.

Separated by a channel in the west, **North Caicos** has a few more inhabitants (1300) in the villages of Bottle Creek, Sandy Point, Whitby and Kew. The lush island is known for its agriculture and its wildlife. With a higher annual rainfall than the other islands, the land is fertile enough to grow a variety of fruits and vegetables, including custard apples, sapodilla, papaya, mangoes, bananas, sweetsop, tamarind, pigeon peas, tomatoes, corn and pumpkin. 'North' is bustling with birds and the country's largest flock of flamingos roosts at Flamingo Pond near Kew. You can visit a superb example of loyalist plantation ruins at Wade's Green, featuring a courtyard and jail.

On the cays strung out between North Caicos and Provo are two islands that have been developed as getaway retreats: **Parrot Cay** (open in late 1997/8) and **Pine Cay**, each fringed by a fantastic beach. The silken sands continue through **Water Cay** and **Little Water Cay** to the tip of Providenciales, and are the perfect spots to be dropped off for a 'day on a deserted island'.

Providenciales is the centrepiece of tourist development and has shot from a tiny and barely inhabited backwater to a resort island with a population of 9000 plus. The hotels are mostly strung along the northern shore and its fantastic beach. The main town, with the banks, supermarket, liquor store, some shops and offices and even a Kentucky Fried Chicken is just north of the airport. Tourist centres include Turtle Cove, where there is a small cluster of hotels, restaurants and shops around a marina, and the Grace Bay 'Gold Coast', which features the resort hotels, the casino, a variety of restaurants and a tourist-orientated shopping complex, Ports of Call. Recently, several condominium projects have been initiated along the Grace Bay Beach. Beyond the golf course you come to Leeward (✆ 946 5000, 📠 946 5674, *info@ leeward-provo-tci.com, www.leeward-provo-tci.com*), a newly revitalized resort community undergoing development, including a marina hotel and 'town square' to complement the ambitious residential sales programme under way.

In the far northeast tip of the island is the **Caicos Conch Farm** (✆ 946 5330; *guided tours available for $6/person, 9–3 Mon–Fri*). It was established in 1984 to grow conch commercially, from eggs to adult (a four-year life cycle). It has a current inventory of 1.5 million conch in all stages and is the only such facility in the world. The shop features unique gifts and souvenirs. Conch meat has long been a staple food in the Caribbean and can be found on the islands in conch salad, conch fritters, conch chowder and 'cracked conch'.

West Caicos is also uninhabited now, except by passing flamingos. There is a stunning beach in the northwest and the diving is superb.

✆ (1 649)–   ***Where to Stay***

Providenciales is the primary destination island in the Turks and Caicos and offers a more typical Caribbean holiday package than its sister islands, strong on watersports and relaxation, with some entertainment available. It has developed quite recently, and has a selection of modern resorts, smaller hotels, condominiums, guest houses and private villas.

Grand Turk, on the other hand, is almost entirely a dive destination. Lodging choices include small resorts and hotels, restored Bermudian homes serving as inns and some villa units. Especially worth recommending are some fine old creole coral stone houses with shuttered windows and wooden balconies that have been turned into guest houses. All have a familiar and friendly atmosphere and you get to know the managers and the other guests quickly. On the smaller islands there is little choice of accommodation. All hotels add a 7% government tax and often charge service at 15%.

luxury

Pine Cay is home to the exclusive and expensive **Meridian Club** (@ 946 5128, US ✆ (1 800) 331 9154), which has 12 sumptuous suites on a stunning 2-mile crescent strip of blinding white sand with palm-thatch sun-shades. Watersports, pool, tennis court, bar for cocktails and an elegant restaurant for a five-course dinner; bird-watching trips to the inland lakes or just seclusion if you want it; quite a discerning crowd.

very expensive

The smartest and most comfortable place to stay in **Providenciales** is the **Grace Bay Club**, PO Box 128 (✆ 946 5757, @ 946 5758, US toll free ✆ (1 800) 677 9192), which sits on a magnificent strip of sand on the huge Grace Bay. It is small and elegant with 22 suites in a single Spanish revival palace with balustrades, terracotta floor-tiles and rounded roof tiles, set among palmetto and coconut palms. The rooms are elegant and have fully equipped kitchens and large living areas, with television, VCR, safes, washer/dryer, etc. Also attached is Anacaona, an excellent restaurant (*see* p.762); pool, tennis courts, some watersports, one- and two-bedroom suites and penthouses.

The **Ocean Club** (✆ 966 5880, @ 946 5845, US toll free ✆ (1 800) 328 5285, *oceanclb@caribsurf.com*) is a condo complex with quite a lot of Caribbean style, including large screened balconies and a view down the fantastic beach. Fully equipped apartments, very comfortable with tropical coloured decorations and furnishings; some common facilities including two pools, a beachside bar and grill and an excellent restaurant, the Gecko Grille.

expensive–moderate

In the curve of **Grace Bay** is the **Turquoise Reef Resort & Casino** (✆ 946 5555, @ 946 5522, US toll free (1 800) 992 2015, *turqreef@caribsurf.com*), with 228 rooms, Provo's major resort hotel. Fun, relaxed and not pretentious, with accommodation clustered in ten low-rise structures overlooking a national marine park and a coral reef just off the beach. The social centre is the seaside sun deck, which surrounds a large freshwater pool and jacuzzi, where guests can sip drinks from Buddy's Beach Bar & Grill. On-site scuba center (Dive Provo) and watersports facility, fitness centre, tennis courts, Kids on Vacation club, tour desk, several restaurants, lounge and casino.

Of the more traditional-style hotels, one of the most comfortable is the **Erebus Inn**, PO Box 238 (✆ 946 4240, @ 946 4704), which perches on the cliff above Turtle Cove, from where the bar and pool have an excellent view. Friendly style, 30 neat and comfortable rooms, Sunset Bar & Grill. Two tennis courts, fitness centre, dive packages, shuttle to the beach.

Close by is another small and low-key resort, the **Turtle Cove Inn** (✆ 946 4203, 🖷 946 4141, US toll free ✆ (1 800) 887 0477). It has 32 simple but comfortable rooms overlooking the Turtle Cove marina, with all the dive shops around, several good restaurants (Tiki Hut Bar & Grill and The Terrace), shuttle to the beach.

LeDeck Hotel & Beach Club (✆ 946 5547, 🖷 946 5770, toll free ✆ (1 800) 528 1905, *ledeck@caribsurf.com*) occupies a prime location on Grace Bay Beach. The charming hotel is arranged in a U-shape to open directly on to the beach. Its 25 rooms surround a garden courtyard and each has a balcony. The cosmopolitan clientele is at least 50% European and between them, the managers speak five languages. On-site dive facility, oceanfront restaurant serving European/French cuisine.

You can find well-priced apartments at **Treasure Beach Villas** (✆ 946 4325, 🖷 946 4108) on Grace Bay, directly in front of an excellent snorkelling reef. There are 18 quiet, fully equipped units with common facilities including a pool and tennis courts.

All-inclusive resorts include the **Club Med Turkoise** (✆ 946 5500, US ✆ (1 800) 258 2633) and the recently acquired **Sandals Beaches** (✆ (1 800) BEACHES) property. Both offer a complete program of sports, dining, entertainment and activities and are located on the 12-mile north-side beach.

North Caicos has a couple of hotels, of which the most comfortable and friendly is the **Prospect of Whitby Hotel** (now Club Vacanze) (✆ 946 7119 🖷 946 7114), with 28 rooms set in long, low blocks on a fine strip of sand with casuarina pines. Pool, tennis, some watersports and scuba. The **Pelican Beach Hotel** (✆ 946 7112, 🖷 946 7139) stands on miles of sand a little further up the beach. It is quiet, with a restaurant and bar, and 14 passable rooms.

moderate–cheap

There is a friendly and amusing guest house on Grace Bay; the **Columbus Slept Here Bed and Breakfast**, PO Box 273, (✆/🖷 946 5878). Contentious title, but that's all part of the fun. Just three rooms. There is nowhere really cheap to stay on Provo.

On **North Caicos** you can go to **Jo Anne's Bed and Breakfast** (✆/🖷 946 7301) just off Whitby beach in the north of the island, friendly and easygoing.

In **Middle Caicos**, you can stay at the cottages at **Blue Horizon Resort** ✆ 946 6141 🖷 946 6139, *bhresort@caribsurf.com*) overlooking Mudjin Harbour Beach; four studio cottages with kitchens, screened porches, living/dining areas, fantastic sea views. There are some guest houses; try **Maria Taylor** (✆ 946 6118) or the very simple rooms at **Arthur's Guest House** (✆ 946 6122).

The most comfortable place to stay in **South Caicos** is the **Club Caribe Beach Resort** (✆ 946 3444, US ✆ (1 800) 581 2582), with 16 rooms set on a superb strip of sand and others on the waterfront. Quiet and comfortable.

Grand Turk and Salt Cay

The **Salt Raker Inn** (✆ 946 2260, 🖷 946 2817, *www.microplan.com/~paradise*; *moderate*) on historic Duke Street in Cockburn Town is the one of the most charming hotels on Grand Turk. Some of the 12 rooms are set in a classic island seafarer's home with wooden walls and floors, others are in suites around the very attractive garden with palms, palmetto and sprays of bougainvillea. Most modern comforts, air-conditioning, cable TV and a fridge, in old Caribbean style and atmosphere.

Another haunt with the best historic West Indian style is the circa-1840s **Turks Head Inn** (✆ 946 2466, ✉ 946 2825; *moderate–cheap*), also on the shore road in town. There are just seven rooms, of which the best are the four upstairs, which have some antique furniture and a balcony with a superb sea view. Excellent bar and covered restaurant.

A larger hotel, more typical of Caribbean resorts, is the **Sitting Pretty Hotel** (✆ 946 2666, ✉ 946 2668, US toll free ✆ (1 800) 577 3872, *GTHotels@caribsurf.com*; *expensive–moderate*), a bit pre-fab, but comfortable, some rooms set above the beach and others in the main house across the road; restaurant, pool and bar, some rooms with kitchenettes.

The **Guanahani Beach Resort** (✆ 946 2666, ✉ 946 2668, US toll free ✆ (1 800) 577 3872, *GTHotels@caribsurf.com; moderate–cheap*) has 16 air-conditioned rooms set in two blocks above spectacular Pillory Beach, just to the north of the town. All mod cons, a restaurant and watersports.

Salt Cay has just a few places to stay—small and quiet guest houses. **Windmills Plantation** (✆ 946 6962, ✉ 946 6930, US ✆ (1 800) 822 7715; *very expensive*) is set on 2½ miles of superb beach, a fantastic retreat on an already secluded island. There are just eight rooms and suites around the central bar and pool area, each decorated in bright Caribbean pastel colours with period antiques and reproduction furniture made with Costa Rican mahogany. Some watersports, very expensive.

If money is a concern, you can contact **Castaways Beach House** (✆ 946 6921, ✉ 946 6922, US ✆ (315) 536 7061; *moderate*) with six, fully furnished one bedroom apartments on the beach, low-key, or **Mount Pleasant Guest House** (✆/✉ 946 6927, US toll free ✆ (1 800) 441 4419; *moderate–cheap*), with eight air-conditioned rooms with TV in newly refurbished historic inn, horseback riding, bicycles, on-site dive facility, restaurant with gourmet dining, bar and lounge.

✆ *(1 649)–*   **Eating Out**

Seafood is the speciality in the islands, including lobster (in season), conch and local fish, which are brought in straight from the seas. Remember that almost everything else is imported by boat or plane and the full menu may not always be available. Ask about  daily specials. Some finer dining has appeared recently, but there are also plenty of enjoyable dining rooms in the low-key inns. Besides such specialties as conch 'n' grits, boiled fish with johnnycake and turtle stew, islanders are fond of spicy fried chicken, jerk pork, souse and stewed beef, and almost all native meals are accompanied by peas 'n' rice, macaroni and cheese and potato salad.

Categories are arranged according to the price of a main dish: *expensive*—US$20 and above; *moderate*—between US$10 and $20; *cheap*—US$10 and below.

expensive

Anacaona (✆ 946 5050) has one of the most attractive settings for a restaurant in the whole Caribbean. You dine under conical, palm-thatch palapas. The gourmet fare is Mediterranean/Caribbean, encompassing the best of local ingredients (and some freshly imported from Miami) with unexpected tastes from around the world: lobster flavoured with saffron and Caribbean snapper with ginger and lime butter. Followed by luscious puddings and then truffles.

Gecko Grill (✆ 946 5885), at the Ocean Club, serves the 'flavors of the world with an island twist' in an 'Art Gecko dining room oozing with tropical sophistication' or outdoors on the patio, decorated with thousands of twinkling lights in the surrounding trees. Grouper Macadamia is a house speciality, and all dishes are liberally seasoned by the talented kitchen team's dedication to originality and detail. Well-stocked bar, excellent wine list, monthly Gourmet Club.

moderate

At the Turtle Cove Inn is the **Tiki Hut Cabana Bar & Grill** (✆ 941 5341); lively dockside dining featuring Colorado Black Angus beef, gourmet pizza, fresh fish and pasta combos. Upstairs is **The Terrace** (✆ 946 4763), a not-to-be-missed fine dining experience, reasonably priced (by Provo standards). One owner was the former chef at Anacaona, and now lets his creativity flourish and experience shine with wonderful conch and seafood dishes. Reservations a must.

In the Turtle Cove area you will also find the legendary **Banana Boat Caribbean Grill** (✆ 941 5706), which is set on a bright and breezy wooden deck hung with nauticalia. Easy atmosphere, featuring Black Angus, fresh fish, Caribbean cuisine and excellent tropical drinks. Every Tuesday is Seafood Night, with 12 types of seafood prepared three ways, punctuated with live local entertainment.

Another good choice for lunch or dinner is the **Caicos Café** (✆ 946 5278) in Grace Bay, next to the Ports of Call shopping complex. Chef Perrik prepares fresh grilled seafood, steak, lamb and chicken.

moderate–cheap

Another very popular meeting place is **Hey Jose's Caribbean Cantina** (✆ 946 4812) in Central Square on the Leeward Highway. Hardly the setting for a romantic dinner, but a lively crowd and Mexican food in a modern air-conditioned dining room. The same can be said for the **Lone Star Bar & Grill** (✆ 946 5832) in Ports of Call at Grace Bay. This rambunctious sports bar dishes out Tex-Mex and gringo fare. A local band plays in the Ports of Call courtyard on Friday nights.

In the western part of the island, in Blue Hills, you will find excellent native food at the **Pub on the Bay** (✆ 941 5309), where there is an easy mix of locals and visitors. A modern building on the road itself, but also a couple of shaded decks on the beach. After the turn to Blue Hills from Leeward Highway, you will see a small building surrounded by shiny pink conch shells. This is **Bugaloo's on the Beach**, where the snack bar's namesake will prepare a tangy conch salad that couldn't be

fresher—the conch are pulled from the water, shelled and diced to order. At the Leeward Marina, you can get reliable seafood and local fare at **Gilley's at Leeward** (✆ 946 5094); the setting is especially romantic in the evenings. **Dora's** (✆ 946 4558) on the Leeward Highway has good island seafood and native dishes in a modern concrete building, open all day and night, often a crowd. Monday and Thursday seafood buffet. On the road to the airport you will find **Fast Eddies** (✆ 941 3176), a typical local restaurant with good seafood or the **Where It's At** restaurant (✆ 946 4185), for Jamaican and native food. Even simpler for a lunchtime snack of fried chicken wings is **Sweet T's** at the Texaco Station.

Nightlife is fairly limited, and includes local bands playing traditional island music at bars and restaurants (ask about when and where at the hotel desk), the island's only casino, Port Royale, at the Turquoise Reef Resort and some nightclubs. The Bacchus Club at the **Bella Luna Restaurant** (✆ 946 5214) in the 'glass house' is a drinking and dancing club on Fridays nights. On Saturday nights, party-seeking residents often cough up the stiff entry fee ($30) and mingle at the **Club Med Turkoise** (✆ 946 5500), where there is often a band and disco. Don't miss a walk along the beach at night—stargazing is extraordinary, and there is no personal security problem, although standard safety precautions should be taken.

On the smaller islands you will be dependent on the hotel dining rooms or local snack bars. In North Caicos you can get an excellent lunch or dinner by reservation at the **Ocean Beach Hotel** (✆ 946 7113) on Whitby Beach, or try **Club Titters** in Bottle Creek or **Papa Grunt's Seafood Restaurant** (✆ 946 7301) in Whitby Plaza. In South Caicos you can get generous portions of southern-styled fish, lobster and conch at the **Club Carib Sunset Bar & Restaurant** (✆ 946 3444) and local fish and chicken at the **Eastern Inn** (✆ 946 3301), near the harbour.

Grand Turk

Most of the small inns have good kitchens, turning out some international food, but mostly good local fare. Try the **Secret Garden at the Salt Raker Inn** (✆ 946 2260; *expensive–moderate*), which is a gathering point anyway, for the lobster tail in spiced melted butter and banana puddings. Wed and Sat night feature a barbecue, with live music and sing-a-long on Wed and Sun. The pub at the **Turks Head Inn** (✆ 946 2466) is the best place to catch up on local gossip and enjoy after-dinner guitar and piano music. The **Water's Edge** (✆ 946 1680; *moderate–cheap*) has dressed up a concrete house into a very attractive restaurant right above the waves, decorated with coloured lights and palm trees; international fare including pastas and steaks.

You will find good local fare (and slot machines) at **Touch of Class** (✆ 946 2071) on Airport Road and at the **Regal Begal**, Overback Salina. (Cracked conch is not to be missed.) The best conch fritters are made by **Peanuts** and sold from a bright blue shack on Front Street next to Town Dock, along with Dragon Stout beer. Don't miss some of Peanuts' Rhythm Pills!

Grand Turk can be quite an active place on Friday and Saturday night. Try **Tropix** for a young crowd and some dancing, or if you fancy watching a bit of dominoes and politics in action, check out **Town Tigers**.

By air: At this time, Providenciales is the main airport of entry into the Turks and Caicos. Domestic air service is provided to all of the inhabited islands on a daily basis by local air carriers. There is a departure tax of US$15.

By air from Europe: There are no direct flights from Europe to the Turks and Caicos Islands, so you are advised to change in Miami.

By air from North America: American Airlines (℡ 941 3587, toll free ℡ (1 800) 433 7300) offers twice daily B727 jet service between Providenciales and Miami. In season, there are weekly charter flights from a number of North American destinations, including Boston, Detroit, New York, Montreal and Toronto. Lynx Air International (℡ 888 LYNX AIR) flies between Providenciales, Grand Turk and Fort Lauderdale.

By air from the Bahamas and other Caribbean islands: Connections to Providenciales can be made via Nassau and Freeport via BahamasAir and SkyKing (℡ 941 KING, *king@caribsurf.com*), while Air Jamaica connects between Montego Bay and Providenciales three times weekly. Flights are available on SkyKing and InterIsland Airways (℡ 941 5481, *interi@caribsurf.com*) to other Caribbean destinations including the Dominican Republic, Haiti and Cuba. You may be able to charter one of the inter-island planes, *see* above.

tourist information

UK: Morris Kevan International, 47 Chase Side, Enfield, Middlesex EN2 6NB (℡ (0181) 364 5188, ✆ 367 9949).

USA and Canada: Trombone Associates Inc, 420 Madison Avenue, New York, NY 10017 (℡ (212) 223 2323, ✆ 223 0260) or PO Box 594023, Miami, FL 33159. There is a general freephone for the USA (℡ (1 800) 241 0824).

On-island, contact the Turks and Caicos Tourist Board on Pond Street, PO Box 128, Grand Turk (℡ 946 2321, ✆ 946 2733, *www.ttg.co.uk/t&c/index.htm*), where they keep hours of Mon-Thurs 8–4.30 and Fri till 4. There is also a tourist board office in Providenciales at 17 Turtle Cove Landing (℡ 946 4970, ✆ 941 5494).

The full-colour magazine *Times of the Islands* (℡ 946 4788, ✆ 946 4703, *timespub@carib-surf.com*) is published quarterly and contains some features on local culture, ecology, lifestyle and development, offering advice for sun-worshippers and investors alike. There is also a free monthly visitor's guide, *Where, When, How Providenciales* (℡ 946 4815, ✆ 941 3497, *advantge@caribsurf.com*) and a similar publication produced quarterly for Grand Turk and Salt Cay. There are two newspapers, the *Free Press* (bi-weekly) and the *Turks and Caicos News* (semi-monthly).

There is a good choice of health care services available, especially on Providenciales. In a **medical emergency**, you can call an ambulance at 999 or 911 or the M.B.S. Group Medical Practice on Leeward Highway (℡ 946 4242/4222/5252). There is a hospital on Grand Turk (℡ 946 2333) and air ambulance service is available to the USA and Nassau.

The **IDD code** for the Turks and Caicos is ℡ (1 649) followed by a seven-figure island number. On island, dial the seven digits.

festivals

Local island festivals include sail and boat races, beauty pageants, local bands and a chance to sample native dishes. These include: the **South Caicos Regatta** at the end of May, **Fun in the Sun** on Salt Cay in June, the **Provo Summer Festival** in July, the **North Caicos Festarama** also in July and **Cactusfest** held at the end of August in Grand Turk. A **deep-sea fishing tournament** is held in July, drawing sportsfishermen from around the US and Caribbean to a two-week orgy of fishing and parties. As a British Crown Colony, the islands recognize many of the official celebrations, including the **Queen's Birthday** in June.

money

The currency of the Turks and Caicos is the US$, though some smaller local coins are issued. Major credit cards and traveller's cheques are usually accepted in any tourist area. If you go off the beaten track or to one of the less inhabited islands, you should take sufficient cash.

Banks (Bank of Nova Scotia and Barclay's): Open Mon–Thurs, 8.30–2.30, until 5 on Fri.

Shops: Open Mon–Sat 9–5, usually with a long Caribbean lunch-break.

shopping

Souvenir shoppers will find Caribbean paintings (Bamboo Gallery at Market Place) and crafts (Maison Creole next to Ports of Call), T-shirts (Tourist Shoppe at Central Square), shells (Caicos Conch Farm), some locally made handicrafts (Greensleeves and Paradise Gifts at Central Square) and videotapes and books about the islands (Unicorn Bookstore at Market Place). Provo's largest shopping complex, Ports of Call, is located across from the Turquoise Reef Resort. In the atmosphere of an old Caribbean seaside town, shoppers can browse through an ever-increasing collection of retail shops and restaurants. Hotel boutiques carry a selection of resort wear, postcards and sundries. Duty-free outlets, including Royal Jewels and Goldsmith Duty Free Shops sell liquor, jewellery, perfume and Cuban cigars.

watersports

You can rent watersports equipment at the major hotels, including windsurfers, sailboats, kayaks and sea cycles. Two unique ways to see Provo by air include parasailing and tandem skydiving from 10,000ft up (Rainbow Flyers, ✆ 941 3888).

Sailing: Charter sail tours including ½ day, full day and sunset cruises aboard monohull, catamaran and trihull vessels can be arranged at hotel desks or through Sail Provo (✆ 946 4783, *charter@caribsurf.com*), *Minx* (✆ 946 5122) or *Beluga* (✆ 946 4396). A day-long sail to French Cay, a nature sanctuary with excellent snorkelling, can be taken on the *Caicos Sol* (✆ 941 2501), expensive. Small boat rentals are available for exploration of Provo's virgin south shore or Grace Bay and the Caicos Cays.

Fishing: Quite popular, close to the shore for feisty reef fish, including those in the much-prized snapper and grouper families, or over the deep-sea channels, where you might hook a yellow tuna or a marlin. Both Silver Deep (✆ 946 5612) and J & B Tours (✆ 946 5047) offer experienced guides, tackle and comfortable boats for reef fishing; moderate. Some restaurants will cook your catch for you! Bonefishing, casting in the sandy shallow flats, is also extremely popular and can be arranged through the same companies. To go out into the deep, try the 43ft *Hatteras Sakitumi* (✆ 946 4065), docked at Turtle Cove. There is an annual international billfishing tournament in July.

In Grand Turk, call Sand Dollar Tours (© 946 2018) or Sea Captivations (© 946 1407).

Scuba diving: Divers return year after year to the submarine walls (which drop sheer) around Grand Turk, at North West Point in Providenciales and at West Caicos. Elsewhere there are pinnacles of coral surrounded by an expanse of sand and ravines plied by flotillas of tiny fish and scoured by a barracuda, even the odd coral-encrusted anchor offshore. Beds of soft corals are near the surface—like tussocks of wool that float on the currents—and lower down are forests of gorgonians and black coral. Lobsters scrabble on the sea-bed (they are one of the islands' major exports) and above them groupers and yellowtail snapper hang around with vibrant blue butterfly fish and the odd long, thin trumpetfish. Turtles cruise by and in the winter months, migrating humpback whales swim through the Columbus Passage. The Grand Turk Wall starts in 35ft of water in places and has ledges and overhangs to explore just below the lip. Off Providenciales there are fish of all kinds, particularly impressive on the wall at the North West Point, where there are ravines, undercuts and chimney tunnels. Other dive sites include West Caicos, where stingrays, loggerhead turtles, hammerhead sharks and even whales have been seen, and South Caicos, pretty much virgin territory.

Divers must present their certification cards, but if you have not dived before, introductory courses are easily available. There is a recompression chamber in Providenciales (© 946 4242). Many of the dive operations are run out of the hotels. On Providenciales, the Turtle Cove area is a centre for dive operators. Here, try Turtle In Divers (©/⊕ 941 5389, US toll free © (1 800) 359 3483), Flamingo Divers (©/⊕ 946 4193, US toll free © (1 800) 234 7768, *flamingo@caribsurf.com*), Art Pickering's Provo Turtle Divers (© 946 4232, ⊕ 941 5296, US toll free © (1 800) 328 5285, *proturtl@caribsurf.com*) and Caicos Adventures (©/⊕ 941 3346, US toll free © (1 800) 513 5822, *divucrzy@ caribsurf.com*). In the main resort area, contact Dive Provo (© 946 5040, ⊕ 946 5936, US toll free © (1 800) 234-7768, *divprovo@caribsurf.com*).

On Salt Cay, where you can dive the wreck of the Endymion, an 18th century British warship, contact Salt Cay Divers (©/⊕ 946 6927). In Grand Turk, you can choose from Blue Water Divers (©/⊕ 946 2432, *mrolling@caribsurf.com*, *www.microplan.com/ ~paradise*), Oasis Divers (©/⊕ 946 1128, US toll free © (1 800) 892 3995) or SeaEye Diving (©/⊕ 946 1407, *CI@caribsurf.com*, *www.interlog.com/~reefnet/GTurk*). On South Caicos, go with the Club Carib (© 946 3444, US toll free © (1 800) 581 2582).

There are also two live-aboard dive boats based in the Turks and Caicos waters, the *Sea Dancer* (US © (305) 669 9391, ⊕ 669 9475, US toll free © (1 800) 932 6237) and the *Turks & Caicos Aggressor* (US © (504) 385 2416, ⊕ 384 0817).

other sports

Golf: There is a 6529-yard 18-hole championship golf course, Provo Golf Club © 946 5991, ⊕ 946 5992, *provogolf@caribsurf.com*) near the hotels at the northeastern end of Providenciales, a surprisingly green area cut into the scrubland, which was recently rated as one of the ten best in the Caribbean. Also a driving range.

Tennis: Courts are available at many of the hotels—check any front desk.

Cricket: You will occasionally see cricket matches played by the local teams.

The Bahamas

The Bahamas are favourite subjects for satellite photographers—700 emerald-green islands and cays scattered over 100,000 square miles of absurdly blue sea. The water is gin-clear and glistens over the banks of sand that stretch for miles and miles. In places you must walk hundreds of yards into the sea to get as deep as your waist. The activity is there too—the reefs are superb and make bewildering diving, and the fishing and sailing are world-renowned. Since Columbus first made land in 1492, these cays have been plied by generations of pirates and gun-runners, and more recently rum- and drug-runners.

For the purposes of tourism the islands are divided into three separate groups. **Nassau, Cable Beach** and **Paradise Island** are on the senior island of New Providence at the heart of the Bahamas, where the capital Nassau is situated. To the north is **Freeport/Lucaya** on Grand Bahama island, a complete resort area that has sprung up from a barren and virtually uninhabited island 30 years ago. The 697 other islands are known as the **Out Islands** and they are less developed and mostly far gentler in their lifestyle, ideal for an isolated island break. The only problem is choosing which ones to go to. They include islands such as Bimini, the Abacos, Eleuthera, the Exumas and Andros.

Named by the Spaniards after the *baja-mar* (the shallow sea) in which they lie, the Bahamas are not geographically in the Caribbean. These splinters and fragments of land stretch from just north of the Greater Antilles (Haiti and Cuba), across the Tropic of Capricorn, and up alongside the coast of Florida, separated from the USA only by the 50 miles of the Gulf Stream. In all there are about 3000 of them if you include the rocks, fringing reefs and the ribbons of sand that just make it above the surf.

The Bahamas are low-lying, coral limestone outcrops that sit on top of the Great Bahama Bank (stretching from Bimini to Cat Island and Ragged Island) and the Little Bahama Bank (in the north, with Grand Bahama and the Abacos). Most do not make it above 50ft—the highest point among them is 206ft, on Cat Island. They are not really that lush and are mostly covered with scrub and wispy casuarina pine trees. There are many inland lakes, usually salt water. Altogether the islands cover about 5380 square miles.

The 270,000 Bahamians do not consider themselves West Indians (despite their claim that Columbus discovered the Indies on San Salvador). They have a long-standing association with the USA, and this is clearly audible in their voices—there is an American drawl on the West Indian English. Most of the islanders are of African descent, but in contrast with other Caribbean islands, white Bahamians (informally known as 'Conkie Joes') make up a high 15 per cent of the population. One or two communities have remained determinedly white since they arrived here as loyalists in the late 1700s. There is also a large number of expatriates resident in the islands.

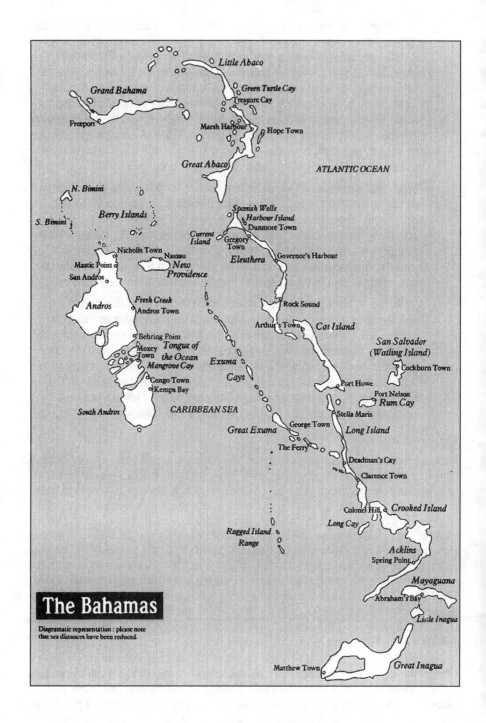

The Bahamas

Diagramatic representation : please note
that sea distances have been reduced.

The Bahamas were a colony of Britain until they took their Independence in 1973 and the connection with Britain still rings clear in parts of Bahamian life. You will actually come across garden fêtes here. The parliamentary system is based on the British model and the policemen are recognizable in their uniforms of black serge and red stripe, complete with white helmet. But in recent years the Bahamians have been strongly influenced by the States. The cars, many of them left-hand drive even though the Bahamians drive on the left, are big American cruisers, and though they have trouble in the tight streets of Nassau, a quick look at Freeport will show them more at ease on the boulevards of the recent development there.

Traditionally commerce has come from outside the islands, as the Bahamas are not fertile. The Bahamians have muddled along, scraping a living from the land, but there have been successive waves of prosperity, many of them brought by wars or carried on the wrong side of the law. The monuments to the different eras are visible in Nassau, from the early stone and timber houses of the Bahamian gun-runners on the hill to the Nassau mansions that have been built on the prosperity of Prohibition and most lately tourism.

The Bahamas have a highly developed tourist industry and the islands see over 3 million tourists a year, one-third of whom arrive by cruise ship (as many as ten a day can call at Nassau). About two-thirds of the work force are employed in tourism one way or another and some 70 per cent of GNP is derived from the industry. The Bahamas offer an extraordinary variety to the visitor. In the traditional centres you can take in glitz and gambling in the vast pink palaces of Cable Beach and Freeport. And yet just a few nautical miles away are the idyllic castaway cays of the Out Islands.

Suggested Itinerary

If you are travelling independently around the Bahamas it will probably be necessary to spend some time in Nassau (most flights arrive there). To see the real Bahamas you must get beyond here, but if you need to change planes (or mail-boats) in Nassau, there are good bars and restaurants to occupy you while you wait. Two weeks gives enough time to see a variety of the Bahamian islands. Start with a trip to one of the more developed Out Islands, perhaps Harbour Island or North Eleuthera or to the lovely cays off the Abacos. Great Exuma is also worth a visit—from here you can reach the superb Exuma Cays. If you cannot persuade a yachtsman to take you on down to the other islands you may have to return to Nassau and set off again, but the further south you go from here, the more remote the islands become. For a taste of small-island life, try Andros, Cat Island, Long Island or San Salvador. Another option, to help you see as much as possible, is to fly in or out of the Bahamas through Bimini, Eleuthera or the Abacos.

Bahamian History

The recorded history of the New World begins on one of the Bahamian islands. On 12 October 1492, after more than a month at sea sailing into the unknown, Columbus made land on the island of *Guanahani*—and named it San Salvador or 'Holy Saviour'. He landed with the banners of Ferdinand and Isabella and immediately claimed the island for Spain, greeted by no doubt dumbstruck native islanders, the *Lucayan* Indians. They were fascinated by the bells and mirrors that Columbus gave them in return for food, beads and the gold ornaments that they wore through their noses. It was the gold that attracted his attention, and the Indians explained that it came from the south. Soon afterwards Columbus sailed off to search for it, touching other islands before leaving Bahamian waters and heading for Cuba.

The Lucayans (an Arawak tribe) had lived in the Bahamas for around 500 years before the arrival of the Europeans, living off fish and turtles and growing a small amount of cassava. Columbus noticed scars on their bodies, received in raids by the Carib Indians from the islands farther south. There were about 40,000 Lucayans when the Spaniards first came to the Bahamas, but within 40 years there were none left—they had all been transported off the island to work in the gold mines in Hispaniola.

The Bahamas, rejected as *islas inutilas* (useless islands), were simply left alone by the Spaniards for the next hundred years. They were avoided because the *bajamar* was a treacherous sea in which to sail. Many ships were to founder over the next four centuries and 'wrecking' became one of the principal Bahamian industries in an otherwise barren place. There are even stories of the islanders putting out false lighthouses to lure passing ships on to the reefs. Others were more open about their profligacy. Pirates discovered the islands in the 16th century and they would lie in wait for the Spanish *flota*, the yearly fleet which collected in Havana harbour and set off into the Gulf Stream for Spain, loaded with the riches of the Spanish Main. Just as they are today, the coves and bays were the perfect hideaways for small sailing vessels.

The first British interest in the island came in one of the many royal grants, in which chunks of uninhabited land were handed out as favours in the courts of Europe. Charles I granted the Bahamas to Sir Robert Heath in 1629, in addition to the Carolinas on the American mainland, just as the French king was to grant other islands a few years later. Settlement was another matter, and it was not until 20 years later that the first serious attempt was ventured from Bermuda. Religious troubles, mirroring the disputes in England itself, led a group of Puritans under the governor William Sayle to leave Bermuda in 1648 for the Bahamas, settling an island that they called Eleuthera (from the Greek word for freedom). The colony had difficulties from the start and most of the settlers returned to Bermuda, but it was at this time that Sayle discovered by accident a fine harbour on another island, which he called New Providence.

New Providence soon became the important island in the group and the pirates and privateers swarmed to it in the late 1600s. Pirates like Charles Vane and Blackbeard, Benjamin Hornigold and Jack Rackham with his two women companions, Anne Bonney and Mary Read, made their way up here from Port Royal in Jamaica and from the Virgin Islands. Working for the British as 'privateers' or on their own account, they looted any Spanish ship or settlement they could find and returned with their loot to Nassau. In revenge, the Spaniards sacked the town four times in 25 years. The town flew the British flag, but it was almost completely lawless, and so in 1717, the British sent out a governor to bring it under control. When he arrived Woodes Rogers was popular, with the merchants and pirates alike, but within months he had stopped piracy, persuading the freebooters to become privateers only in time of war, and hanging those who did not want to give up the trade.

And so the Bahamas took shape, muddling through in times of peace, but flourishing as an entrepôt when there was a war. In the American War of Independence the 3000 Bahamians did not side openly with the rebelling mainland colonists, but there was an undercover trade of arms and gunpowder through the islands. Some took to the seas as privateers on the hunt for American shipping. Nassau was captured in 1766 by the colonist fleet and all the island's military supplies shipped off to the colonies.

Following the war, the population of the islands trebled as 8000 loyalists fled for the Bahamas, setting up cotton estates on the Out Islands, which prospered for a while. To work the plantations they brought slaves, whose descendants form the majority of today's Bahamian population. As their plantations failed the white settlers left the islands, simply leaving the slaves to fend for themselves. Emancipation was declared in 1833.

In the American Civil War Nassau saw another wave of prosperity as blockade runners made the dash over to the coast of the States with boatloads of arms. It lasted just four years and then the islands were eclipsed again, and so the Bahamians continued to scrape a living growing sisal and fruits, and collecting sponges from the sea-bed. Prohibition in the States, from 1920 to 1933, turned the wharves of Nassau into a forest of bootleg barrels and casks waiting for the run across to Florida in fast boats. It took a few years before the coast guard could hope to catch them. The tradition was revived for a while recently as the islands were used as a stopover on the drugs trail from South America, for shipment of marijuana and cocaine, but now the DEA and Royal Bahamas Defence Force is better equipped to deal with it.

The Bahamian tourist industry has mushroomed over the last 40 years, to the point today where there are ten times as many visitors each year as the entire population of the islands. After the Second World War, Hog Island was sexily renamed Paradise Island and it exploded with hotels. Freeport was conceptualized in the fifties and then appeared in the 'pine barren' of Grand Bahama. Bahamians flooded into the centres from other islands to get a piece of the action. Tourism, the mainstay of the economy, is worth over a billion dollars annually and employs over two-thirds of the workforce. Other industries include offshore finance and agriculture, fishing and some light industry in Freeport on Grand Bahama. There is still visible poverty in certain parts of the Bahamas, but the situation is better than in most Caribbean islands, and far better than it was 40 years ago. Considerable money is invested in the country by expatriates who have built houses in estates like Lyford Cay outside Nassau and increasingly throughout the islands.

Traditionally the colonial Bahamas were administered by a small group of mainly white Bahamians called the 'Bay Street Boys', but after the Second World War their predominance came to an end. Universal suffrage did not come until 1962 when their power began to be shared with the Bahamian blacks. Independence came on 10 July 1973. For many years the Bahamas were led by the charismatic leader of the Progressive Liberal Party, Sir Lynden Pindling, despite occasional scandals that implicated him in corruption. He was finally ousted in 1992. The country is now led by the Hon. Hubert Ingraham of the Free National Movement, which holds 34 of the 40 seats in the Bahamas parliament The country is a member of the British Commonwealth and is headed by a Governor General, Sir Orville Turnquest.

Diving

Washed by currents on all sides, the Bahamas have superbly clear waters with excellent diving. The corals and fish are basically the same as in other Caribbean islands, but there are more of certain fish and some corals are able to grow larger here. There are shallow reefs on the slopes close to shore off some of the islands; canyons and pinnacles that rise close to the water's surface; and walls, where the Bahama banks drop sheer down to the deep ocean floor—the resting-place of many wrecks that were beyond the famed Bahamian 'wreckers'. 'Blue holes' are a curious feature—they are cylindrical holes up to 200ft across which descend to 90ft below the surface of the sea. In a strong tide they can generate a vortex as water is sucked in and out from below.

Visibility is excellent, often over 100ft, and it reveals fantastic landscapes of corals: gorgonians like vast fans standing among the fingers and branches of fur-covered corals, bouquets of flower corals and layers of carpet anemone. The fishlife is bewildering. You will come across single rays cruising and groupers loitering, or stopping off at cleaning stations to have their teeth picked by shrimps. Luxuriously coloured angelfish twitch as they glide past and trumpetfish hang vertically beneath the surface of the water.

Diving is available at all the main centres and there are some spectacular reefs right off Nassau itself (these have been used in a number of film sets). You can actually join shark-feeding time there. If you go farther afield into the Out Islands, there is excellent variety. Off the eastern coast of Andros is the third-largest barrier reef in the world, where the colours of the corals and sponges are supreme. Off the Abacos and Eleuthera, wreck dives include the wrecks not only of ships, but of two trains that went down while they were being transported. You could also take a ride in the tidal race at Current Cut off Eleuthera. Lessons are available in all the resorts.

New Providence

The island of New Providence is small (just 21 by 7 miles), but it has always been the hub of Bahamian life. It lies in the northern area of the islands and is the site of the Bahamian capital, Nassau. 170,000 people, two-thirds of the Bahamas population live on New Providence, most of them in Nassau, which has flourished periodically over the centuries as an entrepôt because of its magnificent harbour.

The island is the engine-room of Bahamian tourism, and the three main resort areas now see as many as 1¼ million tourists a year. You can see the successive generations of hotels, each one fading as a newer and more exciting one is built. The old colonial houses on the hill, which are now old-time hotels of 'character', were overtaken in the thirties by Art Deco piles and in the fifties by high-rise hotels downtown. The newest and most exciting are the pastel palaces on Cable Beach, with the cabarets and gambling halls with their acres of slot machines.

With all the cruise ships and straw-hat vendors, Nassau has a pretty fearsome tourist race, but there is a more sophisticated side to it too. There are good restaurants and a large expatriate crowd. And there are a few more noticeably 'West Indian' parts of the island—'over the hill' in Nassau and in outlying towns on the island.

Getting Around

Endless minibuses link downtown Nassau and Cable Beach and ply around the town itself, but only occasionally does one run further to the residential areas out on the island (until about 6.30pm). The Nassau terminal is at the western end of Bay Street, beneath the British Colonial Beach Resort. Stand at the stops and flag them down, fare

75¢. Around the town itself, you might just prefer to travel by horse-drawn carriage, about $5 per person for half an hour.

Hotels often transfer guests from the **airport** on arrival and departure and many run a complimentary safari bus service into town. **Hitchhiking** is illegal, although in the Out Islands it is sometimes the only practical means of transport. **Ferries** run across the harbour from the dock in downtown Nassau to Paradise Island for a couple of dollars. A minibus circles Paradise Island every 30 minutes.

Taxis are always available at the airport, along Bay Street and at the hotels. Fares are fixed by the government and theoretically metered. From the **airport** you can expect to pay $12 to Cable Beach, downtown Nassau—$17 and Paradise Island—$20 (plus $2 toll). If you hire a taxi by the hour for a trip around the island, negotiate a rate of around $25.

Car rental is convenient and the cars are easily available, but expensive at anything from $50 per day. You will be required to leave a hefty deposit by credit card imprint. Drive on the left and avoid downtown Nassau if humanly possible. The big name companies have desks at the airport and major hotels: Avis (✆ 327 7121, 326 6380) on West Bay Street; Budget (✆ 327 9000, 327 7956); Hertz (✆ 377 8684); and National (✆ 327 7301). **Scooters** can be rented at around $25–35 per day. Drivers and passengers must wear crash helmets by law. Try Holiday Scooter Rental (✆ 322 3552) or Bowe's Scooter Rental (✆ 326 8329).

Island tours, visiting the few sights beyond Nassau, or sailing away for a day's snorkelling or a sunset cruise, can be booked through the front desks of most large hotels or direct with Majestic Tours (✆ 322 2606), Happy Tours (✆ 323 5818) or Tropical Travel Tours (✆ 322 3802).

Beaches

Lighthouse Beach: Within a shout of downtown Nassau, on the western esplanade leading out of town, crowded but close.

Cable Beach: A bus-ride away, where there are all the sporting activities on offer.

Paradise Beach: A ferry-ride over on Paradise Island—another active beach on the west of the island (*adm*), or if you want to be a little less crowded, there is a beach farther round on the northern shore.

Elsewhere on New Providence Island, many of the smaller beaches are privately owned by the hotels, but you might go to **Adelaide Beach** or **South Beach**, where there is a beach bar, on the south shore, or **Delaport Point** or **Love Beach** beyond the Cable Beach area. They are not usually deserted, but you will not be one of a thousand.

beach bars

Traveller's Rest is on the West Bay Road approaching Lyford Cay, a pleasant place for hanging out with a view of the sea through the sea grape and palm trees, and you might also try **Tamarind Hill**. Very popular with the locals at the weekends and on holidays is the **Montagu Beach bar** on Montagu beach east of town.

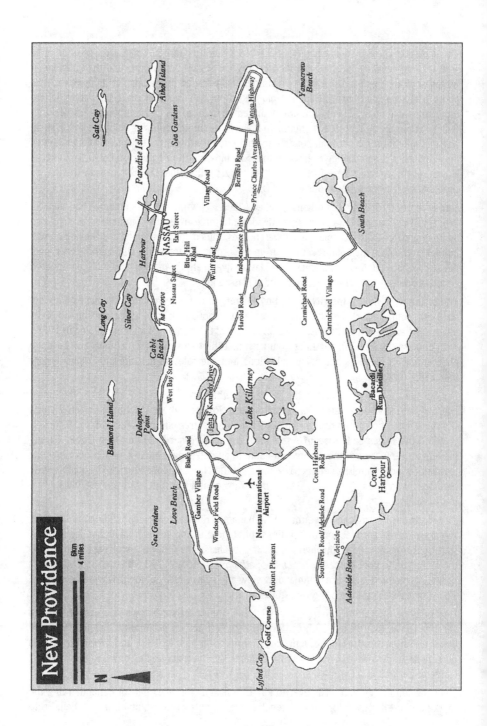

New Providence

The capital of the Bahamas has always centred around its harbour as the source of its prosperity. Large ocean-going ships and local boats have always put in here, and then occasional waves of pirates, gun-runners and rum-runners have traded in the port, bringing extra prosperity while the good times lasted. The old waterfront buildings look on to Bay Street, where the commercial buzz still continues, now driven by shiploads of cruise-trippers—*hackers* tout their goods in the street (usually offering to braid your hair nowadays or sell you a conch shell) and the warehouses contain air-conditioned boutiques with cut-price bargains. You will even hear the cruise liners calling their passengers by blowing their foghorns. The inhabitants of Nassau are not always very forthcoming, but most will oblige if you approach them. You should also be careful about your valuables.

Settled in 1666, the city was originally called Charles Town, but it was renamed Nassau after William III of Orange Nassau. The town divides into three areas: the commercial district down by the waterfront with its colonnaded warehouses, the colonial mansions and the large townhouses built by the merchants, set back from the activity on top of the cliff, and the area 'over the hill', where the poorer inhabitants of Nassau live in streets of clapboard and now modern concrete houses—an extremely lively part of Nassau life.

The commercial hub of the city is still **Bay Street**, an outsize shopping precinct as it always has been, running parallel to the waterfront, just a short walk from the cruise ship dock. Its heart is the **straw market** (constructed on the site of the traditional market building in 1974), with endless stalls selling anything from rush matting to a straw hat, carvings and beads to plait into your hair. Its activity is infectious and the saleswomen are persuasive—more mercantile mayhem.

Not far down Bay Street, close to the cruise ship wharf and Rawson Square, is the traditional heart of the Bahamas government in **Parliament Square**, where a statue of Queen Victoria sits surrounded on three sides by neoclassical buildings dressed up in Nassau pink. Here you will find the Bahamas **House of Assembly**, the old Treasury and Supreme Court. Taking Parliament Street out of the square you come to an octagonal building, which once was the town prison, decommissioned in 1879 and now the Nassau public library. The alcoves with the books were the original cells. The *surreys* (horses and traps) that you see everywhere are tourist taxis.

The **National Historical Museum**, in the Bahamas Historical Society building on Elizabeth Avenue, houses a collection of paintings, photographs and maps from Bahamian history, starting in Arawak times, through pirates and loyalists. The **Queen's staircase** leads to the top of the cliff to **Fort Fincastle** (*open 9–5; adm free*), built in 1793 with the shape of a ship's prow. It is restored and has a commanding view and a few hefty cannon that were never used. The view is better still from the watertower nearby.

Farther along the clifftop, where many of Nassau's finest old stone town houses with louvred verandas were built in the 19th century (like the attractive restaurant, Graycliff), you will come to **Government House**, a neoclassical mansion built in 1801 and dressed in Nassau pink, now the residence of the Governor General. On the stairs leading down to the street is a statue of Columbus.

Near the toll bridge that leads over to Paradise Island is a lively part of Bahamian life, the market, where fruit vendors sit and conch salesmen extract the animal from its shell. Fruits and ground provisions are shipped in from the Out Islands and sold here on the dock. The mail boats also dock here.

There is not much to see on **Paradise Island** itself unless you are a student of the tourist industry—the best reason to go over is for the beaches. However, the island, which was called Hog Island until 1961, is quite pretty and some of the hotels are set in attractive grounds. The one sight to aim for is the **Cloisters** in Versailles Gardens (near the Ocean Club in the east of the island), where a walkway of stairs and statuary lead down to a 14th-century cloister that has ended up thousands of miles from its monastery in Lourdes. The toll to **Paradise Island** costs *25c for walkers (theoretically) and $2 for cars.*

Bahamian theatre is on view at most times of the year at the **Dundas Centre for the Performing Arts** on Mackey Street in eastern Nassau.

Around the Island

Leaving downtown Nassau to the west you reach the seafront on the Western Esplanade. To the left is the lumbering **Fort Charlotte** on the hill (*open daily; adm free*), built at the beginning of the 19th century; it once manned a fearsome 42 cannon, but they never fired a shot in anger.

Behind the fortress are the **Nassau Botanical Gardens** (*✆ 323 5975; open daily 9–4.30; adm*) where trails lead through the 16 acres of flowering trees and shrubs, a cactus garden, and past ponds of tropical fish to a grotto. Nearby the **Ardastra Gardens** (*✆ 323 5806; open daily 9–5; adm*) show off the Bahamian national birds, the pink flamingos, to their best advantage when they perform a bit of precision marching at the orders of their drill sergeant. In the 5 acres of tropical luxuriance there is an aviary of birds and a few animals. **Crystal Cay** (*open daily; adm exp*), visible by its space-age needle off Silver Cay, has a good aquarium and underwater observatory as well as other fishy things to view scattered around a shady garden, including a shark tank. Good for the kids (there is a 'hands-on' pool).

Cable Beach is called so because the Bahamas' first cable link to Florida was made from here, along the magnificent stretch of sand. It is the Bahamas' most built-up resort area, ever-increasing since hotels first appeared here in the 1950s. Travelling further west, you pass many expensive private houses and other condominium developments before reaching **Lyford Cay** on the western tip of the island, an exclusive and extremely rich housing estate mainly peopled by expatriates. It is private.

The south of the island is less densely populated, though there are a few local Bahamian towns like Adelaide that the tourism race seems to have passed by. Some were settled by emancipated slaves, others by Africans who were being transported on Spanish slave ships caught by the British Navy after the abolition of the slave trade in 1807. In the east of the island is the **Retreat** (*✆ 323 1317; tours Tues–Thurs; adm*), the headquarters of the Bahamas National Trust, where there are some 200 species of palms and other exotic plants in the 5 acres of garden.

✆ (1 242)–   ***Where to Stay***

Nassau, Cable Beach and Paradise Island is the largest resort area in the Bahamas, and it has around 4000 rooms for rent in all, in hotels ranging from the most modern, massive, pastel-pink palaces of Cable Beach, through the tower block hotels of the seventies and early eighties to small and comfortable guest houses, the family homes of the last century, built 'on the hill' in Nassau. If you feel like splashing out, you'll find the Caribbean's most expensive hotel room (almost a whole floor in fact, complete with robot servant and thunderstorm light-show) in the Marriott-Crystal Palace on Cable Beach—a snip at $25,000 a night, but you'll be pleased to hear that they'll throw it in free if you are a high roller on the casino downstairs ($100,000 stake). There is a 6% government tax on hotel rooms and there are various supplementary energy and service charges.

luxury–expensive

The **Ocean Club Golf and Tennis Resort**, on the north side of Paradise Island (✆ 326 2501, ✆ 363 2424, US toll free ✆ (1 800) 321 3000) has the finest setting in the area, with its 71 villas with their own jacuzzi and rooms on either side of the charming main courtyard laid with coral flagstones, sprouting with small palms, a fountain and pool and gingerbread trimmings. In the luxuriant gardens are the tennis courts and swimming-pool, and a walkway leading down to the resurrected French cloister. All mod cons, cable TV, beach nearby.

One of the most attractive hotels on Cable Beach is the couples-only **Sandals Royal Bahamian** (✆ 327 6400, ✆ 327 1894, US toll free ✆ (1 800) 543 4300), with a neoclassical façade dressed in Nassau pink on the outside. But there is also 20th-century comfort in the satellite television, health spa, weights and cabaret. 170 rooms and villas linked by coral paving stones in the manicured garden, private beach. If you like all the activity of a humming casino hotel on the beach you can try the huge **Marriott-Crystal Palace** (✆ 327 6200, ✆ 327 6459, US toll free ✆ (1 800) 222 7466), with its five towers of pastel pink, lavender and fuchsia (it looks spectacular at night when it is all lit up). It is vast, as bright inside as out, with 860 rooms, eight restaurants, 24-hour room service, endless activities, waterslide, beached ship bar. Alternatively, the **Atlantis Resort and Casino** (✆ 363 3000, ✆ 363 3524) is a vast complex with so many facilities that some guests never venture outside. It is home to the world's largest outdoor aquarium, with sting-rays, sharks and rare tropical fish, set in a 14-acre waterscape, complete with waterfalls, lagoons and a quarter-mile long Lazy River Ride for tubing. It has 1085 rooms and 62 suites, 12 restaurants, 8 bars, casino and numerous activities, including an ocean-front 18-hole golf course. A new $350 million development is due to open in late 1998, which will double the size of the resort.

Set in its own grand and luxurious landscaped gardens on the south coast of the island is the **South Ocean Hotel** (✆ 362 4391, ✆ 362 4728). The 250 rooms are set in wings around the central great house and there are plenty of sports (there is a golf course) and watersports, including diving, on the beach just across the road. Country club luxury; the hustle of Nassau is miles away. In downtown Nassau the **Graycliff Hotel** on West Hill Street (✆ 322 2796, ✆ 326 6110) has a completely different feel. There is an elegant atmosphere, set in one of the Nassau's magnificent old town houses: downstairs is the restaurant, but on the creaking wooden floors upstairs, behind the breezy screened balconies, and in the explosive walled garden are 14 sumptuous rooms—including Hibiscus, Jasmine and Mandarino, all dressed up in traditional colonial style.

Not far off is the **Buena Vista Hotel,** on Delancy Street (✆ 322 2811, ✉ 322 5811), also set in an old colonial town house. There are just a few rooms upstairs, comfortable and decorated in old style. **Casuarinas of Cable Beach**, PO Box N-4016, Nassau, (✆ 327 8153, ✉ 327 8152, US toll free ✆ (1 800) 327 3012), is reasonably priced if you want to stay at the quieter end of Cable Beach. It is a bit pre-fab, but it is friendly. The rooms are set around the pool and gardens, with air-conditioning and satellite television.

A charming and very low hotel, untypical for the up-beat Bahamas is the **Orange Hill Beach Inn** (✆ 327 7157, ✉ 327 5186). The 32 air-conditioned rooms are quite simple (some have kitchenettes, others full kitchens and all have televisions), standing in a modern block above the pool and garden, just across the road from the beach. But it is the main house, with bar and restaurant which is fun, where everyone meets, to read, swap diving stories and watch videos. Friendly and helpful.

cheap

The **Parthenon Hotel** (✆ 322 2643) on West Street, just out of the downtown area of Nassau, has 18 neat and clean rooms. The best place for cheap accommodation is in Nassau, where there is a number of reasonable guest houses: try the **Diplomat Inn**, 4 Delancy Street (✆ 325 2688), a nice old town-house on the hill in town: kitchen available and bar. **Mignon Guest House** on Market Street in central Nassau (✆ 322 4771) has six air-conditioned rooms. The tourism desk at the airport is also a good source of information about cheap accommodation.

✆ (1 242)–   Eating Out

There are some good restaurants to be found in the islands, and you should look beyond the hotels, which tend to serve standard international fare. Like so many other things in the Bahamas, there is a West Indian lilt, but the accent is also distinctly American. There are the familiar fast-food restaurants such as McDonald's and KFC but also a strong influence from the American South—you will even find *grits* here. The top restaurants serve gourmet food, ingredients imported from the States as well as local fish and seafood, but traditional Caribbean dishes are readily found—rice 'n' peas is peas 'n' rice here—and the Bahamians do a mean seasoned chicken. Goat and tropical vegetables find their way in from the Out Islands and are then served up curried and stewed. *Souse* is a watery stew in which you will find vegetables and odd-looking parts of animals, e.g. 'pig foot'. And the Bahamians make good use of seafood, of the lobsters and crabs (stoned crab and cracked conch), and of the fish that they trawl in the shallows and haul out of the deep, from grouper to kingfish. *Kalik*, named after the cowbells used in the carnival processions, is the beer of the Bahamas and it is quite good—light and quite bitter for a lager, always served chilled.

Nassau has the largest selection of restaurants (many of the best local Bahamian eateries are 'behind the hill'). Most restaurants add service at 15%, 'for your convenience...' Categories are arranged according to the price of a main dish: *expensive*—US$20 and above; *moderate*—between US$10 and $20; *cheap*—US$10 and below.

expensive

The **Graycliff** Restaurant (✆ 322 2796) has a magnificent setting in an old town house on West Hill Street, and serves probably the finest food in Nassau. Before the meal you take cocktails in the drawing room, to a piano accompaniment, and then you move into one of the three dining rooms, candlelit with huge windows and polished wooden floors and tables, air-conditioned inside or on the verandas. It is pleasantly formal for an evening out; the menu is French—*Dover sole à la ciboulette* or grilled spiny lobster *aux deux sauces*. The wine list is like a Bible and to follow you can have a brandy or try an aged Caribbean rum. Not far off is the **Buena Vista** restaurant (✆ 322 2811), also set in a West Indian town house with a large and airy dining room. The cuisine is French and the menu long—Bahamian fish and seafood in creole style, Norwegian salmon, and a speciality of veal with chanterelles and mushrooms.

On Paradise Island the smartest restaurant is the **Café Martinique**, which luxuriates in its sophisticated setting of red deep-pile carpets and patterned wallpaper, over-looking the lagoon. Try *macédonie de poissons* or shrimps in a garlic and herb sauce. 'Jacket required', but they have a stock at the door just in case. It is also known for its Sunday brunch. Back over the channel, in Lakeview Drive off East Bay Street you will find **Sun and...** (✆ 393 1205) in a modern Nassau villa. The tables stand around the courtyard garden, overlooking the fountain and ornamental pool. The menu is French and continental with some Bahamian dishes—*tournedos rossini* with Madeira truffle sauce or roast duck with raspberry sauce. *Closed Mon.*

moderate

There are plenty of touristy spots around town, lively restaurant bars where you can grab a burger and a beer at lunch and hear a band over a more substantial meal in the evening. The best is probably **Green Shutters**, with a pub-style restaurant and saloon bar with studded leather seats and hunting scene table mats. Bangers and mash and fish 'n' chips as well as burgers, quite a lively drinking crowd in the early evening. You might also try **Pick A Dilly** on Parliament Square in the centre of town. Grills, seafood and pastas and of course daiquiris, made with just about every tropical fruit imaginable.

If you would like something a little more Bahamian, there are some great local restaurants. The **Shoal**, on Nassau Street by the Texaco garage, has a classic West Indian setting—an air-conditioned dining room with thick carpets and formica on the walls. And the best in local food—Bahamian broiled crawfish, or stew-fish and johnny cake, all washed down with a *Kalik* beer.

The **Three Queens Restaurant and Lounge** on Wulff Road is also popular with the Bahamians and serves good local fare. You sit on bench seats and will be served superb scorched conch and other traditional West Indian meals such as curry chicken. You can't miss the great-value **23 Delancy Street**, the former residence of the Anglican bishop in the Bahamas; it is pink. And the atmosphere is somewhat less austere than it would have been as a clerical seat. It is a fun bar and restaurant, with a pool table and the sports channel playing on the television and good local food on offer—chicken and fish, steamed conch or curry mutton, or souse. You can always try one of the beach bars if you are travelling around the island.

cheap

If you want to go yet more local, you can find some superb and authentic Bahamian takeaway food in small shacks in Nassau. You should be quite careful at night if you go 'over the hill'. Try the **Dirty's** on Boyd Road or best of all **Rosalee's**, where you are served through an iron grille. The thing to have is a conch snack—conch cracked (beaten and then covered in batter), which usually comes swimming in tomato sauce and with chips. The closest to Paradise Island is **Johnson's** on Shirley Street. At **Bertha's Go-go Ribs** on Mackey Street you can take away ribs cooked in Bertha's secret mellow sauce. You can also get an excellent scorched conch to take away at the stalls near the Crystal Cay bridge.

Bars and Nightlife

You will find that many of the bars around Nassau fill up with sunburnt tourists making whoopee, so if you want something a bit more sophisticated, perhaps a cocktail in colonial surroundings, you might try one of the smarter restaurants. The best is probably the **Rock and Roll Café**, which is set in a huge former private house right above the sand in Cable Beach. There is a good mix of rock and roll and old rock, with a hip crowd of tourists and some locals, barmen and women wear bandanas. Lunch and dinner, but more importantly the bars are open till late; some live music. Otherwise, you can head for a boozy early evening scrum at the **Poop Deck**, above the marina on East Bay Street. It collects a lively crowd of tourists and some locals, testing out their exotic cocktails. **Captain Nemo's** is another lively bar and snack-style restaurant. More tourists on a blow-out and more exotic cocktails. Hip chicks and dudes in sun-glasses (a permanent fixture even at night it seems) gravitate around **Hammerheads** next to the IBM building in the east of town, and you might also try the **Deep End**: MTV and light beer. There are plenty of local bars around the island.

If you feel like going dancing you can try **Roselawn Café** in Parliament Square, **The Ritz**, the **Zoo**, **Enigma** on Bay St, **Club 601** on West Bay St, or the best club **Waterloo** out on East Bay Street, where there are bars and a dance floor set around a pool and garden with statues and balustrades—an easy mix of ages, of locals and tourists, and music from across the Caribbean and the States. There are discotheques, cabaret shows and casinos in the large hotels on Paradise Island and Cable Beach.

Grand Bahama

The tourist area of Freeport/Lucaya is unlike anything else in the Caribbean or the Bahamas. It is visibly American in style, with wide tree-lined boulevards and spacious suburbs, satellite dishes and air-conditioned supermarkets. Freeport/Lucaya is run by a company, the Grand Bahama Port Authority.

The island of Grand Bahama itself is the fourth largest of the Bahamian islands and, with 44,000 inhabitants, its city Freeport has become the second largest in the country. But 40 years ago none of the Freeport/Lucaya area existed. The resort was simply dreamt up and created in the early sixties.

Until 1955 there were no more than 1000 islanders on Grand Bahama, a few lumbermen and fishermen, except during the Civil War and Prohibition, when the village of West End was one of the prime gun- and rum-running centres and had around 400 boats. Otherwise, the islanders scraped a living by catching sponges and cutting wood.

The tourist resort of Freeport was the brainchild of American financier Wallace Groves, to whom the Bahamian government signed over 50,000 acres of land for development as a duty-free port in 1955, with agreements over tax exemptions for 35 years. Industry came—oil refining and bunkering. As tourism boomed the company began to build hotels on the island's magnificent beaches and Freeport/Lucaya took off. The resort sells itself on the ticket of a truly 20th-century cure for your woes—endless watersports by day, and gambling, glitz and cabaret at night.

Getting Around

Within the Freeport/Lucaya area there are **buses**, some of which run beyond the central area to the local villages: Eight Mile Rock, West End and East End. They do not run to the airport, but many hotels have a shuttle service for arriving guests, and buses down to the beach or to the shopping areas. **Taxis** are easily found in the tourist centres and through hotel lobbies or through Freeport Taxi (✆ 352 6666). To hire a taxi by the hour costs $25–30.

Island **tours** to the island's few sights can be arranged (again through any hotel lobby, where they will pick you up) with Executive Tours (✆ 352 8858), Sun Island Tours (✆ 352 4811) or Reef Tours (✆ 373 5880). If you would like to tour by plane, contact Taino Air (✆ 352 8885).

Plenty of **rental cars** are available for a deposit and a steep rental charge ($55–70 per day). Remember to drive on the left. Hire firms, some of which have offices in the hotels, include Avis in Freeport (✆ 352 7675) and at the airport (✆ 352 7666), Hertz (✆ 352 3297), National at the Xanadu Beach (✆ 352 9308) and at the airport (✆ 352 9308), and Star (✆ 352 5953) also at the airport.

Scooters, again steep at around $30 per day or $45 for a two-seater, can be hired at Bowe's in the Grand Bahama Beach Resort (✆ 373 1333) and at all the major resorts.

Beaches

The southern shore of Grand Bahama is ribboned with strips of idyllic white sand interspersed among the coral limestone coast, and the beaches in the Freeport/Lucaya area have become built up with hotels.

best beaches

Silver Point Beach in Lucaya and the **Xanadu Beach**: The most developed and the best for watersports (see p.807–8 for companies).

William's Town: South of Freeport, a cracking beach beyond the tourist hotels, a superb suntrap with casuarina trees down to the sand and with excellent snorkelling and swimming. There are no jetskis or windsurfers for hire there, but you can get a drink and a snack in the town.

Mather Town Beach: Just to the east of Lucaya, a stunning stretch of beach that runs for miles.

Fortune Beach: Off Midshipman Road, south of the Garden of the Groves.

Barbary Beach: The other side of the Lucayan Waterway, more perfect white sand and isolation.

Gold Rock Beach: Can be reached from the Lucayan National Park (no facilities).

Freeport/Lucaya

There are very few sights on the island, but in Freeport you will definitely come across the **International Bazaar**, an odd conglomeration of buildings in imitation of styles from all over the world, from a Japanese arch of welcome to a Turkish bazaar. You can eat and shop here. It feels a little odd and soulless, but most people do not worry because they are on the hunt for bargains. Occasionally there is some entertainment. The real centre of the town of Freeport is **Churchill Square**, near the Port Authority Building, where you should buy groceries if you are catering for yourself.

There is a botanical garden in the area. The **Garden of the Groves** (*✆ 352 4045; open daily except Wed 10–5; adm*) is set in 12 acres of Bahamian greenery laced with lagoons, streams and with a hanging garden at the entrance. The plant species are named.

UNEXSO in the Port Lucaya area is a **diving school**, or perhaps a diving college, where there are courses in diving for beginners and instructors and even in dive medicine. The **Dolphin Experience**, where you can cavort with several bottlenose dolphins who are kept in captivity while being studied, is now in Sanctuary Bay. Learn about dolphin communication. They are eventually to be let back into the wild if they wish to go. **Port Lucaya** is a shopping complex and marina.

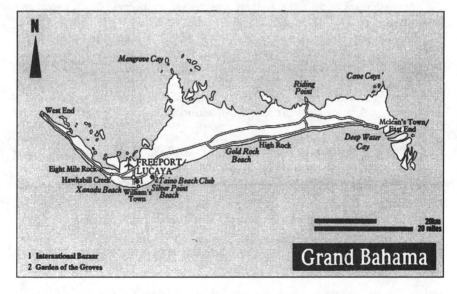

Beyond Freeport to the east you come into the pine barren, endless pine forest with just a few local towns which are a bit more typical of the rest of the Bahamas and where you can usually get a meal or a drink. At the **Lucayan National Park and Caverns**, trails lead through the scrub to a couple of limestone sinkholes, Ben's Cave and Burial Mound Cave. Beyond the park you come to the old Gold Rock missile tracking station, the first down-orbit of Cape Canaveral, and eventually the road comes to McLean's Town at the east end.

To the west of Freeport is Hawksbill Creek, the centre of Grand Bahama industry, where the liners and tankers put in. The town of Eight-Mile Rock is strung along 8 miles of coral shoreline and you will see some of the attractive old Bahamian homes that were here before the recent concrete development. At West End you can still see the remnants of the old warehouses and decaying piers from the days of Prohibition, where the boats tied up before making the dash over to the coast of Florida loaded up with liquor.

✆ *(1 242)–*

Where to Stay
expensive

If you like a large and active resort, try low-rise **Princess Country Club** (✆ 352 6721, ✆ 352 6842, ✆ (1 800) 223 1818) in Freeport, across the road from the International Bazaar and the Moorish casino. It hums: with 565 rooms, five dining rooms, multiple jacuzzis, golf, nightclub. If you want something a little more tranquil, try the adjacent **Princess Tower** (✆ 352 9661). Both are part of the **Bahamas Princess Resort and Casino**, set on 2500 acres of tropical grounds, with extensive facilities including 12 tennis courts, two 18-hole championship golf courses, a full range of watersports, children's activities, and good restaurants.

If you would prefer to be on the beach itself, try the **Clarion Atlantik Beach and Golf Resort**, PO Box F-42500 (✆373 1066, ✆ 373 6659), on Lucaya Beach, whose programme of activities includes golf, watersports, tennis, and windsurfing, with its own shopping arcade and restaurants. Alternatively, the **Lucayan Beach Resort and Casino** (✆ 373 7777, ✆ 373 2826, US toll free ✆ (1 800) 772 1227) boasts a great location, opening on to a two-mile stretch of white beach, and offers a full range of facilities: 248 rooms, endless watersports, tennis, fishing, restaurants, shopping arcades. **Grand Bahama/ Flamingo Beach Resort** (✆ 373 1333, ✆ 373 2396), renovated in 1996, offers 500 rooms, most with private balconies, in a good location just across from the Port Lucaya Marketplace. Facilities include tennis courts, swimming pool, sailing, children's playground, restaurants.

moderate

Port Lucaya Resort and Yacht Club (✆ 373 6618, ✆ 373 6652) has its own marina with slips for 50 boats; a series of two-storey buildings surround the Olympic-size swimming pool, jacuzzi and landscaped garden. **Pelican Bay** (✆ 373 9550, ✆ 373 9551), next to Port Lucaya Marketplace, has 48 rooms, with all mod cons, private balcony, hot tub and pool bar. Activities include safaris and ocean kayaking. The **Bell Channel Inn**, PO Box F-3817 (✆ 373 1053, ✆ 373 2886), has 32 comfortable air-conditioned rooms with televisions in a modern block in the town area.

Next to the Bell Channel is the **Victoria Inn**, PO Box F-1261 (✆ 373 3040, US toll free ✆ (1 800) 451 8891), which has 40 rooms in a semi-circle around a pool. All modern comforts, cable television and telephones. You could also try the **Royal Islander**, PO Box F-42549 (✆ 351 6000, ✆ 351 3546), near the International Bazaar.

✆ *(1 242)–*   **Eating Out**

There is a quite a variety of restaurants in Freeport/Lucaya (many of them in the International Bazaar, of course). There is also a number of places to eat out on the beaches during the day. Remember that service at 10–15% will be added to your bill.

Categories are arranged according to the price of a main dish: *expensive*—US$20 and above; *moderate*—between US$10 and $20; *cheap*—US$10 and below.

expensive–moderate

The **Stoned Crab** (✆ 373 1442) is a popular restaurant on the seafront on Taino Beach, to the east of Freeport/Lucaya, with a breezy terrace and an air-conditioned dining room beneath a pyramid roof. Lobster *al pesto* and other exotic seafood creations, a pleasant place for a dinner for two.

Ruby Swiss (✆ 352 8507) can be found near the International Bazaar and has a subdued, candlelit setting in a modern building. The menu is European—seafood *fettuccine au Pernod* or coconut-fried shrimp. Two popular restaurants are **Pier One** (✆ 352 6674), on stilts in Freeport Harbour, where you can get seafood and fish specialities, and the **Captain's Charthouse** (✆ 373 3900), on East Sunrise and Coral Road, good for a grouper *menuire* or a lobster scampi.

moderate

The **Taino Beach Surfside Restaurant and Lounge** has an easy, slightly rustic air right above the beach, its ceiling hung with driftwood, nets and blown-up puffer fish. It serves seafood: fried shrimps and steamed grouper. (On the beach nearby you can get an excellent seasoned conch cooked to order; on the call of a conch shell, no less, *cheap*.) **Scorpio**, on Explorer's Way, is a good stop for a game of pool and a local meal (eat in or takeaway). **Freddy's Place** (✆ 352 2931) in the village of Hunters is a favourite with the Bahamians, serving conch, snappers and broiled lobster. Or try **Captain Kenny's** (✆ 351 4759) near the International Bazaar. At Smith's Point is **Outrigger's** (✆ 373 4811), where you can get a well-priced beachside meal, scorched conch or steamed grouper.

cheap

And you can get the best of island food at **Mama Flo's White Wave Club**—a classic rum shop, serving fried fish and chicken dinner. You can have a simple burger and a beer at **Le Beach Shack Sand Bar** on Mather Town Beach. At West End you can get an excellent chicken at the **Chicken Nest**.

The Out Islands

The Out Islands comprise the Bahamian out-islands and their hundreds of cays and sandbars that just make it above the waves. They leave the casinos and cabarets of New Providence and Grand Bahama far behind. Instead you will find a more traditional Bahamas—pretty and well-kept houses painted bright colours with shingle roofs, set in gardens of tropical flowers and surrounded by white picket fences.

Houses are mostly built in concrete now, but in the remoter islands you will still just see poorer clay houses with thatched roofs and little ovens built away from the house. In the most barren areas, where the topsoil is so thin that it cannot support much growth, the islanders have developed a system of planting in holes in the ground. They make a compost in there in which they plant. Traditionally self-sufficient and more remote from the capital than the few miles of sea would imply, the Out Islands are now populated in many cases with older folk, as the younger generations have gone off to Nassau in search of work.

Scattered in splinters and shards over the *baja-mar*, most of the islands rise no more than 100ft from the sea. Many are just a couple of miles wide, but they can stretch for a hundred miles. On their sheltered coastlines the beaches are superb—they descend gently into shallows of warm and crystal clear water, rising again as sandbars a few hundred yards offshore before descending into deep green or blue. Fly over them and the views are fantastic—back on land you can walk for miles and hardly see a soul.

As travellers begin to look beyond the glitz and high-rise tourism of Nassau and Freeport/ Lucaya, the Out Islands are steadily beginning to open up. A few of the islands have developed around their pretty waterfront towns and there are a few small and very low key retreats on isolated cays, ideal for a break from the humdrum in wonderful, seemingly uncharted territory.

But besides the superb natural surroundings and the gentle island lifestyle, certain islands have gained renown for their sports—Bimini is known for its deep-sea fishing and the Abacos and the Exumas have superb sailing. Andros has recently gained a reputation as a dive-site. In the east is San Salvador, supposedly Columbus's first landfall in the New World. Alternatively, you may just want to get away to the tranquillity of a tropical island idyll.

Getting There and Around

Most of the Out Islands are served by once- or twice-daily flights from Nassau (the Abacos are also served from Freeport), but a few have direct flights from the US mainland: Marsh Harbour and Treasure Cay (both in **the Abacos**) have flights from Miami, Fort Lauderdale, Orlando, Tampa and West Palm Beach; Governor's Harbour (**Eleuthera**) and **Bimini** are served from Miami and Fort Lauderdale; George Town in **the Exumas** from Miami, Fort Lauderdale and Key West; and **Andros** from Miami. Airlines include American Eagle (US and Bahamas toll free ✆ (1 800) 433 7300) and Gulf Stream (US ✆ (305) 871 1200, toll free ✆ (1 800) 992 8532).

In the **Out Islands** there are rarely any buses, but you can often catch a pick-up. Activity tends to centre around the arrival of the boat or the plane and so there are usually people around. Alternatively, hitch. It is perhaps polite to offer something towards petrol, though it usually won't be accepted. People often walk or go by boat as much as they travel by car. **Taxis**, either boats or cars, are usually available at all the main airstrips. If not, ask around and one will either be found or you will be offered a lift by someone going your way. The taxi drivers often also operate as tour guides around the islands and they will be happy to take you out for about $25 per hour for a full car. **Hire cars** and **boats** are available in the larger resorts and tend to be expensive, as are **scooters**. **Bicycles** are also on hire in many places. If you are sailing by and want to stop in for a meal, many restaurants can be called up on VHF channel 16.

The Abacos

In the northeast of the Bahamian archipelago are the Abaco Islands and their offshore cays, stretched in a 140-mile curve around the east of Grand Bahama. They have a population of over 11,000 and outside the two major resorts of Nassau and Freeport they are the most developed area of the Bahamas. There are two main areas, each served by an airport, to which a string of smaller islands is linked by water-taxi: Marsh Harbour in the south with nearby Hope Town on Elbow Cay; and farther north Treasure Cay and Green Turtle Cay. Walker's Cay, which has its own airstrip, is a self-contained resort 10 miles off Little Abaco Island in the far northwest of the island group. The Abacos are very popular with sailors and have about half of the 60 marinas in the Bahamas.

Marsh Harbour, long the site of a lumbering industry as well as the Abacos' traditional lifeline of shipbuilding, is the third largest town in the Bahamas. As well as building ships, the islanders traditionally helped to destroy them with their other invisible industry, 'wrecking', in which they would clean up after passing ships had been washed on to the reefs. Eventually things were regularized when the lighthouse at Hope Town was built in the 1830s, despite the islanders' best efforts at sabotage. The east coast of Great Abaco (in the south) is fringed by a string of cays, many of which were settled, along with the mainland, by loyalists following the American War of Independence. These islands are still the focus of much of Abaco life. Abaconian 'loyalty' came to the fore once again as the Bahamas headed towards Independence in 1973, when there was a movement to remain part of Britain rather than go along with Nassau.

Marsh Harbour is set on a north-facing cove about midway down Great Abaco. It is a modern town and has local shops and tourist restaurants and there are many vacation villas around the area. Above the town stand the yellow turrets of the house of Dr Evans Cottman, author of *Out Island Doctor*. From here, ferries will take you out to the other islands. There is a tourist information office in the Percy Archer building in town. There are two underwater parks off the Marsh Harbour area, at Sandy Cay in the south and at Fowl Cay next to Man O' War Cay.

Elbow Cay and its very attractive settlement of **Hope Town** are easily reached from Marsh Harbour. There is a charming and slow atmosphere here, with pretty clapboard houses and gardens festooned with blooms and surrounded by white picket fences. Hope Town is best known for the 120ft pink and white lighthouse that stands above the town. The **Wyannie Malone Historical Museum,** restored as it was in the last century, gives a good idea of the old-time life of the Abaconians right down to the rocking chair and the broom-making press. There are bicycles, and golf carts, for hire (© 366 0332) to explore the ribbon of land that leads north and south of the town.

Man O' War Cay has a slightly unreal feel about it, untypical of the Bahamas. The small community of 250 is almost entirely white—until Independence, the islanders would demand that black Bahamians left the island at sundown. They are proud and polite, and their island, one of the traditional boat-building areas of the Abacos, is clearly prosperous. No alcohol is sold on the island and there is just one hotel and a couple of places to eat, including Schooner's Landing. You will still see some of the traditional hulls taking shape in the dock-yards. Offshore, Sandy Cay is excellent for snorkelling.

Great Guana Cay, with a population of around 100, is visited principally for its fantastic 7 miles of beach, where there is excellent swimming and snorkelling, and for its drink, the *Guana Grabber*, a concoction of rums and juices. You can also swim with the dolphins.

Back on the main island, about 30 miles northeast of Marsh Harbour is the resort area of **Treasure Cay** and the surrounding settlements. Despite the name, which implies an island, it is set on a peninsula of Great Abaco, overlooking a fantastic 3-mile beach.

A couple of miles offshore is **Green Turtle Cay**, 2 miles by 4, where the town of New Plymouth is situated—more clapboard houses with gingerbread fretwork set in flowering gardens, and on the ocean shore another superb beach. The **Albert Lowe Museum** is in a Victorian home in the town and it traces the history of the island back to the loyalists. Model boats built by Albert Lowe himself are on view alongside works by his artist son, Alton. There are Boston Whalers in which you can explore the smaller islands around.

Walker's Cay, the most northerly point in the Bahamas, has been a game-fishing haunt since 1939.

© (1 242)–   ***Where to Stay***

In **Marsh Harbour** on Great Abaco there is a string of hotels. The **Abaco Beach Resort and Boat Harbour**, PO Box 511 (*©* 367 2158, *@* 367 2819, US toll free *©* (1 800) 468 4799; *expensive*) is the most upbeat and active. It has about 80 rooms in blocks over-looking the pool and the passable beach, with tennis and watersports, boat rental, evening entertainment. Another good place to stay is the **Abaco Towns by the Sea**, PO Box 486 (*©* 367 2221, *@* 367 2227, US toll free *©* (1 800) 468 9876; *expensive*), a low-key resort with the 68 villas hidden in the hibiscus, casuarina pines and palms between the sea of Abaco and Marsh Harbour. The villas are dressed up in high Caribbean pastel and are well equipped with full kitchens and terraces. All the watersports are on offer and there is a central swimming pool.

The **Conch Inn Resort** and marina, PO Box 434 (*©* 367 2800, *@* 367 2980; *moderate*) has just 10 rooms in a sandy palm garden in Marsh Harbour. Quite simple but comfortable enough and with a friendly crowd passing through; air-conditioned, pool and all the sports are available nearby. If you want a **cheaper** place to stay, try the **Ambassador's Inn Hotel**, PO Box 484 (*©* 367 2022; *cheap*); classic West Indian pre-fab air-conditioned comfort. And finally there is the **Traveller's Rest** in town, in a modern house in a residential street of Marsh Harbour, with just four rooms; air-conditioned, with kitchen facilities and satellite television.

To the south of Marsh Harbour you will find **Casuarina Point**, PO Box AB-20092 (*©/@* 366 2150; *moderate*). The rooms are in a simple wooden house above a lagoon—comfortable with balconies, an original central bar and dining room with walls hung with fishing nets. Some bonefishing, eco-opportunities.

On **Elbow Cay**, a 20-minute ferry ride from Marsh Harbour, you will find isolated beach-club comfort in the **Sea Spray Resort** and Villas, White Sound (✆ 366 0065, ✉ 366 0383; *moderate*), set between the Sea of Abaco and the Atlantic. Just five clapboard villas in pretty pastel colours overlooking the beach. Another good spot on Elbow Cay is the **Abaco Inn** (✆ 366 0133, ✉ 366 0113, US toll free ✆ (1 800) 327 0787; *moderate*), a small retreat just out of Hope Town. There are 12 rooms, standing among the windswept greenery above the beach, each with a hammock on its private terrace. Pool, tennis, and watersports. Rooms have a full kitchen. In **Hope Town** itself you will find **Hope Town Harbour Lodge** (✆ 366 0095, ✉ 366 0286, US toll free ✆ (1 800) 316 7844; *moderate*). There are 21 rooms in this house, dressed in pastel grey and pink, with a lovely view over the harbour, and in cottages on the north shore. Good beach, bar filled with ship-wreckage, friendly and fun atmosphere.

There is also a number of villas around the town where you can stay, some set in the pretty clapboard houses of old Bahamas, and there are two other excellent places to stay: **Hope Town Hideaways** (✆/✉ 366 0224; *expensive–moderate*), which are just a small collection of four villas set in a supreme garden of tropical blooms. Comfortable, with complete kitchens and a deck out front. An excellent hideaway as the name suggests.

Another appealing retreat is the **Club Soleil Resort** nearby (✆ 366 0003, ✉ 366 0254; *moderate*). Just six rooms with pastel decoration; minibars, television and video, and outside a pool with sunning decks surrounded by flowers. On **Man O' War Cay** there are rooms at the **Schooner's Landing Resort** (✆ 365 6072; *expensive*). The **Guana Beach Club Resort**, PO Box 474 (✆ 359 6194, ✉ 367 3590; *moderate*), is another retreat on an isolated cay off the main island. Just 15 rooms standing above the beach (all 7 miles of it), with windsurfers and small sailboats on offer.

A short ferry trip offshore at **Treasure Cay** is **Green Turtle Cay**, where you will find the **Green Turtle Club and Marina** (✆ 365 4271, ✉ 365 4272, US toll free ✆ (1 800) 327 0787; *moderate*), a low-key club-style hotel on the waterfront. The hotel rings with colonial echoes in the decoration and hardwood floors and dark-stained antique-style beds and overhead fans. Rooms and villas look over the harbour, but there are beaches a few minutes' walk away. A trusty retreat. The **Bluff House Club and Marina** (✆ 365 4247, ✉ 365 4248; *moderate*) stands above the sea and beach on a cliff: 25 air-conditioned rooms in a block and in suites and villas. Tennis, pool and bar and a library with a view.

A charming place to stay is the **New Plymouth Club and Inn** (✆ 365 4161, ✉ 365 4138; *moderate*), which is in one of New Plymouth's picture-postcard town houses. The atmosphere of the inn fits the colonial elegance of the building itself. Low-key and comfortable in an enchanting gingerbread setting. Just nine rooms in old-time Bahamian style, some sports, beaches nearby, but a congenial atmosphere centred on relaxing on the pool terrace or at the Galleon Bar. Finally at the northwestern limit of the Abaco Cays you will find a very comfortable hotel on Walker's Cay. The **Walker's Cay Hotel and Marina** (✆ in Miami 352 5252, ✆ (305) 359 1414, US toll free ✆ (1

800) 432 2092; *expensive–moderate*) is set on its own 100-acre island, and is particularly popular for deep-sea fishing, for which it holds many records. There are 62 rooms and two restaurants and the island has its own airstrip for easy access. Also scuba diving, tennis and a friendly crowd passing through the marina.

© (1 242)–   ***Eating Out***

There is a clutch of nice restaurants in Marsh Harbour where you will find a crowd of people onshore from the yachts eating and drinking. **Mangoes** (© 367 2366, VHF channel 16; *moderate*) has a charming setting on the harbour waterfront, where you dine on the veranda or in the air-conditioned interior. Local and international fare such as crawfish and pizzas. **Wally's** (*moderate*) also has a good setting, in a classic gingerbread house on Bay Street. Bahamian food and some concessions to continental style—seafood fritters followed by catch of the day in a local sauce—lively, sometimes live music in the evenings. The **Bay View** (*moderate*) has a good setting on a pink and green deck above the harbour—seafood and steaks. The **Jib Room**, across the harbour (*moderate*), is also popular, known for its rib night on Wednesdays. You will find the best in local cuisine, seafood and chicken and fish dishes at **Mother Merle's Fish Net** in Dundas Town; very much a family restaurant, set in a large wooden house. The **Golden Grouper** in Dove Plaza is another popular spot in Marsh Harbour for a local meal, including a stew or a souse. You might also try **Cynthia's Kitchen** which offers turtle steaks and peas 'n' rice, eaten in or taken away. You can grab a beer with a lively crowd of yachties at **Below Deck** and there is dancing to all the Caribbean rhythms at the **New Oasis Club** in Dundas Town. **Touch of Class** is a discotheque in Treasure Cay.

In **Elbow Cay** a number of lively restaurants overlook the harbour. The finest dining can be found at the hotels, try the Club Soleil and Hope Town Harbour Lodge, both of which serve international fare. International dishes and a sailing crowd can be found at **Cap'n Jack's**, a bright pink and white house on the waterfront—ribs, wings and fritters as well as some more substantial platters, moderate. Another popular gathering place is **Harbour's Edge**, where you can get a game of pool and a wetsuit for your beer, local fare, but some concessions to stateside burgers and steaks. Both have some entertainment at the weekends.

In **Green Turtle Cay** you will get a fine meal at the **Captain's Table** in the old-time Bahamian setting of the New Plymouth Inn. You start off with cocktails at the bar and then retreat to the dining room for grilled local catch, crawfish or rack of lamb with local vegetables. **Roosters Rest** has good local food—souse or a stew goat as well as cracked conch; and you can get other Bahamian specialities, perhaps a plate of peas 'n' rice with shrimps at **Laurie's Kitchen**.

The Berry Islands

The Berry islands are scattered over 40 miles of the Great Bahama Bank to the northwest of Nassau, en route from the capital to the American mainland and a regular stop-off for the cruise ships and yachts. A population of shorebirds (noddies and terns) and just 500 people is scattered across the islands, mainly living in Bullock's Harbour on Great Harbour Cay in the north. Many of the islands are private estates (Wallace Groves of Freeport fame owns Little Whale Cay). There are airstrips in Great Harbour Cay and Chub Cay. **Diving** in the nearby Tongue of the Ocean is superb, and is available through Chub Cay Undersea Adventures (US ✆ (305) 763 2188). Fishing is excellent, also from Chub Cay.

✆ *(1 242)–*   **Where to Stay and Eat**

The **Great Harbour Cay Club** (US ✆ 313 689 1580, 🖅 689 1594, US toll free ✆ (1 800) 343 7256; *expensive–moderate*) has just 16 rooms in beachfront villas. The hotel also services the passing yachts and so there is plenty of activity and an easygoing feel. Sports for those not sailing include tennis, a 9-hole golf course and bicycles. The **Tamboo Club** attached to the hotel is probably the best bet for a meal; you dine on the waterfront on ribs and chicken dishes. **Basil's** bar and restaurant catches a crowd of yachties who are making whoopee either at the very beginning or end of their trip. Burgers and snacks and plenty of beer.

At the other end of the Berry Islands is the **Chub Cay Club** (✆ 325 1490, 🖅 322 5199, US res ✆ (1 800) 662 8555; *expensive–moderate*), which also sees a number of yachts passing through. There are 15 rooms overlooking the swimming-pool. Also tennis and of course excellent fishing and diving.

Bimini

The string of the Bimini Islands, famed as the game-fishing capital of the world, are the westernmost of the Bahamian islands and they lie a bare 50 miles from downtown Miami. In between the two is the Gulf Stream, which has carved out its path over the millennia, and it is here that the biggest marlin and giant tuna are to be found. In the past the islands have been rich and raw—drug money poured through at one stage not long ago (Bimini is one of the traditional staging posts en route to the States), and it would become quite riotous as fishermen, fresh from the day's fight on the seas, would return and booze at night. Bimini is the setting of the novel *Islands in the Stream* by Ernest Hemingway, who visited often in the thirties. It is all a bit tamer now, and it is a pretty nice spot for a few days, though it is expensive. It can get quite lively at the weekends when the Florida vacationers drop in for a break.

South Bimini was one of Ponce de León's stop-offs on his hunt for the Fountain of Youth, and he supposedly came here in 1513 before discovering Florida. The northern island is the main fishing haunt. The inner coastline around Alice Town is furred with marinas, and all the bars are inland. Most of the islanders live in Bailey Town on the King's Highway leading north. A superb white-sand beach runs along the west coast of the island. You will find watersports at the Anchorage and if you want to be a little more isolated you can go to Paradise Beach and Radio Beach farther north. There is a **museum** (*adm free*) devoted to Hemingway in the Compleat Angler Hotel; the walls are hung with pictures of the great man showing off his catches and there are illustrations and excerpts from the *Old Man and the Sea* as well as general fishing memorabilia. Cays to the south of Bimini include Gun Cay and Cat Cay, a private club, founded in the 1930s. There is a bank in Alice Town (*open Mon–Fri 9–1*). **Pan Am Air Bridge** (✆ (1 800) 424 2557) serves the islands (twice daily from Miami and Paradise Island) and there is an airstrip on South Bimini which operates during daylight hours. There are also many marinas on the islands.

Deep-sea fishing is obviously the biggest sport on the island and marinas include the Bimini Big Game Fishing Club (✆ 347 2391), the Blue Water Resort (✆ 347 2166) and Weech's Bimini Dock (✆ 347 2028) in Alice Town.

Bimini holds a host of **fishing tournaments** through the year, including the March Hemingway Billfish Tournament and the April Championship Billfish Tournament (both part of the Bahamas Billfish Championship). In June the Bimini Big Game Fishing Club holds the Blue Marlin Tournament and in July is the Jimmy Albury Blue Marlin Tournament. Two all-fish tournaments are held in August and there are competitions to catch wahoo in November.

Diving is another growing sport on Bimini. Contact Bimini Undersea Adventures (USA ✆ (305) 736 2188). Dive-sites include the reef to the west of the island and a wreck known as the concrete ship.

✆ *(1 242)–*   ## Where to Stay and Eat

The most modern and comfortable hotel is the **Bimini Big Game Fishing Club**, PO Box 669 (✆ 809 347 3391, US toll free ✆ (1 800) 327 4149; *expensive–moderate*) on the sheltered shore of Alice Town, North Bimini. There are 49 rooms overlooking the central pool in the courtyard; diving, and endless fishing packages. The **Bimini Blue Water Resort**, PO Box 601 (✆ 347 2166, ✉ 347 2293; *moderate*) also in Alice Town, has a bit more traditional island charm with an attractive old timber-frame house and an ocean view towards Miami and the sunset. There are 12 air-conditioned rooms in suites and in a cottage. Close to all the activity of the town.

The **Compleat Angler** (✆/✉ 347 2122; *moderate–cheap*) also offers the best in Bimini charm, just a few rooms in one of the island's classic buildings. The interior is lined with wood and the walls are strung with nauticalia (and the exhibits of the Hemingway Museum). Rooms are quite simple, with a couple of good bars downstairs, which can get quite lively, and evening entertainment in season. You can find **cheaper** rooms at **Weech's Marina** (✆ 347 2028), located on the dock, but the cheapest deal is at **Brown's Hotel**, just up from the seaplane terminal.

You will find a string of **restaurants** and **bars** in Alice Town in North Bimini, none of them that cheap. Elsewhere you will be dependent on the hotels. At the **Red Lion Pub** (*moderate*) you sit in a wooden-walled dining room, where a lively crowd collects, boozing and watching the television while they tuck into baked turtle or a platterful of shrimps in fluffy batter. The **Fisherman's Paradise** (*moderate*) is a classic West Indian restaurant, air-conditioned and modern and a liming point for a few locals. Chicken or fish.

Activity at the **Island Bar** centres around the pool table—loud, and quite fun, judging by all the satisfied customers who have left their calling cards attached to the beams. The **Sand Bar** is lower-key and good for a beer or two; set in a small shack with sand on the floor. The **Compleat Angler** bar is also excellent, particularly when they have live music—the whole town stops in for a beer and a dance.

At 100 miles by 40, Andros is the largest island in the Bahamas, and it has a population of 8400, the third largest. It lies just 20 miles from New Providence, across the Tongue of the Ocean, a 6000ft trench that cuts into the Great Bahama Bank. The island is flat and crossed in places by 'bights' (channels), and inland there are many 'blue holes'. It is so low that parts of it are mangrove flats, forested swamp impenetrable except to terns, whistling tree ducks, the island's 6ft iguana and the island gremlin, the *chickcharnie*. This tiny character supposedly has three fingers, three toes, red eyes and hangs upside-down in trees, and he has been attributed with a mischievous turn of mind if you do not believe in him. The island was first settled by loyalists who grew cotton, and later sponges and sisal (for rope) were the mainstays of the economy. In recent years the government has encouraged agriculture and farming of livestock on Andros. The settlements are scattered along the east coast, where there are superb, pristine beaches. There are airports at San Andros and Andros Town on the northern island, at Moxey Town on Mangrove Cay and Congo Town on the southern island.

A mile off the island's eastern shore the sea floor drops sheer for 6000ft into the Tongue of the Ocean. On its submarine 'wall' is the third largest barrier reef in the world, 140 miles of corals and sponges plied by surgeonfish, soldierfish and angelfish. **Diving** is possible at a number of resorts on the island, including the **Small Hope Bay Lodge** just north of Andros Town (✆ 368 2014) and **Andros Undersea Adventures** near San Andros in the north (USA ✆ (305) 736 2188). **Windsurfers** and limited other watersports are available through the hotels. Bone-fishing, casting in the shallow sandy flats, is reputed to be some of the best in the world.

✆ (1 242)–   ***Where to Stay and Eat***

In **Nicholl's Town** near San Andros the most comfortable place to stay is the **Conch Sound Resort Inn**, PO Box 23029 (✆ 329 2060; *moderate*). It is a bit pre-fab, but friendly, just six rooms with satellite television and ceiling fans or air-conditioning. Another retreat is the **Andros Beach Hotel** (✆ 329 2582; *moderate–cheap*), with 24 simple rooms on a superb strip of sand. Sports include scuba and of course fishing. At **Donna Lee's Guest House** (✆ 329 2194; *cheap*) there are 12 rooms which are within a short walk of the beach.

All the hotels have restaurants that double as bars for the tourists and the locals; mostly native fare and seafood—conch fritters followed by grilled local catch, hauled in that afternoon, perhaps by you. **Lilley's Bar** (*moderate–cheap*) is a local favourite, as is **Rumours** (*moderate*), between Nicholl's Town and San Andros, where there is live music and dancing in the evenings.

At **Fresh Creek** the **Lighthouse Yacht Club** (✆ 368 2305, ✉ 368 2300; *moderate*) is centred around sailing and there is a small marina there. There are 20 rooms and villas on the beach and watersports including scuba and fishing, and restaurant over-looking the marina. A charming small hotel, the **Small Hope Bay Lodge** (✆ 368 2014, ✉ 368 2015, US toll free ✆ (1 800) 223 6961; *expensive*), a classic Caribbean retreat, with a speciality in diving. There are just 20 rooms, built of local coral rock and island pine wood, each overlooking the sand and the sea. The atmosphere is extremely low-key, particularly as most people have been out diving all day and are building up their strength for the following day's activity. There is an all-inclusive rate. You can find a cheaper rate at the **Chickcharnie Hotel** (✆ 368 2025; *moderate–cheap*) on the waterfront; eight rooms and a restaurant (*cheap*). If you want a local meal in the area, you can try the **Land Mark Restaurant**, where you can pick up some peas 'n' rice or a curry goat.

Not far off, the **Cargill Creek Lodge** (✆ 329 5129, ✉ 329 5046, US ✆ (1 800) 942 6799; *expensive*) specializes in fishing and has a fleet of boats to take you off to the deep waters and the bonefishing flats. Also diving. There is a pool and central sunning area. The air-conditioned rooms look out to sea and have televisions. Also try the **Andros Island Bonefish Club** (✆/✉ 329 5167), which offers all-inclusive packages for fishermen.

A good local restaurant in this area is the **Gateway Restaurant and Bar**, where you can get a grilled fish or a burger. In **Mangrove Cay** you can stay quite cheaply at the **Mangrove Beach Hotel and Resort** (✆ 369 0004; *moderate–cheap*), 20 rooms in a modern block among the palms right on the beach. **Cool Breeze Cottages** (✆ 329 4465; *cheap*) are just four cottages on the beach.

On **South Andros** you will find one of the Bahamas' more luxurious hotels, the **Emerald Palms by the Sea** (✆ 329 4461, ✉ 329 4467, US res ✆ (1 800) 835 1018; *moderate*). High Caribbean comfort on the 5-mile, palm-backed ocean-front—just 20 rooms with four-poster beds and muslin netting, also a fine restaurant. Sports include tennis, windsurfing, small sailing boats and scuba, or just sunning by the freshwater pool with a book from the library.

For a *cheap* room you can try the **Royal Palm Lodge** (✆ 329 4608), or the **Rahming Guest House**. **Dina's** (*cheap*) offers good native food, as does the **L & M Restaurant** (*moderate–cheap*).

Eleuthera

Eleuthera was the first of the Bahamas to be settled, when the company of Eleutherian Adventurers arrived in 1648, escaping religious persecution in Bermuda and England. They called their island *Eleutheria* after the Greek word for freedom. The settlement was quickly overtaken by New Providence (about 50 miles to the east), but Eleuthera has flourished steadily, helped by an influx of loyalists in the 1780s, making a living from agriculture and the sea. Today Eleuthera is among the most developed of the Out Islands with regard to tourism.

The island is 100 miles long and barely more than 2 miles wide, and on its sheltered side the beaches and sandbars stretch for tens of miles into the jade-green water. On the ocean side the waves barrel in, and are big enough to surf on. Eleuthera is quite fertile, traditionally a farming area, nowadays mainly producing pineapples and tomatoes, though you will still see grain silos along the road.

There are three airstrips: North Eleuthera which serves the north of the island and the offshore islands of Harbour Island and Spanish Wells, Governor's Harbour which serves the centre of the island, and Rock Sound for the south. Make sure to get off at the correct one because it can be a 100-mile drive to the other end of the island. There is a tourist information office in Governor's Harbour (© 332 2142) and Harbour Island (© 333 2261).

Harbour Island with its inhabitants, the 'Brilanders', was once the second most prosperous place in the Bahamas after Nassau, but the docks are quiet now compared with when the ship-building industry was at its height. Dunmore Town is a pretty, slumberstruck village that lines the protected shore of the island—sugary pink gingerbread houses sit snug behind the white picket fences as they always have, only now they are accompanied by satellite dishes. Some of the hotels are set in these old antique houses and so they are quaint and comfortable. The islanders are laid back, and only too happy for you to join in their musings. The famous Pink Beach, miles of sand a delicate shade of pink, is on the ocean side of the island.

Another offshore island close by, **Spanish Wells**, is almost as picturesque, and has the beaches to match Harbour Island, but it has a different feel altogether. The islanders are among the richest in the Bahamas because of the fishing industry. They fish mainly for lobster or craw fish, sailing off for three weeks at a time in their refrigerated boats, scouring the Bahamian waters as far south as Cuba, reaping vast profits. They reappear and make whoopee back home before setting off again a couple of weeks later.

But the island, just three miles long and less than a mile across, has an untypical feel for the Bahamas because there are very few black faces. Until quite recently black Bahamians, even the doctor, would be asked to leave the island at sunset.

On the main island of **North Eleuthera** you can visit Preacher's Cave, where the early settlers are supposed to have worshipped. Current Cut is a popular dive at the change of the tide because the water races through it at around seven knots. Heading south past Gregory Town, a fishing village, you come to the 'Glass Window' (named after a natural bridge that has collapsed), where the difference between the ocean and the protected leeward coast is most clearly visible). At Hatchet Bay there is a more extensive underground cave system, which culminates in a clifftop 70ft above the sea.

Governor's Harbour is another tired town of timber houses set on the curve of Cupid's Bay, now overlooked by the island's Club Med. Not far off, the Windermere Island Club is one of the Bahamas' most exclusive resorts, favoured by royalty from the world over. **Rock Sound** is the largest settlement on Eleuthera and a good place to stock up, but still little more than a village of fading gingerbread houses above the bay. Not far off is one of Eleuthera's famous 'Blue Holes', an inland lake connected to the ocean deep underwater.

Watersports (windsurfers, dinghies and waterskiing) and **tennis courts** are available through the hotels, which will often allow outsiders to use their equipment if it is available. **Bonefishing** is good off the northern resorts and if you wish to take a day's **deep-sea fishing**, contact the resorts, including Spanish Wells Beach Resort (© 332 2645), or the Cotton Bay Club (© 334 2156).

Divers can check out the tidal race at Current Cut and explore the wreck of the train that was on its way to Cuba on the Devil's Backbone reef off the north coast of the island. Contact the Romora Bay Club (℘ 333 2324) and Valentine's Dive Centre (℘ 333 2309), both on Harbour Island, and the Spanish Wells Dive Centre (℘ 332 2645). Also the Cotton Bay Club near Rock Sound, where there is a golf course.

Where to Stay and Eat

Harbour Island, off the northeast coast of Eleuthera, is a charmed spot, with some extremely smart hotels and guest houses set in the old Bahamian island-homes or hidden in luxurious gardens.

Named after the east coast beach, **Pink Sands Resort**, PO Box 87 (℘ 333 2030, ℘ 333 2060; *very expensive–expensive*), is approached through a rickety gate, but once into the garden, the informal luxury of the place is immediately upon you. It has 35 rooms are scattered across the grounds and on the beach itself. There is a good library and a delightful dining room and you can expect extra pampering at moments like afternoon tea. Watersports are available, but the atmosphere is low-key.

The **Coral Sands Hotel** (℘ 333 2320, ℘ 333 2368, US res toll free ℘ (1 800) 468 2799; *moderate*) stands on 3 miles of pink sand beach close to Dunmore Town; 33 rooms and an easy, relaxed air.

The **Romora Bay Club**, PO Box 146 (℘ 333 2325, US toll free ℘ (1 800) 327 8286; *moderate*) is an active hotel which offers diving and other watersports just a short walk from Pink Sands beach. There are 37 rooms with air-conditioning and ceiling fans and a central area with a dining terrace slung with greenery.

The **Runaway Hill Club**, PO Box 31 (℘ 333 2150, US toll free ℘ (1 800) 327 0787; *expensive*) is a charming inn of just eight rooms set in a traditional Bahamian house, not far from the centre of Dunmore Town. In its own garden, it is quiet and isolated from the buzz if that's what you want.

Not far off, **Valentine's Yacht Club and Inn**, PO Box 1 (℘ 333 2142, ℘ 333 2135, US toll free ℘ (1 800) 327 0787; *moderate*) is busy town hotel where passing yachtsmen gather. It is a neat inn, with cottages gathered around an old town house and its tropical garden courtyard. The marina is right over the road and there is evening entertainment in season.

There are one or two cheaper places to stay on Harbour Island, including the **Landing** (℘ 333 2707; *moderate–cheap*); and **Tingum Village** (℘ 333 2161; *cheap*), with 12 simple rooms in cottages, a bar and dining room.

The restaurants have some good dining rooms, but at the Tingum Village, Rubi Percentie cooks the best in local food at **Ma Rubi's** (*moderate*)—excellent conch fritters and grilled lobster and shrimp. Otherwise you might try the **Harbour Lounge** on the waterfront or **Angela's Starfish Restaurant** for local seafood. **Willy's Tavern** is a fun bar for a beer or a cocktail and **The Reach** is a favourite with the passing yacht-folk, on the waterfront opposite Valentine's.

Gusty's, with sand strewn on the floor, is a local bar, where you can get a beer and catch up on the latest sports news on the satellite television, and you can occasionally see a band at **Seagrapes**, the discotheque.

On the island of **Spanish Wells** there are two main hotels. On the eastern shore is the **Spanish Wells Beach Resort**, PO Box 31 (✆ 333 4298, ✆ 333 4565; *moderate*), with 21 airy and simple rooms overlooking a massive expanse of fantastic sand and waist-deep water. There is a restaurant and a lively local bar, where the fishermen collect when they are home from the seas.

The **Spanish Wells Yacht Haven** (✆ 333 4255, ✆ 333 4649; *moderate–cheap*) overlooks the harbour side of the island and has its own bar and dining room. Fishing and diving trips leave from the dock below. Cheaper rooms can be found at the **St George's Hotel**, PO Box 48 (✆ 333 4075; *cheap*). Eating out is limited to the other hotels, though you will be able to pick up a lunchtime snack from the local bakery.

At the western tip of **Eleuthera** itself you will find the **Current Club** (✆ 392 5474, US ✆ (1 800) 832 2772; *moderate*). There are just 18 suites in modern villas and a central club house with a restaurant that specializes in seafood dishes. Fishing and diving are on offer and of course the beach is right there if you just want to soak up a few rays.

In **Gregory Town** you will find the **Cove Eleuthera**, PO Box 1548 (✆/✆ 335 5142; *moderate*), where there are 24 rooms dressed up in Caribbean pastel colours and white rattan furniture. Pool and tennis court and a restaurant.

Not far off, at Hatchet Bay you will find the **Rainbow Inn** (✆/✆ 332 0294, US toll free ✆ (1 800) 327 0787; *moderate*), which is set on an expanse of white sand beach, lost among the palm trees. Surfing when the waves are up and tennis, or a pool bar if you are feeling lazy.

At **Governor's Harbour** you can find one or two less expensive places to stay. The **Cigatoo Inn**, PO Box 86 (✆ 332 2343, ✆ 332 2159, US toll free ✆ (1 800) 327 0787; *moderate–cheap*) has 26 rooms in a modern block and a restaurant. Some sports on the superb beach. And at the **Laughing Bird Apartments** (✆ 332 2012, ✆ 332 2358; *moderate–cheap*) there are comfortable rooms, scuba and tennis. You can eat out at the **Buccaneer Club**, which offers local Bahamian food for lunch and dinner. *Closed Sun.*

One of the Bahamas' smartest hotels is at the **Windermere Island Club** (✆ 332 6003, ✆ 332 6002, US toll free ✆ (1 800) 237 1236; *expensive*), which is hidden away on its own island 18 miles north of Rock Sound. Its sophisticated castaway seclusion on 5 miles of pristine private beach was popular with the British royal family. The hotel is currently closed, however, as is the famous **Cotton Bay Club**, PO Box 28 (✆ 334 6101, ✆ 334 6082, US toll free ✆ (1 800) 334 3523; *very expensive*) at Rock Sound, another sumptuous enclave of low-key luxury where you could expect high-grade pampering. Both may re-open in the future, so do check with your travel agent. At the other end of the scale, you can get a room at **Edwina's Place**, PO Box 30 (✆ 334 2094; *cheap*), just one mile from the airport, with dining room, pool, and beach nearby. An even cheaper option is **Hilton's Haven Motel** (✆ 334 4231; *cheap*), simple rooms in a modern block, with a restaurant and a lively bar. Try the **Haven Restaurant**, good for a local meal of grilled fish or curry goat, and the **Hide Out** bar, where a local crowd of limers stops in for a beer.

Exuma Cays

The 350 or so Exuma cays are strung out over more than 100 miles of magnificent sea, starting 50 miles from Nassau and heading southeasterly towards Great Exuma and Little Exuma in the south, where most of the population lives. Most are uninhabited and some, just sandbars, disappear with the 1ft tides. Others, like Allen's Cay, are just home to a crowd of iguanas. In the string of islands Staniel Cay, Farmer Cay and Black Point each have a marina and a small yacht club. You may hear stories of Norman's Cay, which was used as a smuggling base by cocaine barons until it was raided by the DEA. All that remains are a few buildings, rusting cars with bullet holes and an airstrip. The DEA maintains an air-balloon on a wire from the old airport in Georgetown and watches the seaborne traffic for miles around.

The Exumas are famed for their sailing and the islands see quite lively crowds on yachts during the winter season. The Out Islands Regatta, held each year in April, pits traditional Bahamian sailing vessels against one another, and the whole of Georgetown comes alive with open-air parties in the evenings. Elizabeth Harbour is a magnificent stretch of stunning blue water seven miles by two and rimmed with classic Bahamian beaches. It is well worth hiring a Boston whaler to explore it. Alternatively, take a ride over to Stocking Island, where you will find a beach bar and miles of deserted sand. There are also excellent snorkelling grounds. Exuma is also known for its bonefishing, on the huge expanse of knee-to-waist-deep water on the sheltered leeward coast of the island. The Exuma **Land and Sea Park** is based around Warderick Wells Cay.

The airstrip is at Moss Town, 10 miles north of the main settlement; on Great Exuma in the south, the largest island and home to most of the 3500 population (about one-third of whom have the name Rolle). A few people live on Staniel Cay about midway up the chain.

George Town is set around a lagoon on one side and on the magnificent Elizabeth Harbour. There is a scattering of houses around the one-way ring road, a local market and a straw market under the trees near the neoclassical, pastel-pink government building. Across the harbour you can see a tall obelisk on Stocking, erected to guide ships in to load up with salt in the last century. They would fly flags or burn fires on it when there was salt for sale. There are a few other small settlements and isolated private villas on Great Exuma, and across the bridge to Little Exuma you will find the Ferry, home of Gloria Patience, alias Shark Lady, who sells shark-teeth necklaces made from her own catches when out fishing. The islands have some small agriculture, but the main industry is tourism.

Cars can be hired from Exuma Transport (✆ 336 2101) and there are plenty of **taxis** for hire. If you walk you will find that people often stop to offer you a lift. There is a **tourist information** office in town (✆ 336 2430, ✆ 336 2431). For **watersports** (scuba diving, Boston whalers) contact Exuma Fantasea (✆/✆ 226 3483). Bonefishing can be arranged through Club Peace and Plenty. There are also marina facilities and limited sports on Staniel Cay, Farmer Cay and Black Point.

✆ (1 242)–

Where to Stay and Eat

Most of the hotels in the Exumas are on Great Exuma in the far south where a clutch of small resorts lies along the seashore of George Town and Elizabeth Harbour. Those that are not on the beach have shuttle buses to ferry you around. The **Club Peace and Plenty**, PO Box

29055 (✆ 336 2551, 📠 336 2093, US toll free ✆ (1 800) 525 2210; *moderate*) has an old-time Bahamian charm in a pretty pink building, with the 35 rooms set around a courtyard and looking on to the water. It is named after the ship that brought colonists here in 1783, and the name expresses the theme of the hotel well: quiet and comfortable, if a little faded now; there is air-conditioning, but no televisions or telephones.

It has a more modern counterpoart, the **Peace and Plenty Beach Inn** (✆ 336 2250, 📠 336 2253; *moderate*), 16 bright and breezy rooms with white tiles, pastel decoration and wicker chairs—air-conditioning, telephones, television in the rooms, right above the beach. Lively restaurant and bar. In a converted holiday home right next door is **Coconut Cove** (✆ 336 2659, 📠 336 2658; *expensive–moderate*). Its 11 rooms are set around a pretty courtyard, with restaurant and bar on a wooden deck overlooking the blue of Elizabeth Harbour. Air-conditioned rooms with televisions.

Regatta Point, PO Box 6 (✆ 336 2206, 📠 336 2046, US toll free ✆ (1 800) 327 0787; *moderate*) sits on its own peninsula just out of George Town, a secluded resort, but still within a shout of all the activity of the town, if you can call it that. Just a few apartments with fully equipped kitchens, with terraces and balconies looking through the palms.

The **Two Turtles Inn** (✆ 336 2545, 📠 336 2528; *moderate–cheap*) is another pleasant out-island inn in George Town. There are 14 air-conditioned rooms around the stone courtyard. **Marshall's** and **Helena's** have *cheap* and simple rooms in town.

Finally, the **Staniel Cay Yacht Club** (✆ 335 2024, 📠 335 2044; *expensive*) is situated on its own island, Staniel Cay, about halfway along the string of the Exuma Cays. The hotel, with just six rooms in cottages, sees plenty of passing yachts and so it has a lively crowd at times. Diving and fishing available and simple isolation if that's what you're there for. All-inclusive rate. Sailors who want to stop in for dinner should contact the kitchen well in advance.

The best food is really in the hotels—try the Peace and Plenty dining rooms and Coconut Cove—but you will also find some good local eateries in George Town. Try **Eddie's Edgewater Club** (*moderate–cheap*) is a classic West Indian bar/restaurant where you will find all the variations on conch and local catch with peas 'n' rice. Also try **Tino's Lounge** (*cheap*), for good local fare and a video.

Also **Sam's Place** (*moderate*), on an upstairs deck above the harbour, quiet but pleasant, burgers and local fish and seafood. To the south of the town is a pleasant hideaway on the cliffs, with a superb beach nearby, **La Shanté**; simple fare by day, livelier at night. There is occasionally a band at the **Silver Dollar**, which collects a crowd of domino players in the evenings. In the day, you might wish to go over to the very popular **Stocking Island Beach Club**, which will keep you topped up with beer and rum punch while you spend the day lazing around in the sun.

Cat Island

Cat Island is a sliver of land, 45 miles by one on average, that lies northwest–southeast, across the prevailing ocean winds, ribboned on both coasts by pristine beaches. Named after the British sea captain Catt, the island has a line of cliffs (at 206ft, Mt Alvernia is the highest in the Bahamas) and it is fertile, as the walls and the derelict houses of its former plantation prosperity show at a glance. But if it was developed for cotton and sisal a hundred years ago, Cat Island is one of the least developed of the Bahamian islands today. Old-time Bahamian life continues here, small plantations cut out of the hillside, and traditions such as *obeah*, the West Indian magic, of which you will still see the signs hanging in the trees.

There are three airstrips on Cat Island; near Port Howe in the south, Fernandez Bay in the centre and the main airstrip in the north at Arthur's Town, to which Bahamasair flies.

Arthur's Town is the most populous on the island, and it is much the same as when Sidney Poitier grew up here. It is the commercial centre, but there is not much to see. You are best to set off along the island where you will find the traditional Bahamian thatch-roofed cottages and their outdoor ovens set in the tropical gardens.

The Bight is a large cove with two seafront villages (New Bight and Old Bight) linked by a stunning beach. Pigeon Bay Cottage is the ruin of a 19th-century estate house nearby, and on top of Mt Alvernia above the town you will find the Hermitage, a monastery built in miniature by Father Jerome, who designed many of the Bahamian churches, including the Augustinian monastery on New Providence. He came to live as a hermit on Cat Island in his last years. South of the Bight the road passes the Deveaux Mansion, an impressive ruined plantation house, and heads towards Columbus Point and the small town of Port Howe, famed as a wrecking town in years past. Hawks Nest Creek in the southwest has a large number of herons. Hire cars and sports, including tennis, diving and deep-sea fishing, are available through the few hotels on the island.

© (1 242)– **Where to Stay and Eat**

Fernandez Bay Village (US © 305 792 1905; *expensive–moderate*) is the smartest hotel on the island and it is a classic castaway resort, set on its own magnificent beach. There are just 11 rooms in villas overlooking the sea, with full kitchen facilities, though there is a restaurant if you want it. Some watersports are offered. The hotel can arrange transportation from the USA.

There is a slightly cheaper alternative in the **Bridge Inn** (© 354 5013, © 354 5041, US © (305) 634 1014; *moderate*) which has 12 airy rooms in a modern block just up from the beach, each with satellite television. The bar and restaurant are a gathering point for all comers. The **Hotel Greenwood Inn** (© 354 5053, US res © (1 800) 825 5099) also has rooms at the same price, as well as offering diving and boat rentals. The **Orange Creek Inn** (© 354 4110; *cheap*) has simple rooms looking over one of the islands magnificent beaches at Orange Creek. If you want to eat out you can try **Pilot Harbour**, overlooking the harbour, where you can get a grilled local fish in creole sauce.

Long Island

Long Island, which stretches southeast from the tip of the Exuma Cays and cuts the Tropic of Cancer, is 57 miles long and 4 wide at most. In the north are rugged headlands and at the southern tip of the island the hills subside into salt flats. There are over 40 small communities, many of them white Bahamians or 'Conkie Joes', scattered along its almost entirely undeveloped western coastline of reefs and beaches, of which the largest are Deadman's Cay, midway down the island and Clarence Town, set on a beautiful harbour farther south. The main airstrips are at Stella Maris in the north and Deadman's Cay.

Though some of the 3500 islanders work in the tourist industry, most are involved with fishing and farming. The produce, much of which is grown in fertile 'pot holes' in the limestone ground, is sold to the government and shipped out on the weekly boat to Nassau.

The beaches around the Stella Maris Inn and up to the north of the island at Cape Santa Maria are spectacular and they have the best of the Bahamas' superbly clear water. Travelling south you will see that the island is littered with the walls and the skeletons of former plantation prosperity. Deadman's Cay is the best place for provisions. Clarence Town, which is still the island capital, is dominated by two of Father Jerome's churches (*see* Cat Island). St Paul's Anglican Church was topped when he turned Catholic and constructed St Peter's Catholic Church.

℗ *(1 242)–*   ***Where to Stay and Eat***

One of the best places to stay is the **Cape Santa Maria Beach Resort** (℗/✉ 357 1006, US toll free ℗ (1 800) 663 7090; *expensive*). With six cottages, a clubhouse and a good restaurant, the complex fronts a four-mile stretch of white beach. All rooms have fans and a/c, but no phone or TV. Free beach equipment, also snorkelling gear, sailboards, and bikes.

The **Stella Maris Resort Club**, PO Box 105 (℗ 336 2106, US toll free ℗ (1 800) 426 0466; *expensive–moderate*), has 60 rooms and self-catering units in low pre-fab buildings scattered around a sandy garden of pines and palms. There are three pools, and a bar and dining room in the central area, which can get lively because the property has a marina too. Windsurfing, sailing, fishing and diving are on offer and you can hire cars from them to explore the island. **Thomson Bay Inn** (call *Batelco*, ℗ 323 4911 and ask for 'Deadman's Cay') offers simple and *cheap* rooms.

For a meal outside the hotels try **Conchy's** in the Stella Maris shopping centre or **Salty's Bar**, where you will get a dish of Bahamian peas 'n' rice. At **Sabrina's** in Burnt Ground Village you can also get local Bahamian fare.

San Salvador

San Salvador takes its name (the Saviour) from Columbus's first landfall in the New World on 12 October 1492. Just 12 miles by 5, San Salvador is out on its own, a little farther into the Atlantic than the other islands, and historians decided that what the Indian inhabitants called *Guanahani* was the best site for Columbus's island (in the meantime it had become known as Watling's Island, the lair of a pirate). Just as there are other islands that dispute the claim, so there are four sites on the island that vie for the title of the first bay where he put in and you will see several monuments commemorating them. Long Bay with its simple white cross has the most favoured claim.

For all the controversy, the island is inhabited by only a few hundred people, undeveloped and much like the other out-islands. It is mainly flat, with a series of inland lakes, and offshore reefs that the Navigator had to avoid. There is one airstrip on the island, just north of the main village of Cockburn Town (pronounced 'Co'burn'). There is a spectacular view of the island from the 160ft lighthouse on Dixon Hill in the northeast. On the hill above the south coast is

'Watling's Castle', supposedly the pirate's lookout. In fact it is one of the plantation houses of the American loyalists who settled the island in the late 1700s.

A few **sports** are available through the Riding Rock Inn, including a tennis court, diving with three boats, and a dark-room for film shot on the dives. There is a Club Med, which opened at the time of the quincentenniel celebrations, and there are also marina facilities.

✆ *(1 242)–*   ***Where to Stay and Eat***

 If **Club Med** is your thing you can try that. Alternatively stay at the **Riding Rock Inn** (✆ 332 2631, US toll free ✆ (1 800) 272 1492; *moderate*) is on the beach north of Cockburn Town, with 24 air-conditioned rooms and villas around the freshwater pool, dining room and bar; tennis, full diving operation and fishing. Cheaper options are the smaller **Ocean View Villas** (✆ 323 4911 via the Batelco operator) in the town which have kitchenettes. You can eat out at the **Ocean View Club**, where the island limers gather for a beer, and the **Halem Square Club**, where you can get some conch fritters and a lobster platter and some live music at the weekends.

Rum Cay

About 35 miles from San Salvador, and supposedly Columbus's second island stop, which he named after the Virgin Mary, Rum Cay is another former pirate haunt surrounded by spectacular reefs. Just ten miles by four and with a population of under 100, it is perhaps the most slumberstruck and friendliest of them all. Port Nelson, the only village, is hidden among the palms on the southeast coast and the island is fringed with supreme sand. Apart from piracy, salt manufacture was the only industry. The reefs are as spectacular as they are dangerous for shipping—a shipload of rum that foundered here gave the island its name, and there is a superb dive to the HMS *Conqueror*, wrecked in 1861, which lies in just 25ft of water. There are marina facilities at the head of the harbour. Watch out for the wild boars. The **Rum Cay Club** has its own airstrip. Otherwise you are dependent on the mail boat. **Watersports** can also be arranged through the club.

✆ *(1 242)–*   ***Where to Stay and Eat***

You can stay cheaply at **Dolores** and there is good local fare at **Kaye's Bar** next to the pier in Port Nelson and at the **Ocean View**.

Crooked Island—Acklins

About 300 miles southeast of Nassau, Long Cay, Crooked Island and Acklins enclose on three sides the stunning Bight of Acklins, where crystal clear water runs on to sandbars and palm-lined beaches. The population of the Crooked Island district (500 on Crooked Island and 600 on Acklins) is far lower now than it was a century ago when the islands were a major port of call. Life here is gentle and friendly. Long Cay has about 20 inhabitants, most of whom are fishermen by trade.

The twice-weekly flight from Nassau touches both major islands: Colonel Hill on Crooked Island and Spring Point on Acklins. There is a twice-daily boat link from one island to the other across The Going Through, the strait that divides Lovely Bay and the Ferry (Crooked Island). The reefs are excellent and diving can be arranged through the hotel Pittsdown Point Landings on Crooked Island. Bonefishing in the bay is also excellent.

✆ (1 242)–   *Where to Stay and Eat*

At Landrail Point is **Pittstown Point Landings** (✆ 336 2507, US res ✆ (513) 732 2593; *moderate*), which has 14 rooms set on a magnificent beach (one of a number on the island). It is very low key, with an honour bar and huts on the beaches where you cook up your own catch at lunchtime. Boating, snorkelling and scuba on offer. At Colonel Hill is the **Crooked Island Beach Inn** (✆ 336 2096; *moderate–cheap*), 11 rooms with ceiling fans in beach cottages; kitchenettes, but also a dining room and some sports. **T and S** guest house (*cheap*) is 3 miles from the airstrip at Cabbage Hill and has five simple rooms and a communal kitchen. At Landrail Point, try **Wilfred and Hanna Gibson's Restaurant**.

Mayaguana

Mayaguana is rarely visited except as a stopover for yachts headed south to the Caribbean. And then only for shelter in Abraham's Bay, the capital village on the south coast, because there are no organized facilities there. Life is extremely slow for the 600 or so islanders, many of whom have left because there is no work other than farming. There is a twice-weekly flight to Inagua. There is a guest house and bar, **Reggie Satellite Lounge**, which collects anybody who is out liming at the time.

The Inaguas

Most southerly of the Bahamas, Great Inagua is just within sight of Cuba to the south, about 60 miles across the Old Bahama Channel. The island is remote, over 350 miles away from the bustling centre of Nassau, and less than 1000 people live there. Its remoteness and size (at 35 miles by 25 it is the third largest of all the Bahamas) have meant that it has become the last resort of a large colony of birds, including spoonbills, ducks and most spectacular, pink flamingos; an estimated 60,000 of these birds, which now survive in just a few places in the Americas, are protected in the Inagua National Park, set around Inagua's inland lakes. Trips can be arranged through the Bahamas National Trust (Nassau ✆ 323 1317).

The traditional industry on this low, windswept island is salt manufacture, and miles of brilliant white salt flats of the Morton Salt Company make up the second largest in the world. The main town is Matthew Town in the southwest, where the airport is located for the twice-weekly flights to Nassau. You might also be able to arrange a ride on the ships of the Morton Salt Company, based in Port Canaveral, Fort Lauderdale.

✆ (1 242)–   *Where to Stay and Eat*

There are a couple of guest houses in Matthew Town, 1 mile from Great Inagua airstrip, both with simple rooms, with a dining room and beach nearby. The **Main House** (✆ 339 1267, ✆ 339 1265; *cheap*) has six rooms and **Walkine's Guest House** (✆ 339 1500; *cheap*) has five.

By air: The main centre for air arrivals is New Providence, for Nassau, Cable Beach and Paradise Island, and for onward local flights to the Out Islands. Grand Bahama is also quite a big destination (for Freeport/Lucaya) and there are plenty of direct flights to there from the main American airports. A few of the other islands have direct scheduled flights from the American mainland, principally the Abacos, Eleuthera and the Exumas, plus San Salvador. It is also possible to charter a light plane from Florida to almost any of the islands. Bahamasair is the national carrier and they can be contacted on (USA toll free ✆ (1 800) 222 4262). There is a departure tax of $15, or $18 out of Freeport.

By air from Europe: British Airways fly three times a week from London Gatwick (Tues, Wed, Fri). AOM fly weekly (Fri) from Paris Orly-Sud. Lauda Air offers a weekly flight (Wed) from Milan. There are also plenty of daily links from all over Europe to Miami, where you can transfer. Miami to Nassau is 35 minutes flying time and flights leave for Nassau and Freeport until late on in the evening. The Out Islands are not so easy to get to in the same day.

By air from the USA: The major carriers into the Bahamas from the USA are Delta, US Air and American Airlines; other airlines include Bahamasair, Trinity, Gulf Stream and Pan Am Air Bridge (which has scheduled flights into Paradise Island). Connections for Nassau can be made in Miami, Fort Lauderdale, Orlando and West Palm Beach in Florida and also New York, which have several flights a day into Nassau and Freeport. There are direct flights to Nassau from many other US cities, among them Atlanta (twice daily), Chicago (daily), Dallas (daily), Indianapolis (twice daily), Orlando (daily), Philadelphia (twice daily), Tampa (twice daily) and Washington (daily).

Some of these flights also touch **Freeport**, which in addition is served from: Cincinatti (twice weekly), Cleveland (twice weekly), Key West (daily). For flights direct into the Out Islands, *see* p.786.

Finally, if none of the above happens to be convenient, there are a number of air charter companies that fly light planes ideally suited for a short hop down to the islands. Contact Congo Air (✆ 377 8329), Chalks (✆ (305) 359 7980) or Reliable Air (✆ 327 7335, 377 8910). There is also a seaplane service, Pan Am Air Bridge (USA ✆ (305) 373 1120, US toll free ✆ (1 800) 424 2557), which links the coast of Florida (Watson Island off Miami and Fort Lauderdale), with several points in the Bahamas including Paradise Island and Bimini. Charters are also available.

By air from Canada: There are two weekly flights on Air Canada to Nassau from Toronto and one from Montreal. Charter companies also fly to the Bahamas from these two cities.

By air from other Caribbean islands: There is a daily link to Providenciales in the Turks and Caicos Islands on TCA (Turks and Caicos Airways) and there is a twice-weekly service to Kingston, Jamaica on Air Jamaica.

There are **ports of entry** for sailors in the following islands: **the Abacos:** Green Turtle Cay, Marsh Harbour, Sandy Point, Treasure Cay, Walker's Cay. **Berry Islands:** Chub Cay, Harbour Cay. **Bimini:** Alice Town, at any marina facility. **Andros:** Congo Town, Fresh Creek, San Andros. **Eleuthera:** Cape Eleuthera, Governor's Harbour, Harbour Island, Hatchet Bay, Rock Sound. **Exuma Cays:** George Town. **Cat Island:** Cat Cay Club at

Government Dock. **Long Island**: Stella Maris. **San Salvador**: Cockburn Town. **Mayaguana**: Government Dock.

getting between the Bahamas

Bahamasair (US toll free ℘ (1 800) 222 4262) flies from Nassau to about twenty different islands dotted around the archipelago. The more isolated islands are served only a couple of times a week, but to most there are a couple of flights each day. Hotels usually have a connecting motorboat if you need to make a hop to an offshore cay. All flights are routed via Nassau and so if you wish to travel from one Out island to another, you will find that you have to return to the capital.

The same goes for the **mail boats**, which do a weekly run from Nassau to an island with the mail, the stores, and any locals heading home, accompanied by their goats and chickens. Spaces on mail boats are offered on a first-come, first-served basis and they leave from Potter's Cay docks in downtown Nassau, close to the bridge over to Paradise Island (℘ 393 1064). The boats are fun to travel on, though they can take up anything to 24 hrs to reach their destination. Typical one-way fares are: from **Nassau** to the Abacos—about $30, Grand Bahama—$45, Andros—$25, South Andros—$25, Bimini—$35, the Exumas—$35–40, Cat Island—$35, Rum Cay—$30, San Salvador—$30, Mayaguana and Inagua—$45. Finally, you might consider hitching a lift on a yacht by turning up at the marina and asking around.

tourist information

UK: 3 The Billings, Walnut Tree Close, Guildford, Surrey GU1 4UL (℘ (01483) 448 900, ✆ 448 990).

France: 60 rue St Lazare, 75009 Paris (℘ 1 45 26 62 62, ✆ 1 48 74 06 05).

Germany: Leipziger Straße 67d, D-60487 Frankfurt am Main (℘ (069) 970 8340, 970 83434).

Italy: Via Cusani 10, 20121 Milan (℘ 2 720 22526, ✆ 2 720 23123).

USA: 150 East 52nd Street, 28th Floor North, **New York**, NY 10022 (℘ (212) 758 2777, ✆ 753 6531); 8600 W. Bryn Mawr Avenue, Suite 820, **Chicago** Illinois 60631 (℘ (312) 693 1500, ✆ 693 1114); 3450 Wilshire Boulevard, Suite 208, **Los Angeles**, California 90010 (℘ (213) 385 0033, ✆ 383 3966); and 1 Turnberry Place, 19495 Biscayne Blvd, Suite 80, Aventura, **Florida** 33180 (℘ (305) 932 0051, ✆ 682 8758).

Canada: 1130 Sherbrooke Street West, Suite 750, **Montreal**, Quebec H3A 2M8 (℘ (1 800) 667 3777, ✆ 514 448 5116) or 121 Bloor Street East, Suite 1101, **Toronto**, Ontario M4W 3M5 (℘ (416) 968 2999, ✆ 968 6711).

In the Bahamas themselves there are tourist information booths at Nassau International airport; in arrivals (℘ 377 6806) and departures (℘ 377 6782)—they can be very helpful, but if you are not having any luck, you can always take away an armful of brochures for ideas. Downtown there is an office at Rawson Square on Bay Street (℘ 322 7801). Hotels will also help out usually. Most hotel rooms in the Bahamas can be booked through the **Bahamas Reservation Service** (USA and Canada toll free ℘ (1 800) 327 0787, UK and Europe in London ℘ 0171 434 9915, *sales@bahamasreservations.co.uk*). Information about Freeport/Lucaya and the Out Islands is available from the main office in Nassau, but in Grand Bahama there are also tourist offices at the airport, at the cruise-ship dock, in the International Bazaar and at Port Lucaya. The main office is in the International Bazaar (✆ 352 8044, ✉ 352 2714) and is very helpful.

There are two daily newspapers published in Nassau—the *Nassau Guardian*, which appears in the morning, and the evening *Tribune*. A wide selection of US dailies are flown in on the day of release. There is a proliferation of tourist literature, where some quite useful information is hidden. *What To Do* contains mainly adverts about jewellery, watches and even advice on which perfume might be best suited to your sign of the zodiac, along with a little practical advice. There are a couple of dining magazines. The Out Islands issue the *Getaway* magazine which contains some features and some practical information on things other than shopping.

There is direct dialling to and from the major Bahamian islands. The **IDD code** is ✆ (1 242), followed by a seven-digit number. Hotels sometimes add a hefty service charge to your bill for telephone calls. You may wish to avoid this by going direct to the **Batelco** Bahamas Telecom office in the main towns.

In a medical **emergency**, contact the Princess Margaret Hospital on Shirley Street, Nassau (✆ 322 2861) or, in Grand Bahama, the Rand Memorial Hospital on East Atlantic Drive, Freeport (✆ 352 6735).

festivals

Junkanoo is celebrated at the turn of the year, with masquerades in the streets on 26 December and 1 January to Bahamian *Goombay* and other Caribbean rhythms, mainly in Nassau and Freeport, but also with smaller events in the Out Islands. The festival **Goombay** itself runs over the summer months starting in June with a wider series of cultural events as well as more carnival parades through the streets. Independence Day is celebrated on 10 July and Discovery Day on 12 October.

Sailing regattas are some of the liveliest events in the Bahamas. As well as races there are onshore parties with barbecues and jump-ups. Local boats and crews vie with one another at the Out islands Regatta in Exuma in April, but all-comers can compete at Regatta Time in Abaco from April into June, and then at the Green Turtle Cay Regatta and the All Eleuthera Regatta in July. The Long Island Regatta is held in May, Andros Regatta in August and North Eleuthera Regatta on Discovery Day in October.

money

The Bahamian dollar and the US dollar, set at par with one another, are both valid currencies in the Bahamas. You may receive change in either currency or even both, including Bahamian $3 and 50c notes, though these are nearly finished now. You are best to exchange money in the banks, but hotels will change money at a slightly worse rate. Traveller's cheques and credit cards are accepted almost everywhere in the hotels, restaurants and shops. If you go off the beaten track then take cash with you. Personal cheques are not readily accepted. Tipping runs at a high 15%.

Banks: In Nassau and Grand Bahama, banks keep hours of 9.30–3, Mon–Fri (until 5pm on Fri). In the smaller islands you may find that the bank only opens for a few hours a couple of times a week.

Shops: Open Mon–Sat, 9–5 (later in the hotels), but they often close one afternoon in the week.

watersports

New Providence

General: Nassau offers a full gamut of watersports—most hotels have **windsurfers** on offer to their guests. Otherwise, go to the concessionaires on Cable Beach or Paradise Island. **Parasailing** can also be arranged through many of the beach concessionaires, as can a **jetski. Waterskiing** is easy to arrange, or you may choose a more stately ride on a **pedalo**. You can keep children quiet with a ride on an aqua-sausage for a high-speed view of the harbour. **Glass-bottom boat** tours can be made from the Nassau Dock.

Sailing: Many hotels also have sailing **dinghies** for hire, but if you prefer something a little more organized there are endless yacht tours on offer, from an outing of snorkelling, boozing, dancing and swimming with the dolphins (try the *Calypso*, ② 363 3577), or a picnic trip to Rose Island (Sea Island Adventures (② 325 3910) or Topsail Yacht Charters (② 393 0820). For a full-blooded day's yachting check with the Nassau Yacht Haven (② 322 8173). **Deep-sea fishing** trips are easily arranged through the above marinas; contact *Chubasco* (② 327 8148). Rates run from $300 for a half-day with tackle and bait provided (6 people) to $600 for the full day.

Scuba diving: Shops on the island include Bahama Divers on East Bay Street (② 326 5644), Coral Harbour Divers at the west end (② 326 4171) and Dive Dive Dive (② 362 1401) at the Smuggler's Rest Resort. If you are not a diver, you can still take an underwater walk with a sealed helmet through Underwater Wonderland (② 322 8234) at Nassau Yacht Haven. Also the Atlantis Submarine (② 356 3842) allows you a close inspection of the corals in the dry, expensive.

Grand Bahama

Major watersports operators outside the hotels include Reef Tours (② 373 5880), Executive Tours (② 352 8858) or Forbes Charter (② 352 7142). **Windsurfers** are on hire from all the beach hotels. Try Paradise Watersports (② 352 2887), Mistral also have a school at the Atlantik Beach Hotel in Lucaya (② 373 1444). Small sailing **dinghies** are also available through the major hotels, as is **parasailing** at the Atlantik and Radisson Resort on Lucaya Beach, and **waterskiing. Glass-bottom boat** tours can be fixed up through the tour companies and hotels.

Sailing: Yacht tours can also be arranged with the big operators, anything from a day's roistering with rum-punch in hand to a hard day's yachting. Contact the tour companies for the booze cruises: on the *Jolly Roger* (② 373 3923), or *Pat and Diane* (② 373 8681). Sailors will find plenty of marinas.

Deep-sea fishing: There are also a number of boats for hire in which you can trawl the fishing grounds off the island. A boat with tackle and bait for half a day comes at $400 and a full day at $650.

Snorkelling: Good in many places on the south coast, but it is particularly good at Peterson Cay east of the resort areas.

Scuba diving: Operators include UNEXSO, the Underwater Explorer's Society, based at Lucaya marina (© 373 1244), where you can arrange to swim with dolphins (© 373 1250), Sun Odyssey (© 373 8211) at the Atlantik Beach and Deep Water Cay Club at the East End (USA © 305 684 3958). If you would like a look at the corals in the dry, there is a semi-submersible submarine, the *Seaworld Explorer* (© 373 7863).

The Abacos

Sailing: This is the main sport on the Abacos and you will find facilities on all the islands mentioned above. Abaco Bahamas Charters work out of Hope Town and the big bareboat operators Sunsail work out of Marsh Harbour and The Moorings at Treasure Cay. The islands hold their regattas in late June and July.

Windsurfing: Available in the main hotels in the Abacos (ask around).

Scuba diving: Can be arranged through a number of dive shops; Hopetown (© 366 0029), also boat rentals; Man O' War Cay (© 365 6072) at Schooner's Landing.

Deep-sea fishing: Easy to arrange in the Abacos throughthe centres: Green Turtle Cay Club (© 367 2572), the Elbow Cay Club (© 367 2748) and Great Guana Cay (© 367 2207). Rates at around $600 for a full day.

other sports

Tennis: On land there are plenty of tennis courts in the hotels, often free to guests. If you are travelling independently you can try the hotels (fee usually around $8 per hour), or go to the Nassau Squash and Raquet Club on Independence Drive (© 323 1854).

Golf: There are three golf courses on **New Providence** open to visitors on the island (fees $30–35), at Cable Beach Hotel (© 327 6000), the South Ocean Golf Club in the south-west of the island (© 326 4391) and on the eastern end of Paradise Island (© 326 3926). There are a number of golf courses on **Grand Bahama**: try the Lucayan Golf and Country Club (© 373 4500), set around Lucaya, or the Fortune Hills Golf Course (© 373 4500). The Bahama Princess Emerald and the Ruby courses are closed to the International Bazaar area (© 352 6721). On the **Abacos**, try the Treasure Cay Resort (© 367 2570).

Riding: Horses are available if you would like to explore the pine barren interior of New Providence or take a canter along the beach, through Happy Trails (© 326 1820), $25 per hour. (There is even **bungee jumping** if that's your thing). On Grand Bahama, riding is available through Pinetree Stables on Beachway Drive in Freeport (© 373 3600; closed Mon). You can expect to canter along Grand Bahama's fantastic beaches.

Index

2½ years' exposure to a 100% targeted audience of independent business and leisure travellers

covering more than 100 destinations around the world

"It's difficult to praise the Cadogan books too highly… good writing, amusing comment and invaluable advice"

The Independent

To find out how you can reach this audience call Rebecca Fraser on 0171 287 6555 or fax 0171 734 1733

CADOGAN

Accommodation

Caribbean Chapters, 102 St John's Wood Terrace, London NW8 6PL.
Tel: 0171 722 0722, Fax: 0171 722 9140.
Luxury villas throughout the Caribbean islands, most with pools and staff.

Palmer & Parker Holidays, The Beacon, Penn Buckinghamshire HP10 8ND.
Tel: 01494 815411, Fax: 01494 814184.
Expensive villas in Barbados, Jamaica, and St Lucia.

Cruising

Norwegian Cruise Line, 1 Derry Street, Kensington, London W8 5NN.
Reservations: Tel: 0800 181560, Fax: 0171 938 4515.

Tour Operators

British Virgin Islands Club, 66 High Street, Walton on Thames, Surrey
KT12 1BU. Tel: 01932 220477, Fax: 01932 229346, E-Mail: bvic@vch.co.uk

British Virgin Islands Holidays Ltd, 11–19 Hockerill Street, Bishops
Stortford, Hertfordshire CM23 2DH. Tel: 01279 656111, Fax: 01279 506616,
E-Mail: bvihols@dial.pipex.com

Calypso Gold, 178b High Street, Teddington, Middlesex TW11 8HU.
Tel: 0181 977 9655, Fax: 0181 977 9225, E-Mail: info@calypsogold.com
Experts in tailor-made breaks around the region. 2, 3 & 4 star accommodations
offered. Flights in economy and club class cabins. Cricket holidays our speciality.

Caribbean à la Carte, The Owners' Syndicate, 79 Balham Park Road,
London SW12 8EB. Tel: 0181 767 7926, Fax: 0181 767 5328,
E-Mail: ownerssyndicate@compuserve.com
Acclaimed Caribbean specialists for the discerning traveller not wishing to follow
the crowd. We offer the best choice of private villas, small inns, hotels and yachts
on twenty-five islands at direct rates. Price watch guarantee. Fully bonded.
ATOL: 4049. ABTOT: 5019. AITO.

Harlequin Worldwide Travel Limited, Connoisseurs of Caribbean Holidays,
Harlequin House, 2 North Road, South Ockendon, Essex RM15 6QJ.
Tel: 01708 852780, Fax: 01708 854952,
E-Mail: harlequin@harlequin-holidays.co.uk
ABTA: V2541. ATOL: 2890.

Antigua
NELSON'S DOCKYARD AT ENGLISH HARBOUR

14 TWIN BEDDED ROOMS WITH
PRIVATE BATH AND SHOWER.
FREE TRANSPORTATION TO NEARBY
BEACHES (5 MINS BY BOAT OR CAR).
CLOSES ANNUALLY – SEPTEMBER THRU
MID OCTOBER FOR REFURBISHING.
USE OF SUNFISH AND SNORKELLING
EQUIPMENT AT SISTER PROPERTY.

Falmouth Harbour
Beach Apartments

23 STUDIOS WITH FULLY EQUIPPED KITCHENS,
PRIVATE BATH AND SHOWER, CEILING FAN, PRI-
VATE VERANDA FOR OUTDOOR DINING, MAID
SERVICE.

The Flamboyant Hotel

Grenada
Beach/Hillside Location
with 60 Air-conditioned Bedrooms,
Satellite TV,
Radio and Direct Dial Telephone

◆ Beachside Terrace Restaurant and Bar –
Caribbean and Continental Cuisine
◆ Freshwater swimming pool and sundeck
◆ Games room
(*table tennis, billiards/pool & darts*)
◆ Kayaks and Paddle Boats
◆ Manager's Rum Punch Party (*Mondays*)

Entertainment – Mondays (*crab races*),
Wednesdays (*steel band*),
Fridays (*Strolling Extempo Calypsonian*)

Additional feature for the low season
Flamboyant Summer Inclusive

 For information and reservations on these properties contact:
The Caribbean Centre, 3 The Green, Richmond, Surrey TW9 1PL
Tel: 0181-940 3399 Fax: 0181-940 7424

RESORT AND **MARINA**

British Virgin Islands
BVI Headquarters for Diving ❑ Sailing ❑ Windsurfing
❑ Mountain Biking ❑ Nanny Cay is set on its own 25 acre
peninsula on the south coast of Tortola, 3 miles from the
capital, Road Town and 10 miles from the airport.

All 41 rooms are air-conditioned and feature a fully-equipped
kitchenette, coffee machine, bath with shower, balcony or patio
overlooking the sea, marina or tropical gardens,
direct dial telephone, radio and cable TV

Suites

St Lucia
30 air-conditioned suites, balcony or terrace/patio, cable TV and
direct dial telephone ❑ The Mortar & Pestle Restaurant & Bar
❑ Freshwater swimming pool ❑ Mini-Mart ❑ Beauty Salon
❑ Cosmetology & Body Therapy Salon
❑ Pottery Shop ❑ Kayaks ❑ Manager's Rum Punch Sunset
Cruise Party on board the Trivial Pursuit motor yacht
(Tuesdays 1730 to 1830) ❑ Stay 7 nights pay for 6

Grand View
BEACH HOTEL

St Vincent

*Located at Villa Point on the South Coast with
spectacular views of the ocean and the
neighbouring Grenadine Islands.*

*The family-run hotel is set in eight acres
of beautiful, landscaped tropical gardens*

■ 19 spacious air-conditioned
guest rooms with private bathrooms,
phone and satellite TV ■ Freshwater
swimming pool with swim-up bar
■ Restaurant ■ Sundown Bar with
occasional entertainment
■ Beach Bar

The Grand View Club
offers Tennis, Squash Courts
and a complete Fitness Centre

HAYES and JARVIS
(TRAVEL) LIMITED

*Far and away
a better choice*

Caribbean

*With over 40 years' experience in selling
long haul holidays Hayes & Jarvis is the
obvious choice for your 1998 holiday in
the Caribbean.*

*Our 1997/8 brochure offers excellent
value for money with nothing but the
highest standards.*

Prices start from £399

**Call us for a brochure on
0181 748 5050**

ABTA
V1464

1275

**Hayes and Jarvis (Travel) Ltd
152 King Street, London W6 OQU**

Holidays for

The BAREFOOT TRAVELLER

Tailor made holidays to suit your budget
**BAHAMAS
TRINIDAD & TOBAGO
CURAÇAO & BONAIRE
CAYMAN ISLANDS**
for individuals or groups

SCUBA DIVING SPECIALISTS
including learn to dive holidays

*plus BIRD WATCHING in
Trinidad & Tobago*

Tel: 0181 741 4319

Website http://www.dukes-court-travel.com/barefoot

204 King Street, London W6 0RA

IATA

ATOL
3045

Dukes Court Travel Ltd T/A Holidays for the Barefoot Traveller

**Need help with a
Tailor-Made itinerary?
Call BRS**
The experts in selling
The Bahamas -
With access to over 100 hotels
and villas throughout the
700 Islands of The Bahamas
A range of prices to suit all.
We make the reservations for
you and can arrange some trans-
fers or interesting excursions.
Call us now
Tel: + 44 (0) 171 434 9915
Fax: + 44 (0) 171 734 6460
USA Tel: 1 800 2224262
Email
sales@bahamasreservations.co.uk

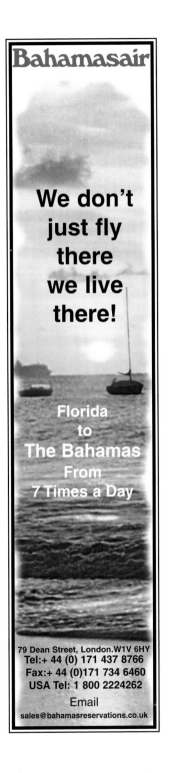

Bahamasair

We don't just fly there we live there!

Florida to The Bahamas From 7 Times a Day

79 Dean Street, London.W1V 6HY
Tel:+ 44 (0) 171 437 8766
Fax:+ 44 (0)171 734 6460
USA Tel: 1 800 2224262

Email

sales@bahamasreservations.co.uk

UNIQUE

H O T E L S

THE VERY BEST OF THE CARIBBEAN

Unique Hotels offer the very best in Caribbean destinations.

Whatever you're looking for, from your own private island or romantic honeymoon hideaway, to a dedicated sports resort, we have the perfect solution.

Experience Unique Hotels and the Caribbean will never be quite the same again.

UNIQUE

H O T E L S

The Old Warehouse, Old Market, Nailsworth,
Gloucestershire GL6 0DU England

Tel: 01453 835801 Fax: 01453 835525
Telex: 43205 UNIHOT G

Email res@uniqueuk.telme.com

CADOGAN

over 80 guides
covering the world

Inside tips, the best places to eat and stay, more history, culture and art... taking you deep into the heart of the destination.

"Absolute gems!"
Sunday Times

"Invaluable advice"
The Independent

"The best written series of all"
Sunday Times

"Sophisticated, beautifully written"
American Bookseller magazine

"Understated, humorous writing"
NY Daily News

"Entertaining companions with sharp insights... The series has received plaudits worldwide for intelligence, originality and a slightly irreverent sense of fun."
Saturday Telegraph

"the outstanding series for the independent traveller who doesn't want to follow the crowd..."
Daily Telegraph

From all good bookshops.

For a catalogue telephone:

✆ (0171) 287 6555 (UK)

✆ (860) 395 0312 (US)

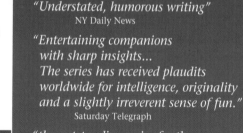

Also Available...

Country Guides

Antarctica
Belize
Central Asia
China: The Silk Routes
Egypt
France: Southwest France;
    Dordogne, Lot & Bordeaux
France: Southwest France;
    Gascony & the Pyrenees
France: Provence
France: Côte d'Azur
France: The South of France
France: The Loire
Germany
Germany: Bavaria
Guatemala
India
India: South India
India: Goa
Ireland
Ireland: Southwest Ireland
Ireland: Northern Ireland
Italy
Italy: The Bay of Naples and Southern Italy
Italy: Lombardy, Milan and the Italian Lakes
Italy: Tuscany
Italy: Three Cities—Rome, Florence and Venice
Japan
Morocco
Portugal
Portugal: The Algarve
Scotland
Scotland's Highlands and Islands
South Africa
Spain
Spain: Southern Spain
Spain: Northern Spain
Syria & Lebanon
Tunisia
Turkey: Western Turkey
Zimbabwe, Botswana and Namibia

City Guides

Amsterdam
Brussels, Bruges, Ghent & Antwerp
Florence, Siena, Pisa & Lucca
London
Moscow & St Petersburg
Paris
Prague
Rome
Venice & the Veneto

Island Guides

Bali
The Caribbean and Bahamas
The Caribbean: NE Caribbean;
    The Leeward Islands
The Caribbean: SE Caribbean;
    The Windward Islands
The Caribbean: Jamaica
Crete
Cyprus
Greece: The Greek Islands
Greece: The Cyclades
Greece: The Dodecanese
Greece: The Ionian Islands
Madeira & Porto Santo
Malta, Comino & Gozo
Sicily

Plus...

Healthy Travel: Bugs, Bites & Bowels
Travel by Cargo Ship
Five Minutes off the Motorway
Henry Kelly in the West of Ireland
London Markets

For every kind of person there's a different

SuperClubs®

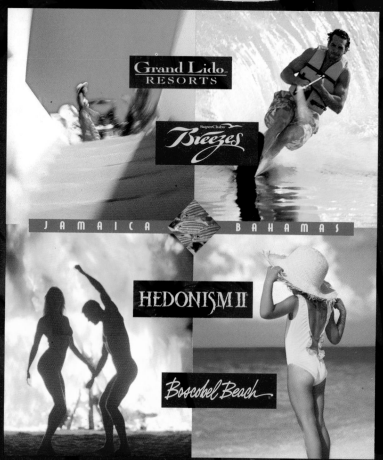

Grand Lido RESORTS

SuperClubs **Breezes**

JAMAICA   BAHAMAS

HEDONISM II

Boscobel Beach

THE CARIBBEAN'S ONLY SUPER-INCLUSIVE® RESORTS.

For more information, call your travel agent or SuperClubs
in N. America at: 1-800-GO-SUPER or (954) 925-0925. Or Fax: (954) 925-0334.
In the U.K. at: (01749) 677200. Or Fax: (01749) 677577.

SuperClubs is represented worldwide by International Lifestyles, Inc.